Collins
School
Dictionary

HarperCollins Publishers
Westerhill Road
Bishopbriggs
Glasgow
G64 2QT

Fourth edition 2009

Reprint 10 9 8 7 6 5

© HarperCollins Publishers 1999, 2002,
2006, 2009

UK paperback
ISBN 978-0-00-728979-0

UK hardback
ISBN 978-0-00-728980-6

Australian edition
ISBN 978-0-7322-8906-5

Collins® is a registered trademark of
HarperCollins Publishers Limited

www.collinslanguage.com

A catalogue record for this book is
available from the British Library

Designed by Wolfgang Homola

Typeset by Wordcraft, Glasgow

Printed in China by South China
Printing Co. Ltd

Acknowledgements
We would like to thank those authors and
publishers who kindly gave permission
for copyright material to be used in
the **Collins Word Web**. We would also
like to thank Times Newspapers Ltd for
providing valuable data.

Editorial Staff

Introduction

Being able to read, understand and write good English are vital and fundamental skills that underpin success in exams and, ultimately, success in the world beyond school. A dictionary is an essential tool for all students who want to achieve success, because if you know how to use a dictionary effectively you can improve your performance in all subjects, not just English. This is why literacy strategies all over the world set ambitious targets for students to acquire dictionary skills at every stage of their education.

Collins School Dictionary has been researched with teachers and students to ensure that it includes the information on language that students need to allow them to improve their performance in English and all other school subjects, and to achieve exam success. It provides:

● Essential information on what words mean, how they are used, spelling, grammar and punctuation, so that students can use language well, communicate with others and express their ideas more effectively

● Comprehensive coverage of core vocabulary from a wide range of curriculum subjects

● A supplementary section following the main dictionary, outlining key spelling rules and listing words that are commonly confused or misspelled, so that students can identify and master the trickiest spelling problems

Collins School Dictionary is exceptionally easy to use. It is relevant to school work in all subjects, accessible and student-friendly, and offers essential help on the route to success.

How To Use The Dictionary

Collins School Dictionary is easy to use and understand. Below are some
entries showing the dictionary's main features, along with an explanation
of what they are.

The entry word •──── **facetious** [*Said fas-see-shuss*] ────── How to say the
word

ADJECTIVE witty or amusing but in a
rather silly or inappropriate way • *He*
didn't appreciate my facetious ────── An example of the
suggestion. word being used

Word history
panel explains
where the word
comes from
● **WORD HISTORY:** from Latin
● *facetiae* meaning 'witty remarks'

famished ADJECTIVE INFORMAL ────── Advice on when to
very hungry. use the word

Other forms of
the word give help
with spelling
fish, fishes, fishing, fished **NOUN ❶** a
cold-blooded creature living in water ────── What the word
that has a spine, gills, fins, and a scaly means
skin. **❷** Fish is the flesh of fish eaten
as food ▷ **VERB ❸** To fish is to try to

Change in part of •──── catch fish for food or sport. **❹** If you
speech arrow fish for information, you try to get it in
an indirect way. **fishing NOUN**
fisherman NOUN ────── Other words that
come from the
● **USAGE NOTE:** The plural of the entry word
● noun *fish* can be either *fish* or *fishes*,
● but *fish* is more common

Usage note gives
more information
on how the word is
used

The word's part
of speech
folly, follies **NOUN** Folly is a foolish
act or foolish behaviour.
● **SIMILAR WORDS:** foolishness,
● stupidity

Similar words list
shows other words
with the same
meaning

full stop, full stops **NOUN** the
punctuation mark (.) used at the end
of a sentence and after an
abbreviation or initial.
▶ SEE GRAMMAR BOX BELOW

Grammar box gives
more information on
the way English
works

See page viii for a
full list of grammar
boxes in the
dictionary

WHAT DOES THE FULL STOP DO?	
The **full stop** (.) marks the end of any sentence which is not a question or an exclamation: *The train is leaving.*	*Dr. Jenkins* *J.R. Hartley*
A full stop is also used after an abbreviation or initial: *etc.*	A full stop is also used after an expression that stands by itself but is not a complete sentence: *Good morning.*

Spelling tips give help with finding words in the dictionary

Some words which sound as if they might begin with *s*, actually begin with *c*, for example *centre* and *cynic*. Some words which sound as if they might begin with *sh* actually begin with *ch*, for example *chute*. Some words which sound as if they might begin with *ch* are spelt with *c* alone, for example *cello*.

compare, compares, comparing, compared **VERB ❶** EXAM TERM
When you compare things, you look at them together and see in what ways they are different or similar. **❷** If you compare one thing to another, you say it is like the other thing • *His voice is often compared to Michael Stipe's.*

Words used in exam questions are highlighted

D & T = Design and technology

ICT = Information and communication technology

PE = Physical education

PSHE = Personal, social and health education

RE = Religious education

Core vocabulary from all curriculum subjects

comparison, comparisons **NOUN** ENGLISH When you make a comparison, you consider two things together and see in what ways they are different or similar.

fabric, fabrics **NOUN** D & T
❶ cloth • *tough fabric for tents.* **❷** The fabric of a building is its walls, roof, and other parts. **❸** The fabric of a society or system is its structure, laws, and customs • *the democratic fabric of American society.*

-ful **SUFFIX ❶** '-ful' is used to form adjectives with the meaning 'full of' • *careful.* **❷** '-ful' is used to form nouns which mean 'the amount needed to fill' • *spoonful.*

Comprehensive coverage of prefixes and suffixes help with learning new words and spelling

centi- **PREFIX** 'Centi-' is used to form words that have 'hundred' as part of their meaning • *centimetre.*

Spelling notes give help with tricky words

▷ SPELLING NOTE: *p*AL up with the princip*AL* and princip*AL* staff (princip*al*)

vii

Grammar Boxes

Throughout the dictionary there are 'grammar boxes' that contain rules and advice on English grammar, as well as helpful examples. In the list below, we have grouped these into useful families so that teachers and students can find all of the relevant information about particular aspects of English grammar.

Aa

THE INDEFINITE ARTICLE

The word *a* is known as the **indefinite article**. You use it before a singular noun to refer to any example of that noun, or to avoid being specific about which example you mean:

a school
a woman

The word *an* is used instead of *a* when a word begins with a vowel sound:

an elephant
an umpire

The word *an* is also used instead of *a* when words sound as though they begin with a vowel:

an hour
an honour

The word *a* is used instead of *an* when words that begin with a vowel sound as though they begin with a consonant:

a union
a European

Also look at the grammar box at **the**.

a or **an** **ADJECTIVE** The indefinite article 'a', or 'an' if the next sound is a vowel, is used when you are talking about one of something • *an apple* • *There was a car parked behind the hedge.*
▶ SEE GRAMMAR BOX ABOVE

a- or **an-** **PREFIX** ❶ When 'a-' comes before an adjective it adds the meaning 'without' or 'opposite to'. 'An-' is the form used before a vowel • *amoral.* ❷ When 'a-' comes at the beginning of certain words it adds the meaning 'towards' or 'in the state of' • *aback* • *asleep.*

aardvark, aardvarks **NOUN** an ant-eating African animal with a long snout.

● **WORD HISTORY:** from obsolete
● Afrikaans meaning 'earth pig'

aback **ADVERB** If you are taken aback, you are very surprised.

abacus, abacuses **NOUN** a frame with beads that slide along rods, used for counting.

abalone, abalones [*Said ab-a-**lone**-ee*] **NOUN** a shellfish which can be eaten.

abandon, abandons, abandoning, abandoned **VERB** ❶ If you abandon someone or something, you leave them or give them up for good ▷ **NOUN** ❷ If you do something with abandon, you do it in an uncontrolled way • *He began to laugh with abandon.*

▷ SPELLING NOTE: *an ELegant angEL (angel)*

A

B
C
D
E
F
G
H
I
J
K
L
M
N
O
P
Q
R
S
T
U
V
W
X
Y
Z

abandoned **ADJECTIVE**
abandonment **NOUN**
● **SIMILAR WORDS:** ❶ desert,
● forsake, leave

abate, abates, abating, abated **VERB**
If something abates, it becomes less
• *His anger abated.*

abattoir, abattoirs [*Said ab-a-twahr*]
NOUN a place where animals are
killed for meat.

abbey, abbeys **NOUN** a church with
buildings attached to it in which
monks or nuns live.

abbot, abbots **NOUN** the monk or
priest in charge of a monastery.

abbreviate, abbreviates,
abbreviating, abbreviated **VERB** To
abbreviate something is to make it
shorter.

abbreviation, abbreviations
NOUN a short form of a word or
phrase. An example is 'W', which is
short for 'West'.

abdicate, abdicates, abdicating,
abdicated **VERB** If a king or queen
abdicates, he or she gives up being a
king or queen. **abdication NOUN**

abdomen, abdomens **NOUN** the
front part of your body below your
chest, containing your stomach and
intestines. **abdominal ADJECTIVE**

abduct, abducts, abducting,
abducted **VERB** To abduct someone
is to take them away by force.
abduction NOUN

aberration, aberrations **NOUN**
something that is not normal or usual.

abet, abets, abetting, abetted **VERB** If
you abet someone, you help them to

do something • *You've aided and
abetted criminals to evade justice.*

abhor, abhors, abhorring, abhorred
VERB **FORMAL** If you abhor something,
you hate it. **abhorrence NOUN**
abhorrent ADJECTIVE

abide, abides, abiding, abided **VERB**
❶ If you can't abide something, you
dislike it very much. ❷ If you abide by
a decision or law, you act in
agreement with it.

abiding **ADJECTIVE** lasting for ever
• *an abiding interest in history.*

ability, abilities **NOUN** (PSHE) the
intelligence or skill needed to do
something • *the ability to swim.*
● **SIMILAR WORDS:** capability,
● proficiency, skill

abject **ADJECTIVE** very bad • *abject
failure.* **abjectly ADVERB**

ablaze **ADJECTIVE** on fire.

able, abler, ablest **ADJECTIVE** (PSHE)
❶ If you are able to do something,
you can do it. ❷ Someone who is able
is very clever or talented.

-able **SUFFIX** ❶ forming adjectives
which have the meaning 'capable of'
an action • *enjoyable* • *breakable.*
❷ forming adjectives with the
meaning 'able to' or 'causing'
• *comfortable* • *miserable.*
● **USAGE NOTE:** When you are
● writing, it is easy to confuse the
● *-able* suffix with its other form,
● *-ible.* It can be helpful to know that
● the *-able* spelling is much
● commoner than *-ible,* and that you
● cannot make new words using *-ible.*
● Occasionally, it is correct to use
● either ending

▷ SPELLING NOTE: *LEt's measure the angLE (angle)*

ably [Said **ay-blee**] **ADVERB** skilfully and successfully • *He is ably supported by the cast.*

abnormal **ADJECTIVE** not normal or usual. **abnormally** **ADVERB**

abnormality, abnormalities **NOUN** something that is not normal or usual.
  ● **SIMILAR WORDS:** irregularity,
  ● oddity, peculiarity

aboard **PREPOSITION OR ADVERB** on a ship or plane.

abode, abodes **NOUN** OLD-FASHIONED Your abode is the place where you live.

abolish, abolishes, abolishing, abolished **VERB** To abolish something is to do away with it • *the campaign to abolish hunting.* **abolition** **NOUN**
  ● **SIMILAR WORDS:** do away with,
  ● eliminate, end

abominable **ADJECTIVE** very unpleasant or shocking. **abominably** **ADVERB**

Aborigine, Aborigines [Said **ab-or-rij-in-ee**] **NOUN** someone descended from the people who lived in Australia before Europeans arrived. **Aboriginal** **ADJECTIVE**

abort, aborts, aborting, aborted **VERB** ❶ If a plan or activity is aborted, it is stopped before it is finished. ❷ If a pregnant woman aborts, the pregnancy ends too soon and the baby dies.

abortion, abortions **NOUN** If a woman has an abortion, the pregnancy is ended deliberately and the baby dies.

abortive **ADJECTIVE** unsuccessful

• *an abortive bank raid.*

abound, abounds, abounding, abounded **VERB** If things abound, there are very large numbers of them.

about **PREPOSITION OR ADVERB** ❶ of or concerning. ❷ approximately and not exactly ▷ **ADVERB** ❸ in different directions • *There were some bottles scattered about.* ▷ **ADJECTIVE** ❹ present or in a place • *Is Jane about?* ▷ **PHRASE** ❺ If you are **about to** do something, you are just going to do it.

above **PREPOSITION OR ADVERB** ❶ directly over or higher than something • *above the clouds.* ❷ greater than a level or amount • *The temperature didn't rise above freezing point.*

above board **ADJECTIVE** completely open and legal • *They assured me it was above board and properly licensed.*
  ● **WORD HISTORY:** an allusion to
  ● the difficulty of cheating at cards
  ● when other players can see your
  ● hands above the table

abrasion, abrasions **NOUN** ❶ an area where your skin has been broken. ❷ (GEOGRAPHY) erosion caused by the small stones, etc. carried by a river or glacier scraping against a surface.

abrasive **ADJECTIVE** ❶ An abrasive substance is rough and can be used to clean hard surfaces. ❷ Someone who is abrasive is unpleasant and rude.

abreast **ADJECTIVE** ❶ side by side • *youths riding their motorbikes four abreast.* ❷ If you keep abreast of a subject, you know all the most recent facts about it.

a
b
c
d
e
f
g
h
i
j
k
l
m
n
o
p
q
r
s
t
u
v
w
x
y
z

abroad ADVERB (GEOGRAPHY) in a foreign country.

abrupt ADJECTIVE ❶ sudden and quick • *His career came to an abrupt end.* ❷ not friendly or polite. **abruptly** ADVERB **abruptness** NOUN

abscess, abscesses [Said *ab-sess*] NOUN a painful swelling filled with pus.

abseiling NOUN Abseiling is the sport of going down a cliff or a tall building by sliding down ropes.

absent ADJECTIVE Something that is absent is not present in a place or situation. **absence** NOUN

absentee, absentees NOUN someone who is not present when they should be.

absent-minded ADJECTIVE forgetful.

absolute ADJECTIVE ❶ total and complete • *absolute honesty.* ❷ having total power • *the absolute ruler.* **absolutely** ADVERB

absolute zero NOUN (SCIENCE) Absolute zero is the lowest temperature possible, and is equal to o kelvins, or -273.15° centigrade.

absolve, absolves, absolving, absolved VERB To absolve someone of something is to state they are not to blame for it.

absorb, absorbs, absorbing, absorbed VERB (SCIENCE) If something absorbs liquid or gas, it soaks it up.
  ● SIMILAR WORDS: soak up, take in

absorbent ADJECTIVE Absorbent materials soak up liquid easily.

absorption NOUN ❶ the soaking up of a liquid. ❷ great interest in something • *my father's absorption in his business affairs.*

abstain, abstains, abstaining, abstained VERB ❶ If you abstain from something, you do not do it or have it • *The patients had to abstain from alcohol.* ❷ If you abstain in a vote, you do not vote. **abstention** NOUN
  ● SIMILAR WORDS: ❶ forbear,
  ● keep from, refrain

abstinence NOUN Abstinence is deliberately not doing something you enjoy.

abstract ADJECTIVE [Said *ab-strakt*] ❶ An abstract idea is based on thoughts and ideas rather than physical objects or events, for example 'bravery'. ❷ (ART) Abstract art is a style of art which uses shapes rather than images of people or objects. ❸ Abstract nouns refer to qualities or ideas rather than to physical objects, for example 'happiness' or 'a question'. **abstraction** NOUN

absurd ADJECTIVE ridiculous and stupid. **absurdly** ADVERB **absurdity** NOUN
  ● SIMILAR WORDS: ludicrous,
  ● preposterous, ridiculous

abundance NOUN Something that exists in abundance exists in large numbers • *an abundance of wildlife.*
  ● SIMILAR WORDS: plenty,
  ● profusion

abundant ADJECTIVE present in large quantities. **abundantly** ADVERB

abuse, abuses [Said ab-*yoose*]

▷ SPELLING NOTE: *Beautiful Elephants Are Usually Tiny (beautiful)*

NOUN ❶ cruel treatment of someone • *child abuse.* **❷** rude and unkind remarks directed towards someone. **❸** the wrong use of something • *an abuse of power* • *alcohol abuse.*
● **SIMILAR WORDS: ❶** ill-treatment, injury, maltreatment

abuse, abuses, abusing, abused [Said ab-**yooze**] **VERB ❶** If you abuse someone, you speak insultingly to them. **❷** To abuse someone also means to treat them cruelly. **❸** If you abuse something, you use it wrongly or for a bad purpose. **abuser NOUN**
● **SIMILAR WORDS: ❷** ill-treat, maltreat

abusive ADJECTIVE rude and unkind. **abusively ADVERB abusiveness NOUN**

abysmal [Said ab-**biz**-ml] **ADJECTIVE** very bad indeed • *an abysmal performance.* **abysmally ADVERB**

abyss, abysses **NOUN** a very deep hole.
● **WORD HISTORY:** from Greek *abussos* meaning 'bottomless'

acacia, acacias [Said a-**kay**-sha] **NOUN** a type of thorny shrub with small yellow or white flowers.

academic, academics **ADJECTIVE ❶** Academic work is work done in a school, college, or university ▷ **NOUN ❷** someone who teaches or does research in a college or university. **academically ADVERB**

academy, academies **NOUN ❶** a school or college, usually one that specializes in one particular subject • *the Royal Academy of Dramatic Art.* **❷** an organization of scientists,

artists, writers, or musicians.
● **WORD HISTORY:** from Greek *akadēmeia*, the name of the grove where Plato taught

a cappella ADJECTIVE OR ADVERB [MUSIC] without musical accompaniment • *We decided to sing it a cappella* • *an a cappella version of* My Way.
● **WORD HISTORY:** an Italian phrase meaning 'according to (the style of the) chapel'

accelerate, accelerates, accelerating, accelerated **VERB** To accelerate is to go faster.

acceleration NOUN the rate at which the speed of something is increasing.

accelerator, accelerators **NOUN** the pedal in a vehicle which you press to make it go faster.

accent, accents **NOUN ❶** a way of pronouncing a language • *She had an Australian accent.* **❷** a mark placed above or below a letter in some languages, which affects the way the letter is pronounced. **❸** [ENGLISH] stress placed on a particular word, syllable, or note • *In Icelandic the accent usually falls on the first syllable of a word.* **❹** an emphasis on something • *The accent is on action and special effects.*

accentuate, accentuates, accentuating, accentuated **VERB** To accentuate a feature of something is to make it more noticeable.

accept, accepts, accepting, accepted **VERB ❶** If you accept something, you say yes to it or take it from someone. **❷** If you accept a situation,

you realize that it cannot be changed • *He accepts criticism as part of his job.* ❸ If you accept a statement or story, you believe it is true • *The board accepted his explanation.* ❹ If a group accepts you, they treat you as one of the group. **acceptance NOUN**
● **WORD HISTORY:** from Latin *ad* meaning 'to' and *capere* meaning 'to take'

acceptable ADJECTIVE good enough to be accepted. **acceptably ADVERB**

access, accesses, accessing, accessed **NOUN** ❶ the right or opportunity to enter a place or to use something ▷ **VERB** ❷ If you access information from a computer, you get it.

accessible ADJECTIVE ❶ easily reached or seen • *The village was accessible by foot only.* ❷ easily understood or used • *guidebooks which present information in a clear and accessible style.* **accessibility NOUN**

accession NOUN A ruler's accession is the time when he or she becomes the ruler of a country.

accessory, accessories **NOUN** ❶ an extra part. ❷ someone who helps another person commit a crime.

accident, accidents **NOUN** ❶ an unexpected event in which people are injured or killed. ❷ Something that happens by accident happens by chance.

accidental ADJECTIVE happening by chance. **accidentally ADVERB**
● **SIMILAR WORDS:** inadvertent, unintentional, unplanned

acclaimed ADJECTIVE If someone

or something is acclaimed, they are praised enthusiastically.

accolade, accolades **NOUN FORMAL** great praise or an award given to someone.

accommodate, accommodates, accommodating, accommodated **VERB** ❶ If you accommodate someone, you provide them with a place to sleep, live, or work. ❷ If a place can accommodate a number of things or people, it has enough room for them.
● **USAGE NOTE:** *Accommodate* has two *c*s and two *m*s

accommodating ADJECTIVE willing to help and to adjust to new situations.

accommodation NOUN a place provided for someone to sleep, live, or work in.

accompaniment, accompaniments **NOUN** ❶ The accompaniment to a song is the music played to go with it. ❷ An accompaniment to something is another thing that comes with it • *Melon is a good accompaniment to cold meats.*

accompany, accompanies, accompanying, accompanied **VERB** ❶ If you accompany someone, you go with them. ❷ If one thing accompanies another, the two things exist at the same time • *severe pain accompanied by fever.* ❸ If you accompany a singer or musician, you play an instrument while they sing or play the main tune.

accomplice, accomplices **NOUN** a person who helps someone else to commit a crime.

accomplish, accomplishes, accomplishing, accomplished **VERB** If you accomplish something, you succeed in doing it.
  USAGE NOTE: The *com* part of
  accomplish can sound like *kum* or
  kom

accomplished ADJECTIVE very talented at something • *an accomplished cook.*

accomplishment, accomplishments **NOUN** Someone's accomplishments are the skills they have gained.

accord, accords, according, accorded **VERB** ❶ If you accord someone or something a particular treatment, you treat them in that way • *He was accorded a proper respect for his status.* ▷ **NOUN** ❷ agreement ▷ **PHRASE** ❸ If you do something **of your own accord**, you do it willingly and not because you have been forced to do it.

accordance PHRASE If you act **in accordance with** a rule or belief, you act in the way the rule or belief says you should.

according to PREPOSITION
❶ If something is true according to a particular person, that person says that it is true. ❷ If something is done according to a principle or plan, that principle or plan is used as the basis for it.

accordion, accordions **NOUN** a musical instrument like an expanding box. It is played by squeezing the two sides together while pressing the keys on it.

accost, accosts, accosting, accosted **VERB** If someone accosts you, especially someone you do not know, they come up and speak to you • *She says she is accosted when she goes shopping.*

account, accounts, accounting, accounted **NOUN** ❶ a written or spoken report of something. ❷ If you have a bank account, you can leave money in the bank and take it out when you need it ❸ IN PLURAL Accounts are records of money spent and received by a person or business ▷ **PHRASE** ❹ If you **take something into account**, you include it in your planning. ❺ **On account of** means because of ▷ **VERB** ❻ To account for something is to explain it • *This might account for her strange behaviour.* ❼ If something accounts for a particular amount of something, it is that amount • *The brain accounts for three per cent of body weight.*

accountable ADJECTIVE If you are accountable for something, you are responsible for it and have to explain your actions • *The committee is accountable to Parliament.*
accountability NOUN

accountancy NOUN the job of keeping or inspecting financial accounts.

accountant, accountants **NOUN** a person whose job is to keep or inspect financial accounts.

accounting NOUN the keeping and checking of financial accounts.

accrue, accrues, accruing, accrued **VERB** If money or interest accrues, it increases gradually.

a
b
c
d
e
f
g
h
i
j
k
l
m
n
o
p
q
r
s
t
u
v
w
x
y
z

accumulate, accumulates, accumulating, accumulated **VERB** If you accumulate things or they accumulate, they collect over a period of time.

accurate **ADJECTIVE** (SCIENCE) completely correct or precise. **accurately** **ADVERB** **accuracy** **NOUN**
- **SIMILAR WORDS:** correct, exact, precise

accuse, accuses, accusing, accused **VERB** If you accuse someone of doing something wrong, you say they have done it. **accusation** **NOUN** **accuser** **NOUN**

accustom, accustoms, accustoming, accustomed **VERB** If you accustom yourself to something new or different, you get used to it.

accustomed **ADJECTIVE** used to something.

ace, aces **NOUN** ❶ In a pack of cards, a card with a single symbol on it ▷ **ADJECTIVE** ❷ INFORMAL good or skilful • *My sister is an ace squash player.*

acerbic [Said as-**ser**-bik] **ADJECTIVE** FORMAL Acerbic remarks are harsh and bitter.

ache, aches, aching, ached **VERB** ❶ If you ache, you feel a continuous dull pain in a part of your body. ❷ If you are aching for something, you want it very much ▷ **NOUN** ❸ a continuous dull pain.

achieve, achieves, achieving, achieved **VERB** (PSHE) If you achieve something, you successfully do it or cause it to happen.

- **USAGE NOTE:** The *i* comes before the *e* in *achieve*
- **SIMILAR WORDS:** accomplish, attain, fulfil

achievement, achievements **NOUN** something you succeed in doing, especially after a lot of effort.

acid, acids **NOUN** (SCIENCE) ❶ a chemical liquid with a pH value of less than 7 and which turns litmus paper red. Strong acids can damage skin, cloth, and metal ▷ **ADJECTIVE** ❷ Acid tastes are sharp or sour. **acidic** **ADJECTIVE** **acidity** **NOUN**

acid rain **NOUN** (GEOGRAPHY) rain polluted by acid in the atmosphere which has come from factories.

acknowledge, acknowledges, acknowledging, acknowledged **VERB** ❶ If you acknowledge a fact or situation, you agree or admit it is true. ❷ If you acknowledge someone, you show that you have seen and recognized them. ❸ If you acknowledge a message, you tell the person who sent it that you have received it. **acknowledgment** or **acknowledgement** **NOUN**
- **USAGE NOTE:** *Acknowledgment* and *acknowledgement* are both correct spellings
- **SIMILAR WORDS:** ❶ accept, admit, grant

acne [Said ak-nee] **NOUN** lumpy spots that cover someone's face.

acorn, acorns **NOUN** the fruit of the oak tree, consisting of a pale oval nut in a cup-shaped base.

acoustic [Said a-**koo**-stik] **ADJECTIVE** ❶ relating to sound or hearing. ❷ An acoustic guitar is not made louder with an electric amplifier.

acoustics PLURAL NOUN The acoustics of a room are its structural features which are responsible for how clearly you can hear sounds made in it.

acquaintance, acquaintances NOUN someone you know slightly but not well.

acquainted ADJECTIVE If you are acquainted with someone, you know them slightly but not well.
● USAGE NOTE: You say that you are
● *acquainted with* someone

acquire, acquires, acquiring, acquired VERB If you acquire something, you obtain it.

acquisition, acquisitions NOUN something you have obtained.

acquit, acquits, acquitting, acquitted VERB ❶ If someone is acquitted of a crime, they have been tried in a court and found not guilty. ❷ If you acquit yourself well on a particular occasion, you behave or perform well. **acquittal** NOUN

acre, acres NOUN a unit for measuring areas of land. One acre is equal to 4840 square yards or about 4047 square metres.
● WORD HISTORY: from Old English
● *æcer* meaning 'field'

acrid ADJECTIVE sharp and bitter • *the acrid smell of burning plastic.*

acrimony [Said **ak**-rim-on-ee] NOUN FORMAL bitterness and anger. **acrimonious** ADJECTIVE

acrobat, acrobats NOUN an entertainer who performs gymnastic tricks. **acrobatic** ADJECTIVE **acrobatics** PLURAL NOUN
● WORD HISTORY: from Greek
● *akrobates* meaning 'someone who
● walks on tiptoe'

acronym, acronyms NOUN a word made up of the initial letters of a phrase. An example of an acronym is 'BAFTA', which stands for 'British Academy of Film and Television Arts'.

across PREPOSITION OR ADVERB ❶ going from one side of something to the other. ❷ on the other side of a road or river.

acrylic, acrylics [Said a-**kril**-lik] NOUN ❶ Acrylic is a type of man-made cloth. ❷ ART Acrylics, or acrylic paints, are thick artists' paints which can be used like oil paints or thinned down with water.

act, acts, acting, acted VERB ❶ If you act, you do something • *It would be irresponsible not to act swiftly.* ❷ If you act in a particular way, you behave in that way. ❸ If a person or thing acts as something else, it has the function or does the job of that thing • *She was able to act as an interpreter.* ❹ If you act in a play or film, you play a part ▷ NOUN ❺ a single thing someone does • *It was an act of disloyalty to the King.* ❻ An Act of Parliament is a law passed by the government. ❼ In a play, ballet, or opera, an act is one of the main parts it is divided into.
● SIMILAR WORDS: ❹ perform,
● play ❺ action, deed ❻ bill,
● decree, law

acting NOUN the profession of performing in plays or films.

action, actions NOUN ❶ the

A
B
C
D
E
F
G
H
I
J
K
L
M
N
O
P
Q
R
S
T
U
V
W
X
Y
Z

THE ACTIVE VOICE

The **active** voice and the **passive** voice are two different ways of presenting information in a sentence. When a sentence is written in the **active** voice, the subject of the verb is doing the action. This is the most natural way of presenting information:
Anna is feeding the cat.
The cat chased a mouse.

Also look at the grammar box at **passive**.

---

process of doing something. ❷ something that is done. ❸ a physical movement. ❹ In law, an action is a legal proceeding • *a libel action.*

activate, activates, activating, activated **VERB** To activate something is to make it start working.
● **SIMILAR WORDS:** set in motion,
● start

active ADJECTIVE ❶ (PE) full of energy. ❷ busy and hardworking. ❸ In grammar, a verb in the active voice is one where the subject does the action, rather than having it done to them. **actively ADVERB**
▶ SEE GRAMMAR BOX ABOVE

activist, activists **NOUN** a person who tries to bring about political and social change.

activity, activities **NOUN** ❶ Activity is a situation in which a lot of things are happening at the same time. ❷ (PE) something you do for pleasure • *sport and leisure activities.*

actor, actors **NOUN** a man or woman whose profession is acting.

actress, actresses **NOUN** a woman whose profession is acting.

actual ADJECTIVE real, rather than imaginary or guessed at • *That is the official figure: the actual figure is much higher.* **actually ADVERB**
● **USAGE NOTE:** Don't use *actual* or
● *actually* when they don't add
● anything to the meaning of a
● sentence. Say *it's a fact* rather than
● *it's an actual fact*

acumen NOUN the ability to make good decisions quickly • *business acumen.*

acupuncture NOUN the treatment of illness or pain by sticking small needles into specific places in a person's body.
● **WORD HISTORY:** from Latin *acus*
● meaning 'needle' added to
● 'puncture'

acute ADJECTIVE ❶ severe or intense • *an acute shortage of accommodation.* ❷ very intelligent • *an acute mind.* ❸ An acute angle is less than 90°. ❹ In French and some other languages, an acute accent is a line sloping upwards from left to right placed over a vowel to indicate a change in pronunciation, as in the word *café.*

ad, ads **NOUN** INFORMAL an advertisement.

AD You use 'AD' in dates to indicate the number of years after the birth of Jesus Christ.

▷ SPELLING NOTE: *The government licenSes Schnapps (licenses)*

ad- PREFIX 'Ad-' means 'near' or 'next to' • *adjoining* • *adverb*.

adage, adages [Said *ad-dij*] NOUN a saying that expresses some general truth about life.

adagio [Said *ad-ah-jee-oh*] ADVERB (MUSIC) In music, adagio is an instruction to play or sing something slowly.

adamant ADJECTIVE If you are adamant, you are determined not to change your mind. **adamantly** ADVERB

Adam's apple, Adam's apples NOUN the larynx, a lump at the front of the neck which is more obvious in men than in women and young boys.
● WORD HISTORY: from the story
● that a piece of the forbidden apple
● got stuck in Adam's throat

adapt, adapts, adapting, adapted VERB ❶ If you adapt to a new situation, you change so you can deal with it successfully. ❷ If you adapt something, you change it so it is suitable for a new purpose or situation. ❸ (SCIENCE) If a plant or animal adapts, it gradually changes over generations to become better suited to its environment. **adaptable** ADJECTIVE **adaptation** NOUN

adaptor, adaptors; *also spelt* **adapter** NOUN a type of electric plug which can be used to connect two or more plugs to one socket.

add, adds, adding, added VERB
❶ If you add something to a number of things, you put it with the things. ❷ If you add numbers together or add them up, you work out the total.

adder, adders NOUN a small poisonous snake.

addict, addicts NOUN (PSHE) someone who cannot stop taking harmful drugs. **addicted** ADJECTIVE **addiction** NOUN

addictive ADJECTIVE If a drug is addictive, the people who take it cannot stop.

addition, additions NOUN
❶ something that has been added to something else. ❷ (MATHS) the process of adding numbers together.
● SIMILAR WORDS: ❶ extra,
● supplement

additional ADJECTIVE extra or more • *They made the decision to take on additional staff.* **additionally** ADVERB

additive, additives NOUN something added to something else, usually in order to improve it. • *food additives.*

address, addresses, addressing, addressed NOUN ❶ the number of the house where you live, together with the name of the street and the town or village. ❷ a speech given to a group of people ▷ VERB ❸ If a letter is addressed to you, it has your name and address written on it. ❹ If you address a problem or task, you start to deal with it.

adept ADJECTIVE very skilful at doing something • *She is adept at motivating others.*

adequate ADJECTIVE enough in amount or good enough for a purpose • *an adequate diet.* **adequately** ADVERB **adequacy** NOUN

▷ SPELLING NOTE: *have a plEce of plE (piece)*

A
B
C
D
E
F
G
H
I
J
K
L
M
N
O
P
Q
R
S
T
U
V
W
X
Y
Z

● **SIMILAR WORDS:** enough,
● satisfactory, sufficient

adhere, adheres, adhering, adhered
VERB ❶ If one thing adheres to
another, it sticks firmly to it. ❷ If you
adhere to a rule or agreement, you do
what it says. ❸ If you adhere to an
opinion or belief, you firmly hold that
opinion or belief. **adherence NOUN**

adherent, adherents **NOUN** An
adherent of a belief is someone who
holds that belief.

adhesive, adhesives **NOUN** ❶ any
substance used to stick two things
together, for example glue
▷ **ADJECTIVE** ❷ Adhesive substances
are sticky and able to stick to things.

adjacent [Said ad-jay-sent]
ADJECTIVE FORMAL ❶ If two things
are adjacent, they are next to each
other • a hotel adjacent to the beach.
❷ (MATHS) Adjacent angles share

one side and have the same point
opposite to their bases.

adjective, adjectives **NOUN**
(ENGLISH) a word that adds to the
description given by a noun. For
example, in 'They live in a large white
Georgian house', 'large', 'white', and
'Georgian' are all adjectives.
adjectival ADJECTIVE
▶ SEE GRAMMAR BOX BELOW

adjoining **ADJECTIVE** If two rooms
are next to each other and are
connected, they are adjoining.

adjourn, adjourns, adjourning,
adjourned **VERB** ❶ If a meeting or
trial is adjourned, it stops for a time
• The case was adjourned until
September. ❷ If people adjourn to
another place, they go there together
after a meeting • We adjourned to the
lounge. **adjournment NOUN**

adjust, adjusts, adjusting, adjusted

WHAT IS AN ADJECTIVE?

An adjective is a word that tells you
something about a noun. Adjectives
are sometimes called "describing
words".

Adjectives may indicate how many of
a person or thing there are:

three men
some fish

Adjectives may describe feelings or
qualities:

a *happy* child
a *strange* girl

Adjectives may describe size, age,
temperature, or measurement:

a *large* envelope
an *old* jacket

Adjectives may indicate colour:

red socks
dark hair

Adjectives may indicate nationality or
origin:

my *Indian* cousin
a *northern* accent

Adjectives may indicate the material
from which something is made:

a *wooden* box
denim trousers

▷ SPELLING NOTE: *plaice* the fish has a glittering 'EYE' (I) (pla*i*ce)

VERB ❶ If you adjust something, you change its position or alter it in some other way. **❷** If you adjust to a new situation, you get used to it.
adjustment NOUN adjustable ADJECTIVE

ad-lib, ad-libs, ad-libbing, ad-libbed
VERB ❶ If you ad-lib, you say something that has not been prepared beforehand • *I ad-lib on radio but use a script on TV.* ▷ **NOUN ❷** a comment that has not been prepared beforehand.
● **WORD HISTORY:** short for Latin *ad*
● *libitum* meaning 'according to
● desire'

administer, administers, administering, administered **VERB**
❶ To administer an organization is to be responsible for managing it. **❷** To administer the law or administer justice is to put it into practice and apply it. **❸** If medicine is administered to someone, it is given to them.

administration, administrations
NOUN ❶ Administration is the work of organizing and supervising an organization. **❷** Administration is also the process of administering something • *the administration of criminal justice.* **❸** The administration is the group of people that manages an organization or a country.
administrative ADJECTIVE administrator NOUN

admirable ADJECTIVE very good and deserving to be admired.
admirably ADVERB

admiral, admirals **NOUN** the commander of a navy.
● **WORD HISTORY:** from Arabic *amir*
● meaning 'commander'

admiration NOUN a feeling of great liking and respect.

admire, admires, admiring, admired
VERB If you admire someone or something, you respect and approve of them. **admirer NOUN admiring ADJECTIVE admiringly ADVERB**

admission, admissions **NOUN ❶** If you are allowed admission to a place, you are allowed to go in. **❷** If you make an admission of something, you agree, often reluctantly, it is true • *It was an admission of guilt.*

admit, admits, admitting, admitted
VERB ❶ If you admit something, you agree, often reluctantly, it is true.
❷ To admit someone or something to a place or organization is to allow them to enter it. **❸** If you are admitted to hospital, you are taken there to stay until you are better.

admittedly ADVERB People use 'admittedly' to show that what they are saying contrasts with something they have already said or are about to say, and weakens their argument • *My studies, admittedly only from books, taught me much.*

adolescent, adolescents **NOUN**
(SCIENCE) a young person who is no longer a child but who is not yet an adult. **adolescence NOUN**
● **WORD HISTORY:** from Latin
● *adolescere* meaning 'to grow up'

adopt, adopts, adopting, adopted
VERB ❶ If you adopt a child that is not your own, you take him or her into your family as your son or daughter.
❷ FORMAL If you adopt a particular attitude, you start to have it.
adoption NOUN

▷ SPELLING NOTE: *I went to see (C) the doctor's new practiCe (practice)*

A
B
C
D
E
F
G
H
I
J
K
L
M
N
O
P
Q
R
S
T
U
V
W
X
Y
Z

adorable ADJECTIVE sweet and attractive.

adore, adores, adoring, adored VERB If you adore someone, you feel deep love and admiration for them. **adoration** NOUN

adorn, adorns, adorning, adorned VERB To adorn something is to decorate it • *The cathedral is adorned with statues.* **adornment** NOUN

adrenalin or **adrenaline** [Said a-**dren**-al-in] NOUN a substance which is produced by your body when you are angry, scared, or excited and which makes your heart beat faster.

adrift ADJECTIVE OR ADVERB If a boat is adrift or goes adrift, it floats on the water without being controlled.

adulation [Said ad-yoo-**lay**-shn] NOUN great admiration and praise for someone. **adulatory** ADJECTIVE

adult, adults NOUN a mature and fully developed person or animal.

adultery NOUN sexual intercourse between a married person and someone he or she is not married to. **adulterer** NOUN **adulterous** ADJECTIVE

adulthood NOUN the time during someone's life when they are an adult.

advance, advances, advancing, advanced VERB ❶ To advance is to move forward. ❷ To advance a cause or interest is to help it to be successful. ❸ If you advance someone a sum of money, you lend it to them ▷ NOUN ❹ Advance in something is progress in it • *scientific advance.* ❺ a sum of money lent to someone ▷ ADJECTIVE ❻ happening

before an event • *The event received little advance publicity.* ▷ PHRASE ❼ If you do something **in advance**, you do it before something else happens • *We booked the room well in advance.*
- SIMILAR WORDS:
- ❹ development, progress

advantage, advantages NOUN ❶ a benefit or something that puts you in a better position ▷ PHRASE ❷ If you **take advantage of** someone, you treat them unfairly for your own benefit. ❸ If you **take advantage of** something, you make use of it.

advantageous ADJECTIVE likely to benefit you in some way • *an advantageous marriage.*

advent NOUN ❶ The advent of something is its start or its coming into existence • *The advent of the submarine changed naval warfare.* ❷ Advent is the season just before Christmas in the Christian calendar.

adventure, adventures NOUN a series of events that are unusual and exciting.

adventurer, adventurers NOUN someone who enjoys doing dangerous and exciting things.

adventurous ADJECTIVE willing to take risks and do new and exciting things. **adventurously** ADVERB

adverb, adverbs NOUN (ENGLISH) a word that adds information about a verb or a following adjective or other adverb, for example, 'slowly', 'now', and 'here' which say how, when, or where something is done. **adverbial** ADJECTIVE
▶ SEE GRAMMAR BOX ON PAGE 15

▷ SPELLING NOTE: *You must practiSe your Ss (practise)*

WHAT IS AN ADVERB?

An adverb is a word that gives information about a verb. Many adverbs end with the letters -ly.

Adverbs of manner answer the question "how?":
*She runs **quickly**.*
*She sings **badly**.*

Adverbs of place answer the question "where?":
*We travelled **northwards**.*
*I live **here**.*

Adverbs of time answer the question "when?":
*You must stop **immediately**.*

*I arrived **yesterday**.*

Adverbs of degree answer the question "to what extent?":
*I **really** hope you will stay.*
*I play golf **fairly** often.*

Adverbs of frequency answer the question "how often?":
*We **sometimes** meet for lunch.*
*You **never** answer my questions.*

Sometimes adverbs can refer to the whole sentence rather than just the verb:
***Fortunately**, she was not badly hurt.*

adversary, adversaries *[Said ad-ver-sar-ee]* NOUN someone who is your enemy or who opposes what you are doing.

adverse ADJECTIVE not helpful to you or opposite to what you want or need • *The return flight was delayed by adverse weather conditions.* **adversely** ADVERB

adversity, adversities NOUN a time of danger or difficulty.

advert, adverts NOUN INFORMAL an advertisement.

advertise, advertises, advertising, advertised VERB (ENGLISH) ❶ If you advertise something, you tell people about it in a newspaper or poster, or on TV. ❷ To advertise is to make an announcement in a newspaper or poster, or on TV. **advertiser** NOUN **advertising** NOUN

advertisement, advertisements *[Said ad-ver-tiss-ment]* NOUN

(ENGLISH) an announcement about something in a newspaper or poster, or on TV.
● **SIMILAR WORDS:** ad, advert,
● commercial

advice NOUN a suggestion from someone about what you should do.
● **USAGE NOTE:** The noun *advice* is
● spelt with a 'c' and the verb *advise*
● is spelt with an 's'
● **SIMILAR WORDS:** counsel,
● guidance, suggestion

advisable ADJECTIVE sensible and likely to achieve the result you want • *It is advisable to buy the visa before travelling.* **advisably** ADVERB **advisability** NOUN

advise, advises, advising, advised VERB ❶ If you advise someone to do something, you tell them you think they should do it. ❷ FORMAL If you advise someone of something, you inform them of it. **advisory** ADJECTIVE

a
b
c
d
e
f
g
h
i
j
k
l
m
n
o
p
q
r
s
t
u
v
w
x
y
z

▷ SPELLING NOTE: *pAL up with the principAL and principAL staff (principal)*

A
B
C
D
E
F
G
H
I
J
K
L
M
N
O
P
Q
R
S
T
U
V
W
X
Y
Z

● **USAGE NOTE:** The verb *advise* is
● spelt with an '*s*' and the noun
● *advice* is spelt with a '*c*'
● **SIMILAR WORDS:** ❶ counsel,
● recommend, suggest

adviser, advisers **NOUN** a person
whose job is to give advice.

advocate, advocates, advocating,
advocated **VERB** ❶ If you advocate a
course of action or plan, you support it
publicly ▷ **NOUN** ❷ An advocate of
something is someone who supports
it publicly. ❸ FORMAL a lawyer who
represents clients in court. **advocacy**
NOUN

aerial, aerials [*Said air-ee-al*]
ADJECTIVE ❶ Aerial means
happening in the air • *aerial combat*.
▷ **NOUN** ❷ a piece of wire for
receiving television or radio signals.

aerial top dressing NOUN In
Australia and New Zealand, the
spreading of fertilizer from an aeroplane
onto land in remote country areas.

aero- PREFIX 'Aero-' means involving
the air, the atmosphere, or aircraft
• *aerobatics*.

aerobics NOUN a type of fast
physical exercise, which increases the
oxygen in your blood and strengthens
your heart and lungs. **aerobic**
ADJECTIVE

aerodynamic ADJECTIVE having
a streamlined shape that moves easily
through the air.

aeroplane, aeroplanes **NOUN** a
vehicle with wings and engines that
enable it to fly.

aerosol, aerosols **NOUN** (SCIENCE) a
small metal container in which liquid

is kept under pressure so that it can be
forced out as a spray.
● **USAGE NOTE:** *Aerosol* starts with
● *aer* and not with *air*

aerospace ADJECTIVE involved in
making and designing aeroplanes and
spacecraft.

aesthetic or **esthetic** [*Said
eess-thet-ik*] **ADJECTIVE** (D & T)
FORMAL relating to the appreciation of
beauty or art. **aesthetically ADVERB**
aesthetics NOUN

afar NOUN LITERARY From afar means
from a long way away.

affable ADJECTIVE pleasant and
easy to talk to. **affably ADVERB**
affability NOUN

affair, affairs **NOUN** ❶ an event or
series of events • *The funeral was a sad
affair.* ❷ To have an affair is to have a
secret sexual or romantic relationship,
especially when one of the people is
married ❸ IN PLURAL Your affairs are
your private and personal life • *Why
had he meddled in her affairs?*

affect, affects, affecting, affected
VERB ❶ If something affects you, it
influences you in some way.
❷ FORMAL If you affect a particular
way of behaving, you behave in that
way • *He affected an Italian accent.*
● **USAGE NOTE:** Do not confuse the
● spelling of the verb *affect* with the
● noun *effect*. Something that *affects*
● you has an *effect* on you

affectation, affectations **NOUN** An
affectation is behaviour that is not
genuine but is put on to impress
people.

affection, affections **NOUN** ❶ a

feeling of love and fondness for someone ❷ IN PLURAL Your affections are feelings of love you have for someone.

affectionate ADJECTIVE full of fondness for someone • *an affectionate embrace.* **affectionately** ADVERB

affiliate, affiliates, affiliating, affiliated VERB If a group affiliates itself to another, larger group, it forms a close association with it • *organizations affiliated to the ANC.* **affiliation** NOUN

affinity, affinities NOUN a close similarity or understanding between two things or people • *There are affinities between the two poets.*

affirm, affirms, affirming, affirmed VERB If you affirm an idea or belief, you clearly indicate your support for it • *We affirm our commitment to broadcast quality programmes.* **affirmation** NOUN

affirmative ADJECTIVE An affirmative word or gesture is one that means yes.

afflict, afflicts, afflicting, afflicted VERB If illness or pain afflicts someone, they suffer from it • *She was afflicted by depression.* **affliction** NOUN

affluent ADJECTIVE having a lot of money and possessions. **affluence** NOUN

afford, affords, affording, afforded VERB ❶ If you can afford to do something, you have enough money or time to do it. ❷ If you cannot afford something to happen, it would be harmful or embarrassing for you if it happened • *We cannot afford to be complacent.*

affordable ADJECTIVE If something is affordable, most people have enough money to buy it • *the availability of affordable housing.*

affray, affrays NOUN FORMAL a noisy and violent fight.

affront, affronts, affronting, affronted VERB ❶ If you are affronted by something, you are insulted and angered by it ▷ NOUN ❷ something that is an insult • *Our prisons are an affront to civilized society.*
● **USAGE NOTE:** Notice that *affront*,
● the noun, is followed by *to*

afield ADVERB Far afield means a long way away • *competitors from as far afield as Russia and China.*

afloat ADVERB OR ADJECTIVE ❶ floating on water. ❷ successful and making enough money • *Companies are struggling hard to stay afloat.*

afoot ADJECTIVE OR ADVERB happening or being planned, especially secretly • *Plans are afoot to build a new museum.*

afraid ADJECTIVE ❶ If you are afraid, you are very frightened. ❷ If you are afraid something might happen, you are worried it might happen.
● **SIMILAR WORDS:** ❶ fearful,
● frightened, scared

afresh ADVERB again and in a new way • *The couple moved abroad to start life afresh.*

Africa NOUN Africa is the second

a
b
c
d
e
f
g
h
i
j
k
l
m
n
o
p
q
r
s
t
u
v
w
x
y
z

largest continent. It is almost surrounded by sea, with the Atlantic on its west side, the Mediterranean to the north and the Indian Ocean and the Red Sea to the east.

African, Africans **ADJECTIVE**
❶ belonging or relating to Africa
▷ **NOUN ❷** someone, especially a Black person, who comes from Africa.

African-American, African-Americans **NOUN** an American whose ancestors came from Africa.

Afrikaans [Said af-rik-**ahns**] **NOUN** a language spoken in South Africa, similar to Dutch.

Afrikaner, Afrikaners **NOUN** a white South African with Dutch ancestors.

aft ADVERB OR ADJECTIVE towards the back of a ship or boat.

after PREPOSITION OR ADVERB
❶ later than a particular time, date, or event. **❷** behind and following someone or something • *They ran after her.*
● **SIMILAR WORDS: ❶** afterwards,
● following, later

afterlife NOUN The afterlife is a life some people believe begins when you die.

aftermath, aftermaths **NOUN** The aftermath of a disaster is the situation that comes after it.

afternoon, afternoons **NOUN** the part of the day between noon and about six o'clock.

aftershave NOUN a pleasant-smelling liquid men put on their faces after shaving.

afterthought, afterthoughts **NOUN** something you do or say as an addition to something else you have already done or said.

afterwards ADVERB after an event or time.

again ADVERB ❶ happening one more time • *He looked forward to becoming a father again.* **❷** returning to the same state or place as before • *there and back again.*
● **SIMILAR WORDS: ❶** anew, once
● more

against PREPOSITION ❶ touching and leaning on • *He leaned against the wall.* **❷** in opposition to • *the Test match against England.* **❸** in preparation for or in case of something • *precautions against fire.* **❹** in comparison with • *The pound is now at its lowest rate against the dollar.*

age, ages, ageing or aging, aged **NOUN**
❶ The age of something or someone is the number of years they have lived or existed. **❷** Age is the quality of being old • *a wine capable of improving with age.* **❸** a particular period in history • *the Iron Age.* **❹** IN PLURAL INFORMAL Ages means a very long time • *He's been talking for ages.*
▷ **VERB ❺** To age is to grow old or to appear older.
● **USAGE NOTE:** *Ageing* and *aging*
● are both correct spellings

aged [rhymes with **raged**] **ADJECTIVE** having a particular age • *people aged 16 to 24.*

aged [Said **ay**-dgid] **ADJECTIVE** very old • *an aged invalid.*
● **SIMILAR WORDS:** elderly, old

agency, agencies **NOUN** an

organization or business which provides certain services • *a detective agency.*

agenda, agendas NOUN a list of items to be discussed at a meeting.

agent, agents NOUN ❶ someone who arranges work or business for other people, especially actors or singers. ❷ someone who works for their country's secret service.

aggravate, aggravates, aggravating, aggravated VERB ❶ To aggravate a bad situation is to make it worse. ❷ INFORMAL If someone or something aggravates you, they make you annoyed. **aggravating** ADJECTIVE **aggravation** NOUN
  ● USAGE NOTE: Some people think
  ● that using *aggravate* to mean
  ● 'annoy' is wrong

aggregate, aggregates NOUN a total that is made up of several smaller amounts.

aggression NOUN violent and hostile behaviour.

aggressive ADJECTIVE full of hostility and violence. **aggressively** ADVERB **aggressiveness** NOUN
  ● SIMILAR WORDS: belligerent,
  ● hostile

aggressor, aggressors NOUN a person or country that starts a fight or a war.

aggrieved ADJECTIVE upset and angry about the way you have been treated.

aghast [Said a-*gast*] ADJECTIVE shocked and horrified.

agile ADJECTIVE (PE) able to move quickly and easily • *He is as agile as a cat.* **agilely** ADVERB **agility** NOUN

agitate, agitates, agitating, agitated VERB ❶ If you agitate for something, you campaign energetically to get it. ❷ If something agitates you, it worries you. **agitation** NOUN **agitator** NOUN

agnostic, agnostics NOUN someone who believes we cannot know definitely whether God exists or not. **agnosticism** NOUN
  ● WORD HISTORY: from Greek
  ● *agnōstos* meaning 'unknown'

ago ADVERB in the past • *She bought her flat three years ago.*

agog ADJECTIVE excited and eager to know more about an event or situation • *She was agog to hear his news.*

agonizing or **agonising** ADJECTIVE extremely painful, either physically or mentally • *an agonizing decision.*

agony NOUN very great physical or mental pain.
  ● SIMILAR WORDS: pain, suffering,
  ● torment

agoraphobia [Said a-gor-a-*foe*-bee-a] NOUN the fear of open spaces. **agoraphobic** ADJECTIVE
  ● WORD HISTORY: from Greek
  ● *agora* meaning 'market place' +
  ● *phobia*

agrarian [Said ag-*rare*-ee-an] ADJECTIVE FORMAL relating to farming and agriculture • *agrarian economies.*

agree, agrees, agreeing, agreed VERB ❶ If you agree with someone, you

▷ SPELLING NOTE: *Rhythmical Hounds Yap To Heavy Music (rhythm)*

a
b
c
d
e
f
g
h
i
j
k
l
m
n
o
p
q
r
s
t
u
v
w
x
y
z

A
B
C
D
E
F
G
H
I
J
K
L
M
N
O
P
Q
R
S
T
U
V
W
X
Y
Z

have the same opinion as them. ❷ If you agree to do something, you say you will do it. ❸ If two stories or totals agree, they are the same. ❹ Food that doesn't agree with you makes you ill.
● **SIMILAR WORDS:** ❶ be of the
● same opinion, concur ❷ comply,
● consent

agreeable ADJECTIVE ❶ pleasant or enjoyable. ❷ If you are agreeable to something, you are willing to allow it or to do it • *She was agreeable to the project.* **agreeably ADVERB**

agreement, agreements **NOUN**
❶ a decision that has been reached by two or more people. ❷ Two people who are in agreement have the same opinion about something.

agriculture NOUN (HISTORY)
Agriculture is farming. **agricultural ADJECTIVE**

aground ADVERB If a boat runs aground, it becomes stuck in a shallow stretch of water.

ahead ADVERB ❶ in front • *He looked ahead.* ❷ more advanced than someone or something else • *We are five years ahead of the competition.* ❸ in the future • *I haven't had time to think far ahead.*

aid, aids, aiding, aided **NOUN** ❶ Aid is money, equipment, or services provided for people in need • *food and medical aid.* ❷ something that makes a task easier • *teaching aids.* ▷ **VERB** ❸ FORMAL If you aid a person or an organization, you help or support them.

aide, aides **NOUN** an assistant to an important person, especially in the government or the army • *one of the*

Prime Minister's closest aides.

AIDS NOUN a disease which destroys the body's natural system of immunity to diseases. AIDS is an abbreviation for 'acquired immune deficiency syndrome'.

ailing ADJECTIVE ❶ sick or ill, and not getting better. ❷ getting into difficulties, especially with money • *an ailing company.*

ailment, ailments **NOUN** a minor illness.

aim, aims, aiming, aimed **VERB** ❶ If you aim an object or weapon at someone or something, you point it at them. ❷ If you aim to do something, you are planning or hoping to do it ▷ **NOUN** ❸ Your aim is what you intend to achieve. ❹ If you take aim, you point an object or weapon at someone or something.
● **SIMILAR WORDS:** ❶ point
● ❷ intend, mean, plan ❸ goal,
● intention, objective

aimless ADJECTIVE having no clear purpose or plan. **aimlessly ADVERB aimlessness NOUN**

air, airs, airing, aired **NOUN** ❶ Air is the mixture of oxygen and other gases which we breathe and which forms the earth's atmosphere. ❷ An air someone or something has is the impression they give • *an air of defiance.* ❸ 'Air' is used to refer to travel in aircraft • *I have to travel by air a great deal.* ▷ **VERB** ❹ If you air your opinions, you talk about them to other people.

airborne ADJECTIVE in the air and flying • *The wreckage was spotted by airborne searchers.*

▷ SPELLING NOTE: *there's SAND in my SANDwich (sandwich)*

air-conditioning NOUN a system of providing cool, clean air in buildings. **air-conditioned** ADJECTIVE

aircraft NOUN any vehicle which can fly.

airfield, airfields NOUN an open area of ground with runways where small aircraft take off and land.

air force, air forces NOUN the part of a country's armed services that fights using aircraft.

air gun, air guns NOUN a gun which uses air pressure to fire pellets.

air hostess, air hostesses NOUN a woman whose job is to look after passengers on an aircraft.

airless ADJECTIVE having no wind or fresh air.

airlift, airlifts NOUN an operation to move people or goods by air, especially in an emergency.

airline, airlines NOUN a company which provides air travel.

airliner, airliners NOUN a large passenger plane.

airmail NOUN the system of sending letters and parcels by air.

airman, airmen NOUN a man who serves in his country's air force.

airport, airports NOUN a place where people go to catch planes.

air quality NOUN (GEOGRAPHY) a measurement of how much pollution there is in the air.

air raid, air raids NOUN an attack by enemy aircraft, in which bombs are dropped onto the ground.

air resistance NOUN (SCIENCE) the friction which slows down something moving through the air.
● SIMILAR WORDS: drag

airship, airships NOUN a large, light aircraft, consisting of a rigid balloon filled with gas and powered by an engine, with a passenger compartment underneath.

airstrip, airstrips NOUN a stretch of land that has been cleared for aircraft to take off and land.

airtight ADJECTIVE not letting air in or out.

airy, airier, airiest ADJECTIVE full of fresh air and light. **airily** ADVERB

aisle, aisles [rhymes with **mile**] NOUN a long narrow gap that people can walk along between rows of seats or shelves.

ajar ADJECTIVE A door or window that is ajar is slightly open.

akin ADJECTIVE FORMAL similar • The taste is akin to veal.

alabaster NOUN a type of smooth stone used for making ornaments.

alacrity NOUN FORMAL eager willingness • He seized this offer with alacrity.

alarm, alarms, alarming, alarmed NOUN ❶ a feeling of fear and worry • The cat sprang back in alarm. ❷ an automatic device used to warn people of something • a car alarm. ▷ VERB ❸ If something alarms you, it makes you worried and anxious. **alarming** ADJECTIVE

a
b
c
d
e
f
g
h
i
j
k
l
m
n
o
p
q
r
s
t
u
v
w
x
y
z

▷ SPELLING NOTE: On WEDNESday Wayne WED NESta (Wednesday)

A
B
C
D
E
F
G
H
I
J
K
L
M
N
O
P
Q
R
S
T
U
V
W
X
Y
Z

alas ADVERB unfortunately or regrettably • *But, alas, it would not be true.*

Albanian, Albanians **ADJECTIVE** ❶ belonging or relating to Albania ▷ **NOUN** ❷ someone who comes from Albania. ❸ Albanian is the main language spoken in Albania.

albatross, albatrosses **NOUN** a large white sea bird.

albeit [Said awl-*bee*-it] **CONJUNCTION** FORMAL although • *He was making progress, albeit slowly.*

albino, albinos **NOUN** a person or animal with very white skin, white hair, and pink eyes.

album, albums **NOUN** ❶ a CD, cassette, or record with a number of songs on it. ❷ a book in which you keep a collection of things such as photographs or stamps.

alchemy [Said al-*kem*-ee] **NOUN** a medieval science that attempted to change ordinary metals into gold. **alchemist NOUN**

alcheringa [Said al-cher-*ring*-ga] **NOUN** Alcheringa is the same as Dreamtime.

alcohol NOUN Alcohol is any drink that can make people drunk; also the colourless flammable liquid found in these drinks, produced by fermenting sugar.

alcoholic, alcoholics **ADJECTIVE** ❶ An alcoholic drink contains alcohol ▷ **NOUN** ❷ someone who is addicted to alcohol. **alcoholism NOUN**

alcove, alcoves **NOUN** an area of a room which is set back slightly from the main part.
● **WORD HISTORY:** from Arabic
● *al-qubbah* meaning 'arch'

ale NOUN a type of beer.

alert, alerts, alerting, alerted **ADJECTIVE** ❶ paying full attention to what is happening • *The criminal was spotted by an alert member of the public.* ▷ **NOUN** ❷ a situation in which people prepare themselves for danger • *The troops were on a war alert.* ▷ **VERB** ❸ If you alert someone to a problem or danger, you warn them of it. **alertness NOUN**
● **SIMILAR WORDS:** ❶ attentive,
● vigilant, watchful

A level, A levels **NOUN** an advanced exam taken by students in many British schools and colleges, usually following GCSEs.

algae [Said al-*jee*] **PLURAL NOUN** plants that grow in water or on damp surfaces.

algebra NOUN a branch of mathematics in which symbols and letters are used instead of numbers to express relationships between quantities. **algebraic ADJECTIVE**
● **WORD HISTORY:** from Arabic
● *al-jabr* meaning 'reunion'

Algerian, Algerians **ADJECTIVE** ❶ belonging or relating to Algeria ▷ **NOUN** ❷ someone who comes from Algeria.

alias, aliases [Said *ay*-lee-ass] **NOUN** a false name • *Leonard Nimoy, alias Mr Spock.*

alibi, alibis [Said al-li-*bye*] **NOUN** An alibi is evidence proving you were somewhere else at the time when a crime was committed.

alien, aliens [Said *ay-lee-an*]
ADJECTIVE ❶ not normal to you • *a
totally alien culture.* ▷ **NOUN
❷** someone who is not a citizen of the
country in which he or she lives. **❸** In
science fiction, an alien is a creature
from outer space.

alienate, alienates, alienating,
alienated **VERB** If you alienate
someone, you do something that
makes them stop being sympathetic
to you • *The Council's approach
alienated many local residents.*
alienation NOUN

alight, alights, alighting, alighted
ADJECTIVE ❶ Something that is
alight is burning ▷ **VERB ❷** If a bird
or insect alights somewhere, it lands
there. **❸** FORMAL When passengers
alight from a vehicle, they get out of it
at the end of a journey.

align, aligns, aligning, aligned [Said
a-line] **VERB ❶** If you align yourself
with a particular group, you support
them. **❷** If you align things, you place
them in a straight line. **alignment
NOUN**

alike ADJECTIVE ❶ Things that are
alike are similar in some way
▷ **ADVERB ❷** If people or things are
treated alike, they are treated in a
similar way.

alimony [Said *al-li-mon-ee*] **NOUN**
money someone has to pay regularly
to their wife or husband after they are
divorced.

alive ADJECTIVE ❶ living. **❷** lively
and active.
● **SIMILAR WORDS: ❶** animate,
● living

alkali, alkalis [Said *al-kal-eye*] **NOUN**
(SCIENCE) a chemical substance that
turns litmus paper blue. **alkaline
ADJECTIVE alkalinity NOUN**

alkali metal NOUN (SCIENCE) a
metal such as sodium or potassium
that forms an alkaline solution in
water and belongs to group 1A of the
periodic table.

alkane, alkanes **NOUN** (SCIENCE) a
type of hydrocarbon with the general
formula C_nH_{2n+2} that has no multiple
bonds between carbon atoms.

alkene, alkenes **NOUN** (SCIENCE) a
type of hydrocarbon with the general
formula C_nH_{2n} that has a double bond
between two carbon atoms.

**all ADJECTIVE, PRONOUN, OR
ADVERB ❶** used when referring to
the whole of something • *Why did he
have to say all that?* • *She managed to
finish it all.* ▷ **ADVERB ❷** 'All' is also
used when saying the two sides in a
game or contest have the same score
• *The final score was six points all.*

Allah PROPER NOUN the Muslim
name for God.

allay, allays, allaying, allayed **VERB** To
allay someone's fears or doubts is to
stop them feeling afraid or doubtful.

allege, alleges, alleging, alleged [Said
a-lej] **VERB** If you allege that
something is true, you say it is true
but do not provide any proof • *It is
alleged that she died as a result of
neglect.* **allegation NOUN alleged
ADJECTIVE**

allegiance, allegiances [Said
al-lee-jenss] **NOUN** loyal support for a
person or organization.

a
b
c
d
e
f
g
h
i
j
k
l
m
n
o
p
q
r
s
t
u
v
w
x
y
z

▷ SPELLING NOTE: *Elaine and Emily shout EE when they mEEt to grEEt each other (-ee-)*

allegory, allegories [Said al-li-gor-ee] **NOUN** a piece of writing or art in which the characters and events are symbols for something else. Allegories usually make some moral, religious, or political point. For example, George Orwell's novel 'Animal Farm' is an allegory in that the animals who revolt in the farmyard are symbols of the political leaders in the Russian Revolution.

allegro ADVERB (MUSIC) In music, allegro is an instruction to play or sing something quickly.

allergy, allergies [Said al-er-jee] **NOUN** a sensitivity someone has to something, so that they become ill when they eat it or touch it • an allergy to cows' milk.

alleviate, alleviates, alleviating, alleviated **VERB** To alleviate pain or a problem is to make it less severe • measures to alleviate poverty. **alleviation NOUN**

alley, alleys **NOUN** a narrow passage between buildings.

alliance, alliances **NOUN** a group of people, organizations, or countries working together for similar aims.
● **SIMILAR WORDS:** association,
● league, union

alligator, alligators **NOUN** a large animal, similar to a crocodile.
● **WORD HISTORY:** from Spanish el
● lagarto meaning 'lizard'

alliteration NOUN (ENGLISH) LITERARY the use of several words together which all begin with the same sound, for example 'around the ragged rock the ragged rascal ran'. **alliterative ADJECTIVE**

allocate, allocates, allocating, allocated **VERB** If you allocate something, you decide it should be given to a person or place, or used for a particular purpose • funds allocated for nursery education. **allocation NOUN**

allot, allots, allotting, allotted **VERB** If something is allotted to you, it is given to you as your share • Space was allotted for visitors' cars.

allotment, allotments **NOUN** ❶ a piece of land which people can rent to grow vegetables on. ❷ a share of something.

allow, allows, allowing, allowed **VERB** ❶ If you allow something, you say it is all right or let it happen. ❷ If you allow a period of time or an amount of something, you set it aside for a particular purpose • Allow four hours for the paint to dry. **allowable ADJECTIVE**
● **USAGE NOTE:** Do not confuse the
● spellings of the past tense form
● allowed and the adverb aloud, which
● sound the same

allowance, allowances **NOUN** ❶ money given regularly to someone for a particular purpose • a petrol allowance. ▷ **PHRASE** ❷ If you **make allowances** for something, you take it into account • The school made allowances for Muslim cultural customs.

alloy, alloys **NOUN** a mixture of two or more metals.

all right or **alright ADJECTIVE** ❶ If something is all right, it is acceptable. ❷ If someone is all right, they are safe and not harmed. ❸ You say 'all right' to agree to something.

allude, alludes, alluding, alluded
VERB If you allude to something, you refer to it in an indirect way.
● **USAGE NOTE:** You *allude to*
● something. Do not confuse *allude*
● with *elude*

allure NOUN The allure of something is an exciting quality that makes it attractive • *the allure of foreign travel.*
alluring ADJECTIVE

allusion, allusions **NOUN** (ENGLISH) an indirect reference to or comment about something • *English literature is full of classical allusions.*

alluvium NOUN (GEOGRAPHY)
Alluvium is a fine, fertile soil consisting of mud and silt that has been deposited by flowing water on a plain or at the mouth of a river.
alluvial ADJECTIVE

ally, allies, allying, allied **NOUN** ❶ a person or country that helps and supports another ▷ **VERB** ❷ If you ally yourself with someone, you agree to help and support each other.
● **SIMILAR WORDS:** ❶ friend,
● helper, partner ❷ associate, join,
● unite

almanac, almanacs **NOUN** a book published every year giving information about a particular subject.

almighty ADJECTIVE ❶ very great or serious • *I've just had an almighty row with the chairman.* ▷ **PROPER NOUN** ❷ The Almighty is another name for God.

almond, almonds **NOUN** a pale brown oval nut.

almost ADVERB very nearly • *Prices have almost doubled.*

● **SIMILAR WORDS:** just about,
● nearly, practically

alms PLURAL NOUN OLD-FASHIONED
Alms are gifts of money, food, or clothing to poor people.

aloft ADVERB up in the air or in a high position • *He held aloft the trophy.*

alone ADJECTIVE OR ADVERB not with other people or things • *He just wanted to be alone.*
● **SIMILAR WORDS:** by oneself,
● solitary, unaccompanied

along PREPOSITION ❶ moving, happening, or existing continuously from one end to the other of something, or at various points beside it • *Put rivets along the top edge.*
▷ **ADVERB** ❷ moving forward • *We marched along, singing as we went.*
❸ with someone • *Why could she not take her along?* ▷ **PHRASE** ❹ **All along** means from the beginning of a period of time right up to now • *You've known that all along.*

alongside PREPOSITION OR ADVERB ❶ next to something • *They had a house in the park alongside the river.* ▷ **PREPOSITION** ❷ If you work alongside other people, you are working in the same place and cooperating with them • *He was thrilled to work alongside Robert De Niro.*
● **USAGE NOTE:** Do not use *of* after
● *alongside*

aloof ADJECTIVE distant from someone or something • *She always stayed aloof from public life.*

aloud ADVERB When you read or speak aloud, you speak loudly enough for other people to hear you.

▷ SPELLING NOTE: *King IAn went to ParlIAment in a carrIAge for his marrIAge (-ia-)*

A
B
C
D
E
F
G
H
I
J
K
L
M
N
O
P
Q
R
S
T
U
V
W
X
Y
Z

USAGE NOTE: Do not confuse the spellings of *aloud* and *allowed*, the past tense form of *allow*.

alphabet, alphabets NOUN (LIBRARY) a set of letters in a fixed order that is used in writing a language. **alphabetical** ADJECTIVE **alphabetically** ADVERB

alpine ADJECTIVE existing in or relating to high mountains • *alpine flowers*.

already ADVERB having happened before the present time or earlier than expected • *She has already gone to bed.*

alright another spelling of **all right**.
USAGE NOTE: Some people think that *all right* is the only correct spelling and that *alright* is wrong

Alsatian, Alsatians [Said al-**say**-shn] NOUN a large wolflike dog.

also ADVERB in addition to something that has just been mentioned.

altar, altars NOUN a holy table in a church or temple.

alter, alters, altering, altered VERB If something alters or if you alter it, it changes. **alteration** NOUN
USAGE NOTE: Do not confuse the spellings of *alter* and *altar*

altercation, altercations NOUN FORMAL a noisy disagreement.

alternate, alternates, alternating, alternated VERB [Said **ol**-tern-ate]
❶ If one thing alternates with another, the two things regularly occur one after the other
▷ ADJECTIVE ❷ [Said ol-**tern**-at] If something happens on alternate days,

it happens on the first day but not the second, and happens again on the third day but not the fourth, and so on.
❸ (MATHS) Alternate angles are two angles on opposite sides of a line that crosses two other lines. **alternately** ADVERB **alternation** NOUN

alternating current, alternating currents NOUN (SCIENCE) a current that regularly changes its direction, so that the electrons flow first one way and then the other.

alternative, alternatives NOUN
❶ something you can do or have instead of something else
• *alternatives to prison such as community service.* ▷ ADJECTIVE
❷ Alternative plans or actions can happen or be done instead of what is already happening or being done. **alternatively** ADVERB
USAGE NOTE: If there are more than two choices in a situation you should say *there are three choices* rather than *there are three alternatives* because the strict meaning of *alternative* is a choice between two things

although CONJUNCTION in spite of the fact that • *He wasn't well-known in America, although he did make a film there.*

altitude, altitudes NOUN (GEOGRAPHY) The altitude of something is its height above sea level • *The mountain range reaches an altitude of 1330 metres.*

alto, altos (MUSIC) NOUN ❶ An alto is a person who sings the second highest part in four-part harmony
▷ ADJECTIVE ❷ An alto musical

instrument has a range of notes that are of medium pitch.

altogether ADVERB ❶ entirely • *She wasn't altogether sorry to be leaving.* ❷ in total; used of amounts • *I get paid £1000 a month altogether.*

aluminium NOUN (SCIENCE) Aluminium is a light silvery-white metallic element. It is used to make aircraft and other equipment, usually in the form of aluminium alloys.

always ADVERB all the time or for ever • *She's always moaning.*

am the first person singular, present tense of **be**.

a.m. used to specify times between 12 midnight and 12 noon, eg *I get up at 6 a.m.* It is an abbreviation for the Latin phrase 'ante meridiem', which means 'before noon'.

amalgamate, amalgamates, amalgamating, amalgamated VERB If two organizations amalgamate, they join together to form one new organization. **amalgamation** NOUN

amandla NOUN In South Africa, amandla is a political slogan which calls for power for Black people.

amass, amasses, amassing, amassed VERB If you amass something such as money or information, you collect large quantities of it • *He amassed a huge fortune.*

amateur, amateurs NOUN someone who does something as a hobby rather than as a job.

amateurish ADJECTIVE not skilfully made or done. **amateurishly** ADVERB

amaze, amazes, amazing, amazed VERB If something amazes you, it surprises you very much.
● SIMILAR WORDS: astonish, astound, stun, surprise

amazement NOUN complete surprise.

amazing ADJECTIVE very surprising or remarkable. **amazingly** ADVERB

ambassador, ambassadors NOUN a person sent to a foreign country as the representative of his or her own government.

amber NOUN ❶ a hard, yellowish-brown substance used for making jewellery ▷ NOUN OR ADJECTIVE ❷ orange-brown.

ambi- PREFIX 'Ambi-' means 'both'. For example, something which is *ambiguous* can have two meanings.
● WORD HISTORY: from Latin *ambo* meaning 'both'

ambidextrous ADJECTIVE Someone who is ambidextrous is able to use both hands equally skilfully.

ambience NOUN FORMAL The ambience of a place is its atmosphere.

ambient ADJECTIVE ❶ surrounding • *low ambient temperatures.* ❷ creating a relaxing atmosphere • *ambient music.*

ambiguous ADJECTIVE A word or phrase that is ambiguous has more than one meaning. **ambiguously** ADVERB **ambiguity** NOUN

ambition, ambitions NOUN ❶ If you have an ambition to achieve something, you want very much to achieve it • *His ambition is to be an*

a
b
c
d
e
f
g
h
i
j
k
l
m
n
o
p
q
r
s
t
u
v
w
x
y
z

actor. **2** a great desire for success, power, and wealth • *He's talented and full of ambition.*

ambitious ADJECTIVE
1 Someone who is ambitious has a strong desire for success, power, and wealth. **2** An ambitious plan is a large one and requires a lot of work • *an ambitious rebuilding schedule.*

ambivalent ADJECTIVE having or showing two conflicting attitudes or emotions. **ambivalence** NOUN

amble, ambles, ambling, ambled VERB If you amble, you walk slowly and in a relaxed manner.

ambulance, ambulances NOUN a vehicle for taking sick and injured people to hospital.

ambush, ambushes, ambushing, ambushed VERB **1** To ambush someone is to attack them after hiding and lying in wait for them ▷ NOUN **2** an attack on someone after hiding and lying in wait for them.

amen INTERJECTION Amen is said at the end of a Christian prayer. It means 'so be it'.

amenable [Said am-**mee**-na-bl] ADJECTIVE willing to listen to suggestions, or to cooperate with someone • *Both brothers were amenable to the arrangement.* **amenably** ADVERB **amenability** NOUN

amend, amends, amending, amended VERB To amend something that has been written or said is to alter it slightly • *Our constitution had to be amended.* **amendment** NOUN

amends PLURAL NOUN If you make

amends for something bad you have done, you say you are sorry and try to make up for it.

amenity, amenities [Said am-**mee**-nit-ee] NOUN GEOGRAPHY
Amenities are things that are available for the public to use, such as sports facilities or shopping centres.

America NOUN America refers to the United States, or to the whole of North, South, and Central America.

American, Americans ADJECTIVE
1 belonging or relating to the United States, or to the whole of North, South, and Central America ▷ NOUN
2 someone who comes from the United States.

amethyst, amethysts NOUN a type of purple semiprecious stone.
● **WORD HISTORY:** from Greek
● *amethustos* meaning 'not drunk'. It
● was thought to prevent intoxication

amiable ADJECTIVE pleasant and friendly **amiably** ADVERB **amiability** NOUN

amicable ADJECTIVE fairly friendly • *an amicable divorce.* **amicably** ADVERB

amid or **amidst** PREPOSITION
FORMAL surrounded by • *She enjoys cooking amid her friends.*
● **USAGE NOTE:** The form *amidst* is a
● bit old-fashioned and *amid* is more
● often used

amino acid, amino acids NOUN
SCIENCE An amino acid is a compound containing an amino group, which forms a part of protein molecules.

amiss ADJECTIVE If something is

amiss, there is something wrong.

ammonia NOUN Ammonia is a colourless, strong-smelling gas or liquid.

ammunition NOUN anything that can be fired from a gun or other weapon, for example bullets.

amnesia NOUN loss of memory.

amnesty, amnesties NOUN an official pardon for political or other prisoners.

amniotic ADJECTIVE (SCIENCE) The amniotic sac is the protective membrane surrounding a baby in its mother's womb. It is filled with amniotic fluid, which protects the baby.

amoeba, amoebas or amoebae [Said am-**mee**-ba]; also spelt **ameba** NOUN the smallest kind of living creature, consisting of one cell. Amoebas reproduce by dividing into two.

amok [Said a-**muk**] PHRASE If a person or animal **runs amok**, they behave in a violent and uncontrolled way.
● WORD HISTORY: a Malay word

among or **amongst** PREPOSITION ❶ surrounded by • The bike lay among piles of chains and pedals. ❷ in the company of • He was among friends. ❸ between more than two • The money will be divided among seven charities.
● USAGE NOTE: If there are more than two things, you should use among. If there are only two things you should use between. The form amongst is a bit old-fashioned and among is more often used

amoral ADJECTIVE Someone who is amoral has no moral standards by which to live.
● USAGE NOTE: Do not confuse amoral and immoral. You use amoral to talk about people with no moral standards, but immoral for people who are aware of moral standards but choose to go against them

amorous ADJECTIVE passionately affectionate • an amorous relationship. **amorously** ADVERB **amorousness** NOUN

amount, amounts, amounting, amounted (MATHS) NOUN ❶ An amount of something is how much there is of it ▷ VERB ❷ If something amounts to a particular total, all the parts of it add up to that total • Her vocabulary amounted to only 50 words.
● SIMILAR WORDS: ❶ extent, number, quantity

amp, amps NOUN An amp is the same as an ampere.

ampere, amperes [Said am-pair] NOUN a unit which is used for measuring electric current.

ampersand, ampersands NOUN the character &, meaning 'and'.

amphetamine, amphetamines NOUN a drug that increases people's energy and makes them excited. It can have dangerous and unpleasant side effects.

amphibian, amphibians NOUN (SCIENCE) a creature that lives partly on land and partly in water, for example a frog or a newt.

amphibious ADJECTIVE An

a b c d e f g h i j k l m n o p q r s t u v w x y z

▷ SPELLING NOTE: Beautiful Elephants Are Usually Tiny ([beaut]iful)

amphibious animal, such as a frog, lives partly on land and partly in the water.
● **WORD HISTORY:** from Greek *amphibios* meaning 'having a double life'

amphitheatre, amphitheatres **NOUN** (HISTORY) An amphitheatre is a large, semicircular open area with sloping sides covered with rows of seats. Amphitheatres were built originally by the Greeks and Romans for theatrical performances.

ample ADJECTIVE If there is an ample amount of something, there is more than enough of it. **amply ADVERB**

amplifier, amplifiers **NOUN** a piece of equipment in a radio or stereo system which causes sounds or signals to become louder.

amplify, amplifies, amplifying, amplified **VERB** If you amplify a sound, you make it louder. **amplification NOUN**

amplitude NOUN (SCIENCE) In physics, the amplitude of a wave is how far its curve moves away from its normal position.

amputate, amputates, amputating, amputated **VERB** To amputate an arm or a leg is to cut it off as a surgical operation. **amputation NOUN**

Amrit NOUN ❶ In the Sikh religion, Amrit is a special mixture of sugar and water used in rituals. ❷ The Amrit or Amrit ceremony takes place when someone is accepted as a full member of the Sikh community, and drinks Amrit as part of the ceremony.

amuse, amuses, amusing, amused **VERB** ❶ If something amuses you, you think it is funny. ❷ If you amuse yourself, you find things to do which stop you from being bored. **amused ADJECTIVE amusing ADJECTIVE**

amusement, amusements **NOUN** ❶ Amusement is the state of thinking something is funny. ❷ Amusement is also the pleasure you get from being entertained or from doing something interesting. ❸ Amusements are ways of passing the time pleasantly.

an ADJECTIVE 'An' is used instead of 'a' in front of words that begin with a vowel sound.
● **USAGE NOTE:** You use *an* in front of abbreviations that start with a vowel sound when they are read out loud: *an MA; an OBE*

-an SUFFIX '-an' comes at the end of nouns and adjectives which show where or what someone or something comes from or belongs to • *American* • *Victorian* • *Christian*.

anabolism NOUN (SCIENCE) a metabolic process in which energy is used to make complex molecules from simpler ones. **anabolic ADJECTIVE**

anachronism, anachronisms *[Said an-ak-kron-izm]* **NOUN** something that belongs or seems to belong to another time. **anachronistic ADJECTIVE**
● **WORD HISTORY:** from Greek *anakhronismos* meaning 'mistake in time'

anaemia *[Said a-nee-mee-a]* **NOUN** a medical condition resulting from too few red cells in a person's blood.

People with anaemia look pale and feel very tired. **anaemic** ADJECTIVE

anaesthetic, anaesthetics [Said an-niss-**thet**-ik] NOUN a substance that stops you feeling pain. A general anaesthetic stops you from feeling pain in the whole of your body by putting you to sleep, and a local anaesthetic makes just one part of your body go numb.

anaesthetist, anaesthetists NOUN a doctor who is specially trained to give anaesthetics.

anaesthetize, anaesthetizes, anaesthetizing, anaesthetized; also spelt **anesthetize** or **anaesthetise** VERB To anaesthetize someone is to give them an anaesthetic to make them unconscious.

anagram, anagrams NOUN a word or phrase formed by changing the order of the letters of another word or phrase. For example, 'triangle' is an anagram of 'integral'.

anal [Said ay-nl] ADJECTIVE relating to the anus.

analgesic, analgesics [Said an-al-**jee**-sik] NOUN a substance that relieves pain.

analogy, analogies [Said an-**al**-o-jee] NOUN a comparison showing that two things are similar in some ways. **analogous** ADJECTIVE

analyse, analyses, analysing, analysed VERB (EXAM TERM) To analyse something is to break it down into parts, or investigate it carefully, so that you can describe its main aspects, or find out what it consists of.

analysis, analyses NOUN the process of investigating something in order to understand it or find out what it consists of • a full analysis of the problem.

analyst, analysts NOUN a person whose job is to analyse things to find out about them.

analytic or **analytical** ADJECTIVE using logical reasoning • Planning in detail requires an acute analytical mind. **analytically** ADVERB

anarchy [Said **an**-nar-kee] NOUN a situation where nobody obeys laws or rules.
- **WORD HISTORY:** from Greek
- anarkhos meaning 'without a ruler'

anatomy, anatomies NOUN ❶ the study of the structure of the human body or of the bodies of animals. ❷ An animal's anatomy is the structure of its body. **anatomical** ADJECTIVE **anatomically** ADVERB

ANC NOUN one of the main political parties in South Africa. ANC is an abbreviation for 'African National Congress'.

ancestor, ancestors NOUN Your ancestors are the members of your family who lived many years ago and from whom you are descended. **ancestral** ADJECTIVE
- **SIMILAR WORDS:** forebear,
- forefather

ancestry, ancestries NOUN Your ancestry consists of the people from whom you are descended • a French citizen of Greek ancestry.

anchor, anchors, anchoring, anchored NOUN ❶ a heavy, hooked object at the end of a chain, dropped

▷ SPELLING NOTE: there's a rAKE in the brAKEs (brake)

from a boat into the water to keep the boat in one place ▷ **VERB** ❷ To anchor a boat or another object is to stop it from moving by dropping an anchor or attaching it to something solid.

anchorage, anchorages **NOUN** a place where a boat can safely anchor.

anchovy, anchovies **NOUN** a type of small edible fish with a very strong salty taste.

ancient [*Said* ayn-shent] **ADJECTIVE** ❶ existing or happening in the distant past • *ancient Greece*. ❷ very old or having a very long history • *an ancient monastery*.

ancillary [*Said* an-sil-lar-ee] **ADJECTIVE** The ancillary workers in an institution are the people such as cooks and cleaners, whose work supports the main work of the institution.
  ● **WORD HISTORY:** from Latin *ancilla* meaning 'maidservant'

and CONJUNCTION You use 'and' to link two or more words or phrases together.

andante, andantes (MUSIC) **ADVERB** ❶ In music, andante is an instruction to play or sing something at a moderately slow tempo ▷ **NOUN** ❷ a piece of music that should be performed at a moderately slow tempo.
  ● **WORD HISTORY:** an Italian word

androgynous [*Said* an-droj-in-uss] **ADJECTIVE** FORMAL having both male and female characteristics.

android, androids **NOUN** In science fiction, an android is a robot that looks like a human being.

anecdote, anecdotes **NOUN** a short, entertaining story about a person or event. **anecdotal ADJECTIVE**

anemometer, anemometers **NOUN** (SCIENCE) an instrument used for recording the speed and direction of winds.

anemone, anemones [*Said* an-em-on-ee] **NOUN** a plant with red, purple, or white flowers.

anew ADVERB If you do something anew, you do it again • *They left their life in Britain to start anew in France.*

angel, angels **NOUN** Angels are spiritual beings some people believe live in heaven and act as messengers for God. **angelic ADJECTIVE**

anger, angers, angering, angered **NOUN** ❶ the strong feeling you get when you feel someone has behaved in an unfair or cruel way ▷ **VERB** ❷ If something angers you, it makes you feel angry.
  ● **SIMILAR WORDS:** ❶ fury, rage, wrath ❷ enrage, infuriate, madden

angina [*Said* an-jy-na] **NOUN** a brief but very severe heart pain, caused by lack of blood supply to the heart. It is also known as 'angina pectoris'.

angle, angles **NOUN** ❶ (MATHS) the distance between two lines at the point where they join together. Angles are measured in degrees. ❷ the direction from which you look at something • *He had painted the vase from all angles.* ❸ An angle on something is a particular way of considering it • *She told the same story* *from a German angle.*

angler, anglers **NOUN** someone who fishes with a fishing rod as a hobby. **angling NOUN**

Anglican, Anglicans **NOUN OR ADJECTIVE** (a member of) one of the churches belonging to the Anglican Communion, a group of Protestant churches which includes the Church of England.

Anglo-Saxon, Anglo-Saxons **NOUN** ❶ The Anglo-Saxons were a race of people who settled in England from the fifth century AD and were the dominant people until the Norman invasion in 1066. They were composed of three West Germanic tribes, the Angles, Saxons, and Jutes. ❷ Anglo-Saxon is another name for **Old English.**

Angolan, Angolans *[Said ang-goh-ln]* **ADJECTIVE** ❶ belonging or relating to Angola ▷ **NOUN** ❷ someone who comes from Angola.

angora ADJECTIVE ❶ An angora goat or rabbit is a breed with long silky hair ▷ **NOUN** ❷ Angora is this hair, usually mixed with other fibres to make clothing.
  ● **WORD HISTORY:** from *Angora*, the
  ● former name of Ankara in Turkey

angry, angrier, angriest **ADJECTIVE** very cross or annoyed. **angrily ADVERB**
  ● **SIMILAR WORDS:** enraged, furious,
  ● infuriated, mad

angst NOUN a feeling of anxiety and worry.

anguish NOUN extreme suffering. **anguished ADJECTIVE**

angular ADJECTIVE Angular things have straight lines and sharp points • *He has an angular face and pointed chin.*

animal, animals **NOUN** any living being except a plant, or any mammal except a human being.
  ● **WORD HISTORY:** from Latin *anima*
  ● meaning 'life' or 'soul'

animal welfare NOUN (SCIENCE) actions taken to make sure that animals are well cared for, given enough food, and not made to suffer any unnecessary pain.

animate, animates, animating, animated **VERB** To animate something is to make it lively and interesting.

animated ADJECTIVE lively and interesting • *an animated conversation.*

animation NOUN ❶ a method of film-making in which a series of drawings are photographed. When the film is projected, the characters in the drawings appear to move. ❷ Someone who has animation shows liveliness in the way they speak and act • *The crowd showed no sign of animation.* **animator NOUN**

animosity, animosities **NOUN** a feeling of strong dislike and anger towards someone.

aniseed NOUN a substance made from the seeds of a Mediterranean plant and used as a flavouring in sweets, drinks, and medicine.

ankle, ankles **NOUN** the joint which connects your foot to your leg.

annex, annexes, annexing, annexed; *also spelt* **annexe NOUN** ❶ an extra

▷ SPELLING NOTE: *LEt's measure the angLE (angle)*

building which is joined to a larger main building. **②** an extra part added to a document ▷ **VERB** **③** If one country annexes another, it seizes the other country and takes control of it. **annexation NOUN**

annihilate, annihilates, annihilating, annihilated [Said an-**nye**-ill-ate] **VERB** If something is annihilated, it is completely destroyed. **annihilation NOUN**

anniversary, anniversaries **NOUN** a date which is remembered because something special happened on that date in a previous year.

announce, announces, announcing, announced **VERB** If you announce something, you tell people about it publicly or officially • *The team was announced on Friday morning.*
● **SIMILAR WORDS:** broadcast, make
● known, proclaim

announcement, announcements **NOUN** a statement giving information about something.

announcer, announcers **NOUN** someone who introduces programmes on radio and television.

annoy, annoys, annoying, annoyed **VERB** If someone or something annoys you, they irritate you and make you fairly angry. **annoyed ADJECTIVE**
● **SIMILAR WORDS:** bother,
● exasperate, irritate, vex

annoyance NOUN **①** a feeling of irritation. **②** something that causes irritation.

annual, annuals **ADJECTIVE**
① happening or done once a year
• *their annual conference.*

② happening or calculated over a period of one year • *the United States' annual budget for national defence.*
▷ **NOUN** **③** a book or magazine published once a year. **④** a plant that grows, flowers, and dies within one year. **annually ADVERB**

annuity, annuities **NOUN** a fixed sum of money paid to someone every year from an investment or insurance policy.

annul, annuls, annulling, annulled **VERB** If a marriage or contract is annulled, it is declared invalid, so that legally it is considered never to have existed. **annulment NOUN**

anoint, anoints, anointing, anointed **VERB** To anoint someone is to put oil on them as part of a ceremony. **anointment NOUN**

anomaly, anomalies [Said an-**nom**-al-ee] **NOUN** Something is an anomaly if it is unusual or different from what is normal. **anomalous ADJECTIVE**

anon. an abbreviation for anonymous.

anonymous ADJECTIVE If something is anonymous, nobody knows who is responsible for it • *The police received an anonymous phone call.* **anonymously ADVERB anonymity NOUN**

anorak, anoraks **NOUN** a warm waterproof jacket, usually with a hood.
● **WORD HISTORY:** an Inuit word

anorexia NOUN a psychological illness in which the person refuses to eat because they are frightened of becoming fat. **anorexic ADJECTIVE**

● **WORD HISTORY:** from Greek *an-* +
orexis meaning 'no appetite'

another **ADJECTIVE OR PRONOUN**
Another thing or person is an
additional thing or person.

answer, answers, answering,
answered **VERB** ❶ If you answer
someone, you reply to them using
words or actions or in writing ▷ **NOUN**
❷ the reply you give when you answer
someone. ❸ a solution to a problem.
● **SIMILAR WORDS:** ❶ reply,
● respond, retort ❷ reply, response,
● retort

answerable **ADJECTIVE** If you are
answerable to someone for
something, you are responsible for it
• *He must be made answerable for these
terrible crimes.*

answering machine, answering
machines **NOUN** a machine which
records phone calls while you are out.

ant, ants **NOUN** Ants are small insects
that live in large groups.

-ant **SUFFIX** '-ant' is used to form
adjectives • *important.*

antagonism **NOUN** hatred or
hostility.

antagonist, antagonists **NOUN** an
enemy or opponent.

antagonistic **ADJECTIVE**
Someone who is antagonistic towards
you shows hate or hostility.
antagonistically **ADVERB**

antagonize, antagonizes,
antagonizing, antagonized; *also spelt*
antagonise **VERB** If someone is
antagonized, they are made to feel
anger and hostility.

Antarctic **NOUN** The Antarctic is
the region south of the Antarctic
Circle.

Antarctic Circle **NOUN** The
Antarctic Circle is an imaginary circle
around the southern part of the world.

ante- **PREFIX** 'Ante-' means 'before'.
For example, *antenatal* means 'before
birth'.
● **WORD HISTORY:** from Latin *ante*,
● meaning 'before'

antecedent, antecedents *[Said
an-tis-**see**-dent]* **NOUN** ❶ An
antecedent of a thing or event is
something which happened or existed
before it and is related to it in some
way • *the prehistoric antecedents of the
horse.* ❷ Your antecedents are your
ancestors, the relatives from whom
you are descended.

antelope, antelopes **NOUN** an
animal which looks like a deer.

antenatal **ADJECTIVE** concerned
with the care of pregnant women and
their unborn children • *an antenatal
clinic.*

antenna, antennae or antennas
NOUN ❶ The antennae of insects
and certain other animals are the two
long, thin parts attached to their
heads which they use to feel with. The
plural is 'antennae'. ❷ In Australian,
New Zealand, and American English,
an antenna is a radio or television
aerial. The plural is 'antennas'.

anthem, anthems **NOUN** a hymn
written for a special occasion.

anther, anthers **NOUN** in a flower,
the part of the stamen that makes
pollen grains.

a
b
c
d
e
f
g
h
i
j
k
l
m
n
o
p
q
r
s
t
u
v
w
x
y
z

▷ SPELLING NOTE: *The government licenSes Schnapps (licenses)*

anthology, anthologies NOUN
(LIBRARY) a collection of writings by various authors published in one book.

anthropo- PREFIX 'Anthropo-' means involving or to do with human beings • *anthropology.*

anthropology NOUN the study of human beings and their society and culture. **anthropological** ADJECTIVE **anthropologist** NOUN

anti- PREFIX 'Anti-' means opposed to or opposite to something • *antiwar marches.*
● WORD HISTORY: from Greek
● *anti-* meaning 'opposite' or
● 'against'

antibiotic, antibiotics NOUN a drug or chemical used in medicine to kill bacteria and cure infections.

antibody, antibodies NOUN a substance produced in the blood which can kill the harmful bacteria that cause disease.

anticipate, anticipates, anticipating, anticipated VERB If you anticipate an event, you are expecting it and are prepared for it • *She had anticipated his visit.* **anticipation** NOUN

anticlimax, anticlimaxes NOUN something that disappoints you because it is not as exciting as expected, or because it occurs after something that was very exciting.

anticlockwise ADJECTIVE OR ADVERB moving in the opposite direction to the hands of a clock.

antics PLURAL NOUN funny or silly ways of behaving.

anticyclone, anticyclones NOUN
(GEOGRAPHY) An anticyclone is an area of high air pressure which causes settled weather.

antidote, antidotes NOUN a chemical substance that acts against the effect of a poison.

antihistamine, antihistamines NOUN a drug used to treat an allergy.

antipathy NOUN a strong feeling of dislike or hostility towards something or someone.

antiperspirant, antiperspirants NOUN a substance which stops you sweating when you put it on your skin.

antipodes [Said an-**tip**-pod-eez] PLURAL NOUN any two points on the earth's surface that are situated directly opposite each other. In Britain, Australia and New Zealand are sometimes called the Antipodes as they are opposite Britain on the globe. **antipodean** ADJECTIVE
● WORD HISTORY: from Greek
● *antipous* meaning 'with the feet
● opposite'

antiquarian ADJECTIVE relating to or involving old and rare objects
• *antiquarian books.*

antiquated ADJECTIVE very old-fashioned • *an antiquated method of teaching.*

antique, antiques [Said an-**teek**] NOUN ❶ an object from the past that is collected because of its value or beauty ▷ ADJECTIVE ❷ from or concerning the past • *antique furniture.*

antiquity, antiquities NOUN

❶ Antiquity is the distant past, especially the time of the ancient Egyptians, Greeks, and Romans. **❷** Antiquities are interesting works of art and buildings from the distant past.

anti-Semitism NOUN hatred of Jewish people. **anti-Semitic** ADJECTIVE **anti-Semite** NOUN

antiseptic ADJECTIVE Something that is antiseptic kills germs.

antisocial ADJECTIVE **❶** An antisocial person is unwilling to meet and be friendly with other people. **❷** Antisocial behaviour is annoying or upsetting to other people • *Smoking in public is antisocial.*

antithesis, antitheses *[Said an-tith-iss-iss]* NOUN FORMAL The antithesis of something is its exact opposite • *Work is the antithesis of leisure.*

antivenene, antivenenes NOUN a substance which reduces the effect of a venom, especially a snake venom.

antler, antlers NOUN A male deer's antlers are the branched horns on its head.

antonym, antonyms NOUN a word which means the opposite of another word. For example, 'hot' is the antonym of 'cold'.

anus, anuses NOUN the hole between the buttocks.

anvil, anvils NOUN a heavy iron block on which hot metal is beaten into shape.

anxiety, anxieties NOUN nervousness or worry.

anxious ADJECTIVE **❶** If you are

anxious, you are nervous or worried. **❷** If you are anxious to do something or anxious that something should happen, you very much want to do it or want it to happen • *She was anxious to have children.* **anxiously** ADVERB

any ADJECTIVE OR PRONOUN **❶** one, some, or several • *Do you have any paperclips I could borrow?* **❷** even the smallest amount or even one • *He was unable to tolerate any dairy products.* **❸** whatever or whichever, no matter what or which • *Any type of cooking oil will do.*

anybody PRONOUN any person.

anyhow ADVERB **❶** in any case. **❷** in a careless way • *They were all shoved in anyhow.*

anyone PRONOUN any person.

anything PRONOUN any object, event, situation, or action.

anyway ADVERB in any case.

anywhere ADVERB in, at, or to any place.

Anzac, Anzacs NOUN **❶** In World War I, an Anzac was a soldier with the Australia and New Zealand Army Corps. **❷** an Australian or New Zealand soldier.

aorta *[Said ay-or-ta]* NOUN the main artery in the body, which carries blood away from the heart.

apart ADVERB OR ADJECTIVE **❶** When something is apart from something else, there is a space or a distance between them • *The couple separated and lived apart for four years* • *The gliders landed about seventy metres apart.* ▷ ADVERB **❷** If you

▷ SPELLING NOTE: *pla*i*ce the fish has a glittering 'EYE' (I) (pla*i*ce)*

a b c d e f g h i j k l m n o p q r s t u v w x y z

take something apart, you separate it into pieces.

apartheid *[Said ap-**par**-tide]* **NOUN** In South Africa apartheid was the government policy and laws which kept people of different races apart. It was abolished in 1994.

apartment, apartments **NOUN** a set of rooms for living in, usually on one floor of a building.

apathetic **ADJECTIVE** not interested in anything.
● **SIMILAR WORDS:** indifferent, uninterested

apathy *[Said **ap**-path-ee]* **NOUN** a state of mind in which you do not care about anything.

ape, apes, aping, aped **NOUN ❶** Apes are animals with a very short tail or no tail. They are closely related to man. Apes include chimpanzees, gorillas, and gibbons ▷ **VERB ❷** If you ape someone's speech or behaviour, you imitate it.

aphid, aphids **NOUN** a small insect that feeds by sucking the juices from plants.

aphrodisiac, aphrodisiacs **NOUN** a food, drink, or drug which makes people want to have sex.

apiece **ADVERB** If people have a particular number of things apiece, they have that number each.

aplomb *[Said uh-**plom**]* **NOUN** If you do something with aplomb, you do it with great confidence.

apocalypse *[Said uh-**pok**-ka-lips]* **NOUN** The Apocalypse is the end of the world. **apocalyptic** **ADJECTIVE**

● **WORD HISTORY:** from Greek *apokaluptein* meaning 'to reveal'; the way the world will end is considered to be revealed in the last book of the Bible, called 'Apocalypse' or 'Revelation'

apocryphal **ADJECTIVE** A story that is apocryphal is generally believed not to have really happened.

apolitical *[Said ay-poll-**it**-i-kl]* **ADJECTIVE** not interested in politics.

apologetic **ADJECTIVE** showing or saying you are sorry. **apologetically** **ADVERB**

apologize, apologizes, apologizing, apologized; *also spelt* **apologise** **VERB** When you apologize to someone, you say you are sorry for something you have said or done.

apology, apologies **NOUN** something you say or write to tell someone you are sorry.

apostle, apostles **NOUN** The Apostles are the twelve followers who were chosen by Christ.

apostrophe, apostrophes *[Said ap-**poss**-troff-ee]* **NOUN** a punctuation mark used to show that one or more letters have been missed out of a word, for example "he's" for "he is". Apostrophes are also used with -s at the end of a noun to show that what follows belongs to or relates to the noun, for example *my brother's books*. If the noun already has an -s at the end, for example because it is plural, you just add the apostrophe, eg *my brothers' books*, referring to more than one brother.
▶ SEE GRAMMAR BOX ON PAGE 39

WHAT DOES THE APOSTROPHE DO?

The **apostrophe** (') is used to show possession. It is usually added to the end of a word and followed by an *s*:

Matthew's book
children's programmes

If a plural word already ends in -*s*, the apostrophe follows that letter:

my parents' generation
seven years' bad luck

You should not use an apostrophe to form plurals or possessive pronouns: *a pound of tomatoes* [not *tomato's*]

I happen to be a fan of hers [not *her's*]

You can, however, add an apostrophe to form the plural of a number, letter, or symbol:

P's and Q's
7's
£'s

The apostrophe is also used to show that a letter or letters have been omitted:

rock'n'roll
Who's next?

---

appal, appals, appalling, appalled
VERB If something appals you, it shocks you because it is very bad.

appalling ADJECTIVE so bad as to be shocking • *She escaped with appalling injuries.*

apparatus NOUN (SCIENCE) The apparatus for a particular task is the equipment used for it.

apparent ADJECTIVE ❶ seeming real rather than actually being real • *an apparent hit and run accident.* ❷ obvious • *It was apparent that he had lost interest.* **apparently ADVERB**
● **SIMILAR WORDS:** ❶ ostensible,
● seeming

apparition, apparitions **NOUN** something you think you see but that is not really there • *a ghostly apparition on the windscreen.*

appeal, appeals, appealing, appealed
VERB ❶ If you appeal for something, you make an urgent request for it
• *The police appealed for witnesses to come forward.* ❷ If you appeal to

someone in authority against a decision, you formally ask them to change it. ❸ If something appeals to you, you find it attractive or interesting
▷ **NOUN** ❹ a formal or serious request • *an appeal for peace.* ❺ The appeal of something is the quality it has which people find attractive or interesting • *the rugged appeal of the Rockies.* **appealing ADJECTIVE**

appear, appears, appearing, appeared **VERB** ❶ When something which you could not see appears, it moves (or you move) so that you can see it. ❷ When something new appears, it begins to exist. ❸ When an actor or actress appears in a film or show, they take part in it. ❹ If something appears to be a certain way, it seems or looks that way • *He appeared to be searching for something.*
● **SIMILAR WORDS:** ❶ come into
● view, emerge, show up

appearance, appearances **NOUN** ❶ The appearance of someone in a place is their arrival there, especially when it is unexpected. ❷ The appearance of something new is the time when it begins to exist • *the appearance of computer technology.* ❸ Someone's or something's appearance is the way they look to other people • *His gaunt appearance had sparked fears for his health.*

appease, appeases, appeasing, appeased **VERB** If you try to appease someone, you try to calm them down when they are angry, for example by giving them what they want. **appeasement NOUN**

appendage, appendages **NOUN** a less important part attached to a main part.

appendicitis [Said app-end-i-*site-uss*] **NOUN** a painful illness in which a person's appendix becomes infected.

appendix, appendices or appendixes **NOUN** ❶ a small closed tube forming part of your digestive system. ❷ An appendix to a book is extra information placed after the end of the main text.

● **USAGE NOTE:** The plural of the
● part of the body is *appendixes*. The
● plural of the extra section in a book
● is *appendices*

appetite, appetites **NOUN** ❶ Your appetite is your desire to eat. ❷ If you have an appetite for something, you have a strong desire for it and enjoyment of it • *She had lost her appetite for air travel.*

appetizing or **appetising** **ADJECTIVE** Food that is appetizing looks and smells good, and makes you look forward to eating it.

applaud, applauds, applauding,

applauded **VERB** ❶ When a group of people applaud, they clap their hands in approval or praise. ❷ When an action or attitude is applauded, people praise it.

applause NOUN (DRAMA) Applause is clapping by a group of people.

apple, apples **NOUN** a round fruit with smooth skin and firm white flesh.

appliance, appliances **NOUN** any machine in your home you use to do a job like cleaning or cooking • *kitchen appliances.*

applicable ADJECTIVE Something that is applicable to a situation is relevant to it • *The rules are applicable to everyone.*

applicant, applicants **NOUN** someone who is applying for something • *We had problems recruiting applicants for the post.*

application, applications **NOUN** ❶ a formal request for something, usually in writing. ❷ The application of a rule, system, or skill is the use of it in a particular situation.

apply, applies, applying, applied **VERB** ❶ If you apply for something, you formally ask for it, usually by writing a letter. ❷ If you apply a rule or skill, you use it in a situation • *He applied his mind to the problem.* ❸ If something applies to a person or a situation, it is relevant to that person or situation • *The legislation applies only to people living in England and Wales.* ❹ If you apply something to a surface, you put it on • *She applied lipstick to her mouth.*

▷ SPELLING NOTE: *pAL up with the principAL and principAL staff (princip**al**)*

appoint, appoints, appointing, appointed **VERB** ❶ If you appoint someone to a job or position, you formally choose them for it. ❷ If you appoint a time or place for something to happen, you decide when or where it will happen. **appointed ADJECTIVE**

appointment, appointments **NOUN** ❶ An arrangement you have with someone to meet them. ❷ The appointment of a person to do a particular job is the choosing of that person to do it. ❸ a job or a position of responsibility • *He applied for an appointment in Russia.*
● **SIMILAR WORDS:** ❶ date,
● engagement, meeting

apposite [*Said* **app**-o-zit] **ADJECTIVE** well suited for a particular purpose • *He went before Cameron could think of anything apposite to say.*

appraise, appraises, appraising, appraised **VERB** If you appraise something, you think about it carefully and form an opinion about it. **appraisal NOUN**

appreciable [*Said* a-**pree**-shuh-bl] **ADJECTIVE** large enough to be noticed • *an appreciable difference.* **appreciably ADVERB**

appreciate, appreciates, appreciating, appreciated **VERB** ❶ If you appreciate something, you like it because you recognize its good qualities • *He appreciates fine wines.* ❷ If you appreciate a situation or problem, you understand it and know what it involves. ❸ If you appreciate something someone has done for you, you are grateful to them for it • *I really appreciate you coming to visit me.* ❹ If

something appreciates over a period of time, its value increases • *The property appreciated by 50% in two years.* **appreciation NOUN**
● **SIMILAR WORDS:** ❶ prize, rate
● highly, value

appreciative ADJECTIVE ❶ understanding and enthusiastic • *They were a very appreciative audience.* ❷ thankful and grateful • *I am particularly appreciative of the help my family and friends have given me.* **appreciatively ADVERB**

apprehend, apprehends, apprehending, apprehended **VERB** FORMAL ❶ When the police apprehend someone, they arrest them and take them into custody. ❷ If you apprehend something, you understand it fully • *They were unable to apprehend his hidden meaning.*

apprehensive ADJECTIVE afraid something bad may happen • *I was very apprehensive about the birth.* **apprehensively ADVERB apprehension NOUN**

apprentice, apprentices **NOUN** a person who works for a period of time with a skilled craftsman in order to learn a skill or trade. **apprenticeship NOUN**
● **WORD HISTORY:** from Old French
● *aprendre* meaning 'to learn'

approach, approaches, approaching, approached **VERB** ❶ To approach something is to come near or nearer to it. ❷ When a future event approaches, it gradually gets nearer • *As winter approached, tents were set up to accommodate refugees.* ❸ If you approach someone about something, you ask them about it. ❹ If you

▷ SPELLING NOTE: *LEarn the principLEs (princip*le*)*

A
B
C
D
E
F
G
H
I
J
K
L
M
N
O
P
Q
R
S
T
U
V
W
X
Y
Z

approach a situation or problem in a particular way, you think about it or deal with it in that way ▷ **NOUN** ❺ The approach of something is the process of it coming closer • *the approach of spring.* ❻ An approach to a situation or problem is a way of thinking about it or dealing with it. ❼ a road or path that leads to a place. **approaching ADJECTIVE**

appropriate, appropriates, appropriating, appropriated **ADJECTIVE** ❶ suitable or acceptable for a particular situation • *He didn't think jeans were appropriate for a vice-president.* ▷ **VERB** ❷ FORMAL If you appropriate something which does not belong to you, you take it without permission. **appropriately ADVERB appropriation NOUN**

approval NOUN (PSHE) ❶ Approval is agreement given to a plan or request • *The plan will require approval from the local authority.* Approval is also admiration • *She looked at James with approval.*
  ● **SIMILAR WORDS:** ❶ agreement, ● consent, permission

approve, approves, approving, approved **VERB** (PSHE) ❶ If you approve of something or someone, you think that thing or person is acceptable or good. ❷ If someone in a position of authority approves a plan or idea, they formally agree to it. **approved ADJECTIVE approving ADJECTIVE**
  ● **SIMILAR WORDS:** ❶ commend, ● favour, like ❷ agree to, authorize, ● pass, permit

approximate ADJECTIVE (MATHS) almost exact • *What was the*

approximate distance between the cars? **approximately ADVERB**
  ● **SIMILAR WORDS:** close, near

apricot, apricots **NOUN** a small, soft, yellowish-orange fruit.
  ● **WORD HISTORY:** from Latin *praecox* meaning 'early ripening'

April NOUN the fourth month of the year. April has 30 days.

apron, aprons **NOUN** a piece of clothing worn over the front of normal clothing to protect it.

apse, apses **NOUN** a domed recess in the east wall of a church.

apt ADJECTIVE ❶ suitable or relevant • *a very apt description.* ❷ having a particular tendency • *They are apt to jump to the wrong conclusions.*

aptitude NOUN Someone's aptitude for something is their ability to learn it quickly and to do it well • *I have a natural aptitude for painting.*

aqua- PREFIX 'Aqua-' means 'water'.

aquarium, aquaria or aquariums **NOUN** a glass tank filled with water in which fish are kept.

Aquarius NOUN Aquarius is the eleventh sign of the zodiac, represented by a person carrying water. People born between January 20th and February 18th are born under this sign.

aquatic ADJECTIVE ❶ An aquatic animal or plant lives or grows in water. ❷ involving water • *aquatic sports.*

aqueduct, aqueducts **NOUN** a long bridge with many arches carrying a water supply over a valley.

▷ SPELLING NOTE: *Psychiatrists Seldom Yell Callously Hard (psychiatrist)*

Arab, Arabs **NOUN** a member of a group of people who used to live in Arabia but who now live throughout the Middle East and North Africa.

Arabic NOUN a language spoken by many people in the Middle East and North Africa.

arable ADJECTIVE Arable land is used for growing crops.

arbiter, arbiters **NOUN** the person who decides about something.
● SIMILAR WORDS: judge, referee,
● adjudicator

arbitrary ADJECTIVE An arbitrary decision or action is one that is not based on a plan or system. **arbitrarily ADVERB**

arbitrate, arbitrates, arbitrating, arbitrated **VERB** When someone arbitrates between two people or groups who are in disagreement, they consider the facts and decide who is right. **arbitration NOUN arbitrator NOUN**

arc, arcs **NOUN** ❶ a smoothly curving line. ❷ in geometry, a section of the circumference of a circle.
● USAGE NOTE: Do not confuse the
● spellings of *arc* and *ark*

arcade, arcades **NOUN** a covered passage with shops or market stalls along one or both sides.

arcane ADJECTIVE mysterious and difficult to understand.

arch, arches, arching, arched **NOUN** ❶ a structure that has a curved top supported on either side by a pillar or wall. ❷ the curved part of bone at the top of the foot ▷ **VERB** ❸ When something arches, it forms a curved

line or shape ▷ **ADJECTIVE** ❹ most important • *my arch enemy.*

arch- PREFIX 'Arch-' means 'most important' or 'chief' • *archangel.*

archaeology or **archeology** [Said ar-kee-**ol**-loj-ee] **NOUN** the study of the past by digging up and examining the remains of buildings, tools, and other things.
archaeological ADJECTIVE
archaeologist NOUN
● WORD HISTORY: from Greek
● *arkhaios* meaning 'ancient'

archaic [Said ar-**kay**-ik] **ADJECTIVE** very old or old-fashioned.

archangel, archangels [Said ark-**ain**-jel] **NOUN** an angel of the highest rank.

archbishop, archbishops **NOUN** a bishop of the highest rank in a Christian Church.

archdeacon, archdeacons **NOUN** an Anglican clergyman ranking just below a bishop.

archeology another spelling of **archaeology**.

archer, archers **NOUN** someone who shoots with a bow and arrow.

archery NOUN a sport in which people shoot at a target with a bow and arrow.

archetype, archetypes [Said **ark**-i-type] **NOUN** An archetype is anything that is a perfect example of its kind • *He is the archetype of a first class athlete.* **archetypal ADJECTIVE**

archipelago, archipelagos [Said ar-kip-**pel**-lag-oh] **NOUN** a group of small islands.

a
b
c
d
e
f
g
h
i
j
k
l
m
n
o
p
q
r
s
t
u
v
w
x
y
z

▷ SPELLING NOTE: *the QUeen stood on the QUay (quay)*

● **WORD HISTORY:** from Italian
● *arcipelago* meaning 'chief sea';
● originally referring to the Aegean
● Sea

architect, architects [Said
ar-kit-tekt] NOUN (ART) a person
who designs buildings.

architecture NOUN (ART) the art
or practice of designing buildings.
architectural ADJECTIVE

archive, archives [Said *ar-kive*]
NOUN Archives are collections of
documents and records about the
history of a family or some other
group of people.

arctic NOUN ❶ The Arctic is the
region north of the Arctic Circle
▷ ADJECTIVE ❷ Arctic means very
cold indeed • *arctic conditions.*
● **WORD HISTORY:** from Greek
● *arktos* meaning 'bear'; originally it
● referred to the northern
● constellation of the Great Bear

Arctic Circle NOUN The Arctic
Circle is an imaginary circle around the
northern part of the world.

ardent ADJECTIVE full of
enthusiasm and passion. **ardently**
ADVERB

ardour NOUN a strong and
passionate feeling of love or
enthusiasm.

arduous [Said *ard-yoo-uss*]
ADJECTIVE tiring and needing a lot of
effort • *the arduous task of rebuilding
the country.*

are the plural form of the present
tense of **be**.

area, areas NOUN ❶ a particular part

of a place, country, or the world • *a
built-up area of the city.* ❷ The area of
a piece of ground or a surface is the
amount of space it covers, measured
in square metres or square feet.
❸ (MATHS) The area of a geometric
object is the amount of space
enclosed within its lines.
● **SIMILAR WORDS:** ❶ district,
● region, zone

arena, arenas NOUN ❶ a place
where sports and other public events
take place. ❷ A particular arena is the
centre of attention or activity in a
particular situation • *the political
arena.*
● **WORD HISTORY:** from Latin
● *harena* meaning 'sand', hence the
● sandy centre of an amphitheatre
● where gladiators fought

Argentinian, Argentinians [Said
ar-jen-tin-ee-an] ADJECTIVE
❶ belonging or relating to Argentina
▷ NOUN ❷ someone who comes
from Argentina.

arguable ADJECTIVE An arguable
idea or point is not necessarily true or
correct and should be questioned.
arguably ADVERB

argue, argues, arguing, argued VERB
❶ If you argue with someone about
something, you disagree with them
about it, sometimes in an angry way.
❷ If you argue that something is the
case, you give reasons why you think it
is so • *She argued that her client had
been wrongly accused.*

argument, arguments NOUN ❶ a
disagreement between two people
which causes a quarrel. ❷ a point or a
set of reasons you use to try to
convince people about something.

▷ SPELLING NOTE: *Rhythmical Hounds Yap To Heavy Music (rhythm)*

argumentative ADJECTIVE An argumentative person is always disagreeing with other people.

aria, arias *[Said ah-ree-a]* NOUN a song sung by one of the leading singers in an opera.

arid ADJECTIVE Arid land is very dry because it has very little rain.

Aries *[Said air-reez]* NOUN Aries is the first sign of the zodiac, represented by a ram. People born between March 21st and April 19th are born under this sign.

arise, arises, arising, arose, arisen VERB ❶ When something such as an opportunity or problem arises, it begins to exist. ❷ FORMAL To arise also means to stand up from a sitting, kneeling, or lying position.

aristocracy, aristocracies NOUN a class of people who have a high social rank and special titles.

aristocrat, aristocrats NOUN someone whose family has a high social rank, and who has a title. **aristocratic** ADJECTIVE

arithmetic NOUN the part of mathematics which is to do with the addition, subtraction, multiplication, and division of numbers. **arithmetical** ADJECTIVE **arithmetically** ADVERB
● **WORD HISTORY:** from Greek *arithmos* meaning 'number'

ark NOUN In the Bible, the ark was the boat built by Noah for his family and the animals during the Flood.
● **USAGE NOTE:** Do not confuse the spellings of *arc* and *ark*

arm, arms, arming, armed NOUN

❶ Your arms are the part of your body between your shoulder and your wrist. ❷ The arms of a chair are the parts on which you rest your arms. ❸ An arm of an organization is a section of it • *the political arm of the armed forces.* ❹ IN PLURAL Arms are weapons used in a war ▷ VERB ❺ To arm someone is to provide them with weapons.

armada, armadas *[Said ar-mah-da]* NOUN a large fleet of warships.

armadillo, armadillos NOUN a mammal from South America which is covered with strong bony plates like armour.
● **WORD HISTORY:** a Spanish word meaning 'little armed man'

Armageddon NOUN In Christianity, Armageddon is the final battle between good and evil at the end of the world.
● **WORD HISTORY:** from Hebrew *har megiddon*, the mountain district of Megiddo, the site of many battles

armament, armaments NOUN Armaments are the weapons and military equipment that belong to a country.

armchair, armchairs NOUN a comfortable chair with a support on each side for your arms.

armed ADJECTIVE A person who is armed is carrying a weapon or weapons.

armistice, armistices *[Said ar-miss-tiss]* NOUN an agreement in a war to stop fighting in order to discuss peace.

armour NOUN In the past, armour was metal clothing worn for

▷ SPELLING NOTE: *A Rude Idiot Thought He Might Eat Toffee In Church* (<u>arithmetic</u>)

protection in battle.

armoured ADJECTIVE covered with thick steel for protection from gunfire and other missiles • *an armoured vehicle.*

armoury, armouries NOUN a place where weapons are stored.

armpit, armpits NOUN the area under your arm where your arm joins your shoulder.

army, armies NOUN a large group of soldiers organized into divisions for fighting on land.

aroma, aromas NOUN a strong, pleasant smell. **aromatic** ADJECTIVE

aromatherapy NOUN a type of therapy that involves massaging the body with special fragrant oils.

around PREPOSITION ❶ placed at various points in a place or area • *There are many seats around the building.* ❷ from place to place inside an area • *We walked around the showroom.* ❸ at approximately the time or place mentioned • *The attacks began around noon.* ▷ ADVERB ❹ here and there • *His papers were scattered around.*

arouse, arouses, arousing, aroused VERB If something arouses a feeling in you, it causes you to begin to have this feeling • *His death still arouses very painful feelings.* **arousal** NOUN

arpeggio, arpeggios [Said ar-**pej**-ee-oh] NOUN In music, an arpeggio is a chord in which the notes are played very quickly one after the other.

● WORD HISTORY: from Italian
● *arpeggiare* meaning 'to play the
● harp'

arrange, arranges, arranging, arranged VERB ❶ If you arrange to do something, you make plans for it. ❷ If you arrange something for someone, you make it possible for them to have it or do it • *The bank has arranged a loan for her.* ❸ If you arrange objects, you set them out in a particular position • *He started to arrange the books in piles.* **arrangement** NOUN

array, arrays NOUN An array of different things is a large number of them displayed together.

arrears PLURAL NOUN ❶ Arrears are amounts of money you owe • *mortgage arrears.* ▷ PHRASE ❷ If you are paid **in arrears**, you are paid at the end of the period for which the payment is due.

arrest, arrests, arresting, arrested VERB ❶ If the police arrest someone, they take them into custody to decide whether to charge them with an offence ▷ NOUN ❷ An arrest is the act of taking a person into custody.

arrival, arrivals NOUN ❶ the act or time of arriving • *The arrival of the train was delayed.* ❷ something or someone that has arrived • *The tourist authority reported record arrivals over Christmas.*

arrive, arrives, arriving, arrived VERB ❶ When you arrive at a place, you reach it at the end of your journey. ❷ When a letter or a piece of news arrives, it is brought to you • *A letter arrived at her lawyer's office.* ❸ When you arrive at an idea or decision you reach it. ❹ When a moment, event, or new thing arrives, it begins to happen • *The Easter holidays arrived.*

▷ SPELLING NOTE: *On WEDNESday Wayne WED NESta (Wednesday)*

arrogant ADJECTIVE Someone who is arrogant behaves as if they are better than other people. **arrogantly** ADVERB **arrogance** NOUN

arrow, arrows NOUN a long, thin weapon with a sharp point at one end, shot from a bow.

arsenal, arsenals NOUN a place where weapons and ammunition are stored or produced.
● **WORD HISTORY:** from Italian
● *arsenale* meaning 'dockyard',
● originally in Venice

arsenic NOUN a very strong poison which can kill people.

arson NOUN the crime of deliberately setting fire to something, especially a building.

art, arts NOUN ❶ Art is the creation of objects such as paintings and sculptures, which are thought to be beautiful or which express a particular idea; also used to refer to the objects themselves. ❷ An activity is called an art when it requires special skill or ability • *the art of diplomacy.* ❸ IN PLURAL The arts are literature, music, painting, and sculpture, considered together.

artefact, artefacts [Said *ar-tif-fact*] NOUN any object made by people.

artery, arteries NOUN ❶ Your arteries are the tubes that carry blood from your heart to the rest of your body. ❷ a main road or major section of any system of communication or transport.

artesian well, artesian wells NOUN (GEOGRAPHY) An artesian well is a well in which water is continually

forced upwards under pressure.

artful ADJECTIVE clever and skilful, often in a cunning way. **artfully** ADVERB

arthritis NOUN a condition in which the joints in someone's body become swollen and painful. **arthritic** ADJECTIVE

artichoke, artichokes NOUN ❶ the round green partly edible flower head of a thistle-like plant; the flower head is made up of clusters of leaves that have a soft fleshy part that is eaten as a vegetable. ❷ A Jerusalem artichoke is a small yellowish-white vegetable that grows underground and looks like a potato.

article, articles NOUN ❶ (LIBRARY) a piece of writing in a newspaper or magazine. ❷ a particular item • *an article of clothing.* ❸ In English grammar, 'a' and 'the' are sometimes called articles: 'a' (or 'an') is the indefinite article; 'the' is the definite article.

articulate, articulates, articulating, articulated ADJECTIVE ❶ If you are articulate, you are able to express yourself well in words ▷ VERB ❷ When you articulate your ideas or feelings, you express in words what you think or feel • *She could not articulate her grief.* ❸ When you articulate a sound or word, you speak it clearly. **articulation** NOUN

artificial ADJECTIVE ❶ created by people rather than occurring naturally • *artificial colouring.* ❷ pretending to have attitudes and feelings which other people realize are not real • *an artificial smile.* **artificially** ADVERB

a
b
c
d
e
f
g
h
i
j
k
l
m
n
o
p
q
r
s
t
u
v
w
x
y
z

▷ SPELLING NOTE: Eddy Ant thinks mEAt is a grEAt trEAt to EAt (-ea-)

artillery NOUN ❶ Artillery consists of large, powerful guns such as cannons. ❷ The artillery is the branch of an army which uses large, powerful guns.

artist, artists NOUN ❶ a person who draws or paints or produces other works of art. ❷ a person who is very skilled at a particular activity.

artiste, artistes [Said ar-**teest**] NOUN a professional entertainer, for example a singer or a dancer.

artistic ADJECTIVE ❶ able to create good paintings, sculpture, or other works of art. ❷ concerning or involving art or artists. **artistically** ADVERB

artistry NOUN Artistry is the creative skill of an artist, writer, actor, or musician • *a supreme demonstration of his artistry as a cellist.*

arty, artier, artiest ADJECTIVE INFORMAL interested in painting, sculpture, and other works of art.

as CONJUNCTION ❶ at the same time that • *She waved at fans as she arrived for the concert.* ❷ in the way that • *They had talked as only the best of friends can.* ❸ because • *As I won't be back tonight, don't bother to cook a meal.* ❹ You use the structure **as... as** when you are comparing things that are similar • *It was as big as four football pitches.* ▷ PREPOSITION ❺ You use 'as' when you are saying what role someone or something has • *She worked as a waitress.* ❻ You use **as if** or **as though** when you are giving a possible explanation for something • *He looked at me as if I were mad.*

asbestos NOUN a grey heat-resistant material used in the past to make fireproof articles.

ASBO NOUN an abbreviation for 'antisocial behaviour order': an order from a judge preventing people who have been persistently annoying or upsetting other people from continuing to do so.

ascend, ascends, ascending, ascended VERB FORMAL To ascend is to move or lead upwards • *We finally ascended to the brow of a steep hill.*

ascendancy NOUN FORMAL If one group has ascendancy over another, it has more power or influence than the other.

ascendant ADJECTIVE ❶ rising or moving upwards ▷ PHRASE ❷ Someone or something **in the ascendant** is increasing in power or popularity.

ascent, ascents NOUN an upward journey, for example up a mountain.

ascertain, ascertains, ascertaining, ascertained [Said ass-er-**tain**] VERB FORMAL If you ascertain that something is the case, you find out it is the case • *He had ascertained that she had given up smoking.*

ascribe, ascribes, ascribing, ascribed VERB ❶ If you ascribe an event or state of affairs to a particular cause, you think that it is the cause of it • *His stomach pains were ascribed to his intake of pork.* ❷ If you ascribe a quality to someone, you think they have it.

ash, ashes NOUN ❶ the grey or black

▷ SPELLING NOTE: *Elaine and Emily shout EE when they mEEt to grEEt each other (-ee-)*

powdery remains of anything that has been burnt. ❷ a tree with grey bark and hard tough wood used for timber.

ashamed ADJECTIVE ❶ feeling embarrassed or guilty. ❷ If you are ashamed of someone, you feel embarrassed to be connected with them.

ashen ADJECTIVE grey or pale • *Her face was ashen with fatigue.*

ashore ADVERB on land or onto the land.

ashtray, ashtrays NOUN a small dish for ash from cigarettes and cigars.

Asia NOUN Asia is the largest continent. It has Europe on its western side, with the Arctic to the north, the Pacific to the east, and the Indian Ocean to the south. Asia includes several island groups, including Japan, Indonesia, and the Philippines.

Asian, Asians ADJECTIVE ❶ belonging or relating to Asia ▷ NOUN ❷ someone who comes from India, Pakistan, Bangladesh, or from some other part of Asia.

aside, asides ADVERB ❶ If you move something aside, you move it to one side ▷ NOUN ❷ a comment made away from the main conversation or dialogue that all those talking are not meant to hear.

ask, asks, asking, asked VERB ❶ If you ask someone a question, you put a question to them for them to answer. ❷ If you ask someone to do something or give you something, you tell them you want them to do it or to give it to you. ❸ If you ask someone's permission or forgiveness, you try to

obtain it. ❹ If you ask someone somewhere, you invite them there • *Not everybody had been asked to the wedding.*

askew ADJECTIVE not straight.

asleep ADJECTIVE sleeping.

AS level, AS levels NOUN an exam taken by students in many British schools and colleges, more advanced than GCSE but less advanced than A level.

asparagus NOUN a vegetable that has long shoots which are cooked and eaten.

aspect, aspects NOUN ❶ An aspect of something is one of its features • *Exam results illustrate only one aspect of a school's success.* ❷ The aspect of a building is the direction it faces • *The southern aspect of the cottage faces over fields.*

asphalt NOUN a black substance used to make road surfaces and playgrounds.

aspiration, aspirations NOUN Someone's aspirations are their desires and ambitions.

aspire, aspires, aspiring, aspired VERB If you aspire to something, you have an ambition to achieve it • *He aspired to work in music journalism.* **aspiring** ADJECTIVE

aspirin, aspirins NOUN ❶ a white drug used to relieve pain, fever, and colds. ❷ a tablet of this drug.

ass, asses NOUN a donkey.

assailant, assailants NOUN someone who attacks another person.

a
b
c
d
e
f
g
h
i
j
k
l
m
n
o
p
q
r
s
t
u
v
w
x
y
z

▷ SPELLING NOTE: *'i' before 'e' except after 'c'*

assassin, assassins **NOUN** someone who has murdered a political or religious leader.

- **WORD HISTORY:** from Arabic *hashshashin* meaning 'people who eat hashish'; the name comes from a medieval Muslim sect who ate hashish and went about murdering Crusaders

assassinate, assassinates, assassinating, assassinated **VERB** To assassinate a political or religious leader is to murder him or her. **assassination NOUN**

assault, assaults, assaulting, assaulted **NOUN** ❶ A violent attack on someone ▷ **VERB** ❷ To assault someone is to attack them violently.

assegai, assegais [Said *ass-i-guy*]; also spelt **assagai NOUN** In South African English, a sharp, light spear.

assemble, assembles, assembling, assembled **VERB** ❶ To assemble is to gather together. ❷ If you assemble something, you fit the parts of it together.

assembly, assemblies **NOUN** ❶ a group of people who have gathered together for a meeting. ❷ The assembly of an object is the fitting together of its parts • *DIY assembly of units.*

assent, assents, assenting, assented [Said *as-sent*] **NOUN** ❶ If you give your assent to something, you agree to it ▷ **VERB** ❷ If you assent to something, you agree to it.

assert, asserts, asserting, asserted **VERB** ❶ If you assert a fact or belief, you state it firmly and forcefully. ❷ If you assert yourself, you speak and

behave in a confident and direct way, so that people pay attention to you.

assertion, assertions **NOUN** a statement or claim.

assertive ADJECTIVE If you are assertive, you speak and behave in a confident and direct way, so that people pay attention to you. **assertively ADVERB assertiveness NOUN**

assess, assesses, assessing, assessed **VERB** (EXAM TERM) If you assess something, you consider it carefully and make a judgment about it. **assessment NOUN**

- **SIMILAR WORDS:** appraise, judge, size up

assessor, assessors **NOUN** someone whose job is to assess the value of something.

asset, assets **NOUN** ❶ a person or thing considered useful • *He will be a great asset to the club.* ❷ IN PLURAL The assets of a person or company are all the things they own that could be sold to raise money.

assign, assigns, assigning, assigned **VERB** ❶ To assign something to someone is to give it to them officially or to make them responsible for it. ❷ If someone is assigned to do something, they are officially told to do it.

- **SIMILAR WORDS:** ❶ allocate, allot, give ❷ appoint, choose, select

assignation, assignations [Said *ass-ig-nay-shn*] **NOUN** LITERARY a secret meeting with someone, especially a lover.

▷ SPELLING NOTE: *King IAn went to ParlIAment in a carrIAge for his marrIAge (-ia-)*

assignment, assignments NOUN a job someone is given to do.

assimilate, assimilates, assimilating, assimilated VERB ❶ If you assimilate ideas or experiences, you learn and understand them. ❷ When people are assimilated into a group, they become part of it. **assimilation** NOUN

assist, assists, assisting, assisted VERB To assist someone is to help them do something. **assistance** NOUN

assistant, assistants NOUN someone whose job is to help another person in their work.

associate, associates, associating, associated VERB ❶ If you associate one thing with another, you connect the two things in your mind. ❷ If you associate with a group of people, you spend a lot of time with them ▷ NOUN ❸ Your associates are the people you work with or spend a lot of time with.
● SIMILAR WORDS: ❶ connect,
● link, relate ❷ consort, mix,
● socialize

association, associations NOUN ❶ an organization for people who have similar interests, jobs, or aims. ❷ Your association with a person or group is the connection or involvement you have with them. ❸ An association between two things is a link you make in your mind between them • *The place contained associations for her.*

assonance NOUN (ENGLISH) the use of similar vowel or consonant sounds in words near to each other or in the same word, for example 'a long storm'.

assorted ADJECTIVE Assorted things are different in size and colour • *assorted swimsuits.*

assortment, assortments NOUN a group of similar things that are different sizes and colours • *an amazing assortment of old toys.*

assume, assumes, assuming, assumed VERB ❶ If you assume that something is true, you accept it is true even though you have not thought about it • *I assumed that he would turn up.* ❷ To assume responsibility for something is to put yourself in charge of it.
● SIMILAR WORDS: ❶ believe,
● presume, suppose, take for granted
● ❷ accept, shoulder, take on

assumption, assumptions NOUN ❶ a belief that something is true, without thinking about it. ❷ Assumption of power or responsibility is the taking of it.

assurance, assurances NOUN ❶ something said which is intended to make people less worried • *She was emphatic in her assurances that she wanted to stay.* ❷ Assurance is a feeling of confidence • *He handled the car with ease and assurance.* ❸ Life assurance is a type of insurance that pays money to your dependants when you die.

assure, assures, assuring, assured VERB If you assure someone that something is true, you tell them it is true.

asterisk, asterisks NOUN a star-shaped symbol (*) used in

▷ SPELLING NOTE: *an ELegant angEL (angel)*

a
b
c
d
e
f
g
h
i
j
k
l
m
n
o
p
q
r
s
t
u
v
w
x
y
z

printing and writing.
- **WORD HISTORY:** from Greek
- *asterikos* meaning 'small star'

astern ADVERB OR ADJECTIVE
NAUTICAL backwards or at the back.

asteroid, asteroids NOUN one of the large number of very small planets that move around the sun between the orbits of Jupiter and Mars.

asthma [Said *ass-ma*] NOUN a disease of the chest which causes wheezing and difficulty in breathing. **asthmatic** ADJECTIVE

astonish, astonishes, astonishing, astonished VERB If something astonishes you, it surprises you very much. **astonished** ADJECTIVE
astonishing ADJECTIVE
astonishingly ADVERB
astonishment NOUN

astound, astounds, astounding, astounded VERB If something astounds you, it shocks and amazes you. **astounded** ADJECTIVE
astounding ADJECTIVE

astray PHRASE ❶ To **lead someone astray** is to influence them to do something wrong. ❷ If something **goes astray**, it gets lost • *The money had gone astray*.

astride PREPOSITION with one leg on either side of something • *He is pictured astride his new motorbike*.

astringent, astringents [Said *ass-trin-jent*] NOUN a liquid that makes skin less greasy and stops bleeding.

astro- PREFIX 'Astro-' means 'involving the stars and planets'. For example, *astrology* is predicting the

future from the positions and movements of the stars and planets, and *astronomy* is the scientific study of the stars and planets.

astrology NOUN the study of the sun, moon, and stars in order to predict the future. **astrological** ADJECTIVE **astrologer** NOUN

astronaut, astronauts NOUN a person who operates a spacecraft.
- **WORD HISTORY:** from Greek
- *astron* meaning 'star' and *nautēs*
- meaning 'sailor'

astronomical ADJECTIVE
❶ involved with or relating to astronomy. ❷ extremely large in amount • *astronomical legal costs*.
astronomically ADVERB

astronomy NOUN the scientific study of stars and planets.
astronomer NOUN

astute ADJECTIVE clever and quick at understanding situations and behaviour • *an astute diplomat*.

asunder ADVERB LITERARY If something is torn asunder, it is violently torn apart.

asylum, asylums [Said *ass-eye-lum*] NOUN ❶ OLD-FASHIONED a hospital for mental patients. ❷ Political asylum is protection given by a government to someone who has fled from their own country for political reasons.

asymmetrical or **asymmetric** [Said *ay-sim-met-ri-kl*] ADJECTIVE unbalanced or with one half not exactly the same as the other half. **asymmetry** NOUN

at PREPOSITION ❶ used to say

▷ SPELLING NOTE: *LEt's measure the angLE (angle)*

where someone or something is • *Bert met us at the airport.* ❷ used to mention the direction something is going in • *He threw his plate at the wall.* ❸ used to say when something happens • *The game starts at 3 o'clock.* ❹ used to mention the rate or price of something • *The shares were priced at fifty pence.*

atheist, atheists *[Said ayth-ee-ist]* NOUN someone who believes there is no God. **atheistic** ADJECTIVE **atheism** NOUN

athlete, athletes NOUN PE someone who is good at sport and takes part in sporting events.

athletic ADJECTIVE PE ❶ strong, healthy, and good at sports. ❷ involving athletes or athletics • *I lost two years of my athletic career because of injury.*

athletics PLURAL NOUN Sporting events such as running, jumping, and throwing are called athletics.

Atlantic NOUN The Atlantic is the ocean separating North and South America from Europe and Africa.

atlas, atlases NOUN GEOGRAPHY a book of maps.
⬤ **WORD HISTORY:** from the giant
⬤ *Atlas* in Greek mythology, who
⬤ supported the sky on his shoulders

atmosphere, atmospheres NOUN ❶ SCIENCE GEOGRAPHY the air and other gases that surround a planet; also the air in a particular place • *a musty atmosphere.* ❷ the general mood of a place • *a relaxed atmosphere.* ❸ ENGLISH the mood created by the writer of a novel or play. **atmospheric** ADJECTIVE

atom, atoms NOUN the smallest part of an element that can take part in a chemical reaction.

atomic ADJECTIVE relating to atoms or to the power released by splitting atoms • *atomic energy.*

atomic bomb, atomic bombs NOUN an extremely powerful bomb which explodes because of the energy that comes from splitting atoms.

atomic number, atomic numbers NOUN SCIENCE The atomic number of a chemical element is a number used to classify it, which is equal to the number of protons in the nucleus of the atom of the element.

atone, atones, atoning, atoned VERB FORMAL If you atone for something wrong you have done, you say you are sorry and try to make up for it.

atrocious ADJECTIVE extremely bad.

atrocity, atrocities NOUN an extremely cruel and shocking act.

attach, attaches, attaching, attached VERB If you attach something to something else, you join or fasten two things together.

attaché, attachés *[Said at-tash-ay]* NOUN a member of staff in an embassy • *the Russian Cultural Attaché.*

attached ADJECTIVE If you are attached to someone, you are very fond of them.

attachment, attachments NOUN ❶ Attachment to someone is a feeling of love and affection for them. ❷ Attachment to a cause or ideal is a

a
b
c
d
e
f
g
h
i
j
k
l
m
n
o
p
q
r
s
t
u
v
w
x
y
z

▷ SPELLING NOTE: *A Rude Idiot Thought He Might Eat Toffee In Church (arithmetic)*

strong belief in it and support for it.
❸ a piece of equipment attached to a
tool or machine to do a particular job.
❹ an extra document attached to or
included with another document. ❺ a
file that is attached to an e-mail.

attack, attacks, attacking, attacked
VERB ❶ To attack someone is to use
violence against them so as to hurt or
kill them. ❷ If you attack someone or
their ideas, you criticize them strongly
• *He attacked the government's
economic policies.* ❸ If a disease or
chemical attacks something, it
damages or destroys it • *fungal
diseases that attack crops.* ❹ In a game
such as football or hockey, to attack is
to get the ball into a position from
which a goal can be scored ▷ **NOUN**
❺ An attack is violent physical action
against someone. ❻ An attack on
someone or on their ideas is strong
criticism of them. ❼ An attack of an
illness is a short time in which you
suffer badly with it. **attacker NOUN**
  ● **SIMILAR WORDS:** ❶ assault, set
  ● upon ❷ censure, criticize
  ● ❺ assault, onslaught

attain, attains, attaining, attained
VERB FORMAL If you attain
something, you manage to achieve it
• *I eventually attained the rank of
major.* **attainable ADJECTIVE
attainment NOUN**

attempt, attempts, attempting,
attempted **VERB** ❶ If you attempt to
do something, you try to do it or
achieve it, but may not succeed • *They
attempted to escape.* ▷ **NOUN** ❷ an
act of trying to do something • *He
made no attempt to go for the ball.*

attend, attends, attending, attended

VERB ❶ If you attend an event, you
are present at it. ❷ To attend school,
church, or hospital is to go there
regularly. ❸ If you attend to
something, you deal with it • *We have
business to attend to first.* **attendance
NOUN**

attendant, attendants **NOUN**
someone whose job is to serve people
in a place such as a garage or
cloakroom.

attention NOUN Attention is the
thought or care you give to something
• *The woman needed medical attention.*

attentive ADJECTIVE paying close
attention to something • *an attentive
audience.* **attentively ADVERB
attentiveness NOUN**

attest, attests, attesting, attested
VERB FORMAL To attest something is
to show or declare it is true.
attestation NOUN

attic, attics **NOUN** a room at the top
of a house immediately below the
roof.

attire NOUN FORMAL Attire is
clothing • *We will be wearing
traditional wedding attire.*

attitude, attitudes **NOUN** Your
attitude to someone or something is
the way you think about them and
behave towards them.

attorney, attorneys [*Said at-**turn**-
ee*] **NOUN** In America, an attorney is
the same as a lawyer.

attract, attracts, attracting, attracted
VERB ❶ If something attracts people,
it interests them and makes them
want to go to it • *The trials have
attracted many leading riders.* ❷ If

someone attracts you, you like and admire them • *He was attracted to her outgoing personality.* ❸ If something attracts support or publicity, it gets it. ❹ (SCIENCE) If something attracts objects to it, it has a force that pulls them towards it.

attraction, attractions NOUN ❶ Attraction is a feeling of liking someone or something very much. ❷ something people visit for interest or pleasure • *The temple is a major tourist attraction.* ❸ a quality that attracts someone or something • *the attraction of moving to seaside resorts.* ❹ (SCIENCE) In physics, attraction is a force that pulls two objects toward each other.

attractive ADJECTIVE ❶ interesting and possibly advantageous • *an attractive proposition.* ❷ pleasant to look at or be with • *an attractive woman* • *an attractive personality.* **attractively** ADVERB **attractiveness** NOUN
● SIMILAR WORDS: ❶ appealing, tempting ❷ charming, lovely, pleasant

attribute, attributes, attributing, attributed VERB *[Said a-**trib**-yoot]* ❶ If you attribute something to a person or thing, you believe it was caused or created by that person or thing • *Water pollution was attributed to the use of fertilizers* • *a painting attributed to Raphael.* ▷ NOUN *[Said a-trib-yoot]* ❷ a quality or feature someone or something has. **attribution** NOUN **attributable** ADJECTIVE

attrition NOUN ❶ Attrition is the constant wearing down of an enemy.

❷ (GEOGRAPHY) the process by which rocks gradually become smaller and smoother as they rub against one another in moving water.

attuned ADJECTIVE accustomed or well adjusted to something • *His eyes quickly became attuned to the dark.*

aubergine, aubergines *[Said oh-ber-jeen]* NOUN a dark purple, pear-shaped fruit that is eaten as a vegetable. It is also called an eggplant.

auburn ADJECTIVE Auburn hair is reddish brown.

auction, auctions, auctioning, auctioned NOUN ❶ a public sale in which goods are sold to the person who offers the highest price ▷ VERB ❷ To auction something is to sell it in an auction.

auctioneer, auctioneers NOUN the person in charge of an auction.

audacious ADJECTIVE very daring • *an audacious escape from jail.* **audaciously** ADVERB **audacity** NOUN

audi- PREFIX 'Audi-' means involving hearing or sound • *audible* • *auditorium.*

audible ADJECTIVE loud enough to be heard • *She spoke in a barely audible whisper.* **audibly** ADVERB **audibility** NOUN

audience, audiences NOUN ❶ the group of people who are watching or listening to a performance. ❷ a private or formal meeting with an important person • *an audience with the Queen.*

audio ADJECTIVE used in recording and reproducing sound • *audio equipment.*

audit, audits, auditing, audited VERB **❶** To audit a set of financial accounts is to examine them officially to check they are correct ▷ NOUN **❷** an official examination of an organization's accounts. **auditor** NOUN

audition, auditions NOUN a short performance given by an actor or musician, so that a director can decide whether they are suitable for a part in a play or film or for a place in an orchestra.

auditorium, auditoriums or auditoria NOUN the part of a theatre where the audience sits.

augment, augments, augmenting, augmented VERB FORMAL To augment something is to add something to it.

August NOUN the eighth month of the year. August has 31 days.
● **WORD HISTORY:** from the name
● of the Roman emperor *Augustus*

aunt, aunts NOUN Your aunt is the sister of your mother or father, or the wife of your uncle.

au pair, au pairs [Said oh *pair*] NOUN a young foreign girl who lives with a family to help with the children and housework and sometimes to learn the language.
● **WORD HISTORY:** a French
● expression meaning 'on equal
● terms'

aura, auras NOUN an atmosphere that surrounds a person or thing • She has a great aura of calmness.

aural [rhymes with *floral*] ADJECTIVE relating to or done through the sense of hearing • *an aural comprehension test.*

aurora borealis [Said aw-**roh**-ra bor-ee-**ay**-liss] NOUN (SCIENCE) The aurora borealis consists of bands of glowing coloured light sometimes seen in the sky in the Arctic. It is caused by charged particles discharged from the sun hitting the earth's atmosphere at an acute angle. A similar phenomenon in the Antarctic is called the **aurora australis**.
● **WORD HISTORY:** from Latin
● meaning 'northern dawn'

auspices [Said **aw**-spiss-eez] PLURAL NOUN FORMAL If you do something under the auspices of a person or organization, you do it with their support • *military intervention under the auspices of the United Nations.*

auspicious ADJECTIVE FORMAL favourable and seeming to promise success • *It was an auspicious start to the month.*

austere ADJECTIVE plain and simple, and without luxury • *an austere grey office block.* **austerity** NOUN

Australasia [Said ost-ral-**lay**-sha] NOUN Australasia consists of Australia, New Zealand, and neighbouring islands in the Pacific. **Australasian** ADJECTIVE

Australia NOUN Australia is the smallest continent and the largest island in the world, situated between the Indian Ocean and the Pacific.

Australian, Australians ADJECTIVE
❶ belonging or relating to Australia
▷ NOUN ❷ someone who comes
from Australia.

Austrian, Austrians ADJECTIVE
❶ belonging or relating to Austria
▷ NOUN ❷ someone who comes
from Austria.

authentic ADJECTIVE real and
genuine. **authenticity** NOUN

author, authors NOUN (ENGLISH)
The author of a book is the person
who wrote it.
● USAGE NOTE: Use *author* to talk
● about both men and women
● writers, as *authoress* is now felt to
● be insulting

authoritarian ADJECTIVE
believing in strict obedience • *thirty
years of authoritarian government*.
authoritarianism NOUN

authoritative ADJECTIVE
❶ having authority • *his deep,
authoritative voice*. ❷ accepted as
being reliable and accurate • *an
authoritative biography of the President*.
authoritatively ADVERB

authority, authorities NOUN
❶ Authority is the power to control
people • *the authority of the state*. ❷
(GEOGRAPHY) In Britain, an authority
is a local government department
• *local health authorities*. ❸ Someone
who is an authority on something
knows a lot about it • *the world's
leading authority on fashion*. ❹ IN
PLURAL The authorities are the people
who have the power to make
decisions.

authorize, authorizes, authorizing,
authorized; *also spelt* **authorise** VERB

To authorize something is to give
official permission for it to happen.
authorization NOUN

autism NOUN a mental condition
which some children are born with, in
which they do not respond normally to
other people. **autistic** ADJECTIVE

auto- PREFIX 'Auto-' means 'self'.
For example, an *automatic* machine
works by itself without needing to be
operated by hand.

autobiography, autobiographies
NOUN Someone's autobiography is an
account of their life which they have
written themselves.
autobiographical ADJECTIVE

autograph, autographs NOUN the
handwritten signature of a famous
person.

automated ADJECTIVE If a factory
or way of making things is automated,
it works using machinery rather than
people. **automation** NOUN

automatic ADJECTIVE ❶ An
automatic machine is programmed to
perform tasks without needing a
person to operate it • *The plane was
flying on automatic pilot*. ❷ Automatic
actions or reactions take place without
involving conscious thought. ❸ A
process or punishment that is
automatic always happens as a direct
result of something • *The penalty for
murder is an automatic life sentence*.
automatically ADVERB

automobile, automobiles NOUN
AMERICAN OR FORMAL a car.

autonomous [*Said aw-ton-nom-
uss*] ADJECTIVE An autonomous
country governs itself rather than

A
B
C
D
E
F
G
H
I
J
K
L
M
N
O
P
Q
R
S
T
U
V
W
X
Y
Z

being controlled by anyone else.
autonomy NOUN

autopsy, autopsies NOUN a medical examination of a dead body to discover the cause of death.

autotrophic ADJECTIVE (SCIENCE) a term used to describe organisms that can make food from inorganic materials.

autumn, autumns NOUN the season between summer and winter. **autumnal** ADJECTIVE

auxiliary, auxiliaries NOUN ❶ a person employed to help other members of staff • *nursing auxiliaries.* ▷ ADJECTIVE ❷ Auxiliary equipment is used when necessary in addition to the main equipment • *Auxiliary fuel tanks were stored in the bomb bay.*

auxiliary verb, auxiliary verbs NOUN In grammar, an auxiliary verb is a verb which forms tenses of other verbs or questions. For example in 'He has gone', 'has' is the auxiliary verb and in 'Do you understand?', 'do' is the auxiliary verb.

avail PHRASE If something you do is **of no avail** or **to no avail**, it is not successful or helpful.

available ADJECTIVE ❶ Something that is available can be obtained • *Artichokes are available in supermarkets.* ❷ Someone who is available is ready for work or free for people to talk to • *She will no longer be available at weekends.* **availability** NOUN
● SIMILAR WORDS: ❷ accessible

avalanche, avalanches [Said *av-a-lahnsh*] NOUN a huge mass of

snow and ice that falls down a mountain side.

avant-garde [Said *av-vong-gard*] ADJECTIVE extremely modern or experimental, especially in art, literature, or music.

avarice NOUN FORMAL greed for money and possessions. **avaricious** ADJECTIVE

avenge, avenges, avenging, avenged VERB If you avenge something harmful someone has done to you or your family, you punish or harm the other person in return • *He was prepared to avenge the death of his friend.* **avenger** NOUN

avenue, avenues NOUN a street, especially one with trees along it.

average, averages, averaging, averaged NOUN ❶ (MATHS) a result obtained by adding several amounts together and then dividing the total by the number of different amounts • *Six pupils were examined in a total of 39 subjects, an average of 6.5 subjects per pupil.* ▷ ADJECTIVE ❷ Average means standard or normal • *the average American teenager.* ▷ VERB ❸ To average a number is to produce that number as an average over a period of time • *Monthly sales averaged more than 110,000.* ▷ PHRASE ❹ You say **on average** when mentioning what usually happens in a situation • *Men are, on average, taller than women.*
● SIMILAR WORDS: ❷ normal, ordinary, typical, usual

averse ADJECTIVE unwilling to do something • *He was averse to taking painkillers.*

aversion, aversions **NOUN** If you have an aversion to someone or something, you dislike them very much.

avert, averts, averting, averted **VERB** ❶ If you avert an unpleasant event, you prevent it from happening. ❷ If you avert your eyes from something, you turn your eyes away from it.

aviary, aviaries **NOUN** a large cage or group of cages in which birds are kept.

aviation **NOUN** the science of flying aircraft.

aviator, aviators **NOUN** OLD-FASHIONED a pilot of an aircraft.

avid **ADJECTIVE** eager and enthusiastic for something. **avidly** **ADVERB**

avocado, avocados **NOUN** a pear-shaped fruit, with dark green skin, soft greenish yellow flesh, and a large stone.

avoid, avoids, avoiding, avoided **VERB** ❶ If you avoid doing something, you make a deliberate effort not to do it. ❷ If you avoid someone, you keep away from them. **avoidable** **ADJECTIVE** **avoidance** **NOUN**

● SIMILAR WORDS: ❶ dodge,
● refrain from, shirk ❷ dodge, evade,
● keep away from

avowed **ADJECTIVE** ❶ FORMAL If you are an avowed supporter or opponent of something, you have declared that you support it or oppose it. ❷ An avowed belief or aim is one you hold very strongly.

avuncular **ADJECTIVE** friendly and helpful in manner towards younger

people, rather like an uncle.

await, awaits, awaiting, awaited **VERB** ❶ If you await something, you expect it. ❷ If something awaits you, it will happen to you in the future.

awake, awakes, awaking, awoke, awoken **ADJECTIVE** ❶ Someone who is awake is not sleeping ▷ **VERB** ❷ When you awake, you wake up. ❸ If you are awoken by something, it wakes you up.

awaken, awakens, awakening, awakened **VERB** If something awakens an emotion or interest in you, you start to feel this emotion or interest.

award, awards, awarding, awarded **NOUN** ❶ a prize or certificate for doing something well. ❷ a sum of money an organization gives to students for training or study ▷ **VERB** ❸ If you award someone something, you give it to them formally or officially.

aware **ADJECTIVE** ❶ If you are aware of something, you realize it is there. ❷ If you are aware of something, you know about it. **awareness** **NOUN**
● SIMILAR WORDS: conscious
● of, knowing about, mindful of

awash **ADJECTIVE OR ADVERB** covered with water • *After the downpour the road was awash.*

away **ADVERB** ❶ moving from a place • *I saw them walk away.* ❷ at a distance from a place • *Our nearest vet is 12 kilometres away.* ❸ in its proper place • *He put his chequebook away.* ❹ not at home, school, or work • *She had been away from home for years.*

▷ SPELLING NOTE: *I want to see (C) your licenCe (licence)*

awe NOUN FORMAL a feeling of great respect mixed with amazement and sometimes slight fear.

awesome ADJECTIVE
1 Something that is awesome is very impressive and frightening.
2 INFORMAL Awesome also means excellent or outstanding.

awful ADJECTIVE **1** very unpleasant or very bad. **2** INFORMAL very great • *It took an awful lot of courage.* **awfully** ADVERB
● SIMILAR WORDS: **1** appalling, ● dreadful, terrible

awkward ADJECTIVE **1** clumsy and uncomfortable • *an awkward gesture.* **2** embarrassed or nervous • *He was a shy, awkward young man.* **3** difficult to deal with • *My lawyer is in an awkward situation.*
● WORD HISTORY: from Old Norse ● *ofugr* meaning 'turned the wrong ● way'

awning, awnings NOUN a large roof of canvas or plastic attached to a building or vehicle.

awry [Said a-**rye**] ADJECTIVE wrong or not as planned • *Why had their plans gone so badly awry?*

axe, axes, axing, axed NOUN **1** a tool with a handle and a sharp blade, used for chopping wood ▷ VERB **2** To axe something is to end it.

axiom, axioms NOUN a statement or saying that is generally accepted to be true.

axis, axes [Said ak-**siss**] NOUN (MATHS) **1** an imaginary line through the centre of something, around which it moves. **2** one of the two sides of a graph.

axle, axles NOUN the long bar that connects a pair of wheels on a vehicle.

ayatollah, ayatollahs NOUN an Islamic religious leader in Iran.

azure [Said az-**yoor**] ADJECTIVE LITERARY bright blue.

Bb

babble, babbles, babbling, babbled **VERB** When someone babbles, they talk in a confused or excited way.

baboon, baboons **NOUN** An African monkey with a pointed face, large teeth, and a long tail.
- **WORD HISTORY:** from Old French
- *baboue* meaning 'grimace'

baby, babies **NOUN** a child in the first year or two of its life. **babyhood NOUN** **babyish ADJECTIVE**
- **SIMILAR WORDS:** babe, infant

baby-sit, baby-sits, baby-sitting, baby-sat **VERB** To baby-sit for someone means to look after their children while that person is out. **baby-sitter NOUN** **baby-sitting NOUN**

baccalaureate, baccalaureates [Said back-uh-law-ree-it] **NOUN** an internationally recognized course of study made up of several different subjects, offered by some schools as an alternative to A levels.

bach, baches, baching, bached [Said batch] **NOUN** ❶ In New Zealand, a small holiday cottage ▷ **VERB** ❷ INFORMAL In Australian and New Zealand English, to bach is to live and keep a house on your own, especially when you are not used to it.

bachelor, bachelors **NOUN** a man who has never been married.

back, backs, backing, backed **ADVERB** ❶ When people or things move back, they move in the opposite direction from the one they are facing. ❷ When people or things go back to a place or situation, they return to it • *She went back to sleep.* ❸ If you get something back, it is returned to you. ❹ If you do something back to someone, you do to them what they have done to you • *I smiled back at them.* ❺ Back also means in the past • *It happened back in the early eighties.* ▷ **NOUN** ❻ the rear part of your body. ❼ the part of something that is behind the front ▷ **ADJECTIVE** ❽ The back parts of something are the ones near the rear • *an animal's back legs.* ▷ **VERB** ❾ If a building backs onto something, its back faces in that direction. ❿ When a car backs, it moves backwards. ⓫ To back a person or organization means to support or finance that person or organization.

back down VERB If you back down on a demand or claim, you withdraw and give up.

back out VERB If you back out of a promise or commitment, you decide not to do what you promised to do.

back up VERB ❶ If you back up a claim or story, you produce evidence to show that it is true. ❷ If you back someone up, you help and support them.

backbencher, backbenchers
NOUN A backbencher is a Member of Parliament who is not a government minister and who does not have an official position as a spokesperson for an opposition party.

backbone, backbones NOUN
❶ the column of linked bones along the middle of a person's or animal's back. ❷ strength of character.

backdate, backdates, backdating, backdated VERB If an arrangement is backdated, it is valid from a date earlier than the one on which it is completed or signed.

backdrop, backdrops NOUN the background to a situation or event • The visit occurred against the backdrop of the political crisis.

backer, backers NOUN The backers of a project are the people who give it financial help.

backfire, backfires, backfiring, backfired VERB ❶ If a plan backfires, it fails. ❷ When a car backfires, there is a small but noisy explosion in its exhaust pipe.

background, backgrounds NOUN
❶ the circumstances which help to explain an event or caused it to happen. ❷ the kind of home you come from and your education and experience • a rich background. ❸ If sounds are in the background, they are there but no one really pays any attention to them • She could hear voices in the background.

backhand, backhands NOUN OR ADJECTIVE (PE) Backhand is a stroke in tennis, squash, or badminton made in front of your body with the back of

your hand facing in the direction that you hit the ball.

backing NOUN support or help • The project got government backing.

backlash, backslashes NOUN a hostile reaction to a new development or a new policy.

backlog, backlogs NOUN a number of things which have not yet been done, but which need to be done.

backpack, backpacks NOUN a large bag that hikers or campers carry on their backs.

backside, backsides NOUN INFORMAL the part of your body that you sit on.

backstroke NOUN (PE) Backstroke is a swimming stroke in which you lie on your back, kick your legs, and move your arms back over your head.

backward ADJECTIVE
❶ Backward means directed behind you • without a backward glance. ❷ A backward country or society is one that does not have modern industries or technology. ❸ A backward child is one who is unable to learn as quickly as other children of the same age.
backwardness NOUN

backwards ADVERB
❶ Backwards means behind you • Lucille looked backwards. ❷ If you do something backwards, you do it the opposite of the usual way • He instructed them to count backwards from one hundred.

bacon NOUN meat from the back or sides of a pig, which has been salted or smoked.

▷ SPELLING NOTE: have a plEce of plE (pie*ce*)

bacteria PLURAL NOUN Bacteria are very tiny organisms which can cause disease. **bacterial** ADJECTIVE
● USAGE NOTE: The word *bacteria* is
● plural. The singular form is
● *bacterium*

bad, worse, worst ADJECTIVE
❶ Anything harmful or upsetting can be described as bad • *I have some bad news* • *Is the pain bad?* ❷ insufficient or of poor quality • *bad roads.* ❸ evil or immoral in character or behaviour • *a bad person.* ❹ lacking skill in something • *I was bad at sports.* ❺ Bad language consists of swearwords. ❻ If you have a bad temper, you become angry easily. **badness** NOUN
● SIMILAR WORDS: ❸ evil, sinful,
● wicked, wrong

bade a form of the past tense of **bid**.

badge, badges NOUN a piece of plastic or metal with a design or message on it that you can pin to your clothes.

badger, badgers, badgering, badgered NOUN ❶ a wild animal that has a white head with two black stripes on it ▷ VERB ❷ If you badger someone, you keep asking them questions or pestering them to do something.

badly ADVERB in an inferior or unimpressive way.

badminton NOUN (PE)
Badminton is a game in which two or four players use rackets to hit a shuttlecock over a high net. It was first played at Badminton House in Gloucestershire.

Bafana bafana PLURAL NOUN In South Africa, Bafana bafana is a name for the South African national soccer team.

baffle, baffles, baffling, baffled VERB If something baffles you, you cannot understand or explain it • *The symptoms baffled the doctors.* **baffled** ADJECTIVE **baffling** ADJECTIVE

bag, bags NOUN ❶ a container for carrying things in ❷ IN PLURAL INFORMAL Bags of something is a lot of it • *bags of fun.*

baggage NOUN the suitcases and bags that you take on a journey.

baggy, baggier, baggiest ADJECTIVE Baggy clothing hangs loosely.

bagpipes PLURAL NOUN (MUSIC) a musical instrument played by squeezing air out of a leather bag through pipes, on which a tune is played.

bail, bails, bailing, bailed NOUN ❶ Bail is a sum of money paid to a court to allow an accused person to go free until the time of the trial • *He was released on bail.* ▷ VERB ❷ If you bail water from a boat, you scoop it out.

bailiff, bailiffs NOUN ❶ a law officer who makes sure that the decisions of a court are obeyed. ❷ a person employed to look after land or property for the owner.

Baisakhi [Said buy-**sah**-kee] NOUN a Sikh festival celebrated every April.

bait, baits, baiting, baited NOUN ❶ a small amount of food placed on a hook or in a trap, to attract a fish or wild animal so that it gets caught. ❷ something used to tempt a person to do something ▷ VERB ❸ If you

a **b** c d e f g h i j k l m n o p q r s t u v w x y z

▷ SPELLING NOTE: *plaice the fish has a glittering 'EYE' (I) (plaice)*

bait a hook or trap, you put some food on it to catch a fish or wild animal.

baize NOUN a smooth woollen material, usually green, used for covering snooker tables.

bake, bakes, baking, baked VERB ❶ To bake food means to cook it in an oven without using liquid or fat. ❷ To bake earth or clay means to heat it until it becomes hard.

baker, bakers NOUN a person who makes and sells bread and cakes.

bakery, bakeries NOUN a building where bread and cakes are baked and sold.

bakkie, bakkies [Said **buck**-ee] NOUN In South African English, a bakkie is a small truck.

balaclava, balaclavas NOUN A balaclava is a close-fitting woollen hood that covers every part of your head except your face. Balaclava is the name of a place in Russia; at a battle there in the Crimean War in 1854, British soldiers wore these hoods to protect themselves from the cold.

balance, balances, balancing, balanced VERB ❶ When someone or something balances, they remain steady and do not fall over ▷ NOUN ❷ Balance is the state of being upright and steady. ❸ Balance is also a situation in which all the parts involved have a stable relationship with each other • *the chemical balance of the brain*. ❹ The balance in someone's bank account is the amount of money in it.

balcony, balconies NOUN ❶ a platform on the outside of a building

with a wall or railing round it. ❷ an area of upstairs seats in a theatre or cinema.

bald, balder, baldest ADJECTIVE ❶ A bald person has little or no hair on their head. ❷ A bald statement or question is made in the simplest way without any attempt to be polite.
baldly ADVERB **baldness** NOUN
● WORD HISTORY: from Middle
● English *ballede* meaning 'having a
● white patch'

bale, bales, baling, baled NOUN ❶ a large bundle of something, such as paper or hay, tied tightly ▷ VERB ❷ If you bale water from a boat, you remove it using a container; also spelt **bail**.

balk, balks, balking, balked; *also spelt* **baulk** VERB If you balk at something, you object to it and may refuse to do it • *He balked at the cost.*

ball, balls NOUN ❶ a round object, especially one used in games such as cricket and soccer. ❷ The ball of your foot or thumb is the rounded part where your toes join your foot or your thumb joins your hand. ❸ a large formal social event at which people dance.
● SIMILAR WORDS: ❶ globe, orb,
● sphere

ballad, ballads NOUN ❶ (ENGLISH) a long song or poem which tells a story. ❷ a slow, romantic pop song.
● WORD HISTORY: from Old French
● *ballade* meaning 'song for dancing
● to'

ballast NOUN any heavy material placed in a ship to make it more stable.

ballerina, ballerinas **NOUN** a woman ballet dancer.

ballet [Said **bal**-lay] **NOUN** Ballet is a type of artistic dancing based on precise steps.

balloon, balloons **NOUN** ❶ a small bag made of thin rubber that you blow into until it becomes larger and rounder. ❷ a large, strong bag filled with gas or hot air, which travels through the air carrying passengers in a compartment underneath.
- **WORD HISTORY:** from Italian *ballone* meaning 'large round object'

ballot, ballots, balloting, balloted **NOUN** ❶ a secret vote in which people select a candidate in an election, or express their opinion about something ▷ **VERB** ❷ When a group of people are balloted, they are asked questions to find out what they think about a particular problem or question.
- **WORD HISTORY:** from Italian *ballotta* meaning 'little round object'; in medieval Venice votes were cast by dropping black or white pebbles or balls into a box

ballpoint, ballpoints **NOUN** a pen with a small metal ball at the end which transfers the ink onto the paper.

ballroom, ballrooms **NOUN** a very large room used for dancing or formal balls.

balm [Said **bahm**] **NOUN** OLD-FASHIONED Balm is a soothing ointment made from a fragrant oily resin produced by certain kinds of tropical trees. Another word for balm is **balsam**.

balmy, balmier, balmiest **ADJECTIVE** mild and pleasant • *balmy summer evenings.*

balsa **NOUN** Balsa is very lightweight wood.

balustrade, balustrades **NOUN** a railing or wall on a balcony or staircase.

bamboo **NOUN** Bamboo is a tall tropical plant with hard, hollow stems used for making furniture. It is a species of giant grass. The young shoots can be eaten.

ban, bans, banning, banned **VERB** ❶ If something is banned, or if you are banned from doing it or using it, you are not allowed to do it or use it ▷ **NOUN** ❷ If there is a ban on something, it is not allowed.
- **SIMILAR WORDS:** ❶ forbid, outlaw, prohibit ❷ disqualification, embargo, prohibition

banal [Said ba-**nahl**] **ADJECTIVE** very ordinary and not at all interesting • *He made some banal remark.*
banality NOUN
- **WORD HISTORY:** Old French *banal* referred to military service which all tenants had to do; hence the word came to mean 'common to everyone' or 'ordinary'

banana, bananas **NOUN** a long curved fruit with a yellow skin.
- **WORD HISTORY:** from a West African language, via Portuguese

band, bands **NOUN** ❶ a group of musicians who play jazz or pop music together, or a group who play brass instruments together. ❷ a group of people who share a common purpose • *a band of rebels.* ❸ a narrow strip of

a
b
c
d
e
f
g
h
i
j
k
l
m
n
o
p
q
r
s
t
u
v
w
x
y
z

something used to hold things together or worn as a decoration • *an elastic band* • *a headband*.

bandage, bandages, bandaging, bandaged **NOUN** ❶ a strip of cloth wrapped round a wound to protect it ▷ **VERB** ❷ If you bandage a wound, you tie a bandage round it.

bandicoot, bandicoots **NOUN** a small Australian marsupial with a long pointed muzzle and a long tail.

bandit, bandits **NOUN** OLD-FASHIONED a member of an armed gang who rob travellers.
  ● **WORD HISTORY:** from Italian
  ● *bandito* meaning 'man who has
  ● been banished or outlawed'

bandstand, bandstands **NOUN** a platform, usually with a roof, where a band can play outdoors.

bandwagon **PHRASE** To **jump on the bandwagon** means to become involved in something because it is fashionable or likely to be successful.

bandy, bandies, bandying, bandied **VERB** If a name is bandied about, many people mention it.
  ● **WORD HISTORY:** from Old French
  ● *bander* meaning 'to hit a tennis ball
  ● back and forth'

bane **NOUN** LITERARY Someone or something that is the bane of a person or organization causes a lot of trouble for them • *the bane of my life*.
  ● **WORD HISTORY:** from Old English
  ● *bana* meaning 'murderer'

bang, bangs, banging, banged **VERB** ❶ If you bang something, you hit it or put it somewhere violently, so that it makes a loud noise • *He banged down*

the receiver. ❷ If you bang a part of your body against something, you accidentally bump it ▷ **NOUN** ❸ a sudden, short, loud noise. ❹ a hard or painful bump against something.

Bangladeshi, Bangladeshis *[Said bang-glad-**desh**-ee]* **ADJECTIVE** ❶ belonging or relating to Bangladesh ▷ **NOUN** ❷ someone who comes from Bangladesh.

bangle, bangles **NOUN** an ornamental band worn round someone's wrist or ankle.

banish, banishes, banishing, banished **VERB** ❶ To banish someone means to send them into exile. ❷ To banish something means to get rid of it • *It will be a long time before cancer is banished*. **banishment NOUN**
  ● **SIMILAR WORDS:** ❶ exile, expel,
  ● outlaw

banister, banisters; also spelt bannister **NOUN** a rail supported by posts along the side of a staircase.

banjo, banjos or banjoes **NOUN** a musical instrument, like a small guitar with a round body.

bank, banks, banking, banked **NOUN** ❶ a business that looks after people's money. ❷ a bank of something is a store of it kept ready for use • *a blood bank*. ❸ the raised ground along the edge of a river or lake • *a path along the canal bank*. ❹ the sloping side of an area of raised ground ▷ **VERB** ❺ When you bank money, you pay it into a bank. ❻ If you bank on something happening, you expect it and rely on it. **banker NOUN banking NOUN**

bank holiday, bank holidays **NOUN** a public holiday, when banks are officially closed.

banknote, banknotes **NOUN** a piece of paper money.

bankrupt, bankrupts, bankrupting, bankrupted **ADJECTIVE** ❶ People or organizations that go bankrupt do not have enough money to pay their debts ▷ **NOUN** ❷ someone who has been declared bankrupt ▷ **VERB** ❸ To bankrupt someone means to make them bankrupt • *Restoring the house nearly bankrupted them.* **bankruptcy NOUN**

banksia, banksias **NOUN** an evergreen Australian tree or shrub with yellow flowers.

banner, banners **NOUN** a long strip of cloth with a message or slogan on it.

bannister another spelling of **banister**.

banquet, banquets **NOUN** a grand formal dinner, often followed by speeches.

banter NOUN Banter is friendly joking and teasing.

baobab, baobabs [*Said **bay-oh-bab***] **NOUN** a small fruit tree with a very thick trunk which grows in Africa and northern Australia.

baptism, baptisms **NOUN** (RE) a ceremony in which someone is baptized.

Baptist, Baptists **NOUN** a member of a Protestant church who believes that people should be baptized when they are adults rather than babies.

baptize, baptizes, baptizing, baptized; *also spelt* **baptise VERB** When someone is baptized water is sprinkled on them, or they are immersed in water, as a sign that they have become a Christian.

bar, bars, barring, barred **NOUN** ❶ a counter or room where alcoholic drinks are served. ❷ a long, straight piece of metal. ❸ a piece of something made in a rectangular shape • *a bar of soap.* ❹ The bars in a piece of music are the many short parts of equal length that the piece is divided into. ❺ (GEOGRAPHY) In meteorology, a bar is a unit of pressure, equivalent to 100,000 newtons per square metre ▷ **VERB** ❻ If you bar a door, you place something across it to stop it being opened. ❼ If you bar someone's way, you stop them going somewhere by standing in front of them.

barb, barbs **NOUN** a sharp curved point on the end of an arrow or fish-hook.

barbarian, barbarians **NOUN** a member of a wild or uncivilized people.

● **WORD HISTORY:** from Greek
● *barbaros* meaning 'foreigner',
● originally 'person saying *bar-bar*'

barbaric ADJECTIVE cruel or brutal **barbarity NOUN**

barbecue, barbecues, barbecuing, barbecued **NOUN** ❶ a grill with a charcoal fire on which you cook food, usually outdoors; also an outdoor party where you eat food cooked on a barbecue ▷ **VERB** ❷ When food is barbecued, it is cooked over a charcoal grill.

a
b
c
d
e
f
g
h
i
j
k
l
m
n
o
p
q
r
s
t
u
v
w
x
y
z

▷ SPELLING NOTE: L**E**arn the princip**LE**s (princip**l**e)

● **WORD HISTORY:** from a Caribbean
● word meaning 'framework'

barbed ADJECTIVE A barbed remark
is one that seems straightforward but
is really unkind or spiteful.

barbed wire NOUN Barbed wire is
strong wire with sharp points sticking
out of it, used to make fences.

barber, barbers **NOUN** a man who
cuts men's hair.

barbiturate, barbiturates **NOUN** a
drug that people take to make them
calm or to put them to sleep.

bar code, bar codes **NOUN** a small
pattern of numbers and lines on
something you buy in a shop, which
can be electronically scanned at a
checkout to give the price.

bard, bards **NOUN** LITERARY A bard is
a poet. Some people call Shakespeare
the Bard.

bare, barer, barest; bares, baring,
bared **ADJECTIVE** ❶ If a part of your
body is bare, it is not covered by any
clothing. ❷ If something is bare, it
has nothing on top of it or inside it
• *bare floorboards* • *a small bare office.*
❸ When trees are bare, they have no
leaves on them. ❹ The bare
minimum or bare essentials means
the very least that is needed • *They
were fed the bare minimum.* ▷ **VERB**
❺ If you bare something, you uncover
or show it.

● **SIMILAR WORDS:** ❶ naked,
● nude, uncovered ❷ plain, stark

barefoot ADJECTIVE OR ADVERB
not wearing anything on your feet.

barely ADVERB only just • *The girl
was barely sixteen.*

● **USAGE NOTE:** Do not use *barely*
● with negative words like *not*: *she*
● *was barely sixteen* rather than *she*
● *was not barely sixteen*

bargain, bargains, bargaining,
bargained **NOUN** ❶ an agreement in
which two people or groups discuss
and agree what each will do, pay, or
receive in a matter which involves
them both. ❷ something which is
sold at a low price and which is good
value ▷ **VERB** ❸ When people
bargain with each other, they discuss
and agree terms about what each will
do, pay, or receive in a matter which
involves both.

barge, barges, barging, barged **NOUN**
❶ a boat with a flat bottom used for
carrying heavy loads, especially on
canals ▷ **VERB** ❷ INFORMAL If you
barge into a place, you push into it in a
rough or rude way.

baritone, baritones **NOUN** (MUSIC)
A baritone is a man with a fairly deep
singing voice, between that of a tenor
and a bass.

bark, barks, barking, barked **VERB**
❶ When a dog barks, it makes a short,
loud noise, once or several times
▷ **NOUN** ❷ the short, loud noise that
a dog makes. ❸ the tough material
that covers the outside of a tree.

barley NOUN a cereal that is grown
for food and is also used for making
beer and whisky.

bar mitzvah NOUN A Jewish boy's
bar mitzvah is a ceremony that takes
place on his 13th birthday, after which
he is regarded as an adult.

● **WORD HISTORY:** a Hebrew phrase
● meaning 'son of the law'

▷ SPELLING NOTE: *Psychiatrists Seldom Yell Callously Hard (psychiatrist)*

barmy, barmier, barmiest **ADJECTIVE** INFORMAL mad or very foolish.

barn, barns **NOUN** a large farm building used for storing crops or animal food.

barnacle, barnacles **NOUN** a small shellfish that fixes itself to rocks and to the bottom of boats.

barometer, barometers **NOUN** an instrument that measures air pressure and shows when the weather is changing.

baron, barons **NOUN** a member of the lowest rank of the nobility.
baronial ADJECTIVE

baroness, baronesses **NOUN** a woman who has the rank of baron, or who is the wife of a baron.

baronet, baronets **NOUN** A baronet is a man who is given the title 'baronet' by the King or Queen, and who can pass this title on to his son. Baronets are addressed as 'Sir'.
baronetcy NOUN

baroque [Said ba-**rok**] **ADJECTIVE** (HISTORY) Baroque describes an elaborate, highly ornamental style of architecture and art popular in Europe in the 17th and 18th centuries.

barracks PLURAL NOUN a building where soldiers live.

barracuda, barracudas **NOUN** a large, fierce tropical fish with sharp teeth.

barrage, barrages **NOUN** ❶ A barrage of questions or complaints is a lot of them all coming at the same time. ❷ A barrage is continuous artillery fire over a wide area, to prevent the enemy from moving.
● SIMILAR WORDS: ❶ deluge, stream, torrent ❷ bombardment, fusillade, volley

barrel, barrels **NOUN** ❶ a wooden container with rounded sides and flat ends. ❷ The barrel of a gun is the long tube through which the bullet is fired.

barren ADJECTIVE ❶ Barren land has soil of such poor quality that plants cannot grow on it. ❷ A barren woman or female animal is not able to have babies.
● SIMILAR WORDS: ❶ desert, empty, unproductive ❷ infertile, sterile

barricade, barricades, barricading, barricaded **NOUN** ❶ a temporary barrier put up to stop people getting past ▷ VERB ❷ If you barricade yourself inside a room or building, you put something heavy against the door to stop people getting in.

barrier, barriers **NOUN** ❶ a fence or wall that prevents people or animals getting from one area to another. ❷ If something is a barrier, it prevents two people or groups from agreeing or communicating, or prevents something from being achieved • Cost is a major barrier to using the law.
● SIMILAR WORDS: barricade, fence, wall

barrister, barristers **NOUN** a lawyer who is qualified to represent people in the higher courts.

barrow, barrows **NOUN** ❶ the same as a **wheelbarrow**. ❷ a large cart from which fruit or other goods are sold in the street.

▷ SPELLING NOTE: the QUeen stood on the QUay (quay)

barter, barters, bartering, bartered **VERB** ❶ If you barter goods, you exchange them for other goods, rather than selling them for money ▷ **NOUN** ❷ Barter is the activity of exchanging goods.

base, bases, basing, based **NOUN** ❶ the lowest part of something, which often supports the rest. ❷ A place which part of an army, navy, or air force works from. ❸ In chemistry, a base is any compound that reacts with an acid to form a salt. ❹ (MATHS) In mathematics, a base is a system of counting and expressing numbers. The decimal system uses base 10, and the binary system uses base 2. ❺ (MATHS) The base of a triangle is the side that is horizontal. ❻ (MATHS) The base of a trapezoid is either of the parallel sides ▷ **VERB** ❼ To base something on something else means to use the second thing as a foundation or starting point of the first • The opera is based on a work by Pushkin. ❽ If you are based somewhere, you live there or work from there.
● **SIMILAR WORDS:** ❶ bottom, ● foot, stand, support

baseball NOUN Baseball is a team game played with a bat and a ball, similar to rounders.

basement, basements **NOUN** a floor of a building built completely or partly below the ground.

bases NOUN ❶ [Said *bay*-seez] the plural of **basis**. ❷ [Said *bay*-siz] the plural of **base**.

bash, bashes, bashing, bashed **VERB** INFORMAL If you bash someone or bash into them, you hit them hard.

bashful ADJECTIVE shy and easily embarrassed.

basic ADJECTIVE ❶ The basic aspects of something are the most necessary ones • the basic necessities of life. ❷ Something that is basic has only the necessary features without any extras or luxuries • The accommodation is pretty basic but perfectly clean. **basically ADVERB**
● **SIMILAR WORDS:** ❶ essential, ● necessary, vital

basics PLURAL NOUN The basics of something are the things you need to know or understand • the basics of map-reading.

basil NOUN Basil is a herb used for flavouring in cooking.

basilica, basilicas **NOUN** an oblong church with a rounded end called an apse.
● **WORD HISTORY:** from Greek ● *basilikē* meaning 'royal hall'

basin, basins **NOUN** ❶ a round wide container which is open at the top. ❷ The basin of a river is a bowl of land from which water runs into the river.

basis, bases **NOUN** ❶ The basis of something is the essential main principle from which it can be developed • The same colour theme is used as the basis for several patterns. ❷ The basis for a belief is the facts that support it • There is no basis for this assumption.
● **SIMILAR WORDS:** ❶ base, ● foundation ❷ foundation, ground, ● support

bask, basks, basking, basked **VERB** If you bask in the sun, you sit or lie in it, enjoying its warmth.

▷ SPELLING NOTE: *Rhythmical Hounds Yap To Heavy Music (rhythm)*

basket, baskets **NOUN** a container made of thin strips of cane woven together.

basketball **NOUN** Basketball is a game in which two teams try to score goals by throwing a large ball through one of two circular nets suspended high up at each end of the court.

bass, basses [rhymes with **lace**] **NOUN** (MUSIC) ❶ A bass is a man who sings the lowest part in four-part harmony. ❷ A bass is also a musical instrument that provides the rhythm and lowest part in the harmonies. A bass may be either a large guitar or a very large member of the violin family: see **double bass**.

bass, basses [rhymes with **gas**] **NOUN** a type of edible sea fish.

basset hound, basset hounds **NOUN** a smooth-haired dog with a long body and ears, and short legs.

bassoon, bassoons **NOUN** a large woodwind instrument.

bastard, bastards **NOUN** ❶ OFFENSIVE, MAINLY AMERICAN People sometimes call someone a bastard when they dislike them or are very angry with them. ❷ OLD-FASHIONED A bastard is someone whose parents were not married when he or she was born.

baste, bastes, basting, basted **VERB** When you baste meat that is roasting, you pour hot fat over it so that it does not become dry while cooking.

bastion, bastions **NOUN** LITERARY something that protects a system or way of life • The country is the last bastion of communism.

bat, bats, batting, batted **NOUN** ❶ a specially shaped piece of wood with a handle, used for hitting the ball in a game such as cricket or table tennis. ❷ a small flying animal, active at night, that looks like a mouse with wings ▷ **VERB** ❸ In certain sports, when someone is batting, it is their turn to try to hit the ball and score runs.

batch, batches **NOUN** a group of things of the same kind produced or dealt with together.

bated **PHRASE** With bated breath means very anxiously.

bath, baths **NOUN** a long container which you fill with water and sit in to wash yourself.

bathe, bathes, bathing, bathed **VERB** ❶ When you bathe, you swim or play in open water. ❷ When you bathe a wound, you wash it gently. ❸ LITERARY If a place is bathed in light, a lot of light reaches it • The room was bathed in spring sunshine. **bather NOUN bathing NOUN**

bathroom, bathrooms **NOUN** a room with a bath or shower, a washbasin, and often a toilet in it.

baths **PLURAL NOUN** The baths is a public swimming pool.

baton, batons **NOUN** ❶ a light, thin stick that a conductor uses to direct an orchestra or choir. ❷ In athletics, the baton is a short stick passed from one runner to another in a relay race. ❸ A baton is also a short stick used by policemen in some countries as a weapon, lighter than a truncheon.

batsman, batsmen **NOUN** In

a
b
c
d
e
f
g
h
i
j
k
l
m
n
o
p
q
r
s
t
u
v
w
x
y
z

▷ SPELLING NOTE: there's SAND in my SANDwich (*sandwich*)

cricket, the batsman is the person who is batting.

battalion, battalions **NOUN** an army unit consisting of three or more companies.

batten, battens, battening, battened **NOUN** a strip of wood that is fixed to something to strengthen it or hold it firm.
batten down VERB If you batten something down, you make it secure by fixing battens across it.

batter, batters, battering, battered **VERB** ❶ To batter someone or something means to hit them many times • *The waves kept battering the life raft.* ▷ **NOUN** ❷ Batter is a mixture of flour, eggs, and milk, used to make pancakes, or to coat food before frying it. **battering NOUN**

battery, batteries **NOUN** ❶ a device, containing two or more cells, for storing and producing electricity, for example in a torch or a car. ❷ a large group of things or people ▷ **ADJECTIVE** ❸ A battery hen is one of a large number of hens kept in small cages for the mass production of eggs.

battle, battles **NOUN** ❶ (HISTORY) a fight between armed forces or a struggle between two people or groups with conflicting aims • *the battle between town and country.* ❷ A battle for something difficult is a determined attempt to obtain or achieve it • *the battle for equality.*

battlefield, battlefields **NOUN** a place where a battle is or has been fought.

battlements PLURAL NOUN
(HISTORY) The battlements of a castle consist of a wall built round the top, with gaps through which guns or arrows could be fired.

battleship, battleships **NOUN** a large, heavily armoured warship.

batty, battier, battiest **ADJECTIVE** INFORMAL crazy or eccentric.

bauble, baubles **NOUN** a pretty but cheap ornament or piece of jewellery.

bawdy, bawdier, bawdiest **ADJECTIVE** a bawdy joke or song contains humorous references to sex.
● **WORD HISTORY:** from Middle
● English *baude* meaning 'brothel
● keeper'

bawl, bawls, bawling, bawled **VERB** ❶ INFORMAL To bawl at someone means to shout at them loudly and harshly. ❷ When a child is bawling, it is crying very loudly and angrily.

bay, bays, baying, bayed **NOUN** ❶ a part of a coastline where the land curves inwards. ❷ a space or area used for a particular purpose • *a loading bay.* ❸ Bay is a kind of tree similar to the laurel, with leaves used for flavouring in cooking ▷ **PHRASE** ❹ If you **keep something at bay**, you prevent it from reaching you • *Eating oranges keeps colds at bay.* ▷ **VERB** ❺ When a hound or wolf bays, it makes a deep howling noise.
● **SIMILAR WORDS:** ❶ cove, gulf,
● inlet

bayonet, bayonets **NOUN** a sharp blade that can be fixed to the end of a rifle and used for stabbing.
● **WORD HISTORY:** named after
● *Bayonne* in France, where it
● originated

▷ SPELLING NOTE: *On WEDNESday Wayne WED NESta (Wednesday)*

THE VERB BE

The verb **to be** has a lot of unusual forms, and does not follow the usual rules.

The main form is *be*. This is used with an auxiliary verb to make compound tenses, and after the preposition *to*:
*She will **be** five years old in April.*

The verb forms *am*, *are*, and *is* are used to talk about the present time. *Am* is used for the first person singular; *are* is used for the second person and for all plural forms; *is* is used for the third person singular:
*I **am** exhausted.*
*You **are** very welcome.*
*Robbie **is** always cheerful.*
*They **are** a pair of rascals.*

The present participle is *being*. This

form is used with an auxiliary verb to make compound tenses:
*Matthew **was being** very helpful.*

The verb forms *was* and *were* talk about past time. *Was* is used for the first and third person singular; *were* is used for the second person and for all plural forms:
*I **was** exhausted.*
*You **were** very welcome.*
*Robbie **was** always cheerful.*
*They **were** a pair of rascals.*

The past participle is *been*. This form is used with an auxiliary verb to make compound tenses:
*I **shall have been** here five years in April.*
*Robbie **has been** polite at all times.*

a
b
c
d
e
f
g
h
i
j
k
l
m
n
o
p
q
r
s
t
u
v
w
x
y
z

bazaar, bazaars **NOUN** ❶ an area with many small shops and stalls, especially in Eastern countries. ❷ a sale to raise money for charity.

BC BC means 'before Christ'. You use '*BC*' in dates to indicate the number of years before the birth of Jesus Christ • *in 49 BC*.

be, am, is, are; being; was, were; been
AUXILIARY VERB ❶ 'Be' is used with a present participle to form the continuous tense • *Crimes of violence are increasing.* ❷ 'Be' is also used to say that something will happen • *We are going to America next month.* ❸ 'Be' is used to form the passive voice • *The walls were being repaired.* ▷ **VERB** ❹ 'Be' is used to give more information about the subject of a sentence • *Her name is Melanie.*
▶ SEE GRAMMAR BOX ABOVE

be- **PREFIX** ❶ 'Be-' is used to form verbs from nouns and adds the meaning 'treat as'. For example, to *befriend* someone is to make friends with them. ❷ 'Be-' is also sometimes used to form verbs from verbs when it is used for emphasis or to mean 'covering completely'. For example, to *besmear* means to smear all over.

beach, beaches **NOUN** an area of sand or pebbles beside the sea.
  ● **SIMILAR WORDS:** seashore,
  ● seaside, shore

beach nourishment NOUN
(GEOGRAPHY) a process in which sand lost by coastal erosion is replaced by transporting material from another area to the beach.

beacon, beacons **NOUN** In the past, a beacon was a light or fire on a hill,

▷ SPELLING NOTE: *Eddy Ant thinks mEAt is a grEAt trEAt to EAt (-ea-)*

bead, beads **NOUN** ❶ Beads are small pieces of coloured glass or wood with a hole through the middle, strung together to make necklaces. ❷ Beads of liquid are drops of it.

beady, beadier, beadiest **ADJECTIVE** Beady eyes are small and bright like beads.

beagle, beagles **NOUN** a short-haired dog with long ears and short legs.

beak, beaks **NOUN** A bird's beak is the hard part of its mouth that sticks out.

beaker, beakers **NOUN** ❶ a cup for drinking out of, usually made of plastic and without a handle. ❷ a glass container with a lip which is used in laboratories.

beam, beams, beaming, beamed **NOUN** ❶ a broad smile. ❷ A beam of light is a band of light that shines from something such as a torch. ❸ a long, thick bar of wood or metal, especially one that supports a roof ▷ **VERB** ❹ If you beam, you smile because you are happy.

bean, beans **NOUN** Beans are the seeds or pods of a climbing plant, which are eaten as a vegetable; also used of some other seeds, for example the seeds from which coffee is made.

bear, bears, bearing, bore, borne **NOUN** ❶ a large, strong wild animal with thick fur and sharp claws ▷ **VERB** ❷ FORMAL To bear something means to carry it or support its weight • *The ice wasn't thick enough to bear their weight.* ❸ If something bears a mark or typical feature, it has it • *The room bore all the signs of a violent struggle.*

❹ If you bear something difficult, you accept it and are able to deal with it • *He bore his last illness with courage.* ❺ If you can't bear someone or something, you dislike them very much. ❻ FORMAL When a plant or tree bears flowers, fruit, or leaves, it produces them. **bearable ADJECTIVE**

beard, beards **NOUN** the hair that grows on the lower part of a man's face. **bearded ADJECTIVE**

bearer, bearers **NOUN** The bearer of something is the person who carries or presents it • *the bearer of bad news.*

bearing NOUN ❶ If something has a bearing on a situation, it is relevant to it. ❷ the way in which a person moves or stands.

beast, beasts **NOUN** ❶ OLD-FASHIONED a large wild animal. ❷ INFORMAL If you call someone a beast, you mean that they are cruel or spiteful.

beastly, beastlier, beastliest **ADJECTIVE** INFORMAL, OLD-FASHIONED cruel or spiteful.

beat, beats, beating, beat, beaten **VERB** ❶ To beat someone or something means to hit them hard and repeatedly • *He threatened to beat her.* ❷ If you beat someone in a race or game, you defeat them or do better than them. ❸ When a bird or insect beats its wings, it moves them up and down. ❹ When your heart is beating, it is pumping blood with a regular rhythm. ❺ If you beat eggs, cream, or butter, you mix them vigorously using a fork or a whisk ▷ **NOUN** ❻ The beat of your heart is its regular pumping action. ❼ (MUSIC) The beat of a piece of music is its main rhythm. ❽ A police officer's beat is the area which he or she patrols.

beat up VERB To beat someone up means to hit or kick them repeatedly. **beater NOUN beating NOUN**

● SIMILAR WORDS: ❶ batter, hit, ● strike ❷ conquer, defeat, vanquish

Beaufort scale [Said boh-fort] **NOUN** (GEOGRAPHY) The Beaufort scale is a scale for measuring the speed of wind, ranging from 0 (calm) to 12 (hurricane force). It was devised by Sir Francis Beaufort (1774–1857), an English admiral.

beaut, beauts INFORMAL **NOUN** ❶ In Australian and New Zealand English, a beaut is an outstanding person or thing ▷ ADJECTIVE ❷ In Australian and New Zealand English, beaut means good or excellent • *a beaut house*.

beautiful ADJECTIVE very attractive or pleasing • *a beautiful girl* • *beautiful music*. **beautifully ADVERB**

● SIMILAR WORDS: attractive, ● gorgeous, lovely

beauty, beauties **NOUN** ❶ Beauty is the quality of being beautiful. ❷ OLD-FASHIONED a very attractive woman. ❸ The beauty of an idea or plan is what makes it attractive or worthwhile • *The beauty of the fund is its simplicity*.

beaver, beavers **NOUN** an animal with a big, flat tail and webbed feet. Beavers build dams.

because CONJUNCTION ❶ 'Because' is used with a clause that gives the reason for something • *I went home because I was tired.*

▷ PHRASE ❷ Because of is used with a noun that gives the reason for something • *He quit playing because of a knee injury.*

beck PHRASE If you are at someone's **beck and call**, you are always available to do what they ask.

beckon, beckons, beckoning, beckoned **VERB** ❶ If you beckon to someone, you signal with your hand that you want them to come to you. ❷ If you say that something beckons, you mean that you find it very attractive • *A career in journalism beckons.*

become, becomes, becoming, became, become **VERB** To become something means to start feeling or being that thing • *I became very angry* • *He became an actor.*

bed, beds **NOUN** ❶ a piece of furniture that you lie on when you sleep. ❷ A bed in a garden is an area of ground in which plants are grown. ❸ The bed of a sea or river is the ground at the bottom of it.

bedclothes PLURAL NOUN the sheets and covers that you put over you when you get into bed.

bedding NOUN Bedding is sheets, blankets, and other covers that are used on beds.

bedlam NOUN You can refer to a noisy and disorderly place or situation as bedlam • *The delay caused bedlam at the station.*

● WORD HISTORY: from *Bedlam*, a ● shortened form of the Hospital of ● St. Mary of Bethlehem in London, ● which was an institution for the ● insane or mentally ill

a
b
c
d
e
f
g
h
i
j
k
l
m
n
o
p
q
r
s
t
u
v
w
x
y
z

▷ SPELLING NOTE: *Beautiful Elephants Are Usually Tiny* (*beautiful*)

A
B
C
D
E
F
G
H
I
J
K
L
M
N
O
P
Q
R
S
T
U
V
W
X
Y
Z

bedpan, bedpans **NOUN** a container used as a toilet by people who are too ill to get out of bed.

bedraggled ADJECTIVE A bedraggled person or animal is in a messy or untidy state.

bedridden ADJECTIVE Someone who is bedridden is too ill or disabled to get out of bed.

bedrock NOUN ❶ Bedrock is the solid rock under the soil. ❷ The bedrock of something is the foundation and principles on which it is based • *His life was built on the bedrock of integrity.*

bedroom, bedrooms **NOUN** a room used for sleeping in.

bedspread, bedspreads **NOUN** a cover put over a bed, on top of the sheets and blankets.

bedstead, bedsteads **NOUN** the metal or wooden frame of an old-fashioned bed.

bee, bees **NOUN** a winged insect that can sting, makes honey and lives in large groups.

beech, beeches **NOUN** a tree with a smooth grey trunk and shiny leaves.

beef NOUN Beef is the meat of a cow, bull, or ox.

beefy, beefier, beefiest **ADJECTIVE** INFORMAL A beefy person is strong and muscular.

beehive, beehives **NOUN** a container in which bees live and make their honey.

beeline PHRASE INFORMAL If you **make a beeline** for a place, you go

there as quickly and directly as possible.

been the past participle of **be**.

beer, beers **NOUN** an alcoholic drink made from malt and flavoured with hops.

beet, beets **NOUN** a plant with an edible root and leaves, such as sugar beet or beetroot.

beetle, beetles **NOUN** a flying insect with hard wings which cover its body when it is not flying.

beetroot, beetroots **NOUN** the round, dark red root of a type of beet, eaten as a vegetable.

befall, befalls, befalling, befell, befallen **VERB** OLD-FASHIONED If something befalls you, it happens to you • *A similar fate befell my cousin.*

before ADVERB, PREPOSITION, OR CONJUNCTION ❶ 'Before' is used to refer to a previous time • *Apply the ointment before going to bed.*
▷ **ADVERB** ❷ If you have done something before, you have done it on a previous occasion • *Never before had he seen such poverty.* ▷ **PREPOSITION** ❸ FORMAL Before also means in front of • *They stopped before a large white villa.*
● **SIMILAR WORDS:** ❶ earlier than, prior to ❷ previously

beforehand ADVERB before • *It had been agreed beforehand that they would spend the night there.*

befriend, befriends, befriending, befriended **VERB** If you befriend someone, you act in a kind and helpful way and so become friends with them.

beg, begs, begging, begged **VERB**

▷ SPELLING NOTE: *King IAn went to ParlIAment in a carrIAge for his marrIAge (-ia-)*

❶ When people beg, they ask for food or money, because they are very poor. **❷** If you beg someone to do something, you ask them very anxiously to do it.
- **SIMILAR WORDS: ❷** beseech, implore, plead

beggar, beggars **NOUN** someone who lives by asking people for money or food.

begin, begins, beginning, began, begun **VERB** If you begin to do something, you start doing it. When something begins, it starts.
- **SIMILAR WORDS:** commence, start

beginner, beginners **NOUN** someone who has just started learning to do something and cannot do it very well yet.
- **SIMILAR WORDS:** learner, novice

beginning, beginnings **NOUN** The beginning of something is the first part of it or the time when it starts • *They had now reached the beginning of the city.*
- **USAGE NOTE:** Remember that *beginning* has one *g* and two *ns*

begonia, begonias [Said be-**go**-nya] **NOUN** a plant with brightly coloured flowers.

begrudge, begrudges, begrudging, begrudged **VERB** If you begrudge someone something, you are angry or envious because they have it • *No one could begrudge him the glory.*

beguiling [rhymes with **smiling**] **ADJECTIVE** charming, but often in a deceptive way.

behalf PHRASE To do something on **behalf of** someone or something

means to do it for their benefit or as their representative.

behave, behaves, behaving, behaved **VERB ❶** If you behave in a particular way, you act in that way • *They were behaving like animals.* **❷** To behave yourself means to act correctly or properly.

behaviour NOUN Your behaviour is the way in which you behave.

behead, beheads, beheading, beheaded **VERB** To behead someone means to cut their head off.

beheld the past tense of **behold**.

behind PREPOSITION ❶ at the back of • *He was seated behind the desk.* **❷** responsible for or causing • *He was the driving force behind the move.* **❸** supporting someone • *The whole country was behind him.*
▷ **ADVERB ❹** If you stay behind, you remain after other people have gone. **❺** If you leave something behind, you do not take it with you.

behold INTERJECTION LITERARY You say 'behold' when you want someone to look at something. **beholder NOUN**

beige, beiges [Said *bayj*] **NOUN OR ADJECTIVE** pale creamy-brown.

being, beings **❶** Being is the present participle of **be**. **NOUN ❷** Being is the state or fact of existing • *The party came into being in 1923.* **❸** a living creature, either real or imaginary • *alien beings from a distant galaxy.*

belated ADJECTIVE FORMAL A belated action happens later than it should have done • *a belated birthday present.* **belatedly ADVERB**

belch, belches, belching, belched
VERB ❶ If you belch, you make a
sudden noise in your throat because
air has risen up from your stomach.
❷ If something belches smoke or fire,
it sends it out in large amounts
• *Smoke belched from the steelworks.*
▷ **NOUN** ❸ the noise you make when
you belch.

beleaguered **ADJECTIVE**
❶ struggling against difficulties or
criticism • *the beleaguered meat
industry.* ❷ besieged by an enemy
• *the beleaguered garrison.*

belfry, belfries **NOUN** the part of a
church tower where the bells are.

Belgian, Belgians **ADJECTIVE**
❶ belonging or relating to Belgium
▷ **NOUN** ❷ someone who comes
from Belgium.

belief, beliefs **NOUN** ❶ a feeling of
certainty that something exists or is
true. ❷ one of the principles of a
religion or moral system.
● **SIMILAR WORDS:** ❷ creed,
● doctrine, faith

believable **ADJECTIVE** possible or
likely to be the case.

believe, believes, believing, believed
VERB ❶ If you believe that
something is true, you accept that it is
true. ❷ If you believe someone, you
accept that they are telling the truth.
❸ If you believe in things such as God
and miracles, you accept that they
exist or happen. ❹ If you believe in
something such as a plan or system,
you are in favour of it • *They really
believe in education.* **believer NOUN**

belittle, belittles, belittling, belittled
VERB If you belittle someone or

something, you make them seem
unimportant • *He belittled my opinions.*
● **SIMILAR WORDS:** deprecate,
● disparage, scoff at

bell, bells **NOUN** ❶ a cup-shaped
metal object with a piece inside that
swings and hits the sides, producing a
ringing sound. ❷ an electrical device
that rings or buzzes in order to attract
attention.

bellbird, bellbirds **NOUN** an
Australian or New Zealand bird that
makes a sound like a bell.

belligerent **ADJECTIVE** aggressive
and keen to start a fight or an
argument. **belligerence NOUN**

bellow, bellowing, bellowed **VERB**
❶ When an animal such as a bull
bellows, it makes a loud, deep roaring
noise. ❷ If someone bellows, they
shout in a loud, deep voice.

bellows **PLURAL NOUN** Bellows are
a piece of equipment used for blowing
air into a fire to make it burn more
fiercely.

belly, bellies **NOUN** ❶ Your belly is
your stomach or the front of your body
below your chest. ❷ An animal's belly
is the underneath part of its body.

belong, belongs, belonging, belonged
VERB ❶ If something belongs to you,
it is yours and you own it. ❷ To
belong to a group means to be a
member of it. ❸ If something belongs
in a particular place, that is where it
should be • *It did not belong in the
music room.*

belongings **PLURAL NOUN** Your
belongings are the things that you own.

beloved [Said bil-**luv**-id] **ADJECTIVE**

▷ SPELLING NOTE: *LEt's measure the angLE (angle)*

A beloved person or thing is one that you feel great affection for.
● **SIMILAR WORDS:** adored, dear, loved, precious

below PREPOSITION OR ADVERB
❶ If something is below a line or the surface of something else, it is lower down • *six inches below soil level.*
❷ Below also means at or to a lower point, level, or rate • *The temperature fell below the legal minimum.*

belt, belts, belting, belted NOUN ❶ a strip of leather or cloth that you fasten round your waist to hold your trousers or skirt up. ❷ In a machine, a belt is a circular strip of rubber that drives moving parts or carries objects along.
❸ a specific area of a country • *Poland's industrial belt.* ▷ VERB
❹ INFORMAL To belt someone means to hit them very hard.

bemused ADJECTIVE If you are bemused, you are puzzled or confused.

bench, benches NOUN ❶ a long seat that two or more people can sit on. ❷ a long, narrow table for working at, for example in a laboratory.
● **SIMILAR WORDS:** ❶ form, pew, seat

bend, bends, bending, bent VERB
❶ When you bend something, you use force to make it curved or angular.
❷ When you bend, you move your head and shoulders forwards and downwards ▷ NOUN ❸ a curved part of something.
● **SIMILAR WORDS:** ❶ *and* ❸ arch, bow, curve

bene- PREFIX 'Bene-' means 'good' or 'well'. For example, something *beneficial* makes you well or produces

a good result, and a *benevolent* person is kind and good to others.

beneath PREPOSITION, ADJECTIVE OR ADVERB ❶ an old-fashioned word for **underneath**.
▷ PREPOSITION ❷ If someone thinks something is beneath them, they think that it is too unimportant for them to bother with it.

benefactor, benefactors NOUN a person who helps to support a person or institution by giving money.
● **SIMILAR WORDS:** patron, sponsor, supporter

beneficial ADJECTIVE Something that is beneficial is good for people • *the beneficial effects of exercise.*
beneficially ADVERB
● **SIMILAR WORDS:** advantageous, favourable, helpful

beneficiary, beneficiaries NOUN A beneficiary of something is someone who receives money or other benefits from it.

benefit, benefits, benefiting, benefited NOUN ❶ The benefits of something are the advantages that it brings to people • *the benefits of relaxation.* ❷ Benefit is money given by the government to people who are unemployed or ill ▷ VERB ❸ If you benefit from something or something benefits you, it helps you.
● **USAGE NOTE:** *benefit* is spelt with two es, not two is
● **SIMILAR WORDS:** ❶ advantage, good, help ❸ gain, profit

benevolent ADJECTIVE kind and helpful. **benevolence** NOUN
benevolently ADVERB

benign [Said be-**nine**] ADJECTIVE

a
b
c
d
e
f
g
h
i
j
k
l
m
n
o
p
q
r
s
t
u
v
w
x
y
z

▷ SPELLING NOTE: *A Rude Idiot Thought He Might Eat Toffee In Church (arithmetic)*

① Someone who is benign is kind and gentle. **②** A benign tumour is one that will not cause death or serious illness. **benignly ADVERB**

bent ① Bent is the past participle and past tense of **bend**. **PHRASE ②** If you are **bent on** doing something, you are determined to do it.

bequeath, bequeaths, bequeathing, bequeathed **VERB FORMAL** If someone bequeaths money or property to you, they give it to you in their will, so that it is yours after they have died.

bequest, bequests **NOUN FORMAL** money or property that has been left to someone in a will.

berate, berates, berating, berated **VERB FORMAL** If you berate someone, you scold them angrily • *He berated them for getting caught.*

bereaved ADJECTIVE FORMAL You say that someone is bereaved when a close relative of theirs has recently died. **bereavement NOUN**

bereft ADJECTIVE LITERARY If you are bereft of something, you no longer have it • *The government seems bereft of ideas.*

beret, berets [*Said* **ber**-ray] **NOUN** a circular flat hat with no brim.

berm, berms **NOUN ①** a narrow path at the edge of a slope, road, or canal. **②** In New Zealand English, a strip of grass between the road and the footpath in areas where people live.

berry, berries **NOUN** Berries are small, round fruits that grow on bushes or trees.

berserk PHRASE If someone **goes** berserk, they lose control of themselves and become very violent.

● **WORD HISTORY:** from Icelandic
● *berserkr*, a kind of Viking who wore
● a shirt (*serkr*) made from the skin of
● a bear (*björn*). They worked
● themselves into a frenzy before
● battle

berth, berths **NOUN ①** a space in a harbour where a ship stays when it is being loaded or unloaded. **②** In a boat or caravan, a berth is a bed.

beseech, beseeches, beseeching, beseeched or besought **VERB LITERARY** If you beseech someone to do something, you ask them very earnestly to do it • *Her eyes beseeched him to show mercy.* **beseeching ADJECTIVE**

beset ADJECTIVE FORMAL If you are beset by difficulties or doubts, you have a lot of them.

beside PREPOSITION If one thing is beside something else, they are next to each other.

● **SIMILAR WORDS:** adjacent to,
● alongside, next to

besiege, besieges, besieging, besieged **VERB ①** When soldiers besiege a place, they surround it and wait for the people inside to surrender. **②** If you are besieged by people, many people want something from you and continually bother you.

besought a past tense and past participle of **beseech**.

best ADJECTIVE OR ADVERB ① the superlative of **good** and **well ADVERB ②** The thing that you like best is the thing that you prefer to everything else ▷ **NOUN ③** the thing

most preferred.
● **SIMILAR WORDS:** ❶ finest,
● supreme, top

best man NOUN The best man at a wedding is the man who acts as the bridegroom's attendant.

bestow, bestows, bestowing, bestowed VERB FORMAL If you bestow something on someone, you give it to them.

bet, bets, betting, bet VERB ❶ If you bet on the result of an event, you will win money if something happens and lose money if it does not ▷ NOUN ❷ the act of betting on something, or the amount of money that you agree to risk ▷ PHRASE INFORMAL ❸ You say I bet to indicate that you are sure that something is or will be so • *I bet the answer is no.* betting NOUN

betray, betrays, betraying, betrayed VERB ❶ If you betray someone who trusts you, you do something which harms them, such as helping their enemies. ❷ If you betray your feelings or thoughts, you show them without intending to. betrayal NOUN betrayer NOUN
● **SIMILAR WORDS:** ❶ be disloyal
● to, double-cross ❷ give away,
● reveal

betrothal, betrothals NOUN OLD-FASHIONED an engagement to be married. betrothed ADJECTIVE OR NOUN

better ADJECTIVE OR ADVERB ❶ the comparative of **good** and **well** ADVERB ❷ If you like one thing better than another, you like it more than the other thing ▷ ADJECTIVE ❸ If you are better after an illness,

you are no longer ill.
● **SIMILAR WORDS:** ❶ finer,
● greater, superior

between PREPOSITION OR ADVERB ❶ If something is between two other things, it is situated or happens in the space or time that separates them • *flights between Europe and Asia.* ❷ A relationship or difference between two people or things involves only those two.
● **USAGE NOTE:** If there are two
● things you should use *between*. If
● there are more than two things you
● should use *among*

beverage, beverages NOUN FORMAL a drink.

bevy, bevies NOUN a group of people • *a bevy of lawyers.*

beware VERB If you tell someone to beware of something, you are warning them that it might be dangerous or harmful.

bewilder, bewilders, bewildering, bewildered VERB If something bewilders you, it is too confusing or difficult for you to understand. bewildered ADJECTIVE bewildering ADJECTIVE bewilderment NOUN

bewitch, bewitches, bewitching, bewitched VERB ❶ To bewitch someone means to cast a spell on them. ❷ If something bewitches you, you are so delighted by it that you cannot pay attention to anything else. bewitched ADJECTIVE bewitching ADJECTIVE

beyond PREPOSITION ❶ If something is beyond a certain place, it is on the other side of it • *Beyond the*

a
b
c
d
e
f
g
h
i
j
k
l
m
n
o
p
q
r
s
t
u
v
w
x
y
z

▷ SPELLING NOTE: *Betty Eats Cakes And Uses Seven Eggs (because)*

hills was the Sahara. ❷ If something continues beyond a particular point, it continues further than that point • *an education beyond the age of 16.* ❸ If someone or something is beyond understanding or help, they cannot be understood or helped.

bi- PREFIX 'Bi-' means 'two' or 'twice' • *bicycle* • *bigamy.*

biannual ADJECTIVE occurring twice a year. **biannually ADVERB**

bias NOUN (HISTORY) Someone who shows bias favours one person or thing unfairly.
● **SIMILAR WORDS:** favouritism, partiality, prejudice

biased or **biassed ADJECTIVE** favouring one person or thing unfairly • *biased attitudes.*
● **SIMILAR WORDS:** one-sided, prejudiced

bib, bibs **NOUN** a piece of cloth or plastic which is worn under the chin of very young children when they are eating, to keep their clothes clean.

Bible, Bibles **NOUN** (RE) The Bible is the sacred book of the Christian religion. **biblical ADJECTIVE**
● **WORD HISTORY:** from Greek *biblia* meaning 'the books'

bicentenary, bicentenaries **NOUN** The bicentenary of an event is its two-hundredth anniversary.

biceps, biceps **NOUN** (PE) The large muscle on your upper arm.
● **WORD HISTORY:** from Latin *bi* + *caput* meaning 'two-headed' (because the muscle has two points of origin)

bicker, bickers, bickering, bickered

VERB When people bicker, they argue or quarrel about unimportant things.

bicycle, bicycles **NOUN** a two-wheeled vehicle which you ride by pushing two pedals with your feet.

bid, bids, bidding, bade, bidden, bid **NOUN** ❶ an attempt to obtain or do something • *He made a bid for freedom.* ❷ an offer to buy something for a certain sum of money ▷ **VERB** ❸ If you bid for something, you offer to pay a certain sum of money for it. ❹ OLD-FASHIONED If you bid someone a greeting or a farewell, you say it to them.
● **USAGE NOTE:** When *bid* means 'offer to pay a certain sum of money' (sense 3), the past tense and past participle is *bid*. When *bid* means 'say a greeting or farewell' (sense 4), the past tense is *bade* and the past participle is *bidden*

biddy-biddy, biddy-biddies **NOUN** a prickly low-growing plant found in New Zealand.

bide, bides, biding, bided **PHRASE** If you **bide your time**, you wait for a good opportunity before doing something.

bidet, bidets [*Said bee-day*] **NOUN** a low basin in a bathroom which is used for washing your bottom in.
● **WORD HISTORY:** a French word meaning 'small horse'

big, bigger, biggest **ADJECTIVE** ❶ of a large size. ❷ of great importance. **biggish ADJECTIVE bigness NOUN**
● **SIMILAR WORDS:** enormous, huge, large

bigamy NOUN Bigamy is the crime of marrying someone when you are

already married to someone else.
bigamist NOUN

bigot, bigots NOUN someone who
has strong and unreasonable opinions
which they refuse to change. **bigoted**
ADJECTIVE **bigotry** NOUN

bike, bikes NOUN INFORMAL a bicycle
or motorcycle.

bikini, bikinis NOUN a small
two-piece swimming costume worn
by women.

● **WORD HISTORY:** after *Bikini* atoll,
● from a comparison between the
● devastating effect of the atom-
● bomb test there and the effect
● caused by women wearing bikinis

bilateral ADJECTIVE A bilateral
agreement is one made between two
groups or countries.

bile NOUN Bile is a bitter yellow liquid
produced by the liver which helps the
digestion of fat.

bilge NOUN the lowest part of a ship,
where dirty water collects.

bilingual ADJECTIVE involving or
using two languages • *bilingual street
signs.*

bill, bills NOUN ❶ a written
statement of how much is owed for
goods or services. ❷ a formal
statement of a proposed new law that
is discussed and then voted on in
Parliament. ❸ a notice or a poster.
❹ A bird's bill is its beak.
● **SIMILAR WORDS:** ❶ charges,
● invoice

billabong, billabongs NOUN In
Australia, a billabong is a lagoon or
pool formed from part of a river.

billboard, billboards NOUN a large
board on which advertisements are
displayed.

billet, billets, billeting, billeted VERB
When soldiers are billeted in a
building, arrangements are made for
them to stay there.

billiards NOUN Billiards is a game
in which a long cue is used to move
balls on a table.

billion, billions NOUN a thousand
million. Formerly, a billion was a
million million.
● **USAGE NOTE:** As the meaning of
● *billion* has changed from one
● million million to one thousand
● million, a writer may mean either of
● these things when using it,
● depending on when the book or
● article was written

billow, billows, billowing, billowed
VERB ❶ When things made of cloth
billow, they swell out and flap slowly
in the wind. ❷ When smoke or cloud
billows, it spreads upwards and
outwards ▷ NOUN ❸ a large wave.

billy or **billycan**, billies or billycans
NOUN In Australian and New Zealand
English, a metal pot for boiling water
over a camp fire.

bin, bins NOUN a container, especially
one that you put rubbish in.

binary [Said *by-nar-ee*] ADJECTIVE
(ICT) The binary system expresses
numbers using only two digits, 0 and 1.

bind, binds, binding, bound VERB
❶ If you bind something, you tie rope
or string round it so that it is held
firmly. ❷ If something binds you to a
course of action, it makes you act in

a
b
c
d
e
f
g
h
i
j
k
l
m
n
o
p
q
r
s
t
u
v
w
x
y
z

A
B
C
D
E
F
G
H
I
J
K
L
M
N
O
P
Q
R
S
T
U
V
W
X
Y
Z

that way • *He was bound by that decision.*

bindi-eye, bindi-eyes **NOUN** a small Australian plant with prickly fruits.

binding, bindings **ADJECTIVE** ❶ If a promise or agreement is binding, it must be obeyed ▷ **NOUN** ❷ The binding of a book is its cover.

binge, binges **NOUN** INFORMAL a wild bout of drinking or eating too much.

bingo **NOUN** Bingo is a game in which players aim to match the numbers that someone calls out with the numbers on the card that they have been given.

binoculars **PLURAL NOUN** Binoculars are an instrument with lenses for both eyes, which you look through in order to see objects far away.

bio- **PREFIX** 'Bio-' means 'life' or 'living things'. For example, a *biography* is the story of someone's life and *biology* is the study of living things.

biochemistry **NOUN** Biochemistry is the study of the chemistry of living things. **biochemical ADJECTIVE** **biochemist NOUN**

biodegradable **ADJECTIVE** If something is biodegradable, it can be broken down into its natural elements by the action of bacteria • *biodegradable cleaning products.*

biodiversity **NOUN** the existence of a wide variety of plant and animal species in a particular area.

biography, biographies **NOUN** the history of someone's life, written by someone else. **biographer NOUN** **biographical ADJECTIVE**

biology **NOUN** Biology is the study

of living things. **biological ADJECTIVE** **biologically ADVERB** **biologist NOUN**

biometric **ADJECTIVE** relating to biometrics • *a biometric passport.*

biometrics **NOUN** the use of mathematical measurements to analyse physical characteristics, especially to identify people.

bionic **ADJECTIVE** having a part of the body that works electronically.

biopsy, biopsies **NOUN** an examination under a microscope of tissue from a living body to find out the cause of a disease.

biosphere **NOUN** (SCIENCE) The biosphere is the part of the earth's surface and atmosphere where life exists.

birch, birches **NOUN** a tall deciduous tree with thin branches and thin bark.

bird, birds **NOUN** an animal with two legs, two wings, and feathers.

birth, births **NOUN** ❶ The birth of a baby is when it comes out of its mother's womb at the beginning of its life. ❷ The birth of something is its beginning • *The era saw the birth of modern art.*

birthday, birthdays **NOUN** Your birthday is the anniversary of the date on which you were born.

birthmark, birthmarks **NOUN** a mark on someone's skin that has been there since they were born.

biscuit, biscuits **NOUN** a small flat cake made of baked dough.
   ● **WORD HISTORY:** from Old French
   ● *bes* + *cuit* meaning 'twice-cooked'

▷ SPELLING NOTE: *I always visit my FRIend on a FRIday (Friday)*

bisect, bisects, bisecting, bisected **VERB** To bisect a line or area means to divide it in half.

bisexual **ADJECTIVE** sexually attracted to both men and women.

bishop, bishops **NOUN** ❶ a high-ranking clergyman in some Christian Churches. ❷ In chess, a bishop is a piece that is moved diagonally across the board.

bison, bison **NOUN** a large hairy animal related to cattle.

bistro, bistros [Said **bee**-stroh] **NOUN** a small informal restaurant.

bit, bits ❶ Bit is the past tense of bite. **NOUN** ❷ A bit of something is a small amount of it • a bit of coal. ▷ **PHRASE** INFORMAL ❸ **A bit** means slightly or to a small extent • That's a bit tricky.
● **SIMILAR WORDS:** ❷ fragment,
● part, piece

bitch, bitches **NOUN** ❶ a female dog. ❷ OFFENSIVE, MAINLY AMERICAN If someone refers to a woman as a bitch, it means that they think she behaves in a spiteful way. **bitchy** **ADJECTIVE**

bite, bites, biting, bit, bitten **VERB** ❶ To bite something or someone is to cut it or cut through it with the teeth ▷ **NOUN** ❷ a small amount that you bite off something with your teeth. ❸ the injury you get when an animal or insect bites you.

bitter, bitterer, bitterest **ADJECTIVE** ❶ If someone is bitter, they feel angry and resentful. ❷ A bitter disappointment or experience makes people feel angry or unhappy for a long time afterwards. ❸ In a bitter argument or war, people argue or fight fiercely and angrily • a bitter power struggle. ❹ A bitter wind is an extremely cold wind. ❺ Something that tastes bitter has a sharp, unpleasant taste. **bitterly** **ADVERB** **bitterness** **NOUN**
● **SIMILAR WORDS:**
● ❶ acrimonious, resentful, sour
● ❺ acid, sharp, sour

bivouac, bivouacs [Said **biv**-oo-ak] **NOUN** a temporary camp in the open air.

bizarre [Said biz-**zahr**] **ADJECTIVE** very strange or eccentric.

blab, blabs, blabbing, blabbed **VERB** INFORMAL When someone blabs, they give away secrets by talking carelessly.

black, blacker, blackest; blacks **NOUN OR ADJECTIVE** ❶ Black is the darkest possible colour, like tar or soot. ▷ **ADJECTIVE** ❷ Someone who is Black is a member of a dark-skinned race. ❸ Black coffee or tea has no milk or cream added to it. ❹ Black humour involves jokes about death or suffering. **blackness** **NOUN**
● **USAGE NOTE:** When you are
● writing about a person or people,
● *Black* should start with a capital
● letter
● **SIMILAR WORDS:** ❶ dark, jet,
● pitch-black

blackberry, blackberries **NOUN** Blackberries are small black fruits that grow on prickly bushes called brambles.

blackbird, blackbirds **NOUN** a common European bird, the male of which has black feathers and a yellow beak.

A
B
C
D
E
F
G
H
I
J
K
L
M
N
O
P
Q
R
S
T
U
V
W
X
Y
Z

blackboard, blackboards **NOUN** a dark-coloured board in a classroom, which teachers write on using chalk.

black box, black boxes **NOUN** an electronic device in an aircraft which collects and stores information during flights.

blackcurrant, blackcurrants **NOUN** Blackcurrants are very small dark purple fruits that grow in bunches on bushes.

blacken, blackens, blackening, blackened **VERB** To blacken something means to make it black • *The smoke from the chimney blackened the roof.*

blackhead, blackheads **NOUN** a very small black spot on the skin caused by a pore being blocked with dirt.

blacklist, blacklists, blacklisting, blacklisted **NOUN** ❶ a list of people or organizations who are thought to be untrustworthy or disloyal ▷ **VERB** ❷ When someone is blacklisted, they are put on a blacklist.

blackmail, blackmails, blackmailing, blackmailed **VERB** ❶ If someone blackmails another person, they threaten to reveal an unpleasant secret about them unless that person gives them money or does something for them ▷ **NOUN** ❷ Blackmail is the action of blackmailing people. **blackmailer NOUN**

black market NOUN If something is bought or sold on the black market, it is bought or sold illegally.

blackout, blackouts **NOUN** If you have a blackout, you lose consciousness for a short time.

blacksmith, blacksmiths **NOUN** a person whose job is making things out of iron, such as horseshoes.

Black Stone NOUN (RE) the sacred stone in the Kaaba in Mecca. Muslims believe that the stone was given by God.

bladder, bladders **NOUN** the part of your body where urine is held until it leaves your body.

blade, blades **NOUN** ❶ The blade of a weapon or cutting tool is the sharp part of it. ❷ The blades of a propeller are the thin, flat parts that turn round. ❸ A blade of grass is a single piece of it.

blame, blames, blaming, blamed **VERB** ❶ If someone blames you for something bad that has happened, they believe you caused it ▷ **NOUN** ❷ The blame for something bad that happens is the responsibility for letting it happen.
  ● **SIMILAR WORDS:** ❶ accuse, hold
  ● responsible

blameless ADJECTIVE Someone who is blameless has not done anything wrong.

blanch, blanches, blanching, blanched **VERB** If you blanch, you suddenly become very pale.

bland, blander, blandest **ADJECTIVE** tasteless, dull or boring • *a bland diet* • *bland pop music.* **blandly ADVERB**

blank, blanker, blankest; blanks **ADJECTIVE** ❶ Something that is blank has nothing on it • *a blank sheet of paper.* ❷ If you look blank, your face shows no feeling or interest ▷ **NOUN** ❸ If your mind is a blank, you cannot think of anything or remember anything.

blanket, blankets **NOUN** ❶ a large rectangle of thick cloth that is put on a bed to keep people warm. ❷ A blanket of something such as snow is a thick covering of it.

blare, blares, blaring, blared **VERB** To blare means to make a loud, unpleasant noise • *The radio blared pop music.*

blaspheme, blasphemes, blaspheming, blasphemed **VERB** When people blaspheme, they are disrespectful about God or religion.
● **WORD HISTORY:** from Greek
● *blapsis* meaning 'evil' and *phēmein*
● meaning 'to speak'

blasphemy, blasphemies **NOUN** Blasphemy is speech or behaviour that shows disrespect for God or religion. **blasphemous ADJECTIVE**

blast, blasts, blasting, blasted **VERB** ❶ When people blast a hole in something they make a hole with an explosion ▷ **NOUN** ❷ a big explosion, especially one caused by a bomb. ❸ a sudden strong rush of wind or air.

blatant ADJECTIVE If you describe something you think is bad as blatant, you mean that rather than hide it, those responsible actually seem to be making it obvious • *a blatant disregard for the law.*

blaze, blazes, blazing, blazed **NOUN** ❶ a large, hot fire. ❷ A blaze of light or colour is a great or strong amount of it • *a blaze of red.* ❸ A blaze of publicity or attention is a lot of it ▷ **VERB** ❹ If something blazes it burns or shines brightly.

blazer, blazers **NOUN** a kind of jacket, often in the colours of a school or sports team.

bleach, bleaches, bleaching, bleached **VERB** ❶ To bleach material or hair means to make it white, usually by using a chemical ▷ **NOUN** ❷ Bleach is a chemical that is used to make material white or to clean thoroughly and kill germs.

bleak, bleaker, bleakest **ADJECTIVE** ❶ If a situation is bleak, it is bad and seems unlikely to improve. ❷ If a place is bleak, it is cold, bare, and exposed to the wind.

bleary, blearier, bleariest **ADJECTIVE** If your eyes are bleary, they are red and watery, usually because you are tired.

bleat, bleats, bleating, bleated **VERB** ❶ When sheep or goats bleat, they make a high-pitched cry ▷ **NOUN** ❷ the high-pitched cry that a sheep or goat makes.

bleed, bleeds, bleeding, bled **VERB** When you bleed, you lose blood as a result of an injury.

bleep, bleeps **NOUN** a short high-pitched sound made by an electrical device such as an alarm.

blemish, blemishes **NOUN** a mark that spoils the appearance of something.

blend, blends, blending, blended **VERB** ❶ When you blend substances, you mix them together to form a single substance. ❷ When colours or sounds blend, they combine in a pleasing way ▷ **NOUN** ❸ A blend of things is a mixture of them, especially one that is pleasing. ❹ a word formed by joining together the beginning and the end of two other words; for

a
b
c
d
e
f
g
h
i
j
k
l
m
n
o
p
q
r
s
t
u
v
w
x
y
z

▷ SPELLING NOTE: *have a pIEce of pIE (piece)*

example, 'brunch' is a blend of 'breakfast' and 'lunch'.

blender, blenders **NOUN** a machine used for mixing liquids and foods at high speed.

bless, blesses, blessing, blessed or blest **VERB** When a priest blesses people or things, he or she asks for God's protection for them.

● **WORD HISTORY:** from Old English *blædsian* meaning 'to sprinkle with sacrificial blood'

blessed **ADJECTIVE** [Said **blest**] If someone is blessed with a particular quality or skill, they have it • *He was blessed with a sense of humour.* **blessedly** **ADVERB**

blessing, blessings **NOUN**
● something good that you are thankful for • *Good health is the greatest blessing.* ▷ **PHRASE** ● If something is done **with someone's blessing**, they approve of it and support it.

blew the past tense of **blow**.

blight, blights, blighting, blighted **NOUN** ● something that damages or spoils other things • *the blight of the recession.* ▷ **VERB** ● When something is blighted, it is seriously harmed • *His life had been blighted by sickness.*

blind, blinder, blindest; blinds, blinding, blinded **ADJECTIVE**
● Someone who is blind cannot see.
● If someone is blind to a particular fact, they do not understand it ▷ **VERB** ● If something blinds you, you become unable to see, either for a short time or permanently ▷ **NOUN**
● a roll of cloth or paper that you pull down over a window to keep out the

light. **blindly** **ADVERB** **blindness** **NOUN**

blindfold, blindfolds, blindfolding, blindfolded **NOUN** ● a strip of cloth tied over someone's eyes so that they cannot see ▷ **VERB** ● To blindfold someone means to cover their eyes with a strip of cloth.

blinding **ADJECTIVE** A blinding light is so bright that it hurts your eyes • *There was a blinding flash.*

blindingly **ADVERB** INFORMAL If something is blindingly obvious, it is very obvious indeed.

bling, blinger, blingest INFORMAL
● **NOUN** jewellery that looks expensive in a vulgar way.
● ▷ **ADJECTIVE** flashy; expensive-looking in a vulgar way.

blink, blinks, blinking, blinked **VERB** When you blink, you close your eyes quickly for a moment.

blinkers PLURAL NOUN Blinkers are two pieces of leather placed at the side of a horse's eyes so that it can only see straight ahead.

bliss NOUN Bliss is a state of complete happiness. **blissful** **ADJECTIVE** **blissfully** **ADVERB**

blister, blisters, blistering, blistered **NOUN** ● a small bubble on your skin containing watery liquid, caused by a burn or rubbing ▷ **VERB** ● If someone's skin blisters, blisters appear on it as result of burning or rubbing.

blithe, blither, blithest **ADJECTIVE** casual and done without serious thought • *a blithe disregard for their safety.* **blithely** **ADVERB** **blitheness** **NOUN**

▷ SPELLING NOTE: *plaice the fish has a glittering 'EYE' (I) (plaice)*

blitz, blitzes, blitzing, blitzed **NOUN**
(HISTORY) **❶** a bombing attack by enemy aircraft on a city ▷ **VERB**
❷ When a city is blitzed, it is bombed by aircraft and is damaged or destroyed.

blizzard, blizzards **NOUN** a heavy snowstorm with strong winds.

bloated ADJECTIVE Something that is bloated is much larger than normal, often because there is a lot of liquid or gas inside it.

blob, blobs **NOUN** a small amount of a thick or sticky substance.

bloc, blocs **NOUN** A group of countries or political parties with similar aims acting together is often called a bloc • *the world's largest trading bloc.*

block, blocks, blocking, blocked **NOUN** **❶** A block of flats or offices is a large building containing flats or offices. **❷** In a town, a block is an area of land with streets on all its sides • *He lives a few blocks down.* **❸** A block of something is a large rectangular piece of it ▷ **VERB** **❹** To block a road or channel means to put something across it so that nothing can get through. **❺** If something blocks your view, it is in the way and prevents you from seeing what you want to see. **❻** If someone blocks something, they prevent it from happening • *The council blocked his plans.*
● **SIMILAR WORDS:** **❸** bar, chunk,
● piece **❹**, **❺** *and* **❻** obstruct

blockade, blockades, blockading, blockaded **NOUN** **❶** an action that prevents goods from reaching a place ▷ **VERB** **❷** When a place is blockaded, supplies are prevented

from reaching it.

blockage, blockages **NOUN** When there is a blockage in a pipe or tunnel, something is clogging it.
● **SIMILAR WORDS:** impediment,
● obstruction, stoppage

blog, blogs **NOUN** INFORMAL short for weblog: a person's online diary that he or she puts on the Internet so that other people can read it.

blogger, bloggers **NOUN** INFORMAL a person who keeps a blog.

bloke, blokes **NOUN** INFORMAL a man.

blonde or **blond**, blonder, blondest; blondes or blonds **ADJECTIVE** **❶** Blonde hair is pale yellow in colour. The spelling 'blond' is used when referring to men ▷ **NOUN** **❷** A blonde, or blond, is a person with light-coloured hair.

blood NOUN **❶** Blood is the red liquid that is pumped by the heart round the bodies of human beings and other mammals ▷ **PHRASE** **❷** If something cruel is done **in cold blood**, it is done deliberately and without showing any emotion.

bloodhound, bloodhounds **NOUN** a large dog with an excellent sense of smell.

bloodless ADJECTIVE **❶** If someone's face or skin is bloodless, it is very pale. **❷** In a bloodless coup or revolution, nobody is killed.

blood pressure NOUN Your blood pressure is a measure of the force with which your blood is being pumped round your body.

a
b
c
d
e
f
g
h
i
j
k
l
m
n
o
p
q
r
s
t
u
v
w
x
y
z

▷ SPELLING NOTE: *I went to see (C) the doctor's new practiCe (practice)*

bloodshed NOUN When there is bloodshed, people are killed or wounded.

bloodshot ADJECTIVE If a person's eyes are bloodshot, the white parts have become red.

blood sport, blood sports NOUN any sport that involves deliberately killing or injuring animals.

bloodstained ADJECTIVE covered with blood.

bloodstream NOUN the flow of blood through your body.

bloodthirsty ADJECTIVE Someone who is bloodthirsty enjoys using or watching violence.

blood transfusion, blood transfusions NOUN a process in which blood is injected into the body of someone who has lost a lot of blood.

blood vessel, blood vessels NOUN Blood vessels are the narrow tubes in your body through which your blood flows.

bloody, bloodier, bloodiest ADJECTIVE OR ADVERB ❶ Bloody is a common swearword, used to express anger or annoyance ▷ ADJECTIVE ❷ A bloody event is one in which a lot of people are killed • *a bloody revolution*. ❸ Bloody also means covered with blood • *a bloody gash on his head*.

bloom, blooms, blooming, bloomed NOUN ❶ a flower on a plant ▷ VERB ❷ When a plant blooms, it produces flowers. ❸ When something like a feeling blooms, it grows • *Romance can bloom where you least expect it.*

blossom, blossoms, blossoming, blossomed NOUN ❶ Blossom is the growth of flowers that appears on a tree before the fruit ▷ VERB ❷ When a tree blossoms, it produces blossom.

blot, blots, blotting, blotted NOUN ❶ a drop of ink that has been spilled on a surface. ❷ A blot on someone's reputation is a mistake or piece of bad behaviour that spoils their reputation. **blot out** VERB To blot something out means to be in front of it and prevent it from being seen • *The smoke blotted out the sky.*

blotch, blotches NOUN a stain or a patch of a different colour. **blotchy** ADJECTIVE

blouse, blouses NOUN a light shirt, worn by a girl or a woman.

blow, blows, blowing, blew, blown VERB ❶ When the wind blows, the air moves. ❷ If something blows or is blown somewhere, the wind moves it there. ❸ If you blow a whistle or horn, you make a sound by blowing into it ▷ NOUN ❹ If you receive a blow, someone or something hits you. ❺ something that makes you very disappointed or unhappy • *Marc's death was a terrible blow.* **blow up** VERB To blow something up means to destroy it with an explosion. ❷ To blow up a balloon or a tyre means to fill it with air.

blubber NOUN The blubber of animals such as whales and seals is the layer of fat that protects them from the cold.

bludge, bludges, bludging, bludged VERB INFORMAL ❶ In Australian and New Zealand English, to bludge is to scrounge or cadge. ❷ In Australian and New Zealand English, to bludge is also to avoid work or responsibilities.

bludgeon, bludgeons, bludgeoning, bludgeoned **VERB** To bludgeon someone means to hit them several times with a heavy object.

blue, bluer, bluest; blues **ADJECTIVE OR NOUN** ❶ Blue is the colour of the sky on a clear, sunny day ▷ **PHRASE** ❷ If something happens **out of the blue**, it happens suddenly and unexpectedly ▷ **ADJECTIVE** ❸ Blue films and jokes are about sex. **bluish** or **blueish ADJECTIVE**

bluebell, bluebells **NOUN** a woodland plant with blue, bell-shaped flowers.

bluebottle, bluebottles **NOUN** ❶ a large fly with a shiny dark-blue body. ❷ In Australia and New Zealand, a bluebottle is also a small stinging jellyfish.

blue-collar ADJECTIVE Blue-collar workers do physical work as opposed to office work.

blueprint, blueprints **NOUN** a plan of how something is expected to work • *the blueprint for successful living.*

blues NOUN The blues is a type of music which is similar to jazz, but is always slow and sad.

bluff, bluffs, bluffing, bluffed **NOUN** ❶ an attempt to make someone wrongly believe that you are in a strong position ▷ **VERB** ❷ If you are bluffing, you are trying to make someone believe that you are in a position of strength.

blunder, blunders, blundering,

blundered **VERB** ❶ If you blunder, you make a silly mistake ▷ **NOUN** ❷ a silly mistake.

blunt, blunter, bluntest **ADJECTIVE** ❶ A blunt object has a rounded point or edge, rather than a sharp one. ❷ If you are blunt, you say exactly what you think, without trying to be polite.
● **SIMILAR WORDS:** ❷ forthright,
● outspoken, straightforward

blur, blurs, blurring, blurred **NOUN** ❶ a shape or area which you cannot see clearly because it has no distinct outline or because it is moving very fast ▷ **VERB** ❷ To blur the differences between things means to make them no longer clear • *The dreams blurred confusingly with her memories.* **blurred ADJECTIVE**

blurt out, blurts out, blurting out, blurted out **VERB** If you blurt something out, you say it suddenly, after trying to keep it a secret.

blush, blushes, blushing, blushed **VERB** ❶ If you blush, your face becomes red, because you are embarrassed or ashamed ▷ **NOUN** ❷ the red colour on someone's face when they are embarrassed or ashamed.

bluster, blusters, blustering, blustered **VERB** ❶ When someone blusters, they behave aggressively because they are angry or frightened ▷ **NOUN** ❷ Bluster is aggressive behaviour by someone who is angry or frightened.

blustery ADJECTIVE Blustery weather is rough and windy.

boa, boas **NOUN** ❶ A boa, or a boa constrictor, is a large snake that kills

a
b
c
d
e
f
g
h
i
j
k
l
m
n
o
p
q
r
s
t
u
v
w
x
y
z

▷ SPELLING NOTE: *pAL up with the principAL and principAL staff (principal)*

its prey by coiling round it and crushing it. ❷ a woman's long thin scarf of feathers or fur.

boar, boars NOUN a male wild pig, or a male domestic pig used for breeding.

board, boards, boarding, boarded NOUN ❶ a long, flat piece of wood. ❷ the group of people who control a company or organization. ❸ Board is the meals provided when you stay somewhere • *The price includes full board.* ▷ VERB ❹ If you board a ship or aircraft, you get on it or in it ▷ PHRASE ❺ If you are **on board** a ship or aircraft, you are on it or in it.

boarder, boarders NOUN a pupil who lives at school during term.

boarding school, boarding schools NOUN a school where the pupils live during the term.

boardroom, boardrooms NOUN a room where the board of a company meets.

boast, boasts, boasting, boasted VERB ❶ If you boast about your possessions or achievements, you talk about them proudly ▷ NOUN ❷ something that you say which shows that you are proud of what you own or have done.
  SIMILAR WORDS: ❶ blow your own trumpet, brag, crow

boastful ADJECTIVE tending to brag about things.

boat, boats NOUN a small vehicle for travelling across water.

bob, bobs, bobbing, bobbed VERB ❶ When something bobs, it moves up and down ▷ NOUN ❷ a woman's hair style in which her hair is cut to be level with her chin.

bobbin, bobbins NOUN a small round object on which thread or wool is wound.

bobby, bobbies NOUN INFORMAL, OLD-FASHIONED a policeman.

bode, bodes, boding, boded PHRASE LITERARY If something **bodes ill**, or **bodes well**, it makes you think that something bad, or good, will happen.

bodice, bodices NOUN the upper part of a dress.

bodily ADJECTIVE ❶ relating to the body • *bodily contact.* ▷ ADVERB ❷ involving the whole of someone's body • *He was carried bodily up the steps.*

body, bodies NOUN ❶ Your body is either all your physical parts, or just the main part not including your head, arms, and legs. ❷ a person's dead body. ❸ the main part of a car or aircraft, not including the engine. ❹ A body of people is also an organized group.
  SIMILAR WORDS: ❶ build, figure, form, physique

bodyguard, bodyguards NOUN a person employed to protect someone.

bodywork NOUN the outer part of a motor vehicle.

boer, boers [Said boh-er] NOUN In South Africa, a boer is a white farmer, especially one who is descended from the Dutch people who went to live in South Africa.

boerewors [Said boo-rih-vorse] NOUN In South Africa, boerewors is a type of meat sausage.

bog, bogs NOUN an area of land

which is always wet and spongy.

boggle, boggles, boggling, boggled **VERB** If your mind boggles at something, you find it difficult to imagine or understand.

bogus **ADJECTIVE** not genuine • *a bogus doctor.*

bohemian [Said boh-**hee**-mee-an] **ADJECTIVE** Someone who is bohemian does not behave in the same way as most other people in society, and is usually involved in the arts.

boil, boils, boiling, boiled **VERB** ❶ When a hot liquid boils, bubbles appear in it and it starts to give off steam. ❷ When you boil a kettle, you heat it until the water in it boils. ❸ When you boil food, you cook it in boiling water ▷ **NOUN** ❹ a red swelling on your skin.

boiler, boilers **NOUN** a piece of equipment which burns fuel to provide hot water.

boiling **ADJECTIVE** INFORMAL very hot.

boiling point, boiling points **NOUN** (SCIENCE) the temperature at which a liquid starts to boil and turn to vapour.

boisterous **ADJECTIVE** Someone who is boisterous is noisy and lively.
● **SIMILAR WORDS:** loud, noisy, rowdy, unruly

bold, bolder, boldest **ADJECTIVE** ❶ confident and not shy or embarrassed • *He was not bold enough to ask them.* ❷ not afraid of risk or danger. ❸ clear and noticeable • *bold colours.* **boldly** **ADVERB** **boldness** **NOUN**

bollard, bollards **NOUN** a short, thick post used to keep vehicles out of a road.

bolster, bolsters, bolstering, bolstered **VERB** To bolster something means to support it or make it stronger • *She relied on others to bolster her self-esteem.*

bolt, bolts, bolting, bolted **NOUN** ❶ a metal bar that you slide across a door or window in order to fasten it. ❷ a metal object which screws into a nut and is used to fasten things together ▷ **VERB** ❸ If you bolt a door or window, you fasten it using a bolt. If you bolt things together, you fasten them together using a bolt. ❹ To bolt means to escape or run away. ❺ To bolt food means to eat it very quickly.

bomb, bombs, bombing, bombed **NOUN** ❶ a container filled with material that explodes when it hits something or is set off by a timer ▷ **VERB** ❷ When a place is bombed, it is attacked with bombs.

bombard, bombards, bombarding, bombarded **VERB** ❶ To bombard a place means to attack it with heavy gunfire or bombs. ❷ If you are bombarded with something you are made to face a great deal of it • *I was bombarded with criticism.* **bombardment** **NOUN**

bomber, bombers **NOUN** an aircraft that drops bombs.

bombshell, bombshells **NOUN** a sudden piece of shocking or upsetting news.

bona fide [Said boh-na **fie**-dee] **ADJECTIVE** genuine • *We are happy to donate to bona fide charities.*

a b c d e f g h i j k l m n o p q r s t u v w x y z

A B C D E F G H I J K L M N O P Q R S T U V W X Y Z

● **WORD HISTORY:** a Latin
● expression meaning 'in good faith'

bond, bonds, bonding, bonded **NOUN**
❶ a close relationship between
people. ❷ LITERARY Bonds are chains
or ropes used to tie a prisoner up. ❸ a
certificate which records that you have
lent money to a business and that it
will repay you the loan with interest.
❹ In chemistry, a bond is the means
by which atoms or groups of atoms
are combined in molecules. ❺ Bonds
are also feelings or obligations that
force you to behave in a particular way
• *the social bonds of community.*
▷ **VERB** ❻ When two things bond or
are bonded, they become closely
linked or attached.
● **SIMILAR WORDS:** ❶ connection,
● link, tie

bondage NOUN Bondage is the
condition of being someone's slave.

bone, bones **NOUN** Bones are the
hard parts that form the framework of
a person's or animal's body. **boneless**
ADJECTIVE

bonfire, bonfires **NOUN** a large fire
made outdoors, often to burn rubbish.
● **WORD HISTORY:** from 'bone' +
● 'fire'; bones were used as fuel in the
● Middle Ages

bonnet, bonnets **NOUN** ❶ the
metal cover over a car's engine. ❷ a
baby's or woman's hat tied under the
chin.

bonny, bonnier, bonniest **ADJECTIVE**
In Scotland and Northern England,
nice to look at.

bonus, bonuses **NOUN** ❶ an
amount of money added to your usual
pay. ❷ Something that is a bonus is a

good thing that you get in addition to
something else • *The view from the*
hotel was an added bonus.

bony, bonier, boniest **ADJECTIVE**
Bony people or animals are thin, with
very little flesh covering their bones.

boo, boos, booing, booed **NOUN** ❶ a
shout of disapproval ▷ **VERB**
❷ When people boo, they shout 'boo'
to show their disapproval.

boobook, boobooks **NOUN** a small
brown Australian owl with a spotted
back and wings.

book, books, booking, booked **NOUN**
❶ a number of pages held together
inside a cover ▷ **VERB** ❷ When you
book something such as a room, you
arrange to have it or use it at a
particular time.

bookcase, bookcases **NOUN** a piece
of furniture with shelves for books.

bookie, bookies **NOUN** INFORMAL a
bookmaker.

booking, bookings **NOUN** an
arrangement to book something such
as a hotel room.

book-keeping NOUN Book-
keeping is the keeping of a record of
the money spent and received by a
business.

booklet, booklets **NOUN** a small
book with a paper cover.

bookmaker, bookmakers **NOUN** a
person who makes a living by taking
people's bets and paying them when
they win.

bookmark, bookmarks **NOUN** a
piece of card which you put between
the pages of a book to mark the place

▷ SPELLING NOTE: *the QUeen stood on the QUay (quay)*

where you stopped reading.

boom, booms, booming, boomed
NOUN ➊ a rapid increase in
something • *the baby boom.* ➋ a loud
deep echoing sound ▷ **VERB**
➌ When something booms, it
increases rapidly • *Sales are booming.*
➍ To boom means to make a loud
deep echoing sound.

boomerang, boomerangs **NOUN** a
curved wooden missile that can be
thrown so that it returns to the
thrower, originally used as a weapon
by Australian Aborigines.

boon, boons **NOUN** Something that
is a boon makes life better or easier
• *Credit cards have been a boon to
shoppers.*

boost, boosts, boosting, boosted
VERB ➊ To boost something means
to cause it to improve or increase
• *The campaign had boosted sales.*
▷ **NOUN** ➋ an improvement or
increase • *a boost to the economy.*
booster NOUN

boot, boots, booting, booted **NOUN**
➊ Boots are strong shoes that come
up over your ankle and sometimes
your calf. ➋ the covered space in a
car, usually at the back, for carrying
things in ▷ **VERB** ➌ INFORMAL If you
boot something, you kick it ▷ **PHRASE**
➍ **To boot** means also or in addition
• *The story was compelling and well
written to boot.*

booth, booths **NOUN** ➊ a small
partly enclosed area • *a telephone
booth.* ➋ a stall where you can buy
goods.

booty NOUN Booty is valuable things
taken from a place, especially by

soldiers after a battle.

booze, boozes, boozing, boozed
INFORMAL **NOUN ➊** Booze is alcoholic
drink ▷ **VERB** ➋ When people booze,
they drink alcohol. **boozer NOUN
boozy ADJECTIVE**

border, borders, bordering, bordered
NOUN ➊ the dividing line between
two places or things. ➋ a strip or
band round the edge of something
• *plain tiles with a bright border.* ➌ a
long flower bed in a garden ▷ **VERB**
➍ To border something means to
form a boundary along the side of it
• *Tall poplar trees bordered the fields.*

borderline ADJECTIVE only just
acceptable as a member of a class or
group • *a borderline case.*

bore, bores, boring, bored **VERB ➊** If
something bores you, you find it dull
and not at all interesting. ➋ If you
bore a hole in something, you make it
using a tool such as a drill ▷ **NOUN**
➌ someone or something that bores
you.

bored ADJECTIVE If you are bored,
you are impatient because you do not
find something interesting or because
you have nothing to do.

● **USAGE NOTE:** You can say that you
● are *bored with* or *bored by* someone
● or something, but you should not
● say *bored of*

boredom NOUN a lack or interest.

boring ADJECTIVE dull and lacking
interest.
● **SIMILAR WORDS:** dull, tedious,
● uninteresting

born VERB ➊ When a baby is born, it
comes out of its mother's womb at

a
b
c
d
e
f
g
h
i
j
k
l
m
n
o
p
q
r
s
t
u
v
w
x
y
z

A
B
C
D
E
F
G
H
I
J
K
L
M
N
O
P
Q
R
S
T
U
V
W
X
Y
Z

the beginning of its life ▷ **ADJECTIVE**
❷ You use 'born' to mean that
someone has a particular quality from
birth • *He was a born pessimist.*

borne the past participle of **bear**.

borough, boroughs [*Said bur-uh*]
NOUN a town, or a district within a
large town, that has its own council.

borrow, borrows, borrowing,
borrowed **VERB** If you borrow
something that belongs to someone
else, they let you have it for a period of
time. **borrower NOUN**
● **USAGE NOTE:** You *borrow*
● something *from* a person, not *off*
● them. Do not confuse *borrow* and
● *lend*. If you *borrow* something, you
● get it from another person for a
● while; if you *lend* something,
● someone gets it from you for a while

Bosnian, Bosnians **ADJECTIVE**
❶ belonging to or relating to Bosnia
▷ **NOUN** **❷** someone who comes
from Bosnia.

bosom, bosoms **NOUN** **❶** A
woman's bosom is her breasts
▷ **ADJECTIVE** **❷** A bosom friend is a
very close friend.

boss, bosses, bossing, bossed **NOUN**
❶ Someone's boss is the person in
charge of the place where they work
▷ **VERB** **❷** If someone bosses you
around, they keep telling you what to do.

bossy, bossier, bossiest **ADJECTIVE** A
bossy person enjoys telling other
people what to do. **bossiness NOUN**
● **SIMILAR WORDS:** dictatorial,
● domineering, overbearing

botany NOUN Botany is the
scientific study of plants. **botanic** or

botanical ADJECTIVE **botanist**
NOUN

botch, botches, botching, botched
VERB INFORMAL If you botch
something, you do it badly or clumsily.
● **SIMILAR WORDS:** bungle, mess up

both ADJECTIVE OR PRONOUN
'Both' is used when saying something
about two things or people.
● **USAGE NOTE:** You can use *of* after
● *both*, but it is not essential. *Both the
● boys* means the same as *both of the
● boys*

bother, bothers, bothering, bothered
VERB **❶** If you do not bother to do
something, you do not do it because it
takes too much effort or it seems
unnecessary. **❷** If something bothers
you, you are worried or concerned
about it. If you do not bother about it,
you are not concerned about it • *She is
not bothered about money.* **❸** If you
bother someone, you interrupt them
when they are busy ▷ **NOUN**
❹ Bother is trouble, fuss, or difficulty.
bothersome ADJECTIVE

bottle, bottles, bottling, bottled
NOUN **❶** a glass or plastic container
for keeping liquids in ▷ **VERB** **❷** To
bottle something means to store it in
bottles.

bottleneck, bottlenecks **NOUN** a
narrow section of road where traffic
has to slow down or stop

bottle store, bottle stores **NOUN**
In Australian, New Zealand, and South
African English, a bottle store is a shop
that sells sealed alcoholic drinks which
can be drunk elsewhere.

bottom, bottoms **NOUN** **❶** The
bottom of something is its lowest part.

❷ Your bottom is your buttocks
▷ **ADJECTIVE** ❸ The bottom thing in a series of things is the lowest one.
bottomless ADJECTIVE

bough, boughs *[rhymes with now]*
NOUN a large branch of a tree.

bought the past tense and past participle of **buy**.
● **USAGE NOTE:** Do not confuse *bought* and *brought*. *Bought* comes from *buy* and *brought* comes from *bring*

boulder, boulders **NOUN** a large rounded rock.

boulevard, boulevards *[Said boo-le-vard]* **NOUN** a wide street in a city, usually with trees along each side.

bounce, bounces, bouncing, bounced **VERB** ❶ When an object bounces, it springs back from something after hitting it. ❷ To bounce also means to move up and down • *Her long black hair bounced as she walked.* ❸ If a cheque bounces, the bank refuses to accept it because there is not enough money in the account.
● **SIMILAR WORDS:** ❶ rebound, recoil, ricochet

bouncy, bouncier, bounciest
ADJECTIVE ❶ Someone who is bouncy is lively and enthusiastic.
❷ Something that is bouncy is capable of bouncing or being bounced on • *a bouncy ball* • *a bouncy castle.*

bound, bounds, bounding, bounded
ADJECTIVE ❶ If you say that something is bound to happen, you mean that it is certain to happen. ❷ If a person or a vehicle is bound for a place, they are going there. ❸ If

someone is bound by an agreement or regulation, they must obey it ▷ **NOUN**
❹ a large leap ❺ IN PLURAL Bounds are limits which restrict or control something • *Their enthusiasm knew no bounds.* ▷ **PHRASE** ❻ If a place is **out of bounds**, you are forbidden to go there ▷ **VERB** ❼ When animals or people bound, they move quickly with large leaps • *He bounded up the stairway.* ❽ Bound is also the past tense and past participle of **bind**.

boundary, boundaries **NOUN**
something that indicates the farthest limit of anything • *the city boundary* • *the boundaries of taste.*

boundless ADJECTIVE without end or limit • *her boundless energy.*

bountiful ADJECTIVE LITERARY freely available in large amounts • *a bountiful harvest.*

bounty NOUN ❶ LITERARY Bounty is a generous supply • *autumn's bounty of fruits.* ❷ Someone's bounty is their generosity in giving a lot of something.

bouquet, bouquets *[Said boo-kay]*
NOUN an attractively arranged bunch of flowers.

bourgeois *[Said boor-jhwah]*
ADJECTIVE typical of fairly rich middle-class people.

bourgeoisie *[Said boor-jhwah-zee]*
NOUN the fairly rich middle-class people in a society.

bout, bouts **NOUN** ❶ If you have a bout of something such as an illness, you have it for a short time • *a bout of flu.* ❷ If you have a bout of doing something, you do it enthusiastically for a short time. ❸ a boxing or

a
b
c
d
e
f
g
h
i
j
k
l
m
n
o
p
q
r
s
t
u
v
w
x
y
z

wrestling match • *his last bout.*

boutique, boutiques [*Said boo-teek*] NOUN a small shop that sells fashionable clothes.

bovine ADJECTIVE TECHNICAL relating to cattle.

bow, bows, bowing, bowed [*rhymes with now*] VERB ① When you bow, you bend your body or lower your head as a sign of respect or greeting. ② If you bow to something, you give in to it • *He bowed to public pressure.* ▷ NOUN ③ the movement you make when you bow. ④ the front part of a ship.

bow, bows [*rhymes with low*] NOUN ① a knot with two loops and two loose ends. ② a long thin piece of wood with horsehair stretched along it, which you use to play a violin. ③ a long flexible piece of wood used for shooting arrows.

bowel, bowels [*rhymes with towel*] NOUN Your bowels are the tubes leading from your stomach, through which waste passes before it leaves your body.

bowerbird, bowerbirds NOUN a bird found in Australia, the male of which builds a shelter during courtship.

bowl, bowls, bowling, bowled [*rhymes with mole*] NOUN ① a round container with a wide uncovered top, used for holding liquid or for serving food. ② the hollow, rounded part of something • *a toilet bowl.* ③ (PE) a large heavy ball used in the game of bowls or tenpin bowling ▷ VERB ④ (PE) In cricket, to bowl means to throw the ball towards the batsman.

bowler NOUN

bowling NOUN Bowling is a game in which you roll a heavy ball down a narrow track towards a group of wooden objects called pins and try to knock them down.

bowls NOUN Bowls is a game in which the players try to roll large wooden balls as near as possible to a small ball.

bow tie, bow ties [*rhymes with low*] NOUN a man's tie in the form of a bow, often worn at formal occasions.

box, boxes, boxing, boxed NOUN ① a container with a firm base and sides and usually a lid. ② On a form, a box is a rectangular space which you have to fill in. ③ In a theatre, a box is a small separate area where a few people can watch the performance together ▷ VERB ④ To box means to fight someone according to the rules of boxing.

boxer, boxers NOUN ① a person who boxes. ② a type of medium-sized, smooth-haired dog with a flat face.

boxing NOUN Boxing is a sport in which two people fight using their fists, wearing padded gloves.

box office, box offices NOUN the place where tickets are sold in a theatre or cinema.

boy, boys NOUN a male child. **boyhood** NOUN **boyish** ADJECTIVE
● SIMILAR WORDS: lad, youngster, ● youth

boycott, boycotts, boycotting, boycotted VERB ① If you boycott an organization or event, you refuse to have anything to do with it ▷ NOUN

▷ SPELLING NOTE: *Eddy Ant thinks mEAt is a grEAt trEAt to EAt (-ea-)*

❷ the boycotting of an organization or event • *a boycott of the elections.*

● **WORD HISTORY:** from the name of Captain C.C. Boycott (1832–1897), an Irish land agent, who offended the tenants, so that they refused to pay their rents

● **SIMILAR WORDS: ❶** ban, black, embargo

boyfriend, boyfriends **NOUN** Someone's boyfriend is the man or boy with whom they are having a romantic relationship.

bra, bras **NOUN** a piece of underwear worn by a woman to support her breasts.

braaivleis or **braai**, braaivleises or braais *[Said bry-flayss]* **NOUN** In South African English, a braaivleis is a picnic where meat is cooked on an open fire.

brace, braces, bracing, braced **VERB** **❶** When you brace yourself, you stiffen your body to steady yourself • *The ship lurched and he braced himself.* **❷** If you brace yourself for something unpleasant, you prepare yourself to deal with it • *The police are braced for violent reprisals.* ▷ **NOUN** **❸** an object fastened to something to straighten or support it • *a neck brace.* **❹** IN PLURAL Braces are a pair of straps worn over the shoulders and fastened to the trousers to hold them up.

bracelet, bracelets **NOUN** a chain or band worn around someone's wrist as an ornament.

bracing ADJECTIVE Something that is bracing makes you feel fit and full of energy • *the bracing sea air.*

bracken NOUN Bracken is a plant like a large fern that grows on hills and in woods.

bracket, brackets **NOUN** **❶** Brackets are a pair of written marks, ( ) or [ ], placed round a word or sentence that is not part of the main text, or to show that the items inside the brackets belong together. **❷** a range between two limits, for example of ages or prices • *the four-figure price bracket.* **❸** a piece of metal or wood fastened to a wall to support something such as a shelf.
▶ SEE GRAMMAR BOX BELOW

brag, brags, bragging, bragged **VERB** When someone brags, they boast

---

WHAT DO BRACKETS DO?

Brackets ( ) enclose material that has been added to the text, but could be omitted and still leave a meaningful sentence. In formal writing this sort of material is usually marked off with commas or dashes, and brackets are used for giving references or translations of foreign phrases:
Buddhism is discussed in Chapter 7 (see pages 152–197).
The boat was called "La Ardilla Roja" (The Red Squirrel).

Square brackets [ ] are used to enclose remarks and explanations which are inserted by a writer to make a quotation clearer:
The minister said, "I think that five million [pounds] should do it."

---

a
b
c
d
e
f
g
h
i
j
k
l
m
n
o
p
q
r
s
t
u
v
w
x
y
z

▷ SPELLING NOTE: *Elaine and Emily shout EE when they mEEt to grEEt each other (-ee-)*

braggart | 100

about their achievements • *Both leaders bragged they could win by a landslide.*

braggart, braggarts **NOUN** someone who brags.

Brahma [Said **brah-ma**] **PROPER NOUN** Brahma is a Hindu god and is one of the Trimurti.

Brahman [Said **brah-men**] **NOUN** In the Hindu religion Brahman is the ultimate and impersonal divine reality of the universe.

brahmin, brahmins [Said **brah-min**] **NOUN** a member of the highest or priestly caste in Hindu society.

braid, braids, braiding, braided **NOUN** ❶ Braid is a strip of decorated cloth used to decorate clothes or curtains. ❷ a length of hair which has been plaited and tied ▷ **VERB** ❸ To braid hair or thread means to plait it.

Braille **NOUN** Braille is a system of printing for blind people in which letters are represented by raised dots that can be felt with the fingers.

brain, brains **NOUN** ❶ Your brain is the mass of nerve tissue inside your head that controls your body and enables you to think and feel; also used to refer to your mind and the way that you think • *I admired his legal brain.* ❷ IN PLURAL If you say that someone has brains, you mean that they are very intelligent.

brainchild **NOUN** INFORMAL Someone's brainchild is something that they have invented or created.

brainwash, brainwashes, brainwashing, brainwashed **VERB** If people are brainwashed into believing

something, they accept it without question because they are told it repeatedly. **brainwashing NOUN**

brainwave, brainwaves **NOUN** INFORMAL a clever idea you think of suddenly.

brainy, brainier, brainiest **ADJECTIVE** INFORMAL clever.

braise, braises, braising, braised **VERB** To braise food means to fry it for a short time, then cook it slowly in a little liquid.

brake, brakes, braking, braked **NOUN** ❶ a device for making a vehicle stop or slow down ▷ **VERB** ❷ When a driver brakes, he or she makes a vehicle stop or slow down by using its brakes.
● **USAGE NOTE:** Do not confuse the spellings of *brake* and *break*, or *braking* and *breaking*

bramble, brambles **NOUN** a wild, thorny bush that produces blackberries.

bran NOUN Bran is the ground husks that are left over after flour has been made from wheat grains.

branch, branches, branching, branched **NOUN** ❶ The branches of a tree are the parts that grow out from its trunk. ❷ A branch of an organization is one of a number of its offices or shops. ❸ A branch of a subject is one of its areas of study or activity • *specialists in certain branches of medicine.* ▷ **VERB** ❹ A road that branches off from another road splits off from it to lead in a different direction.

brand, brands, branding, branded **NOUN** ❶ A brand of something is a particular kind or make of it • *a*

popular brand of chocolate. ▷ **VERB**
2 When an animal is branded, a mark is burned on its skin to show who owns it.

brandish, brandishes, brandishing, brandished **VERB** LITERARY If you brandish something, you wave it vigorously • *He brandished his sword over his head.*

brand-new ADJECTIVE completely new.

brandy, brandies **NOUN** a strong alcoholic drink, usually made from wine.
● **WORD HISTORY:** from Dutch
● *brandewijn* meaning 'burnt wine'

brash, brasher, brashest **ADJECTIVE** If someone is brash, they are overconfident or rather rude.

brass NOUN OR ADJECTIVE
1 Brass is a yellow-coloured metal made from copper and zinc. **2** In an orchestra, the brass section consists of brass wind instruments such as trumpets and trombones.

brassière, brassières **NOUN** FORMAL a bra.

brat, brats **NOUN** INFORMAL A badly behaved child may be referred to as a brat.

bravado [*Said bra-vah-doh*] **NOUN** Bravado is a display of courage intended to impress other people.

brave, braver, bravest; braves, braving, braved **ADJECTIVE 1** A brave person is willing to do dangerous things and does not show any fear ▷ **VERB 2** If you brave an unpleasant or dangerous situation, you face up to it in order to do something • *His fans braved the rain to*

hear him sing. **bravely ADVERB**
● **SIMILAR WORDS: 1** courageous,
● daring, fearless, plucky

bravery NOUN the quality of being courageous.

bravo INTERJECTION People shout 'Bravo!' to express appreciation when something has been done well.

brawl, brawls, brawling, brawled **NOUN 1** a rough fight ▷ **VERB**
2 When people brawl, they take part in a rough fight.

brawn NOUN Brawn is physical strength. **brawny ADJECTIVE**

bray, brays, braying, brayed **VERB**
1 When a donkey brays, it makes a loud, harsh sound ▷ **NOUN 2** the sound a donkey makes.

brazen ADJECTIVE When someone's behaviour is brazen, they show that they do not care if other people think they are behaving wrongly. **brazenly ADVERB**

brazier, braziers **NOUN** a metal container in which coal or charcoal is burned to keep people warm out of doors.

Brazilian, Brazilians **ADJECTIVE**
1 belonging or relating to Brazil
▷ **NOUN 2** someone who comes from Brazil.

breach, breaches, breaching, breached **VERB 1** FORMAL If you breach an agreement or law, you break it. **2** To breach a barrier means to make a gap in it • *The river breached its banks.* ▷ **NOUN 3** A breach of an agreement or law is an action that breaks it • *a breach of contract.* **4** a gap or break.

▷ SPELLING NOTE: *King IAn went to ParlIAment in a carrIAge for his marrIAge (-ia-)*

● SIMILAR WORDS:
● ❸ contravention, infringement,
● violation

bread NOUN a food made from flour and water, usually raised with yeast, and baked.

breadth NOUN The breadth of something is the distance between its two sides.

breadwinner, breadwinners NOUN the person who earns the money in a family.

break, breaks, breaking, broke, broken VERB ❶ When an object breaks, it is damaged and separates into pieces. ❷ If you break a rule or promise you fail to keep it. ❸ When a boy's voice breaks, it becomes permanently deeper. ❹ When a wave breaks, it falls and becomes foam ▷ NOUN ❺ a short period during which you rest or do something different. **breakable** ADJECTIVE
break down VERB ❶ When a machine or a vehicle breaks down, it stops working. ❷ When a discussion or relationship breaks down, it ends because of problems or disagreements.
break up VERB If something breaks up, it ends • *Their marriage broke up.*
● USAGE NOTE: Do not confuse the
● spellings of *break* and *brake*, or
● *breaking* and *braking*
● SIMILAR WORDS: ❶ crack,
● fracture, separate, snap ❷ breach,
● contravene, disobey, violate

breakage, breakages NOUN the act of breaking something or a thing that has been broken.

breakaway ADJECTIVE A breakaway group is one that has separated from a larger group.

breakdown, breakdowns NOUN
❶ The breakdown of something such as a system is its failure • *a breakdown in communications.* ❷ the same as a nervous breakdown. ❸ If a driver has a breakdown, their car stops working. ❹ A breakdown of something complex is a summary of its important points • *He demanded a breakdown of the costs.*

breaker, breakers NOUN Breakers are big sea waves.

breakfast, breakfasts NOUN the first meal of the day.

break-in, break-ins NOUN the illegal entering of a building, especially by a burglar.

breakneck ADJECTIVE INFORMAL Someone or something that is travelling at breakneck speed is travelling dangerously fast.

breakthrough, breakthroughs NOUN a sudden important development • *a medical breakthrough.*

breakwater, breakwaters NOUN a wall extending into the sea which protects a coast from the force of the waves.

bream, breams NOUN an edible fish.

breast, breasts NOUN A woman's breasts are the two soft, fleshy parts on her chest, which produce milk after she has had a baby.

breaststroke NOUN PE
Breaststroke is a swimming stroke in which you lie on your front, moving your arms horizontally through the water and kicking both legs up and

▷ SPELLING NOTE: *you'll brEAK that Electrical Aerial, Kitty (break)*

A
B
C
D
E
F
G
H
I
J
K
L
M
N
O
P
Q
R
S
T
U
V
W
X
Y
Z

down at the same time.

breath, breaths NOUN ❶ Your breath is the air you take into your lungs and let out again when you breathe ▷ PHRASE ❷ If you are **out of breath**, you are breathing with difficulty after doing something energetic. ❸ If you say something **under your breath**, you say it in a very quiet voice.

breathe, breathes, breathing, breathed VERB When you breathe, you take air into your lungs and let it out again.

breathless ADJECTIVE If you are breathless, you are breathing fast or with difficulty. **breathlessly** ADVERB **breathlessness** NOUN

breathtaking ADJECTIVE If you say that something is breathtaking, you mean that it is very beautiful or exciting.

bred the past tense and past participle of **breed**.

breeches [Said **brit-chiz**] PLURAL NOUN Breeches are trousers reaching to just below the knee, nowadays worn especially for riding.

breed, breeds, breeding, bred NOUN ❶ A breed of a species of domestic animal is a particular type of it ▷ VERB ❷ Someone who breeds animals or plants keeps them in order to produce more animals or plants with particular qualities. ❸ When animals breed, they mate and produce offspring.
● SIMILAR WORDS: ❸ multiply,
● procreate, reproduce

breeze, breezes NOUN a gentle wind.

brevity NOUN FORMAL Brevity means shortness • *the brevity of his report.*

brew, brews, brewing, brewed VERB ❶ If you brew tea or coffee, you make it in a pot by pouring hot water over it. ❷ To brew beer means to make it, by boiling and fermenting malt. ❸ If an unpleasant situation is brewing, it is about to happen • *Another scandal is brewing.* **brewer** NOUN

brewery, breweries NOUN a place where beer is made, or a company that makes it.

briar, briars NOUN a wild rose that grows on a dense prickly bush.

bribe, bribes, bribing, bribed NOUN ❶ a gift or money given to an official to persuade them to make a favourable decision ▷ VERB ❷ To bribe someone means to give them a bribe. **bribery** NOUN

bric-a-brac NOUN Bric-a-brac consists of small ornaments or pieces of furniture of no great value.
● WORD HISTORY: from an obsolete
● French phrase *à bric et à brac*
● meaning 'at random'

brick, bricks NOUN Bricks are rectangular blocks of baked clay used in building.

bricklayer, bricklayers NOUN a person whose job is to build with bricks.

bride, brides NOUN a woman who is getting married or who has just got married. **bridal** ADJECTIVE

bridegroom, bridegrooms NOUN a man who is getting married or who has just got married.

bridesmaid, bridesmaids NOUN a

woman who helps and accompanies a bride on her wedding day.

bridge, bridges **NOUN** ❶ a structure built over a river, road, or railway so that vehicles and people can cross. ❷ the platform from which a ship is steered and controlled. ❸ the hard ridge at the top of your nose. ❹ Bridge is a card game for four players based on whist.

bridle, bridles **NOUN** a set of straps round a horse's head and mouth, which the rider uses to control the horse.

brief, briefer, briefest; briefs, briefing, briefed **ADJECTIVE** ❶ Something that is brief lasts only a short time ▷ **VERB** ❷ D & T When you brief someone on a task, you give them all the necessary instructions and information about it. **briefly ADVERB**
● **SIMILAR WORDS:** ❶ fleeting, momentary, quick, short

briefcase, briefcases **NOUN** a small flat case for carrying papers.

briefing, briefings **NOUN** a meeting at which information and instructions are given.

brier another spelling of **briar**.

brigade, brigades **NOUN** an army unit consisting of three battalions.

brigadier, brigadiers [Said brig-ad-**ear**] **NOUN** an army officer of the rank immediately above colonel.

brigalow, brigalows **NOUN** a type of Australian acacia tree that grows in the bush.

bright, brighter, brightest **ADJECTIVE** ❶ strong and startling • a bright light. ❷ clever • my brightest student.

❸ cheerful • a bright smile. **brightly ADVERB brightness NOUN**
● **SIMILAR WORDS:** ❶ brilliant, dazzling, shining, vivid

brighten, brightens, brightening, brightened **VERB** ❶ If something brightens, it becomes brighter • The weather had brightened. ❷ If someone brightens, they suddenly look happier. **brighten up VERB** To brighten something up means to make it more attractive and cheerful.

brilliant ADJECTIVE ❶ A brilliant light or colour is extremely bright. ❷ A brilliant person is extremely clever. ❸ A brilliant career is extremely successful. **brilliantly ADVERB brilliance NOUN**

brim, brims **NOUN** ❶ the wide part of a hat is the part that sticks outwards at the bottom ▷ **PHRASE** ❷ If a container is filled **to the brim**, it is filled right to the top.

brine NOUN Brine is salt water.

bring, brings, bringing, brought **VERB** ❶ If you bring something or someone with you when you go to a place, you take them with you • You can bring a friend to the party. ❷ To bring something to a particular state means to cause it to be like that • Bring the vegetables to the boil. **bring about VERB** To bring something about means to cause it to happen • We must try to bring about a better world. **bring up VERB** ❶ To bring up children means to look after them while they grow up. ❷ If you bring up a subject, you introduce it into the conversation • She brought up the subject at dinner.

▷ SPELLING NOTE: A Rude Idiot Thought He Might Eat Toffee In Church (<u>arithmetic</u>)

brinjal, brinjals **NOUN** In Indian and South African English, an aubergine.

brink NOUN If you are on the brink of something, you are just about to do it or experience it.

brisk, brisker, briskest **ADJECTIVE** ❶ A brisk action is done quickly and energetically • *A brisk walk restores your energy.* ❷ If someone's manner is brisk, it shows that they want to get things done quickly and efficiently. **briskly ADVERB briskness NOUN**

bristle, bristles, bristling, bristled **NOUN** ❶ Bristles are strong animal hairs used to make brushes ▷ **VERB** ❷ If the hairs on an animal's body bristle, they rise up, because it is frightened. **bristly ADJECTIVE**

British ADJECTIVE belonging or relating to the United Kingdom of Great Britain and Northern Ireland.

Briton, Britons **NOUN** someone who comes from the United Kingdom of Great Britain and Northern Ireland.

brittle ADJECTIVE An object that is brittle is hard but breaks easily.

broach, broaches, broaching, broached **VERB** When you broach a subject, you introduce it into a discussion.

broad, broader, broadest **ADJECTIVE** ❶ wide • *a broad smile.* ❷ having many different aspects or concerning many different people • *A broad range of issues was discussed.* ❸ general rather than detailed • *the broad concerns of the movement.* ❹ If someone has a broad accent, the way that they speak makes it very clear where they come from • *She spoke in a broad Irish accent.*

broadband NOUN Broadband is a digital system used on the Internet and in other forms of telecommunication which can process and transfer information input from various sources, such as from telephones, computers or televisions.

broad bean, broad beans **NOUN** Broad beans are light-green beans with thick flat edible seeds.

broadcast, broadcasts, broadcasting, broadcast **NOUN** ❶ a programme or announcement on radio or television ▷ **VERB** ❷ To broadcast something means to send it out by radio waves, so that it can be seen on television or heard on radio. **broadcaster NOUN broadcasting NOUN**

broaden, broadens, broadening, broadened **VERB** ❶ When something broadens, it becomes wider • *His smile broadened.* ❷ To broaden something means to cause it to involve more things or concern more people • *We must broaden the scope of this job.*

broadly ADVERB true to a large extent or in most cases • *There are broadly two schools of thought on this.*

broad-minded ADJECTIVE Someone who is broad-minded does not disapprove of behaviour or attitudes that many other people disapprove of.
  ● **SIMILAR WORDS:** liberal,
  ● open-minded, tolerant

broadsheet, broadsheets **NOUN** a newspaper with large pages and long news stories.

brocade NOUN Brocade is a heavy,

▷ SPELLING NOTE: *Beautiful Elephants Are Usually Tiny (*<u>beautiful</u>*)*

A
B
C
D
E
F
G
H
I
J
K
L
M
N
O
P
Q
R
S
T
U
V
W
X
Y
Z

expensive material, often made of silk, with a raised pattern.

broccoli NOUN Broccoli is a green vegetable, similar to cauliflower.

brochure, brochures [Said *broh-sher*] NOUN a booklet which gives information about a product or service.

brogue, brogues [Said *broag*] NOUN ❶ a strong accent, especially an Irish one. ❷ Brogues are thick leather shoes.
● **WORD HISTORY:** from Irish Gaelic
● *bróg* meaning 'boot' or 'shoe'

broke ❶ the past tense of **break**. **ADJECTIVE** ❷ in pieces. ❸ not kept. ❹ INFORMAL If you are broke, you have no money.

broker, brokers NOUN a person whose job is to buy and sell shares for other people.

brolga, brolgas NOUN a large grey Australian crane with a red-and-green head.

brolly, brollies NOUN INFORMAL an umbrella.

bronchitis NOUN Bronchitis is an illness in which the two tubes which connect your windpipe to your lungs become infected, making you cough.

bronchus, bronchi NOUN (SCIENCE) one of the two tubes that carry air from your windpipe into your lungs.

brontosaurus, brontosauruses NOUN a type of very large, plant-eating dinosaur.

bronze NOUN Bronze is a yellowish-brown metal which is a mixture of copper and tin; also the yellowish-

brown colour of this metal.

brooch, brooches [*rhymes with coach*] NOUN a piece of jewellery with a pin at the back for attaching to clothes.

brood, broods, brooding, brooded NOUN ❶ a family of baby birds ▷ VERB ❷ If you brood about something, you keep thinking about it in a serious or unhappy way.

brook, brooks NOUN a stream.

broom, brooms NOUN ❶ a long-handled brush. ❷ Broom is a shrub with yellow flowers.

broth NOUN Broth is soup, usually with vegetables in it.

brothel, brothels NOUN a house where men pay to have sex with prostitutes.

brother, brothers NOUN Your brother is a boy or man who has the same parents as you. **brotherly** ADJECTIVE

brotherhood, brotherhoods NOUN ❶ Brotherhood is the affection and loyalty that brothers or close male friends feel for each other. ❷ a group of men with common interests or beliefs.

brother-in-law, brothers-in-law NOUN Someone's brother-in-law is the brother of their husband or wife, or their sister's husband.

brought the past tense and past participle of **bring**.
● **USAGE NOTE:** Do not confuse
● *brought* and *bought*. *Brought* comes
● from *bring* and *bought* comes from
● *buy*

brow, brows NOUN ❶ Your brow is

your forehead. ❷ Your brows are your eyebrows. ❸ The brow of a hill is the top of it.

brown, browner, brownest; browns **ADJECTIVE OR NOUN** Brown is the colour of earth or wood.

brownie, brownies **NOUN** a junior member of the Guides.

browse, browses, browsing, browsed **VERB** ❶ If you browse through a book, you look through it in a casual way. ❷ If you browse in a shop, you look at the things in it for interest rather than because you want to buy something.

browser, browsers **NOUN** a piece of computer software that lets you look at websites on the World Wide Web.

bruise, bruises, bruising, bruised **NOUN** ❶ a purple mark that appears on your skin after something has hit it ▷ **VERB** ❷ If something bruises you, it hits you so that a bruise appears on your skin.

brumby, brumbies **NOUN** In Australia and New Zealand, a wild horse.

brunette, brunettes **NOUN** a girl or woman with dark brown hair.

brunt **PHRASE** If you **bear the brunt** of something unpleasant, you are the person who suffers most • *Women bear the brunt of crime.*

brush, brushes, brushing, brushed **NOUN** ❶ an object with bristles which you use for cleaning things, painting, or tidying your hair ▷ **VERB** ❷ If you brush something, you clean it or tidy it with a brush. ❸ To brush against something means to touch it

while passing it • *Her lips brushed his cheek.*

brusque, brusquer, brusquest *[Said broosk]* **ADJECTIVE** Someone who is brusque deals with people quickly and without considering their feelings. **brusquely ADVERB**

brussels sprout, brussels sprouts **NOUN** Brussels sprouts are vegetables that look like tiny cabbages.

brutal ADJECTIVE Brutal behaviour is cruel and violent • *the victim of a brutal murder.* **brutally ADVERB brutality NOUN**

brute, brutes **NOUN** ❶ a rough and insensitive man ▷ **ADJECTIVE** ❷ Brute force is strength alone, without any skill • *You have to use brute force to open the gates.* **brutish ADJECTIVE**

bubble, bubbles, bubbling, bubbled **NOUN** ❶ a ball of air in a liquid. ❷ a hollow, delicate ball of soapy liquid ▷ **VERB** ❸ When a liquid bubbles, bubbles form in it. ❹ If you are bubbling with something like excitement, you are full of it. **bubbly ADJECTIVE**

bubonic plague *[Said byoo-bon-ik]* **NOUN** (HISTORY) Bubonic plague is a disease transmitted by fleas on rats. Until a cure was discovered in the 19th century, it was a widespread cause of epidemics and death. Swellings, called buboes, appeared in the armpits and groin of people who caught it.

buck, bucks, bucking, bucked **NOUN** ❶ the male of various animals, including the deer and the rabbit ▷ **VERB** ❷ If a horse bucks, it jumps

▷ SPELLING NOTE: *there's a rAKE in the brAKES (brake)*

into the air with its feet off the ground.

bucket, buckets **NOUN** a deep round container with an open top and a handle.

buckle, buckles, buckling, buckled **NOUN** **1** a fastening on the end of a belt or strap ▷ **VERB** **2** If you buckle a belt or strap, you fasten it. **3** If something buckles, it becomes bent because of severe heat or pressure.

bud, buds, budding, budded **NOUN** **1** a small, tight swelling on a tree or plant, which develops into a flower or a cluster of leaves ▷ **VERB** **2** When a tree or plant buds, new buds appear on it.

Buddha **PROPER NOUN** (RE) The Buddha is the title of Gautama Siddhartha, a religious teacher living in the 6th century BC in India and founder of Buddhism. Buddha means 'the enlightened one'.

Buddhism **NOUN** (RE) Buddhism is a religion, founded by the Buddha, which teaches that the way to end suffering is by overcoming your desires. **Buddhist** **NOUN OR ADJECTIVE**

budding **ADJECTIVE** just beginning to develop • *a budding artist*.

budge, budges, budging, budged **VERB** If something will not budge, you cannot move it.

budgerigar, budgerigars **NOUN** a small brightly coloured pet bird.

budget, budgets, budgeting, budgeted **NOUN** **1** a plan showing how much money will be available and how it will be spent ▷ **VERB** **2** If you budget for something, you plan your

money carefully, so that you are able to afford it. **budgetary** **ADJECTIVE**

budgie, budgies **NOUN** INFORMAL a budgerigar.

buff, buffs **ADJECTIVE** **1** a pale brown colour ▷ **NOUN** **2** INFORMAL someone who knows a lot about a subject • *a film buff*.

buffalo, buffaloes **NOUN** a wild animal like a large cow with long curved horns.

buffer, buffers **NOUN** **1** Buffers on a train or at the end of a railway line are metal discs on springs that reduce shock when they are hit. **2** something that prevents something else from being harmed • *keep savings as a buffer against unexpected cash needs*.

buffet, buffets [*Said boof-ay*] **NOUN** **1** a café at a station. **2** a meal at which people serve themselves.

buffet, buffets, buffeting, buffeted [*Said buff-it*] **VERB** If the wind or sea buffets a place or person, it strikes them violently and repeatedly.

bug, bugs, bugging, bugged **NOUN** **1** an insect, especially one that causes damage. **2** a small error in a computer program which means that the program will not work properly. **3** INFORMAL a virus or minor infection • *a stomach bug*. ▷ **VERB** **4** If a place is bugged, tiny microphones are hidden there to pick up what people are saying.

bugle, bugles **NOUN** (MUSIC) a brass musical instrument that looks like a small trumpet. **bugler** **NOUN**

build, builds, building, built **VERB**

▷ SPELLING NOTE: *you'll brEAK that Electrical Aerial, Kitty (br<u>eak</u>)*

❶ To build something such as a house means to make it from its parts. **❷** To build something such as an organization means to develop it gradually ▷ **NOUN ❸** Your build is the shape and size of your body.
builder NOUN
● **SIMILAR WORDS: ❶** assemble, construct, erect

building, buildings **NOUN** a structure with walls and a roof.

building society, building societies **NOUN** a business in which some people invest their money, while others borrow from it to buy a house.

bulb, bulbs **NOUN ❶** the glass part of an electric lamp. **❷** an onion-shaped root that grows into a flower or plant.

Bulgarian, Bulgarians **ADJECTIVE ❶** belonging or relating to Bulgaria ▷ **NOUN ❷** someone who comes from Bulgaria. **❸** the main language spoken in Bulgaria.

bulge, bulges, bulging, bulged **VERB ❶** If something bulges, it swells out from a surface ▷ **NOUN ❷** a lump on a normally flat surface.

bulimia NOUN (SCIENCE) an eating disorder in which a person is very afraid of getting fat, so they make themselves vomit after eating.

bulk, bulks **NOUN ❶** a large mass of something • *The book is more impressive for its bulk than its content.* **❷** The bulk of something is most of it • *the bulk of the world's great poetry.* ▷ **PHRASE ❸** To buy something **in bulk** means to buy it in large quantities.

bulky, bulkier, bulkiest **ADJECTIVE** large and heavy • *a bulky package.*
● **SIMILAR WORDS:** cumbersome, large, unwieldy

bull, bulls **NOUN** the male of some species of animals, including the cow family, elephants and whales.

bulldog, bulldogs **NOUN** a squat dog with a broad head and muscular body.

bulldozer, bulldozers **NOUN** a powerful tractor with a broad blade in front, which is used for moving earth or knocking things down.

bullet, bullets **NOUN** a small piece of metal fired from a gun.

bulletin, bulletins **NOUN ❶** a short news report on radio or television. **❷** a leaflet or small newspaper regularly produced by a group or organization.
● **WORD HISTORY:** from Italian *bulletino* meaning 'small Papal edict'

bullion NOUN Bullion is gold or silver in the form of bars.

bullock, bullocks **NOUN** a young castrated bull.

bullroarer, bullroarers **NOUN** a wooden slat attached to a string that is whirled round to make a roaring noise. Bullroarers are used especially by Australian Aborigines.

bully, bullies, bullying, bullied **NOUN ❶** someone who uses their strength or power to hurt or frighten other people ▷ **VERB ❷** If you bully someone, you frighten or hurt them deliberately. **❸** If someone bullies you into doing something, they make you do it by using force or threats.

bump, bumps, bumping, bumped
VERB ❶ If you bump or bump into
something, you knock it with a jolt
▷ **NOUN** ❷ a soft or dull noise made
by something knocking into
something else. ❸ a raised, uneven
part of a surface. **bumpy ADJECTIVE**
● **SIMILAR WORDS:** ❸ bulge, lump,
● protuberance

bumper, bumpers **NOUN**
❶ Bumpers are bars on the front and
back of a vehicle which protect it if
there is a collision ▷ **ADJECTIVE** ❷ A
bumper crop or harvest is larger than
usual.

bun, buns **NOUN** a small, round
cake.

bunch, bunches, bunching, bunched
NOUN ❶ a group of people. ❷ a
number of flowers held or tied
together. ❸ a group of things. ❹ a
group of bananas or grapes growing
on the same stem ▷ **VERB** ❺ When
people bunch together or bunch up,
they stay very close to each other.

bundle, bundles, bundling, bundled
NOUN ❶ a number of things tied
together or wrapped up in a cloth
▷ **VERB** ❷ If you bundle someone or
something somewhere, you push
them there quickly and roughly.

bung, bungs, bunging, bunged **NOUN**
❶ a stopper used to close a hole in
something such as a barrel ▷ **VERB**
❷ INFORMAL If you bung something
somewhere, you put it there quickly
and carelessly.

bungalow, bungalows **NOUN** a
one-storey house.
● **WORD HISTORY:** from Hindi
● *bangla* meaning 'of Bengal'

bungle, bungles, bungling, bungled
VERB To bungle something means to
fail to do it properly.

bunion, bunions **NOUN** a painful
lump on the first joint of a person's big
toe.

bunk, bunks **NOUN** a bed fixed to a
wall in a ship or caravan.

bunker, bunkers **NOUN** ❶ On a golf
course, a bunker is a large hole filled
with sand. ❷ A coal bunker is a
storage place for coal. ❸ an
underground shelter with strong walls
to protect it from bombing.

bunting NOUN Bunting is strips of
small coloured flags displayed on
streets and buildings on special
occasions.

bunyip, bunyips **NOUN** a legendary
monster said to live in swamps and
lakes in Australia.

buoy, buoys [*Said* **boy**] **NOUN** a
floating object anchored to the
bottom of the sea, marking a channel
or warning of danger.

buoyant ADJECTIVE ❶ able to
float. ❷ lively and cheerful • *She was
in a buoyant mood.* **buoyancy NOUN**

burble, burbles, burbling, burbled
VERB To burble means to makes a
soft bubbling sound • *The water
burbled over the gravel.*

burden, burdens **NOUN** ❶ a heavy
load. ❷ If something is a burden to
you, it causes you a lot of worry or
hard work. **burdensome ADJECTIVE**
● **SIMILAR WORDS:** ❶ load, weight
● ❷ millstone, trouble, worry

bureau, bureaux [*Said* **byoo**-roh]

▷ SPELLING NOTE: *I want to see (C) your licenCe (licence)*

NOUN ❶ an office that provides a service • *an employment bureau.* ❷ a writing desk with shelves and drawers • *an antique bureau.*

bureaucracy NOUN Bureaucracy is the complex system of rules and procedures which operates in government departments.
bureaucratic ADJECTIVE

bureaucrat, bureaucrats **NOUN** A bureaucrat is a person who works in a government department, especially one who follows rules and procedures strictly.

burgeoning ADJECTIVE growing or developing rapidly • *a burgeoning political crisis.*

burglar, burglars **NOUN** a thief who breaks into a building. **burglary NOUN**

burgle, burgles, burgling, burgled **VERB** If your house is burgled, someone breaks into it and steals things.

burial, burials **NOUN** (RE) a ceremony held when a dead person is buried.

burly, burlier, burliest **ADJECTIVE** A burly man has a broad body and strong muscles.
● **SIMILAR WORDS:** brawny, well-built

burn, burns, burning, burned or burnt **VERB** ❶ If something is burning, it is on fire. ❷ To burn something means to destroy it with fire. ❸ If you burn yourself or are burned, you are injured by fire or by something hot ▷ **NOUN** ❹ an injury caused by fire or by something hot.

● **USAGE NOTE:** You can write either *burned* or *burnt* as the past form of *burn*
● **SIMILAR WORDS:** ❶ be on fire, blaze ❷ incinerate, set on fire

burp, burps, burping, burped **VERB** ❶ If you burp, you make a noise because air from your stomach has been forced up through your throat ▷ **NOUN** ❷ the noise that you make when you burp.

burrow, burrows, burrowing, burrowed **NOUN** ❶ a tunnel or hole in the ground dug by a small animal ▷ **VERB** ❷ When an animal burrows, it digs a burrow.

bursary, bursaries **NOUN** a sum of money given to someone to help fund their education.

burst, bursts, bursting, burst **VERB** ❶ When something bursts, it splits open because of pressure from inside it. ❷ If you burst into a room, you enter it suddenly. ❸ To burst means to happen or come suddenly and with force • *The aircraft burst into flames.* ❹ INFORMAL If you are bursting with something, you find it difficult to keep it to yourself • *We were bursting with joy.* ▷ **NOUN** ❺ A burst of something is a short period of it • *He had a sudden burst of energy.*
● **SIMILAR WORDS:** ❺ outbreak, rush, spate

bury, buries, burying, buried **VERB** ❶ When a dead person is buried, their body is put into a grave and covered with earth. ❷ To bury something means to put it in a hole in the ground and cover it up. ❸ If something is buried under something, it is covered by it • *My bag was buried* *under a pile of old newspapers.*

bus, buses **NOUN** a large motor vehicle that carries passengers.
● **WORD HISTORY:** from Latin *omnibus* meaning 'for all'; buses were originally called omnibuses

bush, bushes **NOUN** ❶ a thick plant with many stems branching out from ground level. ❷ In Australia and South Africa, an area of land in its natural state outside of city areas is called the bush. ❸ In New Zealand, the bush is land covered with rain forest.

bushman, bushmen **NOUN** ❶ In Australia and New Zealand, someone who lives or travels in the bush. ❷ In New Zealand, a bushman is also someone whose job it is to clear the bush for farming.

Bushman, Bushmen **NOUN** A Bushman is a member of a group of people in southern Africa who live by hunting and gathering food.

bushranger, bushrangers **NOUN** In Australia and New Zealand in the past, an outlaw living in the bush.

bushy, bushier, bushiest **ADJECTIVE** Bushy hair or fur grows very thickly • *bushy eyebrows.*

business, businesses **NOUN** ❶ Business is work relating to the buying and selling of goods and services. ❷ an organization which produces or sells goods or provides a service. ❸ You can refer to any event, situation, or activity as a business • *This whole business has upset me.*
businessman NOUN
businesswoman NOUN
● **SIMILAR WORDS:** ❷ company, establishment, firm, organization

businesslike ADJECTIVE dealing with things in an efficient way.

busker, buskers **NOUN** someone who plays music or sings for money in public places.

bust, busts, busting, bust or busted **NOUN** ❶ a statue of someone's head and shoulders • *a bust of Beethoven.* ❷ A woman's bust is her chest and her breasts ▷ **VERB** ❸ INFORMAL If you bust something, you break it ▷ **PHRASE** ❹ INFORMAL If a business **goes bust**, it becomes bankrupt and closes down.

bustle, bustles, bustling, bustled **VERB** ❶ When people bustle, they move in a busy, hurried way ▷ **NOUN** ❷ Bustle is busy, noisy activity.

busy, busier, busiest; busies, busying, busied **ADJECTIVE** ❶ If you are busy, you are in the middle of doing something. ❷ A busy place is full of people doing things or moving about • *a busy seaside resort.* ▷ **VERB** ❸ If you busy yourself with something, you occupy yourself by doing it. **busily ADVERB**
● **SIMILAR WORDS:** ❶ employed, engaged, occupied

but CONJUNCTION ❶ used to introduce an idea that is opposite to what has gone before • *I don't miss teaching but I miss the pupils.* ❷ used when apologizing • *I'm sorry, but I can't come tonight.* ❸ except • *We can't do anything but wait.*

butcher, butchers **NOUN** a shopkeeper who sells meat.

butler, butlers **NOUN** the chief male

servant in a rich household.
● **WORD HISTORY:** from Old French
● *bouteillier* meaning 'a dealer in
● bottles'

butt, butts, butting, butted **NOUN**
❶ The butt of a weapon is the thick
end of its handle. ❷ If you are the
butt of teasing, you are the target of it
▷ **VERB** ❸ If you butt something, you
ram it with your head.
butt in VERB If you butt in, you join
in a private conversation or activity
without being asked to.

butter, butters, buttering, buttered
NOUN ❶ Butter is a soft fatty food
made from cream, which is spread on
bread and used in cooking ▷ **VERB**
❷ To butter bread means to spread
butter on it.

buttercup, buttercups **NOUN** a
wild plant with bright yellow flowers.

butterfly, butterflies **NOUN** a type
of insect with large colourful wings.

buttocks PLURAL NOUN Your
buttocks are the part of your body that
you sit on.

button, buttons, buttoning, buttoned
NOUN ❶ Buttons are small, hard
objects sewn on to clothing, and used
to fasten two surfaces together. ❷ a
small object on a piece of equipment
that you press to make it work
▷ **VERB** ❸ If you button a piece of
clothing, you fasten its buttons.

buttonhole, buttonholes **NOUN**
❶ a hole that you push a button
through to fasten a piece of clothing.
❷ a flower worn in your lapel.

buxom ADJECTIVE A buxom woman
is large, healthy, and attractive.

buy, buys, buying, bought **VERB** If
you buy something, you obtain it by
paying money for it. **buyer NOUN**

buzz, buzzes, buzzing, buzzed **VERB**
❶ If something buzzes, it makes a
humming sound, like a bee ▷ **NOUN**
❷ the sound something makes when
it buzzes.

buzzard, buzzards **NOUN** a large
brown and white bird of prey.

buzzer, buzzers **NOUN** a device that
makes a buzzing sound, to attract
attention.

by PREPOSITION ❶ used to indicate
who or what has done something
• *The statement was issued by his
solicitor.* ❷ used to indicate how
something is done • *He frightened her
by hiding behind the door.* ❸ located
next to • *I sat by her bed.* ❹ before a
particular time • *It should be ready by
next spring.* ▷ **PREPOSITION OR
ADVERB** ❺ going past • *We drove by
his house.*

by-election, by-elections **NOUN**
an election held to choose a new
member of parliament after the
previous member has resigned or died.

bygone ADJECTIVE LITERARY
happening or existing a long time ago
• *the ceremonies of a bygone era.*

bypass, bypasses **NOUN** a main road
which takes traffic round a town
rather than through it.

bystander, bystanders **NOUN**
someone who is not included or
involved in something but is there to
see it happen.

byte, bytes **NOUN** ICT a unit of
storage in a computer.

▷ SPELLING NOTE: *plaice the fish has a glittering 'EYE' (I) (plaice)*

Cc

Some words which sound as if they might begin with s, actually begin with c, for example *centre* and *cynic*. Some words which sound as if they might begin with *sh* actually begin with *ch*, for example *chute*. Some words which sound as if they might begin with *ch* are spelt with *c* alone, for example *cello*.

cab, cabs NOUN ❶ a taxi. ❷ In a lorry, bus, or train, the cab is where the driver sits.
● WORD HISTORY: from French *cabriolet* meaning 'light two-wheeled carriage'. Cabs were originally horse-drawn

cabaret, cabarets [Said **kab**-bar-ray] NOUN a show consisting of dancing, singing, or comedy acts.
● WORD HISTORY: from French *cabaret* meaning 'tavern'

cabbage, cabbages NOUN a large green or reddish purple leafy vegetable.
● WORD HISTORY: from Norman French *cabache* meaning 'head'

cabbage tree, cabbage trees NOUN a palm-like tree found in New Zealand with a tall bare trunk and big bunches of spiky leaves; also a similar tree found in eastern Australia.

cabin, cabins NOUN ❶ a room in a ship where a passenger sleeps. ❷ a small house, usually in the country and often made of wood. ❸ the area where the passengers or the crew sit in a plane.

cabinet, cabinets NOUN ❶ a small cupboard. ❷ The cabinet in a government is a group of ministers who advise the leader and decide policies.

cable, cables NOUN ❶ a strong, thick rope or chain. ❷ a bundle of wires with a rubber covering, which carries electricity. ❸ a message sent abroad by using electricity.

cable car, cable cars NOUN a vehicle pulled by a moving cable, for taking people up and down mountains.

cable television NOUN a television service people can receive from underground wires which carry the signals.

cacao, cacaos [Said ka-**kah**-oh] NOUN A cacao is a type of small tropical evergreen tree, whose berries are used to produce chocolate and cocoa.

cache, caches [Said kash] NOUN a store of things hidden away • *a cache of guns.*

cachet [Said kash-shay] NOUN FORMAL Cachet is the status and respect something has • *the cachet of* *shopping at Harrods.*

cackle, cackles, cackling, cackled
VERB ❶ If you cackle, you laugh
harshly ▷ **NOUN** ❷ a harsh laugh.

cacophony [Said kak-**koff**-fon-nee]
NOUN FORMAL a loud, unpleasant
noise • *a cacophony of barking dogs.*
● **WORD HISTORY:** from Greek *kakos*
● + *phōnē* meaning 'bad sound'

cactus, cacti or cactuses **NOUN** a
thick, fleshy plant that grows in
deserts and is usually covered in
spikes.

cad, cads **NOUN** OLD-FASHIONED a
man who treats people unfairly.

caddie, caddies; also spelt **caddy**
NOUN ❶ a person who carries golf
clubs for a golf player. ❷ A tea caddy
is a box for keeping tea in.

cadence, cadences **NOUN** The
cadence of someone's voice is the way
it goes up and down as they speak.

cadet, cadets **NOUN** a young person
being trained in the armed forces or
police.

cadge, cadges, cadging, cadged **VERB**
If you cadge something off someone,
you get it from them and don't give
them anything in return • *I cadged a
lift ashore.*

caesarean, caesareans [Said
siz-**air**-ee-an] ; also spelt **caesarian** or
cesarean NOUN A caesarean or
caesarean section is an operation in
which a baby is lifted out of a woman's
womb through a cut in her abdomen.

café, cafés [Said **kaf**-fay] **NOUN** ❶ a
place where you can buy light meals
and drinks. ❷ In South African

English, a café is a corner shop or
grocer's shop.

cafeteria, cafeterias [Said
kaf-fit-**ee**-ree-ya] **NOUN** a restaurant
where you serve yourself.

caffeine or **caffein** [Said **kaf**-feen]
NOUN Caffeine is a chemical in coffee
and tea which makes you more active.

cage, cages **NOUN** a box made of wire
or bars in which birds or animals are
kept. **caged ADJECTIVE**

cagey, cagier, cagiest [Said **kay**-jee]
ADJECTIVE INFORMAL cautious and
not open • *They're very cagey when
they talk to me.*

cagoule, cagoules [Said ka-**gool**]
NOUN a lightweight waterproof jacket
with a hood.

cahoots PHRASE INFORMAL If you
are **in cahoots** with someone, you are
working closely with them on a secret
plan.

cairn, cairns **NOUN** a pile of stones
built as a memorial or a landmark.
● **WORD HISTORY:** from Gaelic *carn*
● meaning 'heap of stones' or 'hill'

cajole, cajoles, cajoling, cajoled **VERB**
If you cajole someone into doing
something, you persuade them to do
it by saying nice things to them.

cake, cakes, caking, caked **NOUN**
❶ a sweet food made by baking flour,
eggs, fat, and sugar. ❷ a block of a
hard substance such as soap ▷ **VERB**
❸ If something cakes or is caked, it
forms or becomes covered with a solid
layer • *caked with mud.*
● **WORD HISTORY:** from Old Norse
● *kaka* meaning 'oatcake'

▷ SPELLING NOTE: *You must practiSe your Ss (practise)*

calamity, calamities **NOUN** an event that causes disaster or distress. **calamitous ADJECTIVE**

calcium [Said kal-see-um] **NOUN** (SCIENCE) Calcium is a soft white element found in bones and teeth. Its atomic number is 20 and its symbol is Ca.

calculate, calculates, calculating, calculated **VERB** (MATHS) If you calculate something, you work it out, usually by doing some arithmetic. **calculation NOUN**
- **WORD HISTORY:** from Latin
- *calculus* meaning 'stone' or 'pebble'.
- The Romans used pebbles to count
- with

calculated ADJECTIVE deliberately planned to have a particular effect.

calculating ADJECTIVE carefully planning situations to get what you want • *Toby was always a calculating type.*

calculator, calculators **NOUN** a small electronic machine used for doing mathematical calculations.

calculus NOUN Calculus is a branch of mathematics concerned with amounts that can change and rates of change.

calendar, calendars **NOUN** ❶ a chart showing the date of each day in a particular year. ❷ a system of dividing time into fixed periods of days, months, and years • *the Jewish calendar.*
- **WORD HISTORY:** from Latin
- *kalendae*, the day of the month on
- which interest on debts was due

calf, calves **NOUN** ❶ a young cow,

bull, elephant, whale, or seal. ❷ the thick part at the back of your leg below your knee.

calibre, calibres [Said kal-lib-ber] **NOUN** ❶ the ability or intelligence someone has • *a player of her calibre.* ❷ The calibre of a gun is the width of the inside of the barrel of the gun.

call, calls, calling, called **VERB** ❶ If someone or something is called a particular name, that is their name • *a man called Jeffrey.* ❷ If you call people or situations something, you use words to describe your opinion of them • *They called me crazy.* ❸ If you call someone, you telephone them. ❹ If you call or call out something, you say it loudly • *He called out his daughter's name.* ❺ If you call on someone, you pay them a short visit • *Don't hesitate to call on me.* ▷ **NOUN** ❻ If you get a call from someone, they telephone you or pay you a visit. ❼ a cry or shout • *a call for help.* ❽ a demand for something • *The call for art teachers was small.*
call off VERB If you call something off, you cancel it.
call up VERB If someone is called up, they are ordered to join the army, navy, or air force.
- **SIMILAR WORDS:** ❶ christen,
- label, name

call box, call boxes **NOUN** a telephone box.

call centre, call centres **NOUN** an office in which most staff are employed to answer telephone calls on behalf of a particular company or organization.

calling NOUN ❶ a profession or career. ❷ If you have a calling to a particular job, you have a strong feeling that you should do it.

callous ADJECTIVE cruel and not concerned with other people's feelings. **callously** ADVERB **callousness** NOUN
● SIMILAR WORDS: hardhearted,
● heartless, unfeeling

calm, calmer, calmest; calms, calming, calmed ADJECTIVE
❶ Someone who is calm is quiet and does not show any worry or excitement. ❷ If the weather or the sea is calm, it is still because there is no strong wind ▷ NOUN ❸ Calm is a state of quietness and peacefulness • *He liked the calm of the evening.*
▷ VERB ❹ To calm someone means to make them less upset or excited. **calmly** ADVERB **calmness** NOUN
● SIMILAR WORDS: ❶ composed,
● cool, self-possessed
● ❸ peacefulness, quiet ❹ quieten,
● soothe

calorie, calories NOUN a unit of measurement for the energy food and drink gives you • *Chocolate cake is high in calories.*

calves the plural of **calf**.

calypso, calypsos [*Said kal-**lip**-soh*] NOUN a type of song from the West Indies, accompanied by a rhythmic beat, about something happening at the time.

calyx, calyxes or calyces [*Said **kay**-lix*] NOUN TECHNICAL In a flower, a calyx is the ring of petal-like sepals that protects the developing bud.

camaraderie [*Said kam-mer-**rah**-der-ree*] NOUN Camaraderie is a feeling of trust and friendship between a group of people.

camber, cambers NOUN a slight downwards slope from the centre of a road to each side of it.

camel, camels NOUN a large mammal with either one or two humps on its back. Camels live in hot desert areas and are sometimes used for carrying things.
● WORD HISTORY: from Hebrew
● *gamal*

cameo, cameos NOUN ❶ a small but important part in a play or film played by a well-known actor or actress. ❷ a brooch with a raised stone design on a flat stone of another colour.

camera, cameras NOUN a piece of equipment used for taking photographs or for filming.
● WORD HISTORY: from Latin
● *camera* meaning 'vault'

camomile NOUN Camomile is a plant with a strong smell and daisy-like flowers which are used to make herbal tea.
● WORD HISTORY: from Greek
● *khamaimēlon* meaning 'apple on
● the ground'

camouflage, camouflages, camouflaging, camouflaged [*Said kam-mof-flahj*] NOUN
❶ Camouflage is a way of avoiding being seen by having the same colour or appearance as the surroundings
▷ VERB ❷ To camouflage something is to hide it by giving it the same colour or appearance as its surroundings.

camp, camps, camping, camped NOUN ❶ a place where people live in

a b **c** d e f g h i j k l m n o p q r s t u v w x y z

tents or stay in tents on holiday. ❷ a collection of buildings for a particular group of people such as soldiers or prisoners. ❸ a group of people who support a particular idea or belief • *the pro-government camp.* ▷ VERB ❹ If you camp, you stay in a tent. **camper** NOUN **camping** NOUN

campaign, campaigns, campaigning, campaigned *[Said kam-*pane*]* NOUN ❶ a set of actions aiming to achieve a particular result • *a campaign to educate people.* ▷ VERB ❷ To campaign means to carry out a campaign • *He has campaigned against smoking.* **campaigner** NOUN

camp-drafting NOUN In Australia, camp-drafting is a competition in which men on horseback select cattle or sheep from a herd or flock.

campus, campuses NOUN the area of land and the buildings that make up a university or college.

can, could VERB ❶ If you can do something, it is possible for you to do it or you are allowed to do it • *You can go to the cinema.* ❷ Also, you have the ability to do it • *I can speak Italian.*

can, cans, canning, canned NOUN ❶ a metal container, often a sealed one with food or drink inside ▷ VERB ❷ To can food or drink is to seal it in cans.

Canadian, Canadians ADJECTIVE ❶ belonging or relating to Canada ▷ NOUN ❷ someone who comes from Canada.

canal, canals NOUN a long, narrow man-made stretch of water.

canary, canaries NOUN a small yellow bird.

can-can, can-cans NOUN a lively dance in which women kick their legs high in the air to fast music.

cancel, cancels, cancelling, cancelled VERB ❶ If you cancel something that has been arranged, you stop it from happening. ❷ If you cancel a cheque or an agreement, you make sure that it is no longer valid. **cancellation** NOUN

cancer, cancers NOUN ❶ a serious disease in which abnormal cells in a part of the body increase rapidly, causing growths. ❷ Cancer is also the fourth sign of the zodiac, represented by a crab. People born between June 21st and July 22nd are born under this sign. **cancerous** ADJECTIVE
● WORD HISTORY: from Latin *cancer* meaning 'crab'

candelabra or **candelabrum**, candelabras NOUN an ornamental holder for a number of candles.

candid ADJECTIVE honest and frank. **candidly** ADVERB **candour** NOUN

candidate, candidates NOUN ❶ a person who is being considered for a job. ❷ a person taking an examination. **candidacy** NOUN
● WORD HISTORY: from Latin *candidatus* meaning 'white-robed'.
● In Rome, a candidate wore a white toga

candied ADJECTIVE covered or cooked in sugar • *candied fruit.*

candle, candles NOUN a stick of hard wax with a wick through the middle. The lighted wick gives a flame that provides light.

candlestick, candlesticks **NOUN** a holder for a candle.

candy, candies **NOUN** In America, candy is sweets.
 ● **WORD HISTORY:** from Arabic *qand* meaning 'cane sugar'

cane, canes, caning, caned **NOUN**
 ❶ Cane is the long, hollow stems of a plant such as bamboo. ❷ Cane is also strips of cane used for weaving things such as baskets. ❸ a long narrow stick, often one used to beat people as a punishment ▷ **VERB** ❹ To cane someone means to beat them with a cane as a punishment.

canine [Said kay-nine] **ADJECTIVE** relating to dogs.

canister, canisters **NOUN** a container with a lid, used for storing foods such as sugar or tea.

cannabis **NOUN** Cannabis is a drug made from the hemp plant, which some people smoke.

canned **ADJECTIVE** ❶ Canned food is kept in cans. ❷ Canned music or laughter on a television or radio show is recorded beforehand.

cannibal, cannibals **NOUN** a person who eats other human beings; also used of animals that eat animals of their own type. **cannibalism** **NOUN**

cannon, cannons or cannon **NOUN** a large gun, usually on wheels, used in battles to fire heavy metal balls.

cannot **VERB** Cannot is the same as can not • *She cannot come home yet.*

canny, cannier, canniest **ADJECTIVE**

clever and cautious • *canny business people.* **cannily** **ADVERB**

canoe, canoes [Said ka-noo] **NOUN** a small, narrow boat that you row using a paddle. **canoeing** **NOUN**

canon, canons **NOUN** ❶ a member of the clergy in a cathedral. ❷ a basic rule or principle • *the canons of political economy.*

canopy, canopies **NOUN** a cover for something, used for shelter or decoration • *a frilly canopy over the bed.*
 ● **WORD HISTORY:** from Greek *kōnōpeion* meaning 'bed with a mosquito net'

cantankerous **ADJECTIVE** Cantankerous people are quarrelsome and bad-tempered.

canteen, canteens **NOUN** ❶ the part of a workplace where the workers can go to eat. ❷ A canteen of cutlery is a set of cutlery in a box.

canter, canters, cantering, cantered **VERB** When a horse canters, it moves at a speed between a gallop and a trot.

cantilever, cantilevers **NOUN** a long beam or bar fixed at only one end and supporting a bridge or other structure at the other end.

canton, cantons **NOUN** a political and administrative region of a country, especially in Switzerland.

canvas, canvases **NOUN** ❶ Canvas is strong, heavy cloth used for making things such as sails and tents. ❷ a piece of canvas on which an artist does a painting.

canvass, canvasses, canvassing, canvassed **VERB** ❶ If you canvass

a b c d e f g h i j k l m n o p q r s t u v w x y z

people or a place, you go round trying to persuade people to vote for a particular candidate or party in an election. ❷ If you canvass opinion, you find out what people think about a particular subject by asking them.

canyon, canyons **NOUN** a narrow river valley with steep sides.

cap, caps, capping, capped **NOUN** ❶ a soft, flat hat, often with a peak at the front. ❷ The top of a bottle. ❸ Caps are small explosives used in toy guns ▷ **VERB** ❹ To cap something is to cover it with something. ❺ If you cap a story or a joke that someone has just told, you tell a better one.

capable ADJECTIVE ❶ able to do something • *a man capable of extreme violence.* ❷ skilful or talented • *She was a very capable woman.* **capably ADVERB** **capability NOUN**

capacity, capacities [Said kap-*pas-sit-tee*] **NOUN** ❶ the maximum amount that something can hold or produce • *a seating capacity of eleven thousand.* ❷ a person's power or ability to do something • *his capacity for consuming hamburgers.* ❸ someone's position or role • *in his capacity as councillor.*

cape, capes **NOUN** ❶ a short cloak with no sleeves. ❷ a large piece of land sticking out into the sea • *the Cape of Good Hope.*

caper, capers **NOUN** ❶ Capers are the flower buds of a spiky Mediterranean shrub, which are pickled and used to flavour food. ❷ a light-hearted practical joke • *Jack wouldn't tolerate such capers.*

capillary, capillaries [Said kap-*pill-lar-ree*] **NOUN** Capillaries are very thin blood vessels.

capital, capitals **NOUN** ❶ The capital of a country is the city where the government meets. ❷ Capital is the amount of money or property owned or used by a business. ❸ Capital is also a sum of money that you save or invest in order to gain interest. ❹ A capital or capital letter is a larger letter used at the beginning of a sentence or a name.

capitalism NOUN Capitalism is an economic and political system where businesses and industries are not owned and run by the government, but by individuals who can make a profit from them. **capitalist ADJECTIVE OR NOUN**

capitalize, capitalizes, capitalizing, capitalized; also spelt **capitalise VERB** If you capitalize on a situation, you use it to get an advantage.

capital punishment NOUN Capital punishment is legally killing someone as a punishment for a crime they have committed.

capitulate, capitulates, capitulating, capitulated **VERB** To capitulate is to give in and stop fighting or resisting • *The Finns did not finally capitulate until the end of March 1940.* **capitulation NOUN**

cappuccino, cappuccinos [Said kap-poot-*sheen*-oh] **NOUN** coffee made with frothy milk.

capricious [Said kap-*prish*-uss] **ADJECTIVE** often changing unexpectedly • *the capricious English weather.*

SPELLING NOTE: *Rhythmical Hounds Yap To Heavy Music (rhythm)*

Capricorn NOUN Capricorn is the tenth sign of the zodiac, represented by a goat. People born between December 22nd and January 19th are born under this sign.
● **WORD HISTORY:** from Latin *caper* meaning 'goat' and *cornu* meaning 'horn'

capsize, capsizes, capsizing, capsized VERB If a boat capsizes, it turns upside down.

capsule, capsules NOUN ❶ a small container with medicine inside which you swallow. ❷ the part of a spacecraft in which astronauts travel.

captain, captains, captaining, captained NOUN ❶ the officer in charge of a ship or aeroplane. ❷ an army officer of the rank immediately above lieutenant. ❸ a navy officer of the rank immediately above commander. ❹ the leader of a sports team • *captain of the cricket team.* ▷ VERB ❺ If you captain a group of people, you are their leader.

caption, captions NOUN a title printed underneath a picture or photograph.

captivate, captivates, captivating, captivated VERB To captivate someone is to fascinate or attract them so that they cannot take their attention away • *I was captivated by her.* **captivating** ADJECTIVE

captive, captives NOUN ❶ a person who has been captured and kept prisoner ▷ ADJECTIVE ❷ imprisoned or enclosed • *a captive bird.* **captivity** NOUN

captor, captors NOUN someone who has captured a person or animal.

capture, captures, capturing, captured VERB ❶ To capture someone is to take them prisoner. ❷ To capture a quality or mood means to succeed in representing or describing it • *capturing the mood of the riots.* ▷ NOUN ❸ The capture of someone or something is the action of taking them prisoner • *the fifth anniversary of his capture.*

car, cars NOUN ❶ a four-wheeled road vehicle with room for a small number of people. ❷ a railway carriage used for a particular purpose • *the buffet car.*

carafe, carafes [*Said kar-**raf**]* NOUN a glass bottle for serving water or wine.
● **WORD HISTORY:** from Arabic *gharrafah* meaning 'vessel for liquid'

caramel, caramels NOUN ❶ a chewy sweet made from sugar, butter, and milk. ❷ Caramel is burnt sugar used for colouring or flavouring food.

carat, carats NOUN ❶ a unit for measuring the weight of diamonds and other precious stones. ❷ a unit for measuring the purity of gold.

caravan, caravans NOUN ❶ a vehicle pulled by a car in which people live or spend their holidays. ❷ a group of people and animals travelling together, usually across a desert.
● **WORD HISTORY:** from Persian *karwan*

carbohydrate, carbohydrates NOUN (D & T) Carbohydrate is a substance that gives you energy. It is found in foods like sugar and bread.

carbon NOUN (SCIENCE) Carbon is a chemical element that is pure in

a
b
c
d
e
f
g
h
i
j
k
l
m
n
o
p
q
r
s
t
u
v
w
x
y
z

diamonds and also found in coal. All living things contain carbon. Its atomic number is 6 and its symbol is C.

carbonated ADJECTIVE carbonated drinks contain bubbles of carbon dioxide that make them fizzy.

carbon dioxide NOUN (SCIENCE) Carbon dioxide is a colourless, odourless gas that humans and animals breathe out. It is used in industry, for example in making fizzy drinks and in fire extinguishers.

carbon monoxide NOUN (SCIENCE) Carbon monoxide is a colourless, poisonous gas formed when carbon burns in a very small amount of air.

carburettor, carburettors [Said *kahr-bur-ret-ter*] NOUN the part of the engine in a vehicle in which air and petrol are mixed together.

carcass, carcasses; *also spelt* carcase NOUN the body of a dead animal.

carcinogen, carcinogens [Said *kahr-sin-ne-jen*] NOUN (SCIENCE) A carcinogen is a substance that produces cancer. **carcinogenic** ADJECTIVE

card, cards NOUN ❶ a piece of stiff paper or plastic with information or a message on it • *a birthday card.*
❷ Cards can mean playing cards • *a poor set of cards with which to play.*
❸ When you play cards, you play any game using playing cards. ❹ Card is strong, stiff paper.
● **WORD HISTORY:** from Greek
● *khartēs* meaning 'papyrus leaf'

cardboard NOUN Cardboard is thick, stiff paper.

cardiac ADJECTIVE MEDICAL relating to the heart • *cardiac disease.*

cardigan, cardigans NOUN a knitted jacket that fastens up the front.

cardinal, cardinals NOUN ❶ a high-ranking member of the Roman Catholic clergy who chooses and advises the Pope ▷ ADJECTIVE
❷ extremely important • *a cardinal principle of law.*
● **WORD HISTORY:** from Latin *cardo*
● meaning 'hinge'. When something
● is important, other things hinge on
● it

care, cares, caring, cared VERB ❶ If you care about something, you are concerned about it and interested in it. ❷ If you care about someone, you feel affection towards them. ❸ If you care for someone, you look after them ▷ NOUN ❹ Care is concern or worry.
❺ Care of someone or something is treatment for them or looking after them • *the care of the elderly.* ❻ If you do something with care, you do it with close attention.

career, careers, careering, careered NOUN ❶ the series of jobs that someone has in life, usually in the same occupation • *a career in insurance.* ▷ VERB ❷ To career somewhere is to move very quickly, often out of control • *His car careered off the road.*

carefree ADJECTIVE having no worries or responsibilities • *the carefree life of the rich.*

careful ADJECTIVE ❶ acting sensibly and with care • *Be careful*

what you say to him. ❷ complete and well done • *It needs very careful planning.* **carefully ADVERB**
● **SIMILAR WORDS:** ❶ cautious,
● prudent

careless ADJECTIVE ❶ done badly without enough attention • *careless driving.* ❷ relaxed and unconcerned • *careless laughter.* **carelessly ADVERB carelessness NOUN**
● **SIMILAR WORDS:** ❶ slapdash,
● sloppy

caress, caresses, caressing, caressed **VERB** ❶ If you caress someone, you stroke them gently and affectionately ▷ **NOUN** ❷ a gentle, affectionate stroke.
● **SIMILAR WORDS:** ❶ fondle,
● stroke

caretaker, caretakers **NOUN** ❶ a person who looks after a large building such as a school ▷ **ADJECTIVE** ❷ having an important position for a short time until a new person is appointed • *O'Leary was named caretaker manager.*

cargo, cargoes **NOUN** the goods carried on a ship or plane.

Caribbean NOUN The Caribbean consists of the Caribbean Sea east of Central America and the islands in it.

caricature, caricatures, caricaturing, caricatured **NOUN** ❶ a drawing or description of someone that exaggerates striking parts of their appearance or personality ▷ **VERB** ❷ To caricature someone is to give a caricature of them.

carjack, carjacks, carjacking, carjacked **VERB** If a car is carjacked,

its driver is attacked and robbed, or the car is stolen.

carnage [*Said kahr-nij*] **NOUN** Carnage is the violent killing of large numbers of people.

carnal ADJECTIVE FORMAL sexual and sensual rather than spiritual • *carnal pleasure.*

carnation, carnations **NOUN** a plant with a long stem and white, pink, or red flowers.

carnival, carnivals **NOUN** a public festival with music, processions, and dancing.

carnivore, carnivores **NOUN** an animal that eats meat. **carnivorous ADJECTIVE**

carol, carols **NOUN** a religious song sung at Christmas time.

carousel, carousels [*Said kar-ros-sel*] **NOUN** a merry-go-round.

carp, carps, carping, carped **NOUN** ❶ a large edible freshwater fish ▷ **VERB** ❷ To carp means to complain about unimportant things.

carpel, carpels **NOUN** the seed-bearing female part of a flower.

carpenter, carpenters **NOUN** a person who makes and repairs wooden structures. **carpentry NOUN**

carpet, carpets, carpeting, carpeted **NOUN** ❶ a thick covering for a floor, usually made of a material like wool ▷ **VERB** ❷ To carpet a floor means to cover it with a carpet.

carriage, carriages **NOUN** ❶ one of the separate sections of a passenger train. ❷ an old-fashioned vehicle for

a
b
c
d
e
f
g
h
i
j
k
l
m
n
o
p
q
r
s
t
u
v
w
x
y
z

▷ SPELLING NOTE: *Eddy Ant thinks mEAt is a grEAt trEAt to EAt (-ea-)*

carrying passengers, usually pulled by horses. ❸ a machine part that moves and supports another part • *a typewriter carriage.* ❹ Someone's carriage is the way they hold their head and body when they move.

carriageway, carriageways NOUN one of the sides of a road which traffic travels along in one direction only.

carrier, carriers NOUN ❶ a vehicle that is used for carrying things • *a troop carrier.* ❷ A carrier of a germ or disease is a person or animal that can pass it on to others.

carrier bag, carrier bags NOUN a bag made of plastic or paper, which is used for carrying shopping.

carrion NOUN Carrion is the decaying flesh of dead animals.

carrot, carrots NOUN a long, thin orange root vegetable.

carry, carries, carrying, carried VERB ❶ To carry something is to hold it and take it somewhere. ❷ When a vehicle carries people, they travel in it. ❸ A person or animal that carries a germ can pass it on to other people or animals • *I still carry the disease.* ❹ If a sound carries, it can be heard far away • *Jake's voice carried over the cheering.* ❺ In a meeting, if a proposal is carried, it is accepted by a majority of the people there.

carry away VERB If you are carried away, you are so excited by something that you do not behave sensibly.

carry on VERB To carry on doing something means to continue doing it.

carry out VERB To carry something out means to do it and complete it

• *The conversion was carried out by a local builder.*

● SIMILAR WORDS: ❷ bear,
● convey, take

carrying capacity, carrying capacities NOUN (GEOGRAPHY) the number of people or the amount of livestock that an area can support in terms of available food.

cart, carts NOUN a vehicle with wheels, used to carry goods and often pulled by horses or cattle.

cartilage NOUN Cartilage is a strong, flexible substance found around the joints and in the nose and ears.

carton, cartons NOUN a cardboard or plastic container.

cartoon, cartoons NOUN ❶ a drawing or a series of drawings which are funny or make a point. ❷ a film in which the characters and scenes are drawn. **cartoonist** NOUN
● WORD HISTORY: from Italian
● *cartone* meaning 'sketch on stiff
● paper'

cartridge, cartridges NOUN ❶ a tube containing a bullet and an explosive substance, used in guns. ❷ a plastic container full of ink that you put in a printer or a pen.

cartwheel, cartwheels NOUN an acrobatic movement in which you throw yourself sideways onto one hand and move round in a circle with arms and legs stretched until you land on your feet again.

carve, carves, carving, carved VERB ❶ To carve an object means to cut it out of a substance such as stone or wood. ❷ To carve meat means to cut

A
B
C
D
E
F
G
H
I
J
K
L
M
N
O
P
Q
R
S
T
U
V
W
X
Y
Z

▷ SPELLING NOTE: *Elaine and Emily shout EE when they mEEt to grEEt each other (-ee-)*

a number of slices from it.

carving, carvings **NOUN** a carved object.

cascade, cascades, cascading, cascaded **NOUN** ❶ a waterfall or group of waterfalls ▷ **VERB** ❷ To cascade means to flow downwards quickly • *Gallons of water cascaded from the attic.*

case, cases **NOUN** ❶ a particular situation, event, or example • *a clear case of mistaken identity.* ❷ a container for something, or a suitcase • *a camera case.* ❸ Doctors sometimes refer to a patient as a case. ❹ Police detectives refer to a crime they are investigating as a case. ❺ In an argument, the case for an idea is the reasons used to support it. ❻ In law, a case is a trial or other inquiry. ❼ In grammar, the case of a noun or pronoun is the form of it which shows its relationship with other words in a sentence • *the accusative case.*
▷ **PHRASE** ❽ You say **in case** to explain something that you do because a particular thing might happen • *I didn't want to shout in case I startled you.* ❾ You say **in that case** to show that you are assuming something said before is true • *In that case we won't do it.*
● **SIMILAR WORDS:** ❶ instance, circumstance, circumstances, situation

casement, casements **NOUN** a window that opens on hinges at one side.

cash, cashes, cashing, cashed **NOUN** ❶ Cash is money in notes and coins rather than cheques ▷ **VERB** ❷ If you cash a cheque, you take it to a bank

and exchange it for money.
● **WORD HISTORY:** from Italian
● *cassa* meaning 'money-box'

cashew, cashews *[Said **kash**-oo]*
NOUN a curved, edible nut.

cash flow NOUN Cash flow is the money that a business makes and spends.

cashier, cashiers **NOUN** the person that customers pay in a shop or get money from in a bank.

cashmere NOUN Cashmere is very soft, fine wool from goats.

cash register, cash registers **NOUN** a machine in a shop which records sales, and where the money is kept.

casing, casings **NOUN** a protective covering for something.

casino, casinos *[Said kass-ee-noh]*
NOUN a place where people go to play gambling games.

cask, casks **NOUN** a wooden barrel.

casket, caskets **NOUN** a small box for jewellery or other valuables.
● **WORD HISTORY:** from Old French
● *cassette* meaning 'little box'

casserole, casseroles **NOUN** a dish made by cooking a mixture of meat and vegetables slowly in an oven; also used to refer to the pot a casserole is cooked in.

cassette, cassettes **NOUN** a small flat container with magnetic tape inside, which is used for recording and playing back sounds.

cassette recorder, cassette recorders **NOUN** a machine used for

a
b
c
d
e
f
g
h
i
j
k
l
m
n
o
p
q
r
s
t
u
v
w
x
y
z

A
B
C
D
E
F
G
H
I
J
K
L
M
N
O
P
Q
R
S
T
U
V
W
X
Y
Z

recording and playing cassettes.

cassock, cassocks **NOUN** a long robe that is worn by some members of the clergy.

cassowary, cassowaries **NOUN** a large bird found in Australia with black feathers and a brightly coloured neck. Cassowaries cannot fly.

cast, casts, casting, cast **NOUN** ❶ all the people who act in a play or film. ❷ an object made by pouring liquid into a mould and leaving it to harden • *the casts of classical sculptures.* ❸ a stiff plaster covering put on broken bones to keep them still so that they heal properly ▷ **VERB** ❹ To cast actors is to choose them for roles in a play or film. ❺ When people cast their votes in an election, they vote. ❻ To cast something is to throw it. ❼ If you cast your eyes somewhere, you look there • *I cast my eyes down briefly.* ❽ To cast an object is to make it by pouring liquid into a mould and leaving it to harden • *An image of him has been cast in bronze.*

cast off VERB If you cast off, you untie the rope fastening a boat to a harbour or shore.

castanets PLURAL NOUN Castanets are a Spanish musical instrument consisting of two small round pieces of wood that are clicked together with the fingers.
● **WORD HISTORY:** from Spanish
● *castañetas* meaning 'little
● chestnuts'

castaway, castaways **NOUN** a person who has been shipwrecked.

caste, castes **NOUN** ❶ one of the four classes into which Hindu society

is divided. ❷ Caste is a system of social classes decided according to family, wealth, and position.

caster sugar or **castor sugar** **NOUN** Caster sugar is very fine white sugar used in cooking.

castigate, castigates, castigating, castigated **VERB** FORMAL To castigate someone is to criticize them severely.

cast iron NOUN ❶ Cast iron is iron which is made into objects by casting ▷ **ADJECTIVE** ❷ A cast-iron excuse or guarantee is absolutely certain and firm.

castle, castles **NOUN** ❶ (HISTORY) a large building with walls or ditches round it to protect it from attack. ❷ In chess, a castle is the same as a rook.

cast-off, cast-offs **NOUN** a piece of outgrown or discarded clothing that has been passed on to someone else.

castor, castors; *also spelt* **caster** **NOUN** a small wheel fitted to furniture so that it can be moved easily.

castor oil NOUN Castor oil is a thick oil that comes from the seeds of the castor oil plant. It is used as a laxative.

castrate, castrates, castrating, castrated **VERB** To castrate a male animal is to remove its testicles so that it can no longer produce sperm. **castration NOUN**

casual ADJECTIVE ❶ happening by chance without planning • *a casual remark.* ❷ careless or without interest • *a casual glance over his shoulder.* ❸ Casual clothes are suitable for informal occasions. ❹ Casual work is not regular or permanent. **casually ADVERB casualness NOUN**

▷ SPELLING NOTE: *King IAn went to ParlIAment in a carrIAge for his marrIAge (-ia-)*

● **SIMILAR WORDS:** ❷ careless,
● nonchalant, offhand

casualty, casualties **NOUN** a person
killed or injured in an accident or war
• *Many of the casualties were office
workers.*

casuarina, casuarinas [*Said
kass-you-a-**rine**-a*] **NOUN** an
Australian tree with jointed green
branches.

cat, cats **NOUN** ❶ a small furry
animal with whiskers, a tail and sharp
claws, often kept as a pet. ❷ any of
the family of mammals that includes
lions and tigers.

catabolism **NOUN** (SCIENCE) a
metabolic process in which complex
molecules are broken down into
simpler ones and energy is released.
**catabolic ADJECTIVE catabolically
ADVERB**

catacomb, catacombs [*Said
kat-a-koom*] **NOUN** Catacombs are
underground passages where dead
bodies are buried.

catalogue, catalogues, cataloguing,
catalogued **NOUN** ❶ a book
containing pictures and descriptions
of goods that you can buy in a shop or
through the post. ❷ (LIBRARY) a list
of things such as the objects in a
museum or the books in a library
▷ **VERB** ❸ To catalogue a collection
of things means to list them in a
catalogue.

catalyst, catalysts [*Said **kat**-a-list*]
NOUN ❶ something that causes a
change to happen • *the catalyst which
provoked civil war.* ❷ (SCIENCE) a
substance that speeds up a chemical
reaction without changing itself.

catalytic converter, catalytic
converters **NOUN** (SCIENCE) a device
that is fitted to a car's exhaust to
reduce the pollution coming from it.

catamaran, catamarans **NOUN** a
sailing boat with two hulls connected
to each other.
● **WORD HISTORY:** from Tamil
● *kattumaram* meaning 'tied logs'

catapult, catapults, catapulting,
catapulted **NOUN** ❶ a Y-shaped
object with a piece of elastic tied
between the two top ends, used for
shooting small stones ▷ **VERB** ❷ To
catapult something is to throw it
violently through the air. ❸ If
someone is catapulted into a
situation, they find themselves
unexpectedly in that situation • *Tony
has been catapulted into the limelight.*

cataract, cataracts **NOUN** ❶ an
area of the lens of someone's eye that
has become white instead of clear, so
that they cannot see properly. ❷ a
large waterfall.

catarrh [*Said kat-**tahr**] **NOUN**
Catarrh is a condition in which you get
a lot of mucus in your nose and throat.

catastrophe, catastrophes [*Said
kat-**tass**-trif-fee*] **NOUN** a terrible
disaster. **catastrophic ADJECTIVE**

catch, catches, catching, caught
VERB ❶ If you catch a ball moving in
the air, you grasp hold of it when it
comes near you. ❷ To catch an
animal means to trap it • *I caught ten
fish.* ❸ When the police catch
criminals, they find them and arrest
them. ❹ If you catch someone doing
something they should not be doing,
you discover them doing it • *He caught*

▷ SPELLING NOTE: *an ELegant angEL (angel)*

catching | 128

me playing the church organ. ❺ If you catch a bus or train, you get on it and travel somewhere. ❻ If you catch a cold or a disease, you become infected with it. ❼ If something catches on an object, it sticks to it or gets trapped • *The white fibres caught on the mesh.* ▷ NOUN ❽ a device that fastens something. ❾ a problem or hidden complication in something.

● SIMILAR WORDS: ❷ capture, ● snare, trap ❸ apprehend, arrest, ● capture ❻ contract, develop, go ● down with

catch on VERB ❶ If you catch on to something, you understand it. ❷ If something catches on, it becomes popular • *This drink has never really caught on in New Zealand.*

catch out VERB To catch someone out is to trick them or trap them.

catch up VERB ❶ To catch up with someone in front of you is to reach the place where they are by moving slightly faster than them. ❷ To catch up with someone is also to reach the same level or standard as them.

catching ADJECTIVE tending to spread very quickly • *Measles is catching.*

catchment area, catchment areas NOUN A catchment area is the area that a school, hospital, or other institution serves.

catchy, catchier, catchiest ADJECTIVE attractive and easily remembered • *a catchy little tune.*

catechism, catechisms [Said *kat-ik-kizm*] NOUN a set of questions and answers about the main beliefs of a religion.

categorical ADJECTIVE absolutely

certain and direct • *a categorical denial.* **categorically** ADVERB

categorize, categorizes, categorizing, categorized; *also spelt* **categorise** VERB To categorize things is to arrange them in different categories.

category, categories NOUN a set of things with a particular characteristic in common • *Occupations can be divided into four categories.*

cater, caters, catering, catered VERB To cater for people is to provide them with what they need, especially food.

caterer, caterers NOUN a person or business that provides food for parties and groups.

caterpillar, caterpillars NOUN the larva of a butterfly or moth. It looks like a small coloured worm and feeds on plants.

● WORD HISTORY: from Old French ● *catepelose* meaning 'hairy cat'

catharsis, catharses [Said *kath-ar-siss*] NOUN FORMAL Catharsis is the release of strong emotions and feelings through expressing them through drama or literature.

cathedral, cathedrals NOUN (HISTORY) an important church with a bishop in charge of it.

cathode-ray tube, cathode-ray tubes NOUN (SCIENCE) A cathode-ray tube is a tube used in televisions and computers, in which an image is produced by sending a beam of electrons onto a fluorescent screen.

Catholic, Catholics NOUN OR ADJECTIVE ❶ (HISTORY) (a) Roman Catholic ▷ ADJECTIVE ❷ If a person has catholic interests, they have a

▷ SPELLING NOTE: *LEt's measure the angLE (angle)*

wide range of interests. **Catholicism**
NOUN
- **WORD HISTORY:** from Greek
katholikos meaning 'universal'
- **USAGE NOTE:** When *Catholic*
begins with a capital letter, it refers
to the religion. When it begins with
a small letter, it means 'covering a
wide range'

cattle **PLURAL NOUN** Cattle are
cows and bulls kept by farmers.

catty, cattier, cattiest **ADJECTIVE**
unpleasant and spiteful. **cattiness**
NOUN

catwalk, catwalks **NOUN** a narrow
pathway that people walk along, for
example over a stage.

Caucasian, Caucasians [Said
kaw-kayz-yn] **NOUN** a person
belonging to the race of people with
fair or light-brown skin.
- **WORD HISTORY:** from *Caucasia*, a
region in the former USSR

caught the past tense and past
participle of **catch**.

cauldron, cauldrons **NOUN** a large,
round metal cooking pot, especially
one that sits over a fire.

cauliflower, cauliflowers **NOUN** a
large, round, white vegetable
surrounded by green leaves.

cause, causes, causing, caused
NOUN ❶ The cause of something is
the thing that makes it happen • *the
most common cause of back pain.* ❷ an
aim or principle which a group of
people are working for • *dedication to
the cause of peace.* ❸ If you have
cause for something, you have a
reason for it • *They gave us no cause to*

believe that. ▷ **VERB** ❹ To cause
something is to make it happen • *This
can cause delays.* **causal ADJECTIVE**
- **WORD HISTORY:** from Latin *causa*
meaning 'cause' or 'reason'

causeway, causeways **NOUN** a
raised path or road across water or
marshland.
- **WORD HISTORY:** from Latin
calciatus meaning 'paved with
limestone'

caustic ADJECTIVE ❶ A caustic
chemical can destroy substances
• *caustic liquids such as acids.* ❷ bitter
or sarcastic • *your caustic sense of
humour.*

caution, cautions, cautioning,
cautioned **NOUN** ❶ Caution is great
care which you take to avoid danger
• *You will need to proceed with caution.*
❷ a warning • *Sutton was let off with a
caution.* ▷ **VERB** ❸ If someone
cautions you, they warn you, usually
not to do something again • *A man
has been cautioned by police.*
cautionary ADJECTIVE

cautious ADJECTIVE acting very
carefully to avoid danger • *a cautious
approach.* **cautiously ADVERB**

cavalcade, cavalcades **NOUN** a
procession of people on horses or in
cars or carriages.

cavalier [Said *kav-val-eer*]
ADJECTIVE arrogant and behaving
without sensitivity • *a cavalier attitude
to women.*

cavalry NOUN The cavalry is the part
of an army that uses armoured
vehicles or horses.

cave, caves, caving, caved **NOUN** ❶ a

a b **c** d e f g h i j k l m n o p q r s t u v w x y z

▷ SPELLING NOTE: *A Rude Idiot Thought He Might Eat Toffee In Church (<u>arithmetic</u>)*

large hole in rock, that is underground or in the side of a cliff ▷ **VERB** ② If a roof caves in, it collapses inwards.

caveman, cavemen **NOUN** Cavemen were people who lived in caves in prehistoric times.

cavern, caverns **NOUN** a large cave.

cavernous **ADJECTIVE** large, deep, and hollow • *a cavernous warehouse.*

caviar or **caviare** [Said *kav-vee-ar*] **NOUN** Caviar is the tiny salted eggs of a fish called the sturgeon.

cavity, cavities **NOUN** a small hole in something solid • *There were dark cavities in his back teeth.*

cavort, cavorts, cavorting, cavorted **VERB** When people cavort, they jump around excitedly.

caw, caws, cawing, cawed **VERB** When a crow or rook caws, it makes a harsh sound.

cc an abbreviation for 'cubic centimetres'.

CD an abbreviation for 'compact disc'.

CD-ROM CD-ROM is a method of storing video, sound, or text on a compact disc which can be played on a computer using a laser. CD-ROM is an abbreviation for 'Compact Disc Read-Only Memory'.

cease, ceases, ceasing, ceased **VERB** ① If something ceases, it stops happening. ② If you cease to do something, or cease doing it, you stop doing it.

cease-fire, cease-fires **NOUN** an agreement between groups that are fighting each other to stop for a period

and discuss making peace.

ceaseless **ADJECTIVE** going on without stopping • *the ceaseless movement of the streets.* **ceaselessly** **ADVERB**

cedar, cedars **NOUN** a large evergreen tree with wide branches and needle-shaped leaves.

cede, cedes, ceding, ceded [Said *seed*] **VERB** To cede something is to give it up to someone else • *Haiti was ceded to France in 1697.*

ceiling, ceilings **NOUN** the top inside surface of a room.

celebrate, celebrates, celebrating, celebrated **VERB** ① If you celebrate or celebrate something, you do something special and enjoyable because of it • *a party to celebrate the end of the exams.* ② (RE) When a priest celebrates Mass, he performs the ceremonies of the Mass.

celebrated **ADJECTIVE** famous • *the celebrated Italian mountaineer.*

celebration, celebrations **NOUN** an event in honour of a special occasion. **celebratory** **ADJECTIVE**

celebrity, celebrities **NOUN** a famous person.

celery **NOUN** Celery is a vegetable with long pale green stalks.

celestial [Said *sil-lest-yal*] **ADJECTIVE** FORMAL concerning the sky or heaven • *The telescope is pointed at a celestial object.*

celibate [Said *sel-lib-bit*] **ADJECTIVE** Someone who is celibate does not marry or have sex. **celibacy** **NOUN**

▷ SPELLING NOTE: *Beautiful Elephants Are Usually Tiny (beautiful)*

cell, cells NOUN ❶ ⟨SCIENCE⟩ In biology, a cell is the smallest part of an animal or plant that can exist by itself. Each cell contains a nucleus. ❷ a small room where a prisoner is kept in a prison or police station. ❸ a small group of people set up to work together as part of a larger organization. ❹ ⟨D & T⟩ a device that converts chemical energy to electricity.

cellar, cellars NOUN a room underneath a building, often used to store wine.

cello, cellos [Said chel-loh] NOUN ⟨MUSIC⟩ a large musical stringed instrument which you play sitting down, holding the instrument upright with your knees. **cellist** NOUN

Cellophane NOUN ⟨D & T⟩ TRADEMARK Cellophane is thin, transparent plastic material used to wrap food or other things to protect them.

cellphone, cellphones NOUN a small portable telephone.

cellular ADJECTIVE Cellular means relating to the cells of animals or plants.

cellular phone, cellular phones NOUN the same as cellphone.

celluloid [Said sel-yul-loyd] NOUN Celluloid is a type of plastic which was once used to make photographic film.

Celsius [Said sel-see-yuss] NOUN Celsius is a scale for measuring temperature in which water freezes at 0 degrees (0° C) and boils at 100 degrees (100° C). Celsius is the same as 'Centigrade'.

Celtic [Said kel-tik] ADJECTIVE A Celtic language is one of a group of languages that includes Gaelic and Welsh.

cement, cements, cementing, cemented NOUN ❶ Cement is a fine powder made from limestone and clay, which is mixed with sand and water to make concrete ▷ VERB ❷ To cement things is to stick them together with cement or cover them with cement. ❸ Something that cements a relationship makes it stronger • to cement relations between them.

cemetery, cemeteries NOUN an area of land where dead people are buried.

cenotaph, cenotaphs [Said sen-not-ahf] NOUN a monument built in memory of dead people, especially soldiers buried elsewhere.
● **WORD HISTORY:** from Greek kenos + taphos meaning 'empty tomb'

censor, censors, censoring, censored NOUN ❶ a person officially appointed to examine books or films and to ban parts that are considered unsuitable ▷ VERB ❷ If someone censors a book or film, they cut or ban parts of it that are considered unsuitable for the public. **censorship** NOUN

censure, censures, censuring, censured [Said sen-sher] NOUN ❶ Censure is strong disapproval of something ▷ VERB ❷ To censure someone is to criticize them severely.

census, censuses NOUN an official survey of the population of a country.

cent, cents NOUN a unit of currency. In the USA, a cent is worth one hundredth of a dollar; in Europe, it is worth one hundredth of a Euro.

centaur, centaurs *[Said sen-tawr]*
NOUN a creature in Greek mythology
with the top half of a man and the
lower body and legs of a horse.

centenary, centenaries *[Said
sen-teen-er-ee]* **NOUN** the 100th
anniversary of something.

centi- **PREFIX** 'Centi-' is used to
form words that have 'hundred' as
part of their meaning • *centimetre.*

Centigrade Centigrade is another
name for **Celsius**.
● **USAGE NOTE:** Scientists say and
● write *Celsius* rather than *Centigrade*

centilitre, centilitres **NOUN** a unit
of liquid volume equal to one
hundredth of a litre.

centime, centimes *[Said sonn-team]*
NOUN a unit of currency used in
Switzerland and some other countries,
and formerly used in France and
Belgium.

centimetre, centimetres **NOUN**
(MATHS) a unit of length equal to ten
millimetres or one hundredth of a metre.

centipede, centipedes **NOUN** a
long, thin insect-like creature with
many pairs of legs.

central **ADJECTIVE** ❶ in or near the
centre of an object or area • *central
ceiling lights.* ❷ main or most
important • *the central idea of this
work.* **centrally** **ADVERB** **centrality**
NOUN

Central America **NOUN** Central
America is another name for the
Isthmus of Panama, the land joining
North America to South America.

central heating **NOUN** Central
heating is a system of heating a
building in which water or air is heated
in a tank and travels through pipes
and radiators round the building.

centralize, centralizes, centralizing,
centralized; *also spelt* **centralise**
VERB To centralize a system is to
bring the organization of it under the
control of one central group.
centralization **NOUN**

centre, centres, centring, centred
NOUN ❶ the middle of an object or
area. ❷ a building where people go
for activities, meetings, or help • *a
health centre.* ❸ Someone or
something that is the centre of
attention attracts a lot of attention
▷ **VERB** ❹ To centre something is to
move it so that it is balanced or at the
centre of something else. ❺ If
something centres on or around a
particular thing, that thing is the main
subject of attention • *The discussion
centred on his request.*
● **SIMILAR WORDS:** ❶ heart,
● middle

centrifugal *[Said sen-trif-yoo-gl]*
ADJECTIVE (SCIENCE) In physics,
centrifugal force is the force that
makes rotating objects move
outwards.
● **WORD HISTORY:** from Latin
● *centrum + fugere* meaning 'to flee
● from the centre'

centripetal *[Said sen-trip-pe-tl]*
ADJECTIVE (SCIENCE) In physics,
centripetal force is the force that
makes rotating objects move inwards.
● **WORD HISTORY:** from Latin
● *centrum + petere* meaning 'to seek
● the centre'

▷ SPELLING NOTE: *there's a rAKE in the brAKEs (bra<u>ke</u>)*

centurion, centurions **NOUN** an ancient Roman officer in charge of a hundred soldiers.

century, centuries **NOUN** ❶ a period of one hundred years. ❷ In cricket, a century is one hundred runs scored by a batsman.

ceramic, ceramics [Said sir-**ram**-mik] **NOUN** ❶ Ceramic is a hard material made by baking clay to a very high temperature. ❷ Ceramics is the art of making objects out of clay.

cereal, cereals **NOUN** ❶ a food made from grain, often eaten with milk for breakfast. ❷ a plant that produces edible grain, such as wheat or oats.

cerebral [Said ser-**reb**-ral] **ADJECTIVE** FORMAL relating to the brain • *She died from a massive cerebral haemorrhage.*

cerebral palsy NOUN Cerebral palsy is an illness caused by damage to a baby's brain, which makes its muscles and limbs very weak.

ceremonial ADJECTIVE relating to a ceremony • *ceremonial dress.* **ceremonially ADVERB**

ceremony, ceremonies **NOUN** ❶ a set of formal actions performed at a special occasion or important public event • *his recent coronation ceremony.* ❷ Ceremony is very formal and polite behaviour • *He hung up without ceremony.*

certain ADJECTIVE ❶ definite or reliable • *He is certain to be in Italy.* ❷ having no doubt in your mind. ❸ You use 'certain' to refer to a specific person or thing • *certain*

aspects of the job. ❹ You use 'certain' to suggest that a quality is noticeable but not obvious • *There's a certain resemblance to Joe.*

certainly ADVERB ❶ without doubt • *My boss was certainly interested.* ❷ of course • *'Will you be there?' – 'Certainly'.*

certainty, certainties **NOUN** ❶ Certainty is the state of being certain. ❷ something that is known without doubt • *There are no certainties and no guarantees.*

certificate, certificates **NOUN** a document stating particular facts, for example of someone's birth or death • *a marriage certificate.*

certify, certifies, certifying, certified **VERB** ❶ To certify something means to declare formally that it is true • *certifying the cause of death.* ❷ To certify someone means to declare officially that they are insane.

cervix, cervixes or cervices **NOUN** TECHNICAL the entrance to the womb at the top of the vagina. **cervical ADJECTIVE**

cessation NOUN FORMAL The cessation of something is the stopping of it • *a swift cessation of hostilities.*

cf. cf. means 'compare'. It is written after something in a text to mention something else which the reader should compare with what has just been written.

CFC, CFCs **NOUN** CFCs are manufactured chemicals that are used in aerosol sprays. They damage the ozone layer. CFC is an abbreviation for 'chlorofluorocarbon'.

▷ SPELLING NOTE: *you'll brEAK that Electrical Aerial, Kitty (br*<u>*eak*</u>*)*

chaff NOUN Chaff is the outer parts of grain separated from the seeds by beating.

chaffinch, chaffinches NOUN a small European bird with black and white wings.

chagrin [Said shag-rin] NOUN FORMAL Chagrin is a feeling of annoyance or disappointment.

chain, chains, chaining, chained NOUN ❶ a number of metal rings connected together in a line • a bicycle chain. ❷ a number of things in a series or connected to each other • a chain of shops. ▷ VERB ❸ If you chain one thing to another, you fasten them together with a chain • They had chained themselves to railings.

chain saw, chain saws NOUN a large saw with teeth fixed in a chain that is driven round by a motor.

chain-smoke, chain-smokes, chain-smoking, chain-smoked VERB To chain-smoke is to smoke cigarettes continually.

chair, chairs, chairing, chaired NOUN ❶ a seat with a back and four legs for one person. ❷ the person in charge of a meeting who decides when each person may speak ▷ VERB ❸ The person who chairs a meeting is in charge of it.

chair lift, chair lifts NOUN a line of chairs that hang from a moving cable and carry people up and down a mountain.

chairman, chairmen NOUN ❶ the person in charge of a meeting who decides when each person may speak. ❷ the head of a company or committee. **chairperson** NOUN **chairwoman** NOUN **chairmanship** NOUN

● **USAGE NOTE:** Some people don't
● like to use *chairman* when talking
● about a woman. You can use *chair*
● or *chairperson* to talk about a man
● or a woman

chalet, chalets [Said shall-lay] NOUN a wooden house with a sloping roof, especially in a mountain area or a holiday camp.

chalice, chalices [Said chal-liss] NOUN (RE) a gold or silver cup used in churches to hold the Communion wine.

chalk, chalks, chalking, chalked NOUN ❶ (ART) Chalk is a soft white rock. Small sticks of chalk are used for writing or drawing on a blackboard ▷ VERB ❷ To chalk up a result is to achieve it • He chalked up his first win. **chalky** ADJECTIVE

challenge, challenges, challenging, challenged NOUN ❶ something that is new and exciting but requires a lot of effort • It's a new challenge at the right time in my career. ❷ a suggestion from someone to compete with them. ❸ A challenge to something is a questioning of whether it is correct or true • a challenge to authority. ▷ VERB ❹ If someone challenges you, they suggest that you compete with them in some way. ❺ If you challenge something, you question whether it is correct or true. **challenger** NOUN **challenging** ADJECTIVE

● **SIMILAR WORDS:** ❺ dispute,
● question

chamber, chambers NOUN ❶ a large room, especially one used for formal meetings • *the Council Chamber.* ❷ a group of people chosen to decide laws or administrative matters. ❸ a hollow place or compartment inside something, especially inside an animal's body or inside a gun • *the chambers of the heart.*

chambermaid, chambermaids
NOUN a woman who cleans and tidies rooms in a hotel.

chameleon, chameleons [Said kam-**mee**-lee-on] NOUN a lizard which is able to change the colour of its skin to match the colour of its surroundings.
● **WORD HISTORY:** from Greek
● *khamai* + *leōn* meaning 'ground
● lion'

chamois leather, chamois leathers [Said **sham**-mee] NOUN a soft leather cloth used for polishing.

champagne, champagnes [Said sham-**pain**] NOUN Champagne is a sparkling white wine made in France.

champion, champions, championing, championed NOUN
❶ a person who wins a competition.
❷ someone who supports or defends a cause or principle • *a champion of women's causes.* ▷ VERB ❸ Someone who champions a cause or principle supports or defends it.

championship, championships
NOUN a competition to find the champion of a sport.

chance, chances, chancing, chanced
NOUN ❶ The chance of something happening is how possible or likely it is • *There's a chance of rain later.* ❷ an opportunity to do something • *Your chance to be a TV star!* ❸ a possibility

that something dangerous or unpleasant may happen • *Don't take chances, he's armed.* ❹ Chance is also the way things happen unexpectedly without being planned • *I only found out by chance.* ▷ VERB ❺ If you chance something, you try it although you are taking a risk.
● **SIMILAR WORDS:** ❹ accident,
● coincidence, luck

chancellor, chancellors NOUN
❶ the head of government in some European countries. ❷ In Britain, the Chancellor is the Chancellor of the Exchequer. ❸ the honorary head of a university.

Chancellor of the Exchequer NOUN In Britain, the minister responsible for finance and taxes.

chandelier, chandeliers [Said shan-del-**leer**] NOUN an ornamental light fitting which hangs from the ceiling.

change, changes, changing, changed
NOUN ❶ a difference or alteration in something • *Steven soon noticed a change in Penny's attitude.* ❷ a replacement of something by something else • *a change of clothes.*
❸ Change is money you get back when you have paid more than the actual price of something ▷ VERB
❹ When something changes or when you change it, it becomes different • *It changed my life.* ❺ If you change something, you exchange it for something else. ❻ When you change, you put on different clothes. ❼ To change money means to exchange it for smaller coins of the same total value, or to exchange it for foreign

a
b
c
d
e
f
g
h
i
j
k
l
m
n
o
p
q
r
s
t
u
v
w
x
y
z

currency • *Can I change money here?*

changeable ADJECTIVE likely to change all the time.
  ● SIMILAR WORDS: erratic,
  ● inconstant, variable

changeover, changeovers NOUN a change from one system or activity to another • *the changeover between day and night.*

channel, channels, channelling, channelled NOUN ❶ a wavelength used to receive programmes broadcast by a television or radio station; also the station itself • *I was watching another channel.* ❷ a passage along which water flows or along which something is carried. ❸ The Channel or the English Channel is the stretch of sea between England and France. ❹ a method of achieving something • *We have tried to do things through the right channels.* ▷ VERB ❺ To channel something such as money or energy means to direct it in a particular way • *Their efforts are being channelled into worthy causes.*

chant, chants, chanting, chanted NOUN ❶ a group of words repeated over and over again • *a rousing chant.* ❷ a religious song sung on only a few notes ▷ VERB ❸ If people chant a group of words, they repeat them over and over again • *Crowds chanted his name.*

Chanukah another spelling of Hanukkah.

chaos *[Said kay-oss]* NOUN Chaos is a state of complete disorder and confusion. **chaotic** ADJECTIVE

chap, chaps, chapping, chapped NOUN ❶ INFORMAL a man ▷ VERB

❷ If your skin chaps, it becomes dry and cracked, usually as a result of cold or wind.

chapel, chapels NOUN ❶ a section of a church or cathedral with its own altar. ❷ a type of small church.
  ● WORD HISTORY: from Latin
  ● *capella* meaning 'small cloak';
  ● originally used of the place where St
  ● Martin's cloak was kept as a relic

chaperone, chaperones *[Said shap-per-rone]* ; also spelt **chaperon** NOUN an older woman who accompanies a young unmarried woman on social occasions, or any person who accompanies a group of younger people.

chaplain, chaplains NOUN a member of the Christian clergy who regularly works in a hospital, school, or prison. **chaplaincy** NOUN

chapter, chapters NOUN ❶ one of the parts into which a book is divided. ❷ a particular period in someone's life or in history.

char, chars, charring, charred VERB If something chars, it gets partly burned and goes black. **charred** ADJECTIVE

character, characters NOUN ❶ all the qualities which combine to form the personality or atmosphere of a person or place. ❷ A person or place that has character has an interesting, attractive, or admirable quality • *an inn of great character and simplicity.* ❸ (ENGLISH) The characters in a film, play, or book are the people in it. ❹ a person • *an odd character.* ❺ a letter, number, or other written symbol.
  ● SIMILAR WORDS: ❶ nature,
  ● personality, quality

characteristic, characteristics
NOUN ❶ a quality that is typical of a particular person or thing • *Silence is the characteristic of the place.*
❷ [SCIENCE] a feature that is typical of a particular living thing
▷ **ADJECTIVE** ❸ Characteristic means typical of a particular person or thing • *Two things are very characteristic of his driving.*
characteristically ADVERB

characterize, characterizes, characterizing, characterized; *also spelt* **characterise VERB** A quality that characterizes something is typical of it • *a condition characterized by muscle stiffness.*

characterless ADJECTIVE dull and uninteresting • *a tiny characterless flat.*

charade, charades [*Said* shar-**rahd**] **NOUN** a ridiculous and unnecessary activity or pretence.
● **WORD HISTORY:** from Provençal
● *charrado* meaning 'chat'

charcoal NOUN [SCIENCE] Charcoal is a black form of carbon made by burning wood without air, used as a fuel and also for drawing.

charge, charges, charging, charged
VERB ❶ If someone charges you money, they ask you to pay it for something you have bought or received • *The company charged £150 on each loan.* ❷ To charge someone means to accuse them formally of having committed a crime. ❸ To charge a battery means to pass an electrical current through it to make it store electricity. ❹ To charge somewhere means to rush forward, often to attack someone • *The rhino*

charged at her. ▷ **NOUN** ❺ the price that you have to pay for something.
❻ a formal accusation that a person is guilty of a crime and has to go to court. ❼ To have charge or be in charge of someone or something means to be responsible for them and be in control of them. ❽ an explosive put in a gun or other weapon. ❾ An electrical charge is the amount of electricity that something carries.

charger, chargers **NOUN** a device for charging or recharging batteries.

chariot, chariots **NOUN** a two-wheeled open vehicle pulled by horses.

charisma [*Said* kar-**riz**-ma] **NOUN** Charisma is a special ability to attract or influence people by your personality. **charismatic ADJECTIVE**

charity, charities **NOUN** ❶ an organization that raises money to help people who are ill, poor, or disabled. ❷ Charity is money or other help given to poor, disabled, or ill people • *to help raise money for charity.* ❸ Charity is also a kind, sympathetic attitude towards people. **charitable ADJECTIVE**

charlatan, charlatans [*Said* shar-**lat**-tn] **NOUN** someone who pretends to have skill or knowledge that they do not really have.

charm, charms, charming, charmed
NOUN ❶ Charm is an attractive and pleasing quality that some people and things have • *a man of great personal charm.* ❷ a small ornament worn on a bracelet. ❸ a magical spell or an object that is supposed to bring good luck ▷ **VERB** ❹ If you charm

a b **c** d e f g h i j k l m n o p q r s t u v w x y z

▷ SPELLING NOTE: *have a pIEce of pIE (piece)*

someone, you use your charm to
please them.

charmer, charmers **NOUN** someone
who uses their charm to influence
people.

charming ADJECTIVE very pleasant
and attractive • *a rather charming
man.* **charmingly ADVERB**

chart, charts, charting, charted
NOUN ❶ a diagram or table showing
information • *He noted the score on his
chart.* ❷ a map of the sea or stars
▷ **VERB** ❸ If you chart something,
you observe and record it carefully.

charter, charters, chartering,
chartered **NOUN** ❶ a document
stating the rights or aims of a group or
organization, often written by the
government • *the new charter for
commuters.* ▷ **VERB** ❷ To charter
transport such as a plane or boat is to
hire it for private use. **chartered
ADJECTIVE**

chase, chases, chasing, chased **VERB**
❶ If you chase someone or
something, you run after them in
order to catch them. ❷ If you chase
someone, you force them to go
somewhere else ▷ **NOUN** ❸ the
activity of chasing or hunting
someone or something • *a high-speed
car chase.*
● **SIMILAR WORDS:** ❶ hunt,
● pursue

chasm, chasms [*Said* **kazm**] **NOUN**
❶ a deep crack in the earth's surface.
❷ a very large difference between two
ideas or groups of people • *the chasm
between rich and poor in America.*

chassis, chassis [*Said* **shas-ee**]
NOUN the frame on which a car or

other vehicle is built.
● **USAGE NOTE:** The plural of *chassis*
● is also *chassis*

chaste [*Said* **chayst**] **ADJECTIVE**
OLD-FASHIONED not having sex with
anyone outside marriage. **chastity
NOUN**

chastise, chastises, chastising,
chastised **VERB** FORMAL If someone
chastises you, they criticize you or
punish you for something that you
have done.

chat, chats, chatting, chatted **NOUN**
❶ a friendly talk with someone,
usually about things that are not very
important ▷ **VERB** ❷ When people
chat, they talk to each other in a
friendly way.
chat up VERB INFORMAL If you chat
up someone, you talk to them in a
friendly way, because you are
attracted to them.
● **SIMILAR WORDS:** ❶ and
● ❷ gossip, natter, talk

chateau, chateaux [*Said* **shat-toe**]
NOUN a large country house or castle
in France.

chatroom, chatrooms **NOUN** an
Internet site where users have group
discussions using e-mail.

chatter, chatters, chattering,
chattered **VERB** ❶ When people
chatter, they talk very fast. ❷ If your
teeth are chattering, they are knocking
together and making a clicking noise
because you are cold ▷ **NOUN**
❸ Chatter is a lot of fast unimportant
talk.

chatty, chattier, chattiest **ADJECTIVE**
talkative and friendly.

▷ SPELLING NOTE: *plaice* the fish has a glittering 'EYE' (I) (*plaice*)

chauffeur, chauffeurs [Said *show-fur*] NOUN a person whose job is to drive another person's car.

chauvinist, chauvinists NOUN ❶ a person who thinks their country is always right. ❷ A male chauvinist is a man who believes that men are superior to women. **chauvinistic** ADJECTIVE **chauvinism** NOUN

cheap, cheaper, cheapest ADJECTIVE ❶ costing very little money. ❷ inexpensive but of poor quality. ❸ A cheap joke or cheap remark is unfair and unkind. **cheaply** ADVERB
- SIMILAR WORDS: ❶ inexpensive, reasonable

cheat, cheats, cheating, cheated VERB ❶ If someone cheats, they do wrong or unfair things to win or get something that they want. ❷ If you are cheated of or out of something, you do not get what you are entitled to ▷ NOUN ❸ a person who cheats.
- SIMILAR WORDS: ❶ con, deceive, swindle

check, checks, checking, checked VERB ❶ To check something is to examine it in order to make sure that everything is all right. ❷ To check the growth or spread of something is to make it stop • *a policy to check fast population growth.* ▷ NOUN ❸ an inspection to make sure that everything is all right. ❹ Checks are different coloured squares which form a pattern ▷ PHRASE ❺ If you keep something **in check**, you keep it under control • *She kept her emotions in check.* ▷ ADJECTIVE ❻ Check or checked means marked with a pattern of squares • *check design.*
check out VERB If you check something out, you inspect it and find out whether everything about it is right.

checkmate NOUN In chess, checkmate is a situation where one player cannot stop their king being captured and so loses the game.
- WORD HISTORY: from Arabic *shah mat* meaning 'the King is dead'

checkout, checkouts NOUN a counter in a supermarket where the customers pay for their goods.

checkpoint, checkpoints NOUN a place where traffic has to stop in order to be checked.

checkup, checkups NOUN an examination by a doctor to see if you are healthy.

cheek, cheeks NOUN ❶ Your cheeks are the sides of your face below your eyes. ❷ Cheek is speech or behaviour that is rude or disrespectful • *an expression of sheer cheek.*
- SIMILAR WORDS:
- ❷ impertinence, impudence, insolence

cheeky, cheekier, cheekiest ADJECTIVE rather rude and disrespectful.

cheer, cheers, cheering, cheered VERB ❶ When people cheer, they shout with approval or in order to show support for a person or team ▷ NOUN ❷ a shout of approval or support.
cheer up VERB When you cheer up, you feel more cheerful.

cheerful ADJECTIVE ❶ happy and in good spirits • *I had never seen her so cheerful.* ❷ bright and pleasant-looking • *a cheerful and charming place.* **cheerfully** ADVERB **cheerfulness** NOUN

cheerio INTERJECTION Cheerio is a friendly way of saying goodbye.

cheery, cheerier, cheeriest ADJECTIVE happy and cheerful • *He gave me a cheery nod.*

cheese, cheeses NOUN a hard or creamy food made from milk.

cheesecake, cheesecakes NOUN a dessert made of biscuit covered with cream cheese.

cheetah, cheetahs NOUN a wild animal like a large cat with black spots.
● WORD HISTORY: from Sanskrit
● *citra + kaya* meaning 'speckled
● body'

chef, chefs NOUN a head cook in a restaurant or hotel.

chemical, chemicals NOUN
(SCIENCE) ❶ Chemicals are substances manufactured by chemistry ▷ ADJECTIVE ❷ involved in chemistry or using chemicals • *chemical weapons.* **chemically** ADVERB

chemist, chemists NOUN ❶ a person who is qualified to make up drugs and medicines prescribed by a doctor. ❷ a shop where medicines and cosmetics are sold. ❸ a scientist who does research in chemistry.

chemistry NOUN Chemistry is the scientific study of substances and the ways in which they change when they are combined with other substances.

chemotherapy [*Said keem-oh-ther-a-pee*] NOUN Chemotherapy is a way of treating diseases such as cancer by using chemicals.

cheque, cheques NOUN a printed form on which you write an amount of money that you have to pay. You sign the cheque and your bank pays the money from your account.

chequered [*Said chek-kerd*] ADJECTIVE ❶ covered with a pattern of squares. ❷ A chequered career is a varied career that has both good and bad parts.

cherish, cherishes, cherishing, cherished VERB ❶ If you cherish something, you care deeply about it and want to keep it or look after it lovingly. ❷ If you cherish a memory or hope, you have it in your mind and care deeply about it • *I cherish the good memories I have of him.*

cherry, cherries NOUN ❶ a small, juicy fruit with a red or black skin and a hard stone in the centre. ❷ a tree that produces cherries.

cherub, cherubs or cherubim NOUN an angel, shown in pictures as a plump, naked child with wings. **cherubic** ADJECTIVE

chess NOUN Chess is a board game for two people in which each player has 16 pieces and tries to move his or her pieces so that the other player's king cannot escape.

chessboard, chessboards NOUN A chessboard is a board divided into 64 squares of two alternating colours on which chess is played.

chest, chests NOUN ❶ the front part of your body between your shoulders and your waist. ❷ a large wooden box with a hinged lid.

chestnut, chestnuts NOUN
❶ Chestnuts are reddish-brown nuts that grow inside a prickly green outer covering. ❷ a tree that produces these nuts ▷ ADJECTIVE
❸ Something that is chestnut is reddish-brown.

chest of drawers, chests of drawers NOUN a piece of furniture with drawers in it, used for storing clothes.

chew, chews, chewing, chewed VERB
When you chew something, you use your teeth to break it up in your mouth before swallowing it. **chewy** ADJECTIVE

chewing gum NOUN Chewing gum is a kind of sweet that you chew for a long time, but which you do not swallow.

chic, chicer, chicest [Said **sheek**]
ADJECTIVE elegant and fashionable • a chic restaurant.

chick, chicks NOUN a young bird.

chicken, chickens, chickening, chickened NOUN ❶ a bird kept on a farm for its eggs and meat; also the meat of this bird • roast chicken.
▷ VERB ❷ INFORMAL If you chicken out of something, you do not do it because you are afraid.

chickenpox NOUN Chickenpox is an illness which produces a fever and blister-like spots on the skin.

chicory NOUN Chicory is a plant with bitter leaves that are used in salads.

chide, chides, chiding, chided VERB

OLD-FASHIONED To chide someone is to tell them off.

chief, chiefs NOUN ❶ the leader of a group or organization ▷ ADJECTIVE
❷ most important • the chief source of oil. **chiefly** ADVERB

chieftain, chieftains NOUN the leader of a tribe or clan.

chiffon [Said **shif**-fon] NOUN
Chiffon is a very thin lightweight cloth made of silk or nylon.

chihuahua, chihuahuas [Said chi-**wah**-wah] NOUN a breed of very small dog with short hair and pointed ears.

chilblain, chilblains NOUN a sore, itchy swelling on a finger or toe.

child, children NOUN ❶ a young person who is not yet an adult.
❷ Someone's child is their son or daughter.
● SIMILAR WORDS: ❶ baby, kid, ● youngster

childbirth NOUN Childbirth is the act of giving birth to a child.

childhood, childhoods NOUN
Someone's childhood is the time when they are a child.

childish ADJECTIVE immature and foolish • I don't have time for childish arguments. **childishly** ADVERB **childishness** NOUN
● USAGE NOTE: If you call someone childish, you think they are immature or foolish. If you call them childlike, you think they are innocent like a young child
● SIMILAR WORDS: immature, infantile, juvenile

a b c d e f g h i j k l m n o p q r s t u v w x y z

childless ADJECTIVE having no children.

childlike ADJECTIVE like a child in appearance or behaviour • *childlike enthusiasm.*

childminder, childminders NOUN a person who is qualified and paid to look after other people's children while they are at work.

Chilean, Chileans ADJECTIVE ❶ belonging or relating to Chile ▷ NOUN ❷ someone who comes from Chile.

chill, chills, chilling, chilled VERB ❶ To chill something is to make it cold • *Chill the cheesecake.* ❷ If something chills you, it makes you feel worried or frightened • *The thought chilled her.* ▷ NOUN ❸ a feverish cold. ❹ a feeling of cold • *the chill of the night air.*

chilli, chillies NOUN the red or green seed pod of a type of pepper which has a very hot, spicy taste.

chilly, chillier, chilliest ADJECTIVE ❶ rather cold • *the chilly November breeze.* ❷ unfriendly and without enthusiasm • *a chilly reception.*

chilly-bin, chilly-bins NOUN INFORMAL In New Zealand English, a container for keeping food and drink cool that can be carried.

chime, chimes, chiming, chimed VERB When a bell chimes, it makes a clear ringing sound.

chimney, chimneys NOUN a vertical pipe or other hollow structure above a fireplace or furnace through which smoke from a fire escapes.

chimpanzee, chimpanzees NOUN a small ape with dark fur that lives in forests in Africa.

chin, chins NOUN the part of your face below your mouth.

china, chinas NOUN ❶ China is items like cups, saucers, and plates made from very fine clay. ❷ INFORMAL In South African English, a china is a friend.

Chinese ADJECTIVE ❶ belonging or relating to China ▷ NOUN ❷ someone who comes from China. ❸ Chinese refers to any of a group of related languages and dialects spoken by Chinese people.

chink, chinks NOUN ❶ a small, narrow opening • *a chink in the roof.* ❷ a short, light, ringing sound, like one made by glasses touching each other.

chintz NOUN Chintz is a type of brightly patterned cotton fabric.
● **WORD HISTORY:** from Hindi *chint*
● meaning 'brightly coloured'

chip, chips, chipping, chipped NOUN ❶ Chips are thin strips of fried potato. ❷ In electronics, a chip is a tiny piece of silicon inside a computer which is used to form electronic circuits. ❸ a small piece broken off an object, or the mark made when a piece breaks off. ❹ In some gambling games, chips are counters used to represent money ▷ VERB ❺ If you chip an object, you break a small piece off it.

chipboard NOUN Chipboard is a material made from wood scraps pressed together into hard sheets.

chipmunk, chipmunks NOUN a

small rodent with a striped back.

chiropodist, chiropodists [Said kir-**rop**-pod-dist] NOUN a person whose job is treating people's feet. **chiropody** NOUN

chirp, chirps, chirping, chirped VERB When a bird chirps, it makes a short, high-pitched sound.

chisel, chisels, chiselling, chiselled NOUN ❶ a tool with a long metal blade and a sharp edge at the end which is used for cutting and shaping wood, stone, or metal ▷ VERB ❷ To chisel wood, stone, or metal is to cut or shape it using a chisel.

chivalry [Said shiv-**val**-ree] NOUN Chivalry is polite and helpful behaviour, especially by men towards women. **chivalrous** ADJECTIVE
● WORD HISTORY: from Latin
● *caballarius* meaning 'horseman'

chive, chives NOUN Chives are grasslike hollow leaves that have a mild onion flavour.

chlorine [Said **klaw**-reen] NOUN (SCIENCE) Chlorine is a chemical element which is a poisonous greenish-yellow gas with a strong, unpleasant smell. It is used to disinfect water and to make bleach. Its atomic number is 17 and its symbol is Cl.

chloroform [Said **klor**-rof-form] NOUN Chloroform is a colourless liquid with a strong, sweet smell used in cleaning products.

chlorophyll [Said **klor**-rof-fil] NOUN (SCIENCE) Chlorophyll is a green substance in plants which enables them to use the energy from sunlight in order to grow.

chock-a-block or **chock-full** ADJECTIVE completely full.

chocolate, chocolates NOUN
❶ Chocolate is a sweet food made from cacao seeds. ❷ a sweet made of chocolate ▷ ADJECTIVE ❸ dark brown.
● WORD HISTORY: from Aztec *xococ*
● + *atl* meaning 'bitter water'

choice, choices NOUN ❶ a range of different things that are available to choose from • *a wider choice of treatments.* ❷ something that you choose • *You've made a good choice.* ❸ Choice is the power or right to choose • *I had no choice.*
● SIMILAR WORDS: ❶ range,
● selection, variety

choir, choirs [Said **kwire**] NOUN (MUSIC) a group of singers, for example in a church.

choke, chokes, choking, choked VERB ❶ If you choke, you stop being able to breathe properly, usually because something is blocking your windpipe • *the diner who choked on a fish bone.* ❷ If things choke a place, they fill it so much that it is blocked or clogged up • *The canal was choked with old tyres.*

choko, chokos NOUN a fruit that is shaped like a pear and used as a vegetable in Australia and New Zealand.

cholera [Said **kol**-ler-ra] NOUN Cholera is a serious disease causing severe diarrhoea and vomiting. It is caused by infected food or water.

cholesterol [Said kol-**less**-ter-rol] NOUN Cholesterol is a substance found in all animal fats, tissues, and

a
b
c
d
e
f
g
h
i
j
k
l
m
n
o
p
q
r
s
t
u
v
w
x
y
z

blood. Some types are unhealthy.

chook, chooks **NOUN** INFORMAL In Australian and New Zealand English, a chicken.

choose, chooses, choosing, chose, chosen **VERB** To choose something is to decide to have it or do it • *He chose to live in Kenya.*
- **SIMILAR WORDS:** opt for, pick, select

choosy, choosier, choosiest **ADJECTIVE** fussy and difficult to satisfy • *You can't be too choosy about jobs.*

chop, chops, chopping, chopped **VERB** ❶ To chop something is to cut it with quick, heavy strokes using an axe or a knife ▷ **NOUN** ❷ a small piece of lamb or pork containing a bone, usually cut from the ribs.

chopper, choppers **NOUN** INFORMAL a helicopter.

choppy, choppier, choppiest **ADJECTIVE** Choppy water has a lot of waves because it is windy.

chopstick, chopsticks **NOUN** Chopsticks are a pair of thin sticks used by people in the Far East for eating food.

choral **ADJECTIVE** relating to singing by a choir • *choral music.*

chord, chords **NOUN** (MUSIC) a group of three or more musical notes played together.

chore, chores **NOUN** an uninteresting job that has to be done • *the chore of cleaning.*

choreography [*Said kor-ree-og-raf-fee*] **NOUN** Choreography is the art

of composing dance steps and movements. **choreographer** **NOUN**

chortle, chortles, chortling, chortled **VERB** To chortle is to laugh with amusement.

chorus, choruses, chorusing, chorused (MUSIC) **NOUN** ❶ a large group of singers; also a piece of music for a large group of singers. ❷ a part of a song which is repeated after each verse ▷ **VERB** ❸ If people chorus something, they all say or sing it at the same time.
- **WORD HISTORY:** from Greek *khoros*, the group of actors who gave the commentary in Classical plays

Christ **PROPER NOUN** Christ is the name for Jesus. Christians believe that Jesus is the son of God.

christen, christens, christening, christened **VERB** When a baby is christened, it is named by a member of the clergy in a religious ceremony.

Christian, Christians **NOUN** (RE) ❶ a person who believes in Jesus Christ and his teachings ▷ **ADJECTIVE** ❷ relating to Christ and his teachings • *the Christian faith.* ❸ good, kind, and considerate. **Christianity** **NOUN**

Christian name, Christian names **NOUN** the name given to someone when they were born or christened.

Christmas, Christmases **NOUN** (RE) the Christian festival celebrating the birth of Christ, falling on December 25th.

chromatic [*Said kro-ma-tik*] **ADJECTIVE** (MUSIC) A chromatic scale is one which is based on an octave of 12 semitones.

chromatography NOUN
(SCIENCE) a technique used to
discover the components of mixtures
of gases or liquids. It involves passing
the mixture through a material that
absorbs the components at different
rates.

chrome [Said **krome**] NOUN
Chrome is metal plated with
chromium, a hard grey metal.

chromosome, chromosomes
NOUN (SCIENCE) In biology, a
chromosome is a part of a cell which
contains genes that determine the
characteristics of an animal or plant.

chronic [Said **kron-nik**] ADJECTIVE
lasting a very long time or never
stopping • *a chronic illness.*
chronically ADVERB

chronicle, chronicles, chronicling,
chronicled NOUN ❶ a record of a
series of events described in the order
in which they happened ▷ VERB
❷ To chronicle a series of events is to
record or describe them in the order in
which they happened.

chronological [Said **kron-nol-loj-
i-kl**] ADJECTIVE (HISTORY) arranged
in the order in which things happened
• *Tell me the whole story in chronological
order.* **chronologically** ADVERB

chronology [Said **kron-nol-loj-jee**]
NOUN (HISTORY) The chronology of
events is the order in which they
happened.
 ● **WORD HISTORY:** from Greek
 ● *khronos* meaning 'time' and *legein*
 ● meaning 'to say'

chrysalis, chrysalises [Said

kriss-sal-liss] NOUN a butterfly or
moth when it is developing from being
a caterpillar to being a fully grown adult.

chrysanthemum,
chrysanthemums [Said *kriss-**an**-thim-
mum*] NOUN a plant with large,
brightly coloured flowers.

chubby, chubbier, chubbiest
ADJECTIVE plump and round • *his
chubby cheeks.*

chuck, chucks, chucking, chucked
VERB INFORMAL To chuck something
is to throw it casually.

chuckle, chuckles, chuckling,
chuckled VERB When you chuckle,
you laugh quietly.

chug, chugs, chugging, chugged
VERB When a machine or engine
chugs, it makes a continuous dull
thudding sound.

chum, chums NOUN INFORMAL a
friend.

chunk, chunks NOUN a thick piece
of something.
 ● **SIMILAR WORDS:** hunk, lump,
 ● piece

chunky, chunkier, chunkiest
ADJECTIVE Someone who is chunky
is broad and heavy but usually short.

church, churches NOUN ❶ a
building where Christians go for
religious services and worship. ❷ In
the Christian religion, a church is one
of the groups with their own particular
beliefs, customs, and clergy • *the
Catholic Church.*
 ● **WORD HISTORY:** from Greek
 ● *kuriakon* meaning 'master's house'

Church of England NOUN The

A
B
C
D
E
F
G
H
I
J
K
L
M
N
O
P
Q
R
S
T
U
V
W
X
Y
Z

Church of England is the Anglican church in England, where it is the state church, with the King or Queen as its head.

churchyard, churchyards NOUN an area of land around a church, often used as a graveyard.

churn, churns NOUN a container used for making milk or cream into butter.

chute, chutes [Said **shoot**] NOUN a steep slope or channel used to slide things down • *a rubbish chute*.

chutney, chutneys NOUN Chutney is a strong-tasting thick sauce made from fruit, vinegar, and spices.

cider, ciders NOUN Cider is an alcoholic drink made from apples.

cigar, cigars NOUN a roll of dried tobacco leaves which people smoke.
● **WORD HISTORY:** from Mayan *sicar* meaning 'to smoke'

cigarette, cigarettes NOUN a thin roll of tobacco covered in thin paper which people smoke.

cinder, cinders NOUN Cinders are small pieces of burnt material left after something such as wood or coal has burned.

cinema, cinemas NOUN ❶ a place where people go to watch films. ❷ Cinema is the business of making films.

cinnamon NOUN Cinnamon is a sweet spice which comes from the bark of an Asian tree.

cipher, ciphers [Said **sy**-fer]; also spelt **cypher** NOUN a secret code or system of writing.

circa [Said **sir**-ka] PREPOSITION FORMAL about or approximately; used especially before dates • *portrait of a lady, circa 1840*.

circle, circles, circling, circled NOUN ❶ a completely regular round shape. Every point on its edge is the same distance from the centre. ❷ a group of people with the same interest or profession • *a character well known in yachting circles*. ❸ an area of seats on an upper floor of a theatre ▷ VERB ❹ To circle is to move round and round as though going round the edge of a circle • *A police helicopter circled above*.

circuit, circuits [Said **sir**-kit] NOUN ❶ any closed line or path, often circular, for example a racing track; also the distance round this path • *three circuits of the 26-lap race remaining*. ❷ (SCIENCE) An electrical circuit is a complete route around which an electric current can flow. A **closed circuit** is a complete electrical circuit around which current can flow; a **parallel circuit** is a closed circuit in which the current divides into two or more paths before coming back together to complete the circuit; a **series circuit** is an electrical circuit in which the separate elements are connected one after the other so that the same current flows through them all.

circular, circulars ADJECTIVE ❶ in the shape of a circle. ❷ A circular argument or theory is not valid because it uses a statement to prove a conclusion and the conclusion to prove the statement ▷ NOUN ❸ a letter or advert sent to a lot of people at the same time. **circularity** NOUN

▷ SPELLING NOTE: *there's SAND in my SANDwich (sandwich)*

circulate, circulates, circulating, circulated **VERB** ❶ (SCIENCE) When something circulates or when you circulate it, it moves easily around an area • *an open position where the air can circulate freely.* ❷ When you circulate something among people, you pass it round or tell it to all the people • *We circulate a regular newsletter.*

circulation, circulations **NOUN** ❶ The circulation of something is the act of circulating it or the action of it circulating • *traffic circulation.* ❷ The circulation of a newspaper or magazine is the number of copies that are sold of each issue. ❸ (SCIENCE) Your circulation is the movement of blood through your body • *the cramped seating position affected her circulation.*

circumcise, circumcises, circumcising, circumcised **VERB** If a boy or man is circumcised, the foreskin at the end of his penis is removed. This is carried out mainly as part of a Muslim or Jewish religious ceremony. **circumcision NOUN**

circumference, circumferences **NOUN** (MATHS) The circumference of a circle is its outer line or edge; also the length of this line.

circumstance, circumstances **NOUN** ❶ The circumstances of a situation or event are the conditions that affect what happens • *He did well in the circumstances.* ❷ Someone's circumstances are their position and conditions in life • *Her circumstances had changed.*

circus, circuses **NOUN** a show given by a travelling group of entertainers such as clowns, acrobats, and specially trained animals.

cirrus NOUN (GEOGRAPHY) Cirrus is a type of thin cloud high up in the sky.

cistern, cisterns **NOUN** a tank in which water is stored, for example one in the roof of a house or above a toilet.

citadel, citadels **NOUN** a fortress in or near a city.

cite, cites, citing, cited **VERB** ❶ FORMAL If you cite something, you quote it or refer to it • *He cited a letter written by Newall.* ❷ If someone is cited in a legal action, they are officially called to appear in court.

citizen, citizens **NOUN** (HISTORY) The citizens of a country or city are the people who live in it or belong to it • *American citizens.*

citizenship NOUN the status of being a citizen, with all the rights and duties that go with it • *I'm applying for Australian citizenship.*

citrus fruit, citrus fruits **NOUN** Citrus fruits are juicy, sharp-tasting fruits such as oranges, lemons, and grapefruit.

city, cities **NOUN** a large town where many people live and work.

civic ADJECTIVE relating to a city or citizens • *the Civic Centre.*

civil ADJECTIVE ❶ relating to the citizens of a country • *civil rights.* ❷ relating to people or things that are not connected with the armed forces • *the history of civil aviation.* ❸ polite. **civilly ADVERB civility NOUN**

civil engineering NOUN Civil engineering is the design and

▷ SPELLING NOTE: On WEDNESday Wayne WED NESta (Wednesday)

construction of roads, bridges, and public buildings.

civilian, civilians NOUN a person who is not in the armed forces.

civilization, civilizations; *also spelt* **civilisation** NOUN (HISTORY) ❶ a society which has a highly developed organization and culture • *the tale of a lost civilization.* ❷ Civilization is an advanced state of social organization and culture.

civilized ADJECTIVE ❶ A civilized society is one with a developed social organization and way of life. ❷ A civilized person is polite and reasonable.

civil servant, civil servants NOUN a person who works in the civil service.

civil service NOUN The civil service is the government departments responsible for the administration of a country.

civil war, civil wars NOUN a war between groups of people who live in the same country.

cl an abbreviation for 'centilitres'.

clad ADJECTIVE LITERARY Someone who is clad in particular clothes is wearing them.

claim, claims, claiming, claimed VERB ❶ If you claim that something is the case, you say that it is the case • *He claims to have lived in the same house all his life.* ❷ If you claim something, you ask for it because it belongs to you or you have a right to it • *Cartier claimed the land for the King of France.* ▷ NOUN ❸ a statement that something is the case, or that you have a right to something • *She will make a claim for damages.*
- SIMILAR WORDS: ❶ allege, assert, maintain

claimant, claimants NOUN someone who is making a claim, especially for money.

clairvoyant, clairvoyants ADJECTIVE ❶ able to know about things that will happen in the future ▷ NOUN ❷ a person who is, or claims to be, clairvoyant.
- WORD HISTORY: from French *clair* + *voyant* meaning 'clear-seeing'

clam, clams NOUN a kind of shellfish.

clamber, clambers, clambering, clambered VERB If you clamber somewhere, you climb there with difficulty.

clammy, clammier, clammiest ADJECTIVE unpleasantly damp and sticky • *clammy hands.*

clamour, clamours, clamouring, clamoured VERB ❶ If people clamour for something, they demand it noisily or angrily • *We clamoured for an explanation.* ▷ NOUN ❷ Clamour is noisy or angry shouts or demands by a lot of people.

clamp, clamps, clamping, clamped NOUN ❶ an object with movable parts that are used to hold two things firmly together ▷ VERB ❷ To clamp things together is to fasten them or hold them firmly with a clamp.
clamp down on VERB To clamp down on something is to become stricter in controlling it • *The Queen has clamped down on all expenditure.*

clan, clans NOUN a group of families related to each other by being descended from the same ancestor.

clandestine ADJECTIVE secret and hidden • *a clandestine meeting with friends.*

clang, clangs, clanging, clanged VERB When something metal clangs or when you clang it, it makes a loud, deep sound.

clank, clanks, clanking, clanked VERB If something metal clanks, it makes a loud noise.

clap, claps, clapping, clapped VERB ❶ When you clap, you hit your hands together loudly to show your appreciation. ❷ If you clap someone on the back or shoulder, you hit them in a friendly way. ❸ If you clap something somewhere, you put it there quickly and firmly • *I clapped a hand over her mouth.* ▷ NOUN ❹ a sound made by clapping your hands. ❺ A clap of thunder is a sudden loud noise of thunder.

clapper, clappers NOUN A clapper is a small piece of metal that hangs inside a bell and strikes the side to make the bell sound.

claret, clarets NOUN a type of red wine, especially one from the Bordeaux region of France.

clarify, clarifies, clarifying, clarified VERB (EXAM TERM) To clarify something is to make it clear and easier to understand • *Discussion will clarify your thoughts.* **clarification** NOUN

clarinet, clarinets NOUN (MUSIC) a woodwind instrument with a straight tube and a single reed in its mouthpiece.

clarity NOUN The clarity of something is its clearness.

clash, clashes, clashing, clashed VERB ❶ If people clash with each other, they fight or argue. ❷ Ideas or styles that clash are so different that they do not go together. ❸ If two events clash, they happen at the same time so you cannot go to both. ❹ When metal objects clash, they hit each other with a loud noise ▷ NOUN ❺ a fight or argument. ❻ A clash of ideas, styles, or events is a situation in which they do not go together. ❼ a loud noise made by metal objects when they hit each other.

clasp, clasps, clasping, clasped VERB ❶ To clasp something means to hold it tightly or fasten it • *He clasped his hands.* ▷ NOUN ❷ a fastening such as a hook or catch.

class, classes, classing, classed NOUN ❶ A class of people or things is a group of them of a particular type or quality • *the old class of politicians.* ❷ a group of pupils or students taught together, or a lesson that they have together. ❸ Someone who has class is elegant in appearance or behaviour. ❹ (SCIENCE) A class is a major division of living organisms that is smaller than a phylum and larger than an order ▷ VERB ❺ To class something means to arrange it in a particular group or to consider it as belonging to a particular group • *They are officially classed as visitors.*
● SIMILAR WORDS: ❶ category, ● group, kind, type

classic, classics ADJECTIVE ❶ typical and therefore a good model or example of something • *a classic* case of misuse. ❷ of very high quality • *one of the classic films of all time.* ❸ simple in style and form • *the classic dinner suit.* ▷ **NOUN** ❹ something of the highest quality • *one of the great classics of rock music.* ❺ Classics is the study of Latin and Greek, and the literature of ancient Greece and Rome.

classical **ADJECTIVE** ❶ traditional in style, form, and content • *classical ballet.* ❷ Classical music is serious music considered to be of lasting value. ❸ characteristic of the style of ancient Greece and Rome • *Classical friezes decorate the walls.* **classically** **ADVERB**

classified **ADJECTIVE** officially declared secret by the government • *access to classified information.*

classify, classifies, classifying, classified (**LIBRARY**) **VERB** To classify things is to arrange them into groups with similar characteristics • *We can classify the differences into three groups.* **classification** **NOUN**

classroom, classrooms **NOUN** a room in a school where pupils have lessons.

classy, classier, classiest **ADJECTIVE** INFORMAL stylish and elegant.

clatter, clatters, clattering, clattered **VERB** ❶ When things clatter, they hit each other with a loud rattling noise ▷ **NOUN** ❷ a loud rattling noise made by hard things hitting each other.

clause, clauses **NOUN** ❶ a section of a legal document. ❷ (**ENGLISH**) In grammar, a clause is a group of words with a subject and a verb, which may be a complete sentence or one of the parts of a sentence.
▶ SEE GRAMMAR BOX ON PAGE 151

claustrophobia *[Said klos-trof-foe-bee-ya]* **NOUN** Claustrophobia is a fear of being in enclosed spaces. **claustrophobic** **ADJECTIVE**

claw, claws, clawing, clawed **NOUN** ❶ An animal's claws are hard, curved nails at the end of its feet. ❷ The claws of a crab or lobster are the two jointed parts, used for grasping things ▷ **VERB** ❸ If an animal claws something, it digs its claws into it.

clay **NOUN** Clay is a type of earth that is soft and sticky when wet and hard when baked dry. It is used to make pottery and bricks.

clean, cleaner, cleanest; cleans, cleaning, cleaned **ADJECTIVE** ❶ free from dirt or marks. ❷ clean from germs or infection. ❸ If humour is clean it is not rude and does not involve bad language. ❹ A clean movement is skilful and accurate. ❺ Clean also means free from fault or error • *a clean driving licence.* ▷ **VERB** ❻ To clean something is to remove dirt from it. **cleanly** **ADVERB** **cleaner** **NOUN**

cleanliness *[Said klen-lin-ness]* **NOUN** Cleanliness is the practice of keeping yourself and your surroundings clean.

cleanse, cleanses, cleansing, cleansed *[Said klenz]* **VERB** To cleanse something is to make it completely free from dirt.

clear, clearer, clearest; clears, clearing, cleared **ADJECTIVE** ❶ easy to understand, see, or hear • *He made*

WHAT IS A CLAUSE?

A **clause** is a group of words which form part of a sentence and express an idea or describe a situation. A clause often gives information about the main idea or situation:
*Matthew ate a cake **which was covered in chocolate***.
*Anna crossed the street **after looking carefully in both directions***.

MAIN CLAUSES AND SUBORDINATE CLAUSES

Clauses can be either **main clauses** or **subordinate clauses**.

A **main clause** is the core of a sentence. It would make sense if it stood on its own. Every sentence contains a main clause:
***Matthew ate a cake** which was covered in chocolate*.
After looking carefully in both

*directions, **Anna crossed the road***.

A **subordinate clause** is a less important part of a sentence. It would not make sense on its own, but gives information about the main clause:
***After looking carefully**, Anna crossed the road*.
*Anna had to cross the road, **which was often very busy***.

RELATIVE CLAUSES

Relative clauses give additional information about a person or thing mentioned in the main clause.

Relative clauses are introduced by a relative pronoun — *who, whom, whose, which* or *that*:
*Robbie has a cat **who likes fish***.
*Anna has one sister, **whose name is Rosie***.

it clear he did not want to talk. ❷ easy to see through • *a clear liquid*. ❸ free from obstructions or unwanted things • *clear of snow*. ▷ **VERB** ❹ To clear an area is to remove unwanted things from it. ❺ If you clear a fence or other obstacle, you jump over it without touching it. ❻ When fog or mist clears, it disappears. ❼ If someone is cleared of a crime, they are proved to be not guilty. **clearly ADVERB**
clear up VERB ❶ If you clear up, you tidy a place and put things away. ❷ When a problem or misunderstanding is cleared up, it is solved or settled.

● **SIMILAR WORDS:** ❶ evident, obvious, plain

clearance NOUN ❶ Clearance is the removal of old buildings in an area. ❷ If someone is given clearance to do something, they get official permission to do it.

clearing, clearings **NOUN** an area of bare ground in a forest.

cleavage, cleavages **NOUN** the space between a woman's breasts.

cleaver, cleavers **NOUN** a knife with a large square blade, used especially by butchers.

cleft, clefts **NOUN** a narrow opening in a rock.

cleft palate, cleft palates **NOUN** (SCIENCE) Someone with a cleft palate

▷ SPELLING NOTE: *King IAn went to ParlIAment in a carrIAge for his marrIAge (-ia-)*

A
B
C
D
E
F
G
H
I
J
K
L
M
N
O
P
Q
R
S
T
U
V
W
X
Y
Z

was born with a narrow opening along the roof of their mouth which makes it difficult for them to speak.

clementine, clementines **NOUN** a type of small citrus fruit that is a cross between an orange and a tangerine.

clench, clenches, clenching, clenched **VERB** ❶ When you clench your fist, you curl your fingers up tightly. ❷ When you clench your teeth, you squeeze them together tightly.

clergy **PLURAL NOUN** The clergy are the ministers of the Christian Church.

clergyman, clergymen **NOUN** a male member of the clergy.

clerical **ADJECTIVE** ❶ relating to work done in an office • *clerical jobs with the City Council.* ❷ relating to the clergy.

clerihew, clerihews **NOUN** (ENGLISH) a kind of humorous poem that has two rhyming couplets and an irregular metre.

clerk, clerks *[Said klahrk]* **NOUN** a person who keeps records or accounts in an office, bank, or law court.

clever, cleverer, cleverest **ADJECTIVE** ❶ intelligent and quick to understand things. ❷ very effective or skilful • *a clever plan.* **cleverly** **ADVERB** **cleverness** **NOUN**
● SIMILAR WORDS: ❶ bright,
● intelligent, smart

clianthus *[Said klee-an-thuss]* **NOUN** A clianthus is a plant found in Australia and New Zealand which has clusters of scarlet flowers.

cliché, clichés *[Said klee-shay]* **NOUN** (ENGLISH) an idea or phrase which is no longer effective because it has been used so much.

click, clicks, clicking, clicked **VERB** ❶ When something clicks or when you click it, it makes a short snapping sound. ❷ When you click on an area of a computer screen, you point the cursor at it and press one of the buttons on the mouse in order to make something happen ▷ **NOUN** ❸ a sound of something clicking • *I heard the click of a bolt.*

client, clients **NOUN** someone who pays a professional person or company for a service.

clientele *[Said klee-on-tell]* **PLURAL NOUN** The clientele of a place is its customers.

cliff, cliffs **NOUN** a steep high rock face by the sea.

climate, climates **NOUN** ❶ (GEOGRAPHY) The climate of a place is the typical weather conditions there • *The climate was dry in the summer.* ❷ the general attitude and opinion of people at a particular time • *the American political climate.* **climatic** **ADJECTIVE**

climax, climaxes **NOUN** (ENGLISH) The climax of a process, story, or piece of music is the most exciting moment in it, usually near the end.
● WORD HISTORY: from Greek
● *klimax* meaning 'ladder'

climb, climbs, climbing, climbed **VERB** ❶ To climb is to move upwards. ❷ If you climb somewhere, you move there with difficulty • *She climbed out of the driving seat.* ▷ **NOUN** ❸ a movement upwards • *this long climb up the slope* • *the rapid climb in*

▷ SPELLING NOTE: an ELegant angEL (ang**el**)

murders. **climber NOUN**

clinch, clinches, clinching, clinched
VERB If you clinch an agreement or
an argument, you settle it in a definite
way • *Peter clinched a deal.*

cling, clings, clinging, clung **VERB** To
cling to something is to hold onto it or
stay closely attached to it • *still
clinging to old-fashioned values.*

clingfilm NOUN TRADEMARK a clear
thin plastic used for wrapping food.

clinic, clinics **NOUN** a building where
people go for medical treatment.

clinical ADJECTIVE ❶ relating to
the medical treatment of patients
• *clinical tests.* **❷** Clinical behaviour or
thought is logical and unemotional
• *the cold, clinical attitudes of his
colleagues.* **clinically ADVERB**

clip, clips, clipping, clipped **NOUN**
❶ a small metal or plastic object used
for holding things together. **❷** a short
piece of a film shown by itself ▷ **VERB**
❸ If you clip things together, you
fasten them with clips. **❹** If you clip
something, you cut bits from it to
shape it • *clipped hedges.*

clippers PLURAL NOUN Clippers
are tools used for cutting.

clipping, clippings **NOUN** an article
cut from a newspaper or magazine.

clique, cliques [rhymes with **seek**]
NOUN a small group of people who
stick together and do not mix with
other people.

clitoris, clitorises [Said **klit**-tor-riss]
NOUN a small highly sensitive piece
of flesh near the opening of a
woman's vagina.

cloak, cloaks, cloaking, cloaked
NOUN ❶ a wide, loose coat without
sleeves ▷ **VERB ❷** To cloak
something is to cover or hide it • *a
land permanently cloaked in mist.*

cloakroom, cloakrooms **NOUN** a
room for coats or a room with toilets
and washbasins in a public building.

clock, clocks **NOUN ❶** a device that
measures and shows the time
▷ **PHRASE ❷** If you work **round the
clock**, you work all day and night.

clockwise ADJECTIVE OR ADVERB
in the same direction as the hands on
a clock.

clockwork NOUN ❶ Toys that
work by clockwork move when they
are wound up with a key ▷ **PHRASE
❷** If something happens **like
clockwork**, it happens with no
problems or delays.

clog, clogs, clogging, clogged **VERB**
❶ To clog something is to block it
• *pavements clogged up with people.*
▷ **NOUN ❷** Clogs are heavy wooden
shoes.

cloister, cloisters **NOUN** a covered
area in a monastery or a cathedral for
walking around a square.

clone, clones, cloning, cloned
(SCIENCE) **NOUN ❶** In biology, a
clone is an animal or plant that has
been produced artificially from the
cells of another animal or plant and is
therefore identical to it ▷ **VERB ❷** To
clone an animal or plant is to produce
it as a clone.

close, closes, closing, closed; closer,
closest **VERB ❶** To close something
is to shut it. **❷** To close a road or

a
b
c
d
e
f
g
h
i
j
k
l
m
n
o
p
q
r
s
t
u
v
w
x
y
z

▷ SPELLING NOTE: *LEt's measure the angLE (angle)*

entrance is to block it so that no-one can go in or out. ❸ If a shop closes at a certain time, then it does not do business after that time ▷ **ADJECTIVE OR ADVERB** ❹ near to something • *a restaurant close to their home.* ▷ **ADJECTIVE** ❺ People who are close to each other are very friendly and know each other well. ❻ You say the weather is close when it is uncomfortably warm and there is not enough air. **closely ADVERB closeness NOUN closed ADJECTIVE close down VERB** If a business closes down, all work stops there permanently.

● **SIMILAR WORDS:** ❹ near, nearby

closed shop, closed shops **NOUN** a factory or other business whose employees have to be members of a trade union.

closet, closets, closeting, closeted **NOUN** ❶ a cupboard ▷ **VERB** ❷ If you are closeted somewhere, you shut yourself away alone or in private with another person ▷ **ADJECTIVE** ❸ Closet beliefs or habits are kept private and secret • *a closet romantic.*

close-up, close-ups **NOUN** a detailed close view of something, especially a photograph taken close to the subject.

closure, closures [Said **klohz**-yur] **NOUN** ❶ The closure of a business is the permanent shutting of it. ❷ The closure of a road is the blocking of it so it cannot be used.

clot, clots, clotting, clotted **NOUN** ❶ a lump, especially one that forms when blood thickens ▷ **VERB** ❷ When a substance such as blood clots, it thickens and forms a lump.

cloth, cloths **NOUN** ❶ Cloth is fabric made by a process such as weaving. ❷ a piece of material used for wiping or protecting things.

clothe, clothes, clothing, clothed **VERB** To clothe someone is to give them clothes to wear.

clothes PLURAL NOUN the things people wear on their bodies.

clothing NOUN the clothes people wear.

cloud, clouds, clouding, clouded **NOUN** ❶ a mass of water vapour, smoke, or dust that forms in the air and is seen floating in the sky ▷ **VERB** ❷ If something clouds or is clouded, it becomes cloudy or difficult to see through • *The sky clouded over.* ❸ Something that clouds an issue makes it more confusing.

cloudy, cloudier, cloudiest **ADJECTIVE** ❶ full of clouds • *the cloudy sky.* ❷ difficult to see through • *a glass of cloudy liquid.*
● **SIMILAR WORDS:** ❶ dull, ● overcast

clout NOUN INFORMAL Someone who has clout has influence.

clove, cloves **NOUN** ❶ Cloves are small, strong-smelling dried flower buds from a tropical tree, used as a spice in cooking. ❷ A clove of garlic is one of the separate sections of the bulb.

clover NOUN Clover is a small plant with leaves made up of three similar parts.

clown, clowns, clowning, clowned **NOUN** ❶ a circus performer who wears funny clothes and make-up and does silly things to make people laugh ▷ **VERB ②** If you clown, you do silly things to make people laugh.

cloying ADJECTIVE unpleasantly sickly, sweet, or sentimental • *something less cloying than whipped cream.*

club, clubs, clubbing, clubbed **NOUN ①** an organization of people with a particular interest, who meet regularly; also the place where they meet. **②** a thick, heavy stick used as a weapon. **③** a stick with a shaped head that a golf player uses to hit the ball. **④** Clubs is one of the four suits in a pack of playing cards. It is marked by a black symbol in the shape of a clover leaf ▷ **VERB ⑤** To club someone is to hit them hard with a heavy object.
club together VERB If people club together, they all join together to give money to buy something.
● **SIMILAR WORDS: ①** association,
● group, society

cluck, clucks, clucking, clucked **VERB** When a hen clucks, it makes a short, repeated, high-pitched sound.

clue, clues **NOUN** something that helps to solve a problem or mystery.

clump, clumps, clumping, clumped **NOUN ①** a small group of things close together ▷ **VERB ②** If you clump about, you walk with heavy footsteps.

clumsiness NOUN awkwardness in the way someone or something moves.

clumsy, clumsier, clumsiest **ADJECTIVE ①** moving awkwardly and carelessly. **②** said or done without thought or tact • *his clumsy attempts to*

catch her out. **clumsily ADVERB**
● **SIMILAR WORDS: ①** awkward,
● gauche, ungainly

cluster, clusters, clustering, clustered **NOUN ①** A cluster of things is a group of them together • *a cluster of huts at the foot of the mountains.* ▷ **VERB ②** If people cluster together, they stay together in a close group.

clutch, clutches, clutching, clutched **VERB ①** If you clutch something, you hold it tightly or seize it **②** IN PLURAL If you are in someone's clutches, they have power or control over you.

clutter, clutters, cluttering, cluttered **NOUN ①** Clutter is an untidy mess ▷ **VERB ②** Things that clutter a place fill it and make it untidy.

cm an abbreviation for 'centimetres'.

CO- PREFIX 'Co-' means 'together' • *Paula is now co-writing a book with Pierre.*

coach, coaches, coaching, coached **NOUN ①** a long motor vehicle used for taking passengers on long journeys. **②** a section of a train that carries passengers. **③** a four-wheeled vehicle with a roof pulled by horses, which people used to travel in. **④** a person who coaches a sport or a subject ▷ **VERB ⑤** If someone coaches you, they teach you and help you to get better at a sport or a subject.
● **SIMILAR WORDS: ④** instructor,
● trainer **⑤** instruct, train

coal, coals **NOUN ①** Coal is a hard black rock obtained from under the earth and burned as a fuel. **②** Coals are burning pieces of coal.

▷ SPELLING NOTE: *Beautiful Elephants Are Usually Tiny (beautiful)*

coalition, coalitions **NOUN** a temporary alliance, especially between different political parties forming a government.

coarse, coarser, coarsest **ADJECTIVE** ❶ Something that is coarse is rough in texture, often consisting of large particles • *a coarse blanket*. ❷ Someone who is coarse talks or behaves in a rude or rather offensive way. **coarsely ADVERB coarseness NOUN**

coast, coasts, coasting, coasted **NOUN** ❶ the edge of the land where it meets the sea ▷ **VERB** ❷ A vehicle that is coasting is moving without engine power. **coastal ADJECTIVE**

coastguard, coastguards **NOUN** an official who watches the sea near a coast to get help for sailors when they need it, and to prevent smuggling.

coastline, coastlines **NOUN** the outline of a coast, especially its appearance as seen from the sea or air.

coat, coats, coating, coated **NOUN** ❶ a piece of clothing with sleeves which you wear over your other clothes. ❷ An animal's coat is the fur or hair on its body. ❸ A coat of paint or varnish is a layer of it ▷ **VERB** ❹ To coat something means to cover it with a thin layer of a something • *walnuts coated with chocolate*.

coat hanger, coat hangers **NOUN** a curved piece of wood, metal, or plastic that you hang clothes on.

coating, coatings **NOUN** a layer of something.

coax, coaxes, coaxing, coaxed **VERB** If you coax someone to do something,

you gently persuade them to do it.
● **SIMILAR WORDS:** cajole,
● persuade, talk into, wheedle

cobalt NOUN Cobalt is a hard silvery-white metal which is used for producing a blue dye.

cobble, cobbles **NOUN** Cobbles or cobblestones are stones with a rounded surface that were used in the past for making roads.

cobbler, cobblers **NOUN** a person who makes or mends shoes.

cobra, cobras [*Said koh-bra*] **NOUN** a type of large poisonous snake from Africa and Asia.

cobweb, cobwebs **NOUN** the very thin net that a spider spins for catching insects.

cocaine NOUN Cocaine is an addictive drug.

coccyx, coccyxes [*Said kok-siks*] **NOUN** (SCIENCE) In anatomy, the coccyx is the small triangular bone at the bottom of the spine in humans and some apes.

cock, cocks **NOUN** an adult male chicken; also used of any male bird.

cockatoo, cockatoos **NOUN** a type of parrot with a crest, found in Australia and New Guinea.

cockerel, cockerels **NOUN** a young cock.

Cockney, Cockneys **NOUN** a person born in the East End of London.

cockpit, cockpits **NOUN** The place in a small plane where the pilot sits.

cockroach, cockroaches **NOUN** a large dark-coloured insect that is often found in dirty rooms.

cocktail, cocktails NOUN an alcoholic drink made from several ingredients.

cocky, cockier, cockiest; cockies INFORMAL ADJECTIVE ❶ cheeky or too self-confident ▷ NOUN ❷ in Australian English, a cockatoo. ❸ in Australian and New Zealand English, a farmer, especially one whose farm is small. **cockiness** NOUN

cocoa NOUN Cocoa is a brown powder made from the seeds of a tropical tree and used for making chocolate; also a hot drink made from this powder.

coconut, coconuts NOUN a very large nut with white flesh, milky juice, and a hard hairy shell.

cocoon, cocoons NOUN a silky covering over the larvae of moths and some other insects.
- **WORD HISTORY:** from Provençal *coucoun* meaning 'eggshell'

cod, cod NOUN a large edible fish.
- **USAGE NOTE:** The plural of *cod* is also *cod*

coda, codas NOUN (MUSIC) a passage of music at the end of a section, for example at the end of a movement in a concerto.
- **WORD HISTORY:** an Italian word meaning 'tail'

code, codes NOUN ❶ a system of replacing the letters or words in a message with other letters or words, so that nobody can understand the message unless they know the system. ❷ a group of numbers and letters which is used to identify

something • *the telephone code for Melbourne.* **coded** ADJECTIVE

coexist, coexists, coexisting, coexisted VERB When two or more things coexist, they exist together in the same place or at the same time. **coexistence** NOUN **coexistent** ADJECTIVE

coffee NOUN Coffee is a substance made by roasting and grinding the beans of a tropical shrub; also a hot drink made from this substance.
- **WORD HISTORY:** from Arabic *qahwah* meaning 'wine' or 'coffee'

coffin, coffins NOUN a box in which a dead body is buried or cremated.

cog, cogs NOUN a wheel with teeth which turns another wheel or part of a machine.

cognac, cognacs [Said **kon**-yak] NOUN Cognac is a kind of brandy.

coherent ADJECTIVE ❶ If something such as a theory is coherent, its parts fit together well and do not contradict each other. ❷ If someone is coherent, what they are saying makes sense and is not jumbled or confused. **coherence** NOUN

cohesive ADJECTIVE If something is cohesive, its parts fit together well • *The team must work as a cohesive unit.* **cohesion** NOUN

coil, coils, coiling, coiled NOUN ❶ a length of rope or wire wound into a series of loops; also one of the loops ▷ VERB ❷ If something coils, it turns into a series of loops.

coin, coins, coining, coined NOUN ❶ a small metal disc which is used as

a
b
c
d
e
f
g
h
i
j
k
l
m
n
o
p
q
r
s
t
u
v
w
x
y
z

money ▷ **VERB** ❷ If you coin a word or a phrase, you invent it.

coinage NOUN The coinage of a country is the coins that are used there.

coincide, coincides, coinciding, coincided **VERB** ❶ If two events coincide, they happen at about the same time. ❷ When two people's ideas or opinions coincide, they agree • *What she said coincided exactly with his own thinking.*

coincidence, coincidences **NOUN** ❶ what happens when two similar things occur at the same time by chance • *I had moved to London, and by coincidence, Helen had too.* ❷ the fact that two things are surprisingly the same. **coincidental ADJECTIVE coincidentally ADVERB**

coke NOUN Coke is a grey fuel produced from coal.

colander, colanders [*Said* **kol***-an-der*] **NOUN** a bowl-shaped container with holes in it, used for washing or draining food.

cold, colder, coldest; colds **ADJECTIVE** ❶ having a low temperature. ❷ Someone who is cold does not show much affection ▷ **NOUN** ❸ You can refer to cold weather as the cold • *She was complaining about the cold.* ❹ a minor illness in which you sneeze and may have a sore throat. **coldly ADVERB coldness NOUN**

cold-blooded ADJECTIVE ❶ Someone who is cold-blooded does not show any pity • *two cold-blooded killers.* ❷ A cold-blooded animal has a body temperature that changes according to the temperature of its surrounding environment.

cold war NOUN Cold war is a state of extreme unfriendliness between countries not actually at war.

coleslaw NOUN Coleslaw is a salad of chopped cabbage and other vegetables in mayonnaise.
● **WORD HISTORY:** from Dutch
● *koolsla* meaning 'cabbage salad'

colic NOUN Colic is pain in a baby's stomach.

collaborate, collaborates, collaborating, collaborated **VERB** When people collaborate, they work together to produce something • *The two bands have collaborated in the past.* **collaboration NOUN collaborator NOUN**

collage, collages [*Said* **kol***-lahj*] **NOUN** (ART) a picture made by sticking pieces of paper or cloth onto a surface.

collapse, collapses, collapsing, collapsed **VERB** ❶ If something such as a building collapses, it falls down suddenly. If a person collapses, they fall down suddenly because they are ill. ❷ If something such as a system or a business collapses, it suddenly stops working • *50,000 small firms collapsed last year.* ▷ **NOUN** ❸ The collapse of something is what happens when it stops working • *the collapse of his marriage.*

collapsible ADJECTIVE A collapsible object can be folded flat when it is not in use • *a collapsible ironing board.*

collar, collars **NOUN** ❶ The collar of a shirt or coat is the part round the neck which is usually folded over. **2** a leather band round the neck of a dog or cat.

collarbone, collarbones NOUN (SCIENCE) Your collarbones are the two long bones which run from the base of your neck to your shoulders.

collateral NOUN Collateral is money or property which is used as a guarantee that someone will repay a loan, and which the lender can take if the loan is not repaid.

colleague, colleagues NOUN A person's colleagues are the people he or she works with.

collect, collects, collecting, collected VERB **1** To collect things is to gather them together for a special purpose or as a hobby • *collecting money for charity*. **2** If you collect someone or something from a place, you call there and take them away • *We had to collect her from school.* **3** When things collect in a place, they gather there over a period of time • *Food collects in holes in the teeth.* **collector** NOUN

collected ADJECTIVE calm and self-controlled.

collection, collections NOUN **1** (ART) a group of things acquired over a period of time • *a collection of paintings*. **2** Collection is the collecting of something • *tax collection*. **3** the organized collecting of money, for example for charity, or the sum of money collected.
● **SIMILAR WORDS:**
● **1** accumulation, compilation, set

collective, collectives ADJECTIVE **1** involving every member of a group of people • *The wine growers took a collective decision.* ▷ NOUN **2** a group of people who share the responsibility both for running something and for doing the work. **collectively** ADVERB

collective noun, collective nouns NOUN a noun that refers to a single unit made up of a number of things, for example 'flock' and 'swarm'.

college, colleges NOUN **1** a place where students study after they have left school. **2** a name given to some secondary schools. **3** one of the institutions into which some universities are divided. **4** In New Zealand English, a college can also refer to a teacher training college.

collide, collides, colliding, collided VERB If a moving object collides with something, it hits it.

collie, collies NOUN a dog that is used for rounding up sheep.

colliery, collieries NOUN a coal mine.

collision, collisions NOUN A collision occurs when a moving object hits something.
● **SIMILAR WORDS:** crash, impact,
● smash

colloquial [Said kol-*loh*-kwee-al] ADJECTIVE Colloquial words and phrases are informal and used especially in conversation. **colloquially** ADVERB **colloquialism** NOUN

cologne [Said kol-*lone*] NOUN Cologne is a kind of weak perfume.

colon, colons NOUN **1** the punctuation mark (:). **2** part of your intestine.
▶ SEE GRAMMAR BOX ON PAGE 160

a
b
c
d
e
f
g
h
i
j
k
l
m
n
o
p
q
r
s
t
u
v
w
x
y
z

▷ SPELLING NOTE: *I always visit my FRIend on a FRIday (Friday)*

WHAT DOES THE COLON DO?

The **colon** (:) and the **semicolon** (;) are often confused and used incorrectly.

The **colon** is used to introduce a list:
I bought fruit: pears, apples, grapes and plums.

The colon can also be used to introduce a quotation:
He received a message which read: "You

can't fool all of the people all of the time."

Another use of the colon is to introduce an explanation of a statement:
They did not enjoy the meal: the food was cold.

Also look at the grammar box at **semicolon**.

---

colonel, colonels [Said **kur**-nl] NOUN an army officer with a fairly high rank.

colonial ADJECTIVE ❶ relating to a colony. ❷ In Australia, colonial is used to relate to the period of Australian history before the Federation in 1901.

colonize, colonizes, colonizing, colonized; *also spelt* colonise VERB (HISTORY) When people colonize a place, they go to live there and take control of it • *the Europeans who colonized North America.* When a lot of animals colonize a place, they go there and make it their home • *Toads are colonizing the whole place.*
colonization NOUN **colonist** NOUN

colony, colonies NOUN (HISTORY) ❶ a country controlled by a more powerful country. ❷ a group of people who settle in a country controlled by their homeland.

colossal ADJECTIVE very large indeed.

colour, colours, colouring, coloured NOUN ❶ (ART) the appearance something has as a result of reflecting

light. ❷ a substance used to give colour. ❸ Someone's colour is the normal colour of their skin. ❹ Colour is also a quality that makes something interesting or exciting • *bringing more culture and colour to the city.* ▷ VERB ❺ If you colour something, you give it a colour. ❻ If something colours your opinion, it affects the way you think about something. **coloured** ADJECTIVE **colourless** ADJECTIVE **colouring** NOUN
● SIMILAR WORDS: ❶ hue, shade, ● tint

colour blind ADJECTIVE Someone who is colour blind cannot distinguish between colours.

colourful ADJECTIVE ❶ full of colour. ❷ interesting or exciting. **colourfully** ADVERB

colt, colts NOUN a young male horse.

column, columns NOUN ❶ a tall solid upright cylinder, especially one supporting a part of a building. ❷ a group of people moving in a long line.

columnist, columnists NOUN a journalist who writes a regular article in a newspaper or magazine.

▷ SPELLING NOTE: *I want to see (C) your licenCe (licence)*

coma, comas **NOUN** Someone who is in a coma is in a state of deep unconsciousness.

comb, combs, combing, combed **NOUN** ❶ a flat object with pointed teeth used for tidying your hair ▷ **VERB** ❷ When you comb your hair, you tidy it with a comb. ❸ If you comb a place, you search it thoroughly to try to find someone or something.

combat, combats, combating, combated **NOUN** ❶ Combat is fighting • *his first experience of combat.* ▷ **VERB** ❷ To combat something means to try to stop it happening or developing • *a way to combat crime.*

combination, combinations **NOUN** ❶ a mixture of things • *a combination of charm and skill.* ❷ a series of letters or numbers used to open a special lock.

combine, combines, combining, combined **VERB** ❶ To combine things is to cause them to exist together • *to combine a career with being a mother.* ❷ To combine things also means to join them together to make a single thing • *Combine all the ingredients.* ❸ If something combines two qualities or features, it has them both • *a film that combines great charm and scintillating performances.*

combustion **NOUN** (SCIENCE) Combustion is the act of burning something or the process of burning.

come, comes, coming, came, come **VERB** ❶ To come to a place is to move there or arrive there. ❷ To come to a place also means to reach as far as that place • *The sea water came up to his waist.* ❸ 'Come' is used

to say that someone or something reaches a particular state • *They came to power in 1997* • *We had come to a decision.* ❹ When a particular time or event comes, it happens • *The peak of his career came early in 1990.* ❺ If you come from a place, you were born there or it is your home ▷ **PHRASE** ❻ A time or event **to come** is a future time or event • *The public will thank them in years to come.*

come about **VERB** The way something comes about is the way it happens • *The discussion came about because of the proposed changes.*

come across **VERB** If you come across something, you find it by chance.

come off **VERB** If something comes off, it succeeds • *His rescue plan had come off.*

come on **VERB** If something is coming on, it is making progress • *Let's go and see how the grapes are coming on.*

come up **VERB** If something comes up in a conversation or meeting, it is mentioned or discussed.

come up with **VERB** If you come up with a plan or idea, you suggest it.

comeback, comebacks **NOUN** To make a comeback means to be popular or successful again.

comedian, comedians **NOUN** an entertainer whose job is to make people laugh.

comedienne, comediennes *[Said kom-mee-dee-en]* **NOUN** a female comedian.

comedy, comedies **NOUN** a light-hearted play or film with a happy ending.

a
b
c
d
e
f
g
h
i
j
k
l
m
n
o
p
q
r
s
t
u
v
w
x
y
z

▷ SPELLING NOTE: *The government licenSes Schnapps (licenses)*

A B C D E F G H I J K L M N O P Q R S T U V W X Y Z

● **WORD HISTORY:** from Greek
● *kōmos* meaning 'village festival' and
● *aeidein* meaning 'to sing'

comet, comets **NOUN** an object that travels around the sun leaving a bright trail behind it.

comfort, comforts, comforting, comforted **NOUN** ❶ Comfort is the state of being physically relaxed • *He settled back in comfort.* ❷ Comfort is also a feeling of relief from worries or unhappiness • *The thought is a great comfort to me.* ❸ IN PLURAL Comforts are things which make your life easier and more pleasant • *all the comforts of home.* ▷ **VERB** ❹ To comfort someone is to make them less worried or unhappy.

comfortable ADJECTIVE ❶ If you are comfortable, you are physically relaxed. ❷ Something that is comfortable makes you feel relaxed • *a comfortable bed.* ❸ If you feel comfortable in a particular situation, you are not afraid or embarrassed. **comfortably ADVERB**

comic ADJECTIVE ❶ funny • *a comic monologue.* ▷ **NOUN** ❷ someone who tells jokes. ❸ a magazine that contains stories told in pictures.

comical ADJECTIVE funny • *a comical sight.*

comma, commas **NOUN** (ENGLISH) the punctuation mark (,).
▶ SEE GRAMMAR BOX BELOW

WHAT DOES THE COMMA DO?

The **comma** (,) indicates a short pause between different elements within a sentence. This happens, for example, when a sentence consists of two main clauses joined by a conjunction:
Anna likes swimming, but Matthew prefers fishing.

A comma may also separate an introductory phrase or a subordinate clause from the main clause in a sentence:
After a month of sunshine, it rained on Thursday.

However, a short introductory phrase does not need to be followed by a comma:
After lunch the classes continued.

When words such as *therefore*, *however*, and *moreover* are put into a

sentence to show how a train of thought is progressing, they should be marked off by commas:
We are confident, however, that the operation will be successful.

The comma also separates items in a list or series:
I made this soup with carrots, leeks, and potatoes.

Commas separate the name of a person or people being addressed from the rest of the sentence:
Thank you, ladies and gentlemen, for your attention.

The comma also separates words in quotation marks from the rest of the sentence, if there is no question or exclamation mark at the end of the quotation:
"This is a terrific picture," she said.

▷ SPELLING NOTE: *have a plEce of plE (piece)*

WHAT IS A COMMAND?

Commands are used to give orders, instructions, or warnings.

Commands are made by putting the verb at the start of the sentence. The verb is used in its **imperative form** which is the basic form without any endings added:
Come over here.

Commands do not need a subject, as people who are being told to do something already know who they

are. So commands may consist of a single verb: *Stop!*

The negative form of a command is introduced by *do not* or *don't*:
Don't put that on the table.

Commands often end with an exclamation mark rather than a full stop, especially if they express urgency:
Run for your life!

command, commands, commanding, commanded **VERB**
① To command someone to do something is to order them to do it. **②** If you command something such as respect, you receive it because of your personal qualities. **③** An officer who commands part of an army or navy is in charge of it ▷ **NOUN** **④** an order to do something. **⑤** Your command of something is your knowledge of it and your ability to use this knowledge • *a good command of English.*
● **SIMILAR WORDS: ①** direct, order
▶ SEE GRAMMAR BOX ABOVE

commandant, commandants
[Said **kom-man-dant**] **NOUN** an army officer in charge of a place or group of people.

commander, commanders **NOUN** an officer in charge of a military operation or organization.

commandment, commandments **NOUN** RE The commandments are the ten rules of behaviour that, according to the Old Testament, people should

obey to live properly.

commando, commandos **NOUN** Commandos are soldiers who have been specially trained to carry out raids.

commemorate, commemorates, commemorating, commemorated **VERB** **①** An object that commemorates a person or an event is intended to remind people of that person or event. **②** If you commemorate an event, you do something special to show that you remember it. **commemorative ADJECTIVE commemoration NOUN**

commence, commences, commencing, commenced **VERB** FORMAL To commence is to begin. **commencement NOUN**

commend, commends, commending, commended **VERB** To commend someone or something is to praise them • *He has been commended for his work.* **commendation NOUN commendable ADJECTIVE**

comment, comments, commenting,

▷ SPELLING NOTE: *plaice the fish has a glittering 'EYE' (I) (plaice)*

commented VERB ❶ If you comment on something, you make a remark about it ▷ NOUN ❷ a remark about something • *She received many comments about her appearance.*
● SIMILAR WORDS: ❶ observe, ● remark

commentary, commentaries NOUN a description of an event which is broadcast on radio or television while the event is happening.

commentator, commentators NOUN someone who gives a radio or television commentary.

commerce NOUN Commerce is the buying and selling of goods.

commercial, commercials ADJECTIVE ❶ relating to commerce. ❷ Commercial activities involve producing goods on a large scale in order to make money • *the commercial fishing world.* ▷ NOUN ❸ an advertisement on television or radio. **commercially** ADVERB

commission, commissions, commissioning, commissioned VERB ❶ If someone commissions a piece of work, they formally ask someone to do it • *a study commissioned by the government.* ▷ NOUN ❷ a piece of work that has been commissioned. ❸ Commission is money paid to a salesman each time a sale is made. ❹ an official body appointed to investigate or control something.

commit, commits, committing, committed VERB ❶ To commit a crime or sin is to do it. ❷ If you commit yourself, you state an opinion or state that you will do something. ❸ If someone is committed to

hospital or prison, they are officially sent there. **committal** NOUN
● SIMILAR WORDS: ❶ do, perform, ● perpetrate

commitment, commitments NOUN ❶ RE Commitment is a strong belief in an idea or system. ❷ something that regularly takes up some of your time • *business commitments.*

committed ADJECTIVE A committed person has strong beliefs • *a committed feminist.*

committee, committees NOUN a group of people who make decisions on behalf of a larger group.

commodity, commodities NOUN FORMAL Commodities are things that are sold.

common, commoner, commonest; commons ADJECTIVE ❶ Something that is common exists in large numbers or happens often • *a common complaint.* ❷ If something is common to two or more people, they all have it or use it • *I realized we had a common interest.* ❸ 'Common' is used to indicate that something is of the ordinary kind and not special. ❹ If you describe someone as common, you mean they do not have good taste or good manners ▷ NOUN ❺ an area of grassy land where everyone can go ▷ PHRASE ❻ If two things or people have something **in common**, they both have it. **commonly** ADVERB
● SIMILAR WORDS: ❶ customary, ● frequent ❹ coarse, vulgar

commoner, commoners NOUN someone who is not a member of the nobility.

commonplace ADJECTIVE
Something that is commonplace
happens often • *Foreign holidays have
become commonplace.*

common sense NOUN Your
common sense is your natural ability
to behave sensibly and make good
judgments.

Commonwealth NOUN ❶ The
Commonwealth is an association of
countries around the world that are or
used to be ruled by Britain. ❷ a
country made up of a number of
states • *the Commonwealth of Australia.*

commotion, commotions NOUN A
commotion is a lot of noise and
excitement.

communal ADJECTIVE shared by a
group of people • *a communal canteen.*

commune, communes *[Said
kom-yoon]* NOUN a group of people
who live together and share
everything.

communicate, communicates,
communicating, communicated
VERB ❶ If you communicate with
someone, you keep in touch with
them. ❷ If you communicate
information or a feeling to someone,
you make them aware of it.
● SIMILAR WORDS: ❷ convey,
● make known

communication,
communications NOUN ❶ (PSHE)
Communication is the process by
which people or animals exchange
information ❷ IN PLURAL
Communications are the systems by
which people communicate or
broadcast information, especially
using electricity or radio waves

▷ NOUN ❸ FORMAL a letter or
telephone call.

communicative ADJECTIVE
Someone who is communicative is
willing to talk to people.

communion NOUN
❶ Communion is the sharing of
thoughts and feelings. ❷ (RE) In
Christianity, Communion is a religious
service in which people share bread
and wine in remembrance of the
death and resurrection of Jesus Christ.

communism NOUN Communism
is the doctrine that the state should
own the means of production and that
there should be no private property.
communist ADJECTIVE OR NOUN

community, communities NOUN
all the people living in a particular
area; also used to refer to particular
groups within a society • *the heart of
the local community* • *the Asian community.*

commute, commutes, commuting,
commuted VERB People who
commute travel a long distance to
work every day. **commuter** NOUN

compact ADJECTIVE taking up very
little space • *a compact microwave.*

compact disc, compact discs
NOUN a music or video recording in
the form of a plastic disc which is
played using a laser on a special
machine, and gives good quality
sound or pictures.

companion, companions NOUN
someone you travel or spend time
with. **companionship** NOUN
● WORD HISTORY: from Latin
● *com-* meaning 'together' and *panis*
● meaning 'bread'. A companion was

A
B
C
D
E
F
G
H
I
J
K
L
M
N
O
P
Q
R
S
T
U
V
W
X
Y
Z

WHAT IS A COMPARATIVE?

Many adjectives have three different forms. These are known as the **positive**, the **comparative**, and the **superlative**. The comparative and superlative are used when you make comparisons.

The **positive** form of an adjective is given as the entry in the dictionary. It is used when there is no comparison between different objects: *Matthew is tall*.

The **comparative** form is usually made by adding the ending *-er* to the positive form of the adjective. It shows that something possesses a quality to a greater extent than the thing it is being compared with: *Matthew is **taller** than Anna*.

You can also make comparisons by using the words *more* or *less* with the positive (not the comparative) form of the adjective:

*Matthew is **more energetic** than Robbie.*

IRREGULAR COMPARATIVE FORMS

When the comparative and superlative of an adjective are not formed in the regular way, the irregular forms of the adjective are shown in the dictionary after the main entry.

Many adjectives — especially ones that have more than one syllable and do not end in *-y* — do not have separate spelling forms for the comparative and superlative. For these adjectives comparisons must be made using *more, less, most,* and *least*:
beautiful → more beautiful → most beautiful
boring → less boring → least boring

Look also at the grammar box at **superlative**.

- originally someone you shared a
- meal with

company, companies NOUN ❶ a business that sells goods or provides a service • *the record company*. ❷ a group of actors, opera singers, or dancers • *the Royal Shakespeare Company*. ❸ If you have company, you have a friend or visitor with you • *I enjoyed her company*.

comparable [Said **kom**-pra-bl] ADJECTIVE If two things are comparable, they are similar in size or quality • *The skill is comparable to playing the violin*. **comparably** ADVERB

- SIMILAR WORDS: equal,
- equivalent, on a par

comparative, comparatives ADJECTIVE ❶ You add comparative to indicate that something is true only when compared with what is normal • *eight years of comparative calm*. ▷ NOUN ❷ In grammar, the comparative is the form of an adjective which indicates that the person or thing described has more of a particular quality than someone or something else. For example, 'quicker', 'better', and 'easier' are all comparatives. **comparatively** ADVERB
▶ SEE GRAMMAR BOX ABOVE

▷ SPELLING NOTE: *pAL up with the principAL and principAL staff (principal)*

compare, compares, comparing, compared VERB ❶ (EXAM TERM) When you compare things, you look at them together and see in what ways they are different or similar. ❷ If you compare one thing to another, you say it is like the other thing • *His voice is often compared to Michael Stipe's.*

comparison, comparisons NOUN (ENGLISH) When you make a comparison, you consider two things together and see in what ways they are different or similar.

compartment, compartments NOUN ❶ a section of a railway carriage. ❷ one of the separate parts of an object • *a special compartment inside your vehicle.*

compass, compasses NOUN ❶ an instrument with a magnetic needle for finding directions ❷ IN PLURAL Compasses are a hinged instrument for drawing circles.
  ● USAGE NOTE: The proper name for the drawing instrument is *a pair of compasses*

compassion NOUN pity and sympathy for someone who is suffering.
  ● WORD HISTORY: from Latin *compati* meaning 'to suffer with'

compassionate ADJECTIVE feeling or showing sympathy and pity for others. **compassionately** ADVERB

compatible ADJECTIVE If people or things are compatible, they can live or work together successfully. **compatibility** NOUN

compatriot, compatriots NOUN Your compatriots are people from the same country as you.

compel, compels, compelling, compelled VERB To compel someone to do something is to force them to do it.

compelling ADJECTIVE ❶ If a story or event is compelling, it is extremely interesting • *a compelling novel.* ❷ A compelling argument or reason makes you believe that something is true or should be done • *compelling new evidence.*

compensate, compensates, compensating, compensated VERB ❶ To compensate someone is to give them money to replace something lost or damaged. ❷ If one thing compensates for another, it cancels out its bad effects • *The trip more than compensated for the hardship.* **compensatory** ADJECTIVE
  ● SIMILAR WORDS: ❶ recompense, refund ❷ make up for

compensation, compensations NOUN something that makes up for loss or damage.

compere, comperes, compering, compered *[Said kom-pare]* NOUN ❶ the person who introduces the guests or performers in a show ▷ VERB ❷ To compere a show is to introduce the guests or performers.

compete, competes, competing, competed VERB ❶ When people or firms compete, each tries to prove that they or their products are the best. ❷ If you compete in a contest or game, you take part in it.

competent ADJECTIVE Someone who is competent at something can do it satisfactorily • *a very competent*

a
b
c
d
e
f
g
h
i
j
k
l
m
n
o
p
q
r
s
t
u
v
w
x
y
z

engineer. **competently ADVERB competence NOUN**

competition, competitions **NOUN** ❶ When there is competition between people or groups, they are all trying to get something that not everyone can have • *There's a lot of competition for places.* ❷ an event in which people take part to find who is best at something. ❸ When there is competition between firms, each tries to get people to buy its own goods.

competitive ADJECTIVE ❶ A competitive situation is one in which people or firms are competing with each other • *a crowded and competitive market.* ❷ A competitive person is eager to be more successful than others. ❸ Goods sold at competitive prices are cheaper than other goods of the same kind. **competitively ADVERB**

competitor, competitors **NOUN** a person or firm that is competing to become the most successful.

compilation, compilations **NOUN** A compilation is a book, record, or programme consisting of several items that were originally produced separately.

compile, compiles, compiling, compiled **VERB** When someone compiles a book or report, they make it by putting together several items.

complacent ADJECTIVE If someone is complacent, they are unconcerned about a serious situation and do nothing about it. **complacency NOUN**

complain, complains, complaining, complained **VERB** ❶ If you complain, you say that you are not satisfied with something. ❷ If you complain of pain or illness, you say that you have it.
- **SIMILAR WORDS:** ❶ find fault,
- grumble, moan

complaint, complaints **NOUN** If you make a complaint, you complain about something.

complement, complements, complementing, complemented **VERB** ❶ If one thing complements another, the two things go well together • *The tiled floor complements the pine furniture.* ▷ **NOUN** ❷ If one thing is a complement to another, it goes well with it. ❸ In grammar, a complement is a word or phrase that gives information about the subject or object of a sentence. For example, in the sentence 'Rover is a dog', 'is a dog' is a complement. **complementary ADJECTIVE**

complementary angle, complementary angles **NOUN** (MATHS) A complementary angle is either of the two angles that together make up 90°.

complete, completes, completing, completed **ADJECTIVE** ❶ to the greatest degree possible • *a complete mess.* ❷ If something is complete, none of it is missing • *a complete set of tools.* ❸ When a task is complete, it is finished • *The planning stage is now complete.* ▷ **VERB** ❹ If you complete something, you finish it. ❺ If you complete a form, you fill it in. **completely ADVERB completion NOUN**
- **SIMILAR WORDS:** ❶ absolute,
- thorough, total ❷ entire, full,
- whole

▷ SPELLING NOTE: *Psychiatrists Seldom Yell Callously Hard (psychiatrist)*

complex, complexes ADJECTIVE
❶ Something that is complex has many different parts • *a very complex problem.* ▷ NOUN **❷** A complex is a group of buildings, roads, or other things connected with each other in some way • *a hotel and restaurant complex.* **❸** If someone has a complex, they have an emotional problem because of a past experience • *an inferiority complex.* **complexity** NOUN

● SIMILAR WORDS: **❶** complicated,
● intricate, involved

complexion, complexions NOUN
the quality of the skin on your face • *Plenty of fresh air helps to give you a healthy glowing complexion.*

complicate, complicates, complicating, complicated VERB To complicate something is to make it more difficult to understand or deal with.

complicated ADJECTIVE
Something that is complicated has so many parts or aspects that it is difficult to understand or deal with.

complication, complications NOUN something that makes a situation more difficult to deal with • *One possible complication was that it was late in the year.*

compliment, compliments, complimenting, complimented NOUN **❶** If you pay someone a compliment, you tell them you admire something about them ▷ VERB **❷** If you compliment someone, you pay them a compliment.

complimentary ADJECTIVE **❶** If you are complimentary about

something, you express admiration for it. **❷** A complimentary seat, ticket, or publication is given to you free.

comply, complies, complying, complied VERB If you comply with an order or rule, you obey it. **compliance** NOUN

component, components NOUN
D & T The components of something are the parts it is made of.

compose, composes, composing, composed VERB **❶** If something is composed of particular things or people, it is made up of them. **❷** To compose a piece of music, letter, or speech means to write it. **❸** If you compose yourself, you become calm after being excited or upset.

composed ADJECTIVE calm and in control of your feelings.

composer, composers NOUN
someone who writes music.

composition, compositions NOUN **❶** The composition of something is the things it consists of • *the composition of the ozone layer.* **❷** MUSIC The composition of a poem or piece of music is the writing of it. **❸** MUSIC a piece of music or writing.

compost NOUN Compost is a mixture of decaying plants and manure added to soil to help plants grow.

composure NOUN Someone's composure is their ability to stay calm • *Jarvis was able to recover his composure.*

compound, compounds, compounding, compounded NOUN

a
b
c
d
e
f
g
h
i
j
k
l
m
n
o
p
q
r
s
t
u
v
w
x
y
z

▷ SPELLING NOTE: *the QUeen stood on the QUay (quay)*

A
B
C
D
E
F
G
H
I
J
K
L
M
N
O
P
Q
R
S
T
U
V
W
X
Y
Z

❶ an enclosed area of land with buildings used for a particular purpose • *the prison compound.* ❷ SCIENCE In chemistry, a compound is a substance consisting of two or more different substances or chemical elements ▷ **VERB** ❸ To compound something is to put together different parts to make a whole. ❹ To compound a problem is to make it worse by adding to it • *Water shortages were compounded by taps left running.*

comprehend, comprehends, comprehending, comprehended **VERB** FORMAL To comprehend something is to understand or appreciate it • *He did not fully comprehend what was puzzling me.* **comprehension NOUN**

comprehensible ADJECTIVE able to be understood.

comprehensive, comprehensives **ADJECTIVE** ❶ Something that is comprehensive includes everything necessary or relevant • *a comprehensive guide.* ▷ **NOUN** ❷ a school where children of all abilities are taught together. **comprehensively ADVERB**

compress, compresses, compressing, compressed **VERB** To compress something is to squeeze it or shorten it so that it takes up less space • *compressed air.* **compression NOUN**

comprise, comprises, comprising, comprised **VERB** FORMAL What something comprises is what it consists of • *The district then comprised 66 villages.*
● **USAGE NOTE:** You do not need *of* after *comprise.* For example, you say

● *the library comprises 500,000 books*

compromise, compromises, compromising, compromised **NOUN** ❶ an agreement in which people accept less than they originally wanted • *In the end they reached a compromise.* ▷ **VERB** ❷ When people compromise, they agree to accept less than they originally wanted. **compromising ADJECTIVE**

compulsion, compulsions **NOUN** a very strong desire to do something.

compulsive ADJECTIVE ❶ You use 'compulsive' to describe someone who cannot stop doing something • *a compulsive letter writer.* ❷ If you find something such as a book or television programme compulsive, you cannot stop reading or watching it.

compulsory ADJECTIVE If something is compulsory, you have to do it • *School attendance is compulsory.*
● **SIMILAR WORDS:** mandatory,
● obligatory

computer, computers **NOUN** an electronic machine that can quickly make calculations or store and find information.

computer-aided design NOUN Computer-aided design is the use of computers and computer graphics to help design things.

computerize, computerizes, computerizing, computerized; *also spelt* **computerise VERB** When a system or process is computerized, the work is done by computers.

computing NOUN Computing is the use of computers and the writing of programs for them.

▷ SPELLING NOTE: *Rhythmical Hounds Yap To Heavy Music (rhythm)*

comrade, comrades **NOUN** A soldier's comrades are his fellow soldiers, especially in battle. **comradeship NOUN**

con, cons, conning, conned INFORMAL **VERB** ❶ If someone cons you, they trick you into doing or believing something ▷ **NOUN** ❷ a trick in which someone deceives you into doing or believing something.

concave ADJECTIVE A concave surface curves inwards, rather than being level or bulging outwards.

conceal, conceals, concealing, concealed **VERB** To conceal something is to hide it • *He had concealed his gun.* **concealment NOUN**

concede, concedes, conceding, conceded [Said kon-*seed*] **VERB** ❶ If you concede something, you admit that it is true • *I conceded that he was entitled to his views.* ❷ When someone concedes defeat, they accept that they have lost something such as a contest or an election.

conceit NOUN Conceit is someone's excessive pride in their appearance or abilities.
  ● **SIMILAR WORDS:** pride,
  ● self-importance

conceited ADJECTIVE Someone who is conceited is too proud of their appearance or abilities.
  ● **SIMILAR WORDS:** bigheaded, full
  ● of oneself, self-important

conceivable ADJECTIVE If something is conceivable, you can believe that it could exist or be true • *It's conceivable that you also met her.* **conceivably ADVERB**

conceive, conceives, conceiving, conceived **VERB** ❶ If you can conceive of something, you can imagine it or believe it • *Could you conceive of doing such a thing yourself?* ❷ If you conceive something such as a plan, you think of it and work out how it could be done. ❸ When a woman conceives, she becomes pregnant.

concentrate, concentrates, concentrating, concentrated **VERB** ❶ If you concentrate on something, you give it all your attention. ❷ When something is concentrated in one place, it is all there rather than in several places • *They are mostly concentrated in the urban areas.* **concentration NOUN**

concentrated ADJECTIVE A concentrated liquid has been made stronger by having water removed from it • *concentrated apple juice.*

concentration camp, concentration camps **NOUN** a prison camp, especially one set up by the Nazis during World War Two.

concept, concepts **NOUN** an abstract or general idea • *the concept of tolerance.* **conceptual** ADJECTIVE **conceptually** ADVERB

conception, conceptions **NOUN** ❶ Your conception of something is the idea you have of it. ❷ Conception is the process by which a woman becomes pregnant.

concern, concerns, concerning, concerned **NOUN** ❶ Concern is a feeling of worry about something or someone • *public concern about violence.* ❷ If something is your

a b **c** d e f g h i j k l m n o p q r s t u v w x y z

A
B
C
D
E
F
G
H
I
J
K
L
M
N
O
P
Q
R
S
T
U
V
W
X
Y
Z

concern, it is your responsibility. **3** a business • *a large manufacturing concern.* ▷ **VERB** **4** If something concerns you or if you are concerned about it, it worries you. **5** You say that something concerns you if it affects or involves you • *It concerns you and me.* ▷ **PHRASE** **6** If something is **of concern** to you, it is important to you. **concerned ADJECTIVE**

● **SIMILAR WORDS:** **5** be relevant
● to, involve, regard

concerning **PREPOSITION** You use 'concerning' to show what something is about • *documents concerning arms sales to Iraq.*

concert, concerts **NOUN** a public performance by musicians.

concerted **ADJECTIVE** A concerted action is done by several people together • *concerted action to cut interest rates.*

concerto, concertos or concerti [Said kon-*cher*-toe] **NOUN** (MUSIC) a piece of music for a solo instrument and an orchestra.

concession, concessions **NOUN** If you make a concession, you agree to let someone have or do something • *Her one concession was to let me come into the building.*

conch, conches **NOUN** a shellfish with a large, brightly coloured shell; also the shell itself.

concise **ADJECTIVE** giving all the necessary information using as few words as necessary • *a concise guide.*

● **SIMILAR WORDS:** brief, short,
● succinct

conclude, concludes, concluding,

concluded **VERB** **1** If you conclude something, you decide that it is so because of the other things that you know • *An inquiry concluded that this was untrue.* **2** When you conclude something, you finish it • *At that point I intend to conclude the interview.* **concluding ADJECTIVE**

conclusion, conclusions **NOUN** **1** a decision made after thinking carefully about something. **2** the finish or ending of something.

conclusive **ADJECTIVE** Facts that are conclusive show that something is certainly true. **conclusively ADVERB**

concoct, concocts, concocting, concocted **VERB** **1** If you concoct an excuse or explanation, you invent one. **2** If you concoct something, you make it by mixing several things together. **concoction NOUN**

concourse, concourses **NOUN** a wide hall in a building where people walk about or gather together.

concrete **NOUN** **1** Concrete is a solid building material made by mixing cement, sand, and water ▷ **ADJECTIVE** **2** definite, rather than general or vague • *I don't really have any concrete plans.* **3** real and physical, rather than abstract • *concrete evidence.*

concubine, concubines [Said *kong*-kyoo-bine] **NOUN** OLD-FASHIONED A man's concubine is his mistress.

concur, concurs, concurring, concurred **VERB** FORMAL To concur is to agree • *She concurred with me.*

concurrent **ADJECTIVE** If things

▷ SPELLING NOTE: *On WEDNESday Wayne WED NESta* (<u>Wednesday</u>)

are concurrent, they happen at the same time. **concurrently ADVERB**

concussed ADJECTIVE confused or unconscious because of a blow to the head. **concussion NOUN**

condemn, condemns, condemning, condemned **VERB** ❶ If you condemn something, you say it is bad and unacceptable • *Teachers condemned the new plans.* ❷ If someone is condemned to a punishment, they are given it • *She was condemned to death.* ❸ If you are condemned to something unpleasant, you must suffer it • *Many women are condemned to poverty.* ❹ When a building is condemned, it is going to be pulled down because it is unsafe. **condemnation NOUN**
● **SIMILAR WORDS:** ❶ censure,
● criticize, disapprove ❷ sentence
● ❸ doom

condensation NOUN (SCIENCE)
Condensation is a coating of tiny drops formed on a surface by steam or vapour.

condense, condenses, condensing, condensed **VERB** ❶ If you condense a piece of writing or a speech, you shorten it. ❷ (SCIENCE) When a gas or vapour condenses, it changes into a liquid.

condescending ADJECTIVE If you are condescending, you behave in a way that shows you think you are superior to other people.
● **SIMILAR WORDS:** patronizing,
● superior

condition, conditions, conditioning, conditioned **NOUN** ❶ the state someone or something is in ❷ IN PLURAL The conditions in which

something is done are the location and other factors likely to affect it • *The very difficult conditions continued to affect our performance.* ❸ a requirement that must be met for something else to be possible • *He had been banned from drinking alcohol as a condition of bail.* ❹ You can refer to an illness or other medical problem as a condition • *a heart condition.*
▷ **PHRASE** ❺ If you are **out of condition**, you are unfit ▷ **VERB** ❻ If someone is conditioned to behave or think in a certain way, they do it as a result of their upbringing or training.
● **SIMILAR WORDS:** ❸ prerequisite,
● requirement, stipulation

conditional ADJECTIVE If one thing is conditional on another, it can only happen if the other thing happens • *You feel his love is conditional on you pleasing him.*

condolence, condolences **NOUN** Condolence is sympathy expressed for a bereaved person.

condom, condoms **NOUN** a rubber sheath worn by a man on his penis or by a woman inside her vagina as a contraceptive.

condominium, condominiums **NOUN** In Canadian, Australian, and New Zealand English, an apartment block in which each apartment is owned by the person who lives in it.

condone, condones, condoning, condoned **VERB** If you condone someone's bad behaviour, you accept it and do not try to stop it • *We cannot condone violence.*

conducive [Said kon-**joo**-siv] **ADJECTIVE** If something is conducive

▷ SPELLING NOTE: *Eddy Ant thinks mEAt is a grEAt trEAt to EAt (-ea-)*

to something else, it makes it likely to happen • *a situation that is conducive to relaxation.*

conduct, conducts, conducting, conducted **VERB** ❶ To conduct an activity or task is to carry it out • *He seemed to be conducting a conversation.* ❷ FORMAL The way you conduct yourself is the way you behave. ❸ (MUSIC) When someone conducts an orchestra or choir, they stand in front of it and direct it. ❹ (SCIENCE) If something conducts heat or electricity, heat or electricity can pass through it ▷ **NOUN** ❺ If you take part in the conduct of an activity or task, you help to carry it out. ❻ Your conduct is your behaviour.

conductor, conductors **NOUN** ❶ (MUSIC) someone who conducts an orchestra or choir. ❷ someone who moves round a bus or train selling tickets. ❸ (SCIENCE) a substance that conducts heat or electricity.

cone, cones **NOUN** ❶ a regular three-dimensional shape with a circular base and a point at the top. ❷ A fir cone or pine cone is the fruit of a fir or pine tree.

confectionery NOUN Confectionery is sweets.

confederation, confederations **NOUN** an organization formed for business or political purposes.

confer, confers, conferring, conferred **VERB** When people confer, they discuss something in order to make a decision.

conference, conferences **NOUN** a meeting at which formal discussions take place.

confess, confesses, confessing, confessed **VERB** If you confess to something, you admit it • *Your son has confessed to his crimes.*
● **SIMILAR WORDS:** admit, own up

confession, confessions **NOUN** ❶ If you make a confession, you admit you have done something wrong. ❷ Confession is the act of confessing something, especially a religious act in which people confess their sins to a priest.
● **SIMILAR WORDS:**
● ❶ acknowledgment, admission

confessional, confessionals **NOUN** (RE) a small room in some churches where people confess their sins to a priest.

confetti NOUN Confetti is small pieces of coloured paper thrown over the bride and groom at a wedding.
● **WORD HISTORY:** from Italian
● *confetto* meaning 'a sweet'

confidant, confidants *[Said kon-fid-dant]* **NOUN** FORMAL a person you discuss your private problems with.
● **USAGE NOTE:** When the person
● you discuss your private problems
● with is a girl or a woman, the word
● is spelt *confidante*

confide, confides, confiding, confided **VERB** If you confide in or to someone, you tell them a secret • *Marian confided in me that she was very worried.*

confidence, confidences **NOUN** ❶ If you have confidence in someone, you feel you can trust them. ❷ Someone who has confidence is sure of their own abilities or qualities.

❸ a secret you tell someone.

confident ADJECTIVE ❶ If you are confident about something, you are sure it will happen the way you want it to. ❷ People who are confident are sure of their own abilities or qualities. **confidently** ADVERB
● SIMILAR WORDS: ❶ certain,
● positive, sure ❷ assured,
● self-assured

confidential ADJECTIVE Confidential information is meant to be kept secret. **confidentially** ADVERB **confidentiality** NOUN

confine, confines, confining, confined VERB ❶ If something is confined to one place, person, or thing, it exists only in that place or affects only that person or thing. ❷ If you confine yourself to doing or saying something, it is the only thing you do or say • *They confined themselves to discussing the weather.* ❸ If you are confined to a place, you cannot leave it • *She was confined to bed for two days.* ❹ IN PLURAL The confines of a place are its boundaries • *outside the confines of the prison.* **confinement** NOUN

confined ADJECTIVE A confined space is small and enclosed by walls.

confirm, confirms, confirming, confirmed VERB ❶ To confirm something is to say or show that it is true • *Police confirmed that they had received a call.* ❷ If you confirm an arrangement or appointment, you say it is definite. ❸ (RE) When someone is confirmed, they are formally accepted as a member of a Christian church. **confirmation** NOUN
● SIMILAR WORDS: ❶ prove, verify

confirmed ADJECTIVE You use 'confirmed' to describe someone who has a belief or way of life that is unlikely to change • *a confirmed bachelor.*

confiscate, confiscates, confiscating, confiscated VERB To confiscate something is to take it away from someone as a punishment.

conflict, conflicts, conflicting, conflicted NOUN [Said kon-*flikt*] ❶ Conflict is disagreement and argument • *conflict between workers and management.* ❷ (HISTORY) a war or battle. ❸ When there is a conflict of ideas or interests, people have different ideas or interests which cannot all be satisfied ▷ VERB [Said kon-*flikt*] ❹ When ideas or interests conflict, they are different and cannot all be satisfied.
● SIMILAR WORDS:
● ❶ disagreement, dissension
● ❷ battle, clash ❹ be
● incompatible, clash, disagree

confluence, confluences NOUN (GEOGRAPHY) the place where two rivers join.

conform, conforms, conforming, conformed VERB ❶ If you conform, you behave the way people expect you to. ❷ If something conforms to a law or to someone's wishes, it is what is required or wanted. **conformist** NOUN OR ADJECTIVE

confront, confronts, confronting, confronted VERB ❶ If you are confronted with a problem or task, you have to deal with it. ❷ If you confront someone, you meet them face to face like an enemy. ❸ If you confront someone with evidence or a fact, you present it to them in order to accuse

▷ SPELLING NOTE: 'i' before 'e' except after 'c'

a b **c** d e f g h i j k l m n o p q r s t u v w x y z

A
B
C
D
E
F
G
H
I
J
K
L
M
N
O
P
Q
R
S
T
U
V
W
X
Y
Z

them of something.

confrontation, confrontations
NOUN a serious dispute or fight • *a confrontation between police and fans.*

confuse, confuses, confusing, confused **VERB** ❶ If you confuse two things, you mix them up and think one of them is the other • *You are confusing facts with opinion.* ❷ To confuse someone means to make them uncertain about what is happening or what to do. ❸ To confuse a situation means to make it more complicated.
● **SIMILAR WORDS:** ❷ baffle,
● bewilder

confused **ADJECTIVE** ❶ uncertain about what is happening or what to do. ❷ in an untidy mess.

confusing **ADJECTIVE** puzzling or bewildering.

confusion **NOUN** a bewildering state or untidy mess.

congeal, congeals, congealing, congealed [Said kon-*jeel*] **VERB** When a liquid congeals, it becomes very thick and sticky.

congenial [Said kon-*jeen*-yal] **ADJECTIVE** If something is congenial, it is pleasant and suits you • *We wanted to talk in congenial surroundings.*

congenital **ADJECTIVE** MEDICAL If someone has a congenital disease or handicap, they have had it from birth but did not inherit it.

congested **ADJECTIVE** ❶ When a road is congested, it is so full of traffic that normal movement is impossible. ❷ If your nose is congested, it is

blocked and you cannot breathe properly. **congestion** **NOUN**

conglomerate, conglomerates **NOUN** a large business organization consisting of several companies.

congratulate, congratulates, congratulating, congratulated **VERB** If you congratulate someone, you express pleasure at something good that has happened to them, or praise them for something they have achieved. **congratulation** **NOUN** **congratulatory** **ADJECTIVE**

congregate, congregates, congregating, congregated **VERB** When people congregate, they gather together somewhere.

congregation, congregations **NOUN** the congregation are the people attending a service in a church.

congress, congresses **NOUN** a large meeting held to discuss ideas or policies • *a medical congress.*

conical **ADJECTIVE** shaped like a cone.

conifer, conifers **NOUN** any type of evergreen tree that produces cones. **coniferous** **ADJECTIVE**

conjecture **NOUN** Conjecture is guesswork about something • *There was no evidence, only conjecture.*

conjugate, conjugates, conjugating, conjugated [Said *kon*-joo-gate] **VERB** (ENGLISH) When you conjugate a verb, you list the different forms of it you use with the pronouns 'I', 'you' (singular), 'he', 'she', 'it', 'you' (plural), and 'they'.

conjunction, conjunctions **NOUN**

▷ SPELLING NOTE: *King IAn went to ParlIAment in a carrIAge for his marrIAge (-ia-)*

WHAT IS A CONJUNCTION?

A conjunction is a word that joins two words or two parts of a sentence together. Conjunctions are sometimes called "joining words".

Co-ordinating conjunctions join items of equal importance:
*I ordered fish **and** chips.*

Contrasting conjunctions are a type of co-ordinating conjunction which are used to join opposites or contrasting items:
*He was not walking **but** running.*

Correlative conjunctions are pairs of conjunctions, such as *either... or,* or *both... and,* each of which introduces a separate item in the sentence:
*She speaks **both** French **and** German.*
*You can drink **either** tea **or** coffee.*

Subordinating conjunctions join additional items to the main part of the sentence:
*He was happy **because** he had finished his work.*
*I will come **if** I have time.*

❶ ⟮ENGLISH⟯ In grammar, a conjunction is a word that links two other words or two clauses, for example 'and', 'but', 'while', and 'that' ▷ **PHRASE** ❷ If two or more things are done **in conjunction**, they are done together.
▶ SEE GRAMMAR BOX ABOVE

conjurer, conjurers **NOUN** someone who entertains people by doing magic tricks.

conker, conkers **NOUN** Conkers are hard brown nuts from a horse chestnut tree.

connect, connects, connecting, connected **VERB** ❶ To connect two things is to join them together. ❷ If you connect something with something else, you think of them as being linked • *High blood pressure is closely connected to heart disease.*

connection, connections; *also spelt* **connexion NOUN** ❶ a link or relationship between things.
❷ ⟮SCIENCE⟯ the point where two wires or pipes are joined together • *a*

loose connection. ❸ IN PLURAL Someone's connections are the people they know • *He had powerful connections in the army.*

connective, connectives **NOUN** ⟮ENGLISH⟯ a word or short phrase that connects clauses, phrases or words.

connoisseur, connoisseurs *[Said kon-nis-sir]* **NOUN** someone who knows a lot about the arts, or about food or drink • *a great connoisseur of champagne.*
  ● **WORD HISTORY:** from Old French
  ● *connoistre* meaning 'to know'

connotation, connotations **NOUN** ⟮ENGLISH⟯ The connotations of a word or name are what it makes you think of • *a grey man for whom grey has no connotation of dullness.*

conquer, conquers, conquering, conquered **VERB** ❶ To conquer people is to take control of their country by force. ❷ If you conquer something difficult or dangerous, you succeed in controlling it • *Conquer your fear!* **conqueror NOUN**

▷ SPELLING NOTE: *an ELegant angEL (angel)*

conquest, conquests NOUN
❶ Conquest is the conquering of a country or group of people.
❷ Conquests are lands captured by conquest.

conscience, consciences NOUN
the part of your mind that tells you what is right and wrong.

conscientious [Said kon-shee-en-shus] ADJECTIVE Someone who is conscientious is very careful to do their work properly. **conscientiously** ADVERB

  SIMILAR WORDS: careful,
  meticulous, thorough

conscious ADJECTIVE ❶ If you are conscious of something, you are aware of it • She was not conscious of the time. ❷ A conscious action or effort is done deliberately • I made a conscious decision not to hide.
❸ Someone who is conscious is awake, rather than asleep or unconscious • Still conscious, she was taken to hospital. **consciously** ADVERB **consciousness** NOUN

consecrated ADJECTIVE A consecrated building or place is one that has been officially declared to be holy.

consecutive ADJECTIVE
Consecutive events or periods of time happen one after the other • eight consecutive games.

consensus NOUN Consensus is general agreement among a group of people • The consensus was that it could be done.

  USAGE NOTE: There are three ss in
  consensus; do not confuse the
  spelling with census. You should not

  say consensus of opinion, as
  consensus already has of opinion in
  its meaning

consent, consents, consenting, consented NOUN ❶ Consent is permission to do something • Thomas reluctantly gave his consent to my writing this book. ❷ Consent is also agreement between two or more people • By common consent it was the best game of these championships.
▷ VERB ❸ If you consent to something, you agree to it or allow it.

consequence, consequences NOUN ❶ The consequences of something are its results or effects • the dire consequences of major war.
❷ FORMAL If something is of consequence, it is important.

consequent ADJECTIVE
Consequent describes something as being the result of something else • an earthquake in 1980 and its consequent damage. **consequently** ADVERB

conservation NOUN Conservation is the preservation of the environment. **conservationist** NOUN OR ADJECTIVE

conservative, conservatives NOUN ❶ In Britain, a member or supporter of the Conservative Party, a political party that believes that the government should interfere as little as possible in the running of the economy ▷ ADJECTIVE ❷ In Britain, Conservative views and policies are those of the Conservative Party.
❸ Someone who is conservative is not willing to accept changes or new ideas. ❹ A conservative estimate or guess is a cautious or moderate one.

▷ SPELLING NOTE: LEt's measure the angLE (angle)

conservatively ADVERB
conservatism NOUN

conservatory, conservatories
NOUN a room with glass walls and a glass roof in which plants are kept.

conserve, conserves, conserving, conserved VERB If you conserve a supply of something, you make it last • *the only way to conserve energy.*

consider, considers, considering, considered VERB ❶ If you consider something to be the case, you think or judge it to be so • *The manager does not consider him an ideal team member.* ❷ (EXAM TERM) To consider something is to think about it carefully • *If an offer were made, we would consider it.* ❸ If you consider someone's needs or feelings, you take account of them.
● SIMILAR WORDS:
● ❷ contemplate, think about

considerable ADJECTIVE A considerable amount of something is a lot of it • *a considerable sum of money.* **considerably** ADVERB

considerate ADJECTIVE Someone who is considerate pays attention to other people's needs and feelings.

consideration, considerations
NOUN ❶ Consideration is careful thought about something • *a decision demanding careful consideration.* ❷ If you show consideration for someone, you take account of their needs and feelings. ❸ something that has to be taken into account • *Money was also a consideration.*
● SIMILAR WORDS: ❶ deliberation,
● thought

considered ADJECTIVE A

considered opinion or judgment is arrived at by careful thought.

considering CONJUNCTION OR
PREPOSITION You say 'considering' to indicate that you are taking something into account • *I know that must sound callous, considering that I was married to the man for seventeen years.*

consign, consigns, consigning, consigned VERB FORMAL To consign something to a particular place is to send or put it there.

consignment, consignments
NOUN A consignment of goods is a load of them being delivered somewhere.

consist, consists, consisting, consisted VERB What something consists of is its different parts or members • *The brain consists of millions of nerve cells.*

consistency, consistencies NOUN
❶ Consistency is the quality of being consistent. ❷ The consistency of a substance is how thick or smooth it is • *the consistency of single cream.*

consistent ADJECTIVE ❶ If you are consistent, you keep doing something the same way • *one of our most consistent performers.* ❷ If something such as a statement or argument is consistent, there are no contradictions in it. **consistently** ADVERB

console, consoles, consoling, consoled VERB [Said con-**sole**] ❶ To console someone who is unhappy is to make them more cheerful ▷ NOUN [Said **con**-sole] ❷ a panel with switches or knobs for operating a machine. **consolation** NOUN

▷ SPELLING NOTE: *A Rude Idiot Thought He Might Eat Toffee In Church (arithmetic)*

A
B
C
D
E
F
G
H
I
J
K
L
M
N
O
P
Q
R
S
T
U
V
W
X
Y
Z

consolidate, consolidates, consolidating, consolidated **VERB** To consolidate something you have gained or achieved is to make it more secure. **consolidation NOUN**

consonant, consonants **NOUN** (ENGLISH) A sound such as 'p' or 'm' which you make by stopping the air flowing freely through your mouth.
● **WORD HISTORY:** from Latin *consonare* meaning 'to sound at the same time'

consort, consorts, consorting, consorted **VERB** [Said con-*sort*] ❶ FORMAL If you consort with someone, you spend a lot of time with them ▷ **NOUN** [Said con-*sort*] ❷ the wife or husband of the king or queen.

consortium, consortia or consortiums **NOUN** a group of businesses working together.

conspicuous ADJECTIVE If something is conspicuous, people can see or notice it very easily. **conspicuously ADVERB**

conspiracy, conspiracies **NOUN** When there is a conspiracy, a group of people plan something illegal, often for a political purpose.

conspirator, conspirators **NOUN** someone involved in a conspiracy.

conspire, conspires, conspiring, conspired **VERB** ❶ When people conspire, they plan together to do something illegal, often for a political purpose. ❷ LITERARY When events conspire towards a particular result, they seem to work together to cause it • *Circumstances conspired to doom the business.*

constable, constables **NOUN** a police officer of the lowest rank.
● **WORD HISTORY:** from Latin *comes stabuli* meaning 'officer of the stable'

constabulary, constabularies **NOUN** a police force.

constant ADJECTIVE ❶ Something that is constant happens all the time or is always there • *a city under constant attack.* ❷ If an amount or level is constant, it stays the same. ❸ People who are constant stay loyal to a person or idea. **constantly ADVERB constancy NOUN**
● **SIMILAR WORDS:** ❷ fixed, steady, unchanging

constellation, constellations **NOUN** a group of stars.

consternation NOUN Consternation is anxiety or dismay • *There was some consternation when it began raining.*

constipated ADJECTIVE Someone who is constipated is unable to pass solid waste from their bowels. **constipation NOUN**

constituency, constituencies **NOUN** a town or area represented by an MP.

constituent, constituents **NOUN** ❶ An MP's constituents are the voters who live in his or her constituency. ❷ The constituents of something are its parts • *the major constituents of bone.*

constitute, constitutes, constituting, constituted **VERB** If a group of things constitute something, they are what it consists of • *Jewellery constitutes 80 per cent of the stock.*

constitution, constitutions NOUN
1 HISTORY The constitution of a country is the system of laws which formally states people's rights and duties. **2** Your constitution is your health • *a very strong constitution.*
constitutional ADJECTIVE
constitutionally ADVERB

constrained ADJECTIVE If a person feels constrained to do something, they feel that they should do that.

constraint, constraints NOUN something that limits someone's freedom of action • *constraints on trade union power.*

constrict, constricts, constricting, constricted VERB To constrict something is to squeeze it tightly. **constriction** NOUN

construct, constructs, constructing, constructed VERB To construct something is to build or make it.

construction, constructions NOUN **1** The construction of something is the building or making of it • *the construction of the harbour.* **2** something built or made • *a shoddy modern construction built of concrete.*

constructive ADJECTIVE Constructive criticisms and comments are helpful. **constructively** ADVERB

consul, consuls NOUN an official who lives in a foreign city and who looks after people there who are citizens of his or her own country. **consular** ADJECTIVE

consulate, consulates NOUN the place where a consul works.

consult, consults, consulting,

consulted VERB **1** If you consult someone, you ask for their opinion or advice. **2** When people consult each other, they exchange ideas and opinions. **3** If you consult a book or map, you look at it for information.

consultancy, consultancies NOUN an organization whose members give expert advice on a subject.

consultant, consultants NOUN **1** an experienced doctor who specializes in one type of medicine. **2** someone who gives expert advice • *a management consultant.*

consultation, consultations NOUN **1** a meeting held to discuss something. **2** Consultation is discussion or the seeking of advice • *There has to be much better consultation with the public.* **consultative** ADJECTIVE

consume, consumes, consuming, consumed VERB **1** FORMAL If you consume something, you eat or drink it. **2** To consume fuel or energy is to use it up.

consumer, consumers NOUN someone who buys things or uses services • *two new magazines for teenage consumers.*

consumerism NOUN Consumerism is the belief that a country will have a strong economy if its people buy a lot of goods and spend a lot of money.

consuming ADJECTIVE A consuming passion or interest is more important to you than anything else.

consummate, consummates, consummating, consummated [Said

a b **c** d e f g h i j k l m n o p q r s t u v w x y z

▷ SPELLING NOTE: *Betty Eats Cakes And Uses Seven Eggs (because)*

kons-yum-mate VERB ❶ To consummate something is to make it complete. ❷ FORMAL If two people consummate a marriage or relationship, they make it complete by having sex ▷ ADJECTIVE *[Said kon-**sum**-mit]* ❸ You use 'consummate' to describe someone who is very good at something • *a consummate politician.*
consummation NOUN

consumption NOUN The consumption of fuel or food is the using of it, or the amount used.

contact, contacts, contacting, contacted ❶ If you are in contact with someone, you regularly talk to them or write to them. ❷ When things are in contact, they are touching each other. ❸ someone you know in a place or organization from whom you can get help or information ▷ VERB ❹ If you contact someone, you telephone them or write to them.
● SIMILAR WORDS: ❹ get in touch
● with, reach

contact lens, contact lenses NOUN Contact lenses are small plastic lenses that you put in your eyes instead of wearing glasses, to help you see better.

contagious ADJECTIVE A contagious disease can be caught by touching people or things infected with it.

contain, contains, containing, contained VERB ❶ If a substance contains something, that thing is a part of it • *Alcohol contains sugar.* ❷ The things a box or room contains are the things inside it. ❸ FORMAL To

contain something also means to stop it increasing or spreading • *efforts to contain the disease.* **containment** NOUN

container, containers NOUN ❶ something such as a box or a bottle that you keep things in. ❷ a large sealed metal box for transporting things.
● SIMILAR WORDS: ❶ holder,
● receptacle

contaminate, contaminates, contaminating, contaminated VERB If something is contaminated by dirt, chemicals, or radiation, it is made impure and harmful • *foods contaminated with lead.*
contamination NOUN

contemplate, contemplates, contemplating, contemplated VERB ❶ To contemplate is to think carefully about something for a long time. ❷ If you contemplate doing something, you consider doing it • *I never contemplated marrying Charles.* ❸ If you contemplate something, you look at it for a long time • *He contemplated his drawings.* **contemplation** NOUN **contemplative** ADJECTIVE

contemporary, contemporaries ADJECTIVE ❶ produced or happening now • *contemporary literature.* ❷ produced or happening at the time you are talking about • *contemporary descriptions of Lizzie Borden.* ▷ NOUN ❸ Someone's contemporaries are other people living or active at the same time as them • *Shakespeare and his contemporaries.*

contempt NOUN If you treat someone or something with contempt, you show that you have no

▷ SPELLING NOTE: *there's a rAKE in the brAKEs (brake)*

respect for them at all.

contemptible ADJECTIVE not
worthy of any respect • *this
contemptible piece of nonsense.*

contemptuous ADJECTIVE
showing contempt. **contemptuously**
ADVERB

contend, contends, contending,
contended VERB ❶ To contend with
a difficulty is to deal with it • *They had
to contend with injuries.* ❷ FORMAL If
you contend that something is true,
you say firmly that it is true. ❸ When
people contend for something, they
compete for it. **contender** NOUN

content, contents, contenting,
contented NOUN [Said con-tent]
❶ IN PLURAL The contents of
something are the things inside it
❷ (LIBRARY) The content of an article
or speech is what is expressed in it.
❸ Content is the proportion of
something that a substance contains
• *White bread is inferior in vitamin
content.* ▷ ADJECTIVE [Said con-tent]
❹ happy and satisfied with your life.
❺ willing to do or have something
• *He would be content to telephone her.*
▷ VERB [Said con-tent] ❻ If you
content yourself with doing
something, you do it and do not try to
do anything else • *He contented himself
with an early morning lecture.*

contented ADJECTIVE happy and
satisfied with your life. **contentedly**
ADVERB **contentment** NOUN

contention, contentions NOUN
FORMAL Someone's contention is the
idea or opinion they are expressing • *It
is our contention that the 1980s mark a
turning point in planning.*

contest, contests, contesting,
contested NOUN [Said con-test] ❶ a
competition or game • *a boxing
contest.* ❷ a struggle for power • *a
presidential contest.* ▷ VERB [Said
con-test] ❸ If you contest a
statement or decision, you object to it
formally.
● SIMILAR WORDS: ❶ competition,
● game, match

contestant, contestants NOUN
someone taking part in a competition.
● SIMILAR WORDS: competitor,
● player

context, contexts NOUN ❶ The
context of something consists of
matters related to it which help to
explain it • *English history is treated in
a European context.* ❷ (ENGLISH) The
context of a word or sentence consists
of the words or sentences before and
after it.

continent, continents NOUN ❶ a
very large area of land, such as Africa
or Asia. ❷ The Continent is the
mainland of Europe. **continental**
ADJECTIVE

contingency, contingencies [Said
kon-tin-jen-see] NOUN something
that might happen in the future • *I
need to examine all possible contingencies.*

contingent, contingents NOUN
❶ a group of people representing a
country or organization • *a strong
South African contingent.* ❷ a group of
police or soldiers.

continual ADJECTIVE
❶ happening all the time without
stopping • *continual headaches.*
❷ happening again and again • *the
continual snide remarks.* **continually**

▷ SPELLING NOTE: *you'll brEAK that Electrical Aerial, Kitty (break)*

ADVERB
● **SIMILAR WORDS:** constant,
● incessant

continuation, continuations
NOUN ❶ The continuation of
something is the continuing of it • *the
continuation of the human race.*
❷ Something that is a continuation of
an event follows it and seems like a
part of it • *a meeting which was a
continuation of a conference.*

continue, continues, continuing,
continued **VERB** ❶ If you continue to
do something, you keep doing it. ❷ If
something continues, it does not stop.
❸ You also say something continues
when it starts again after stopping
• *She continued after a pause.*
● **SIMILAR WORDS:** ❷ *and* ❸ carry
● on, go on, proceed

continuous ADJECTIVE
❶ Continuous means happening or
existing without stopping. ❷ (MATHS)
A continuous line or surface has no
gaps or holes in it. A continuous set of
data has an unlimited amount of
numbers or items in it. **continuously
ADVERB continuity NOUN**

contorted ADJECTIVE twisted into
an unnatural, unattractive shape.

contour, contours **NOUN** ❶ The
contours of something are its general
shape. ❷ (GEOGRAPHY) On a map, a
contour is a line joining points of
equal height.

contra- PREFIX 'Contra-' means
'against' or 'opposite to' • *contraflow*
• *contraindication.*

contraception NOUN
Contraception is methods of
preventing pregnancy.

contraceptive, contraceptives
NOUN a device or pill for preventing
pregnancy.

contract, contracts, contracting,
contracted **NOUN** [*Said con-trakt*]
❶ a written legal agreement about
the sale of something or work done for
money ▷ **VERB** [*Said con-trakt*]
❷ When something contracts, it gets
smaller or shorter. ❸ **FORMAL** If you
contract an illness, you get it • *Her
husband contracted a virus.*
contractual ADJECTIVE

contraction, contractions **NOUN**
❶ contracting. ❷ (ENGLISH) a
shortened form of a word or words, for
example *I'm* for *I am.*

contractor, contractors **NOUN** a
person or company who does work for
other people or companies • *a building
contractor.*

contradict, contradicts,
contradicting, contradicted **VERB**
(HISTORY) If you contradict someone,
you say that what they have just said
is not true, and that something else is.
**contradiction NOUN contradictory
ADJECTIVE**

contraption, contraptions **NOUN**
a strange-looking machine or piece of
equipment.

contrary ADJECTIVE ❶ Contrary
ideas or opinions are opposed to each
other and cannot be held by the same
person ▷ **PHRASE** ❷ You say **on the
contrary** when you are contradicting
what someone has just said.

contrast, contrasts **NOUN** ❶ a
great difference between things • *the
real contrast between the two poems.*
❷ If one thing is a contrast to

▷ SPELLING NOTE: *I always visit my FRIend on a FRIday (Friday)*

another, it is very different from it • *I couldn't imagine a greater contrast to Maxwell.*

contrast, contrasts, contrasting, contrasted **VERB** ❶ [EXAM TERM] If you contrast things, you describe or emphasize the differences between them. ❷ If one thing contrasts with another, it is very different from it • *The interview contrasted completely with the one she gave after Tokyo.*

contravene, contravenes, contravening, contravened **VERB** FORMAL If you contravene a law or rule, you do something that it forbids.

contribute, contributes, contributing, contributed **VERB** ❶ If you contribute to something, you do things to help it succeed • *The elderly have much to contribute to the community.* ❷ If you contribute money, you give it to help to pay for something. ❸ If something contributes to an event or situation, it is one of its causes • *The dry summer has contributed to perfect conditions.*
contribution NOUN **contributor** NOUN **contributory** ADJECTIVE
● SIMILAR WORDS: ❷ donate, give

contrive, contrives, contriving, contrived **VERB** FORMAL If you contrive to do something difficult, you succeed in doing it • *Anthony contrived to escape with a few companions.*

contrived ADJECTIVE Something that is contrived is unnatural • *a contrived compliment.*

control, controls, controlling, controlled **NOUN** ❶ Control of a country or organization is the power to make the important decisions about how it is run. ❷ Your control over something is your ability to make it work the way you want it to. ❸ The controls on a machine are knobs or other devices used to work it ▷ **VERB** ❹ To control a country or organization means to have the power to make decisions about how it is run. ❺ To control something such as a machine or system means to make it work the way you want it to. ❻ [PSHE] If you control yourself, you make yourself behave calmly when you are angry or upset ▷ **PHRASE** ❼ If something is **out of control**, nobody has any power over it. **controller** NOUN
● SIMILAR WORDS: ❻ hold back, ● restrain

controversial ADJECTIVE Something that is controversial causes a lot of discussion and argument, because many people disapprove of it.

controversy, controversies *[Said kon-triv-ver-see or kon-trov-ver-see]* NOUN discussion and argument because many people disapprove of something.
● WORD HISTORY: from Latin ● *controversus* meaning 'turned in an ● opposite direction'
● USAGE NOTE: Notice that there ● are two ways to say *controversy*. The ● first way is older, and the second is ● becoming more common

conundrum, conundrums NOUN FORMAL a puzzling problem.

conurbation, conurbations NOUN [GEOGRAPHY] FORMAL A conurbation is a very large urban area formed by towns spreading towards each other.

convalesce, convalesces, convalescing, convalesced **VERB**

▷ SPELLING NOTE: *I want to see (C) your licenCe (licence)*

When people convalesce, they rest and regain their health after an illness or operation.

convection NOUN Convection is the process by which heat travels through gases and liquids.

convene, convenes, convening, convened VERB ❶ FORMAL To convene a meeting is to arrange for it to take place. ❷ When people convene, they come together for a meeting.

convenience, conveniences NOUN ❶ The convenience of something is the fact that it is easy to use or that it makes something easy to do. ❷ something useful.

convenient ADJECTIVE If something is convenient, it is easy to use or it makes something easy to do. **conveniently** ADVERB
● SIMILAR WORDS: handy, useful

convent, convents NOUN a building where nuns live, or a school run by nuns.

convention, conventions NOUN ❶ an accepted way of behaving or doing something. ❷ a large meeting of an organization or political group • *the Democratic Convention*.

conventional ADJECTIVE ❶ You say that people are conventional when there is nothing unusual about their way of life. ❷ Conventional methods are the ones that are usually used. **conventionally** ADVERB

converge, converges, converging, converged VERB To converge is to meet or join at a particular place.

conversation, conversations NOUN If you have a conversation with someone, you spend time talking to them. **conversational** ADJECTIVE **conversationalist** NOUN

converse, converses, conversing, conversed VERB [*Said con-verse*] ❶ FORMAL When people converse, they talk to each other ▷ NOUN [*Said con-verse*] ❷ The converse of something is its opposite • *Don't you think that the converse might also be possible?* **conversely** ADVERB

convert, converts, converting, converted VERB [*Said con-vert*] ❶ To convert one thing into another is to change it so that it becomes the other thing. ❷ MATHS If you convert a unit or measurement, you express it in terms of another unit or scale of measurement. For example, you can convert inches to centimetres by multiplying by 2.54. ❸ If someone converts you, they persuade you to change your religious or political beliefs ▷ NOUN [*Said con-vert*] ❹ someone who has changed their religious or political beliefs. **conversion** NOUN **convertible** ADJECTIVE

convex ADJECTIVE A convex surface bulges outwards, rather than being level or curving inwards.

convey, conveys, conveying, conveyed VERB ❶ To convey information or ideas is to cause them to be known or understood. ❷ FORMAL To convey someone or something to a place is to transport them there.

conveyor belt, conveyor belts NOUN a moving strip used in factories for moving objects along.

convict, convicts, convicting, convicted **VERB** [Said kon-**vikt**] **①** To convict someone of a crime is to find them guilty ▷ **NOUN** [Said **kon**-vikt] **②** someone serving a prison sentence.

conviction, convictions **NOUN** **①** a strong belief or opinion. **②** The conviction of someone is what happens when they are found guilty in a court of law.

convince, convinces, convincing, convinced **VERB** To convince someone of something is to persuade them that it is true.
● **SIMILAR WORDS**: persuade, sway

convincing **ADJECTIVE**
'Convincing' is used to describe things or people that can make you believe something is true • *a convincing argument*. **convincingly ADVERB**
● **SIMILAR WORDS**: credible,
● persuasive, plausible

convoluted [Said kon-vol-**yoo**-tid] **ADJECTIVE** Something that is convoluted has many twists and bends • *the convoluted patterns of these designs.*

convoy, convoys **NOUN** a group of vehicles or ships travelling together.

convulsion, convulsions **NOUN** If someone has convulsions, their muscles move violently and uncontrollably.

coo, coos, cooing, cooed **VERB** When pigeons and doves coo, they make a soft flutelike sound.

cook, cooks, cooking, cooked **VERB** **①** To cook food is to prepare it for eating by heating it ▷ **NOUN** **②** someone who prepares and cooks

food, often as their job.

cooker, cookers **NOUN** a device for cooking food.

cookery NOUN Cookery is the activity of preparing and cooking food.

cookie, cookies **NOUN** **①** a sweet biscuit. **②** a small file placed on a user's computer by a website, containing information about the user's preferences that will be used on any future visits he or she may make to the site.

cool, cooler, coolest; cools, cooling, cooled **ADJECTIVE** **①** Something cool has a low temperature but is not cold. **②** If you are cool in a difficult situation, you stay calm and unemotional ▷ **VERB** **③** When something cools or when you cool it, it becomes less warm. **coolly ADVERB** **coolness NOUN**

coolabah, coolabahs; *also spelt* **coolibar NOUN** an Australian eucalypt that grows along rivers.

coop, coops **NOUN** a cage for chickens or rabbits.

cooperate, cooperates, cooperating, cooperated [Said koh-**op**-er-rate] **VERB** **①** When people cooperate, they work or act together. **②** To cooperate also means to do what someone asks. **cooperation NOUN**

cooperative, cooperatives [Said koh-**op**-er-ut-tiv] **NOUN** **①** a business or organization run by the people who work for it, and who share its benefits or profits ▷ **ADJECTIVE** **②** A cooperative activity is done by people working together. **③** Someone who is cooperative does what you ask.

a
b
c
d
e
f
g
h
i
j
k
l
m
n
o
p
q
r
s
t
u
v
w
x
y
z

▷ SPELLING NOTE: *have a pIEce of pIE (piece)*

A
B
C
D
E
F
G
H
I
J
K
L
M
N
O
P
Q
R
S
T
U
V
W
X
Y
Z

coordinate, coordinates, coordinating, coordinated [Said koh-**or**-din-ate] **VERB ❶** To coordinate an activity is to organize the people or things involved in it • to coordinate the campaign. **❷** IN PLURAL (MATHS) Coordinates are a pair of numbers or letters that tell you how far along and up or down a point is on a grid. **coordination NOUN coordinator NOUN**

cop, cops **NOUN** INFORMAL a policeman.

cope, copes, coping, coped **VERB** If you cope with a problem or task, you deal with it successfully • couldn't cope with such a volume of work.

copious ADJECTIVE FORMAL existing or produced in large quantities • I wrote copious notes for the solicitor.

copper, coppers **NOUN ❶** (SCIENCE) Copper is a reddish-brown metallic element. Its atomic number is 29 and its symbol is Cu. **❷** Coppers are brown metal coins of low value. **❸** INFORMAL A copper is also a policeman.

copse, copses **NOUN** a small group of trees growing close together.

copulate, copulates, copulating, copulated **VERB** FORMAL To copulate is to have sex. **copulation NOUN**

copy, copies, copying, copied **NOUN ❶** something made to look like something else. **❷** A copy of a book, newspaper, or record is one of many identical ones produced at the same time ▷ **VERB ❸** If you copy what someone does, you do the same thing.

❹ If you copy something, you make a copy of it. **copier NOUN**
● **SIMILAR WORDS: ❶** duplicate,
● replica, reproduction **❹** duplicate,
● reproduce

copyright, copyrights **NOUN** (LIBRARY) If someone has the copyright on a piece of writing or music, it cannot be copied or performed without their permission.

coral, corals **NOUN** Coral is a hard substance that forms in the sea from the skeletons of tiny animals called corals.

cor anglais, cors anglais [Said kohr ong-**glay**] **NOUN** (MUSIC) A cor anglais is a woodwind instrument with a double reed. It has a slightly lower pitch than an oboe.

cord, cords **NOUN ❶** Cord is strong, thick string. **❷** Electrical wire covered in rubber or plastic is also called cord.

cordial, cordials **ADJECTIVE ❶** warm and friendly • the cordial greeting. ▷ **NOUN ❷** a sweet drink made from fruit juice.

cordon, cordons, cordoning, cordoned **NOUN ❶** a line or ring of police or soldiers preventing people entering or leaving a place ▷ **VERB ❷** If police or soldiers cordon off an area, they stop people entering or leaving by forming themselves into a line or ring.

corduroy NOUN Corduroy is a thick cloth with parallel raised lines on the outside.

core, cores **NOUN ❶** the hard central part of a fruit such as an apple. **❷** the most central part of an object or place

▷ SPELLING NOTE: plaice the fish has a glittering 'EYE' (I) (plaice)

• *the earth's core.* ❸ the most important part of something • *the core of Asia's problems.*

cork, corks NOUN ❶ Cork is the very light, spongelike bark of a Mediterranean tree. ❷ a piece of cork pushed into the end of a bottle to close it.

corkscrew, corkscrews NOUN a device for pulling corks out of bottles.

cormorant, cormorants NOUN a dark-coloured bird with a long neck.

corn, corns NOUN ❶ Corn refers to crops such as wheat and barley and to their seeds. ❷ a small painful area of hard skin on your foot.

cornea, corneas [*Said kor-nee-a*] NOUN the transparent skin that covers the outside of your eyeball.

corner, corners, cornering, cornered NOUN ❶ a place where two sides or edges of something meet • *a small corner of one shelf* • *a street corner.* ▷ VERB ❷ To corner a person or animal is to get them into a place they cannot escape from.

cornet, cornets NOUN (MUSIC) a small brass instrument used in brass and military bands.

cornflour NOUN Cornflour is a fine white flour made from maize and used in cooking to thicken sauces.

cornflower, cornflowers NOUN a small plant with bright flowers, usually blue.

cornice, cornices NOUN a decorative strip of plaster, wood, or stone along the top edge of a wall.

corny, cornier, corniest ADJECTIVE very obvious or sentimental and not at all original • *corny old love songs.*

corolla, corollas NOUN (SCIENCE) a flower's corolla is all of its petals considered as a unit.

coronary, coronaries NOUN If someone has a coronary, blood cannot reach their heart because of a blood clot.

coronation, coronations NOUN the ceremony at which a king or queen is crowned.

coroner, coroners NOUN an official who investigates the deaths of people who have died in a violent or unusual way.

coronet, coronets NOUN a small crown.

corporal, corporals NOUN an officer of low rank in the army or air force.

corporal punishment NOUN Corporal punishment is the punishing of people by beating them.

corporate ADJECTIVE FORMAL belonging to or done by all members of a group together • *a corporate decision.*

corporation, corporations NOUN ❶ a large business. ❷ a group of people responsible for running a city.

corps, corps [*rhymes with* **more**] NOUN ❶ a part of an army with special duties • *the engineering Corps.* ❷ a small group of people who do a special job • *the world press corps.*
● USAGE NOTE: The plural of *corps* is
● also *corps*

corpse, corpses NOUN a dead body.

a
b
c
d
e
f
g
h
i
j
k
l
m
n
o
p
q
r
s
t
u
v
w
x
y
z

▷ SPELLING NOTE: *I went to see (C) the doctor's new practiCe (practice)*

A
B
C
D
E
F
G
H
I
J
K
L
M
N
O
P
Q
R
S
T
U
V
W
X
Y
Z

corpuscle, corpuscles *[Said kor-pus-sl]* NOUN (SCIENCE) a red or white blood cell.

correa, correas NOUN an Australian shrub with large green and white flowers.

correct, corrects, correcting, corrected ADJECTIVE ❶ If something is correct, there are no mistakes in it. ❷ The correct thing in a particular situation is the right one • *Each has the correct number of coins.* ❸ Correct behaviour is considered to be socially acceptable ▷ VERB ❹ If you correct something which is wrong, you make it right. **correctly** ADVERB **corrective** ADJECTIVE OR NOUN
● SIMILAR WORDS: ❹ emend,
● rectify

correction, corrections NOUN the act of making something right.

correlate, correlates, correlating, correlated VERB If two things correlate or are correlated, they are closely connected or strongly influence each other • *Obesity correlates with increased risk of stroke and diabetes.* **correlation** NOUN

correspond, corresponds, corresponding, corresponded VERB ❶ If one thing corresponds to another, it has a similar purpose, function, or status. ❷ (MATHS) If numbers or amounts correspond, they are the same. ❸ When people correspond, they write to each other.

correspondence, correspondences NOUN ❶ Correspondence is the writing of letters; also the letters written. ❷ If there is a correspondence between

two things, they are closely related or very similar.

correspondent, correspondents NOUN a newspaper, television, or radio reporter.

corresponding ADJECTIVE ❶ You use 'corresponding' to describe a change that results from a change in something else • *the rise in interest rates and corresponding fall in house values.* ❷ You also use 'corresponding' to describe something which has a similar purpose or status to something else • *Alfard is the corresponding Western name for the star.* **correspondingly** ADVERB

corresponding angle, corresponding angles NOUN (MATHS) Corresponding angles occur where a line crosses two or more parallel lines. They are the equivalent angles on the same side of the intersection.

corridor, corridors NOUN a passage in a building or train.

corroboree, corroborees NOUN an Australian Aboriginal gathering or dance that is festive or warlike.

corrode, corrodes, corroding, corroded VERB (SCIENCE) When metal corrodes, it is gradually destroyed by a chemical or rust. **corrosion** NOUN **corrosive** ADJECTIVE

corrugated ADJECTIVE Corrugated metal or cardboard is made in parallel folds to make it stronger.
● WORD HISTORY: from Latin
● *corrugare* meaning 'to wrinkle up'

corrupt, corrupts, corrupting, corrupted ADJECTIVE ❶ Corrupt

▷ SPELLING NOTE: *You must practiSe your Ss (practise)*

people act dishonestly or illegally in return for money or power • *corrupt ministers.* ▷ **VERB ②** To corrupt someone means to make them dishonest. **③** To corrupt someone also means to make them immoral. **corruptible ADJECTIVE**
● **SIMILAR WORDS: ①** crooked,
● dishonest **②** deprave

corruption NOUN Corruption is dishonesty and illegal behaviour by people in positions of power.
● **SIMILAR WORDS:** depravity,
● immorality, vice

corset, corsets **NOUN** Corsets are stiff underwear worn by some women round their hips and waist to make them look slimmer.

cortex, cortices **NOUN** The cortex of the brain or other organ is its outer layer.

cosine, cosines **NOUN** (MATHS) In mathematics a cosine is a function of an angle. If B is the right angle in a right-angled triangle ABC, the cosine of the angle at A is AB divided by AC.

cosmetic, cosmetics **NOUN ①** Cosmetics are substances such as lipstick and face powder which improve a person's appearance ▷ **ADJECTIVE ②** Cosmetic changes improve the appearance of something without changing its basic nature.

cosmic ADJECTIVE belonging or relating to the universe.

cosmopolitan ADJECTIVE A cosmopolitan place is full of people from many countries.
● **WORD HISTORY:** from Greek
● *kosmos* meaning 'universe' and
● *politēs* meaning 'citizen'

cosmos NOUN The cosmos is the universe.

cosset, cossets, cosseting, cosseted **VERB** If you cosset someone, you spoil them and protect them too much.

cost, costs, costing, cost **NOUN ①** The cost of something is the amount of money needed to buy it, do it, or make it. **②** The cost of achieving something is the loss or injury in achieving it • *the total cost in human misery.* ▷ **VERB ③** You use 'cost' to talk about the amount of money you have to pay for things • *The air fares were going to cost a lot.* **④** If a mistake costs you something, you lose that thing because of the mistake • *a reckless gamble that could cost him his job.*

costly, costlier, costliest **ADJECTIVE** expensive • *a costly piece of furniture.*

costume, costumes **NOUN ①** (DRAMA) a set of clothes worn by an actor. **②** Costume is the clothing worn in a particular place or during a particular period • *eighteenth-century costume.*

cosy, cosier, cosiest; cosies **ADJECTIVE ①** warm and comfortable • *her cosy new flat.* **②** Cosy activities are pleasant and friendly • *a cosy chat.* ▷ **NOUN ③** a soft cover put over a teapot to keep the tea warm. **cosily ADVERB cosiness NOUN**

cot, cots **NOUN** a small bed for a baby, with bars or panels round it to stop the baby falling out.

cottage, cottages **NOUN** a small house in the country.

cottage cheese NOUN Cottage

cheese is a type of soft white lumpy cheese.

cotton, cottons NOUN ❶ Cotton is cloth made from the soft fibres of the cotton plant. ❷ Cotton is also thread used for sewing.

cotton wool NOUN Cotton wool is soft fluffy cotton, often used for dressing wounds.

couch, couches, couching, couched NOUN ❶ a long, soft piece of furniture which more than one person can sit on ▷ VERB ❷ If a statement is couched in a particular type of language, it is expressed in that language • *a comment couched in impertinent terms.*

cough, coughs, coughing, coughed [Said *koff*] VERB ❶ When you cough, you force air out of your throat with a sudden harsh noise ▷ NOUN ❷ an illness that makes you cough a lot; also the noise you make when you cough.

could VERB ❶ You use 'could' to say that you were able or allowed to do something • *He could hear voices* • *She could come and go as she wanted.* ❷ You also use 'could' to say that something might happen or might be the case • *It could rain.* ❸ You use 'could' when you are asking for something politely • *Could you tell me the name of that film?*

coulomb, coulombs [Said *koo*-lom] (SCIENCE) NOUN a unit used to measure electric charge.

council, councils NOUN ❶ a group of people elected to look after the affairs of a town, district, or county. ❷ Some other groups have Council as

part of their name • *the World Gold Council.*

councillor, councillors NOUN an elected member of a local council.

counsel, counsels, counselling, counselled NOUN ❶ FORMAL To give someone counsel is to give them advice ▷ VERB ❷ To counsel people is to give them advice about their problems. **counselling** NOUN **counsellor** NOUN

count, counts, counting, counted VERB ❶ To count is to say all the numbers in order up to a particular number. ❷ If you count all the things in a group, you add them up to see how many there are. ❸ What counts in a situation is whatever is most important. ❹ To count as something means to be regarded as that thing • *I'm not sure whether this counts as harassment.* ❺ If you can count on someone or something, you can rely on them ▷ NOUN ❻ a number reached by counting. ❼ FORMAL If something is wrong on a particular count, it is wrong in that respect. ❽ a European nobleman.
 ● SIMILAR WORDS: ❷ add up,
 ● calculate, reckon

countdown, countdowns NOUN the counting aloud of numbers in reverse order before something happens, especially before a spacecraft is launched.

countenance, countenances NOUN FORMAL Someone's countenance is their face.

counter, counters, countering, countered NOUN ❶ a long, flat surface over which goods are sold in a shop. ❷ a small, flat, round object used in board games ▷ **VERB** ❸ If you counter something that is being done, you take action to make it less effective • *I countered that argument with a reference to our sales report.*

counteract, counteracts, counteracting, counteracted **VERB** To counteract something is to reduce its effect by producing an opposite effect.

counterfeit, counterfeits, counterfeiting, counterfeited *[Said kown-ter-fit]* **ADJECTIVE** ❶ Something counterfeit is not genuine but has been made to look genuine to deceive people • *counterfeit money.* ▷ **VERB** ❷ To counterfeit something is to make a counterfeit version of it.

counterpart, counterparts **NOUN** The counterpart of a person or thing is another person or thing with a similar function in a different place • *Unlike his British counterpart, the French mayor is an important personality.*

countess, countesses **NOUN** the wife of a count or earl, or a woman with the same rank as a count or earl.

counting **PREPOSITION** You say 'counting' when including something in a calculation • *nearly 4000 of us, not counting women and children.*

countless **ADJECTIVE** too many to count • *There had been countless demonstrations.*
- **SIMILAR WORDS:** incalculable,
- innumerable

country, countries **NOUN** [GEOGRAPHY] ❶ one of the political areas the world is divided into. ❷ The country is land away from towns and

cities. ❸ 'Country' is used to refer to an area with particular features or associations • *the heart of wine country.*
- **SIMILAR WORDS:** ❶ nation, state

countryman, countrymen **NOUN** Your countrymen are people from your own country.

countryside **NOUN** The countryside is land away from towns and cities.

county, counties **NOUN** [GEOGRAPHY] a region with its own local government.
- **WORD HISTORY:** from Old French
- *conté* meaning 'land belonging to a
- count'

coup, coups *[rhymes with you]*; also spelt **coup d'état** *[Said koo day-tah]* **NOUN** [HISTORY] When there is a coup, a group of people seize power in a country.
- **WORD HISTORY:** from French
- *coup* meaning 'a blow'

couple, couples, coupling, coupled **NOUN** ❶ two people who are married or having a sexual or romantic relationship. ❷ A couple of things or people means two of them • *a couple of weeks ago.* ▷ **VERB** ❸ If one thing is coupled with another, the two things are done or dealt with together • *Its stores offer high quality coupled with low prices.*

couplet, couplets **NOUN** [ENGLISH] two lines of poetry together, especially two that rhyme.

coupon, coupons **NOUN** ❶ a piece of printed paper which, when you hand it in, entitles you to pay less than usual for something. ❷ a form you fill in to ask for or supply information or

▷ SPELLING NOTE: *Psychiatrists Seldom Yell Callously Hard (*psychiatrist*)*

a
b
c
d
e
f
g
h
i
j
k
l
m
n
o
p
q
r
s
t
u
v
w
x
y
z

A
B
C
D
E
F
G
H
I
J
K
L
M
N
O
P
Q
R
S
T
U
V
W
X
Y
Z

to enter a competition.

courage NOUN Courage is the quality shown by people who do things knowing they are dangerous or difficult. **courageous** ADJECTIVE **courageously** ADVERB

courgette, courgettes [Said koor-**jet**] NOUN a type of small marrow with dark green skin. Courgettes are also called **zucchini**.

courier, couriers [Said **koo**-ree-er] NOUN ❶ someone employed by a travel company to look after people on holiday. ❷ someone employed to deliver special letters quickly.

course, courses NOUN ❶ a series of lessons or lectures. ❷ a series of medical treatments • *a course of injections.* ❸ one of the parts of a meal. ❹ A course or a course of action is one of the things you can do in a situation. ❺ a piece of land where a sport such as golf is played. ❻ the route a ship or aircraft takes. ❼ If something happens in the course of a period of time, it happens during that period • *Ten people died in the course of the day.* ▷ PHRASE ❽ If you say of course, you are showing that something is totally expected or that you are sure about something • *Of course she wouldn't do that.*

court, courts, courting, courted NOUN ❶ a place where legal matters are decided by a judge and jury or a magistrate. The judge and jury or magistrate can also be referred to as the court. ❷ a place where a game such as tennis or badminton is played. ❸ the place where a king or queen lives and carries out ceremonial duties ▷ VERB ❹ OLD-FASHIONED If a man

and woman are courting, they are spending a lot of time together because they intend to get married.

courteous [Said **kur**-tee-yuss] ADJECTIVE Courteous behaviour is polite and considerate.

courtesy NOUN Courtesy is polite, considerate behaviour.

courtier, courtiers NOUN Courtiers were noblemen and noblewomen at the court of a king or queen.

court-martial, court-martials, court-martialling, court-martialled NOUN ❶ a military trial ▷ VERB ❷ If a member of the armed forces is court-martialled, he or she is tried by a court martial.

courtship NOUN FORMAL Courtship is the activity of courting or the period of time during which a man and a woman are courting.

courtyard, courtyards NOUN a flat area of ground surrounded by buildings or walls.

cousin, cousins NOUN Your cousin is the child of your uncle or aunt.

covalent bond, covalent bonds NOUN (SCIENCE) a chemical bond in which the atoms in a molecule share two electrons.

cove, coves NOUN a small bay.

covenant, covenants [Said **kuv**-vi-nant] NOUN a formal written agreement or promise.

cover, covers, covering, covered VERB ❶ If you cover something, you put something else over it to protect it or hide it. ❷ If something covers something else, it forms a layer over it

▷ SPELLING NOTE: *the QUeen stood on the QUay (quay)*

• *Tears covered his face.* ❸ If you cover a particular distance, you travel that distance • *He covered 52 kilometres in 210 laps.* ▷ NOUN ❹ something put over an object to protect it or keep it warm. ❺ The cover of a book or magazine is its outside. ❻ Insurance cover is a guarantee that money will be paid if something is lost or harmed. ❼ In the open, cover consists of trees, rocks, or other places where you can shelter or hide.

cover up VERB If you cover up something you do not want people to know about, you hide it from them • *He lied to cover up his crime.*
cover-up NOUN

coverage NOUN The coverage of something in the news is the reporting of it.

covering, coverings NOUN a layer of something which protects or conceals something else • *A morning blizzard left a covering of snow.*

covert [Said *kuv-vert*] ADJECTIVE FORMAL Covert activities are secret, rather than open. **covertly** ADVERB

covet, covets, coveting, coveted [Said *kuv-vit*] VERB FORMAL If you covet something, you want it very much.

cow, cows NOUN a large animal kept on farms for its milk.

coward, cowards NOUN someone who is easily frightened and who avoids dangerous or difficult situations. **cowardice** NOUN

cowardly ADJECTIVE easily scared.

cowboy, cowboys NOUN a man employed to look after cattle in America.

cower, cowers, cowering, cowered VERB When someone cowers, they crouch or move backwards because they are afraid.
● SIMILAR WORDS: cringe, shrink

cox, coxes NOUN a person who steers a boat.

coy, coyer, coyest ADJECTIVE If someone is coy, they pretend to be shy and modest. **coyly** ADVERB

coyote, coyotes [Said *koy-ote-ee*] NOUN a North American animal like a small wolf.

crab, crabs NOUN a sea creature with four pairs of legs, two pincers, and a flat, round body covered by a shell.

crack, cracks, cracking, cracked VERB ❶ If something cracks, it becomes damaged, with lines appearing on its surface. ❷ If you crack a joke, you tell it. ❸ If you crack a problem or code, you solve it ▷ NOUN ❹ one of the lines appearing on something when it cracks. ❺ a narrow gap ▷ ADJECTIVE ❻ A crack soldier or sportsman is highly trained and skilful.
● SIMILAR WORDS: ❺ break, fracture, gap

cracker, crackers NOUN ❶ a thin, crisp biscuit that is often eaten with cheese. ❷ a paper-covered tube that pulls apart with a bang and usually has a toy and paper hat inside.

cracking NOUN (SCIENCE) In chemistry, cracking is when large molecules break down into smaller ones because of the breaking of the bonds between their carbon atoms.

crackle, crackles, crackling, crackled VERB ❶ If something crackles, it makes a rapid series of short, harsh noises ▷ **NOUN** ❷ a short, harsh noise.

cradle, cradles, cradling, cradled **NOUN** ❶ a box-shaped bed for a baby ▷ **VERB** ❷ If you cradle something in your arms or hands, you hold it there carefully.

craft, crafts **NOUN** ❶ an activity such as weaving, carving, or pottery. ❷ a skilful occupation • *the writer's craft.* ❸ a boat, plane, or spacecraft.
● **USAGE NOTE:** When *craft* means 'a boat, plane, or spacecraft' (sense 3), the plural is *craft*

craftsman, craftsmen **NOUN** a man who makes things skilfully with his hands. **craftsmanship NOUN craftswoman NOUN**

crafty, craftier, craftiest **ADJECTIVE** Someone who is crafty gets what they want by tricking people in a clever way.

crag, crags **NOUN** a steep rugged rock or peak.

craggy, craggier, craggiest **ADJECTIVE** A craggy mountain or cliff is steep and rocky.

cram, crams, cramming, crammed **VERB** If you cram people or things into a place, you put more in than there is room for.
● **SIMILAR WORDS:** pack, squeeze, stuff

cramp, cramps **NOUN** Cramp or cramps is a pain caused by a muscle contracting.

cramped ADJECTIVE If a room or building is cramped, it is not big enough for the people or things in it.

cranberry, cranberries **NOUN** Cranberries are sour-tasting red berries, often made into a sauce.

crane, cranes, craning, craned **NOUN** ❶ a machine that moves heavy things by lifting them in the air. ❷ a large bird with a long neck and long legs ▷ **VERB** ❸ If you crane your neck, you extend your head in a particular direction to see or hear something better.

crank, cranks, cranking, cranked **NOUN** ❶ INFORMAL someone with strange ideas who behaves in an odd way. ❷ a device you turn to make something move • *The adjustment is made by turning the crank.* ▷ **VERB** ❸ If you crank something, you make it move by turning a handle. **cranky ADJECTIVE**

cranny, crannies **NOUN** a very narrow opening in a wall or rock • *nooks and crannies.*

crash, crashes, crashing, crashed **NOUN** ❶ an accident in which a moving vehicle hits something violently. ❷ a sudden loud noise • *the crash of the waves on the rocks.* ❸ the sudden failure of a business or financial institution ▷ **VERB** ❹ When a vehicle crashes, it hits something and is badly damaged.

crash helmet, crash helmets **NOUN** a helmet worn by motor cyclists for protection when they are riding.

crate, crates **NOUN** a large box used for transporting or storing things.

crater, craters **NOUN** (GEOGRAPHY) a wide hole in the ground caused by something hitting it or by the explosion of a bomb.

cravat, cravats NOUN a piece of cloth a man can wear round his neck tucked into his shirt collar.
- WORD HISTORY: from Serbo-Croat *Hrvat* meaning 'Croat'. Croat soldiers wore cravats during the Thirty Years' War

crave, craves, craving, craved VERB If you crave something, you want it very much • *I crave her approval.* **craving** NOUN

crawl, crawls, crawling, crawled VERB ❶ When you crawl, you move forward on your hands and knees. ❷ When a vehicle crawls, it moves very slowly. ❸ INFORMAL If a place is crawling with people or things, it is full of them • *The place is crawling with drunks.* **crawler** NOUN

crayfish, crayfishes or crayfish NOUN a small shellfish like a lobster.

crayon, crayons NOUN a coloured pencil or a stick of coloured wax.

craze, crazes NOUN something that is very popular for a short time.

crazy, crazier, craziest ADJECTIVE INFORMAL ❶ very strange or foolish • *The guy is crazy* • *a crazy idea.* ❷ If you are crazy about something, you are very keen on it • *I was crazy about dancing.* **crazily** ADVERB **craziness** NOUN

creak, creaks, creaking, creaked VERB ❶ If something creaks, it makes a harsh sound when it moves or when you stand on it ▷ NOUN ❷ a harsh squeaking noise. **creaky** ADJECTIVE

cream, creams NOUN ❶ Cream is a thick, yellowish-white liquid taken from the top of milk. ❷ Cream is also a substance people can rub on their skin to make it soft ▷ ADJECTIVE ❸ yellowish-white. **creamy** ADJECTIVE

crease, creases, creasing, creased NOUN ❶ an irregular line that appears on cloth or paper when it is crumpled. ❷ a straight line on something that has been pressed or folded neatly ▷ VERB ❸ To crease something is to make lines appear on it. **creased** ADJECTIVE

create, creates, creating, created VERB ❶ To create something is to cause it to happen or exist • *This is absolutely vital but creates a problem.* ❷ When someone creates a new product or process, they invent it. **creator** NOUN **creation** NOUN

creative ADJECTIVE ❶ Creative people are able to invent and develop original ideas. ❷ Creative activities involve the inventing and developing of original ideas • *creative writing.* **creatively** ADVERB **creativity** NOUN

creature, creatures NOUN any living thing that moves about.

crèche, crèches [Said **kresh**] NOUN a place where small children are looked after while their parents are working.

credence NOUN FORMAL If something gives credence to a theory or story, it makes it easier to believe.

credentials PLURAL NOUN Your credentials are records of your past achievements or other things in your background that show that you are qualified for something.

credible ADJECTIVE If someone or something is credible, you can believe or trust them. **credibility** NOUN

credit, credits, crediting, credited NOUN ❶ If you are allowed credit, you can take something and pay for it later • *to buy goods on credit.* ❷ If you get the credit for something, people praise you for it. ❸ If you say someone is a credit to their family or school, you mean that their family or school should be proud of them ❹ IN PLURAL The list of people who helped make a film, record, or television programme is called the credits ▷ PHRASE ❺ If someone or their bank account is **in credit**, their account has money in it ▷ VERB ❻ If you are credited with an achievement, people believe that you were responsible for it.

creditable ADJECTIVE satisfactory or fairly good • *a creditable performance.*

credit card, credit cards NOUN a plastic card that allows someone to buy goods on credit.

creditor, creditors NOUN Your creditors are the people you owe money to.

creed, creeds NOUN ❶ a religion. ❷ any set of beliefs • *the feminist creed.*

creek, creeks NOUN a narrow inlet where the sea comes a long way into the land.
● **WORD HISTORY:** from Old Norse
● *kriki* meaning 'nook'

creep, creeps, creeping, crept VERB

To creep is to move quietly and slowly.

creepy, creepier, creepiest ADJECTIVE INFORMAL strange and frightening • *a creepy feeling.*

cremate, cremates, cremating, cremated VERB When someone is cremated, their dead body is burned during a funeral service. **cremation** NOUN

crematorium, crematoriums or crematoria NOUN a building in which the bodies of dead people are burned.

crepe [Said **krayp**] NOUN ❶ Crepe is a thin ridged material made from cotton, silk, or wool. ❷ Crepe is also a type of rubber with a rough surface.

crescendo, crescendos [Said **krish-en-doe**] NOUN (MUSIC) When there is a crescendo in a piece of music, the music gets louder.

crescent, crescents NOUN a curved shape that is wider in its middle than at the ends, which are pointed.

cress NOUN Cress is a plant with small, strong-tasting leaves. It is used in salads.

crest, crests NOUN ❶ The crest of a hill or wave is its highest part. ❷ a tuft of feathers on top of a bird's head. ❸ a small picture or design that is the emblem of a noble family, a town, or an organization. **crested** ADJECTIVE

crevice, crevices NOUN a narrow crack or gap in rock.

crew, crews NOUN ❶ The crew of a ship, aeroplane, or spacecraft are the people who operate it. ❷ people with special technical skills who work together • *the camera crew.*

crib, cribs, cribbing, cribbed VERB ❶ INFORMAL If you crib, you copy what someone else has written and pretend it is your own work ▷ NOUN ❷ OLD-FASHIONED a baby's cot.

crib-wall, crib-walls NOUN in New Zealand English, a wooden wall built against a bank of earth to support it.

crick, cricks NOUN a pain in your neck or back caused by muscles becoming stiff.

cricket, crickets NOUN ❶ Cricket is an outdoor game played by two teams who take turns at scoring runs by hitting a ball with a bat. ❷ a small jumping insect that produces sounds by rubbing its wings together. **cricketer** NOUN

crime, crimes NOUN an action for which you can be punished by law • *a serious crime.*
● SIMILAR WORDS: misdemeanour,
● offence

criminal, criminals NOUN ❶ someone who has committed a crime ▷ ADJECTIVE ❷ involving or related to crime • *criminal activities.* **criminally** ADVERB
● SIMILAR WORDS: ❶ crook,
● lawbreaker, offender

criminology NOUN the scientific study of crime and criminals. **criminologist** NOUN

crimson NOUN OR ADJECTIVE dark purplish-red.

cringe, cringes, cringing, cringed VERB If you cringe, you back away from someone or something because you are afraid or embarrassed.

crinkle, crinkles, crinkling, crinkled

VERB ❶ If something crinkles, it becomes slightly creased or folded ▷ NOUN ❷ Crinkles are small creases or folds.

cripple, cripples, crippling, crippled VERB ❶ To cripple someone is to injure them severely. ❷ To cripple a company or country is to prevent it from working. **crippled** ADJECTIVE **crippling** ADJECTIVE

crisis, crises [Said kry-*seez* in the plural] NOUN a serious or dangerous situation.

crisp, crisper, crispest; crisps ADJECTIVE ❶ Something that is crisp is pleasantly fresh and firm • *crisp lettuce leaves.* ❷ If the air or the weather is crisp, it is pleasantly fresh, cold, and dry • *crisp wintry days.* ▷ NOUN ❸ Crisps are thin slices of potato fried until they are hard and crunchy.

crispy, crispier, crispiest ADJECTIVE Crispy food is pleasantly hard and crunchy • *a crispy salad.*

criterion, criteria [Said kry-*teer*-ee-on] NOUN a standard by which you judge or decide something.
● USAGE NOTE: *Criteria* is the plural
● of *criterion*, and needs to be used
● with a plural verb

critic, critics NOUN ❶ someone who writes reviews of books, films, plays, or musical performances. ❷ A critic of a person or system is someone who criticizes them publicly • *the government's critics.*

critical ADJECTIVE ❶ A critical time is one which is very important in determining what happens in the future • *critical months in the history of*

A
B
C
D
E
F
G
H
I
J
K
L
M
N
O
P
Q
R
S
T
U
V
W
X
Y
Z

the world. ❷ A critical situation is a very serious one • *Rock music is in a critical state.* ❸ If an ill or injured person is critical, they are in danger of dying. ❹ If you are critical of something or someone, you express severe judgments or opinions about them. ❺ If you are critical, you examine and judge something carefully • *a critical look at the way he led his life.* **critically ADVERB**

criticism, criticisms **NOUN** ❶ When there is criticism of someone or something, people express disapproval of them. ❷ If you make a criticism, you point out a fault you think someone or something has.

criticize, criticizes, criticizing, criticized; *also spelt* **criticise VERB** If you criticize someone or something, you say what you think is wrong with them.
● **SIMILAR WORDS:** disparage, find
● fault with

croak, croaks, croaking, croaked **VERB** ❶ When animals and birds croak, they make harsh, low sounds ▷ **NOUN** ❷ a harsh, low sound.

Croatian, Croatians **ADJECTIVE** ❶ belonging to or relating to Croatia ▷ **NOUN** ❷ someone who comes from Croatia. ❸ Croatian is the form of Serbo-Croat spoken in Croatia.

crochet [*Said* **kroh-shay**] **NOUN** Crochet is a way of making clothes and other things out of thread using a needle with a small hook at the end.

crockery NOUN Crockery is plates, cups, and saucers.

crocodile, crocodiles **NOUN** a large scaly meat-eating reptile which lives

in tropical rivers.

crocus, crocuses **NOUN** Crocuses are yellow, purple, or white flowers that grow in early spring.

croft, crofts **NOUN** a small piece of land, especially in Scotland, which is farmed by one family. **crofter NOUN**

croissant, croissants [*Said* **krwah-son**] **NOUN** a light, crescent-shaped roll eaten at breakfast.
● **WORD HISTORY:** from French
● *croissant* meaning 'crescent'

crony, cronies **NOUN OLD-FASHIONED** Your cronies are the friends you spend a lot of time with.

crook, crooks **NOUN** ❶ INFORMAL a criminal. ❷ The crook of your arm or leg is the soft inside part where you bend your elbow or knee ▷ **ADJECTIVE** ❸ In Australian English, crook means ill.

crooked [*Said* **kroo-kid**] **ADJECTIVE** ❶ bent or twisted. ❷ Someone who is crooked is dishonest.

croon, croons, crooning, crooned **VERB** To croon is to sing or hum quietly and gently • *He crooned a love song.*
● **WORD HISTORY:** from Old Dutch
● *kronen* meaning 'to groan'

crop, crops, cropping, cropped **NOUN** ❶ Crops are plants such as wheat and potatoes that are grown for food. ❷ the plants collected at harvest time • *You should have two crops in the year.* ▷ **VERB** ❸ To crop someone's hair is to cut it very short.

croquet [*Said* **kroh-kay**] **NOUN** Croquet is a game in which the players use long-handled mallets to hit balls through metal arches pushed into a lawn.

cross, crosses, crossing, crossed; crosser, crossest **VERB** ❶ If you cross something such as a room or a road, you go to the other side of it. ❷ Lines or roads that cross meet and go across each other. ❸ If a thought crosses your mind, you think of it. ❹ If you cross your arms, legs, or fingers, you put one on top of the other ▷ **NOUN** ❺ a vertical bar or line crossed by a shorter horizontal bar or line; also used to describe any object shaped like this. ❻ RE The Cross is the cross-shaped structure on which Jesus Christ was crucified. A cross is also any symbol representing Christ's Cross. ❼ a written mark shaped like an X • *I drew a small bicycle and put a cross by it.* ❽ Something that is a cross between two things is neither one thing nor the other, but a mixture of both ▷ **ADJECTIVE** ❾ Someone who is cross is rather angry. **crossly ADVERB**

crossbow, crossbows **NOUN** a weapon consisting of a small bow fixed at the end of a piece of wood.

cross-country NOUN ❶ Cross-country is the sport of running across open countryside, rather than on roads or on a track ▷ **ADVERB OR ADJECTIVE** ❷ across country.

cross-eyed ADJECTIVE A cross-eyed person has eyes that seem to look towards each other.

crossfire NOUN Crossfire is gunfire crossing the same place from opposite directions.

crosshatching NOUN ART

Crosshatching is drawing an area of shade in a picture using two or more sets of parallel lines.

crossing, crossings **NOUN** ❶ a place where you can cross a road safely. ❷ a journey by ship to a place on the other side of the sea.

cross-legged ADJECTIVE If you are sitting cross-legged, you are sitting on the floor with your knees pointing outwards and your feet tucked under them.

cross section, cross sections **NOUN** A cross section of a group of people is a representative sample of them.

crossword, crosswords **NOUN** a puzzle in which you work out the answers to clues and write them in the white squares of a pattern of black and white squares.

crotch, crotches **NOUN** the part of your body between the tops of your legs.

crotchet, crotchets **NOUN** MUSIC A crotchet is a musical note equal to two quavers or half a minim.

crouch, crouches, crouching, crouched **VERB** If you are crouching, you are leaning forward with your legs bent under you.

crow, crows, crowing, crowed **NOUN** ❶ a large black bird which makes a loud, harsh noise ▷ **VERB** ❷ When a cock crows, it utters a loud squawking sound.

crowbar, crowbars **NOUN** a heavy iron bar used as a lever or for forcing things open.

▷ SPELLING NOTE: *King IAn went to ParlIAment in a carrIAge for his marrIAge (-ia-)*

a
c
d
e
f
g
h
i
j
k
l
m
n
o
p
q
r
s
t
u
v
w
x
y
z

crowd, crowds, crowding, crowded
NOUN ❶ a large group of people gathered together ▷ **VERB** ❷ When people crowd somewhere, they gather there close together or in large numbers.
● **SIMILAR WORDS:** ❶ mass, mob,
● multitude, throng

crowded **ADJECTIVE** A crowded place is full of people.

crown, crowns, crowning, crowned
NOUN ❶ a circular ornament worn on a royal person's head. ❷ The crown of something such as your head is the top part of it ▷ **VERB** ❸ When a king or queen is crowned, a crown is put on their head during their coronation ceremony. ❹ When something crowns an event, it is the final part of it • *The news crowned a dreadful week.*

crucial [*Said kroo-shl*] **ADJECTIVE** If something is crucial, it is very important in determining how something else will be in the future.
● **WORD HISTORY:** from Latin *crux* meaning 'a cross'
● **SIMILAR WORDS:** critical, decisive,
● vital

crucifix, crucifixes **NOUN** (RE) a cross with a figure representing Jesus Christ being crucified on it.

crucify, crucifies, crucifying, crucified **VERB** (RE) To crucify someone is to tie or nail them to a large wooden cross and leave them there to die.
crucifixion **NOUN**

crude, cruder, crudest **ADJECTIVE**
❶ rough and simple • *a crude weapon* • *a crude method of entry.* ❷ A crude person speaks or behaves in a rude

and offensive way • *You can be quite crude at times.* **crudely** **ADVERB**
crudity **NOUN**
● **SIMILAR WORDS:** ❶ makeshift,
● primitive ❷ coarse, vulgar

cruel, crueller, cruellest **ADJECTIVE** Cruel people deliberately cause pain or distress to other people or to animals.
cruelly **ADVERB**
● **SIMILAR WORDS:** brutal, callous,
● unkind

cruelty **NOUN** cruel behaviour.

cruise, cruises, cruising, cruised
NOUN ❶ a holiday in which you travel on a ship and visit places ▷ **VERB** ❷ When a vehicle cruises, it moves at a constant moderate speed.

cruiser, cruisers **NOUN** ❶ a motor boat with a cabin you can sleep in. ❷ a large, fast warship.

crumb, crumbs **NOUN** Crumbs are very small pieces of bread or cake.

crumble, crumbles, crumbling, crumbled **VERB** When something crumbles, it breaks into small pieces.

crumbly, crumblier, crumbliest **ADJECTIVE** Something crumbly easily breaks into small pieces.

crumpet, crumpets **NOUN** a round, flat, breadlike cake which you eat toasted.

crumple, crumples, crumpling, crumpled **VERB** To crumple paper or cloth is to squash it so that it is full of creases and folds.

crunch, crunches, crunching, crunched **VERB** If you crunch something, you crush it noisily, for example between your teeth or under your feet • *steps crunching the gravel.*

crunchy, crunchier, crunchiest **ADJECTIVE** Crunchy food is hard or crisp and makes a noise when you eat it.

crusade, crusades **NOUN** a long and determined attempt to achieve something • *the crusade for human rights.* **crusader NOUN**

crush, crushes, crushing, crushed **VERB** ❶ To crush something is to destroy its shape by squeezing it. ❷ To crush a substance is to turn it into liquid or powder by squeezing or grinding it. ❸ To crush an army or political organization is to defeat it completely ▷ **NOUN** ❹ a dense crowd of people.

crust, crusts **NOUN** ❶ the hard outside part of a loaf. ❷ a hard layer on top of something • *The snow had a fine crust on it.*

crustacean, crustaceans [Said *kruss-**tay**-shn*] **NOUN** (SCIENCE) A crustacean is a creature with a shell and several pairs of legs. Crabs, lobsters, and shrimps are crustaceans.

crusty, crustier, crustiest **ADJECTIVE** ❶ Something that is crusty has a hard outside layer. ❷ Crusty people are impatient and irritable.

crutch, crutches **NOUN** a support like a long stick which you lean on to help you walk when you have an injured foot or leg.

crux, cruxes **NOUN** the most important or difficult part of a problem or argument.

cry, cries, crying, cried **VERB** ❶ When you cry, tears appear in your eyes.

❷ To cry something is to shout it or say it loudly • *'See you soon!' they cried.* ▷ **NOUN** ❸ If you have a cry, you cry for a period of time. ❹ a shout or other loud sound made with your voice. ❺ a loud sound made by some birds • *the cry of a seagull.*
● **SIMILAR WORDS:** ❶ sob, weep

crypt, crypts **NOUN** an underground room beneath a church, usually used as a burial place.
● **WORD HISTORY:** from Greek *kruptein* meaning 'to hide'

cryptic ADJECTIVE A cryptic remark or message has a hidden meaning.

crystal, crystals **NOUN** ❶ a piece of a mineral that has formed naturally into a regular shape. ❷ Crystal is a type of transparent rock, used in jewellery. ❸ Crystal is also a kind of very high quality glass. **crystalline ADJECTIVE**

crystallize, crystallizes, crystallizing, crystallized; also spelt **crystallise VERB** ❶ If a substance crystallizes, it turns into crystals. ❷ If an idea crystallizes, it becomes clear in your mind.

cub, cubs **NOUN** ❶ Some young wild animals are called cubs • *a lion cub.* ❷ The Cubs is an organization for young boys before they join the Scouts.

Cuban, Cubans [Said **kyoo**-ban] **ADJECTIVE** ❶ belonging or relating to Cuba ▷ **NOUN** ❷ someone who comes from Cuba.

cube, cubes, cubing, cubed (MATHS) **NOUN** ❶ a three-dimensional shape with six equally-sized square surfaces. ❷ If you multiply a number by itself

a
b
c
d
e
f
g
h
i
j
k
l
m
n
o
p
q
r
s
t
u
v
w
x
y
z

twice, you get its cube ▷ **VERB** ❸ To cube a number is to multiply it by itself twice.

cubic ADJECTIVE (MATHS) used in measurements of volume • *cubic centimetres.*

cubicle, cubicles **NOUN** a small enclosed area in a place such as a sports centre, where you can dress and undress.

cuboid, cuboids **NOUN** ❶ (MATHS) a three-dimensional shape with six rectangular faces ▷ **ADJECTIVE** ❷ shaped like a cube • *a cuboid structure.*

cuckoo, cuckoos **NOUN** a grey bird with a two-note call that lays its eggs in other birds' nests.

cucumber, cucumbers **NOUN** a long, thin, green-skinned fruit eaten raw in salads.

cuddle, cuddles, cuddling, cuddled **VERB** ❶ If you cuddle someone, you hold them affectionately in your arms ▷ **NOUN** ❷ If you give someone a cuddle, you hold them affectionately in your arms.

cuddly, cuddlier, cuddliest **ADJECTIVE** Cuddly people, animals, or toys are soft or pleasing in some way so that you want to cuddle them.

cue, cues **NOUN** ❶ something said or done by a performer that is a signal for another performer to begin • *Chris never misses a cue.* ❷ a long stick used to hit the balls in snooker and billiards.

cuff, cuffs **NOUN** the end part of a sleeve.

cufflink, cufflinks **NOUN** Cufflinks are small objects for holding shirt cuffs together.

cuisine, cuisines *[Said kwiz-een]* **NOUN** The cuisine of a region is the style of cooking that is typical of it.
● **WORD HISTORY:** from French *cuisine* meaning 'kitchen'

cul-de-sac, cul-de-sacs *[Said kul-des-sak]* **NOUN** a road that does not lead to any other roads because one end is blocked off.

culinary ADJECTIVE FORMAL connected with the kitchen or cooking.
● **WORD HISTORY:** from Latin *culina* meaning 'kitchen'

cull, culls, culling, culled **VERB** ❶ If you cull things, you gather them from different places or sources • *information culled from movies.* ▷ **NOUN** ❷ When there is a cull, weaker animals are killed to reduce the numbers in a group.

culminate, culminates, culminating, culminated **VERB** To culminate in something is to finally develop into it • *a campaign that culminated in a stunning success.* **culmination NOUN**

culprit, culprits **NOUN** someone who has done something harmful or wrong.

cult, cults **NOUN** ❶ A cult is a religious group with special rituals, usually connected with the worship of a particular person. ❷ 'Cult' is used to refer to any situation in which someone or something is very popular with a large group of people • *the American sports car cult.*

▷ SPELLING NOTE: *A Rude Idiot Thought He Might Eat Toffee In Church* (*arithmetic*)

cultivate, cultivates, cultivating, cultivated **VERB** ❶ To cultivate land is to grow crops on it. ❷ If you cultivate a feeling or attitude, you try to develop it in yourself or other people. **cultivation NOUN**

culture, cultures **NOUN** ❶ Culture refers to the arts and to people's appreciation of them • *He was a man of culture.* ❷ The culture of a particular society is its ideas, customs, and art • *Japanese culture.* ❸ In science, a culture is a group of bacteria or cells grown in a laboratory. **cultured ADJECTIVE cultural ADJECTIVE**

cumulative ADJECTIVE Something that is cumulative keeps being added to.

cunjevoi, cunjevois [*Said* **kun-jiv-voi**] **NOUN** a very small Australian sea creature that lives on rocks.

cunning ADJECTIVE ❶ Someone who is cunning uses clever and deceitful methods to get what they want ▷ **NOUN** ❷ Cunning is the ability to get what you want using clever and deceitful methods. **cunningly ADVERB**
● **SIMILAR WORDS:** ❶ crafty, sly, ● wily

cup, cups, cupping, cupped **NOUN** ❶ a small, round container with a handle, which you drink out of. ❷ a large metal container with two handles, given as a prize ▷ **VERB** ❸ If you cup your hands, you put them together to make a shape like a cup.

cupboard, cupboards **NOUN** a piece of furniture with doors and shelves.

curable ADJECTIVE If a disease or illness is curable, it can be cured.

curate, curates **NOUN** a clergyman who helps a vicar or a priest.

curator, curators **NOUN** the person in a museum or art gallery in charge of its contents.

curb, curbs, curbing, curbed **VERB** ❶ To curb something is to keep it within limits • *policies designed to curb inflation.* ▷ **NOUN** ❷ If a curb is placed on something, it is kept within limits • *the curb on spending.*

curdle, curdles, curdling, curdled **VERB** When milk curdles, it turns sour.

curds PLURAL NOUN Curds are the thick white substance formed when milk turns sour.

cure, cures, curing, cured **VERB** ❶ To cure an illness is to end it. ❷ To cure a sick or injured person is to make them well. ❸ If something cures you of a habit or attitude, it stops you having it. ❹ To cure food, tobacco, or animal skin is to treat it in order to preserve it ▷ **NOUN** ❺ A cure for an illness is something that cures it.
● **SIMILAR WORDS:** ❷ heal, make ● better

curfew, curfews **NOUN** If there is a curfew, people must stay indoors between particular times at night.

curiosity, curiosities **NOUN** ❶ Curiosity is the desire to know about something. ❷ something unusual and interesting.

curious ADJECTIVE ❶ Someone who is curious wants to know more about something. ❷ Something that

▷ SPELLING NOTE: *Beautiful Elephants Are Usually Tiny (beautiful)*

is curious is unusual and hard to explain. **curiously ADVERB**
● **SIMILAR WORDS: ❶** inquiring,
● inquisitive, nosy

curl, curls, curling, curled **NOUN**
❶ Curls are lengths of hair shaped in tight curves and circles. ❷ a curved or spiral shape • *the curls of morning fog.*
▷ **VERB** ❸ If something curls, it moves in a curve or spiral. **curly ADJECTIVE**

curler, curlers **NOUN** Curlers are plastic or metal tubes that women roll their hair round to make it curly.

curlew, curlews [Said *kur-lyoo*] **NOUN** a large brown bird with a long curved beak and a loud cry.

currant, currants **NOUN** ❶ Currants are small dried grapes often put in cakes and puddings. ❷ Currants are also blackcurrants or redcurrants.
● **WORD HISTORY:** sense 1 is from
● Middle English *rayson of Corannte*
● meaning 'Corinth raisin'

currawong, currawongs **NOUN** an Australian bird like a crow.

currency, currencies **NOUN** ❶ A country's currency is its coins and banknotes, or its monetary system generally • *foreign currency* • *a strong economy and a weak currency.* ❷ If something such as an idea has currency, it is used a lot at a particular time.

current, currents **NOUN**
❶ (GEOGRAPHY) a strong continuous movement of the water in a river or in the sea. ❷ (GEOGRAPHY) An air current is a flowing movement in the air. ❸ (SCIENCE) An electric current is a flow of electricity through a wire or

circuit ▷ **ADJECTIVE** ❹ Something that is current is happening, being done, or being used now. **currently ADVERB**

current affairs PLURAL NOUN Current affairs are political and social events discussed in newspapers and on television and radio.

curriculum, curriculums or curricula [Said *kur-rik-yoo-lum*] **NOUN** the different courses taught at a school or university.

curriculum vitae, curricula vitae [Said *vee-tie*] **NOUN** Someone's curriculum vitae is a written account of their personal details, education, and work experience which they send when they apply for a job.

curried ADJECTIVE Curried food has been flavoured with hot spices • *curried lamb.*

curry, curries, currying, curried **NOUN** ❶ Curry is an Indian dish made with hot spices ▷ **PHRASE** ❷ To **curry favour** with someone means to try to please them by flattering them or doing things to help them.
● **WORD HISTORY:** sense 1 is from
● Tamil *kari* meaning 'sauce'; sense 2
● is from Old French *correer* meaning
● 'to make ready'

curse, curses, cursing, cursed **VERB**
❶ To curse is to swear because you are angry. ❷ If you curse someone or something, you say angry things about them using rude words ▷ **NOUN**
❸ what you say when you curse.
❹ something supernatural that is supposed to cause unpleasant things to happen to someone. ❺ a thing or person that causes a lot of distress

• *the curse of recession.* **cursed ADJECTIVE**

cursor, cursors **NOUN** an arrow or box on a computer monitor which indicates where the next letter or symbol is.

cursory ADJECTIVE When you give something a cursory glance or examination, you look at it briefly without paying attention to detail.

curt, curter, curtest **ADJECTIVE** If someone is curt, they speak in a brief and rather rude way. **curtly ADVERB**

curtail, curtails, curtailing, curtailed **VERB** FORMAL To curtail something is to reduce or restrict it • *Injury curtailed his career.*

curtain, curtains **NOUN** **1** a hanging piece of material which can be pulled across a window for privacy or to keep out the light. **2** (DRAMA) a large piece of material which hangs in front of the stage in a theatre until a performance begins.

curtsy, curtsies, curtsying, curtsied; also spelt **curtsey VERB** **1** When a woman curtsies, she lowers her body briefly, bending her knees, to show respect ▷ **NOUN** **2** the movement a woman makes when she curtsies • *She gave a mock curtsy.*

curve, curves, curving, curved **NOUN** **1** a smooth, gradually bending line ▷ **VERB** **2** When something curves, it moves in a curve or has the shape of a curve • *The track curved away below him* • *His mouth curved slightly.* **curved ADJECTIVE**

cushion, cushions, cushioning, cushioned **NOUN** **1** a soft object put

on a seat to make it more comfortable ▷ **VERB** **2** To cushion something is to reduce its effect • *We might have helped to cushion the shock for her.*

custard NOUN Custard is a sweet yellow sauce made from milk and eggs or milk and a powder.

custodian, custodians **NOUN** the person in charge of a collection in an art gallery or a museum.

custody NOUN **1** To have custody of a child means to have the legal right to keep it and look after it • *She won custody of her younger son.* ▷ **PHRASE** **2** Someone who is **in custody** is being kept in prison until they can be tried in a court. **custodial ADJECTIVE**

custom, customs **NOUN** **1** a traditional activity • *an ancient Chinese custom.* **2** something usually done at a particular time or in particular circumstances by a person or by the people in a society • *It was also my custom to do Christmas shows.* **3** Customs is the place at a border, airport, or harbour where you have to declare any goods you are bringing into a country. **4** FORMAL If a shop or business has your custom, you buy things or go there regularly • *Banks are desperate to get your custom.*
  ● **SIMILAR WORDS: 1** convention, tradition **2** habit, practice

customary ADJECTIVE usual • *his customary modesty* • *her customary greeting.* **customarily ADVERB**

custom-built or **custom-made ADJECTIVE** Something that is custom-built or custom-made is made to someone's special requirements.

A
B
C
D
E
F
G
H
I
J
K
L
M
N
O
P
Q
R
S
T
U
V
W
X
Y
Z

customer, customers NOUN ❶ A shop's or firm's customers are the people who buy its goods. ❷ INFORMAL You can use 'customer' to refer to someone when describing what they are like to deal with • *a tough customer*.
● SIMILAR WORDS: ❶ buyer, client, ● consumer

customize, customizes, customizing, customized; *also spelt* **customise** VERB To customize a car means to alter its appearance to make it look unusual.

cut, cuts, cutting, cut VERB ❶ If you cut something, you use a knife, scissors, or some other sharp tool to mark it or remove parts of it. ❷ If you cut yourself, you injure yourself on a sharp object. ❸ If you cut the amount of something, you reduce it • *Some costs could be cut.* ❹ When writing is cut, parts of it are not printed or broadcast. ❺ To cut from one scene or shot to another in a film is to go instantly to the other scene or shot ▷ NOUN ❻ a mark or injury made with a knife or other sharp tool. ❼ a reduction • *another cut in interest rates.* ❽ a part in something written that is not printed or broadcast. ❾ a large piece of meat ready for cooking ▷ ADJECTIVE ❿ Well cut clothes have been well designed and made • *this beautifully cut coat.*
cut back VERB To cut back or cut back on spending means to reduce it.
cutback NOUN
cut down VERB If you cut down on an activity, you do it less often • *cutting down on smoking.*
cut off VERB ❶ To cut someone or something off means to separate

them from things they are normally connected with • *The President had cut himself off from the people.* ❷ If a supply of something is cut off, you no longer get it • *The water had been cut off.* ❸ If your telephone or telephone call is cut off, it is disconnected.
cut out VERB ❶ If you cut out something you are doing, you stop doing it • *Cut out drinking.* ❷ If an engine cuts out, it suddenly stops working.

cute, cuter, cutest ADJECTIVE pretty or attractive.

cuticle, cuticles NOUN Cuticles are the pieces of skin that cover the base of your fingernails and toenails.

cutlass, cutlasses NOUN a curved sword that was used by sailors.

cutlery NOUN Cutlery is knives, forks, and spoons.

cutlet, cutlets NOUN a small piece of meat which you fry or grill.

cutting, cuttings NOUN ❶ something cut from a newspaper or magazine. ❷ a part cut from a plant and used to grow a new plant ▷ ADJECTIVE ❸ A cutting remark is unkind and likely to hurt someone.

CV an abbreviation for **curriculum vitae**.

cyanide [*Said* **sigh**-*an-nide*] NOUN Cyanide is an extremely poisonous chemical.

cyber- PREFIX Words that begin with 'cyber-' have something to do with computers in their meaning. For example a *cybercafé* is a place where computers are provided for customers to use.

▷ SPELLING NOTE: *you'll* brEAK *that* Electrical Aerial, Kitty (*break*)

● **WORD HISTORY:** from Greek
● *kybernētēs* meaning 'a steerman'

cyberpet, cyberpets **NOUN** an
electronic toy that imitates the
activities of a pet, and needs to be fed
and entertained.

cyberspace NOUN all of the data
stored in a large computer, seen as a
three-dimensional model.

cycle, cycles, cycling, cycled **VERB**
❶ When you cycle, you ride a bicycle
▷ **NOUN** **❷** a bicycle or a motorcycle.
❸ a series of events which is repeated
again and again in the same order
• *the cycle of births and deaths.*
❹ (SCIENCE) a single complete series
of movements or events in an
electrical, electronic, mechanical, or
organic process. **❺** a series of songs
or poems intended to be performed or
read together.
● **WORD HISTORY:** from Greek
● *kuklos* meaning 'ring' or 'wheel'

cyclical or **cyclic ADJECTIVE**
happening over and over again in
cycles • *a clear cyclical pattern.*

cyclist, cyclists **NOUN** someone who
rides a bicycle.

cyclone, cyclones **NOUN** a violent
tropical storm.

cygnet, cygnets *[Said **sig**-net]* **NOUN**
a young swan.

cylinder, cylinders **NOUN ❶** a
regular three-dimensional shape with
two equally-sized flat circular ends
joined by a curved surface. **❷** the part
in a motor engine in which the piston
moves backwards and forwards.
cylindrical ADJECTIVE

cymbal, cymbals **NOUN** a circular

brass plate used as a percussion
instrument. Cymbals are clashed
together or hit with a stick.

cynic, cynics *[Said **sin**-nik]* **NOUN** a
cynical person.
● **WORD HISTORY:** from Greek
● *kunikos* meaning 'dog-like'

cynical ADJECTIVE believing that
people always behave selfishly or
dishonestly. **cynically ADVERB**
cynicism NOUN

cypher another spelling of **cipher.**

cypress, cypresses **NOUN** a type of
evergreen tree with small dark green
leaves and round cones.

cyst, cysts *[Said **sist**]* **NOUN** a growth
containing liquid that can form under
your skin or inside your body.

cytoplasm *[Said **sigh**-toh-plazm]*
NOUN (SCIENCE) all the substances
and structures inside a cell except the
nucleus.

czar another spelling of **tsar.**

czarina another spelling of **tsarina.**

Czech, Czechs *[Said **chek**]*
ADJECTIVE ❶ belonging or relating
to the Czech Republic ▷ **NOUN**
❷ someone who comes from the
Czech Republic. **❸** Czech is the
language spoken in the Czech
Republic.

Czechoslovak, Czechoslovaks
*[Said chek-oh-**slow**-vak]* **ADJECTIVE**
❶ belonging or relating to the
country that used to be
Czechoslovakia ▷ **NOUN ❷** someone
who came from the country that used
to be Czechoslovakia.

▷ SPELLING NOTE: *I always visit my FRIend on a FRIday (Friday)*

Dd

A
B
C
D
E
F
G
H
I
J
K
L
M
N
O
P
Q
R
S
T
U
V
W
X
Y
Z

Words that sound as if they should start with *di* are often spelt with *de* instead, for example *determination* and *dessert*.

dab, dabs, dabbing, dabbed **VERB** ❶ If you dab something, you touch it with quick light strokes • *He dabbed some disinfectant on to the gash.* ▷ **NOUN** ❷ a small amount of something that is put on a surface • *a dab of perfume.*

dabble, dabbles, dabbling, dabbled **VERB** If you dabble in something, you work or play at it without being seriously involved in it • *All his life he dabbled in poetry.*

dachshund, dachshunds *[Said daks-hoond]* **NOUN** a small dog with a long body and very short legs.
● **WORD HISTORY:** a German word
● meaning 'badger-dog'

dad or **daddy**, dads or daddies **NOUN** INFORMAL Your dad or your daddy is your father.

daddy-long-legs NOUN a harmless flying insect with very long legs.

daffodil, daffodils **NOUN** a plant with a yellow trumpet-shaped flower.

daft, dafter, daftest **ADJECTIVE** stupid and not sensible.
● **WORD HISTORY:** from Old English

● *gedæfte* meaning 'gentle'

dagga NOUN INFORMAL In South African English, dagga is cannabis.

dagger, daggers **NOUN** a weapon like a short knife.

dahlia, dahlias *[Said dale-ya]* **NOUN** a type of brightly coloured garden flower.

daily ADJECTIVE ❶ occurring every day • *our daily visit to the gym.* ❷ of or relating to a single day or to one day at a time • *the average daily wage.*

dainty, daintier, daintiest **ADJECTIVE** very delicate and pretty. **daintily ADVERB**

dairy, dairies **NOUN** ❶ a shop or company that supplies milk and milk products. ❷ in New Zealand, a small shop selling groceries, often outside of usual opening hours ▷ **ADJECTIVE** ❸ Dairy products are foods made from milk, such as butter, cheese, cream, and yogurt. ❹ A dairy farm is one which keeps cattle to produce milk.
● **USAGE NOTE:** Do not confuse the
● order of the vowels in *dairy* and
● *diary*

dais, daises *[Said day-is]* **NOUN** a raised platform, normally at one end of a hall and used by a speaker.

daisy, daisies **NOUN** a small wild flower with a yellow centre and small

white petals.
- **WORD HISTORY:** from Old English
- *dæges eage* meaning 'day's eye',
- because the daisy opens in the
- daytime and closes at night

dale, dales NOUN a valley.

dalmatian, dalmatians NOUN a large dog with short smooth white hair and black or brown spots.

dam, dams NOUN a barrier built across a river to hold back water.

damage, damages, damaging, damaged VERB ❶ To damage something means to harm or spoil it ▷ NOUN ❷ Damage to something is injury or harm done to it. ❸ Damages is the money awarded by a court to compensate someone for loss or harm. **damaging** ADJECTIVE

dame, dames NOUN the title given to a woman who has been awarded the OBE or one of the other British orders of chivalry.

damn, damns, damning, damned [Said *dam*] VERB ❶ To damn something or someone means to curse or condemn them ▷ INTERJECTION ❷ 'Damn' is a swearword. **damned** ADJECTIVE

damnation [Said *dam-nay-shun*] NOUN Damnation is eternal punishment in Hell after death.

damp, damper, dampest ADJECTIVE ❶ slightly wet ▷ NOUN ❷ Damp is slight wetness, especially in the air or in the walls of a building. **dampness** NOUN

dampen, dampens, dampening, dampened VERB ❶ If you dampen something, you make it slightly wet.

❷ To dampen something also means to reduce its liveliness or strength
• *The whole episode has rather dampened my enthusiasm.*

damper PHRASE To **put a damper on** something means to stop it being enjoyable.

damson, damsons NOUN a small blue-black plum; also the tree that the fruit grows on.
- **WORD HISTORY:** from Latin
- *prunum Damascenum* meaning
- 'Damascus plum'

dance, dances, dancing, danced VERB ❶ To dance means to move your feet and body rhythmically in time to music ▷ NOUN ❷ a series of rhythmic movements or steps in time to music. ❸ a social event where people dance with each other. **dancer** NOUN **dancing** NOUN

dandelion, dandelions NOUN a wild plant with yellow flowers which form a ball of fluffy seeds.

dandruff NOUN Dandruff is small, loose scales of dead skin in someone's hair.

D and T an abbreviation for 'Design and Technology'.

dandy, dandies NOUN OLD-FASHIONED a man who always dresses in very smart clothes.

Dane, Danes NOUN someone who comes from Denmark.

danger, dangers NOUN ❶ Danger is the possibility that someone may be harmed or killed. ❷ something or someone that can hurt or harm you.
- **SIMILAR WORDS:** ❶ hazard, peril
- risk

▷ SPELLING NOTE: *The government licenSes Schnapps (licenses)*

a b c **d** e f g h i j k l m n o p q r s t u v w x y z

A
B
C
D
E
F
G
H
I
J
K
L
M
N
O
P
Q
R
S
T
U
V
W
X
Y
Z

dangerous ADJECTIVE able to or likely to cause hurt or harm.
dangerously ADVERB
- SIMILAR WORDS: hazardous,
- perilous, unsafe

dangle, dangles, dangling, dangled VERB When something dangles or when you dangle it, it swings or hangs loosely.

Danish ADJECTIVE ❶ belonging or relating to Denmark ▷ NOUN ❷ Danish is the main language spoken in Denmark.

dank, danker, dankest ADJECTIVE A dank place is unpleasantly damp and chilly.

dapper ADJECTIVE slim and neatly dressed.
- WORD HISTORY: from Old Dutch
- *dapper* meaning 'active' or 'nimble'

dappled ADJECTIVE marked with patches of a different or darker shade.

dare, dares, daring, dared VERB ❶ To dare someone means to challenge them to do something in order to prove their courage. ❷ To dare to do something means to have the courage to do it ▷ NOUN ❸ a challenge to do something dangerous.
- USAGE NOTE: When *dare* is used
- in a question or with a negative, it
- does not add an s: *dare she come?*;
- *he dare not come*

daredevil, daredevils NOUN a person who enjoys doing dangerous things.

daring ADJECTIVE ❶ bold and willing to take risks ▷ NOUN ❷ the courage required to do things which are dangerous.

dark, darker, darkest ADJECTIVE ❶ If it is dark, there is not enough light to see properly. ❷ Dark colours or surfaces reflect little light and so look deep-coloured or dull. ❸ 'Dark' is also used to describe thoughts or ideas which are sinister or unpleasant ▷ NOUN ❹ The dark is the lack of light in a place. **darkly** ADVERB
darkness NOUN
- SIMILAR WORDS: ❶ dim, murky

darken, darkens, darkening, darkened VERB If something darkens, or if you darken it, it becomes darker than it was.

darkroom, darkrooms NOUN a room from which daylight is shut out so that photographic film can be developed.

darling, darlings NOUN ❶ Someone who is lovable or a favourite may be called a darling ▷ ADJECTIVE ❷ much admired or loved • *his darling daughter.*

darn, darns, darning, darned VERB ❶ To darn a hole in a garment means to mend it with crossing stitches ▷ NOUN ❷ a part of a garment that has been darned.

dart, darts, darting, darted NOUN ❶ a small pointed arrow. ❷ Darts is a game in which the players throw darts at a round board divided into numbered sections ▷ VERB ❸ To dart about means to move quickly and suddenly from one place to another.

dash, dashes, dashing, dashed VERB ❶ To dash somewhere means to rush there. ❷ If something is dashed against something else, it strikes it or is thrown violently against it. ❸ If

a
b
c
d
e
f
g
h
i
j
k
l
m
n
o
p
q
r
s
t
u
v
w
x
y
z

WHAT DOES THE DASH DO?

The **dash** (—) marks an abrupt change in the flow of a sentence, either showing a sudden change of subject, or marking off extra information. The dash can also show that a speech has been cut off suddenly:
I'm not sure — what was the question again?
"Go ahead and — " He broke off as Robbie seized his arm.

hopes or ambitions are dashed, they are ruined or frustrated ▷ **NOUN** **④** a sudden movement or rush. **⑤** a small quantity of something. **⑥** the punctuation mark (—) which shows a change of subject, or which may be used instead of brackets.
▶ SEE GRAMMAR BOX ABOVE

dashboard, dashboards **NOUN** the instrument panel in a motor vehicle.

dashing **ADJECTIVE** A dashing man is stylish and confident • *He was a dashing figure in his younger days.*

dasyure, dasyures *[Said dass-ee-your]* **NOUN** a small marsupial that lives in Australia and eats meat.

data **NOUN** **①** information, usually in the form of facts or statistics. **②** (ICT) any information put into a computer and which the computer works on or processes.
● **WORD HISTORY:** from Latin *data* meaning 'things given'
● **USAGE NOTE:** *Data* is really a plural word, but it is usually used as a singular

database, databases **NOUN** (ICT) a collection of information stored in a computer.

date, dates, dating, dated **NOUN** **①** a particular day or year that can be named. **②** If you have a date, you

have an appointment to meet someone; also used to refer to the person you are meeting. **③** a small dark-brown sticky fruit with a stone inside, which grows on palm trees ▷ **VERB** **④** If you are dating someone, you have a romantic relationship with them. **⑤** If you date something, you find out the time when it began or was made. **⑥** If something dates from a particular time, that is when it happened or was made ▷ **PHRASE** **⑦** If something is **out of date**, it is old-fashioned or no longer valid.

dated **ADJECTIVE** no longer fashionable.

datum the singular form of **data**.

daub, daubs, daubing, daubed **VERB** If you daub something such as mud or paint on a surface, you smear it there.

daughter, daughters **NOUN** Someone's daughter is their female child.

daughter-in-law, daughters-in-law **NOUN** Someone's daughter-in-law is the wife of their son.

daunt, daunts, daunting, daunted **VERB** If something daunts you, you feel worried about whether you can succeed in doing it • *He was not the type of man to be daunted by adversity.*
daunting **ADJECTIVE**

▷ SPELLING NOTE: *plaice the fish has a glittering 'EYE' (I) (plaice)*

dauphin, dauphins *[Said **doe**-fan]* NOUN (HISTORY) The dauphin was the name given to the eldest son of the King of France from the 14th to the 19th century.

dawn, dawns, dawning, dawned NOUN **1** the time in the morning when light first appears in the sky. **2** the beginning of something • *the dawn of the radio age.* ▷ VERB **3** If day is dawning, morning light is beginning to appear. **4** If an idea or fact dawns on you, you realize it.

day, days NOUN **1** one of the seven 24-hour periods of time in a week, measured from one midnight to the next. **2** Day is the period of light between sunrise and sunset. **3** You can refer to a particular day or days meaning a particular period in history • *in Gladstone's day.*

daybreak NOUN Daybreak is the time in the morning when light first appears in the sky.

daydream, daydreams, daydreaming, daydreamed NOUN **1** a series of pleasant thoughts about things that you would like to happen ▷ VERB **2** When you daydream, you drift off into a daydream.

daylight NOUN **1** Daylight is the period during the day when it is light. **2** Daylight is also the light from the sun.

day-to-day ADJECTIVE happening every day as part of ordinary routine life.

day trip, day trips NOUN a journey for pleasure to a place and back again on the same day.

daze PHRASE If you are in a daze, you are confused and bewildered.

dazed ADJECTIVE If you are dazed, you are stunned and unable to think clearly.

dazzle, dazzles, dazzling, dazzled VERB **1** If someone or something dazzles you, you are very impressed by their brilliance. **2** If a bright light dazzles you, it blinds you for a moment. **dazzling** ADJECTIVE

de- PREFIX When 'de-' is added to a noun or verb, it changes the meaning to its opposite • *de-ice.*

deacon, deacons NOUN **1** In the Church of England or Roman Catholic Church, a deacon is a member of the clergy below the rank of priest. **2** In some other churches, a deacon is a church official appointed to help the minister. **deaconess** NOUN

dead ADJECTIVE **1** no longer living or supporting life. **2** no longer used or no longer functioning • *a dead language.* **3** If part of your body goes dead, it loses sensation and feels numb ▷ NOUN **4** the middle part of night or winter, when it is most quiet and at its darkest or coldest.

dead end, dead ends NOUN a street that is closed off at one end.

deadline, deadlines NOUN a time or date before which something must be completed.

deadlock, deadlocks NOUN a situation in which neither side in a dispute is willing to give in.
● SIMILAR WORDS: impasse,
● stalemate

▷ SPELLING NOTE: *I went to see (C) the doctor's new practiCe (practice)*

deadly, deadlier, deadliest
ADJECTIVE ❶ likely or able to cause
death ▷ **ADVERB OR ADJECTIVE**
❷ 'Deadly' is used to emphasize how
serious or unpleasant a situation is
• *He is deadly serious.*

deadpan **ADJECTIVE OR ADVERB**
showing no emotion or expression.

deaf, deafer, deafest **ADJECTIVE**
❶ partially or totally unable to hear.
❷ refusing to listen or pay attention
to something • *He was deaf to all pleas
for financial help.* **deafness** **NOUN**

deafen, deafens, deafening, deafened
VERB If you are deafened by a noise,
it is so loud that you cannot hear
anything else.

deafening **ADJECTIVE** If a noise is
deafening, it is so loud that you
cannot hear anything else.

deal, deals, dealing, dealt **NOUN**
❶ an agreement or arrangement,
especially in business ▷ **VERB** ❷ If
you deal with something, you do what
is necessary to sort it out • *He must
learn to deal with stress.* ❸ If you deal
in a particular type of goods, you buy
and sell those goods. ❹ If you deal
someone or something a blow, you
hurt or harm them • *Competition from
abroad dealt a heavy blow to the
industry.*

dealer, dealers **NOUN** a person or
firm whose business involves buying
or selling things.

dealings **PLURAL NOUN** Your
dealings with people are the relations
you have with them or the business
you do with them.

dean, deans **NOUN** ❶ In a university

or college, a dean is a person
responsible for administration or for
the welfare of students. ❷ In the
Church of England, a dean is a
clergyman who is responsible for
administration.
- **WORD HISTORY:** from Latin
- *decanus* meaning 'someone in
- charge of ten people'

dear, dears; dearer, dearest **NOUN**
❶ 'Dear' is used as a sign of affection
• *What's the matter, dear?*
▷ **ADJECTIVE** ❷ much loved • *my
dear son.* ❸ Something that is dear is
very expensive. ❹ You use 'dear' at
the beginning of a letter before the
name of the person you are writing to.
dearly **ADVERB**
- **SIMILAR WORDS:** ❷ beloved,
- cherished ❸ costly, expensive

dearth [Said **derth**] **NOUN** a
shortage of something.

death, deaths **NOUN** Death is the
end of the life of a person or animal.

debacle, debacles [Said day-**bah**-kl]
NOUN FORMAL a sudden disastrous
failure.

debase, debases, debasing, debased
VERB To debase something means to
reduce its value or quality.

debatable **ADJECTIVE** not
absolutely certain • *The justness of
these wars is debatable.*
- **SIMILAR WORDS:** doubtful,
- questionable

debate, debates, debating, debated
NOUN ❶ Debate is argument or
discussion • *There is much debate as to
what causes depression.* ❷ a formal
discussion in which opposing views
are expressed ▷ **VERB** ❸ When

a
b
c
d
e
f
g
h
i
j
k
l
m
n
o
p
q
r
s
t
u
v
w
x
y
z

▷ SPELLING NOTE: *You must practiSe your Ss (practise)*

people debate something, they discuss it in a fairly formal manner. **❹** If you are debating whether or not to do something, you are considering it • *He was debating whether or not he should tell her.*

debilitating ADJECTIVE FORMAL If something is debilitating, it makes you very weak • *a debilitating illness.*

debit, debits, debiting, debited VERB **❶** to take money from a person's bank account ▷ NOUN **❷** a record of the money that has been taken out of a person's bank account.

debrief, debriefs, debriefing, debriefed VERB When someone is debriefed, they are asked to give a report on a task they have just completed. **debriefing** NOUN

debris [*Said day-bree*] NOUN Debris is fragments or rubble left after something has been destroyed.
● WORD HISTORY: from Old French
● *débriser* meaning 'to shatter'

debt, debts [*Said det*] NOUN **❶** a sum of money that is owed to one person by another. **❷** Debt is the state of owing money.

debtor, debtors NOUN a person who owes money.

debut, debuts [*Said day-byoo*] NOUN a performer's first public appearance.

debutante, debutantes [*Said deb-yoo-tant*] NOUN OLD-FASHIONED a girl from the upper classes who has started going to social events.

dec- or **deca-** PREFIX Words beginning with 'dec-' or 'deca-' have 'ten' in their meaning • *decathlon.*

decade, decades NOUN a period of ten years.

decadence NOUN Decadence is a decline in standards of morality and behaviour. **decadent** ADJECTIVE

decaffeinated [*Said dee-kaf-in-ate-ed*] ADJECTIVE Decaffeinated coffee or tea has had most of the caffeine removed.

decagon, decagons NOUN (MATHS) a shape with ten straight sides.

decanter, decanters NOUN a glass bottle with a stopper, from which wine and other drinks are served.

decapitate, decapitates, decapitating, decapitated VERB To decapitate someone means to cut off their head.

decathlon, decathlons [*Said de-cath-lon*] NOUN a sports contest in which athletes compete in ten different events.
● WORD HISTORY: from Greek *deka*
● meaning 'ten' and *athlon* meaning
● 'contest'

decay, decays, decaying, decayed VERB **❶** When things decay, they rot or go bad ▷ NOUN **❷** Decay is the process of decaying.

deceased FORMAL ADJECTIVE **❶** A deceased person is someone who has recently died ▷ NOUN **❷** The deceased is someone who has recently died.

deceit NOUN Deceit is behaviour that is intended to mislead people into believing something that is not true. **deceitful** ADJECTIVE

deceive, deceives, deceiving,

deceived **VERB** If you deceive someone, you make them believe something that is not true.

decelerate, decelerates, decelerating, decelerated **VERB** If something decelerates, it slows down. **deceleration NOUN**

December NOUN December is the twelfth and last month of the year. It has 31 days.
● **WORD HISTORY:** from Latin *December* meaning 'the tenth month'

decency NOUN ❶ Decency is behaviour that is respectable and follows accepted moral standards. ❷ Decency is also behaviour which shows kindness and respect towards people • *No one had the decency to tell me to my face.*

decent ADJECTIVE ❶ of an acceptable standard or quality • *He gets a decent pension.* ❷ Decent people are honest and respectable • *a decent man.* **decently ADVERB**
● **SIMILAR WORDS:** ❷ respectable

decentralize, decentralizes, decentralizing, decentralized; *also spelt* **decentralise VERB** To decentralize an organization means to reorganize it so that power is transferred from one main administrative centre to smaller local units. **decentralization NOUN**

deception, deceptions **NOUN** ❶ something that is intended to trick or deceive someone. ❷ Deception is the act of deceiving someone.

deceptive ADJECTIVE likely to make people believe something that is not true. **deceptively ADVERB**

● **SIMILAR WORDS:** false, ● misleading

decibel, decibels **NOUN** (SCIENCE) a unit of the intensity of sound.

decide, decides, deciding, decided **VERB** If you decide to do something, you choose to do it.
● **SIMILAR WORDS:** make up one's ● mind, reach a decision, come to a ● decision

deciduous ADJECTIVE Deciduous trees lose their leaves each autumn.

decimal, decimals **ADJECTIVE** (MATHS) ❶ The decimal system expresses numbers using all the digits from 0 to 9 ▷ **NOUN** ❷ a fraction in which a dot called a decimal point is followed by numbers representing tenths, hundredths, and thousandths. For example, 0.5 represents $5/10$ (or $1/2$); 0.05 represents $5/100$ (or $1/20$).

decimate, decimates, decimating, decimated **VERB** To decimate a group of people or animals means to kill or destroy a large number of them.

decipher, deciphers, deciphering, deciphered **VERB** If you decipher a piece of writing or a message, you work out its meaning.

decision, decisions **NOUN** a choice or judgment that is made about something • *The editor's decision is final.*
● **SIMILAR WORDS:** judgment, ● resolution

decisive [Said dis-**sigh**-siv] **ADJECTIVE** ❶ having great influence on the result of something • *It was the decisive moment of the race.* ❷ A decisive person is able to make

▷ SPELLING NOTE: *LEarn the principLEs (principle)*

A
B
C
D
E
F
G
H
I
J
K
L
M
N
O
P
Q
R
S
T
U
V
W
X
Y
Z

decisions firmly and quickly.
decisively ADVERB **decisiveness** NOUN

deck, decks NOUN ❶ a floor or platform built into a ship, or one of the two floors on a bus. ❷ a pack of cards.

deck chair, deck chairs NOUN a light folding chair, made from canvas and wood and used outdoors.

declaration, declarations NOUN a firm, forceful statement, often an official announcement • *a declaration of war.*
  ● SIMILAR WORDS: assertion,
  ● statement

declare, declares, declaring, declared VERB ❶ If you declare something, you state it forcefully or officially. ❷ If you declare goods or earnings, you state what you have bought or earned, in order to pay tax or duty.
  ● SIMILAR WORDS: ❶ announce,
  ● proclaim, state

decline, declines, declining, declined VERB ❶ If something declines, it becomes smaller or weaker. ❷ If you decline something, you politely refuse to accept it or do it ▷ NOUN ❸ a gradual weakening or decrease • *a decline in the birth rate.*

decode, decodes, decoding, decoded VERB If you decode a coded message, you convert it into ordinary language.
decoder NOUN

decommission, decommissions, decommissioning, decommissioned VERB When something such as a nuclear reactor or large machine is decommissioned, it is taken to pieces or removed from service because it is

no longer going to be used.

decompose, decomposes, decomposing, decomposed VERB If something decomposes, it decays through chemical or bacterial action.

decor [*Said day-kor*] NOUN The decor of a room or house is the style in which it is decorated and furnished.

decorate, decorates, decorating, decorated VERB ❶ If you decorate something, you make it more attractive by adding some ornament or colour to it. ❷ If you decorate a room or building, you paint or wallpaper it.
  ● SIMILAR WORDS: ❶ adorn,
  ● ornament

decoration, decorations NOUN ❶ Decorations are features added to something to make it more attractive. ❷ The decoration in a building or room is the style of the furniture and wallpaper.

decorative ADJECTIVE intended to look attractive.

decorator, decorators NOUN a person whose job is painting and putting up wallpaper in rooms and buildings.

decorum [*Said dik-ore-um*] NOUN FORMAL Decorum is polite and correct behaviour.

decoy, decoys NOUN a person or object that is used to lead someone or something into danger.

decrease, decreases, decreasing, decreased VERB ❶ If something decreases or if you decrease it, it becomes less in quantity or size ▷ NOUN ❷ a lessening in the

amount of something; also the
amount by which something becomes
less. **decreasing ADJECTIVE**

decree, decrees, decreeing, decreed
VERB ❶ If someone decrees
something, they state formally that it
will happen ▷ **NOUN ❷** an official
decision or order, usually by
governments or rulers.

decrepit ADJECTIVE broken or
worn out by use or old age.
decrepitude NOUN

dedicate, dedicates, dedicating,
dedicated **VERB** If you dedicate
yourself to something, you devote
your time and energy to it.
dedication NOUN
● **SIMILAR WORDS:** commit, devote

deduce, deduces, deducing, deduced
VERB If you deduce something, you
work it out from other facts that you
know are true.
● **SIMILAR WORDS:** conclude,
● reason

deduct, deducts, deducting,
deducted **VERB** To deduct an amount
from a total amount means to
subtract it from the total.

deduction, deductions **NOUN**
❶ an amount which is taken away
from a total. **❷** a conclusion that you
have reached because of other things
that you know are true.

deed, deeds **NOUN ❶** something
that is done. **❷** a legal document,
especially concerning the ownership
of land or buildings.

deem, deems, deeming, deemed
VERB FORMAL If you deem something
to be true, you judge or consider it to

be true • *His ideas were deemed
unacceptable.*

deep, deeper, deepest **ADJECTIVE**
❶ situated or extending a long way
down from the top surface of
something, or a long way inwards • *a
deep hole.* **❷** great or intense • *deep
suspicion.* **❸** low in pitch • *a deep
voice.* **❹** strong and fairly dark in
colour • *The wine was deep ruby in
colour.* **deeply ADVERB**

deepen, deepens, deepening,
deepened **VERB** If something
deepens or is deepened, it becomes
deeper or more intense.

deer NOUN a large, hoofed mammal
that lives wild in parts of Britain.

deface, defaces, defacing, defaced
VERB If you deface a wall or notice,
you spoil it by writing or drawing on it
• *She spitefully defaced her sister's
poster.*

default, defaults, defaulting,
defaulted **VERB ❶** If someone
defaults on something they have
legally agreed to do, they fail to do it
• *He defaulted on repayment of the loan.*
▷ **PHRASE ❷** If something happens
by default, it happens because
something else which might have
prevented it has failed to happen.

defeat, defeats, defeating, defeated
VERB ❶ If you defeat someone or
something, you win a victory over
them, or cause them to fail ▷ **NOUN**
❷ the state of being beaten or of
failing or an occasion on which
someone is beaten or fails to achieve
something • *He was gracious in defeat.*

defecate, defecates, defecating,
defecated **VERB** To defecate means

to get rid of waste matter from the bowels through the anus.

defect, defects, defecting, defected
NOUN ❶ a fault or flaw in something
▷ VERB ❷ If someone defects, they leave their own country or organization and join an opposing one. **defection** NOUN

defective ADJECTIVE imperfect or faulty • *defective eyesight*.

defence, defences NOUN
❶ Defence is action that is taken to protect someone or something from attack. ❷ any arguments used in support of something that has been criticized or questioned. ❸ the case presented, in a court of law, by a lawyer for the person on trial; also the person on trial and his or her lawyers.
❹ (HISTORY) A country's defences are its military resources, such as its armed forces and weapons.

defend, defends, defending, defended VERB ❶ To defend someone or something means to protect them from harm or danger.
❷ If you defend a person or their ideas and beliefs, you argue in support of them. ❸ To defend someone in court means to represent them and argue their case for them. ❹ In a game such as football or hockey, to defend means to try to prevent goals being scored by your opponents.

defendant, defendants NOUN a person who has been accused of a crime in a court of law.

defender, defenders NOUN ❶ a person who protects someone or something from harm or danger.
❷ a person who argues in support of

something. ❸ a person who tries to stop goals being scored in certain sports.

defensible ADJECTIVE able to be defended against criticism or attack.

defensive ADJECTIVE ❶ intended or designed for protection • *defensive weapons*. ❷ Someone who is defensive feels unsure and threatened by other people's opinions and attitudes • *Don't get defensive, I was only joking about your cooking.*
defensively ADVERB
defensiveness NOUN

defer, defers, deferring, deferred VERB ❶ If you defer something, you delay or postpone it until a future time. ❷ If you defer to someone, you agree with them or do what they want because you respect them.

deference [Said def-er-ense] NOUN Deference is polite and respectful behaviour. **deferential** ADJECTIVE

defiance NOUN Defiance is behaviour which shows that you are not willing to obey or behave in the expected way • *a gesture of defiance.*
defiant ADJECTIVE **defiantly** ADVERB

deficiency, deficiencies NOUN a lack of something • *vitamin deficiency.*

deficient ADJECTIVE lacking in something.

deficit, deficits [Said def-iss-it] NOUN the amount by which money received by an organization is less than money spent.

define, defines, defining, defined VERB (EXAM TERM) If you define something, you say clearly what it is or what it means • *Culture can be defined in hundreds of ways.*

definite ADJECTIVE ❶ firm and unlikely to be changed • *The answer is a definite 'yes'.* ❷ certain or true rather than guessed or imagined • *definite proof.* **definitely** ADVERB

definition, definitions NOUN a statement explaining the meaning of a word or idea.

definitive ADJECTIVE ❶ final and unable to be questioned or altered • *a definitive answer.* ❷ most complete, or the best of its kind • *a definitive history of science fiction.* **definitively** ADVERB

deflate, deflates, deflating, deflated VERB ❶ If you deflate something such as a tyre or balloon, you let out all the air or gas in it. ❷ If you deflate someone, you make them seem less important.

deflation NOUN Deflation is a reduction in economic activity that leads to lower levels of industrial output, trade, investment, and prices.

deflect, deflects, deflecting, deflected VERB To deflect something means to turn it aside or make it change direction. **deflection** NOUN

deforestation NOUN (GEOGRAPHY) Deforestation is the cutting down of all the trees in an area.

deform, deforms, deforming, deformed VERB To deform something means to put it out of shape or spoil its appearance • *Badly fitting shoes can deform the feet.* **deformed** ADJECTIVE **deformity** NOUN

deformed ADJECTIVE disfigured or abnormally shaped.

defraud, defrauds, defrauding, defrauded VERB If someone defrauds you, they cheat you out of something that should be yours.

defrost, defrosts, defrosting, defrosted VERB ❶ If you defrost a freezer or refrigerator, you remove the ice from it. ❷ If you defrost frozen food, you let it thaw out.

deft, defter, deftest ADJECTIVE Someone who is deft is quick and skilful in their movements. **deftly** ADVERB

defunct ADJECTIVE no longer existing or functioning.

defuse, defuses, defusing, defused VERB ❶ To defuse a dangerous or tense situation means to make it less dangerous or tense. ❷ To defuse a bomb means to remove its fuse or detonator so that it cannot explode.

defy, defies, defying, defied VERB ❶ If you defy a person or a law, you openly refuse to obey. ❷ FORMAL If you defy someone to do something that you think is impossible, you challenge them to do it.

● SIMILAR WORDS: ❶ disregard, ● flout, resist

degenerate, degenerates, degenerating, degenerated VERB ❶ If something degenerates, it becomes worse • *The election campaign degenerated into farce.* ▷ ADJECTIVE ❷ having low standards of morality ▷ NOUN ❸ someone whose standards of morality are so low that people find their behaviour shocking or disgusting.

▷ SPELLING NOTE: there's SAND in my SANDwich (*sand*wich)

degradation | 222

degeneration NOUN

degradation NOUN Degradation is a state of poverty and misery.

degrade, degrades, degrading, degraded VERB If something degrades people, it humiliates them and makes them feel that they are not respected. **degrading** ADJECTIVE
● SIMILAR WORDS: debase, demean

degree, degrees NOUN ❶ an amount of a feeling or quality • *a degree of pain.* ❷ a unit of measurement of temperature; often written as ° after a number • *20° C.* ❸ (MATHS) a unit of measurement of angles in mathematics, and of latitude and longitude • *The yacht was 20° off course.* ❹ a course of study at a university or college; also the qualification awarded after passing the course.

dehydrate, dehydrates, dehydrating, dehydrated VERB ❶ If something is dehydrated, water is removed or lost from it. ❷ If someone is dehydrated, they are weak or ill because they have lost too much water from their body. **dehydrated** ADJECTIVE **dehydration** NOUN

deign, deigns, deigning, deigned [Said *dane*] VERB FORMAL If you deign to do something, you do it even though you think you are too important to do such a thing.

deity, deities NOUN a god or goddess.

deja vu [Said *day-ja voo*] NOUN Deja vu is the feeling that you have already experienced in the past exactly the same sequence of events as is happening now.

● WORD HISTORY: from French *déja vu* meaning literally 'already seen'

dejected ADJECTIVE miserable and unhappy • *She returned with a dejected expression.* **dejection** NOUN

delay, delays, delaying, delayed VERB ❶ If you delay doing something, you put it off until a later time. ❷ If something delays you, it hinders you or slows you down ▷ NOUN ❸ Delay is time during which something is delayed.
● SIMILAR WORDS: ❶ postpone, put off

delectable ADJECTIVE very pleasing or delightful.

delegate, delegates, delegating, delegated NOUN ❶ a person appointed to vote or to make decisions on behalf of a group of people ▷ VERB ❷ If you delegate duties, you give them to someone who can then act on your behalf.

delegation, delegations NOUN ❶ a group of people chosen to represent a larger group of people. ❷ Delegation is the giving of duties, responsibilities, or power to someone who can then act on your behalf.

delete, deletes, deleting, deleted VERB (ICT) To delete something means to cross it out or remove it • *He had deleted the computer file by mistake.* **deletion** NOUN

deliberate, deliberates, deliberating, deliberated [Said *di-lib-er-at*] ADJECTIVE ❶ done on purpose or planned in advance • *It was a deliberate insult.* ❷ careful and not hurried in speech and action • *She was very deliberate in her movements.*

▷ SPELLING NOTE: On WEDNESday Wayne WED NESta (Wednesday)

▷ VERB [Said di-**lib**-er-ayt] ❸ If you deliberate about something, you think about it seriously and carefully. **deliberately** ADVERB
- SIMILAR WORDS: ❶ intentional,
- planned

deliberation, deliberations NOUN Deliberation is careful consideration of a subject.

delicacy, delicacies NOUN ❶ Delicacy is grace and attractiveness. ❷ Something said or done with delicacy is said or done tactfully so that nobody is offended. ❸ Delicacies are rare or expensive foods that are considered especially nice to eat.

delicate ADJECTIVE ❶ fine, graceful, or subtle in character • *a delicate fragrance*. ❷ fragile and needing to be handled carefully • *delicate antique lace*. ❸ precise or sensitive, and able to notice very small changes • *a delicate instrument*. **delicately** ADVERB

delicatessen, delicatessens NOUN a shop selling unusual or imported foods.
- WORD HISTORY: from German
- *Delikatessen* meaning 'delicacies'

delicious ADJECTIVE very pleasing, especially to taste. **deliciously** ADVERB
- SIMILAR WORDS: delectable,
- scrumptious

delight, delights, delighting, delighted NOUN ❶ Delight is great pleasure or joy ▷ VERB ❷ If something delights you or if you are delighted by it, it gives you a lot of pleasure. **delighted** ADJECTIVE

delightful ADJECTIVE very pleasant and attractive.

delinquent, delinquents NOUN a young person who commits minor crimes. **delinquency** NOUN

delirious ADJECTIVE ❶ unable to speak or act in a rational way because of illness or fever. ❷ wildly excited and happy. **deliriously** ADVERB

deliver, delivers, delivering, delivered VERB ❶ If you deliver something to someone, you take it to them and give them it. ❷ To deliver a lecture or speech means to give it.

delivery, deliveries NOUN ❶ Delivery or a delivery is the bringing of letters or goods to a person or firm. ❷ Someone's delivery is the way in which they give a speech.

dell, dells NOUN LITERARY a small wooded valley.

delta, deltas NOUN a low, flat area at the mouth of a river where the river has split into several branches to enter the sea.

delude, deludes, deluding, deluded VERB To delude people means to deceive them into believing something that is not true.

deluge, deluges, deluging, deluged NOUN ❶ a sudden, heavy downpour of rain ▷ VERB ❷ To be deluged with things means to be overwhelmed by a great number of them.

delusion, delusions NOUN a mistaken or misleading belief or idea.

de luxe [Said de luks] ADJECTIVE rich, luxurious, or of superior quality.

delve, delves, delving, delved VERB If

a
b
c
d
e
f
g
h
i
j
k
l
m
n
o
p
q
r
s
t
u
v
w
x
y
z

you delve into something, you seek
out more information about it.

demand, demands, demanding,
demanded **VERB** ❶ If you demand
something, you ask for it forcefully
and urgently. ❷ If a job or situation
demands a particular quality, it needs
it • *This situation demands hard work.*
▷ **NOUN** ❸ a forceful request for
something. ❹ If there is a demand for
something, a lot of people want to buy
it or have it.
● **USAGE NOTE:** The verb *demand* is
● either followed by *of* or *from*: *at least*
● *one important decision was*
● *demanded of me; he had demanded*
● *an explanation from Daphne*

demean, demeans, demeaning,
demeaned **VERB** If you demean
yourself, you do something which
makes people have less respect for
you. **demeaning ADJECTIVE**

demeanour NOUN Your
demeanour is the way you behave and
the impression that this creates.

demented ADJECTIVE Someone
who is demented behaves in a wild or
violent way.

dementia [Said dee-**men**-sha]
NOUN MEDICAL Dementia is a serious
illness of the mind.

demi- PREFIX 'Demi-' means 'half'.

demise [Said dee-**myz**] **NOUN**
FORMAL Someone's demise is their
death.

demo, demos **NOUN** INFORMAL a
demonstration.

democracy, democracies **NOUN**
Democracy is a system of government
in which the people choose their

leaders by voting for them in elections.

democrat, democrats **NOUN** a
person who believes in democracy,
personal freedom, and equality.

democratic ADJECTIVE having
representatives elected by the people.
democratically ADVERB
● **WORD HISTORY:** from Greek
● *dēmos* meaning 'the people' and
● *kratos* meaning 'power'

demography NOUN Demography
is the study of the changes in the size
and structure of populations.
demographic ADJECTIVE

demolish, demolishes, demolishing,
demolished **VERB** To demolish a
building means to pull it down or
break it up. **demolition NOUN**

demon, demons **NOUN** ❶ an evil
spirit or devil ▷ **ADJECTIVE** ❷ skilful,
keen, and energetic • *a demon squash
player.* **demonic ADJECTIVE**

demonstrate, demonstrates,
demonstrating, demonstrated **VERB**
❶ (EXAM TERM) To demonstrate a
fact or theory means to prove or show
it to be true. ❷ If you demonstrate
something to somebody, you show
and explain it by using or doing the
thing itself • *She demonstrated how to
apply the make-up.* ❸ If people
demonstrate, they take part in a
march or rally to show their opposition
or support for something.

demonstration, demonstrations
NOUN ❶ a talk or explanation to
show how to do or use something.
❷ Demonstration is proof that
something exists or is true. ❸ a public
march or rally in support of or
opposition to something.

▷ SPELLING NOTE: *Elaine and Emily shout EE when they mEEt to grEEt each other (-ee-)*

demonstrator NOUN

demoralize, demoralizes, demoralizing, demoralized; *also spelt* **demoralise** VERB If something demoralizes someone, it makes them feel depressed and lose their confidence.

demote, demotes, demoting, demoted VERB A person who is demoted is put in a lower rank or position, often as a punishment. **demotion** NOUN

demure ADJECTIVE Someone who is demure is quiet, shy, and behaves very modestly. **demurely** ADVERB

den, dens NOUN ❶ the home of some wild animals such as lions or foxes. ❷ a secret place where people meet.

denial, denials NOUN ❶ A denial of something is a statement that it is untrue • *He published a firm denial of the report.* ❷ The denial of a request or something to which you have a right is the refusal of it • *the denial of human rights.*

denigrate, denigrates, denigrating, denigrated VERB FORMAL To denigrate someone or something means to criticize them in order to damage their reputation.

denim, denims NOUN ❶ Denim is strong cotton cloth, used for making clothes ❷ IN PLURAL Denims are jeans made from denim.
   ● WORD HISTORY: from French
   ● *serge de Nîmes*, meaning 'serge (a
   ● type of cloth) from Nîmes'

denomination, denominations NOUN ❶ a particular group which

has slightly different religious beliefs from other groups within the same faith. ❷ a unit in a system of weights, values, or measures • *a high denomination note.*

denominator, denominators NOUN (MATHS) In maths, the denominator is the bottom part of a fraction.

denote, denotes, denoting, denoted VERB If one thing denotes another, it is a sign of it or it represents it • *Formerly, a tan denoted wealth.*

denouement, denouements *[Said day-noo-mon]* NOUN (ENGLISH) The denouement of a story is the explanation at the end of it of something that has previously been unclear or kept secret.

denounce, denounces, denouncing, denounced VERB ❶ If you denounce someone or something, you express very strong disapproval of them • *He publicly denounced government nuclear policy.* ❷ If you denounce someone, you give information against them • *He was denounced as a dangerous agitator.*

dense, denser, densest ADJECTIVE ❶ thickly crowded or packed together • *the dense crowd.* ❷ difficult to see through • *dense black smoke.* **densely** ADVERB

density, densities NOUN the degree to which something is filled or occupied • *a very high population density.*

dent, dents, denting, dented VERB ❶ To dent something means to damage it by hitting it and making a hollow in its surface ▷ NOUN ❷ a

▷ SPELLING NOTE: *'i' before 'e' except after 'c'*

hollow in the surface of something.

dental ADJECTIVE relating to the teeth.

dentist, dentists NOUN a person who is qualified to treat people's teeth.

dentistry NOUN Dentistry is the branch of medicine concerned with disorders of the teeth.

dentures PLURAL NOUN Dentures are false teeth.

denunciation, denunciations NOUN A denunciation of someone or something is severe public criticism of them.

deny, denies, denying, denied VERB ❶ If you deny something that has been said, you state that it is untrue. ❷ If you deny that something is the case, you refuse to believe it • *He denied the existence of God*. ❸ If you deny someone something, you refuse to give it to them • *They were denied permission to attend*.
● SIMILAR WORDS: ❶ contradict,
● gainsay

deodorant, deodorants NOUN a substance or spray used to hide the smell of perspiration.

depart, departs, departing, departed VERB When you depart, you leave. **departure** NOUN

department, departments NOUN one of the sections into which an organization is divided • *the marketing department*. **departmental** ADJECTIVE

depend, depends, depending, depended VERB ❶ If you depend on

someone or something, you trust them and rely on them. ❷ If one thing depends on another, it is influenced by it • *Success depends on the quality of the workforce*.
● SIMILAR WORDS: ❶ count on,
● rely on, trust

dependable ADJECTIVE reliable and trustworthy.

dependant, dependants NOUN (PSHE) someone who relies on another person for financial support.

dependence NOUN Dependence is a constant need that someone has for something or someone in order to survive or operate properly • *He was flattered by her dependence on him*.

dependency, dependencies NOUN ❶ (PSHE) Dependency is relying on someone or something to give you what you need • *drug dependency*. ❷ a country or area controlled by another country.

dependent ADJECTIVE reliant on someone or something.

depict, depicts, depicting, depicted VERB To depict someone or something means to represent them in painting or sculpture.

deplete, depletes, depleting, depleted VERB To deplete something means to reduce greatly the amount of it available. **depletion** NOUN

deplorable ADJECTIVE shocking or regrettable • *deplorable conditions*.

deplore, deplores, deploring, deplored VERB If you deplore something, you condemn it because you feel it is wrong.

deploy, deploys, deploying, deployed **VERB** To deploy troops or resources means to organize or position them so that they can be used effectively. **deployment NOUN**

depopulation NOUN (GEOGRAPHY) Depopulation is when the population of an area or town is reduced • *the depopulation of rural areas.*

deport, deports, deporting, deported **VERB** If a government deports someone, it sends them out of the country because they have committed a crime or because they do not have the right to be there. **deportation NOUN**

depose, deposes, deposing, deposed **VERB** If someone is deposed, they are removed from a position of power.

deposit, deposits, depositing, deposited **VERB** ❶ If you deposit something, you put it down or leave it somewhere. ❷ If you deposit money or valuables, you put them somewhere for safekeeping. ❸ (GEOGRAPHY) If something is deposited on a surface, a layer of it is left there as a result of chemical or geological action ▷ **NOUN** ❹ a sum of money given in part payment for goods or services.

deposition, depositions **NOUN** ❶ (GEOGRAPHY) Deposition is the geological process which causes layers of minerals to be formed in the ground over a period of time. ❷ A deposition is a formal written statement of evidence, given under oath.

depot, depots [*Said dep-oh*] **NOUN** a place where large supplies of materials or equipment may be stored.

depraved ADJECTIVE morally bad.

depress, depresses, depressing, depressed **VERB** ❶ If something depresses you, it makes you feel sad and gloomy. ❷ If wages or prices are depressed, their value falls. **depressive ADJECTIVE**

depressant, depressants **NOUN** a drug which reduces nervous activity and so has a calming effect.

depressed ADJECTIVE ❶ unhappy and gloomy. ❷ A place that is depressed has little economic activity and therefore low incomes and high unemployment • *depressed industrial areas.*
  ● **SIMILAR WORDS:** ❶ dejected, despondent, low-spirited

depression, depressions **NOUN** ❶ a state of mind in which someone feels unhappy and has no energy or enthusiasm. ❷ a time of industrial and economic decline. ❸ (GEOGRAPHY) In meteorology, a depression is a mass of air that has low pressure and often causes rain. ❹ (GEOGRAPHY) A depression in the surface of something is a part which is lower than the rest.

deprive, deprives, depriving, deprived **VERB** If you deprive someone of something, you take it away or prevent them from having it. **deprived ADJECTIVE deprivation NOUN**

depth, depths **NOUN** ❶ The depth of something is the measurement or distance between its top and bottom, or between its front and back. ❷ The depth of something such as emotion is its intensity • *He was astonished by*

a
b
c
d
e
f
g
h
i
j
k
l
m
n
o
p
q
r
s
t
u
v
w
x
y
z

▷ SPELLING NOTE: *an ELegant angEL (angel)*

the depth of her hostility.

deputation, deputations **NOUN** a small group of people sent to speak or act on behalf of others.

deputy, deputies **NOUN** Someone's deputy is a person appointed to act in their place.

deranged **ADJECTIVE** mad, or behaving in a wild and uncontrolled way.

derby, derbies [*Said dar-bee*] **NOUN** A local derby is a sporting event between two teams from the same area.

derelict **ADJECTIVE** abandoned and falling into ruins.

deride, derides, deriding, derided **VERB** To deride someone or something means to mock or jeer at them with contempt.

derision **NOUN** Derision is an attitude of contempt or scorn towards something or someone.

derivation, derivations **NOUN** The derivation of something is its origin or source.

derivative, derivatives **NOUN** ❶ something which has developed from an earlier source ▷ **ADJECTIVE** ❷ not original, but based on or copied from something else • *The record was not deliberately derivative.*

derive, derives, deriving, derived **VERB** ❶ FORMAL If you derive something from someone or something, you get it from them • *He derived so much joy from music.* ❷ If something derives from something else, it develops from it.

derogatory **ADJECTIVE** critical and scornful • *He made derogatory remarks about them.*

descant, descants **NOUN** (MUSIC) The descant to a tune is another tune played at the same time and at a higher pitch.

descend, descends, descending, descended **VERB** ❶ To descend means to move downwards. ❷ If you descend on people or on a place, you arrive unexpectedly.

descendant, descendants **NOUN** A person's descendants are the people in later generations who are related to them.

descended **ADJECTIVE** If you are descended from someone who lived in the past, your family originally derived from them.

descent, descents **NOUN** ❶ a movement or slope from a higher to a lower position or level. ❷ Your descent is your family's origins.

describe, describes, describing, described **VERB** To describe someone or something means to give an account or a picture of them in words.

description, descriptions **NOUN** an account or picture of something in words. **descriptive** **ADJECTIVE**

desert, deserts [*Said dez-ert*] **NOUN** (GEOGRAPHY) a region of land with very little plant life, usually because of low rainfall.

desert, deserts, deserting, deserted [*Said dez-zert*] **VERB** To desert a person means to leave or abandon them • *His clients had deserted him.* **desertion** **NOUN**

▷ SPELLING NOTE: *LEt's measure the angLE (angle)*

deserter, deserters NOUN someone who leaves the armed forces without permission.

deserve, deserves, deserving, deserved VERB If you deserve something, you are entitled to it or earn it because of your qualities, achievements, or actions • *He deserved a rest.*
● SIMILAR WORDS: be worthy of,
● justify, merit

deserving ADJECTIVE worthy of being helped, rewarded, or praised • *a deserving charity.*

design, designs, designing, designed
D&T VERB ❶ To design something means to plan it, especially by preparing a detailed sketch or drawings from which it can be built or made ▷ NOUN ❷ a drawing or plan from which something can be built or made. ❸ The design of something is its shape and style. **designer** NOUN

designate, designates, designating, designated [Said *dez-ig-nate*] VERB
❶ To designate someone or something means to formally label or name them • *The room was designated a no smoking area.* ❷ If you designate someone to do something, you appoint them to do it • *He designated his son as his successor.*

designation, designations NOUN a name or title.

designing ADJECTIVE crafty and cunning.

desirable ADJECTIVE ❶ worth having or doing • *a desirable job.* ❷ sexually attractive. **desirability** NOUN

desire, desires, desiring, desired
VERB ❶ If you desire something, you want it very much ▷ NOUN ❷ a strong feeling of wanting something.
❸ Desire for someone is a strong sexual attraction to them.
● SIMILAR WORDS: ❶ long for,
● want, wish for ❷ longing, want,
● wish

desist, desists, desisting, desisted VERB FORMAL To desist from doing something means to stop doing it.

desk, desks NOUN ❶ a piece of furniture designed for working at or writing on. ❷ a counter or table behind which a receptionist sits.

desktop ADJECTIVE of a convenient size to be used on a desk or table • *a desktop computer.*

desolate ADJECTIVE ❶ deserted and bleak • *a desolate mountainous region.* ❷ lonely, very sad, and without hope • *He was desolate without her.* **desolation** NOUN

despair, despairs, despairing, despaired NOUN ❶ Despair is a total loss of hope ▷ VERB ❷ If you despair, you lose hope • *He despaired of finishing it.* **despairing** ADJECTIVE
● SIMILAR WORDS: ❶ desperation,
● hopelessness

despatch another spelling of **dispatch**.

desperate ADJECTIVE ❶ If you are desperate, you are so worried or frightened that you will try anything to improve your situation • *a desperate attempt to save their marriage.* ❷ A desperate person is violent and dangerous. ❸ A desperate situation is

a b c d e f g h i j k l m n o p q r s t u v w x y z

▷ SPELLING NOTE: *A Rude Idiot Thought He Might Eat Toffee In Church (*arithmetic*)*

A
B
C
D
E
F
G
H
I
J
K
L
M
N
O
P
Q
R
S
T
U
V
W
X
Y
Z

extremely dangerous or serious.
desperately ADVERB **desperation**
NOUN

despicable ADJECTIVE deserving
contempt.

despise, despises, despising,
despised VERB If you despise
someone or something, you dislike
them very much.

despite PREPOSITION in spite of
• *He fell asleep despite all the coffee he'd
drunk.*
● SIMILAR WORDS: in spite of,
● regardless of

despondent ADJECTIVE dejected
and unhappy. **despondency** NOUN

dessert, desserts [*Said diz-ert*]
NOUN a sweet food served after the
main course of a meal.
● WORD HISTORY: from French
● *desservir* meaning 'to clear the table
● after a meal'

destination, destinations NOUN a
place to which someone or something
is going or is being sent.

destined ADJECTIVE meant or
intended to happen • *I was destined for
fame and fortune.*

destiny, destinies NOUN ❶ Your
destiny is all the things that happen to
you in your life, especially when they
are considered to be outside human
control. ❷ Destiny is the force which
some people believe controls
everyone's life.

destitute ADJECTIVE without
money or possessions, and therefore
in great need. **destitution** NOUN

destroy, destroys, destroying,

destroyed VERB ❶ To destroy
something means to damage it so
much that it is completely ruined.
❷ To destroy something means to put
an end to it • *The holiday destroyed
their friendship.*
● SIMILAR WORDS: ❶ demolish,
● ruin, wreck

destruction NOUN Destruction is
the act of destroying something or the
state of being destroyed.
● SIMILAR WORDS: devastation,
● ruin

destructive ADJECTIVE causing or
able to cause great harm, damage, or
injury. **destructiveness** NOUN

desultory [*Said dez-ul-tree*]
ADJECTIVE passing from one thing to
another in a fitful or random way • *A
desultory, embarrassed chatter began
again.*

detach, detaches, detaching,
detached VERB To detach something
means to remove it • *The hood can be
detached.* **detachable** ADJECTIVE

detached ADJECTIVE ❶ separate
or standing apart • *a detached house.*
❷ having no real interest or emotional
involvement in something • *He
observed me with a detached curiosity.*

detachment, detachments NOUN
❶ Detachment is the feeling of not
being personally involved with
something • *A stranger can view your
problems with detachment.* ❷ a small
group of soldiers sent to do a special
job.

detail, details NOUN ❶ an individual
fact or feature of something • *We
discussed every detail of the
performance.* ❷ Detail is all the small

features that make up the whole of something • *Look at the detail.*
detailed ADJECTIVE

detain, detains, detaining, detained **VERB** ❶ To detain someone means to force them to stay • *She was being detained for interrogation.* ❷ If you detain someone, you delay them • *I mustn't detain you.*

detect, detects, detecting, detected **VERB** ❶ If you detect something, you notice it • *I detected a glimmer of interest in his eyes.* ❷ To detect something means to find it • *Cancer can be detected by X-rays.* **detectable ADJECTIVE**

detection NOUN ❶ Detection is the act of noticing, discovering, or sensing something. ❷ Detection is also the work of investigating crime.

detective, detectives **NOUN** a person, usually a police officer, whose job is to investigate crimes.

detector, detectors **NOUN** an instrument which is used to detect the presence of something • *a metal detector.*

detention NOUN The detention of someone is their arrest or imprisonment.

deter, deters, deterring, deterred **VERB** To deter someone means to discourage or prevent them from doing something by creating a feeling of fear or doubt • *99 per cent of burglars are deterred by the sight of an alarm box.*

detergent, detergents **NOUN** a chemical substance used for washing or cleaning things.

deteriorate, deteriorates, deteriorating, deteriorated **VERB** If something deteriorates, it gets worse • *My father's health has deteriorated lately.* **deterioration NOUN**

determination NOUN Determination is great firmness, after you have made up your mind to do something • *They shared a determination to win the war.*

determine, determines, determining, determined **VERB** ❶ If something determines a situation or result, it causes it or controls it • *The track surface determines his tactics in a race.* ❷ To determine something means to decide or settle it firmly • *The date has still to be determined.* ❸ To determine something means to find out or calculate the facts about it • *He bit the coin to determine whether it was genuine.*
● **SIMILAR WORDS:** ❷ decide,
● settle ❸ ascertain, find out, verify

determined ADJECTIVE firmly decided • *She was determined not to repeat her error.* **determinedly ADVERB**
● **SIMILAR WORDS:** intent on,
● resolute

determiner, determiners **NOUN** (ENGLISH) a word that can go before a noun or noun group to show, for instance, which thing you are referring to or whether you are referring to one thing or several. For example, in 'my house', 'the windows', 'this red book', and 'each time', 'my', 'the', 'this', and 'each' can be called determiners.

deterrent, deterrents **NOUN** something that prevents you from doing something by making you afraid

a
b
c
d
e
f
g
h
i
j
k
l
m
n
o
p
q
r
s
t
u
v
w
x
y
z

of what will happen if you do it
• *Capital punishment was no deterrent to domestic murders.* **deterrence** NOUN

detest, detests, detesting, detested VERB If you detest someone or something, you strongly dislike them.

detonate, detonates, detonating, detonated VERB To detonate a bomb or mine means to cause it to explode. **detonator** NOUN

detour, detours NOUN an alternative, less direct route.

detract, detracts, detracting, detracted VERB To detract from something means to make it seem less good or valuable.

detriment NOUN Detriment is disadvantage or harm • *a detriment to their health.* **detrimental** ADJECTIVE

deuce, deuces [Said *joos*] NOUN In tennis, deuce is the score of forty all.

devalue, devalues, devaluing, devalued VERB To devalue something means to lower its status, importance, or worth. **devaluation** NOUN

devastate, devastates, devastating, devastated VERB To devastate an area or place means to damage it severely or destroy it. **devastation** NOUN

devastated ADJECTIVE very shocked or upset • *The family are devastated by the news.*

develop, develops, developing, developed VERB When something develops or is developed, it grows or becomes more advanced • *The sneezing developed into a full blown*

cold. ❷ To develop an area of land means to build on it. ❸ To develop an illness or a fault means to become affected by it.

developer, developers NOUN a person or company that builds on land.

development, developments NOUN ❶ Development is gradual growth or progress. ❷ The development of land or water is the process of making it more useful or profitable by the expansion of industry or housing • *the development of the old docks.* ❸ a new stage in a series of events • *developments in technology.* **developmental** ADJECTIVE

deviant, deviants ADJECTIVE ❶ Deviant behaviour is unacceptable or different from what people consider as normal ▷ NOUN ❷ someone whose behaviour or beliefs are different from what people consider to be acceptable. **deviance** NOUN

deviate, deviates, deviating, deviated VERB To deviate means to differ or depart from what is usual or acceptable. **deviation** NOUN

device, devices NOUN ❶ a machine or tool that is used for a particular purpose • *a device to warn you when the batteries need changing.* ❷ a plan or scheme • *a device to pressurise him into selling.*

devil, devils NOUN ❶ In Christianity and Judaism, the Devil is the spirit of evil and enemy of God. ❷ an evil spirit.

devious ADJECTIVE insincere and dishonest. **deviousness** NOUN

▷ SPELLING NOTE: *there's a rAKE in the brAKEs (brake)*

devise, devises, devising, devised
VERB To devise something means to work it out • *Besides diets, he devised punishing exercise routines.*

devoid **ADJECTIVE** lacking in a particular thing or quality • *His glance was devoid of expression.*

devolution **NOUN** Devolution is the transfer of power from a central government or organization to local government departments or smaller organizations.

devote, devotes, devoting, devoted
VERB If you devote yourself to something, you give all your time, energy, or money to it • *She has devoted herself to women's causes.*

devoted **ADJECTIVE** very loving and loyal.

devotee, devotees **NOUN** a fanatical or enthusiastic follower of something.

devotion **NOUN** Devotion to someone or something is great love or affection for them. **devotional** **ADJECTIVE**

devour, devours, devouring, devoured **VERB** If you devour something, you eat it hungrily or greedily.

devout **ADJECTIVE** deeply and sincerely religious • *a devout Buddhist.* **devoutly** **ADVERB**

dew **NOUN** Dew is drops of moisture that form on the ground and other cool surfaces at night.

dexterity **NOUN** Dexterity is skill or agility in using your hands or mind • *He had learned to use the crutches with dexterity.* **dexterous** **ADJECTIVE**

dharma *[Said dar-ma]* **NOUN** In the Buddhist religion, dharma is ideal truth as set out in the teaching of the Buddha.
● **WORD HISTORY:** a Sanskrit word

diabetes *[Said dy-a-bee-tiss]* **NOUN** Diabetes is a disease in which someone has too much sugar in their blood, because they do not produce enough insulin to absorb it. **diabetic** **NOUN OR ADJECTIVE**

diabolic **ADJECTIVE** extremely wicked or cruel.

diabolical **ADJECTIVE** ❶ INFORMAL dreadful and very annoying • *The pain was diabolical.* ❷ extremely wicked and cruel.

diadem, diadems **NOUN** A diadem is a small jewelled crown or headband, usually worn by royalty.

diagnose, diagnoses, diagnosing, diagnosed **VERB** To diagnose an illness or problem means to identify exactly what is wrong.

diagnosis, diagnoses **NOUN** the identification of what is wrong with someone who is ill. **diagnostic** **ADJECTIVE**

diagonal **ADJECTIVE** in a slanting direction. **diagonally** **ADVERB**

diagram, diagrams **NOUN** a drawing that shows or explains something.

dial, dials, dialling, dialled **NOUN**
❶ the face of a clock or meter, with divisions marked on it so that a time or measurement can be recorded and read. ❷ a part of a device, such as a radio, used to control or tune it
▷ **VERB** ❸ To dial a telephone number means to press the number

a
b
c
d
e
f
g
h
i
j
k
l
m
n
o
p
q
r
s
t
u
v
w
x
y
z

A
B
C
D
E
F
G
H
I
J
K
L
M
N
O
P
Q
R
S
T
U
V
W
X
Y
Z

keys to select the required number.

dialect, dialects **NOUN** a form of a language spoken in a particular geographical area.

dialogue, dialogues **NOUN**
❶ ENGLISH In a novel, play, or film, dialogue is conversation. ❷ Dialogue is communication or discussion between people or groups of people
• *The union sought dialogue with the council.*

dialysis **NOUN** Dialysis is a treatment used for some kidney diseases, in which blood is filtered by a special machine to remove waste products.
 ● **WORD HISTORY:** from Greek
 ● *dialuein* meaning 'to rip apart'

diameter, diameters **NOUN**
 MATHS The diameter of a circle is the length of a straight line drawn across it through its centre.

diamond, diamonds **NOUN** ❶ a precious stone made of pure carbon. ❷ MATHS a shape with four straight sides of equal length forming two opposite angles less than 90° and two opposite angles greater than 90°. ❸ Diamonds is one of the four suits in a pack of playing cards. It is marked by a red diamond-shaped symbol ▷ **ADJECTIVE** ❹ A diamond anniversary is the 60th anniversary of an event.

diaphragm, diaphragms *[Said dy-a-fram]* **NOUN** SCIENCE In mammals, the diaphragm is the muscular wall that separates the lungs from the stomach.

diarrhoea *[Said dy-a-ree-a]* **NOUN** Diarrhoea is a condition in which the

faeces are more liquid and frequent than usual.

diary, diaries **NOUN** a book which has a separate space or page for each day of the year on which to keep a record of appointments. **diarist** **NOUN**
 ● **USAGE NOTE:** Do not confuse the
 ● order of the vowels in *diary* and
 ● *dairy*

dice, dices, dicing, diced **NOUN** ❶ a small cube which has each side marked with dots representing the numbers one to six ▷ **VERB** ❷ To dice food means to cut it into small cubes. **diced ADJECTIVE**

dictate, dictates, dictating, dictated **VERB** ❶ If you dictate something, you say or read it aloud for someone else to write down. ❷ To dictate something means to command or state what must happen • *What we wear is largely dictated by our daily routine.* **dictation NOUN**

dictator, dictators **NOUN** HISTORY a ruler who has complete power in a country, especially one who has taken power by force. **dictatorial** **ADJECTIVE**

diction **NOUN** Someone's diction is the clarity with which they speak or sing.

dictionary, dictionaries **NOUN** LIBRARY a book in which words are listed alphabetically and explained, or equivalent words are given in another language.
 ● **WORD HISTORY:** from Latin *dictio*
 ● meaning 'phrase' or 'word'

didgeridoo, didgeridoos **NOUN** an Australian musical wind instrument made in the shape of a long wooden tube.

die, dies, dying, died VERB ❶ When people, animals, or plants die, they stop living. ❷ When something dies, dies away, or dies down, it gradually fades away • *The footsteps died away.* ▷ NOUN ❸ a dice.

die out VERB When something dies out, it ceases to exist.

● SIMILAR WORDS: ❶ expire, pass
● away, perish

diesel [Said **dee**-zel] NOUN ❶ a heavy fuel used in trains, buses, and lorries. ❷ a vehicle with a diesel engine.

diesel engine, diesel, engines NOUN (SCIENCE) A diesel engine is an internal-combustion engine in which the fuel is ignited by hot air produced by compression in the cylinders. It is named after Rudolf Diesel, who invented it in 1892.

diet, diets NOUN (D & T)
❶ Someone's diet is the usual food that they eat • *a vegetarian diet.* ❷ a special restricted selection of foods that someone eats to improve their health or regulate their weight.
dietary ADJECTIVE
● WORD HISTORY: from Greek
● *diaita* meaning 'mode of living'
dieter NOUN

dietician, dieticians; also spelt **dietitian** NOUN a person trained to advise people about healthy eating.

differ, differs, differing, differed VERB
❶ If two or more things differ, they are unlike each other. ❷ If people differ, they have opposing views or disagree about something.

difference, differences NOUN
❶ The difference between things is the way in which they are unlike each other. ❷ The difference between two numbers is the amount by which one is less than another. ❸ A difference in someone or something is a significant change in them • *You wouldn't believe the difference in her.*
● SIMILAR WORDS: ❶ disparity,
● dissimilarity, distinction

different ADJECTIVE ❶ unlike something else. ❷ unusual and out of the ordinary. ❸ distinct and separate, although of the same kind • *The lunch supports a different charity each year.*
differently ADVERB
● USAGE NOTE: You should say that
● one thing is *different from* another
● thing. Some people think that
● *different to* is incorrect. *Different*
● *than* is American
● SIMILAR WORDS: ❶ dissimilar,
● unlike

differentiate, differentiates, differentiating, differentiated VERB
❶ To differentiate between things means to recognize or show how one is unlike the other. ❷ Something that differentiates one thing from another makes it distinct and unlike the other.
differentiation NOUN

difficult ADJECTIVE ❶ not easy to do, understand, or solve • *a very difficult decision to make.* ❷ hard to deal with, especially because of being unreasonable or unpredictable • *a difficult child.*
● SIMILAR WORDS: ❶ demanding,
● hard, laborious

difficulty, difficulties NOUN ❶ a problem • *The central difficulty is his*

a
b
c
d
e
f
g
h
i
j
k
l
m
n
o
p
q
r
s
t
u
v
w
x
y
z

drinking. ❷ Difficulty is the fact or quality of being difficult.

diffident ADJECTIVE timid and lacking in self-confidence. **diffidently** ADVERB **diffidence** NOUN

diffract, diffracts, diffracting, diffracted VERB (SCIENCE) When rays of light or sound waves diffract, they break up after hitting an obstacle. **diffraction** NOUN

diffuse, diffuses, diffusing, diffused VERB ❶ [Said dif-yooz] (SCIENCE) If something diffuses, it spreads out or scatters in all directions. ❷ (SCIENCE) If particles of a gas, liquid, or solid diffuse, they mix together, especially by moving from an area where they are very concentrated to one where there are fewer of them ▷ ADJECTIVE [Said dif-yoos] ❸ spread out over a wide area. **diffusion** NOUN

dig, digs, digging, dug VERB ❶ If you dig, you break up soil or sand, especially with a spade or garden fork. ❷ To dig something into an object means to push, thrust, or poke it in ▷ NOUN ❸ a prod or jab, especially in the ribs. ❹ INFORMAL A dig at someone is a spiteful or unpleasant remark intended to hurt or embarrass them ❺ IN PLURAL Digs are lodgings in someone else's house.

digest, digests, digesting, digested VERB (SCIENCE) ❶ To digest food means to break it down in the gut so that it can be easily absorbed and used by the body. ❷ If you digest information or a fact, you understand it and take it in. **digestible** ADJECTIVE

digestion, digestions NOUN

(SCIENCE) ❶ Digestion is the process of digesting food. ❷ Your digestion is your ability to digest food • Camomile tea aids poor digestion. **digestive** ADJECTIVE

digger, diggers NOUN In Australian English, digger is a friendly name to call a man.

digit, digits [Said dij-it] NOUN ❶ FORMAL Your digits are your fingers or toes. ❷ (MATHS) a written symbol for any of the numbers from 0 to 9.

digital ADJECTIVE displaying information, especially time, by numbers, rather than by a pointer moving round a dial • a digital watch. **digitally** ADVERB

dignified ADJECTIVE full of dignity.

dignitary, dignitaries NOUN a person who holds a high official position.

dignity NOUN Dignity is behaviour which is serious, calm, and controlled • She conducted herself with dignity.

digression, digressions NOUN A digression in speech or writing is leaving the main subject for a while.

dilapidated ADJECTIVE falling to pieces and generally in a bad condition • a dilapidated castle.

dilate, dilates, dilating, dilated VERB To dilate means to become wider and larger • The pupil of the eye dilates in the dark. **dilated** ADJECTIVE **dilation** NOUN

dilemma, dilemmas NOUN a situation in which a choice has to be made between alternatives that are equally difficult or unpleasant.

● **WORD HISTORY:** from Greek
● *di-* meaning 'two' and *lemma*
● meaning 'assumption'
● **USAGE NOTE:** A *dilemma* involves
● a difficult choice between two
● things. If there are more than two
● choices you should say *problem* or
● *difficulty*

diligent ADJECTIVE hard-working,
and showing care and perseverance.
diligently ADVERB diligence NOUN
● **SIMILAR WORDS:** conscientious,
● hard-working, industrious

dill NOUN Dill is a herb with yellow
flowers and a strong sweet smell.

dilly bag, dilly bags **NOUN** In
Australian English, a dilly bag is a
small bag used to carry food.

dilute, dilutes, diluting, diluted **VERB**
To dilute a liquid means to add water
or another liquid to it to make it less
concentrated. **dilution NOUN**

dim, dimmer, dimmest; dims,
dimming, dimmed **ADJECTIVE**
❶ badly lit and lacking in brightness.
❷ very vague and unclear in your
mind • *dim recollections.* ❸ INFORMAL
stupid or mentally dull • *He is rather
dim.* ▷ **VERB** ❹ If lights dim or are
dimmed, they become less bright.
dimly ADVERB dimness NOUN

dimension, dimensions **NOUN**
❶ A dimension of a situation is an
aspect or factor that influences the
way you understand it • *This process
had a domestic and a foreign dimension.*
❷ You can talk about the size or
extent of something as its dimensions
• *It was an explosion of major
dimensions.* ❸ (ART) The dimensions
of something are also its

measurements, for example its length,
breadth, height, or diameter.

diminish, diminishes, diminishing,
diminished **VERB** If something
diminishes or if you diminish it, it
becomes reduced in size or
importance.

diminuendo, diminuendos **NOUN**
(MUSIC) ❶ a gradual decrease in
loudness ▷ **ADVERB** ❷ gradually
decreasing in loudness.
● **WORD HISTORY:** an Italian word
● meaning 'getting smaller'

diminutive ADJECTIVE very small.

dimmer switch, dimmer switches
NOUN a switch that allows you to
adjust the brightness of an electric
light.

dimple, dimples **NOUN** a small
hollow in someone's cheek or chin.

din, dins **NOUN** a loud and unpleasant
noise.

dinar, dinars [Said **dee**-nar] **NOUN** a
unit of currency in several countries in
Southern Europe, North Africa and the
Middle East.

dine, dines, dining, dined **VERB**
FORMAL To dine means to eat dinner in
the evening • *We dined together in the
hotel.*

diner, diners **NOUN** ❶ a person who
is having dinner in a restaurant. ❷ a
small restaurant or railway restaurant
car.

dinghy, dinghies [Said **ding**-ee]
NOUN a small boat which is rowed,
sailed, or powered by outboard motor.

dingo, dingoes **NOUN** an Australian
wild dog.

dingy, dingier, dingiest *[Said din-jee]* **ADJECTIVE** dusty, dark, and rather depressing • *a dingy bedsit.*

dinkum **ADJECTIVE** INFORMAL In Australian and New Zealand English, dinkum means genuine or right • *a fair dinkum offer.*

dinner, dinners **NOUN** ❶ the main meal of the day, eaten either in the evening or at lunchtime. ❷ a formal social occasion in the evening, at which a meal is served.

dinosaur, dinosaurs *[Said dy-no-sor]* **NOUN** a large reptile which lived in prehistoric times.
● **WORD HISTORY:** from Greek
● *deinos + sauros* meaning 'fearful
● lizard'

dint **PHRASE** **By dint of** means by means of • *He succeeds by dint of hard work.*

diocese, dioceses **NOUN** a district controlled by a bishop. **diocesan** **ADJECTIVE**

dip, dips, dipping, dipped **VERB** ❶ If you dip something into a liquid, you lower it or plunge it quickly into the liquid. ❷ If something dips, it slopes downwards or goes below a certain level • *The sun dipped below the horizon.* ❸ To dip also means to make a quick, slight downward movement • *She dipped her fingers into the cool water.* ▷ **NOUN** ❹ a rich creamy mixture which you scoop up with biscuits or raw vegetables and eat • *an avocado dip.* ❺ INFORMAL a swim.

diphthong, diphthongs **NOUN** (ENGLISH) A diphthong is a vowel in which the speaker's tongue changes position while it is being pronounced,

so that the vowel sounds like a combination of two other vowels.

diploma, diplomas **NOUN** a certificate awarded to a student who has successfully completed a course of study.
● **WORD HISTORY:** from Greek
● *diploma* meaning 'folded paper' or
● 'letter of recommendation'

diplomacy **NOUN** ❶ Diplomacy is the managing of relationships between countries. ❷ Diplomacy is also skill in dealing with people without offending or upsetting them. **diplomatic** **ADJECTIVE** **diplomatically** **ADVERB**

diplomat, diplomats **NOUN** an official who negotiates and deals with another country on behalf of his or her own country.

dire, direr, direst **ADJECTIVE** disastrous, urgent, or terrible • *people in dire need.*

direct, directs, directing, directed **ADJECTIVE** ❶ moving or aimed in a straight line or by the shortest route • *the direct route.* ❷ straightforward, and without delay or evasion • *his direct manner.* ❸ without anyone or anything intervening • *Schools can take direct control of their own funding.* ❹ exact • *the direct opposite.* ▷ **VERB** ❺ To direct something means to guide and control it. ❻ To direct people or things means to send them, tell them, or show them the way. ❼ To direct a film, a play, or a television programme means to organize the way it is made and performed.
● **SIMILAR WORDS:** ❷ frank, open,
● straightforward

▷ SPELLING NOTE: *plaice the fish has a glittering 'EYE' (I) (pla*i*ce)*

direct current NOUN (SCIENCE)
Direct current is a term used in physics to refer to an electric current that always flows in the same direction.

direction, directions NOUN ❶ the general line that someone or something is moving or pointing in. ❷ Direction is the controlling and guiding of something • *He was chopping vegetables under the chef's direction.* ❸ IN PLURAL Directions are instructions that tell you how to do something or how to get somewhere.

directive, directives NOUN an instruction that must be obeyed • *a directive banning cigarette advertising.*

directly ADVERB in a straight line or immediately • *He looked directly at Rose.*

director, directors NOUN ❶ a member of the board of a company or institution. ❷ (DRAMA) the person responsible for the making and performance of a programme, play, or film. **directorial** ADJECTIVE

directorate, directorates NOUN a board of directors of a company or organization.

directory, directories NOUN ❶ a book which gives lists of facts, such as names and addresses, and is usually arranged in alphabetical order. ❷ (ICT) another name for **folder**.

direct speech NOUN (ENGLISH) the reporting of what someone has said by quoting the exact words.

dirge, dirges NOUN a slow, sad piece of music, sometimes played or sung at funerals.

dirt NOUN ❶ Dirt is any unclean substance, such as dust, mud, or stains. ❷ Dirt is also earth or soil.
● SIMILAR WORDS: ❶ filth, grime, ● muck

dirty, dirtier, dirtiest ADJECTIVE ❶ marked or covered with dirt. ❷ unfair or dishonest • *a dirty fight.* ❸ about sex in a way that many people find offensive • *dirty jokes.*
● SIMILAR WORDS: ❶ filthy, ● grubby, mucky, unclean

dis- PREFIX 'Dis-' is added to the beginning of a word to form a word that means the opposite • *discontented.*

disability, disabilities NOUN a physical or mental condition or illness that restricts someone's way of life.

disable, disables, disabling, disabled VERB If something disables someone, it injures or harms them physically or mentally and severely affects their life. **disablement** NOUN

disabled ADJECTIVE lacking one or more physical powers, such as the ability to walk or to coordinate one's movements.

disadvantage, disadvantages NOUN an unfavourable or harmful circumstance. **disadvantaged** ADJECTIVE
● SIMILAR WORDS: drawback, ● handicap

disaffected ADJECTIVE If someone is disaffected with an idea or organization, they no longer believe in it or support it • *disaffected voters.*

disagree, disagrees, disagreeing, disagreed VERB ❶ If you disagree

a b c **d** e f g h i j k l m n o p q r s t u v w x y z

▷ SPELLING NOTE: *I went to see (C) the doctor's new practiCe (practice)*

with someone, you have a different
view or opinion from theirs. ❷ If you
disagree with an action or proposal,
you disapprove of it and believe it is
wrong • *He detested her and disagreed
with her policies.* ❸ If food or drink
disagrees with you, it makes you feel
unwell.
● **SIMILAR WORDS:** ❶ differ,
● dispute, dissent

disagreeable ADJECTIVE
unpleasant or unhelpful and
unfriendly • *a disagreeable odour.*

disagreement, disagreements
NOUN ❶ a dispute about something.
❷ an objection to something.

disappear, disappears,
disappearing, disappeared VERB ❶ If
something or someone disappears,
they go out of sight or become lost.
❷ To disappear also means to stop
existing or happening • *The pain has
disappeared.* **disappearance** NOUN
● **SIMILAR WORDS:** fade away,
● vanish

disappoint, disappoints,
disappointing, disappointed VERB If
someone or something disappoints
you, it fails to live up to what you
expected of it.

disappointed ADJECTIVE sad
because something has not happened.

disappointment,
disappointments NOUN ❶ a feeling
of being disappointed. ❷ something
that disappoints you.

disapproval NOUN the belief that
something is wrong or inappropriate.

disapprove, disapproves,
disapproving, disapproved VERB To

disapprove of something or someone
means to believe they are wrong or
bad • *Everyone disapproved of their
marrying so young.* **disapproving**
ADJECTIVE

disarm, disarms, disarming,
disarmed VERB ❶ To disarm means
to get rid of weapons. ❷ If someone
disarms you, they overcome your
anger or doubt by charming or
soothing you • *Mahoney was almost
disarmed by the frankness.* **disarming**
ADJECTIVE

disarmament NOUN
Disarmament is the reducing or
getting rid of military forces and
weapons.

disarray NOUN Disarray is a state of
disorder and confusion • *Our army was
in disarray and practically weaponless.*

disassemble, disassembles,
disassembling, disassembled VERB
D & T To disassemble a structure or
object which has been made up or
built from several smaller parts is to
separate its parts from one another.

disaster, disasters NOUN ❶ an
event or accident that causes great
distress or destruction. ❷ a complete
failure. **disastrous** ADJECTIVE
disastrously ADVERB
● **SIMILAR WORDS:** ❶ calamity,
● catastrophe

disband, disbands, disbanding,
disbanded VERB When a group of
people disbands, it officially ceases to
exist.

disc, discs; also spelt **disk** NOUN ❶ a
flat round object • *a tax disc* • *a
compact disc.* ❷ one of the thin
circular pieces of cartilage which

▷ SPELLING NOTE: *You must practiSe your Ss (practise)*

separate the bones in your spine.
3 (ICT) in computing, another
spelling of **disk**.

discard, discards, discarding,
discarded **VERB** To discard something
means to get rid of it, because you no
longer want it or find it useful.
● **SIMILAR WORDS:** dump, get rid
● of, throw away

discern, discerns, discerning,
discerned *[Said dis-**ern**]* **VERB**
FORMAL To discern something means
to notice or understand it clearly • *The
film had no plot that I could discern.*

discernible **ADJECTIVE** able to be
seen or recognized • *no discernible
talent.*

discerning **ADJECTIVE** having
good taste and judgment.
discernment NOUN

discharge, discharges, discharging,
discharged **VERB** **1** If something
discharges or is discharged, it is given
or sent out • *Oil discharged into the
world's oceans.* **2** To discharge
someone from hospital means to
allow them to leave. **3** If someone is
discharged from a job, they are
dismissed from it ▷ **NOUN** **4** a
substance that is released from the
inside of something • *a thick nasal
discharge.* **5** a dismissal or release
from a job or an institution.

disciple, disciples *[Said dis-**sigh**-pl]*
NOUN (RE) a follower of someone or
something, especially one of the
twelve men who were followers and
helpers of Christ.

discipline, disciplines, disciplining,
disciplined **NOUN** **1** (PSHE)
Discipline is making people obey rules

and punishing them when they break
them. **2** (PSHE) Discipline is the
ability to behave and work in a
controlled way ▷ **VERB** (PSHE) **3** If
you discipline yourself, you train
yourself to behave and work in an
ordered way. **4** To discipline
someone means to punish them.
**disciplinary ADJECTIVE disciplined
ADJECTIVE**

disc jockey, disc jockeys **NOUN**
someone who introduces and plays
pop records on the radio or at a night
club.

disclose, discloses, disclosing,
disclosed **VERB** To disclose
something means to make it known or
allow it to be seen. **disclosure NOUN**

disco, discos **NOUN** a party or a club
where people go to dance to pop
records.

discomfort, discomforts **NOUN**
1 Discomfort is distress or slight
pain. **2** Discomfort is also a feeling of
worry or embarrassment.
3 Discomforts are things that make
you uncomfortable.

disconcert, disconcerts,
disconcerting, disconcerted **VERB** If
something disconcerts you, it makes
you feel uneasy or embarrassed.
disconcerting ADJECTIVE

disconnect, disconnects,
disconnecting, disconnected **VERB**
1 To disconnect something means to
detach it from something else. **2** If
someone disconnects your fuel supply
or telephone, they cut you off.

discontent NOUN Discontent is a
feeling of dissatisfaction with
conditions or with life in general • *He*

was aware of the discontent this policy had caused. **discontented ADJECTIVE**

discontinue, discontinues, discontinuing, discontinued **VERB** To discontinue something means to stop doing it.

discord NOUN Discord is unpleasantness or quarrelling between people.

discount, discounts, discounting, discounted **NOUN** ❶ a reduction in the price of something ▷ **VERB** ❷ If you discount something, you reject it or ignore it • *I haven't discounted her connection with the kidnapping case.*

discourage, discourages, discouraging, discouraged **VERB** To discourage someone means to take away their enthusiasm to do something. **discouraging ADJECTIVE discouragement NOUN**

● SIMILAR WORDS: demoralize,
● dishearten, put off

discourse, discourses FORMAL **NOUN** ❶ a formal talk or piece of writing intended to teach or explain something. ❷ Discourse is serious conversation between people on a particular subject.

discover, discovers, discovering, discovered **VERB** When you discover something, you find it or find out about it. **discovery NOUN discoverer NOUN**

discredit, discredits, discrediting, discredited **VERB** ❶ To discredit someone means to damage their reputation. ❷ To discredit an idea means to cause it to be doubted or not believed.

discreet ADJECTIVE If you are discreet, you avoid causing embarrassment when dealing with secret or private matters. **discreetly ADVERB**

discrepancy, discrepancies **NOUN** a difference between two things which ought to be the same • *discrepancies in his police interviews.*

discrete ADJECTIVE ❶ FORMAL separate and distinct • *two discrete sets of nerves.* ❷ (MATHS) A discrete line or set of data is made up of a limited number of separate points or items.

discretion NOUN ❶ Discretion is the quality of behaving with care and tact so as to avoid embarrassment or distress to other people • *You can count on my discretion.* ❷ Discretion is also freedom and authority to make decisions and take action according to your own judgment • *Class teachers have very limited discretion in decision-making.* **discretionary ADJECTIVE**

discriminate, discriminates, discriminating, discriminated **VERB** ❶ To discriminate between things means to recognize and understand the differences between them. ❷ To discriminate against a person or group means to treat them unfairly, usually because of their race, colour, or sex. ❸ To discriminate in favour of a person or group means to treat them more favourably than others. **discrimination NOUN discriminatory ADJECTIVE**

discursive ADJECTIVE (ENGLISH) FORMAL moving from one topic to another in a rambling or unmethodical way.

▷ SPELLING NOTE: *LEarn the principLEs (principle)*

discus, discuses NOUN a disc-shaped object with a heavy middle, thrown by athletes.

discuss, discusses, discussing, discussed VERB ❶ When people discuss something, they talk about it in detail. ❷ (EXAM TERM) To discuss a question is to look at the points or arguments of both sides and try to reach your own opinion.

discussion, discussions NOUN (PSHE) a conversation or piece of writing in which a subject is considered in detail.
● **SIMILAR WORDS:** conversation,
● discourse, talk

disdain NOUN Disdain is a feeling of superiority over or contempt for someone or something • *The candidates shared an equal disdain for the press.* **disdainful** ADJECTIVE

disease, diseases NOUN (HISTORY & SCIENCE) an unhealthy condition in people, animals, or plants. **diseased** ADJECTIVE

disembark, disembarks, disembarking, disembarked VERB To disembark means to land or unload from a ship, aircraft, or bus.

disembodied ADJECTIVE
❶ separate from or existing without a body • *a disembodied skull.* ❷ seeming not to be attached to or to come from anyone • *disembodied voices.*

disenchanted ADJECTIVE disappointed with something, and no longer believing that it is good or worthwhile • *She is very disenchanted with the marriage.* **disenchantment** NOUN

disfigure, disfigures, disfiguring, disfigured VERB To disfigure something means to spoil its appearance • *Graffiti or posters disfigured every wall.*

disgrace, disgraces, disgracing, disgraced NOUN ❶ Disgrace is a state in which people disapprove of someone. ❷ If something is a disgrace, it is unacceptable • *The overcrowded prisons were a disgrace.* ❸ If someone is a disgrace to a group of people, their behaviour makes the group feel ashamed • *You're a disgrace to the school.* ▷ VERB ❹ If you disgrace yourself or disgrace someone else, you cause yourself or them to be strongly disapproved of by other people.
● **SIMILAR WORDS:** ❶ dishonour,
● shame ❹ discredit, dishonour,
● shame

disgraceful ADJECTIVE If something is disgraceful, people disapprove of it strongly and think that those who are responsible for it should be ashamed. **disgracefully** ADVERB
● **SIMILAR WORDS:** scandalous,
● shameful, shocking

disgruntled ADJECTIVE discontented or in a bad mood.

disguise, disguises, disguising, disguised VERB ❶ To disguise something means to change its appearance so that people do not recognize it. ❷ To disguise a feeling means to hide it • *I tried to disguise my relief.* ▷ NOUN ❸ something you wear or something you do to alter your appearance so that you cannot be recognized by other people.

▷ SPELLING NOTE: *Psychiatrists Seldom Yell Callously Hard (*<u>psychiatrist</u>*)*

a
b
c
d
e
f
g
h
i
j
k
l
m
n
o
p
q
r
s
t
u
v
w
x
y
z

A
B
C
D
E
F
G
H
I
J
K
L
M
N
O
P
Q
R
S
T
U
V
W
X
Y
Z

disgust, disgusts, disgusting, disgusted **NOUN** ❶ Disgust is a strong feeling of dislike or disapproval ▷ **VERB** ❷ To disgust someone means to make them feel a strong sense of dislike or disapproval. **disgusted ADJECTIVE**
● **SIMILAR WORDS:** ❶ loathing,
● repugnance, revulsion ❷ revolt,
● sicken

disgusting ADJECTIVE very unpleasant and offensive.

dish, dishes **NOUN** ❶ a shallow container for cooking or serving food. ❷ food of a particular kind or food cooked in a particular way • *two fish dishes to choose from.*

disheartened ADJECTIVE If you are disheartened, you feel disappointed.

dishevelled [Said dish-*ev*-ld] **ADJECTIVE** If someone looks dishevelled, their clothes or hair look untidy.

dishonest ADJECTIVE not truthful or able to be trusted. **dishonestly ADVERB**

dishonesty NOUN Dishonesty is behaviour which is meant to deceive people, either by not telling the truth or by cheating.

disillusion, disillusions, disillusioning, disillusioned **VERB** If something or someone disillusions you, you discover that you were mistaken about something you valued, and so you feel disappointed with it. **disillusionment NOUN**

disillusioned ADJECTIVE If you are disillusioned with something, you

are disappointed because it is not as good as you had expected.

disinfectant, disinfectants **NOUN** a chemical substance that kills germs.

disintegrate, disintegrates, disintegrating, disintegrated **VERB** ❶ If something disintegrates, it becomes weakened and is not effective • *My confidence disintegrated.* ❷ If an object disintegrates, it breaks into many pieces and so is destroyed. **disintegration NOUN**

disinterest NOUN ❶ Disinterest is a lack of interest. ❷ Disinterest is also a lack of personal involvement in a situation.

disinterested ADJECTIVE If someone is disinterested, they are not going to gain or lose from the situation they are involved in, and so can act in a way that is fair to both sides • *a disinterested judge.*
● **USAGE NOTE:** Some people use
● *disinterested* to mean 'not
● interested', but the word they
● should use is *uninterested*

disjointed ADJECTIVE If thought or speech is disjointed, it jumps from subject to subject and so is difficult to follow.

disk, disks **NOUN** ❶ ICT In a computer, the disk is the part where information is stored • *The program takes up 2.5 megabytes of disk space.* ❷ another spelling of **disc.**

dislike, dislikes, disliking, disliked **VERB** ❶ If you dislike something or someone, you think they are unpleasant and do not like them ▷ **NOUN** ❷ Dislike is a feeling that you have when you do not like

▷ SPELLING NOTE: *the QUeen stood on the QUay (quay)*

someone or something.
● **SIMILAR WORDS:** ❷ aversion,
● distaste

dislocate, dislocates, dislocating, dislocated **VERB** To dislocate your bone or joint means to put it out of place.

dislodge, dislodges, dislodging, dislodged **VERB** To dislodge something means to move it or force it out of place.

dismal [Said diz-mal] **ADJECTIVE** rather gloomy and depressing • dismal weather. **dismally ADVERB**
● **WORD HISTORY:** from Latin dies
● mali meaning 'evil days'

dismantle, dismantles, dismantling, dismantled **VERB** To dismantle something means to take it apart.

dismay, dismays, dismaying, dismayed **NOUN** ❶ Dismay is a feeling of fear and worry ▷ **VERB** ❷ If someone or something dismays you, it fills you with alarm and worry.

dismember, dismembers, dismembering, dismembered **VERB** **FORMAL** To dismember a person or animal means to cut or tear their body into pieces.

dismiss, dismisses, dismissing, dismissed **VERB** ❶ If you dismiss something, you decide to ignore it because it is not important enough for you to think about. ❷ To dismiss an employee means to ask that person to leave their job. ❸ If someone in authority dismisses you, they tell you to leave. **dismissal NOUN**

dismissive ADJECTIVE If you are dismissive of something or someone,

you show that you think they are of little importance or value • a dismissive gesture.

disobey, disobeys, disobeying, disobeyed **VERB** To disobey a person or an order means to deliberately refuse to do what you are told.

disorder, disorders **NOUN**
❶ Disorder is a state of untidiness.
❷ Disorder is also a lack of organization • The men fled in disorder.
❸ a disease • a stomach disorder.
● **SIMILAR WORDS:** ❷ chaos,
● confusion

disorganized or **disorganised ADJECTIVE** If something is disorganized, it is confused and badly prepared or badly arranged. **disorganization NOUN**

disown, disowns, disowning, disowned **VERB** To disown someone or something means to refuse to admit any connection with them.

disparaging ADJECTIVE critical and scornful • disparaging remarks.

disparate ADJECTIVE **FORMAL** Things that are disparate are utterly different from one another. **disparity NOUN**

dispatch, dispatches, dispatching, dispatched; also spelt **despatch VERB** ❶ To dispatch someone or something to a particular place means to send them there for a special reason • The president dispatched him on a fact-finding visit. ▷ **NOUN** ❷ an official written message, often sent to an army or government headquarters.

dispel, dispels, dispelling, dispelled **VERB** To dispel fears or beliefs means

▷ SPELLING NOTE: Rhythmical Hounds Yap To Heavy Music (rhythm)

to drive them away or to destroy them • *The myths are being dispelled.*

dispensary, dispensaries **NOUN** a place where medicines are prepared and given out.

dispense, dispenses, dispensing, dispensed **VERB** ❶ FORMAL To dispense something means to give it out • *They dispense advice.* ❷ To dispense medicines means to prepare them and give them out. ❸ To dispense with something means to do without it or do away with it • *We'll dispense with formalities.*

dispenser, dispensers **NOUN** a machine or container from which you can get things • *a cash dispenser.*

disperse, disperses, dispersing, dispersed **VERB** ❶ When something disperses, it scatters over a wide area. ❷ When people disperse or when someone disperses them, they move apart and go in different directions. **dispersion NOUN**

dispirited **ADJECTIVE** depressed and having no enthusiasm for anything.

dispiriting **ADJECTIVE** Something dispiriting makes you depressed • *a dispiriting defeat.*

displace, displaces, displacing, displaced **VERB** ❶ If one thing displaces another, it forces the thing out of its usual place and occupies that place itself. ❷ If people are displaced, they are forced to leave their home or country.

displacement **NOUN** ❶ Displacement is the removal of something from its usual or correct

place or position. ❷ (SCIENCE) In physics, displacement is the weight or volume of liquid displaced by an object submerged or floating in it.

display, displays, displaying, displayed **VERB** ❶ If you display something, you show it or make it visible to people. ❷ If you display something such as an emotion, you behave in a way that shows you feel it ▷ **NOUN** ❸ (ART) an arrangement of things designed to attract people's attention.

displease, displeases, displeasing, displeased **VERB** If someone or something displeases you, they make you annoyed, dissatisfied, or offended. **displeasure NOUN**

disposable **ADJECTIVE** designed to be thrown away after use • *disposable nappies.*

disposal **NOUN** Disposal is the act of getting rid of something that is no longer wanted or needed.

dispose, disposes, disposing, disposed **VERB** ❶ To dispose of something means to get rid of it. ❷ If you are not disposed to do something, you are not willing to do it.

disprove, disproves, disproving, disproved **VERB** If someone disproves an idea, belief, or theory, they show that it is not true.

dispute, disputes, disputing, disputed **NOUN** ❶ an argument ▷ **VERB** ❷ To dispute a fact or theory means to question the truth of it.

disqualify, disqualifies, disqualifying, disqualified **VERB** If someone is disqualified from a competition or activity, they are officially stopped from taking part in it • *He was disqualified from driving for 18 months.* **disqualification** NOUN

disquiet NOUN Disquiet is worry or anxiety. **disquieting** ADJECTIVE

disregard, disregards, disregarding, disregarded VERB **①** To disregard something means to pay little or no attention to it ▷ NOUN **②** Disregard is a lack of attention or respect for something • *He exhibited a flagrant disregard of the law.*

disrepair PHRASE If something is **in disrepair** or **in a state of disrepair**, it is broken or in poor condition.

disrespect NOUN Disrespect is contempt or lack of respect • *his disrespect for authority.* **disrespectful** ADJECTIVE

disrupt, disrupts, disrupting, disrupted VERB To disrupt something such as an event or system means to break it up or throw it into confusion • *Strikes disrupted air traffic in Italy.* **disruption** NOUN **disruptive** ADJECTIVE

dissatisfied ADJECTIVE not pleased or not contented. **dissatisfaction** NOUN

dissect, dissects, dissecting, dissected VERB To dissect a plant or a dead body means to cut it up so that it can be scientifically examined. **dissection** NOUN

dissent, dissents, dissenting, dissented NOUN **①** Dissent is strong difference of opinion • *political dissent.* ▷ VERB **②** When people dissent, they express a difference of opinion about something. **dissenting** ADJECTIVE

dissertation, dissertations NOUN a long essay, especially for a university degree.

disservice NOUN To do someone a disservice means to do something that harms them.

dissident, dissidents NOUN someone who disagrees with and criticizes the government of their country.

dissimilar ADJECTIVE If things are dissimilar, they are unlike each other.

dissipate, dissipates, dissipating, dissipated VERB **①** FORMAL When something dissipates or is dissipated, it completely disappears • *The cloud seemed to dissipate there.* **②** If someone dissipates time, money, or effort, they waste it.

dissipated ADJECTIVE Someone who is dissipated shows signs of indulging too much in alcohol or other physical pleasures.

dissolve, dissolves, dissolving, dissolved VERB **①** (SCIENCE) If you dissolve something or if it dissolves in a liquid, it becomes mixed with and absorbed in the liquid. **②** To dissolve an organization or institution means to officially end it.

dissuade, dissuades, dissuading, dissuaded *[Said dis-**wade**]* VERB To dissuade someone from doing something or from believing something means to persuade them not to do it or not to believe it.

distance, distances, distancing, distanced NOUN **①** The distance

a
b
c
d
e
f
g
h
i
j
k
l
m
n
o
p
q
r
s
t
u
v
w
x
y
z

▷ SPELLING NOTE: On WEDNESday Wayne WED NESta (*Wednesday*)

between two points is how far it is between them. ❷ Distance is the fact of being far away in space or time ▷ **VERB** ❸ If you distance yourself from someone or something or are distanced from them, you become less involved with them.

distant ADJECTIVE ❶ far away in space or time. ❷ A distant relative is one who is not closely related to you. ❸ Someone who is distant is cold and unfriendly. **distantly** ADVERB
● SIMILAR WORDS: ❸ aloof,
● reserved, standoffish

distaste NOUN Distaste is a dislike of something which you find offensive.

distasteful ADJECTIVE If you find something distasteful, you think it is unpleasant or offensive.

distil, distils, distilling, distilled **VERB** (SCIENCE) When a liquid is distilled, it is heated until it evaporates and then cooled to enable purified liquid to be collected. **distillation** NOUN

distillery, distilleries NOUN a place where whisky or other strong alcoholic drink is made, using a process of distillation.

distinct ADJECTIVE ❶ If one thing is distinct from another, it is recognizably different from it • *A word may have two quite distinct meanings.* ❷ If something is distinct, you can hear, smell, or see it clearly and plainly • *There was a distinct buzzing noise.* ❸ If something such as a fact, idea, or intention is distinct, it is clear and definite • *She had a distinct feeling that someone was watching them.* **distinctly** ADVERB

distinction, distinctions NOUN

❶ a difference between two things • *a distinction between the body and the soul.* ❷ Distinction is a quality of excellence and superiority • *a man of distinction.* ❸ a special honour or claim • *It had the distinction of being the largest square in Europe.*

distinctive ADJECTIVE Something that is distinctive has a special quality which makes it recognizable • *a distinctive voice.* **distinctively** ADVERB

distinguish, distinguishes, distinguishing, distinguished **VERB** ❶ To distinguish between things means to recognize the difference between them • *I've learned to distinguish business and friendship.* ❷ To distinguish something means to make it out by seeing, hearing, or tasting it • *I heard shouting but was unable to distinguish the words.* ❸ If you distinguish yourself, you do something that makes people think highly of you. **distinguishable** ADJECTIVE **distinguishing** ADJECTIVE

distort, distorts, distorting, distorted **VERB** ❶ If you distort a statement or an argument, you represent it in an untrue or misleading way. ❷ If something is distorted, it is changed so that it seems strange or unclear • *His voice was distorted.* ❸ If an object is distorted, it is twisted or pulled out of shape. **distorted** ADJECTIVE **distortion** NOUN

distract, distracts, distracting, distracted **VERB** If something distracts you, your attention is taken away from what you are doing. **distracted** ADJECTIVE **distractedly**

▷ SPELLING NOTE: *Eddy Ant thinks mEAt is a grEAt trEAt to EAt (-ea-)*

ADVERB distracting ADJECTIVE
● **SIMILAR WORDS:** divert, sidetrack

distraction, distractions **NOUN**
❶ something that takes people's attention away from something. ❷ an activity that is intended to amuse or relax someone.

distraught ADJECTIVE so upset and worried that you cannot think clearly • *He was distraught over the death of his mother.*

distress, distresses, distressing, distressed **NOUN** ❶ Distress is great suffering caused by pain or sorrow. ❷ Distress is also the state of needing help because of difficulties or danger ▷ **VERB** ❸ To distress someone means to make them feel alarmed or unhappy • *Her death had profoundly distressed me.*
● **SIMILAR WORDS:** ❸ trouble,
● upset

distressing ADJECTIVE very worrying or upsetting.

distribute, distributes, distributing, distributed **VERB** ❶ To distribute something such as leaflets means to hand them out or deliver them • *They publish and distribute brochures.* ❷ If things are distributed, they are spread throughout an area or space • *Distribute the cheese evenly on top of the quiche.* ❸ To distribute something means to divide it and share it out among a number of people.
● **SIMILAR WORDS:** ❸ dispense,
● share out

distribution, distributions **NOUN**
❶ Distribution is the delivering of something to various people or organizations • *the distribution of*

vicious leaflets. ❷ Distribution is the sharing out of something to various people • *distribution of power.*

distributor, distributors **NOUN** a company that supplies goods to other businesses who then sell them to the public.

district, districts **NOUN** an area of a town or country • *a residential district.*

district nurse, district nurses **NOUN** a nurse who visits and treats people in their own homes.

distrust, distrusts, distrusting, distrusted **VERB** ❶ If you distrust someone, you are suspicious of them because you are not sure whether they are honest ▷ **NOUN** ❷ Distrust is suspicion. **distrustful ADJECTIVE**

disturb, disturbs, disturbing, disturbed **VERB** ❶ If you disturb someone, you break their peace or privacy. ❷ If something disturbs you, it makes you feel upset or worried. ❸ If something is disturbed, it is moved out of position or meddled with. **disturbing ADJECTIVE**
● **SIMILAR WORDS:** ❷ trouble,
● upset, worry

disturbance, disturbances **NOUN**
❶ Disturbance is the state of being disturbed. ❷ a violent or unruly incident in public.

disuse NOUN Something that has fallen into disuse is neglected or no longer used. **disused ADJECTIVE**

ditch, ditches **NOUN** a channel at the side of a road or field, to drain away excess water.

dither, dithers, dithering, dithered **VERB** To dither means to be unsure

▷ SPELLING NOTE: *Elaine and Emily shout EE when they mEEt to grEEt each other (-ee-)*

and hesitant about what to do.

ditto 'Ditto' means 'the same'. In written lists, 'ditto' is represented by a mark (") to avoid repetition.
● **WORD HISTORY:** from Italian *detto* meaning 'said'

ditty, ditties **NOUN** OLD-FASHIONED a short simple song or poem.

diva, divas **NOUN** a great or leading female singer, especially in opera.
● **WORD HISTORY:** from Latin *diva* meaning 'a goddess'

dive, dives, diving, dived **VERB** ❶ To dive means to jump into water with your arms held straight above your head. ❷ If you go diving, you go down under the surface of the sea or a lake using special breathing equipment. ❸ If an aircraft or bird dives, it flies in a steep downward path, or drops sharply. **diver NOUN diving NOUN**

diverge, diverges, diverging, diverged **VERB** ❶ If opinions or facts diverge, they differ • *Theory and practice sometimes diverged.* ❷ If two things such as roads or paths which have been going in the same direction diverge, they separate and go off in different directions. **divergence NOUN divergent ADJECTIVE**

diverse ADJECTIVE ❶ If a group of things is diverse, it is made up of different kinds of things • *a diverse range of goods and services.* ❷ People, ideas, or objects that are diverse are very different from each other. **diversity NOUN**

diversify, diversifies, diversifying, diversified **VERB** To diversify means to increase the variety of something • *Has the company diversified into new*

areas? **diversification NOUN**

diversion, diversions **NOUN** ❶ a special route arranged for traffic when the usual route is closed. ❷ something that takes your attention away from what you should be concentrating on • *A break for tea created a welcome diversion.* ❸ a pleasant or amusing activity.

divert, diverts, diverting, diverted **VERB** To divert something means to change the course or direction it is following. **diverting ADJECTIVE**

divide, divides, dividing, divided **VERB** ❶ When something divides or is divided, it is split up and separated into two or more parts. ❷ If something divides two areas, it forms a barrier between them. ❸ If people divide over something or if something divides them, it causes strong disagreement between them. ❹ **[MATHS]** In mathematics, when you divide, you calculate how many times one number contains another ▷ **NOUN** ❺ a separation • *the class divide.*

dividend, dividends **NOUN** a portion of a company's profits that is paid to shareholders.

divination NOUN Divination is the foretelling of the future as though by supernatural power.

divine, divines, divining, divined **ADJECTIVE** ❶ having the qualities of a god or goddess ▷ **VERB** ❷ To divine something means to discover it by guessing. **divinely ADVERB**

divinity, divinities **NOUN** ❶ Divinity is the study of religion. ❷ Divinity is the state of being a god. ❸ A Divinity

▷ SPELLING NOTE: *'i' before 'e' except after 'c'*

is a god or goddess.

division, divisions **NOUN**
❶ Division is the separation of something into two or more distinct parts. **❷** (**MATHS**) Division is also the process of dividing one number by another. **❸** a difference of opinion that causes separation between ideas or groups of people • *There were divisions in the Party on economic policy.* **❹** any one of the parts or groups into which something is split • *the Research Division.* **divisional ADJECTIVE**

divisive ADJECTIVE causing hostility between people so that they split into different groups • *Inflation is economically and socially divisive.*

divisor, divisors **NOUN** (**MATHS**) a number by which another number is divided.

divorce, divorces, divorcing, divorced **NOUN** **❶** Divorce is the formal and legal ending of a marriage ▷ **VERB** **❷** When a married couple divorce, their marriage is legally ended. **divorced ADJECTIVE** **divorcee NOUN**

divulge, divulges, divulging, divulged **VERB** To divulge information means to reveal it.

Diwali [*Said dih-wah-lee*] **NOUN** a Hindu religious festival in honour of the goddess of wealth. It is celebrated by feasting, exchanging gifts, and lighting lamps.

DIY NOUN DIY is the activity of making or repairing things yourself. DIY is an abbreviation for 'do-it-yourself'.

dizzy, dizzier, dizziest **ADJECTIVE**

having or causing a whirling sensation. **dizziness NOUN**

DNA NOUN (**SCIENCE**) DNA is deoxyribonucleic acid, which is found in the cells of all living things. It is responsible for passing on characteristics from parents to their children.

do, does, doing, did, done; dos **VERB** **❶** Do is an auxiliary verb, which is used to form questions, negatives, and to give emphasis to the main verb of a sentence. **❷** If someone does a task or activity, they perform it and finish it • *He just didn't want to do any work.* **❸** If you ask what people do, you want to know what their job is • *What will you do when you leave school?* **❹** If you do well at something, you are successful. If you do badly, you are unsuccessful. **❺** If something will do, it is adequate but not the most suitable option • *Home-made stock is best, but cubes will do.* ▷ **NOUN** **❻** INFORMAL a party or other social event.
 ● **SIMILAR WORDS: ❷** carry out,
 ● execute, perform
do up VERB **❶** To do something up means to fasten it. **❷** To do up something old means to repair and decorate it.

docile ADJECTIVE quiet, calm, and easily controlled.

dock, docks, docking, docked **NOUN** **❶** an enclosed area in a harbour where ships go to be loaded, unloaded, or repaired. **❷** In a court of law, the dock is the place where the accused person stands or sits ▷ **VERB** **❸** When a ship docks, it is brought into dock at the end of its voyage.

❹ To dock someone's wages means to deduct an amount from the sum they would normally receive. **❺** To dock an animal's tail means to cut part of it off. **docker NOUN**

doctor, doctors, doctoring, doctored
NOUN ❶ a person who is qualified in medicine and treats people who are ill. **❷** A doctor of an academic subject is someone who has been awarded the highest academic degree • *She is a doctor of philosophy.* ▷ **VERB ❸** To doctor something means to alter it in order to deceive people • *Stamps can be doctored.*

doctorate, doctorates **NOUN** the highest university degree. **doctoral ADJECTIVE**

doctrine, doctrines **NOUN** a set of beliefs or principles held by a group. **doctrinal ADJECTIVE**

document, documents, documenting, documented **NOUN ❶** [HISTORY] a piece of paper which provides an official record of something. **❷** [ICT] a piece of text or graphics stored in a computer as a file that can be amended or altered by document processing software ▷ **VERB ❸** [HISTORY] If you document something, you make a detailed record of it. **documentation NOUN**

documentary, documentaries
NOUN ❶ a radio or television programme, or a film, which gives information on real events ▷ **ADJECTIVE ❷** Documentary evidence is made up of written or official records.

dodge, dodges, dodging, dodged

VERB ❶ If you dodge or dodge something, you move suddenly to avoid being seen, hit, or caught. **❷** If you dodge something such as an issue or accusation, you avoid dealing with it.

dodgy, dodgier, dodgiest **ADJECTIVE** INFORMAL dangerous, risky, or unreliable • *He has a dodgy heart.*

dodo, dodos **NOUN** [SCIENCE] a large, flightless bird which is now extinct.

doe, does **NOUN** a female deer, rabbit, or hare.

does the third person singular of the present tense of **do**.

dog, dogs, dogging, dogged **NOUN ❶** a four-legged, meat-eating animal, kept as a pet, or to guard property or go hunting ▷ **VERB ❷** If you dog someone, you follow them very closely and never leave them.

dog collar, dog collars **NOUN** INFORMAL a white collar with no front opening worn by Christian clergy.

dog-eared ADJECTIVE A book that is dog-eared has been used so much that the corners of the pages are turned down or worn.

dogged [*Said* **dog**-ged] **ADJECTIVE** showing determination to continue with something, even if it is very difficult • *dogged persistence.* **doggedly ADVERB**

doggerel NOUN [ENGLISH] Doggerel is funny or silly verse, often written quickly and not intended to be serious.

dogma, dogmas **NOUN** a belief or

▷ SPELLING NOTE: *an ELegant angEL (angel)*

system of beliefs held by a religious or political group.

dogmatic ADJECTIVE Someone who is dogmatic about something is convinced that they are right about it. **dogmatism** NOUN

dolce [Said dol-chay] ADVERB MUSIC In music, dolce is an instruction to play or sing something gently and sweetly.
● **WORD HISTORY:** an Italian word
● meaning 'sweet'

doldrums INFORMAL PHRASE If you are **in the doldrums**, you are depressed or bored.

dole, doles, doling, doled VERB If you dole something out, you give a certain amount of it to each individual in a group.

doll, dolls NOUN a child's toy which looks like a baby or person.

dollar, dollars NOUN the main unit of currency in Australia, New Zealand, the USA, Canada, and some other countries. A dollar is worth 100 cents.

dollop, dollops NOUN an amount of food, served casually in a lump.

dolphin, dolphins NOUN a mammal which lives in the sea and looks like a large fish with a long snout.

domain, domains NOUN ❶ a particular area of activity or interest • *the domain of science.* ❷ an area over which someone has control or influence • *This reservation was the largest of the Apache domains.*

dome, domes NOUN a round roof. **domed** ADJECTIVE

domestic ADJECTIVE ❶ happening or existing within one particular country • *domestic and foreign politics.* ❷ involving or concerned with the home and family • *routine domestic tasks.*

domesticated ADJECTIVE If a wild animal or plant has been domesticated, it has been controlled or cultivated.

domesticity NOUN FORMAL Domesticity is life at home with your family.

dominance NOUN ❶ Dominance is power or control. ❷ If something has dominance over other similar things, it is more powerful or important than they are • *the dominance of the United States in the film business.* **dominant** ADJECTIVE

dominate, dominates, dominating, dominated VERB ❶ If something or someone dominates a situation or event, they are the most powerful or important thing in it and have control over it • *The civil service dominated public affairs.* ❷ If a person or country dominates other people or places, they have power or control over them. ❸ If something dominates an area, it towers over it • *The valley was dominated by high surrounding cliffs.* **dominating** ADJECTIVE **domination** NOUN

domineering ADJECTIVE Someone who is domineering tries to control other people • *a domineering mother.*

dominion NOUN Dominion is control or authority that a person or a country has over other people.

domino, dominoes NOUN

▷ SPELLING NOTE: *LEt's measure the angLE (angle)*

A
B
C
D
E
F
G
H
I
J
K
L
M
N
O
P
Q
R
S
T
U
V
W
X
Y
Z

Dominoes are small rectangular blocks marked with two groups of spots on one side, used for playing the game called dominoes.

don, dons, donning, donned **NOUN**
❶ a lecturer at Oxford or Cambridge university ▷ **VERB** ❷ LITERARY If you don clothing, you put it on.

donate, donates, donating, donated **VERB** To donate something to a charity or organization means to give it as a gift. **donation NOUN**

done the past participle of **do**.

donkey, donkeys **NOUN** an animal like a horse, but smaller and with longer ears.

donor, donors **NOUN** ❶ someone who gives some of their blood while they are alive or an organ after their death to be used to help someone who is ill • a kidney donor. ❷ someone who gives something such as money to a charity or other organization.

doodle, doodles, doodling, doodled **NOUN** ❶ a drawing done when you are thinking about something else or when you are bored ▷ **VERB** ❷ To doodle means to draw doodles.

doom NOUN Doom is a terrible fate or event in the future which you can do nothing to prevent.

doomed ADJECTIVE If someone or something is doomed to an unpleasant or unhappy experience, they are certain to suffer it • doomed to failure.

doomsday NOUN Doomsday is the end of the world.

door, doors **NOUN** a swinging or

sliding panel for opening or closing the entrance to something; also the entrance itself.

doorway, doorways **NOUN** an opening in a wall for a door.

dope, dopes, doping, doped **NOUN** ❶ Dope is an illegal drug ▷ **VERB** ❷ If someone dopes you, they put a drug into your food or drink.
● **WORD HISTORY:** from Dutch *doop*
● meaning 'sauce'

dormant ADJECTIVE Something that is dormant is not active, growing, or being used • The buds will remain dormant until spring.

dormitory, dormitories **NOUN** a large bedroom where several people sleep.

dormouse, dormice **NOUN** an animal, like a large mouse, with a furry tail.

dorsal ADJECTIVE (SCIENCE) relating to the back of a fish or animal • a dorsal fin.

dosage, dosages **NOUN** the amount of a medicine or a drug that should be taken.

dose, doses **NOUN** a measured amount of a medicine or drug.

dossier, dossiers [Said **doss**-ee-ay] **NOUN** a collection of papers with information on a particular subject or person.

dot, dots, dotting, dotted **NOUN** ❶ a very small, round mark ▷ **VERB** ❷ If things dot an area, they are scattered all over it • Fishing villages dot the coastline. ▷ **PHRASE** ❸ If you arrive somewhere **on the dot**, you arrive there at exactly the right time.

dotcom, dotcoms **NOUN** a company that does most of its business on the Internet.

dote, dotes, doting, doted **VERB** If you dote on someone, you love them very much. **doting ADJECTIVE**

double, doubles, doubling, doubled **ADJECTIVE** ❶ twice the usual size • *a double whisky.* ❷ consisting of two parts • *a double album.* ▷ **VERB** ❸ If something doubles, it becomes twice as large. ❹ To double as something means to have a second job or use as well as the main one • *Their home doubles as an office.* ▷ **NOUN** ❺ Your double is someone who looks exactly like you. ❻ Doubles is a game of tennis or badminton which two people play against two other people. **doubly ADVERB**

double bass, double basses **NOUN** a musical instrument like a large violin, which you play standing up.

double-cross, double-crosses, double-crossing, double-crossed **VERB** If someone double-crosses you, they cheat you by pretending to do what you both planned, when in fact they do the opposite.

double-decker, double-deckers **ADJECTIVE** ❶ having two tiers or layers ▷ **NOUN** ❷ a bus with two floors.

double glazing NOUN Double glazing is a second layer of glass fitted to windows to keep the building quieter or warmer.

doubt, doubts, doubting, doubted **NOUN** ❶ Doubt is a feeling of

uncertainty about whether something is true or possible ▷ **VERB** ❷ If you doubt something, you think that it is probably not true or possible.

● **SIMILAR WORDS:** ❶ misgiving,
● qualm, uncertainty

doubtful ADJECTIVE unlikely or uncertain.

dough [rhymes with **go**] **NOUN** ❶ Dough is a mixture of flour and water and sometimes other ingredients, used to make bread, pastry, or biscuits. ❷ INFORMAL Dough is money.

doughnut, doughnuts **NOUN** a ring of sweet dough cooked in hot fat.

dour, dourer, dourest [rhymes with **poor**] **ADJECTIVE** severe and unfriendly • *a dour portrait of his personality.*

douse, douses, dousing, doused; also spelt **dowse VERB** If you douse a fire, you stop it burning by throwing water over it.

dove, doves **NOUN** a bird like a small pigeon.

dovetail, dovetails, dovetailing, dovetailed **VERB** If two things dovetail together, they fit together closely or neatly.

dowager, dowagers **NOUN** a woman who has inherited a title from her dead husband • *the Empress Dowager.*

dowdy, dowdier, dowdiest **ADJECTIVE** wearing dull and unfashionable clothes.

dowel, dowels **NOUN** D & T A dowel is a short, thin piece of wood or

a
b
c
d
e
f
g
h
i
j
k
l
m
n
o
p
q
r
s
t
u
v
w
x
y
z

▷ SPELLING NOTE: *Beautiful Elephants Are Usually Tiny (*<u>*beautiful*</u>*)*

metal which is fitted into holes in larger pieces of wood or metal to join them together.

down, downs, downing, downed
PREPOSITION OR ADVERB **1** Down means towards the ground, towards a lower level, or in a lower place. **2** If you go down a road or river, you go along it ▷ **ADVERB** **3** If you put something down, you place it on a surface. **4** If an amount of something goes down, it decreases ▷ **ADJECTIVE** **5** If you feel down, you feel depressed ▷ **VERB** **6** If you down a drink, you drink it quickly ▷ **NOUN** **7** Down is the small, soft feathers on young birds.

down beat, down beats **NOUN** (MUSIC) the first beat of a bar of music.

downcast ADJECTIVE **1** feeling sad and dejected. **2** If your eyes are downcast, they are looking towards the ground.

downfall NOUN **1** The downfall of a successful or powerful person or institution is their failure. **2** Something that is someone's downfall is the thing that causes their failure • *His pride may be his downfall.*

downgrade, downgrades, downgrading, downgraded **VERB** If you downgrade something, you give it less importance or make it less valuable.

downhill ADVERB **1** moving down a slope. **2** becoming worse • *The press has gone downhill in the last 10 years.*

download, downloads, downloading, downloaded (ICT)

VERB **1** If you download data you transfer it from the memory of one computer to that of another, especially over the Internet ▷ **NOUN** **2** a piece of data transferred in this way.

downpour, downpours **NOUN** a heavy fall of rain.

downright ADJECTIVE OR ADVERB You use 'downright' to emphasize that something is extremely unpleasant or bad • *Staff are often discourteous and sometimes downright rude.*

downs PLURAL NOUN an area of low grassy hills, especially in the south of England.

downstairs ADVERB **1** going down a staircase towards the ground floor ▷ **ADJECTIVE OR ADVERB** **2** on a lower floor or on the ground floor.

downstream ADJECTIVE OR ADVERB Something that is downstream or moving downstream is nearer or moving nearer to the mouth of a river from a point further up.

down-to-earth ADJECTIVE sensible and practical • *a down-to-earth approach.*

downtrodden ADJECTIVE People who are downtrodden are treated badly by those with power and do not have the ability to fight back.

downturn, downturns **NOUN** a decline in the economy or in the success of a company or industry.

down under INFORMAL **NOUN** **1** Australia or New Zealand ▷ **ADVERB** **2** in or to Australia or New Zealand.

▷ SPELLING NOTE: Betty Eats Cakes And Uses Seven Eggs (*because*)

downwards or **downward**
ADVERB OR ADJECTIVE ❶ If you
move or look downwards, you move or
look towards the ground or towards a
lower level • *His eyes travelled
downwards* • *She slipped on the
downward slope.* ❷ If an amount or
rate moves downwards, it decreases.

downwind ADVERB If something
moves downwind, it moves in the
same direction as the wind • *Sparks
drifted downwind.*

dowry, dowries **NOUN** A woman's
dowry is money or property which her
father gives to the man she marries.

doze, dozes, dozing, dozed **VERB**
❶ When you doze, you sleep lightly
for a short period ▷ **NOUN** ❷ a short,
light sleep.

dozen, dozens **NOUN** A dozen things
are twelve of them.

Dr [*Said dock-ter*] ❶ 'Dr' is short for
'Doctor' and is used before the name
of someone with the highest form of
academic degree or who practises
medicine. ❷ 'Dr' is short for 'drive'.

drab, drabber, drabbest **ADJECTIVE**
dull and unattractive. **drabness**
NOUN
● **SIMILAR WORDS:** dreary, dull

draft, drafts, drafting, drafted **NOUN**
❶ an early rough version of it of a
document or speech ▷ **VERB**
❷ When you draft a document or
speech, you write the first rough
version of it. ❸ To draft people
somewhere means to move them
there so that they can do a specific job
• *Various different presenters were
drafted in.* ❹ In Australian and New
Zealand English, to draft cattle or

sheep is to select some from a herd or
flock.

drag, drags, dragging, dragged **VERB**
❶ If you drag a heavy object
somewhere, you pull it slowly and
with difficulty. ❷ If you drag someone
somewhere, you make them go
although they may be unwilling. ❸ If
things drag behind you, they trail
along the ground as you move along.
❹ If an event or a period of time
drags, it is boring and seems to last a
long time ▷ **NOUN** ❺ Drag is the
resistance to the motion of a body
passing through air or a fluid.
● **SIMILAR WORDS:** ❶ draw, haul,
● pull

dragon, dragons **NOUN** In stories
and legends, a dragon is a fierce
animal like a large lizard with wings
and claws that breathes fire.

dragonfly, dragonflies **NOUN** a
colourful insect which is often found
near water.

dragoon, dragoons, dragooning,
dragooned **NOUN** ❶ Dragoons are
soldiers. Originally, they were
mounted infantry soldiers ▷ **VERB**
❷ If you dragoon someone into
something, you force them to do it.

drain, drains, draining, drained **VERB**
❶ If you drain something, you cause
liquid to flow out of it. ❷ If you drain
a glass, you drink all its contents. ❸ If
liquid drains somewhere, it flows
there. ❹ If something drains strength
or resources, it gradually uses them up
• *The prolonged boardroom battle
drained him of energy and money.*
▷ **NOUN** ❺ a pipe or channel that
carries water or sewage away from a
place. ❻ a metal grid in a road,

A
B
C
D
E
F
G
H
I
J
K
L
M
N
O
P
Q
R
S
T
U
V
W
X
Y
Z

through which rainwater flows.

drainage NOUN ❶ Drainage is the system of pipes, drains, or ditches used to drain water or other liquid away from a place. ❷ Drainage is also the process of draining water away, or the way in which a place drains • *To grow these well, all you need is good drainage.*

drainage basin, drainage basins NOUN (GEOGRAPHY) the area of land from which rainwater drains into a particular river or reservoir.

drake, drakes NOUN a male duck.

drama, dramas NOUN ❶ a serious play for the theatre, television, or radio. ❷ Drama is plays and the theatre in general • *Japanese drama.* ❸ You can refer to the exciting events or aspects of a situation as drama • *the drama of real life.*

dramatic ADJECTIVE A dramatic change or event happens suddenly and is very noticeable • *a dramatic departure from tradition.* **dramatically** ADVERB

dramatist, dramatists NOUN (DRAMA) a person who writes plays.

drape, drapes, draping, draped VERB If you drape a piece of cloth, you arrange it so that it hangs down or covers something in loose folds.

drastic ADJECTIVE A drastic course of action is very severe and is usually taken urgently • *It's time for drastic action.* **drastically** ADVERB

● SIMILAR WORDS: extreme, radical

draught, draughts [Said *draft*] NOUN ❶ a current of cold air. ❷ an amount of liquid that you swallow.

❸ Draughts is a game for two people played on a chessboard with round pieces ▷ ADJECTIVE ❹ Draught beer is served straight from barrels rather than in bottles.

draughtsman, draughtsmen NOUN a person who prepares detailed drawings or plans.

draughty, draughtier, draughtiest ADJECTIVE A place that is draughty has currents of cold air blowing through it.

draw, draws, drawing, drew, drawn VERB ❶ When you draw, you use a pen or crayon to make a picture or diagram. ❷ To draw near means to move closer. To draw away or draw back means to move away. ❸ If you draw something in a particular direction, you pull it there smoothly and gently • *He drew his feet under the chair.* ❹ If you draw a deep breath, you breathe in deeply. ❺ If you draw the curtains, you pull them so that they cover or uncover the window. ❻ If something such as water or energy is drawn from a source, it is taken from it. ❼ If you draw a conclusion, you arrive at it from the facts you know. ❽ If you draw a distinction or a comparison between two things, you point out that it exists ▷ NOUN ❾ the result of a game or competition in which nobody wins. **draw up** VERB To draw up a plan, document, or list means to prepare it and write it out.

drawback, drawbacks NOUN a problem that makes something less acceptable or desirable • *Shortcuts usually have a drawback.*

drawbridge, drawbridges NOUN a

bridge that can be pulled up or lowered.

drawer, drawers **NOUN** a sliding box-shaped part of a piece of furniture used for storing things.

drawing, drawings **NOUN** ❶ a picture made with a pencil, pen, or crayon. ❷ Drawing is the skill or work of making drawings.

drawing pin, drawing pins **NOUN** ⟨**D & T**⟩ A drawing pin is a short nail with a broad, flat top.

drawing room, drawing rooms **NOUN** OLD-FASHIONED a room in a house where people relax or entertain guests.

drawl, drawls, drawling, drawled **VERB** If someone drawls, they speak slowly with long vowel sounds.

drawn Drawn is the past participle of draw.

dread, dreads, dreading, dreaded **VERB** ❶ If you dread something, you feel very worried and frightened about it • *He was dreading the journey.* ▷ **NOUN** ❷ Dread is a feeling of great fear or anxiety. **dreaded ADJECTIVE**

dreadful ADJECTIVE very bad or unpleasant. **dreadfully ADVERB**
● **SIMILAR WORDS:** atrocious,
● awful, terrible

dream, dreams, dreaming, dreamed or dreamt **NOUN** ❶ a series of events that you experience in your mind while asleep. ❷ a situation or event which you often think about because you would very much like it to happen • *his dream of winning the lottery.* ▷ **VERB** ❸ When you dream, you see events in your mind while you are

asleep. ❹ When you dream about something happening, you often think about it because you would very much like it to happen. ❺ If someone dreams up a plan or idea, they invent it. ❻ If you say you would not dream of doing something, you are emphasizing that you would not do it • *I wouldn't dream of giving the plot away.* ▷ **ADJECTIVE** ❼ too good to be true • *a dream holiday.* **dreamer NOUN**

Dreamtime NOUN In Australian Aboriginal legends, Dreamtime is the time when the world was being made and the first people were created.

dreamy, dreamier, dreamiest **ADJECTIVE** Someone with a dreamy expression looks as if they are thinking about something very pleasant.

dreary, drearier, dreariest **ADJECTIVE** dull or boring.

dregs PLURAL NOUN The dregs of a liquid are the last drops left at the bottom of a container, and any sediment left with it.

drenched ADJECTIVE soaking wet.

dress, dresses, dressing, dressed **NOUN** ❶ a piece of clothing for women or girls made up of a skirt and top attached. ❷ Dress is any clothing worn by men or women ▷ **VERB** ❸ When you dress, you put clothes on. ❹ If you dress for a special occasion, you put on formal clothes. ❺ To dress a wound means to clean it up and treat it.

dresser, dressers **NOUN** a piece of kitchen or dining room furniture with cupboards or drawers in the lower part and open shelves in the top part.

a b c **d** e f g h i j k l m n o p q r s t u v w x y z

▷ SPELLING NOTE: *I always visit my FRIend on a FRIday (Friday)*

A
B
C
D
E
F
G
H
I
J
K
L
M
N
O
P
Q
R
S
T
U
V
W
X
Y
Z

dressing gown, dressing gowns
NOUN an item of clothing shaped like
a coat and put on over nightwear.

dressing room, dressing rooms
NOUN a room used for getting
changed and putting on make-up,
especially a backstage room at a
theatre.

dress rehearsal, dress rehearsals
NOUN the last rehearsal of a show or
play, using costumes, scenery, and
lighting.

dribble, dribbles, dribbling, dribbled
VERB ❶ When liquid dribbles down a
surface, it trickles down it in drops or a
thin stream. ❷ If a person or animal
dribbles, saliva trickles from their
mouth. ❸ In sport, to dribble a ball
means to move it along by repeatedly
tapping it with your foot or a stick
▷ **NOUN** ❹ a small quantity of liquid
flowing in a thin stream or drops.

drift, drifts, drifting, drifted **VERB**
❶ When something drifts, it is carried
along by the wind or by water.
❷ When people drift, they move
aimlessly from one place or activity to
another. ❸ If you drift off to sleep,
you gradually fall asleep ▷ **NOUN**
❹ A snow drift is a pile of snow
heaped up by the wind. ❺ The drift of
an argument or a speech is its main
point. **drifter NOUN**

drill, drills, drilling, drilled **NOUN**
❶ (D & T) a tool for making holes
• *an electric drill*. ❷ Drill is a routine
exercise or routine training • *lifeboat
drill*. ▷ **VERB** ❸ (D & T) To drill into
something means to make a hole in it
using a drill. ❹ If you drill people, you
teach them to do something by
repetition.

drink, drinks, drinking, drank, drunk
VERB ❶ When you drink, you take
liquid into your mouth and swallow it.
❷ To drink also means to drink
alcohol • *He drinks little and eats
carefully*. ▷ **NOUN** ❸ an amount of
liquid suitable for drinking. ❹ an
alcoholic drink. **drinker NOUN**
● **SIMILAR WORDS:** ❶ imbibe, sip,
● swallow ❷ booze, tipple

drip, drips, dripping, dripped **VERB**
❶ When liquid drips, it falls in small
drops. ❷ When an object drips, drops
of liquid fall from it ▷ **NOUN** ❸ a
drop of liquid falling from something.
❹ a device for allowing liquid food to
enter the bloodstream of a person
who cannot eat properly because they
are ill.

drive, drives, driving, drove, driven
VERB ❶ To drive a vehicle means to
operate it and control its movements.
❷ If something or someone drives
you to do something, they force you to
do it • *The illness of his daughter drove
him to religion*. ❸ If you drive a post or
nail into something, you force it in by
hitting it with a hammer. ❹ If
something drives a machine, it
supplies the power that makes it work
▷ **NOUN** ❺ a journey in a vehicle.
❻ a private road that leads from a
public road to a person's house.
❼ Drive is energy and determination.
driver NOUN driving NOUN

drive-in, drive-ins **NOUN** a
restaurant, cinema, or other
commercial place that is specially
designed for customers to use while
staying in their cars.

drivel NOUN Drivel is nonsense • *He
is still writing mindless drivel*.

▷ SPELLING NOTE: *I want to see (C) your licenCe (licence)*

drizzle NOUN Drizzle is light rain.

dromedary, dromedaries NOUN a camel which has one hump.

drone, drones, droning, droned VERB ❶ If something drones, it makes a low, continuous humming noise. ❷ If someone drones on, they keep talking or reading aloud in a boring way ▷ NOUN ❸ a continuous low dull sound.

drool, drools, drooling, drooled VERB If someone drools, saliva dribbles from their mouth without them being able to stop it.

droop, droops, drooping, drooped VERB If something droops, it hangs or sags downwards with no strength or firmness.

drop, drops, dropping, dropped VERB ❶ If you drop something, you let it fall. ❷ If something drops, it falls straight down. ❸ If a level or amount drops, it becomes less. ❹ If your voice drops, or if you drop your voice, you speak more quietly. ❺ If you drop something that you are doing or dealing with, you stop doing it or dealing with it • *She dropped the subject and never mentioned it again.* ❻ If you drop a hint, you give someone a hint in a casual way. ❼ If you drop something or someone somewhere, you deposit or leave them there ▷ NOUN ❽ A drop of liquid is a very small quantity of it that forms or falls in a round shape. ❾ a decrease • *a huge drop in income.* ❿ the distance between the top and bottom of something tall, such as a cliff or building • *It is a sheer drop to the foot of the cliff.*

droplet, droplets NOUN a small drop.

droppings PLURAL NOUN Droppings are the faeces of birds and small animals.

drought, droughts [rhymes with *shout*] NOUN (GEOGRAPHY) a long period during which there is no rain.

drove, droves, droving, droved ❶ Drove is the past tense of **drive**. VERB ❷ To drove cattle or sheep is to drive them over a long distance.

drown, drowns, drowning, drowned VERB ❶ When someone drowns or is drowned, they die because they have gone under water and cannot breathe. ❷ If a noise drowns a sound, it is louder than the sound and makes it impossible to hear it.

drowsy, drowsier, drowsiest ADJECTIVE feeling sleepy.

drudgery NOUN Drudgery is hard boring work.

drug, drugs, drugging, drugged NOUN ❶ a chemical given to people to treat disease. ❷ Drugs are chemical substances that some people smoke, swallow, inhale, or inject because of their stimulating effects ▷ VERB ❸ To drug a person or animal means to give them a drug to make them unconscious. ❹ To drug food or drink means to add a drug to it in order to make someone unconscious.
drugged ADJECTIVE

druid, druids [Said *droo-id*] NOUN a priest of an ancient religion in Northern Europe.

drum, drums, drumming, drummed NOUN ❶ a musical instrument

a
b
c
d
e
f
g
h
i
j
k
l
m
n
o
p
q
r
s
t
u
v
w
x
y
z

▷ SPELLING NOTE: *The government licenSes Schnapps (licenSes)*

consisting of a skin stretched tightly over a round frame. **❷** an object or container shaped like a drum • *an oil drum.* **❸** INFORMAL In Australian English, the drum is information or advice • *The manager gave me the drum.* ▷ VERB **❹** If something is drumming on a surface, it is hitting it regularly, making a continuous beating sound. **❺** If you drum something into someone, you keep saying it to them until they understand it or remember it. **drummer** NOUN

drumstick, drumsticks NOUN **❶** a stick used for beating a drum. **❷** A chicken drumstick is the lower part of the leg of a chicken, which is cooked and eaten.

drunk, drunks **❶** Drunk is the past participle of **drink**. ADJECTIVE **❷** If someone is drunk, they have drunk so much alcohol that they cannot speak clearly or behave sensibly ▷ NOUN **❸** a person who is drunk, or who often gets drunk. **drunken** ADJECTIVE **drunkenly** ADVERB **drunkenness** NOUN

● SIMILAR WORDS: **❷** inebriated,
● intoxicated

dry, drier or dryer, driest; dries, drying, dried ADJECTIVE **❶** Something that is dry contains or uses no water or liquid. **❷** Dry bread or toast is eaten without a topping. **❸** Dry sherry or wine does not taste sweet. **❹** Dry also means plain and sometimes boring • *the dry facts.* **❺** Dry humour is subtle and sarcastic ▷ VERB **❻** When you dry something, or when it dries, liquid is removed from it.

dry up VERB **❶** If something dries up, it becomes completely dry.

❷ INFORMAL If you dry up, you forget what you were going to say, or find that you have nothing left to say. **dryness** NOUN **drily** ADVERB

● SIMILAR WORDS: **❶** arid,
● dehydrated, parched

dry-clean, dry-cleans, dry-cleaning, dry-cleaned VERB When clothes are dry-cleaned, they are cleaned with a liquid chemical rather than with water.

dryer, dryers; *also spelt* **drier** NOUN a device for removing moisture from something by heating or by hot air • *a hair dryer.*

dual ADJECTIVE having two parts, functions, or aspects • *a dual-purpose trimmer.*

dub, dubs, dubbing, dubbed VERB **❶** If something is dubbed a particular name, it is given that name • *Smiling has been dubbed 'nature's secret weapon'.* **❷** If a film is dubbed, the voices on the soundtrack are not those of the actors, but those of other actors speaking in a different language.

dubious [Said **dyoo**-bee-uss] ADJECTIVE **❶** not entirely honest, safe, or reliable • *dubious sales techniques.* **❷** doubtful • *I felt dubious about the entire proposition.* **dubiously** ADVERB

● SIMILAR WORDS:
● **❶** questionable, suspect

duchess, duchesses NOUN a woman who has the same rank as a duke, or who is a duke's wife or widow.

duchy, duchies [Said **dut**-shee] NOUN the land owned and ruled by a duke or duchess.

▷ SPELLING NOTE: *have a pIEce of pIE (piece)*

duck, ducks, ducking, ducked **NOUN**
① a bird that lives in water and has webbed feet and a large flat bill
▷ **VERB** **②** If you duck, you move your head quickly downwards in order to avoid being hit by something. **③** If you duck a duty or responsibility, you avoid it. **④** To duck someone means to push them briefly under water.

duckling, ducklings **NOUN** a young duck.

duct, ducts **NOUN** **①** a pipe or channel through which liquid or gas is sent. **②** a bodily passage through which liquid such as tears can pass.

ductile **ADJECTIVE** Material that is ductile is soft enough to be shaped, moulded, or drawn out into threads • *Copper is a ductile metal.*

dud, duds **NOUN** something which does not function properly.

due, dues **ADJECTIVE** **①** expected to happen or arrive • *The baby is due at Christmas.* **②** If you give something due consideration, you give it the consideration it needs ▷ **PHRASE** **③** Due to means because of • *Headaches can be due to stress.* ▷ **ADVERB** **④** Due means exactly in a particular direction • *about a mile due west.* **⑤** IN PLURAL Dues are sums of money that you pay regularly to an organization you belong to.

duel, duels **NOUN** **①** a fight arranged between two people using deadly weapons, to settle a quarrel. **②** Any contest or conflict between two people can be referred to as a duel.

duet, duets **NOUN** (MUSIC) a piece of music sung or played by two people.

dug Dug is the past tense and past participle of **dig**.

dugong, dugongs **NOUN** an animal like a whale that lives in warm seas.

dugout, dugouts **NOUN** **①** a canoe made by hollowing out a log. **②** MILITARY a shelter dug in the ground for protection.

duke, dukes **NOUN** a nobleman with a rank just below that of a prince.
● **WORD HISTORY:** from Latin *dux* meaning 'leader'

dull, duller, dullest; dulls, dulling, dulled **ADJECTIVE** **①** not at all interesting in any way. **②** slow to learn or understand. **③** not bright, sharp, or clear. **④** A dull day or dull sky is very cloudy. **⑤** Dull feelings are weak and not intense • *He should have been angry but felt only dull resentment.* ▷ **VERB** **⑥** If something dulls or is dulled, it becomes less bright, sharp, or clear. **dully** **ADVERB** **dullness** **NOUN**
● **SIMILAR WORDS:** **④** cloudy, overcast

duly **ADVERB** **①** FORMAL If something is duly done, it is done in the correct way • *I wish to record my support for the duly elected council.* **②** If something duly happens, it is something that you expected to happen • *Two chicks duly emerged from their eggs.*

dumb, dumber, dumbest **ADJECTIVE** **①** unable to speak. **②** INFORMAL slow to understand or stupid.

dumbfounded **ADJECTIVE** speechless with amazement • *She was too dumbfounded to answer.*

dummy, dummies NOUN ❶ a rubber teat which a baby sucks or bites on. ❷ an imitation or model of something which is used for display ▷ ADJECTIVE ❸ imitation or substitute.

dump, dumps, dumping, dumped VERB ❶ When unwanted waste is dumped, it is left somewhere. ❷ If you dump something, you throw it down or put it down somewhere in a careless way ▷ NOUN ❸ GEOGRAPHY a place where rubbish is left. ❹ A storage place, especially used by the military for storing supplies. ❺ INFORMAL You refer to a place as a dump when it is unattractive and unpleasant to live in.

dumpling, dumplings NOUN a small lump of dough that is cooked and eaten with meat and vegetables.

dunce, dunces NOUN a person who cannot learn what someone is trying to teach them.

dune, dunes NOUN A dune or sand dune is a hill of sand near the sea or in the desert.

dung NOUN Dung is the faeces from large animals, sometimes called manure.

dungarees PLURAL NOUN Dungarees are trousers which have a bib covering the chest and straps over the shoulders.

dungeon, dungeons [Said **dun**-jen] NOUN an underground prison.

dunk, dunks, dunking, dunked VERB To dunk something means to dip it briefly into a liquid • He dunked a single tea bag into two cups.

duo, duos NOUN ❶ a pair of musical performers; also a piece of music written for two players. ❷ Any two people doing something together can be referred to as a duo.

duodenum, duodenums [Said dyoo-o-**dee**-num] NOUN (SCIENCE) The duodenum is the first part of the small intestine. **duodenal** ADJECTIVE

dupe, dupes, duping, duped VERB ❶ If someone dupes you, they trick you ▷ NOUN ❷ someone who has been tricked.
  ● **WORD HISTORY:** from Old French
  ● de huppe meaning 'of the hoopoe', a
  ● bird thought to be stupid

duplicate, duplicates, duplicating, duplicated VERB [Said dyoop-lik-ayt] ❶ To duplicate something means to make an exact copy of it ▷ NOUN [Said dyoop-lik-it] ❷ something that is identical to something else ▷ ADJECTIVE [Said dyoop-lik-it] ❸ identical to or an exact copy of • a duplicate key. **duplication** NOUN

durable ADJECTIVE strong and lasting for a long time. **durability** NOUN

duration NOUN The duration of something is the length of time during which it happens or exists.

duress [Said dyoo-**ress**] NOUN If you do something under duress, you are forced to do it, and you do it very unwillingly.

during PREPOSITION happening throughout a particular time or at a particular point in time • The mussels will open naturally during cooking.

▷ SPELLING NOTE: I went to see (C) the doctor's new practiCe (practice)

dusk NOUN Dusk is the time just before nightfall when it is not completely dark.
● **WORD HISTORY:** from Old English *dox* meaning 'dark' or 'swarthy'

dust, dusts, dusting, dusted NOUN ❶ Dust is dry fine powdery material such as particles of earth, dirt, or pollen ▷ VERB ❷ When you dust furniture or other objects, you remove dust from them using a duster. ❸ If you dust a surface with powder, you cover it lightly with the powder.

dustbin, dustbins NOUN a large container for rubbish.

duster, dusters NOUN a cloth used for removing dust from furniture and other objects.

dustman, dustmen NOUN someone whose job is to collect the rubbish from people's houses.

dusty, dustier, dustiest ADJECTIVE covered with dust.

Dutch ADJECTIVE ❶ belonging or relating to Holland ▷ NOUN ❷ Dutch is the main language spoken in Holland.

dutiful ADJECTIVE doing everything you are expected to do. **dutifully** ADVERB

duty, duties NOUN ❶ something you ought to do or feel you should do, because it is your responsibility • *We have a duty as adults to listen to children.* ❷ a task which you do as part of your job ❸ Duty is tax paid to the government on some goods, especially imports.
● **SIMILAR WORDS:** ❶ obligation, ● responsibility

duty-free ADJECTIVE Duty-free goods are sold at airports or on planes or ships at a cheaper price than usual because they are not taxed • *duty-free vodka.*

duvet, duvets [*Said doo-vay*] NOUN a cotton quilt filled with feathers or other material, used on a bed in place of sheets and blankets.

DVD, DVDs NOUN an abbreviation for 'digital video *or* digital versatile disc': a type of compact disc that can store large amounts of video and sound information.

dwarf, dwarfs, dwarfing, dwarfed VERB ❶ If one thing dwarfs another, it is so much bigger that it makes it look very small ▷ ADJECTIVE ❷ smaller than average ▷ NOUN ❸ a person who is much smaller than average size.

dwell, dwells, dwelling, dwelled or dwelt VERB ❶ LITERARY To dwell somewhere means to live there. ❷ If you dwell on something or dwell upon it, you think or write about it a lot.

dwelling, dwellings NOUN FORMAL Someone's dwelling is the house or other place where they live.

dwindle, dwindles, dwindling, dwindled VERB If something dwindles, it becomes smaller or weaker.

dye, dyes, dyeing, dyed VERB ❶ To dye something means to change its colour by applying coloured liquid to it ▷ NOUN ❷ a colouring substance which is used to change the colour of something such as cloth or hair.

dying ADJECTIVE ❶ likely to die

a
b
c
d
e
f
g
h
i
j
k
l
m
n
o
p
q
r
s
t
u
v
w
x
y
z

▷ SPELLING NOTE: *You must practiSe your Ss (practise)*

A
B
C
D
E
F
G
H
I
J
K
L
M
N
O
P
Q
R
S
T
U
V
W
X
Y
Z

soon. ❷ INFORMAL If you are **dying for something**, you want it very much.

dyke, dykes; *also spelt* **dike** NOUN a thick wall that prevents water flooding onto land from a river or from the sea.

dynamic, dynamics ADJECTIVE ❶ A dynamic person is full of energy, ambition, and new ideas. ❷ relating to energy or forces which produce motion

dynamics PLURAL NOUN ❶ (SCIENCE) In physics, dynamics is the study of the forces that change or produce the motion of bodies or particles. ❷ The dynamics of a society or a situation are the forces that cause it to change. ❸ (MUSIC) Dynamics is the various degrees of loudness needed in the performance of a piece

of music, or the symbols used to indicate this in written music.

dynamite NOUN (SCIENCE) Dynamite is an explosive made of nitroglycerine.

dynamo, dynamos NOUN (SCIENCE) a device that converts mechanical energy into electricity.

dynasty, dynasties NOUN (HISTORY) a series of rulers of a country all belonging to the same family.

dysentery [*Said* **diss**-*en*-tree] NOUN an infection of the bowel which causes fever, stomach pain, and severe diarrhoea.

dyslexia [*Said* dis-**lek**-see-a] NOUN Dyslexia is difficulty with reading caused by a slight disorder of the brain. **dyslexic** ADJECTIVE OR NOUN

▷ SPELLING NOTE: *pAL up with the principAL and principAL staff (princip<u>al</u>)*

Ee

a
b
c
d
e
f
g
h
i
j
k
l
m
n
o
p
q
r
s
t
u
v
w
x
y
z

The words *aesthetic*, *oesophagus* and *oestrogen* sound as if they should start with letter *e*, but in British English they are spelt with *ae* and *oe*. These two combinations of letters, which both sound like ee, can come in the middle of words too, for example in *anaesthetic* and *amoeba*.

each ADJECTIVE OR PRONOUN
1 every one taken separately • *Each time she went out, she would buy a plant.* ▷ **PHRASE 2** If people do something to **each other**, each person does it to the other or others • *She and Chris smiled at each other.*
● **USAGE NOTE:** Wherever you use
● *each other* you could also use *one*
● *another*

eager ADJECTIVE wanting very much to do or have something. **eagerly ADVERB eagerness NOUN**

eagle, eagles **NOUN** a large bird of prey.

ear, ears **NOUN 1** the parts of your body on either side of your head with which you hear sounds. **2** An ear of corn or wheat is the top part of the stalk which contains seeds.

eardrum, eardrums **NOUN** Your eardrums are thin pieces of tightly stretched skin inside your ears which vibrate so that you can hear sounds.

earl, earls **NOUN** a British nobleman.
● **WORD HISTORY:** from Old English
● *eorl* meaning 'chieftain'

early, earlier, earliest **ADJECTIVE**
1 before the arranged or expected time • *He wasn't late for our meeting, I was early.* **2** near the beginning of a day, evening, or other period of time • *the early 1970s.* ▷ **ADVERB**
3 before the arranged or expected time • *I arrived early.*
● **SIMILAR WORDS: 1** premature,
● untimely

earmark, earmarks, earmarking, earmarked **VERB** If you earmark something for a special purpose, you keep it for that purpose.
● **WORD HISTORY:** from
● identification marks on the ears of
● domestic or farm animals

earn, earns, earning, earned **VERB**
1 If you earn money, you get it in return for work that you do. **2** If you earn something such as praise, you receive it because you deserve it. **earner NOUN**

earnest ADJECTIVE 1 sincere in what you say or do • *I answered with an earnest smile.* ▷ **PHRASE 2** If something begins **in earnest**, it happens to a greater or more serious extent than before • *The battle began in earnest.* **earnestly ADVERB**

▷ SPELLING NOTE: LEarn the principLEs (princip*le*)

A
B
C
D
E
F
G
H
I
J
K
L
M
N
O
P
Q
R
S
T
U
V
W
X
Y
Z

earnings PLURAL NOUN Your earnings are money that you earn.

earphones PLURAL NOUN small speakers which you wear on your ears to listen to a radio or cassette player.

earring, earrings **NOUN** Earrings are pieces of jewellery that you wear on your ear lobes.

earshot PHRASE If you are **within earshot** of something, you can hear it.

earth, earths **NOUN** ❶ The earth is the planet on which we live. ❷ Earth is the dry land on the surface of the earth, especially the soil in which things grow. ❸ a hole in the ground where a fox lives. ❹ The earth in a piece of electrical equipment is the wire through which electricity can pass into the ground and so make the equipment safe for use.

earthenware NOUN pottery made of baked clay.

earthly, earthlier, earthliest **ADJECTIVE** concerned with life on earth rather than heaven or life after death.

earthquake, earthquakes **NOUN** (SCIENCE) (GEOGRAPHY) a shaking of the ground caused by movement of the earth's crust.

earthworm, earthworms **NOUN** a worm that lives under the ground.

earthy, earthier, earthiest **ADJECTIVE** ❶ looking or smelling like earth. ❷ Someone who is earthy is open and direct, often in a crude way • *earthy language.*

earwig, earwigs **NOUN** a small, thin, brown insect which has a pair of

pincers at the end of its body.
● **WORD HISTORY:** from Old English
● *earwicga* meaning 'ear insect'; it
● was believed to creep into ears

ease, eases, easing, eased **NOUN**
❶ lack of difficulty, worry, or hardship
• *He had sailed through life with relative ease.* ▷ **VERB** ❷ When something eases, or when you ease it, it becomes less severe or less intense • *to ease the pain.* ❸ If you ease something somewhere, you move it there slowly and carefully • *He eased himself into his chair.*
● **SIMILAR WORDS:** ❶ easiness,
● effortlessness ❷ alleviate, relieve

easel, easels **NOUN** (ART) an upright frame which supports a picture that someone is painting.
● **WORD HISTORY:** from Dutch *ezel*
● meaning 'ass' or 'donkey'

easily ADVERB ❶ without difficulty.
❷ without a doubt • *The song is easily one of their finest.*

east NOUN ❶ East is the direction in which you look to see the sun rise.
❷ The east of a place is the part which is towards the east when you are in the centre • *the east of Africa.*
❸ The East is the countries in the south and east of Asia ▷ **ADJECTIVE OR ADVERB** ❹ East means in or towards the east • *The entrance faces east.* ▷ **ADJECTIVE** ❺ An east wind blows from the east.

Easter NOUN (RE) a Christian religious festival celebrating the resurrection of Christ.
● **WORD HISTORY:** from Old English
● *Eostre*, a pre-Christian Germanic
● goddess whose festival was at the
● spring equinox

▷ SPELLING NOTE: Psychiatrists Seldom Yell Callously Hard (*psychi*atrist)

easterly ADJECTIVE ❶ Easterly means to or towards the east. ❷ An easterly wind blows from the east.

eastern ADJECTIVE in or from the east • *a remote eastern corner of the country.*

eastward or **eastwards** ADVERB ❶ Eastward or eastwards means towards the east • *The city expanded eastward.* ▷ ADJECTIVE ❷ The eastward part of something is the east part.

easy, easier, easiest ADJECTIVE ❶ able to be done without difficulty • *It's easy to fall.* ❷ comfortable and without any worries • *an easy life.*
● **USAGE NOTE:** Although *easy* is an
● adjective, it can be used as an
● adverb in fixed phrases like *take it*
● *easy*

eat, eats, eating, ate, eaten VERB ❶ To eat means to chew and swallow food. ❷ When you eat, you have a meal • *We like to eat early.*
eat away VERB If something is eaten away, it is slowly destroyed • *The sea had eaten away at the headland.*

eaves PLURAL NOUN The eaves of a roof are the lower edges which jut out over the walls.

eavesdrop, eavesdrops, eavesdropping, eavesdropped VERB If you eavesdrop, you listen secretly to what other people are saying.
● **WORD HISTORY:** from Old English
● *yfesdrype* meaning 'water dripping
● down from the eaves'; people were
● supposed to stand outside in the
● rain to hear what was being said
● inside the house

ebb, ebbs, ebbing, ebbed VERB ❶ When the sea or the tide ebbs, it flows back. ❷ If a person's feeling or strength ebbs, it gets weaker • *The strength ebbed from his body.*

ebony NOUN ❶ a hard, dark-coloured wood, used for making furniture ▷ NOUN OR ADJECTIVE ❷ very deep black.

ebullient ADJECTIVE FORMAL lively and full of enthusiasm. **ebullience** NOUN

EC NOUN The EC is an old name for the European Union. EC is an abbreviation for 'European Community'.

eccentric, eccentrics [Said ik-**sen**-trik] ADJECTIVE ❶ having habits or opinions which other people think are odd or peculiar ▷ NOUN ❷ someone who is eccentric. **eccentricity** NOUN **eccentrically** ADVERB
● **SIMILAR WORDS:** ❶ odd,
● peculiar, strange ❷ crank, oddball,
● weirdo

ecclesiastical [Said ik-leez-ee-**ass**-ti-kl] ADJECTIVE of or relating to the Christian church.
● **WORD HISTORY:** from Greek
● *ekklēsia* meaning 'assembly' or
● 'church'

echelon, echelons [Said **esh**-el-on] NOUN a level of power or responsibility in an organization • *obeying orders from a higher echelon.*

echidna, echidnas or echidnae [Said ik-**kid**-na] NOUN a small, spiny mammal that lays eggs and has a long snout and claws, found in Australia.

a
b
c
d
e
f
g
h
i
j
k
l
m
n
o
p
q
r
s
t
u
v
w
x
y
z

A
B
C
D
E
F
G
H
I
J
K
L
M
N
O
P
Q
R
S
T
U
V
W
X
Y
Z

echo, echoes, echoing, echoed **NOUN**
❶ a sound which is caused by sound waves reflecting off a surface. ❷ a repetition, imitation, or reminder of something • *Echoes of the past are everywhere.* ▷ **VERB** ❸ If a sound echoes, it is reflected off a surface so that you can hear it again after the original sound has stopped.

eclipse, eclipses **NOUN** An eclipse occurs when one planet passes in front of another and hides it from view for a short time.

eco- **PREFIX** Words beginning with 'eco-' have something to do with ecology or the environment.
● **WORD HISTORY:** from Greek *oikos*
● meaning 'environment'

ecology **NOUN** the relationship between living things and their environment; also used of the study of this relationship. **ecological** **ADJECTIVE** **ecologically** **ADVERB** **ecologist** **NOUN**

economic **ADJECTIVE**
❶ (HISTORY) concerning the management of the money, industry, and trade of a country. ❷ concerning making a profit • *economic to produce.*

economical **ADJECTIVE**
❶ (HISTORY) another word for **economic**. ❷ Something that is economical is cheap to use or operate. ❸ Someone who is economical spends money carefully and sensibly. **economically** **ADVERB**

economics **NOUN** the study of the production and distribution of goods, services, and wealth in a society and the organization of its money, industry, and trade.

economist, economists **NOUN** a person who studies or writes about economics.

economy, economies **NOUN**
❶ (HISTORY) The economy of a country is the system it uses to organize and manage its money, industry, and trade; also used of the wealth that a country gets from business and industry. ❷ Economy is the careful use of things to save money, time, or energy • *Max dished up deftly, with an economy of movement.*
● **WORD HISTORY:** from Greek
● *oikonomia* meaning 'domestic
● management'

ecosystem, ecosystems **NOUN**
TECHNICAL the relationship between plants and animals and their environment.

ecstasy, ecstasies **NOUN** ❶ Ecstasy is a feeling of extreme happiness. ❷ INFORMAL a strong illegal drug that can cause hallucinations. **ecstatic** **ADJECTIVE** **ecstatically** **ADVERB**

ecumenical *[Said ee-kyoo-**men**-i-kl]* **ADJECTIVE** (RE) Within Christianity, the ecumenical movement is the movement that is trying to unite all the various branches of the Church.

eczema *[Said ek-sim-ma or ek-see-ma]* **NOUN** a skin disease that causes the surface of the skin to become rough and itchy.
● **WORD HISTORY:** from Greek
● *ekzein* meaning 'to boil over'

-ed **SUFFIX** '-ed' is used to form the past tense of most English verbs • *jumped* • *tried.*

▷ SPELLING NOTE: *Rhythmical Hounds Yap To Heavy Music (rhythm)*

eddy, eddies NOUN a circular movement in water or air.

edge, edges, edging, edged NOUN ❶ The edge of something is a border or line where it ends or meets something else. ❷ The edge of a blade is its thin, sharp side. ❸ If you have an edge over someone, you have an advantage over them ▷ VERB ❹ If you edge something, you make a border for it • *The veil was edged with matching lace.* ❺ If you edge somewhere, you move there very gradually • *The ferry edged its way out into the river.*
● SIMILAR WORDS: ❶ border,
● brink, margin

edgy, edgier, edgiest ADJECTIVE anxious and irritable • *What's making you feel so edgy?*

edible ADJECTIVE safe and pleasant to eat.

edifice, edifices [Said *ed-if-iss*] NOUN FORMAL a large and impressive building.

edit, edits, editing, edited VERB ❶ If you edit a piece of writing, you correct it so that it is fit for publishing. ❷ To edit a film or television programme means to select different parts of it and arrange them in a particular order. ❸ Someone who edits a newspaper or magazine is in charge of it.

edition, editions NOUN
❶ (ENGLISH) An edition of a book or magazine is a particular version of it printed at one time. ❷ An edition of a television or radio programme is a single programme that is one of a series.

editor, editors NOUN (LIBRARY) ❶ a person who is responsible for the content of a newspaper or magazine. ❷ a person who checks books and makes corrections to them before they are published. ❸ a person who selects different parts of a television programme or a film and arranges them in a particular order. **editorship** NOUN

editorial, editorials ADJECTIVE ❶ involved in preparing a newspaper, book, or magazine for publication. ❷ involving the contents and the opinions of a newspaper or magazine • *an editorial comment.* ▷ NOUN ❸ an article in a newspaper or magazine which gives the opinions of the editor or publisher on a particular topic. **editorially** ADVERB

educate, educates, educating, educated VERB To educate someone means to teach them so that they gain knowledge about something.

educated ADJECTIVE having a high standard of learning and culture.

education NOUN the process of gaining knowledge and understanding through learning or the system of teaching people. **educational** ADJECTIVE **educationally** ADVERB

eel, eels NOUN a long, thin, snakelike fish.

eerie, eerier, eeriest ADJECTIVE strange and frightening • *an eerie silence.* **eerily** ADVERB

effect, effects NOUN ❶ a direct result of someone or something on another person or thing • *the effect of divorce on children.* ❷ An effect that someone or something has is the

a b c d e f g h i j k l m n o p q r s t u v w x y z

overall impression or result that they have • *The effect of the decor was cosy and antique.* ▷ **PHRASE** ❸ If something **takes effect** at a particular time, it starts to happen or starts to produce results at that time • *The law will take effect next year.*
● **USAGE NOTE:** Remember that
● *effect* is a noun and *affect* is a verb

effective ADJECTIVE ❶ working well and producing the intended results. ❷ coming into operation or beginning officially • *The agreement has become effective immediately.*
effectively ADVERB

effeminate ADJECTIVE A man who is effeminate behaves, looks, or sounds like a woman.

effervescent ADJECTIVE ❶ (SCIENCE) An effervescent liquid is fizzy and gives off bubbles of gas. ❷ Someone who is effervescent is lively and enthusiastic.
effervescence NOUN

efficient ADJECTIVE capable of doing something well without wasting time or energy. **efficiently** ADVERB **efficiency** NOUN
● **SIMILAR WORDS:** capable,
● competent, proficient

effigy, effigies [Said *ef-fij-ee*] NOUN a statue or model of a person.

effluent, effluents [Said *ef-loo-ent*] NOUN Effluent is liquid waste that comes out of factories or sewage works.

effluvium, effluvia [Said *ef-floo-vi-um*] NOUN Effluvium is an unpleasant smell or gas that is given off by something, especially something that is decaying.

effort, efforts NOUN ❶ (PSHE) Effort is the physical or mental energy needed to do something. ❷ an attempt or struggle to do something • *I went to keep-fit classes in an effort to fight the flab.*
● **SIMILAR WORDS:** ❶ exertion,
● trouble, work

effortless ADJECTIVE done easily. **effortlessly** ADVERB

eg or **e.g.** Eg means 'for example', and is abbreviated from the Latin expression 'exempli gratia'.

egalitarian ADJECTIVE favouring equality for all people • *an egalitarian country.*

egg, eggs NOUN ❶ an oval or rounded object laid by female birds, reptiles, fishes, and insects. A baby creature develops inside the egg until it is ready to be born. ❷ a hen's egg used as food. ❸ In a female animal, an egg is a cell produced in its body which can develop into a baby if it is fertilized.

eggplant, eggplants NOUN a dark purple pear-shaped fruit eaten as a vegetable. It is also called **aubergine**.

ego, egos [Said *ee-goh*] NOUN Your ego is your opinion of what you are worth • *It'll do her good and boost her ego.*
● **WORD HISTORY:** from Latin *ego*
● meaning 'I'

egocentric ADJECTIVE only thinking of yourself.

egoism or **egotism** NOUN Egoism is behaviour and attitudes which show that you believe that you are more important than other people. **egoist**

or **egotist** NOUN egoistic, egotistic
or **egotistical** ADJECTIVE

Egyptian, Egyptians [Said ij-**jip**-shn]
ADJECTIVE ❶ belonging or relating
to Egypt ▷ NOUN ❷ An Egyptian is
someone who comes from Egypt.

eiderdown, eiderdowns NOUN An
eiderdown is a thick bed covering that
is filled with feathers.

Eid-ul-Adha [Said eed-dool-ah-
duh] NOUN an annual Muslim festival
marking the end of the pilgrimage to
Mecca known as the hajj. Animals are
sacrificed and their meat is shared
among the poor.
● WORD HISTORY: from Arabic id ul
● adha festival of sacrifice

eight, eights the number 8. **eighth**
ADJECTIVE

eighteen the number 18.
eighteenth ADJECTIVE

eighty, eighties the number 80.
eightieth ADJECTIVE

either ADJECTIVE, PRONOUN, OR
CONJUNCTION ❶ one or the other of
two possible alternatives • You can
spell it either way • Either of these
schemes would cost billions of pounds
• Either take it or leave it. ▷ ADJECTIVE
❷ both one and the other • on either
side of the head.
● USAGE NOTE: When either is
● followed by a plural noun, the
● following verb can be plural too:
● either of these books are useful

ejaculate, ejaculates, ejaculating,
ejaculated VERB ❶ (SCIENCE) When
a man ejaculates, he discharges
semen from his penis. ❷ If you
ejaculate, you suddenly say

something. **ejaculation** NOUN
● WORD HISTORY: from Latin jacere
● meaning 'to throw'

eject, ejects, ejecting, ejected VERB If
you eject something or someone, you
forcefully push or send them out • He
was ejected from the club. **ejection**
NOUN
● SIMILAR WORDS: expel, throw out

elaborate, elaborates, elaborating,
elaborated ADJECTIVE ❶ having
many different parts • an elaborate
system of drains. ❷ carefully planned,
detailed, and exact • elaborate plans.
❸ highly decorated and complicated
• elaborate designs. ▷ VERB ❹ If you
elaborate on something, you add more
information or detail about it.
elaborately ADVERB **elaboration**
NOUN
● SIMILAR WORDS: ❸ complicated,
● fancy, ornate

eland, elands NOUN a large African
antelope with twisted horns.

elapse, elapses, elapsing, elapsed
VERB When time elapses, it passes by
• Eleven years elapsed before you got
this job.

elastic ADJECTIVE ❶ able to stretch
easily ▷ NOUN ❷ Elastic is rubber
material which stretches and returns
to its original shape. **elasticity** NOUN

elation NOUN Elation is a feeling of
great happiness. **elated** ADJECTIVE

elbow, elbows, elbowing, elbowed
NOUN ❶ Your elbow is the joint
between the upper part of your arm
and your forearm ▷ VERB ❷ If you
elbow someone aside, you push them
away with your elbow.

a b c d **e** f g h i j k l m n o p q r s t u v w x y z

elder, eldest; elders **ADJECTIVE**
❶ Your elder brother or sister is older than you ▷ **NOUN** ❷ a senior member of a group who has influence or authority. ❸ a bush or small tree with dark purple berries.
● **USAGE NOTE:** The adjectives *elder*
● and *eldest* can only be used when
● talking about the age of people
● within families. You can use *older*
● and *oldest* to talk about the age of
● other people or things

elderly ADJECTIVE ❶ Elderly is a polite way to describe an old person ▷ **NOUN** ❷ The elderly are old people • *Priority is given to services for the elderly.*

elect, elects, electing, elected **VERB**
❶ If you elect someone, you choose them to fill a position, by voting • *He's just been elected president.* ❷ FORMAL If you elect to do something, you choose to do it • *I have elected to stay.* ▷ **ADJECTIVE** ❸ FORMAL voted into a position, but not yet carrying out the duties of the position • *the vice-president elect.*

election, elections **NOUN** the selection of one or more people for an official position by voting. **electoral ADJECTIVE**

electorate, electorates **NOUN** all the people who have the right to vote in an election.

electric ADJECTIVE ❶ powered or produced by electricity. ❷ very tense or exciting • *The atmosphere is electric.*
● **USAGE NOTE:** The word *electric* is
● an adjective and should not be used
● as a noun

electrical ADJECTIVE using or producing electricity • *electrical goods.* **electrically ADVERB**

electrician, electricians **NOUN** a person whose job is to install and repair electrical equipment.

electricity NOUN Electricity is a form of energy used for heating and lighting, and to provide power for machines.
● **WORD HISTORY:** from Greek
● *ēlektron* meaning 'amber'; in early
● experiments, scientists rubbed
● amber in order to get an electrical
● charge

electrified ADJECTIVE connected to a supply of electricity.

electrifying ADJECTIVE Something that is electrifying makes you feel very excited.

electro- PREFIX 'Electro-' means 'electric' or involving electricity.

electrocute, electrocutes, electrocuting, electrocuted **VERB** If someone is electrocuted, they are killed by touching something that is connected to electricity. **electrocution NOUN**

electrode, electrodes **NOUN** a small piece of metal which allows an electric current to pass between a source of power and a piece of equipment.

electrolysis [Said il-ek-**trol**-iss-iss] **NOUN** (SCIENCE) Electrolysis is the process of passing an electric current through a substance in order to produce chemical changes in it.

electrolyte, electrolytes **NOUN** (SCIENCE) a substance that electricity can pass through.

electromotive force NOUN
SCIENCE a force that causes
electricity to flow.

electron, electrons NOUN
SCIENCE ❶ In physics, an electron is
a tiny particle of matter, smaller than
an atom. ❷ An **electron shell** is the
orbit of an electron around the
nucleus of an atom.

electronic ADJECTIVE ICT
having transistors or silicon chips
which control an electric current.
electronically ADVERB

electronics NOUN Electronics is
the technology of electronic devices
such as televisions, and computers;
also the study of how these devices
work.

elegant ADJECTIVE attractive and
graceful or stylish • *an elegant and
beautiful city.* **elegantly** ADVERB
elegance NOUN

elegiac [Said el-lij-**eye**-ak]
ADJECTIVE ENGLISH LITERARY
expressing or showing sadness.

elegy, elegies [Said **el**-lij-ee] NOUN a
sad poem or song about someone
who has died.

element, elements NOUN ❶ a part
of something which combines with
others to make a whole. ❷ SCIENCE
In chemistry, an element is a
substance that is made up of only one
type of atom. ❸ A particular element
within a large group of people is a
section of it which is similar • *criminal
elements.* ❹ An element of a quality is
a certain amount of it • *Their attack
has largely lost the element of surprise.*
❺ The elements of a subject are the
basic and most important points.

❻ The elements are the weather
conditions • *Our open boat is exposed
to the elements.*

elemental ADJECTIVE FORMAL
simple and basic, but powerful
• *elemental emotions.*

elementary ADJECTIVE simple,
basic, and straightforward • *an
elementary course in woodwork.*

elephant, elephants NOUN a very
large four-legged mammal with a long
trunk, large ears, and ivory tusks.

elevate, elevates, elevating, elevated
VERB ❶ To elevate someone to a
higher status or position means to
give them greater status or
importance • *He was elevated to the
rank of major in the army.* ❷ To elevate
something means to raise it up.

elevation, elevations NOUN ❶ The
elevation of someone or something is
the raising of them to a higher level or
position. ❷ The elevation of a place is
its height above sea level or above the
ground.

eleven, elevens ❶ Eleven is the
number 11 NOUN ❷ a team of cricket
or soccer players. **eleventh**
ADJECTIVE

elf, elves NOUN In folklore, an elf is a
small mischievous fairy.

elicit, elicits, eliciting, elicited [Said
il-**iss**-it] VERB ❶ FORMAL If you elicit
information, you find it out by asking
careful questions. ❷ If you elicit a
response or reaction, you make it
happen • *He elicited sympathy from the
audience.*

eligible [Said **el**-lij-i-bl] ADJECTIVE
suitable or having the right

▷ SPELLING NOTE: *'i' before 'e' except after 'c'*

a b c d e f g h i j k l m n o p q r s t u v w x y z

qualifications for something • *You will be eligible for a grant in the future.* **eligibility** NOUN

eliminate, eliminates, eliminating, eliminated VERB ❶ If you eliminate something or someone, you get rid of them • *They eliminated him from their inquiries.* ❷ If a team or a person is eliminated from a competition, they can no longer take part. **elimination** NOUN

elite, elites [Said ill-**eet**] NOUN a group of the most powerful, rich, or talented people in a society.

Elizabethan ADJECTIVE Someone or something that is Elizabethan lived or was made during the reign of Elizabeth I.

elk, elks NOUN a large kind of deer.

ellipse, ellipses NOUN a regular oval shape, like a circle seen from an angle.

ellipsis, ellipses NOUN (ENGLISH) Ellipsis is the omission of parts of a sentence when the sentence can be understood without these parts. An example is 'You coming too?', where 'Are' has been omitted from the beginning of the question.

elm, elms NOUN a tall tree with broad leaves.

elocution NOUN the art or study of speaking clearly or well in public.

elongated ADJECTIVE long and thin.

elope, elopes, eloping, eloped VERB If someone elopes, they run away secretly with their lover to get married.

eloquent ADJECTIVE able to speak or write skilfully and with ease • *an*

eloquent politician. **eloquently** ADVERB **eloquence** NOUN

else ADVERB ❶ other than this or more than this • *Can you think of anything else?* ▷ PHRASE ❷ You say **or else** to introduce a possibility or an alternative • *You have to go with the flow or else be left behind in the rush.*

elsewhere ADVERB in or to another place • *He would rather be elsewhere.*

elude, eludes, eluding, eluded [Said ill-**ood**] VERB ❶ If a fact or idea eludes you, you cannot understand it or remember it. ❷ If you elude someone or something, you avoid them or escape from them • *He eluded the authorities.*

elusive ADJECTIVE difficult to find, achieve, describe, or remember • *the elusive million dollar prize.*

elves the plural of **elf**.

em- PREFIX `Em-' is another form of the prefix en-.
● USAGE NOTE: *em-* is the form
● which is used before the letters *b*,
● *m* and *p*

emaciated [Said im-**may**-see-ate-ed] ADJECTIVE extremely thin and weak, because of illness or lack of food.

e-mail or **email** NOUN ❶ the sending of messages from one computer to another. ❷ a message sent in this way ▷ VERB ❸ If you e-mail someone, you send an e-mail to them.

emancipation NOUN The emancipation of a person means the act of freeing them from harmful or

---

▷ SPELLING NOTE: *King IAn went to ParlIAment in a carrIAge for his marrIAge (-ia-)*

unpleasant restrictions.

embargo, embargoes NOUN an order made by a government to stop trade with another country.

embark, embarks, embarking, embarked VERB ❶ If you embark, you go onto a ship at the start of a journey. ❷ If you embark on something, you start it • *He embarked on a huge spending spree.*

embarrass, embarrasses, embarrassing, embarrassed VERB If you embarrass someone, you make them feel ashamed or awkward • *I won't embarrass you by asking for details.* **embarrassing** ADJECTIVE

embarrassed ADJECTIVE ashamed or awkward.

embarrassment, embarrassments NOUN shame and awkwardness.

embassy, embassies NOUN the building in which an ambassador and his or her staff work; also used of the ambassador and his or her staff.

embedded ADJECTIVE Something that is embedded is fixed firmly and deeply • *glass decorated with embedded threads.*

ember, embers NOUN Embers are glowing pieces of coal or wood from a dying fire.

embittered ADJECTIVE If you are embittered, you are angry and resentful about things that have happened to you.

emblazoned [Said im-**blaze**-nd] ADJECTIVE If something is emblazoned with designs, it is

decorated with them • *vases emblazoned with bold and colourful images.*
● **WORD HISTORY:** originally a heraldic term from Old French *blason* meaning 'shield'

emblem, emblems NOUN an object or a design representing an organization or an idea • *a flower emblem of Japan.*

embody, embodies, embodying, embodied VERB ❶ To embody a quality or idea means to contain it or express it • *A young dancer embodies the spirit of fun.* ❷ If a number of things are embodied in one thing, they are contained in it • *the principles embodied in his report.* **embodiment** NOUN

embossed ADJECTIVE decorated with designs that stand up slightly from the surface • *embossed wallpaper.*

embrace, embraces, embracing, embraced VERB ❶ If you embrace someone, you hug them to show affection or as a greeting. ❷ If you embrace a belief or cause you accept it and believe in it ▷ NOUN ❸ a hug.

embroider, embroiders, embroidering, embroidered VERB If you embroider fabric, you sew a decorative design onto it.

embroidery NOUN Embroidery is decorative designs sewn onto fabric; also the art or skill of embroidery.

embroiled ADJECTIVE If someone is embroiled in an argument or conflict they are deeply involved in it and cannot get out of it • *The two companies are now embroiled in the courts.*

▷ SPELLING NOTE: *an ELegant angEL (angel)*

embryo, embryos *[Said em-bree-oh]* NOUN an animal or human being in the very early stages of development in the womb. **embryonic** ADJECTIVE
● WORD HISTORY: from Greek
● *embruon* meaning 'new-born
● animal'

emerald, emeralds NOUN ❶ a bright green precious stone ▷ NOUN OR ADJECTIVE ❷ bright green.

emerge, emerges, emerging, emerged VERB ❶ If someone emerges from a place, they come out of it so that they can be seen. ❷ If something emerges, it becomes known or begins to be recognized as existing • *It later emerged that he faced bankruptcy proceedings.* **emergence** NOUN **emergent** ADJECTIVE

emergency, emergencies NOUN an unexpected and serious event which needs immediate action to deal with it.
● SIMILAR WORDS: crisis, extremity

EMF the abbreviation for **electromotive force**.

emigrant, emigrants NOUN a person who leaves their native country and goes to live permanently in another one.

emigrate, emigrates, emigrating, emigrated VERB If you emigrate, you leave your native country and go to live permanently in another one.

emigration NOUN (HISTORY) Emigration is the process of emigrating, especially by large numbers of people at various periods of history.

eminence NOUN ❶ Eminence is the quality of being well-known and respected for what you do. ❷ 'Your Eminence' is a title of respect used to address a Roman Catholic cardinal.

eminent ADJECTIVE well-known and respected for what you do • *an eminent scientist.*

eminently ADVERB FORMAL very • *eminently reasonable.*

emir, emirs *[Said em-eer]* NOUN a Muslim ruler or nobleman.

emission, emissions NOUN FORMAL The emission of something such as gas or radiation is the release of it into the atmosphere.

emit, emits, emitting, emitted VERB To emit something means to give it out or release it • *She emitted a long, low whistle.*
● SIMILAR WORDS: exude, give off,
● give out

emoticon, emoticons NOUN a symbol used in e-mail which represents a particular emotion and is made up of normal keyboard characters that are viewed sideways. For example, the symbol (:+(means 'frightened' or 'scared'.

emotion, emotions NOUN (PSHE) a strong feeling, such as love or fear.

emotional ADJECTIVE (PSHE) ❶ causing strong feelings • *an emotional appeal for help.* ❷ to do with feelings rather than your physical condition • *emotional support.* ❸ showing your feelings openly • *The child is in a very emotional state.* **emotionally** ADVERB

emotive ADJECTIVE concerning

emotions, or stirring up strong
emotions • *emotive language*.

empathize, empathizes,
empathizing, empathized; *also spelt*
empathise VERB If you empathize
with someone, you understand how
they are feeling. **empathy NOUN**

emperor, emperors **NOUN** a male
ruler of an empire.

emphasis, emphases **NOUN**
Emphasis is special importance or
extra stress given to something.

emphasize, emphasizes,
emphasizing, emphasized; *also spelt*
emphasise VERB If you emphasize
something, you make it known that it
is very important • *It was emphasized
that the matter was of international
concern.*

emphatic ADJECTIVE expressed
strongly and with force to show how
important something is • *I answered
both questions with an emphatic 'Yes'.*
emphatically ADVERB

empire, empires **NOUN** ❶ a group
of countries controlled by one country.
❷ a powerful group of companies
controlled by one person.

empirical ADJECTIVE (SCIENCE)
based on practical experience rather
than theories.

employ, employs, employing,
employed **VERB** ❶ If you employ
someone, you pay them to work for
you. ❷ If you employ something for a
particular purpose, you make use of it
• *the techniques employed in turning
grapes into wine.*

● **SIMILAR WORDS:** ❶ engage,
● hire, take on

employee, employees **NOUN** a
person who is paid to work for another
person or for an organization.

employer, employers **NOUN**
Someone's employer is the person or
organization that they work for.

employment NOUN (GEOGRAPHY)
Employment is the state of having a
paid job, or the activity of recruiting
people for a job.

empower, empowers, empowering,
empowered **VERB** If you are
empowered to do something, you
have the authority or power to do it.

empress, empresses **NOUN** a
woman who rules an empire, or the
wife of an emperor.

empty, emptier, emptiest; empties,
emptying, emptied **ADJECTIVE**
❶ having nothing or nobody inside.
❷ without purpose, value, or meaning
• *empty promises.* ▷ **VERB** ❸ If you
empty something, or empty its
contents, you remove the contents.
emptiness NOUN
● **SIMILAR WORDS:** ❶ bare, blank,
● vacant ❸ clear, evacuate

emu, emus *[Said ee-myoo]* **NOUN** a
large Australian bird which can run
fast but cannot fly.

emulate, emulates, emulating,
emulated **VERB** If you emulate
someone or something, you imitate
them because you admire them.
emulation NOUN

emulsion, emulsions **NOUN** a
water-based paint.

en- PREFIX ❶ 'En-' means to
surround or cover • *enclose* • *encrusted*.
❷ 'En-' means to cause to be in a

a
b
c
d
e
f
g
h
i
j
k
l
m
n
o
p
q
r
s
t
u
v
w
x
y
z

▷ SPELLING NOTE: *A Rude Idiot Thought He Might Eat Toffee In Church (arithmetic)*

certain state or condition • *enamoured* • *endanger*.

● **WORD HISTORY:** from Latin prefix
● *in-*

enable, enables, enabling, enabled
VERB To enable something to happen means to make it possible.

enact, enacts, enacting, enacted
VERB ❶ If a government enacts a law or bill, it officially passes it so that it becomes law. ❷ If you enact a story or play, you act it out. **enactment**
NOUN

enamel, enamels, enamelling, enamelled **NOUN** ❶ a substance like glass, used to decorate or protect metal or china. ❷ The enamel on your teeth is the hard, white substance that forms the outer part
▷ **VERB** ❸ If you enamel something, you decorate or cover it with enamel.
enamelled ADJECTIVE

enamoured [Said in-**am**-erd]
ADJECTIVE If you are enamoured of someone or something, you like them very much.

encapsulate, encapsulates, encapsulating, encapsulated **VERB** If something encapsulates facts or ideas, it contains or represents them in a small space.

encased ADJECTIVE Something that is encased is surrounded or covered with a substance • *encased in plaster*.

-ence SUFFIX '-ence' is used to form nouns which mean a state, condition or quality • *residence* • *patience*.

enchanted ADJECTIVE If you are enchanted by something or someone,

you are fascinated or charmed by them.

enchanting ADJECTIVE attractive, delightful, or charming • *an enchanting baby*.

encircle, encircles, encircling, encircled **VERB** To encircle something or someone means to completely surround them.

enclave, enclaves **NOUN** a place that is surrounded by areas that are different from it in some important way, for example because the people there are from a different culture • *a Muslim enclave in Bosnia*.

enclose, encloses, enclosing, enclosed **VERB** To enclose an object or area means to surround it with something solid. **enclosed ADJECTIVE**

enclosure, enclosures **NOUN** an area of land surrounded by a wall or fence and used for a particular purpose.

encompass, encompasses, encompassing, encompassed **VERB** To encompass a number of things means to include all of those things • *The book encompassed all aspects of maths*.

encore, encores [Said **ong**-kor]
NOUN a short extra performance given by an entertainer because the audience asks for it.
● **WORD HISTORY:** from French
● *encore* meaning 'again'

encounter, encounters, encountering, encountered **VERB**
❶ If you encounter someone or something, you meet them or are

faced with them • *She was the most gifted child he ever encountered.*
▷ **NOUN ②** a meeting, especially when it is difficult or unexpected.

encourage, encourages, encouraging, encouraged **VERB**
(PSHE) **①** If you encourage someone, you give them courage and confidence to do something. **②** If someone or something encourages a particular activity, they support it • *The government will encourage the creation of nursery places.* **encouraging ADJECTIVE encouragement NOUN**
● **SIMILAR WORDS: ①** hearten, inspire

encroach, encroaches, encroaching, encroached **VERB** If something encroaches on a place or on your time or rights, it gradually takes up or takes away more and more of it. **encroachment NOUN**

encrusted ADJECTIVE covered with a crust or layer of something • *a necklace encrusted with gold.*

encyclopedia, encyclopedias [Said *en-sigh-klop-ee-dee-a*]; also spelt **encyclopaedia NOUN** (LIBRARY) a book or set of books giving information about many different subjects.
● **WORD HISTORY:** from Greek *enkuklios paideia* meaning 'general education'

encyclopedic or **encyclopaedic ADJECTIVE** knowing or giving information about many different things.

end, ends, ending, ended **NOUN**
① The end of a period of time or an event is the last part. **②** The end of

something is the farthest point of it • *the room at the end of the passage.*
③ the purpose for which something is done • *the use of taxpayers' money for overt political ends.* ▷ **VERB ④** If something ends or if you end it, it comes to a finish.

endanger, endangers, endangering, endangered **VERB** To endanger something means to cause it to be in a dangerous and harmful situation • *a driver who endangers the safety of others.*
● **SIMILAR WORDS:** jeopardize, put at risk

endangered species NOUN
(SCIENCE) a plant or animal that is in danger of becoming extinct • *Grey wolves are now an endangered species.*

endear, endears, endearing, endeared **VERB** If someone's behaviour endears them to you, it makes them fond of them. **endearing ADJECTIVE endearingly ADVERB**

endeavour, endeavours, endeavouring, endeavoured [Said *in-dev-er*] **VERB ①** FORMAL If you endeavour to do something, you try very hard to do it ▷ **NOUN ②** an effort to do or achieve something.

endless ADJECTIVE having or seeming to have no end. **endlessly ADVERB**

endorse, endorses, endorsing, endorsed **VERB ①** If you endorse someone or something, you give approval and support to them. **②** If you endorse a document, you write your signature or a comment on it, to show that you approve of it. **endorsement NOUN**

A
B
C
D
E
F
G
H
I
J
K
L
M
N
O
P
Q
R
S
T
U
V
W
X
Y
Z

endoskeleton, endoskeletons
NOUN (SCIENCE) an animal's internal bones.

endothermic ADJECTIVE
(SCIENCE) If a chemical reaction is endothermic, then heat is absorbed.

endowed ADJECTIVE If someone is endowed with a quality or ability, they have it or are given it • *He was endowed with great willpower.*

endurance NOUN Endurance is the ability to put up with a difficult situation for a period of time.

endure, endures, enduring, endured
VERB ❶ If you endure a difficult situation, you put up with it calmly and patiently. **❷** If something endures, it lasts or continues to exist • *The old alliance still endures.*
enduring ADJECTIVE

enema, enemas **NOUN** a liquid that is put into a person's rectum in order to empty their bowels.

enemy, enemies **NOUN** a person or group that is hostile or opposed to another person or group.
● **SIMILAR WORDS:** adversary, foe

energetic ADJECTIVE having or showing energy or enthusiasm.
energetically ADVERB
● **SIMILAR WORDS:** active, lively, vigorous

energy, energies **NOUN ❶** the physical strength to do active things. **❷** the power which drives machinery. **❸** (SCIENCE) In physics, energy is the capacity of a body or system to do work. It is measured in joules.
● **SIMILAR WORDS:** ❶ drive, stamina, vigour

enforce, enforces, enforcing, enforced **VERB** If you enforce a law or a rule, you make sure that it is obeyed.
enforceable ADJECTIVE
enforcement NOUN

engage, engages, engaging, engaged
VERB ❶ If you engage in an activity, you take part in it • *Officials have declined to engage in a debate.* **❷** To engage someone or their attention means to make or keep someone interested in something • *He engaged the driver in conversation.*

engaged ADJECTIVE ❶ When two people are engaged, they have agreed to marry each other. **❷** If someone or something is engaged, they are occupied or busy • *Mr Anderson was otherwise engaged* • *The emergency number was always engaged.*

engagement, engagements **NOUN**
❶ an appointment that you have with someone. **❷** an agreement that two people have made with each other to get married.

engine, engines **NOUN ❶** a machine designed to convert heat or other kinds of energy into mechanical movement. **❷** a railway locomotive.
● **WORD HISTORY:** from Latin
● *ingenium* meaning 'ingenious device'

engineer, engineers, engineering, engineered **NOUN ❶** a person trained in designing and building machinery and electrical devices, or roads and bridges. **❷** a person who repairs mechanical or electrical devices ▷ **VERB ❸** If you engineer an event or situation, you arrange it cleverly, usually for your own advantage.

▷ SPELLING NOTE: *there's a rAKE in the brAKEs (brake)*

engineering NOUN Engineering is the profession of designing and constructing machinery and electrical devices, or roads and bridges.

English ADJECTIVE ❶ belonging or relating to England ▷ NOUN ❷ English is the main language spoken in the United Kingdom, the USA, Canada, Australia, New Zealand, and many other countries.

Englishman, Englishmen NOUN a man who comes from England. **Englishwoman** NOUN

engrave, engraves, engraving, engraved VERB To engrave means to cut letters or designs into a hard surface with a tool.

engraving, engravings NOUN a picture or design that has been cut into a hard surface. **engraver** NOUN

engrossed ADJECTIVE If you are engrossed in something, it holds all your attention • *He was engrossed in a video game.*

engulf, engulfs, engulfing, engulfed VERB To engulf something means to completely cover or surround it • *Black smoke engulfed him.*

enhance, enhances, enhancing, enhanced VERB To enhance something means to make it more valuable or attractive • *an outfit that really enhances his good looks.* **enhancement** NOUN

enigma, enigmas NOUN anything which is puzzling or difficult to understand.

enigmatic ADJECTIVE mysterious, puzzling, or difficult to understand. **enigmatically** ADVERB

enjambment or **enjambement** [*Said in-jam-ment*] NOUN (ENGLISH) In poetry, enjambment is when a sentence or phrase runs from one line of verse over to the next without a pause between lines.

enjoy, enjoys, enjoying, enjoyed VERB ❶ If you enjoy something, you find pleasure and satisfaction in it. ❷ If you enjoy something, you are lucky to have it or experience it • *The mother has enjoyed a long life.*

enjoyable ADJECTIVE giving pleasure or satisfaction • *a highly enjoyable day out.*

enjoyment NOUN Enjoyment is the feeling of pleasure or satisfaction you get from something you enjoy.

enlarge, enlarges, enlarging, enlarged VERB ❶ When you enlarge something, it gets bigger. ❷ If you enlarge on a subject, you give more details about it.

enlargement, enlargements NOUN ❶ An enlargement of something is the action of making it bigger. ❷ something, especially a photograph, which has been made bigger.

enlighten, enlightens, enlightening, enlightened VERB To enlighten someone means to give them more knowledge or understanding of something. **enlightening** ADJECTIVE **enlightenment** NOUN

enlightened ADJECTIVE well-informed and willing to consider different opinions • *an enlightened government.*

a
b
c
d
e
f
g
h
i
j
k
l
m
n
o
p
q
r
s
t
u
v
w
x
y
z

▷ SPELLING NOTE: *you'll brEAK that Electrical Aerial, Kitty (br**eak**)*

A
B
C
D
E
F
G
H
I
J
K
L
M
N
O
P
Q
R
S
T
U
V
W
X
Y
Z

enlist, enlists, enlisting, enlisted
VERB ❶ If someone enlists, they join the army, navy, or air force. ❷ If you enlist someone's help, you persuade them to help you in something you are doing.

enliven, enlivens, enlivening, enlivened **VERB** To enliven something means to make it more lively or more cheerful.

en masse [Said on mass] **ADVERB** If a group of people do something en masse, they do it together and at the same time.

enormity, enormities **NOUN** ❶ The enormity of a problem or difficulty is its great size and seriousness. ❷ something that is thought to be a terrible crime or offence.

enormous **ADJECTIVE** very large in size or amount. **enormously** **ADVERB**

enough **ADJECTIVE OR ADVERB** ❶ as much or as many as required • He did not have enough money for a coffee. ▷ **NOUN** ❷ Enough is the quantity necessary for something • There's not enough to go round. ▷ **ADVERB** ❸ very or fairly • She could manage well enough without me.

enquire, enquires, enquiring, enquired; also spelt **inquire** **VERB** If you enquire about something or someone, you ask about them.

enquiry, enquiries; also spelt **inquiry** **NOUN** ❶ a question that you ask in order to find something out. ❷ an investigation into something that has happened and that needs explaining.

enrage, enrages, enraging, enraged

VERB If something enrages you, it makes you very angry. **enraged** **ADJECTIVE**

enrich, enriches, enriching, enriched **VERB** To enrich something means to improve the quality or value of it • new woods to enrich our countryside. **enriched** **ADJECTIVE** **enrichment** **NOUN**

enrol, enrols, enrolling, enrolled **VERB** If you enrol for something such as a course or a college, you register to join or become a member of it. **enrolment** **NOUN**

en route [Said on root] **ADVERB** If something happens en route to a place, it happens on the way there.

ensconced **ADJECTIVE** If you are ensconced in a particular place, you are settled there firmly and comfortably.

ensemble, ensembles [Said on-som-bl] **NOUN** ❶ a group of things or people considered as a whole rather than separately. ❷ a small group of musicians who play or sing together.

enshrine, enshrines, enshrining, enshrined **VERB** If something such as an idea or a right is enshrined in a society, constitution, or a law, it is protected by it • Freedom of speech is enshrined in the American Constitution.

ensign, ensigns **NOUN** a flag flown by a ship to show what country that ship belongs to.

ensue, ensues, ensuing, ensued [Said en-syoo] **VERB** If something ensues, it happens after another event, usually as a result of it • He entered the house

and an argument ensued. **ensuing**
ADJECTIVE

ensure, ensures, ensuring, ensured
VERB To ensure that something
happens means to make certain that it
happens • *We make every effort to
ensure the information given is correct.*

entangled **ADJECTIVE** If you are
entangled in problems or difficulties,
you are involved in them.

enter, enters, entering, entered **VERB**
❶ To enter a place means to go into
it. ❷ If you enter an organization or
institution, you join and become a
member of it • *He entered Parliament
in 1979.* ❸ If you enter a competition
or examination, you take part in it.
❹ If you enter something in a diary or
a list, you write it down.

enterprise, enterprises **NOUN** ❶ a
business or company. ❷ a project or
task, especially one that involves risk
or difficulty.

enterprising **ADJECTIVE** ready to
start new projects and tasks and full of
boldness and initiative • *an
enterprising company.*

entertain, entertains, entertaining,
entertained **VERB** ❶ If you entertain
people, you keep them amused or
interested. ❷ If you entertain guests,
you receive them into your house and
give them food and hospitality.

entertainer, entertainers **NOUN**
someone whose job is to amuse and
please audiences, for example a
comedian or singer.

entertainment, entertainments
NOUN anything people watch or do
for pleasure.

enthral, enthrals, enthralling,
enthralled *[Said in-thrawl]* **VERB** If
you enthral someone, you hold their
attention and interest completely.
enthralling **ADJECTIVE**

enthuse, enthuses, enthusing,
enthused *[Said inth-yooz]* **VERB** If
you enthuse about something, you
talk about it with enthusiasm and
excitement.

enthusiasm, enthusiasms **NOUN**
Enthusiasm is interest, eagerness, or
delight in something that you enjoy.
● **WORD HISTORY:** from Greek
● *enthousiasmos* meaning 'possessed
● or inspired by the gods'
● **SIMILAR WORDS:** keenness,
● passion, zeal

enthusiastic **ADJECTIVE** showing
great excitement, eagerness, or
approval for something • *She was
enthusiastic about poetry.*
enthusiastically **ADVERB**

entice, entices, enticing, enticed
VERB If you entice someone to do
something, you tempt them to do it
• *We tried to entice the mouse out of the
hole.*

enticing **ADJECTIVE** extremely
attractive and tempting.

entire **ADJECTIVE** all of something
• *the entire month of July.*

entirely **ADVERB** wholly and
completely • *He and I were entirely
different.*

entirety *[Said en-tire-it-tee]*
PHRASE If something happens to
something **in its entirety**, it happens
to all of it • *This message will now be
repeated in its entirety.*

a
b
c
d
e
f
g
h
i
j
k
l
m
n
o
p
q
r
s
t
u
v
w
x
y
z

▷ SPELLING NOTE: *I want to see (C) your licenCe (licence)*

A
B
C
D
E
F
G
H
I
J
K
L
M
N
O
P
Q
R
S
T
U
V
W
X
Y
Z

entitle, entitles, entitling, entitled **VERB** If something entitles you to have or do something, it gives you the right to have or do it. **entitlement NOUN**

entity, entities [Said en-tit-ee] **NOUN** any complete thing that is not divided and not part of anything else.

entomology NOUN (SCIENCE) Entomology is the study of insects. **entomologist NOUN**

entourage, entourages [Said on-too-rahj] **NOUN** a group of people who follow or travel with a famous or important person.

entrails PLURAL NOUN Entrails are the inner parts, especially the intestines, of people or animals.

entrance, entrances [Said en-trunss] **1** The entrance of a building or area is its doorway or gate. **2** A person's entrance is their arrival in a place, or the way in which they arrive • *Each creation is designed for you to make a dramatic entrance.* **3** (DRAMA) In the theatre, an actor makes his or her entrance when he or she comes on to the stage. **4** Entrance is the right to enter a place • *He had gained entrance to the Hall by pretending to be a heating engineer.*

entrance, entrances, entrancing, entranced [Said en-trahnss] **VERB** If something entrances you, it gives you a feeling of wonder and delight. **entrancing ADJECTIVE**

entrant, entrants **NOUN** a person who officially enters a competition or an organization.

entrenched ADJECTIVE If a belief, custom, or power is entrenched, it is firmly established.

entrepreneur, entrepreneurs [Said on-tre-pren-ur] **NOUN** a person who sets up business deals, especially ones in which risks are involved, in order to make a profit. **entrepreneurial ADJECTIVE**

entrust, entrusts, entrusting, entrusted **VERB** If you entrust something to someone, you give them the care and protection of it • *Miss Fry was entrusted with the children's education.*

entry, entries **NOUN** **1** Entry is the act of entering a place. **2** a place through which you enter somewhere. **3** anything which is entered or recorded • *Send your entry to the address below.*
● **SIMILAR WORDS: 2** entrance,
● way in

envelop, envelops, enveloping, enveloped **VERB** To envelop something means to cover or surround it completely • *A dense fog enveloped the area.*

envelope, envelopes **NOUN** a flat covering of paper with a flap that can be folded over to seal it, which is used to hold a letter.

enviable ADJECTIVE If you describe something as enviable, you mean that you wish you had it yourself.

envious ADJECTIVE full of envy. **enviously ADVERB**

environment, environments **NOUN** **1** Your environment is the circumstances and conditions in

which you live or work • *a good environment to grow up in.*
2 SCIENCE The environment is the natural world around us • *the waste which is dumped in the environment.*
environmental ADJECTIVE
environmentally ADVERB
● **USAGE NOTE:** There is an *n* before
● the *m* in *environment*

environmentalist, environmentalists **NOUN** a person who is concerned with the problems of the natural environment, such as pollution.

envisage, envisages, envisaging, envisaged **VERB** If you envisage a situation or state of affairs, you can picture it in your mind as being true or likely to happen.

envoy, envoys **NOUN** a messenger, sent especially from one government to another.

envy, envies, envying, envied **NOUN**
1 Envy is a feeling of resentment you have when you wish you could have what someone else has ▷ **VERB 2** If you envy someone, you wish you had had what they have.

enzyme, enzymes **NOUN** SCIENCE a chemical substance, usually a protein, produced by cells in the body.

ephemeral [*Said if-em-er-al*] **ADJECTIVE** lasting only a short time.

epic, epics **NOUN 1** a long story of heroic events and actions ▷ **ADJECTIVE 2** very impressive or ambitious • *epic adventures.*

epicentre, epicentres **NOUN** GEOGRAPHY The epicentre of an earthquake is the place on the surface

of the earth immediately above where the earthquake started.

epidemic, epidemics **NOUN 1** an occurrence of a disease in one area, spreading quickly and affecting many people. **2** a rapid development or spread of something • *the country's crime epidemic.*

epidermis [*Said ep-pid-der-miss*] **NOUN** SCIENCE The epidermis is the top layer of skin.

epigram, epigrams **NOUN** a short saying which expresses an idea in a clever and amusing way.

epigraph NOUN 1 a quotation at the beginning of a book. **2** an inscription on a monument or building.

epilepsy NOUN Epilepsy is a condition of the brain which causes fits and periods of unconsciousness.
epileptic NOUN OR ADJECTIVE

epilogue, epilogues [*Said ep-ill-og*] **NOUN** ENGLISH An epilogue is a passage added to the end of a book or play as a conclusion.

episcopal [*Said ip-piss-kop-pl*] **ADJECTIVE** RE relating to or involving the activities, duties, and responsibilities of a bishop.

episode, episodes **NOUN 1** an event or period • *After this episode, she found it impossible to trust him.* **2** ENGLISH one of several parts of a novel or drama appearing for example on television • *I never miss an episode of 'Neighbours'.*

epistle, epistles [*Said ip-piss-sl*] **NOUN** FORMAL a letter.

a
b
c
d
e
f
g
h
i
j
k
l
m
n
o
p
q
r
s
t
u
v
w
x
y
z

▷ SPELLING NOTE: *have a piEce of piE (piece)*

A
B
C
D
E
F
G
H
I
J
K
L
M
N
O
P
Q
R
S
T
U
V
W
X
Y
Z

epitaph, epitaphs *[Said ep-it-ahf]* NOUN some words on a tomb about the person who has died.

epithet, epithets NOUN a word or short phrase used to describe some characteristic of a person.

epitome *[Said ip-pit-om-ee]* NOUN FORMAL The epitome of something is the most typical example of its sort • *She was the epitome of the successful woman.*

● USAGE NOTE: Do not use *epitome* to mean 'the peak of something'. It means 'the most typical example of something'

epoch, epochs *[Said ee-pok]* NOUN a long period of time.

eponymous *[Said ip-on-im-uss]* ADJECTIVE FORMAL The eponymous hero or heroine of a play or book is the person whose name forms its title • *the eponymous hero of 'Eric the Viking'.*

equal, equals, equalling, equalled ADJECTIVE ❶ having the same size, amount, value, or standard. ❷ If you are equal to a task, you have the necessary ability to deal with it ▷ NOUN ❸ Your equals are people who have the same ability, status, or rights as you ▷ VERB ❹ If one thing equals another, it is as good or remarkable as the other • *He equalled the course record of 63.* **equally** ADVERB **equality** NOUN

equate, equates, equating, equated VERB If you equate a particular thing with something else, you believe that it is similar or equal • *You can't equate lives with money.*

equation, equations NOUN (MATHS) a mathematical formula

stating that two amounts or values are the same.

equator *[Said ik-way-tor]* NOUN an imaginary line drawn round the middle of the earth, lying halfway between the North and South poles. **equatorial** ADJECTIVE

equestrian *[Said ik-west-ree-an]* ADJECTIVE relating to or involving horses.

equidistant ADJECTIVE Things that are equidistant are at an equal distance from each other or from a central point • *The three houses are equidistant.*

equilateral ADJECTIVE (MATHS) An equilateral triangle has sides that are all the same length.

equilibrium, equilibria NOUN a state of balance or stability in a situation.

equine ADJECTIVE relating to horses.
● WORD HISTORY: from Latin *equus* meaning 'horse'

equinox, equinoxes NOUN one of the two days in the year when the day and night are of equal length, occurring in September and March.
● WORD HISTORY: from Latin *aequinoctium* meaning 'equal night'

equip, equips, equipping, equipped VERB If a person or thing is equipped with something, they have it or are provided with it • *The test boat was equipped with a folding propeller.*
● SIMILAR WORDS: provide, supply

equipment NOUN Equipment is all the things that are needed or used for a particular job or activity.

▷ SPELLING NOTE: *plaice* the fish has a glittering 'EYE' (I) (*plaice*)

● **SIMILAR WORDS:** apparatus, gear,
● tools

equitable ADJECTIVE fair and
reasonable.

equity NOUN Equity is the quality of
being fair and reasonable • *It is
important to distribute income with
some sense of equity.*

equivalent, equivalents ADJECTIVE
❶ equal in use, size, value, or effect
▷ NOUN ❷ something that has the
same use, value, or effect as
something else • *One glass of wine is
the equivalent of half a pint of beer.*
equivalence NOUN
● **SIMILAR WORDS:** ❷ equal,
● match

-er SUFFIX ❶ When '-er' is used to
form some nouns it means 'for' or
'belonging to' • *fastener* • *Highlander.*
❷ '-er' is also used to form nouns
which mean someone or something
that does something • *climber*
• *teacher* • *baker.* ❸ '-er' is used to
make adjectives and adverbs that have
the meaning 'more' • *lighter* • *funnier.*

era, eras *[Said ear-a]* NOUN a period
of time distinguished by a particular
feature • *a new era of prosperity.*

eradicate, eradicates, eradicating,
eradicated VERB To eradicate
something means to get rid of it or
destroy it completely. **eradication**
NOUN

erase, erases, erasing, erased VERB
To erase something means to remove
it.

erect, erects, erecting, erected VERB
❶ To erect something means to put it
up or construct it • *The building was*

erected in 1900. ▷ ADJECTIVE ❷ in a
straight and upright position • *She
held herself erect and looked directly at
him.*
● **SIMILAR WORDS:** ❷ straight,
● upright, vertical

erection, erections NOUN ❶ the
process of erecting something.
❷ anything which has been erected.
❸ When a man has an erection, his
penis is stiff, swollen, and in an
upright position.

ermine NOUN Ermine is expensive
white fur.

erode, erodes, eroding, eroded VERB
If something erodes or is eroded, it is
gradually worn or eaten away and
destroyed.

erosion NOUN (GEOGRAPHY) the
gradual wearing away and destruction
of something • *soil erosion.*

erotic ADJECTIVE involving or
arousing sexual desire. **erotically**
ADVERB **eroticism** NOUN

err, errs, erring, erred VERB If you err,
you make a mistake.

errand, errands NOUN a short trip
you make in order to do a job for
someone.

erratic ADJECTIVE not following a
regular pattern or a fixed course
• *Police officers noticed his erratic
driving.* **erratically** ADVERB

erroneous *[Said ir-rone-ee-uss]*
ADJECTIVE Ideas or methods that are
erroneous are incorrect or only partly
correct. **erroneously** ADVERB

error, errors NOUN a mistake or
something which you have done

▷ SPELLING NOTE: *I went to see (C) the doctor's new practiCe (practice)*

A B C D **E** F G H I J K L M N O P Q R S T U V W X Y Z

wrong • *a spelling error.*

erudite [*Said* **eh**-roo-dite]
ADJECTIVE having great academic knowledge.

erupt, erupts, erupting, erupted
VERB ❶ When a volcano erupts, it violently throws out a lot of hot lava and ash. ❷ When a situation erupts, it starts up suddenly and violently • *A family row erupted.* **eruption NOUN**

escalate, escalates, escalating, escalated **VERB** If a situation escalates, it becomes greater in size, seriousness, or intensity.

escalator, escalators **NOUN** a mechanical moving staircase.

escapade, escapades **NOUN** an adventurous or daring incident that causes trouble.

escape, escapes, escaping, escaped
VERB ❶ To escape means to get free from someone or something. ❷ If you escape something unpleasant or difficult, you manage to avoid it • *He escaped the death penalty.* ❸ If something escapes you, you cannot remember it • *It was an actor whose name escapes me for the moment.*
▷ **NOUN** ❹ an act of escaping from a particular place or situation • *his escape from North Korea.* ❺ a situation or activity which distracts you from something unpleasant • *Television provides an escape.*

escapee, escapees [*Said* is-kay-**pee**]
NOUN someone who has escaped, especially an escaped prisoner.

escapism NOUN avoiding the real and unpleasant things in life by thinking about pleasant or fantastic

things • *Most horror movies are simple escapism.* **escapist ADJECTIVE**

eschew, eschews, eschewing, eschewed [*Said* is-**chew**] **VERB**
FORMAL If you eschew something, you deliberately avoid or keep away from it.

escort, escorts, escorting, escorted
NOUN ❶ a person or vehicle that travels with another in order to protect or guide them. ❷ a person who accompanies another person of the opposite sex to a social event ▷ **VERB**
❸ If you escort someone, you go with them somewhere, especially in order to protect or guide them.

-ese [*Said* -eez] **SUFFIX** '-ese' forms adjectives and nouns which show where a person or thing comes from • *Japanese.*

Eskimo, Eskimos **NOUN** a name that was formerly used for the Inuit people and their language.

especially ADVERB You say especially to show that something applies more to one thing, person, or situation than to any other • *Regular eye tests are important, especially for the elderly.*

espionage [*Said* **ess**-pee-on-ahj]
NOUN Espionage is the act of spying to get secret information, especially to find out military or political secrets.
● **WORD HISTORY:** from French
● *espionner* meaning 'to spy'

espouse, espouses, espousing, espoused **VERB FORMAL** If you espouse a particular policy, cause, or plan, you give your support to it • *They espoused the rights of man.*

▷ SPELLING NOTE: *You must practiSe your Ss (practise)*

espresso NOUN Espresso is strong coffee made by forcing steam through ground coffee.
● WORD HISTORY: from Italian *caffè espresso* meaning 'pressed coffee'
● USAGE NOTE: The second letter of *espresso* is *s* and not *x*

-ess SUFFIX '-ess' added at the end of a noun indicates a female • *lioness*.
● USAGE NOTE: Special words for a woman who does a particular job or activity, such as *actress*, *poetess* and *authoress*, are now used less often because many women prefer to be referred to simply as an *actor*, *poet* or *author*

essay, essays NOUN a short piece of writing on a particular subject, for example one done as an exercise by a student.

essence, essences NOUN ❶ The essence of something is its most basic and most important part, which gives it its identity • *the very essence of being a woman*. ❷ a concentrated liquid used for flavouring food • *vanilla essence*.

essential ADJECTIVE ❶ vitally important and absolutely necessary • *Good ventilation is essential in the greenhouse*. ❷ very basic, important, and typical • *the essential aspects of international banking*. **essentially** ADVERB

essentials PLURAL NOUN things that are very important or necessary • *the bare essentials of furnishing*.

-est SUFFIX '-est' is used to form adjectives and adverbs that have the meaning 'most' • *greatest* • *furthest*.

establish, establishes, establishing,

established VERB ❶ To establish something means to set it up in a permanent way. ❷ If you establish yourself or become established as something, you achieve a strong reputation for a particular activity • *He had just established himself as a film star*. ❸ If you establish a fact or establish the truth of something, you discover it and can prove it • *Our first priority is to establish the cause of her death*. **established** ADJECTIVE
● SIMILAR WORDS: ❶ create, found, set up

establishment, establishments NOUN ❶ The establishment of an organization or system is the act of setting it up. ❷ a shop, business, or some other sort of organization or institution. ❸ The Establishment is the group of people in a country who have power and influence • *lawyers, businessmen and other pillars of the Establishment*.

estate, estates NOUN ❶ a large area of privately owned land in the country, together with all the property on it. ❷ an area of land, usually in or near a city, which has been developed for housing or industry. ❸ LEGAL A person's estate consists of all the possessions they leave behind when they die.

estate agent, estate agents NOUN a person who works for a company that sells houses and land.

esteem NOUN admiration and respect that you feel for another person. **esteemed** ADJECTIVE

estimate, estimates, estimating, estimated VERB ❶ (MATHS) If you estimate an amount or quantity, you calculate it approximately. ❷ If you estimate something, you make a guess about it based on the evidence you have available • *Often it's possible to estimate a person's age just by knowing their name.* ▷ **NOUN** ❸ a guess at an amount, quantity, or outcome, based on the evidence you have available. ❹ a formal statement from a company who may do some work for you, telling you how much it is likely to cost • *Get several estimates before you choose a builder.*

estimation, estimations **NOUN**
❶ an approximate calculation of something that can be measured.
❷ the opinion or impression you form about a person or situation.

estranged **ADJECTIVE** ❶ If someone is estranged from their husband or wife, they no longer live with them. ❷ If someone is estranged from their family or friends, they have quarrelled with them and they no longer keep in touch with them.

estrogen **NOUN** a female sex hormone which regulates the reproductive cycle.

estuary, estuaries *[Said **est**-yoo-ree]* **NOUN** (GEOGRAPHY) the wide part of a river near where it joins the sea and where fresh water mixes with salt water.

etc. a written abbreviation for et cetera.

et cetera *[Said it set-ra]* 'Et cetera' is used at the end of a list to indicate that other items of the same type you have mentioned could have been mentioned if there had been time or space.

● **USAGE NOTE:** As *etc.* means 'and
● the rest', you should not write *and*
● *etc*

etch, etches, etching, etched **VERB**
❶ If you etch a design or pattern on a surface, you cut it into the surface by using acid or a sharp tool. ❷ If something is etched on your mind or memory, it has made such a strong impression on you that you will never forget it. **etched** **ADJECTIVE**

etching, etchings **NOUN** a picture printed from a metal plate that has had a design cut into it.

eternal **ADJECTIVE** lasting forever, or seeming to last forever • *eternal life.* **eternally** **ADVERB**
● **SIMILAR WORDS:** endless,
● everlasting, perpetual

eternity, eternities **NOUN**
❶ Eternity is time without end, or a state of existing outside time, especially the state some people believe they will pass into when they die. ❷ a period of time which seems to go on for ever • *We arrived there after an eternity.*

ether *[Said eeth-er]* **NOUN** a colourless liquid that burns easily. Used in industry as a solvent and in medicine as an anaesthetic.

ethereal *[Said ith-ee-ree-al]* **ADJECTIVE** light and delicate • *misty ethereal landscapes.* **ethereally** **ADVERB**

ethical **ADJECTIVE** in agreement with accepted principles of behaviour that are thought to be right • *teenagers who become vegetarian for ethical reasons.* **ethically** **ADVERB**

▷ SPELLING NOTE: *LEarn the principLEs (principle)*

ethics PLURAL NOUN Ethics are moral beliefs about right and wrong • *The medical profession has a code of ethics.*

Ethiopian, Ethiopians *[Said eeth-ee-oh-pee-an]* ADJECTIVE ❶ belonging to or relating to Ethiopia ▷ NOUN ❷ someone who comes from Ethiopia.

ethnic ADJECTIVE ❶ involving different racial groups of people • *ethnic minorities.* ❷ relating to a particular racial or cultural group, especially when very different from modern western culture • *ethnic food.* **ethnically** ADVERB

ethos *[Said eeth-oss]* NOUN a set of ideas and attitudes that is associated with a particular group of people • *the ethos of journalism.*

etiquette *[Said et-ik-ket]* NOUN a set of rules for behaviour in a particular social situation.

-ette SUFFIX '-ette' is used to form nouns which have 'small' as part of their meaning • *launderette* • *cigarette.*

etymology *[Said et-tim-ol-loj-ee]* NOUN (ENGLISH) Etymology is the study of the origin and changes of form in words.

EU NOUN EU is an abbreviation for 'European Union'.

eucalyptus or **eucalypt**, eucalyptuses or eucalypts NOUN an evergreen tree, grown mostly in Australia; also the wood and oil from this tree.

Eucharist, Eucharists *[Said yoo-kar-rist]* NOUN a religious ceremony in which Christians

remember and celebrate Christ's last meal with his disciples.
● WORD HISTORY: from Greek
● *eucharistia* meaning 'thanksgiving'

eunuch, eunuchs *[Said yoo-nuk]* NOUN a man who has been castrated.

euphemism, euphemisms NOUN a polite word or expression that you can use instead of one that might offend or upset people • *action movies, a euphemism for violence.* **euphemistic** ADJECTIVE **euphemistically** ADVERB

euphoria NOUN a feeling of great happiness. **euphoric** ADJECTIVE

euro, euros NOUN the official unit of currency in some countries of the European Union, replacing their old currencies at the beginning of January 2002.

Europe NOUN Europe is the second smallest continent. It has Asia on its eastern side, with the Arctic to the north, the Atlantic to the west, and the Mediterranean and Africa to the south.

European, Europeans ADJECTIVE ❶ belonging or relating to Europe ▷ NOUN ❷ someone who comes from Europe.

European Union NOUN The group of countries who have joined together under the Treaty of Rome for economic and trade purposes are officially known as the European Union.

euthanasia *[Said yooth-a-nay-zee-a]* NOUN Euthanasia is the act of painlessly killing a dying person in order to stop their suffering.

▷ SPELLING NOTE: Psychiatrists Seldom Yell Callously Hard (<u>psychi</u>atrist)

A
B
C
D
E
F
G
H
I
J
K
L
M
N
O
P
Q
R
S
T
U
V
W
X
Y
Z

● **WORD HISTORY:** from Greek
● *eu-* meaning 'easy' and *thanatos*
● meaning 'death'

evacuate, evacuates, evacuating, evacuated **VERB** If someone is evacuated, they are removed from a place of danger to a place of safety • *A crowd of shoppers had to be evacuated from a store after a bomb scare.* **evacuation NOUN evacuee NOUN**

evade, evades, evading, evaded **VERB** **①** If you evade something or someone, you keep moving in order to keep out of their way • *For two months he evaded police.* **②** If you evade a problem or question, you avoid dealing with it.

evaluate, evaluates, evaluating, evaluated **VERB** (EXAM TERM) If you evaluate something, you assess its strengths and weaknesses.

evaluation, evaluations **NOUN** **①** Evaluation is assessing something's strengths and weaknesses. **②** (D & T) To carry out an evaluation of a design, product or system is to do an assessment to find out how well it works or will work.

evangelical [Said ee-van-**jel**-ik-kl] **ADJECTIVE** Evangelical beliefs are Christian beliefs that stress the importance of the gospels and a personal belief in Christ.

evangelist, evangelists [Said iv-**van**-jel-ist] **NOUN** a person who travels from place to place preaching Christianity. **evangelize VERB evangelism NOUN**

● **WORD HISTORY:** from Greek
● *evangelion* meaning 'good news'

evaporate, evaporates, evaporating,

evaporated **VERB** (SCIENCE) **①** When a liquid evaporates, it gradually becomes less and less because it has changed from a liquid into a gas. **②** If a substance has been evaporated, all the liquid has been taken out so that it is dry or concentrated. **evaporation NOUN**

evasion, evasions **NOUN** deliberately avoiding doing something • *evasion of arrest.*

evasive ADJECTIVE deliberately trying to avoid talking about or doing something • *He was evasive about his past.*

eve, eves **NOUN** the evening or day before an event or occasion • *on the eve of the battle.*

even, evens, evening, evened **ADJECTIVE** **①** flat and level • *an even layer of chocolate.* **②** regular and without variation • *an even temperature.* **③** In maths, numbers that are even can be divided exactly by two • *4 is an even number.* **④** Scores that are even are exactly the same ▷ **ADVERB** **⑤** 'Even' is used to suggest that something is unexpected or surprising • *I haven't even got a bank account.* **⑥** 'Even' is also used to say that something is greater in degree than something else • *This was an opportunity to obtain even more money.* ▷ **PHRASE** **⑦** Even if or even though is used to introduce something that is surprising in relation to the main part of the sentence • *She was too kind to say anything, even though she was jealous.* **evenly ADVERB**

● **SIMILAR WORDS:** **①** flat, level,
● straight **④** equal, level

evening, evenings NOUN the part of the day between late afternoon and the time you go to bed.

event, events NOUN **1** something that happens, especially when it is unusual or important. **2** one of the competitions that are part of an organized occasion, especially in sports ▷ PHRASE **3** If you say **in any event**, you mean whatever happens • In any event we must get on with our own lives.
● SIMILAR WORDS: **1** happening,
● incident, occurrence

eventful ADJECTIVE full of interesting and important events.

eventual ADJECTIVE happening or being achieved in the end • He remained confident of eventual victory.

eventuality, eventualities NOUN a possible future event or result • equipment to cope with most eventualities.

eventually ADVERB in the end • Eventually I got to Berlin.

ever ADVERB **1** at any time • Have you ever seen anything like it? **2** all the time • The President will come under ever more pressure to resign. **3** 'Ever' is used to give emphasis to what you are saying • I'm as happy here as ever I was in England. ▷ PHRASE **4** INFORMAL **Ever so** means very • Thank you ever so much.

evergreen, evergreens NOUN a tree or bush which has green leaves all the year round.

everlasting ADJECTIVE never coming to an end.

every ADJECTIVE **1** 'Every' is used to refer to all the members of a particular group, separately and one by one • We eat out every night. **2** 'Every' is used to mean the greatest or the best possible degree of something • He has every reason to avoid the subject. **3** 'Every' is also used to indicate that something happens at regular intervals • renewable every five years. ▷ PHRASE **4** **Every other** means each alternate • I see Lisa at least every other week.

everybody PRONOUN **1** all the people in a group • He obviously thinks everybody in the place knows him. **2** all the people in the world • Everybody has a hobby.
● USAGE NOTE: Everybody and
● everyone mean the same

everyday ADJECTIVE usual or ordinary • the everyday drudgery of work.

everyone PRONOUN **1** all the people in a group. **2** all the people in the world.
● USAGE NOTE: Everyone and
● everybody mean the same

everything PRONOUN **1** all or the whole of something. **2** the most important thing • When I was 20, friends were everything to me.

everywhere ADVERB in or to all places.

evict, evicts, evicting, evicted VERB To evict someone means to officially force them to leave a place they are occupying. **eviction** NOUN

evidence NOUN **1** Evidence is anything you see, read, or are told which gives you reason to believe something. **2** Evidence is the

▷ SPELLING NOTE: Rhythmical Hounds Yap To Heavy Music (*rhythm*)

A
B
C
D
E
F
G
H
I
J
K
L
M
N
O
P
Q
R
S
T
U
V
W
X
Y
Z

information used in court to attempt to prove or disprove something.

evident ADJECTIVE easily noticed or understood • *His love of nature is evident in his paintings.* **evidently** ADVERB

evil, evils NOUN ❶ Evil is a force or power that is believed to cause wicked or bad things to happen. ❷ a very unpleasant or harmful situation or activity • *the evils of war.* ▷ ADJECTIVE ❸ Someone or something that is evil is morally wrong or bad • *evil deeds.*

evoke, evokes, evoking, evoked VERB To evoke an emotion, memory, or reaction means to cause it • *Enthusiasm was evoked by the appearance of the Prince.*

evolution [Said ee-vol-*oo*-shn] NOUN ❶ Evolution is a process of gradual change taking place over many generations during which living things slowly change as they adapt to different environments. ❷ Evolution is also any process of gradual change and development over a period of time • *the evolution of the European Union.* **evolutionary** ADJECTIVE

evolve, evolves, evolving, evolved VERB ❶ If something evolves or if you evolve it, it develops gradually over a period of time • *I was given a brief to evolve a system of training.* ❷ When living things evolve, they gradually change and develop into different forms over a period of time.

ewe, ewes [Said *yoo*] NOUN a female sheep.

ex- PREFIX 'Ex' means 'former' • *her ex-husband.*

exacerbate, exacerbates, exacerbating, exacerbated [Said ig-*zass*-er-bate] VERB To exacerbate something means to make it worse.

exact, exacts, exacting, exacted ADJECTIVE ❶ correct and complete in every detail • *an exact replica of the Santa Maria.* ❷ accurate and precise, as opposed to approximate • *Mystery surrounds the exact circumstances of his death.* ▷ VERB ❸ FORMAL If somebody or something exacts something from you, they demand or obtain it from you, especially through force • *The navy was on its way to exact a terrible revenge.*

exactly ADVERB ❶ with complete accuracy and precision • *That's exactly what happened.* ❷ You can use 'exactly' to emphasize the truth of a statement, or a similarity or close relationship between one thing and another • *It's exactly the same colour.* ▷ INTERJECTION ❸ an expression implying total agreement.

exaggerate, exaggerates, exaggerating, exaggerated VERB ❶ If you exaggerate, you make the thing you are describing seem better, worse, bigger, or more important than it really is. ❷ To exaggerate something means to make it more noticeable than usual • *His Irish accent was exaggerated for the benefit of the joke he was telling.* **exaggeration** NOUN

exalted ADJECTIVE FORMAL Someone who is exalted is very important.

exam, exams NOUN an official test set to find out your knowledge or skill in a subject.

examination, examinations NOUN
❶ an exam. ❷ If you make an examination of something, you inspect it very carefully • *I carried out a careful examination of the hull.* ❸ A medical examination is a check by a doctor to find out the state of your health.

examine, examines, examining, examined VERB ❶ If you examine something, you inspect it very carefully. ❷ (EXAM TERM) To examine a subject is to look closely at the issues involved and form your own opinion. ❸ To examine someone means to find out their knowledge or skill in a particular subject by testing them. ❹ If a doctor examines you, he or she checks your body to find out the state of your health.

examiner, examiners NOUN a person who sets or marks an exam.

example, examples NOUN
❶ something which represents or is typical of a group or set • *some examples of early Spanish music.* ❷ If you say someone or something is an example to people, you mean that people can imitate and learn from them ▷ PHRASE ❸ You use **for example** to give an example of something you are talking about.
● SIMILAR WORDS: ❶ sample,
● specimen

exasperate, exasperates, exasperating, exasperated VERB If someone or something exasperates you, they irritate you and make you angry. **exasperating** ADJECTIVE **exasperation** NOUN

excavate, excavates, excavating, excavated VERB To excavate means to remove earth from the ground by digging. **excavation** NOUN

exceed, exceeds, exceeding, exceeded VERB To exceed something such as a limit means to go beyond it or to become greater than it • *the first aircraft to exceed the speed of sound.*

exceedingly ADVERB extremely or very much.

excel, excels, excelling, excelled VERB If someone excels in something, they are very good at doing it.

Excellency, Excellencies NOUN a title used to address an official of very high rank, such as an ambassador or a governor.

excellent ADJECTIVE very good indeed. **excellence** NOUN
● SIMILAR WORDS: first-rate,
● outstanding, superb

except PREPOSITION Except or except for means other than or apart from • *All my family were musicians except my father.*

exception, exceptions NOUN somebody or something that is not included in a general statement or rule • *English, like every language, has exceptions to its rules.*

exceptional ADJECTIVE
❶ unusually talented or clever. ❷ unusual and likely to happen very rarely. **exceptionally** ADVERB

excerpt, excerpts NOUN a short piece of writing or music which is taken from a larger piece.

excess, excesses NOUN ❶ Excess is behaviour which goes beyond

a
b
c
d
e
f
g
h
i
j
k
l
m
n
o
p
q
r
s
t
u
v
w
x
y
z

▷ SPELLING NOTE: On WEDNESday Wayne WED NESta (*Wednesday*)

A B C D **E** F G H I J K L M N O P Q R S T U V W X Y Z

---

normally acceptable limits • *a life of excess.* **2** a larger amount of something than is needed, usual, or healthy • *an excess of energy.* ▷ **ADJECTIVE** **3** more than is needed, allowed, or healthy • *excess weight.* ▷ **PHRASE** **4** **In excess of** a particular amount means more than that amount • *a fortune in excess of 150 million pounds.* **5** If you do something **to excess**, you do it too much • *She drank to excess.*

excessive ADJECTIVE too great in amount or degree • *using excessive force.* **excessively ADVERB**

exchange, exchanges, exchanging, exchanged **VERB** **1** To exchange things means to give or receive one thing in return for another • *They exchange small presents on Christmas Eve.* ▷ **NOUN** **2** the act of giving or receiving something in return for something else • *an exchange of letters* • *exchanges of gunfire.* **3** a place where people trade and do business • *the stock exchange.*

exchequer [Said iks-**chek**-er] **NOUN** The exchequer is the department in the government in Britain and other countries which is responsible for money belonging to the state.

excise NOUN Excise is a tax put on

goods produced for sale in the country that produces them.

excitable ADJECTIVE easily excited.

excite, excites, exciting, excited **VERB** **1** If somebody or something excites you, they make you feel very happy and nervous or very interested and enthusiastic. **2** If something excites a particular feeling, it causes somebody to have that feeling • *This excited my suspicion.*
● **SIMILAR WORDS:** **1** arouse, thrill

excited ADJECTIVE happy and unable to relax. **excitedly ADVERB**

excitement NOUN interest and enthusiasm.

exciting ADJECTIVE making you feel happy and enthusiastic.

exclaim, exclaims, exclaiming, exclaimed **VERB** When you exclaim, you cry out suddenly or loudly because you are excited or shocked.

exclamation, exclamations **NOUN** (ENGLISH) a word or phrase spoken suddenly to express a strong feeling.

exclamation mark, exclamation marks **NOUN** a punctuation mark (!) used in writing to express a strong feeling.
▶ SEE GRAMMAR BOX ABOVE

exclude, excludes, excluding,

▷ SPELLING NOTE: *Eddy Ant thinks mEAt is a grEAt trEAt to EAt (-ea-)*

excluded VERB ❶ If you exclude something, you deliberately do not include it or do not consider it. ❷ If you exclude somebody from a place or an activity, you prevent them from entering the place or taking part in the activity. **exclusion** NOUN

exclusive, exclusives ADJECTIVE ❶ available to or for the use of a small group of rich or privileged people • *an exclusive club*. ❷ belonging to a particular person or group only • *exclusive rights to coverage of the Olympic Games.* ▷ NOUN ❸ a story or interview which appears in only one newspaper or on only one television programme. **exclusively** ADVERB

excrement [Said *eks-krim-ment*] NOUN Excrement is the solid waste matter that is passed out of a person's or animal's body through their bowels.

excrete, excretes, excreting, excreted VERB (SCIENCE) When you excrete waste matter from your body, you get rid of it, for example by going to the lavatory or by sweating. **excretion** NOUN **excretory** ADJECTIVE

excruciating [Said *iks-kroo-shee-ate-ing*] ADJECTIVE unbearably painful. **excruciatingly** ADVERB
● WORD HISTORY: from Latin
● *excruciare* meaning 'to torture'

excursion, excursions NOUN a short journey or outing.

excuse, excuses, excusing, excused NOUN ❶ a reason which you give to explain why something has been done, has not been done, or will not be done ▷ VERB ❷ If you excuse yourself or something that you have done, you give reasons defending your actions. ❸ If you excuse somebody for something wrong they have done, you forgive them for it. ❹ If you excuse somebody from a duty or responsibility, you free them from it • *He was excused from standing trial because of ill health.* ▷ PHRASE ❺ You say **excuse me** to try to catch somebody's attention or to apologize for an interruption or for rude behaviour.

execute, executes, executing, executed VERB ❶ To execute somebody means to kill them as a punishment for a crime. ❷ If you execute something such as a plan or an action, you carry it out or perform it • *The crime had been planned and executed in Montreal.* **execution** NOUN

executioner, executioners NOUN a person whose job is to execute criminals.

executive, executives NOUN ❶ a person who is employed by a company at a senior level. ❷ The executive of an organization is a committee which has the authority to make decisions and ensure that they are carried out ▷ ADJECTIVE ❸ concerned with making important decisions and ensuring that they are carried out • *the commission's executive director.*

executor, executors [Said *ig-zek-yoo-tor*] NOUN a person you appoint to carry out the instructions in your will.

exemplary ADJECTIVE ❶ being a good example and worthy of imitation • *an exemplary performance.* ❷ serving as a warning • *an exemplary tale.*

▷ SPELLING NOTE: *Elaine and Emily shout EE when they mEEt to grEEt each other (~ee-)*

A
B
C
D
E
F
G
H
I
J
K
L
M
N
O
P
Q
R
S
T
U
V
W
X
Y
Z

exemplify, exemplifies, exemplifying, exemplified **VERB** ❶ To exemplify something means to be a typical example of it • *This aircraft exemplifies the advantages of European technological cooperation.* ❷ If you exemplify something, you give an example of it.

exempt, exempts, exempting, exempted **ADJECTIVE** ❶ excused from a rule or duty • *people exempt from prescription charges.* ▷ **VERB** ❷ To exempt someone from a rule, duty, or obligation means to excuse them from it. **exemption NOUN**

exercise, exercises, exercising, exercised **NOUN** ❶ PE Exercise is any activity which you do to get fit or remain healthy. ❷ Exercises are also activities which you do to practise and train for a particular skill • *piano exercises* • *a mathematical exercise.* ▷ **VERB** ❸ When you exercise, you do activities which help you to get fit and remain healthy. ❹ If you exercise your rights or responsibilities, you use them.

exert, exerts, exerting, exerted **VERB** ❶ To exert pressure means to apply it. ❷ If you exert yourself, you make a physical or mental effort to do something.

exertion, exertions **NOUN** Exertion is vigorous physical effort or exercise.

exhale, exhales, exhaling, exhaled **VERB** SCIENCE When you exhale, you breathe out.

exhaust, exhausts, exhausting, exhausted **VERB** ❶ To exhaust somebody means to make them very tired • *Several lengths of the pool left*

her exhausted. ❷ If you exhaust a supply of something such as money or food, you use it up completely. ❸ If you exhaust a subject, you talk about it so much that there is nothing else to say about it ▷ **NOUN** ❹ a pipe which carries the gas or steam out of the engine of a vehicle. ❺ GEOGRAPHY Exhaust is the gas or steam produced by the engine of a vehicle. **exhaustion NOUN**

● **SIMILAR WORDS:** ❶ fatigue, tire
● out, wear out

exhaustive ADJECTIVE thorough and complete • *an exhaustive series of tests.* **exhaustively ADVERB**

exhibit, exhibits, exhibiting, exhibited **VERB** ❶ To exhibit things means to show them in a public place for people to see. ❷ If you exhibit your feelings or abilities, you display them so that other people can see them ▷ **NOUN** ❸ anything which is put on show for the public to see.

exhibition, exhibitions **NOUN** ART a public display of works of art, products, or skills.

exhibitor, exhibitors **NOUN** a person whose work is being shown in an exhibition.

exhilarating ADJECTIVE Something that is exhilarating makes you feel very happy and excited.

exile, exiles, exiling, exiled **NOUN** ❶ If somebody lives in exile, they live in a foreign country because they cannot live in their own country, usually for political reasons. ❷ a person who lives in exile ▷ **VERB** ❸ If somebody is exiled, they are sent away from their own country and not allowed ever to return.

exist, exists, existing, existed VERB If something exists, it is present in the world as a real or living thing.

existence NOUN ❶ Existence is the state of being or existing. ❷ a way of living or being • *an idyllic existence.*

exit, exits, exiting, exited NOUN ❶ a way out of a place. ❷ If you make an exit, you leave a place ▷ VERB ❸ To exit means to go out. ❹ (DRAMA) An actor exits when he or she leaves the stage.

exodus NOUN An exodus is the departure of a large number of people from a place.

exoskeleton, exoskeletons NOUN (SCIENCE) An exoskeleton is a hard covering around the outside of the bodies of creatures such as insects and shellfish.

exothermic ADJECTIVE (SCIENCE) If a chemical reaction is exothermic, heat is produced.

exotic ADJECTIVE ❶ attractive or interesting through being unusual • *exotic fabrics.* ❷ coming from a foreign country • *exotic plants.*
● WORD HISTORY: from Greek
● *exotikos* meaning 'foreign'

expand, expands, expanding, expanded VERB ❶ If something expands or you expand it, it becomes larger in number or size. ❷ If you expand on something, you give more details about it • *The minister's speech expanded on the aims which he outlined last month.* **expansion** NOUN

expanse, expanses NOUN a very large or widespread area • *They flew*

over a vast expanse of pine forests.

expansive ADJECTIVE ❶ Something that is expansive is very wide or extends over a very large area • *the expansive countryside.* ❷ Someone who is expansive is friendly, open, or talkative.

expatriate, expatriates [Said eks-**pat**-ree-it] NOUN someone who is living in a country which is not their own.

expect, expects, expecting, expected VERB ❶ If you expect something to happen, you believe that it will happen • *The trial is expected to end today.* ❷ If you are expecting somebody or something, you believe that they are going to arrive or to happen • *The Queen was expecting the chambermaid.* ❸ If you expect something, you believe that it is your right to get it or have it • *He seemed to expect a reply.*
● SIMILAR WORDS: ❶ anticipate,
● look forward to

expectancy NOUN Expectancy is the feeling that something is about to happen, especially something exciting.

expectant ADJECTIVE ❶ If you are expectant, you believe that something is about to happen, especially something exciting. ❷ An expectant mother or father is someone whose baby is going to be born soon.
expectantly ADVERB

expectation, expectations NOUN Expectation or an expectation is a strong belief or hope that something will happen.

expedient, expedients [Said iks-**pee**-dee-ent] NOUN ❶ an action or plan that achieves a particular purpose but that may not be morally acceptable • *Many firms have improved their profitability by the simple expedient of cutting staff.* ▷ **ADJECTIVE** ❷ Something that is expedient is useful or convenient in a particular situation. **expediency NOUN**

expedition, expeditions **NOUN** ❶ an organized journey made for a special purpose, such as to explore; also the party of people who make such a journey. ❷ a short journey or outing • *shopping expeditions.* **expeditionary ADJECTIVE**

expel, expels, expelling, expelled **VERB** ❶ If someone is expelled from a school or club, they are officially told to leave because they have behaved badly. ❷ If a gas or liquid is expelled from a place, it is forced out of it.

expend, expends, expending, expended **VERB** To expend energy, time, or money means to use it up or spend it.

expendable ADJECTIVE no longer useful or necessary, and therefore able to be got rid of.

expenditure NOUN Expenditure is the total amount of money spent on something.

expense, expenses **NOUN** ❶ Expense is the money that something costs • *the expense of installing a burglar alarm.* ❷ IN PLURAL Expenses are the money somebody spends while doing something connected with their work, which is paid back to them by their employer.
● **SIMILAR WORDS:** ❶ cost,
● expenditure, outlay

expensive ADJECTIVE costing a lot

of money. **expensively ADVERB**

experience, experiences, experiencing, experienced **NOUN** ❶ Experience consists of all the things that you have done or that have happened to you. ❷ the knowledge or skill you have in a particular activity. ❸ something that you do or something that happens to you, especially something new or unusual ▷ **VERB** ❹ If you experience a situation or feeling, it happens to you or you are affected by it.
● **SIMILAR WORDS:** ❸ go through,
● undergo

experienced ADJECTIVE skilled or knowledgeable through doing something for a long time.

experiment, experiments, experimenting, experimented **NOUN** ❶ the testing of something, either to find out its effect or to prove something ▷ **VERB** ❷ If you experiment with something, you do a scientific test on it to prove or discover something. **experimentation NOUN experimental ADJECTIVE experimentally ADVERB**

expert, experts **NOUN** ❶ a person who is very skilled at doing something or very knowledgeable about a particular subject ▷ **ADJECTIVE** ❷ having or requiring special skill or knowledge • *expert advice.* **expertly ADVERB**
● **SIMILAR WORDS:** ❶ authority,
● master, specialist

expertise [Said eks-per-*teez*] **NOUN** Expertise is special skill or knowledge.

expire, expires, expiring, expired **VERB** When something expires, it

▷ SPELLING NOTE: *an ELegant angEL (angel)*

reaches the end of the period of time for which it is valid • *My contract expires in the summer.* **expiry** NOUN

explain, explains, explaining, explained **VERB** If you explain something, you give details about it or reasons for it so that it can be understood.
● **SIMILAR WORDS:** clarify,
● elucidate, make clear

explanation, explanations **NOUN** a helpful or clear description. **explanatory** ADJECTIVE

explicit ADJECTIVE shown or expressed clearly and openly • *an explicit death threat.* **explicitly** ADVERB

explode, explodes, exploding, exploded **VERB** ❶ If something such as a bomb explodes, it bursts loudly and with great force, often causing damage. ❷ If somebody explodes, they express strong feelings suddenly or violently • *I half expected him to explode in anger.* ❸ When something increases suddenly and rapidly, it can be said to explode • *Sales of men's toiletries have exploded.*
● **WORD HISTORY:** from Latin
● *explodere* meaning 'to clap someone
● offstage', from *ex* meaning 'out of'
● +*plodere* meaning 'to clap'

exploit, exploits, exploiting, exploited **VERB** ❶ If somebody exploits a person or a situation, they take advantage of them for their own ends • *Critics claim he exploited black musicians.* ❷ If you exploit something, you make the best use of it, often for profit • *exploiting the power of computers.* ▷ **NOUN** ❸ something daring or interesting that somebody

has done • *His courage and exploits were legendary.* **exploitation** NOUN

explore, explores, exploring, explored **VERB** ❶ If you explore a place, you travel in it to find out what it is like. ❷ If you explore an idea, you think about it carefully. **exploration** NOUN **exploratory** ADJECTIVE **explorer** NOUN

explosion, explosions **NOUN** a sudden violent burst of energy, for example one caused by a bomb.

explosive, explosives ADJECTIVE ❶ capable of exploding or likely to explode. ❷ happening suddenly and making a loud noise. ❸ An explosive situation is one which is likely to have serious or dangerous effects ▷ **NOUN** ❹ a substance or device that can explode.

exponent, exponents **NOUN** ❶ An exponent of an idea or plan is someone who puts it forward. ❷ FORMAL An exponent of a skill or activity is someone who is good at it.

export, exports, exporting, exported **VERB** ❶ To export goods means to send them to another country and sell them there ▷ **NOUN** ❷ Exports are goods which are sent to another country and sold. **exporter** NOUN

expose, exposes, exposing, exposed **VERB** ❶ To expose something means to uncover it and make it visible. ❷ To expose a person to something dangerous means to put them in a situation in which it might harm them • *exposed to tobacco smoke.* ❸ To expose a person or situation means to reveal the truth about them.

exposition, expositions **NOUN**

▷ SPELLING NOTE: *LEt's measure the angLE (angle)*

(ENGLISH) a detailed explanation of a particular subject.

exposure, exposures **NOUN**
1 Exposure is the exposing of something. **2** Exposure is the harmful effect on the body caused by very cold weather.

express, expresses, expressing, expressed **VERB** **1** When you express an idea or feeling, you show what you think or feel by saying or doing something. **2** If you express a quantity in a particular form, you write it down in that form • *The result of the equation is usually expressed as a percentage.* ▷ **ADJECTIVE** **3** very fast • *express delivery service.* ▷ **NOUN** **4** a fast train or coach which stops at only a few places.

expression, expressions **NOUN**
1 Your expression is the look on your face which shows what you are thinking or feeling. **2** (ENGLISH) The expression of ideas or feelings is the showing of them through words, actions, or art. **3** a word or phrase used in communicating • *the expression 'nosey parker'.*

expressive **ADJECTIVE** **1** showing feelings clearly. **2** full of expression.

expressway, expressways **NOUN** a road designed for fast-moving traffic.

expulsion, expulsions **NOUN** The expulsion of someone from a place or institution is the act of officially banning them from that place or institution • *the high number of school expulsions.*

exquisite **ADJECTIVE** extremely beautiful and pleasing.

extend, extends, extending, extended **VERB** **1** If something extends for a distance, it continues and stretches into the distance. **2** If something extends from a surface or an object, it sticks out from it. **3** If you extend something, you make it larger or longer.

extension, extensions **NOUN** **1** a room or building which is added to an existing building. **2** an extra period of time for which something continues to exist or be valid • *an extension to his visa.* **3** an additional telephone connected to the same line as another telephone.

extensive **ADJECTIVE** **1** covering a large area. **2** very great in effect • *extensive repairs.* **extensively ADVERB**

extent, extents **NOUN** The extent of something is its length, area, or size.

exterior, exteriors **NOUN** **1** The exterior of something is its outside. **2** Your exterior is your outward appearance.

exterior angle, exterior angles **NOUN** (MATHS) the angle formed between a line extending from one side of a polygon and the side next to it.

exterminate, exterminates, exterminating, exterminated **VERB** When animals or people are exterminated, they are deliberately killed. **extermination NOUN**

external, externals **ADJECTIVE** existing or happening on the outside or outer part of something. **externally ADVERB**

▷ SPELLING NOTE: *A Rude Idiot Thought He Might Eat Toffee In Church* (<u>arithmetic</u>)

extinct ADJECTIVE ❶ An extinct species of animal or plant is no longer in existence. ❷ An extinct volcano no longer erupts. **extinction** NOUN

extinguish, extinguishes, extinguishing, extinguished VERB To extinguish a light or fire means to put it out.

extortionate ADJECTIVE more expensive than you consider to be fair.

extra, extras ADJECTIVE ❶ more than is usual, necessary, or expected ▷ NOUN ❷ anything which is additional. ❸ a person who is hired to play a very small and unimportant part in a film.
● SIMILAR WORDS: ❶ added, ● additional, further

extra- PREFIX 'extra-' means 'outside' or 'beyond' • *extraordinary*.

extract, extracts, extracting, extracted VERB ❶ To extract something from a place means to take it out or get it out, often by force. ❷ If you extract information from someone, you get it from them with difficulty ▷ NOUN (LIBRARY) ❸ a small section taken from a book or piece of music.

extraction NOUN ❶ Your extraction is the country or people that your family originally comes from • *a Malaysian citizen of Australian extraction*. ❷ Extraction is the process of taking or getting something out of a place.

extraordinary ADJECTIVE unusual or surprising.
extraordinarily ADVERB
● SIMILAR WORDS: exceptional, ● remarkable, unusual

extraterrestrial ADJECTIVE (SCIENCE) happening or existing beyond the earth's atmosphere.

extravagant ADJECTIVE ❶ spending or costing more money than is reasonable or affordable. ❷ going beyond reasonable limits.
extravagantly ADVERB
extravagance NOUN

extravaganza, extravaganzas NOUN a spectacular and expensive public show.

extreme, extremes ADJECTIVE ❶ very great in degree or intensity • *extreme caution*. ❷ going beyond what is usual or reasonable • *extreme weather conditions*. ❸ at the furthest point or edge of something • *the extreme north of Spain*. ▷ NOUN ❹ the highest or furthest degree of something. **extremely** ADVERB

extremist, extremists NOUN a person who uses unreasonable or violent methods to bring about political change. **extremism** NOUN

extremity, extremities NOUN The extremities of something are its furthest ends or edges.

extricate, extricates, extricating, extricated VERB To extricate someone from a place or a situation means to free them from it.

extrovert, extroverts NOUN a person who is more interested in other people and the world around them than their own thoughts and feelings.
● WORD HISTORY: from Latin *extra* ● meaning 'outwards' + *vertere* ● meaning 'to turn'

▷ SPELLING NOTE: *Beautiful Elephants Are Usually Tiny* (<u>beautiful</u>)

exuberant ADJECTIVE full of energy and cheerfulness.
exuberantly ADVERB **exuberance** NOUN

exude, exudes, exuding, exuded VERB If someone exudes a quality or feeling, they seem to have it to a great degree.

eye, eyes, eyeing or eying, eyed NOUN ❶ the organ of sight. ❷ the small hole at the end of a needle through which you pass the thread ▷ VERB ❸ To eye something means to look at it carefully or suspiciously.

eyeball, eyeballs NOUN the whole of the ball-shaped part of the eye.

eyebrow, eyebrows NOUN Your eyebrows are the lines of hair which grow on the ridges of bone above your eyes.

eyelash, eyelashes NOUN Your eyelashes are hairs that grow on the edges of your eyelids.

eyelid, eyelids NOUN Your eyelids are the folds of skin which cover your eyes when they are closed.

eyesight NOUN Your eyesight is your ability to see.

eyesore, eyesores NOUN Something that is an eyesore is extremely ugly.

eyewitness, eyewitnesses NOUN a person who has seen an event and can describe what happened.

eyrie, eyries [Said ear-ee] NOUN the nest of an eagle or other bird of prey.

▷ SPELLING NOTE: *Betty Eats Cakes And Uses Seven Eggs (because)*

Ff

a
b
c
d
e
f
g
h
i
j
k
l
m
n
o
p
q
r
s
t
u
v
w
x
y
z

Some words which sound as if they should begin with the letter *f* actually begin with the letters *ph*, for example *pharmacy*, *pharaoh* and *phrase*. The *ph* combination, pronounced like *f*, comes in the middle of some words too, for example *amphetamine* and *emphasis*.

fable, fables **NOUN** a story intended to teach a moral lesson.

fabled ADJECTIVE well-known because many stories have been told about it • *the fabled city of Troy*.

fabric, fabrics **NOUN** D & T ❶ cloth • *tough fabric for tents*. ❷ The fabric of a building is its walls, roof, and other parts. ❸ The fabric of a society or system is its structure, laws, and customs • *the democratic fabric of American society*.

fabricate, fabricates, fabricating, fabricated **VERB** ❶ If you fabricate a story or an explanation, you invent it in order to deceive people. ❷ To fabricate something is to make or manufacture it. **fabrication NOUN**

fabulous ADJECTIVE ❶ wonderful or very impressive • *a fabulous picnic*. ❷ not real, but happening in stories and legends • *fabulous creatures*.

facade, facades [Said *fas-sahd*]

NOUN ❶ the front outside wall of a building. ❷ a false outward appearance • *the facade of honesty*.

face, faces, facing, faced **NOUN** ❶ the front part of your head from your chin to your forehead. ❷ the expression someone has or is making • *a grim face*. ❸ a surface or side of something, especially the most important side • *the north face of Everest*. ❹ the main aspect or general appearance of something • *We have changed the face of language study*. ▷ **VERB** ❺ To face something or someone is to be opposite them or to look at them or towards them • *a room that faces on to the street*. ❻ If you face something difficult or unpleasant, you have to deal with it • *She faced a terrible dilemma*. ▷ **PHRASE** ❼ **On the face of it** means judging by the appearance of something or your initial reaction to it • *On the face of it the palace looks gigantic*.
● **SIMILAR WORDS:**
● ❶ countenance, visage

faceless ADJECTIVE without character or individuality.

face-lift, face-lifts **NOUN** ❶ an operation to tighten the skin on someone's face to make them look younger. ❷ If you give something a face-lift, you clean it or improve its appearance.

▷ SPELLING NOTE: *there's a rAKE in the brAKEs (brake)*

facet, facets [Said **fas**-it] NOUN ❶ a single part or aspect of something • *the many facets of his talent.* ❷ one of the flat, cut surfaces of a precious stone.
 ● **WORD HISTORY:** from French
 ● *facette* meaning 'little face'

facetious [Said fas-**see**-shuss] ADJECTIVE witty or amusing but in a rather silly or inappropriate way • *He didn't appreciate my facetious suggestion.*
 ● **WORD HISTORY:** from Latin
 ● *facetiae* meaning 'witty remarks'

facial [Said **fay**-shal] ADJECTIVE appearing on or being part of the face • *facial expressions.*

facilitate, facilitates, facilitating, facilitated VERB To facilitate something is to make it easier for it to happen • *a process that will facilitate individual development.*

facility, facilities NOUN ❶ a service or piece of equipment which makes it possible to do something • *excellent shopping facilities.* ❷ A facility for something is an ability to do it easily or well • *Few people have a facility for novel-writing.*

fact, facts NOUN ❶ a piece of knowledge or information that is true or something that has actually happened ▷ PHRASES ❷ **In fact, as a matter of fact**, and **in point of fact** mean 'actually' or 'really' and are used for emphasis or when making an additional comment • *Very few people, in fact, have this type of skin.* **factual** ADJECTIVE **factually** ADVERB

faction, factions NOUN a small group of people belonging to a larger group, but differing from the larger group in some aims or ideas • *a conservative faction in the Church.*

fact of life, facts of life NOUN ❶ The facts of life are details about sexual intercourse and how babies are conceived and born. ❷ If you say that something is a fact of life, you mean that it is something that people expect to happen, even though they might find it shocking or unpleasant • *War is a fact of life.*

factor, factors NOUN ❶ something that helps to cause a result • *House dust mites are a major factor in asthma.* ❷ The factors of a number are the whole numbers that will divide exactly into it. For example, 2 and 5 are factors of 10. ❸ If something increases by a particular factor, it is multiplied that number of times • *The amount of energy used has increased by a factor of eight.*
 ● **SIMILAR WORDS:** ❶ cause,
 ● element, part

factory, factories NOUN a building or group of buildings where goods are made in large quantities.

faculty, faculties NOUN ❶ Your faculties are your physical and mental abilities • *My mental faculties are as sharp as ever.* ❷ In some universities, a Faculty is a group of related departments • *the Science Faculty.*

fad, fads NOUN a temporary fashion or craze • *the latest exercise fad.*

fade, fades, fading, faded VERB If something fades, the intensity of its colour, brightness, or sound is gradually reduced.

faeces or **feces** [Said **fee**-seez]

▷ SPELLING NOTE: *you'll brEAK that Electrical Aerial, Kitty (br*e*ak)*

PLURAL NOUN the solid waste substances discharged from a person's or animal's body.

fag, fags **NOUN** INFORMAL a cigarette.

Fahrenheit [Said *far-ren-hite*] **NOUN** a scale of temperature in which the freezing point of water is 32° and the boiling point is 212°.

fail, fails, failing, failed **VERB** **❶** If someone fails to achieve something, they are not successful. **❷** If you fail an exam, your marks are too low and you do not pass. **❸** If you fail to do something that you should have done, you do not do it • *They failed to phone her.* **❹** If something fails, it becomes less effective or stops working properly • *The power failed* • *His grandmother's eyesight began to fail.* ▷ **NOUN** **❺** In an exam, a fail is a piece of work that is not good enough to pass ▷ **PHRASE** **❻** **Without fail** means definitely or regularly • *Every Sunday her mum would ring without fail.*
● **SIMILAR WORDS: ❶** be
● unsuccessful, flop

failing, failings **NOUN** **❶** a fault in something or someone ▷ **PREPOSITION** **❷** used to introduce an alternative • *Failing that, get a market stall.*

failure, failures **NOUN** **❶** lack of success • *Not all conservation programmes ended in failure.* **❷** an unsuccessful person, thing, or action • *The venture was a complete failure.* **❸** Your failure to do something is not doing something that you were expected to do • *a statement explaining his failure to turn up as a speaker.* **❹** a weakness in something.

● **SIMILAR WORDS: ❷** flop, loser,
● washout

faint, fainter, faintest; faints, fainting, fainted **ADJECTIVE** **❶** A sound, colour, or feeling that is faint is not very strong or intense. **❷** If you feel faint, you feel weak, dizzy, and unsteady ▷ **VERB** **❸** If you faint, you lose consciousness. **faintly ADVERB**
● **SIMILAR WORDS: ❸** black out,
● pass out, swoon

fair, fairer, fairest; fairs **ADJECTIVE** **❶** reasonable and just • *fair and prompt trials for political prisoners.* **❷** quite large • *a fair size envelope.* **❸** moderately good or likely to be correct • *He had a fair idea of what to expect.* **❹** having light coloured hair or pale skin. **❺** with pleasant and dry weather • *Ireland's fair weather months.* ▷ **NOUN** **❻** a form of entertainment that takes place outside, with stalls, sideshows, and machines to ride on. **❼** an exhibition of goods produced by a particular industry • *International Wine and Food Fair.* **fairly ADVERB fairness NOUN**
● **SIMILAR WORDS: ❶** impartial,
● just, unbiased

fairground, fairgrounds **NOUN** an outdoor area where a fair is set up.

fairway, fairways **NOUN** the area of trimmed grass between a tee and a green on a golf course.

fairy, fairies **NOUN** In stories, fairies are small, supernatural creatures with magical powers.

fairy tale, fairy tales **NOUN** a story of magical events.

faith, faiths **NOUN** **❶** Faith is a feeling of confidence, trust or

▷ SPELLING NOTE: *I always visit my FRIend on a FRIday (Friday)*

optimism about something. ❷ RE someone's faith is their religion.

faithful ADJECTIVE ❶ loyal to someone or something and remaining firm in support of them. ❷ accurate and truthful • *a faithful copy of an original.* **faithfully** ADVERB **faithfulness** NOUN
● SIMILAR WORDS: ❶ loyal,
● steadfast, trusty

fake, fakes, faking, faked NOUN ❶ an imitation of something made to trick people into thinking that it is genuine ▷ ADJECTIVE ❷ imitation and not genuine • *fake fur.* ▷ VERB ❸ If you fake a feeling, you pretend that you are experiencing it.
● SIMILAR WORDS: ❶ copy,
● imitation, sham ❷ artificial, false,
● phoney ❸ feign, pretend, simulate

falcon, falcons NOUN a bird of prey that can be trained to hunt other birds or small animals.

fall, falls, falling, fell, fallen VERB ❶ If someone or something falls or falls over, they drop towards the ground. ❷ If something falls somewhere, it lands there • *The spotlight fell on her.* ❸ If something falls in amount or strength, it becomes less • *Steel production fell about 25%.* ❹ If a person or group in a position of power falls, they lose their position and someone else takes control. ❺ Someone who falls in battle is killed. ❻ If, for example, you fall asleep, fall ill, or fall in love, you change quite quickly to that new state. ❼ If you fall for someone, you become strongly attracted to them and fall in love. ❽ If you fall for a trick or lie, you are deceived by it.

❾ Something that falls on a particular date occurs on that date ▷ NOUN ❿ If you have a fall, you accidentally fall over. ⓫ A fall of snow, soot, or other substance is a quantity of it that has fallen to the ground. ⓬ A fall in something is a reduction in its amount or strength. ⓭ In America, autumn is called the fall.

fall down VERB An argument or idea that falls down on a particular point is weak on that point and as a result will be unsuccessful.

fall out VERB If people fall out, they disagree and quarrel.

fall through VERB If an arrangement or plan falls through, it fails or is abandoned.

fallacy, fallacies *[Said fal-lass-ee]* NOUN something false that is generally believed to be true.

fallopian tube, fallopian tubes *[Said fal-loh-pee-an]* NOUN one of two tubes in a woman's body along which the eggs pass from the ovaries to the uterus.

fallout NOUN radioactive particles that fall to the earth after a nuclear explosion.

fallow ADJECTIVE Land that is fallow is not being used for crop growing so that it has the chance to rest and improve.

false, falser, falsest ADJECTIVE ❶ untrue or incorrect • *I think that's a false argument.* ❷ not real or genuine but intended to seem real • *false hair.* ❸ unfaithful or deceitful. **falsely** ADVERB **falsity** NOUN

falsehood, falsehoods NOUN ❶ the quality or fact of being untrue

▷ SPELLING NOTE: *I want to see (C) your licenCe (licence)*

• *the difference between truth and falsehood.* ❷ a lie.

falsetto, falsettos NOUN (MUSIC) A falsetto is a man's very high-pitched speaking or singing voice.

falsify, falsifies, falsifying, falsified VERB If you falsify something, you change it in order to deceive people. **falsification** NOUN

falter, falters, faltering, faltered VERB If someone or something falters, they hesitate or become unsure or unsteady • *Her voice faltered.*

fame NOUN the state of being very well-known.
● SIMILAR WORDS: prominence, renown, repute

famed ADJECTIVE very well-known • *an area famed for its beauty.*

familiar ADJECTIVE ❶ well-known or easy to recognize • *familiar faces.* ❷ knowing or understanding something well • *Most children are familiar with stories.* **familiarity** NOUN **familiarize** VERB
● SIMILAR WORDS:
● ❶ recognizable, well-known

family, families NOUN ❶ a group consisting of parents and their children; also all the people who are related to each other, including aunts and uncles, cousins, and grandparents. ❷ (SCIENCE) a group of related species of animals or plants. It is smaller than an order and larger than a genus. **familial** ADJECTIVE

family planning NOUN the practice of controlling the number of children you have, usually by using contraception.

family tree, family trees NOUN A family tree is a chart showing all the people in a family and their relationship to others over many generations.

famine, famines NOUN a serious shortage of food which may cause many deaths.

famished ADJECTIVE INFORMAL very hungry.

famous ADJECTIVE very well-known.
● SIMILAR WORDS: prominent, renowned, well-known

famously ADVERB OLD-FASHIONED If people get on famously, they enjoy each other's company very much.

fan, fans, fanning, fanned NOUN ❶ If you are a fan of someone or something, you like them very much and are very enthusiastic about them. ❷ a hand-held or mechanical object which creates a draught of cool air when it moves ▷ VERB ❸ To fan someone or something is to create a draught in their direction • *The gentle wind fanned her from all sides.*
fan out VERB If things or people fan out, they move outwards in different directions.
● SIMILAR WORDS: ❶ admirer, enthusiast, supporter

fanatic, fanatics NOUN a person who is very extreme in their support for a cause or in their enthusiasm for a particular activity. **fanaticism** NOUN
● WORD HISTORY: from Latin *fanaticus* meaning 'possessed by a god'

fanatical ADJECTIVE If you are fanatical about something, you are

a b c d e **f** g h i j k l m n o p q r s t u v w x y z

A
B
C
D
E
F
G
H
I
J
K
L
M
N
O
P
Q
R
S
T
U
V
W
X
Y
Z

very extreme in your enthusiasm or support for it. **fanatically ADVERB**
● **SIMILAR WORDS:** obsessive,
● overenthusiastic

fancy, fancies, fancying, fancied; fancier, fanciest **VERB** ❶ If you fancy something, you want to have it or do it • *She fancied living in Canada.*
▷ **ADJECTIVE** ❷ special and elaborate • *dressed up in some fancy clothes.* **fanciful ADJECTIVE**
● **SIMILAR WORDS:** ❷ elaborate,
● ornate

fancy dress NOUN clothing worn for a party at which people dress up to look like a particular character or animal.

fanfare, fanfares **NOUN** a short, loud, musical introduction to a special event, usually played on trumpets.

fang, fangs **NOUN** Fangs are long, pointed teeth.

fantail, fantails **NOUN** ❶ a pigeon with a large tail that can be opened out like a fan. ❷ In Australia and New Zealand, a fantail is also a small, insect-eating bird with a fan-shaped tail.

fantasize, fantasizes, fantasizing, fantasized; *also spelt* **fantasise VERB** If you fantasize, you imagine pleasant but unlikely events or situations.

fantastic ADJECTIVE ❶ wonderful and very pleasing • *a fantastic view of the sea.* ❷ extremely large in degree or amount • *fantastic debts.* ❸ strange and difficult to believe • *fantastic animals found nowhere else on earth.* **fantastically ADVERB**
● **SIMILAR WORDS:** ❶ marvellous,
● wonderful

fantasy, fantasies **NOUN** ❶ an imagined story or situation. ❷ Fantasy is the activity of imagining things or the things that you imagine • *She can't distinguish between fantasy and reality.* ❸ (LIBRARY) In books and films, fantasy is the people or situations in books or films which are created in the writer's imagination and do not reflect reality.
● **WORD HISTORY:** from Greek
● *phantasia* meaning 'imagination'

far, farther, farthest; further, furthest **ADVERB** ❶ If something is far away from other things, it is a long distance away. ❷ Far also means very much or to a great extent or degree • *far more important.* ▷ **ADJECTIVE** ❸ Far means very distant • *in the far south of Africa.* ❹ Far also describes the more distant of two things rather than the nearer one • *the far corner of the goal.* ▷ **PHRASE** ❺ By far and far and away are used to say that something is the best • *Walking is by far the best way to get around.* ❻ So far means up to the present moment • *So far, it's been good news.* ❼ As far as, so far as, and in so far as mean to the degree or extent that something is true • *As far as I know he is progressing well.*
● **USAGE NOTE:** When you are
● talking about a physical distance
● you can use *farther* and *farthest* or
● *further* and *furthest*. If you are
● talking about extra effort or time,
● use *further* and *furthest*: *a further*
● *delay is likely*
● **SIMILAR WORDS:**
● ❷ considerably, much ❸ distant,
● remote

farce, farces **NOUN** ❶ a humorous

play in which ridiculous and unlikely situations occur. ❷ a disorganized and ridiculous situation. **farcical** **ADJECTIVE**

fare, fares, faring, fared **NOUN** ❶ the amount charged for a journey on a bus, train, or plane ▷ **VERB** ❷ How someone fares in a particular situation is how they get on • *The team have not fared well in this tournament.*

Far East **NOUN** The Far East consists of the countries of East Asia, including China, Japan, and Malaysia. **Far Eastern** **ADJECTIVE**

farewell **INTERJECTION** ❶ Farewell means goodbye ▷ **ADJECTIVE** ❷ A farewell act is performed by or for someone who is leaving a particular job or career • *a farewell speech.*

far-fetched **ADJECTIVE** unlikely to be true.

farm, farms, farming, farmed **NOUN** ❶ an area of land together with buildings, used for growing crops and raising animals ▷ **VERB** ❷ Someone who farms uses land to grow crops and raise animals. **farmer** **NOUN** **farming** **NOUN**
● **WORD HISTORY:** from Old French *ferme* meaning 'rented land'

farmhouse, farmhouses **NOUN** the main house on a farm.

farmyard, farmyards **NOUN** an area surrounded by farm buildings.

fascinate, fascinates, fascinating, fascinated **VERB** If something fascinates you, it interests you so much that you think about it and nothing else. **fascinating** **ADJECTIVE**

● **SIMILAR WORDS:** absorb, enthral, intrigue

fascism [*Said fash-izm*] **NOUN** an extreme right-wing political ideology or system of government with a powerful dictator and state control of most activities. Nationalism is encouraged and political opposition is not allowed. **fascist** **NOUN OR** **ADJECTIVE**

fashion, fashions, fashioning, fashioned **NOUN** ❶ a style of dress or way of behaving that is popular at a particular time. ❷ The fashion in which someone does something is the way in which they do it ▷ **VERB** ❸ If you fashion something, you make or shape it.
● **SIMILAR WORDS:** ❶ style, trend, vogue

fashionable **ADJECTIVE** Something that is fashionable is very popular with a lot of people at the same time. **fashionably** **ADVERB**
● **SIMILAR WORDS:** in, in vogue, popular, trendy

fast, faster, fastest; fasts, fasting, fasted **ADJECTIVE** ❶ moving or done at great speed. ❷ If a clock is fast, it shows a time that is later than the real time ▷ **ADVERB** ❸ quickly and without delay. ❹ Something that is held fast is firmly fixed ▷ **PHRASE** ❺ If you are **fast asleep**, you are in a deep sleep ▷ **VERB** ❻ If you fast, you eat no food at all for a period of time, usually for religious reasons ▷ **NOUN** ❼ a period of time during which someone does not eat food.
● **SIMILAR WORDS:** ❶ quick, rapid, speedy, swift

fasten, fastens, fastening, fastened

● a b c d e f g h i j k l m n o p q r s t u v w x y z

A B C D E F G H I J K L M N O P Q R S T U V W X Y Z

VERB ❶ To fasten something is to close it or attach it firmly to something else. **❷** If you fasten your hands or teeth around or onto something, you hold it tightly with them. **fastener NOUN fastening NOUN**
● **SIMILAR WORDS: ❶** fix, secure

fast food NOUN hot food that is prepared and served quickly after you have ordered it.

fastidious ADJECTIVE extremely choosy and concerned about neatness and cleanliness.

fast-track, fast-tracks, fast-tracking, fast-tracked **VERB** To fast-track something is to make it happen or put it into effect as quickly as possible, usually giving it priority over other things.

fat, fatter, fattest; fats **ADJECTIVE ❶** Someone who is fat has too much weight on their body. **❷** large or great • *a fat pile of letters.* ▷ **NOUN ❸** Fat is the greasy, cream-coloured substance that animals and humans have under their skin, which is used to store energy and to help keep them warm. **❹** Fat is also the greasy solid or liquid substance obtained from animals and plants and used in cooking. **fatness NOUN fatty ADJECTIVE**
● **SIMILAR WORDS: ❶** overweight,
● plump, podgy, tubby

fatal ADJECTIVE ❶ causing death • *fatal injuries.* **❷** very important or significant and likely to have an undesirable effect • *The mistake was fatal to my plans.* **fatally ADVERB**
● **SIMILAR WORDS: ❶** deadly,
● lethal, mortal

fatality, fatalities **NOUN** a death

caused by accident or violence.

fate, fates **NOUN ❶** Fate is a power that is believed to control events. **❷** Someone's fate is what happens to them • *She was resigned to her fate.*
● **SIMILAR WORDS: ❶** destiny,
● providence

fateful ADJECTIVE having an important, often disastrous, effect • *fateful political decisions.*

father, fathers, fathering, fathered **NOUN ❶** A person's father is their male parent. **❷** The father of something is the man who invented or started it • *the father of Italian painting.* **❸** 'Father' is used to address a priest in some Christian churches. **❹** Father is another name for God ▷ **VERB ❺** LITERARY When a man fathers a child, he makes a woman pregnant. **fatherly ADJECTIVE fatherhood NOUN**

father-in-law, fathers-in-law **NOUN** A person's father-in-law is the father of their husband or wife.

fathom, fathoms, fathoming, fathomed **NOUN ❶** a unit for measuring the depth of water. It is equal to 6 feet or about 1.83 metres ▷ **VERB ❷** If you fathom something, you understand it after careful thought • *Daisy tries to fathom what it means.*

fatigue, fatigues, fatiguing, fatigued [*Said fat-eeg*] **NOUN ❶** Fatigue is extreme tiredness ▷ **VERB ❷** If you are fatigued by something, it makes you extremely tired.

fault, faults, faulting, faulted **NOUN ❶** If something bad is your fault, you are to blame for it. **❷** a weakness or

▷ SPELLING NOTE: *I went to see (C) the doctor's new practiCe (practise)*

imperfection in someone or something. ❸ a large crack in rock caused by movement of the earth's crust ▷ **PHRASE** ❹ If you are **at fault**, you are mistaken or are to blame for something • *If you were at fault, you accept it.* ▷ **VERB** ❺ If you fault someone, you criticize them for what they are doing because they are not doing it well. **faultless ADJECTIVE**

● **SIMILAR WORDS:** ❷ defect,
● failing, flaw

faulty, faultier, faultiest **ADJECTIVE** containing flaws or errors.

fauna [*Said* **faw**-na] **NOUN** (GEOGRAPHY) The fauna of a particular area is all the animals found in that area • *the flora and fauna of Africa.*

favour, favours, favouring, favoured **NOUN** ❶ If you regard someone or something with favour, you like or support them. ❷ If you do someone a favour, you do something helpful for them ▷ **PHRASE** ❸ Something that is **in someone's favour** is a help or advantage to them • *The arguments seemed to be in our favour.* ❹ If you are **in favour of** something, you agree with it and think it should happen ▷ **VERB** ❺ If you favour something or someone, you prefer that person or thing.

favourable ADJECTIVE ❶ of advantage or benefit to someone. ❷ positive and expressing approval. **favourably ADVERB**

favourite, favourites **ADJECTIVE** ❶ Your favourite person or thing is the one you like best ▷ **NOUN** ❷ Someone's favourite is the person or thing they like best. ❸ the animal

or person expected to win in a race or contest.

favouritism NOUN Favouritism is behaviour in which you are unfairly more helpful or more generous to one person than to other people.

fawn, fawns, fawning, fawned **NOUN OR ADJECTIVE** ❶ pale yellowish-brown ▷ **NOUN** ❷ a very young deer ▷ **VERB** ❸ To fawn on someone is to seek their approval by flattering them.

fax, faxes **NOUN** an exact copy of a document sent electronically along a telephone line.

fear, fears, fearing, feared **NOUN** ❶ Fear is an unpleasant feeling of danger. ❷ a thought that something undesirable or unpleasant might happen • *You have a fear of failure.* ▷ **VERB** ❸ If you fear someone or something, you are frightened of them. ❹ If you fear something unpleasant, you are worried that it is likely to happen • *Artists feared that their pictures would be forgotten.* **fearless ADJECTIVE fearlessly ADVERB**

● **SIMILAR WORDS:** ❶ dread, fright,
● terror

fearful ADJECTIVE ❶ afraid and full of fear. ❷ extremely unpleasant or worrying • *The world's in such a fearful mess.* **fearfully ADVERB**

fearsome ADJECTIVE terrible or frightening • *a powerful, fearsome weapon.*

feasible ADJECTIVE possible and likely to happen • *The proposal is just not feasible.* **feasibility NOUN**

feast, feasts **NOUN** a large and

▷ SPELLING NOTE: *You must practiSe your Ss (practise)*

special meal for many people.

feat, feats **NOUN** an impressive and difficult achievement • *It was an astonishing feat for Leeds to score six away from home.*

feather, feathers **NOUN** one of the light fluffy things covering a bird's body. **feathery ADJECTIVE**

feature, features, featuring, featured **NOUN** ❶ an interesting or important part or characteristic of something. ❷ Someone's features are the various parts of their face. ❸ (SCIENCE) a characteristic that is typical of a particular living thing. ❹ a special article or programme dealing with a particular subject. ❺ the main film in a cinema programme ▷ **VERB** ❻ To feature something is to include it or emphasize it as an important part or subject. **featureless ADJECTIVE**

February **NOUN** February is the second month of the year. It has 28 days, except in a leap year, when it has 29 days.

● **WORD HISTORY:** from *Februa*, a Roman festival of purification

fed the past tense and past participle of **feed**.

federal ADJECTIVE relating to a system of government in which a group of states is controlled by a central government, but each state has its own local powers • *The United States of America is a federal country.*

federation, federations **NOUN** a group of organizations or states that have joined together for a common purpose.

fed up ADJECTIVE INFORMAL

unhappy or bored • *I'm really fed up with this kind of behaviour.*

fee, fees **NOUN** a charge or payment for a job, service, or activity.

feeble, feebler, feeblest **ADJECTIVE** weak or lacking in power or influence • *feeble and stupid arguments.*

feed, feeds, feeding, fed **VERB** ❶ To feed a person or animal is to give them food. ❷ When an animal or baby feeds, it eats. ❸ To feed something is to supply what is needed for it to operate or exist • *The information was fed into a computer database.* ▷ **NOUN** ❹ Feed is food for animals or babies.

feedback NOUN ❶ Feedback is comments and information about the quality or success of something. ❷ Feedback is also a condition in which some of the power, sound, or information produced by electronic equipment goes back into it.

feel, feels, feeling, felt **VERB** ❶ If you feel an emotion or sensation, you experience it • *I felt a bit ashamed.* ❷ If you feel that something is the case, you believe it to be so • *She feels that she is in control of her life.* ❸ If you feel something, you touch it. ❹ If something feels warm or cold, for example, you experience its warmth or coldness through the sense of touch • *Real marble feels cold to the touch.* ❺ To feel the effect of something is to be affected by it • *The shock waves of this fire will be felt by people from all over the world.* ▷ **NOUN** ❻ The feel of something is how it feels to you when you touch it • *skin with a velvety smooth feel.* ▷ **PHRASE** ❼ If you **feel like** doing something, you want to do it.

▷ SPELLING NOTE: *pAL up with the principAL and principAL staff (principal)*

WHAT IS THE FEMININE?

Feminine nouns denote female people and animals:
The girl put on her coat. → *girl is* **feminine**

It is customary to refer to countries and vehicles as if they were feminine:
The ship came into view, her sails swelling in the breeze.

Common nouns may be either masculine or feminine. Other words in the sentence may tell us if they are male or female:
The doctor parked his car.
The doctor parked her car.

Also look at the grammar boxes at **gender**, **masculine** and **neuter**.

● **SIMILAR WORDS:** ❶ be aware of, experience ❷ believe, consider, think

feeler, feelers **NOUN** the two thin antennae on an insect's head with which it senses things around it.

feeling, feelings **NOUN** ❶ an emotion or reaction • *feelings of envy*. ❷ a physical sensation • *a feeling of pain*. ❸ Feeling is the ability to experience the sense of touch in your body • *He had no feeling in his hands*. ❹ IN PLURAL Your feelings about something are your general attitudes or thoughts about it • *He has strong feelings about our national sport*.

feet the plural of **foot**.

feign, feigns, feigning, feigned [*rhymes with* **rain**] **VERB** If you feign an emotion or state, you pretend to experience it • *I feigned a headache*.

feline [*Said* **fee**-*line*] **ADJECTIVE** belonging or relating to the cat family.

fell, fells, felling, felled ❶ the past tense of **fall**. **VERB** ❷ To fell a tree is to cut it down.

fellow, fellows **NOUN** ❶ INFORMAL, OLD-FASHIONED a man • *I knew a fellow by that name.* ❷ a senior

member of a learned society or a university college. ❸ Your fellows are the people who share work or an activity with you ▷ **ADJECTIVE** ❹ You use 'fellow' to describe people who have something in common with you • *his fellow editors*.

fellowship, fellowships **NOUN** ❶ a feeling of friendliness that a group of people have when they are doing things together. ❷ a group of people that join together because they have interests in common • *the Dickens Fellowship*. ❸ an academic post at a university which involves research.

felt ❶ the past tense and past participle of **feel**. **NOUN** ❷ D & T Felt is a thick cloth made by pressing short threads together.

female, females **NOUN** ❶ a person or animal that belongs to the sex that can have babies or young ▷ **ADJECTIVE** ❷ concerning or relating to females.

feminine **ADJECTIVE** ❶ relating to women or considered to be typical of women. ❷ belonging to a particular class of nouns in some languages, such as French, German, and Latin. **femininity** **NOUN**
▶ SEE GRAMMAR BOX ABOVE

▷ SPELLING NOTE: LEarn the principLEs (principle)

feminism NOUN Feminism is the belief that women should have the same rights and opportunities as men. **feminist** NOUN OR ADJECTIVE

femur, femurs or femora [Said *fee-mer*] NOUN (SCIENCE) Your femur is the large bone in the upper part of your leg.

fen, fens NOUN The fens are an area of low, flat, very wet land in the east of England.

fence, fences, fencing, fenced NOUN ❶ a wooden or wire barrier between two areas of land. ❷ a barrier or hedge for the horses to jump over in horse racing or show jumping ▷ VERB ❸ To fence an area of land is to surround it with a fence. ❹ When two people fence, they use special swords to fight each other as a sport.

fend, fends, fending, fended PHRASE ❶ If you have to **fend for yourself**, you have to look after yourself ▷ VERB ❷ If you fend off an attack or unwelcome questions or attention, you defend and protect yourself.

ferment, ferments, fermenting, fermented VERB When wine, beer, or fruit ferments, a chemical change takes place in it, often producing alcohol. **fermentation** NOUN

fern, ferns NOUN a plant with long feathery leaves and no flowers.

ferocious ADJECTIVE violent and fierce • *ferocious dogs* • *ferocious storms*. **ferociously** ADVERB **ferocity** NOUN
● **WORD HISTORY:** from Latin *ferox* meaning 'like a wild animal'

ferret, ferrets NOUN a small, fierce animal related to the weasel and kept for hunting rats and rabbits.
● **WORD HISTORY:** from Old French
● *furet* meaning 'little thief'

ferry, ferries, ferrying, ferried NOUN ❶ a boat that carries people and vehicles across short stretches of water ▷ VERB ❷ To ferry people or goods somewhere is to transport them there, usually on a short, regular journey.

fertile ADJECTIVE ❶ capable of producing offspring or plants. ❷ creative • *fertile minds*. **fertility** NOUN

fertilize, fertilizes, fertilizing, fertilized; *also spelt* **fertilise** VERB ❶ (SCIENCE) When an egg, plant, or female is fertilized, the process of reproduction begins by sperm joining with the egg, or by pollen coming into contact with the reproductive part of a plant. ❷ To fertilize land is to put manure or chemicals onto it to feed the plants.

fertilizer, fertilizers; *also spelt* **fertiliser** NOUN (GEOGRAPHY) a substance put onto soil to improve plant growth.

fervent ADJECTIVE showing strong, sincere, and enthusiastic feeling • *a fervent nationalist*. **fervently** ADVERB

fervour NOUN a very strong feeling for or belief in something.
● **WORD HISTORY:** from Latin *fervor*
● meaning 'heat'

fester, festers, festering, festered VERB If a wound festers it becomes infected and produces pus.
● **WORD HISTORY:** from Latin *fistula*
● meaning 'ulcer'

▷ SPELLING NOTE: *Psychiatrists Seldom Yell Callously Hard (psychiatrist)*

festival, festivals **NOUN** ❶ an organized series of events and performances • *the Cannes Film Festival*. ❷ RE a day or period of religious celebration.

festive **ADJECTIVE** full of happiness and celebration • *a festive time of singing and dancing*.

festivity, festivities **NOUN** celebration and happiness • *the wedding festivities*.

festooned **ADJECTIVE** If something is festooned with objects, the objects are hanging across it in large numbers • *trees festooned with Christmas lights*.

fetch, fetches, fetching, fetched **VERB** ❶ If you fetch something, you go to where it is and bring it back. ❷ If something fetches a particular sum of money, it is sold for that amount • *Portraits fetch the highest prices*.

fetching **ADJECTIVE** attractive in appearance • *a fetching purple frock*.

fete, fetes, feting, feted [*rhymes with date*] **NOUN** ❶ an outdoor event with competitions, displays, and goods for sale ▷ **VERB** ❷ Someone who is feted receives a public welcome or entertainment as an honour.

feud, feuds, feuding, feuded [*Said fyood*] **NOUN** ❶ a long-term and very bitter quarrel, especially between families ▷ **VERB** ❷ When people feud, they take part in a feud.

feudalism **NOUN** Feudalism is a social and political system that was common in the Middle Ages in Europe. Under this system, ordinary people were given land and protection by a lord, and in return they worked and fought for him. **feudal** **ADJECTIVE**

fever, fevers **NOUN** ❶ Fever is a condition occurring during illness, in which the patient has a very high body temperature. ❷ A fever is extreme excitement or agitation • *a fever of impatience*.

feverish **ADJECTIVE** ❶ in a state of extreme excitement or agitation • *increasingly feverish activity*. ❷ suffering from a high body temperature. **feverishly** **ADVERB**

few, fewer, fewest **ADJECTIVE OR NOUN** ❶ used to refer to a small number of things • *I saw him a few moments ago* • *one of only a few*. ▷ **PHRASES** ❷ **Quite a few** or **a good few** means quite a large number of things.
● **USAGE NOTE:** You use *fewer* to talk about things that can be counted: *fewer than five visits*. When you are talking about amounts that can't be counted you should use *less*

fiancé, fiancés [*Said fee-on-say*] **NOUN** A woman's fiancé is the man to whom she is engaged.

fiancée, fiancées **NOUN** A man's fiancée is the woman to whom he is engaged.

fiasco, fiascos [*Said fee-ass-koh*] **NOUN** an event or attempt that fails completely, especially in a ridiculous or disorganized way • *The game ended in a complete fiasco*.

fib, fibs, fibbing, fibbed **NOUN** ❶ a small, unimportant lie ▷ **VERB** ❷ If you fib, you tell a small lie.

a
b
c
d
e
f
g
h
i
j
k
l
m
n
o
p
q
r
s
t
u
v
w
x
y
z

▷ SPELLING NOTE: *the QUeen stood on the QUay (quay)*

A
B
C
D
E
F
G
H
I
J
K
L
M
N
O
P
Q
R
S
T
U
V
W
X
Y
Z

fibre, fibres **NOUN** ❶ **D&T** a thin thread of a substance used to make cloth. ❷ Fibre is also a part of plants that can be eaten but not digested; it helps food pass quickly through the body. **fibrous ADJECTIVE**

fibreglass NOUN **D&T** Fibreglass is a material made from thin threads of glass. It can be mixed with plastic to make boats, cars, and furniture, and is often used as an insulating material.

fibre optics NOUN Fibre optics is the use of long, thin threads of glass to carry information in the form of light.

fibula, fibulae or fibulas **NOUN** **SCIENCE** Your fibula is the outer and thinner of the two bones between your knee and your ankle.

fickle ADJECTIVE A fickle person keeps changing their mind about who or what they like or want.

fiction, fictions **NOUN** ❶ Fiction is stories about people and events that have been invented by the author. ❷ something that is not true. **fictional ADJECTIVE fictitious ADJECTIVE**

fiddle, fiddles, fiddling, fiddled **VERB** ❶ If you fiddle with something, you keep moving it or touching it restlessly. ❷ INFORMAL If someone fiddles something such as an account, they alter it dishonestly to get money for themselves ▷ **NOUN** ❸ INFORMAL a dishonest action or scheme to get money. ❹ a violin. **fiddler NOUN**

fiddly, fiddlier, fiddliest **ADJECTIVE** small and difficult to do or use • *fiddly nuts and bolts.*

fidelity NOUN Fidelity is remaining firm in your beliefs, friendships, or loyalty to another person.

fidget, fidgets, fidgeting, fidgeted **VERB** ❶ If you fidget, you keep changing your position because of nervousness or boredom ▷ **NOUN** ❷ someone who fidgets. **fidgety ADJECTIVE**

field, fields, fielding, fielded **NOUN** ❶ an area of land where crops are grown or animals are kept. ❷ **PE** an area of land where sports are played • *a hockey field.* ❸ A coal field, oil field, or gold field is an area where coal, oil, or gold is found. ❹ a particular subject or area of interest • *He was doing well in his own field of advertising.* ▷ **ADJECTIVE** ❺ A field trip or a field study involves research or activity in the natural environment rather than theoretical or laboratory work. ❻ In an athletics competition, the field events are the events such as the high jump and the javelin which do not take place on a running track ▷ **VERB** ❼ In cricket, when you field the ball, you stop it after the batsman has hit it. ❽ To field questions is to answer or deal with them skilfully.

fielder, fielders **NOUN** In cricket, the fielders are the team members who stand at various parts of the pitch and try to get the batsmen out or to prevent runs from being scored.

field marshal, field, marshals **NOUN** an army officer of the highest rank.

fieldwork NOUN Fieldwork is the study of something in the environment where it naturally lives or occurs, rather than in a class or laboratory.

fiend, fiends [Said **feend**] NOUN ❶ a devil or evil spirit. ❷ a very wicked or cruel person. ❸ INFORMAL someone who is very keen on a particular thing • *a fitness fiend.*

fierce, fiercer, fiercest ADJECTIVE ❶ very aggressive or angry. ❷ extremely strong or intense • *a sudden fierce pain* • *a fierce storm.* **fiercely** ADVERB
● SIMILAR WORDS: ❶ ferocious, ● savage, wild

fiery, fierier, fieriest ADJECTIVE ❶ involving fire or seeming like fire • *a huge fiery sun.* ❷ showing great anger, energy, or passion • *a fiery debate.*

fifteen the number 15. **fifteenth** ADJECTIVE

fifth, fifths ADJECTIVE ❶ The fifth item in a series is the one counted as number five ▷ NOUN ❷ one of five equal parts.

fifty, fifties the number 50. **fiftieth** ADJECTIVE

fifty-fifty ADVERB ❶ divided equally into two portions ▷ ADJECTIVE ❷ just as likely not to happen as to happen • *You've got a fifty-fifty chance of being right.*

fig, figs NOUN a soft, sweet fruit full of tiny seeds that grows in hot countries.

fight, fights, fighting, fought VERB ❶ When people fight, they take part in a battle, a war, a boxing match, or in some other attempt to hurt or kill someone. ❷ To fight for something is to try in a very determined way to

achieve it • *I must fight for respect.* ▷ NOUN ❸ a situation in which people hit or try to hurt each other. ❹ a determined attempt to prevent or achieve something • *the fight for independence.* ❺ an angry disagreement.
● SIMILAR WORDS: ❶ battle, come ● to blows, struggle ❸ battle, ● conflict, struggle

fighter, fighters NOUN someone who physically fights another person.

figurative ADJECTIVE (ENGLISH) If you use a word or expression in a figurative sense, you use it with a more abstract or imaginative meaning than its ordinary one. **figuratively** ADVERB

figure, figures, figuring, figured NOUN ❶ a written number or the amount a number stands for. ❷ a geometrical shape. ❸ a diagram or table in a written text. ❹ the shape of a human body, sometimes one that you cannot see properly • *his slim and supple figure* • *A human figure leaped at him.* ❺ a person • *He was a major figure in the trial.* ▷ VERB ❻ To figure in something is to appear or be included in it • *the many people who have figured in his life.* ❼ INFORMAL If you figure that something is the case, you guess or conclude this • *We figure the fire broke out around four in the morning.*

figurehead, figureheads NOUN the leader of a movement or organization who has no real power.

figure of speech, figures of speech NOUN (ENGLISH) A figure of speech is an expression such as a simile or idiom in which the words are

▷ SPELLING NOTE: *there's SAND in my SANDwich (__sand__wich)*

A
B
C
D
E
F
G
H
I
J
K
L
M
N
O
P
Q
R
S
T
U
V
W
X
Y
Z

not used in their literal sense.

filament, filaments **NOUN**
(SCIENCE) ❶ A filament is a very fine wire or thread, especially the wire that produces light in a light bulb. ❷ In a flower, the filament is the stalk of a stamen.

file, files, filing, filed **NOUN** ❶ a box or folder in which a group of papers or records is kept; also used of the information kept in the file. ❷ In computing, a file is a stored set of related data with its own name. ❸ a line of people one behind the other. ❹ (D & T) a long steel tool with a rough surface, used for smoothing and shaping hard materials ▷ **VERB** ❺ When someone files a document, they put it in its correct place with similar documents. ❻ When a group of people file somewhere, they walk one behind the other in a line. ❼ If you file something, you smooth or shape it with a file.

fill, fills, filling, filled **VERB** ❶ If you fill something or if it fills up, it becomes full. ❷ If something fills a need, it satisfies the need • *Ella had in some small way filled the gap left by Molly's absence.* ❸ To fill a job vacancy is to appoint someone to do that job ▷ **NOUN** ❹ If you have had your fill of something, you do not want any more.
fill in VERB ❶ If you fill in a form, you write information in the appropriate spaces. ❷ If you fill someone in, you give them information to bring them up to date.

fillet, fillets, filleting, filleted **NOUN** ❶ a strip of tender, boneless beef, veal, or pork. ❷ a piece of fish with the bones removed ▷ **VERB** ❸ To

fillet meat or fish is to prepare it by cutting out the bones.

filling, fillings **NOUN** ❶ the soft food mixture inside a sandwich, cake, or pie. ❷ a small amount of metal or plastic put into a hole in a tooth by a dentist.

filly, fillies **NOUN** a female horse or pony under the age of four.

film, films, filming, filmed **NOUN** ❶ a series of moving pictures projected onto a screen and shown at the cinema or on television. ❷ a thin flexible strip of plastic used in a camera to record images when exposed to light. ❸ a very thin layer of powder or liquid on a surface. ❹ Plastic film is a very thin sheet of plastic used for wrapping things ▷ **VERB** ❺ If you film someone, you use a video camera to record their movements on film.

filter, filters, filtering, filtered **NOUN** ❶ a device that allows some substances, lights, or sounds to pass through it, but not others • *a filter against the harmful rays of the sun.* ▷ **VERB** ❷ To filter a substance is to pass it through a filter. ❸ If something filters somewhere, it gets there slowly or faintly • *Traffic filtered into the city.* **filtration NOUN**

filth NOUN ❶ Filth is disgusting dirt and muck. ❷ People often use the word filth to refer to very bad language or to sexual material that is thought to be crude and offensive. **filthy ADJECTIVE**
● **SIMILAR WORDS:** ❶ dirt, muck,
● squalor

fin, fins **NOUN** a thin, flat structure on

the body of a fish, used to help guide it through the water.

final, finals **ADJECTIVE** ❶ last in a series or happening at the end of something. ❷ A decision that is final cannot be changed or questioned ▷ **NOUN** ❸ the last game or contest in a series which decides the overall winner ❹ IN PLURAL Finals are the last and most important examinations of a university or college course.
● **SIMILAR WORDS:** ❶ concluding,
● last

finale, finales [Said fin-**nah**-lee] **NOUN** the last section of a piece of music or show.

finalist, finalists **NOUN** a person taking part in the final of a competition.

finalize, finalizes, finalizing, finalized; also spelt **finalise VERB** If you finalize something, you complete all the arrangements for it.

finally ADVERB If something finally happens, it happens after a long delay.
● **SIMILAR WORDS:** at last,
● eventually

finance, finances, financing, financed **VERB** ❶ To finance a project or a large purchase is to provide the money for it ▷ **NOUN** ❷ Finance for something is the money or loans used to pay for it. ❸ Finance is also the management of money, loans, and investments.

financial ADJECTIVE relating to or involving money. **financially ADVERB**

financier, financiers **NOUN** a person who deals with the finance for large business concerns.

finch, finches **NOUN** a small bird with a short strong beak.

find, finds, finding, found **VERB** ❶ If you find someone or something, you discover them, either as a result of searching or by coming across them unexpectedly. ❷ If you find that something is the case, you become aware of it or realize it • *I found my fists were clenched.* ❸ Something that is found in a particular place typically lives or exists there. ❹ When a court or jury finds a person guilty or not guilty, they decide that the person is guilty or innocent • *He was found guilty and sentenced to life imprisonment.* ▷ **NOUN** ❺ If you describe something or someone as a find, you mean that you have recently discovered them and they are valuable or useful. **finder NOUN**

find out VERB ❶ If you find out something, you learn or discover something that you did not know. ❷ If you find someone out, you discover that they have been doing something they should not have been doing.
● **SIMILAR WORDS:** ❶ come
● across, discover

findings PLURAL NOUN Someone's findings are the conclusions they reach as a result of investigation.

fine, finer, finest; fines, fining, fined **ADJECTIVE** ❶ very good or very beautiful • *a fine school* • *fine clothes.* ❷ satisfactory or suitable • *Pasta dishes are fine if not served with a rich sauce.* ❸ very narrow or thin. ❹ A fine detail, adjustment, or distinction is very delicate, exact, or subtle.

a b c d e f g h i j k l m n o p q r s t u v w x y z

⑤ When the weather is fine, it is not raining and is bright or sunny ▷ **NOUN** **⑥** a sum of money paid as a punishment ▷ **VERB** **⑦** Someone who is fined has to pay a sum of money as a punishment.

finery **NOUN** Finery is very beautiful clothing and jewellery.

finesse [Said fin-ness] **NOUN** If you do something with finesse, you do it with skill and subtlety.

finger, fingers, fingering, fingered **NOUN** **①** Your fingers are the four long jointed parts of your hands, sometimes including the thumbs ▷ **VERB** **②** If you finger something you feel it with your fingers.

fingernail, fingernails **NOUN** Your fingernails are the hard coverings at the ends of your fingers.

fingerprint, fingerprints **NOUN** a mark made showing the pattern on the skin at the tip of a person's finger.

finish, finishes, finishing, finished **VERB** **①** When you finish something, you reach the end of it and complete it. **②** When something finishes, it ends or stops ▷ **NOUN** **③** The finish of something is the end or last part of it. **④** (D & T) The finish that something has is the texture or appearance of its surface • *a healthy, glossy finish*.

● **SIMILAR WORDS:** **①** complete,
● conclude, end **③** close,
● conclusion, end

finite [Said fie-nite] **ADJECTIVE** having a particular size or limit which cannot be increased • *There's only finite money to spend.*

Finn, Finns **NOUN** someone who comes from Finland.

Finnish **ADJECTIVE** **①** belonging or relating to Finland ▷ **NOUN** **②** Finnish is the main language spoken in Finland.

fir, firs **NOUN** a tall pointed evergreen tree that has thin needle-like leaves and produces cones.

fire, fires, firing, fired **NOUN** **①** Fire is the flames produced when something burns. **②** a pile or mass of burning material. **③** a piece of equipment that is used as a heater • *a gas fire*. ▷ **VERB** **④** If you fire a weapon or fire a bullet, you operate the weapon so that the bullet or missile is released. **⑤** If you fire questions at someone, you ask a lot of questions quickly. **⑥** INFORMAL If an employer fires someone, he or she dismisses that person from their job ▷ **PHRASE** **⑦** If someone **opens fire**, they start shooting.

firearm, firearms **NOUN** a gun.

fire brigade, fire brigades **NOUN** the organization which has the job of putting out fires.

fire engine, fire engines **NOUN** a large vehicle that carries equipment for putting out fires.

fire escape, fire escapes **NOUN** an emergency exit or staircase for use if there is a fire.

fire extinguisher, fire extinguishers **NOUN** a metal cylinder containing water or foam for spraying onto a fire.

firefighter, firefighters **NOUN** a person whose job is to put out fires

▷ SPELLING NOTE: *Elaine and Emily shout EE when they mEEt to grEEt each other (-ee-)*

and rescue trapped people.

firefly, fireflies NOUN an insect that glows in the dark.

fireplace, fireplaces NOUN the opening beneath a chimney where a fire can be lit.

fireproof ADJECTIVE resistant to fire.

fire station, fire stations NOUN a building where fire engines are kept and where firefighters wait to be called out.

firework, fireworks NOUN a small container of gunpowder and other chemicals which explodes and produces coloured sparks or smoke when lit.

firing squad, firing squads NOUN a group of soldiers ordered to shoot a person condemned to death.

firm, firmer, firmest; firms ADJECTIVE ❶ Something that is firm does not move easily when pressed or pushed, or when weight is put on it. ❷ A firm grasp or push is one with controlled force or pressure. ❸ A firm decision is definite. ❹ Someone who is firm behaves with authority that shows they will not change their mind ▷ NOUN ❺ a business selling or producing something. **firmly** ADVERB **firmness** NOUN

first ADJECTIVE ❶ done or in existence before anything else. ❷ more important than anything else • *Her cheese won first prize.* ▷ ADVERB ❸ done or occurring before anything else ▷ NOUN ❹ something that has never happened or been done before. **firstly** ADVERB

● SIMILAR WORDS: ❷ chief,
● foremost, principal

first aid NOUN First aid is medical treatment given to an injured person.

first class ADJECTIVE
❶ Something that is first class is of the highest quality or standard.
❷ First-class accommodation on a train, aircraft, or ship is the best and most expensive type of accommodation. ❸ First-class postage is quick but more expensive.

first-hand ADJECTIVE First-hand knowledge or experience is gained directly rather than from books or other people.

First Lady, First Ladies NOUN The First Lady of a country is the wife of a president.

first person NOUN (ENGLISH) In English grammar, the first person is the 'I' or 'we' form of the pronoun or the verb.

first-person narrator NOUN (ENGLISH) a first-person narrator is the principal character in a story and uses the pronoun *I*.

first-rate ADJECTIVE excellent.

fiscal ADJECTIVE involving government or public money, especially taxes.
● WORD HISTORY: from Latin *fiscus*
● meaning 'money-bag' or 'treasury'

fish, fishes, fishing, fished NOUN ❶ a cold-blooded creature living in water that has a spine, gills, fins, and a scaly skin. ❷ Fish is the flesh of fish eaten as food ▷ VERB ❸ To fish is to try to catch fish for food or sport. ❹ If you fish for information, you try to get it in

a
b
c
d
e
f
g
h
i
j
k
l
m
n
o
p
q
r
s
t
u
v
w
x
y
z

▷ SPELLING NOTE: *'i' before 'e' except after 'c'*

an indirect way. **fishing** NOUN
fisherman NOUN

- **USAGE NOTE:** The plural of the
- noun *fish* can be either *fish* or *fishes*,
- but *fish* is more common

fishery, fisheries NOUN an area of
the sea where fish are caught
commercially.

fishmonger, fishmongers NOUN a
shopkeeper who sells fish; also the
shop itself.

fishy, fishier, fishiest ADJECTIVE
❶ smelling of fish. **❷** INFORMAL
suspicious or doubtful • *He spotted
something fishy going on.*

fission [rhymes with **mission**] NOUN
❶ Fission is the splitting of something
into parts. **❷** Fission is also nuclear
fission.

fissure, fissures NOUN a deep crack
in rock.

fist, fists NOUN a hand with the
fingers curled tightly towards the
palm.

fit, fits, fitting, fitted; fitter, fittest
VERB ❶ Something that fits is the
right shape or size for a particular
person or position. **❷** If you fit
something somewhere, you put it
there carefully or securely • *Very
carefully he fitted the files inside the
compartment.* **❸** If something fits a
particular situation, person, or thing, it
is suitable or appropriate • *a sentence
that fitted the crime.* ▷ NOUN **❹** The
fit of something is how it fits • *This
bolt must be a good fit.* **❺** If someone
has a fit, their muscles suddenly start
contracting violently and they may
lose consciousness. **❻** A fit of
laughter, coughing, anger, or panic is a

sudden uncontrolled outburst
▷ ADJECTIVE **❼** good enough or
suitable • *Housing fit for frail elderly
people.* **❽** Someone who is fit is
healthy and has strong muscles as a
result of regular exercise. **fitness**
NOUN

- **SIMILAR WORDS: ❸** match, suit
- **❺** convulsion, seizure, spasm

fitful ADJECTIVE happening at
irregular intervals and not continuous
• *a fitful breeze.* **fitfully** ADVERB

fitter, fitters NOUN a person who
assembles or installs machinery.

fitting, fittings ADJECTIVE **❶** right
or suitable • *a fitting reward for his
efforts.* ▷ NOUN **❷** a small part that is
fixed to a piece of equipment or
furniture. **❸** If you have a fitting, you
try on a garment that is being made to
see if it fits properly.

five the number 5.

fix, fixes, fixing, fixed VERB **❶** If you
fix something somewhere, you attach
it or put it there securely. **❷** If you fix
something broken, you mend it. **❸** If
you fix your attention on something,
you concentrate on it. **❹** If you fix
something, you make arrangements
for it • *The opening party is fixed for the
24th September.* **❺** INFORMAL To fix
something is to arrange the outcome
unfairly or dishonestly ▷ NOUN
❻ INFORMAL something that has been
unfairly or dishonestly arranged.
❼ INFORMAL If you are in a fix, you are
in a difficult situation. **❽** an injection
of a drug such as heroin. **fixed**
ADJECTIVE **fixedly** ADVERB

- **SIMILAR WORDS: ❷** mend, repair

fixation, fixations NOUN an extreme

and obsessive interest in something.

fixture, fixtures NOUN ❶ a piece of furniture or equipment that is fixed into position in a house. ❷ a sports event due to take place on a particular date.

fizz, fizzes, fizzing, fizzed VERB Something that fizzes makes a hissing sound.

fizzle, fizzles, fizzling, fizzled VERB Something that fizzles makes a weak hissing or spitting sound.

fizzy, fizzier, fizziest ADJECTIVE Fizzy drinks have carbon dioxide in them to make them bubbly.

fjord, fjords [Said fee-**ord**]; also spelt **fiord** NOUN a long narrow inlet of the sea between very high cliffs, especially in Norway.
● WORD HISTORY: a Norwegian
● word

flab NOUN Flab is large amounts of surplus fat on someone's body.

flabbergasted ADJECTIVE extremely surprised.

flabby, flabbier, flabbiest ADJECTIVE Someone who is flabby is rather fat and unfit, with loose flesh on their body.

flag, flags, flagging, flagged NOUN ❶ a rectangular or square cloth which has a particular colour and design, and is used as the symbol of a nation or as a signal ▷ VERB ❷ If you or your spirits flag, you start to lose energy or enthusiasm.

flagrant [Said **flay**-grant] ADJECTIVE very shocking and bad in an obvious way • He was guilty of a

flagrant defiance of the rules.

flagship, flagships NOUN ❶ a ship carrying the commander of the fleet. ❷ the most modern or impressive product or asset of an organization.

flail, flails, flailing, flailed VERB If someone's arms or legs flail about, they move in a wild, uncontrolled way.

flair NOUN Flair is a natural ability to do something well or stylishly.

flak NOUN ❶ Flak is anti-aircraft fire. ❷ If you get flak for doing something, you get a lot of severe criticism.
● WORD HISTORY: from the first
● letters of the parts of German
● Fliegerabwehrkanone meaning
● 'anti-aircraft gun'

flake, flakes, flaking, flaked NOUN ❶ a small thin piece of something ▷ VERB ❷ When something such as paint flakes, small thin pieces of it come off. **flaky** ADJECTIVE flaked ADJECTIVE

flamboyant ADJECTIVE showy and confident, or behaving in a very showy and confident way. **flamboyance** NOUN

flame, flames NOUN ❶ a flickering tongue or blaze of fire. ❷ A flame of passion, desire, or anger is a sudden strong feeling.

flamenco NOUN Flamenco is a type of very lively, fast Spanish dancing, accompanied by guitar music.

flamingo, flamingos or flamingoes NOUN a long-legged wading bird with pink feathers and a long neck.

flammable ADJECTIVE likely to catch fire and burn easily.

▷ SPELLING NOTE: an ELegant angEL (angel)

● **USAGE NOTE:** Although *flammable*
● and *inflammable* both mean 'likely
● to catch fire', *flammable* is used
● more often as people sometimes
● think that *inflammable* means 'not
● likely to catch fire'

flan, flans **NOUN** an open sweet or
savoury tart with a pastry or cake base.

flank, flanks, flanking, flanked **NOUN**
❶ the side of an animal between the
ribs and the hip ▷ **VERB** ❷ Someone
or something that is flanked by a
particular thing or person has them at
their side • *flanked by four bodyguards.*

flannel, flannels **NOUN** ❶ Flannel is
a lightweight woollen fabric. ❷ a
small square of towelling, used for
washing yourself. In Australian English
it is called a **washer**.

flap, flaps, flapping, flapped **VERB**
❶ Something that flaps moves up and
down or from side to side with a
snapping sound ▷ **NOUN** ❷ a loose
piece of something such as paper or
skin that is attached at one edge.

flare, flares, flaring, flared **NOUN** ❶ a
device that produces a brightly
coloured flame, used especially as an
emergency signal ▷ **VERB** ❷ If a fire
flares, it suddenly burns much more
vigorously. ❸ If violence or a conflict
flares or flares up, it suddenly starts or
becomes more serious.

flash, flashes, flashing, flashed **NOUN**
❶ a sudden short burst of light
▷ **VERB** ❷ If a light flashes, it shines
for a very short period, often
repeatedly. ❸ Something that flashes
past moves or happens so fast that
you almost miss it. ❹ If you flash
something, you show it briefly

• *Michael Jackson flashed his face at the
crowd.* ▷ **PHRASE** ❺ Something that
happens **in a flash** happens suddenly
and lasts a very short time.

flashback, flashbacks **NOUN** a
scene in a film, play, or book that
returns to events in the past.

flashlight, flashlights **NOUN** a
large, powerful torch.

flashy, flashier, flashiest **ADJECTIVE**
expensive and fashionable in
appearance, in a vulgar way • *flashy
clothes.*

flask, flasks **NOUN** a bottle used for
carrying alcoholic or hot drinks around
with you.

flat, flats; flats, flatting, flatted; flatter,
flattest **NOUN** ❶ a self-contained set
of rooms, usually on one level, for
living in. ❷ In music, a flat is a note or
key a semitone lower than that
described by the same letter. It is
represented by the symbol (♭)
▷ **VERB** ❸ In Australian and New
Zealand English, to flat is to live in a
flat • *flatting in London.* ▷ **ADJECTIVE**
❹ Something that is flat is level and
smooth. ❺ A flat object is not very tall
or deep • *a low flat building.* ❻ A flat
tyre or ball has not got enough air in it.
❼ A flat battery has lost its electrical
charge. ❽ A flat refusal or denial is
complete and firm. ❾ Something that
is flat is without emotion or interest.
❿ A flat rate or price is fixed and the
same for everyone • *The company
charges a flat fee for its advice.* ⓫ A
musical instrument or note that is flat
is slightly too low in pitch ▷ **ADVERB**
⓬ Something that is done in a
particular time flat, takes exactly that
time • *They would find them in two*

minutes flat. **flatly** ADVERB **flatness** NOUN
● SIMILAR WORDS: ❸ even, level

flat character NOUN (ENGLISH) A flat character is a character in a story who plays a minor role, does not seem complicated or realistic, and does not undergo any kind of change during the story.

flatfish NOUN a sea fish with a wide flat body, such as a plaice or sole.

flathead, flatheads NOUN a common Australian edible fish.

flatten, flattens, flattening, flattened VERB If you flatten something or if it flattens, it becomes flat or flatter.

flatter, flatters, flattering, flattered VERB ❶ If you flatter someone, you praise them in an exaggerated way, either to please them or to persuade them to do something. ❷ If you are flattered by something, it makes you feel pleased and important • *He was very flattered because she liked him.* ❸ If you flatter yourself that something is the case, you believe, perhaps mistakenly, something good about yourself or your abilities. ❹ Something that flatters you makes you appear more attractive.
flattering ADJECTIVE
● SIMILAR WORDS: ❶ butter up, praise

flattery NOUN Flattery is flattering words or behaviour.

flatting PHRASE In New Zealand English, to **go flatting** is to leave home and live with others in a shared house or flat.

flatulence NOUN Flatulence is the uncomfortable state of having too much gas in your stomach or intestine.

flaunt, flaunts, flaunting, flaunted VERB If you flaunt your possessions or talents, you display them too obviously or proudly.
● USAGE NOTE: Be careful not to confuse *flaunt* with *flout*, which means 'disobey'

flautist, flautists NOUN someone who plays the flute.

flavour, flavours, flavouring, flavoured NOUN ❶ (D&T) The flavour of food is its taste. ❷ (D&T) The flavour of something is its distinctive characteristic or quality ▷ VERB ❸ (D&T) If you flavour food with a spice or herb, you add it to the food to give it a particular taste. **flavouring** NOUN

flaw, flaws NOUN ❶ a fault or mark in a piece of fabric or glass, or in a decorative pattern. ❷ a weak point or undesirable quality in a theory, plan, or person's character. **flawed** ADJECTIVE **flawless** ADJECTIVE
● SIMILAR WORDS: ❶ blemish, spot ❷ fault, weakness

flax NOUN Flax is a plant used for making rope and cloth.

flay, flays, flaying, flayed VERB ❶ To flay a dead animal is to cut off its skin. ❷ To flay someone is to criticize them severely • *The team's supporters will flay them alive for this performance.*

flea, fleas NOUN a small wingless jumping insect which feeds on blood.

fleck, flecks NOUN a small coloured mark or particle. **flecked** ADJECTIVE

▷ SPELLING NOTE: *A Rude Idiot Thought He Might Eat Toffee In Church (arithmetic)*

A B C D E F G H I J K L M N O P Q R S T U V W X Y Z

fled the past tense and past participle of **flee**.

fledgling, fledglings **NOUN** ❶ a young bird that is learning to fly ▷ **ADJECTIVE** ❷ Fledgling means new, or young and inexperienced • *the fledgling American President.*

flee, flees, fleeing, fled **VERB** To flee from someone or something is to run away from them.

fleece, fleeces, fleecing, fleeced **NOUN** ❶ A sheep's fleece is its coat of wool ▷ **VERB** ❷ To fleece someone is to swindle them or charge them too much money.

fleet, fleets **NOUN** a group of ships or vehicles owned by the same organization or travelling together.

fleeting **ADJECTIVE** lasting for a very short time.

Flemish **NOUN** Flemish is a language spoken in many parts of Belgium.

flesh **NOUN** ❶ Flesh is the soft part of the body. ❷ The flesh of a fruit or vegetable is the soft inner part that you eat. **fleshy ADJECTIVE**

flew the past tense of **fly**.

flex, flexes, flexing, flexed **NOUN** ❶ a length of wire covered in plastic, which carries electricity to an appliance ▷ **VERB** ❷ If you flex your muscles, you bend and stretch them.

flexible **ADJECTIVE** ❶ able to be bent easily without breaking. ❷ able to adapt to changing circumstances. **flexibility NOUN**

flick, flicks, flicking, flicked **VERB** ❶ If you flick something, you move it sharply with your finger. ❷ If something flicks somewhere, it moves with a short sudden movement • *His foot flicked forward.* ▷ **NOUN** ❸ a sudden quick movement or sharp touch with the finger • *a sideways flick of the head.*

flicker, flickers, flickering, flickered **VERB** ❶ If a light or a flame flickers, it shines and moves unsteadily ▷ **NOUN** ❷ a short unsteady light or movement of light • *the flicker of candlelight.* ❸ A flicker of a feeling is a very brief experience of it • *a flicker of interest.*

flight, flights **NOUN** ❶ a journey made by aeroplane. ❷ Flight is the action of flying or the ability to fly. ❸ Flight is also the act of running away. ❹ A flight of stairs or steps is a set running in a single direction.

flight attendant, flight attendants **NOUN** a person who looks after passengers on an aircraft.

flightless **ADJECTIVE** Flightless birds, such as penguins and ostriches, are birds that cannot fly.

flimsy, flimsier, flimsiest **ADJECTIVE** ❶ made of something very thin or weak and not providing much protection. ❷ not very convincing • *flimsy evidence.*

flinch, flinches, flinching, flinched **VERB** If you flinch, you make a sudden small movement in fear or pain.
● **SIMILAR WORDS:** cringe, recoil,
● wince

fling, flings, flinging, flung **VERB** ❶ If you fling something, you throw it with a lot of force ▷ **NOUN** ❷ a short period devoted to pleasure and free from any restrictions or rules.

flint, flints NOUN Flint is a hard greyish-black form of quartz. It produces a spark when struck with steel.

flip, flips, flipping, flipped VERB ❶ If you flip something, you turn or move it quickly and sharply • *He flipped over the first page.* ❷ If you flip something, you hit it sharply with your finger or thumb.

flippant ADJECTIVE showing an inappropriate lack of seriousness • *a flippant attitude to money.* **flippancy** NOUN

flipper, flippers NOUN ❶ one of the broad, flat limbs of sea animals, for example seals or penguins, used for swimming. ❷ Flippers are broad, flat pieces of rubber that you can attach to your feet to help you swim.

flirt, flirts, flirting, flirted VERB ❶ If you flirt with someone, you behave as if you are sexually attracted to them but without serious intentions. ❷ If you flirt with an idea, you consider it without seriously intending to do anything about it ▷ NOUN ❸ someone who often flirts with people. **flirtation** NOUN **flirtatious** ADJECTIVE

flit, flits, flitting, flitted VERB To flit somewhere is to fly or move there with quick, light movements.

float, floats, floating, floated VERB ❶ Something that floats is supported by water. ❷ Something that floats through the air moves along gently, supported by the air. ❸ If a company is floated, shares are sold to the public for the first time and the company

gains a listing on the stock exchange ▷ NOUN ❹ a light object that floats and either supports something or someone or regulates the level of liquid in a tank or cistern. ❺ In Australian English, a float is also a vehicle for transporting horses.

flock, flocks, flocking, flocked NOUN ❶ a group of birds, sheep, or goats ▷ VERB ❷ If people flock somewhere, they go there in large numbers.

flog, flogs, flogging, flogged VERB ❶ INFORMAL If you flog something, you sell it. ❷ To flog someone is to beat them with a whip or stick. **flogging** NOUN

flood, floods, flooding, flooded NOUN ❶ a large amount of water covering an area that is usually dry. ❷ A flood of something is a large amount of it suddenly occurring • *a flood of angry language.* ▷ VERB ❸ If liquid floods an area, or if a river floods, the water or liquid overflows, covering the surrounding area. ❹ If people or things flood into a place, they come there in large numbers • *Refugees have flooded into Austria in the last few months.*
 ● SIMILAR WORDS: ❶ deluge,
 ● spate, torrent ❷ stream, torrent

floodgates PHRASE To **open the floodgates** is suddenly to give a lot of people the opportunity to do something they could not do before.

floodlight, floodlights NOUN a very powerful outdoor lamp used to light up public buildings and sports grounds. **floodlit** ADJECTIVE

floor, floors, flooring, floored NOUN

❶ the part of a room you walk on.
❷ one of the levels in a building • *the top floor of a factory.* **❸** the ground at the bottom of a valley, forest, or the sea ▷ **VERB ❹** If a remark or question floors you, you are completely unable to deal with it or answer it.

floorboard, floorboards **NOUN** one of the long planks of wood from which a floor is made.

flop, flops, flopping, flopped **VERB ❶** If someone or something flops, they fall loosely and rather heavily. **❷** INFORMAL Something that flops fails ▷ **NOUN ❸** INFORMAL something that is completely unsuccessful.

floppy, floppier, floppiest **ADJECTIVE** tending to hang downwards in a rather loose way • *a floppy, outsize jacket.*
● **SIMILAR WORDS:** droopy, limp

floppy disk, floppy disks; *also spelt* **floppy disc NOUN** a small flexible magnetic disk on which computer data is stored.

floral ADJECTIVE patterned with flowers or made from flowers • *floral cotton dresses.*

florid [*rhymes with* **horrid**] **ADJECTIVE ❶** highly elaborate and extravagant • *florid language.* **❷** having a red face.

florist, florists **NOUN** a person or shop selling flowers.

floss NOUN Dental floss is soft silky threads or fibre which you use to clean between your teeth.

flotation, flotations **NOUN ❶** The flotation of a business is the issuing of

shares in order to launch it or to raise money. **❷** Flotation is the act of floating.

flotilla, flotillas *[Said flot-**til**-la]* **NOUN** a small fleet or group of small ships.
● **WORD HISTORY:** from Spanish
● *flotilla* meaning 'little fleet'

flotsam NOUN Flotsam is rubbish or wreckage floating at sea or washed up on the shore.

flounce, flounces, flouncing, flounced **VERB ❶** If you flounce somewhere, you walk there with exaggerated movements suggesting that you are feeling angry or impatient about something • *She flounced out of the office.* ▷ **NOUN ❷** a big frill around the bottom of a dress or skirt.

flounder, flounders, floundering, floundered **VERB ❶** To flounder is to struggle to move or stay upright, for example in water or mud. **❷** If you flounder in a conversation or situation, you find it difficult to decide what to say or do ▷ **NOUN ❸** a type of edible flatfish.

flour NOUN (D & T) Flour is a powder made from finely ground grain, usually wheat, and used for baking and cooking. **floured ADJECTIVE floury ADJECTIVE**

flourish, flourishes, flourishing, flourished **VERB ❶** Something that flourishes develops or functions successfully or healthily. **❷** If you flourish something, you wave or display it so that people notice it ▷ **NOUN ❸** a bold sweeping or waving movement.

flout, flouts, flouting, flouted **VERB** If

you flout a convention or law, you deliberately disobey it.

● **USAGE NOTE:** Be careful not to confuse *flout* with *flaunt*, which means 'display obviously'

flow, flows, flowing, flowed **VERB** ❶ If something flows, it moves or happens in a steady continuous stream ▷ **NOUN** ❷ A flow of something is a steady continuous movement of it; also the rate at which it flows • *a steady flow of complaints.*

flow chart, flow charts **NOUN** (D & T) a diagram showing the sequence of steps that lead to various results.

flower, flowers, flowering, flowered **NOUN** ❶ (SCIENCE) the part of a plant containing the reproductive organs from which the fruit or seeds develop. A **complete flower** is a flower that has all the flower parts, particularly the stamens and pistils; an **incomplete flower** is a flower without one or more of the main flower parts; a **perfect flower** is a flower that has both stamens and pistils ▷ **VERB** ❷ When a plant flowers, it produces flowers.

flowery **ADJECTIVE** Flowery language is full of elaborate expressions.

flown the past participle of **fly**.

flu **NOUN** Flu is an illness similar to a very bad cold, which causes headaches, sore throat, weakness, and aching muscles. Flu is short for 'influenza'.

fluctuate, fluctuates, fluctuating, fluctuated **VERB** Something that fluctuates is irregular and changeable

• *fluctuating between feeling well and not so well.*

flue, flues **NOUN** a pipe which takes fumes and smoke away from a stove or boiler.

fluent **ADJECTIVE** ❶ able to speak a foreign language correctly and without hesitation. ❷ able to express yourself clearly and without hesitation. **fluently** **ADVERB**

fluff, fluffs, fluffing, fluffed **NOUN** ❶ Fluff is soft, light, woolly threads or fibres bunched together ▷ **VERB** ❷ If you fluff something up or out, you brush or shake it to make it seem larger and lighter • *Fluff the rice up with a fork before serving.* **fluffy** **ADJECTIVE**

fluid, fluids **NOUN** ❶ a liquid ▷ **ADJECTIVE** ❷ Fluid movement is smooth and flowing. ❸ A fluid arrangement or plan is flexible and without a fixed structure. **fluidity** **NOUN**

fluke, flukes **NOUN** an accidental success or piece of good luck.

flung the past tense of **fling**.

fluorescent [Said floo-er-**ess**-nt] **ADJECTIVE** ❶ having a very bright appearance when light is shone on it, as if it is shining itself • *fluorescent yellow dye.* ❷ A fluorescent light is in the form of a tube and shines with a hard bright light.

fluoride **NOUN** Fluoride is a mixture of chemicals that is meant to prevent tooth decay.

flurry, flurries **NOUN** a short rush of activity or movement.

a
b
c
d
e
f
g
h
i
j
k
l
m
n
o
p
q
r
s
t
u
v
w
x
y
z

▷ SPELLING NOTE: *you'll brEAK that Electrical Aerial, Kitty (break)*

flush, flushes, flushing, flushed; flusher, flushest **NOUN** ❶ A flush is a rosy red colour • *The flowers are cream with a pink flush.* ❷ In cards, a flush is a hand all of one suit ▷ **VERB** ❸ If you flush, your face goes red. ❹ If you flush a toilet or something such as a pipe, you force water through it to clean it ▷ **ADJECTIVE** ❺ INFORMAL Someone who is flush has plenty of money. ❻ Something that is flush with a surface is level with it or flat against it.

flustered **ADJECTIVE** If you are flustered, you feel confused, nervous, and rushed.

flute, flutes **NOUN** a musical wind instrument consisting of a long metal tube with holes and keys. It is held sideways to the mouth and played by blowing across a hole in its side.

fluted **ADJECTIVE** decorated with long grooves.

flutter, flutters, fluttering, fluttered **VERB** ❶ If something flutters, it flaps or waves with small, quick movements ▷ **NOUN** ❷ If you are in a flutter, you are excited and nervous. ❸ INFORMAL A flutter is a small bet.

flux **NOUN** Flux is a state of constant change • *stability in a world of flux.*

fly, flies, flying, flew, flown **NOUN** ❶ an insect with two pairs of wings. ❷ The front opening on a pair of trousers is the fly or the flies. ❸ The fly or fly sheet of a tent is either a flap at the entrance or an outer layer providing protection from rain ▷ **VERB** ❹ When a bird, insect, or aircraft flies, it moves through the air. ❺ If someone or something flies, they

move or go very quickly. ❻ If you fly at someone or let fly at them, you attack or criticize them suddenly and aggressively. **flying ADJECTIVE OR NOUN flyer NOUN**

fly-fishing **NOUN** Fly-fishing is a method of fishing using imitation flies as bait.

flying fox, flying foxes **NOUN** ❶ a large bat that eats fruit, found in Australia and Africa. ❷ In Australia and New Zealand, a cable car used to carry people over rivers and gorges.

flying saucer, flying saucers **NOUN** a large disc-shaped spacecraft which some people claim to have seen.

flyover, flyovers **NOUN** a structure carrying one road over another at a junction or intersection.

foal, foals, foaling, foaled **NOUN** ❶ a young horse ▷ **VERB** ❷ When a female horse foals, she gives birth.

foam, foams, foaming, foamed **NOUN** ❶ Foam is a mass of tiny bubbles. ❷ D & T Foam is light spongy material used, for example, in furniture or packaging ▷ **VERB** ❸ When something foams, it forms a mass of small bubbles.
  ● **SIMILAR WORDS:** ❶ bubbles,
  ● froth

fob off, fobs off, fobbing off, fobbed off **VERB** INFORMAL If you fob someone off, you provide them with something that is not very good or not adequate.

focus, focuses or focusses, focusing or focussing, focused or focussed; focuses or foci **VERB** ❶ If you focus

Sidebar alphabet: A B C D E F G H I J K L M N O P Q R S T U V W X Y Z your eyes or an instrument on an object, you adjust them so that the image is clear ▷ **NOUN** ❷ The focus of something is its centre of attention • *The focus of the conversation had moved around during the meal.* **focal ADJECTIVE**

- **USAGE NOTE:** When you add the
- verb endings to *focus*, you can
- either add them straight to *focus*
- (*focuses, focusing, focused*), or you
- can put another *s* at the end of
- *focus* before adding the endings
- (*focusses, focussing, focussed*). Either
- way is correct, but the first way is
- much more common. The plural of
- the noun is either *focuses* or *foci*,
- but *focuses* is the commoner

fodder NOUN Fodder is food for farm animals or horses.

foe, foes **NOUN** an enemy.

foetus, foetuses [*Said fee-tus*]; *also spelt* **fetus NOUN** an unborn child or animal in the womb. **foetal ADJECTIVE**

fog, fogs, fogging, fogged **NOUN** ❶ Fog is a thick mist of water droplets suspended in the air ▷ **VERB** ❷ If glass fogs up, it becomes clouded with steam or condensation. **foggy ADJECTIVE**

foil, foils, foiling, foiled **VERB** ❶ If you foil someone's attempt at something, you prevent them from succeeding ▷ **NOUN** ❷ Foil is thin, paper-like sheets of metal used to wrap food. ❸ Something that is a good foil for something else contrasts with it and makes its good qualities more noticeable. ❹ a thin, light sword with a button on the tip, used in fencing.

foist, foists, foisting, foisted **VERB** If you foist something on someone, you force or impose it on them.

fold, folds, folding, folded **VERB** ❶ If you fold something, you bend it so that one part lies over another. ❷ INFORMAL If a business folds, it fails and closes down. ❸ In cooking, if you fold one ingredient into another, you mix it in gently ▷ **NOUN** ❹ a crease or bend in paper or cloth. ❺ a small enclosed area for sheep.

- **SIMILAR WORDS:** ❶ bend,
- crease, double over

folder, folders **NOUN** ❶ a thin piece of folded cardboard for keeping loose papers together. ❷ In computing, a folder is a named area of computer disk where you can group together files and subdirectories. It is also called a **directory**.

foliage NOUN Foliage is leaves and plants.

folk, folks **NOUN** ❶ Folk or folks are people ▷ **ADJECTIVE** ❷ Folk music, dance, or art is traditional or representative of the ordinary people of an area.

folklore NOUN Folklore is the traditional stories and beliefs of a community.

follicle, follicles **NOUN** a small sac or cavity in the body • *hair follicles.*

follow, follows, following, followed **VERB** ❶ If you follow someone, you move along behind them. If you follow a path or a sign, you move along in that direction. ❷ Something that follows a particular thing happens after it. ❸ Something that follows is true or logical as a result of something

a b c d e **f** g h i j k l m n o p q r s t u v w x y z

A
B
C
D
E
F
G
H
I
J
K
L
M
N
O
P
Q
R
S
T
U
V
W
X
Y
Z

else being the case • *Just because she is pretty, it doesn't follow that she can sing.* ❹ If you follow instructions or advice, you do what you are told. ❺ If you follow an explanation or the plot of a story, you understand each stage of it.

follower, followers **NOUN** The followers of a person or belief are the people who support them.
● **SIMILAR WORDS:** adherent,
● supporter

folly, follies **NOUN** Folly is a foolish act or foolish behaviour.
● **SIMILAR WORDS:** foolishness,
● stupidity

fond, fonder, fondest **ADJECTIVE**
❶ If you are fond of someone or something, you like them. ❷ A fond hope or belief is thought of with happiness but is unlikely to happen.
fondly ADVERB fondness NOUN
● **SIMILAR WORDS:** ❶ affectionate,
● loving

fondle, fondles, fondling, fondled **VERB** To fondle something is to stroke it affectionately.

font, fonts **NOUN** a large stone bowl in a church that holds the water for baptisms.

food, foods **NOUN** Food is any substance consumed by an animal or plant to provide energy.
● **SIMILAR WORDS:** fare,
● nourishment

food chain, food chains **NOUN** a series of living things which are linked because each one feeds on the next one in the series. For example, a plant may be eaten by a rabbit which may be eaten by a fox.

foodstuff, foodstuffs **NOUN** anything used for food.

food technology NOUN Food technology is the study of foods and what they consist of, and their effect on the body.

fool, fools, fooling, fooled **NOUN** ❶ someone who behaves in a silly or stupid way. ❷ a dessert made from fruit, eggs, cream, and sugar whipped together ▷ **VERB** ❸ If you fool someone, you deceive or trick them.

foolhardy ADJECTIVE foolish and involving too great a risk.

foolish ADJECTIVE very silly or unwise. **foolishly ADVERB foolishness NOUN**

foolproof ADJECTIVE Something that is foolproof is so well designed or simple to use that it cannot fail.

foot, feet **NOUN** ❶ the part of your body at the end of your leg. ❷ the bottom, base, or lower end of something • *the foot of the mountain.* ❸ a unit of length equal to 12 inches or about 30.5 centimetres. ❹ In poetry, a foot is the basic unit of rhythm containing two or three syllables ▷ **ADJECTIVE** ❺ A foot brake, pedal, or pump is operated by your foot.

footage NOUN Footage is a length of film • *library footage of prison riots.*

foot-and-mouth disease NOUN (SCIENCE) Foot-and-mouth disease is a serious infectious disease affecting cattle, sheep, pigs, and goats which causes swellings around the animal's hooves and mouth.

football, footballs **NOUN**

▷ SPELLING NOTE: *The government licenSes Schnapps (licenSes)*

① Football is any game in which the ball can be kicked, such as soccer, Australian Rules, rugby union, and American football. **②** a ball used in any of these games. **footballer NOUN**

foothills PLURAL NOUN Foothills are hills at the base of mountains.

foothold, footholds **NOUN ①** a place where you can put your foot when climbing. **②** a position from which further progress can be made.

footing NOUN ① Footing is a secure grip by or for your feet • *He missed his footing and fell flat.* **②** a footing is the basis or nature of a relationship or situation • *Steps to put the nation on a war footing.*

footman, footmen **NOUN** a male servant in a large house who wears uniform.

footnote, footnotes **NOUN** a note at the bottom of a page or an additional comment giving extra information.

footpath, footpaths **NOUN** a path for people to walk on.

footprint, footprints **NOUN** a mark left by a foot or shoe.

footstep, footsteps **NOUN** the sound or mark made by someone walking.

for PREPOSITION ① meant to be given to or used by a particular person, or done in order to help or benefit them • *private beaches for their exclusive use.* **②** 'For' is used when explaining the reason, cause, or purpose of something • *This is my excuse for going to Italy.* **③** You use 'for' to express a quantity, time, or

distance • *I'll play for ages* • *the only house for miles around.* **④** If you are for something, you support it or approve of it • *votes for or against independence.*

forage, forages, foraging, foraged **VERB** When a person or animal forages, they search for food.

foray, forays **NOUN ①** a brief attempt to do or get something • *her first foray into acting.* **②** an attack or raid by soldiers.

forbid, forbids, forbidding, forbade, forbidden **VERB** If you forbid someone to do something, you order them not to do it. **forbidden ADJECTIVE**

force, forces, forcing, forced **VERB ①** To force someone to do something is to make them do it. **②** To force something is to use violence or great strength to move or open it ▷ **NOUN ③** a pressure to do something, sometimes with the use of violence or great strength. **④** The force of something is its strength or power • *The force of the explosion shook buildings.* **⑤** a person or thing that has a lot of influence or effect • *She became the dominant force in tennis.* **⑥** an organized group of soldiers or police. **⑦** (SCIENCE) In physics, force is a pushing or pulling influence that changes a body from a state of rest to one of motion, or changes its rate of motion ▷ **PHRASE ⑧** A law or rule that is **in force** is currently valid and must be obeyed.
● **SIMILAR WORDS: ①** compel,
● drive, make

forceful ADJECTIVE powerful and convincing • *a forceful, highly political lawyer.* **forcefully ADVERB**

a
b
c
d
e
f
g
h
i
j
k
l
m
n
o
p
q
r
s
t
u
v
w
x
y
z

▷ SPELLING NOTE: *have a pIEce of pIE (piece)*

forceps PLURAL NOUN Forceps are a pair of long tongs or pincers used by a doctor or surgeon.

forcible ADJECTIVE ❶ involving physical force or violence. ❷ convincing and making a strong impression • *a forcible reminder.* **forcibly** ADVERB

ford, fords, fording, forded NOUN ❶ a shallow place in a river where it is possible to cross on foot or in a vehicle ▷ VERB ❷ To ford a river is to cross it on foot or in a vehicle.

fore PHRASE Someone or something that comes **to the fore** becomes important or popular.

forearm, forearms NOUN the part of your arm between your elbow and your wrist.

forebear, forebears NOUN Your forebears are your ancestors.

foreboding, forebodings NOUN a strong feeling of approaching disaster.

forecast, forecasts, forecasting, forecast or forecasted NOUN ❶ a prediction of what will happen, especially a statement about what the weather will be like ▷ VERB ❷ To forecast an event is to predict what will happen.

forecourt, forecourts NOUN an open area at the front of a petrol station or large building.

forefather, forefathers NOUN Your forefathers are your ancestors.

forefinger, forefingers NOUN the finger next to your thumb.

forefront NOUN The forefront of something is the most important and progressive part of it.

forego, foregoes, foregoing, forewent, foregone; *also spelt* **forgo** VERB If you forego something pleasant, you give it up or do not insist on having it.

foregoing a FORMAL PHRASE You can say **the foregoing** when talking about something that has just been said • *The foregoing discussion has highlighted the difficulties.*

foregone conclusion, foregone conclusions NOUN A foregone conclusion is a result or conclusion that is bound to happen.

foreground NOUN (ART) In a picture, the foreground is the part that seems nearest to you.

forehand, forehands NOUN OR ADJECTIVE a stroke in tennis, squash, or badminton made with the palm of your hand facing in the direction that you hit the ball.

forehead, foreheads NOUN the area at the front of your head, above your eyebrows and below your hairline.

foreign ADJECTIVE ❶ belonging to or involving countries other than your own • *foreign coins* • *foreign travel.* ❷ unfamiliar or uncharacteristic • *Such daft enthusiasm was foreign to him.* ❸ A foreign object has got into something, usually by accident, and should not be there • *a foreign object in my eye.* **foreigner** NOUN
  ● SIMILAR WORDS: ❷ alien,
  ● unfamiliar

foreman, foremen NOUN ❶ a person in charge of a group of workers, for example on a building site. ❷ The foreman of a jury is the

A B C D E F G H I J K L M N O P Q R S T U V W X Y Z

spokesman for the other jurors.

foremost ADJECTIVE The foremost of a group of things is the most important or the best.

forensic ADJECTIVE ❶ relating to or involving the scientific examination of objects involved in a crime. **❷** relating to or involving the legal profession.

forerunner, forerunners **NOUN** The forerunner of something is the person who first introduced or achieved it, or the first example of it.

foresee, foresees, foreseeing, foresaw, foreseen **VERB** If you foresee something, you predict or expect that it will happen. **foreseeable ADJECTIVE**

foresight NOUN Foresight is the ability to know what is going to happen in the future.

foreskin, foreskins **NOUN** A man's foreskin is the fold of skin covering the end of his penis.

forest, forests **NOUN** a large area of trees growing close together.

forestry NOUN Forestry is the study and work of growing and maintaining forests.

foretaste, foretastes **NOUN** a slight taste or experience of something in advance.

foretell, foretells, foretelling, foretold **VERB** If you foretell something, you predict that it will happen.

forever ADVERB permanently or continually.

forewarn, forewarns, forewarning,

forewarned VERB If you forewarn someone, you warn them in advance about something.

foreword, forewords **NOUN** an introduction in a book.

forfeit, forfeits, forfeiting, forfeited **VERB ❶** If you forfeit something, you have to give it up as a penalty ▷ **NOUN ❷** something that you have to give up or do as a penalty.

forge, forges, forging, forged **NOUN ❶** a place where a blacksmith works making metal goods by hand ▷ **VERB ❷** To forge metal is to hammer and bend it into shape while hot. **❸** To forge a relationship is to create a strong and lasting relationship. **❹** Someone who forges money, documents, or paintings makes illegal copies of them. **❺** To forge ahead is to progress quickly.

forgery, forgeries **NOUN** Forgery is the crime of forging money, documents, or paintings; also something that has been forged. **forger NOUN**

forget, forgets, forgetting, forgot, forgotten **VERB ❶** If you forget something, you fail to remember or think about it. **❷** If you forget yourself, you behave in an unacceptable, uncontrolled way. **forgetful ADJECTIVE**

forget-me-not, forget-me-nots **NOUN** a small plant with tiny blue flowers.

forgive, forgives, forgiving, forgave, forgiven **VERB** If you forgive someone for doing something bad, you stop feeling angry and resentful towards them. **forgiving ADJECTIVE**

a b c d e **f** g h i j k l m n o p q r s t u v w x y z

▷ SPELLING NOTE: *I went to see (C) the doctor's new practiCe (practice)*

● **SIMILAR WORDS:** absolve, excuse,
● pardon

forgiveness NOUN the act of
forgiving.

forgo another spelling of **forego**.

fork, forks, forking, forked **NOUN** ❶ a
pronged instrument used for eating
food. ❷ a large garden tool with three
or four prongs. ❸ a y-shaped junction
or division in a road, river, or branch
▷ **VERB** ❹ To fork something is to
move or turn it with a fork.
fork out VERB INFORMAL If you fork
out for something, you pay for it, often
unwillingly.

forlorn ADJECTIVE ❶ lonely,
unhappy and pitiful. ❷ desperate and
without any expectation of success • *a
forlorn fight for a draw.* **forlornly
ADVERB**

form, forms, forming, formed **NOUN**
❶ A particular form of something is a
type or kind of it • *a new form of
weapon.* ❷ The form of something is
the shape or pattern of something • *a
brooch in the form of a bright green
lizard.* ❸ a sheet of paper with
questions and spaces for you to fill in
the answers. ❹ a class in a school
▷ **VERB** ❺ The things that form
something are the things it consists of
• *events that were to form the basis of
her novel.* ❻ When someone forms
something or when it forms, it is
created, organized, or started.

formal ADJECTIVE ❶ correct,
serious, and conforming to accepted
conventions • *a very formal letter of
apology.* ❷ official and publicly
recognized • *the first formal agreement
of its kind.* **formally ADVERB**

formaldehyde *[Said for-**mal**-di-
hide]* **NOUN** Formaldehyde is a
poisonous, strong-smelling gas, used
for preserving specimens in biology.

formality, formalities **NOUN** an
action or process that is carried out as
part of an official procedure.

format, formats **NOUN** the way in
which something is arranged or
presented.

formation, formations **NOUN**
❶ The formation of something is the
process of developing and creating it.
❷ the pattern or shape of something.

formative ADJECTIVE having an
important and lasting influence on
character and development • *the
formative days of his young manhood.*

former ADJECTIVE ❶ happening or
existing before now or in the past • *a
former tennis champion.* ▷ **NOUN**
❷ You use 'the former' to refer to the
first of two things just mentioned • *If I
had to choose between happiness and
money, I would have the former.*
formerly ADVERB

formidable ADJECTIVE very
difficult to deal with or overcome, and
therefore rather frightening or
impressive • *formidable enemies.*
● **SIMILAR WORDS:** daunting,
● intimidating

formula, formulae or formulas
NOUN ❶ (MATHS) a group of letters,
numbers, and symbols which stand
for a mathematical or scientific rule.
❷ (SCIENCE) a list of quantities of
substances that when mixed make
another substance, for example in
chemistry. ❸ a plan or set of rules for
dealing with a particular problem • *my*

▷ SPELLING NOTE: *You must practiSe your Ss (practise)*

secret formula for keeping in trim.

formulate, formulates, formulating, formulated **VERB** If you formulate a plan or thought, you create it and express it in a clear and precise way.

fornication **NOUN** FORMAL Fornication is the sin of having sex with someone when you are not married to them.

forsake, forsakes, forsaking, forsook, forsaken **VERB** To forsake someone or something is to give up or abandon them.

fort, forts **NOUN** **①** a strong building built for defence ▷ **PHRASE** **②** If you **hold the fort** for someone, you manage their affairs while they are away.

forte, fortes [Said **for**-tay] **ADVERB** **①** (MUSIC) In music, forte is an instruction to play or sing something loudly **NOUN** **②** If something is your forte, you are particularly good at doing it.
● **SIMILAR WORDS:** **②** speciality,
● strong point

forth **ADVERB** **①** out and forward from a starting place • *Christopher Columbus set forth on his epic voyage of discovery.* **②** into view • *he brought forth a slim volume of his newly published verse.*

forthcoming **ADJECTIVE**
① planned to happen soon • *their forthcoming holiday.* **②** given or made available • *Medical aid might be forthcoming.* **③** willing to give information • *He was not too forthcoming about this.*

forthright **ADJECTIVE** Someone

who is forthright is direct and honest about their opinions and feelings.

fortification, fortifications **NOUN** Fortifications are buildings, walls, and ditches used to protect a place.

fortissimo (MUSIC) In music, fortissimo is an instruction to play or sing something very loudly.

fortitude **NOUN** Fortitude is calm and patient courage.

fortnight, fortnights **NOUN** a period of two weeks. **fortnightly** **ADVERB OR ADJECTIVE**

fortress, fortresses **NOUN** a castle or well-protected town built for defence.

fortuitous [Said for-**tyoo**-it-uss] **ADJECTIVE** happening by chance or good luck • *a fortuitous winning goal.*

fortunate **ADJECTIVE** **①** Someone who is fortunate is lucky. **②** Something that is fortunate brings success or advantage. **fortunately** **ADVERB**

fortune, fortunes **NOUN** **①** Fortune or good fortune is good luck. **②** A fortune is a large amount of money ▷ **PHRASE** **③** If someone **tells your fortune**, they predict your future.

forty, forties the number 40. **fortieth** **ADJECTIVE**

forum, forums **NOUN** **①** a place or meeting in which people can exchange ideas and discuss public issues. **②** a square in Roman towns where people met to discuss things.

forward, forwards, forwarding, forwarded **ADVERB OR ADJECTIVE** **①** Forward or forwards means in the

front or towards the front • *A photographer moved forward to capture the moment.* ❷ Forward means in or towards a future time • *a positive atmosphere of looking forward and making fresh starts.* ❸ Forward or forwards also means developing or progressing • *The new committee would push forward government plans.*
▷ **ADVERB** ❹ If someone or something is put forward, they are suggested as being suitable for something ▷ **VERB** ❺ If you forward a letter that you have received, you send it on to the person to whom it is addressed at their new address
▷ **NOUN** ❻ In a game such as football or hockey, a forward is a player in an attacking position.
● **SIMILAR WORDS:** ❸ ahead, on

fossick, fossicks, fossicking, fossicked **VERB** ❶ In Australian and New Zealand English, to fossick for gold nuggets or precious stones is to look for them in rivers or old mines. ❷ In Australian and New Zealand English, to fossick for something is to search for it.

fossil, fossils **NOUN** (SCIENCE) the remains or impression of an animal or plant from a previous age, preserved in rock. **fossilize VERB**

fossil fuel, fossil fuels **NOUN** (GEOGRAPHY) Fossil fuels are fuels such as coal, oil, and natural gas, which have been formed by rotting animals and plants from millions of years ago.

foster, fosters, fostering, fostered **VERB** ❶ If someone fosters a child, they are paid to look after the child for a period, but do not become its legal parent. ❷ If you foster something such as an activity or an idea, you help its development and growth by encouraging people to do or think it • *to foster and maintain this goodwill.* **foster child NOUN foster home NOUN foster parent NOUN**

fought the past tense and past participle of **fight**.

foul, fouler, foulest; fouls, fouling, fouled **ADJECTIVE** ❶ Something that is foul is very unpleasant, especially because it is dirty, wicked, or obscene ▷ **VERB** ❷ To foul something is to make it dirty, especially with faeces • *Dogs must not be allowed to foul the pavement.* ▷ **NOUN** ❸ In sport, a foul is an act of breaking the rules.

found, founds, founding, founded ❶ Found is the past tense and past participle of **find**. **VERB** ❷ If someone founds an organization or institution, they start it and set it up.

foundation, foundations **NOUN** ❶ The foundation of a belief or way of life is the basic ideas or attitudes on which it is built. ❷ a solid layer of concrete or bricks in the ground, on which a building is built to give it a firm base. ❸ an organization set up by money left in someone's will for research or charity.

founder, founders, foundering, foundered **NOUN** ❶ The founder of an institution or organization is the person who sets it up ▷ **VERB** ❷ If something founders, it fails.

foundry, foundries **NOUN** a factory where metal is melted and cast.

fountain, fountains **NOUN** an ornamental structure consisting of a

▷ SPELLING NOTE: *LEarn the principLEs (principle)*

jet of water forced into the air by a pump.

fountain pen, fountain pens NOUN a pen which is supplied with ink from a container inside the pen.

four, fours ❶ the number 4 PHRASE ❷ If you are **on all fours**, you are on your hands and knees.

four-poster, four-posters NOUN a bed with a tall post at each corner supporting a canopy and curtains.

fourteen the number 14. **fourteenth** ADJECTIVE

fourth The fourth item in a series is the one counted as number four.

fowl, fowls NOUN a bird such as chicken or duck that is kept or hunted for its meat or eggs.

fox, foxes, foxing, foxed NOUN ❶ a dog-like wild animal with reddish-brown fur, a pointed face and ears, and a thick tail ▷ VERB ❷ If something foxes you, it is too confusing or puzzling for you to understand.

foxglove, foxgloves NOUN a plant with a tall spike of purple or white trumpet-shaped flowers.

foxhound, foxhounds NOUN a dog trained for hunting foxes.

foyer, foyers [Said *foy-ay*] NOUN a large area just inside the main doors of a cinema, hotel, or public building.

fracas [Said *frak-ah*] NOUN a rough noisy quarrel or fight.

fraction, fractions NOUN ❶ (MATHS) In arithmetic, a fraction is a part of a whole number. A **proper**

fraction is a fraction in which the number above the line is lower than the number below it; an **improper fraction** has the greater number above the line • *¾ is a proper fraction.* ❷ a tiny proportion or amount of something • *an area a fraction of the size of London.* **fractional** ADJECTIVE **fractionally** ADVERB

fractious ADJECTIVE When small children are fractious, they become upset or angry very easily, often because they are very tired.

fracture, fractures, fracturing, fractured NOUN ❶ a crack or break in something, especially a bone ▷ VERB ❷ If something fractures, it breaks.

fragile ADJECTIVE easily broken or damaged • *fragile glass* • *a fragile relationship.* **fragility** NOUN
  ● SIMILAR WORDS: breakable, ● delicate, frail

fragment, fragments, fragmenting, fragmented NOUN ❶ a small piece or part of something ▷ VERB ❷ If something fragments, it breaks into small pieces or different parts. **fragmentation** NOUN **fragmented** ADJECTIVE

fragmentary ADJECTIVE made up of small pieces, or parts that are not connected • *fragmentary notes in a journal.*

fragrance, fragrances NOUN a sweet or pleasant smell.
  ● SIMILAR WORDS: aroma, ● perfume, scent

fragrant ADJECTIVE Something that is fragrant smells sweet or pleasant.

a
b
c
d
e
f
g
h
i
j
k
l
m
n
o
p
q
r
s
t
u
v
w
x
y
z

▷ SPELLING NOTE: *Psychiatrists Seldom Yell Callously Hard (psychiatrist)*

frail, frailer, frailest **ADJECTIVE**
❶ Someone who is frail is not strong or healthy. ❷ Something that is frail is easily broken or damaged. **frailty NOUN**

frame, frames, framing, framed
NOUN ❶ the structure surrounding a door, window, or picture. ❷ an arrangement of connected bars over which something is built. ❸ The frames of a pair of glasses are the wire or plastic parts that hold the lenses. ❹ Your frame is your body • *his large frame.* ❺ one of the many separate photographs of which a cinema film is made up ▷ **VERB** ❻ To frame a picture is to put it into a frame • *I've framed pictures I've pulled out of magazines.* ❼ The language something is framed in is the language used to express it.

framework, frameworks **NOUN**
❶ (D & T) a structure acting as a support or frame. ❷ a set of rules, beliefs, or ideas which you use to decide what to do.

franc, francs **NOUN** the main unit of currency in Switzerland. A franc is worth 100 centimes.

franchise, franchises **NOUN** ❶ The franchise is the right to vote in an election • *a franchise that gave the vote to less than 2% of the population.* ❷ the right given by a company to someone to allow them to sell its goods or services.

frank, franker, frankest **ADJECTIVE** If you are frank, you say things in an open and honest way. **frankly ADVERB frankness NOUN**
● **SIMILAR WORDS:** candid, honest, ● open

frantic ADJECTIVE If you are frantic, you behave in a wild, desperate way because you are anxious or frightened. **frantically ADVERB**

fraternal ADJECTIVE 'Fraternal' is used to describe friendly actions and feelings between groups of people • *an affectionate fraternal greeting.*

fraternity, fraternities **NOUN**
❶ Fraternity is friendship between groups of people. ❷ a group of people with something in common • *the golfing fraternity.*

fraud, frauds **NOUN** ❶ Fraud is the crime of getting money by deceit or trickery. ❷ something that deceives people in an illegal or immoral way. ❸ Someone who is not what they pretend to be.

fraudulent ADJECTIVE dishonest or deceitful • *fraudulent cheques.*

fraught ADJECTIVE If something is fraught with problems or difficulties, it is full of them • *Modern life was fraught with hazards.*

fray, frays, fraying, frayed **VERB** ❶ If cloth or rope frays, its threads or strands become worn and it is likely to tear or break ▷ **NOUN** ❷ a fight or argument.

freak, freaks **NOUN** ❶ someone whose appearance or behaviour is very unusual ▷ **ADJECTIVE OR NOUN** ❷ A freak event is very unusual and unlikely to happen • *a freak allergy to peanuts.*

freckle, freckles **NOUN** Freckles are small, light brown spots on someone's skin, especially their face. **freckled ADJECTIVE**

▷ SPELLING NOTE: *the QUeen stood on the QUay (quay)*

free, freer, freest; frees, freeing, freed
ADJECTIVE ❶ not controlled or
limited • *the free flow of aid* • *free
trade.* ❷ Someone who is free is no
longer a prisoner. ❸ To be free of
something unpleasant is not to have it
• *She wanted her aunt's life to be free of
worry.* ❹ If someone is free, they are
not busy or occupied. If a place, seat,
or machine is free, it is not occupied
or not being used • *Are you free for
dinner?* ❺ If something is free, you
can have it without paying for it
▷ **VERB** ❻ If you free someone or
something that is imprisoned,
fastened, or trapped, you release
them.
● **SIMILAR WORDS:** ❷ at liberty,
● liberated ❺ complimentary, gratis
● ❻ liberate, release

freedom NOUN ❶ If you have the
freedom to do something, you have
the scope or are allowed to do it • *We
have the freedom to decide our own
futures.* ❷ When prisoners gain their
freedom, they escape or are released.
❸ When there is freedom from
something unpleasant, people are not
affected by it • *freedom from guilt.*
● **SIMILAR WORDS:** ❷ liberty,
● release

freehold, freeholds **NOUN** the right
to own a house or piece of land for life
without conditions.

freelance ADJECTIVE OR ADVERB
A freelance journalist or photographer
is not employed by one organization,
but is paid for each job he or she
does.

freely ADVERB Freely means without
restriction • *the pleasure of being able
to walk about freely.*

free-range ADJECTIVE Free-range
eggs are laid by hens that can move
and feed freely on an area of open
ground.

freestyle NOUN Freestyle refers to
sports competitions, especially
swimming, in which competitors can
use any style or method.

freeway, freeways **NOUN** In
Australia, South Africa, and the United
States, a road-designed for fast-
moving traffic.

free will PHRASE If you do
something **of your own free will**,
you do it by choice and not because
you are forced to.

freeze, freezes, freezing, froze, frozen
VERB ❶ **SCIENCE** When a liquid
freezes, it becomes solid because it is
very cold. ❷ If you freeze, you
suddenly become very still and quiet.
❸ **DRAMA** To freeze the action in a
film is to stop the film at a particular
frame. ❹ If you freeze food, you put it
in a freezer to preserve it. ❺ When
wages or prices are frozen, they are
officially prevented from rising
▷ **NOUN** ❻ an official action taken to
prevent wages or prices from rising.
❼ a period of freezing weather.

freezer, freezers **NOUN** a large
refrigerator which freezes and stores
food for a long time.

freeze-thaw cycle, freeze-thaw
cycles **NOUN** **GEOGRAPHY** the
continuous process, for example in
rocks on high mountains, of the
freezing and thawing of water which
results in the rocks cracking and
eroding.

freezing ADJECTIVE extremely cold.

a
b
c
d
e
f
g
h
i
j
k
l
m
n
o
p
q
r
s
t
u
v
w
x
y
z

▷ SPELLING NOTE: *Rhythmical Hounds Yap To Heavy Music (rhythm)*

freight NOUN Freight is goods moved by lorries, ships, or other transport; also the moving of these goods.

French ADJECTIVE ❶ belonging or relating to France ▷ NOUN ❷ French is the main language spoken in France, and is also spoken by many people in Belgium, Switzerland, and Canada.

French bean, French beans NOUN French beans are green pods eaten as a vegetable, which grow on a climbing plant with white or mauve flowers.

French horn, French horns NOUN a brass musical wind instrument consisting of a tube wound in a circle.

Frenchman, Frenchmen NOUN a man who comes from France. **Frenchwoman** NOUN

french window, french windows NOUN French windows are glass doors that lead into a garden or onto a balcony.

frenetic ADJECTIVE Frenetic behaviour is wild and excited.

frenzy, frenzies NOUN If someone is in a frenzy, their behaviour is wild and uncontrolled. **frenzied** ADJECTIVE

frequency, frequencies NOUN ❶ The frequency of an event is how often it happens • He was not known to call anyone with great frequency. ❷ (SCIENCE) The frequency of a sound or radio wave is the rate at which it vibrates. ❸ (MATHS) In statistics, the frequency of a particular class is the number of individuals in it.

frequent, frequents, frequenting, frequented ADJECTIVE [Said *free-kwuhnt*] ❶ often happening • His visits were frequent • They move at frequent intervals. ▷ VERB [Said *frih-kwent*] ❷ If you frequent a place, you go there often. **frequently** ADVERB

fresco, frescoes NOUN a picture painted on a plastered wall while the plaster is still wet.

fresh, fresher, freshest ADJECTIVE ❶ A fresh thing replaces a previous one, or is added to it • footprints filled in by fresh snow • fresh evidence. ❷ Fresh food is newly made or obtained, and not tinned or frozen. ❸ Fresh water is not salty, for example the water in a stream. ❹ If the weather is fresh, it is fairly cold and windy. ❺ If you are fresh from something, you have experienced it recently • a teacher fresh from college. **freshly** ADVERB **freshness** NOUN

freshwater ADJECTIVE ❶ A freshwater lake or pool contains water that is not salty. ❷ A freshwater creature lives in a river, lake, or pool.

fret, frets, fretting, fretted VERB ❶ If you fret about something, you worry about it ▷ NOUN ❷ The frets on a stringed instrument, such as a guitar, are the metal ridges across its neck. **fretful** ADJECTIVE

Freudian slip, Freudian slips NOUN something that you say or do that reveals your unconscious thoughts.

friar, friars NOUN a member of a Catholic religious order.

friction NOUN ❶ (SCIENCE) the force that stops things from moving freely when they rub against each other. ❷ Friction between people is disagreement and quarrels.

Friday, Fridays **NOUN** the day between Thursday and Saturday.
- **WORD HISTORY:** from Old English *Frigedæg* meaning 'Freya's day'.
- Freya was the Norse goddess of love

fridge, fridges **NOUN** the same as a **refrigerator**.

friend, friends **NOUN** Your friends are people you know well and like to spend time with.
- **SIMILAR WORDS:** chum,
- companion, mate, pal

friendly, friendlier, friendliest **ADJECTIVE** ❶ If you are friendly to someone, you behave in a kind and pleasant way to them. ❷ People who are friendly with each other like each other and enjoy spending time together. **friendliness NOUN**
- **SIMILAR WORDS:** ❶ amicable,
- cordial, genial

friendship, friendships **NOUN** ❶ Your friendships are the special relationships that you have with your friends. ❷ Friendship is the state of being friends with someone.
- **SIMILAR WORDS:** ❷ friendliness,
- goodwill

frieze, friezes **NOUN** ❶ a strip of decoration or carving along the top of a wall or column. ❷ (ART) a picture on a long strip of paper which is hung along a wall.

frigate, frigates **NOUN** a small, fast warship.

fright NOUN Fright is a sudden feeling of fear.

frighten, frightens, frightening, frightened **VERB** If something frightens you, it makes you afraid.

frightened ADJECTIVE having feelings of fear about something.

frightening ADJECTIVE causing someone to feel fear.

frightful ADJECTIVE very bad or unpleasant • *a frightful bully*.

frigid ADJECTIVE Frigid behaviour is cold and unfriendly • *frigid stares*.

frill, frills **NOUN** a strip of cloth with many folds, attached to something as a decoration. **frilly ADJECTIVE**

fringe, fringes **NOUN** ❶ the hair that hangs over a person's forehead. ❷ a decoration on clothes and other objects, consisting of a row of hanging strips or threads. ❸ The fringes of a place are the parts farthest from its centre • *the western fringe of the Amazon basin*. **fringed ADJECTIVE**

frisk, frisks, frisking, frisked **VERB** INFORMAL If someone frisks you, they search you quickly with their hands to see if you are hiding a weapon in your clothes.

frisky, friskier, friskiest **ADJECTIVE** A frisky animal or child is energetic and wants to have fun.

fritter, fritters, frittering, frittered **NOUN** ❶ Fritters consist of food dipped in batter and fried • *apple fritters*. ▷ **VERB** ❷ If you fritter away your time or money, you waste it on unimportant things.

frivolous ADJECTIVE Someone who is frivolous behaves in a silly or light-hearted way, especially when

a
b
c
d
e
f
g
h
i
j
k
l
m
n
o
p
q
r
s
t
u
v
w
x
y
z

▷ SPELLING NOTE: *I always visit my FRIend on a FRIday (Friday)*

A
B
C
D
E
F
G
H
I
J
K
L
M
N
O
P
Q
R
S
T
U
V
W
X
Y
Z

they should be serious or sensible.
frivolity NOUN
● **SIMILAR WORDS:** flippant, silly

frizzy, frizzier, frizziest **ADJECTIVE**
Frizzy hair has stiff, wiry curls.

frock, frocks **NOUN** OLD-FASHIONED a dress.

frog, frogs **NOUN** a small amphibious creature with smooth skin, prominent eyes, and long back legs which it uses for jumping.

frolic, frolics, frolicking, frolicked **VERB** When animals or children frolic, they run around and play in a lively way.
● **WORD HISTORY:** from Dutch *vrolijk* meaning 'joyful'
● **SIMILAR WORDS:** frisk, play, romp

from PREPOSITION ❶ You use 'from' to say what the source, origin, or starting point of something is • *a call from a public telephone* • *people from a city 100 miles away.* ❷ If you take something from an amount, you reduce the amount by that much • *A sum of money was wrongly taken from his account.* ❸ You also use 'from' when stating the range of something • *a score from one to five.*

frond, fronds **NOUN** Fronds are long feathery leaves.

front, fronts, fronting, fronted **NOUN** ❶ The front of something is the part that faces forward. ❷ In a war, the front is the place where two armies are fighting. ❸ In meteorology, a front is the line where a mass of cold air meets a mass of warm air. ❹ A front is an outward appearance, often one that is false • *I put up a brave front* • *He's no more than a respectable front*

for some very dubious happenings.
▷ **PHRASE** ❺ **In front** means ahead or further forward. ❻ If you do something **in front of** someone, you do it when they are present. **frontal ADJECTIVE**

frontage, frontages **NOUN** The frontage of a building is the wall that faces a street.

frontier, frontiers **NOUN** a border between two countries.

frontispiece, frontispieces **NOUN** a picture opposite the title page of a book.

frost, frosts **NOUN** When there is a frost, the temperature outside falls below freezing.

frostbite NOUN Frostbite is damage to your fingers, toes, or ears caused by extreme cold.

frosty, frostier, frostiest **ADJECTIVE** ❶ If it is frosty, the temperature outside is below freezing point. ❷ If someone is frosty, they are unfriendly or disapproving.

froth, froths, frothing, frothed **NOUN** ❶ Froth is a mass of small bubbles on the surface of a liquid ▷ **VERB** ❷ If a liquid froths, small bubbles appear on its surface. **frothy ADJECTIVE**

frown, frowns, frowning, frowned **VERB** ❶ If you frown, you move your eyebrows closer together, because you are annoyed, worried, or concentrating ▷ **NOUN** ❷ a cross expression on someone's face.

froze the past tense of **freeze**.

frozen ❶ Frozen is the past participle of **freeze**. **ADJECTIVE** ❷ If you say

▷ SPELLING NOTE: *Eddy Ant thinks mEAt is a grEAt trEAt to EAt (-ea-)*

are frozen, you mean you are extremely cold.
● **SIMILAR WORDS:** chilled, ice-cold, icy

fructose [Said **fruck**-toes] **NOUN** Fructose is a type of sugar found in many fruits and in honey.

frugal ADJECTIVE ❶ Someone who is frugal spends very little money. ❷ A frugal meal is small and cheap. **frugality NOUN**
● **SIMILAR WORDS:** ❶ economical, thrifty

fruit, fruits **NOUN** ❶ the part of a plant that develops after the flower and contains the seeds. Many fruits are edible ❷ IN PLURAL The fruits of something are its good results • *the fruits of his labours*.

fruitful ADJECTIVE Something that is fruitful has good and useful results • *a fruitful experience*.

fruitless ADJECTIVE Something that is fruitless does not achieve anything • *a fruitless effort*.

fruit machine, fruit machines **NOUN** a coin-operated gambling machine which pays out money when a particular series of symbols, usually fruit, appears on a screen.

fruit salad, fruit salads **NOUN** a mixture of pieces of different fruits served in a juice as a dessert.

fruity, fruitier, fruitiest **ADJECTIVE** Something that is fruity smells or tastes of fruit.

frustrate, frustrates, frustrating, frustrated **VERB** ❶ If something frustrates you, it prevents you doing what you want and makes you upset and angry • *Everyone gets frustrated with their work.* ❷ To frustrate something such as a plan is to prevent it • *She hopes to frustrate the engagement of her son.* **frustrated ADJECTIVE frustrating ADJECTIVE frustration NOUN**
● **SIMILAR WORDS:** ❷ foil, thwart

fry, fries, frying, fried **VERB** When you fry food, you cook it in a pan containing hot fat or oil.

fuchsia, fuchsias [Said **fyoo**-sha] **NOUN** a plant or small bush with pink, purple, or white flowers that hang downwards.

fudge, fudges, fudging, fudged **NOUN** ❶ Fudge is a soft brown sweet made from butter, milk, and sugar ▷ **VERB** ❷ If you fudge something, you avoid making clear or definite decisions or statements about it • *He was carefully fudging his message.*

fuel, fuels, fuelling, fuelled **NOUN** ❶ Fuel is a substance such as coal or petrol that is burned to provide heat or power ▷ **VERB** ❷ A machine or vehicle that is fuelled by a substance works by burning the substance as a fuel • *power stations fuelled by wood.*

fug NOUN A fug is an airless, smoky atmosphere.

fugitive, fugitives [Said **fyoo**-jit-tiv] **NOUN** someone who is running away or hiding, especially from the police.

-ful SUFFIX ❶ '-ful' is used to form adjectives with the meaning 'full of' • *careful.* ❷ '-ful' is used to form nouns which mean 'the amount needed to fill' • *spoonful.*

fulcrum, fulcrums or fulcra **NOUN**

a b c d e f g h i j k l m n o p q r s t u v w x y z

▷ SPELLING NOTE: *Elaine and Emily shout EE when they mEEt to grEEt each other (-ee-)*

| **WHAT DOES THE FULL STOP DO?** |

The **full stop** (.) marks the end of any sentence which is not a question or an exclamation:
The train is leaving.

A full stop is also used after an abbreviation or initial:
etc.

Dr. Jenkins
J.R. Hartley

A full stop is also used after an expression that stands by itself but is not a complete sentence:
Good morning.

⟨ D & T ⟩ the point at which something is balancing or pivoting.

fulfil, fulfils, fulfilling, fulfilled **VERB**
❶ If you fulfil a promise, hope, or duty, you carry it out or achieve it.
❷ If something fulfils you, it gives you satisfaction. **fulfilling ADJECTIVE**
fulfilment NOUN

full, fuller, fullest **ADJECTIVE**
❶ containing or having as much as it is possible to hold • *His room is full of posters.* ❷ complete or whole • *They had taken a full meal* • *a full 20 years later.* ❸ loose and made from a lot of fabric • *full sleeves.* ❹ rich and strong • *a full, fruity wine.* ▷ **ADVERB**
❺ completely and directly • *Turn the taps full on.* ▷ **PHRASE** ❻ Something that has been done or described **in full** has been dealt with completely.
fullness NOUN fully ADVERB
● SIMILAR WORDS: ❶ filled,
● loaded, packed

full-blooded ADJECTIVE having great commitment and enthusiasm • *a full-blooded sprint for third place.*

full-blown ADJECTIVE complete and fully developed • *a full-blown love of music.*

full moon, full moons **NOUN** A full moon is the moon when it appears as a complete circle.

full stop, full stops **NOUN** the punctuation mark (.) used at the end of a sentence and after an abbreviation or initial.
▶ SEE GRAMMAR BOX ABOVE

full-time ADJECTIVE ❶ involving work for the whole of each normal working week ▷ **NOUN** ❷ In games such as football, full time is the end of the match.

fully-fledged ADJECTIVE completely developed • *I was a fully-fledged and mature human being.*

fulsome ADJECTIVE exaggerated and elaborate, and often sounding insincere • *His most fulsome praise was reserved for his mother.*

fumble, fumbles, fumbling, fumbled **VERB** If you fumble, you feel or handle something clumsily.

fume, fumes, fuming, fumed **NOUN**
❶ Fumes are unpleasant-smelling gases and smoke, often toxic, that are produced by burning and by some chemicals ▷ **VERB** ❷ If you are fuming, you are very angry.

fun NOUN ❶ Fun is pleasant, enjoyable and light-hearted activity ▷ **PHRASE** ❷ If you **make fun** of

▷ SPELLING NOTE: *'i' before 'e' except after 'c'*

someone, you tease them or make jokes about them.

function, functions, functioning, functioned **NOUN** ❶ The function of something or someone is their purpose or the job they have to do. ❷ a large formal dinner, reception, or party. ❸ (MATHS) A function is a variable whose value depends on the value of other independent variables. 'y is a function of x' is written y = f(x) ▷ **VERB** ❹ When something functions, it operates or works.

functional ADJECTIVE ❶ relating to the way something works. ❷ designed for practical use rather than for decoration or attractiveness • *Feminine clothing has never been designed to be functional.* ❸ working properly • *fully functional smoke alarms.*

fund, funds, funding, funded **NOUN** ❶ an amount of available money, usually for a particular purpose • *a pension fund.* ❷ A fund of something is a lot of it • *He had a fund of hilarious tales on the subject.* ▷ **VERB** ❸ Someone who funds something provides money for it • *research funded by pharmaceutical companies.*
● **SIMILAR WORDS:** ❸ finance,
● subsidize

fundamental, fundamentals **ADJECTIVE** ❶ basic and central • *the fundamental right of freedom of choice* • *fundamental changes.* ▷ **NOUN** ❷ The fundamentals of something are its most basic and important parts • *teaching small children the fundamentals of road safety.*

fundi, fundis **NOUN** In South Africa, an expert.

funeral, funerals [*Said fyoo-ner-al*] **NOUN** (RE) a ceremony or religious service for the burial or cremation of a dead person.

funereal [*Said few-nee-ree-al*] **ADJECTIVE** depressing and gloomy.

funfair, funfairs **NOUN** a place of entertainment with things like amusement arcades and rides.

fungicide, fungicides **NOUN** a chemical used to kill or prevent fungus.

fungus, fungi or funguses **NOUN** (SCIENCE) a plant such as a mushroom or mould that does not have leaves and grows on other living things. **fungal ADJECTIVE**

funk, funks, funking, funked **VERB** ❶ INFORMAL, OLD-FASHIONED If you funk something, you fail to do it because of fear • **NOUN** ❷ Funk is a style of music with a strong rhythm based on jazz and blues.

funnel, funnels, funnelling, funnelled **NOUN** ❶ an open cone narrowing to a tube, used to pour substances into containers. ❷ a metal chimney on a ship or steam engine ▷ **VERB** ❸ If something is funnelled somewhere, it is directed through a narrow space into that place.

funny, funnier, funniest **ADJECTIVE** ❶ strange or puzzling • *You get a lot of funny people coming into the libraries.* ❷ causing amusement or laughter • *a funny old film.* **funnily ADVERB**
● **SIMILAR WORDS:** ❶ odd,
● peculiar, strange ❷ amusing,
● comical, humorous

fur, furs **NOUN** ❶ Fur is the soft thick body hair of many animals. ❷ a coat

▷ SPELLING NOTE: King IAn went to ParlIAment in a carrIAge for his marrIAge (-ia-)

a
b
c
d
e
f
g
h
i
j
k
l
m
n
o
p
q
r
s
t
u
v
w
x
y
z

made from an animal's fur. **furry**
ADJECTIVE

furious ADJECTIVE ❶ extremely
angry. **❷** involving great energy,
effort, or speed • *the furious speed of
technological development.* **furiously**
ADVERB

furlong, furlongs **NOUN** a unit of
length equal to 220 yards or about
201.2 metres. Furlong originally referred
to the length of the average furrow.

furnace, furnaces **NOUN** a container
for a very large, hot fire used, for
example, in the steel industry for
melting ore.

furnish, furnishes, furnishing,
furnished **VERB ❶** If you furnish a
room, you put furniture into it.
❷ FORMAL If you furnish someone
with something, you supply or provide
it for them.

furnishings PLURAL NOUN The
furnishings of a room or house are the
furniture and fittings in it.

furniture NOUN Furniture is
movable objects such as tables, chairs
and wardrobes.

furore [Said fyoo-**roh**-ree] **NOUN** an
angry and excited reaction or protest.
● **WORD HISTORY:** from Italian
furore meaning 'rage'

furrow, furrows, furrowing, furrowed
NOUN ❶ a long, shallow trench
made by a plough ▷ **VERB ❷** When
someone furrows their brow, they frown.

further, furthers, furthering,
furthered **❶** a comparative form of
far. ADJECTIVE ❷ additional or more
• *There was no further rain.* ▷ **VERB**
❸ If you further something, you help

it to progress • *He wants to further his
acting career.*
● **SIMILAR WORDS: ❸** advance,
● promote

further education NOUN
Further education is education at a
college after leaving school, but not at
a university.

furthermore ADVERB FORMAL
used to introduce additional
information • *There is no record of such
a letter. Furthermore it is company policy
never to send such letters.*

furthest a superlative form of **far.**

furtive ADJECTIVE secretive, sly,
and cautious • *a furtive smile.*
furtively ADVERB

fury NOUN Fury is violent or extreme
anger.

fuse, fuses, fusing, fused **NOUN ❶** a
safety device in a plug or electrical
appliance consisting of a piece of wire
which melts to stop the electric
current if a fault occurs. **❷** a long cord
attached to some types of simple
bomb which is lit to detonate ▷ **VERB**
❸ When an electrical appliance fuses,
it stops working because the fuse has
melted to protect it. **❹** If two things
fuse, they join or become combined
• *Christianity slowly fused with existing
beliefs.*

fuselage, fuselages [Said **fyoo**-zil-
ahj] **NOUN** the main part of an
aeroplane or rocket.

fusion NOUN ❶ Fusion is what
happens when two substances join by
melting together. **❷** Fusion is also
nuclear fusion ▷ **ADJECTIVE**
❸ Fusion is used to refer to food or a

▷ SPELLING NOTE: *an ELegant angEL (angel)*

TALKING ABOUT THE FUTURE

There is no simple future tense in English. To talk about an event that will happen in the future, we usually use **compound tenses**.

The auxiliary verbs *will* and *shall* are used before the basic form of the verb to show that an action will happen:
*His father **will cook** the dinner.*
*I **shall cook** the dinner.*

You can also talk about the future by putting the verbs *will have* or *shall have* before the verb, and adding the ending *-ed*. This form shows that an action will be completed in the future:
*His father **will have cooked** the dinner.*
*I **shall have cooked** the dinner.*

You can also talk about the future by using the phrase *be about to* or *be going to* in front of the dictionary form of the verb. This shows that the action will take place very soon:
*He **is about to cook** the dinner.*
*I **am going to cook** the dinner.*

You can sometimes use a form of the present tense to talk about future events, but only if the sentence contains a clear reference to the future:
*His father **is cooking** the dinner tonight.*
*The plane **leaves** at three o'clock.*

Also see the grammar box at **tense**.

style of cooking that brings together ingredients or cooking techniques from several different countries.

fuss, fusses, fussing, fussed **NOUN** ❶ Fuss is unnecessarily anxious or excited behaviour ▷ **VERB** ❷ If someone fusses, they behave with unnecessary anxiety and concern for unimportant things.
● **SIMILAR WORDS:** ❶ bother,
● commotion, palaver

fussy, fussier, fussiest **ADJECTIVE** ❶ likely to fuss a lot • *He was unusually fussy about keeping things perfect.* ❷ with too much elaborate detail or decoration • *fussy chiffon evening wear.*
● **SIMILAR WORDS:** ❶ finicky,
● particular

futile **ADJECTIVE** having no chance of success • *a futile attempt to calm the storm.* **futility** **NOUN**

● **SIMILAR WORDS:** useless, vain

future, futures **NOUN** ❶ The future is the period of time after the present. ❷ Something that has a future is likely to succeed • *She sees no future in a modelling career.* ▷ **ADJECTIVE** ❸ relating to or occurring at a time after the present • *to predict future events.* ❹ ⟨**ENGLISH**⟩ The future tense of a verb is the form used to express something that will happen in the future.
▶ SEE GRAMMAR BOX ABOVE

futuristic **ADJECTIVE** very modern and strange, as if belonging to a time in the future • *futuristic cars.*

fuzz **NOUN** short fluffy hair. **fuzzy** **ADJECTIVE**

fuzz **PLURAL NOUN** INFORMAL The fuzz are the police.

▷ SPELLING NOTE: *LEt's measure the angLE (angle)*

Gg

Some words which sound as if they might begin with *g* alone, are actually spelt with the letters *gh*, for example *ghastly* and *ghost*. Some words which sound as if they might begin with the letter *n*, are spelt with *gn*, for example *gnaw*, *gnome* and *gnu*. Also take care with the spelling of words that start with *gu-* followed by the vowels *a*, *e* or *i*, because the *u* is not pronounced, for example *guarantee*, *guard*, *guerrilla* and *guile*.

g an abbreviation for 'grams'.

gabble, gabbles, gabbling, gabbled **VERB** If you gabble, you talk so fast that it is difficult for people to understand you.

gable, gables **NOUN** Gables are the triangular parts at the top of the outside walls at each end of a house.

gadget, gadgets **NOUN** a small machine or tool. **gadgetry NOUN**
● **SIMILAR WORDS:** contraption,
● device

Gaelic [*Said* gay-lik] **NOUN** a language spoken in some parts of Scotland and Ireland.

gaffe, gaffes [*Said* gaf] **NOUN** a social blunder or mistake.

gaffer, gaffers **NOUN** INFORMAL a boss.

gag, gags, gagging, gagged **NOUN**
❶ a strip of cloth that is tied round someone's mouth to stop them speaking. ❷ INFORMAL a joke told by a comedian ▷ **VERB** ❸ To gag someone means to put a gag round their mouth. ❹ If you gag, you choke and nearly vomit.

gaggle, gaggles **NOUN** ❶ a group of geese. ❷ INFORMAL a noisy group • *a gaggle of schoolboys*.

gaiety [*Said* gay-yet-tee] **NOUN** liveliness and fun.

gaily ADVERB in a happy and cheerful way.

gain, gains, gaining, gained **VERB**
❶ If you gain something, you get it gradually • *I spent years at night school trying to gain qualifications.* ❷ If you gain from a situation, you get some advantage from it. ❸ If you gain on someone, you gradually catch them up ▷ **NOUN** ❹ an increase • *a gain in speed.* ❺ an advantage that you get for yourself • *People use whatever influence they have for personal gain.*

gait, gaits **NOUN** Someone's gait is their way of walking • *an awkward gait.*

gala, galas **NOUN** a special public celebration or performance.

▷ SPELLING NOTE: *you'll brEAK that Electrical Aerial, Kitty (br**eak**)*

galah, galahs NOUN **①** an Australian cockatoo with a pink breast and a grey back and wings. **②** INFORMAL In Australian English, a galah is also a stupid person.

galaxy, galaxies NOUN (SCIENCE) A galaxy is an enormous group of stars that extends over many millions of miles. The galaxy to which the earth's solar system belongs is called the Milky Way. **galactic** ADJECTIVE

galaxy, galaxies NOUN an enormous group of stars that extends over many millions of miles. **galactic** ADJECTIVE

gale, gales NOUN an extremely strong wind.

gall, galls, galling, galled [rhymes with **ball**] NOUN **①** If someone has the gall to do something, they have enough courage or impudence to do it • He even has the gall to visit her. ▷ VERB **②** If something galls you, it makes you extremely annoyed.

gallant ADJECTIVE **①** brave and honourable • They have put up a gallant fight for pensioners' rights. **②** polite and considerate towards women. **gallantly** ADVERB **gallantry** NOUN

gall bladder, gall bladders NOUN an organ in your body which stores bile and which is next to your liver.

galleon, galleons NOUN a large sailing ship used in the sixteenth and seventeenth centuries.

gallery, galleries NOUN **①** (ART) a building or room where works of art are shown. **②** In a theatre or large hall, the gallery is a raised area at the back or sides • the public gallery in Parliament.

galley, galleys NOUN **①** a kitchen in a ship or aircraft. **②** a ship, driven by oars, used in ancient and medieval times.

Gallic [Said gal-lik] ADJECTIVE FORMAL OR LITERARY French.

gallon, gallons NOUN a unit of liquid volume equal to eight pints or about 4.55 litres.

gallop, gallops, galloping, galloped VERB **①** When a horse gallops, it runs very fast, so that during each stride all four feet are off the ground at the same time ▷ NOUN **②** a very fast run.

gallows NOUN A gallows is a framework on which criminals used to be hanged.

gallstone, gallstones NOUN a small painful lump that can develop in your gall bladder.

galore ADJECTIVE in very large numbers • chocolates galore.
● **WORD HISTORY:** from Irish Gaelic
● go leór meaning 'to sufficiency'

galoshes PLURAL NOUN Galoshes are waterproof rubber shoes which you wear over your ordinary shoes to stop them getting wet.

galvanized or **galvanised** ADJECTIVE Galvanized metal has been coated with zinc by an electrical process to protect it from rust.

gambit, gambits NOUN something which someone to gain an advantage in a situation • Commentators are calling the plan a *clever political gambit.*

● **WORD HISTORY:** from Italian *gambetto* meaning 'a tripping up'

gamble, gambles, gambling, gambled **VERB** ❶ When people gamble, they bet money on the result of a game or race. ❷ If you gamble something, you risk losing it in the hope of gaining an advantage • *The company gambled everything on the new factory.* ▷ **NOUN** ❸ If you take a gamble, you take a risk in the hope of gaining an advantage. **gambler NOUN gambling NOUN**
● **SIMILAR WORDS:** ❶ bet, wager

game, games; gamer, gamest **NOUN** ❶ an enjoyable activity with a set of rules which is played by individuals or teams against each other. ❷ an enjoyable imaginative activity played by small children • *childhood games of cowboys and Indians.* ❸ You might describe something as a game when it is designed to gain advantage • *the political game.* ❹ Game is wild animals or birds that are hunted for sport or for food ❺ IN PLURAL Games are sports played at school or in a competition ▷ **ADJECTIVE** ❻ INFORMAL Someone who is game is willing to try something unusual or difficult. **gamely ADVERB**
● **SIMILAR WORDS:** ❶ amusement, pastime

gamekeeper, gamekeepers **NOUN** a person employed to look after game animals and birds on a country estate.

gamete, gametes [Said *gam-meet*] **NOUN** SCIENCE In biology, a gamete is a cell that can unite with another during reproduction to form a new organism.

gammon NOUN Gammon is cured meat from a pig, similar to bacon.

gamut [Said *gam-mut*] **NOUN** FORMAL The gamut of something is the whole range of things that can be included in it • *the whole gamut of human emotions.*

gander, ganders **NOUN** a male goose.

gang, gangs, ganging, ganged **NOUN** ❶ a group of people who join together for some purpose, for example to commit a crime ▷ **VERB** ❷ INFORMAL If people gang up on you, they join together to oppose you.

gangplank, gangplanks **NOUN** a plank used for boarding and leaving a ship or boat.

gangrene [Said *gang*-green] **NOUN** Gangrene is decay in the tissues of part of the body, caused by inadequate blood supply. **gangrenous ADJECTIVE**

gangster, gangsters **NOUN** a violent criminal who is a member of a gang.

gannet, gannets **NOUN** a large sea bird which dives to catch fish.

gaol another spelling of **jail**.

gap, gaps **NOUN** ❶ a space between two things or a hole in something solid. ❷ a period of time. ❸ A gap between things, people, or ideas is a great difference between them • *the gap between fantasy and reality.*
● **SIMILAR WORDS:** ❶ hole, opening, space

gape, gapes, gaping, gaped **VERB** ❶ If you gape at someone or something, you stare at them with

your mouth open in surprise.
❷ Something that gapes is wide open • *gaping holes in the wall.*

garage, garages NOUN ❶ a building where a car can be kept. ❷ a place where cars are repaired and where petrol is sold.

garb NOUN FORMAL Someone's garb is their clothes • *his usual garb of a dark suit.*

garbage NOUN ❶ Garbage is rubbish, especially household rubbish. ❷ If you say something is garbage, you mean it is nonsense.
  ● WORD HISTORY: from Anglo-
  ● French *garbelage* meaning 'removal
  ● of discarded matter'

garbled ADJECTIVE Garbled messages are jumbled and the details may be wrong.

garden, gardens NOUN ❶ an area of land next to a house, where flowers, fruit, or vegetables are grown ❷ IN PLURAL Gardens are a type of park in a town or around a large house.
gardening NOUN

gardener, gardeners NOUN a person who looks after a garden as a job or as a hobby.

gargle, gargles, gargling, gargled VERB When you gargle, you rinse the back of your throat by putting some liquid in your mouth and making a bubbling sound without swallowing.

gargoyle, gargoyles NOUN a stone carving below the roof of an old building, in the shape of an ugly person or animal and often having a water spout at the mouth.

garish [Said **gair**-rish] ADJECTIVE

bright and harsh to look at • *garish bright red boots.*

garland, garlands NOUN a circle of flowers and leaves which is worn around the neck or head.

garlic NOUN Garlic is the small white bulb of an onion-like plant which has a strong taste and smell and is used in cooking.

garment, garments NOUN a piece of clothing.

garnet, garnets NOUN a type of gemstone, usually red in colour.

garnish, garnishes, garnishing, garnished NOUN ❶ something such as a sprig of parsley, that is used in cooking for decoration ▷ VERB ❷ To garnish food means to decorate it with a garnish.

garret, garrets NOUN an attic.

garrison, garrisons NOUN a group of soldiers stationed in a town in order to guard it; also used of the buildings in which these soldiers live.

garrotte, garrottes, garrotting, garrotted [Said gar-**rot**]; also spelt **garotte** VERB To garrotte someone means to strangle them with a piece of wire.

garter, garters NOUN a piece of elastic worn round the top of a stocking to hold it up.

gas, gases; gasses, gassing, gassed NOUN ❶ (SCIENCE) any airlike substance that is not liquid or solid, such as oxygen or the gas used as a fuel in heating. ❷ In American English, gas is petrol ▷ VERB ❸ To gas people or animals means to kill

them with poisonous gas.
● **USAGE NOTE:** The plural of the
● noun *gas* is *gases*. The verb forms of
● *gas* are spelt with a double *s*

gas chamber, gas chambers
NOUN a room in which people or
animals are killed with poisonous gas.

gash, gashes, gashing, gashed **NOUN**
❶ a long, deep cut ▷ **VERB** ❷ If you
gash something, you make a long,
deep cut in it.

gas mask, gas masks **NOUN** a large
mask with special filters attached
which people wear over their face to
protect them from poisonous gas.

gasoline NOUN In American
English, gasoline is petrol.

gasp, gasps, gasping, gasped **VERB**
❶ If you gasp, you quickly draw in
your breath through your mouth
because you are surprised or in pain
▷ **NOUN** ❷ a sharp intake of breath
through the mouth.

gastric ADJECTIVE occurring in the
stomach or involving the stomach
• *gastric pain*.

gate, gates **NOUN** ❶ a barrier which
can open and shut and is used to close
the entrance to a garden or field.
❷ The gate at a sports event is the
number of people who have attended.

gateau, gateaux [Said **gat**-toe]
NOUN a rich layered cake with cream
in it.

gatecrash, gatecrashes,
gatecrashing, gatecrashed **VERB** If
you gatecrash a party, you go to it
when you have not been invited.

gateway, gateways **NOUN** ❶ an
entrance through a wall or fence
where there is a gate. ❷ Something
that is considered to be the entrance
to a larger or more important thing
can be described as the gateway to
it • *New York is the gateway to
America.*

gather, gathers, gathering, gathered
VERB ❶ When people gather, they
come together in a group. ❷ If you
gather a number of things, you bring
them together in one place. ❸ If
something gathers speed or strength,
it gets faster or stronger. ❹ If you
gather something, you learn it, often
from what someone says.
● **SIMILAR WORDS:** ❶ assemble,
● congregate ❷ amass, assemble,
● collect

gathering, gatherings **NOUN** a
meeting of people who have come
together for a particular purpose.

gauche [Said **gohsh**] **ADJECTIVE**
FORMAL socially awkward.
● **WORD HISTORY:** from French
● *gauche* meaning 'left-handed'

gaudy, gaudier, gaudiest [Said
gaw-dee] **ADJECTIVE** very colourful
in a vulgar way.
● **SIMILAR WORDS:** bright, flashy,
● garish

gauge, gauges, gauging, gauged [Said
gayj] **VERB** ❶ If you gauge
something, you estimate it or
calculate it • *He gauged the wind at
over 30 knots.* ▷ **NOUN** ❷ a piece of
equipment that measures the amount
of something • *a rain gauge.*
❸ something that is used as a
standard by which you judge a
situation • *They see profit as a gauge of*

efficiency. ❹ On railways, the gauge is the distance between the two rails on a railway line.

gaunt ADJECTIVE A person who looks gaunt is thin and bony.

gauntlet, gauntlets NOUN
❶ Gauntlets are long thick gloves worn for protection, for example by motorcyclists ▷ PHRASE ❷ If you **throw down the gauntlet**, you challenge someone. ❸ If you **run the gauntlet**, you have an unpleasant experience in which you are attacked or criticized by people.

gave the past tense of **give**.

gay, gayer, gayest; gays ADJECTIVE
❶ Someone who is gay is homosexual. ❷ OLD-FASHIONED Gay people or places are lively and full of fun ▷ NOUN ❸ a homosexual person.

● **USAGE NOTE:** The most common
● meaning of *gay* now is
● 'homosexual'. In some older books
● it may have its old-fashioned
● meaning of 'lively and full of fun'.
● The noun *gaiety* is related to this
● older meaning of *gay*. The noun
● that means 'the state of being
● homosexual' is *gayness*

gaze, gazes, gazing, gazed VERB If you gaze at something, you look steadily at it for a long time.

gazelle, gazelles NOUN a small antelope found in Africa and Asia.

gazette, gazettes NOUN a newspaper or journal.

GB an abbreviation for **Great Britain**.

GCSE, GCSEs In Britain, the GCSE is an examination taken by school students

aged fifteen and sixteen. GCSE is an abbreviation for 'General Certificate of Secondary Education'.

gear, gears, gearing, geared NOUN ❶ D & T a piece of machinery that controls the rate at which energy is converted into movement. Gears in vehicles control the speed and power of the vehicle. ❷ PE The gear for an activity is the clothes and equipment that you need for it ▷ VERB ❸ If someone or something is geared to a particular event or purpose, they are prepared for it.

geek, geeks INFORMAL NOUN a person who is obsessive about an interest or hobby, especially computers • *I never thought of you as a computer geek.*

geese the plural of **goose**.

Geiger counter, Geiger counters [Said **gy**-ger] NOUN SCIENCE A Geiger counter is a scientific instrument used to detect and measure radioactivity.

geisha, geishas [Said **gay**-sha] NOUN GEOGRAPHY A geisha is a Japanese woman whose job is to entertain men, for example by dancing and making conversation.

gel, gels, gelling, gelled [Said **jel**] NOUN ❶ a smooth soft jelly-like substance • *shower gel.* ▷ VERB ❷ If a liquid gels, it turns into a gel. ❸ If a vague thought or plan gels, it becomes more definite.

gelatine or **gelatin** [Said **jel**-lat-tin] NOUN a clear tasteless substance, obtained from meat and bones, used to make liquids firm and jelly-like.

a
b
c
d
e
f
g
h
i
j
k
l
m
n
o
p
q
r
s
t
u
v
w
x
y
z

▷ SPELLING NOTE: *plaice the fish has a glittering 'EYE' (I) (plaice)*

A
B
C
D
E
F
G
H
I
J
K
L
M
N
O
P
Q
R
S
T
U
V
W
X
Y
Z

WHAT IS GENDER?

When we talk about the "gender" of a noun, we mean whether it is referred to as *he*, *she*, or *it*. There are three genders: **masculine** (things referred to as *he*), **feminine** (things referred to as *she*), and **neuter** (things referred to as *it*).

Masculine nouns refer to male people and animals:
The boy put on his coat. → *boy* is **masculine**

Feminine nouns denote female people and animals:
The girl put on her coat. → *girl* is **feminine**

It is customary to refer to countries and vehicles as if they were feminine:
The ship came into view, her sails swelling in the breeze.

Neuter nouns refer to inanimate objects and abstract ideas:
The kettle will switch itself off. → *kettle* is **neuter**

Common nouns may be either masculine or feminine. Other words in the sentence may tell us if they are male or female:
The doctor parked his car.
The doctor parked her car.

---

gelding, geldings *[Said **gel**-ding]*
NOUN a horse which has been castrated.

gem, gems NOUN ❶ a jewel or precious stone. ❷ You can describe something or someone that is extremely good or beautiful as a gem • *A gem of a novel.*

Gemini *[Said **jem**-in-nye]* NOUN Gemini is the third sign of the zodiac, represented by a pair of twins. People born between May 21st and June 20th are born under this sign.

gemsbok, gemsbok or gemsboks; *also spelt* **gemsbuck** NOUN In South African English, a gemsbok is an oryx, a type of large antelope with straight horns.

gen NOUN INFORMAL The gen on something is information about it.

gender, genders NOUN ❶ (PSHE) Gender is the sex of a person or

animal • *the female gender.* ❷ the classification of nouns as masculine, feminine, and neuter in certain languages.
▶ SEE GRAMMAR BOX ABOVE

gene, genes *[Said **jeen**]* NOUN one of the parts of a living cell which controls the physical characteristics of an organism and which are passed on from one generation to the next.

genealogy, genealogies *[Said jeen-nee-**al**-loj-ee]* NOUN Genealogy is the study of the history of families, or the history of a particular family.

general, generals ADJECTIVE ❶ relating to the whole of something or to most things in a group • *your general health.* ❷ true, suitable, or relevant in most situations • *the general truth of science.* ❸ including or involving a wide range of different things • *a general hospital.* ❹ having complete responsibility over a wide area of work or a large number of

---

▷ SPELLING NOTE: *I went to see (C) the doctor's new practiCe (practice)*

people • *the general secretary.* ▷ NOUN
❺ an officer of very high rank
▷ PHRASE ❻ **In general** means
usually. **generally** ADVERB
● **SIMILAR WORDS:** ❶ overall
● ❷ common, universal, widespread

general election, general
elections NOUN an election for a new
government, which all the people of a
country may vote in.

generalize, generalizes,
generalizing, generalized; *also spelt*
generalise VERB To generalize
means to say that something is true in
most cases, ignoring minor details.
generalization NOUN

general practitioner, general
practitioners NOUN a doctor who
works in the community rather than in
a hospital.

generate, generates, generating,
generated VERB To generate
something means to create or
produce it • *using wind power to
generate electricity.*

generation, generations NOUN all
the people of about the same age; also
the period of time between one
generation and the next, usually
considered to be about 25-30 years.

generator, generators NOUN a
machine which produces electricity
from another form of energy such as
wind or water power.

generic ADJECTIVE A generic term
is a name that applies to all the
members of a group of similar things.

generosity NOUN the willingness
to give money, time, or help.

generous ADJECTIVE ❶ PSHE A

generous person is very willing to give
money or time. ❷ Something that is
generous is very large • *a generous
waist.* **generously** ADVERB
generosity NOUN
● **SIMILAR WORDS:** ❶ lavish,
● liberal ❷ abundant, ample, lavish

genesis, geneses NOUN FORMAL The
genesis of something is its beginning.

genetically modified
ADJECTIVE SCIENCE Genetically
modified plants and animals have had
one or more genes changed, for
example so that they grow larger or
resist diseases better.

genetics NOUN Genetics is the
science of the way that characteristics
are passed on from generation to
generation by means of genes.
genetic ADJECTIVE **genetically**
ADVERB

genial ADJECTIVE cheerful, friendly,
and kind. **genially** ADVERB

genie, genies [*Said jee-nee*] NOUN a
magical being that obeys the wishes
of the person who controls it.
● **WORD HISTORY:** from Arabic *jinni*
● meaning 'demon'

genitals PLURAL NOUN The
genitals are the reproductive organs.
The technical name is **genitalia**.
genital ADJECTIVE

genius, geniuses NOUN ❶ a highly
intelligent, creative, or talented
person. ❷ Genius is great
intelligence, creativity, or talent • *a
poet of genius.*

genocide [*Said jen-nos-side*] NOUN
FORMAL Genocide is the systematic
murder of all members of a particular

a
b
c
d
e
f
g
h
i
j
k
l
m
n
o
p
q
r
s
t
u
v
w
x
y
z

▷ SPELLING NOTE: *You must practiSe your Ss (practise)*

A
B
C
D
E
F
G
H
I
J
K
L
M
N
O
P
Q
R
S
T
U
V
W
X
Y
Z

race or group • *genocide of the Jews.*

genome, genomes [*Said* **jee**-nome] **NOUN** all of the genes contained in a single cell of an organism.

genre, genres [*Said* **jahn**-ra] **NOUN** (ENGLISH & LIBRARY) FORMAL a particular style in literature or art.

genteel **ADJECTIVE** very polite and refined.

Gentile, Gentiles [*Said* **jen**-tile] **NOUN** a person who is not Jewish.

gentility **NOUN** Gentility is excessive politeness and refinement.

gentle, gentler, gentlest **ADJECTIVE** mild and calm; not violent or rough • *a gentle man.* **gently** **ADVERB** **gentleness** **NOUN**

gentleman, gentlemen **NOUN** a man who is polite and well-educated; also a polite way of referring to any man. **gentlemanly** **ADJECTIVE**

gentry **PLURAL NOUN** The gentry are people from the upper classes.

genuine [*Said* **jen**-yoo-in] **ADJECTIVE** ❶ real and not false or pretend • *a genuine smile* • *genuine silver.* ❷ A genuine person is sincere and honest. **genuinely** **ADVERB** **genuineness** **NOUN**

genus, genera [*Said* **jee**-nuss] **NOUN** (SCIENCE) In biology, a genus is a class of animals or closely related plants. It is smaller than a family and larger than a species.

geo- **PREFIX** 'Geo-' means 'earth' • *geography* • *geologist.*
● **WORD HISTORY:** from Greek *gē*
● *meaning 'earth'*

geography **NOUN** the study of the physical features of the earth, together with the climate, natural resources and population in different parts of the world. **geographic** or **geographical** **ADJECTIVE** **geographically** **ADVERB**
● **WORD HISTORY:** from Greek *gē*
● *meaning 'earth' and -graphia*
● *meaning 'writing'*

geology **NOUN** the study of the earth's structure, especially the layers of rock and soil that make up the surface of the earth. **geological** **ADJECTIVE** **geologist** **NOUN**

geometric or **geometrical** **ADJECTIVE** ❶ consisting of regular lines and shapes, such as squares, triangles, and circles • *bold geometric designs.* ❷ involving geometry.

geometry **NOUN** Geometry is the branch of mathematics that deals with lines, angles, curves, and spaces.

Georgian **ADJECTIVE** belonging to or typical of the time from 1714 to 1830, when George I to George IV reigned in Britain.

geranium, geraniums **NOUN** a plant with red, pink, or white flowers.

gerbil, gerbils [*Said* **jer**-bil] **NOUN** a small rodent with long back legs, often kept as a pet.

geriatric [*Said* jer-ree-**at**-rik] **ADJECTIVE** ❶ relating to the medical care of old people • *a geriatric nurse.* ❷ Someone or something that is geriatric is very old • *a geriatric donkey.* ▷ **NOUN** ❸ an old person, especially as a patient. **geriatrics** **NOUN**

germ, germs **NOUN** ❶ a very small organism that causes disease.

❷ FORMAL The germ of an idea or plan is the beginning of it.

German, Germans ADJECTIVE ❶ belonging or relating to Germany ▷ NOUN ❷ someone who comes from Germany. ❸ German is the main language spoken in Germany and Austria and is also spoken by many people in Switzerland.

Germanic ADJECTIVE ❶ typical of Germany or the German people. ❷ The Germanic group of languages includes English, Dutch, German, Danish, Swedish, and Norwegian.

German measles NOUN
(SCIENCE) German measles is a contagious disease that gives you a sore throat and red spots.

germinate, germinates, germinating, germinated VERB ❶ When a seed germinates, it starts to grow. ❷ When an idea or plan germinates, it starts to develop. **germination** NOUN

gerrymander, gerrymanders, gerrymandering, gerrymandered VERB To gerrymander is to change political boundaries in an area so that a particular party or politician gets a bigger share of votes in an election.

gestation [Said jes-**tay**-shn] NOUN TECHNICAL Gestation is the time during which a foetus is growing inside its mother's womb.

gesticulate, gesticulates, gesticulating, gesticulated [Said jes-**stik**-yoo-late] VERB If you gesticulate, you move your hands and arms around while you are talking. **gesticulation** NOUN

gesture, gestures, gesturing, gestured NOUN ❶ a movement of your hands or head that conveys a message or feeling. ❷ an action symbolizing something • a gesture of support. ▷ VERB ❸ If you gesture, you move your hands or head in order to communicate a message or feeling.

get, gets, getting, got VERB ❶ Get often means the same as become • People draw the curtains once it gets dark. ❷ If you get into a particular situation, you put yourself in that situation • We are going to get into a hopeless muddle. ❸ If you get something done, you do it or you persuade someone to do it • You can get your homework done in time. ❹ If you get somewhere, you go there • I must get home. ❺ If you get something, you fetch it or are given it • I'll get us all a cup of coffee • I got your message. ❻ If you get a joke or get the point of something, you understand it. ❼ If you get a train, bus, or plane, you travel on it • You can get a bus.

get across VERB If you get an idea across, you make people understand it.

get at VERB ❶ If someone is getting at you, they are criticizing you in an unkind way. ❷ If you ask someone what they are getting at, you are asking them to explain what they mean.

get away with VERB If you get away with something dishonest, you are not found out or punished for doing it.

get by VERB If you get by, you have just enough money to live on.

get on VERB ❶ If two people get on well together, they like each other's company. ❷ If you get on with a task,

a
b
c
d
e
f
g
h
i
j
k
l
m
n
o
p
q
r
s
t
u
v
w
x
y
z

▷ SPELLING NOTE: L**E**arn the princip**LE**s (principl**e**) you do it • *Get on with your homework.*

get over with VERB If you want to get something unpleasant over with, you want it to be finished quickly.

get through VERB ❶ If you get through to someone, you make them understand what you are saying. ❷ If you get through to someone on the telephone, you succeed in talking to them.

● **SIMILAR WORDS: ❶** become, grow **❺** acquire, obtain, procure

getaway, getaways **NOUN** an escape made by criminals.

Gethsemane NOUN (RE) the garden in Jerusalem where Christ was betrayed by Judas Iscariot on the night before his Crucifixion.

get-together, get-togethers **NOUN** INFORMAL an informal meeting or party.

geyser, geysers [*Said gee-zer*] **NOUN** a spring through which hot water and steam gush up in spurts.

● **WORD HISTORY:** from Old Norse
● *geysa* meaning 'to gush'

Ghanaian, Ghanaians [*Said gah-nay-an*] **ADJECTIVE ❶** belonging or relating to Ghana ▷ **NOUN ❷** someone who comes from Ghana.

ghastly, ghastlier, ghastliest **ADJECTIVE** extremely horrible and unpleasant • *a ghastly crime* • *ghastly food.*

gherkin, gherkins **NOUN** a small pickled cucumber.

ghetto, ghettoes or ghettos **NOUN** a part of a city where many poor people of a particular race live.

● **WORD HISTORY:** from Italian
● *borghetto* meaning 'settlement
● outside the city walls'

ghost, ghosts **NOUN** the spirit of a dead person, believed to haunt people or places.

● **SIMILAR WORDS:** phantom,
● spectre, spirit

ghoulish [*Said gool-ish*] **ADJECTIVE** very interested in unpleasant things such as death and murder.

giant, giants **NOUN ❶** a huge person in a myth or legend ▷ **ADJECTIVE ❷** much larger than other similar things • *giant prawns* • *a giant wave.*

gibberish NOUN Gibberish is speech that makes no sense at all.

gibbon, gibbons **NOUN** an ape with very long arms.

gibe, gibes; *also spelt* jibe **NOUN** an insulting remark.

gidday INTERJECTION In Australia and New Zealand, a term for hello.

giddy, giddier, giddiest **ADJECTIVE** If you feel giddy, you feel unsteady on your feet usually because you are ill.
giddily ADVERB

gift, gifts **NOUN ❶** a present. ❷ a natural skill or ability • *a gift for comedy.*

gifted ADJECTIVE having a special ability • *gifted tennis players.*

gig, gigs **NOUN** a rock or jazz concert.

gigantic ADJECTIVE extremely large.

giggle, giggles, giggling, giggled **VERB ❶** To giggle means to laugh in a nervous or embarrassed way

▷ **NOUN ②** a short, nervous laugh. **giggly ADJECTIVE**

gilded ADJECTIVE Something which is gilded is covered with a thin layer of gold.

gill, gills **NOUN ①** [Said gil] The gills of a fish are the organs on its sides which it uses for breathing. **②** [Said jil] a unit of liquid volume equal to one quarter of a pint or about 0.142 litres.

gilt, gilts **NOUN ①** a thin layer of gold ▷ **ADJECTIVE ②** covered with a thin layer of gold • a gilt writing-table.

gimmick, gimmicks **NOUN** a device that is not really necessary but is used to attract interest • All pop stars need a good gimmick. **gimmicky ADJECTIVE**

gin NOUN Gin is a strong, colourless alcoholic drink made from grain and juniper berries.

ginger NOUN ① Ginger is a plant root with a hot, spicy flavour, used in cooking ▷ **ADJECTIVE ②** bright orange or red • ginger hair.

gingerbread NOUN Gingerbread is a sweet, ginger-flavoured cake.

gingerly ADVERB If you move gingerly, you move cautiously • They walked gingerly down the stairs.

gingham NOUN Gingham is checked cotton cloth.
● **WORD HISTORY:** from Malay
● ginggang meaning 'striped
● cloth'

gipsy another spelling of **gypsy**.

giraffe, giraffes **NOUN** a tall, four-legged African mammal with a very long neck.

girder, girders **NOUN** a large metal beam used in the construction of a bridge or a building.

girdle, girdles **NOUN** a woman's corset.

girl, girls **NOUN** a female child. **girlish ADJECTIVE girlhood NOUN**

girlfriend, girlfriends **NOUN** Someone's girlfriend is the woman or girl with whom they are having a romantic or sexual relationship.

giro, giros [Said jie-roh] **NOUN ①** Giro is a system of transferring money from one account to another through a bank or post office. **②** in Britain, a cheque received regularly from the government by unemployed or sick people.

girth NOUN The girth of something is the measurement round it.

gist [Said jist] **NOUN** the general meaning or most important points in a piece of writing or speech.

give, gives, giving, gave, given **VERB ①** If you give someone something, you hand it to them or provide it for them • I gave her a tape • George gave me my job. **②** 'Give' is also used to express physical actions and speech • He gave a fierce smile • Rosa gave a lovely performance. **③** If you give a party or a meal, you are the host at it. **④** If something gives, it collapses under pressure ▷ **NOUN ⑤** If material has give, it will bend or stretch when pulled or put under pressure ▷ **PHRASE ⑥** You use **give or take** to indicate that an amount you are mentioning is not exact • About two years, give or take a month or so. **⑦** If something **gives way** to

something else, it is replaced by it.
8 If something **gives way**, it collapses.

give in VERB If you give in, you admit that you are defeated.

give out VERB If something gives out, it stops working • *the electricity gave out.*

give up VERB **1** If you give something up, you stop doing it • *I can't give up my job.* **2** If you give up, you admit that you cannot do something. **3** If you give someone up, you let the police know where they are hiding.

● SIMILAR WORDS: **1** grant,
● present, provide

given 1 the past participle of **give**.
ADJECTIVE **2** fixed or specified • *My style can change at any given moment.*

glacé [Said *glass-say*] ADJECTIVE Glacé fruits are fruits soaked and coated with sugar • *glacé cherries.*

glaciation [Said *glay-see-ay-shn*] NOUN In geography, glaciation is the condition of being covered with sheet ice.

glacier, glaciers [Said *glass-yer*] NOUN a huge frozen river of slow-moving ice.

glad, gladder, gladdest ADJECTIVE happy and pleased. **gladly** ADVERB **gladness** NOUN

glade, glades NOUN a grassy space in a forest.

gladiator, gladiators NOUN In ancient Rome, gladiators were slaves trained to fight in arenas to provide entertainment.
● WORD HISTORY: from Latin
● *gladius* meaning 'sword'

gladiolus, gladioli NOUN a garden plant with spikes of brightly coloured flowers on a long stem.

glamour NOUN The glamour of a fashionable or attractive person or place is the charm and excitement that they have • *the glamour of Paris.*
glamorous ADJECTIVE

glance, glances, glancing, glanced VERB **1** If you glance at something, you look at it quickly. **2** If one object glances off another, it hits it at an angle and bounces away in another direction ▷ NOUN **3** a quick look.

gland, glands NOUN an organ in your body, such as the thyroid gland and the sweat glands, which either produce chemical substances for your body to use, or which help to get rid of waste products from your body.
glandular ADJECTIVE

glare, glares, glaring, glared VERB **1** If you glare at someone, you look at them angrily ▷ NOUN **2** a hard, angry look. **3** Glare is extremely bright light.

glass, glasses NOUN **1** Glass is a hard, transparent substance that is easily broken, used to make windows and bottles. **2** a container for drinking out of, made from glass • *a glass of milk.*

glasses PLURAL NOUN Glasses are two lenses in a frame, which some people wear over their eyes to improve their eyesight.

glassy ADJECTIVE **1** smooth and shiny like glass • *glassy water.* **2** A glassy look shows no feeling or expression.

glaze, glazes, glazing, glazed NOUN
❶ A glaze on pottery or on food is a smooth shiny surface ▷ VERB **❷** To glaze pottery or food means to cover it with a glaze. **❸** To glaze a window means to fit a sheet of glass into a window frame.
glaze over VERB If your eyes glaze over, they lose all expression, usually because you are bored.

glazed ADJECTIVE Someone who has a glazed expression looks bored.

gleam, gleams, gleaming, gleamed VERB **❶** If something gleams, it shines and reflects light ▷ NOUN **❷** a pale shining light.

glean, gleans, gleaning, gleaned VERB To glean information means to collect it from various sources.

glee NOUN OLD-FASHIONED Glee is joy and delight. **gleeful** ADJECTIVE **gleefully** ADVERB

glen, glens NOUN a deep, narrow valley, especially in Scotland or Ireland.

glide, glides, gliding, glided VERB **❶** To glide means to move smoothly • *cygnets gliding up the stream.* **❷** When birds or aeroplanes glide, they float on air currents.

glider, gliders NOUN an aeroplane without an engine, which flies by floating on air currents.

glimmer, glimmers, glimmering, glimmered NOUN **❶** a faint, unsteady light. **❷** A glimmer of a feeling or quality is a faint sign of it • *a glimmer of intelligence.*

glimpse, glimpses, glimpsing, glimpsed NOUN **❶** a brief sight of something • *They caught a glimpse of*
their hero. ▷ VERB **❷** If you glimpse something, you see it very briefly.

glint, glints, glinting, glinted VERB **❶** If something glints, it reflects quick flashes of light ▷ NOUN **❷** a quick flash of light. **❸** A glint in someone's eye is a brightness expressing some emotion • *A glint of mischief in her blue-grey eyes.*

glisten, glistens, glistening, glistened [Said *gliss*-sn] VERB If something glistens, it shines or sparkles.

glitter, glitters, glittering, glittered VERB **❶** If something glitters, it shines in a sparkling way • *a glittering crown.* ▷ NOUN **❷** Glitter is sparkling light.

gloat, gloats, gloating, gloated VERB If you gloat, you cruelly show your pleasure about your own success or someone else's failure • *Their rivals were gloating over their triumph.*

global ADJECTIVE concerning the whole world • *a global tour.*

globalization NOUN **❶** the process by which a company expands so that it can do business internationally. **❷** the process by which cultures throughout the world become more and more similar for a variety of reasons including increased global business and better international communications.

global warming NOUN (GEOGRAPHY) an increase in the world's overall temperature believed to be caused by the greenhouse effect

globe, globes NOUN **❶** a ball-shaped object, especially one with a map of the earth on it. **❷** (GEOGRAPHY) You

a
b
c
d
e
f
g
h
i
j
k
l
m
n
o
p
q
r
s
t
u
v
w
x
y
z

▷ SPELLING NOTE: *there's SAND in my SANDwich (sandwich)*

can refer to the world as the globe. **❸** In South African, Australian, and New Zealand English, a globe is an electric light bulb.

gloom NOUN **❶** Gloom is darkness or dimness. **❷** Gloom is also a feeling of unhappiness or despair.

gloomy, gloomier, gloomiest ADJECTIVE **❶** dark and depressing. **❷** feeling very sad. **gloomily** ADVERB

glorify, glorifies, glorifying, glorified VERB If you glorify someone or something, you make them seem better than they really are • *Their aggressive music glorifies violence.* **glorification** NOUN

glorious ADJECTIVE **❶** beautiful and impressive to look at • *glorious beaches.* **❷** very pleasant and giving a feeling of happiness • *glorious sunshine.* **❸** involving great fame and success • *a glorious career.* **gloriously** ADVERB

glory, glories, glorying, gloried NOUN **❶** Glory is fame and admiration for an achievement. **❷** something considered splendid or admirable • *the true glories of the Alps.* ▷ VERB **❸** If you glory in something, you take great delight in it.

glory box, glory boxes NOUN OLD-FASHIONED In Australian and New Zealand English, a chest in which a young woman stores household goods and linen for her marriage.

gloss, glosses, glossing, glossed NOUN **❶** Gloss is a bright shine on a surface. **❷** Gloss is also an attractive appearance which may hide less attractive qualities • *to put a positive gloss on the events.* **❸** If you gloss over a problem or fault, you try to ignore it or deal with it very quickly.

glossary, glossaries NOUN LIBRARY a list of explanations of specialist words, usually found at the back of a book.

glossy, glossier, glossiest ADJECTIVE smooth and shiny • *glossy lipstick* • *glossy paper.*
● SIMILAR WORDS: lustrous, shiny

glove, gloves NOUN Gloves are coverings which you wear over your hands for warmth or protection.

glow, glows, glowing, glowed NOUN **❶** a dull, steady light. **❷** a strong feeling of pleasure or happiness ▷ VERB **❸** If something glows, it shines with a dull, steady light • *A light glowed behind the curtains.* **❹** If you are glowing, you look very happy or healthy.

glower, glowers, glowering, glowered [rhymes with *shower*] VERB If you glower, you stare angrily.
● SIMILAR WORDS: glare, scowl

glowing ADJECTIVE A glowing description praises someone or something very highly • *a glowing character reference.*

glucose NOUN Glucose is a type of sugar found in plants and that animals and people make in their bodies from food to provide energy.

glue, glues, gluing or glueing, glued NOUN **❶** a substance used for sticking things together ▷ VERB **❷** If you glue one object to another, you stick them together using glue.

glum, glummer, glummest

▷ SPELLING NOTE: *On WEDNESday Wayne WED NESta (Wednesday)*

ADJECTIVE miserable and depressed.
glumly ADVERB

glut, gluts **NOUN** a greater quantity of
things than is needed.

gluten [Said **gloo-ten**] **NOUN** a
sticky protein found in cereal grains,
such as wheat.

glutton, gluttons **NOUN** ❶ a person
who eats too much. ❷ If you are a
glutton for something, such as
punishment or hard work, you seem
very eager for it. **gluttony NOUN**

gnarled [Said **narld**] **ADJECTIVE**
old, twisted, and rough • *gnarled
fingers.*

gnat, gnats [Said **nat**] **NOUN** a tiny
flying insect that bites.

gnaw, gnaws, gnawing, gnawed [Said
naw] **VERB** ❶ To gnaw something
means to bite at it repeatedly. ❷ If a
feeling gnaws at you, it keeps worrying
you • *a question gnawed at him.*

gnome, gnomes [Said **nome**] **NOUN**
a tiny old man in fairy stories.

gnu, gnus [Said **noo**] **NOUN** a large
African antelope.

go, goes, going, went, gone **VERB** ❶ If
you go somewhere, you move or travel
there. ❷ You can use 'go' to mean
become • *She felt she was going mad.*
❸ You can use 'go' to describe the
state that someone or something is in
• *Our arrival went unnoticed.* ❹ If
something goes well, it is successful.
If it goes badly, it is unsuccessful. ❺ If
you are going to do something, you
will do it. ❻ If a machine or clock
goes, it works and is not broken.
❼ You use 'go' before giving the
sound something makes or before

quoting a song or saying • *The bell
goes ding-dong.* ❽ If something
goes on something or to someone, it is
allotted to them. ❾ If one thing goes
with another, they are appropriate
together. ❿ If one number goes into
another, it can be divided into it. ⓫ If
you go back on a promise or
agreement, you do not do what you
promised or agreed. ⓬ If someone
goes for you, they attack you. ⓭ If
you go in for something, you decide to
do it as your job. ⓮ If you go out with
someone, you have a romantic
relationship with them. ⓯ If you go
over something, you think about it or
discuss it carefully ▷ **NOUN** ⓰ an
attempt at doing something
▷ **PHRASE** ⓱ If someone is always
on the go, they are always busy and
active. ⓲ **To go** means remaining
• *I've got one more year of my course to
go.*

go down VERB ❶ If something
goes down well, people like it. If it
goes down badly, they do not like it.
❷ If you go down with an illness, you
catch it.

go off VERB ❶ If you go off
someone or something, you stop
liking them. ❷ If a bomb goes off, it
explodes.

go on VERB ❶ If you go on doing
something, you continue to do it. ❷ If
you go on about something, you keep
talking about it in a rather boring way.
❸ Something that is going on is
happening.

go through VERB ❶ If you go
through an unpleasant event, you
experience it. ❷ If a law or agreement
goes through, it is approved and
becomes official. ❸ If you go through
with something, you do it even though

it is unpleasant • *She threatened to quit her job but she didn't go though with it.*

goad, goads, goading, goaded **VERB**
If you goad someone, you encourage them to do something by making them angry or excited • *He had goaded the man into near violence.*

go-ahead **NOUN** If someone gives you the go-ahead for something, they give you permission to do it.

goal, goals **NOUN** ❶ the space, in games like football or hockey, into which the players try to get the ball in order to score a point. ❷ an instance of this. ❸ Your goal is something that you hope to achieve.

goalkeeper, goalkeepers **NOUN**
the player, in games like soccer or hockey, who stands in the goal and tries to stop the other team from scoring.

goanna, goannas **NOUN** a large Australian lizard.

goat, goats **NOUN** an animal, like a sheep, with coarse hair, a beard, and horns.

go-away bird, go-away birds **NOUN** In South Africa, a go-away bird is a grey lourie, a type of bird which lives in open grassland.

gob, gobs **NOUN** INFORMAL Your gob is your mouth.

gobble, gobbles, gobbling, gobbled **VERB** ❶ If you gobble food, you eat it very quickly. ❷ When a turkey gobbles, it makes a loud gurgling sound.

● **SIMILAR WORDS:** devour, guzzle,
● wolf

gobbledygook or **gobbledegook** **NOUN**
Gobbledygook is language that is impossible to understand because it is so formal or complicated.

goblet, goblets **NOUN** a glass with a long stem.

goblin, goblins **NOUN** an ugly, mischievous creature in fairy stories.

god, gods **PROPER NOUN** ❶ The name God is given to the being who is worshipped by Christians, Jews, and Muslims as the creator and ruler of the world ▷ **NOUN** ❷ any of the beings that are believed in many religions to have power over an aspect of life or a part of the world • *Dionysus, the Greek god of wine.* ❸ If someone is your god, you admire them very much ❹ IN PLURAL In a theatre, the gods are the highest seats farthest from the stage.

godchild, godchildren **NOUN** If you are someone's godchild, they agreed to be responsible for your religious upbringing when you were baptized in a Christian church. **goddaughter NOUN godson NOUN**

goddess, goddesses **NOUN** a female god.

godparent, godparents **NOUN** A person's godparent is someone who agrees to be responsible for their religious upbringing when they are baptized in a Christian church. **godfather NOUN godmother NOUN**

godsend, godsends **NOUN** something that comes unexpectedly and helps you very much.

▷ SPELLING NOTE: *Elaine and Emily shout EE when they mEEt to grEEt each other (-ee-)*

goggles PLURAL NOUN Goggles are special glasses that fit closely round your eyes to protect them.

going NOUN The going is the conditions that affect your ability to do something • *He found the going very slow indeed.*

gold NOUN ❶ Gold is a valuable, yellow-coloured metal. It is used for making jewellery and as an international currency. **❷** 'Gold' is also used to mean things that are made of gold ▷ **ADJECTIVE ❸** bright yellow.

golden ADJECTIVE ❶ gold in colour • *golden syrup.* **❷** made of gold • *a golden chain.* **❸** excellent or ideal • *a golden hero.*

golden rule, golden rules **NOUN** a very important rule to remember in order to be able to do something successfully.

golden wedding, golden weddings **NOUN** A married couple's golden wedding is their fiftieth wedding anniversary.

goldfish NOUN a small orange-coloured fish, often kept in ponds or bowls.

goldsmith, goldsmiths **NOUN** a person whose job is making jewellery out of gold.

golf NOUN Golf is a game in which players use special clubs to hit a small ball into holes that are spread out over a large area of grassy land. **golfer NOUN**

golf course, golf courses **NOUN** an area of grassy land where people play golf.

gondola, gondolas [*Said* **gon**-*dol-la*] **NOUN** a long narrow boat used in Venice, which is propelled with a long pole.

gone the past participle of **go**.

gong, gongs **NOUN** a flat, circular piece of metal that is hit with a hammer to make a loud sound, often as a signal for something.

good, better, best; goods **ADJECTIVE ❶** pleasant, acceptable, or satisfactory • *good news.* • *a good film.* **❷** skilful or successful • *good at art.* **❸** kind, thoughtful, and loving • *She was grateful to him for being so good to her.* **❹** well-behaved • *Have the children been good?* **❺** used to emphasize something • *a good few million pounds.* ▷ **NOUN ❻** Good is moral and spiritual justice and virtue • *the forces of good and evil.* **❼** Good also refers to anything that is desirable or beneficial as opposed to harmful • *The break has done me good.* **❽** IN PLURAL Goods are objects that people own or that are sold in shops • *leather goods.* ▷ **PHRASE ❾** **For good** means for ever. **❿** **As good as** means almost • *The election is as good as decided.*
● **USAGE NOTE:** *Good* is an adjective,
● and should not be used as an
● adverb. You should say that *a person*
● *did well* not *did good*

goodbye INTERJECTION You say goodbye when you are leaving someone or ending a telephone conversation.

Good Friday NOUN (RE) Good Friday is the Friday before Easter, when Christians remember the crucifixion of Christ.

a
b
c
d
e
f
g
h
i
j
k
l
m
n
o
p
q
r
s
t
u
v
w
x
y
z

▷ SPELLING NOTE: *'i' before 'e' except after 'c'*

A
B
C
D
E
F
G
H
I
J
K
L
M
N
O
P
Q
R
S
T
U
V
W
X
Y
Z

good-natured ADJECTIVE friendly, pleasant and even-tempered.

goodness NOUN ❶ Goodness is the quality of being kind ▷ INTERJECTION ❷ People say 'Goodness!' or 'My goodness!' when they are surprised.

goodwill NOUN Goodwill is kindness and helpfulness • *Messages of goodwill were exchanged.*

goody, goodies NOUN ❶ INFORMAL Goodies are enjoyable things, often food. ❷ You can call a hero in a film or book a goody.

goose, geese NOUN a fairly large bird with webbed feet and a long neck.

gooseberry, gooseberries NOUN a round, green berry that grows on a bush and has a sharp taste.

gore, gores, goring, gored VERB ❶ If an animal gores someone, it wounds them badly with its horns or tusks ▷ NOUN ❷ Gore is clotted blood from a wound.

gorge, gorges, gorging, gorged NOUN ❶ a deep, narrow valley ▷ VERB ❷ If you gorge yourself, you eat a lot of food greedily.

gorgeous ADJECTIVE extremely pleasant or attractive • *a gorgeous man.*

gorilla, gorillas NOUN a very large, strong ape with very dark fur.
● **WORD HISTORY**: from *Gorillai*, the
● Greek name for an African tribe
● with hairy bodies

gorse NOUN Gorse is a dark green wild shrub that has sharp prickles and small yellow flowers.

gory, gorier, goriest ADJECTIVE Gory situations involve people being injured in horrible ways.

gosling, goslings [Said **goz**-ling] NOUN a young goose.

gospel, gospels NOUN ❶ The Gospels are the four books in the New Testament which describe the life and teachings of Jesus Christ. ❷ a set of ideas that someone strongly believes in • *the so-called gospel of work.* ▷ ADJECTIVE ❸ Gospel music is a style of religious music popular among Black Christians in the United States.

gossip, gossips, gossiping, gossiped NOUN ❶ Gossip is informal conversation, often concerning people's private affairs. ❷ Someone who is a gossip enjoys talking about other people's private affairs ▷ VERB ❸ If you gossip, you talk informally with someone, especially about other people.

got ❶ Got is the past tense and past participle of **get**. ❷ You can use 'have got' instead of the more formal 'have' when talking about possessing things • *The director has got a map.* ❸ You can use 'have got to' instead of the more formal 'have to' when talking about something that must be done • *He has got to win.*

Gothic ADJECTIVE (ART) ❶ Gothic buildings have tall pillars, high vaulted ceilings, and pointed arches. ❷ Gothic printing or writing has letters that are very ornate.

gouge, gouges, gouging, gouged [Said **gowj**] VERB ❶ If you gouge a hole in something, you make a hole in it with a pointed object. ❷ If you gouge something out, you force it out of position with your fingers or a sharp tool.

goulash [Said **goo-lash**] NOUN Goulash is a type of rich meat stew, originally from Hungary.

gourd, gourds [Said **goord**] NOUN a large fruit with a hard outside.

gourmet, gourmets [Said **goor-may**] NOUN a person who enjoys good food and drink and knows a lot about it.

gout NOUN Gout is a disease which causes someone's joints to swell painfully, especially in their toes.

govern, governs, governing, governed VERB ❶ To govern a country means to control it. ❷ Something that governs a situation influences it • *Our thinking is as much governed by habit as by behaviour.*

governess, governesses NOUN a woman who is employed to teach the children in a family and who lives with the family.

government, governments NOUN HISTORY ❶ The government is the group of people who govern a country. ❷ Government is the control and organization of a country. **governmental** ADJECTIVE

governor, governors NOUN ❶ a person who controls and organizes a state or an institution. ❷ In Australia, the Governor is the representative of the King or Queen in a State.

governor-general, governors-general NOUN the chief representative of the King or Queen in Australia, New Zealand, and other Commonwealth countries.

gown, gowns NOUN ❶ a long, formal dress. ❷ a long, dark cloak worn by people such as judges and lawyers.

GP an abbreviation for **general practitioner**.

grab, grabs, grabbing, grabbed VERB ❶ If you grab something, you take it or pick it up roughly. ❷ If you grab an opportunity, you take advantage of it eagerly. ❸ INFORMAL If an idea grabs you, it excites you ▷ NOUN ❹ A grab at an object is an attempt to grab it.
  ● SIMILAR WORDS: ❶ and ❷
  ● grasp, seize, snatch

grace, graces, gracing, graced NOUN ❶ Grace is an elegant way of moving. ❷ Grace is also a pleasant, kind way of behaving. ❸ Grace is also a short prayer of thanks said before a meal. ❹ Dukes and archbishops are addressed as 'Your Grace' and referred to as 'His Grace' ▷ VERB ❺ Something that graces a place makes it more attractive. ❻ If someone important graces an event, they kindly agree to be present at it. **graceful** ADJECTIVE **gracefully** ADVERB
  ● SIMILAR WORDS: ❶ elegance,
  ● poise

gracious ADJECTIVE ❶ kind, polite, and pleasant. ▷ INTERJECTION ❷ 'Good gracious' is an exclamation of surprise. **graciously** ADVERB

grade, grades, grading, graded VERB ❶ To grade things means to arrange them according to quality ▷ NOUN ❷ The grade of something is its quality. ❸ the mark that you get for an exam or piece of written work. ❹ Your grade in a company or

▷ SPELLING NOTE: *an ELegant angEL (angel)*

organization is your level of importance or your rank.

gradient, gradients NOUN ❶ a slope or the steepness of a slope. ❷ (MATHS) In maths, the gradient of a side of triangle is the steepness of the line from its height to its base.

gradual ADJECTIVE happening or changing slowly over a long period of time.

gradually ADVERB happening or changing slowly over a long period of time.

graduate, graduates, graduating, graduated NOUN ❶ a person who has completed a first degree at a university or college ▷ VERB ❷ When students graduate, they complete a first degree at a university or college. ❸ To graduate from one thing to another means to progress gradually towards the second thing. **graduation** NOUN

graffiti [Said graf-*fee*-tee] NOUN Graffiti is slogans or drawings scribbled on walls.
● **WORD HISTORY:** from Italian *graffiare* meaning 'to scratch a surface'
● **USAGE NOTE:** Although *graffiti* is a plural in Italian, the language it comes from, in English it can be used as a singular noun or a plural noun

graft, grafts, grafting, grafted NOUN ❶ a piece of living tissue which is used to replace by surgery a damaged or unhealthy part of a person's body. ❷ INFORMAL Graft is hard work ▷ VERB ❸ To graft one thing to another means to attach it.

grain, grains NOUN ❶ a cereal plant, such as wheat, that is grown as a crop and used for food. ❷ Grains are seeds of a cereal plant. ❸ A grain of sand or salt is a tiny particle of it. ❹ The grain of a piece of wood is the pattern of lines made by the fibres in it ▷ PHRASE ❺ If something **goes against the grain**, you find it difficult to accept because it is against your principles.
● **SIMILAR WORDS:** ❸ bit, granule,
● particle

gram, grams; *also spelt* **gramme** NOUN a unit of weight equal to one thousandth of a kilogram.

grammar NOUN (ENGLISH) Grammar is the rules of a language relating to the ways you can combine words to form sentences.

grammar school, grammar schools NOUN ❶ a secondary school for pupils of high academic ability. ❷ In Australia, a private school, usually one controlled by a church.

grammatical ADJECTIVE ❶ relating to grammar • *grammatical knowledge.* ❷ following the rules of grammar correctly • *grammatical sentences.* **grammatically** ADVERB

gran, grans NOUN INFORMAL Your gran is your grandmother.

granary, granaries NOUN ❶ a building for storing grain ▷ ADJECTIVE ❷ TRADEMARK Granary bread contains whole grains of wheat.

grand, grander, grandest ADJECTIVE ❶ magnificent in appearance and size • *a grand house.* ❷ very important • *the grand scheme of your life.* ❸ INFORMAL very pleasant or enjoyable • *It was a grand day.* **4** A grand total is the final complete amount ▷ **NOUN 5** INFORMAL a thousand pounds or dollars. **grandly ADVERB**

● **SIMILAR WORDS: 1** impressive,
● magnificent, splendid

grandad, grandads **NOUN** INFORMAL Your grandad is your grandfather.

grandchild, grandchildren **NOUN** Someone's grandchildren are the children of their son or daughter.

granddaughter, granddaughters **NOUN** Someone's granddaughter is the daughter of their son or daughter.

grandeur [Said **grand**-yer] **NOUN** Grandeur is great beauty and magnificence.

grandfather, grandfathers **NOUN** Your grandfather is your father's father or your mother's father.

grandfather clock, grandfather clocks **NOUN** a clock in a tall wooden case that stands on the floor.

grandiose [Said **gran**-dee-ose] **ADJECTIVE** intended to be very impressive, but seeming ridiculous • *a grandiose gesture of love.*

grandma, grandmas **NOUN** INFORMAL Your grandma is your grandmother.

grandmother, grandmothers **NOUN** Your grandmother is your father's mother or your mother's mother.

grandparent, grandparents **NOUN** Your grandparents are your parents' parents.

grand piano, grand pianos **NOUN**

a large flat piano with horizontal strings.

grandson, grandsons **NOUN** Someone's grandson is the son of their son or daughter.

grandstand, grandstands **NOUN** a structure with a roof and seats for spectators at a sports ground.

granite [Said **gran**-nit] **NOUN** Granite is a very hard rock used in building.

granny, grannies **NOUN** INFORMAL Your granny is your grandmother.

grant, grants, granting, granted **NOUN 1** an amount of money that an official body gives to someone for a particular purpose • *a grant to carry out repairs.* ▷ **VERB 2** If you grant something to someone, you allow them to have it. **3** If you grant that something is true, you admit that it is true ▷ **PHRASES 4** If you **take something for granted**, you believe it without thinking about it. If you **take someone for granted**, you benefit from them without showing that you are grateful.

granule, granules **NOUN** a very small piece of something • *granules of salt.*

grape, grapes **NOUN** a small green or purple fruit, eaten raw or used to make wine.

grapefruit, grapefruits **NOUN** a large, round, yellow citrus fruit.

grapevine, grapevines **NOUN 1** a climbing plant which grapes grow on. **2** If you hear some news on the grapevine, it has been passed on from person to person, usually unofficially.

▷ SPELLING NOTE: *A Rude Idiot Thought He Might Eat Toffee In Church (arithmetic)*

graph | 376

graph, graphs NOUN (MATHS) a diagram in which a line shows how two sets of numbers or measurements are related.

-graph SUFFIX '-graph' means a writer or recorder of some sort or something made by writing, drawing or recording • *telegraph* • *autograph*.

graphic ADJECTIVE ❶ A graphic description is very detailed and lifelike. ❷ relating to drawing or painting. **graphically** ADVERB

graphics PLURAL NOUN (ICT) Graphics are drawings and pictures composed of simple lines and strong colours • *computerized graphics*.

graphite NOUN a black form of carbon that is used in pencil leads.

grapple, grapples, grappling, grappled VERB ❶ If you grapple with someone, you struggle with them while fighting. ❷ If you grapple with a problem, you try hard to solve it.

grasp, grasps, grasping, grasped VERB ❶ If you grasp something, you hold it firmly. ❷ If you grasp an idea, you understand it ▷ NOUN ❸ a firm hold. ❹ Your grasp of something is your understanding of it • *She has a good grasp of Spanish.*

grass, grasses NOUN Grass is the common green plant that grows on lawns and in parks. **grassy** ADJECTIVE

grasshopper, grasshoppers NOUN an insect with long back legs which it uses for jumping and making a high-pitched sound.

grate, grates, grating, grated NOUN ❶ a framework of metal bars in a fireplace ▷ VERB ❷ To grate food means to shred it into small pieces by rubbing it against a grater. ❸ When something grates on something else, it rubs against it making a harsh sound. ❹ If something grates on you, it irritates you.

grateful ADJECTIVE If you are grateful for something, you are glad you have it and want to thank the person who gave it to you. **gratefully** ADVERB
● SIMILAR WORDS: appreciative, thankful

grater, graters NOUN a small metal tool used for grating food.

gratify, gratifies, gratifying, gratified VERB ❶ If you are gratified by something, you are pleased by it. ❷ If you gratify a wish or feeling, you satisfy it.

grating, gratings NOUN ❶ a metal frame with bars across it fastened over a hole in a wall or in the ground ▷ ADJECTIVE ❷ A grating sound is harsh and unpleasant • *grating melodies*.

gratis [Said **grah**-tis] ADVERB OR ADJECTIVE free • *food and drink supplied gratis.*

gratitude NOUN Gratitude is the feeling of being grateful.
● SIMILAR WORDS: appreciation, thankfulness

gratuitous [Said grat-**yoo**-it-tuss] ADJECTIVE unnecessary • *a gratuitous attack.* **gratuitously** ADVERB

grave, graves; graver, gravest [rhymes with **save**] NOUN ❶ a place where a

▷ SPELLING NOTE: *Beautiful Elephants Are Usually Tiny (beautiful)*

corpse is buried ▷ **ADJECTIVE**
2 FORMAL very serious • *grave danger*.

grave [*Said* **grahv**] **ADJECTIVE** In
French and some other languages, a
grave accent is a line sloping
downwards from left to right placed
over a vowel to indicate a change in
pronunciation, as in the word *lèvre* (a
hare).

gravel NOUN Gravel is small stones
used for making roads and paths.

gravestone, gravestones **NOUN** a
large stone placed over someone's
grave, with their name on it.

graveyard, graveyards **NOUN** an
area of land where corpses are
buried.

gravitate, gravitates, gravitating,
gravitated **VERB** When people
gravitate towards something, they go
towards it because they are attracted
by it.

gravitation NOUN (SCIENCE)
Gravitation is the force which causes
objects to be attracted to each other.
gravitational ADJECTIVE

gravity NOUN **1** (SCIENCE) Gravity
is the force that makes things fall
when you drop them. **2** FORMAL The
gravity of a situation is its seriousness.

gravy NOUN Gravy is a brown sauce
made from meat juices.

graze, grazes, grazing, grazed **VERB**
1 When animals graze, they eat
grass. **2** If something grazes a part of
your body, it scrapes against it,
injuring you slightly ▷ **NOUN** **3** a
slight injury caused by something
scraping against your skin.

grease, greases, greasing, greased
NOUN **1** Grease is an oily substance
used for lubricating machines.
2 Grease is also melted animal fat,
used in cooking. **3** Grease is also an
oily substance produced by your skin
and found in your hair ▷ **VERB** **4** If
you grease something, you lubricate it
with grease. **greasy ADJECTIVE**

great, greater, greatest **ADJECTIVE**
1 very large • *a great sea* • *great
efforts.* **2** very important • *a great
artist.* **3** INFORMAL very good • *Paul
had a great time.* **greatly ADVERB**
greatness NOUN

Great Britain NOUN Great Britain
is the largest of the British Isles,
consisting of England, Scotland, and
Wales.

Great Dane, Great Danes **NOUN** a
very large dog with short hair.

great-grandfather, great-
grandfathers **NOUN** Your great-
grandfather is your father's or
mother's grandfather.

great-grandmother, great-
grandmothers **NOUN** Your great-
grandmother is your father's or
mother's grandmother.

greed NOUN Greed is a desire for
more of something than you really
need.

greedy, greedier, greediest
ADJECTIVE wanting more of
something than you really need.
greedily ADVERB **greediness
NOUN**
  ● **SIMILAR WORDS:** grasping,
  ● insatiable, voracious

Greek, Greeks **ADJECTIVE**

a
b
c
d
e
f
g
h
i
j
k
l
m
n
o
p
q
r
s
t
u
v
w
x
y
z

▷ SPELLING NOTE: *Betty Eats Cakes And Uses Seven Eggs (because)*

❶ belonging or relating to Greece ▷ **NOUN ❷** someone who comes from Greece. **❸** Greek is the main language spoken in Greece.

green, greener, greenest; greens **ADJECTIVE OR NOUN ❶** Green is a colour between yellow and blue on the spectrum ▷ **NOUN ❷** an area of grass in the middle of a village. **❸** A putting green or bowling green is a grassy area on which putting or bowls is played. **❹** an area of smooth short grass around each hole on a golf course **❺** IN PLURAL Greens are green vegetables ▷ **ADJECTIVE ❻** (GEOGRAPHY) 'Green' is used to describe political movements which are concerned with environmental issues. **❼** INFORMAL Someone who is green is young and inexperienced.

green belt, green belts **NOUN** (GEOGRAPHY) The green belt is the area of countryside round a city where people are not allowed to build houses and factories.

greenery NOUN Greenery is a lot of trees, bushes, or other green plants together in one place.

greenfly NOUN Greenfly are small green insects that damage plants.

greengrocer, greengrocers **NOUN** a shopkeeper who sells vegetables and fruit.

greenhouse, greenhouses **NOUN** a glass building in which people grow plants that need to be kept warm.

greenhouse effect NOUN (GEOGRAPHY) the gradual rise in temperature in the earth's atmosphere due to heat being absorbed from the sun and being trapped by gases such as carbon dioxide in the air around the earth.

green paper, green papers **NOUN** In Britain, Australia, and New Zealand, a report published by the government containing proposals to be discussed before decisions are made about them.

greenstone NOUN a type of jade found in New Zealand and used for making ornaments, weapons, and tools.

greet, greets, greeting, greeted **VERB ❶** If you greet someone, you say something friendly like 'hello' to them when you meet them. **❷** If you greet something in a particular way, you react to it in that way • *He was greeted with deep suspicion.*
● **SIMILAR WORDS: ❶** hail, salute

greeting, greetings **NOUN** something friendly that you say to someone when you meet them • *Her greeting was warm.*

gregarious [Said grig-**air**-ee-uss] **ADJECTIVE** FORMAL Someone who is gregarious enjoys being with other people.

grenade, grenades **NOUN** a small bomb, containing explosive or tear gas, which can be thrown.
● **WORD HISTORY:** from Spanish
● *granada* meaning 'pomegranate'

grevillea, grevilleas **NOUN** an evergreen Australian tree or shrub.

grew the past tense of grow.

grey, greyer, greyest; greys, greying, greyed **ADJECTIVE OR NOUN ❶** Grey is a colour between black and white ▷ **ADJECTIVE ❷** dull and boring

▷ SPELLING NOTE: *there's a rAKE in the brAKEs (br**a**ke)*

• *He's a bit of a grey man.* ▷ **VERB**
❸ If someone is greying, their hair is going grey. **greyness NOUN**

greyhound, greyhounds **NOUN** a thin dog with long legs that can run very fast.

grid, grids **NOUN** ❶ a pattern of lines crossing each other to form squares. ❷ The grid is the network of wires and cables by which electricity is distributed throughout a country.

grief NOUN ❶ Grief is extreme sadness ▷ **PHRASE** ❷ If someone or something **comes to grief**, they fail or are injured.
● **SIMILAR WORDS:** ❶ heartache,
● sadness, sorrow

grievance, grievances **NOUN** a reason for complaining.

grieve, grieves, grieving, grieved **VERB** ❶ If you grieve, you are extremely sad, especially because someone has died. ❷ If something grieves you, it makes you feel very sad.
● **SIMILAR WORDS:** ❶ lament,
● mourn

grievous ADJECTIVE FORMAL extremely serious • *grievous damage.* **grievously ADVERB**

grill, grills, grilling, grilled **NOUN** ❶ a part on a cooker where food is cooked by strong heat from above. ❷ a metal frame on which you cook food over a fire ▷ **VERB** ❸ If you grill food, you cook it on or under a grill.
❹ INFORMAL If you grill someone, you ask them a lot of questions in a very intense way.

grille, grilles [*rhymes with pill*] **NOUN** a metal framework over a window or piece of machinery, used for protection.

grim, grimmer, grimmest **ADJECTIVE** ❶ If a situation or piece of news is grim, it is very unpleasant and worrying • *There are grim times ahead.* ❷ Grim places are unattractive and depressing. ❸ If someone is grim, they are very serious or stern. **grimly ADVERB**

grimace, grimaces, grimacing, grimaced [*Said grim-***mace**] **NOUN** ❶ a twisted facial expression indicating disgust or pain ▷ **VERB** ❷ When someone grimaces, they make a grimace.

grime NOUN Grime is thick dirt which gathers on the surface of something. **grimy ADJECTIVE**

grin, grins, grinning, grinned **VERB** ❶ If you grin, you smile broadly ▷ **NOUN** ❷ a broad smile ▷ **PHRASE** ❸ If you **grin and bear it**, you accept a difficult situation without complaining.

grind, grinds, grinding, ground **VERB** ❶ If you grind something such as pepper, you crush it into a fine powder. ❷ If you grind your teeth, you rub your upper and lower teeth together ▷ **PHRASE** ❸ If something **grinds to a halt**, it stops • *Progress ground to a halt.*
● **SIMILAR WORDS:** ❶ crush,
● powder, pulverize

grip, grips, gripping, gripped **NOUN** ❶ a firm hold. ❷ a handle on a bat or a racket. ❸ Your grip on a situation is your control over it ▷ **VERB** ❹ If you grip something, you hold it firmly ▷ **PHRASE** ❺ If you **get to grips**

a
b
c
d
e
f
g
h
i
j
k
l
m
n
o
p
q
r
s
t
u
v
w
x
y
z

▷ SPELLING NOTE: *you'll br**EAK** that **E**lectrical **A**erial, **K**itty (br**eak**)*

with a situation or problem, you start to deal with it effectively.

grisly, grislier, grisliest ADJECTIVE very nasty and horrible • *a grisly murder scene*.

grit, grits, gritting, gritted NOUN ❶ Grit consists of very small stones. It is put on icy roads to make them less slippery ▷ VERB ❷ When workmen grit an icy road, they put grit on it ▷ PHRASE ❸ To grit your teeth means to decide to carry on in a difficult situation. **gritty** ADJECTIVE

grizzled ADJECTIVE Grizzled hair is grey. A grizzled person has grey hair.

grizzly bear, grizzly bears NOUN a large, greyish-brown bear from North America.

groan, groans, groaning, groaned VERB ❶ If you groan, you make a long, low sound of pain, unhappiness, or disapproval ▷ NOUN ❷ the sound you make when you groan.

grocer, grocers NOUN a shopkeeper who sells many kinds of food and other household goods.

grocery, groceries NOUN ❶ a grocer's shop ❷ IN PLURAL Groceries are the goods that you buy in a grocer's shop.

grog NOUN INFORMAL In Australian and New Zealand English, grog is any alcoholic drink.

groin, groins NOUN the area where your legs join the main part of your body at the front.

groom, grooms, grooming, groomed NOUN ❶ someone who looks after horses in a stable. ❷ At a wedding,

the groom is the bridegroom ▷ VERB ❸ To groom an animal means to clean its fur. ❹ If you groom someone for a job, you prepare them for it by teaching them the skills they will need.

groove, grooves NOUN a deep line cut into a surface. **grooved** ADJECTIVE

grope, gropes, groping, groped VERB ❶ If you grope for something you cannot see, you search for it with your hands. ❷ If you grope for something such as the solution to a problem, you try to think of it.

gross, grosser, grossest; grosses, grossing, grossed ADJECTIVE ❶ extremely bad • *a gross betrayal*. ❷ Gross speech or behaviour is very rude. ❸ Gross things are ugly • *gross holiday outfits*. ❹ Someone's gross income is their total income before any deductions are made. ❺ The gross weight of something is its total weight including the weight of its container ▷ VERB ❻ If you gross an amount of money, you earn that amount in total. **grossly** ADVERB

grotesque [Said groh-**tesk**] ADJECTIVE ❶ exaggerated and absurd • *It was the most grotesque thing she had ever heard.* ❷ very strange and ugly • *grotesque animal puppets.* **grotesquely** ADVERB
● WORD HISTORY: from Old Italian
● *pittura grottesca* meaning 'cave
● paintings'

grotto, grottoes or grottos NOUN a small cave that people visit because it is attractive.

ground, grounds, grounding,

▷ SPELLING NOTE: *I always visit my FRIend on a FRIday (Friday)*

grounded **NOUN** ❶ The ground is the surface of the earth. ❷ a piece of land that is used for a particular purpose • *the training ground*. ❸ The ground covered by a book or course is the range of subjects it deals with ❹ IN PLURAL The grounds of a large building are the land belonging to it and surrounding it. ❺ FORMAL The grounds for something are the reasons for it • *genuine grounds for caution*. ▷ **VERB** ❻ FORMAL If something is grounded in something else, it is based on it. ❼ If an aircraft is grounded, it has to remain on the ground. ❽ Ground is the past tense and past participle of **grind**.

ground floor, ground floors **NOUN** The ground floor of a building is the floor that is approximately level with the ground.

grounding **NOUN** If you have a grounding in a skill or subject, you have had basic instruction in it.

groundless **ADJECTIVE** not based on reason or evidence • *groundless accusations*.

group, groups, grouping, grouped
NOUN ❶ A group of things or people is a number of them that are linked together in some way. ❷ a number of musicians who perform pop music together ▷ **VERB** ❸ When things or people are grouped together, they are linked together in some way.
  ● **SIMILAR WORDS:** ❶ band,
  ● bunch, crowd, set

grouping, groupings **NOUN** a number of things or people that are linked together in some way.

grouse, grouse **NOUN** a fat brown or grey bird, often shot for sport.

grove, groves **NOUN** LITERARY a group of trees growing close together.

grovel, grovels, grovelling, grovelled
VERB If you grovel, you behave in an unpleasantly humble way towards someone you regard as important.

grow, grows, growing, grew, grown
VERB ❶ To grow means to increase in size or amount. ❷ If a tree or plant grows somewhere, it is alive there. ❸ When people grow plants, they plant them and look after them. ❹ If a man grows a beard or moustache, he lets it develop by not shaving. ❺ To grow also means to pass gradually into a particular state. ❻ If one thing grows from another, it develops from it. ❼ INFORMAL If something grows on you, you gradually get to like it.
grow up VERB When a child grows up, he or she becomes an adult.
  ● **SIMILAR WORDS:** ❶ expand, get
  ● bigger, increase

growl, growls, growling, growled
VERB ❶ When an animal growls, it makes a low rumbling sound, usually because it is angry. ❷ If you growl something, you say it in a low, rough, rather angry voice ▷ **NOUN** ❸ the sound an animal makes when it growls.

grown-up, grown-ups **NOUN**
❶ INFORMAL an adult ▷ **ADJECTIVE**
❷ Someone who is grown-up is adult, or behaves like an adult.

growth, growths **NOUN** ❶ When there is a growth in something, it gets bigger • *the growth of the fishing industry*. ❷ (SCIENCE) Growth is the

a
b
c
d
e
f
g
h
i
j
k
l
m
n
o
p
q
r
s
t
u
v
w
x
y
z

▷ SPELLING NOTE: *I want to see (C) your licenCe (licence)*

---

process by which something develops to its full size. ❸ an abnormal lump that grows inside or on a person, animal, or plant.

● **SIMILAR WORDS:** ❶ expansion, ● increase

grub, grubs **NOUN** ❶ a wormlike insect that has just hatched from its egg. ❷ **INFORMAL** Grub is food.

grubby, grubbier, grubbiest **ADJECTIVE** rather dirty.

grudge, grudges, grudging, grudged **NOUN** ❶ If you have a grudge against someone, you resent them because they have harmed you in the past ▷ **VERB** ❷ If you grudge someone something, you give it to them unwillingly, or are displeased that they have it.

grudging ADJECTIVE done or felt unwillingly • *grudging admiration.* **grudgingly ADVERB**

gruel NOUN Gruel is oatmeal boiled in water or milk.

gruelling ADJECTIVE difficult and tiring • *a gruelling race.*

gruesome ADJECTIVE shocking and horrible • *gruesome pictures.*

gruff, gruffer, gruffest **ADJECTIVE** If someone's voice is gruff, it sounds rough and unfriendly.

grumble, grumbles, grumbling, grumbled **VERB** ❶ If you grumble, you complain in a bad-tempered way ▷ **NOUN** ❷ a bad-tempered complaint.

grumpy, grumpier, grumpiest **ADJECTIVE** bad-tempered and fed-up.

● **SIMILAR WORDS:** ill-tempered, ● irritable

grunt, grunts, grunting, grunted **VERB** ❶ If a person or a pig grunts, they make a short, low, gruff sound ▷ **NOUN** ❷ the sound a person or a pig makes when they grunt.

guarantee, guarantees, guaranteeing, guaranteed **NOUN** ❶ If something is a guarantee of something else, it makes it certain that it will happen. ❷ a written promise that if a product develops a fault it will be replaced or repaired free ▷ **VERB** ❸ If something or someone guarantees something, they make certain that it will happen • *Money may not guarantee success.* **guarantor NOUN**

● **SIMILAR WORDS:** ❶ assurance, ● pledge, promise ❸ ensure, ● promise

guard, guards, guarding, guarded **VERB** ❶ If you guard a person or object, you stay near to them to protect them. ❷ If you guard a person, you stop them making trouble or escaping. ❸ If you guard against something, you are careful to avoid it happening ▷ **NOUN** ❹ a person or group of people who guard a person, object, or place. ❺ a railway official in charge of a train. ❻ Any object which covers something to prevent it causing harm can be called a guard • *a fire guard.*

● **SIMILAR WORDS:** ❶ defend, ● protect, watch over ❸ protector, ● sentry, watchman

guardian, guardians **NOUN** ❶ someone who has been legally appointed to look after an orphaned child. **2** A guardian of something is someone who protects it • *a guardian of the law.* **guardianship NOUN**

guernsey, guernseys **NOUN 1** In Australian and New Zealand English, a jersey. **2** a sleeveless top worn by an Australian Rules football player.

guerrilla, guerrillas [*Said ger-ril-la*]; *also spelt* **guerilla NOUN** a member of a small unofficial army fighting an official army.
  ● **WORD HISTORY:** from Spanish
  ● *guerrilla* meaning 'little war'

guess, guesses, guessing, guessed **VERB 1** If you guess something, you form or express an opinion that it is the case, without having much information ▷ **NOUN 2** (MATHS) an attempt to give the correct answer to something without having much information, or without working it out properly.
  ● **SIMILAR WORDS: 1** conjecture,
  ● suppose **2** conjecture,
  ● speculation, supposition

guest, guests **NOUN 1** someone who stays at your home or who attends an occasion because they have been invited. **2** The guests in a hotel are the people staying there.

guffaw NOUN a loud, coarse laugh.

guidance NOUN Guidance is help and advice.

guide, guides, guiding, guided **NOUN 1** someone who shows you round places, or leads the way through difficult country. **2** a book which gives you information or instructions • *a Sydney street guide.* **3** A Guide is a girl who is a member of an organization that encourages

discipline and practical skills ▷ **VERB 4** If you guide someone in a particular direction, you lead them in that direction. **5** If you are guided by something, it influences your actions or decisions.

guidebook, guidebooks **NOUN** a book which gives information about a place.

guide dog, guide dogs **NOUN** a dog that has been trained to lead a blind person.

guideline, guidelines **NOUN** a piece of advice about how something should be done.

guild, guilds **NOUN** a society of people • *the Screen Writers' Guild.*

guile [*rhymes with* **mile**] **NOUN** Guile is cunning and deceit. **guileless ADJECTIVE**

guillotine, guillotines [*Said gil-lot-teen*] (HISTORY) **NOUN** a machine used for beheading people, especially in the past in France.

guilt NOUN 1 Guilt is an unhappy feeling of having done something wrong. **2** Someone's guilt is the fact that they have done something wrong • *The law will decide their guilt.*

guilty, guiltier, guiltiest **ADJECTIVE 1** If you are guilty of doing something wrong, you did it • *He was guilty of theft.* **2** If you feel guilty, you are unhappy because you have done something wrong. **guiltily ADVERB**

guinea, guineas [*Said gin-ee*] **NOUN** an old British unit of money, worth 21 shillings.

guinea pig, guinea pigs **NOUN 1** a

a
b
c
d
e
f
g
h
i
j
k
l
m
n
o
p
q
r
s
t
u
v
w
x
y
z

▷ SPELLING NOTE: *have a pIEce of pIE (piece)*

small furry animal without a tail, often kept as a pet. ❷ a person used to try something out on • *a guinea pig for a new drug.*

guise, guises [rhymes with *prize*] **NOUN** a misleading appearance • *political statements in the guise of religious talk.*

guitar, guitars **NOUN** a musical instrument with six strings which are strummed or plucked. **guitarist NOUN**

gulf, gulfs **NOUN** ❶ a very large bay. ❷ a wide gap or difference between two things or people.

gull, gulls **NOUN** a sea bird with long wings, white and grey or black feathers, and webbed feet.
  ● **WORD HISTORY:** from Welsh
  ● *gwylan*

gullet, gullets **NOUN** the tube that goes from your mouth to your stomach.

gullible ADJECTIVE easily tricked. **gullibility NOUN**
  ● **SIMILAR WORDS:** credulous, naive

gully, gullies **NOUN** a long, narrow valley.

gulp, gulps, gulping, gulped **VERB** ❶ If you gulp food or drink, you swallow large quantities of it. ❷ If you gulp, you swallow air, because you are nervous ▷ **NOUN** ❸ A gulp of food or drink is a large quantity of it swallowed at one time.

gum, gums **NOUN** ❶ Gum is a soft flavoured substance that people chew but do not swallow. ❷ Gum is also glue for sticking paper. ❸ Your gums are the firm flesh in which your teeth

are set • *healthy teeth and gums.*

gumboot, gumboots **NOUN** Gumboots are long waterproof boots.

gumtree, gumtrees **NOUN** a eucalyptus, or other tree which produces gum.

gun, guns **NOUN** a weapon which fires bullets or shells.

gunfire NOUN Gunfire is the repeated firing of guns.

gunpowder NOUN Gunpowder is an explosive powder made from a mixture of potassium nitrate and other substances.

gunshot, gunshots **NOUN** the sound of a gun being fired.

gunyah, gunyahs **NOUN** In Australia, a hut or shelter in the bush.

guppy, guppies **NOUN** a small, brightly coloured tropical fish.

gurdwara NOUN a Sikh place of worship.
  ● **WORD HISTORY:** from Sanskrit
  ● *guru* meaning 'teacher' + *dvārā*
  ● meaning 'door'

gurgle, gurgles, gurgling, gurgled **VERB** ❶ To gurgle means to make a bubbling sound ▷ **NOUN** ❷ a bubbling sound.

guru, gurus [Said *goo-rooh*] **NOUN** a spiritual leader and teacher, especially in India.
  ● **WORD HISTORY:** from Sanskrit
  ● *guruh* meaning 'weighty' or 'of
  ● importance'

gush, gushes, gushing, gushed **VERB** ❶ When liquid gushes from something, it flows out of it in large

quantities. ❷ When people gush, they express admiration or pleasure in an exaggerated way. **gushing ADJECTIVE**
● **SIMILAR WORDS: ❶** flow, pour,
● spurt, stream

gust, gusts **NOUN** a sudden rush of wind. **gusty ADJECTIVE**

gusto NOUN Gusto is energy and enthusiasm • *Her gusto for life was amazing.*

gut, guts, gutting, gutted **NOUN ❶ IN PLURAL** Your guts are your internal organs, especially your intestines. ❷ **IN PLURAL, INFORMAL** Guts is courage. ▷ **VERB ❸** To gut a dead fish means to remove its internal organs. ❹ If a building is gutted, the inside is destroyed, especially by fire.
● **SIMILAR WORDS: ❶** entrails,
● innards, intestines

gutter, gutters **NOUN ❶** the edge of a road next to the pavement, where rain collects and flows away. ❷ a channel fixed to the edge of a roof, where rain collects and flows away. **guttering NOUN**

guttural [Said **gut**-ter-al] **ADJECTIVE** Guttural sounds are produced at the back of a person's throat and are often considered to be unpleasant.

guy, guys **NOUN ❶ INFORMAL** a man or boy. ❷ a crude model of Guy Fawkes, that is burnt on top of a bonfire on Guy Fawkes Day (November 5).
● **WORD HISTORY:** short for *Guy*
● *Fawkes*, who plotted to blow up the
● British Houses of Parliament

guzzle, guzzles, guzzling, guzzled **VERB** To guzzle something means to drink or eat it quickly and greedily.

gym, gyms **NOUN** (PE) **❶** a gymnasium. ❷ Gym is gymnastics.

gymkhana, gymkhanas [Said jim-**kah**-na] **NOUN** an event in which people take part in horse-riding contests.
● **WORD HISTORY:** from Hindi
● *gend-khana* literally meaning 'ball
● house', because it is where sports
● were held

gymnasium, gymnasiums **NOUN** a room with special equipment for physical exercises.

gymnast, gymnasts **NOUN** someone who is trained in gymnastics. **gymnastic ADJECTIVE**

gymnastics NOUN (PE) Gymnastics is physical exercises, especially ones using equipment such as bars and ropes.

gynaecology or **gynecology** [Said gie-nak-**kol**-loj-ee] **NOUN** Gynaecology is the branch of medical science concerned with the female reproductive system. **gynaecologist NOUN gynaecological ADJECTIVE**

gypsy, gypsies; *also spelt* **gipsy NOUN** a member of a race of people who travel from place to place in caravans.
● **WORD HISTORY:** from 'Egyptian',
● because people used to think
● gypsies came from Egypt

gyrate, gyrates, gyrating, gyrated [Said jy-**rate**] **VERB** To gyrate means to move round in a circle.

a
b
c
d
e
f
g
h
i
j
k
l
m
n
o
p
q
r
s
t
u
v
w
x
y
z

▷ SPELLING NOTE: *I went to see (C) the doctor's new practiCe (practice)*

Hh

Some words which sound as if they might begin with letter *h*, instead begin with the letters *wh*, for example *who, whole, wholly, whom, whore,* and *whose*.

habit, habits **NOUN** ❶ something that you do often • *He got into the habit of eating out.* ❷ something that you keep doing and find it difficult to stop doing • *a 20-a-day smoking habit.* ❸ A monk's or nun's habit is a garment like a loose dress. **habitual ADJECTIVE habitually ADVERB**

habitat, habitats **NOUN** (GEOGRAPHY) the natural home of a plant or animal.

hack, hacks, hacking, hacked **VERB** ❶ If you hack at something, you cut it using rough strokes ▷ **NOUN** ❷ a writer or journalist who produces work fast without worrying about quality.

hacker, hackers **NOUN** INFORMAL someone who uses a computer to break into the computer system of a company or government.

hackles PLURAL NOUN ❶ A dog's hackles are the hairs on the back of its neck which rise when it is angry ▷ **PHRASE** ❷ Something that **makes your hackles rise** makes you angry.

hackneyed ADJECTIVE A hackneyed phrase is meaningless because it has been used too often.
● **SIMILAR WORDS:** clichéd,
● unoriginal

hacksaw, hacksaws **NOUN** a small saw with a narrow blade set in a frame.

haddock NOUN an edible sea fish.

haemoglobin [Said hee-moh-**gloh**-bin] **NOUN** Haemoglobin is a substance in red blood cells which carries oxygen round the body.

haemophilia or **hemophilia** [Said hee-moh-**fil**-lee-a] **NOUN** (SCIENCE) Haemophilia is a disease in which a person's blood does not clot so they bleed for too long when they are injured. **haemophiliac NOUN**

haemorrhage [Said **hem**-er-rij] **NOUN** (SCIENCE) A haemorrhage is serious bleeding especially inside a person's body.

haemorrhoids [Said **hem**-er-roydz] **PLURAL NOUN** (SCIENCE) Haemorrhoids are painful lumps around the anus that are caused by swollen veins.

hag, hags **NOUN** OFFENSIVE an ugly old woman.

haggard ADJECTIVE A person who is haggard looks very tired and ill.

haggis NOUN Haggis is a Scottish dish made of the internal organs of a

▷ SPELLING NOTE: *You must practiSe your Ss (practise)*

sheep, boiled together with oatmeal and spices in a skin.

haggle, haggles, haggling, haggled **VERB** If you haggle with someone, you argue with them, usually about the cost of something.

haiku NOUN (ENGLISH) a type of very short Japanese poem which has 17 syllables.
● **USAGE NOTE:** The plural of *haiku* is *haiku*

hail, hails, hailing, hailed **NOUN**
❶ Hail is frozen rain. ❷ A hail of things is a lot of them falling together • *a hail of bullets* • *a hail of protest.*
▷ **VERB** ❸ When it is hailing, frozen rain is falling. ❹ If someone hails you, they call you to attract your attention or greet you • *He hailed a taxi.*

hair, hairs **NOUN** Hair consists of the long, threadlike strands that grow from the skin of animals and humans.

haircut, haircuts **NOUN** the cutting of someone's hair; also the style in which it is cut.

hairdo, hairdos **NOUN** a hairstyle.

hairdresser, hairdressers **NOUN** someone who is trained to cut and style people's hair; also a shop where this is done. **hairdressing NOUN OR ADJECTIVE**

hairline, hairlines **NOUN** ❶ the edge of the area on your forehead where your hair grows ▷ **ADJECTIVE**
❷ A hairline crack is so fine that you can hardly see it.

hairpin, hairpins **NOUN** ❶ a U-shaped wire used to hold hair in position ▷ **ADJECTIVE** ❷ A hairpin bend is a U-shaped bend in the road.

hair-raising ADJECTIVE very frightening or exciting.

hairstyle, hairstyles **NOUN** Someone's hairstyle is the way in which their hair is arranged or cut.

hairy, hairier, hairiest **ADJECTIVE**
❶ covered in a lot of hair.
❷ INFORMAL difficult, exciting, and rather frightening • *He had lived through many hairy adventures.*

hajj, hajjes [rhymes with **badge**] **NOUN** (RE) The hajj is the pilgrimage to Mecca that every Muslim must make at least once in their life if they are healthy and wealthy enough to do so.

haka, haka or hakas **NOUN** ❶ In New Zealand, a haka is a ceremonial Maori dance made up of various postures and accompanied by a chant.
❷ an imitation of this dance performed by New Zealand sports teams before matches as a challenge.

hake, hakes **NOUN** an edible sea fish related to the cod.

hakea, hakeas **NOUN** a large Australian shrub with bright flowers and hard, woody fruit.

halal ADJECTIVE (RE) Halal meat is from animals that have been killed in the correct way according to Islamic law.

halcyon [Said **hal**-see-on] **ADJECTIVE** ❶ LITERARY peaceful, gentle, and calm • *halcyon colours of yellow and turquoise.* ▷ **PHRASE**
❷ Halcyon days are a happy and carefree time in the past • *halcyon days in the sun.*

half, halves **NOUN, ADJECTIVE, OR**

▷ SPELLING NOTE: *pAL up with the principAL and principAL staff (principal)*

ADVERB ❶ Half refers to one of two equal parts that make up a whole • *the two halves of the brain* • *They chatted for another half hour* • *The bottle was only half full.* ▷ **ADVERB** ❷ You can use 'half' to say that something is only partly true • *I half expected him to explode in anger.*

half-baked ADJECTIVE INFORMAL Half-baked ideas or plans have not been properly thought out.

half board NOUN Half board at a hotel includes breakfast and dinner but not lunch.

half-brother, half-brothers **NOUN** Your half-brother is the son of either your mother or your father but not of your other parent.

half-hearted ADJECTIVE showing no real effort or enthusiasm.

half-pie ADJECTIVE INFORMAL In New Zealand English, half-pie means incomplete or not properly done • *finished in a half-pie way.*

half-sister, half-sisters **NOUN** Your half-sister is the daughter of either your mother or your father but not of your other parent.

half-timbered ADJECTIVE A half-timbered building has a framework of wooden beams showing in the walls.

half-time NOUN Half-time is a short break between two parts of a game when the players have a rest.

halfway ADVERB at the middle of the distance between two points in place or time • *He stopped halfway down the ladder* • *halfway through the term.*

halibut, halibuts **NOUN** a large edible flat fish.

hall, halls **NOUN** ❶ the room just inside the front entrance of a house which leads into other rooms. ❷ a large room or building used for public events • *a concert hall.*

hallmark, hallmarks **NOUN** ❶ The hallmark of a person or group is their most typical quality • *A warm, hospitable welcome is the hallmark of island people.* ❷ an official mark on gold or silver indicating its quality.

hallowed [Said **hal**-lode] **ADJECTIVE** respected as being holy • *hallowed ground.*

Halloween NOUN Halloween is October 31st, and is celebrated by children dressing up, often as ghosts and witches.
● **WORD HISTORY:** from Old English *halig* + *æfen* meaning 'holy evening', the evening before All Saints' Day

hallucinate, hallucinates, hallucinating, hallucinated [Said hal-**loo**-sin-ate] **VERB** If you hallucinate, you see strange things in your mind because of illness or drugs. **hallucination NOUN hallucinatory ADJECTIVE**
● **WORD HISTORY:** from Latin *alucinari* meaning 'to wander in thought'

halo, haloes or halos **NOUN** a circle of light around the head of a holy figure.
● **WORD HISTORY:** from Greek *halos* meaning 'disc shape of the sun or moon'

halogen [Said **hal**-o-jen] **NOUN** (SCIENCE) A halogen is any of the chemical elements fluorine, chlorine, bromine, iodine, and astatine. They form group VIII in the periodic table.

halt, halts, halting, halted **VERB**
❶ To halt when moving means to stop. ❷ To halt development or action means to stop it ▷ **NOUN** ❸ a short standstill.

halter, halters **NOUN** a strap fastened round a horse's head so that it can be led easily.

halve, halves, halving, halved [Said *hahv*] **VERB** ❶ If you halve something, you divide it into two equal parts. ❷ To halve something also means to reduce its size or amount by half.

ham, hams **NOUN** ❶ Ham is meat from the hind leg of a pig, salted and cured. ❷ a bad actor who exaggerates emotions and gestures. ❸ someone who is interested in amateur radio.

hamburger, hamburgers **NOUN** a flat disc of minced meat, seasoned and fried; often eaten in a bread roll.
● **WORD HISTORY:** named after its
● city of origin *Hamburg* in Germany

hammer, hammers, hammering, hammered **NOUN** ❶ a tool consisting of a heavy piece of metal at the end of a handle, used for hitting nails into things ▷ **VERB** ❷ If you hammer something, you hit it repeatedly, with a hammer or with your fist. ❸ If you hammer an idea into someone, you keep repeating it and telling them about it.
❹ INFORMAL If you hammer someone, you criticize or attack them severely.

hammock, hammocks **NOUN** a

piece of net or canvas hung between two supports and used as a bed.

hamper, hampers, hampering, hampered **NOUN** ❶ a rectangular wicker basket with a lid, used for carrying food ▷ **VERB** ❷ If you hamper someone, you make it difficult for them to move or progress.
● **SIMILAR WORDS:** ❷ handicap,
● hinder, impede

hamster, hamsters **NOUN** a small furry rodent which is often kept as a pet.
● **USAGE NOTE:** There is no *p* in
● *hamster*

hamstring, hamstrings **NOUN** PE Your hamstring is a tendon behind your knee joining your thigh muscles to the bones of your lower leg.

hand, hands, handing, handed **NOUN** ❶ Your hand is the part of your body beyond the wrist, with four fingers and a thumb. ❷ Your hand is also your writing style. ❸ The hand of someone in a situation is their influence or the part they play in it • *He had a hand in its design.* ❹ If you give someone a hand, you help them to do something. ❺ When an audience gives someone a big hand, they applaud. ❻ The hands of a clock or watch are the pointers that point to the numbers. ❼ In cards, your hand is the cards you are holding ▷ **VERB** ❽ If you hand something to someone, you give it to them ▷ **PHRASES** ❾ Something that is **at hand**, **to hand**, or **on hand** is available, close by, and ready for use. ❿ You use **on the one hand** to introduce the first part of an argument or discussion with two different points of view. ⓫ You use **on the other**

hand to introduce the second part of an argument or discussion with two different points of view. **12** If you do something **by hand**, you do it using your hands rather than a machine.
hand down VERB Something that is handed down is passed from one generation to another.

handbag, handbags **NOUN** a small bag used mainly by women to carry money and personal items.

handbook, handbooks **NOUN** a book giving information and instructions about something.

handcuff, handcuffs **NOUN** Handcuffs are two metal rings linked by a chain which are locked around a prisoner's wrists.

handful, handfuls **NOUN** **1** A handful of something is the amount of it you can hold in your hand • *He picked up a handful of seeds.* **2** a small quantity • *Only a handful of people knew.* **3** Someone who is a handful is difficult to control • *He is a bit of a handful.*

handicap, handicaps, handicapping, handicapped **NOUN** **1** a physical or mental disability. **2** something that makes it difficult for you to achieve something. **3** In sport, a handicap is a disadvantage or advantage given to competitors according to their skill, in order to give them an equal chance of winning ▷ **VERB** **4** If something handicaps someone, it makes it difficult for them to achieve something.

● **SIMILAR WORDS:** **1** disability, ● impairment

handicraft, handicrafts **NOUN**

Handicrafts are activities such as embroidery or pottery which involve making things with your hands; also the items produced.

handiwork NOUN Your handiwork is something that you have done or made yourself.

handkerchief, handkerchiefs **NOUN** a small square of fabric used for blowing your nose.

handle, handles, handling, handled **NOUN** **1** The handle of an object is the part by which it is held or controlled. **2** a small lever used to open and close a door or window ▷ **VERB** **3** If you handle an object, you hold it in your hands to examine it. **4** If you handle something, you deal with it or control it • *I have learned how to handle pressure.*

handlebar, handlebars **NOUN** Handlebars are the bar and handles at the front of a bicycle, used for steering.

handout, handouts **NOUN** **1** a gift of food, clothing, or money given to a poor person. **2** a piece of paper giving information about something.

hand-picked ADJECTIVE carefully chosen • *a hand-picked team of bodyguards.*

handset, handsets **NOUN** The handset of a telephone is the part that you speak into and listen with.

handshake, handshakes **NOUN** the grasping and shaking of a person's hand by another person.

handsome ADJECTIVE **1** very attractive in appearance. **2** large and generous • *a handsome profit.*

▷ SPELLING NOTE: *the QUeen stood on the QUay (quay)*

handsomely ADVERB
● **SIMILAR WORDS:** ❶ attractive,
● good-looking

handwriting NOUN Someone's
handwriting is their style of writing as
it looks on the page.

handy, handier, handiest **ADJECTIVE**
❶ conveniently near. ❷ easy to
handle or use. ❸ skilful.

hang, hangs, hanging, hung **VERB**
❶ If you hang something somewhere,
you attach it to a high point • *She
hung heavy red velvet curtains in the
sitting room.* ❷ If something is
hanging on something, it is attached
by its top to it • *His jacket hung from a
hook behind the door.* ❸ If a future
event or possibility is hanging over
you, it worries or frightens you • *She
has an eviction notice hanging over her.*
❹ When you hang wallpaper, you
stick it onto a wall. ❺ To hang
someone means to kill them by
suspending them by a rope around the
neck ▷ **PHRASE** ❻ When you **get
the hang of something**, you
understand it and are able to do it.
hang about or **hang around**
VERB ❶ INFORMAL to wait
somewhere. ❷ To hang about or
hang around with someone means to
spend a lot of time with them.
hang on VERB ❶ If you hang on to
something, you hold it tightly or keep
it. ❷ INFORMAL to wait.
hang up VERB When you hang up,
you put down the receiver to end a
telephone call.
● **USAGE NOTE:** When *hang* means
● 'kill someone by suspending them
● by a rope' (sense 5), the past tense
● and past participle are *hanged*: *he
● was hanged for murder in 1959*

hangar, hangars **NOUN** a large
building where aircraft are kept • *The
bombers were still in their hangars.*

hanger, hangers **NOUN** a coat
hanger.

hanger-on, hangers-on **NOUN** an
unwelcome follower of an important
person.

hang-glider, hang-gliders **NOUN**
an aircraft without an engine and
consisting of a large frame covered in
fabric, from which the pilot hangs in a
harness.

hangi, hangi or hangis [*Said* **hung**-*ee*]
NOUN In New Zealand, a Maori oven
made from a hole in the ground lined
with hot stones.

hangover, hangovers **NOUN** a
feeling of sickness and headache after
drinking too much alcohol.

hang-up, hang-ups **NOUN** A
hang-up about something is a
continual feeling of embarrassment or
fear about it • *a hang-up about
speaking in public.*

hanker, hankers, hankering,
hankered **VERB** If you hanker after
something, you continually want it.
hankering NOUN

hanky, hankies **NOUN** a
handkerchief.

Hanukkah or **Chanukah** [*Said
hah-na-ka*] **NOUN** Hanukkah is an
eight-day Jewish festival of lights.
● **WORD HISTORY:** a Hebrew word
● meaning literally 'a dedication'

haphazard [*Said hap-***haz**-*ard*]
ADJECTIVE not organized or planned.
haphazardly ADVERB

▷ SPELLING NOTE: *Rhythmical Hounds Yap To Heavy Music* (rhythm)

● **WORD HISTORY:** from Old Norse
● *hap* meaning 'chance' and Arabic
● *az-zahr* meaning 'gaming dice'

hapless ADJECTIVE LITERARY
unlucky.

happen, happens, happening,
happened VERB ❶ When something
happens, it occurs or takes place. ❷ If
you happen to do something, you do it
by chance. **happening** NOUN
● **SIMILAR WORDS:** ❶ come about,
● occur, take place

happiness NOUN a feeling of great
contentment or pleasure.

happy, happier, happiest ADJECTIVE
❶ feeling, showing, or producing
contentment or pleasure • *a happy
smile* • *a happy atmosphere.*
❷ satisfied that something is right • *I
wasn't very happy about the layout.*
❸ willing • *I would be happy to help.*
❹ fortunate or lucky • *a happy
coincidence.* **happily** ADVERB
● **SIMILAR WORDS:** ❶ blissful,
● content, glad, joyful

happy-go-lucky ADJECTIVE
carefree and unconcerned.

harangue, harangues, haranguing,
harangued *[Said har-rang]* NOUN
❶ a long, forceful, passionate speech
▷ VERB ❷ To harangue someone
means to talk to them at length
passionately and forcefully about
something.
● **WORD HISTORY:** from Old Italian
● *aringa* meaning 'public speech'

harass, harasses, harassing, harassed
[Said har-rass] VERB If someone
harasses you, they trouble or annoy
you continually. **harassed**
ADJECTIVE **harassment** NOUN

harbinger, harbingers *[Said
har-bin-jer]* NOUN a person or thing
that announces or indicates the
approach of a future event • *others see
the shortage of cash as a harbinger of
bankruptcy.*

harbour, harbours, harbouring,
harboured NOUN ❶ a protected area
of deep water where boats can be
moored ▷ VERB ❷ To harbour
someone means to hide them secretly
in your house. ❸ If you harbour a
feeling, you have it for a long time
• *She's still harbouring great bitterness.*
● **WORD HISTORY:** from Old English
● *here + beorg* meaning 'army shelter'

hard, harder, hardest ADJECTIVE
❶ Something that is hard is firm,
solid, or stiff • *a hard piece of cheese.*
❷ requiring a lot of effort • *hard work.*
❸ difficult • *These are hard times.*
❹ Someone who is hard has no
kindness or pity • *Don't be hard on
him.* ❺ A hard colour or voice is harsh
and unpleasant. ❻ Hard evidence or
facts can be proved to be true.
❼ Hard water contains a lot of lime
and does not easily produce a lather.
❽ Hard drugs are very strong illegal
drugs. ❾ Hard drink is strong alcohol
▷ ADVERB ❿ earnestly or intently
• *They tried hard to attract tourists* An
event that follows hard upon
something takes place immediately
afterwards. **hardness** NOUN
● **SIMILAR WORDS:** ❶ firm, rigid,
● solid, stiff

hard and fast ADJECTIVE fixed
and not able to be changed • *hard and
fast rules.*

hardback, hardbacks NOUN a book
with a stiff cover.

▷ SPELLING NOTE: there's SAND in my SANDwich (<u>sand</u>wich)

hard core NOUN The hard core in an organization is the group of people who most resist change.

harden, hardens, hardening, hardened VERB To harden means to become hard or get harder.
hardening NOUN **hardened** ADJECTIVE

hard labour NOUN physical work which is difficult and tiring, used in some countries as a punishment for a crime.

hardly ADVERB ❶ almost not or not quite • *I could hardly believe it.*
❷ certainly not • *It's hardly a secret.*
● USAGE NOTE: You should not use
● *hardly* with a negative word like *not*
● or *no*: *he could hardly hear her*, not
● *he could not hardly hear her*

hard-nosed ADJECTIVE tough, practical, and realistic.

hard of hearing ADJECTIVE not able to hear properly.

hardship, hardships NOUN Hardship is a time or situation of suffering and difficulty.

hard shoulder, hard shoulders NOUN the area at the edge of a motorway where a driver can stop in the event of a breakdown.

hard up ADJECTIVE INFORMAL having hardly any money.

hardware NOUN ❶ Hardware is tools and equipment for use in the home and garden. ❷ ICT Hardware is also computer machinery rather than computer programs.

hard-wearing ADJECTIVE strong, well-made, and long-lasting.

hardwood, hardwoods NOUN strong, hard wood from a tree such as an oak; also the tree itself.

hardy, hardier, hardiest ADJECTIVE tough and able to endure very difficult or cold conditions • *a hardy race of pioneers.*

hare, hares, haring, hared NOUN ❶ an animal like a large rabbit, but with longer ears and legs ▷ VERB ❷ To hare means to run very fast • *He hared off down the corridor.*

harem, harems [Said har-*reem*] NOUN a group of wives or mistresses of one man, especially in Muslim societies; also the place where these women live.

hark, harks, harking, harked VERB ❶ OLD-FASHIONED To hark means to listen. ❷ To hark back to something in the past means to refer back to it or recall it.

harlequin [Said *har*-lik-win] ADJECTIVE having many different colours.

harm, harms, harming, harmed VERB ❶ To harm someone or something means to injure or damage them ▷ NOUN ❷ Harm is injury or damage.
● SIMILAR WORDS: ❶ damage, hurt, injure

harmful ADJECTIVE having a bad effect on something • *Whilst most stress is harmful, some is beneficial.*

harmless ADJECTIVE ❶ safe to use or be near. ❷ unlikely to cause problems or annoyance • *He's harmless really.* **harmlessly** ADVERB

harmonic ADJECTIVE using musical harmony.

harmonica, harmonicas **NOUN** a small musical instrument which you play by blowing and sucking while moving it across your lips.

harmonious [Said har-*moh*-nee-uss] **ADJECTIVE** ❶ showing agreement, peacefulness, and friendship • *a harmonious relationship.* ❷ consisting of parts which blend well together making an attractive whole • *harmonious interior decor.* **harmoniously ADVERB**

harmonize, harmonizes, harmonizing, harmonized; *also spelt* **harmonise VERB** If things harmonize, they fit in with each other or interact in an agreeable way.

harmony, harmonies **NOUN** ❶ Harmony is a state of peaceful agreement and cooperation • *the promotion of racial harmony.* ❷ (MUSIC) Harmony is the structure and relationship of chords in a piece of music. ❸ Harmony is the pleasant combination of two or more notes played at the same time.

harness, harnesses, harnessing, harnessed **NOUN** ❶ a set of straps and fittings fastened round a horse so that it can pull a vehicle, or fastened round someone's body to attach something • *a safety harness.* ▷ **VERB** ❷ If you harness something, you bring it under control to use it • *harnessing public opinion.*

harp, harps, harping, harped **NOUN** ❶ a musical instrument consisting of a triangular frame with vertical strings which you pluck with your fingers ▷ **VERB** ❷ If someone harps on something, they keep talking about it, especially in a boring way.

harpoon, harpoons **NOUN** a barbed spear attached to a rope, thrown or fired from a gun and used for catching whales or large fish.

harpsichord, harpsichords **NOUN** a musical instrument like a small piano, with strings which are plucked when the keys are pressed.

harrowing ADJECTIVE very upsetting or disturbing • *a harrowing experience.*

harsh, harsher, harshest **ADJECTIVE** severe, difficult, and unpleasant • *harsh weather conditions* • *harsh criticism.* **harshly ADVERB** **harshness NOUN**
● **SIMILAR WORDS:** hard, severe,
● tough

harvest, harvests, harvesting, harvested **NOUN** ❶ the cutting and gathering of a crop; also the ripe crop when it is gathered and the time of gathering ▷ **VERB** ❷ To harvest food means to gather it in when it is ripe. **harvester NOUN**
● **WORD HISTORY:** from Old
● German *herbist* meaning 'autumn'

has-been, has-beens **NOUN** INFORMAL a person who is no longer important or successful.

hash, hashes **PHRASE** ❶ If you **make a hash of** a job, you do it badly ▷ **NOUN** ❷ the name for the symbol #. ❸ Hash is a dish made of small pieces of meat and vegetables cooked together. ❹ INFORMAL Hash is also hashish.

hashish [Said *hash*-eesh] **NOUN** Hashish is a drug made from the hemp plant. It is usually smoked, and is illegal in many countries.

▷ SPELLING NOTE: *Eddy Ant thinks mEAt is a grEAt trEAt to EAt (-ea-)*

hassle, hassles, hassling, hassled
NOUN ❶ INFORMAL Something that
is a hassle is difficult or causes trouble
▷ **VERB ❷** If you hassle someone,
you annoy them by repeatedly asking
them to do something.

haste **NOUN** Haste is doing
something quickly, especially too
quickly.

hasten, hastens, hastening, hastened
[Said **hay-sn**] **VERB** To hasten means
to move quickly or do something
quickly.

hasty, hastier, hastiest **ADJECTIVE**
done or happening suddenly and
quickly, often without enough care or
thought. **hastily** **ADVERB**

hat, hats **NOUN** a covering for the
head.

hatch, hatches, hatching, hatched
VERB ❶ When an egg hatches, or
when a bird or reptile hatches, the egg
breaks open and the young bird or
reptile emerges. **❷** To hatch a plot
means to plan it ▷ **NOUN ❸** a
covered opening in a floor or wall.

hatchback, hatchbacks **NOUN** a
car with a door at the back which
opens upwards.

hatchet, hatchets **NOUN ❶** a small
axe ▷ **PHRASE ❷** To **bury the
hatchet** means to resolve a
disagreement and become friends
again.

hate, hates, hating, hated **VERB ❶** If
you hate someone or something, you
have a strong dislike for them
▷ **NOUN ❷** Hate is a strong dislike.
● **SIMILAR WORDS: ❶** detest,
● loathe

hateful **ADJECTIVE** extremely
unpleasant.

hatred [Said **hay-trid**] **NOUN** an
extremely strong feeling of dislike.

hat trick, hat tricks **NOUN** In sport,
a hat trick is three achievements, for
example when a footballer scores
three goals in a match • Crawford
completed his hat trick in the 60th
minute.

haughty, haughtier, haughtiest
[rhymes with **naughty**] **ADJECTIVE**
showing excessive pride • He behaved
in a haughty manner. **haughtily**
ADVERB
● **SIMILAR WORDS:** disdainful,
● proud, supercilious

haul, hauls, hauling, hauled **VERB**
❶ To haul something somewhere
means to pull it with great effort
▷ **NOUN ❷** a quantity of something
obtained • a good haul of fish.
▷ **PHRASE ❸** Something that you
describe as **a long haul** takes a lot of
time and effort to achieve • So women
began the long haul to equality.

haulage [Said **hawl-lij**] **NOUN**
Haulage is the business or cost of
transporting goods by road.

haunches **PLURAL NOUN** Your
haunches are your buttocks and the
tops of your legs • He squatted on his
haunches.

haunt, haunts, haunting, haunted
VERB ❶ If a ghost haunts a place, it
is seen or heard there regularly. **❷** If a
memory or a fear haunts you, it
continually worries you ▷ **NOUN ❸** A
person's favourite haunt is a place
they like to visit often.

▷ SPELLING NOTE: Elaine and Emily shout EE when they mEEt to grEEt each other (-ee-)

haunted ADJECTIVE ❶ regularly visited by a ghost • *a haunted house.* ❷ very worried or troubled • *a haunted expression.*

haunting ADJECTIVE extremely beautiful or sad so that it makes a lasting impression on you • *haunting landscapes.*

have, has, having, had **VERB** ❶ Have is an auxiliary verb, used to form the past tense or to express completed actions • *They have never met* • *I have lost it.* ❷ If you have something, you own or possess it • *We have two tickets for the concert.* ❸ If you have something, you experience it, it happens to you, or you are affected by it • *I have an idea!* • *He had a marvellous time.* ❹ To have a child or baby animal means to give birth to it • *When is she having the baby?* ▷ **PHRASES** ❺ If you **have to** do something, you must do it. If you **had better** do something, you ought to do it.

haven, havens [*Said hay-ven*] **NOUN** a safe place.

havoc NOUN ❶ Havoc is disorder and confusion ▷ **PHRASE** ❷ To **play havoc** with something means to cause great disorder and confusion • *Food allergies often play havoc with the immune system.*

hawk, hawks, hawking, hawked **NOUN** ❶ a bird of prey with short rounded wings and a long tail ▷ **VERB** ❷ To hawk goods means to sell them by taking them around from place to place.

hawthorn, hawthorns **NOUN** a small, thorny tree producing white blossom and red berries.

hay NOUN Hay is grass which has been cut and dried and is used as animal feed.

hay fever NOUN Hay fever is an allergy to pollen and grass, causing sneezing and watering eyes.

haystack, haystacks **NOUN** a large, firmly built pile of hay, usually covered and left out in the open.

hazard, hazards, hazarding, hazarded **NOUN** ❶ (SCIENCE) a substance, object or action which could be dangerous to you ▷ **VERB** ❷ If you hazard something, you put it at risk • *hazarding the health of his crew.* ▷ **PHRASE** ❸ If you **hazard a guess**, you make a guess. **hazardous ADJECTIVE**
● **WORD HISTORY:** from Arabic *az-zahr* meaning 'gaming dice'

haze NOUN If there is a haze, you cannot see clearly because there is moisture or smoke in the air.

hazel, hazels **NOUN** ❶ a small tree producing edible nuts ▷ **ADJECTIVE** ❷ greenish brown in colour.

hazy, hazier, haziest **ADJECTIVE** dim or vague • *hazy sunshine* • *a hazy memory.*

he PRONOUN 'He' is used to refer to a man, boy, or male animal or to any person whose sex is not mentioned.

head, heads, heading, headed **NOUN** ❶ Your head is the part of your body which has your eyes, brain, and mouth in it. ❷ Your head is also your mind and mental abilities • *He has a head for figures.* ❸ The head of something is the top, start, or most important end

• *at the head of the table.* ❹ The head of a group or organization is the person in charge. ❺ The head on beer is the layer of froth on the top. ❻ The head on a computer or tape recorder is the part that can read or write information. ❼ When you toss a coin, the side called heads is the one with the head on it ▷ **VERB** ❽ To head a group or organization means to be in charge • *Bryce heads the help organization.* ❾ To head in a particular direction means to move in that direction • *She is heading for a breakdown.* ❿ To head a ball means to hit it with your head ▷ **PHRASE** ⓫ If you **lose your head**, you panic. ⓬ If you say that someone is **off their head**, you mean that they are mad or very stupid. ⓭ If something is **over someone's head**, it is too difficult for them to understand. ⓮ If you **can't make head nor tail of something**, you cannot understand it.

head off VERB If you head off someone or something, you make them change direction or prevent something from happening • *He hopes to head off a public squabble.*

headache, headaches **NOUN** ❶ a pain in your head. ❷ Something that is a headache is causing a lot of difficulty or worry • *Delays in receiving money owed is a major headache for small firms.*

header, headers **NOUN** A header in soccer is hitting the ball with your head.

heading, headings **NOUN** a piece of writing that is written or printed at the top of a page.

headland, headlands **NOUN** a narrow piece of land jutting out into the sea.

headlight, headlights **NOUN** The headlights on a motor vehicle are the large powerful lights at the front.

headline, headlines **NOUN** ❶ A newspaper headline is the title of a newspaper article printed in large, bold type. ❷ The headlines are the main points of the radio or television news.

headmaster, headmasters **NOUN** a man who is the head teacher of a school.

headmistress, headmistresses **NOUN** a woman who is the head teacher of a school.

headphones PLURAL NOUN Headphones are a pair of small speakers which you wear over your ears to listen to a radio without other people hearing.

headquarters NOUN The headquarters of an organization is the main place or from which it is run.

headroom NOUN Headroom is the amount of space below a roof or surface under which an object must pass or fit.

headstone, headstones **NOUN** a large stone standing at one end of a grave and showing the name of the person buried there.

headstrong ADJECTIVE determined to do something in your own way and ignoring other people's advice.

head teacher, head teachers

▷ SPELLING NOTE: *King IAn went to ParlIAment in a carrIAge for his marrIAge (-ia-)*

A
B
C
D
E
F
G
H
I
J
K
L
M
N
O
P
Q
R
S
T
U
V
W
X
Y
Z

NOUN the teacher who is in charge of a school.

headway **PHRASE** If you are **making headway**, you are making progress.

headwind, headwinds **NOUN** a wind blowing in the opposite direction to the way you are travelling.

heady, headier, headiest **ADJECTIVE** extremely exciting.

heal, heals, healing, healed **VERB** If something heals or if you heal it, it becomes healthy or normal again • *He had a nasty wound which had not healed properly.* **healer** **NOUN**

health **NOUN** ❶ Your health is the condition of your body • *His health is not good.* ❷ Health is also the state of being free from disease and feeling well.
  ● **WORD HISTORY:** from Old English *hǣlth* a toast drunk to a person's wellbeing
  ● **SIMILAR WORDS:** fitness, wellbeing

health food, health foods **NOUN** food which is free from added chemicals and is considered to be good for your health.

healthy, healthier, healthiest **ADJECTIVE** ❶ Someone who is healthy is fit and strong and does not have any diseases. ❷ Something that is healthy is good for you • *a healthy diet.* ❸ An organization or system that is healthy is successful • *a healthy economy.* **healthily** **ADVERB**
  ● **SIMILAR WORDS:** ❶ fit, well

heap, heaps, heaping, heaped **NOUN** ❶ a pile of things ❷ IN PLURAL,

INFORMAL Heaps of something means plenty of it • *His performance earned him heaps of praise.* ▷ **VERB** ❸ If you heap things, you pile them up. ❹ To heap something such as praise on someone means to give them a lot of it.
  ● **SIMILAR WORDS:** ❶ mass, mound, pile

hear, hears, hearing, heard **VERB** ❶ When you hear sounds, you are aware of them because they reach your ears. ❷ When you hear from someone, they write to you or phone you. ❸ When you hear about something, you are informed about it. ❹ When a judge hears a case, he or she listens to it in court in order to make a decision on it ▷ **PHRASE** ❺ If you say that you **won't hear of** something, you mean you refuse to allow it.

hear out **VERB** If you hear someone out, you listen to all they have to say without interrupting.

hearing, hearings **NOUN** ❶ Hearing is the sense which makes it possible for you to be aware of sounds • *My hearing is poor.* ❷ a court trial or official meeting to hear facts about an incident. ❸ If someone gives you a hearing, they let you give your point of view and listen to you.

hearsay **NOUN** Hearsay is information that you have heard from other people rather than something that you know personally to be true.

hearse, hearses [rhymes with *verse*] **NOUN** a large car that carries the coffin at a funeral.

heart, hearts **NOUN** ❶ the organ in your chest that pumps the blood around your body. ❷ Your heart is also thought of as the centre of your emotions. ❸ Heart is courage, determination, or enthusiasm • *They were losing heart.* ❹ The heart of something is the most central and important part of it. ❺ a shape similar to a heart, used especially as a symbol of love. ❻ Hearts is one of the four suits in a pack of playing cards. It is marked by a red heart-shaped symbol.

heartache, heartaches **NOUN** Heartache is very great sadness and emotional suffering.

heart attack, heart attacks **NOUN** a serious medical condition in which the heart suddenly beats irregularly or stops completely.

heartbreak, heartbreaks **NOUN** Heartbreak is great sadness and emotional suffering. **heartbreaking ADJECTIVE**

heartbroken ADJECTIVE very sad and emotionally upset • *She was heartbroken at his death.*

heartburn NOUN Heartburn is a painful burning sensation in your chest, caused by indigestion.

heartening ADJECTIVE encouraging or uplifting • *heartening news.*

heart failure NOUN Heart failure is a serious condition in which someone's heart does not work as well as it should, sometimes stopping completely.

heartfelt ADJECTIVE sincerely and deeply felt • *Our heartfelt sympathy goes out to you.*

hearth, hearths [Said **harth**] **NOUN** A hearth is the floor of a fireplace.

heartless ADJECTIVE cruel and unkind.

heart-rending ADJECTIVE causing great sadness and pity • *a heart-rending story.*

heart-throb, heart-throbs **NOUN** someone who is attractive to a lot of people.

heart-to-heart, heart-to-hearts **NOUN** a discussion in which two people talk about their deepest feelings.

hearty, heartier, heartiest **ADJECTIVE** ❶ cheerful and enthusiastic • *hearty congratulations.* ❷ strongly felt • *a hearty dislike for her teacher.* ❸ A hearty meal is large and satisfying. **heartily ADVERB**

heat, heats, heating, heated **NOUN** ❶ Heat is warmth or the quality of being hot; also the temperature of something that is warm or hot. ❷ Heat is strength of feeling, especially of anger or excitement. ❸ a contest or race in a competition held to decide who will play in the final ▷ **VERB** ❹ To heat something means to raise its temperature ▷ **PHRASE** ❺ When a female animal is **on heat**, she is ready for mating. **heater NOUN**

heath, heaths **NOUN** an area of open land covered with rough grass or heather.

heathen, heathens **NOUN** OLD-FASHIONED someone who does not believe in one of the established religions.

heather NOUN a plant with small

a b c d e f g h i j k l m n o p q r s t u v w x y z

purple or white flowers that grows wild on hills and moorland.

heating NOUN Heating is the equipment used to heat a building; also the process and cost of running the equipment to provide heat.

heatwave, heatwaves NOUN a period of time during which the weather is much hotter than usual.

heave, heaves, heaving, heaved VERB ❶ To heave something means to move or throw it with a lot of effort. ❷ If your stomach heaves, you vomit or suddenly feel sick. ❸ If you heave a sigh, you sigh loudly ▷ NOUN ❹ If you give something a heave, you move or throw it with a lot of effort.

heaven, heavens NOUN ❶ RE a place of happiness where God is believed to live and where good people are believed to go when they die. ❷ If you describe a situation or place as heaven, you mean that it is wonderful • *The cake was pure heaven.* ▷ PHRASE ❸ You say **Good heavens** to express surprise.

heavenly ADJECTIVE ❶ relating to heaven • *a heavenly choir.* ❷ INFORMAL wonderful • *his heavenly blue eyes.*

heavy, heavier, heaviest; heavies ADJECTIVE ❶ great in weight or force • *How heavy are you?* • *a heavy blow.* ❷ great in degree or amount • *heavy casualties.* ❸ solid and thick in appearance • *heavy shoes.* ❹ using a lot of something quickly • *The van is heavy on petrol.* ❺ serious and difficult to deal with or understand • *It all got a bit heavy when the police arrived* • *a heavy speech.* ❻ Food that is heavy is solid and difficult to digest • *a heavy*

meal. ❼ When it is heavy, the weather is hot, humid, and still. ❽ Someone with a heavy heart is very sad ▷ NOUN ❾ INFORMAL a large, strong man employed to protect someone or something. **heavily** ADVERB **heaviness** NOUN

heavy-duty ADJECTIVE Heavy-duty equipment is strong and hard-wearing.

heavy-handed ADJECTIVE showing a lack of care or thought and using too much authority • *heavy-handed police tactics.*

heavyweight, heavyweights NOUN ❶ a boxer in the heaviest weight group. ❷ an important person with a lot of influence.

Hebrew, Hebrews *[Said hee-broo]* NOUN ❶ Hebrew is an ancient language now spoken in Israel, where it is the official language. ❷ In the past, the Hebrews were Hebrew-speaking Jews who lived in Israel ▷ ADJECTIVE ❸ relating to the Hebrews and their customs.

heckle, heckles, heckling, heckled VERB If members of an audience heckle a speaker, they interrupt and shout rude remarks. **heckler** NOUN

hectare, hectares NOUN a unit for measuring areas of land, equal to 10,000 square metres or about 2.471 acres.

hectic ADJECTIVE involving a lot of rushed activity • *a hectic schedule.*

hedge, hedges, hedging, hedged NOUN ❶ a row of bushes forming a barrier or boundary ▷ VERB ❷ If you hedge against something unpleasant

▷ SPELLING NOTE: *A Rude Idiot Thought He Might Eat Toffee In Church (arithmetic)*

happening, you protect yourself. **❸** If you hedge, you avoid answering a question or dealing with a problem ▷ **PHRASE ❹** If you **hedge your bets**, you support two or more people or courses of action to avoid the risk of losing a lot.

hedgehog, hedgehogs **NOUN** a small, brown animal with sharp spikes covering its back.

hedonism [Said *hee-dn-izm*] **NOUN** Hedonism is the belief that gaining pleasure is the most important thing in life. **hedonistic ADJECTIVE**

heed, heeds, heeding, heeded **VERB ❶** If you heed someone's advice, you pay attention to it ▷ **NOUN ❷** If you take or pay heed to something, you give it careful attention.
● **SIMILAR WORDS: ❶** listen to,
● mind, pay attention to

heel, heels, heeling, heeled **NOUN ❶** the back part of your foot. **❷** The heel of a shoe or sock is the part that fits over your heel ▷ **VERB ❸** To heel a pair of shoes means to put a new piece on the heel ▷ **PHRASE ❹** A person or place that looks **down at heel** looks untidy and in poor condition.

heeler, heelers **NOUN** In Australia, a dog that herds cattle by biting at their heels.

hefty, heftier, heftiest **ADJECTIVE** of great size, force, or weight • *a hefty fine* • *hefty volumes.*

height, heights **NOUN ❶** The height of an object is its measurement from the bottom to the top. **❷** a high position or place • *Their nesting rarely takes place at any great height.* **❸** The

height of something is its peak, or the time when it is most successful or intense • *the height of the tourist season* • *at the height of his career.* **❹** (MATHS) In maths, the height of a triangle is the point where two sides meet at a peak opposite the base.

heighten, heightens, heightening, heightened **VERB** If something heightens a feeling or experience, it increases its intensity.

heinous [Said *hay-nuss* or *hee-nuss*] **ADJECTIVE** evil and terrible • *heinous crimes.*

heir, heirs [Said *air*] **NOUN** A person's heir is the person who is entitled to inherit their property or title.

heiress, heiresses [Said *air-iss*] **NOUN** a female with the right to inherit property or a title.

heirloom, heirlooms [Said *air-loom*] **NOUN** something belonging to a family that has been passed from one generation to another.

helicopter, helicopters **NOUN** an aircraft with rotating blades above it which enable it to take off vertically, hover, and fly.
● **WORD HISTORY:** from Greek
● *heliko* + *pteron* meaning 'spiral
● wing'

helium [Said *hee-lee-um*] **NOUN** Helium is a gas that is lighter than air and that is used to fill balloons.

hell NOUN ❶ (RE) Hell is the place where souls of evil people are believed to go to be punished after death. **❷** INFORMAL If you say that something is hell, you mean it is very unpleasant

a b c d e f g h i j k l m n o p q r s t u v w x y z

A
B
C
D
E
F
G
H
I
J
K
L
M
N
O
P
Q
R
S
T
U
V
W
X
Y
Z

▷ **INTERJECTION** ❸ 'Hell' is also a swearword.

hell-bent ADJECTIVE determined to do something whatever the consequences.

hellish ADJECTIVE INFORMAL very unpleasant.

hello INTERJECTION You say 'Hello' as a greeting or when you answer the phone.

helm, helms **NOUN** ❶ The helm on a boat is the position from which it is steered and the wheel or tiller ▷ **PHRASE** ❷ **At the helm** means in a position of leadership or control.

helmet, helmets **NOUN** a hard hat worn to protect the head.

help, helps, helping, helped **VERB** ❶ To help someone means to make something easier or better for them ▷ **NOUN** ❷ If you need or give help, you need or give assistance. ❸ someone or something that helps you • *He really is a good help.* ▷ **PHRASE** ❹ If you **help yourself** to something, you take it. ❺ If you **can't help** something, you cannot control it or change it • *I can't help feeling sorry for him.*

helper, helpers **NOUN** a person who gives assistance.

helpful ADJECTIVE ❶ If someone is helpful, they help you by doing something for you. ❷ Something that is helpful makes a situation more pleasant or easier to tolerate. **helpfully ADVERB**
● **SIMILAR WORDS:** ❶ cooperative, ● supportive ❷ beneficial, useful

helping, helpings **NOUN** an amount

of food that you get in a single serving.

helpless ADJECTIVE ❶ unable to cope on your own • *a helpless child.* ❷ weak or powerless • *helpless despair.* **helplessly ADVERB helplessness NOUN**

hem, hems, hemming, hemmed **NOUN** ❶ The hem of a garment is an edge which has been turned over and sewn in place ▷ **VERB** ❷ To hem something means to make a hem on it.
hem in VERB If someone is hemmed in, they are surrounded and prevented from moving.

hemisphere, hemispheres [*Said hem-iss-feer*] **NOUN** one half of the earth, the brain, or a sphere.

hemp NOUN Hemp is a tall plant, some varieties of which are used to make rope, and others to produce the drug cannabis.

hen, hens **NOUN** a female chicken; also any female bird.

hence ADVERB ❶ FORMAL for this reason • *It sells more papers, hence more money is made.* ❷ from now or from the time mentioned • *The convention is due to start two weeks hence.*

henceforth ADVERB FORMAL from this time onward • *His life henceforth was to revolve around her.*

henchman, henchmen **NOUN** The henchmen of a powerful person are the people employed to do violent or dishonest work for that person.

hepatitis NOUN Hepatitis is a serious infectious disease causing inflammation of the liver.

▷ SPELLING NOTE: *Betty Eats Cakes And Uses Seven Eggs (because)*

her PRONOUN OR ADJECTIVE 'Her' is used to refer to a woman, girl or female animal that has already been mentioned, or to show that something belongs to a particular female.

herald, heralds, heralding, heralded NOUN ❶ In the past, a herald was a messenger ▷ VERB ❷ Something that heralds a future event is a sign of that event.

herb, herbs NOUN a plant whose leaves are used in medicine or to flavour food. **herbal** ADJECTIVE **herbalist** NOUN

herbicide, herbicides NOUN (SCIENCE) a chemical used to kill plants, especially weeds.

herbivore, herbivores NOUN an animal that eats only plants.

herd, herds, herding, herded NOUN ❶ a large group of animals ▷ VERB ❷ To herd animals or people means to make them move together as a group.

here ADVERB ❶ at, to, or in the place where you are, or the place mentioned or indicated ▷ PHRASE ❷ **Here and there** means in various unspecified places • *dense forests broken here and there by small towns.*

hereafter ADVERB FORMAL after this time or point • *the South China Morning Post (referred to hereafter as SCMP).*

hereby ADVERB FORMAL used in documents and statements to indicate that a declaration is official • *All leave is hereby cancelled.*

hereditary ADJECTIVE passed on to a child from a parent • *A hereditary disease afflicted the family.*

heredity NOUN Heredity is the process by which characteristics are passed from parents to their children through the genes.

herein ADVERB FORMAL in this place or document.

heresy, heresies [Said **herr**-ess-ee] NOUN Heresy is belief or behaviour considered to be wrong because it disagrees with what is generally accepted, especially with regard to religion. **heretic** NOUN **heretical** ADJECTIVE

herewith ADVERB FORMAL with this letter or document • *I herewith return your cheque.*

heritage NOUN the possessions or traditions that have been passed from one generation to another.

hermit, hermits NOUN a person who lives alone with a simple way of life, especially for religious reasons.
  ● **WORD HISTORY:** from Greek
  ● *erēmitēs* meaning 'living in the
  ● desert'

hernia, hernias [Said **her**-nee-a] NOUN a medical condition in which part of the intestine sticks through a weak point in the surrounding tissue.

hero, heroes NOUN ❶ the main male character in a book, film, or play. ❷ a person who has done something brave or good.

heroic ADJECTIVE brave, courageous, and determined. **heroically** ADVERB

heroin [Said **herr**-oh-in] NOUN Heroin is a powerful drug formerly

a b c d e f g **h** i j k l m n o p q r s t u v w x y z

▷ SPELLING NOTE: *there's a rAKE in the brAKEs (brake)*

used as an anaesthetic and now taken illegally by some people for pleasure.

heroine, heroines [Said herr-oh-in] NOUN ❶ the main female character in a book, film, or play. ❷ a woman who has done something brave or good.

heroism [Said herr-oh-i-zm] NOUN Heroism is great courage and bravery.

heron, herons NOUN a wading bird with very long legs and a long beak and neck.

herpes [Said her-peez] NOUN Herpes is a virus which causes painful red spots on the skin.

herring, herrings NOUN a silvery fish that lives in large shoals in northern seas.

hers PRONOUN 'Hers' refers to something that belongs to or relates to a woman, girl, or female animal.

herself PRONOUN ❶ 'Herself' is used when the same woman, girl, or female animal does an action and is affected by it • She pulled herself out of the water. ❷ 'Herself' is used to emphasize 'she'.

hertz NOUN A hertz is a unit of frequency equal to one cycle per second.

hesitant ADJECTIVE If you are hesitant, you do not do something immediately because you are uncertain or worried. **hesitantly** ADVERB
● SIMILAR WORDS: irresolute,
● uncertain, unsure

hesitate, hesitates, hesitating, hesitated VERB To hesitate means to

pause or show uncertainty. **hesitation** NOUN

hessian NOUN Hessian is a thick, rough fabric used for making sacks.

heterosexual, heterosexuals [Said het-roh-seks-yool] ADJECTIVE ❶ involving a sexual relationship between a man and a woman • heterosexual couples. ▷ NOUN ❷ a person who is sexually attracted to people of the opposite sex.

hewn ADJECTIVE carved from a substance • a cave, hewn out of the hillside.

hexagon, hexagons NOUN (MATHS) a shape with six straight sides; a **regular hexagon** has six straight sides of the same length. **hexagonal** ADJECTIVE

hexameter, hexameters NOUN (ENGLISH) a line of verse that has six metrical feet.

heyday [Said hay-day] NOUN The heyday of a person or thing is the period when they are most successful or popular • Hollywood in its heyday.

hi INTERJECTION 'Hi!' is an informal greeting.

hiatus, hiatuses [Said high-ay-tuss] NOUN FORMAL a pause or gap.

hibernate, hibernates, hibernating, hibernated VERB Animals that hibernate spend the winter in a state like deep sleep. **hibernation** NOUN
● WORD HISTORY: from Latin
● hibernare meaning 'to spend the
● winter'

hibiscus, hibiscuses [Said hie-bis-kuss] NOUN a type of tropical shrub with brightly coloured flowers.

hiccup, hiccups, hiccupping, hiccupped [Said **hik-kup**] NOUN
❶ Hiccups are short, uncontrolled choking sounds in your throat that you sometimes get if you have been eating or drinking too quickly. ❷ INFORMAL a minor problem ▷ VERB ❸ When you hiccup, you make these little choking sounds.

hide, hides, hiding, hid, hidden VERB
❶ To hide something means to put it where it cannot be seen, or to prevent it from being discovered • *He was unable to hide his disappointment.*
▷ NOUN ❷ the skin of a large animal.
● SIMILAR WORDS: ❶ conceal, ● disguise

hideous [Said **hid-ee-uss**] ADJECTIVE extremely ugly or unpleasant. **hideously** ADVERB

hideout, hideouts NOUN a hiding place.

hierarchy, hierarchies [Said **high-er-ar-kee**] NOUN a system in which people or things are ranked according to how important they are. **hierarchical** ADJECTIVE

hi-fi, hi-fis NOUN a set of stereo equipment on which you can play compact discs and tapes.

high, higher, highest; highs ADJECTIVE ❶ tall or a long way above the ground. ❷ great in degree, quantity, or intensity • *high interest rates* • *There is a high risk of heart disease.* ❸ towards the top of a scale of importance or quality • *high fashion.* ❹ close to the top of a range of sound or notes • *the human voice reaches a very high pitch.* ❺ INFORMAL Someone

who is high on a drug is affected by having taken it ▷ ADVERB ❻ at or to a height ▷ NOUN ❼ a high point or level • *Morale reached a new high.*
❽ INFORMAL Someone who is on a high is in a very excited and optimistic mood.
● SIMILAR WORDS: ❶ lofty, tall, ● towering

highbrow ADJECTIVE concerned with serious, intellectual subjects.

higher education NOUN Higher education is education at universities and colleges.

high jump NOUN The high jump is an athletics event involving jumping over a high bar.

highlands PLURAL NOUN Highlands are mountainous or hilly areas of land.

highlight, highlights, highlighting, highlighted VERB ❶ If you highlight a point or problem, you emphasize and draw attention to it ▷ NOUN ❷ The highlight of something is the most interesting part of it • *His show was the highlight of the Festival.*
❸ ART a lighter area of a painting, showing where light shines on things. ❹ Highlights are also light-coloured streaks in someone's hair.

highly ADVERB ❶ extremely • *It is highly unlikely I'll be able to replace it.*
❷ towards the top of a scale of importance, admiration, or respect • *She thought highly of him* • *highly qualified personnel.*

high-minded ADJECTIVE Someone who is high-minded has strong moral principles.

▷ SPELLING NOTE: *I always visit my FRIend on a FRIday (Friday)*

Highness NOUN 'Highness' is used in titles and forms of address for members of the royal family other than a king or queen • *Her Royal Highness, Princess Alexandra.*

high-pitched ADJECTIVE A high-pitched sound is high and often rather shrill.

high-rise ADJECTIVE High-rise buildings are very tall.

high school, high schools NOUN a secondary school.

high technology NOUN High technology is the development and use of advanced electronics and computers.

high tide NOUN On a coast, high tide is the time, usually twice a day, when the sea is at its highest level.

high-water mark NOUN (GEOGRAPHY) The high-water mark is the highest level reached by the sea at high tide or a river in a flood.

highway, highways NOUN a road along which vehicles have the right to pass.

highwayman, highwaymen NOUN In the past, highwaymen were robbers on horseback who used to rob travellers.

hijack, hijacks, hijacking, hijacked VERB If someone hijacks a plane or vehicle, they illegally take control of it during a journey. **hijacking** NOUN

hike, hikes, hiking, hiked NOUN ❶ a long country walk ▷ VERB ❷ To hike means to walk long distances in the country. **hiker** NOUN

hilarious ADJECTIVE very funny.

hilariously ADVERB
● SIMILAR WORDS: funny,
● humorous, uproarious

hilarity NOUN Hilarity is great amusement and laughter • *His antics caused great hilarity.*

hill, hills NOUN a rounded area of land higher than the land surrounding it. **hilly** ADJECTIVE

hillbilly, hillbillies NOUN someone who lives in the country away from other people, especially in remote areas in the southern United States.

hilt, hilts NOUN The hilt of a sword or knife is its handle.

him PRONOUN You use 'him' to refer to a man, boy, or male animal that has already been mentioned, or to any person whose sex is not known.

himself PRONOUN ❶ 'Himself' is used when the same man, boy, or male animal does an action and is affected by it • *He discharged himself from hospital.* ❷ 'Himself' is used to emphasize 'he'.

hind, hinds [rhymes with **blind**] ADJECTIVE ❶ used to refer to the back part of an animal • *the hind legs.* ▷ NOUN ❷ a female deer.

hinder, hinders, hindering, hindered [Said **hin-der**] VERB If you hinder someone or something, you get in their way and make things difficult for them.

Hindi [Said **hin-dee**] NOUN Hindi is a language spoken in northern India.

hindrance, hindrances NOUN ❶ Someone or something that is a hindrance causes difficulties or is an obstruction. ❷ Hindrance is the act of hindering someone or something.

hindsight NOUN Hindsight is the ability to understand an event after it has actually taken place • *With hindsight, I realized how odd he is.*

Hindu, Hindus [*Said hin-doo*] NOUN (RE) a person who believes in Hinduism, an Indian religion which has many gods and believes that people have another life on earth after death. Hinduism NOUN

hinge, hinges, hinging, hinged NOUN ❶ the movable joint which attaches a door or window to its frame ▷ VERB ❷ Something that hinges on a situation or event depends entirely on that situation or event • *Victory or defeat hinged on her final putt.*

hint, hints, hinting, hinted NOUN ❶ an indirect suggestion. ❷ a helpful piece of advice ▷ VERB ❸ If you hint at something, you suggest it indirectly.
● SIMILAR WORDS: ❶ clue,
● indication, suggestion ❸ imply,
● insinuate, suggest

hinterland, hinterlands NOUN The hinterland of a coastline or a port is the area of land behind it or around it.

hip, hips NOUN Your hips are the two sides of your body between your waist and your upper legs.

hippo, hippos NOUN INFORMAL a hippopotamus.

hippopotamus, hippopotamuses or hippopotami NOUN a large African animal with thick wrinkled skin and short legs, that lives near rivers.
● WORD HISTORY: from Greek *hippo*
● + *potamos* meaning 'river horse'

hippy, hippies; *also spelt* **hippie** NOUN In the 1960s and 1970s hippies were people who rejected conventional society and tried to live a life based on peace and love.

hire, hires, hiring, hired VERB ❶ If you hire something, you pay money to be able to use it for a period of time. ❷ If you hire someone, you pay them to do a job for you ▷ PHRASE ❸ Something that is **for hire** is available for people to hire.

hirsute [*Said hir-syoot*] ADJECTIVE FORMAL hairy.

his ADJECTIVE OR PRONOUN 'His' refers to something that belongs or relates to a man, boy, or male animal that has already been mentioned, and sometimes also to any person whose sex is not known.

hiss, hisses, hissing, hissed VERB ❶ To hiss means to make a long 's' sound, especially to show disapproval or aggression ▷ NOUN ❷ a long 's' sound.

histogram, histograms NOUN (MATHS) a graph consisting of rectangles of varying sizes, that shows the frequency of values of a quantity.

historian, historians NOUN a person who studies and writes about history.

historic ADJECTIVE important in the past or likely to be seen as important in the future.

historical ADJECTIVE ❶ occurring in the past, or relating to the study of the past • *historical events.*
❷ describing or representing the past

• *historical novels.* **historically**
ADVERB

history, histories **NOUN** History is
the study of the past. A history is a
record of the past • *The village is
steeped in history* • *my family history.*

histrionic, histrionics *[Said
hiss-tree-**on**-ik]* **ADJECTIVE**
① Histrionic behaviour is very
dramatic and full of exaggerated
emotion. **②** FORMAL relating to drama
and acting • *a young man of marked
histrionic ability.*

histrionics PLURAL NOUN
Histrionics are histrionic behaviour.

hit, hits, hitting, hit **VERB** **①** If you hit
someone, you strike them forcefully,
usually causing hurt or damage. **②** If
you hit an object, you collide with it.
③ To hit a ball or other object means
to make it move by hitting it with
something. **④** If something hits you,
it affects you badly and suddenly • *The
recession has hit the tourist industry
hard.* **⑤** If something hits a particular
point or place, it reaches it • *The book
hit Britain just at the right time.* **⑥** If
you hit on an idea or solution, you
suddenly think of it ▷ **NOUN** **⑦** a
person or thing that is popular and
successful. **⑧** the action of hitting
something • *Give it a good hard hit
with the hammer.* ▷ **PHRASE**
⑨ INFORMAL If you **hit it off** with
someone, you become friendly with
them the first time you meet them.

hit and miss **ADJECTIVE**
happening in an unpredictable way or
without being properly organized.

hit-and-run **ADJECTIVE** A
hit-and-run car accident is one in

which the person who has caused the
damage drives away without stopping.

hitch, hitches, hitching, hitched
NOUN **①** a slight problem or difficulty
• *The whole process was completed
without a hitch.* ▷ **VERB** **②** INFORMAL
If you hitch, you travel by getting lifts
from passing vehicles • *America is no
longer a safe place to hitch round.*

hitchhiking **NOUN** Hitchhiking is
travelling by getting free lifts from
passing vehicles.

hi tech **ADJECTIVE** designed using
the most modern methods and
equipment, especially electronic
equipment.

hither OLD-FASHIONED **ADVERB**
① used to refer to movement towards
the place where you are ▷ **PHRASE**
② Something that moves **hither and
thither** moves in all directions.

hitherto **ADVERB** FORMAL until now
• *What he was aiming at had not
hitherto been attempted.*

HIV **NOUN** HIV is a virus that reduces
people's resistance to illness and can
cause AIDS. HIV is an abbreviation for
'human immunodeficiency virus'.

hive, hives, hiving, hived **NOUN** **①** a
beehive. **②** A place that is a hive of
activity is very busy with a lot of
people working hard ▷ **VERB** **③** If
part of something such as a business
is hived off, it is transferred to new
ownership • *The company is poised to
hive off its music interests.*

hoard, hoards, hoarding, hoarded
VERB **①** To hoard things means to
save them even though they may no
longer be useful ▷ **NOUN** **②** a store

of things that has been saved or hidden.

● **USAGE NOTE:** Do not confuse *hoard* with *horde*
● **SIMILAR WORDS:** ❶ save, stockpile, store ❷ cache, stash, store

hoarding, hoardings **NOUN** a large advertising board by the side of the road.

hoarse, hoarser, hoarsest **ADJECTIVE** A hoarse voice sounds rough and unclear. **hoarsely ADVERB**

hoax, hoaxes, hoaxing, hoaxed **NOUN** ❶ a trick or an attempt to deceive someone ▷ **VERB** ❷ To hoax someone means to trick or deceive them.

hob, hobs **NOUN** a surface on top of a cooker which can be heated in order to cook things.

hobble, hobbles, hobbling, hobbled **VERB** ❶ If you hobble, you walk awkwardly because of pain or injury. ❷ If you hobble an animal, you tie its legs together to restrict its movement.

hobby, hobbies **NOUN** something that you do for enjoyment in your spare time.

hock, hocks **NOUN** The hock of a horse or other animal is the angled joint in its back leg.

hockey NOUN Hockey is a game in which two teams use long sticks with curved ends to try to hit a small ball into the other team's goal.

hoe, hoes, hoeing, hoed **NOUN** ❶ a long-handled gardening tool with a small square blade, used to remove weeds and break up the soil ▷ **VERB**

❷ To hoe the ground means to use a hoe on it.

hog, hogs, hogging, hogged **NOUN** ❶ a castrated male pig ▷ **VERB** ❷ INFORMAL If you hog something, you take more than your share of it, or keep it for too long ▷ **PHRASE** ❸ INFORMAL If you **go the whole hog**, you do something completely or thoroughly in a bold or extravagant way.

hoist, hoists, hoisting, hoisted **VERB** ❶ To hoist something means to lift it, especially using a crane or other machinery ▷ **NOUN** ❷ a machine for lifting heavy things.

hokey-pokey NOUN In New Zealand, hokey-pokey is a kind of brittle toffee.

hold, holds, holding, held **VERB** ❶ To hold something means to carry or keep it in place, usually with your hand or arms. ❷ Someone who holds power, office, or an opinion has it or possesses it. ❸ If you hold something such as a meeting or an election, you arrange it and cause it to happen. ❹ If something holds, it is still available or valid • *The offer still holds.* ❺ If you hold someone responsible for something, you consider them responsible for it. ❻ If something holds a certain amount, it can contain that amount • *The theatre holds 150 people.* ❼ If you hold something such as theatre tickets, a telephone call, or the price of something, you keep or reserve it for a period of time • *The line is engaged – will you hold?* ❽ To hold something down means to keep it or to keep it under control • *How could I have children and hold down a job like*

a
b
c
d
e
f
g
h
i
j
k
l
m
n
o
p
q
r
s
t
u
v
w
x
y
z

this? **9** If you hold on to something, you continue it or keep it even though it might be difficult • *They are keen to hold on to their culture.* **10** To hold something back means to prevent it, keep it under control, or not reveal it • *She failed to hold back the tears.* ▷ **NOUN** **11** If someone or something has a hold over you, they have power, control, or influence over you • *The party has a considerable hold over its own leader.* **12** a way of holding something or the act of holding it • *He grabbed the rope and got a hold on it.* **13** the place where cargo or luggage is stored in a ship or a plane. **holder** **NOUN**

holdall, holdalls **NOUN** a large, soft bag for carrying clothing.

hole, holes, holing, holed **NOUN** **1** an opening or hollow in something. **2** INFORMAL If you are in a hole, you are in a difficult situation. **3** INFORMAL A hole in a theory or argument is a weakness or error in it. **4** In golf, a hole is one of the small holes into which you have to hit the ball ▷ **VERB** **5** When you hole the ball in golf, you hit the ball into one of the holes.

● **SIMILAR WORDS:** **1** aperture, gap, opening

Holi **NOUN** (RE) Holi is a Hindu festival celebrated in spring.

holiday, holidays, holidaying, holidayed **NOUN** **1** a period of time spent away from home for enjoyment. **2** a time when you are not working or not at school ▷ **VERB** **3** When you holiday somewhere, you take a holiday there • *She is currently holidaying in Italy.*

● **WORD HISTORY:** from Old English *haligdæg* meaning 'holy day'

holidaymaker, holidaymakers **NOUN** a person who is away from home on holiday.

holiness **NOUN** **1** Holiness is the state or quality of being holy. **2** 'Your Holiness' and 'His Holiness' are titles used to address or refer to the Pope or to leaders of some other religions.

hollow, hollows, hollowing, hollowed **ADJECTIVE** **1** Something that is hollow has space inside it rather than being solid. **2** An opinion or situation that is hollow has no real value or worth • *a hollow gesture.* **3** A hollow sound is dull and has a slight echo • *the hollow sound of his footsteps on the stairs.* ▷ **NOUN** **4** a hole in something or a part of a surface that is lower than the rest • *It is a pleasant village in a lush hollow.* ▷ **VERB** **5** To hollow means to make a hollow • *They hollowed out crude dwellings from the soft rock.*

holly **NOUN** Holly is an evergreen tree or shrub with spiky leaves. It often has red berries in winter.

holocaust, holocausts *[Said hol-o-kawst]* **NOUN** **1** a large-scale destruction or loss of life, especially the result of war or fire. **2** The Holocaust was the mass murder of the Jews in Europe by the Nazis during World War II.

● **WORD HISTORY:** from Greek *holos* + *kaustos* meaning 'completely burnt'

holster, holsters **NOUN** a holder for a hand gun, worn at the side of the body or under the arm.

▷ SPELLING NOTE: *I went to see (C) the doctor's new practiCe (practice)*

holy, holier, holiest **ADJECTIVE**
① relating to God or to a particular religion • *the holy city.* **②** Someone who is holy is religious and leads a pure and good life.
● **SIMILAR WORDS: ①** hallowed, sacred **②** devout, pious

homage [Said *hom-ij*] **NOUN**
Homage is an act of respect and admiration • *The thronging crowds paid homage to their assassinated president.*

home, homes **NOUN** **①** Your home is the building or place in which you live or feel you belong. **②** a building in which elderly or ill people live and are looked after • *He has been confined to a nursing home since his stroke.*
▷ **ADJECTIVE** **③** connected with or involving your home or country • *He gave them his home phone number* • *The government is expanding the home market.*
● **SIMILAR WORDS: ①** abode, dwelling, residence

homeland, homelands **NOUN** Your homeland is your native country.

homeless ADJECTIVE **①** having no home **②** IN PLURAL The homeless are people who have no home.
homelessness NOUN

homely, homelier, homeliest **ADJECTIVE** simple, ordinary and comfortable • *The room was small and homely.*

homeopathy [Said *home-ee-op-path-ee*] **NOUN** Homeopathy is a way of treating illness by giving the patient tiny amounts of a substance that would normally cause illness in a healthy person. **homeopathic ADJECTIVE**

homeowner, homeowners **NOUN**

a person who owns the home in which he or she lives.

homesick ADJECTIVE unhappy because of being away from home and missing family and friends.

homespun ADJECTIVE not sophisticated or complicated • *The book is simple homespun philosophy.*

homestead, homesteads **NOUN** a house and its land and other buildings, especially a farm.

home truth, home truths **NOUN** Home truths are unpleasant facts about yourself that you are told by someone else.

homeward or **homewards ADJECTIVE OR ADVERB** towards home • *the homeward journey.*

homework NOUN **①** Homework is school work given to pupils to be done in the evening at home. **②** Homework is also research and preparation • *You certainly need to do your homework before buying a horse.*

homicide, homicides **NOUN** Homicide is the crime of murder.
homicidal ADJECTIVE

homing ADJECTIVE A homing device is able to guide itself to a target. An animal with a homing instinct is able to guide itself home.

homonym, homonyms **NOUN**
(ENGLISH) Homonyms are words which are pronounced or spelt in the same way but which have different meanings. For example, *swift* is an adjective meaning 'fast', and the name for a type of bird; *meat* is the flesh of animals, and *meet* is a verb meaning 'encounter'.

a b c d e f g h i j k l m n o p q r s t u v w x y z

▷ SPELLING NOTE: *You must practiSe your Ss (practiSe)*

A B C D E F G H I J K L M N O P Q R S T U V W X Y Z

homophone, homophones **NOUN**
(ENGLISH) Homophones are words
with different meanings which are
pronounced in the same way but are
spelt differently. For example, 'write'
and 'right' are homophones.

homo sapiens [Said *hoh-moh
sap-ee-enz*] **NOUN** FORMAL Homo
sapiens is the scientific name for
human beings.
● **WORD HISTORY:** from Latin *homo*
● meaning 'man' and *sapiens*
● meaning 'wise'

homosexual, homosexuals **NOUN**
❶ a person who is sexually attracted
to someone of the same sex
▷ **ADJECTIVE** ❷ sexually attracted to
people of the same sex.
homosexuality NOUN

hone, hones, honing, honed **VERB**
❶ If you hone a tool, you sharpen it.
❷ If you hone a quality or ability, you
develop and improve it • *He had a
sharply honed sense of justice.*

honest **ADJECTIVE** truthful and
trustworthy. **honestly ADVERB**
● **SIMILAR WORDS:** honourable,
● trustworthy, truthful

honesty NOUN Honesty is the
quality of being truthful and
trustworthy.
● **SIMILAR WORDS:** honour,
● integrity, truthfulness

honey NOUN ❶ Honey is a sweet,
edible, sticky substance produced by
bees. ❷ 'Honey' means 'sweetheart'
or 'darling' • *What is it, honey?*

honeycomb, honeycombs **NOUN** a
wax structure consisting of rows of
six-sided cells made by bees for
storage of honey and the eggs.

honeyeater, honeyeaters **NOUN** a
small Australian bird that feeds on
nectar from flowers.

honeymoon, honeymoons **NOUN**
a holiday taken by a couple who have
just got married.

honeysuckle NOUN Honeysuckle
is a climbing plant with fragrant pink
or cream flowers.

hongi [Said *hong-ee*] **NOUN** In New
Zealand, hongi is a Maori greeting in
which people touch noses.

honk, honks, honking, honked **NOUN**
❶ a short, loud sound like that made
by a car horn or a goose ▷ **VERB**
❷ When something honks, it makes a
short, loud sound.

honorary ADJECTIVE An honorary
title or job is given as a mark of
respect, and does not involve the
usual qualifications or work • *She was
awarded an honorary degree.*

honour, honours, honouring,
honoured **NOUN** ❶ Your honour is
your good reputation and the respect
that other people have for you • *This is
a war fought by men totally without
honour.* ❷ an award or privilege given
as a mark of respect. ❸ Honours is a
class of university degree which is
higher than a pass or ordinary degree
▷ **PHRASE** ❹ If something is done **in
honour of** someone, it is done out of
respect for them • *Egypt celebrated
frequent minor festivals in honour of the
dead.* ▷ **VERB** ❺ If you honour
someone, you give them special praise
or attention, or an award. ❻ If you
honour an agreement or promise, you
do what was agreed or promised • *Try
to find out if there is enough cash to*

▷ SPELLING NOTE: *pAL up with the principAL and principAL staff (principal)*

honour the existing pledges.

honourable ADJECTIVE worthy of respect or admiration • *He should do the honourable thing and resign.*

hood, hoods NOUN ❶ a loose covering for the head, usually part of a coat or jacket. ❷ a cover on a piece of equipment or vehicle, usually curved and movable • *The mechanic had the hood up to work on the engine.* **hooded** ADJECTIVE

-hood SUFFIX '-hood' is added at the end of words to form nouns that indicate a state or condition • *childhood* • *priesthood.*

hoof, hooves or hoofs NOUN the hard bony part of certain animals' feet.

hook, hooks, hooking, hooked NOUN ❶ a curved piece of metal or plastic that is used for catching, holding, or hanging things • *picture hooks.* ❷ a curving movement, for example of the fist in boxing, or of a golf ball ▷ VERB ❸ If you hook one thing onto another, you attach it there using a hook ▷ PHRASE ❹ If you are **let off the hook**, something happens so that you avoid punishment or a difficult situation.

hooked ADJECTIVE addicted to something; also obsessed by something • *hooked on alcohol* • *I'm hooked on exercise.*

hooligan, hooligans NOUN a destructive and violent young person. **hooliganism** NOUN
● SIMILAR WORDS: delinquent, ● ruffian, yob

hoop, hoops NOUN a large ring, often used as a toy.

hooray INTERJECTION another spelling of **hurray**.

hoot, hoots, hooting, hooted VERB ❶ To hoot means to make a long 'oo' sound like an owl • *hooting with laughter.* ❷ If a car horn hoots, it makes a loud honking noise ▷ NOUN ❸ a sound like that made by an owl or a car horn.

hoover, hoovers, hoovering, hoovered NOUN ❶ TRADEMARK a vacuum cleaner ▷ VERB ❷ When you hoover, you use a vacuum cleaner to clean the floor.

hooves a plural of **hoof**.

hop, hops, hopping, hopped VERB ❶ If you hop, you jump on one foot. ❷ When animals or birds hop, they jump with two feet together. ❸ INFORMAL If you hop into or out of something, you move there quickly and easily • *You only have to hop on the ferry to get there.* ▷ NOUN ❹ a jump on one leg. ❺ Hops are flowers of the hop plant, which are dried and used for making beer.

hope, hopes, hoping, hoped VERB ❶ If you hope that something will happen or hope that it is true, you want it to happen or be true ▷ NOUN ❷ Hope is a wish or feeling of desire and expectation • *There was little hope of recovery.* **hopeful** ADJECTIVE **hopefully** ADVERB
● USAGE NOTE: Some people do not ● like the use of *hopeful* to mean 'it is ● hoped', for example *hopefully, we ● can get a good result on Saturday.* ● Although it is very common in ● speech, it should be avoided in ● written work

▷ SPELLING NOTE: L*Earn* the princi*PLE*s (princi*ple*)

A
B
C
D
E
F
G
H
I
J
K
L
M
N
O
P
Q
R
S
T
U
V
W
X
Y
Z

hopeless ADJECTIVE ❶ having no hope • *She shook her head in hopeless bewilderment.* ❷ certain to fail or be unsuccessful. ❸ bad or inadequate • *I'm hopeless at remembering birthdays* • *hopeless parents.* **hopelessly** ADVERB **hopelessness** NOUN

hopper, hoppers NOUN a large, funnel-shaped container for storing things such as grain or sand.

horde, hordes *[rhymes with **bored**]* NOUN a large group or number of people or animals • *hordes of tourists.*
● USAGE NOTE: Do not confuse
● *horde* with *hoard*

horizon, horizons *[Said hor-**eye**-zn]* NOUN ❶ the distant line where the sky seems to touch the land or sea. ❷ Your horizons are the limits of what you want to do or are interested in • *Travel broadens your horizons.*
▷ PHRASE ❸ If something is **on the horizon**, it is almost certainly going to happen or be done in the future • *Political change was on the horizon.*

horizontal *[Said hor-riz-**zon**-tl]* ADJECTIVE (MATHS) flat and parallel with the horizon or with a line considered as a base • *a patchwork of vertical and horizontal black lines.* **horizontally** ADVERB

hormone, hormones NOUN a chemical made by one part of your body that stimulates or has a specific effect on another part of your body. **hormonal** ADJECTIVE

horn, horns NOUN ❶ one of the hard, pointed growths on the heads of animals such as goats. ❷ a musical instrument made of brass, consisting of a pipe or that is narrow at one end

and wide at the other. ❸ On vehicles, a horn is a warning device which makes a loud noise.

hornet, hornets NOUN a type of very large wasp.

horoscope, horoscopes *[Said hor-ros-kope]* NOUN a prediction about what is going to happen to someone, based on the position of the stars when they were born.
● WORD HISTORY: from Greek *hora* + *skopos* meaning 'hour observer'

horrendous ADJECTIVE very unpleasant and shocking • *horrendous injuries.*

horrible ADJECTIVE
❶ disagreeable and unpleasant • *A horrible nausea rose within him.*
❷ causing shock, fear, or disgust • *horrible crimes.* **horribly** ADVERB
● SIMILAR WORDS:
● ❶ disagreeable, nasty, unpleasant
● ❷ dreadful, ghastly, shocking

horrid ADJECTIVE very unpleasant indeed • *We were all so horrid to him.*

horrific ADJECTIVE so bad or unpleasant that people are horrified • *a horrific attack.*

horrify, horrifies, horrifying, horrified VERB If something horrifies you, it makes you feel dismay or disgust • *a crime trend that will horrify parents.* **horrifying** ADJECTIVE

horror, horrors NOUN ❶ a strong feeling of alarm, dismay, and disgust • *He gazed in horror at the knife.* ❷ If you have a horror of something, you fear it very much • *a horror of fire.*

horse, horses NOUN ❶ a large animal with a mane and long tail, on

▷ SPELLING NOTE: *Psychiatrists Seldom Yell Callously Hard (psychiatrist)*

which people can ride. ❷ a piece of gymnastics equipment with four legs, used for jumping over.

horseback NOUN OR ADJECTIVE You refer to someone who is riding a horse as someone **on horseback**, or a horseback rider.

horsepower NOUN Horsepower is a unit used for measuring how powerful an engine is, equal to about 746 watts.

horseradish NOUN Horseradish is the white root of a plant made into a hot-tasting sauce, often served cold with beef.

horseshoe, horseshoes NOUN a U-shaped piece of metal, nailed to the hard surface of a horse's hoof to protect it; also anything of this shape, often regarded as a good luck symbol.

horsey or **horsy**, horsier, horsiest ADJECTIVE ❶ very keen on horses and riding. ❷ having a face similar to that of a horse.

horticulture NOUN Horticulture is the study and practice of growing flowers, fruit, and vegetables. **horticultural** ADJECTIVE

hose, hoses, hosing, hosed NOUN ❶ a long flexible tube through which liquid or gas can be passed • *He left the garden hose on.* ▷ VERB ❷ If you hose something, you wash or water it using a hose • *The street cleaners need to hose the square down.*

hosiery [Said **hoze**-ee-yer-ee] NOUN Hosiery consists of tights, socks, and similar items, especially in shops.

hospice, hospices [Said **hoss**-piss]

NOUN a hospital which provides care for people who are dying.

hospitable ADJECTIVE friendly, generous, and welcoming to guests or strangers. **hospitality** NOUN

hospital, hospitals NOUN a place where sick and injured people are treated and cared for.

host, hosts, hosting, hosted NOUN ❶ The host of an event is the person that welcomes guests and provides food or accommodation for them • *He is a most generous host who takes his guests to the best restaurants in town.* ❷ a plant or animal with smaller plants or animals living on or in it. ❸ A host of things is a large number of them • *a host of close friends.* ❹ In the Christian church, the Host is the consecrated bread used in Mass or Holy Communion ▷ VERB ❺ To host an event means to organize it or act as host at it.

hostage, hostages NOUN a person who is illegally held prisoner and threatened with injury or death unless certain demands are met by other people.

hostel, hostels NOUN a large building in which people can stay or live • *a hostel for battered women.*

hostess, hostesses NOUN a woman who welcomes guests or visitors and provides food or accommodation for them.

hostile ADJECTIVE ❶ unfriendly, aggressive, and unpleasant • *a hostile audience.* ❷ relating to or involving the enemies of a country • *hostile territory.*

▷ SPELLING NOTE: *the QUeen stood on the QUay (quay)*

hostility, hostilities **NOUN**
aggression or unfriendly behaviour
towards a person or thing.

hot, hotter, hottest **ADJECTIVE**
❶ having a high temperature • *a hot
climate.* ❷ very spicy and causing a
burning sensation in your mouth • *a
hot curry.* ❸ new, recent, and exciting
• *hot news from tinseltown.*
❹ dangerous or difficult to deal with
• *Animal testing is a hot issue.* **hotly**
ADVERB

hotbed, hotbeds **NOUN** A hotbed of
some type of activity is a place that
seems to encourage it • *The city was a
hotbed of rumour.*

hot dog, hot dogs **NOUN** a sausage
served in a roll split lengthways.

hotel, hotels **NOUN** a building where
people stay, paying for their room and
meals.

hothouse, hothouses **NOUN** ❶ a
large heated greenhouse. ❷ a place
or situation of intense intellectual or
emotional activity • *a hothouse of
radical socialist ideas.*

hot seat NOUN INFORMAL Someone
who is in the hot seat has to make
difficult decisions for which they will
be held responsible.

hound, hounds, hounding, hounded
NOUN ❶ a dog, especially one used
for hunting or racing ▷ **VERB** ❷ If
someone hounds you, they constantly
pursue or trouble you.

hour, hours **NOUN** ❶ a unit of time
equal to 60 minutes, of which there
are 24 in a day. ❷ The hour for
something is the time when it
happens • *The hour for launching*
approached. ❸ The hour is also the
time of day • *What are you doing up at
this hour?* ❹ an important or difficult
time • *The hour has come* • *He is the
hero of the hour.* ❺ IN PLURAL The
hours that you keep are the times that
you usually go to bed and get up.
hourly ADJECTIVE OR ADVERB

house, houses, housing, housed
NOUN *[Said hows]* ❶ a building
where a person or family lives. ❷ a
building used for a particular purpose
• *an auction house* • *the opera house.*
❸ In a theatre or cinema, the house is
the part where the audience sits; also
the audience itself • *The show had a
packed house calling for more.* ▷ **VERB**
[Said howz] ❹ To house something
means to keep it or contain it • *The
west wing housed a store of valuable
antiques.*

houseboat, houseboats **NOUN** a
small boat which people live on that is
tied up at a particular place on a river
or canal.

household, households **NOUN**
❶ all the people who live as a group in
a house or flat ▷ **PHRASE**
❷ Someone who is **a household
name** is very well-known.
householder NOUN

housekeeper, housekeepers
NOUN a person who is employed to
do the cooking and cleaning in a
house.

House of Commons NOUN The
House of Commons is the more
powerful of the two parts of the British
Parliament. Its members are elected
by the public.

House of Lords NOUN The House

▷ SPELLING NOTE: *Rhythmical Hounds Yap To Heavy Music (rhythm)*

of Lords is the less powerful of the two parts of the British Parliament. Its members are unelected and come from noble families or are appointed by the Queen as an honour for a life of public service

House of Representatives
NOUN ❶ In Australia, the House of Representatives is the larger of the two parts of the Federal Parliament. ❷ In New Zealand, the House of Representatives is the Parliament.

housewife, housewives NOUN a married woman who does the chores in her home, and does not have a paid job.

housing NOUN Housing is the buildings in which people live • *the serious housing shortage.*

hovel, hovels NOUN a small hut or house that is dirty or badly in need of repair.

hover, hovers, hovering, hovered VERB ❶ When a bird, insect, or aircraft hovers, it stays in the same position in the air. ❷ If someone is hovering they are hesitating because they cannot decide what to do • *He was hovering nervously around the sick animal.*

hovercraft, hovercraft or hovercrafts NOUN a vehicle which can travel over water or land supported by a cushion of air.

how ADVERB ❶ 'How' is used to ask about, explain, or refer to the way in which something is done, known, or experienced • *How did this happen?* • *He knew how quickly rumours could spread.* ❷ 'How' is used to ask about or refer to a measurement or quantity

• *How much is it for the weekend?* • *I wonder how old he is.* ❸ 'How' is used to emphasize the following word or statement • *How odd!*

however ADVERB ❶ You use 'however' when you are adding a comment that seems to contradict or contrast with what has just been said • *For all his compassion, he is, however, surprisingly restrained.* ❷ You use 'however' to say that something makes no difference to a situation • *However hard she tried, nothing seemed to work.*

howl, howls, howling, howled VERB ❶ To howl means to make a long, loud wailing noise such as that made by a dog when it is upset • *A distant coyote howled at the moon* • *The wind howled through the trees.* ▷ NOUN ❷ a long, loud wailing noise.

HQ an abbreviation for **headquarters**.

hub, hubs NOUN ❶ the centre part of a wheel. ❷ the most important or active part of a place or organization • *The kitchen is the hub of most households.*

hubbub NOUN Hubbub is great noise or confusion • *the general hubbub of conversation.*

huddle, huddles, huddling, huddled VERB ❶ If you huddle up or are huddled, you are curled up with your arms and legs close to your body. ❷ When people or animals huddle together, they sit or stand close to each other, often for warmth ▷ NOUN ❸ A huddle of people or things is a small group of them.

hue, hues NOUN ❶ LITERARY a colour or a particular shade of a colour

▷ SPELLING NOTE: *there's SAND in my SANDwich (sandwich)*

huff | 418

▷ **PHRASE ❷** If people raise a **hue and cry**, they are very angry about something and protest.

huff **PHRASE** If you are **in a huff**, you are sulking or offended about something. **huffy ADJECTIVE**

hug, hugs, hugging, hugged **VERB** ❶ If you hug someone, you put your arms round them and hold them close to you. ❷ To hug the ground or a stretch of water or land means to keep very close to it • *The road hugs the coast for hundreds of miles.* ▷ **NOUN** ❸ If you give someone a hug, you hold them close to you.
● **WORD HISTORY:** from Old Norse
● *hugga* meaning 'to comfort' or
● 'console'

huge, huger, hugest **ADJECTIVE** extremely large in amount, size, or degree • *a huge success* • *a huge crowd.* **hugely ADVERB**
● **SIMILAR WORDS:** enormous,
● gigantic, vast

hui, hui or huis [Said **hoo-ee**] **NOUN** ❶ In New Zealand, a meeting of Maori people. ❷ INFORMAL In New Zealand English, a party.

hulk, hulks **NOUN** ❶ a large, heavy person or thing. ❷ the body of a ship that has been wrecked or abandoned. **hulking ADJECTIVE**

hull, hulls **NOUN** The hull of a ship is the main part of its body that sits in the water.

hum, hums, humming, hummed **VERB** ❶ To hum means to make a continuous low noise • *The generator hummed faintly.* ❷ If you hum, you sing with your lips closed ▷ **NOUN** ❸ a continuous low noise • *The hum*

was coming from the fridge.

human, humans **ADJECTIVE** ❶ relating to, concerning, or typical of people • *Intolerance appears deeply ingrained in human nature.* ▷ **NOUN** ❷ a person. **humanly ADVERB**

human being, human beings **NOUN** a person.

Human Development Index **NOUN** (GEOGRAPHY) a way of measuring how much a country has developed by gathering data about things such as life expectancy, adult literacy, and standard of living, and comparing them with data about the same things in other countries.

humane ADJECTIVE showing kindness and sympathy towards others • *Medicine is regarded as the most humane of professions.* **humanely ADVERB**

humanism NOUN Humanism is the belief in mankind's ability to achieve happiness and fulfilment without the need for religion.

humanitarian, humanitarians **NOUN** ❶ a person who works for the welfare of mankind ▷ **ADJECTIVE** ❷ concerned with the welfare of mankind • *humanitarian aid.* **humanitarianism NOUN**

humanity NOUN ❶ Humanity is people in general • *I have faith in humanity.* ❷ Humanity is also the condition of being human • *He denies his humanity.* ❸ Someone who has humanity is kind and sympathetic.

human rights PLURAL NOUN Human rights are the rights of individuals to freedom and justice.

▷ SPELLING NOTE: *On WEDNESday Wayne WED NESta (Wednesday)*

humble, humbler, humblest; humbles, humbling, humbled
ADJECTIVE ❶ A humble person is modest and thinks that he or she has very little value. ❷ Something that is humble is small or not very important • *Just a splash of wine will transform a humble casserole.* ▷ **VERB** ❸ To humble someone means to make them feel humiliated. **humbly ADVERB humbled ADJECTIVE**
● **SIMILAR WORDS:** ❶ modest,
● unassuming

humbug, humbugs **NOUN** ❶ a hard black and white striped sweet that tastes of peppermint. ❷ Humbug is speech or writing that is obviously dishonest or untrue • *hypocritical humbug.*

humdrum ADJECTIVE ordinary, dull, and boring • *humdrum domestic tasks.*

humerus, humeri [Said hyoo-mer-us] **NOUN** (SCIENCE) Your humerus is the long bone in the upper part of your arm.

humid ADJECTIVE If it is humid, the air feels damp, heavy, and warm.

humidity NOUN Humidity is the amount of moisture in the air, or the state of being humid.

humiliate, humiliates, humiliating, humiliated **VERB** To humiliate someone means to make them feel ashamed or appear stupid to other people. **humiliation NOUN**
● **SIMILAR WORDS:** embarrass,
● mortify, shame

humility NOUN Humility is the quality of being modest and humble.

hummingbird, hummingbirds **NOUN** a small bird with powerful wings that make a humming noise as they beat.

humour, humours, humouring, humoured **NOUN** ❶ Humour is the quality of being funny • *They discussed it with tact and humour.* ❷ Humour is also the ability to be amused by certain things • *Helen's got a peculiar sense of humour.* ❸ Someone's humour is the mood they are in • *He hasn't been in a good humour lately.* ▷ **VERB** ❹ If you humour someone, you are especially kind to them and do whatever they want. **humorous ADJECTIVE**
● **SIMILAR WORDS:** ❶ comedy,
● funniness, wit

hump, humps, humping, humped **NOUN** ❶ a small, rounded lump or mound • *a camel's hump.* ▷ **VERB** ❷ INFORMAL If you hump something heavy, you carry or move it with difficulty.

hunch, hunches, hunching, hunched **NOUN** ❶ a feeling or suspicion about something, not based on facts or evidence ▷ **VERB** ❷ If you hunch your shoulders, you raise your shoulders and lean forwards.

hunchback, hunchbacks **NOUN** OLD-FASHIONED someone who has a large hump on their back.

hundred, hundreds the number 100. **hundredth ADJECTIVE**

Hungarian, Hungarians [Said hung-**gair**-ee-an] **ADJECTIVE** ❶ belonging or relating to Hungary ▷ **NOUN** ❷ someone who comes from Hungary. ❸ Hungarian is the

▷ SPELLING NOTE: *Eddy Ant thinks mEAt is a grEAt trEAt to EAt (-ea-)*

main language spoken in Hungary.

hunger, hungers, hungering, hungered **NOUN** ❶ Hunger is the need to eat or the desire to eat. ❷ A hunger for something is a strong need or desire for it • *a hunger for winning.* ▷ **VERB** ❸ If you hunger for something, you want it very much.

hunger strike, hunger strikes **NOUN** a refusal to eat anything at all, especially by prisoners, as a form of protest.

hungry, hungrier, hungriest **ADJECTIVE** needing or wanting to eat • *People are going hungry.* **hungrily ADVERB**

hunk, hunks **NOUN** A hunk of something is a large piece of it.

hunt, hunts, hunting, hunted **VERB** ❶ To hunt means to chase wild animals to kill them for food or for sport. ❷ If you hunt for something, you search for it ▷ **NOUN** ❸ the act of hunting • *Police launched a hunt for an abandoned car.* **hunter NOUN hunting ADJECTIVE OR NOUN**

huntaway, huntaways **NOUN** In Australia and New Zealand, a dog trained to drive sheep forward.

hurdle, hurdles **NOUN** ❶ one of the frames or barriers that you jump over in an athletics race called hurdles • *She won the four hundred metre hurdles.* ❷ a problem or difficulty • *Several hurdles exist for anyone seeking to do postgraduate study.*

hurl, hurls, hurling, hurled **VERB** ❶ To hurl something means to throw it with great force. ❷ If you hurl insults at someone, you insult them aggressively and repeatedly.

hurray, hurrah or **hooray INTERJECTION** an exclamation of excitement or approval.

hurricane, hurricanes **NOUN** (GEOGRAPHY) A hurricane is a violent wind or storm, usually force 12 or above on the Beaufort scale.

hurry, hurries, hurrying, hurried **VERB** ❶ To hurry means to move or do something as quickly as possible • *She hurried through the empty streets.* ❷ To hurry something means to make it happen more quickly • *You can't hurry nature.* ▷ **NOUN** ❸ Hurry is the speed with which you do something quickly • *He was in a hurry to leave.* **hurried ADJECTIVE hurriedly ADVERB**

● **SIMILAR WORDS:** ❶ dash, fly, ● rush ❸ haste, rush

hurt, hurts, hurting, hurt **VERB** ❶ To hurt someone means to cause them physical pain. ❷ If a part of your body hurts, you feel pain there. ❸ If you hurt yourself, you injure yourself. ❹ To hurt someone also means to make them unhappy by being unkind or thoughtless towards them • *I didn't want to hurt his feelings.* ▷ **ADJECTIVE** ❺ If someone feels hurt, they feel unhappy because of someone's unkindness towards them • *He felt hurt by all the lies.* **hurtful ADJECTIVE**

hurtle, hurtles, hurtling, hurtled **VERB** To hurtle means to move or travel very fast indeed, especially in an uncontrolled way.

husband, husbands **NOUN** A woman's husband is the man she is married to.

▷ SPELLING NOTE: *Elaine and Emily shout EE when they mEEt to grEEt each other (-ee-)*

husbandry NOUN ❶ Husbandry is the art or skill of farming.
❷ Husbandry is also the art or skill of managing something carefully and economically.

hush, hushes, hushing, hushed **VERB** ❶ If you tell someone to hush, you are telling them to be quiet. ❷ To hush something up means to keep it secret, especially something dishonest involving important people • *The government has hushed up a series of scandals.* ▷ **NOUN** ❸ If there is a hush, it is quiet and still • *A graveyard hush fell over the group.* **hushed ADJECTIVE**

husk, husks **NOUN** Husks are the dry outer coverings of grain or seed.

husky, huskier, huskiest; huskies **ADJECTIVE** ❶ A husky voice is rough or hoarse ▷ **NOUN** ❷ a large, strong dog with a thick coat, often used to pull sledges across snow.

hustle, hustles, hustling, hustled **VERB** To hustle someone means to make them move by pushing and jostling them • *The guards hustled him out of the car.*

hut, huts **NOUN** a small, simple building, with one or two rooms.

hutch, hutches **NOUN** a wooden box with wire mesh at one side, in which small pets can be kept.

hyacinth, hyacinths [*Said high-as-sinth*] **NOUN** a spring flower with many small, bell-shaped flowers.

hybrid, hybrids **NOUN** ❶ a plant or animal that has been bred from two different types of plant or animal.
❷ anything that is a mixture of two different other things.

hydra, hydras or hydrae **NOUN** a microscopic freshwater creature that has a slender tubular body and tentacles round the mouth.

hydrangea, hydrangeas [*Said high-drain-ja*] **NOUN** a garden shrub with large clusters of pink or blue flowers.

hydraulic [*Said high-drol-lik*] **ADJECTIVE** operated by water or other fluid which is under pressure.

hydro- PREFIX 'Hydro-' means 'water'. For example, *hydroelectricity* is electricity made using water power.
● **WORD HISTORY:** from Greek
● *hudōr* meaning 'water'

hydrocarbon, hydrocarbons **NOUN** (SCIENCE) A hydrocarbon is a chemical compound that is a mixture of hydrogen and carbon.

hydrogen NOUN Hydrogen is the lightest gas and the simplest chemical element.

hydrology NOUN (GEOGRAPHY) the study of the distribution and use of water on the earth and in its atmosphere.

hydrolysis [*Said high-drol-iss-iss*] **NOUN** (SCIENCE) In chemistry, hydrolysis is a process of decomposition in which a compound reacts with water to produce other compounds.

hyena, hyenas [*Said high-ee-na*]; also spelt **hyaena NOUN** a wild doglike animal of Africa and Asia that hunts in packs.

hygiene [*Said high-jeen*] **NOUN**

a b c d e f g h i j k l m n o p q r s t u v w x y z

▷ SPELLING NOTE: *'i' before 'e' except after 'c'*

WHAT DOES THE HYPHEN DO?

The **hyphen** (-) separates the different parts of certain words. A hyphen is often used when there would otherwise be an awkward combination of letters, or confusion with another word:
Anna was re-elected president.

She adopted a no-nonsense approach.

In printed texts, the hyphen also divides a word that will not fit at the end of a line and has to be continued on the next line.

D & T Hygiene is the practice of keeping yourself and your surroundings clean, especially to stop the spread of disease. **hygienic ADJECTIVE**

hymn, hymns NOUN (RE) a Christian song in praise of God.

hyper- PREFIX 'Hyper-' means 'very much' or 'excessively' • *hyperactive*.
● **WORD HISTORY:** from Greek
● *huper* meaning 'over'

hyperactive ADJECTIVE A hyperactive person is unable to relax and is always in a state of restless activity.

hyperbole [Said high-**per**-bol-lee] NOUN Hyperbole is a style of speech or writing which uses exaggeration.

hyperlink, hyperlinks NOUN a word, phrase, or picture in a computer document which a user may click to move to another part of the document, or to another document.

hypertension NOUN Hypertension is a medical condition in which a person has high blood pressure.

hypertext, hypertexts NOUN computer software that allows users to create, store, and view text and move between related items easily.

hyphen, hyphens NOUN a punctuation mark used to join together words or parts of words, as for example in the word 'left-handed'. **hyphenate VERB hyphenation NOUN**
▶ SEE GRAMMAR BOX ABOVE

hypnosis [Said hip-**noh**-siss] NOUN Hypnosis is an artificially produced state of relaxation in which the mind is very receptive to suggestion.
● **WORD HISTORY:** from Greek
● *hupnos* meaning 'sleep'

hypnotize, hypnotizes, hypnotizing, hypnotized; *also spelt* **hypnotise** VERB To hypnotize someone means to put them into a state in which they seem to be asleep but can respond to questions and suggestions. **hypnotic ADJECTIVE hypnotism NOUN hypnotist NOUN**

hypochondriac, hypochondriacs [Said high-pok-**kon**-dree-ak] NOUN a person who continually worries about their health, being convinced that they are ill when there is actually nothing wrong with them.

hypocrisy, hypocrisies NOUN Hypocrisy is pretending to have beliefs or qualities that you do not really have, so that you seem a better person than you are. **hypocritical**

▷ SPELLING NOTE: *King IAn went to ParlIAment in a carrIAge for his marrIAge (-ia-)*

ADJECTIVE hypocrite NOUN

hypodermic, hypodermics NOUN a medical instrument with a hollow needle, used for giving people injections, or taking blood samples.

hypotenuse, hypotenuses [Said high-**pot**-tin-yooz] NOUN (MATHS) In a triangle that has a right angle, the hypotenuse is the longest side and is opposite the right angle.

hypothermia NOUN (SCIENCE) Hypothermia is a condition in which a person is very ill because their body temperature has been unusually low for a long time.

hypothesis, hypotheses NOUN an explanation or theory which has not yet been proved to be correct.

hypothetical ADJECTIVE based on assumption rather than on fact.

hysterectomy, hysterectomies [Said his-ter-**rek**-tom-ee] NOUN an operation to remove a woman's womb.

hysteria [Said hiss-**teer**-ee-a] NOUN Hysteria is a state of uncontrolled excitement or panic.

hysterical ADJECTIVE ❶ Someone who is hysterical is in a state of uncontrolled excitement or panic. ❷ INFORMAL Something that is hysterical is extremely funny. **hysterically** ADVERB **hysterics** NOUN

● SIMILAR WORDS: ❶ frantic, ● frenzied

a
b
c
d
e
f
g
h
i
j
k
l
m
n
o
p
q
r
s
t
u
v
w
x
y
z

Ii

I PRONOUN A speaker or writer uses 'I' to refer to himself or herself • *I like the colour.*

iambic ADJECTIVE (ENGLISH) If a line of verse is iambic, it is made up of rhythmic units called *iambs*, which have one unstressed syllable followed by a stressed one.

ibis, ibises [*Said* **eye**-*biss*] NOUN a large wading bird with a long, thin, curved bill that lives in warm countries.

-ible SUFFIX another form of the suffix **-able**.

-ic or **-ical** SUFFIX '-ic' and '-ical' form adjectives from nouns. For example, *ironic* or *ironical* formed from *irony*.

ice, ices, icing, iced NOUN ❶ water that has frozen solid. ❷ an ice cream ▷ VERB ❸ If you ice cakes, you cover them with icing. ❹ If something ices over or ices up, it becomes covered with a layer of ice ▷ PHRASE ❺ If you do something to **break the ice**, you make people feel relaxed and comfortable.

Ice Age, Ice Ages NOUN a period of time lasting thousands of years when a lot of the earth's surface was covered with ice.

iceberg, icebergs NOUN a large mass of ice floating in the sea.

● WORD HISTORY: from Dutch
● *ijsberg* meaning 'ice mountain'

icecap, icecaps NOUN a layer of ice and snow that permanently covers the North or South Pole.

ice cream, ice creams NOUN a very cold sweet food made from frozen cream.

ice cube, ice cubes NOUN Ice cubes are small cubes of ice put in drinks to make them cold.

ice hockey NOUN a type of hockey played on ice, with two teams of six players.

Icelandic NOUN the main language spoken in Iceland.

ice-skate, ice-skates, ice-skating, ice-skated ❶ a boot with a metal blade on the bottom, which you wear when skating on ice ▷ VERB ❷ If you ice-skate, you move about on ice wearing ice-skates.

icicle, icicles [*Said* **eye**-*sik-kl*] NOUN a piece of ice shaped like a pointed stick that hangs down from a surface.

icing NOUN a mixture of powdered sugar and water or egg whites, used to decorate cakes.

icon, icons [*Said* **eye**-*kon*] NOUN ❶ (ICT) a picture on a computer screen representing a program that can be activated by moving the cursor

▷ SPELLING NOTE: *LEt's measure the angLE (angle)*

over it. **❷** in the Orthodox Churches, a holy picture of Christ, the Virgin Mary, or a saint.
● **WORD HISTORY:** from Greek *eikōn* meaning 'likeness' or 'image'

ICT an abbreviation for 'Information and Communication Technology'.

icy, icier, iciest **ADJECTIVE**
❶ Something which is icy is very cold • *an icy wind*. **❷** An icy road has ice on it. **icily ADVERB**

id NOUN In psychology, your id is your basic instincts and unconscious thoughts.

idea, ideas **NOUN** **❶** a plan, suggestion, or thought that you have after thinking about a problem. **❷** an opinion or belief • *old-fashioned ideas about women*. **❸** An idea of something is what you know about it • *They had no idea of their position.*
● **SIMILAR WORDS:** **❶** impression, thought **❷** belief, notion, opinion

ideal, ideals **NOUN** **❶** a principle or idea that you try to achieve because it seems perfect to you. **❷** Your ideal of something is the person or thing that seems the best example of it
▷ **ADJECTIVE** **❸** The ideal person or thing is the best possible person or thing for the situation.

idealism [Said eye-**dee**-il-izm] **NOUN** behaviour that is based on a person's ideals. **idealist NOUN** **idealistic ADJECTIVE**

idealize, idealizes, idealizing, idealized; *also spelt* **idealise VERB** If you idealize someone or something, you regard them as being perfect. **idealization NOUN**

ideally ADVERB **❶** If you say that ideally something should happen, you mean that you would like it to happen but you know that it is not possible. **❷** Ideally means perfectly • *The hotel is ideally placed for business travellers.*

identical ADJECTIVE exactly the same. **identically ADVERB**

identification NOUN **❶** The identification of someone or something is the act of identifying them. **❷** Identification is a document such as a driver's licence or passport, which proves who you are.

identify, identifies, identifying, identified **VERB** **❶** To identify someone or something is to recognize them or name them. **❷** If you identify with someone, you understand their feelings and ideas. **identifiable ADJECTIVE**

identity, identities **NOUN** the characteristics that make you who you are.

ideology, ideologies **NOUN** a set of political beliefs. **ideological ADJECTIVE ideologically ADVERB**

idiom, idioms **NOUN** (ENGLISH) a group of words whose meaning together is different from all the words taken individually. For example, 'It is raining cats and dogs' is an idiom.
● **WORD HISTORY:** from Greek *idiōma* meaning 'special phraseology'

idiosyncrasy, idiosyncrasies [Said id-ee-oh-**sing**-krass-ee] **NOUN** Someone's idiosyncrasies are their own habits and likes or dislikes. **idiosyncratic ADJECTIVE**

idiot, idiots **NOUN** someone who is stupid or foolish.
- **WORD HISTORY:** from Greek *idiōtēs* meaning 'ignorant person'
- **SIMILAR WORDS:** fool, halfwit, moron

idiotic ADJECTIVE extremely foolish or silly.
- **SIMILAR WORDS:** foolish, senseless, stupid

idle, idles, idling, idled **ADJECTIVE** If you are idle, you are doing nothing. **idleness NOUN idly ADVERB**
- **WORD HISTORY:** from Saxon *idal* meaning 'worthless' or 'empty'

idol, idols *[Said eye-doll]* **NOUN** ❶ a famous person who is loved and admired by fans. ❷ a picture or statue which is worshipped as if it were a god.

idyll, idylls *[Said id-ill]* **NOUN** a situation which is peaceful and beautiful. **idyllic ADJECTIVE**

i.e. i.e. means 'that is', and is used before giving more information. It is an abbreviation for the Latin expression 'id est'.

if CONJUNCTION ❶ on the condition that • *I shall stay if I can.* ❷ whether • *I asked her if she wanted to go.*

igloo, igloos **NOUN** a dome-shaped house built out of blocks of snow by the Inuit, or Eskimo, people.

igneous *[Said ig-nee-uss]* **ADJECTIVE** (GEOGRAPHY) Igneous rocks are formed by hot liquid rock cooling and going hard.
- **WORD HISTORY:** from Latin *igneus* meaning 'fiery'

ignite, ignites, igniting, ignited **VERB** If you ignite something or if it ignites, it starts burning.
- **WORD HISTORY:** from Latin *ignis* meaning 'fire'

ignition, ignitions **NOUN** In a car, the ignition is the part of the engine where the fuel is ignited.

ignominious ADJECTIVE shameful or considered wrong • *It was an ignominious end to a brilliant career.* **ignominiously ADVERB ignominy NOUN**

ignoramus, ignoramuses *[Said ig-nor-ray-muss]* **NOUN** an ignorant person.
- **WORD HISTORY:** from the character *Ignoramus*, an uneducated lawyer in a 17th-century play by Ruggle. In Latin *ignoramus* means 'we do not know'

ignorant ADJECTIVE ❶ If you are ignorant of something, you do not know about it • *He was completely ignorant of the rules.* ❷ Someone who is ignorant does not know about things in general • *I thought of asking, but didn't want to seem ignorant.* **ignorantly ADVERB ignorance NOUN**
- **SIMILAR WORDS:** ❶ unaware, unconscious, uninformed

ignore, ignores, ignoring, ignored **VERB** If you ignore someone or something, you deliberately do not take any notice of them.

iguana, iguanas *[Said ig-wah-na]* **NOUN** a large, tropical lizard.

il- PREFIX 'il-' means 'not' or 'the opposite of', and is the form of 'in-' that is used before the letter *l*

▷ SPELLING NOTE: *Beautiful Elephants Are Usually Tiny (beautiful)*

• illegible • illegitimate • illiterate.

ill, ills **ADJECTIVE** ❶ unhealthy or sick. ❷ harmful or unpleasant • *ill effects.* ❸ IN PLURAL Ills are difficulties or problems.
● **WORD HISTORY:** from Norse *illr* meaning 'bad'
● **SIMILAR WORDS:** ❶ sick, unhealthy, unwell

ill at ease PHRASE If you feel **ill at ease**, you feel unable to relax.

illegal ADJECTIVE forbidden by the law. **illegally** ADVERB **illegality** NOUN
● **SIMILAR WORDS:** criminal, illicit, unlawful

illegible *[Said il-lej-i-bl]* ADJECTIVE Writing which is illegible is unclear and very difficult to read.

illegitimate *[Said il-lij-it-tim-it]* ADJECTIVE A person who is illegitimate was born to parents who were not married at the time. **illegitimacy** NOUN

ill-fated ADJECTIVE doomed to end unhappily • *his ill-fated attempt on the world record.*

illicit *[Said il-liss-it]* ADJECTIVE not allowed by law or not approved of by society • *illicit drugs.*

illiterate ADJECTIVE unable to read or write. **illiteracy** NOUN

illness, illnesses NOUN ❶ Illness is the experience of being ill. ❷ a particular disease • *the treatment of common illnesses.*
● **SIMILAR WORDS:** ❷ ailment, disease, malady, sickness

illogical ADJECTIVE An illogical feeling or action is not reasonable or sensible. **illogically** ADVERB

ill-treat, ill-treats, ill-treating, ill-treated VERB If you ill-treat someone or something you hurt or damage them or treat them cruelly. **ill-treatment** NOUN

illuminate, illuminates, illuminating, illuminated VERB To illuminate something is to shine light on it to make it easier to see.

illumination, illuminations NOUN ❶ Illumination is lighting. ❷ Illuminations are the coloured lights put up to decorate a town, especially at Christmas.

illusion, illusions NOUN ❶ a false belief which you think is true • *Their hopes proved to be an illusion.* ❷ ART a false appearance of reality which deceives the eye • *Painters create the illusion of space.*

illusory *[Said ill-yoo-ser-ee]* ADJECTIVE seeming to be true, but actually false • *an illusory truce.*

illustrate, illustrates, illustrating, illustrated VERB ❶ EXAM TERM If you illustrate a point, you explain it or make it clearer, often by using examples. ❷ If you illustrate a book, you put pictures in it. **illustrator** NOUN **illustrative** ADJECTIVE

illustration, illustrations NOUN ❶ an example or a story which is used to make a point clear. ❷ a picture in a book.

illustrious ADJECTIVE An illustrious person is famous and respected.

ill will NOUN Ill will is a feeling of

a
b
c
d
e
f
g
h
i
j
k
l
m
n
o
p
q
r
s
t
u
v
w
x
y
z

▷ SPELLING NOTE: *Betty Eats Cakes And Uses Seven Eggs (because)*

A
B
C
D
E
F
G
H
I
J
K
L
M
N
O
P
Q
R
S
T
U
V
W
X
Y
Z

hostility • *no ill will towards us.*

im- PREFIX 'im-' means 'not' or 'the opposite of', and is the form of 'in-' which is used before the letters *b, m* and *p* • *imbalance* • *immature* • *impatient.*

image, images NOUN **①** a mental picture of someone or something. **②** the appearance which a person, group, or organization presents to the public.

imagery NOUN (ENGLISH) The imagery of a poem or book is the descriptive language used in it.

imaginary ADJECTIVE Something that is imaginary exists only in your mind, not in real life.

imagination, imaginations NOUN the ability to form new and exciting ideas.

imaginative ADJECTIVE Someone who is imaginative can easily form new or exciting ideas in their mind. **imaginatively** ADVERB

imagine, imagines, imagining, imagined VERB **①** If you imagine something, you form an idea of it in your mind, or you think you have seen or heard it but you have not really. **②** If you imagine that something is the case, you believe it is the case • *I imagine that's what you aim to do.* **imaginable** ADJECTIVE
● SIMILAR WORDS: **①** conceive,
● envisage, picture, visualize
● **②** believe, suppose, think

imam [*Said ih-mam*] NOUN a person who leads a group in prayer in a mosque.

imbalance, imbalances NOUN If

there is an imbalance between things, they are unequal • *the imbalance between rich and poor.*

imbecile, imbeciles [*Said im-bis-seel*] NOUN a stupid person.

imitate, imitates, imitating, imitated VERB To imitate someone or something is to copy them. **imitator** NOUN **imitative** ADJECTIVE
● SIMILAR WORDS: copy, mimic

imitation, imitations NOUN a copy of something else.

immaculate [*Said im-mak-yoo-lit*] ADJECTIVE **①** completely clean and tidy • *The flat was immaculate.* **②** without any mistakes at all • *his usual immaculate guitar accompaniment.* **immaculately** ADVERB

immaterial ADJECTIVE Something that is immaterial is not important.

immature ADJECTIVE **①** Something that is immature has not finished growing or developing. **②** A person who is immature does not behave in a sensible adult way. **immaturity** NOUN

immediate ADJECTIVE **①** Something that is immediate happens or is done without delay. **②** Your immediate relatives and friends are the ones most closely connected or related to you.

immediately ADVERB **①** If something happens immediately it happens right away. **②** Immediately means very near in time or position • *immediately behind the house.*

immemorial ADJECTIVE If something has been happening from

▷ SPELLING NOTE: *there's a rAKE in the brAKEs (brake)*

time immemorial, it has been happening longer than anyone can remember.

immense ADJECTIVE very large or huge. **immensely** ADVERB **immensity** NOUN

immerse, immerses, immersing, immersed VERB ❶ If you are immersed in an activity you are completely involved in it. ❷ If you immerse something in a liquid, you put it into the liquid so that it is completely covered. **immersion** NOUN

immigrant, immigrants NOUN (HISTORY) someone who has come to live permanently in a new country. **immigrate** VERB **immigration** NOUN

imminent ADJECTIVE If something is imminent, it is going to happen very soon. **imminently** ADVERB **imminence** NOUN
  ● SIMILAR WORDS: coming,
  ● impending, near

immobile ADJECTIVE not moving. **immobility** NOUN

immoral ADJECTIVE (RE) If you describe someone or their behaviour as immoral, you mean that they do not fit in with most people's idea of what is right and proper. **immorality** NOUN
  ● USAGE NOTE: Do not confuse
  ● *immoral* and *amoral*. You use
  ● *immoral* to talk about people who
  ● are aware of moral standards, but
  ● go against them. *Amoral* applies to
  ● people with no moral standards

immortal ADJECTIVE
❶ Something that is immortal is

famous and will be remembered for a long time • *Emily Bronte's immortal love story.* ❷ In stories, someone who is immortal will never die.

immortality NOUN (RE) Immortality is never dying. In many religions, people believe that the soul or some other essential part of a person lives forever or continues to exist in some form.

immovable or **immoveable** ADJECTIVE Something that is immovable is fixed and cannot be moved. **immovably** ADVERB

immune [Said im-*yoon*] ADJECTIVE ❶ If you are immune to a particular disease, you cannot catch it. ❷ If someone or something is immune to something, they are able to avoid it or are not affected by it • *The captain was immune to prosecution.* **immunity** NOUN

immune system NOUN Your body's immune system consists of your white blood cells, which fight disease by producing antibodies or germs to kill germs which come into your body.

immunize, immunizes, immunizing, immunized; *also spelt* **immunise** VERB (SCIENCE) To immunize a person or animal means to make them immune to a particular disease, usually by giving them an injection. **immunization** NOUN

imp, imps NOUN a small mischievous creature in fairy stories. **impish** ADJECTIVE

impact, impacts NOUN ❶ The impact that someone or something has is the impression that they make

a
b
c
d
e
f
g
h
i
j
k
l
m
n
o
p
q
r
s
t
u
v
w
x
y
z

▷ SPELLING NOTE: *you'll brEAK that Electrical Aerial, Kitty (break)*

or the effect that they have. **❷** Impact is the action of one object hitting another, usually with a lot of force • *The aircraft crashed into a ditch, exploding on impact.*

impair, impairs, impairing, impaired **VERB** To impair something is to damage it so that it stops working properly • *Travel had made him weary and impaired his judgement.*

impale, impales, impaling, impaled **VERB** If you impale something, you pierce it with a sharp object.

impart, imparts, imparting, imparted **VERB** FORMAL To impart information to someone is to pass it on to them.

impartial **ADJECTIVE** Someone who is impartial has a view of something which is fair or not biased. **impartially** **ADVERB** **impartiality** **NOUN**
● SIMILAR WORDS: fair, neutral, ● objective

impasse [*Said am-pass*] **NOUN** a difficult situation in which it is impossible to find a solution.
● WORD HISTORY: from French ● *impasse* meaning 'dead end'

impassioned **ADJECTIVE** full of emotion • *an impassioned plea.*

impassive **ADJECTIVE** showing no emotion. **impassively** **ADVERB**

impasto **NOUN** ART a technique of painting with thick paint so that brush strokes or palette knife marks can be seen.
● WORD HISTORY: an Italian word, ● from *pasta* meaning 'paste'

impatient **ADJECTIVE** **❶** Someone who is impatient becomes annoyed

easily or is quick to lose their temper when things go wrong. **❷** If you are impatient to do something, you are eager and do not want to wait • *He was impatient to get back.* **impatiently** **ADVERB** **impatience** **NOUN**

impeccable [*Said im-pek-i-bl*] **ADJECTIVE** excellent, without any faults. **impeccably** **ADVERB**

impede, impedes, impeding, impeded **VERB** If you impede someone, you make their progress difficult.

impediment, impediments **NOUN** something that makes it difficult to move, develop, or do something properly • *a speech impediment.*

impelled **ADJECTIVE** If you feel impelled to do something, you feel strongly that you must do it.

impending **ADJECTIVE** FORMAL You use 'impending' to describe something that is going to happen very soon • *a sense of impending doom.*

impenetrable **ADJECTIVE** impossible to get through.

imperative **ADJECTIVE** **❶** Something that is imperative is extremely urgent or important ▷ **NOUN** **❷** In grammar, an imperative is the form of a verb that is used for giving orders.

imperfect **ADJECTIVE** **❶** Something that is imperfect has faults or problems ▷ **NOUN** **❷** In grammar, the imperfect is a tense used to describe continuous or repeated actions which happened in the past. **imperfectly** **ADVERB** **imperfection** **NOUN**

▷ SPELLING NOTE: *I always visit my FRIend on a FRIday (Friday)*

● **SIMILAR WORDS:** ❶ faulty,
● flawed

imperial ADJECTIVE ❶ (HISTORY)
Imperial means relating to an empire
or an emperor or empress • *the
Imperial Palace.* ❷ The imperial
system of measurement is the
measuring system which uses inches,
feet, and yards, ounces and pounds,
and pints and gallons.

imperialism NOUN (HISTORY) a
system of rule in which a rich and
powerful nation controls other
nations. **imperialist** ADJECTIVE OR
NOUN

imperious ADJECTIVE proud and
domineering • *an imperious manner.*
imperiously ADVERB

impersonal ADJECTIVE
Something that is impersonal
makes you feel that individuals and
their feelings do not matter
• *impersonal cold rooms.* **impersonally**
ADVERB
● **SIMILAR WORDS:** detached,
● dispassionate, inhuman

impersonate, impersonates,
impersonating, impersonated VERB If
you impersonate someone, you
pretend to be that person.
impersonation NOUN
impersonator NOUN

impertinent ADJECTIVE
disrespectful and rude • *impertinent
questions.* **impertinently** ADVERB
impertinence NOUN

impetuous ADJECTIVE If you are
impetuous, you act quickly without
thinking • *an impetuous gamble.*
impetuously ADVERB **impetuosity**
NOUN

impetus NOUN ❶ An impetus is
the stimulating effect that something
has on a situation, which causes it to
develop more quickly. ❷ In physics,
impetus is the force that starts an
object moving and resists changes in
speed or direction.

impinge, impinges, impinging,
impinged VERB If something
impinges on your life, it has an effect
on you and influences you • *My private
life doesn't impinge on my professional
life.*

implacable [Said im-**plak**-a-bl]
ADJECTIVE Someone who is
implacable is being harsh and refuses
to change their mind. **implacably**
ADVERB

implant, implants, implanting,
implanted VERB ❶ To implant
something into a person's body is to
put it there, usually by means of an
operation ▷ NOUN ❷ something that
has been implanted into someone's
body.

implausible ADJECTIVE very
unlikely • *implausible stories.*
implausibly ADVERB

implement, implements,
implementing, implemented VERB
❶ If you implement something such
as a plan, you carry it out • *The
government has failed to implement
promised reforms.* ▷ NOUN ❷ An
implement is a tool. **implementation**
NOUN

implicate, implicates, implicating,
implicated VERB If you are implicated
in a crime, you are shown to be
involved in it.

implication, implications NOUN

▷ SPELLING NOTE: *I want to see (C) your licenCe (licence)*

something that is suggested or implied but not stated directly.

implicit [Said im-**pliss**-it] ADJECTIVE ❶ expressed in an indirect way • *implicit criticism.* ❷ If you have an implicit belief in something, you have no doubts about it • *He had implicit faith in her noble intentions.* **implicitly** ADVERB

implore, implores, imploring, implored VERB If you implore someone to do something, you beg them to do it.

imply, implies, implying, implied VERB If you imply that something is the case, you suggest it in an indirect way.

import, imports, importing, imported VERB ❶ If you import something from another country, you bring it into your country or have it sent there ▷ NOUN ❷ a product that is made in another country and sent to your own country for use there. **importation** NOUN **importer** NOUN

important ADJECTIVE ❶ Something that is important is very valuable, necessary, or significant. ❷ An important person has great influence or power. **importantly** ADVERB **importance** NOUN
● SIMILAR WORDS: ❶ momentous,
● significant

impose, imposes, imposing, imposed VERB ❶ If you impose something on people, you force it on them • *The allies had imposed a ban on all flights over Iraq.* ❷ If someone imposes on you, they unreasonably expect you to do something for them. **imposition** NOUN

imposing ADJECTIVE having an impressive appearance or manner • *an imposing building.*

impossible ADJECTIVE Something that is impossible cannot happen, be done, or be believed. **impossibly** ADVERB **impossibility** NOUN

imposter, imposters; *also spelt* **impostor** NOUN a person who pretends to be someone else in order to get things they want.

impotent ADJECTIVE ❶ Someone who is impotent has no power to influence people or events. ❷ A man who is impotent is unable to have or maintain an erection during sexual intercourse. **impotently** ADVERB **impotence** NOUN

impound, impounds, impounding, impounded VERB If something you own is impounded, the police or other officials take it.

impoverished ADJECTIVE Someone who is impoverished is poor.

impractical ADJECTIVE not practical, sensible, or realistic.

impregnable ADJECTIVE A building or other structure that is impregnable is so strong that it cannot be broken into or captured • *An impregnable fortress.*

impregnated ADJECTIVE If something is impregnated with a substance, it has absorbed the substance so that it spreads right through it • *sponges impregnated with detergent and water.*

impresario, impresarios [Said im-pris-**sar**-ee-oh] NOUN a person

▷ SPELLING NOTE: *The government licenSes Schnapps (licenSes)*

who manages theatrical or musical events or companies.

impress, impresses, impressing, impressed **VERB** ❶ If you impress someone, you make them admire or respect you. ❷ If you impress something on someone, you make them understand the importance of it.

impression, impressions **NOUN** ❶ An impression of someone or something is the way they look or seem to you. ❷ If you **make an impression**, you have a strong effect on people you meet.

impressionable **ADJECTIVE** easy to influence • *impressionable teenagers.*

impressionism **NOUN** a style of painting which is concerned with the impressions created by light and shapes, rather than with exact details. **impressionist NOUN**

impressive **ADJECTIVE** If something is impressive, it impresses you • *an impressive display of old-fashioned American cars.*

imprint, imprints, imprinting, imprinted **NOUN** ❶ If something leaves an imprint on your mind, it has a strong and lasting effect. ❷ the mark left by the pressure of one object on another ▷ **VERB** ❸ If something is imprinted on your memory, it is firmly fixed there.

imprison, imprisons, imprisoning, imprisoned **VERB** If you are imprisoned, you are locked up, usually in a prison. **imprisonment NOUN**

improbable **ADJECTIVE** not probable or likely to happen.

improbably ADVERB
● **SIMILAR WORDS:** doubtful,
● unlikely

impromptu *[Said im-**prompt**-yoo]* **ADJECTIVE** An impromptu action is one done without planning or organization.
● **WORD HISTORY:** from Latin *in promptu* meaning 'in readiness'
● **SIMILAR WORDS:** improvised, off the cuff, unprepared

improper **ADJECTIVE** ❶ rude or shocking • *improper behaviour.* ❷ illegal or dishonest • *improper dealings.* ❸ not suitable or correct • *an improper diet.* **improperly ADVERB**

improve, improves, improving, improved **VERB** If something improves or if you improve it, it gets better or becomes more valuable.
● **SIMILAR WORDS:** better, enhance

improvement, improvements **NOUN** the fact or process of getting better.

improvise, improvises, improvising, improvised **VERB** ❶ If you improvise something, you make or do something without planning in advance, and with whatever materials are available. ❷ (DRAMA) (MUSIC) When musicians or actors improvise, they make up the music or words as they go along. **improvised ADJECTIVE improvisation NOUN**

impudence **NOUN** disrespectful talk or behaviour towards someone.

impudent **ADJECTIVE** If someone is impudent, something they say or do is cheeky and lacking in respect. **impudently ADVERB**

a
b
c
d
e
f
g
h
i
j
k
l
m
n
o
p
q
r
s
t
u
v
w
x
y
z

▷ SPELLING NOTE: *have a plEce of plE (pie*ce)

impulse, impulses NOUN a strong urge to do something • *She felt a sudden impulse to confide in her.*

impulsive ADJECTIVE If you are impulsive, you do things suddenly, without thinking about them carefully. **impulsively** ADVERB

impure ADJECTIVE Something which is impure contains small amounts of other things, such as dirt.

impurity, impurities NOUN ❶ Impurity is the quality of being impure • *the impurity of the water.* ❷ If something contains impurities, it contains small amounts of dirt or other substances that should not be there.

in PREPOSITION OR ADVERB 'In' is used to indicate position, direction, time, and manner • *boarding schools in England* • *in the past few years.*

in- PREFIX ❶ 'In-' is added to the beginning of some words to form a word with the opposite meaning • *insincere.* ❷ 'In-' also means in, into, or in the course of • *infiltrate.*

inability NOUN a lack of ability to do something.

inaccessible ADJECTIVE impossible or very difficult to reach.

inaccurate ADJECTIVE not accurate or correct.

inadequate ADJECTIVE ❶ If something is inadequate, there is not enough of it. ❷ not good enough in quality for a particular purpose. ❸ If someone feels inadequate, they feel they do not possess the skills necessary to do a particular job or to cope with life in general.

inadequately ADVERB **inadequacy** NOUN
● SIMILAR WORDS: ❶ insufficient, ● meagre

inadvertent ADJECTIVE not intentional • *the murder had been inadvertent.* **inadvertently** ADVERB

inane ADJECTIVE silly or stupid. **inanely** ADVERB **inanity** NOUN

inanimate ADJECTIVE An inanimate object is not alive.

inappropriate ADJECTIVE not suitable for a particular purpose or occasion • *It was quite inappropriate to ask such questions.* **inappropriately** ADVERB
● SIMILAR WORDS: out of place, ● unfitting, unsuitable

inarticulate ADJECTIVE If you are inarticulate, you are unable to express yourself well or easily in speech.

inasmuch CONJUNCTION 'Inasmuch as' means 'to the extent that' • *She's giving herself a hard time inasmuch as she feels guilty.*

inaudible ADJECTIVE not loud enough to be heard. **inaudibly** ADVERB

inaugurate, inaugurates, inaugurating, inaugurated [Said in-*awg*-yoo-rate] VERB ❶ To inaugurate a new scheme is to start it. ❷ To inaugurate a new leader is to officially establish them in their new position in a special ceremony • *Albania's Orthodox Church inaugurated its first archbishop in 25 years.* **inauguration** NOUN **inaugural** ADJECTIVE

inborn ADJECTIVE An inborn quality

▷ SPELLING NOTE: *plaice the fish has a glittering 'EYE' (I) (plaice)*

is one that you were born with.

incandescent ADJECTIVE
Something which is incandescent
gives out light when it is heated.
incandescence NOUN
● **WORD HISTORY:** from Latin
● *candescere* meaning 'to glow white'

incapable ADJECTIVE ❶ Someone
who is incapable of doing something
is not able to do it • *He is incapable of
changing a fuse.* ❷ An incapable
person is weak and helpless.

incarcerate, incarcerates,
incarcerating, incarcerated [Said
in-**kar**-ser-rate] **VERB** To incarcerate
someone is to lock them up.
incarceration NOUN

Incarnation NOUN The
Incarnation is the Christian belief that
God took human form in Jesus Christ.

incendiary [Said in-**send**-yer-ee]
ADJECTIVE An incendiary weapon is
one which sets fire to things
• *incendiary bombs.*

incense NOUN Incense is a spicy
substance which is burned to create a
sweet smell, especially during
religious services.

incensed ADJECTIVE If you are
incensed by something, it makes you
extremely angry.

incentive, incentives **NOUN**
something that encourages you to do
something.

inception NOUN FORMAL The
inception of a project is the start of it.
● **WORD HISTORY:** from Latin
● *incipere* meaning 'to take up' or 'to
● begin'

incessant ADJECTIVE continuing
without stopping • *her incessant
talking.* **incessantly ADVERB**

incest NOUN Incest is the crime of
two people who are closely related
having sex with each other.
incestuous ADJECTIVE

inch, inches, inching, inched **NOUN**
❶ a unit of length equal to about 2.54
centimetres ▷ **VERB** ❷ To inch
forward is to move forward slowly.
● **WORD HISTORY:** from Latin *uncia*
● meaning 'twelfth part'; there are
● twelve inches to the foot

incident, incidents **NOUN** an event
• *a shooting incident.*

incidental ADJECTIVE occurring as
a minor part of something • *vivid
incidental detail.* **incidentally
ADVERB**

incinerate, incinerates,
incinerating, incinerated **VERB** If you
incinerate something, you burn it.
incineration NOUN

incinerator, incinerators **NOUN** a
furnace for burning rubbish.

incipient ADJECTIVE beginning to
happen or appear • *incipient panic.*

incision, incisions **NOUN** a sharp
cut, usually made by a surgeon
operating on a patient.

incisive ADJECTIVE Incisive
language is clear and forceful.

incisor, incisors **NOUN** (SCIENCE) An
incisor is a flat tooth with a sharp
cutting edge at the front of your
mouth.

incite, incites, inciting, incited **VERB**
If you incite someone to do

▷ SPELLING NOTE: *I went to see (C) the doctor's new practiCe (practice)*

something, you encourage them to do it by making them angry or excited. **incitement** NOUN

- SIMILAR WORDS: encourage,
- provoke, spur

inclination, inclinations NOUN If you have an inclination to do something, you want to do it.

incline, inclines, inclining, inclined VERB **❶** If you are inclined to behave in a certain way, you often behave that way or you want to behave that way ▷ NOUN **❷** a slope.

include, includes, including, included VERB If one thing includes another, it has the second thing as one of its parts. **including** PREPOSITION

- SIMILAR WORDS: contain,
- incorporate

inclusion NOUN The inclusion of one thing in another is the act of making it part of the other thing.

inclusive ADJECTIVE A price that is inclusive includes all the goods and services that are being offered, with no extra charge for any of them.

incognito [Said in-kog-**nee**-toe] ADVERB If you are travelling incognito, you are travelling in disguise.

- WORD HISTORY: from Latin in- +
- cognitus meaning 'not known'

incoherent ADJECTIVE If someone is incoherent, they are talking in an unclear or rambling way. **incoherently** ADVERB **incoherence** NOUN

income, incomes NOUN the money a person earns.

income tax NOUN Income tax is a part of someone's salary which they have to pay regularly to the government.

incoming ADJECTIVE coming in • incoming trains • an incoming phone call.

incomparable ADJECTIVE Something that is incomparable is so good that it cannot be compared with anything else. **incomparably** ADVERB

- SIMILAR WORDS: matchless,
- unequalled, unparalleled

incompatible ADJECTIVE Two things or people are incompatible if they are unable to live or exist together because they are completely different. **incompatibility** NOUN

incompetent ADJECTIVE Someone who is incompetent does not have the ability to do something properly. **incompetently** ADVERB **incompetence** NOUN

incomplete ADJECTIVE not complete or finished. **incompletely** ADVERB

incomprehensible ADJECTIVE not able to be understood.

inconceivable ADJECTIVE impossible to believe.

inconclusive ADJECTIVE not leading to a decision or to a definite result.

incongruous ADJECTIVE Something that is incongruous seems strange because it does not fit in to a place or situation. **incongruously** ADVERB

▷ SPELLING NOTE: You must practiSe your Ss (practise)

A B C D E F G H I J K L M N O P Q R S T U V W X Y Z

inconsequential ADJECTIVE
Something that is inconsequential is
not very important.

inconsistent ADJECTIVE
Someone or something which is
inconsistent is unpredictable and
behaves differently in similar
situations. **inconsistently** ADVERB
inconsistency NOUN

inconspicuous ADJECTIVE not
easily seen or obvious.
inconspicuously ADVERB

incontinent ADJECTIVE Someone
who is incontinent is unable to control
their bladder or bowels.

inconvenience, inconveniences,
inconveniencing, inconvenienced
NOUN ❶ If something causes
inconvenience, it causes difficulty or
problems ▷ VERB ❷ To
inconvenience someone is to cause
them trouble, difficulty or problems.
inconvenient ADJECTIVE
inconveniently ADVERB

incorporate, incorporates,
incorporating, incorporated VERB If
something is incorporated into
another thing, it becomes part of that
thing. **incorporation** NOUN

incorrect ADJECTIVE wrong or
untrue. **incorrectly** ADVERB

increase, increases, increasing,
increased VERB ❶ If something
increases, it becomes larger in amount
▷ NOUN ❷ a rise in the number,
level, or amount of something.
increasingly ADVERB

incredible ADJECTIVE ❶ totally
amazing. ❷ impossible to believe.
incredibly ADVERB

● **SIMILAR WORDS:** ❶ amazing,
● unbelievable ❷ amazing,
● unbelievable

incredulous ADJECTIVE If you are
incredulous, you are unable to believe
something because it is very surprising
or shocking. **incredulously** ADVERB
incredulity NOUN

increment, increments NOUN the
amount by which something
increases, or a regular increase in
someone's salary. **incremental**
ADJECTIVE

incriminate, incriminates,
incriminating, incriminated VERB If
something incriminates you, it
suggests that you are involved in a
crime.

incubate, incubates, incubating,
incubated [Said in-kyoo-bate] VERB
When eggs incubate, they are kept
warm until they are ready to hatch.
incubation NOUN

incubator, incubators NOUN a
piece of hospital equipment in which
sick or weak newborn babies are kept
warm.

incumbent, incumbents FORMAL
ADJECTIVE ❶ If it is incumbent on
you to do something, it is your duty to
do it ▷ NOUN ❷ the person in a
particular official position.

incur, incurs, incurring, incurred
VERB If you incur something
unpleasant, you cause it to happen.

incurable ADJECTIVE ❶ An
incurable disease is one which cannot
be cured. ❷ An incurable habit is one
which cannot be changed • *Your
boyfriend is an incurable romantic.*

a
b
c
d
e
f
g
h
i
j
k
l
m
n
o
p
q
r
s
t
u
v
w
x
y
z

▷ SPELLING NOTE: *pAL up with the principAL and principAL staff (principal)*

incurably ADVERB

indebted ADJECTIVE If you are indebted to someone, you are grateful to them.

indecent ADJECTIVE Something that is indecent is shocking or rude, usually because it concerns nakedness or sex. **indecently** ADVERB **indecency** NOUN

indeed ADVERB You use 'indeed' to strengthen a point that you are making • *The desserts are very good indeed.*

indefatigable [Said in-dif-**fat**-ig-a-bl] ADJECTIVE People who never get tired of doing something are indefatigable.

indefinite ADJECTIVE ❶ If something is indefinite, no time to finish has been decided • *an indefinite strike.* ❷ Indefinite also means vague or not exact • *indefinite words and pictures.* **indefinitely** ADVERB

indefinite article, indefinite articles NOUN the grammatical term for 'a' and 'an'.

indelible ADJECTIVE unable to be removed • *indelible ink.* **indelibly** ADVERB

indemnity NOUN FORMAL Indemnity is protection against damage or loss.

indentation, indentations NOUN a dent or a groove in a surface or on the edge of something.

independence NOUN ❶ Independence is not relying on anyone else. ❷ (HISTORY) A nation or state gains its independence when it stops being ruled or governed by another country and has its own government and laws.

independent ADJECTIVE ❶ Something that is independent happens or exists separately from other people or things • *Results are assessed by an independent panel.* ❷ Someone who is independent does not need other people's help • *a fiercely independent woman.* ❸ An independent nation is one that is not ruled or governed by another country. **independently** ADVERB
  ● SIMILAR WORDS:
  ● ❶ and ❸ autonomous, self-
  ● governing

indeterminate ADJECTIVE not certain or definite • *some indeterminate point in the future.*

index, indices; indexes, indexing, indexed NOUN ❶ (ENGLISH) An index is an alphabetical list at the back of a book, referring to items in the book. ❷ (LIBRARY) An index is also a set of cards listing all the books in a library, arranged alphabetically. ❸ (MATHS) In maths, an index is a small number placed to the right of another number to indicate the number of times the number is to be multiplied by itself ▷ VERB ❹ To index a book or collection of information means to provide an index for it. ❺ To index one thing to another means to arrange them so that they increase and decrease at the same time.

index finger, index fingers NOUN your first finger, next to your thumb.

Indian, Indians ADJECTIVE ❶ belonging or relating to India

▷ **NOUN** ❷ someone who comes from India. ❸ someone descended from the people who lived in North, South, or Central America before Europeans arrived.

indicate, indicates, indicating, indicated **VERB** ❶ If something indicates something, it shows that it is true • *a gesture which clearly indicates his relief.* ❷ If you indicate something to someone, you point to it. ❸ If you indicate a fact, you mention it. ❹ If the driver of a vehicle indicates, they give a signal to show which way they are going to turn.

● **SIMILAR WORDS:** ❶ denote,
● show, signify

indication, indications **NOUN** a sign of what someone feels or what is likely to happen.

indicative ADJECTIVE ❶ If something is indicative of something else, it is a sign of that thing • *Clean, pink tongues are indicative of a good, healthy digestion.* ▷ **NOUN** ❷ If a verb is used in the indicative, it is in the form used for making statements.

indicator, indicators **NOUN** ❶ something which tells you what something is like or what is happening. ❷ A car's indicators are the lights at the front and back which are used to show when it is turning left or right. ❸ a substance used in chemistry that shows if another substance is an acid or alkali by changing colour when it comes into contact with it.

indict, indicts, indicting, indicted [Said in-**dite**] **VERB** FORMAL To indict someone is to charge them officially with a crime. **indictment NOUN**

indictable ADJECTIVE

indifferent ADJECTIVE ❶ If you are indifferent to something, you have no interest in it. ❷ If something is indifferent, it is of a poor quality or low standard • *a pair of rather indifferent paintings.* **indifferently ADVERB indifference NOUN**

indigenous [Said in-**dij**-in-uss] **ADJECTIVE** If something is indigenous to a country, it comes from that country • *a plant indigenous to Asia.*

indigestion NOUN Indigestion is a pain you get when you find it difficult to digest food.

indignant ADJECTIVE If you are indignant, you feel angry about something that you think is unfair. **indignantly ADVERB**

indignation NOUN Indignation is anger about something that you think is unfair.

indignity, indignities **NOUN** something that makes you feel embarrassed or humiliated • *the indignity of having to flee angry protesters.*

indigo, indigos or indigoes **NOUN OR ADJECTIVE** dark violet-blue.

indirect ADJECTIVE Something that is indirect is not done or caused directly by a particular person or thing, but by someone or something else. **indirectly ADVERB**
● **SIMILAR WORDS:** circuitous,
● roundabout

indiscriminate ADJECTIVE not involving careful thought or choice • *an indiscriminate bombing campaign.*

▷ SPELLING NOTE: *Psychiatrists Seldom Yell Callously Hard (psychiatrist)*

indiscriminately ADVERB

indispensable ADJECTIVE If something is indispensable, you cannot do without it • *A good pair of walking shoes is indispensable.*

indistinct ADJECTIVE not clear • *indistinct voices.* **indistinctly** ADVERB

individual, individuals ADJECTIVE ❶ relating to one particular person or thing • *Each family needs individual attention.* ❷ Someone who is individual behaves quite differently from the way other people behave ▷ NOUN ❸ a person, different from any other person • *wealthy individuals.* **individually** ADVERB

individualist, individualists NOUN someone who likes to do things in their own way. **individualistic** ADJECTIVE

individuality NOUN If something has individuality, it is different from all other things, and therefore is very interesting and noticeable.

indomitable ADJECTIVE FORMAL impossible to overcome • *an indomitable spirit.*

Indonesian, Indonesians [Said in-don-*nee*-zee-an] ADJECTIVE ❶ belonging or relating to Indonesia ▷ NOUN ❷ someone who comes from Indonesia. ❸ Indonesian is the official language of Indonesia.

indoor ADJECTIVE situated or happening inside a building.

indoors ADVERB If something happens indoors, it takes place inside a building.

induce, induces, inducing, induced VERB ❶ To induce a state is to cause it • *His manner was rough and suspicious but he did not induce fear.* ❷ If you induce someone to do something, you persuade them to do it.

inducement, inducements NOUN something offered to encourage someone to do something.

indulge, indulges, indulging, indulged VERB ❶ If you indulge in something, you allow yourself to do something that you enjoy. ❷ If you indulge someone, you let them have or do what they want, often in a way that is not good for them.

indulgence, indulgences NOUN ❶ something you allow yourself to have because it gives you pleasure. ❷ Indulgence is the act of indulging yourself or another person.

indulgent ADJECTIVE If you are indulgent, you treat someone with special kindness • *a rich, indulgent father.* **indulgently** ADJECTIVE

industrial ADJECTIVE relating to industry.

industrial action NOUN Industrial action is action such as striking taken by workers in protest over pay or working conditions.

industrialist, industrialists NOUN a person who owns or controls a lot of factories.

Industrial Revolution NOUN The Industrial Revolution took place in Britain in the late eighteenth and early nineteenth century, when machines began to be used more in factories

A B C D E F G H I J K L M N O P Q R S T U V W X Y Z

▷ SPELLING NOTE: *the QUeen stood on the QUay (quay)*

and more goods were produced as a result.

industrious ADJECTIVE An industrious person works very hard.

industry, industries NOUN
❶ Industry is the work and processes involved in manufacturing things in factories. ❷ all the people and processes involved in manufacturing a particular thing.

inedible ADJECTIVE too nasty or poisonous to eat.

inefficient ADJECTIVE badly organized, wasteful, and slow • *a corrupt and inefficient administration.* **inefficiently** ADVERB **inefficiency** NOUN

inept ADJECTIVE without skill • *an inept lawyer.* **ineptitude** NOUN

inequality, inequalities NOUN a difference in size, status, wealth, or position, between different things, groups, or people.

inert ADJECTIVE ❶ Something that is inert does not move and appears lifeless • *an inert body lying on the floor.* ❷ In chemistry, an inert gas does not react with other substances. The inert gases are also called **noble gases**.

inertia [Said in-*ner*-sha] NOUN If you have a feeling of inertia, you feel very lazy and unwilling to do anything.

inevitable ADJECTIVE certain to happen. **inevitably** ADVERB **inevitability** NOUN

inexhaustible ADJECTIVE Something that is inexhaustible will never be used up • *an inexhaustible supply of ideas.*

inexorable ADJECTIVE FORMAL Something that is inexorable cannot be prevented from continuing • *the inexorable increase in the number of cars.* **inexorably** ADVERB

inexpensive ADJECTIVE not costing much.

inexperienced ADJECTIVE lacking experience of a situation or activity • *inexperienced drivers.* **inexperience** NOUN
● SIMILAR WORDS: new, raw,
● unpractised

inexplicable ADJECTIVE If something is inexplicable, you cannot explain it • *For some inexplicable reason I still felt uneasy.* **inexplicably** ADVERB

inextricably ADVERB If two or more things are inextricably linked, they cannot be separated.

infallible ADJECTIVE never wrong • *No machine is infallible.* **infallibility** NOUN

infamous [Said in-*fe*-muss] ADJECTIVE well-known because of something bad or evil • *a book about the country's most infamous murder cases.*

infant, infants NOUN ❶ a baby or very young child ▷ ADJECTIVE ❷ designed for young children • *an infant school.* **infancy** NOUN **infantile** ADJECTIVE
● WORD HISTORY: from Latin *infans*
● meaning 'unable to speak'

infantry NOUN In an army, the infantry are soldiers who fight on foot rather than in tanks or on horses.

infatuated ADJECTIVE If you are

a b c d e f g h i j k l m n o p q r s t u v w x y z

A
B
C
D
E
F
G
H
I
J
K
L
M
N
O
P
Q
R
S
T
U
V
W
X
Y
Z

infatuated with someone, you have such strong feelings of love or passion that you cannot think sensibly about them. **infatuation** NOUN

infect, infects, infecting, infected **VERB** To infect someone or something is to cause disease in them.

infection, infections NOUN ❶ a disease caused by germs • *a chest infection.* ❷ Infection is the state of being infected • *a very small risk of infection.*

infectious ADJECTIVE spreading from one person to another • *an infectious disease.*
   ● **SIMILAR WORDS:** catching,
   ● contagious

infer, infers, inferring, inferred **VERB** If you infer something, you work out that it is true on the basis of information that you already have.
   inference NOUN
   ● **USAGE NOTE:** Do not use *infer* to
   ● mean the same as *imply*

inferior, inferiors ADJECTIVE
   ❶ having a lower position than something or someone else. ❷ of low quality • *inferior quality cassette tapes.*
   ▷ NOUN ❸ Your inferiors are people in a lower position than you.
   inferiority NOUN

infernal ADJECTIVE very unpleasant • *an infernal bore.*
   ● **WORD HISTORY:** from Latin
   ● *infernus* meaning 'hell'

inferno, infernos NOUN a very large dangerous fire.

infertile ADJECTIVE ❶ Infertile soil is of poor quality and plants cannot

grow well in it. ❷ Someone who is infertile cannot have children.

infested ADJECTIVE Something that is infested has a large number of animals or insects living on it and causing damage • *The flats are damp and infested with rats.* **infestation** NOUN

infidelity, infidelities NOUN Infidelity is being unfaithful to your husband, wife, or lover.

infighting NOUN Infighting is quarrelling or rivalry between members of the same organization.

infiltrate, infiltrates, infiltrating, infiltrated **VERB** If people infiltrate an organization, they gradually enter it in secret to spy on its activities.
   infiltration NOUN

infinite ADJECTIVE without any limit or end • *an infinite number of possibilities.* **infinitely** ADVERB
   ● **SIMILAR WORDS:** limitless,
   ● never-ending

infinitive, infinitives NOUN In grammar, the infinitive is the base form of the verb. It often has 'to' in front of it, for example 'to go' or 'to see'.

infinity NOUN ❶ Infinity is a number that is larger than any other number and can never be given an exact value. ❷ Infinity is also a point that can never be reached, further away than any other point • *skies stretching on into infinity.*

infirm ADJECTIVE weak or ill.
   infirmity NOUN

infirmary, infirmaries NOUN a hospital.

inflamed ADJECTIVE If part of your body is inflamed, it is red and swollen, usually because of infection.

inflammable ADJECTIVE An inflammable material burns easily.
- USAGE NOTE: Although
- *inflammable* and *flammable* both
- mean 'likely to catch fire',
- *flammable* is used more often as
- people sometimes think that
- *inflammable* means 'not likely to
- catch fire'

inflammation NOUN Inflammation is painful redness or swelling of part of the body.

inflammatory ADJECTIVE Inflammatory actions are likely to make people very angry.

inflate, inflates, inflating, inflated VERB When you inflate something, you fill it with air or gas to make it swell. **inflatable** ADJECTIVE

inflation NOUN Inflation is an increase in the price of goods and services in a country. **inflationary** ADJECTIVE

inflection, inflections; also spelt **inflexion** NOUN a change in the form of a word that shows its grammatical function, for example a change that makes a noun plural.

inflexible ADJECTIVE fixed and unable to be altered • *an inflexible routine*.

inflict, inflicts, inflicting, inflicted VERB If you inflict something unpleasant on someone, you make them suffer it.

influence, influences, influencing, influenced NOUN ❶ Influence is power that a person has over other people. ❷ An influence is also the effect that someone or something has • *under the influence of alcohol*. ▷ VERB ❸ To influence someone or something means to have an effect on them.
- WORD HISTORY: from Latin
- *influentia* meaning 'power flowing
- from the stars'
- SIMILAR WORDS: ❶ hold, power,
- pull

influential ADJECTIVE Someone who is influential has a lot of influence over people.

influenza NOUN FORMAL Influenza is flu.

influx NOUN a steady arrival of people or things • *a large influx of tourists*.

inform, informs, informing, informed VERB ❶ If you inform someone of something, you tell them about it. ❷ If you inform on a person, you tell the police about a crime they have committed. **informant** NOUN
- SIMILAR WORDS: ❶ notify, tell
- ❷ betray, grass, shop

informal ADJECTIVE relaxed and casual • *an informal meeting*. **informally** ADVERB **informality** NOUN

information NOUN If you have information on or about something, you know something about it.
- SIMILAR WORDS: data, facts

informative ADJECTIVE Something that is informative gives you useful information.

informer, informers NOUN

a
b
c
d
e
f
g
h
i
j
k
l
m
n
o
p
q
r
s
t
u
v
w
x
y
z

▷ SPELLING NOTE: *On WEDNESday Wayne WED NESta (Wednesday)*

someone who tells the police that another person has committed a crime.

infrastructure, infrastructures **NOUN** (GEOGRAPHY) The infrastructure of a country consists of things like factories, schools, and roads, which show how much money the country has and how strong its economy is.

infringe, infringes, infringing, infringed **VERB** ❶ If you infringe a law, you break it. ❷ To infringe people's rights is to not allow them the rights to which they are entitled. **infringement NOUN**

infuriate, infuriates, infuriating, infuriated **VERB** If someone infuriates you, they make you very angry. **infuriating ADJECTIVE**

infuse, infuses, infusing, infused **VERB** ❶ If you infuse someone with a feeling such as enthusiasm or joy, you fill them with it. ❷ If you infuse a substance such as a herb or medicine, you pour hot water onto it and leave it for the water to absorb the flavour. **infusion NOUN**

ingenious [Said in-**jeen**-yuss] **ADJECTIVE** very clever and using new ideas • his ingenious invention. **ingeniously ADVERB**

ingenuity [Said in-jen-**yoo**-it-ee] **NOUN** Ingenuity is cleverness and skill at inventing things or working out plans.

ingot, ingots **NOUN** a brick-shaped lump of metal, especially gold.

ingrained ADJECTIVE If habits and beliefs are ingrained, they are difficult

to change or destroy.

ingredient, ingredients **NOUN** (D & T) Ingredients are the things that something is made from, especially in cookery.

inhabit, inhabits, inhabiting, inhabited **VERB** If you inhabit a place, you live there.

inhabitant, inhabitants **NOUN** The inhabitants of a place are the people who live there.
● **SIMILAR WORDS:** citizen, dweller, resident

inhale, inhales, inhaling, inhaled **VERB** When you inhale, you breathe in. **inhalation NOUN**

inherent ADJECTIVE Inherent qualities or characteristics in something are a natural part of it • her inherent common sense. **inherently ADVERB**

inherit, inherits, inheriting, inherited **VERB** ❶ If you inherit money or property, you receive it from someone who has died. ❷ If you inherit a quality or characteristic from a parent or ancestor, it is passed on to you at birth. **inheritor NOUN**

inheritance, inheritances **NOUN** something that is passed on from another person.

inhibit, inhibits, inhibiting, inhibited **VERB** If you inhibit someone from doing something, you prevent them from doing it.

inhibited ADJECTIVE People who are inhibited find it difficult to relax and to show their emotions.

inhibition, inhibitions **NOUN**

▷ SPELLING NOTE: *Eddy Ant thinks mEAt is a grEAt trEAt to EAt (-ea-)*

Inhibitions are feelings of fear or embarrassment that make it difficult for someone to relax and to show their emotions.

inhospitable ADJECTIVE ❶ An inhospitable place is unpleasant or difficult to live in. ❷ If someone is inhospitable, they do not make people who visit them feel welcome.

inhuman ADJECTIVE not human or not behaving like a human • *the inhuman killing of their enemies.*

inhumane ADJECTIVE extremely cruel. **inhumanity** NOUN

inimitable ADJECTIVE If you have an inimitable characteristic, no-one else can imitate it • *her inimitable sense of style.*

initial, initials [Said in-**nish**-l] ADJECTIVE ❶ first, or at the beginning • *Shock and dismay were my initial reactions.* ▷ NOUN ❷ the first letter of a name. **initially** ADVERB

initiate, initiates, initiating, initiated [Said in-**nish**-ee-ate] VERB ❶ If you initiate something, you make it start or happen. ❷ If you initiate someone into a group or club, you allow them to become a member of it, usually by means of a special ceremony. **initiation** NOUN

initiative, initiatives [Said in-**nish**-at-ive] NOUN ❶ an attempt to get something done. ❷ If you have initiative, you decide what to do and then do it, without needing the advice of other people.

inject, injects, injecting, injected VERB ❶ If a doctor or nurse injects you with a substance, they use a needle and syringe to put the substance into your body. ❷ If you inject something new into a situation, you add it. **injection** NOUN

injunction, injunctions NOUN an order issued by a court of law to stop someone doing something.

injure, injures, injuring, injured VERB To injure someone is to damage part of their body.

injury, injuries NOUN (PE) hurt or damage, especially to part of a person's body or to their feelings • *He suffered acute injury to his pride* • *The knee injury forced him to retire from the professional game.*

injustice, injustices NOUN ❶ Injustice is lack of justice and fairness. ❷ If you do someone an injustice, you judge them too harshly.

ink NOUN Ink is the coloured liquid used for writing or printing.

inkling, inklings NOUN a vague idea about something.

inlaid ADJECTIVE decorated with small pieces of wood, metal, or stone • *decorative plates inlaid with brass.* **inlay** NOUN

inland ADJECTIVE ❶ near the middle of a country, away from the sea ▷ ADVERB ❷ towards the middle of a country, away from the sea.

in-law, in-laws NOUN Your in-laws are members of your husband's or wife's family.

inlet, inlets NOUN a narrow bay.

inmate, inmates NOUN someone who lives in a prison or psychiatric hospital.

▷ SPELLING NOTE: *Elaine and Emily shout EE when they mEEt to grEEt each other (-ee-)*

inn, inns **NOUN** a small old country pub or hotel.

innards **PLURAL NOUN** The innards of something are its inside parts.

innate **ADJECTIVE** An innate quality is one that you were born with • *an innate sense of fairness.* **innately** **ADVERB**

inner **ADJECTIVE** contained inside a place or object • *an inner room.*

innermost **ADJECTIVE** deepest and most secret • *our innermost feelings.*

innings **NOUN** In cricket, an innings is a period when a particular team is batting.

innocence **NOUN** inexperience of evil or unpleasant things.

innocent **ADJECTIVE** ❶ not guilty of a crime. ❷ without experience of evil or unpleasant things • *an innocent child.* **innocently** **ADVERB**

innocuous [Said in-**nok**-yoo-uss] **ADJECTIVE** not harmful.

innovation, innovations **NOUN** (D & T) a completely new idea, product, or system of doing things.

innuendo, innuendos or innuendoes [Said in-yoo-**en**-doe] **NOUN** an indirect reference to something rude or unpleasant.
● **WORD HISTORY:** from Latin
● *innuendo* meaning 'by hinting', from
● *innuere* meaning 'to convey by a
● nod'

innumerable **ADJECTIVE** too many to be counted • *innumerable cups of tea.*

inoculate, inoculates, inoculating, inoculated **VERB** (SCIENCE) To inoculate someone means to inject them with a weak form of a disease in order to protect them from that disease. **inoculation** **NOUN**

inorganic **ADJECTIVE** (SCIENCE) Inorganic substances are substances which do not form part of living things and have no life of their own, for example rocks and water.

inorganic chemistry **NOUN** (SCIENCE) Inorganic chemistry is the study of the elements and their compounds, except those containing carbon.

input, inputs **NOUN** ❶ Input consists of all the money, information, and other resources that are put into a job, project, or company to make it work. ❷ (ICT) In computing, input is information which is fed into a computer.

inquest, inquests **NOUN** an official inquiry to find out what caused a person's death.

inquire, inquires, inquiring, inquired; *also spelt* **enquire** **VERB** If you inquire about something, you ask for information about it. **inquiring** **ADJECTIVE** **inquiry** **NOUN**

inquisition, inquisitions **NOUN** an official investigation, especially one which is very thorough and uses harsh methods of questioning.

inquisitive **ADJECTIVE** Someone who is inquisitive is keen to find out about things. **inquisitively** **ADVERB**

inroads **PLURAL NOUN** If something makes inroads on or into

▷ SPELLING NOTE: *'i' before 'e' except after 'c'*

something, it starts affecting it.

insane ADJECTIVE Someone who is insane is mad. **insanely** ADVERB **insanity** NOUN

insatiable [Said in-saysh-a-bl] ADJECTIVE A desire or urge that is insatiable is very great • *an insatiable curiosity.* **insatiably** ADVERB

inscribe, inscribes, inscribing, inscribed VERB If you inscribe words on an object, you write or carve them on it.

inscription, inscriptions NOUN the words that are written or carved on something.

inscrutable [Said in-skroot-a-bl] ADJECTIVE Someone who is inscrutable does not show what they are really thinking.

insect, insects NOUN (SCIENCE) a small creature with six legs, and usually wings.

insecticide, insecticides NOUN a poisonous chemical used to kill insects.

insecure ADJECTIVE ❶ If you are insecure, you feel unsure of yourself and doubt whether other people like you. ❷ Something that is insecure is not safe or well protected • *People still feel their jobs are insecure.* **insecurity** NOUN

insensitive ADJECTIVE If you are insensitive, you do not notice when you are upsetting people. **insensitivity** NOUN

insert, inserts, inserting, inserted VERB If you insert an object into something, you put it inside.

insertion NOUN

inshore ADJECTIVE at sea but close to the shore • *inshore boats.*

inside, insides NOUN ❶ the part of something that is surrounded by the main part and often hidden • *Tom had to stay inside and work.* ❷ IN PLURAL Your insides are the parts inside your body ▷ ADJECTIVE ❸ surrounded by the main part and often hidden • *an inside pocket.* ▷ PREPOSITION ❹ in or to the interior of • *inside the house.* ▷ PHRASE ❺ **Inside out** means with the inside part facing outwards.
■ USAGE NOTE: Do not use *of* after *inside.* You should write *she was waiting inside the school* and not *inside of the school*

insider, insiders NOUN a person who is involved in a situation and so knows more about it than other people.

insidious ADJECTIVE Something that is insidious is unpleasant and develops slowly without being noticed • *the insidious progress of the disease.* **insidiously** ADVERB

insight, insights NOUN If you gain insight into a problem, you gradually get a deep and accurate understanding of it.

insignia [Said in-sig-nee-a] NOUN the badge or a sign of a particular organization.

insignificant ADJECTIVE small and unimportant. **insignificance** NOUN

insincere ADJECTIVE Someone who is insincere pretends to have feelings which they do not really have.

▷ SPELLING NOTE: *King IAn went to ParlIAment in a carrIAge for his marrIAge (-ia-)*

A
B
C
D
E
F
G
H
I
J
K
L
M
N
O
P
Q
R
S
T
U
V
W
X
Y
Z

insinuate, insinuates, insinuating, insinuated **VERB** If you insinuate something unpleasant, you hint about it. **insinuation NOUN**

insipid ADJECTIVE ❶ An insipid person or activity is dull and boring. ❷ Food that is insipid has very little taste.
● **SIMILAR WORDS:** ❶ bland,
● colourless, uninteresting

insist, insists, insisting, insisted **VERB** If you insist on something, you demand it forcefully. **insistent ADJECTIVE insistence NOUN**

insolent ADJECTIVE very rude and disrespectful. **insolently ADVERB insolence NOUN**

insoluble [Said in-**soll**-yoo-bl] **ADJECTIVE** ❶ impossible to solve • an insoluble problem. ❷ unable to dissolve • substances which are insoluble in water.

insolvent ADJECTIVE unable to pay your debts. **insolvency NOUN**

insomnia NOUN Insomnia is difficulty in sleeping. **insomniac NOUN**

inspect, inspects, inspecting, inspected **VERB** To inspect something is to examine it carefully to check that everything is all right. **inspection NOUN**

inspector, inspectors **NOUN** ❶ someone who inspects things. ❷ a police officer just above a sergeant in rank.

inspire, inspires, inspiring, inspired **VERB** ❶ (DRAMA) If something inspires you, it gives you new ideas and enthusiasm to do something.

❷ To inspire an emotion in someone is to make them feel this emotion. **inspired ADJECTIVE inspiring ADJECTIVE inspiration NOUN**

instability NOUN Instability is a lack of stability in a place • political instability.

install, installs, installing, installed **VERB** ❶ If you install a piece of equipment in a place, you put it there so it is ready to be used. ❷ To install someone in an important job is to officially give them that position. ❸ If you install yourself in a place, you settle there and make yourself comfortable. **installation NOUN**

instalment, instalments **NOUN** ❶ If you pay for something in instalments, you pay small amounts of money regularly over a period of time. ❷ one of the parts of a story or television series.

instance, instances **NOUN** ❶ a particular example or occurrence of an event, situation, or person • a serious instance of corruption. ▷ **PHRASE** ❷ You use **for instance** to give an example of something you are talking about.

instant, instants **NOUN** ❶ a moment or short period of time • In an instant they were gone.
▷ **ADJECTIVE** ❷ immediate and without delay • The record was an instant success. **instantly ADVERB**

instantaneous ADJECTIVE happening immediately and without delay • The applause was instantaneous. **instantaneously ADVERB**

instead ADVERB in place of

something • *Take the stairs instead of the lift.*

instigate, instigates, instigating, instigated **VERB** Someone who instigates a situation makes it happen. **instigation NOUN instigator NOUN**

instil, instils, instilling, instilled **VERB** If you instil an idea or feeling into someone, you make them feel or think it.

instinct, instincts **NOUN** a natural tendency to do something • *My first instinct was to protect myself.* **instinctive ADJECTIVE instinctively ADVERB**

institute, institutes, instituting, instituted **NOUN** ❶ an organization for teaching or research ▷ **VERB** ❷ FORMAL If you institute a rule or system, you introduce it.

institution, institutions **NOUN** ❶ a custom or system regarded as an important tradition within a society • *The family is an institution to be cherished.* ❷ a large, important organization, for example a university or bank. **institutional ADJECTIVE**

instruct, instructs, instructing, instructed **VERB** ❶ If you instruct someone to do something, you tell them to do it. ❷ If someone instructs you in a subject or skill, they teach you about it. **instructor NOUN instructive ADJECTIVE instruction NOUN**

instrument, instruments **NOUN** ❶ a tool or device used for a particular job • *a special instrument which cut through the metal.* ❷ (MUSIC) A musical instrument is an object, such as a guitar, piano or flute, played to

make music.

instrumental **ADJECTIVE** ❶ If you are instrumental in doing something, you help to make it happen. ❷ (MUSIC) Instrumental music is performed using only musical instruments, and not voices.

insufficient **ADJECTIVE** not enough for a particular purpose. **insufficiently ADVERB**

insular [Said **inss-yoo-lar**] **ADJECTIVE** Someone who is insular is unwilling to meet new people or to consider new ideas. **insularity NOUN**

insulate, insulates, insulating, insulated **VERB** ❶ If you insulate a person from harmful things, you protect them from those things. ❷ If materials such as feathers, fur, or foam insulate something, they keep it warm by covering it in a thick layer. ❸ (SCIENCE) You insulate an electrical or metal object by covering it with rubber or plastic. This is to stop electricity passing through it and giving you an electric shock. **insulation NOUN insulator NOUN**

insulin [Said **inss-yoo-lin**] **NOUN** Insulin is a substance which controls the level of sugar in the blood. People who have diabetes do not produce insulin naturally and have to take regular doses of it.

insult, insults, insulting, insulted **VERB** ❶ If you insult someone, you offend them by being rude to them ▷ **NOUN** ❷ a rude remark which offends you. **insulting ADJECTIVE**
  ● **SIMILAR WORDS:** ❶ abuse,
  ● affront, offend ❷ abuse, affront,
  ● offence

▷ SPELLING NOTE: *LEt's measure the angLE (angle)*

insure, insures, insuring, insured
VERB ❶ If you insure something or
yourself, you pay money regularly to a
company so that if there is an accident
or damage, the company will pay for
medical treatment or repairs. ❷ If you
do something to insure against
something unpleasant happening, you
do it to prevent the unpleasant thing
from happening or to protect yourself
if it does happen. **insurance NOUN**

insurrection, insurrections **NOUN**
a violent action taken against the
rulers of a country.

intact ADJECTIVE complete, and not
changed or damaged in any way • *The
rear of the aircraft remained intact when
it crashed.*

intake, intakes **NOUN** A person's
intake of food, drink, or air is the
amount they take in.

integer, integers **NOUN** (MATHS) In
mathematics, an integer is any whole
number.

integral ADJECTIVE If something is
an integral part of a whole thing, it is
an essential part.

integrate, integrates, integrating,
integrated **VERB** ❶ If a person
integrates into a group, they become
part of it. ❷ To integrate things is to
combine them so that they become
closely linked or form one thing • *his
plan to integrate the coal and steel
industries.* **integration NOUN**

integrity NOUN ❶ Integrity is the
quality of being honest and following
your principles. ❷ The integrity of a
group of people is their being united
as one whole.

intellect, intellects **NOUN** Intellect
is the ability to understand ideas and
information.

intellectual, intellectuals
ADJECTIVE ❶ involving thought,
ideas, and understanding • *an
intellectual exercise.* ▷ **NOUN**
❷ someone who enjoys thinking
about complicated ideas.
intellectually ADVERB

intelligence NOUN A person's
intelligence is their ability to
understand and learn things quickly
and well.
● **SIMILAR WORDS:** brains, intellect,
● understanding

intelligent ADJECTIVE able to
understand and learn things quickly
and well. **intelligently ADVERB**

intelligentsia [Said in-tell-lee-
*jent-*sya] **NOUN** The intelligentsia are
intellectual people, considered as a
group.

intelligible ADJECTIVE able to be
understood • *few intelligible remarks.*

intend, intends, intending, intended
VERB ❶ If you intend to do
something, you have decided or
planned to do it • *She intended to move
back to Cape Town.* ❷ If something is
intended for a particular use, you have
planned that it should have this use
• *The booklet is intended to be kept
handy.*

intense ADJECTIVE ❶ very great in
strength or amount • *intense heat.*
❷ If a person is intense, they take
things very seriously and have very
strong feelings. **intensely ADVERB**
intensity NOUN

▷ SPELLING NOTE: *A Rude Idiot Thought He Might Eat Toffee In Church (arithmetic)*

intensify, intensifies, intensifying, intensified **VERB** To intensify something is to make it greater or stronger.

intensive **ADJECTIVE** involving a lot of energy or effort over a very short time • *an intensive training course.*

intent, intents **NOUN** ❶ FORMAL A person's intent is their purpose or intention ▷ **ADJECTIVE** ❷ If you are intent on doing something, you are determined to do it. **intently** **ADVERB**

intention, intentions **NOUN** If you have an intention to do something, you have a plan of what you are going to do.

intentional **ADJECTIVE** If something is intentional, it is done on purpose. **intentionally** **ADVERB**

inter- **PREFIX** 'Inter-' means 'between' • *inter-school competitions.*

interact, interacts, interacting, interacted **VERB** The way two people or things interact is the way they work together, communicate, or react with each other. **interaction** **NOUN**

interactive **ADJECTIVE** (ICT) Interactive television, computers and games react to decisions taken by the viewer, user or player.

intercept, intercepts, intercepting, intercepted [Said in-ter-**sept**] **VERB** If you intercept someone or something that is going from one place to another, you stop them.

interchange, interchanges **NOUN** An interchange is the act or process of exchanging things or ideas. **interchangeable** **ADJECTIVE**

intercom, intercoms **NOUN** a device consisting of a microphone and a loudspeaker, which you use to speak to people in another room.

intercourse **NOUN** Intercourse or sexual intercourse is the act of having sex.

interest, interests, interesting, interested **NOUN** ❶ If you have an interest in something or if something is of interest, you want to learn or hear more about it. ❷ Your interests are your hobbies. ❸ If you have an interest in something being done, you want it to be done because it will benefit you. ❹ Interest is an extra payment made to the lender by someone who has borrowed a sum of money, or by a bank or company to someone who has invested money in them. Interest is worked out as a percentage of the sum of money borrowed or invested ▷ **VERB** ❺ Something that interests you attracts your attention so that you want to learn or hear more about it. **interested** **ADJECTIVE**

interesting **ADJECTIVE** making you want to know, learn or hear more. **interestingly** **ADVERB**

interface, interfaces **NOUN** ❶ The interface between two subjects or systems is the area in which they affect each other or are linked. ❷ (ICT) The user interface of a computer program is how it is presented on the computer screen and how easy it is to operate.

interfere, interferes, interfering, interfered **VERB** ❶ If you interfere in a situation, you try to influence it, although it does not really concern

▷ SPELLING NOTE: *Beautiful Elephants Are Usually Tiny (beautiful)*

WHAT IS AN INTERJECTION?

An interjection is a word that expresses a strong emotion, such as anger, surprise, or excitement. Interjections often stand alone rather than as part of a sentence.

Some interjections express greetings:

Hello.
Congratulations!

Some interjections express agreement or disagreement:

Indeed.
No.

Some interjections express pain, anger, or annoyance:

Ouch!
Blast!

Some interjections express approval, pleasure, or excitement:

Bravo!

Hooray!

Some interjections express surprise or relief:

Wow!
Phew!

Sometimes an interjection is more like a noise than a word:

Sh!
Psst!

A group of words can be used together as an interjection:

Happy birthday!
Hey presto!

When an interjection does occur within a sentence, it is usually separated by commas or dashes:
*I turned the key and, **bingo**, the engine started.*

you. ❷ Something that interferes with a situation has a damaging effect on it. **interference** NOUN **interfering** ADJECTIVE
● **WORD HISTORY:** from Old French *s'entreferir* meaning 'to collide'
● **SIMILAR WORDS:** ❶ butt in, intrude, meddle

interim ADJECTIVE intended for use only until something permanent is arranged • *an interim government.*

interior, interiors NOUN ❶ the inside part of something
▷ ADJECTIVE ❷ Interior means inside • *They painted the interior walls white.*

interior angle NOUN (MATHS) the

angle between any two adjacent sides of a polygon.

interjection, interjections NOUN a word or phrase spoken suddenly to express surprise, pain, or anger.
▶ SEE GRAMMAR BOX ABOVE

interlude, interludes *[rhymes with rude]* NOUN a short break from an activity.

intermediary, intermediaries *[Said in-ter-meed-yer-ee]* NOUN someone who tries to get two groups of people to come to an agreement.

intermediate ADJECTIVE An intermediate level occurs in the middle, between two other stages

▷ SPELLING NOTE: *Betty Eats Cakes And Uses Seven Eggs (because)*

• *intermediate students.*

interminable ADJECTIVE If something is interminable, it goes on for a very long time • *an interminable wait for the bus.* **interminably** ADVERB

intermission, intermissions NOUN an interval between two parts of a film or play.

intermittent ADJECTIVE happening only occasionally. **intermittently** ADVERB

internal ADJECTIVE happening inside a person, place, or object. **internally** ADVERB

international, internationals ADJECTIVE (GEOGRAPHY) ❶ involving different countries ▷ NOUN ❷ a sports match between two countries. **internationally** ADVERB

Internet NOUN (ICT) The Internet is a worldwide communication system which people use through computers.

interplay NOUN The interplay between two things is the way they react with one another.

interpret, interprets, interpreting, interpreted VERB ❶ If you interpret what someone says or does, you decide what it means. ❷ If you interpret a foreign language that someone is speaking, you translate it. **interpretation** NOUN **interpreter** NOUN

interrogate, interrogates, interrogating, interrogated VERB If you interrogate someone, you question them thoroughly to get information from them. **interrogation** NOUN **interrogator**

NOUN
● SIMILAR WORDS: cross-examine,
● question

interrogative, interrogatives ADJECTIVE (ENGLISH) ❶ An interrogative sentence is one that is in the form of a question ▷ NOUN ❷ An interrogative is a word such as 'who' or 'why' that is used to ask a question.

interrupt, interrupts, interrupting, interrupted VERB ❶ If you interrupt someone, you start talking while they are talking. ❷ If you interrupt a process or activity, you stop it continuing for a time. **interruption** NOUN

intersect, intersects, intersecting, intersected VERB When two roads intersect, they cross each other. **intersection** NOUN

intersection, intersections NOUN ❶ An intersection is where two roads meet. ❷ (MATHS) In maths, an intersection is the point where two straight lines meet.

interspersed ADJECTIVE If something is interspersed with things, these things occur at various points in it.

interval, intervals NOUN ❶ the period of time between two moments or dates. ❷ a short break during a play or concert. ❸ (MUSIC) In music, an interval is the difference in pitch between two musical notes.
● SIMILAR WORDS: ❷ break,
● interlude, intermission

intervene, intervenes, intervening, intervened VERB If you intervene in a situation, you step in to prevent conflict between people.

▷ SPELLING NOTE: *there's a rAKE in the brAKEs (brake)*

intervention NOUN
  ● SIMILAR WORDS: mediate, step in

intervening ADJECTIVE An intervening period of time is one which separates two events.

interview, interviews, interviewing, interviewed NOUN ❶ a meeting at which someone asks you questions about yourself to see if you are suitable for a particular job. ❷ a conversation in which a journalist asks a famous person questions ▷ VERB ❸ If you interview someone, you ask them questions about themselves.

intestine, intestines NOUN Your intestines are a long tube which carries food from your stomach through to your bowels, and in which the food is digested. **intestinal** ADJECTIVE

intimate, intimates, intimating, intimated ADJECTIVE ❶ If two people are intimate, there is a close relationship between them. ❷ An intimate matter is very private and personal. ❸ An intimate knowledge of something is very deep and detailed ▷ VERB ❹ If you intimate something, you hint at it • *He did intimate that he is considering legal action.* **intimately** ADVERB **intimacy** NOUN **intimation** NOUN

intimidate, intimidates, intimidating, intimidated VERB If you intimidate someone, you frighten them in a threatening way. **intimidated** ADJECTIVE **intimidating** ADJECTIVE **intimidation** NOUN

into PREPOSITION ❶ If something goes into something else, it goes

inside it. ❷ If you bump or crash into something, you hit it. ❸ INFORMAL If you are into something, you like it very much • *Nowadays I'm really into healthy food.*

intolerable ADJECTIVE If something is intolerable, it is so bad that it is difficult to put up with it. **intolerably** ADVERB

intonation NOUN Your intonation is the way that your voice rises and falls as you speak.

intoxicated ADJECTIVE If someone is intoxicated, they are drunk. **intoxicating** ADJECTIVE **intoxication** NOUN

intra- PREFIX 'Intra-' means 'within' or 'inside' • *intra-European conflicts.*

intractable ADJECTIVE FORMAL stubborn and difficult to deal with or control.

intransitive ADJECTIVE An intransitive verb is one that does not have a direct object. For example, 'sings' is intransitive in 'She sings', but not in 'She sings a song'.

intravenous *[Said in-trav-vee-nuss]* ADJECTIVE Intravenous foods or drugs are given to sick people through their veins. **intravenously** ADVERB

intrepid ADJECTIVE not worried by danger • *an intrepid explorer.* **intrepidly** ADVERB

intricate ADJECTIVE Something that is intricate has many fine details • *walls and ceilings covered with intricate patterns.* **intricately** ADVERB **intricacy** NOUN

▷ SPELLING NOTE: *you'll brEAK that Electrical Aerial, Kitty (break)*

intrigue, intrigues, intriguing, intrigued **NOUN** ❶ Intrigue is the making of secret plans, often with the intention of harming other people • *political intrigue.* ▷ **VERB** ❷ If something intrigues you, you are fascinated by it and curious about it. **intriguing ADJECTIVE**

intrinsic ADJECTIVE FORMAL The intrinsic qualities of something are its basic qualities. **intrinsically ADVERB**

introduce, introduces, introducing, introduced **VERB** ❶ If you introduce one person to another, you tell them each other's name so that they can get to know each other. ❷ When someone introduces a radio or television show, they say a few words at the beginning to tell you about it. ❸ If you introduce someone to something, they learn about it for the first time. **introductory ADJECTIVE**

introduction, introductions **NOUN** ❶ The introduction of someone or something is the act of presenting them for the first time. ❷ (ENGLISH) a piece of writing at the beginning of a book, which usually tells you what the book is about.
  ● **SIMILAR WORDS:** ❷ foreword,
  ● opening, preface

introvert, introverts **NOUN** someone who spends more time thinking about their private feelings than about the world around them, and who often finds it difficult to talk to others. **introverted ADJECTIVE**

intrude, intrudes, intruding, intruded **VERB** To intrude on someone or something is to disturb them • *I don't want to intrude on your parents.* **intruder NOUN intrusion NOUN**

intrusive ADJECTIVE
  ● **SIMILAR WORDS:** butt in, trespass

intuition, intuitions [Said *int-yoo-ish-n*] **NOUN** Your intuition is a feeling you have about something that you cannot explain • *My intuition is right about him.* **intuitive ADJECTIVE intuitively ADVERB**

Inuit, Inuits; also spelt **Innuit NOUN** a member of a group of people who live in Northern Canada, Greenland, Alaska, and Eastern Siberia, formerly known as Eskimos.

inundated ADJECTIVE If you are inundated by letters or requests, you receive so many that you cannot deal with them all.

invade, invades, invading, invaded **VERB** ❶ If an army invades a country, it enters it by force. ❷ If someone invades your privacy, they disturb you when you want to be alone. **invader NOUN**

invalid, invalids [Said *in-va-lid*] **NOUN** someone who is so ill that they need to be looked after by someone else.
  ● **WORD HISTORY:** from Latin *invalidus* meaning 'infirm'

invalid [Said *in-val-id*] **ADJECTIVE** ❶ If an argument or result is invalid, it is not acceptable because it is based on a mistake. ❷ If a law, marriage, or election is invalid, it is illegal because it has not been carried out properly. **invalidate VERB**
  ● **WORD HISTORY:** from Latin *invalidus* meaning 'without legal force'

invalidity [Said *in-va-lid-dit-ee*] **NOUN** Invalidity is the condition of being very ill for a very long time.

invaluable ADJECTIVE extremely useful • *This book contains invaluable tips.*

invariably ADVERB If something invariably happens, it almost always happens.

invasion, invasions NOUN ❶ (HISTORY) The invasion of a country or territory is the act of entering it by force. ❷ an unwanted disturbance or intrusion • *an invasion of her privacy.*

invective NOUN FORMAL Invective is abusive language used by someone who is angry.

invent, invents, inventing, invented VERB ❶ If you invent a device or process, you are the first person to think of it or to use it. ❷ If you invent a story or an excuse, you make it up.
inventor NOUN **invention** NOUN **inventive** ADJECTIVE **inventiveness** NOUN
● SIMILAR WORDS: ❶ conceive, ● create, devise

inventory, inventories NOUN a written list of all the objects in a place.

inverse ADJECTIVE (MATHS) FORMAL If there is an inverse relationship between two things, one decreases as the other increases.

invertebrate, invertebrates NOUN (SCIENCE) An invertebrate is a creature which does not have a spine. Some invertebrates, for example crabs, have an external skeleton.

inverted ADJECTIVE upside down or back to front.

inverted comma, inverted commas NOUN Inverted commas are the punctuation marks " " or ' ', used to show where speech begins and ends.
▶ SEE GRAMMAR BOX BELOW

invest, invests, investing, invested VERB ❶ If you invest money, you pay it into a bank or buy shares so that you will receive a profit. ❷ If you invest in something useful, you buy it because it will help you do something better.

WHAT DO INVERTED COMMAS DO?

Inverted commas or **quotation marks** (" " or ' ') mark the beginning and end of a speaker's exact words or thoughts:
"I would like some more," said Matthew.

Inverted commas are not used when a speaker's words are reported indirectly rather than in their exact form:
Matthew said that he would like some more.

Inverted commas can also be used to

indicate the title of a book, piece of music, etc:
The class had been reading 'The Little Prince'.

Inverted commas are also used to draw attention to the fact that a word or phrase is being used in an unusual way, or that a word itself is the subject of discussion:
Braille allows a blind person to "see" with the fingers.
What rhymes with "orange" ?

▷ SPELLING NOTE: *I want to see (C) your licenCe (licence)*

❸ If you invest money, time, or energy in something, you try to make it a success. **investor NOUN investment NOUN**

investigate, investigates, investigating, investigated **VERB** To investigate something is to try to find out all the facts about it. **investigator NOUN investigation NOUN**
- **SIMILAR WORDS:** examine, look into, study

inveterate ADJECTIVE having lasted for a long time and not likely to stop • *an inveterate gambler.*

invincible ADJECTIVE unable to be defeated. **invincibility NOUN**

invisible ADJECTIVE If something is invisible, you cannot see it, because it is hidden, very small, or imaginary. **invisibly ADVERB invisibility NOUN**

invite, invites, inviting, invited **VERB** ❶ If you invite someone to an event, you ask them to come to it. ❷ If you invite someone to do something, you ask them to do it • *Andrew has been invited to speak at the conference.* **inviting ADJECTIVE invitation NOUN**

invoice, invoices **NOUN** a bill for services or goods.

invoke, invokes, invoking, invoked **VERB** ❶ FORMAL If you invoke a law, you use it to justify what you are doing. ❷ If you invoke certain feelings, you cause someone to have these feelings.
- **WORD HISTORY:** from Latin *invocare* meaning 'to call upon'

involuntary ADJECTIVE sudden and uncontrollable • *an involuntary*

gasp. **involuntarily ADVERB**

involve, involves, involving, involved **VERB** (PSHE) If a situation involves someone or something, it includes them as a necessary part. **involvement NOUN**

inward or **inwards ADJECTIVE** ❶ Your inward thoughts and feelings are private ▷ **ADJECTIVE OR ADVERB** ❷ If something moves inward or inwards, it moves towards the inside or centre of something. **inwardly ADVERB**

iodine [Said *eye-oh-deen*] **NOUN** Iodine is a bluish-black substance used in medicine and photography.

iodine solution NOUN (SCIENCE) a liquid containing iodine that is used as a disinfectant.

ion, ions [Said *eye-on*] **NOUN** Ions are electrically charged atoms.

iota NOUN an extremely small amount • *He did not have an iota of proof.*

IQ, IQs **NOUN** Your IQ is your level of intelligence shown by the results of a special test. IQ is an abbreviation for 'intelligence quotient'.

ir- PREFIX 'Ir-' means 'not' or 'the opposite of', and is the form of 'in-' which is used before the letter *r* • *irrational.*

Iranian, Iranians [Said *ir-rain-ee-an*] **ADJECTIVE** ❶ belonging or relating to Iran ▷ **NOUN** ❷ someone who comes from Iran. ❸ Iranian is the main language spoken in Iran. It is also known as Farsi.

Iraqi, Iraqis [Said *ir-ah-kee*]

▷ SPELLING NOTE: *The government licenSes Schnapps (licenses)*

A B C D E F G H I J K L M N O P Q R S T U V W X Y Z

ADJECTIVE ❶ belonging or relating to Iraq ▷ **NOUN** ❷ someone who comes from Iraq.

irate [Said eye-**rate**] **ADJECTIVE** very angry.

iris, irises [Said eye-riss] **NOUN** ❶ the round, coloured part of your eye. ❷ a tall plant with long leaves and large blue, yellow, or white flowers.
● **WORD HISTORY:** from Greek *iris*
● meaning 'rainbow' or 'coloured
● circle'

Irish ADJECTIVE ❶ belonging or relating to the Irish Republic, or to the whole of Ireland ▷ **NOUN** ❷ Irish or Irish Gaelic is a language spoken in some parts of Ireland.

Irishman, Irishmen **NOUN** a man who comes from Ireland.
Irishwoman NOUN

irk, irks, irking, irked **VERB** If something irks you, it annoys you.
irksome ADJECTIVE

iron, irons, ironing, ironed **NOUN**
❶ (SCIENCE) Iron is a strong hard metallic element found in rocks. It is used in making tools and machines, and is also an important component of blood. Its atomic number is 26 and its symbol is Fe. ❷ An iron is a device which heats up and which you rub over clothes to remove creases ▷ **VERB** ❸ If you iron clothes, you use a hot iron to remove creases from them. **ironing NOUN**
iron out VERB If you iron out difficulties, you solve them.

Iron Age NOUN The Iron Age was a time about three thousand years ago when people first started to make tools out of iron.

ironbark, ironbarks **NOUN** an Australian eucalypt with a hard, rough bark.

irony, ironies [Said eye-ron-ee] **NOUN**
❶ (ENGLISH) Irony is a form of humour in which you say the opposite of what you really mean • *This group could be described, without irony, as the fortunate ones.* ❷ There is irony in a situation when there is an unexpected or unusual connection between things or events • *It's a sad irony of life: once you are lost, a map is useless.* **ironic** or **ironical ADJECTIVE ironically ADVERB**

irrational ADJECTIVE Irrational feelings are not based on logical reasons • *irrational fears.* **irrationally ADVERB irrationality NOUN**

irregular ADJECTIVE ❶ not smooth or even. ❷ not forming a regular pattern • *irregular walls.*
❸ (MATHS) Irregular things are uneven or unequal, or are not symmetrical. **irregularly ADVERB irregularity NOUN**
● **SIMILAR WORDS:** haphazard,
● random, variable

irrelevant ADJECTIVE (LIBRARY) not directly connected with a subject • *He either ignored questions or gave irrelevant answers.* **irrelevance NOUN**

irrepressible ADJECTIVE Someone who is irrepressible is lively and cheerful.

irresistible ADJECTIVE ❶ unable to be controlled • *an irresistible urge to yawn.* ❷ extremely attractive • *Women always found him irresistible.* **irresistibly ADVERB**

irrespective ADJECTIVE If you say

something will be done irrespective of certain things, you mean it will be done without taking those things into account.

irresponsible ADJECTIVE An irresponsible person does things without considering the consequences • *an irresponsible driver.* **irresponsibly** ADVERB **irresponsibility** NOUN

● **SIMILAR WORDS:** careless,
● reckless, thoughtless

irrigate, irrigates, irrigating, irrigated VERB To irrigate land is to supply it with water brought through pipes or ditches. **irrigated** ADJECTIVE **irrigation** NOUN

irritable ADJECTIVE easily annoyed.

irritate, irritates, irritating, irritated VERB ❶ If something irritates you, it annoys you. ❷ If something irritates part of your body, it makes it tender, sore, or itchy. **irritant** NOUN **irritation** NOUN

● **SIMILAR WORDS:** ❶ annoy, get
● on one's nerves

is the third person, present tense of be.

-ish SUFFIX '-ish' forms adjectives that mean 'fairly' or 'rather' • *smallish* • *greenish.*

Islam [*Said* **iz**-*lahm*] NOUN (RE) Islam is the Muslim religion, which teaches that there is only one God, Allah, and Mohammed is his prophet. The holy book of Islam is the Koran. **Islamic** ADJECTIVE

● **WORD HISTORY:** from Arabic
● *islam* meaning 'surrender to God'

island, islands [*Said* **eye**-*land*] NOUN a piece of land surrounded on all sides by water. **islander** NOUN

isle, isles [*rhymes with* **mile**] NOUN LITERARY an island.

-ism SUFFIX ❶ '-ism' forms nouns that refer to an action or condition • *criticism* • *heroism.* ❷ '-ism' forms nouns that refer to a political or economic system or a system of beliefs • *Marxism* • *Sikhism.* ❸ '-ism' forms nouns that refer to a type of prejudice • *racism* • *sexism.*

isobar, isobars [*Said* **eye**-*so-bar*] NOUN (GEOGRAPHY) An isobar is a line on a map which joins places of equal air pressure.

isolate, isolates, isolating, isolated VERB ❶ If something isolates you or if you isolate yourself, you are set apart from other people. ❷ If you isolate something, you separate it from everything else. **isolated** ADJECTIVE **isolation** NOUN

isomer, isomers NOUN (SCIENCE) Isomers are compounds which have the same molecular formula but in which the atoms are arranged differently, for example $CH_3CH_2CH_2OH$ and $CH_3CH(OH)CH_3$. **isomeric** ADJECTIVE

isometric ADJECTIVE (MATHS) If two or more things are isometric they have equal dimensions.

isosceles [*Said* **eye**-*soss*-*il-eez*] ADJECTIVE (MATHS) An isosceles triangle has two sides of the same length.

● **WORD HISTORY:** from Greek
● *iso-* meaning 'equal' and *skelos*
● meaning 'leg'

isotherm, isotherms NOUN (GEOGRAPHY) a line on a map which joins places of equal temperature.

a
b
c
d
e
f
g
h
i
j
k
l
m
n
o
p
q
r
s
t
u
v
w
x
y
z

▷ SPELLING NOTE: *plaice the fish has a glittering 'EYE' (I) (plaice)*

A
B
C
D
E
F
G
I
J
K
L
M
N
O
P
Q
R
S
T
U
V
W
X
Y
Z

isotope, isotopes **NOUN** (SCIENCE)
An isotope is one of two or more atoms of the same atomic number that contain different numbers of neutrons.

ISP an abbreviation for 'internet service provider'.

Israeli, Israelis [Said iz-**rail**-ee] **ADJECTIVE** (RE) ❶ belonging or relating to Israel • *a new force in Israeli politics.* ▷ **NOUN** ❷ someone who comes from Israel.

issue, issues, issuing, issued [Said **ish**-yoo] **NOUN** ❶ an important subject that people are talking about. ❷ a particular edition of a newspaper or magazine ▷ **VERB** ❸ If you issue a statement or a warning, you say it formally and publicly. ❹ If someone issues something, they officially give it • *Staff were issued with plastic cards.*
● **SIMILAR WORDS:** ❹ distribute,
● give out

-ist SUFFIX ❶ '-ist' forms nouns and adjectives which refer to someone who is involved in a certain activity, or who believes in a certain system or religion • *chemist* • *motorist* • *Buddhist.* ❷ '-ist' forms nouns and adjectives which refer to someone who has a certain prejudice • *racist.*

isthmus, isthmuses **NOUN** a narrow strip of land connecting two larger areas.

it PRONOUN ❶ 'It' is used to refer to something that has already been mentioned, or to a situation or fact • *It was a difficult decision.* ❷ 'It' is used to refer to people or animals whose sex is not known • *If a baby is thirsty, it feeds more often.* ❸ You use 'it' to make

statements about the weather, time, or date • *It's noon.* • *I see it's starting to rain.*

Italian, Italians **ADJECTIVE** ❶ belonging or relating to Italy ▷ **NOUN** ❷ someone who comes from Italy. ❸ Italian is the main language spoken in Italy.

italics PLURAL NOUN Italics are letters printed in a special sloping way, and are often used to emphasize something. All the examples in this dictionary are in italics. **italic ADJECTIVE**

itch, itches, itching, itched **VERB** ❶ When your skin itches, it has an unpleasant feeling and you want to scratch it. ❷ If you are itching to do something, you are impatient to do it ▷ **NOUN** ❸ an unpleasant feeling on your skin that you want to scratch. **itchy ADJECTIVE**

item, items **NOUN** ❶ one of a collection or list of objects. ❷ a newspaper or magazine article.
● **SIMILAR WORDS:** ❷ article,
● feature, piece

itinerary, itineraries **NOUN** a plan of a journey, showing a route to follow and places to visit • *Is Florence going to feature in your itinerary?*

-itis SUFFIX '-itis' is added to the name of a part of the body to refer to disease or inflammation in that part • *appendicitis* • *tonsillitis.*

its ADJECTIVE OR PRONOUN 'Its' refers to something belonging to or relating to things, children, or animals that have already been mentioned • *The lion lifted its head* • *Heavy rain made the river burst its banks.*

▷ SPELLING NOTE: *I went to see (C) the doctor's new practiCe (practice)*

- **USAGE NOTE:** Many people are
- confused about the difference
- between *its* and *it's*. *Its*, without the
- apostrophe, is the possessive form
- of *it*: *the cat has hurt its paw*. *It's*,
- with the apostrophe, is a short form
- of *it is* or *it has*: *it's green; it's been*
- *snowing again*

itself PRONOUN ❶ 'Itself' is used
when the same thing, child, or animal
does an action and is affected by it
• *Paris prides itself on its luxurious
hotels.* ❷ 'Itself' is used to emphasize
'it'.

-ity SUFFIX '-ity' forms nouns that
refer to a state or condition
• *continuity* • *technicality*.

-ive SUFFIX '-ive' forms adjectives
and some nouns • *massive* • *detective*.

ivory NOUN ❶ the valuable
creamy-white bone which forms the
tusk of an elephant. It is used to make
ornaments ▷ NOUN OR ADJECTIVE
❷ creamy-white.

ivy NOUN an evergreen plant which
creeps along the ground and up walls.

iwi, iwi or iwis NOUN In New Zealand,
a Maori tribe.

-ize or **-ise** SUFFIX '-ize' and '-ise'
forms verbs. Most verbs can be spelt with
either ending, though there are some
that can only be spelt with '-ise', for
example *advertise*, *improvise* and *revise*.

Jj

Many words which sound as if they ought to begin with letter *j* are spelt instead with letter *g*, for example *gender*, *geranium*, *giraffe* and *gym*.

jab, jabs, jabbing, jabbed **VERB** ❶ To jab something means to poke at it roughly ▷ **NOUN** ❷ a sharp or sudden poke. ❸ INFORMAL an injection.

jabiru, jabirus **NOUN** a white-and-green Australian stork with red legs.

jack, jacks, jacking, jacked **NOUN** ❶ a piece of equipment for lifting heavy objects, especially for lifting a car when changing a wheel. ❷ In a pack of cards, a jack is a card whose value is between a ten and a queen ▷ **VERB** ❸ To jack up an object means to raise it, especially by using a jack.

jackal, jackals **NOUN** a wild animal related to the dog.

jackaroo, jackaroos; *also spelt* **jackeroo** **NOUN** In Australia, a young person learning the work of a sheep or cattle station.

jackdaw, jackdaws **NOUN** a bird like a small crow with black and grey feathers.

jacket, jackets **NOUN** ❶ a short coat reaching to the waist or hips. ❷ an outer covering for something • *a book jacket.* ❸ The jacket of a baked potato is its skin.

jackpot, jackpots **NOUN** In a

gambling game, the jackpot is the top prize.

jack up, jacks up, jacking up, jacked up **VERB** INFORMAL In New Zealand English, to jack up is to organize or prepare something.

jade **NOUN** Jade is a hard green stone used for making jewellery and ornaments.

jagged **ADJECTIVE** sharp and spiky.
● **SIMILAR WORDS:** serrated, spiked,
● uneven

jaguar, jaguars **NOUN** a large member of the cat family with spots on its back.

jail, jails, jailing, jailed; *also spelt* **gaol** **NOUN** ❶ a building where people convicted of a crime are locked up ▷ **VERB** ❷ To jail someone means to lock them up in a jail.
● **SIMILAR WORDS:** ❶ nick,
● penitentiary, prison

jailer, jailers; *also spelt* **gaoler** **NOUN** a person who is in charge of the prisoners in a jail.

jam, jams, jamming, jammed **NOUN** ❶ a food, made by boiling fruit and sugar together until it sets. ❷ a situation in which it is impossible to move • *a traffic jam.* ▷ INFORMAL **PHRASE** ❸ If someone is **in a jam**, they are in a difficult situation ▷ **VERB** ❹ If people or things are jammed into a place, they are squeezed together so closely that they can hardly move. **5** To jam something somewhere means to push it there roughly • *He jammed his foot on the brake.* **6** If something is jammed, it is stuck or unable to work properly. **7** To jam a radio signal means to interfere with it and prevent it from being received clearly.

● **SIMILAR WORDS: 3** fix,
● predicament, tight spot

Jamaican, Jamaicans *[Said jam-may-kn]* **ADJECTIVE**
1 belonging or relating to Jamaica
▷ **NOUN 2** someone who comes from Jamaica.

jamboree, jamborees **NOUN** a gathering of large numbers of people enjoying themselves.

Jandal, Jandals **NOUN** TRADEMARK In New Zealand, a sandal with a strap between the big toe and other toes and over the foot.

jangle, jangles, jangling, jangled **VERB 1** If something jangles, it makes a harsh metallic ringing noise ▷ **NOUN 2** the sound made by metal objects striking against each other.

janitor, janitors **NOUN** the caretaker of a building.

January **NOUN** January is the first month of the year. It has 31 days.
● **WORD HISTORY:** from Latin
● *Januarius* meaning 'the month of
● Janus', named after a Roman god

Japanese **ADJECTIVE 1** belonging or relating to Japan ▷ **NOUN**
2 someone who comes from Japan.
3 Japanese is the main language spoken in Japan.

jar, jars, jarring, jarred **NOUN 1** a glass container with a wide top used for storing food ▷ **VERB 2** If something jars on you, you find it unpleasant or annoying.

jargon **NOUN** Jargon consists of words that are used in special or technical ways by particular groups of people, often making the language difficult to understand.

jarrah, jarrahs **NOUN** an Australian eucalypt tree that produces wood used for timber.

jasmine **NOUN** Jasmine is a climbing plant with small sweet-scented white flowers.

jaundice **NOUN** Jaundice is an illness affecting the liver, in which the skin and the whites of the eyes become yellow.

jaundiced **ADJECTIVE** pessimistic and lacking enthusiasm • *He takes a rather jaundiced view of politicians.*

jaunt, jaunts **NOUN** a journey or trip you go on for pleasure.

jaunty, jauntier, jauntiest **ADJECTIVE** expressing cheerfulness and self-confidence • *a jaunty tune.*
jauntily **ADVERB**

javelin, javelins **NOUN** a long spear that is thrown in sports competitions.

jaw, jaws **NOUN 1** A person's or animal's jaw is the bone in which the teeth are set. **2** A person's or animal's mouth and teeth are their jaws.

jay, jays **NOUN** a kind of noisy chattering bird.

jazz, jazzes, jazzing, jazzed **NOUN**
1 Jazz is a style of popular music with

▷ SPELLING NOTE: LEarn the principLEs (principle)

A
B
C
D
E
F
G
H
I
J
K
L
M
N
O
P
Q
R
S
T
U
V
W
X
Y
Z

a forceful rhythm ▷ **VERB**
2 INFORMAL To jazz something up means to make it more colourful or exciting.

jazzy, jazzier, jazziest **ADJECTIVE** INFORMAL bright and showy.

jealous ADJECTIVE 1 If you are jealous, you feel bitterness towards someone who has something that you would like to have. **2** If you are jealous of something you have, you feel you must try to keep it from other people. **jealously ADVERB jealousy NOUN**
● **SIMILAR WORDS: 1** covetous,
● envious **2** possessive

jeans PLURAL NOUN Jeans are casual denim trousers.

jeep, jeeps **NOUN** TRADEMARK a small road vehicle with four-wheel drive.

jeer, jeers, jeering, jeered **VERB 1** If you jeer at someone, you insult them in a loud, unpleasant way ▷ **NOUN 2** Jeers are rude and insulting remarks. **jeering ADJECTIVE**

Jehovah [Said ji-**hove**-ah] **PROPER NOUN** Jehovah is the name of God in the Old Testament.
● **WORD HISTORY:** from adding
● vowels to the Hebrew *JHVH*, the
● sacred name of God

jelly, jellies **NOUN 1** a clear, sweet food eaten as a dessert. **2** a type of clear, set jam.

jellyfish, jellyfishes **NOUN** a sea animal with a clear soft body and tentacles which may sting.

jeopardize, jeopardizes, jeopardizing, jeopardized [Said *jep-par-dyz*]; also spelt **jeopardise**

VERB To jeopardize something means to do something which puts it at risk
• *Elaine jeopardized her health.*

jeopardy NOUN If someone or something is in jeopardy, they are at risk of failing or of being destroyed.

jerk, jerks, jerking, jerked **VERB 1** To jerk something means to give it a sudden, sharp pull. **2** If something jerks, it moves suddenly and sharply ▷ **NOUN 3** a sudden sharp movement. **4** INFORMAL If you call someone a jerk, you mean they are stupid. **jerky ADJECTIVE jerkily ADVERB**

jerkin, jerkins **NOUN** a short sleeveless jacket.

jersey, jerseys **NOUN 1** a knitted garment for the upper half of the body. **2** Jersey is a type of knitted woollen or cotton fabric used to make clothing.

jest, jests, jesting, jested **NOUN 1** a joke ▷ **VERB 2** To jest means to speak jokingly.

jester, jesters **NOUN** In the past, a jester was a man who was kept to amuse the king or queen.

Jesuit, Jesuits [Said *jez*-yoo-it] **NOUN** RE A Jesuit is a priest who is a member of the Roman Catholic Society of Jesus, founded in the sixteenth century by Ignatius Loyola. One of the main aims of the Society is missionary work.

jet, jets, jetting, jetted **NOUN 1** a plane which is able to fly very fast. **2** a stream of liquid, gas, or flame forced out under pressure. **3** Jet is a hard black stone, usually highly polished and used in jewellery and

▷ SPELLING NOTE: *Psychiatrists Seldom Yell Callously Hard* (**psychiatrist**)

ornaments ▷ **VERB** ❹ To jet somewhere means to fly there in a plane, especially a jet.

jet boat, jet boats **NOUN** In New Zealand, a motor boat that is powered by a jet of water at the rear.

jet lag NOUN Jet lag is a feeling of tiredness or confusion that people have after a long flight across different time zones.

jetsam NOUN Jetsam is rubbish left floating on the sea or washed up on the seashore.

jettison, jettisons, jettisoning, jettisoned **VERB** If you jettison something, you throw it away because you no longer want it.

jetty, jetties **NOUN** a wide stone wall or wooden platform at the edge of the sea or a river, where boats can be moored.

Jew, Jews [Said joo] (RE) **NOUN** a person who practises the religion of Judaism, or who is of Hebrew descent. **Jewish ADJECTIVE**
● **WORD HISTORY:** from *Judah*, the name of a Jewish patriarch

jewel, jewels **NOUN** a precious stone used to decorate valuable ornaments or jewellery. **jewelled ADJECTIVE**

jeweller, jewellers **NOUN** a person who makes jewellery or who sells and repairs jewellery and watches.

jewellery NOUN Jewellery consists of ornaments that people wear, such as rings or necklaces, made of valuable metals and sometimes decorated with precious stones.

jib, jibs **NOUN** a small sail towards the front of a sailing boat.

jibe another spelling of **gibe**.

jig, jigs, jigging, jigged **NOUN** ❶ a type of lively folk dance ▷ **VERB** ❷ If you jig, you dance around in a lively bouncy manner.

jiggle, jiggles, jiggling, jiggled **VERB** If you jiggle something, you move it around with quick jerky movements.

jigsaw, jigsaws **NOUN** a puzzle consisting of a picture on cardboard that has been cut up into small pieces, which have to be put together again.

jihad, jihads [Said jee-had] **NOUN** ❶ a holy war waged to defend or further the ideals of Islam. ❷ Jihad also means the personal struggle of a Muslim against against sin.

jilt, jilts, jilting, jilted **VERB** If you jilt someone, you suddenly break off your relationship with them. **jilted ADJECTIVE**

jingle, jingles, jingling, jingled **NOUN** ❶ a short, catchy phrase or rhyme set to music and used to advertise something on radio or television. ❷ the sound of something jingling ▷ **VERB** ❸ When something jingles, it makes a tinkling sound like small bells.

jinks PLURAL NOUN High jinks is boisterous and mischievous behaviour.

jinx, jinxes **NOUN** someone or something that is thought to bring bad luck • *He was beginning to think he was a jinx.*

jinxed ADJECTIVE If something is jinxed it is considered to be unlucky • *I think this house is jinxed.*

a
b
c
d
e
f
g
h
i
j
k
l
m
n
o
p
q
r
s
t
u
v
w
x
y
z

▷ SPELLING NOTE: *the QUeen stood on the QUay (quay)*

jitters PLURAL NOUN INFORMAL If you have got the jitters, you are feeling very nervous. **jittery** ADJECTIVE

job, jobs NOUN ❶ the work that someone does to earn money. ❷ a duty or responsibility • *It is a captain's job to lead from the front.* ▷ PHRASE ❸ If something is **just the job**, it is exactly right or exactly what you wanted.
● SIMILAR WORDS:
● ❶ employment, occupation, work

job centre, job centres NOUN a government office where people can find out about job vacancies.

jobless ADJECTIVE without any work.

jockey, jockeys, jockeying, jockeyed NOUN ❶ someone who rides a horse in a race ▷ VERB ❷ To jockey for a position means to manoeuvre in order to gain an advantage over other people.

jocular ADJECTIVE A jocular comment is intended to make people laugh.

jodhpurs [Said *jod-purz*] PLURAL NOUN Jodhpurs are close-fitting trousers worn when riding a horse.
● WORD HISTORY: from *Jodhpur*,
● the name of a town in N. India

joey, joeys NOUN INFORMAL In Australian English, a young kangaroo or other young animal.

jog, jogs, jogging, jogged VERB ❶ To jog means to run slowly and rhythmically, often as a form of exercise. ❷ If you jog something, you knock it slightly so that it shakes or moves. ❸ If someone or something jogs your memory, they remind you of something ▷ NOUN ❹ a slow run.

jogger NOUN jogging NOUN

join, joins, joining, joined VERB ❶ When two things join, or when one thing joins another, they come together. ❷ If you join a club or organization, you become a member of it or start taking part in it. ❸ To join two things means to fasten them together ▷ NOUN ❹ a place where two things are fastened together.
join up VERB If someone joins up, they become a member of the armed forces.
● SIMILAR WORDS: ❶ *and* ❸ connect, link, unite ❷ enlist, enrol, sign up

joiner, joiners NOUN a person who makes wooden window frames, doors, and furniture.

joinery NOUN Joinery is the work done by a joiner.

joint, joints, jointing, jointed ADJECTIVE ❶ shared by or belonging to two or more people • *a joint building society account.* ▷ NOUN ❷ (SCIENCE) a part of the body where two bones meet and are joined together so that they can move, for example a knee or hip. ❸ (D & T) a place where two things are fixed together. ❹ a large piece of meat suitable for roasting. ❺ INFORMAL any place of entertainment, such as a nightclub or pub ▷ VERB ❻ To joint meat means to cut it into large pieces according to where the bones are. **jointly** ADVERB **jointed** ADJECTIVE

joist, joists NOUN a large beam used to support floors or ceilings.

joke, jokes, joking, joked NOUN ❶ something that you say or do to

make people laugh, such as a funny
story. ❷ anything that you think is
ridiculous and not worthy of respect
• *The decision was a joke.* ▷ VERB ❸ If
you are joking, you are teasing
someone. **jokingly ADVERB**
● SIMILAR WORDS: ❶ gag, jest
● ❸ jest, kid

joker, jokers NOUN In a pack of
cards, a joker is an extra card that does
not belong to any of the four suits, but
is used in some games.

jolly, jollier, jolliest ADJECTIVE
❶ happy, cheerful, and pleasant
▷ ADVERB ❷ INFORMAL Jolly also
means very • *jolly good fun.*

jolt, jolts, jolting, jolted VERB ❶ To
jolt means to move or shake roughly
and violently. ❷ If you are jolted by
something, it gives you an unpleasant
surprise ▷ NOUN ❸ a sudden jerky
movement. ❹ an unpleasant shock or
surprise.

jostle, jostles, jostling, jostled VERB
To jostle means to push roughly
against people in a crowd.

jot, jots, jotting, jotted VERB ❶ If you
jot something down, you write it
quickly in the form of a short informal
note ▷ NOUN ❷ a very small
amount. **jotting NOUN**

jotter, jotters NOUN a pad or
notebook.

joule, joules *[rhymes with school]*
NOUN (SCIENCE) A joule is a unit of
energy or work. A watt is equal to one
joule per second. The joule is named
after the English physicist J.P. Joule
(1818–1889).

journal, journals NOUN ❶ a

magazine that deals with a particular
subject, trade, or profession. ❷ a
diary which someone keeps regularly.

journalism NOUN Journalism is
the work of collecting, writing, and
publishing news in newspapers,
magazines, and on television and
radio. **journalist NOUN journalistic
ADJECTIVE**

journey, journeys, journeying,
journeyed NOUN ❶ the act of
travelling from one place to another
▷ VERB ❷ FORMAL To journey
somewhere means to travel there • *He
intended to journey up the Amazon.*

joust, jousts NOUN In medieval
times, a joust was a competition
between knights fighting on
horseback, using lances.

jovial ADJECTIVE cheerful and
friendly. **jovially ADVERB joviality
NOUN**

joy, joys NOUN ❶ Joy is a feeling of
great happiness. ❷ INFORMAL Joy also
means success or luck • *Any joy with
your insurance claim?* ❸ something
that makes you happy or gives you
pleasure.

joyful ADJECTIVE ❶ causing
pleasure and happiness. ❷ Someone
who is joyful is extremely happy.
joyfully ADVERB

joyous ADJECTIVE FORMAL joyful.
joyously ADVERB

joyride, joyrides NOUN a drive in a
stolen car for pleasure. **joyriding
NOUN joyrider NOUN**

joystick, joysticks NOUN a lever in
an aircraft which the pilot uses to
control height and direction.

jube, jubes NOUN INFORMAL In Australian and New Zealand English, a fruit-flavoured jelly sweet.

jubilant ADJECTIVE feeling or expressing great happiness or triumph. **jubilantly** ADVERB

jubilation NOUN Jubilation is a feeling of great happiness and triumph.

jubilee, jubilees NOUN a special anniversary of an event such as a coronation • *Queen Elizabeth's Silver Jubilee in 1977.*
- WORD HISTORY: from Hebrew *yobhel* meaning 'ram's horn'; rams' horns were blown during festivals and celebrations

Judaism [Said joo-day-i-zm] NOUN RE Judaism is the religion of the Jewish people. It is based on a belief in one God, and draws its laws and authority from the Old Testament. **Judaic** ADJECTIVE

judder, judders, juddering, juddered VERB To judder means to shake and vibrate noisily and violently.

judder bar, judder bars NOUN In New Zealand English, a bump built across a road to stop drivers from going too fast. In Britain it is called a **sleeping policeman**.

judge, judges, judging, judged NOUN ❶ the person in a law court who decides how the law should be applied to people who appear in the court. ❷ someone who decides the winner in a contest or competition ▷ VERB ❸ If you judge someone or something, you form an opinion about them based on the evidence that you have. ❹ To judge a contest or competition means

to decide on the winner.
- SIMILAR WORDS: ❷ adjudicator, referee, umpire ❹ adjudicate, referee, umpire

judgment, judgments; also spelt **judgement** NOUN an opinion or decision based on evidence.
- USAGE NOTE: *Judgment* and *judgement* are both correct spellings

judicial ADJECTIVE relating to judgment or to justice • *a judicial review.*

judiciary NOUN The judiciary is the branch of government concerned with justice and the legal system.

judicious ADJECTIVE sensible and showing good judgment. **judiciously** ADVERB

judo NOUN Judo is a sport in which two people try to force each other to the ground using special throwing techniques.

jug, jugs NOUN a container with a lip or spout used for holding or serving liquids.

juggernaut, juggernauts NOUN a large heavy lorry.
- WORD HISTORY: from Hindi *Jagannath*, the name of a huge idol of the god Krishna, which every year is wheeled through the streets of Puri in India

juggle, juggles, juggling, juggled VERB To juggle means to throw objects into the air, catching them in sequence, and tossing them up again so there are several in the air at one time. **juggler** NOUN

jugular, jugulars NOUN The jugular or jugular vein is one of the veins in the neck which carry blood from the head back to the heart.

juice, juices **NOUN** ❶ Juice is the liquid that can be squeezed or extracted from fruit or other food. ❷ Juices in the body are fluids • *gastric juices*.

juicy, juicier, juiciest **ADJECTIVE** ❶ Juicy food has a lot of juice in it. ❷ Something that is juicy is interesting, exciting, or scandalous • *a juicy bit of gossip*.

jukebox, jukeboxes **NOUN** a large record player found in cafés and pubs which automatically plays a selected record when coins are inserted.

July NOUN July is the seventh month of the year. It has 31 days.
● **WORD HISTORY:** from Latin *Julius*, the month of July, named after Julius Caesar by the Romans

jumble, jumbles, jumbling, jumbled **NOUN** ❶ an untidy muddle of things. ❷ Jumble consists of articles for a jumble sale ▷ **VERB** ❸ To jumble things means to mix them up untidily.

jumble sale, jumble sales **NOUN** an event at which cheap second-hand clothes and other articles are sold to raise money, usually for a charity.

jumbo, jumbos **NOUN** ❶ A jumbo or jumbo jet is a large jet aeroplane that can carry several hundred passengers ▷ **ADJECTIVE** ❷ very large • *jumbo packs of elastic bands*.
● **WORD HISTORY:** from *Jumbo*, the name of a famous 19th-century elephant

jumbuck, jumbucks **NOUN** OLD-FASHIONED In Australian English, a sheep.

jump, jumps, jumping, jumped **VERB** ❶ To jump means to spring off the ground using your leg muscles. ❷ To jump something means to spring off the ground and move over or across it. ❸ If you jump at something such as an opportunity, you accept it eagerly. ❹ If you jump on someone, you criticize them suddenly and forcefully. ❺ If someone jumps, they make a sudden sharp movement of surprise. ❻ If an amount or level jumps, it suddenly increases ▷ **NOUN** ❼ a spring into the air, sometimes over an object.
● **SIMILAR WORDS:** ❶ and ❼
● bound, leap, spring

jumper, jumpers **NOUN** a knitted garment for the top half of the body.

jumpy, jumpier, jumpiest **ADJECTIVE** nervous and worried.

junction, junctions **NOUN** a place where roads or railway lines meet or cross.

June NOUN June is the sixth month of the year. It has 30 days.
● **WORD HISTORY:** from Latin *Junius*, the month of June, probably from the name of an important Roman family

jungle, jungles **NOUN** ❶ a dense tropical forest. ❷ a tangled mass of plants or other objects.

junior, juniors **ADJECTIVE** ❶ Someone who is junior to other people has a lower position in an organization. ❷ Junior also means younger. ❸ relating to childhood • *a junior school*. ▷ **NOUN** ❹ someone who holds an unimportant position in an organization.

▷ SPELLING NOTE: *Eddy Ant thinks mEAt is a grEAt trEAt to EAt (-ea-)*

A
B
C
D
E
F
G
H
I
J
K
L
M
N
O
P
Q
R
S
T
U
V
W
X
Y
Z

juniper, junipers **NOUN** an evergreen shrub with purple berries used in cooking and medicine.

junk, junks **NOUN** ❶ Junk is old or second-hand articles which are sold cheaply or thrown away. ❷ If you think something is junk, you think it is worthless rubbish. ❸ a Chinese sailing boat with a flat bottom and square sails.

junk food **NOUN** Junk food is food low in nutritional value which is eaten as well as or instead of proper meals.

junkie, junkies **NOUN** INFORMAL a drug addict.

Jupiter **NOUN** Jupiter is the largest planet in the solar system and the fifth from the sun.

jurisdiction **NOUN** ❶ FORMAL Jurisdiction is the power or right of the courts to apply laws and make legal judgments • *The Court held that it did not have the jurisdiction to examine the merits of the case.* ❷ Jurisdiction is power or authority • *The airport was under French jurisdiction.*

juror, jurors **NOUN** a member of a jury.

jury, juries **NOUN** a group of people in a court of law who have been selected to listen to the facts of a case on trial, and to decide whether the accused person is guilty or not.

just **ADJECTIVE** ❶ fair and impartial • *She arrived at a just decision.* ❷ morally right or proper • *a just reward.* ▷ **ADVERB** ❸ If something has just happened, it happened a very short time ago. ❹ If you just do something, you do it by a very small amount • *They only just won.* ❺ simply or only • *It was just an excuse not to mow the lawn.* ❻ exactly • *It's just what she wanted.* ▷ **PHRASE** ❼ In South African English, **just now** means in a little while. **justly** **ADVERB**

justice, justices **NOUN** ❶ Justice is fairness and reasonableness. ❷ The system of justice in a country is the way in which laws are maintained by the courts. ❸ a judge or magistrate.

justify, justifies, justifying, justified **VERB** ❶ If you justify an action or idea, you prove or explain why it is reasonable or necessary. ❷ ICT To justify text that you have typed or keyed into a computer is to adjust the spaces between the words so each full line in a paragraph fills the space between the left and right hand margins of the page. **justification** **NOUN** **justifiable** **ADJECTIVE**

jut, juts, jutting, jutted **VERB** If something juts out, it sticks out beyond or above a surface or edge.
● **SIMILAR WORDS:** project,
● protrude, stick out

jute **NOUN** Jute is a strong fibre made from the bark of an Asian plant, used to make rope and sacking.

juvenile, juveniles **ADJECTIVE** ❶ suitable for young people. ❷ childish and rather silly • *a juvenile game.* ▷ **NOUN** ❸ a young person not old enough to be considered an adult.

juxtapose, juxtaposes, juxtaposing, juxtaposed **VERB** If you juxtapose things or ideas, you put them close together, often to emphasize the difference between them. **juxtaposition** **NOUN**

▷ SPELLING NOTE: *Elaine and Emily shout EE when they mEEt to grEEt each other (-ee-)*

Kk

Some words that begin with a
k- sound are spelt with the letters
ch-, for example *chlorophyll*,
chlorine, and *choir*. Some words that
begin with a k- sound are spelt with
letter q, for example *quite* and *quiet*.

Kaaba NOUN (RE) a cube-shaped
building inside the mosque at Mecca,
which contains the Black Stone which
Muslims believe God gave to Abraham.
It is the most holy site in Islam and
Muslims turn towards it when they pray.

kai NOUN INFORMAL In New Zealand,
another name for food.

kaleidoscope, kaleidoscopes *[Said
kal-**eye**-dos-skope]* NOUN a toy
consisting of a tube with a hole at one
end. When you look through the hole
and twist the other end of the tube, you
can see a changing pattern of colours.
● **WORD HISTORY:** from Greek *kalos*
● meaning 'beautiful',*eidos* meaning
● 'shape', and *skopein* meaning 'to
● look at'

kamikaze NOUN In the Second
World War, a kamikaze was a Japanese
pilot who flew an aircraft loaded with
explosives directly into an enemy
target knowing he would be killed
doing so.
● **WORD HISTORY:** from Japanese
● *kami* meaning 'divine' + *kaze*
● meaning 'wind'

kangaroo, kangaroos NOUN a
large Australian animal with very
strong back legs which it uses for
jumping.

karate *[Said kar-**rat**-ee]* NOUN
Karate is a sport in which people fight
each other using only their hands,
elbows, feet, and legs.
● **WORD HISTORY:** from
● Japanese *kara* + *te* meaning 'empty
● hand'

karma NOUN In Buddhism and
Hinduism, karma is actions you take
which affect you in your present and
future lives.

Karoo, Karoos; *also spelt* **Karroo**
NOUN In South Africa, the Karoos are
areas of very dry land.

karri, karris NOUN an Australian
eucalypt that produces a dark red
wood used for building.

katipo, katipo or katipos NOUN a
small, poisonous spider with a red or
orange stripe on its back, found in
New Zealand.

kauri, kauri or kauris NOUN a large
tree found in New Zealand which
produces wood used for building and
making furniture.

kayak, kayaks *[Said **ky**-ak]* NOUN a
covered canoe with a small opening
for the person sitting in it, originally
used by the Inuit people.

▷ SPELLING NOTE: 'i' before 'e' except after 'c'

kea, kea or keas [Said **kay-ah**] NOUN
1 a large, greenish parrot found in New Zealand. **2** In New Zealand, Keas are the youngest members of the Scouts.

kebab, kebabs NOUN pieces of meat or vegetable stuck on a stick and grilled.

keel, keels, keeling, keeled NOUN
1 the specially shaped bottom of a ship which supports the sides and sits in the water ▷ VERB **2** If someone or something keels over, they fall down sideways.

keen, keener, keenest ADJECTIVE
1 Someone who is keen shows great eagerness and enthusiasm. **2** If you are keen on someone or something, you are attracted to or fond of them.
3 quick to notice or understand things. **4** Keen senses let you see, hear, smell, and taste things very clearly or strongly. **keenly** ADVERB **keenness** NOUN
● SIMILAR WORDS: **1** avid, eager,
● enthusiastic

keep, keeps, keeping, kept VERB
1 To keep someone or something in a particular condition means to make them stay in that condition • *We'll walk to keep warm.* **2** If you keep something, you have it and look after it. **3** To keep something also means to store it in the usual place. **4** If you keep doing something, you do it repeatedly or continuously • *I kept phoning the hospital.* **5** If you keep a promise, you do what you promised to do. **6** If you keep a secret, you do not tell anyone else. **7** If you keep a diary, you write something in it every day.
8 If you keep someone from going

somewhere, you delay them so that they are late. **9** To keep someone means to provide them with money, food, and clothing ▷ NOUN **10** Your keep is the cost of the food you eat, your housing, and your clothing • *He does not contribute towards his keep.*
11 (HISTORY) the main tower inside the walls of a castle.

keep up VERB If you keep up with other people, you move or work at the same speed as they do.
● SIMILAR WORDS: **2** hold,
● maintain, preserve

keeper, keepers NOUN **1** a person whose job is to look after the animals in a zoo. **2** a goalkeeper in soccer or hockey.

keeping NOUN **1** If something is in your keeping, it has been given to you to look after for a while ▷ PHRASE
2 If one thing is **in keeping with** another, the two things are suitable or appropriate together.

keepsake, keepsakes NOUN something that someone gives you to remind you of a particular person or event.
● SIMILAR WORDS: memento,
● souvenir

keg, kegs NOUN a small barrel.

kelpie, kelpies; also spelt **kelpy** NOUN a smooth-haired Australian sheepdog with upright ears.

kennel, kennels NOUN **1** a shelter for a dog. **2** A kennels is a place where dogs can be kept for a time, or where they are bred.

Kenyan, Kenyans [Said **keen-yan**] ADJECTIVE **1** belonging or relating to Kenya ▷ NOUN **2** someone who

▷ SPELLING NOTE: *King IAn went to ParlIAment in a carrIAge for his marrIAge (-ia-)*

comes from Kenya.

kerb, kerbs **NOUN** the raised edge at the point where a pavement joins onto a road.

kernel, kernels **NOUN** the part of a nut that is inside the shell.

kerosene **NOUN** Kerosene is the same as paraffin.

kestrel, kestrels **NOUN** a type of small falcon.

ketchup **NOUN** Ketchup is a cold sauce, usually made from tomatoes.

kettle, kettles **NOUN** a metal container with a spout, in which you boil water.

key, keys, keying, keyed **NOUN** ❶ a shaped piece of metal that fits into a hole so that you can unlock a door, wind something that is clockwork, or start a car. ❷ The keys on a typewriter, piano, or cash register are the buttons that you press to use it. ❸ an explanation of the symbols used in a map or diagram. ❹ (MUSIC) In music, a key is a scale of notes ▷ **VERB** ❺ (ICT) If you key in information on a computer keyboard, you type it.

keyboard, keyboards **NOUN** (ICT) a row of levers or buttons on a piano, typewriter, or computer.

Key Stage, Key Stages **NOUN** In England and Wales, one of the four age-group divisions to which each level of the National Curriculum applies (5–7; 7–11; 11–14; 14–16).

kg an abbreviation for 'kilograms'.

khaki [Said **kah**-kee] **NOUN** ❶ Khaki is a strong yellowish-brown material, used especially for military uniforms ▷ **NOUN OR ADJECTIVE** ❷ yellowish-brown.
  ● **WORD HISTORY:** from Urdu kaki meaning 'dusty'

khanda, khandas [Said **kun**-dah] **NOUN** a sword used by Sikhs in the Amrit ceremony.

kia ora [Said ki-**or**-ah] **INTERJECTION** In New Zealand, 'kia ora' is a Maori greeting.

kibbutz, kibbutzim [Said kib-**boots**] **NOUN** a place of work in Israel, for example a farm or factory, where the workers live together and share all the duties and income.

kick, kicks, kicking, kicked **VERB** ❶ If you kick something, you hit it with your foot ▷ **NOUN** ❷ If you give something a kick, you hit it with your foot. ❸ INFORMAL If you get a kick out of doing something, you enjoy doing it very much.
kick off **VERB** When players kick off, they start a soccer or rugby match.
kick-off **NOUN**

kid, kids, kidding, kidded **NOUN** ❶ INFORMAL a child. ❷ a young goat ▷ **VERB** ❸ If you kid people, you tease them by deceiving them in fun.

kidnap, kidnaps, kidnapping, kidnapped **VERB** To kidnap someone is to take them away by force and demand a ransom in exchange for returning them. **kidnapper NOUN** **kidnapping NOUN**
  ● **SIMILAR WORDS:** abduct, seize

kidney, kidneys **NOUN** Your kidneys are two organs in your body that remove waste products from your blood.

a
b
c
d
e
f
g
h
i
j
k
l
m
n
o
p
q
r
s
t
u
v
w
x
y
z

▷ SPELLING NOTE: an ELegant angEL (angel)

kill, kills, killing, killed **VERB ❶** To kill a person, animal, or plant is to make them die. **❷** If something is killing you, it is causing you severe pain or discomfort • *My arms are killing me.* ▷ **NOUN ❸** The kill is the moment when a hunter kills an animal. **killer NOUN**

● **SIMILAR WORDS: ❶** murder, slay

kiln, kilns **NOUN** (ART) an oven for baking china or pottery until it becomes hard and dry.

kilo, kilos **NOUN** a kilogram.

kilogram, kilograms **NOUN** (MATHS) A kilogram is a unit of weight equal to 1000 grams.

kilohertz NOUN a unit of measurement of radio waves equal to one thousand hertz.

kilometre, kilometres **NOUN** (MATHS) a unit of distance equal to one thousand metres.

kilowatt, kilowatts **NOUN** a unit of power equal to one thousand watts.

kilt, kilts **NOUN** a tartan skirt worn by men as part of Scottish Highland dress.

kimono, kimonos **NOUN** a long, loose garment with wide sleeves and a sash, worn in Japan.

kin PLURAL NOUN Your kin are your relatives.
● **SIMILAR WORDS:** family, kindred, ● relatives

kind, kinds; kinder, kindest **NOUN** **❶** A particular kind of thing is something of the same type or sort as other things • *that kind of film.* ▷ **ADJECTIVE ❷** Someone who is

kind is considerate and generous towards other people. **kindly ADVERB**

● **USAGE NOTE:** When you use *kind* in its singular form, the adjective before it should also be singular: *that kind of dog.* When you use the plural form *kinds*, the adjective before it should be plural: *those kinds of dog; those kinds of dogs*
● **SIMILAR WORDS: ❶** class, sort, ● type **❷** considerate, generous

kindergarten, kindergartens **NOUN** a school for children who are too young to go to primary school.
● **WORD HISTORY:** from German ● *Kinder + Garten* meaning 'children's ● garden'

kindle, kindles, kindling, kindled **VERB ❶** If you kindle a fire, you light it. **❷** If something kindles a feeling in you, it causes you to have that feeling.

kindling NOUN Kindling is bits of dry wood or paper that you use to start a fire.

kindness NOUN the quality of being considerate towards other people.

kindred ADJECTIVE If you say that someone is a kindred spirit, you mean that they have the same interests or opinions as you.

kinetic, kinetics **ADJECTIVE** **❶** relating to movement ▷ **NOUN ❷** (SCIENCE) Kinetics is the scientific study of the way energy behaves when something moves.

kinetic energy NOUN (SCIENCE) Kinetic energy is the energy that is produced when something moves.

A B C D E F G H I J K L M N O P Q R S T U V W X Y Z

▷ SPELLING NOTE: *LEt's measure the angLE (angle)*

king, kings NOUN **❶** HISTORY a man who is the head of state in a country, and who inherited his position from his parents. **❷** a chess piece which can only move one square at a time. **❸** In a pack of cards, a king is a card with a picture of a king on it.

kingdom, kingdoms NOUN **❶** HISTORY a country that is governed by a king or queen. **❷** SCIENCE The largest divisions of the living organisms in the natural world are called kingdoms • *the animal kingdom.*

kingfisher, kingfishers NOUN a brightly coloured bird that lives near water and feeds on fish.

king-size or **king-sized** ADJECTIVE larger than the normal size • *a king-size bed.*

kink, kinks NOUN a dent or curve in something which is normally straight.

kinky ADJECTIVE INFORMAL having peculiar sexual tastes.

kinship NOUN Kinship is a family relationship to other people.

kiosk, kiosks [Said kee-osk] NOUN a covered stall on a street where you can buy newspapers, sweets, or cigarettes.

● **WORD HISTORY:** from Turkish
● *kösk* meaning 'pavilion'

kip, kips, kipping, kipped INFORMAL NOUN **❶** a period of sleep ▷ VERB **❷** When you kip, you sleep.

kipper, kippers NOUN a smoked herring.

kirk, kirks NOUN In Scotland, a kirk is a church.

kiss, kisses, kissing, kissed VERB **❶** When you kiss someone, you touch them with your lips as a sign of love or affection ▷ NOUN **❷** When you give someone a kiss, you kiss them.

kiss of life NOUN The kiss of life is a method of reviving someone by blowing air into their lungs.

kit, kits NOUN **❶** a collection of things that you use for a sport or other activity. **❷** a set of parts that you put together to make something.

kitchen, kitchens NOUN a room used for cooking and preparing food.

kite, kites NOUN **❶** a frame covered with paper or cloth which is attached to a piece of string, and which you fly in the air. **❷** a shape with four sides, with two pairs of the same length, and none of the sides parallel to each other. **❸** a large bird of prey with a long tail and long wings.

kitset, kitsets NOUN In New Zealand English, a set of parts which you assemble yourself to make an item such as a house or a piece of furniture.

kitten, kittens NOUN a young cat.

kitty, kitties NOUN a fund of money that has been given by a group of people who will use it to pay for or do things together.

kiwi, kiwi or kiwis [Said kee-wee] NOUN **❶** a type of bird found in New Zealand. Kiwis cannot fly. **❷** someone who comes from New Zealand. The plural of this sense is 'kiwis'.

kiwi fruit, kiwi fruits NOUN a fruit with a brown hairy skin and green flesh.

a
b
c
d
e
f
g
h
i
j
k
l
m
n
o
p
q
r
s
t
u
v
w
x
y
z

▷ SPELLING NOTE: *A Rude Idiot Thought He Might Eat Toffee In Church (arithmetic)*

kloof | 476

kloof, kloofs **NOUN** In South Africa, a kloof is a narrow valley.

km an abbreviation for 'kilometres'.

knack **NOUN** an ability to do something difficult whilst making it look easy • *the knack of making friends.*

knead, kneads, kneading, kneaded **VERB** If you knead dough, you press it and squeeze it with your hands before baking it.

knee, knees **NOUN** the joint in your leg between your ankle and your hip.

kneecap, kneecaps **NOUN** Your kneecaps are the bones at the front of your knees.

kneel, kneels, kneeling, knelt **VERB** When you kneel, you bend your legs and lower your body until your knees are touching the ground.

knell, knells **NOUN** LITERARY the sound of a bell rung to announce a death or at a funeral.

knickers **PLURAL NOUN** Knickers are underpants worn by women and girls.

knick-knacks **PLURAL NOUN** Knick-knacks are small ornaments.

knife, knives; knifes, knifing, knifed **NOUN** ❶ (D & T) a sharp metal tool that you use to cut things ▷ **VERB** ❷ To knife someone is to stab them with a knife.

knight, knights, knighting, knighted **NOUN** ❶ a man who has been given the title 'Sir' by the King or Queen. ❷ (HISTORY) In medieval Europe, a knight was a man who served a monarch or lord as a mounted soldier. ❸ a chess piece that is usually in the

shape of a horse's head ▷ **VERB** ❹ To knight a man is to give him the title 'Sir'. **knighthood** **NOUN**

knit, knits, knitting, knitted **VERB** ❶ If you knit a piece of clothing, you make it by working lengths of wool together, either using needles held in the hand, or with a machine. ❷ If you knit your brows, you frown. **knitting** **NOUN**

knob, knobs **NOUN** ❶ a round handle. ❷ a round switch on a machine • *the knobs of a radio.*

knobkerrie, knobkerries **NOUN** In South Africa, a knobkerrie is a club or stick with a rounded end.

knock, knocks, knocking, knocked **VERB** ❶ If you knock on something, you strike it with your hand or fist. ❷ If you knock a part of your body against something, you bump into it quite forcefully. ❸ INFORMAL To knock someone is to criticize them ▷ **NOUN** ❹ a firm blow on something solid • *There was a knock at the door.* **knock out VERB** To knock someone out is to hit them so hard that they become unconscious.

knocker, knockers **NOUN** a metal lever attached to a door, which you use to knock on the door.

knockout, knockouts **NOUN** ❶ a punch in boxing which knocks a boxer unconscious. ❷ a competition in which competitors are eliminated in each round until a winner is left.

knoll, knolls *[rhymes with **roll**]* **NOUN** LITERARY a gently sloping hill with a rounded top.

knot, knots, knotting, knotted **NOUN**

A B C D E F G H I J **K** L M N O P Q R S T U V W X Y Z

▷ SPELLING NOTE: *Beautiful Elephants Are Usually Tiny (beautiful)*

① a fastening made by looping a piece of string around itself and pulling the ends tight. **②** a small lump visible on the surface of a piece of wood. **③** A knot of people is a small group of them. **④** TECHNICAL a unit of speed used for ships and aircraft ▷ VERB **⑤** If you knot a piece of string, you tie a knot in it.

know, knows, knowing, knew, known VERB **①** If you know a fact, you have it in your mind and you do not need to learn it. **②** People you know are not strangers because you have met them and spoken to them ▷ INFORMAL PHRASE **③** If you are **in the know**, you are one of a small number of people who share a secret.

know-how NOUN Know-how is the ability to do something that is quite difficult or technical.

knowing ADJECTIVE A knowing look is one that shows that you know or understand something that other people do not. **knowingly** ADVERB

knowledge NOUN Knowledge is all the information and facts that you know.

knowledgeable ADJECTIVE Someone who is knowledgeable knows a lot about a subject • *She was very knowledgeable about Irish mythology.*

knuckle, knuckles NOUN Your knuckles are the joints at the end of your fingers where they join your hand.

koala, koalas NOUN an Australian animal with grey fur and small tufted ears. Koalas live in trees and eat eucalyptus leaves.

kohanga reo or **kohanga**, kohanga reo NOUN In New Zealand, an infant class where children are taught in Maori.
● WORD HISTORY: a Maori term meaning 'language nest'

kookaburra, kookaburras NOUN a large Australian kingfisher.
● WORD HISTORY: a native Australian word

koppie, koppies [Said *kop-i*]; also spelt **kopje** NOUN In South Africa, a koppie is a small hill with no other hills around it.

Koran or **Qur'an** [Said kaw-*rahn*] NOUN The Koran is the holy book of Islam.
● WORD HISTORY: from Arabic *kara'a* meaning 'to read'

Korean, Koreans [Said kor-*ree*-an] ADJECTIVE **①** relating or belonging to Korea ▷ NOUN **②** someone who comes from Korea. **③** Korean is the main language spoken in Korea.

kosher [Said *koh*-sher] ADJECTIVE Kosher food has been specially prepared to be eaten according to Jewish law.
● WORD HISTORY: from Hebrew *kasher* meaning 'right' or 'proper'

kowhai, kowhai or kowhais [Said ko-*wigh*] NOUN a small New Zealand tree with clusters of yellow flowers.

kraal, kraals NOUN In South Africa, a kraal is a village in which a tribe lives and which is often surrounded by a fence.

kudu, kudus; also spelt **koodoo** NOUN a large African antelope with curled horns.

▷ SPELLING NOTE: *Betty Eats Cakes And Uses Seven Eggs (because)*

kumara or **kumera**, kumara or kumaras *[Said koo-mih-rah]* **NOUN** In New Zealand English, a kumara is a sweet potato, a vegetable with yellow or orange flesh.

kumquat, kumquats **NOUN** a very small round or oval citrus fruit.

kung fu *[Said kung foo]* **NOUN** Kung fu is a Chinese style of fighting which involves using your hands and feet.

kura kaupapa Maori, kura kaupapa Maori *[Said koo-ra kow-puh-puh]* **NOUN** In New Zealand, a primary school where teaching is based on Maori language and culture.

Kurd, Kurds **NOUN** The Kurds are a group of people who live mainly in eastern Turkey, northern Iraq, and western Iran.

Kurdish ADJECTIVE ❶ belonging or relating to the Kurds • *Kurdish culture.* ▷ **NOUN** ❷ Kurdish is the language spoken by the Kurds.

kwashiorkor NOUN (SCIENCE) severe malnutrition in very young children, caused by lack of protein.
● **WORD HISTORY:** from a
● native word in Ghana

A B C D E F G H I J K L M N O P Q R S T U V W X Y Z

▷ SPELLING NOTE: *there's a rAKE in the brAKEs (brake)*

l an abbreviation for 'litres'.

lab, labs **NOUN** INFORMAL a laboratory.

label, labels, labelling, labelled **NOUN** ❶ a piece of paper or plastic attached to something as an identification ▷ **VERB** ❷ If you label something, you put a label on it.

laboratory, laboratories **NOUN** (SCIENCE) a place where scientific experiments are carried out.

laborious **ADJECTIVE** needing a lot of effort or time. **laboriously** **ADVERB**

Labor Party **NOUN** In Australia, the Labor Party is one of the major political parties.

labour, labours, labouring, laboured **NOUN** ❶ Labour is hard work. ❷ The workforce of a country or industry is sometimes called its labour • *unskilled labour.* ❸ In Britain, the Labour Party is a political party that believes that the government should provide free health care and education for everyone. ❹ New Zealand, the Labour Party is one of the main political parties. ❺ Labour is also the last stage of pregnancy when a woman gives birth to a baby ▷ **VERB** ❻ OLD-FASHIONED To labour means to work hard. **labourer** **NOUN**
● **SIMILAR WORDS:** ❶ toil, work
● ❻ slave, toil, work

labrador, labradors **NOUN** a large dog with short black or golden hair.

labyrinth, labyrinths [*Said lab-er-inth*] **NOUN** a complicated series of paths or passages.

lace, laces, lacing, laced **NOUN** ❶ Lace is a very fine decorated cloth made with a lot of holes in it. ❷ Laces are cords with which you fasten your shoes ▷ **VERB** ❸ When you lace up your shoes, you tie a bow in the laces. ❹ To lace someone's food or drink means to put a small amount of alcohol, a drug, or poison in it • *coffee laced with vodka.* **lacy** **ADJECTIVE**

lack, lacks, lacking, lacked **NOUN** ❶ If there is a lack of something, it is not present when or where it is needed ▷ **VERB** ❷ If something is lacking, it is not present when or where it is needed. ❸ If someone or something is lacking something, they do not have it or do not have enough of it • *Francis was lacking in stamina.*
● **SIMILAR WORDS:** ❶ absence,
● scarcity, shortage

lacklustre [*Said lak-luss-ter*] **ADJECTIVE** not interesting or exciting.

laconic [*Said lak-kon-ik*] **ADJECTIVE** using very few words.
● **WORD HISTORY:** from Greek
● *Lakonikas* meaning 'Spartan'. The
● Spartans were famous for using few
● words

▷ SPELLING NOTE: you'll brEAK that Electrical Aerial, Kitty (br**eak**)

A
B
C
D
E
F
G
H
I
J
K
L
M
N
O
P
Q
R
S
T
U
V
W
X
Y
Z

lacquer, lacquers *[Said **lak**-er]*
NOUN Lacquer is thin, clear paint that
you put on wood to protect it and
make it shiny.

lacrosse NOUN Lacrosse is an
outdoor ball game in which two teams
try to score goals using long sticks
with nets on the end of them.
● **WORD HISTORY:** from Canadian
● French *la crosse* meaning 'the
● hooked stick'

lactic acid NOUN (SCIENCE) Lactic
acid is an acid that is found in sour
milk and is also produced in your
muscles after you have done a lot of
exercise.

lactose NOUN (SCIENCE) Lactose is
the natural sugar that occurs in milk.
It is sometimes used for making
medicines and baby food.

lad, lads **NOUN** a boy or young man.

ladder, ladders, laddering, laddered
NOUN ❶ a wooden or metal frame
used for climbing which consists of
horizontal steps fixed to two vertical
poles. ❷ If your stockings or tights
have a ladder in them, they have a
vertical, ladder-like tear in them
▷ **VERB** ❸ If you ladder your
stockings or tights, you get a ladder in
them.

laden *[Said **lay**-den]* **ADJECTIVE** To
be laden with something means to be
carrying a lot of it • *bushes laden with
ripe fruit.*

ladle, ladles, ladling, ladled **NOUN**
❶ a long-handled spoon with a deep,
round bowl, which you use to serve
soup ▷ **VERB** ❷ If you ladle out food,
you serve it with a ladle.

lady, ladies **NOUN** ❶ a woman,
especially one who is considered to be
well mannered. ❷ Lady is a title used
in front of the name of a woman from
the nobility, such as a lord's wife.

ladybird, ladybirds **NOUN** a small
flying beetle with a round red body
patterned with black spots.

lady-in-waiting, ladies-in-waiting
NOUN a woman who acts as
companion to a queen or princess.

ladylike ADJECTIVE behaving in a
polite and socially correct way.

Ladyship, Ladyships **NOUN** You
address a woman who has the title
'Lady' as 'Your Ladyship'.

lag, lags, lagging, lagged **VERB** ❶ To
lag behind is to make slower progress
than other people. ❷ To lag pipes is
to wrap cloth round them to stop the
water inside freezing in cold weather.

lager, lagers **NOUN** Lager is
light-coloured beer.
● **WORD HISTORY:** from German
● *Lagerbier* meaning 'beer for storing'

lagoon, lagoons **NOUN** an area of
water separated from the sea by reefs
or sand.

laid the past tense and past participle
of **lay**.

lain the past participle of some
meanings of **lie**.

lair, lairs **NOUN** a place where a wild
animal lives.

laird, lairds *[rhymes with **dared**]*
NOUN a landowner in Scotland.

lake, lakes **NOUN** an area of fresh
water surrounded by land.

▷ SPELLING NOTE: *I always visit my FRIend on a FRIday (**Fri**day)*

lama, lamas NOUN a Buddhist priest or monk.

lamb, lambs NOUN ❶ a young sheep. ❷ Lamb is the meat from a lamb.

lame, lamer, lamest ADJECTIVE ❶ Someone who is lame has an injured leg and cannot walk easily. ❷ A lame excuse is not very convincing. **lamely** ADVERB **lameness** NOUN
● SIMILAR WORDS: ❷ feeble,
● flimsy, weak

lament, laments, lamenting, lamented VERB ❶ To lament something means to express sorrow or regret about it ▷ NOUN ❷ an expression of sorrow or regret. ❸ a song or poem expressing grief at someone's death.

lamentable ADJECTIVE disappointing and regrettable.

laminated ADJECTIVE consisting of several thin sheets or layers stuck together • *laminated glass.*

lamp, lamps NOUN a device that produces light.

lamppost, lampposts NOUN a tall column in a street, with a lamp at the top.

lampshade, lampshades NOUN a decorative covering over an electric light bulb which prevents the bulb giving out too harsh a light.

lance, lances, lancing, lanced VERB ❶ To lance a boil or abscess means to stick a sharp instrument into it in order to release the fluid ▷ NOUN ❷ a long spear that used to be used by soldiers on horseback.

land, lands, landing, landed NOUN ❶ Land is an area of ground. ❷ Land is also the part of the earth that is not covered by water. ❸ a country • *our native land.* ▷ VERB ❹ When a plane lands, it arrives back on the ground after a flight. ❺ If you land something you have been trying to get, you succeed in getting it • *She eventually landed a job with a local radio station.* ❻ To land a fish means to catch it while fishing. ❼ If you land someone with something unpleasant, you cause them to have to deal with it.

landing, landings NOUN ❶ a flat area in a building at the top of a flight of stairs. ❷ The landing of an aeroplane is its arrival back on the ground after a flight • *a smooth landing.*

landlady, landladies NOUN a woman who owns a house or small hotel and who lets rooms to people.

landlord, landlords NOUN a man who owns a house or small hotel and who lets rooms to people.

landmark, landmarks NOUN ❶ a noticeable feature in a landscape, which you can use to check your position. ❷ an important stage in the development of something • *The play is a landmark in Japanese theatre.*

landowner, landowners NOUN someone who owns land, especially a large area of the countryside.

landscape, landscapes NOUN ❶ (GEOGRAPHY) The landscape is the view over an area of open land. ❷ (ART) a painting of the countryside.

landslide, landslides NOUN ❶ a large amount of loose earth and rocks falling down a mountain side. ❷ a victory in an election won by a large number of votes.

lane, lanes NOUN ❶ a narrow road, especially in the country. ❷ one of the strips on a road marked with lines to guide drivers.

language, languages NOUN ❶ the system of words that the people of a country use to communicate with each other. ❷ Your language is the style in which you express yourself • *His language is often obscure.* ❸ Language is the study of the words and grammar of a particular language.
● SIMILAR WORDS: ❷ expression,
● speech

languid [*Said* lang-gwid] ADJECTIVE slow and lacking energy. **languidly** ADVERB

languish, languishes, languishing, languished VERB If you languish, you endure an unpleasant situation for a long time • *Many languished in poverty.*

lanky, lankier, lankiest ADJECTIVE Someone who is lanky is tall and thin and moves rather awkwardly.

lantana, lantanas NOUN In Australia, a shrub with yellow or orange flowers which is regarded as a pest in some areas.

lantern, lanterns NOUN a lamp in a metal frame with glass sides.

lap, laps, lapping, lapped NOUN ❶ Your lap is the flat area formed by your thighs when you are sitting down. ❷ one circuit of a running track or racecourse ▷ VERB ❸ When an animal laps up liquid, it drinks using its tongue to get the liquid into

its mouth. ❹ If you lap someone in a race, you overtake them when they are still on the previous lap. ❺ When water laps against something, it gently moves against it in little waves.

lapel, lapels [*Said* lap-**el**] NOUN a flap which is joined on to the collar of a jacket or coat.

lapse, lapses, lapsing, lapsed NOUN ❶ a moment of bad behaviour by someone who usually behaves well. ❷ a slight mistake. ❸ a period of time between two events ▷ VERB ❹ If you lapse into a different way of behaving, you start behaving that way • *The offenders lapsed into a sullen silence.* ❺ If a legal document or contract lapses, it is not renewed on the date when it expires.

lard NOUN Lard is fat from a pig, used in cooking.

larder, larders NOUN a room in which you store food, often next to a kitchen.

large, larger, largest ADJECTIVE ❶ Someone or something that is large is much bigger than average ▷ PHRASE ❷ If a prisoner is **at large**, he or she has escaped from prison.

largely ADVERB to a great extent • *The public are largely unaware of this.*

lark, larks NOUN ❶ a small brown bird with a distinctive song. ❷ If you do something for a lark, you do it in a high-spirited or mischievous way for fun.

larrikin, larrikins NOUN INFORMAL In Australian and New Zealand English, a young person who behaves in a wild or irresponsible way.

larva, larvae **NOUN** an insect, which looks like a short, fat worm, at the stage before it becomes an adult.

laryngitis [Said lar-in-*jie*-tiss] **NOUN** Laryngitis is an infection of the throat which causes you to lose your voice.

larynx, larynxes or larynges **NOUN** the part of your throat containing the vocal cords, through which air passes between your nose and lungs.

lasagne [Said laz-*zan*-ya] **NOUN** Lasagne is an Italian dish made with wide flat sheets of pasta, meat, and cheese sauce.
  ● **WORD HISTORY:** from Latin
  ● *lasanum* meaning 'cooking pot'

laser, lasers **NOUN** a machine that produces a powerful concentrated beam of light which is used to cut very hard materials and in some kinds of surgery.
  ● **WORD HISTORY:** from the first
  ● letters of 'Light Amplification by
  ● Stimulated Emission of Radiation'

lash, lashes, lashing, lashed **NOUN**
❶ Your lashes are the hairs growing on the edge of your eyelids. **❷** a strip of leather at the end of a whip.
❸ Lashes are blows struck with a whip.
lash out VERB To lash out at someone means to criticize them severely.

lass, lasses **NOUN** a girl or young woman.

lasso, lassoes or lassos, lassoing, lassoed [Said las-*soo*] **NOUN** **❶** a length of rope with a noose at one end, used by cowboys to catch cattle and horses ▷ **VERB** **❷** To lasso an animal means to catch it by throwing the noose of a lasso around its neck.

last, lasts, lasting, lasted **ADJECTIVE**
❶ The last thing or event is the most recent one • *last year.* **❷** The last thing that remains is the only one left after all the others have gone • *The last family left in 1950.* ▷ **ADVERB**
❸ If you last did something on a particular occasion, you have not done it since then • *They last met in Rome.*
❹ The thing that happens last in a sequence of events is the final one • *He added the milk last.* ▷ **VERB** **❺** If something lasts, it continues to exist or happen • *Her speech lasted fifty minutes.* **❻** To last also means to remain in good condition • *The mixture will last for up to 2 weeks in the fridge.*
▷ **PHRASE** **❼** At last means after a long time. **lastly ADVERB**

last-ditch ADJECTIVE A last-ditch attempt to do something is a final attempt to succeed when everything else has failed.

latch, latches, latching, latched **NOUN** **❶** a simple door fastening consisting of a metal bar which falls into a hook. **❷** a type of door lock which locks automatically when you close the door and which has to be opened with a key ▷ **VERB**
❸ INFORMAL If you latch onto someone or something, you become attached to them.

late, later, latest **ADJECTIVE OR ADVERB** **❶** Something that happens late happens towards the end of a period of time • *the late evening* • *late in the morning.* **❷** If you arrive late, or do something late, you arrive or do it after the time you were expected to

a b c d e f g h i j k l m n o p q r s t u v w x y z

▷ SPELLING NOTE: have a plEce of plE (*piece*)

> **ADJECTIVE** ❸ A late event happens after the time when it usually takes place • *a late breakfast.* ❹ FORMAL Late means dead • *my late grandmother.*
● **SIMILAR WORDS:** ❷ belated,
● overdue, tardy

lately ADVERB Events that happened lately happened recently.

latent ADJECTIVE A latent quality is hidden at the moment, but may emerge in the future • *a latent talent for art.*

lateral ADJECTIVE relating to the sides of something, or moving in a sideways direction.

lathe, lathes NOUN a machine which holds and turns a piece of wood or metal against a tool to cut or shape it.

lather, lathers NOUN Lather is the foam that you get when you rub soap in water.

Latin, Latins NOUN ❶ Latin is the language of ancient Rome ▷ NOUN OR ADJECTIVE ❷ Latins are people who speak languages closely related to Latin, such as French, Italian, Spanish, and Portuguese.

Latin America NOUN Latin America consists of the countries in North, South, and Central America where Spanish or Portuguese is the main language. **Latin American** ADJECTIVE

latitude, latitudes NOUN
(GEOGRAPHY) The latitude of a place is its distance north or south of the equator measured in degrees.

latrine, latrines [Said lat-**reen**] NOUN a hole or trench in the ground used as a toilet at a camp.

latter ADJECTIVE OR NOUN ❶ You use 'latter' to refer to the second of two things that are mentioned • *They were eating sandwiches and cakes (the latter bought from Mrs Paul's bakery).*
▷ ADJECTIVE ❷ 'Latter' also describes the second or end part of something • *The latter part of his career.*
● **USAGE NOTE:** You use *latter* to talk
● about the second of two items. To
● talk about the last of three or more
● items you should use *last-named*

latterly ADVERB FORMAL Latterly means recently • *It's only latterly that this has become an issue.*

lattice, lattices NOUN a structure made of strips which cross over each other diagonally leaving holes in between.

laudable ADJECTIVE FORMAL deserving praise • *It is a laudable enough aim.*

laugh, laughs, laughing, laughed VERB ❶ When you laugh, you make a noise which shows that you are amused or happy ▷ NOUN ❷ the noise you make when you laugh. **laughter** NOUN

laughable ADJECTIVE quite absurd.

laughing stock NOUN someone who has been made to seem ridiculous.

launch, launches, launching, launched VERB ❶ To launch a ship means to send it into the water for the first time. ❷ To launch a rocket

> SPELLING NOTE: *plaice the fish has a glittering 'EYE' (i) (plaice)*

means to send it into space. ❸ When a company launches a new product, they have an advertising campaign to promote it as they start to sell it ▷ **NOUN** ❹ a motorboat.

launch pad, launch pads **NOUN** A launch pad, or a launching pad, is the place from which space rockets take off.

launder, launders, laundering, laundered **VERB** OLD-FASHIONED To launder clothes, sheets, or towels means to wash and iron them.

laundry, laundries **NOUN** ❶ a business that washes and irons clothes and sheets. ❷ Laundry is also the dirty clothes and sheets that are being washed, or are about to be washed.

laurel, laurels **NOUN** an evergreen tree with shiny leaves.

lava **NOUN** (GEOGRAPHY) Lava is the very hot liquid rock that comes shooting out of an erupting volcano, and becomes solid as it cools.

lavatory, lavatories **NOUN** a toilet.

lavender **NOUN** ❶ Lavender is a small bush with bluish-pink flowers that have a strong, pleasant scent ▷ **ADJECTIVE** ❷ bluish-pink.

lavish, lavishes, lavishing, lavished **ADJECTIVE** ❶ If you are lavish, you are very generous with your time, money, or gifts. ❷ A lavish amount is a large amount ▷ **VERB** ❸ If you lavish money or affection on someone, you give them a lot of it. **lavishly** **ADVERB**

law, laws **NOUN** ❶ The law is the system of rules developed by the government of a country, which regulate what people may and may not do and deals with people who break these rules. ❷ The law is also the profession of people such as lawyers, whose job involves the application of the laws of a country. ❸ one of the rules established by a government or a religion, which tells people what they may or may not do. ❹ a scientific fact which allows you to explain how things work in the physical world. **lawful** **ADJECTIVE** **lawfully** **ADVERB**

law-abiding **ADJECTIVE** obeying the law and not causing any trouble.

lawless **ADJECTIVE** having no regard for the law.

lawn, lawns **NOUN** an area of cultivated grass.

lawnmower, lawnmowers **NOUN** a machine for cutting grass.

lawsuit, lawsuits **NOUN** a civil court case between two people, as opposed to the police prosecuting someone for a criminal offence.

lawyer, lawyers **NOUN** a person who is qualified in law, and whose job is to advise people about the law and represent them in court.

lax, laxer, laxest **ADJECTIVE** careless and not keeping up the usual standards • *a lax accounting system.*

laxative, laxatives **NOUN** something that you eat or drink to stop you being constipated.

lay, lays, laying, laid **VERB** ❶ When you lay something somewhere, you put it down so that it lies there. ❷ If you lay something, you arrange it or

a b c d e f g h i j k l m n o p q r s t u v w x y z

▷ SPELLING NOTE: *I went to see (C) the doctor's new practiCe (practice)*

set it out. ❸ If you lay the table, you put cutlery on the table ready for a meal. ❹ When a bird lays an egg, it produces the egg out of its body. ❺ If you lay a trap for someone, you create a situation in which you will be able to catch them out. ❻ If you lay emphasis on something, you refer to it in a way that shows you think it is very important. ❼ If you lay odds on something, you bet that it will happen ▷ **ADJECTIVE** ❽ You use 'lay' to describe people who are involved with a Christian church but are not members of the clergy • *a lay preacher.* ❾ Lay is the past tense of some senses of **lie**.

lay off VERB ❶ When workers are laid off, their employers tell them not to come to work for a while because there is a shortage of work.
❷ INFORMAL If you tell someone to lay off, you want them to stop doing something annoying.

lay on VERB If you lay on a meal or entertainment, you provide it.
● USAGE NOTE: People often get confused about *lay* and *lie*. The verb *lay* takes an object: *lay the table please; the Queen laid a wreath.* The verb *lie* does not take an object: *the book was lying on the table; I'm going to lie down*

lay-by, lay-bys **NOUN** ❶ an area by the side of a main road where motorists can stop for a short while. ❷ In Australia and New Zealand, lay-by is a system where you pay a deposit on an item in a shop so that it will be kept for you until you pay the rest of the price.

layer, layers **NOUN** a single thickness of something • *layers of clothing.*

layman, laymen **NOUN** ❶ someone who does not have specialized knowledge of a subject • *a layman's guide to computers.* ❷ someone who belongs to the church but is not a member of the clergy.

layout, layouts **NOUN** The layout of something is the pattern in which it is arranged.

laze, lazes, lazing, lazed **VERB** If you laze, you relax and do no work • *We spent a few days lazing around the pool.*

lazy, lazier, laziest **ADJECTIVE** idle and unwilling to work. **lazily ADVERB laziness NOUN**
● SIMILAR WORDS: idle, indolent, slothful

lb an abbreviation for 'pounds' • *3lb of sugar.*

lbw In cricket lbw is an abbreviation for 'leg before wicket', which is a way of dismissing a batsman when his legs prevent the ball from hitting the wicket.

leach, leaches, leaching, leached **VERB** When minerals are leached from rocks, they are dissolved by water which filters through the rock.

lead, leads, leading, led *[rhymes with feed]* **VERB** ❶ If you lead someone somewhere, you go in front of them in order to show them the way. ❷ If one thing leads to another, it causes the second thing to happen. ❸ a person who leads a group of people is in charge of them ▷ **NOUN** ❹ a length of leather or chain attached to a dog's collar, so that the dog can be kept under control. ❺ If the police have a lead, they have a clue which might

help them to solve a crime.
● **SIMILAR WORDS:** ❶ conduct,
● escort, guide

lead *[rhymes with fed]* NOUN Lead is
a soft, grey, heavy metal.

leaden *[Said led-en]* ADJECTIVE
❶ dark grey • *a leaden sky.* ❷ heavy
and slow-moving.

leader, leaders NOUN ❶ someone
who is in charge of a country, an
organization, or a group of people.
❷ the person who is winning in a
competition or race. ❸ a newspaper
article that expresses the newspaper's
opinions.

leadership NOUN ❶ the group of
people in charge of an organization.
❷ Leadership is the ability to be a
good leader.

leading ADJECTIVE particularly
important, respected, or advanced.

leaf, leaves; leafs, leafing, leafed
NOUN ❶ the flat green growth on the
end of a twig or branch of a tree or
other plant ▷ VERB ❷ If you leaf
through a book, magazine, or
newspaper, you turn the pages over
quickly. **leafy** ADJECTIVE

leaflet, leaflets NOUN a piece of
paper with information or advertising
printed on it.

league, leagues *[Said leeg]* NOUN
❶ PE a group of countries, clubs, or
people who have joined together for a
particular purpose or because they
share a common interest • *the League
of Red Cross Societies* • *the Australian
Football League.* ❷ a unit of distance
used in former times, equal to about 3
miles.

leak, leaks, leaking, leaked VERB ❶ If
a pipe or container leaks, it has a hole
which lets gas or liquid escape. ❷ If
liquid or gas leaks, it escapes from a
pipe or container. ❸ If someone in an
organization leaks information, they
give the information to someone who
is not supposed to have it • *The letter
was leaked to the press.* ▷ NOUN ❹ If
a pipe or container has a leak, it has a
hole which lets gas or liquid escape.
❺ If there is a leak in an organization,
someone inside the organization is
giving information to people who are
not supposed to have it. **leaky**
ADJECTIVE

leakage, leakages NOUN an escape
of gas or liquid from a pipe or
container.

lean, leans, leaning, leant or leaned;
leaner, leanest VERB ❶ When you
lean in a particular direction, you bend
your body in that direction. ❷ When
you lean on something, you rest your
body against it for support. ❸ If you
lean on someone, you depend on
them. ❹ If you lean towards
particular ideas, you approve of them
and follow them • *parents who lean
towards strictness.* ▷ ADJECTIVE
❺ having little or no fat • *lean cuts of
meat.* ❻ A lean period is a time when
food or money is in short supply.

leap, leaps, leaping, leapt or leaped
VERB ❶ If you leap somewhere, you
jump over a long distance or high in
the air ▷ NOUN ❷ a jump over a long
distance or high in the air.

leap year, leap years NOUN a year,
occurring every four years, in which
there are 366 days.

learn, learns, learning, learnt or

a b c d e f g h i j k **l** m n o p q r s t u v w x y z

learned VERB ❶ When you learn something, you gain knowledge or a skill through studying or training. ❷ If you learn of something, you find out about it • *She had first learnt of the bomb attack that morning.* **learner** NOUN

● **SIMILAR WORDS:** ❷ discover, find out, hear

learned [*Said* ler-nid] ADJECTIVE A learned person has a lot of knowledge gained from years of study.

learning NOUN Learning is knowledge that has been acquired through serious study.

lease, leases, leasing, leased NOUN ❶ an agreement which allows someone to use a house or flat in return for rent ▷ VERB ❷ To lease property to someone means to allow them to use it in return for rent.

leash, leashes NOUN a length of leather or chain attached to a dog's collar so that the dog can be controlled.

least NOUN ❶ The least is the smallest possible amount of something ▷ ADJECTIVE ❷ as small or as few as possible ▷ ADVERB ❸ Least is a superlative form of **little**. ▷ PHRASE ❹ You use **at least** to show that you are referring to the minimum amount of something, and that you think the true amount is greater • *At least 200 hundred people were injured.*

leather NOUN Leather is the tanned skin of some animals, used to make shoes and clothes. **leathery** ADJECTIVE

leave, leaves, leaving, left VERB ❶ When you leave a place, you go away from it. ❷ If you leave someone somewhere, they stay behind after you go away. ❸ If you leave a job or organization, you stop being part of it • *He left his job shortly after Christmas.* ❹ If someone leaves money or possessions to someone, they arrange for them to be given to them after their death. ❺ In subtraction, when you take one number from another, it leaves a third number ▷ NOUN ❻ a period of holiday or absence from a job.

● **SIMILAR WORDS:** ❶ depart, exit, go

Lebanese ADJECTIVE ❶ belonging or relating to Lebanon ▷ NOUN ❷ someone who comes from Lebanon.

lecherous ADJECTIVE constantly thinking about sex.

lectern, lecterns NOUN a sloping desk which people use to rest books or notes on.

lecture, lectures, lecturing, lectured NOUN ❶ a formal talk intended to teach people about a particular subject. ❷ a talk intended to tell someone off ▷ VERB ❸ Someone who lectures teaches in a college or university.

lecturer, lecturers NOUN a teacher in a college or university.

led the past tense and past participle of **lead**.

ledge, ledges NOUN a narrow shelf on the side of a cliff or rock face, or on the outside of a building, directly under a window. • *She peered over the ledge.*

▷ SPELLING NOTE: *LEarn the principLEs (principle)*

ledger, ledgers **NOUN** a book in which accounts are kept.

lee NOUN ❶ the sheltered side of a place • *the lee of the mountain.* ▷ **ADJECTIVE** ❷ the side of a ship away from the wind.

leech, leeches **NOUN** a small worm that lives in water and feeds by sucking the blood from other animals.

leek, leeks **NOUN** a long vegetable of the onion family, which is white at one end and has green leaves at the other.

leer, leers, leering, leered **VERB** ❶ To leer at someone means to smile at them in an unpleasant or sexually suggestive way ▷ **NOUN** ❷ an unpleasant or sexually suggestive smile.

leeward NOUN ❶ (GEOGRAPHY) an area or direction that is sheltered from the wind ▷ **ADJECTIVE OR ADVERB** ❷ towards or in an area sheltered from the wind • *the leeward side of a boat.*

leeway NOUN If something gives you some leeway, it allows you more flexibility in your plans, for example by giving you time to finish an activity.

left NOUN ❶ The left is one of two sides of something. For example, on a page, English writing begins on the left. ❷ People and political groups who hold socialist or communist views are referred to as the Left. ❸ Left is the past tense and past participle of leave. ▷ **ADJECTIVE OR ADVERB** ❹ Left means on or towards the left side of something • *Turn left down Govan Road.*

left-handed ADJECTIVE OR

ADVERB Someone who is left-handed does things such as writing with their left hand.

leftist, leftists **NOUN OR ADJECTIVE** someone who holds left-wing political views.

leftovers PLURAL NOUN the bits of food which have not been eaten at the end of the meal.

left-wing ADJECTIVE believing more strongly in socialism, or less strongly in capitalism or conservatism, than other members of the same party or group. **left-winger NOUN**

leg, legs **NOUN** ❶ Your legs are the two limbs which stretch from your hips to your feet. ❷ The legs of a pair of trousers are the parts that cover your legs. ❸ The legs of an object such as a table are the parts which rest on the floor and support the object's weight. ❹ A leg of a journey is one part of it. ❺ one of two matches played between two sports teams • *He will miss the second leg of their UEFA Cup tie.*

legacy, legacies **NOUN** ❶ property or money that someone gets in the will of a person who has died. ❷ something that exists as a result of a previous event or time • *the legacy of a Catholic upbringing.*
● **SIMILAR WORDS:** ❶ bequest, inheritance

legal ADJECTIVE ❶ relating to the law • *the Dutch legal system.* ❷ allowed by the law • *The strike was perfectly legal.* **legally ADVERB**

legal aid NOUN Legal aid is a system which provides the services of a lawyer free, or very cheaply, to people who cannot afford the full fees.

legality NOUN The legality of an action means whether or not it is allowed by the law • *They challenged the legality of the scheme.*

legalize, legalizes, legalizing, legalized; *also spelt* **legalise** VERB To legalize something that is illegal means to change the law so that it becomes legal. **legalization** NOUN

legend, legends NOUN ❶ an old story which was once believed to be true, but which is probably untrue. ❷ If you refer to someone or something as a legend, you mean they are very famous • *His career has become a legend.* **legendary** ADJECTIVE

leggings PLURAL NOUN ❶ Leggings are very close-fitting trousers made of stretch material, worn mainly by young women. ❷ Leggings are also a waterproof covering worn over ordinary trousers to protect them.

legible ADJECTIVE Writing that is legible is clear enough to be read.

legion, legions NOUN ❶ In ancient Rome, a legion was a military unit of between 3000 and 6000 soldiers. ❷ a large military force • *the French Foreign Legion.* ❸ Legions of people are large numbers of them.

legislate, legislates, legislating, legislated VERB FORMAL When a government legislates, it creates new laws.

legislation NOUN Legislation is a law or set of laws created by a government.

legislative ADJECTIVE relating to the making of new laws • *a legislative council.*

legislator, legislators NOUN FORMAL a person involved in making or passing laws.

legislature NOUN FORMAL the parliament in a country, which is responsible for making new laws.

legitimate [Said lij-**it**-tim-it] ADJECTIVE Something that is legitimate is reasonable or acceptable according to existing laws or standards • *a legitimate charge for parking the car.* **legitimacy** NOUN **legitimately** ADVERB

leisure [rhymes with **measure**] NOUN ❶ Leisure is time during which you do not have to work, and can do what you enjoy doing ▷ PHRASES ❷ If you do something **at leisure**, or **at your leisure**, you do it at a convenient time.

leisurely ADJECTIVE OR ADVERB A leisurely action is done in an unhurried and calm way.

lekker ADJECTIVE SLANG ❶ In South African English, lekker means pleasant. ❷ In South African English, lekker can also mean tasty.

lemming, lemmings NOUN a small rodent which lives in cold, northern countries. Lemmings were believed in the past to jump off cliffs to their death in large numbers.

lemon, lemons NOUN ❶ a yellow citrus fruit with a sour taste ▷ ADJECTIVE ❷ pale yellow.

lemonade NOUN a sweet, fizzy drink made from lemons, water, and sugar • *a bottle of lemonade.*

lend, lends, lending, lent **VERB** ❶ If you lend someone something, you give it to them for a period of time and then they give it back to you. ❷ If a bank lends money, it gives the money to someone and the money has to be repaid in the future, usually with interest ▷ **PHRASE** ❸ If you **lend someone a hand**, you help them. **lender NOUN**

length, lengths **NOUN** ❶ The length of something is the horizontal distance from one end to the other. ❷ The length of an event or activity is the amount of time it lasts for. ❸ The length of something is also the fact that it is long rather than short • *Despite its length, it is a rewarding read.* ❹ a long piece of something.

lengthen, lengthens, lengthening, lengthened **VERB** To lengthen something means to make it longer.
● **SIMILAR WORDS:** elongate,
● extend, prolong

lengthways or **lengthwise ADVERB** If you measure something lengthways, you measure the horizontal distance from one end to the other.

lengthy, lengthier, lengthiest **ADJECTIVE** Something that is lengthy lasts for a long time.

lenient ADJECTIVE If someone in authority is lenient, they are less severe than expected. **leniently ADVERB leniency NOUN**

lens, lenses **NOUN** ❶ a curved piece of glass designed to focus light in a certain way, for example in a camera, telescope, or pair of glasses. ❷ The

lens in your eye is the part behind the iris, which focuses light.

lent ❶ the past tense and past participle of **lend**. **NOUN** ❷ RE Lent is the period of forty days leading up to Easter, during which Christians give up something they enjoy.

lentil, lentils **NOUN** Lentils are small dried red or brown seeds which are cooked and eaten in soups and curries.

Leo NOUN Leo is the fifth sign of the zodiac, represented by a lion. People born between July 23rd and August 22nd are born under this sign.

leopard, leopards **NOUN** a wild Asian or African big cat, with yellow fur and black or brown spots.

leotard, leotards *[Said lee-eh-tard]* **NOUN** a tight-fitting costume covering the body and legs, which is worn for dancing or exercise.

leper, lepers **NOUN** someone who has leprosy.
● **WORD HISTORY:** from Greek
● *lepros* meaning 'scaly'

leprosy NOUN Leprosy is an infectious disease which attacks the skin and nerves, and which can lead to fingers or toes dropping off.

lesbian, lesbians **NOUN** a homosexual woman. **lesbianism NOUN**

lesion, lesions *[Said lee-shen]* **NOUN** a wound or injury.

less ADJECTIVE OR ADVERB ❶ Less means a smaller amount, or not as much in quality • *They left less than three weeks ago* • *She had become less*

a
b
c
d
e
f
g
h
i
j
k
l
m
n
o
p
q
r
s
t
u
v
w
x
y
z

▷ SPELLING NOTE: *Rhythmical Hounds Yap To Heavy Music (rhythm)*

frightened of him now. ❷ Less is a comparative form of **little**.
▷ **PREPOSITION** ❸ You use 'less' to show that you are subtracting one number from another • *Eight less two leaves six.*
● **USAGE NOTE:** You use *less* to talk about things that can't be counted:*vless time.* When you are talking about amounts that can be counted you should use *fewer*

-less **SUFFIX** '-less' means without • *hopeless* • *fearless.*

lessen, lessens, lessening, lessened **VERB** If something lessens, it is reduced in amount, size, or quality.
● **SIMILAR WORDS:** decrease, diminish, reduce

lesser **ADJECTIVE** smaller in importance or amount than something else.

lesson, lessons **NOUN** ❶ a fixed period of time during which a class of pupils is taught by a teacher. ❷ an experience that makes you understand something important which you had not realized before.

lest **CONJUNCTION** OLD-FASHIONED as a precaution in case something unpleasant or unwanted happens • *I was afraid to open the door lest he should follow me.*

let, lets, letting, let **VERB** ❶ If you let someone do something, you allow them to do it. ❷ If someone lets a house or flat that they own, they rent it out. ❸ You can say 'let's' or 'let us' when you want to suggest doing something with someone else • *Let's go.* ❹ If you let yourself in for something, you agree to do it

although you do not really want to.
let off **VERB** ❶ If someone in authority lets you off, they do not punish you for something you have done wrong. ❷ If you let off a firework or explosive, you light it or detonate it.

lethal *[Said lee-thal]* **ADJECTIVE** able to kill someone • *a lethal weapon.*

lethargic *[Said lith-ar-jik]* **ADJECTIVE** If you feel lethargic, you have no energy or enthusiasm.

lethargy *[Said leth-ar-jee]* **NOUN** Lethargy is a lack of energy and enthusiasm.

letter, letters **NOUN** ❶ Letters are written symbols which go together to make words. ❷ a piece of writing addressed to someone, and usually sent through the post.

letter box, letter boxes **NOUN** ❶ an oblong gap in the front door of a house or flat, through which letters are delivered. ❷ a large metal container in the street, where you post letters.

lettering **NOUN** Lettering is writing, especially when you are describing the type of letters used • *bold lettering.*

lettuce, lettuces **NOUN** a vegetable with large green leaves eaten raw in salad.

leukaemia or **leukemia** *[Said loo-kee-mee-a]* **NOUN** Leukaemia is a serious illness which affects the blood.

level, levels, levelling, levelled **ADJECTIVE** ❶ A surface that is level is smooth, flat, and parallel to the ground ▷ **VERB** ❷ To level a piece of land means to make it flat. ❸ If you level a criticism at someone, you say

or write something critical about them
▷ **ADVERB** ❹ If you draw level with someone, you get closer to them so that you are moving next to them
▷ **NOUN** ❺ a point on a scale which measures the amount, importance, or difficulty of something. ❻ The level of a liquid is the height it comes up to in a container.

level off or **level out VERB** If something levels off or levels out, it stops increasing or decreasing • *Profits are beginning to level off.*
● **SIMILAR WORDS:** ❺ grade,
● position, stage

level crossing, level crossings **NOUN** a place where road traffic is allowed to drive across a railway track.

level-headed ADJECTIVE Someone who is level-headed is sensible and calm in emergencies.

lever, levers **NOUN** ❶ a handle on a machine that you pull in order to make the machine work. ❷ a long bar that you wedge underneath a heavy object and press down on to make the object move.

leverage NOUN Leverage is knowledge or influence that you can use to make someone do something.

leveret, leverets **NOUN** a young hare.

levy, levies, levying, levied *[Said lev-ee]* **NOUN** ❶ FORMAL an amount of money that you pay in tax ❷ When a government levies a tax, it makes people pay the tax and organizes the collection of the money.

lewd, lewder, lewdest *[rhymes with rude]* **ADJECTIVE** sexually coarse and crude.

lexicography NOUN the profession of writing dictionaries.
lexicographer NOUN
● **WORD HISTORY:** from Greek *lexis*
● meaning 'word' and *graphein*
● meaning 'to write'

liability, liabilities **NOUN**
❶ Someone's liability is their responsibility for something they have done wrong. ❷ In business, a company's liabilities are its debts.
❸ INFORMAL If you describe someone as a liability, you mean that they cause a lot of problems or embarrassment.

liable ADJECTIVE ❶ If you say that something is liable to happen, you mean that you think it will probably happen. ❷ If you are liable for something you have done, you are legally responsible for it.
● **USAGE NOTE:** It used to be wrong
● to use *liable* to mean 'probable or
● likely', but that use is now
● considered correct

liaise, liaises, liaising, liaised *[Said lee-aze]* **VERB** To liaise with someone or an organization means to cooperate with them and keep them informed.

liaison, liaisons *[Said lee-aze-on]* **NOUN** Liaison is communication between two organizations or two sections of an organization.

liar, liars **NOUN** a person who tells lies.

libel, libels, libelling, libelled *[Said lie-bel]* **NOUN** ❶ Libel is something written about someone which is not true, and for which the writer can be made to pay damages in court
▷ **VERB** ❷ To libel someone means to write or say something untrue

▷ SPELLING NOTE: *On WEDNESday Wayne WED NESta (Wednesday)*

about them. **libellous** ADJECTIVE
● **WORD HISTORY:** from Latin
● *libellus* meaning 'little book'

liberal, liberals NOUN ❶ someone
who believes in political progress,
social welfare, and individual freedom
▷ ADJECTIVE ❷ Someone who is
liberal is tolerant of a wide range of
behaviour, standards, or opinions.
❸ To be liberal with something
means to be generous with it. ❹ A
liberal quantity of something is a large
amount of it. **liberally** ADVERB
liberalism NOUN

Liberal Democrat, Liberal
Democrats NOUN In Britain, a
member or supporter of the Liberal
Democrats, a political party that
believes that individuals should have
more rights and freedom.

liberate, liberates, liberating,
liberated VERB To liberate people
means to free them from prison or
from an unpleasant situation.
liberation NOUN **liberator** NOUN

liberty NOUN Liberty is the freedom
to choose how you want to live,
without government restrictions.

libido, libidos [Said lib-**bee**-doe]
NOUN Someone's libido is their
sexual drive.
● **WORD HISTORY:** from Latin *libido*
● meaning 'desire'

Libra NOUN Libra is the seventh sign
of the zodiac, represented by a pair of
scales. People born between
September 23rd and October 22nd are
born under this sign.

librarian, librarians NOUN
(LIBRARY) a person who works in, or is
in charge of, a library.

library, libraries NOUN ❶ a building
in which books are kept for people to
come and read or borrow. ❷ a
collection of books, records, or videos.

Libyan, Libyans ADJECTIVE
❶ belonging or relating to Libya
▷ NOUN ❷ someone who comes
from Libya.

lice the plural of **louse**.

licence, licences NOUN ❶ an
official document which entitles you
to carry out a particular activity, for
example to drive a car. ❷ Licence is
the freedom to do what you want,
especially when other people consider
that it is being used irresponsibly.
● **USAGE NOTE:** The noun *licence*
● ends in *ce*

license, licenses, licensing, licensed
VERB To license an activity means to
give official permission for it to be
carried out.
● **USAGE NOTE:** The verb *license*
● ends in *se*

lichen, lichens [Said **lie**-ken] NOUN
Lichen is a green, moss-like growth on
rocks or tree trunks.

lick, licks, licking, licked VERB ❶ If
you lick something, you move your
tongue over it ▷ NOUN ❷ the action
of licking.

lid, lids NOUN the top of a container,
which you open in order to reach what
is inside.

lie, lies, lying, lay, lain VERB ❶ To lie
somewhere means to rest there
horizontally. ❷ If you say where
something lies, you are describing
where it is • *The farm lies between two
valleys.*

▷ SPELLING NOTE: *I want to see (C) your licenCe (licence)*

● **USAGE NOTE:** The past tense of
● this verb *lie* is *lay*. Do not confuse it
● with the verb *lay* meaning 'put'

lie, lies, lying, lied **VERB ❶** To lie
means to say something that is not
true ▷ **NOUN ❷** something you say
which is not true.

lieu *[Said lyoo]* **PHRASE** If one thing
happens **in lieu** of another, it happens
instead of it.

lieutenant, lieutenants *[Said
lef-ten-ent]* **NOUN** a junior officer in
the army or navy.
● **WORD HISTORY:** from Old French
● *lieutenant* meaning literally 'holding
● a place'

life, lives **NOUN ❶** Life is the quality
of being able to grow and develop,
which is present in people, plants, and
animals. **❷** Your life is your existence
from the time you are born until the
time you die. **❸** The life of a machine
is the period of time for which it is
likely to work. **❹** If you refer to the life
in a place, you are talking about the
amount of activity there • *The town
was full of life.* **❺** If criminals are
sentenced to life, they are sent to
prison for the rest of their lives, or
until they are granted parole.

life assurance NOUN Life
assurance is an insurance which
provides a sum of money in the event
of the policy holder's death.

lifeblood NOUN The lifeblood of
something is the most essential part
of it.

lifeboat, lifeboats **NOUN ❶** a boat
kept on shore, which is sent out to
rescue people who are in danger at
sea. **❷** a small boat kept on a ship,

which is used if the ship starts to sink.

life expectancy, life expectancies
NOUN (GEOGRAPHY) Your life
expectancy is the number of years you
can expect to live.

lifeguard, lifeguards **NOUN** a
person whose job is to rescue people
who are in difficulty in the sea or in a
swimming pool.

life jacket, life jackets **NOUN** a
sleeveless inflatable jacket that keeps
you afloat in water.

lifeless ADJECTIVE ❶ Someone
who is lifeless is dead. **❷** If you
describe a place or person as lifeless,
you mean that they are dull.

lifelike ADJECTIVE A picture or
sculpture that is lifelike looks very real
or alive.

lifeline, lifelines **NOUN**
❶ something which helps you to
survive or helps an activity to
continue. **❷** a rope thrown to
someone who is in danger of
drowning.

lifelong ADJECTIVE existing
throughout someone's life • *He had a
lifelong interest in music.*

lifesaver, lifesavers **NOUN** In
Australia and New Zealand, a person
whose job is to rescue people who are
in difficulty in the sea.

life span, life spans **NOUN**
❶ Someone's life span is the length of
time during which they are alive.
❷ The life span of a product or
organization is the length of time it
exists or is useful.

lifetime, lifetimes **NOUN** Your

a b c d e f g h i j k l m n o p q r s t u v w x y z

▷ SPELLING NOTE: *The government licenSes Schnapps (licenses)*

lifetime is the period of time during which you are alive.

lift, lifts, lifting, lifted **VERB ❶** To lift something means to move it to a higher position. **❷** When fog or mist lifts, it clears away. **❸** To lift a ban on something means to remove it. **❹** INFORMAL To lift things means to steal them ▷ NOUN **❺** a machine like a large box which carries passengers from one floor to another in a building. **❻** If you give someone a lift, you drive them somewhere in a car or on a motorcycle.
● **SIMILAR WORDS: ❶** elevate,
● raise

ligament, ligaments **NOUN** a piece of tough tissue in your body which connects your bones.

light, lights, lighting, lighted or lit; lighter, lightest **NOUN ❶** Light is brightness from the sun, fire, or lamps, that enables you to see things. **❷** a lamp or other device that gives out brightness. **❸** If you give someone a light, you give them a match or lighter to light their cigarette ▷ ADJECTIVE **❹** A place that is light is bright because of the sun or the use of lamps. **❺** A light colour is pale. **❻** A light object does not weigh much. **❼** A light task is fairly easy. **❽** Light books or music are entertaining and are not intended to be serious ▷ VERB **❾** To light a place means to cause it to be filled with light. **❿** To light a fire means to make it start burning. **⓫** To light upon something means to find it by accident. **lightly** ADVERB **lightness** NOUN

lighten, lightens, lightening,

lightened **VERB ❶** When something lightens, it becomes less dark. **❷** To lighten a load means to make it less heavy.

lighter, lighters **NOUN** a device for lighting a cigarette or cigar.

light-headed ADJECTIVE If you feel light-headed, you feel slightly dizzy or drunk.

light-hearted ADJECTIVE Someone who is light-hearted is cheerful and has no worries.
● **SIMILAR WORDS:** blithe, carefree,
● happy-go-lucky

lighthouse, lighthouses **NOUN** a tower by the sea, which sends out a powerful light to guide ships and warn them of danger.

lighting NOUN **❶** The lighting in a room or building is the way that it is lit. **❷** (DRAMA) Lighting in the theatre or for a film is the special lights that are directed on the performers or scene.

lightning NOUN Lightning is the bright flashes of light in the sky which are produced by natural electricity during a thunder storm.

lightweight, lightweights **NOUN ❶** a boxer in one of the lighter weight groups ▷ ADJECTIVE **❷** Something that is lightweight does not weigh very much • *a lightweight jacket.*

light year, light years **NOUN** a unit of distance equal to the distance that light travels in a year.

likable or **likeable** ADJECTIVE Someone who is likable is very pleasant and friendly.

▷ SPELLING NOTE: *'i' before 'e' except after 'c'*

like, likes, liking, liked PREPOSITION ❶ If one thing is like another, it is similar to it ▷ NOUN ❷ 'The like' means other similar things of the sort just mentioned • *nappies, prams, cots, and the like.* ▷ PHRASE ❸ If you **feel like** something, you want to do it or have it • *I feel like a walk.* ▷ VERB ❹ If you like something or someone, you find them pleasant.

-like SUFFIX '-like' means resembling or similar to • *a balloonlike object.*

likelihood NOUN If you say that there is a likelihood that something will happen, you mean that you think it will probably happen.

likely, likelier, likeliest ADJECTIVE Something that is likely will probably happen or is probably true.

liken, likens, likening, likened VERB If you liken one thing to another, you say that they are similar.

likeness, likenesses NOUN If two things have a likeness to each other, they are similar in appearance.

likewise ADVERB Likewise means similarly • *She sat down and he did likewise.*

liking NOUN If you have a liking for someone or something, you like them.

lilac NOUN ❶ a shrub with large clusters of pink, white, or mauve flowers ▷ ADJECTIVE ❷ pale mauve.

lilt, lilts NOUN A lilt in someone's voice is a pleasant rising and falling sound in it. **lilting** ADJECTIVE

lily, lilies NOUN a plant with trumpet-shaped flowers of various colours.

limb, limbs NOUN ❶ Your limbs are your arms and legs. ❷ The limbs of a tree are its branches ▷ PHRASE ❸ If you have gone **out on a limb**, you have said or done something risky.

limber up, limbers up, limbering up, limbered up VERB If you limber up, you stretch your muscles before doing a sport.

limbo NOUN ❶ If you are in limbo, you are in an uncertain situation over which you feel you have no control. ❷ The limbo is a West Indian dance in which the dancer has to pass under a low bar while leaning backwards.
● **WORD HISTORY:** sense 1 is from
● Latin *in limbo* meaning 'on the
● border (of Hell)'

lime, limes NOUN ❶ a small, green citrus fruit, rather like a lemon. ❷ A lime tree is a large tree with pale green leaves. ❸ Lime is a chemical substance that is used in cement and as a fertilizer.

limelight NOUN If someone is in the limelight, they are getting a lot of attention.

limerick, limericks NOUN an amusing nonsense poem of five lines.

limestone NOUN Limestone is a white rock which is used for building and making cement.

limit, limits, limiting, limited NOUN ❶ a boundary or an extreme beyond which something cannot go • *the speed limit.* ▷ VERB ❷ To limit something means to prevent it from becoming bigger, spreading, or making progress • *He did all he could to limit the damage.*

a b c d e f g h i j k l m n o p q r s t u v w x y z

▷ SPELLING NOTE: *King IAn went to ParlIAment in a carrIAge for his marrIAge (-ia-)*

limitation, limitations NOUN
❶ The limitation of something is the reducing or controlling of it. ❷ If you talk about the limitations of a person or thing, you are talking about the limits of their abilities.

limited ADJECTIVE Something that is limited is rather small in amount or extent • *a limited number of bedrooms.*

limousine, limousines [Said *lim-o-zeen*] NOUN a large, luxurious car, usually driven by a chauffeur.

limp, limps, limping, limped; limper, limpest VERB ❶ If you limp, you walk unevenly because you have hurt your leg or foot ▷ NOUN ❷ an uneven way of walking ▷ ADJECTIVE ❸ Something that is limp is soft and floppy, and not stiff or firm • *a limp lettuce.*

limpet, limpets NOUN a shellfish with a pointed shell, that attaches itself very firmly to rocks.

line, lines, lining, lined NOUN ❶ a long, thin mark. ❷ a number of people or things positioned one behind the other. ❸ a route along which someone or something moves • *a railway line.* ❹ In a piece of writing, a line is a number of words together • *I often used to change my lines as an actor.* ❺ (MATHS) In maths, a line is the straight, one-dimensional space between two points. ❻ Someone's line of work is the kind of work they do. ❼ The line someone takes is the attitude they have towards something • *He took a hard line with terrorism.* ❽ In a shop or business, a line is a type of product • *That line has been discontinued.* ▷ VERB ❾ To line something means to cover its inside

surface or edge with something • *Cottages lined the edge of the harbour.*

line up VERB ❶ When people line up, they stand in a line. ❷ When you line something up, you arrange it for a special occasion • *A tour is being lined up for July.*

lineage, lineages [Said *lin-ee-ij*] NOUN Someone's lineage is all the people from whom they are directly descended.

linear [Said *lin-ee-ar*] ADJECTIVE arranged in a line or in a strict sequence, or happening at a constant rate.

line dancing NOUN a type of dancing performed by rows of people to country music.

linen NOUN (D & T) ❶ Linen is a type of cloth made from a plant called flax. ❷ Linen is also household goods made of cloth, such as sheets and tablecloths.

liner, liners NOUN a large passenger ship that makes long journeys.

linesman, linesmen NOUN an official at a sports match who watches the lines of the field or court and indicates when the ball goes outside them.

-ling SUFFIX '-ling' means 'small' • *duckling.*

linger, lingers, lingering, lingered VERB To linger means to remain for a long time • *Economic problems lingered in the background.*

lingerie [Said *lan-jer-ee*] NOUN Lingerie is women's nightclothes and underclothes • *Swimwear is on the second floor, next to lingerie.*

A
B
C
D
E
F
G
H
I
J
K
L
M
N
O
P
Q
R
S
T
U
V
W
X
Y
Z

▷ SPELLING NOTE: *an ELegant angEL (angel)*

lingo, lingoes **NOUN** INFORMAL a foreign language.

linguist, linguists **NOUN** (ENGLISH) someone who studies foreign languages or the way in which language works.

linguistic **ADJECTIVE** (ENGLISH) relating to language or to linguistics.

linguistics **NOUN** (ENGLISH) Linguistics is the study of language and of how it works.

lining, linings **NOUN** any material used to line the inside of something.

link, links, linking, linked **NOUN** ❶ a relationship or connection between two things • *the link between sunbathing and skin cancer.* ❷ a physical connection between two things or places • *a high-speed rail link between the cities.* ❸ one of the rings in a chain ▷ **VERB** ❹ To link people, places, or things means to join them together. **linkage NOUN**

lino **NOUN** Lino is the same as linoleum.

linoleum **NOUN** a floor covering with a shiny surface.

lint **NOUN** soft cloth made from linen, used to dress wounds.

lion, lions **NOUN** a large member of the cat family which comes from Africa. Lions have light brown fur, and the male has a long mane. A female lion is called a lioness.

lip, lips **NOUN** ❶ Your lips are the edges of your mouth. ❷ The lip of a jug is the slightly pointed part through which liquids are poured out.

lip-read, lip-reads, lip-reading,

lip-read **VERB** To lip-read means to watch someone's lips when they are talking in order to understand what they are saying. Deaf people often lip-read.

lipstick, lipsticks **NOUN** a coloured substance which women wear on their lips.

liqueur, liqueurs *[Said lik-yoor]* **NOUN** a strong sweet alcoholic drink, usually drunk after a meal.

liquid, liquids (SCIENCE) **NOUN** ❶ any substance which is not a solid or a gas, and which can be poured ▷ **ADJECTIVE** ❷ Something that is liquid is in the form of a liquid • *liquid nitrogen.* ❸ In commerce and finance a person's or company's liquid assets are the things that can be sold quickly to raise cash.

liquidate, liquidates, liquidating, liquidated **VERB** ❶ To liquidate a company means to close it down and to use its assets to pay off its debts. ❷ INFORMAL To liquidate a person means to murder them. **liquidation NOUN liquidator NOUN**

liquor **NOUN** Liquor is any strong alcoholic drink.

liquorice *[Said lik-ker-iss]* **NOUN** Liquorice is a root used to flavour sweets; also the sweets themselves.

lisp, lisps, lisping, lisped **NOUN** ❶ Someone who has a lisp pronounces the sounds 's' and 'z' like 'th' ▷ **VERB** ❷ To lisp means to speak with a lisp.

list, lists, listing, listed **NOUN** ❶ a set of words or items written one below the other ▷ **VERB** ❷ If you list a

a
b
c
d
e
f
g
h
i
j
k
l
m
n
o
p
q
r
s
t
u
v
w
x
y
z

▷ SPELLING NOTE: *LEt's measure the angLE (angle)*

A
B
C
D
E
F
G
H
I
J
K
L
M
N
O
P
Q
R
S
T
U
V
W
X
Y
Z

number of things, you make a list of them.

listen, listens, listening, listened **VERB** If you listen to something, you hear it and pay attention to it. **listener NOUN**

listless ADJECTIVE lacking energy and enthusiasm. **listlessly ADVERB**
● **WORD HISTORY:** from Old English *list* meaning 'desire'

lit a past tense and past participle of **light**.

litany, litanies **NOUN** ❶ a part of a church service in which the priest says or chants prayers and the people give responses. ❷ something, especially a list of things, that is repeated often or in a boring or insincere way • *a tedious litany of complaints.*

literacy NOUN Literacy is the ability to read and write. **literate ADJECTIVE**

literal ADJECTIVE (ENGLISH) ❶ The literal meaning of a word is its most basic meaning. ❷ A literal translation from a foreign language is one that has been translated exactly word for word. **literally ADVERB**
● **USAGE NOTE:** Be careful where
● you use *literally*. It can emphasize
● something without changing the
● meaning: *the house was literally only*
● *five minutes walk away.* However, it
● can make nonsense of some things:
● *he literally swept me off my feet.* This
● sentence is ridiculous unless *he*
● actually took a broom and swept
● the speaker over

literary ADJECTIVE (ENGLISH) connected with literature • *literary critics.*

literature NOUN (ENGLISH) ❶ Literature consists of novels, plays, and poetry. ❷ The literature on a subject is everything that has been written about it.

lithe, lither, lithest **ADJECTIVE** supple and graceful.

litmus NOUN In chemistry, litmus is a substance that turns red under acid and blue under alkali conditions.

litmus test, litmus tests **NOUN** something which is regarded as a simple and accurate test of a particular thing, such as a person's attitude to an issue • *The conflict was seen as a litmus test of Britain's will to remain a major power.*

litre, litres **NOUN** (MATHS) a unit of liquid volume equal to about 1.76 pints.

litter, litters, littering, littered **NOUN** ❶ Litter is rubbish in the street and other public places. ❷ Cat litter is a gravelly substance you put in a container where you want your cat to urinate and defecate. ❸ a number of baby animals born at the same time to the same mother ▷ **VERB** ❹ If things litter a place, they are scattered all over it.

little, less, lesser, least **ADJECTIVE** ❶ small in size or amount ▷ **NOUN** ❷ A little is a small amount or degree • *Would you like a little fruit juice?* ❸ Little also means not much • *He has little to say.* ▷ **ADVERB** ❹ to a small amount or degree • *a little afraid* • *She ate little.*

live, lives, living, lived **VERB** ❶ If you live in a place, that is where your home is. ❷ To live means to be alive. ❸ If something lives up to your

▷ SPELLING NOTE: A Rude Idiot Thought He Might Eat Toffee In Church (<u>arithmetic</u>)

expectations, it is as good as you thought it would be ▷ **ADJECTIVE OR ADVERB** ④ Live television or radio is broadcast while the event is taking place • *a live football match* • *The concert will go out live.* ▷ **ADJECTIVE** ⑤ Live animals or plants are alive, rather than dead or artificial • *a live spider.* ⑥ Something is live if it is directly connected to an electricity supply • *Careful – those wires are live.* ⑦ Live bullets or ammunition have not yet been exploded.
live down VERB If you cannot live down a mistake or failure, you cannot make people forget it.

livelihood, livelihoods **NOUN** Someone's livelihood is their job or the source of their income.

lively, livelier, liveliest **ADJECTIVE** full of life and enthusiasm • *lively conversation.* **liveliness NOUN**
● **SIMILAR WORDS:** brisk, energetic, ● vigorous

liven, livens, livening, livened **VERB** To liven things up means to make them more lively or interesting.

liver, livers **NOUN** ① Your liver is a large organ in your body which cleans your blood and helps digestion. ② Liver is also the liver of some animals, which may be cooked and eaten.
● **WORD HISTORY:** from Greek ● *liparos* meaning 'fat'

livestock NOUN Livestock is farm animals.

livid ADJECTIVE ① extremely angry. ② dark purple or bluish • *livid bruises.*

living ADJECTIVE ① If someone is living, they are alive • *her only living*

relative. ▷ **NOUN** ② The work you do for a living is the work you do in order to earn money to live.

living room, living rooms **NOUN** the room where people relax and entertain in their homes.

lizard, lizards **NOUN** a long, thin, reptile found in hot, dry countries.

llama, llamas **NOUN** a South American animal related to the camel.

load, loads, loading, loaded **NOUN** ① something being carried. ② INFORMAL Loads means a lot • *loads of work.* ▷ **VERB** ③ To load a vehicle or animal means to put a large number of things into it or onto it.

loaf, loaves; loafs, loafing, loafed **NOUN** ① a large piece of bread baked in a shape that can be cut into slices ▷ **VERB** ② To loaf around means to be lazy and not do any work.

loan, loans, loaning, loaned **NOUN** ① a sum of money that you borrow. ② the act of borrowing or lending something • *I am grateful to Jane for the loan of her book.* ▷ **VERB** ③ If you loan something to someone, you lend it to them.

loath *[rhymes with both]* **ADJECTIVE** If you are loath to do something, you are very unwilling to do it.
● **USAGE NOTE:** Do not confuse ● *loath* with *loathe*

loathe, loathes, loathing, loathed **VERB** To loathe someone or something means to feel strong dislike for them. **loathing NOUN loathsome ADJECTIVE**
● **USAGE NOTE:** Do not confuse ● *loathe* with *loath*

a
b
c
d
e
f
g
h
i
j
k
l
m
n
o
p
q
r
s
t
u
v
w
x
y
z

▷ SPELLING NOTE: *Beautiful Elephants Are Usually Tiny (*<u>beautiful</u>*)*

lob, lobs, lobbing, lobbed **VERB** ❶ If you lob something, you throw it high in the air ▷ **NOUN** ❷ In tennis, a lob is a stroke in which the player hits the ball high in the air.

lobby, lobbies, lobbying, lobbied **NOUN** ❶ The lobby in a building is the main entrance area with corridors and doors leading off it. ❷ a group of people trying to persuade an organization that something should be done • *the environmental lobby.* ▷ **VERB** ❸ To lobby an MP or an organization means to try to persuade them to do something, for example by writing them lots of letters.

lobe, lobes **NOUN** ❶ The lobe of your ear is the rounded soft part at the bottom. ❷ any rounded part of something • *the frontal lobe of the brain.*

lobotomy, lobotomies **NOUN** (SCIENCE) A lobotomy is an operation performed on the brain to treat severe mental disorders.

lobster, lobsters **NOUN** an edible shellfish with two front claws and eight legs.

local, locals **ADJECTIVE** ❶ Local means in, near, or belonging to the area in which you live • *the local newspaper.* ❷ A local anaesthetic numbs only one part of your body and does not send you to sleep ▷ **NOUN** ❸ The locals are the people who live in a particular area. ❹ INFORMAL Someone's local is the pub nearest their home • *Is this pub your local?*
locally ADVERB
● **SIMILAR WORDS:** ❶ provincial,
● regional

locality, localities **NOUN** an area of a country or city • *a large map of the locality.*

localized or **localised** **ADJECTIVE** existing or happening in only one place • *localized pain.*

locate, locates, locating, located **VERB** ❶ To locate someone or something means to find out where they are. ❷ If something is located in a place, it is in that place.

location, locations **NOUN** ❶ (GEOGRAPHY) a place, or the position of something. ❷ In South Africa, a location was a small town where only Black people or Coloured people were allowed to live ▷ **PHRASE** ❸ If a film is made **on location**, it is made away from a studio.
● **SIMILAR WORDS:** ❶ place,
● position

loch, lochs **NOUN** In Scottish English, a loch is a lake.

lock, locks, locking, locked **VERB** ❶ If you lock something, you close it and fasten it with a key. ❷ If something locks into place, it moves into place and becomes firmly fixed there ▷ **NOUN** ❸ a device on something which fastens it and prevents it from being opened except with a key. ❹ A lock on a canal is a place where the water level can be raised or lowered to allow boats to go between two parts of the canal which have different water levels. ❺ A lock of hair is a small bunch of hair.

locker, lockers **NOUN** a small cupboard for your personal belongings, for example in a changing room.

▷ SPELLING NOTE: *Betty Eats Cakes And Uses Seven Eggs (because)*

locket, lockets **NOUN** a piece of jewellery consisting of a small case which you can keep a photograph in, and which you wear on a chain round your neck.

locksmith, locksmiths **NOUN** a person who makes or mends locks.

locomotive, locomotives **NOUN** a railway engine.

locus, loci **NOUN** (MATHS) A locus is a set of points whose position satisfies a particular condition. For example, a circle is the locus of points in the plane at the same distance from a central point.

locust, locusts **NOUN** an insect like a large grasshopper, which travels in huge swarms and eats crops.

lodge, lodges, lodging, lodged **NOUN** ❶ a small house in the grounds of a large country house, or a small house used for holidays ▷ **VERB** ❷ If you lodge in someone else's house, you live there and pay them rent. ❸ If something lodges somewhere, it gets stuck there • *The bullet lodged in his pelvis.* ❹ If you lodge a complaint, you formally make it.

lodger, lodgers **NOUN** a person who lives in someone's house and pays rent.

lodgings **PLURAL NOUN** If you live in lodgings, you live in someone else's house and pay them rent.

loft, lofts **NOUN** the space immediately under the roof of a house, often used for storing things.

lofty, loftier, loftiest **ADJECTIVE** ❶ very high • *a lofty hall.* ❷ very noble and important • *lofty ideals.*

❸ proud and superior • *her lofty manner.*

log, logs, logging, logged **NOUN** ❶ a thick branch or piece of tree trunk which has fallen or been cut down. ❷ the captain's official record of everything that happens on board a ship ▷ **VERB** ❸ If you log something, you officially make a record of it, for example in a ship's log. ❹ To log into a computer system means to gain access to it, usually by giving your name and password. To log out means to finish using the system.

logarithm, logarithms **NOUN** (MATHS) In mathematics, every number has a logarithm to a particular base. Logarithms to the base 10 are arranged in tables to make calculations easier. For example, you can add or subtract the logarithms of two numbers instead of multiplying or dividing the numbers.

logic **NOUN** Logic is a way of reasoning involving a series of statements, each of which must be true if the statement before it is true.

logical **ADJECTIVE** ❶ A logical argument uses logic. ❷ A logical course of action or decision is sensible or reasonable in the circumstances • *the logical conclusion.* **logically ADVERB**

logistics **NOUN** FORMAL The logistics of a complicated undertaking is the skilful organization of it.

logo, logos *[Said **loh**-goh]* **NOUN** The logo of an organization is a special design that is put on all its products.
  ● **WORD HISTORY:** from Greek *logos*
  ● meaning 'word'

a
b
c
d
e
f
g
h
i
j
k
l
m
n
o
p
q
r
s
t
u
v
w
x
y
z

▷ SPELLING NOTE: *there's a rAKE in the brAKEs (brake)*

A
B
C
D
E
F
G
H
I
J
K
L
M
N
O
P
Q
R
S
T
U
V
W
X
Y
Z

-logy SUFFIX '-logy' is used to form words that refer to the study of something • *biology* • *geology*.

loin, loins NOUN ❶ OLD-FASHIONED Your loins are the front part of your body between your waist and your thighs, especially your sexual parts. ❷ Loin is a piece of meat from the back or sides of an animal • *loin of pork*.

loiter, loiters, loitering, loitered VERB To loiter means stand about idly with no real purpose.

loll, lolls, lolling, lolled VERB ❶ If you loll somewhere, you sit or lie there in an idle, relaxed way. ❷ If your head or tongue lolls, it hangs loosely.

lollipop, lollipops NOUN a hard sweet on the end of a stick.

lolly, lollies NOUN ❶ a lollipop. ❷ a piece of flavoured ice or ice cream on a stick. ❸ In Australian and New Zealand English, a sweet.

lolly scramble, lolly scrambles NOUN In New Zealand, a lolly scramble is a lot of sweets thrown on the ground for children to pick up.

lone ADJECTIVE A lone person or thing is the only one in a particular place • *a lone climber*.
● SIMILAR WORDS: single, solitary

lonely, lonelier, loneliest ADJECTIVE ❶ If you are lonely, you are unhappy because you are alone. ❷ A lonely place is an isolated one which very few people visit • *a lonely hillside*.
loneliness NOUN

loner, loners NOUN a person who likes to be alone.

lonesome ADJECTIVE lonely and sad.

long, longer, longest; longs, longing, longed ADJECTIVE ❶ continuing for a great amount of time • *There had been no rain for a long time*. ▷ ADJECTIVE ❷ great in length or distance • *a long dress* • *a long road*. ▷ ADVERB ❸ for a certain period of time • *How long will it last?* ❹ for an extensive period of time • *long into the following year*. ▷ PHRASES ❺ If something **no longer** happens, it does not happen any more. ❻ **Before long** means soon. ❼ If one thing is true **as long as** another thing is true, it is true only if the other thing is true ▷ VERB ❽ If you long for something, you want it very much.

longevity [Said lon-*jev*-it-ee] NOUN FORMAL Longevity is long life.

longhand NOUN If you write something in longhand, you do it in your own handwriting rather than using shorthand or a typewriter.

longing, longings NOUN a strong wish for something.

longitude, longitudes NOUN (GEOGRAPHY) The longitude of a place is its distance east or west of a line passing through Greenwich, measured in degrees.

long jump NOUN The long jump is an athletics event in which you jump as far as possible after taking a run.

long-range ADJECTIVE ❶ able to be used over a great distance • *long-range artillery*. ❷ extending a long way into the future • *a long-range weather forecast*.

▷ SPELLING NOTE: *you'll brEAK that Electrical Aerial, Kitty* (br**eak**)

long-sighted ADJECTIVE If you are long-sighted, you have difficulty seeing things that are close.

long-standing ADJECTIVE having existed for a long time • *a long-standing tradition.*

long-suffering ADJECTIVE very patient • *her long-suffering husband.*

long-term ADJECTIVE extending a long way into the future • *a long-term investment.*

long-winded ADJECTIVE long and boring • *a long-winded letter.*

loo, loos NOUN INFORMAL a toilet.

look, looks, looking, looked VERB ❶ If you look at something, you turn your eyes towards it so that you can see it. ❷ If you look at a subject or situation, you study it or judge it. ❸ If you look down on someone, you think that they are inferior to you. ❹ If you are looking forward to something, you want it to happen because you think you will enjoy it. ❺ If you look up to someone, you admire and respect them. ❻ If you describe the way that something or someone looks, you are describing the appearance of it or them ▷ NOUN ❼ If you have a look at something, you look at it. ❽ the way someone or something appears, especially the expression on a person's face. ❾ If you talk about someone's looks, you are talking about how attractive they are ▷ INTERJECTION ❿ You say 'look out' to warn someone of danger.

look after VERB If you look after someone or something, you take care of them.

look for VERB If you look for

someone or something, you try to find them.

look up VERB ❶ To look up information means to find it out in a book. ❷ If you look someone up, you go to see them after not having seen them for a long time. ❸ If a situation is looking up, it is improving.

● SIMILAR WORDS: ❶ gaze, glance, see, watch ❽ glance, glimpse, peek ❾ appearance, expression

lookalike, lookalikes NOUN a person who looks very like someone else • *an Elvis lookalike.*

lookout, lookouts NOUN ❶ someone who is watching for danger, or a place where they watch for danger ▷ PHRASE ❷ If you are **on the lookout** for something, you are watching for it or waiting expectantly for it.

loom, looms, looming, loomed NOUN ❶ a machine for weaving cloth ▷ VERB ❷ If something looms in front of you, it suddenly appears as a tall, unclear, and sometimes frightening shape. ❸ If a situation or event is looming, it is likely to happen soon and is rather worrying.

loony, loonies INFORMAL ADJECTIVE ❶ People or behaviour can be described as loony if they are mad or eccentric ▷ NOUN ❷ a mad or eccentric person.

loop, loops, looping, looped NOUN ❶ a curved or circular shape in something long such as a piece of string ▷ VERB ❷ If you loop rope or string around an object, you place it in a loop around the object.

loophole, loopholes NOUN a small

a b c d e f g h i j k l m n o p q r s t u v w x y z

mistake or omission in the law which allows you to do something that the law really intends that you should not do.

loose, looser, loosest **ADJECTIVE**
① If something is loose, it is not firmly held, fixed, or attached. **②** Loose clothes are rather large and do not fit closely ▷ **ADVERB** **③** To set animals loose means to set them free after they have been tied up or kept in a cage. **loosely ADVERB**
● **USAGE NOTE:** The adjective and
● adverb *loose* is spelt with two *o*s. Do
● not confuse it with the verb *lose*

loosen, loosens, loosening, loosened **VERB** To loosen something means to make it looser.

loot, loots, looting, looted **VERB**
① To loot shops and houses means to steal goods from them during a battle or riot ▷ **NOUN** **②** Loot is stolen money or goods.
● **WORD HISTORY:** from Hindi *lut*
● **SIMILAR WORDS:** **①** pillage,
● plunder, ransack **②** booty, plunder,
● spoils

lop, lops, lopping, lopped **VERB** If you lop something off, you cut it off with one quick stroke.

lopsided ADJECTIVE Something that is lopsided is uneven because its two sides are different sizes or shapes.

lord, lords **NOUN** **①** a nobleman. **②** Lord is a title used in front of the names of some noblemen, and of bishops, archbishops, judges, and some high-ranking officials • *the Lord Mayor of London.* **③** In Christianity, Lord is a name given to God and Jesus Christ.

Lordship, Lordships **NOUN** You address a lord, judge, or bishop as Your Lordship.

lore NOUN The lore of a place, people, or subject is all the traditional knowledge and stories about it.

lorikeet, lorikeets **NOUN** a type of small parrot found in Australia.

lorry, lorries **NOUN** a large vehicle for transporting goods by road.

lory, lories *[Said law-ree]* **NOUN** a small, brightly coloured parrot found in Australia.

lose, loses, losing, lost **VERB** **①** If you lose something, you cannot find it, or you no longer have it because it has been taken away from you • *I lost my airline ticket.* **②** If you lose a relative or friend, they die • *She lost her brother in the war.* **③** If you lose a fight or an argument, you are beaten. **④** If a business loses money, it is spending more money than it is earning. **loser NOUN**
● **USAGE NOTE:** The verb *lose* is spelt
● with one *o*. Do not confuse it with
● the adjective and adverb *loose*

loss, losses **NOUN** **①** The loss of something is the losing of it ▷ **PHRASE** **②** If you are **at a loss**, you do not know what to do.

lost ADJECTIVE **①** If you are lost, you do not know where you are. **②** If something is lost, you cannot find it. **③** Lost is the past tense and past participle of **lose**.

lot, lots **NOUN** **①** A lot of something, or lots of something, is a large amount of it. **②** A lot means very much or very often • *I love him a lot.* **③** an amount

of something or a number of things
• *He bet all his wages and lost the lot.*
❹ In an auction, a lot is one of the
things being sold.
● SIMILAR WORDS: **❶** abundance,
● loads, plenty

lotion, lotions NOUN a liquid that
you put on your skin to protect or
soften it • *suntan lotion.*

lottery, lotteries NOUN a method of
raising money by selling tickets by
which a winner is selected at random.

lotus, lotuses NOUN a large water
lily, found in Africa and Asia.

loud, louder, loudest ADJECTIVE OR
ADVERB **❶** A loud noise has a high
volume of sound • *a loud explosion.*
❷ If you describe clothing as loud,
you mean that it is too bright • *a loud
tie.* **loudly** ADVERB

loudspeaker, loudspeakers NOUN
a piece of equipment that makes your
voice louder when you speak into a
microphone connected to it.

lounge, lounges, lounging, lounged
NOUN **❶** a room in a house or hotel
with comfortable chairs where people
can relax. **❷** The lounge or lounge bar
in a pub or hotel is a more expensive
and comfortably furnished bar
▷ VERB **❸** If you lounge around, you
lean against something or sit or lie
around in a lazy and comfortable way.

lourie, louries [*rhymes with* **Maori**]
NOUN one of two types of bird found
in South Africa. The grey lourie lives in
open grassland and the other more
brightly coloured species lives in
forests and wooded areas.

louse, lice NOUN Lice are small

insects that live on people's bodies
• *head lice.*

lousy, lousier, lousiest ADJECTIVE
INFORMAL **❶** of bad quality or very
unpleasant • *The weather is lousy.* **❷** ill
or unhappy.

lout, louts NOUN a young man who
behaves in an aggressive and rude
way.

lovable or **loveable** ADJECTIVE
having very attractive qualities and
therefore easy to love • *a lovable black
mongrel.*

love, loves, loving, loved VERB **❶** If
you love someone, you have strong
emotional feelings of affection for
them. **❷** If you love something, you
like it very much • *We both love fishing.*
❸ If you would love to do something,
you want very much to do it • *I would
love to live there.* ▷ NOUN **❹** Love is a
strong emotional feeling of affection
for someone or something. **❺** a
strong liking for something. **❻** In
tennis, love is a score of zero
▷ PHRASE **❼** If you are **in love** with
someone, you feel strongly attracted
to them romantically or sexually.
❽ When two people **make love**, they
have sex.
● SIMILAR WORDS: **❶** adore, dote
● on

love affair, love affairs NOUN a
romantic and often sexual relationship
between two people who are not
married to each other.

love life, love lives NOUN a person's
romantic and sexual relationships.

lovely, lovelier, loveliest ADJECTIVE
very beautiful, attractive, and pleasant.
loveliness NOUN

a b c d e f g h i j k l m n o p q r s t u v w x y z

▷ SPELLING NOTE: *The government licenSes Schnapps (licenꜱes)*

lover, lovers NOUN ❶ A person's lover is someone that they have a sexual relationship with but are not married to. ❷ Someone who is a lover of something, for example art or music, is very fond of it.

loving ADJECTIVE feeling or showing love. **lovingly** ADVERB

low, lower, lowest ADJECTIVE ❶ Something that is low is close to the ground, or measures a short distance from the ground to the top • *a low stool.* ❷ Low means small in value or amount. ❸ 'Low' is used to describe people who are considered not respectable • *mixing with low company.* ▷ ADVERB ❹ in a low position, level, or degree ▷ NOUN ❺ a level or amount that is less than before • *Sales hit a new low.*

lowboy, lowboys NOUN In Australian and New Zealand English, a small wardrobe or chest of drawers.

lower, lowers, lowering, lowered VERB ❶ To lower something means to move it downwards. ❷ To lower something also means to make it less in value or amount.

lower case ADJECTIVE (ENGLISH) Lower case letters are the small letters used in printing or on a computer.

lowlands PLURAL NOUN Lowlands are an area of flat, low land. **lowland** ADJECTIVE

lowly, lowlier, lowliest ADJECTIVE low in importance, rank or status.

low tide, low tides NOUN On a coast, low tide is the time, usually twice a day, when the sea is at its lowest level.

loyal ADJECTIVE firm in your friendship or support for someone or something. **loyally** ADVERB **loyalty** NOUN

loyalist, loyalists NOUN a person who remains firm in their support for a government or ruler.

lozenge, lozenges NOUN ❶ a type of sweet with medicine in it, which you suck to relieve a sore throat or cough. ❷ a diamond shape.

LP, LPs NOUN a long-playing record. LP is short for 'long-playing record'.

LSD NOUN LSD is a very powerful drug which causes hallucinations. LSD is an abbreviation for 'lysergic acid diethylamide'.

Ltd an abbreviation for 'limited'; used after the names of limited companies.

lubra, lubras NOUN an Australian Aboriginal woman.

lubricate, lubricates, lubricating, lubricated VERB To lubricate something such as a machine means to put oil or an oily substance onto it, so that it moves smoothly and friction is reduced. **lubrication** NOUN **lubricant** NOUN

lucid ADJECTIVE ❶ Lucid writing or speech is clear and easy to understand. ❷ Someone who is lucid after having been ill or delirious is able to think clearly again.

luck NOUN Luck is anything that seems to happen by chance and not through your own efforts.
● SIMILAR WORDS: chance, fortune

luckless ADJECTIVE unsuccessful or unfortunate • *We reduced our* *luckless opponents to shattered wrecks.*

lucky, luckier, luckiest **ADJECTIVE**
❶ Someone who is lucky has a lot of good luck. ❷ Something that is lucky happens by chance and has good effects or consequences. **luckily**
ADVERB

lucrative ADJECTIVE Something that is lucrative earns you a lot of money • *a lucrative sponsorship deal.*

ludicrous ADJECTIVE completely foolish, unsuitable, or ridiculous.

lug, lugs, lugging, lugged **VERB** If you lug a heavy object around, you carry it with difficulty.

luggage NOUN Your luggage is the bags and suitcases that you take with you when you travel.

lukewarm ADJECTIVE ❶ slightly warm • *a mug of lukewarm tea.* ❷ not very enthusiastic or interested • *The report was given a polite but lukewarm response.*

lull, lulls, lulling, lulled **NOUN** ❶ a pause in something, or a short time when it is quiet and nothing much happens • *There was a temporary lull in the fighting.* ❷ If you are lulled into feeling safe, someone or something causes you to feel safe at a time when you are not safe • *We had been lulled into a false sense of security.*

lullaby, lullabies **NOUN** a song used for sending a baby or child to sleep.

lumber, lumbers, lumbering, lumbered **NOUN** ❶ Lumber is wood that has been roughly cut up. ❷ Lumber is also old unwanted furniture and other items ▷ **VERB** ❸ If you lumber around, you move heavily and clumsily. ❹ INFORMAL If you are lumbered with something, you are given it to deal with even though you do not want it • *Women are still lumbered with the housework.*

luminary, luminaries **NOUN** LITERARY a person who is famous or an expert in a particular subject.

luminous ADJECTIVE Something that is luminous glows in the dark, usually because it has been treated with a special substance • *The luminous dial on her clock.* **luminosity NOUN**

lump, lumps, lumping, lumped **NOUN** ❶ A lump of something is a solid piece of it, of any shape or size • *a big lump of dough.* ❷ a bump on the surface of something ▷ **VERB** ❸ If you lump people or things together, you combine them into one group or consider them as being similar in some way. **lumpy ADJECTIVE**

lump sum, lump sums **NOUN** a large sum of money given or received all at once.

lunacy NOUN ❶ Lunacy is extremely foolish or eccentric behaviour. ❷ OLD-FASHIONED Lunacy is also severe mental illness.

lunar ADJECTIVE relating to the moon.
● **WORD HISTORY:** from Latin *luna* meaning 'moon'

lunatic, lunatics **NOUN** ❶ If you call someone a lunatic, you mean that they are very foolish • *He drives like a lunatic!* ❷ someone who is insane ▷ **ADJECTIVE** ❸ Lunatic behaviour is very stupid, foolish, or dangerous.

▷ SPELLING NOTE: *plaice the fish has a glittering 'EYE' (I) (plaice)*

a
b
c
d
e
f
g
h
i
j
k
l
m
n
o
p
q
r
s
t
u
v
w
x
y
z

lunch, lunches, lunching, lunched
NOUN ❶ a meal eaten in the middle
of the day ▷ **VERB** ❷ When you
lunch, you eat lunch.

luncheon, luncheons [Said
lun-shen] **NOUN** FORMAL Luncheon is
lunch.

lung, lungs **NOUN** Your lungs are the
two organs inside your ribcage with
which you breathe.

lunge, lunges, lunging, lunged **NOUN**
❶ a sudden forward movement • *He
made a lunge for her.* ▷ **VERB** ❷ To
lunge means to make a sudden
movement in a particular direction.

lurch, lurches, lurching, lurched
VERB ❶ To lurch means to make a
sudden, jerky movement ▷ **NOUN**
❷ a sudden, jerky movement.

lure, lures, luring, lured **VERB** ❶ To
lure someone means to attract them
into going somewhere or doing
something ▷ **NOUN** ❷ something
that you find very attractive.

lurid [Said *loo-rid*] **ADJECTIVE**
❶ involving a lot of sensational detail
• *lurid stories in the press.* ❷ very
brightly coloured or patterned.

lurk, lurks, lurking, lurked **VERB** To
lurk somewhere means to remain
there hidden from the person you are
waiting for.

luscious **ADJECTIVE** very tasty
• *luscious fruit.*

lush, lusher, lushest **ADJECTIVE** In a
lush field or garden, the grass or
plants are healthy and growing thickly.

lust, lusts, lusting, lusted **NOUN**
❶ Lust is a very strong feeling of

sexual desire for someone. ❷ A lust
for something is a strong desire to
have it • *a lust for money.* ▷ **VERB**
❸ To lust for or after someone means
to desire them sexually. ❹ If you lust
for or after something, you have a very
strong desire to possess it • *She lusted
after fame.*

lustful **ADJECTIVE** feeling or
expressing strong sexual desire.

lustre [Said *lus-ter*] **NOUN** Lustre is
soft shining light reflected from the
surface of something • *the lustre of
silk.*

lute, lutes **NOUN** an old-fashioned
stringed musical instrument which is
plucked like a guitar.

luxuriant **ADJECTIVE** Luxuriant
plants, trees, and gardens are large,
healthy, and growing strongly.

luxurious **ADJECTIVE** very
expensive and full of luxury.
luxuriously **ADVERB**
● **SIMILAR WORDS:** opulent,
● splendid, sumptuous

luxury, luxuries **NOUN** ❶ Luxury is
great comfort in expensive and
beautiful surroundings • *a life of
luxury.* ❷ something that you enjoy
very much but do not have very often,
usually because it is expensive.
● **SIMILAR WORDS:**
● ❶ extravagance, indulgence, treat

-ly **SUFFIX** ❶ '-ly' forms adjectives
that describe a quality • *friendly.*
❷ '-ly' forms adjectives that refer to
how often something happens or is
done • *yearly.* ❸ '-ly' forms adverbs
that refer to how or in what way
something is done • *quickly* • *nicely.*

▷ SPELLING NOTE: *I went to see (C) the doctor's new practiCe (practice)*

lying NOUN ❶ Lying is telling lies ▷ ADJECTIVE ❷ A lying person often tells lies. ❸ Lying is also the present participle of **lie**.

lynch, lynches, lynching, lynched VERB If a crowd lynches someone, it kills them in a violent way without first holding a legal trial.

lynx, lynxes NOUN a wildcat with a short tail and tufted ears.

lyre, lyres NOUN a stringed instrument rather like a small harp, which was used in ancient Greece.

lyric, lyrics NOUN ❶ (MUSIC) The lyrics of a song are the words ▷ ADJECTIVE ❷ Lyric poetry is written in a simple and direct style, and is usually about love.

lyrical ADJECTIVE poetic and romantic.

a
b
c
d
e
f
g
h
i
j
k
l
m
n
o
p
q
r
s
t
u
v
w
x
y
z

▷ SPELLING NOTE: *You must practiSe your Ss (practise)*

Mm

m an abbreviation for 'metres' or 'miles'.

macabre [Said mak-**kahb**-ra] **ADJECTIVE** A macabre event is strange and horrible • *a macabre horror story.*

macadamia, macadamias [Said ma-ka-**dame**-ee-a] **NOUN** an Australian tree, also grown in New Zealand, that produces edible nuts.

macaroni **NOUN** Macaroni is short hollow tubes of pasta.
- **WORD HISTORY:** an Italian word; from Greek *makaria* meaning 'food made from barley'

macaroon, macaroons **NOUN** a sweet biscuit flavoured with almonds or coconut.

mace, maces **NOUN** an ornamental pole carried by an official during ceremonies as a symbol of authority.

machete, machetes [Said mash-**ett**-ee] **NOUN** a large, heavy knife with a big blade.

machine, machines, machining, machined **NOUN** ❶ (D & T) a piece of equipment that uses electricity or power from an engine to make it work ▷ **VERB** ❷ If you machine something, you make it or work on it using a machine.

machine-gun, machine-guns **NOUN** a gun that works automatically, firing bullets one after the other.

machinery **NOUN** Machinery is machines in general.

machismo [Said mak-**kiz**-moe] **NOUN** Machismo is exaggerated aggressive male behaviour.

macho [Said **mat**-shoh] **ADJECTIVE** A man who is described as macho behaves in an aggressively masculine way.
- **WORD HISTORY:** from Spanish *macho* meaning 'male'

mackerel, mackerels **NOUN** a sea fish with blue and silver stripes.

mackintosh, mackintoshes **NOUN** a raincoat made from specially treated waterproof cloth.

mad, madder, maddest **ADJECTIVE** ❶ Someone who is mad has a mental illness which often causes them to behave in strange ways. ❷ If you describe someone as mad, you mean that they are very foolish • *He said we were mad to share a flat.* ❸ INFORMAL Someone who is mad is angry. ❹ If you are mad about someone or something, you like them very much • *Alan was mad about golf.* **madness NOUN madman NOUN**
- **SIMILAR WORDS:** ❶ crazy, deranged, insane ❷ daft, foolish

madam **NOUN** 'Madam' is a very formal way of addressing a woman.

▷ SPELLING NOTE: *pAL up with the principAL and principAL staff (principal)*

maddening ADJECTIVE irritating or frustrating • *She had many maddening habits.*

madly ADVERB If you do something madly, you do it in a fast, excited way.

madrigal, madrigals NOUN a song sung by several people without instruments.

Mafia NOUN The Mafia is a large crime organization operating in Sicily, Italy, and the USA.

magazine, magazines NOUN ❶ (LIBRARY) a weekly or monthly publication with articles and photographs. ❷ a compartment in a gun for cartridges.
● **WORD HISTORY:** from Arabic
● *makhzan* meaning 'storehouse'

magenta [*Said maj-jen-ta*] NOUN OR ADJECTIVE dark reddish-purple.

maggot, maggots NOUN a creature that looks like a small worm and lives on decaying things. Maggots turn into flies.

magic NOUN ❶ In fairy stories, magic is a special power that can make impossible things happen. ❷ Magic is the art of performing tricks to entertain people.

magical ADJECTIVE wonderful and exciting. **magically** ADVERB

magician, magicians NOUN ❶ a person who performs tricks as entertainment. ❷ In fairy stories, a magician is a man with magical powers.

magistrate, magistrates NOUN an official who acts as a judge in a law court that deals with less serious crimes.

magma NOUN (GEOGRAPHY) Magma is a hot liquid within the earth's crust which forms igneous rock when it solidifies.

magnanimous ADJECTIVE generous and forgiving.

magnate, magnates NOUN someone who is very rich and powerful in business.

magnet, magnets NOUN (SCIENCE) a piece of iron which attracts iron or steel towards it, and which points towards north if allowed to swing freely. A **permanent magnet** is a magnet that is still magnetic when the magnetic field that produced it is taken away; a **temporary magnet** is a magnet that loses its magnetism when the magnetic field that produced it is taken away. **magnetic** ADJECTIVE **magnetism** NOUN

magnetic field NOUN (SCIENCE) the area around a magnet inside which a magnetic force is felt.

magnificent ADJECTIVE extremely beautiful or impressive. **magnificently** ADVERB **magnificence** NOUN

magnify, magnifies, magnifying, magnified VERB When a microscope or lens magnifies something, it makes it appear bigger than it actually is. **magnification** NOUN

magnifying glass, magnifying glasses NOUN a lens which makes things appear bigger than they really are.

magnitude NOUN The magnitude of something is its great size or importance.

a b c d e f g h i j k l **m** n o p q r s t u v w x y z

▷ SPELLING NOTE: *LEarn the principLEs (principle)*

A
B
C
D
E
F
G
H
I
J
K
L
M
N
O
P
Q
R
S
T
U
V
W
X
Y
Z

magnolia, magnolias **NOUN** a tree which has large white or pink flowers in spring.

magpie, magpies **NOUN** a large black and white bird with a long tail.

mahogany **NOUN** Mahogany is a hard reddish brown wood used for making furniture.

maid, maids **NOUN** a female servant.

maiden, maidens **NOUN** ❶ LITERARY a young woman ▷ **ADJECTIVE** ❷ first • *a maiden voyage.*

maiden name, maiden names **NOUN** the surname a woman had before she married.

mail, mails, mailing, mailed **NOUN** ❶ Your mail is the letters and parcels delivered to you by the post office ▷ **VERB** ❷ If you mail a letter, you send it by post.

mail order **NOUN** Mail order is a system of buying goods by post.

maim, maims, maiming, maimed **VERB** To maim someone is to injure them very badly for life • *He was maimed in a dreadful road accident.*

main, mains **ADJECTIVE** ❶ most important • *the main event.* ▷ **NOUN** ❷ The mains are large pipes or wires that carry gas, water or electricity.
● **SIMILAR WORDS:** ❶ chief, major, principal

mainframe, mainframes **NOUN** a large computer which can be used by many people at the same time.

mainland **NOUN** The mainland is the main part of a country in contrast to islands around its coast.

mainly **ADVERB** true in most cases.

mainstay **NOUN** The mainstay of something is the most important part of it.

mainstream **NOUN** The mainstream is the most ordinary and conventional group of people or ideas in a society.

maintain, maintains, maintaining, maintained **VERB** ❶ If you maintain something, you keep it going or keep it at a particular rate or level • *I wanted to maintain our friendship.* ❷ If you maintain someone, you provide them regularly with money for what they need. ❸ To maintain a machine or a building is to keep it in good condition. ❹ If you maintain that something is true, you believe it is true and say so.

maintenance **NOUN** ❶ Maintenance is the process of keeping something in good condition. ❷ Maintenance is also money that a person sends regularly to someone to provide for the things they need.

maize **NOUN** Maize is a tall plant which produces sweet corn.

majesty, majesties ❶ You say 'His Majesty' when you are talking about a king, and 'Her Majesty' when you are talking about a queen **NOUN** ❷ Majesty is great dignity and impressiveness. **majestic ADJECTIVE** **majestically ADVERB**

major, majors **ADJECTIVE** ❶ more important or more significant than other things • *There were over fifty major injuries.* ❷ (MUSIC) A major key is one of the keys in which most European music is written ▷ **NOUN** ❸ an army officer of the rank

▷ SPELLING NOTE: *Psychiatrists Seldom Yell Callously Hard (psychiatrist)*

immediately above captain.

majority, majorities NOUN ❶ The majority of people or things in a group is more than half of the group. ❷ In an election, the majority is the difference between the number of votes gained by the winner and the number gained by the runner-up.
- USAGE NOTE: You should use
- *majority* only to talk about things
- that can be counted: *the majority of*
- *car owners*. To talk about an amount
- that cannot be counted you should
- use *most*: *most of the harvest was*
- *saved*

make, makes, making, made VERB
❶ To make something is to produce or construct it, or to cause it to happen. ❷ To make something is to do it • *He was about to make a speech.* ❸ To make something is to prepare it • *I'll make some salad dressing.* ❹ If someone makes you do something, they force you to do it • *Mum made me clean the bathroom.* ▷ NOUN ❺ The make of a product is the name of the company that manufactured it • *'What make of car do you drive?'* – *'Toyota.'*
make up VERB ❶ If a number of things make up something, they form that thing. ❷ If you make up a story, you invent it. ❸ If you make yourself up, you put make-up on. ❹ If two people make it up, they become friends again after a quarrel.
- SIMILAR WORDS: ❶ create,
- fashion, form, produce ❺ brand,
- kind, type

make-up NOUN ❶ Make-up is coloured creams and powders which women put on their faces to make themselves look more attractive.
❷ Someone's make-up is their character or personality.

making NOUN ❶ The making of something is the act or process of creating or producing it ▷ PHRASE ❷ When you describe someone as something **in the making**, you mean that they are gradually becoming that thing • *a captain in the making.*

maladjusted ADJECTIVE A maladjusted person has psychological or behaviour problems.

malaise [Said mal-**laze**] NOUN FORMAL Malaise is a feeling of dissatisfaction or unhappiness.

malaria [Said mal-**lay**-ree-a] NOUN Malaria is a tropical disease caught from mosquitoes which causes fever and shivering.

Malaysian, Malaysians ADJECTIVE ❶ belonging or relating to Malaysia ▷ NOUN ❷ someone who comes from Malaysia.

male, males NOUN ❶ a person or animal belonging to the sex that cannot give birth or lay eggs ▷ ADJECTIVE ❷ concerning or affecting men rather than women.

male chauvinist, male chauvinists NOUN a man who thinks that men are better than women.

malevolent [Said mal-**lev**-oh-lent] ADJECTIVE FORMAL wanting or intending to cause harm.
malevolence NOUN
- SIMILAR WORDS: malicious,
- spiteful, vindictive

malfunction, malfunctions, malfunctioning, malfunctioned VERB
❶ If a machine malfunctions, it fails

a b c d e f g h i j k l **m** n o p q r s t u v w x y z

to work properly ▷ **NOUN** ❷ the failure of a machine to work properly.

malice NOUN Malice is a desire to cause harm to people.

malicious ADJECTIVE Malicious talk or behaviour is intended to harm someone.

malign, maligns, maligning, maligned **VERB** FORMAL To malign someone is to say unpleasant and untrue things about them.

malignant ADJECTIVE ❶ harmful and cruel. ❷ A malignant disease or tumour could cause death if it is allowed to continue.

mallard, mallards **NOUN** a kind of wild duck. The male has a green head.

malleable ADJECTIVE FORMAL ❶ easily influenced by other people. ❷ If a metal or other substance is malleable, it is soft enough to be made into different shapes • *Gold and silver are the most malleable of all metals.* **malleability NOUN**

mallee, mallees **NOUN** a eucalypt that grows close to the ground in dry areas of Australia.

mallet, mallets **NOUN** a wooden hammer with a square head.

malnutrition NOUN Malnutrition is not eating enough healthy food.

malodorous ADJECTIVE If you describe something as malodorous, you means it smells bad.

malpractice NOUN If someone such as a doctor or lawyer breaks the rules of their profession, their behaviour is called malpractice.

malt NOUN Malt is roasted grain, usually barley, that is used in making beer and whisky.

mammal, mammals **NOUN** (SCIENCE) Animals that give birth to live babies and feed their young with milk from the mother's body are called mammals. Human beings, dogs, and whales are all mammals.

mammary gland, mammary glands **NOUN** (SCIENCE) a gland in female mammals that produces milk.

mammoth, mammoths **ADJECTIVE** ❶ very large indeed • *a mammoth outdoor concert.* ▷ **NOUN** ❷ a huge animal that looked like a hairy elephant with long tusks. Mammoths became extinct a long time ago.

man, men; mans, manning, manned **NOUN** ❶ an adult male human being ❷ IN PLURAL Human beings in general are sometimes referred to as men • *All men are equal.* ▷ **VERB** ❸ To man something is to be in charge of it or operate it • *Two officers were manning the radar screens.*
● **SIMILAR WORDS:** ❶ bloke, chap, guy ❷ humanity, mankind

mana NOUN Mana is authority and influence such as that held by a New Zealand Maori chief.

manacle, manacles **NOUN** Manacles are metal rings or clamps attached to a prisoner's wrists or ankles.

manage, manages, managing, managed **VERB** ❶ If you manage to do something, you succeed in doing it • *We managed to find somewhere to sit.* ❷ If you manage an organization or

business, you are responsible for controlling it.
● **SIMILAR WORDS:** ❶ accomplish, succeed

manageable ADJECTIVE able to be dealt with.

management NOUN ❶ The management of a business is the controlling and organizing of it. ❷ The people who control an organization are called the management.
● **SIMILAR WORDS:**
● ❶ administration, control, running

manager, managers NOUN a person responsible for running a business or organization • *a bank manager.*
● **USAGE NOTE:** In business, the word *manager* can apply to either a man or a woman

manageress, manageresses NOUN a woman responsible for running a business or organization.

managing director, managing directors NOUN a company director who is responsible for the way the company is managed.

mandarin, mandarins NOUN a type of small orange which is easy to peel.

mandate, mandates NOUN FORMAL A government's mandate is the authority it has to carry out particular policies as a result of winning an election.

mandatory ADJECTIVE If something is mandatory, there is a law or rule stating that it must be done • *a mandatory life sentence for murder.*

mandir, mandirs [Said **mun-dir**] NOUN a Hindu temple.

● **WORD HISTORY:** a Hindi word

mandolin, mandolins NOUN a musical instrument like a small guitar with a deep, rounded body.

mane, manes NOUN the long hair growing from the neck of a lion or horse.

manger, mangers NOUN a feeding box in a barn or stable.

mangle, mangles, mangling, mangled VERB ❶ If something is mangled, it is crushed and twisted ▷ NOUN ❷ an old-fashioned piece of equipment consisting of two large rollers which squeeze water out of wet clothes.

mango, mangoes or mangos NOUN a sweet yellowish fruit which grows in tropical countries.

manhole, manholes NOUN a covered hole in the ground leading to a drain or sewer.

manhood NOUN Manhood is the state of being a man rather than a boy.

mania, manias NOUN ❶ a strong liking for something • *my wife's mania for plant collecting.* ❷ a mental illness.
● **WORD HISTORY:** from Greek *mania* meaning 'madness'

maniac, maniacs NOUN a mad person who is violent and dangerous.

manic ADJECTIVE energetic and excited • *a manic attack.*

manicure, manicures, manicuring, manicured VERB ❶ If you manicure your hands, you care for them by softening the skin and shaping and polishing the nails ▷ NOUN ❷ A manicure is a special treatment for the

a
b
c
d
e
f
g
h
i
j
k
l
m
n
o
p
q
r
s
t
u
v
w
x
y
z

▷ SPELLING NOTE: *there's SAND in my SANDwich (sandwich)*

hands and nails. **manicurist** NOUN

manifest, manifests, manifesting, manifested FORMAL ADJECTIVE ❶ obvious or easily seen • *his manifest enthusiasm.* ▷ VERB ❷ To manifest something is to make people aware of it • *Fear can manifest itself in many ways.*

manifestation, manifestations NOUN FORMAL A manifestation of something is a sign that it is happening or exists • *The illness may be a manifestation of stress.*

manifesto, manifestoes or manifestos NOUN a published statement of the aims and policies of a political party.

manipulate, manipulates, manipulating, manipulated VERB ❶ To manipulate people or events is to control or influence them to produce a particular result. ❷ If you manipulate a piece of equipment, you control it in a skilful way. **manipulation** NOUN **manipulator** NOUN **manipulative** ADJECTIVE

mankind NOUN 'Mankind' is used to refer to all human beings • *a threat to mankind.*

manly, manlier, manliest ADJECTIVE having qualities that are typically masculine • *He laughed a deep, manly laugh.*

manna NOUN If something appears like manna from heaven, it appears suddenly as if by a miracle and helps you in a difficult situation.

manner, manners NOUN ❶ The manner in which you do something is the way you do it. ❷ Your manner is

the way in which you behave and talk • *his kind manner.* ❸ IN PLURAL If you have good manners, you behave very politely.

mannerism, mannerisms NOUN a gesture or a way of speaking which is characteristic of a person.

manoeuvre, manoeuvres, manoeuvring, manoeuvred [*Said man-noo-ver*] VERB ❶ If you manoeuvre something into a place, you skilfully move it there • *It took expertise to manoeuvre the boat so close to the shore.* ▷ NOUN ❷ a clever move you make in order to change a situation to your advantage.

manor, manors NOUN a large country house with land.

manpower NOUN Workers can be referred to as manpower.

mansion, mansions NOUN a very large house.

manslaughter NOUN LEGAL Manslaughter is the accidental killing of a person.

mantelpiece, mantelpieces NOUN a shelf over a fireplace.

mantle, mantles NOUN LITERARY To take on the mantle of something is to take on responsibility for it • *He has taken over the mantle of England's greatest living poet.*

mantra, mantras NOUN a word or short piece of sacred text or prayer continually repeated to help concentration.

manual, manuals ADJECTIVE ❶ Manual work involves physical strength rather than mental skill.

▷ SPELLING NOTE: *On WEDNESday Wayne WED NESta (Wednesday)*

2 operated by hand rather than by electricity or by motor • *a manual typewriter.* ▷ **NOUN 3** an instruction book which tells you how to use a machine. **manually ADVERB**

manufacture, manufactures, manufacturing, manufactured D & T **VERB 1** To manufacture goods is to make them in a factory ▷ **NOUN 2** The manufacture of goods is the making of them in a factory • *the manufacture of nuclear weapons.* **manufacturer NOUN**

manure NOUN Manure is animal faeces used to fertilize the soil.

manuscript, manuscripts **NOUN** a handwritten or typed document, especially a version of a book before it is printed.

Manx ADJECTIVE belonging or relating to the Isle of Man.

many ADJECTIVE 1 If there are many people or things, there is a large number of them. **2** You also use 'many' to ask how great a quantity is or to give information about it • *How many tickets do you require?* ▷ **PRONOUN 3** a large number of people or things • *Many are too weak to walk.*

Maori, Maoris **NOUN 1** someone descended from the people who lived in New Zealand before Europeans arrived. **2** Maori is a language spoken by Maoris.

map, maps, mapping, mapped **NOUN 1** a detailed drawing of an area as it would appear if you saw it from above. **2** MATHS the relationship between elements of a set and elements in the same or another set ▷ **VERB 3** If you

map out a plan, you work out in detail what you will do.

maple, maples **NOUN** a tree that has large leaves with five points.

mar, mars, marring, marred **VERB** To mar something is to spoil it • *The game was marred by violence.*

marae, marae or maraes **NOUN** [Said ma-**rye**] In New Zealand, a Maori meeting house; also the enclosed space in front of it.

marathon, marathons **NOUN 1** a race in which people run 26 miles along roads ▷ **ADJECTIVE 2** A marathon task is a large one that takes a long time.

marble, marbles **NOUN 1** Marble is a very hard, cold stone which is often polished to show the coloured patterns in it. **2** Marbles is a children's game played with small coloured glass balls. These balls are also called marbles.

march, marches, marching, marched **NOUN 1** March is the third month of the year. It has 31 days. **2** an organized protest in which a large group of people walk somewhere together ▷ **VERB 3** When soldiers march, they walk with quick regular steps in time with each other. **4** To march somewhere is to walk quickly in a determined way • *He marched out of the room.*

● **WORD HISTORY:** sense 1 is from
● Latin *Martius* (month) of Mars, the
● Roman god of war

mare, mares **NOUN** an adult female horse.

margarine [Said **mar**-jar-reen],

a
b
c
d
e
f
g
h
i
j
k
m
n
o
p
q
r
s
t
u
v
w
x
y
z

margarines **NOUN** Margarine is a substance that is similar to butter but is made from vegetable oil and animal fats.

margin, margins **NOUN** ❶ If you win a contest by a large or small margin, you win it by a large or small amount. ❷ an extra amount that allows you more freedom in doing something • *a small margin of error.* ❸ the blank space at each side on a written or printed page.

marginal **ADJECTIVE** ❶ small and not very important • *a marginal increase.* ❷ A marginal seat or constituency is a political constituency where the previous election was won by a very small majority. **marginally** **ADVERB**

marigold, marigolds **NOUN** a type of yellow or orange garden flower.

marijuana [Said mar-rih-**hwan**-a] **NOUN** Marijuana is an illegal drug which is smoked in cigarettes.

marina, marinas **NOUN** a harbour for pleasure boats and yachts.

marinate, marinates, marinating, marinated; *also spelt* **marinade** **VERB** To marinate food is to soak it in a mixture of oil and vinegar to flavour it before cooking.

marine, marines **NOUN** ❶ a soldier who serves with the navy ▷ **ADJECTIVE** ❷ relating to or involving the sea • *marine life.*

marital **ADJECTIVE** relating to or involving marriage • *marital problems.*

maritime **ADJECTIVE** relating to the sea and ships • *maritime trade.*

marjoram **NOUN** Marjoram is a herb with small, rounded leaves and tiny, pink flowers.

mark, marks, marking, marked **NOUN** ❶ a small stain or damaged area on a surface • *I can't get this mark off the curtain.* ❷ a written or printed symbol • *He made a few marks with his pen.* ❸ a letter or number showing how well you have done in homework or in an exam ▷ **VERB** ❹ If something marks a surface, it damages it in some way. ❺ If you mark something, you write a symbol on it or identify it in some other way. ❻ When a teacher marks your work, he or she decides how good it is and gives it a mark. ❼ To mark something is to be a sign of it • *The accident marked a tragic end to the day.* ❽ In soccer or hockey, if you mark your opposing player, you stay close to them, trying to prevent them from getting the ball.

marked **ADJECTIVE** very obvious • *a marked improvement.* **markedly** **ADVERB**

market, markets, marketing, marketed **NOUN** ❶ a place where goods or animals are bought and sold. ❷ The market for a product is the number of people who want to buy it • *the market for cars.* ▷ **VERB** ❸ To market a product is to sell it in an organized way.
● **SIMILAR WORDS:** ❶ bazaar, fair, ● mart

marketing **NOUN** D&T Marketing is the part of a business concerned with the way a product is sold.

market research **NOUN** D&T Market research is research into what people want and buy.

marksman, marksmen **NOUN** someone who can shoot very accurately.

marlin, marlins **NOUN** a large fish found in tropical seas which has a very long upper jaw.

marmalade **NOUN** Marmalade is a jam made from citrus fruit, usually eaten at breakfast.
- **WORD HISTORY:** from Latin
- *marmelo* meaning 'quince'

maroon **NOUN OR ADJECTIVE** dark reddish-purple.

marooned **ADJECTIVE** If you are marooned in a place, you are stranded there and cannot leave it.

marquee, marquees [Said mar-kee] **NOUN** a very large tent used at a fair or other outdoor entertainment.

marquis, marquises [Said mar-kwiss]; also spelt **marquess** **NOUN** a male member of the nobility of the rank between duke and earl.

marriage, marriages **NOUN** ❶ the relationship between a husband and wife. ❷ (RE) Marriage is the act of marrying someone.
- **SIMILAR WORDS:** ❶ matrimony, wedlock

marrow, marrows **NOUN** a long, thick green-skinned fruit with cream-coloured flesh eaten as a vegetable.

marry, marries, marrying, married **VERB** ❶ When a man and a woman marry, they become each other's husband and wife during a special ceremony. ❷ When a clergyman or

registrar marries a couple, he or she is in charge of their marriage ceremony. **married** **ADJECTIVE**

Mars **NOUN** Mars is the planet in the solar system which is fourth from the sun.

marsh, marshes **NOUN** an area of land which is permanently wet.

marshal, marshals, marshalling, marshalled **VERB** ❶ If you marshal things or people, you gather them together and organize them • *Shipping was being marshalled into convoys.* ▷ **NOUN** ❷ an official who helps to organize a public event.

marshmallow, marshmallows **NOUN** a soft, spongy, pink or white sweet made using gelatine.

marsupial, marsupials [Said mar-syoo-pee-al] **NOUN** an animal that carries its young in a pouch. Koalas and kangaroos are marsupials.
- **WORD HISTORY:** from Greek
- *marsupion* meaning 'purse'

martial [Said mar-shal] **ADJECTIVE** relating to or involving war or soldiers • *martial music.*

martial arts **PLURAL NOUN** The martial arts are the techniques of self-defence that come from the Far East, for example karate or judo.

Martian, Martians [Said mar-shan] **NOUN** an imaginary creature from the planet Mars.

martyr, martyrs, martyring, martyred **NOUN** ❶ someone who suffers or is killed rather than change their beliefs ▷ **VERB** ❷ If someone is martyred, they are killed because of their beliefs. **martyrdom** **NOUN**

▷ SPELLING NOTE: *'i' before 'e' except after 'c'*

marvel, marvels, marvelling,
marvelled **VERB** ❶ If you marvel at
something, it fills you with surprise or
admiration • *Modern designers can only
marvel at his genius.* ▷ **NOUN**
❷ something that makes you feel
great surprise or admiration • *a marvel
of high technology.*

marvellous ADJECTIVE wonderful
or excellent. **marvellously ADVERB**

Marxism NOUN Marxism is a
political philosophy based on the
writings of Karl Marx. It states that
society will develop towards
communism through the struggle
between different social classes.
Marxist ADJECTIVE OR NOUN

marzipan NOUN Marzipan is a
paste made of almonds, sugar, and
egg. It is put on top of cakes or used to
make small sweets.

mascara NOUN Mascara is a
substance that can be used to colour
eyelashes and make them look longer.

mascot, mascots **NOUN** a person,
animal, or toy which is thought to
bring good luck • *Celtic's mascot,
Hoopy the Huddle Hound.*

masculine ADJECTIVE ❶ typical
of men, rather than women • *the
masculine world of motorsport.*
❷ belonging to a particular class of

nouns in some languages, such as
French, German, and Latin.
masculinity NOUN
▶ SEE GRAMMAR BOX ABOVE

mash, mashes, mashing, mashed
VERB If you mash vegetables, you
crush them after they have been
cooked.

mask, masks, masking, masked
NOUN ❶ something you wear over
your face for protection or disguise • *a
surgical mask.* ▷ **VERB** ❷ If you mask
something, you cover it so that it is
protected or cannot be seen.

masochist, masochists *[Said
mass-so-kist]* **NOUN** someone who
gets pleasure from their own suffering.
masochism NOUN
● **WORD HISTORY:** named after the
● Austrian novelist Leopold von
● Sacher Masoch (1836–1895), who
● wrote about masochism

mason, masons **NOUN** a person who
is skilled at making things with stone.

masonry NOUN Masonry is pieces
of stone which form part of a wall or
building.

masquerade, masquerades,
masquerading, masqueraded *[Said
mass-ker-**raid**]* **VERB** If you
masquerade as something, you
pretend to be it • *He masqueraded as a*

▷ SPELLING NOTE: *King IAn went to ParlIAment in a carrIAge for his marrIAge (-ia-)*

doctor in the local clinic.

mass, masses, massing, massed
NOUN ❶ a large amount of
something. ❷ The masses are the
ordinary people in society considered
as a group • *opera for the masses.* ❸ In
physics, the mass of an object is the
amount of physical matter that it has.
❹ In the Roman Catholic Church,
Mass is a religious service in which
people share bread and wine in
remembrance of the death and
resurrection of Jesus Christ
▷ **ADJECTIVE** ❺ involving a large
number of people • *mass
unemployment.* ▷ **VERB** ❻ When
people mass, they gather together in a
large group.

massacre, massacres, massacring,
massacred [Said *mass-ik-ker*] **NOUN**
❶ the killing of a very large number of
people in a violent and cruel way
▷ **VERB** ❷ To massacre people is to
kill large numbers of them in a violent
and cruel way.

massage, massages, massaging,
massaged **VERB** ❶ To massage
someone is to rub their body in order
to help them relax or to relieve pain
▷ **NOUN** ❷ A massage is treatment
which involves rubbing the body.

massive ADJECTIVE extremely large
• *a massive iceberg.* **massively
ADVERB**

mass-produce, mass-produces,
mass-producing, mass-produced
VERB To mass-produce something is
to make it in large quantities • *They
began mass-producing cameras after
the war.*

mast, masts **NOUN** the tall upright

pole that supports the sails of a boat.

master, masters, mastering,
mastered **NOUN** ❶ a man who has
authority over others, such as the
employer of servants, or the owner of
slaves or animals. ❷ If you are master
of a situation, you have control over it
• *He was master of his own destiny.* ❸ a
male teacher at some schools ▷ **VERB**
❹ If you master a difficult situation,
you succeed in controlling it. ❺ If you
master something, you learn how to
do it properly • *She found it easy to
master the game.*

masterful ADJECTIVE showing
control and authority.

masterly ADJECTIVE extremely
clever or well done • *a masterly
exhibition of batting.*

mastermind, masterminds,
masterminding, masterminded **VERB**
❶ If you mastermind a complicated
activity, you plan and organize it
▷ **NOUN** ❷ The mastermind behind
something is the person responsible
for planning it.

masterpiece, masterpieces **NOUN**
an extremely good painting or other
work of art.

masturbate, masturbates,
masturbating, masturbated **VERB** If
someone masturbates, they stroke or
rub their own genitals in order to get
sexual pleasure. **masturbation
NOUN**

mat, mats **NOUN** ❶ a small round or
square piece of cloth, card, or plastic
that is placed on a table to protect it
from plates or glasses. ❷ a small
piece of carpet or other thick material
that is placed on the floor.

a b c d e f g h i j k l m n o p q r s t u v w x y z

▷ SPELLING NOTE: *an ELegant angEL (angel)*

matador, matadors **NOUN** a man who fights and tries to kill bulls as part of a public entertainment, especially in Spain.
  ● **WORD HISTORY:** from Spanish *matar* meaning 'to kill'

match, matches, matching, matched **NOUN** ❶ an organized game of football, cricket, or some other sport. ❷ a small, thin stick of wood that produces a flame when you strike it against a rough surface ▷ **VERB** ❸ If one thing matches another, the two things look the same or have similar qualities.

mate, mates, mating, mated **NOUN** ❶ INFORMAL Your mates are your friends. ❷ The first mate on a ship is the officer who is next in importance to the captain. ❸ An animal's mate is its sexual partner ▷ **VERB** ❹ When a male and female animal mate, they come together sexually in order to breed.

material, materials **NOUN** ❶ (D & T) Material is cloth. ❷ (D & T) a substance from which something is made • *the materials to make red dye.* ❸ (D & T) The equipment for a particular activity can be referred to as materials • *building materials.* ❹ Material for a book, play, or film is the information or ideas on which it is based ▷ **ADJECTIVE** ❺ involving possessions and money • *concerned with material comforts.* **materially ADVERB**

materialism NOUN Materialism is thinking that money and possessions are the most important things in life. **materialistic ADJECTIVE**

materialize, materializes, materializing, materialized; *also spelt* **materialise VERB** If something materializes, it actually happens or appears • *Fortunately, the attack did not materialize.*

maternal ADJECTIVE relating to or involving a mother • *her maternal instincts.*

maternity ADJECTIVE relating to or involving pregnant women and birth • *a maternity hospital.*

mathematics NOUN Mathematics is the study of numbers, quantities, and shapes. **mathematical ADJECTIVE mathematically ADVERB mathematician NOUN**

maths NOUN Maths is mathematics.

Matilda NOUN INFORMAL, OLD-FASHIONED In Australia, Matilda is the pack of belongings carried by a swagman in the bush. The word is now used only in the phrase 'waltzing Matilda', meaning someone who travels in the bush with few possessions.

matinee, matinees [Said *mat-in-nay*]; *also spelt* **matinée NOUN** an afternoon performance of a play or film.

matriarch, matriarchs [Said *may-tree-ark*] **NOUN** (GEOGRAPHY) A matriarch is a woman who is the head of a family in a society in which power passes from mother to daughter. **matriarchy NOUN**

matrimony NOUN FORMAL Matrimony is marriage. **matrimonial ADJECTIVE**

matrix, matrices [Said *may-trix*]

NOUN ❶ FORMAL the framework in which something grows and develops. ❷ In maths, a matrix is a set of numbers or elements set out in rows and columns.

matron, matrons **NOUN** In a hospital, a senior nurse in charge of all the nursing staff used to be known as matron.

matt **ADJECTIVE** A matt surface is dull rather than shiny • *matt black plastic*.

matted **ADJECTIVE** Hair that is matted is tangled with the strands sticking together.

matter, matters, mattering, mattered **NOUN** ❶ something that you have to deal with. ❷ Matter is any substance • *The atom is the smallest divisible particle of matter*. ❸ Books and magazines are reading matter ▷ **VERB** ❹ If something matters to you, it is important ▷ **PHRASE** ❺ If you ask **What's the matter?**, you are asking what is wrong.

● **SIMILAR WORDS:** ❶ affair,
● business, situation, subject

matter-of-fact **ADJECTIVE** showing no emotion.

matting **NOUN** Matting is thick woven material such as rope or straw, used as a floor covering.

mattress, mattresses **NOUN** a large thick pad filled with springs or feathers that is put on a bed to make it comfortable.

mature, matures, maturing, matured **VERB** ❶ When a child or young animal matures, it becomes an adult. ❷ When something matures, it

reaches complete development ▷ **ADJECTIVE** ❸ Mature means fully developed and emotionally balanced. **maturely** **ADVERB** **maturity** **NOUN**

maudlin **ADJECTIVE** Someone who is maudlin is sad and sentimental when they are drunk.

maul, mauls, mauling, mauled **VERB** If someone is mauled by an animal, they are savagely attacked and badly injured by it.

mausoleum, mausoleums [Said maw-sal-**lee**-um] **NOUN** a building which contains the grave of a famous person.

mauve [rhymes with **grove**] **NOUN OR ADJECTIVE** pale purple.

maxim, maxims **NOUN** a short saying which gives a rule for good or sensible behaviour • *Instant action: that's my maxim*.

maximize, maximizes, maximizing, maximized; *also spelt* **maximise** **VERB** To maximize something is to make it as great or effective as possible • *Their objective is to maximize profits*.

maximum **ADJECTIVE** ❶ The maximum amount is the most that is possible • *the maximum recommended intake*. ▷ **NOUN** ❷ The maximum is the most that is possible • *a maximum of fifty men*.

may **VERB** ❶ If something may happen, it is possible that it will happen • *It may happen quite soon*. ❷ If someone may do something, they are allowed to do it • *Please may I be excused?* ❸ You can use 'may' when saying that, although something

a
b
c
d
e
f
g
h
i
j
k
l
m
n
o
p
q
r
s
t
u
v
w
x
y
z

▷ SPELLING NOTE: *A Rude Idiot Thought He Might Eat Toffee In Church (*<u>arithmetic</u>*)*

A
B
C
D
E
F
G
H
I
J
K
L
M
N
O
P
Q
R
S
T
U
V
W
X
Y
Z

is true, something else is also true • *This may be true, but it is only part of the story.* **④** FORMAL You also use 'may' to express a wish that something will happen • *May you live to be a hundred.* ▷ NOUN **⑤** May is the fifth month of the year. It has 31 days.

● USAGE NOTE: It used to be that you used *may* instead of *can* when asking for or giving someone permission to do something: *you may leave the table.* Nowadays *may* is usually only used in polite questions: *may I open the window?*

maybe ADVERB You use 'maybe' when you are stating a possibility that you are not certain about • *Maybe I should lie about my age.*

mayhem NOUN You can refer to a confused and chaotic situation as mayhem • *There was complete mayhem in the classroom.*

mayonnaise [Said may-on-*nayz*] NOUN Mayonnaise is a thick salad dressing made with egg yolks and oil.

mayor, mayors NOUN a person who has been elected to lead and represent the people of a town.

maze, mazes NOUN a system of complicated passages which it is difficult to find your way through • *a maze of dark tunnels.*

MBE, MBEs NOUN a British honour granted by the King or Queen. MBE is an abbreviation for 'Member of the Order of the British Empire' • *Ally McCoist, MBE.*

MD an abbreviation for 'Doctor of Medicine' or 'Managing Director'.

me PRONOUN A speaker or writer uses 'me' to refer to himself or herself.

meadow, meadows NOUN a field of grass.

meagre [Said mee-*ger*] ADJECTIVE very small and poor • *his meagre pension.*

meal, meals NOUN an occasion when people eat, or the food they eat at that time.

mealie, mealies; also spelt **mielie** NOUN In South African English, mealie is maize or an ear of maize.

mean, means, meaning, meant; meaner, meanest VERB **①** If you ask what something means, you want to know what it refers to or what its message is. **②** If you mean what you say, you are serious • *The boss means what he says.* **③** If something means a lot to you, it is important to you. **④** If one thing means another, it shows that the second thing is true or will happen • *Major roadworks will mean long delays.* **⑤** If you mean to do something, you intend to do it • *I meant to phone you, but didn't have time.* **⑥** If something is meant to be true, it is supposed to be true • *I found a road that wasn't meant to be there.* ▷ ADJECTIVE **⑦** Someone who is mean is unwilling to spend much money. **⑧** Someone who is mean is unkind or cruel • *He apologized for being so mean to her.* ▷ NOUN **⑨** IN PLURAL A means of doing something is a method or object which makes it possible • *The tests were marked by means of a computer.* **⑩** IN PLURAL Someone's means are their money and income • *He's obviously a man of means.* **⑪** In mathematics, the mean

is the average of a set of numbers.
meanness NOUN
● **SIMILAR WORDS:** ❺ aim, intend,
● plan ❼ miserly, parsimonious,
● stingy, tight-fisted

meander, meanders, meandering,
meandered [Said mee-an-der] VERB
If a road or river meanders, it has a lot
of bends in it.

meaning, meanings NOUN ❶ The
meaning of a word is what it refers to
or expresses. ❷ The meaning of what
someone says, or of a book or a film, is
the thoughts or ideas that it is
intended to express. ❸ If something
has meaning, it seems to be
worthwhile and to have real purpose.
meaningful ADJECTIVE
meaningfully ADVERB
meaningless ADJECTIVE
● **SIMILAR WORDS:** ❶ gist, sense,
● significance

means test, means tests NOUN a
check of a person's money and
income to see whether they need
money or benefits from the
government or other organization.

meantime PHRASE **In the
meantime** means in the period of
time between two events • *I'll call the
nurse; in the meantime, you must rest.*

meanwhile ADVERB
❶ Meanwhile means while something
else is happening ▷ NOUN ❷ The
meanwhile also means the time
between two events.

measles NOUN Measles is an
infectious illness in which you have
red spots on your skin.

measly ADJECTIVE INFORMAL very
small or inadequate • *He only gave her*
a measly ten cents.

measure, measures, measuring,
measured VERB ❶ (MATHS) When
you measure something, you find out
how big it is. ❷ (MATHS) If something
measures a particular distance, its
length or depth is that distance
• *slivers of glass measuring a few*
millimetres across. ▷ NOUN ❸ A
measure of something is a certain
amount of it • *There has been a*
measure of agreement. ❹ (MATHS) a
unit in which size, speed, or depth is
expressed. ❺ Measures are actions
carried out to achieve a particular
result • *Tough measures are needed to*
maintain order. **measurement** NOUN

measured ADJECTIVE careful and
deliberate • *walking at the same*
measured pace.

measurement, measurements
NOUN ❶ the result that you obtain
when you measure something.
❷ Measurement is the activity of
measuring something. ❸ Your
measurements are the sizes of your
chest, waist, and hips that you use to
buy the correct size of clothes.

meat, meats NOUN Meat is the flesh
of animals that is cooked and eaten.
meaty ADJECTIVE

Mecca NOUN ❶ Mecca is the
holiest city of Islam, to which many
Muslims make pilgrimages. ❷ If a
place is a mecca for people of a
particular kind, many of them go there
because it is of special interest to
them • *The island is a mecca for bird*
lovers.
● **USAGE NOTE:** Most Muslims
● dislike this form and use the Arabic
● Makkah

A
B
C
D
E
F
G
H
I
J
K
L
M
N
O
P
Q
R
S
T
U
V
W
X
Y
Z

mechanic, mechanics **NOUN** ❶ a person who repairs and maintains engines and machines ❷ IN PLURAL The mechanics of something are the way in which it works or is done • *the mechanics of accounting.* ❸ IN PLURAL Mechanics is also the scientific study of movement and the forces that affect objects.

mechanical **ADJECTIVE** ❶ A mechanical device has moving parts and is used to do a physical task. ❷ A mechanical action is done automatically without thinking about it • *He gave a mechanical smile.* **mechanically** **ADVERB**

mechanism, mechanisms **NOUN** ❶ D&T a part of a machine that does a particular task • *a locking mechanism.* ❷ SCIENCE part of your behaviour that is automatic • *the body's defence mechanisms.*

medal, medals **NOUN** a small disc of metal given as an award for bravery or as a prize for sport.

medallion, medallions **NOUN** a round piece of metal worn as an ornament on a chain round the neck.

medallist, medallists **NOUN** a person who has won a medal in sport • *a gold medallist at the Olympics.*

meddle, meddles, meddling, meddled **VERB** To meddle is to interfere and try to change things without being asked.

media **PLURAL NOUN** You can refer to the television, radio, and newspapers as the media.
● USAGE NOTE: Although *media* is a plural noun, it is becoming more common for it to be used as a
singular: *the media is obsessed with violence*

mediaeval another spelling of medieval.

median, medians [Said **mee-dee-an**] **ADJECTIVE** ❶ The median value of a set is the middle value when the set is arranged in order ▷ **NOUN** ❷ In geometry, a straight line drawn from one of the angles of a triangle to the middle point of the opposite side.

mediate, mediates, mediating, mediated **VERB** If you mediate between two groups, you try to settle a dispute between them. **mediation** **NOUN** **mediator** **NOUN**

medical, medicals **ADJECTIVE** ❶ relating to the prevention and treatment of illness and injuries ▷ **NOUN** ❷ a thorough examination of your body by a doctor. **medically** **ADVERB**

medication, medications **NOUN** Medication is a substance that is used to treat illness.

medicinal **ADJECTIVE** relating to the treatment of illness • *a valuable medicinal herb.*

medicine, medicines **NOUN** PE ❶ Medicine is the treatment of illness and injuries by doctors and nurses. ❷ a substance you drink or swallow to help cure an illness.

medieval or **mediaeval** [Said med-dee-ee-vul] **ADJECTIVE** relating to the period between about 1100 AD and 1500 AD, especially in Europe.
● WORD HISTORY: from Latin *medium aevum* meaning 'the middle age'

mediocre [Said meed-dee-**oh**-ker] **ADJECTIVE** of rather poor quality • a mediocre string of performances. **mediocrity NOUN**

meditate, meditates, meditating, meditated **VERB** ❶ If you meditate on something, you think about it very deeply. ❷ If you meditate, you remain in a calm, silent state for a period of time, often as part of a religious training. **meditation NOUN**

Mediterranean NOUN ❶ The Mediterranean is the large sea between southern Europe and northern Africa ▷ **ADJECTIVE** ❷ relating to or typical of the Mediterranean or the European countries adjoining it.

medium, mediums or media **ADJECTIVE** ❶ If something is of medium size or degree, it is neither large nor small • a medium sized hotel. ▷ **NOUN** ❷ a means that you use to communicate something • the medium of television. ❸ a person who claims to be able to speak to the dead and to receive messages from them.

medley, medleys **NOUN** ❶ a mixture of different things creating an interesting effect. ❷ a number of different songs or tunes sung or played one after the other.

meek, meeker, meekest **ADJECTIVE** A meek person is timid and does what other people say. **meekly ADVERB**
  ● **SIMILAR WORDS**: submissive,
  ● timid

meet, meets, meeting, met **VERB** ❶ If you meet someone, you happen to be in the same place as them. ❷ If you meet a visitor you go to be with

them when they arrive. ❸ When a group of people meet, they gather together for a purpose. ❹ If something meets a need, it can fulfil it • services intended to meet the needs of the elderly. ❺ If something meets with a particular reaction, it gets that reaction from people • I was met with silence.

meeting, meetings **NOUN** ❶ an event in which people discuss proposals and make decisions together. ❷ what happens when you meet someone.

mega- PREFIX 'Mega-' means very great.

megabyte, megabytes **NOUN** (ICT) a unit of storage in a computer, equal to 1 048 576 bytes.

megalomaniac, megalomaniacs **NOUN** Someone who is a megalomaniac is always seeking power and enjoys feeling important.

megaphone, megaphones **NOUN** A megaphone is a cone-shaped device that makes your voice sound louder when you speak into it.

melaleuca, melaleucas [Said mel-a-**loo**-ka] **NOUN** an Australian tree or shrub that has black branches and a white trunk.

melancholy ADJECTIVE OR NOUN If you feel melancholy, you feel sad.

mêlée, mêlées [Said **mel**-lay] **NOUN** a situation where there are a lot of people rushing around.

mellow, mellower, mellowest; mellows, mellowing, mellowed **ADJECTIVE** ❶ Mellow light is soft and golden. ❷ A mellow sound is

a b c d e f g h i j k l **m** n o p q r s t u v w x y z

▷ SPELLING NOTE: you'll brEAK that Electrical Aerial, Kitty (br**eak**)

smooth and pleasant to listen to • *his mellow clarinet.* ▷ **VERB ❸** If someone mellows, they become more pleasant or relaxed • *He certainly hasn't mellowed with age.*

melodic ADJECTIVE relating to melody.

melodious ADJECTIVE pleasant to listen to • *soft melodious music.*

melodrama, melodramas NOUN a story or play in which people's emotions are exaggerated.

melodramatic ADJECTIVE behaving in an exaggerated, emotional way.
● **SIMILAR WORDS:** histrionic,
● overdramatic, theatrical

melody, melodies NOUN (MUSIC) a tune.

melon, melons NOUN a large, juicy fruit with a green or yellow skin and many seeds inside.

melt, melts, melting, melted VERB ❶ When something melts or when you melt it, it changes from a solid to a liquid because it has been heated. ❷ If something melts, it disappears • *The crowd melted away* • *Her inhibitions melted.*

melting point, melting points NOUN (SCIENCE) the temperature at which a solid starts to turn to liquid.

member, members NOUN ❶ A member of a group is one of the people or things belonging to the group • *members of the family.* ❷ A member of an organization is a person who has joined the organization ▷ ADJECTIVE ❸ A country belonging to an international organization is

called a member country or a member state.

Member of Parliament, Members of Parliament NOUN a person who has been elected to represent people in a country's parliament.

membership NOUN ❶ Membership of an organization is the state of being a member of it. ❷ The people who belong to an organization are its membership.

membrane, membranes NOUN (SCIENCE) a very thin piece of skin or tissue which connects or covers plant or animal organs or cells • *the nasal membrane.*

memento, mementos NOUN an object which you keep because it reminds you of a person or a special occasion • *a lasting memento of their romance.*

memo, memos NOUN a note from one person to another within the same organization. Memo is short for 'memorandum'.

memoirs [Said *mem-wahrz*] PLURAL NOUN (ENGLISH) If someone writes their memoirs, they write a book about their life and experiences.

memorable ADJECTIVE If something is memorable, it is likely to be remembered because it is special or unusual • *a memorable victory.*
memorably ADVERB

memorandum, memorandums or memoranda NOUN a memo.

memorial, memorials NOUN ❶ a structure built to remind people of a famous person or event • *a war* *memorial.* ▷ **ADJECTIVE** ❷ A memorial event or prize is in honour of someone who has died, so that they will be remembered.

memorize, memorizes, memorizing, memorized; *also spelt* **memorise** **VERB** If you memorize something, you learn it thoroughly so you can remember it exactly.

memory, memories **NOUN** ❶ Your memory is your ability to remember things. ❷ something you remember about the past • *memories of their school days.* ❸ [ICT] the part in which information is stored in a computer.
● **SIMILAR WORDS:** ❶ recall,
● recollection, remembrance

men the plural of **man**.

menace, menaces, menacing, menaced **NOUN** ❶ someone or something that is likely to cause serious harm • *the menace of drugs in sport.* ❷ Menace is the quality of being threatening • *an atmosphere of menace.* ▷ **VERB** ❸ If someone or something menaces you, they threaten to harm you. **menacingly** **ADVERB**

menagerie, menageries *[Said men-naj-er-ree]* **NOUN** a collection of different wild animals.
● **WORD HISTORY:** from French
● *menagerie* meaning 'household
● management', which used to
● include the care of domestic
● animals

mend, mends, mending, mended **VERB** If you mend something that is broken, you repair it.

menial **ADJECTIVE** Menial work is boring and tiring and the people who

do it have low status.

meningitis **NOUN** Meningitis is a serious infectious illness which affects your brain and spinal cord.

menopause **NOUN** The menopause is the time during which a woman gradually stops menstruating. This usually happens when she is about fifty.

menorah, menorahs *[Said mi-naw-rah]* **NOUN** a candelabra that usually has seven parts and is used in Jewish temples.

menstruate, menstruates, menstruating, menstruated **VERB** When a woman menstruates, blood comes from her womb. This normally happens once a month.
menstruation **NOUN** **menstrual** **ADJECTIVE**

-ment **SUFFIX** '-ment' forms nouns which refer to a state or a feeling • *contentment* • *resentment.*

mental **ADJECTIVE** ❶ relating to the process of thinking or intelligence • *mental arithmetic.* ❷ relating to the health of the mind • *mental health.* **mentally** **ADVERB**

mentality, mentalities **NOUN** an attitude or way of thinking • *the traditional military mentality.*

mention, mentions, mentioning, mentioned **VERB** ❶ If you mention something, you talk about it briefly ▷ **NOUN** ❷ a brief comment about someone or something • *He made no mention of his criminal past.*
● **SIMILAR WORDS:** ❶ bring up,
● refer to, touch upon

mentor, mentors **NOUN** Someone's

mentor is a person who teaches them and gives them advice.

menu, menus NOUN **1** a list of the foods you can eat in a restaurant. **2** (ICT) a list of different options shown on a computer screen which the user must choose from.

MEP, MEPs NOUN an abbreviation for 'Member of the European Parliament': a person who has been elected to represent people in the European Parliament.

mercenary, mercenaries NOUN **1** a soldier who is paid to fight for a foreign country ▷ ADJECTIVE **2** Someone who is mercenary is mainly interested in getting money.

merchandise NOUN FORMAL Merchandise is goods that are sold • *He had left me with more merchandise than I could sell.*

merchant, merchants NOUN a trader who imports and exports goods • *a coal merchant.*

merchant navy NOUN The merchant navy is the boats and sailors involved in carrying goods for trade.

merciful ADJECTIVE **1** showing kindness. **2** showing forgiveness. **3** considered to be fortunate as a relief from suffering • *Death came as a merciful release.* **mercifully** ADVERB
● SIMILAR WORDS:
● **2** compassionate, humane, kind

merciless ADJECTIVE showing no kindness or forgiveness. **mercilessly** ADVERB
● SIMILAR WORDS: cruel, heartless,
● ruthless

mercury NOUN **1** Mercury is a

silver-coloured metallic element that is liquid at room temperature. It is used in thermometers. **2** Mercury is also the planet in the solar system which is nearest to the sun.

mercy, mercies NOUN If you show mercy, you show forgiveness and do not punish someone as severely as you could.
● SIMILAR WORDS: compassion,
● kindness, pity

mere, merest ADJECTIVE used to emphasize how unimportant or small something is • *It's a mere 7-minute journey by boat.* **merely** ADVERB

merge, merges, merging, merged VERB When two things merge, they combine together to make one thing • *The firms merged in 1983.* **merger** NOUN

meringue, meringues [Said mer-**rang**] NOUN a type of crisp, sweet cake made with egg whites and sugar.

merino, merinos [Said mer-**ree**-no] NOUN a breed of sheep, common in Australia and New Zealand, with long, fine wool.

merit, merits, meriting, merited NOUN **1** If something has merit, it is good or worthwhile. **2** The merits of something are its advantages or good qualities ▷ VERB **3** If something merits a particular treatment, it deserves that treatment • *He merits a place in the team.*

mermaid, mermaids NOUN In stories, a mermaid is a woman with a fish's tail instead of legs, who lives in the sea.

▷ SPELLING NOTE: *The government licenSes Schnapps (licenses)*

merry, merrier, merriest **ADJECTIVE** happy and cheerful • *He was, for all his shyness, a merry man.* **merrily ADVERB**

merry-go-round, merry-go-rounds **NOUN** a large rotating platform with models of animals or vehicles on it, on which children ride at a fair.

mesh NOUN Mesh is threads of wire or plastic twisted together like a net • *a fence made of wire mesh.*

mesolithic ADJECTIVE (GEOGRAPHY) relating to the middle period of the Stone Age, roughly between 12,000 BC and 3000 BC.

mess, messes, messing, messed **NOUN** ❶ something untidy. ❷ a situation which is full of problems and trouble. ❸ a room or building in which members of the armed forces eat • *the officers' mess.* ▷ **VERB** ❹ If you mess about or mess around, you do things without any particular purpose. ❺ If you mess something up, you spoil it or do it wrong. **messy ADJECTIVE**

message, messages **NOUN** ❶ a piece of information or a request that you send someone or leave for them. ❷ an idea that someone tries to communicate to people, for example in a play or a speech • *the story's anti-drugs message.*

messaging NOUN Messaging or text messaging is the sending and receiving of short pieces of information between mobile phones, using both letters and numbers to produce shortened forms of words.

messenger, messengers **NOUN**

someone who takes a message to someone for someone else.
● **SIMILAR WORDS:** courier,
● emissary, envoy

Messiah [*Said* miss-**eye**-ah] **PROPER NOUN** (RE) ❶ For Jews, the Messiah is the king of the Jews who will be sent by God. ❷ For Christians, the Messiah is Jesus Christ.
● **WORD HISTORY:** from Hebrew
● *mashiach* meaning 'anointed'

Messrs [*Said* mes-**serz**] Messrs is the plural of **Mr.** It is often used in the names of businesses • *Messrs Brown and Humberley, Solicitors.*

met the past tense and past participle of **meet.**

metabolism, metabolisms **NOUN** Your metabolism is the chemical processes in your body that use food for growth and energy. **metabolic ADJECTIVE**

metacarpal, metacarpals **NOUN** (SCIENCE) The metacarpals are the bones in your hand joining your thumb and fingers to your wrist.

metal, metals **NOUN** (SCIENCE) Metal is a chemical element such as iron, steel, copper, or lead. Metals are good conductors of heat and electricity. **metallic ADJECTIVE**

metamorphic ADJECTIVE (GEOGRAPHY) Metamorphic rock is rock that has been altered from its original state by heat or pressure.

metamorphosis, metamorphoses [*Said* met-am-**mor**-fiss-iss] **NOUN** FORMAL When a metamorphosis occurs, a person or thing changes into something completely different • *the*

a
b
c
d
e
f
g
h
i
j
k
l
m
n
o
p
q
r
s
t
u
v
w
x
y
z

▷ SPELLING NOTE: *have a plEce of plE* (piece)

metamorphosis of a larva into an insect.

A B C D E F G H I J K L **M** N O P Q R S T U V W X Y Z

metaphor, metaphors NOUN (ENGLISH) an imaginative way of describing something as another thing, and so suggesting that it has the typical qualities of that other thing. For example, if you wanted to say that someone is shy, you might say they are a mouse. **metaphorical** ADJECTIVE **metaphorically** ADVERB

metatarsal, metatarsals NOUN (SCIENCE) The metatarsals are the bones in your foot joining your toes to your ankle.

meteor, meteors NOUN a piece of rock or metal that burns very brightly when it enters the earth's atmosphere from space.

meteoric ADJECTIVE A meteoric rise to power or success happens very quickly.

meteorite, meteorites NOUN a piece of rock from space that has landed on earth.

meteorological ADJECTIVE (GEOGRAPHY) relating to or involving the weather or weather forecasting. **meteorology** NOUN

meteorologist, meteorologists NOUN (GEOGRAPHY) someone who studies and forecasts the weather.

meter, meters NOUN a device that measures and records something • *a gas meter.*

methane [Said **mee**-thane] NOUN Methane is a colourless gas with no smell that is found in coal gas and produced by decaying vegetable matter. Methane burns easily and can be used as a fuel.

method, methods NOUN ❶ a particular way of doing something • *the traditional method of making wine.* ❷ (SCIENCE) a way that an experiment or test is carried out • *Describe the method as well as the result obtained.*

methodical ADJECTIVE Someone who is methodical does things carefully and in an organized way. **methodically** ADVERB

Methodist, Methodists NOUN OR ADJECTIVE someone who belongs to the Methodist Church, a Protestant church whose members worship God in a way begun by John Wesley and his followers.

meticulous ADJECTIVE A meticulous person does things very carefully and with great attention to detail. **meticulously** ADVERB

metre, metres NOUN ❶ (MATHS) The metre is the SI unit of length. One metre is equal to 100 centimetres. ❷ (ENGLISH) In poetry, metre is the regular and rhythmic arrangement of words and syllables. **metrical** ADJECTIVE

metric ADJECTIVE relating to the system of measurement that uses metres, grams, and litres.

metropolis, metropolises NOUN a very large city.
● WORD HISTORY: from Greek
● *mētēr* + *polis* meaning 'mother city'

metropolitan ADJECTIVE relating or belonging to a large, busy city • *metropolitan districts.*

mettle NOUN If you are on your

mettle, you are ready to do something as well as you can because you know you are being tested or challenged.

mew, mews, mewing, mewed **VERB**
❶ When a cat mews, it makes a short high-pitched noise ▷ **NOUN** ❷ the short high-pitched sound that a cat makes. ❸ A mews is a quiet yard or street surrounded by houses.

Mexican, Mexicans **ADJECTIVE**
❶ belonging or relating to Mexico ▷ **NOUN** ❷ someone who comes from Mexico.

mezzo forte *[Said met-so for-tay]*
ADVERB (MUSIC) In music, mezzo forte is an instruction to play or sing something fairly loudly.
● **WORD HISTORY:** an Italian term;
● 'mezzo' is Italian for 'half'

mezzo piano *[Said met-so pee-an-oh]* **ADVERB** (MUSIC) In music, mezzo piano is an instruction to play or sing something fairly quietly.
● **WORD HISTORY:** an Italian term;
● 'mezzo' is Italian for 'half'

mg an abbreviation for 'milligrams'.

miasma, miasmas or miasmata **NOUN** an unhealthy or unpleasant atmosphere, especially one caused by decaying things.

mice the plural of **mouse**.

micro- **PREFIX** 'Micro-' means very small.

microchip, microchips **NOUN** a small piece of silicon on which electronic circuits for a computer are printed.

microphone, microphones **NOUN** a device that is used to make sounds louder or to record them on a tape recorder.

microprocessor, microprocessors **NOUN** a microchip which can be programmed to do a large number of tasks or calculations.

microscope, microscopes **NOUN** a piece of equipment which magnifies very small objects so that you can study them.

microscopic **ADJECTIVE** very small indeed • *microscopic parasites*.

microwave, microwaves **NOUN** A microwave or microwave oven is a type of oven which cooks food very quickly by radiation.

mid- **PREFIX** 'Mid-' is used to form words that refer to the middle part of a place or period of time • *mid-Atlantic* • *the mid-70s*.

midday **NOUN** Midday is twelve o'clock in the middle of the day.

middle, middles **NOUN** ❶ The middle of something is the part furthest from the edges, ends, or outside surface ▷ **ADJECTIVE** ❷ The middle one in a series or a row is the one that has an equal number of people or things each side of it • *the middle house*.

middle age **NOUN** Middle age is the period of your life when you are between about 40 and 60 years old. **middle-aged** **ADJECTIVE**

Middle Ages **PLURAL NOUN** In European history, the Middle Ages were the period between about 1100 AD and 1500 AD.

middle class, middle classes

a
b
c
d
e
f
g
h
i
j
k
l
m
n
o
p
q
r
s
t
u
v
w
x
y
z

▷ SPELLING NOTE: *I went to see (C) the doctor's new practiCe (practice)*

NOUN The middle classes are the people in a society who are not working-class or upper-class, for example managers and lawyers.

Middle East NOUN The Middle East consists of Iran and the countries in Asia to the west and south-west of Iran.

Middle English NOUN Middle English was the English language from about 1100 AD until about 1450 AD.

middle-of-the-road ADJECTIVE Middle-of-the-road opinions are moderate.

middle school, middle schools NOUN In England and Wales, a middle school is for children aged between about 8 and 12.

middling ADJECTIVE of average quality or ability.

midge, midges NOUN a small flying insect which can bite people.

midget, midgets NOUN a very short person.

midnight NOUN Midnight is twelve o'clock at night.

midriff, midriffs NOUN the middle of your body between your waist and your chest.

midst NOUN If you are in the midst of a crowd or an event, you are in the middle of it.

midsummer ADJECTIVE relating to the period in the middle of summer • *a lovely midsummer morning in July.*

midway ADVERB in the middle of a distance or period of time • *They scored midway through the second half.*

midwife, midwives NOUN a nurse who is trained to help women at the birth of a baby. **midwifery** NOUN

might VERB ❶ If you say something might happen, you mean that it is possible that it will happen • *I might stay a while.* ❷ If you say that someone might do something, you are suggesting that they do it • *You might like to go and see it.* ❸ Might is also the past tense of **may.** ▷ NOUN ❹ LITERARY Might is strength or power • *the full might of the Navy.*
  ● **USAGE NOTE:** You can use *might* or *may* to make a very polite request: *might I ask a favour?; may I ask a favour?*

mightily ADVERB LITERARY to a great degree or extent • *I was mightily relieved by the decision.*

mighty, mightier, mightiest ADJECTIVE LITERARY very powerful or strong • *a mighty army on the march.*

migraine, migraines [Said *mee-grane* or *my-grane*] NOUN a severe headache that makes you feel very ill.
  ● **WORD HISTORY:** from Latin *hemicrania* meaning 'pain in half the head'

migrant worker, migrant workers NOUN (GEOGRAPHY) someone who travels to another country to work, especially harvesting crops on a farm.

migrate, migrates, migrating, migrated VERB ❶ (GEOGRAPHY) If people migrate, they move from one place to another, especially to find work. ❷ (SCIENCE) When birds or animals migrate, they move at a particular season to a different place, usually to breed or to find new feeding grounds • *the birds migrate each year to Mexico.* **migration NOUN migratory ADJECTIVE migrant NOUN OR ADJECTIVE**

mike, mikes **NOUN** INFORMAL a microphone.

mild, milder, mildest **ADJECTIVE** ❶ Something that is mild is not strong and does not have any powerful or damaging effects • *a mild shampoo.* ❷ Someone who is mild is gentle and kind. ❸ Mild weather is warmer than usual • *The region has mild winters and hot summers.* ❹ Mild emotions or attitudes are not very great or extreme • *mild surprise.* **mildly ADVERB**

mildew NOUN Mildew is a soft white fungus that grows on things when they are warm and damp.

mile, miles **NOUN** a unit of distance equal to 1760 yards or about 1.6 kilometres.
● **WORD HISTORY:** from Latin *milia*
● *passuum* meaning 'a thousand
● paces'

mileage, mileages **NOUN** ❶ Your mileage is the distance that you have travelled, measured in miles. ❷ The amount of mileage that you get out of something is how useful it is to you.

militant, militants **ADJECTIVE** ❶ A militant person is very active in trying to bring about extreme political or social change • *a militant socialist.* ▷ **NOUN** ❷ a person who tries to bring about extreme political or social change. **militancy NOUN**

military ADJECTIVE ❶ related to or involving the armed forces of a country • *military bases.* ▷ **NOUN**

❷ The military are the armed forces of a country. **militarily ADVERB**

militia, militias [Said mil-*lish*-a] **NOUN** an organization that operates like an army but whose members are not professional soldiers.

milk, milks, milking, milked **NOUN** ❶ Milk is the white liquid produced by female cows, goats, and some other animals to feed their young. People drink milk and use it to make butter, cheese, and yogurt. ❷ Milk is also the white liquid that a baby drinks from its mother's breasts ▷ **VERB** ❸ When someone milks a cow or a goat, they get milk from it by pulling its udders. ❹ If you milk a situation, you get as much personal gain from it as possible • *They milked money from a hospital charity.*

milk tooth, milk teeth **NOUN** Your milk teeth are your first teeth which fall out and are replaced by the permanent set.

milky, milkier, milkiest **ADJECTIVE** ❶ pale creamy white • *milky white skin.* ❷ containing a lot of milk • *a large mug of milky coffee.*

Milky Way NOUN The Milky Way is a strip of stars clustered closely together, appearing as a pale band in the sky.

mill, mills **NOUN** ❶ a building where grain is crushed to make flour. ❷ a factory for making materials such as steel, wool, or cotton. ❸ a small device for grinding coffee or spices into powder • *a pepper mill.*

millennium, millennia or millenniums **NOUN** FORMAL a period of 1000 years.

a
b
c
d
e
f
g
h
i
j
k
l
m
n
o
p
q
r
s
t
u
v
w
x
y
z

▷ SPELLING NOTE: *pAL up with the principAL and principAL staff (principal)*

millennium bug NOUN a computer software problem caused by the change of date at the start of the year 2000.

miller, millers **NOUN** the person who operates a flour mill.

millibar, millibars **NOUN** (GEOGRAPHY) a unit of atmospheric pressure equal to one thousandth of a bar.

milligram, milligrams **NOUN** a unit of weight equal to one thousandth of a gram.

millilitre, millilitres **NOUN** a unit of liquid volume equal to one thousandth of a litre.

millimetre, millimetres **NOUN** a unit of length equal to one tenth of a centimetre or one thousandth of a metre.

million, millions the number 1,000,000. **millionth**

millionaire, millionaires **NOUN** a very rich person who has property worth millions of pounds or dollars.

millstone, millstones **PHRASE** If something is **a millstone round your neck**, it is an unpleasant problem or responsibility you cannot escape from.

mime, mimes, miming, mimed **NOUN** ❶ Mime is the use of movements and gestures to express something or to tell a story without using speech ▷ **VERB** ❷ If you mime something, you describe or express it using mime.

mimic, mimics, mimicking, mimicked **VERB** ❶ If you mimic someone's actions or voice, you imitate them in

an amusing way ▷ **NOUN** ❷ a person who can imitate other people. **mimicry NOUN**

minaret, minarets **NOUN** a tall, thin tower on a mosque.

mince, minces, mincing, minced **NOUN** ❶ Mince is meat which has been chopped into very small pieces in a special machine ▷ **VERB** ❷ If you mince meat, you chop it into very small pieces. ❸ To mince about is to walk with small quick steps in an affected, effeminate way.

mind, minds, minding, minded **NOUN** ❶ Your mind is your ability to think, together with all the thoughts you have and your memory ▷ **PHRASE** ❷ If you **change your mind**, you change a decision that you have made or an opinion that you have ▷ **VERB** ❸ If you do not mind something, you are not annoyed by it or bothered about it. ❹ If you say that you wouldn't mind something, you mean that you would quite like it • *I wouldn't mind a drink.* ❺ If you mind a child or mind something for someone, you look after it for a while • *My mother is minding the office.*

mindful ADJECTIVE FORMAL If you are mindful of something, you think about it carefully before taking action • *mindful of their needs.*

mindless ADJECTIVE ❶ Mindless actions are regarded as stupid and destructive • *mindless violence.* ❷ A mindless job or activity is simple and repetitive.

mine, mines, mining, mined **PRONOUN** ❶ 'Mine' refers to something belonging or relating to the

A B C D E F G H I J K L M N O P Q R S T U V W X Y Z

▷ SPELLING NOTE: L*Earn* the princip*LEs* (princip*le*)

person who is speaking or writing • *a friend of mine.* ▷ **NOUN** ❷ a series of holes or tunnels in the ground from which diamonds, coal, or other minerals are dug out • *a diamond mine.* ❸ a bomb hidden in the ground or underwater, which explodes when people or things touch it ▷ **VERB** ❹ To mine diamonds, coal, or other minerals is to obtain these substances from underneath the ground. **miner NOUN mining NOUN**

minefield, minefields **NOUN** an area of land or water where mines have been hidden.

mineral, minerals **NOUN** (D & T) a substance such as tin, salt, or coal that is formed naturally in rocks and in the earth • *rich mineral deposits.*

mineral water NOUN Mineral water is water which comes from a natural spring.

minestrone [Said min-nes-**strone**-ee] **NOUN** Minestrone is soup containing small pieces of vegetable and pasta.

● **WORD HISTORY:** from Italian *minestrare* meaning 'to serve'

minesweeper, minesweepers **NOUN** a ship for clearing away underwater mines.

mingle, mingles, mingling, mingled **VERB** ❶ If things mingle, they become mixed together • *His cries mingled with theirs.* ❷ (SCIENCE) to mix so that the parts become united.

mini- **PREFIX** 'Mini-' is used to form nouns referring to something smaller or less important than similar things • *a TV mini-series.*

miniature, miniatures [Said min-nit-cher] **ADJECTIVE** ❶ copying something on a much smaller scale ▷ **NOUN** ❷ a very small detailed painting, often of a person.

minibus, minibuses **NOUN** a van with seats in the back which is used as a small bus.

minim, minims **NOUN** (MUSIC) a musical note (♩) that has a time value equal to half a semibreve. In the United States and Canada, a minim is called a half note.

minimal **ADJECTIVE** very small in quality, quantity, or degree • *He has minimal experience.* **minimally ADVERB**

minimize, minimizes, minimizing, minimized; *also spelt* **minimise** **VERB** If you minimize something, you reduce it to the smallest amount possible • *His route was changed to minimize jet lag.*

minimum **ADJECTIVE** ❶ The minimum amount is the smallest amount that is possible • *a minimum wage.* ▷ **NOUN** ❷ The minimum is the smallest amount that is possible • *a minimum of three weeks.*

minister, ministers **NOUN** ❶ A minister is a person who is in charge of a particular government department • *Portugal's deputy foreign minister.* ❷ A minister in a Protestant church is a member of the clergy.

ministerial **ADJECTIVE** relating to a government minister or ministry • *ministerial duties.*

ministry, ministries **NOUN** ❶ a government department that deals with a particular area of work • *the Ministry of Defence*. ❷ Members of the clergy can be referred to as the ministry • *Her son is in the ministry.*

mink, minks **NOUN** Mink is an expensive fur used to make coats or hats.

minnow, minnows **NOUN** a very small freshwater fish.

minor, minors **ADJECTIVE** ❶ not as important or serious as other things • *a minor injury*. ❷ (MUSIC) A minor key is one of the keys in which most European music is written ▷ **NOUN** ❸ FORMAL a young person under the age of 18 • *laws concerning the employment of minors.*

minority, minorities **NOUN** ❶ The minority of people or things in a group is a number of them forming less than half of the whole • *Only a minority of people want this*. ❷ A minority is a group of people of a particular race or religion living in a place where most people are of a different race or religion • *ethnic minorities.*

minstrel, minstrels **NOUN** a singer and entertainer in medieval times.

mint, mints, minting, minted **NOUN** ❶ Mint is a herb used for flavouring in cooking. ❷ a peppermint-flavoured sweet. ❸ The mint is the place where the official coins of a country are made ▷ **VERB** ❹ When coins or medals are minted, they are made ▷ **ADJECTIVE** ❺ If something is in mint condition, it is in very good condition, like new.

minus (MATHS) ❶ You use 'minus' to show that one number is being subtracted from another • *Ten minus*

six equals four. **ADJECTIVE** ❷ 'Minus' is used when talking about temperatures below 0° C or 0° F.

minuscule [Said *min-nus-kyool*] **ADJECTIVE** very small indeed.

minute, minutes, minuting, minuted [Said *min-nit*] **NOUN** ❶ a unit of time equal to sixty seconds. ❷ The minutes of a meeting are the written records of what was said and decided ▷ **VERB** ❸ To minute a meeting is to write the official notes of it.

minute [Said *my-nyoot*] **ADJECTIVE** extremely small • *a minute amount of pesticide*. **minutely ADVERB**

minutiae [Said *my-nyoo-shee-aye*] **PLURAL NOUN** FORMAL Minutiae are small, unimportant details.

miracle, miracles **NOUN** ❶ (RE) a wonderful and surprising event, believed to have been caused by God. ❷ any very surprising and fortunate event • *My father got a job. It was a miracle.* **miraculous ADJECTIVE miraculously ADVERB**

mirage, mirages [Said *mir-ahj*] **NOUN** an image which you can see in the distance in very hot weather, but which does not actually exist.

mire NOUN LITERARY Mire is swampy ground or mud.

mirror, mirrors, mirroring, mirrored **NOUN** ❶ a piece of glass which reflects light and in which you can see your reflection ▷ **VERB** ❷ To mirror something is to have similar features to it • *His own shock was mirrored on her face.*

mirth NOUN LITERARY Mirth is great amusement and laughter.

mis- PREFIX 'Mis-' means 'wrong' or 'false' • *misbehaviour* • *misconception*.

misbehave, misbehaves, misbehaving, misbehaved **VERB** If a child misbehaves, he or she is naughty or behaves badly. **misbehaviour NOUN**

miscarriage, miscarriages **NOUN** ❶ If a woman has a miscarriage she gives birth to a baby before it is properly formed and it dies. ❷ A miscarriage of justice is a wrong decision made by a court, which causes an innocent person to be punished.

miscellaneous ADJECTIVE A miscellaneous group is made up of people or things that are different from each other.

mischief NOUN Mischief is eagerness to have fun by teasing people or playing tricks. **mischievous ADJECTIVE**

miscible ADJECTIVE (SCIENCE) Liquids that are miscible can be mixed together. **miscibility NOUN**

misconception, misconceptions **NOUN** a wrong idea about something • *Another misconception is that cancer is infectious*.

misconduct NOUN Misconduct is bad or unacceptable behaviour by a professional person • *The Football Association found him guilty of misconduct*.

misdemeanour, misdemeanours [Said miss-dem-**mee**-ner] **NOUN** FORMAL an act that is shocking or unacceptable.

miser, misers **NOUN** a person who enjoys saving money but hates spending it. **miserly ADJECTIVE**

miserable ADJECTIVE ❶ If you are miserable, you are very unhappy. ❷ If a place or a situation is miserable, it makes you feel depressed • *a miserable little flat*. **miserably ADVERB**

● SIMILAR WORDS: ❶ dejected,
● unhappy, wretched ❷ gloomy,
● wretched

misery, miseries **NOUN** Misery is great unhappiness.

misfire, misfires, misfiring, misfired **VERB** If a plan misfires, it goes wrong.

misfit, misfits **NOUN** a person who is not accepted by other people because of being rather strange or eccentric.

misfortune, misfortunes **NOUN** an unpleasant occurrence that is regarded as bad luck • *I had the misfortune to fall off my bike*.

misgiving, misgivings **NOUN** If you have misgivings, you are worried or unhappy about something • *I had misgivings about his methods*.

misguided ADJECTIVE A misguided opinion or action is wrong because it is based on a misunderstanding or bad information.

misinform, misinforms, misinforming, misinformed **VERB** If you are misinformed, you are given wrong or inaccurate information. **misinformation NOUN**

misinterpret, misinterprets, misinterpreting, misinterpreted **VERB** To misinterpret something is to understand it wrongly • *You completely misinterpreted what I wrote*.

a
b
c
d
e
f
g
h
i
j
k
l
m
n
o
p
q
r
s
t
u
v
w
x
y
z

▷ SPELLING NOTE: *Rhythmical Hounds Yap To Heavy Music (rhythm)*

A
B
C
D
E
F
G
H
I
J
K
L
M
N
O
P
Q
R
S
T
U
V
W
X
Y
Z

misjudge, misjudges, misjudging, misjudged **VERB** If you misjudge someone or something, you form an incorrect idea or opinion about them.

mislay, mislays, mislaying, mislaid **VERB** If you mislay something, you lose it because you have forgotten where you put it.

mislead, misleads, misleading, misled **VERB** To mislead someone is to make them believe something which is not true.

misplaced **ADJECTIVE** A misplaced feeling is inappropriate or directed at the wrong thing or person • *misplaced loyalty.*

misprint, misprints **NOUN** a mistake such as a spelling mistake in something that has been printed.

misrepresent, misrepresents, misrepresenting, misrepresented **VERB** To misrepresent someone is to give an inaccurate or misleading account of what they have said or done. **misrepresentation NOUN**

miss, misses, missing, missed **VERB** ❶ If you miss something, you do not notice it • *You can't miss it. It's on the second floor.* ❷ If you miss someone or something, you feel sad that they are no longer with you • *The boys miss their father.* ❸ If you miss a chance or opportunity, you fail to take advantage of it. ❹ If you miss a bus, plane, or train, you arrive too late to catch it. ❺ If you miss something, you fail to hit it when you aim at it • *His shot missed the target and went wide.* ▷ **NOUN** ❻ an act of missing something that you were aiming at. ❼ 'Miss' is used before the name of a

woman or girl who is not married as a form of address • *Did you know Miss Smith?*

missile, missiles **NOUN** a weapon that moves long distances through the air and explodes when it reaches its target; also used of any object thrown as a weapon.

mission, missions **NOUN** ❶ an important task that you have to do. ❷ a group of people who have been sent to a foreign country to carry out an official task • *He became head of the Israeli mission.* ❸ a journey made by a military aeroplane or space rocket to carry out a task. ❹ If you have a mission, there is something that you believe it is your duty to try to achieve. ❺ the workplace of a group of Christians who are working for the Church.

missionary, missionaries **NOUN** a Christian who has been sent to a foreign country to work for the Church.

missive, missives **NOUN** OLD-FASHIONED a letter or message.

mist, mists, misting, misted **NOUN** ❶ Mist consists of a large number of tiny drops of water in the air, which make it hard to see clearly ▷ **VERB** ❷ If your eyes mist, you cannot see very far because there are tears in your eyes. ❸ If glass mists over or mists up, it becomes covered with condensation so that you cannot see through it.

mistake, mistakes, mistaking, mistook, mistaken **NOUN** ❶ an action or opinion that is wrong or is not what you intended ▷ **VERB** ❷ If you mistake someone or something for another person or thing, you wrongly think that they are the other person or thing • *I mistook him for the owner of the house.*

● **SIMILAR WORDS: ❶** blunder, error, miscalculation, slip

mistaken ADJECTIVE **❶** If you are mistaken about something, you are wrong about it. **❷** If you have a mistaken belief or opinion, you believe something which is not true.
mistakenly ADVERB

mister NOUN A man is sometimes addressed in a very informal way as 'mister' • *Where do you live, mister?*

mistletoe [*Said* **mis**-*sel-toe*] NOUN Mistletoe is a plant which grows on trees and has white berries on it. It is used as a Christmas decoration.

mistook the past tense of **mistake**.

mistreat, mistreats, mistreating, mistreated VERB To mistreat a person or animal is to treat them badly and make them suffer.

mistress, mistresses NOUN **❶** A married man's mistress is a woman who is not his wife and who he is having a sexual relationship with. **❷** A school mistress is a female teacher. **❸** A servant's mistress is the woman who is the servant's employer.

mistrust, mistrusts, mistrusting, mistrusted VERB **❶** If you mistrust someone, you do not feel that you can trust them ▷ NOUN **❷** Mistrust is a feeling that you cannot trust someone.

misty, mistier, mistiest ADJECTIVE full of or covered with mist.

misunderstand, misunderstands, misunderstanding, misunderstood VERB If you misunderstand someone, you do not properly understand what they say or do • *He misunderstood the problem.*

misunderstanding, misunderstandings NOUN If two people have a misunderstanding, they have a slight quarrel or disagreement.

misuse, misuses, misusing, misused [*Said* mis-**yoos**] NOUN The misuse of something is the incorrect or dishonest use of it • *the misuse of public money.* [*Said* mis-**yooz**] ▷ VERB To misuse something is to use it incorrectly or dishonestly.

mite, mites NOUN a very tiny creature that lives in the fur of animals.

mitigate, mitigates, mitigating, mitigated VERB FORMAL To mitigate something means to make it less unpleasant, serious, or painful.
mitigation NOUN

mitigating ADJECTIVE FORMAL Mitigating circumstances make a crime easier to understand, and perhaps justify.

mitre, mitres [*Said* **my**-*ter*] NOUN (RE) A mitre is a tall, pointed hat worn by bishops and archbishops on ceremonial occasions.

mitten, mittens NOUN Mittens are gloves which have one section that covers your thumb and another section for the rest of your fingers together.

mix, mixes, mixing, mixed VERB If you mix things, you combine them or

a
b
c
d
e
f
g
h
i
j
k
l
m
n
o
p
q
r
s
t
u
v
w
x
y
z

▷ SPELLING NOTE: On WEDNESday Wayne WED NESta (*Wednesday*)

A
B
C
D
E
F
G
H
I
J
K
L
M
N
O
P
Q
R
S
T
U
V
W
X
Y
Z

shake or stir them together.

mix up VERB If you mix up two things or people, you confuse them • *People often mix us up and greet us by each other's names.*

● SIMILAR WORDS: blend, combine,
● merge, mingle blend, combine,
● merge, mingle

mixed ADJECTIVE ❶ consisting of several things of the same general kind • *a mixed salad.* ❷ involving people from two or more different races • *mixed marriages.* ❸ Mixed education or accommodation is for both males and females • *a mixed comprehensive.*

mixed up ADJECTIVE ❶ If you are mixed up, you are confused • *I'm mixed up about which country I want to play for.* ❷ If you are mixed up in a crime or a scandal, you are involved in it.

mixer, mixers NOUN a machine used for mixing things together • *a cement mixer.*

mixture, mixtures NOUN several different things mixed or shaken together.

● SIMILAR WORDS: blend, medley,
● mix

mix-up, mix-ups NOUN a mistake in something that was planned • *a mix-up with the bookings.*

ml an abbreviation for 'millilitres'.

mm an abbreviation for 'millimetres'.

mnemonic, mnemonics [Said *nim-on-nik*] NOUN ENGLISH A mnemonic is a word or rhyme that helps you to remember things such as scientific facts or spelling rules. 'i

before e, except after c' is an example of a mnemonic

moa, moa or moas NOUN a large, flightless bird that lived in New Zealand and which became extinct in the late 18th century.

moan, moans, moaning, moaned VERB ❶ If you moan, you make a low, miserable sound because you are in pain or suffering. ❷ INFORMAL If you moan about something, you complain about it ▷ NOUN ❸ a low cry of pain or misery.

moat, moats NOUN a wide, water-filled ditch around a building such as a castle.

mob, mobs, mobbing, mobbed NOUN ❶ a large, disorganized crowd of people • *A violent mob attacked the team bus.* ▷ VERB ❷ If a lot of people mob someone, they crowd around the person in a disorderly way • *The band was mobbed by over a thousand fans.*
● WORD HISTORY: from Latin
● *mobile vulgus* meaning 'the fickle
● public'

mobile, mobiles ADJECTIVE ❶ able to move or be moved freely and easily • *a mobile home.* ❷ PE If you are mobile, you are able to travel or move about from one place to another • *a mobile workforce.* ▷ NOUN ❸ a decoration consisting of several small objects which hang from threads and move around when a breeze blows. ❹ a mobile phone. **mobility** NOUN

mobile phone, mobile phones NOUN a small portable telephone.

mobilize, mobilizes, mobilizing, mobilized; *also spelt* **mobilise** VERB ❶ If you mobilize a group of people,

you organize them to do something.
2 If a country mobilizes its armed
forces, it prepares them to fight a war.
mobilization NOUN

moccasin, moccasins **NOUN**
Moccasins are flat, soft leather shoes
with a raised seam above the toe.
● **WORD HISTORY:** from *moccasin*, a
● North American Indian word
● meaning 'shoe'

mock, mocks, mocking, mocked
VERB 1 If you mock someone, you
say something scornful or imitate
their foolish behaviour ▷ **ADJECTIVE**
2 not genuine • *mock surprise* • *a
mock Tudor house.* **3** A mock
examination is one that you do as a
practice before the real examination.
● **SIMILAR WORDS: 1** laugh at,
● make fun of, ridicule

mockery NOUN Mockery is the
expression of scorn or ridicule of
someone.
● **SIMILAR WORDS:** derision,
● ridicule

mode, modes **NOUN 1** A mode of
life or behaviour is a particular way of
living or behaving. **2** In mathematics,
the mode is the biggest in a set of
groups.

model, models, modelling, modelled
NOUN OR ADJECTIVE 1 a copy of
something that shows what it looks
like or how it works • *a model aircraft.*
▷ **NOUN 2** Something that is
described as, for example, a model of
clarity or a model of perfection, is
extremely clear or absolutely perfect.
3 a type or version of a machine
• *Which model of washing machine did
you choose?* **4** a person who poses for
a painter or a photographer. **5** a

person who wears the clothes that are
being displayed at a fashion show
▷ **ADJECTIVE 6** Someone who is
described as, for example, a model
wife or a model student is an excellent
wife or student ▷ **VERB 7** If you
model yourself on someone, you copy
their behaviour because you admire
them. **8** To model clothes is to
display them by wearing them. **9** To
model shapes or figures is to make
them out of clay or wood.
● **SIMILAR WORDS: 2** example,
● ideal, pattern

modem, modems [*Said moe-dem*]
NOUN ⌐ICT⌐ a piece of equipment
that links a computer to the telephone
system so that data can be transferred
from one machine to another via the
telephone line.

moderate, moderates, moderating,
moderated **ADJECTIVE 1** Moderate
views are not extreme, and usually
favour gradual changes rather than
major ones. **2** A moderate amount of
something is neither large nor small
▷ **NOUN 3** a person whose political
views are not extreme ▷ **VERB 4** If
you moderate something or if it
moderates, it becomes less extreme or
violent • *The weather moderated* • *Try
to moderate your temper.* **moderately
ADVERB**

moderation NOUN Moderation is
control of your behaviour that stops
you acting in an extreme way • *a man
of fairness and moderation.*

modern ADJECTIVE 1 relating to
the present time • *modern society.*
2 new and involving the latest ideas
and equipment • *modern technology.*
modernity NOUN

a
b
c
d
e
f
g
h
i
j
k
l
m
n
o
p
q
r
s
t
u
v
w
x
y
z

A
B
C
D
E
F
G
H
I
J
K
L
M
N
O
P
Q
R
S
T
U
V
W
X
Y
Z

modernize, modernizes, modernizing, modernized; *also spelt* **modernise** **VERB** To modernize something is to introduce new methods or equipment to it.

modest **ADJECTIVE** ❶ quite small in size or amount. ❷ Someone who is modest does not boast about their abilities or possessions. ❸ shy and easily embarrassed. **modestly** **ADVERB** **modesty** **NOUN**

modification, modifications **NOUN** a small change made to improve something • *Modifications to the undercarriage were made.*

modify, modifies, modifying, modified **VERB** If you modify something, you change it slightly in order to improve it.

module, modules **NOUN** ❶ one of the parts which when put together form a whole unit or object • *The college provides modules for trainees.* ❷ (ICT) a part of a machine or system that does a particular task. ❸ a part of a spacecraft which can do certain things away from the main body • *the lunar module.* **modular** **ADJECTIVE**

mohair **NOUN** Mohair is very soft, fluffy wool obtained from angora goats.

moist, moister, moistest **ADJECTIVE** slightly wet.

moisten, moistens, moistening, moistened **VERB** If you moisten something, you make it slightly wet.

moisture **NOUN** Moisture is tiny

drops of water in the air or on the ground.

molar, molars **NOUN** Your molars are the large teeth at the back of your mouth.

mole, moles **NOUN** ❶ a dark, slightly raised spot on your skin. ❷ a small animal with black fur. Moles live in tunnels underground. ❸ INFORMAL a member of an organization who is working as a spy for a rival organization.

molecular formula, molecular formulae **NOUN** (SCIENCE) a chemical formula that gives the different types of atom in one molecule of a compound and how many atoms of each type there are. For example, H_2SO_4 is the molecular formula for sulphuric acid, which has two hydrogen atoms, one sulphur atom, and four oxygen atoms.

molecule, molecules **NOUN** the smallest amount of a substance that can exist. **molecular** **ADJECTIVE**

molest, molests, molesting, molested **VERB** To molest a child is to touch the child in a sexual way. This is illegal. **molester** **NOUN**

mollify, mollifies, mollifying, mollified **VERB** To mollify someone is to do something to make them less upset or angry.

mollusc, molluscs **NOUN** an animal with a soft body and no backbone. Snails, slugs, clams, and mussels are all molluscs.

molten **ADJECTIVE** Molten rock or metal has been heated to a very high temperature and has become a thick liquid • *A stream of molten lava was flowing down the mountainside.*

moment, moments NOUN ❶ a very short period of time • *He paused for a moment.* ❷ The moment at which something happens is the point in time at which it happens • *At that moment, the doorbell rang.* ▷ PHRASE ❸ If something is happening **at the moment**, it is happening now.
● SIMILAR WORDS: ❶ instant,
● second

momentary ADJECTIVE
Something that is momentary lasts for only a few seconds • *a momentary lapse of concentration.* **momentarily**
ADVERB
● USAGE NOTE: Some Americans
● say *momentarily* when they mean
● 'very soon', rather than 'for a
● moment'

momentous ADJECTIVE FORMAL
very important, often because of its future effect • *a momentous occasion.*

momentum NOUN ❶ Momentum is the ability that something has to keep developing • *The campaign is gaining momentum.* ❷ Momentum is also the ability that an object has to continue moving as a result of the speed it already has.

monarch, monarchs *[Said mon-nark]* NOUN a queen, king, or other royal person who reigns over a country.

monarchy, monarchies NOUN a system in which a queen or king reigns in a country.

monastery, monasteries NOUN a building in which monks live.
monastic ADJECTIVE

Monday, Mondays NOUN Monday is the day between Sunday and Tuesday.
● WORD HISTORY: from Old English
● *monandæg* meaning 'moon's day'

monetary *[Said mun-net-tree]*
ADJECTIVE FORMAL relating to money, especially the total amount of money in a country.

money NOUN Money is the coins or banknotes that you use to buy something.

mongoose, mongooses NOUN A mongoose is a small animal with a long tail. Mongooses live in hot countries and kill snakes.

mongrel, mongrels NOUN a dog with parents of different breeds.

monitor, monitors, monitoring, monitored VERB ❶ If you monitor something, you regularly check its condition and progress • *Her health will be monitored daily.* ▷ NOUN ❷ a machine used to check or record things. ❸ ICT the visual display unit of a computer. ❹ a school pupil chosen to do special duties by the teacher.

monk, monks NOUN a member of a male religious community.

monkey, monkeys NOUN an animal which has a long tail and climbs trees. Monkeys live in hot countries.

mono- PREFIX 'Mono-' is used at the beginning of nouns and adjectives that have 'one' as part of their meaning • *monopoly* • *monogamy.*

monocle, monocles NOUN a glass lens worn in front of one eye only and held in place by the curve of the eye socket.

a
b
c
d
e
f
g
h
i
j
k
l
m
n
o
p
q
r
s
t
u
v
w
x
y
z

▷ SPELLING NOTE: *King IAn went to ParlIAment in a carrIAge for his marrIAge (-ia-)*

A
B
C
D
E
F
G
H
I
J
K
L
M
N
O
P
Q
R
S
T
U
V
W
X
Y
Z

monogamy NOUN FORMAL
Monogamy is the custom of being
married to only one person at a time.
monogamous ADJECTIVE

monolith, monoliths NOUN
(GEOGRAPHY) A monolith is a very
large upright piece of stone.
monolithic ADJECTIVE

monologue, monologues *[Said
mon-nol-og]* NOUN (ENGLISH) a long
speech by one person during a play or
a conversation.

monomer, monomers NOUN
(SCIENCE) a compound whose
molecules can join together to form a
polymer.

monopoly, monopolies NOUN
control of most of an industry by one
or a few large firms.

monorail, monorails NOUN (D & T)
A monorail is a railway running on a
single rail usually raised above ground
level.

monosyllable, monosyllables
NOUN (ENGLISH) If someone speaks
in monosyllables, they use only words
containing one syllable such as 'yes'
and 'no'. **monosyllabic** ADJECTIVE

monotone, monotones NOUN a
tone which does not vary • *He droned
on in a boring monotone.*

monotonous ADJECTIVE having a
regular pattern which is very dull and
boring • *monotonous work.* **monotony**
NOUN

monotreme, monotremes NOUN
an Australian mammal that has a
single opening in its body.

monounsaturated ADJECTIVE

Monounsaturated oils are made
mainly from vegetable fats and are
considered to be healthier than
saturated oils. **monounsaturate**
NOUN

monsoon, monsoons NOUN the
season of very heavy rain in South-
east Asia.

monster, monsters NOUN ❶ a
large, imaginary creature that looks
very frightening. ❷ a cruel or
frightening person ▷ ADJECTIVE
❸ extremely large • *a monster truck.*
● **WORD HISTORY:** from Latin
● *monstrum* meaning 'omen' or
● 'warning'

monstrosity, monstrosities NOUN
something that is large and extremely
ugly • *a concrete monstrosity in the
middle of the city.*

monstrous ADJECTIVE extremely
shocking or unfair • *a monstrous crime.*
monstrously ADVERB

montage, montages *[Said
mon-tahj]* NOUN a picture or film
consisting of a combination of several
different items arranged to produce an
unusual effect.

month, months NOUN one of the
twelve periods that a year is divided
into.

monthly ADJECTIVE Monthly
describes something that happens or
appears once a month • *monthly staff
meetings.*

monument, monuments NOUN a
large stone structure built to remind
people of a famous person or event • *a
monument to the dead.*

monumental ADJECTIVE ❶ A

▷ SPELLING NOTE: *an ELegant angEL (angel)*

monumental building or sculpture is very large and important. ❷ very large or extreme • *We face a monumental task.*

moo, moos, mooing, mooed **VERB** When a cow moos, it makes a long, deep sound.

mood, moods **NOUN** the way you are feeling at a particular time • *She was in a really cheerful mood.*
● **SIMILAR WORDS:** humour, state of mind, temper

moody, moodier, moodiest **ADJECTIVE** ❶ Someone who is moody is depressed or unhappy • *Tony, despite his charm, could sulk and be moody.* ❷ Someone who is moody often changes their mood for no apparent reason.
● **SIMILAR WORDS:** ❶ morose, sulky, sullen ❷ mercurial, temperamental

moon, moons **NOUN** The moon is an object moving round the earth which you see as a shining circle or crescent in the sky at night. Some other planets have moons.

moonlight, moonlights, moonlighting, moonlighted **NOUN** ❶ Moonlight is the light that comes from the moon at night ▷ **VERB** ❷ **INFORMAL** If someone is moonlighting, they have a second job that they have not informed the tax office about. **moonlit ADJECTIVE**

moor, moors, mooring, moored **NOUN** ❶ a high area of open land ▷ **VERB** ❷ If a boat is moored, it is attached to the land with a rope.

mooring, moorings **NOUN** a place where a boat can be tied.

moose **NOUN** a large North American deer with flat antlers.

moot, moots, mooting, mooted **VERB** **FORMAL** When something is mooted, it is suggested for discussion • *The project was first mooted in 1988.*

mop, mops, mopping, mopped **NOUN** ❶ a tool for washing floors, consisting of a sponge or string head attached to a long handle. ❷ a large amount of loose or untidy hair ▷ **VERB** ❸ To mop a floor is to clean it with a mop. ❹ To mop a surface is to wipe it with a dry cloth to remove liquid.

mope, mopes, moping, moped **VERB** If you mope, you feel miserable and not interested in anything.

moped, mopeds [*Said* **moe***-ped*] **NOUN** a type of small motorcycle.

mopoke, mopokes **NOUN** a small, spotted owl found in Australia and New Zealand. In New Zealand it is called a **morepork**.

moral, morals ❶ **RE** IN PLURAL Morals are values based on beliefs about the correct and acceptable way to behave **ADJECTIVE** ❷ concerned with whether behaviour is right or acceptable • *moral values.* **morality NOUN morally ADVERB**

morale [*Said* mor-**rahl**] **NOUN** Morale is the amount of confidence and optimism that you have • *The morale of the troops was high.*

morbid ADJECTIVE having a great interest in unpleasant things, especially death.

more ADJECTIVE ❶ More means a greater number or extent than something else • *He's got more chips*

▷ SPELLING NOTE: *LEt's measure the angLE (angle)*

than me. **❷** used to refer to an additional thing or amount of something • *He found some more clues.* ▷ **PRONOUN ❸** a greater number or extent ▷ **ADVERB ❹** to a greater degree or extent • *more amused than concerned.* **❺** You can use 'more' in front of adjectives and adverbs to form comparatives • *You look more beautiful than ever.*

moreover ADVERB used to introduce a piece of information that supports or expands the previous statement • *They have accused the government of corruption. Moreover, they have named names.*

morepork, moreporks **NOUN** In New Zealand English, morepork is the same as a mopoke.

morgue, morgues *[Said **morg**]* **NOUN** a building where dead bodies are kept before being buried or cremated.

moribund ADJECTIVE no longer having a useful function and about to come to an end • *a moribund industry.*

morning, mornings **NOUN ❶** the early part of the day until lunchtime. **❷** the part of the day between midnight and noon • *He was born at three in the morning.*

Moroccan, Moroccans *[Said mor-**rok**-an]* **ADJECTIVE ❶** belonging or relating to Morocco ▷ **NOUN ❷** someone who comes from Morocco.

moron, morons **NOUN** INFORMAL a very stupid person. **moronic ADJECTIVE**

morose ADJECTIVE miserable and

bad-tempered • *a morose shrug.*

morphine NOUN Morphine is a drug which is used to relieve pain.

morphology NOUN (ENGLISH) In the study of language, morphology refers to the ways words are constructed with stems, prefixes, and suffixes.

Morse or **Morse code NOUN** Morse or Morse code is a code used for sending messages in which each letter is represented by a series of dots and dashes.

morsel, morsels **NOUN** a small piece of food.

mortal, mortals **ADJECTIVE ❶** unable to live forever • *Remember that you are mortal.* **❷** A mortal wound is one that causes death ▷ **NOUN ❸** an ordinary person.

mortality NOUN ❶ Mortality is the fact that all people must die. **❷** Mortality also refers to the number of people who die at any particular time • *a low infant mortality rate.*

mortar, mortars **NOUN ❶** a short cannon which fires missiles high into the air for a short distance. **❷** Mortar is a mixture of sand, water, and cement used to hold bricks firmly together.

mortgage, mortgages, mortgaging, mortgaged *[Said **mor**-gij]* **NOUN ❶** a loan which you get from a bank or a building society in order to buy a house ▷ **VERB ❷** If you mortgage your house, you use it as a guarantee to a company in order to borrow money from them. They can take the house from you if you do not pay back the money you have borrowed.

mortifying ADJECTIVE
embarrassing or humiliating • *There were some mortifying setbacks.*

mortuary, mortuaries NOUN a special room in a hospital where dead bodies are kept before being buried or cremated.

mosaic, mosaics [*Said moe-**zay**-yik*] NOUN a design made of small coloured stones or pieces of coloured glass set into concrete or plaster.

Moslem another spelling of **Muslim**.

mosque, mosques [*Said **mosk**]* NOUN a building where Muslims go to worship.
● WORD HISTORY: from Arabic
● *masjid* meaning 'temple'

mosquito, mosquitoes or mosquitos [*Said moss-**skee**-toe*] NOUN Mosquitoes are small insects which bite people in order to suck their blood.
● WORD HISTORY: from Spanish
● *mosquito* meaning 'little fly'

moss, mosses NOUN Moss is a soft, low-growing, green plant which grows on damp soil or stone. **mossy** ADJECTIVE

most ADJECTIVE OR PRONOUN
❶ Most of a group of things or people means nearly all of them • *Most people don't share your views.* ❷ The most means a larger amount than anyone or anything else • *She has the most talent.* ▷ ADVERB ❸ You can use 'most' in front of adjectives or adverbs to form superlatives • *the most beautiful women in the world.*

mostly ADVERB 'Mostly' is used to

show that a statement is generally true • *Her friends are mostly men.*

MOT, MOTs NOUN In Britain, an annual test for road vehicles to check that they are safe to drive.

motel, motels NOUN a hotel providing overnight accommodation for people in the middle of a car journey.

moth, moths NOUN an insect like a butterfly which usually flies at night.

mother, mothers, mothering, mothered NOUN ❶ Your mother is the woman who gave birth to you. ❷ Your mother could also be the woman who has looked after you and brought you up ▷ VERB ❸ To mother someone is to look after them and bring them up.

motherhood NOUN Motherhood is the state of being a mother.

mother-in-law, mothers-in-law NOUN Someone's mother-in-law is the mother of their husband or wife.

motif, motifs [*Said moe-**teef**]* NOUN a design which is used as a decoration.

motion, motions, motioning, motioned NOUN ❶ Motion is the process of continually moving or changing position • *the motion of the ship.* ❷ an action or gesture • *Apply with a brush using circular motions.* ❸ a proposal which people discuss and vote on at a meeting ▷ VERB ❹ If you motion to someone, you make a movement with your hand in order to show them what they should do • *I motioned him to proceed.*

motionless ADJECTIVE not moving at all • *He sat motionless.*

a
b
c
d
e
f
g
h
i
j
k
l
m
n
o
p
q
r
s
t
u
v
w
x
y
z

A
B
C
D
E
F
G
H
I
J
K
L
M
N
O
P
Q
R
S
T
U
V
W
X
Y
Z

motivate, motivates, motivating, motivated **VERB** ❶ If you are motivated by something, it makes you behave in a particular way • *He is motivated by duty rather than ambition.* ❷ If you motivate someone, you make them feel determined to do something. **motivated ADJECTIVE motivation NOUN**
● **SIMILAR WORDS:** ❶ drive,
● inspire, prompt

motive, motives **NOUN** (HISTORY) a reason or purpose for doing something • *There was no motive for the attack.*

motley ADJECTIVE A motley collection is made up of people or things of very different types.

motor, motors **NOUN** (D & T) ❶ a part of a vehicle or a machine that uses electricity or fuel to produce movement so that the machine can work ▷ **ADJECTIVE** ❷ concerned with or relating to vehicles with a petrol or diesel engine • *the motor industry.*

motorboat, motorboats **NOUN** a boat with an engine.

motorcycle, motorcycles **NOUN** a two-wheeled vehicle with an engine which is ridden like a bicycle. **motorcyclist NOUN**

motoring ADJECTIVE relating to cars and driving • *a motoring correspondent.*

motorist, motorists **NOUN** a person who drives a car.

motorway, motorways **NOUN** a wide road built for fast travel over long distances.

mottled ADJECTIVE covered with patches of different colours • *mottled leaves.*

motto, mottoes or mottos **NOUN** a short sentence or phrase that is a rule for good or sensible behaviour.

mould, moulds, moulding, moulded **VERB** ❶ To mould someone or something is to influence and change them so they develop in a particular way • *Early experiences mould our behaviour for life.* ❷ (D & T) To mould a substance is to make it into a particular shape • *Mould the mixture into flat round cakes.* ▷ **NOUN** ❸ (D & T) a container used to make something into a particular shape • *a jelly mould.* ❹ Mould is a soft grey or green substance that can form on old food or damp walls. **mouldy ADJECTIVE**

moult, moults, moulting, moulted **VERB** When an animal or bird moults, it loses its hair or feathers so new ones can grow.

mound, mounds **NOUN** ❶ a small man-made hill. ❷ a large, untidy pile • *a mound of blankets.*

mount, mounts, mounting, mounted **VERB** ❶ To mount a campaign or event is to organize it and carry it out. ❷ If something is mounting, it is increasing • *Economic problems are mounting.* ❸ FORMAL To mount something is to go to the top of it • *He mounted the steps.* ❹ If you mount a horse, you climb on its back. ❺ If you mount an object in a particular place, you fix it there to display it ▷ **NOUN** ❻ 'Mount' is also used as part of the name of a mountain • *Mount Everest.*

▷ SPELLING NOTE: *Betty Eats Cakes And Uses Seven Eggs (because)*

mountain, mountains **NOUN** ❶ a very high piece of land with steep sides. ❷ a large amount of something • *mountains of paperwork.*

mountaineer, mountaineers **NOUN** a person who climbs mountains.

mountainous **ADJECTIVE** A mountainous area has a lot of mountains.

mourn, mourns, mourning, mourned **VERB** ❶ If you mourn for someone who has died, you are very sad and think about them a lot. ❷ If you mourn something, you are sad because you no longer have it • *He mourned the end of his marriage.*

mourner, mourners **NOUN** a person who attends a funeral.

mournful **ADJECTIVE** very sad.

mourning **NOUN** If someone is in mourning, they wear special black clothes or behave in a quiet and restrained way because a member of their family has died.

mouse, mice **NOUN** ❶ a small rodent with a long tail. ❷ a small device moved by hand to control the position of the cursor on a computer screen.

mousse, mousses [*Said* **moos**] **NOUN** Mousse is a light, fluffy food made from whipped eggs and cream.

moustache, moustaches [*Said* **mus-stahsh**] **NOUN** A man's moustache is hair growing on his upper lip.
● **WORD HISTORY:** from Greek
● *mustax* meaning 'upper lip'

mouth, mouths, mouthing, mouthed **NOUN** ❶ your lips, or the space behind them where your tongue and teeth are. ❷ The mouth of a cave or a hole is the entrance to it. ❸ The mouth of a river is the place where it flows into the sea ▷ **VERB** ❹ If you mouth something, you form words with your lips without making any sound • *He mouthed 'Thank you' to the jurors.* **mouthful NOUN**

mouthpiece, mouthpieces **NOUN** ❶ the part you speak into on a telephone. ❷ the part of a musical instrument you put to your mouth. ❸ The mouthpiece of an organization is the person who publicly states its opinions and policies.

movable **ADJECTIVE** Something that is movable can be moved from one place to another.

move, moves, moving, moved **VERB** ❶ To move means to go to a different place or position. To move something means to change its place or position. ❷ If you move, or move house, you go to live in a different house. ❸ If something moves you, it causes you to feel a deep emotion • *Her story moved us to tears.* ▷ **NOUN** ❹ a change from one place or position to another • *We were watching his every move.* ❺ an act of moving house. ❻ the act of putting a piece or counter in a game in a different position • *It's your move next.*
● **SIMILAR WORDS:** ❶ budge, go,
● shift, stir

movement, movements **NOUN** ❶ (DRAMA) Movement involves changing position or going from one place to another ❷ IN PLURAL,

a b c d e f g h i j k l **m** n o p q r s t u v w x y z

▷ **SPELLING NOTE:** *there's a rAKE in the brAKEs (brake)*

FORMAL Your movements are everything you do during a period of time • *They asked him for an account of his movements during the previous morning.* ❸ a group of people who share the same beliefs or aims • *the peace movement.* ❹ one of the major sections of a piece of classical music.

moving ADJECTIVE Something that is moving makes you feel deep sadness or emotion. **movingly** ADVERB

mow, mows, mowing, mowed, mown VERB ❶ To mow grass is to cut it with a lawnmower. ❷ To mow down a large number of people is to kill them all violently.

mower, mowers NOUN a machine for cutting grass.

MP, MPs NOUN a person who has been elected to represent people in a country's parliament. MP is an abbreviation for 'Member of Parliament'.

MP3 player, MP3 players NOUN a device that plays audio or video files, often used for listening to music downloaded from the Internet.

mpg an abbreviation for 'miles per gallon'.

mph an abbreviation for 'miles per hour'.

Mr [Said *miss-ter*] NOUN 'Mr' is used before a man's name when you are speaking or referring to him.

Mrs [Said *miss-iz*] NOUN 'Mrs' is used before the name of a married woman when you are speaking or referring to her.

Ms [Said *miz*] NOUN 'Ms' is used before a woman's name when you are speaking or referring to her. Ms does not specify whether a woman is married or not.

MSP, MSPs NOUN an abbreviation for 'Member of the Scottish Parliament': a person who has been elected to represent people in the Scottish Parliament.

much ADVERB ❶ You use 'much' to emphasize that something is true to a great extent • *I feel much better now.* ❷ If something does not happen much, it does not happen very often ▷ ADJECTIVE OR PRONOUN ❸ You use 'much' to ask questions or give information about the size or amount of something • *How much money do you need?*

muck, mucks, mucking, mucked NOUN ❶ INFORMAL Muck is dirt or some other unpleasant substance. ❷ Muck is also manure ▷ VERB ❸ INFORMAL If you muck about, you behave stupidly and waste time. **mucky** ADJECTIVE

mucus [Said *myoo-kuss*] NOUN Mucus is a liquid produced in parts of your body, for example in your nose.

mud NOUN Mud is wet, sticky earth.

muddle, muddles, muddling, muddled NOUN ❶ A muddle is a state of disorder or untidiness • *Our finances are in a muddle.* ▷ VERB ❷ If you muddle things, you mix them up.
● SIMILAR WORDS: ❷ jumble, mix ● up

muddy, muddier, muddiest ADJECTIVE ❶ covered in mud. ❷ A muddy colour is dull and not clear • *a* *mottled, muddy brown.*

muesli [*Said myooz-lee*] **NOUN**
Muesli is a mixture of chopped nuts,
cereal flakes, and dried fruit that you
can eat for breakfast with milk.

muffin, muffins **NOUN** a small,
round cake which you eat hot.

muffled **ADJECTIVE** A muffled
sound is quiet or difficult to hear • *a
muffled explosion.*

mug, mugs, mugging, mugged **NOUN**
❶ a large, deep cup. ❷ INFORMAL
someone who is stupid and easily
deceived ▷ **VERB** ❸ INFORMAL If
someone mugs you, they attack you in
order to steal your money. **mugging**
NOUN **mugger** **NOUN**

muggy, muggier, muggiest
ADJECTIVE Muggy weather is
unpleasantly warm and damp.

mule, mules **NOUN** the offspring of a
female horse and a male donkey.

mulga **NOUN** ❶ Mulga are acacia
shrubs that are found in the desert
regions of Australia. ❷ INFORMAL In
Australian English, mulga is also the
bush or outback.

mull, mulls, mulling, mulled **VERB** If
you mull something over, you think
about it for a long time before making
a decision.

mullet, mullets **NOUN** a common
edible fish found in Australian and
New Zealand waters.

mulloway, mulloways **NOUN** a
large edible fish found in Australian
waters.

multi- **PREFIX** 'Multi-' is used to
form words that refer to something

that has many parts or aspects • *a
multistorey car park.*

multicellular **ADJECTIVE**
(SCIENCE) An organism that is
multicellular has many cells.

multimedia **NOUN** ❶ (ICT) in
computing, you use multimedia to
refer to products which use sound,
pictures, film and ordinary text to
convey information. ❷ in the
classroom, all the things like TV,
computers, and books which are used
as teaching aids are called multimedia.

multinational, multinationals
NOUN a very large company with
branches in many countries.

multiple, multiples **ADJECTIVE**
❶ having or involving many different
functions or things • *He died from
multiple injuries in the crash.* ▷ **NOUN**
❷ The multiples of a number are
other numbers that it will divide into
exactly. For example, 6, 9, and 12 are
multiples of 3.

multiple sclerosis [*Said
skler-roe-siss*] **NOUN** Multiple
sclerosis is a serious disease which
attacks the nervous system, affecting
your ability to move.

multiplication **NOUN**
❶ (MATHS) Multiplication is the
process of multiplying one number by
another. ❷ The multiplication of
things is a large increase in their
number • *the multiplication of
universities.*

multiplicity **NOUN** If there is a
multiplicity of things, there is a large
number or variety of them.

multiply, multiplies, multiplying,

a
b
c
d
e
f
g
h
i
j
k
l
m
n
o
p
q
r
s
t
u
v
w
x
y
z

multiplied **VERB** ❶ When something multiplies, it increases greatly in number • *The trip wore on and the hazards multiplied.* ❷ MATHS When you multiply one number by another, you calculate the total you would get if you added the first number to itself a particular number of times. For example, two multiplied by three is equal to two plus two plus two, which equals six.

multitude, multitudes **NOUN** FORMAL a very large number of people or things.

mum, mums **NOUN** INFORMAL Your mum is your mother.

mumble, mumbles, mumbling, mumbled **VERB** If you mumble, you speak very quietly and indistinctly.

mummy, mummies **NOUN** ❶ INFORMAL Your mummy is your mother. ❷ a dead body which was preserved long ago by being rubbed with special oils and wrapped in cloth.

mumps NOUN Mumps is a disease that causes painful swelling in the neck glands.

munch, munches, munching, munched **VERB** If you munch something, you chew it steadily and thoroughly.

mundane ADJECTIVE very ordinary and not interesting or unusual • *a mundane job.*

municipal [Said *myoo-nis-si-pl*] **ADJECTIVE** belonging to a city or town which has its own local government • *a municipal golf course.*
 ● **WORD HISTORY:** from Latin
 ● *municipium* meaning 'free town'

munitions PLURAL NOUN Munitions are bombs, guns, and other military supplies.

mural, murals **NOUN** a picture painted on a wall.

murder, murders, murdering, murdered **NOUN** ❶ Murder is the deliberate killing of a person ▷ **VERB** ❷ To murder someone is to kill them deliberately. **murderer NOUN**
 ● **SIMILAR WORDS:** ❶ homicide,
 ● killing

murderous ADJECTIVE ❶ likely to murder someone • *murderous gangsters.* ❷ A murderous attack or other action results in the death of many people • *murderous acts of terrorism.*

murky, murkier, murkiest **ADJECTIVE** dark or dirty and unpleasant • *He rushed through the murky streets.*

murmur, murmurs, murmuring, murmured **VERB** ❶ If you murmur, you say something very softly ▷ **NOUN** ❷ something that someone says which can hardly be heard.

muscle, muscles, muscling, muscled **NOUN** ❶ SCIENCE Your muscles are pieces of flesh which you can expand or contract in order to move parts of your body. An **agonistic muscle** is a muscle which is relaxed when another muscle is contracted; an **antagonistic muscle** is a muscle which is contracted when another muscle is relaxed, returning the limb to its original position; an **antagonistic pair of muscles** means two muscles which work together, for example one opening a joint and the other closing it

▷ **VERB** ❷ INFORMAL If you muscle in on something, you force your way into a situation in which you are not welcome.

● **WORD HISTORY:** from Latin *musculus* meaning 'little mouse', because muscles were thought to look like mice

muscular [*Said* musk-*yool-lar*] **ADJECTIVE** ❶ involving or affecting your muscles • *muscular strength.* ❷ Someone who is muscular has strong, firm muscles.

muse, muses, musing, mused **VERB** LITERARY To muse is to think about something for a long time.

museum, museums **NOUN** a building where many interesting or valuable objects are kept and displayed.

mush NOUN A mush is a thick, soft paste.

mushroom, mushrooms, mushrooming, mushroomed **NOUN** ❶ a fungus with a short stem and a round top. Some types of mushroom are edible ▷ **VERB** ❷ If something mushrooms, it appears and grows very quickly • *The mill towns mushroomed into cities.*

mushy, mushier, mushiest **ADJECTIVE** ❶ Mushy fruits or vegetables are too soft • *mushy tomatoes.* ❷ INFORMAL Mushy stories are too sentimental.

music NOUN ❶ Music is a pattern of sounds performed by people singing or playing instruments. ❷ Music is also the written symbols that represent musical sounds • *I taught myself to read music.*

musical, musicals **ADJECTIVE** ❶ relating to playing or studying music • *a musical instrument.* ▷ **NOUN** ❷ a play or film that uses songs and dance to tell the story. **musically ADVERB**

musician, musicians **NOUN** (MUSIC) a person who plays a musical instrument as their job or hobby.

musk NOUN Musk is a substance with a strong, sweet smell. It is used to make perfume. **musky ADJECTIVE**

musket, muskets **NOUN** an old-fashioned gun with a long barrel.

Muslim, Muslims; *also spelt* **Moslem** **NOUN** (RE) ❶ a person who believes in Islam and lives according to its rules ▷ **ADJECTIVE** ❷ relating to Islam.

muslin NOUN Muslin is a very thin cotton material.

mussel, mussels **NOUN** Mussels are a kind of shellfish with black shells.

must VERB ❶ If something must happen, it is very important or necessary that it happens • *You must be over 18.* ❷ If you tell someone they must do something, you are suggesting that they do it • *You must try this pudding: it's delicious.* ▷ **NOUN** ❸ something that is absolutely necessary • *The museum is a must for all visitors.*

mustard NOUN Mustard is a spicy-tasting yellow or brown paste made from seeds.

muster, musters, mustering, mustered **VERB** If you muster something such as energy or support, you gather it together • *as much calm as he could muster.*

a
b
c
d
e
f
g
h
i
j
k
l
m
n
o
p
q
r
s
t
u
v
w
x
y
z

musty, mustier, mustiest **ADJECTIVE** smelling stale and damp • *musty old books.*

mutate, mutates, mutating, mutated **VERB** (SCIENCE) If something mutates, its structure or appearance alters in some way • *Viruses react to change and can mutate fast.* **mutation NOUN mutant NOUN OR ADJECTIVE**

mute **ADJECTIVE** FORMAL not giving out sound or speech • *mute amazement.*

muted **ADJECTIVE** ❶ Muted colours or sounds are soft and gentle. ❷ A muted reaction is not very strong.

muti [*Said* **moo-ti**] **NOUN** INFORMAL In South African English, muti is medicine.

mutilate, mutilates, mutilating, mutilated **VERB** ❶ If someone is mutilated, their body is badly injured • *His leg was badly mutilated.* ❷ If you mutilate something, you deliberately damage or spoil it • *Almost every book had been mutilated.* **mutilation NOUN**

mutiny, mutinies **NOUN** A mutiny is a rebellion against someone in authority.

mutter, mutters, muttering, muttered **VERB** To mutter is to speak in a very low and perhaps cross voice • *Rory muttered something under his breath.*

mutton **NOUN** Mutton is the meat of an adult sheep.

muttonbird, muttonbirds **NOUN** a seabird in the Pacific Ocean that is often hunted for its flesh, which is said to taste like mutton.

mutual **ADJECTIVE** used to describe something that two or more people do to each other or share • *They had a mutual interest in rugby.*
  ● **USAGE NOTE:** It used to be that *mutual* could only be used of something that was shared between two people or groups. Nowadays you can use it to mean 'shared between two or more people or groups'

mutually **ADVERB** Mutually describes a situation in which two or more people feel the same way about each other • *a mutually supportive relationship.*

muzzle, muzzles, muzzling, muzzled **NOUN** ❶ the nose and mouth of an animal. ❷ a cover or a strap for a dog's nose and mouth to prevent it from biting. ❸ the open end of a gun through which the bullets come out ▷ **VERB** ❹ To muzzle a dog is to put a muzzle on it.

my **ADJECTIVE** 'My' refers to something belonging or relating to the person speaking or writing • *I held my breath.*

mynah bird, mynah birds **NOUN** a tropical bird which can mimic speech and sounds.

myriad, myriads [*Said* **mir**-ree-ad] **NOUN OR ADJECTIVE** LITERARY a very large number of people or things.

myrrh [*rhymes with* **purr**] **NOUN** Myrrh is a fragrant substance used in perfume and incense.

myself **PRONOUN** ❶ 'Myself' is used when the person speaking or writing does an action and is affected by it • *I was ashamed of myself.*

▷ SPELLING NOTE: *have a plEce of plE (piece)*

❷ 'Myself' is also used to emphasize 'I' • *I find it a bit odd myself.*

mysterious ADJECTIVE
❶ strange and not well understood.
❷ secretive about something • *Stop being so mysterious.* **mysteriously ADVERB**
● **SIMILAR WORDS: ❷** enigmatic,
● secretive

mystery, mysteries **NOUN** something that is not understood or known about.

mystic, mystics **NOUN ❶** a religious person who spends long hours meditating ▷ **ADJECTIVE ❷** Mystic means the same as mystical.

mystical ADJECTIVE involving spiritual powers and influences • *a mystical experience.* **mysticism NOUN**

mystify, mystifies, mystifying, mystified **VERB** If something mystifies you, you find it impossible to understand.

mystique *[Said mis-steek]* **NOUN** Mystique is an atmosphere of mystery and importance associated with a particular person or thing.

myth, myths **NOUN ❶** an untrue belief or explanation. **❷** (ENGLISH) a story which was made up long ago to explain natural events and religious beliefs • *Viking myths.*

mythical ADJECTIVE imaginary, untrue, or existing only in myths • *a mythical beast.*

mythology NOUN Mythology refers to stories that have been made up in the past to explain natural events or justify religious beliefs. **mythological ADJECTIVE**

Nn

Some words which sound as if they should begin with letter *n*, are spelt with *gn*, for example *gnaw*, *gnome* and *gnu*. Other words that sound as if they ought to begin with letter *n* are actually spelt with *kn*, for example *knee*, *knight*, *knock* and *knot*. Other words that sound as if they ought to begin with letter *n* are actually spelt with *pn*, for example *pneumatic* and *pneumonia*.

naartjie, naartjies *[Said nar-chi]* **NOUN** In South African English, a tangerine.

nag, nags, nagging, nagged **VERB** ❶ If you nag someone, you keep complaining to them about something. ❷ If something nags at you, it keeps worrying you.

nail, nails, nailing, nailed **NOUN** ❶ a small piece of metal with a sharp point at one end, which you hammer into objects to hold them together. ❷ Your nails are the thin hard areas covering the ends of your fingers and toes ▷ **VERB** ❸ If you nail something somewhere, you fit it there using a nail.

naive or **naïve** *[Said ny-eev]* **ADJECTIVE** foolishly believing that things are easier or less complicated than they really are. **naively ADVERB naivety NOUN**

naked ADJECTIVE ❶ not wearing any clothes or not covered by anything. ❷ shown openly • *naked aggression.* **nakedness NOUN**

name, names, naming, named **NOUN** ❶ a word that you use to identify a person, place, or thing. ❷ Someone's name is also their reputation • *My only wish now is to clear my name.* ▷ **VERB** ❸ If you name someone or something, you give them a name or you say their name. ❹ If you name a price or a date, you say what you want it to be.

nameless ADJECTIVE You describe someone or something as nameless when you do not know their name, or when a name has not yet been given to them.

namely ADVERB that is; used to introduce more detailed information about what you have just said • *The state stripped them of their rights, namely the right to own land.*

namesake, namesakes **NOUN** Your namesake is someone with the same name as you • *Audrey Hepburn and her namesake Katharine.*

nanny, nannies **NOUN** a woman whose job is looking after young children.

nap, naps, napping, napped **NOUN** ❶ a short sleep ▷ **VERB** ❷ When you nap, you have a short sleep.

▷ SPELLING NOTE: *I went to see (C) the doctor's new practiCe (practice)*

nape, napes NOUN The nape of your neck is the back of it.

napkin, napkins NOUN a small piece of cloth or paper used to wipe your hands and mouth after eating.

nappy, nappies NOUN a piece of towelling or paper worn round a baby's bottom.

narcotic, narcotics NOUN a drug which makes you sleepy and unable to feel pain.
- **WORD HISTORY:** from Greek *narkoun* meaning 'to make numb'

narrate, narrates, narrating, narrated VERB If you narrate a story, you tell it. **narration** NOUN

narrative, narratives [Said *nar-rat-tiv*] NOUN (ENGLISH) a story or an account of events.

narrator, narrators NOUN ❶ a person who is reading or telling a story out loud. ❷ (ENGLISH) a character in a novel who tells the story.

narrow, narrower, narrowest; narrows, narrowing, narrowed ADJECTIVE ❶ having a small distance from one side to the other • *a narrow stream*. ❷ concerned only with a few aspects of something and ignoring the important points • *people with a narrow point of view*. ❸ A narrow escape or victory is one that you only just achieve ▷ VERB ❹ To narrow means to become less wide. **narrowly** ADVERB

narrow-minded ADJECTIVE unwilling to consider new ideas or opinions.
- **SIMILAR WORDS:** bigoted, intolerant

nasal [Said *nay-zal*] ADJECTIVE ❶ relating to the nose • *the nasal passages*. ❷ Nasal sounds are made by breathing out through your nose as you speak.

nasty, nastier, nastiest ADJECTIVE very unpleasant • *She had suffered a nasty shock*. **nastily** ADVERB **nastiness** NOUN

nation, nations NOUN (GEOGRAPHY) a large group of people sharing the same history and language and usually inhabiting a particular country.

national, nationals (GEOGRAPHY) ADJECTIVE ❶ relating to the whole of a country • *a national newspaper*. ❷ typical of a particular country • *women in Polish national dress*. ▷ NOUN ❸ A national of a country is a citizen of that country • *Turkish nationals*. **nationally** ADVERB

national anthem, national anthems NOUN A country's national anthem is its official song.

nationalism NOUN ❶ Nationalism is a desire for the independence of a country; also a political movement aiming to achieve such independence. ❷ Nationalism is also love of your own country. **nationalist** NOUN **nationalistic** ADJECTIVE

nationality, nationalities NOUN Nationality is the fact of belonging to a particular country.

nationalize, nationalizes, nationalizing, nationalized; *also spelt* **nationalise** VERB To nationalize an industry to bring it under the control and ownership of the state.

a b c d e f g h i j k l m **n** o p q r s t u v w x y z

▷ SPELLING NOTE: *You must practiSe your Ss (practise)*

A
B
C
D
E
F
G
H
I
J
K
L
M
N
O
P
Q
R
S
T
U
V
W
X
Y
Z

nationalization NOUN

National Party NOUN In Australia and New Zealand, the National Party is a major political party.

national service NOUN National service is a compulsory period of service in the armed forces.

nationwide ADJECTIVE OR ADVERB happening all over a country • *a nationwide search.*

native, natives ADJECTIVE ❶ Your native country is the country where you were born. ❷ Your native language is the language that you first learned to speak. ❸ Animals or plants that are native to a place live or grow there naturally and have not been brought there by people ▷ NOUN ❹ A native of a place is someone who was born there.

Nativity NOUN In Christianity, the Nativity is the birth of Christ or the festival celebrating this.

natter, natters, nattering, nattered VERB INFORMAL If you natter, you talk about unimportant things.

natural, naturals ADJECTIVE ❶ normal and to be expected • *It was only natural that he was tempted.* ❷ not trying to pretend or hide anything • *Caitlin's natural manner reassured her.* ❸ D & T existing or happening in nature • *natural disasters.* ❹ A natural ability is one you were born with. ❺ Your natural mother or father is your real mother or father and not someone who has adopted you ▷ NOUN ❻ someone who is born with a particular ability • *She's a natural at bridge.* ❼ In music, a natural is a note that is not a sharp

or a flat. It is represented by the symbol (♮). **naturally** ADVERB
● **SIMILAR WORDS:** ❶ inborn,
● inherent, innate

natural resources PLURAL NOUN GEOGRAPHY materials such as minerals, trees, coal etc. that exist naturally in a country and can be used by its people.

natural selection NOUN SCIENCE Natural selection is Darwin's theory that only the species of animals and plants that are best suited to their environment survive and reproduce, while those that are less well suited die.

nature, natures NOUN ❶ Nature is animals, plants, and all the other things in the world not made by people. ❷ The nature of a person or thing is their basic character • *She liked his warm, generous nature.*
● **WORD HISTORY:** from Latin
● *natura* meaning 'birth'

naughty, naughtier, naughtiest ADJECTIVE ❶ behaving badly. ❷ rude or indecent • *naughty films.* **naughtiness** NOUN

nausea [Said *naw-zee-ah*] NOUN Nausea is a feeling in your stomach that you are going to be sick. **nauseous** ADJECTIVE

nautical [Said *naw-tik-kl*] ADJECTIVE relating to ships or navigation.

nautical mile, nautical miles NOUN GEOGRAPHY A nautical mile is a unit of distance used at sea, equal to 1852 metres.

naval ADJECTIVE relating to or

having a navy • *naval officers* • *naval bases*.

navel, navels **NOUN** the small hollow on the front of your body just below your waist.

navigable **ADJECTIVE** wide enough and deep enough to sail on.

navigate, navigates, navigating, navigated **VERB** ❶ When someone navigates, they work out the direction in which a ship, plane, or car should go, using maps and sometimes instruments. ❷ To navigate a stretch of water means to travel safely across it • *It was the first time I had navigated the ocean.* **navigation NOUN navigator NOUN**

navy, navies **NOUN** ❶ the part of a country's armed forces that fights at sea ▷ **ADJECTIVE** ❷ dark blue.

Nazi, Nazis [*Said naht-see*] **NOUN** The Nazis were members of the National Socialist German Workers' Party, which was led by Adolf Hitler.

NB You write NB to draw attention to what you are going to write next. NB is an abbreviation for the Latin 'nota bene', which means 'note well'.

Neanderthal [*Said nee-an-der-tahl*] **ADJECTIVE** (HISTORY) Neanderthal man was a primitive species of man who lived in Europe before 12,000 BC. The name comes from Neandertal, a German valley where archaeological discoveries were made.

near, nearer, nearest; nears, nearing, neared **PREPOSITION** ❶ not far from ▷ **ADJECTIVE** ❷ not far away in distance. ❸ not far away in time.

❹ You can also use 'near' to mean almost • *a night of near disaster.* ▷ **VERB** ❺ When you are nearing something, you are approaching it and will soon reach it • *The dog began to bark as he neared the porch.*

nearby **ADJECTIVE** ❶ only a short distance away • *a nearby town.* ▷ **ADVERB** ❷ only a short distance away • *a house nearby.*

nearly **ADVERB** not completely but almost.

neat, neater, neatest **ADJECTIVE** ❶ tidy and smart. ❷ A neat alcoholic drink does not have anything added to it • *a small glass of neat vodka.* **neatly ADVERB neatness NOUN**

necessarily **ADVERB** Something that is not necessarily the case is not always or inevitably the case.

necessary **ADJECTIVE** ❶ Something that is necessary is needed or must be done. ❷ **FORMAL** Necessary also means certain or inevitable • *a necessary consequence of war.*

● **SIMILAR WORDS:** ❶ essential,
● needed, requisite

necessity, necessities **NOUN** ❶ Necessity is the need to do something • *There is no necessity for any of this.* ❷ Necessities are things needed in order to live.

neck, necks **NOUN** ❶ the part of your body which joins your head to the rest of your body. ❷ the long narrow part at the top of a bottle.

necklace, necklaces **NOUN** ❶ a piece of jewellery which a woman wears around her neck. ❷ In South

a b c d e f g h i j k l m **n** o p q r s t u v w x y z

▷ SPELLING NOTE: *LEarn the principLEs (principle)*

Africa, a name for a tyre filled with petrol which is placed round a person's neck and set on fire in order to kill that person.

nectar NOUN Nectar is a sweet liquid produced by flowers and attractive to insects.

nectarine, nectarines NOUN a kind of peach with a smooth skin.

née [rhymes with **day**] ADJECTIVE 'Née' is used to indicate what a woman's surname was before she got married • *Sara Black, née Wells.*

need, needs, needing, needed VERB ❶ If you need something, you believe that you must have it or do it ▷ NOUN ❷ Your needs are the things that you need to have. ❸ a strong feeling that you must have or do something • *I just felt the need to write about it.*

● SIMILAR WORDS: ❷ necessity, ● requirement

needle, needles, needling, needled NOUN ❶ a small thin piece of metal with a pointed end and a hole at the other, which is used for sewing. ❷ Needles are also long thin pieces of steel or plastic, used for knitting. ❸ the small pointed part in a record player that touches the record and picks up the sound signals. ❹ the part of a syringe that a doctor or nurse sticks into your body. ❺ the thin piece of metal or plastic on a dial which moves to show a measurement. ❻ The needles of a pine tree are its leaves ▷ VERB ❼ INFORMAL If someone needles you, they annoy or provoke you.

needless ADJECTIVE unnecessary. **needlessly** ADVERB

needy, needier, neediest ADJECTIVE very poor.

negative, negatives ADJECTIVE ❶ A negative answer means 'no'. ❷ Someone who is negative sees only problems and disadvantages • *Why are you so negative about everything?* ❸ If a medical or scientific test is negative, it shows that something has not happened or is not present • *The pregnancy test came back negative.* ❹ (MATHS) A negative number is less than zero. ❺ (SCIENCE) In physics, a negative electric charge has the same polarity as the charge of an electron ▷ NOUN ❻ the image that is first produced when you take a photograph. **negatively** ADVERB

neglect, neglects, neglecting, neglected VERB ❶ If you neglect something, you do not look after it properly. ❷ FORMAL If you neglect to do something, you fail to do it • *He had neglected to give her his address.* ▷ NOUN ❸ Neglect is failure to look after something or someone properly • *Most of her plants died from neglect.* **neglectful** ADJECTIVE

negligent ADJECTIVE not taking enough care • *her negligent driving.* **negligence** NOUN

negligible ADJECTIVE very small and unimportant • *a negligible amount of fat.*

negotiable ADJECTIVE able to be changed or agreed by discussion • *All contributions are negotiable.*

negotiate, negotiates, negotiating, negotiated VERB ❶ When people negotiate, they have formal discussions in order to reach an

A B C D E F G H I J K L M N O P Q R S T U V W X Y Z

agreement about something. ❷ If you negotiate an obstacle, you manage to get over it or round it. **negotiation** NOUN **negotiator** NOUN

Negro, Negroes NOUN OLD-FASHIONED a person with black skin who comes from Africa or whose ancestors came from Africa.

neigh, neighs, neighing, neighed [rhymes with **day**] VERB ❶ When a horse neighs, it makes a loud high-pitched sound ▷ NOUN ❷ a loud sound made by a horse.

neighbour, neighbours NOUN ❶ Your neighbour is someone who lives next door to you or near you. ❷ Your neighbour is also someone standing or sitting next to you • *I got chatting with my neighbour in the studio.*

neighbourhood, neighbourhoods NOUN a district where people live • *a safe neighbourhood.*

neighbouring ADJECTIVE situated nearby • *Children were being bussed to schools in neighbouring areas.*

neither ADJECTIVE OR PRONOUN used to indicate that a negative statement refers to two or more things or people • *It's neither a play nor a musical* • *Neither of them spoke.*
● USAGE NOTE: When *neither* is
● followed by a plural noun, the verb
● can be plural too: *neither of these*
● *books are useful.* When you have
● two singular subjects the verb
● should be singular too: *neither Jack*
● *nor John has done the work*

neo- PREFIX new or modern • *neo-fascism.*

● WORD HISTORY: from Greek *neos*
● meaning 'new'

neolithic ADJECTIVE (GEOGRAPHY) relating to the Stone Age period when people first started farming.

neon [Said **nee**-yon] NOUN (SCIENCE) Neon is a chemical element existing as a gas in very small amounts in the atmosphere. It is used in glass tubes to make bright electric lights and signs. Neon's atomic number is 10 and its symbol is Ne.

nephew, nephews NOUN Someone's nephew is the son of their sister or brother.

Neptune NOUN Neptune is the planet in the solar system which is eighth from the sun.
● WORD HISTORY: from *Neptune*,
● the Roman god of the sea

nerve, nerves NOUN ❶ a long thin fibre that sends messages between your brain and other parts of your body. ❷ If you talk about someone's nerves, you are referring to how able they are to remain calm in a difficult situation • *It needs confidence and strong nerves.* ❸ Nerve is courage • *O'Meara held his nerve to sink the putt.* ❹ INFORMAL Nerve is boldness or rudeness • *He had the nerve to swear at me.* ▷ INFORMAL PHRASE ❺ If someone **gets on your nerves**, they irritate you.

nerve cell, nerve cells NOUN (SCIENCE) A nerve cell is the same as a neuron.

nerve-racking ADJECTIVE making you feel very worried and tense • *a nerve-racking experience.*

▷ SPELLING NOTE: *the QUeen stood on the QUay (quay)*

A
B
C
D
E
F
G
H
I
J
K
L
M
N
O
P
Q
R
S
T
U
V
W
X
Y
Z

nervous ADJECTIVE ❶ worried and frightened. ❷ A nervous illness affects your emotions and mental health. **nervously** ADVERB **nervousness** NOUN
● SIMILAR WORDS:
● ❶ apprehensive, edgy, jumpy

nervous breakdown, nervous breakdowns NOUN an illness in which someone suffers from deep depression and needs psychiatric treatment.

nervous system, nervous systems NOUN Your nervous system is the nerves in your body together with your brain and spinal cord.

-ness SUFFIX '-ness' forms nouns from adjectives • *tenderness* • *happiness.*
● WORD HISTORY: from an Old English suffix

nest, nests, nesting, nested NOUN ❶ a place that a bird makes to lay its eggs in; also a place that some insects and other animals make to rear their young in ▷ VERB ❷ When birds nest, they build a nest and lay eggs in it.

nestle, nestles, nestling, nestled [Said ness-sl] VERB If you nestle somewhere, you settle there comfortably, often pressing up against someone else • *A new puppy nestled in her lap.*

nestling, nestlings NOUN a young bird that has not yet learned to fly and so has not left the nest.

net, nets NOUN ❶ a piece of material made of threads woven together with small spaces in between. ❷ The net is the same as the **Internet**.
▷ ADJECTIVE ❸ A net result or

amount is final, after everything has been considered • *a net profit of £171 million.* ❹ The net weight of something is its weight without its wrapping.

netball NOUN Netball is a game played by two teams of seven players in which each team tries to score goals by throwing a ball through a net at the top of a pole.

netting NOUN Netting is material made of threads or metal wires woven together with small spaces in between.

nettle, nettles NOUN a wild plant covered with little hairs that sting.

network, networks NOUN ❶ a large number of lines or roads which cross each other at many points • *a small network of side roads.* ❷ A network of people or organizations is a large number of them that work together as a system • *the public telephone network.* ❸ A television network is a group of broadcasting stations that all transmit the same programmes at the same time. ❹ ⟨ICT⟩ a group of computers connected to each other.

neuron, neurons NOUN a cell that is part of the nervous system and conducts messages to and from the brain.

neurone, neurones NOUN the same as a **neuron**.

neurosis, neuroses [Said nyoor-**roh**-siss] NOUN Neurosis is mental illness which causes people to have strong and unreasonable fears and worries.

neurotic [Said nyoor-**rot**-ik] ADJECTIVE having strong and

▷ SPELLING NOTE: *Rhythmical Hounds Yap To Heavy Music (rhythm)*

WHAT IS NEUTER?

Neuter nouns refer to inanimate objects and abstract ideas:
The kettle will switch itself off. → kettle is **neuter**

Also look at the grammar boxes at **gender**, **masculine** and **feminine**.

---

unreasonable fears and worries • *He was almost neurotic about being followed.*

neuter, neuters, neutering, neutered [Said *nyoo-ter*] **VERB** ❶ When an animal is neutered, its reproductive organs are removed ▷ **ADJECTIVE** ❷ In some languages, a neuter noun or pronoun is one which is not masculine or feminine.
▶ SEE GRAMMAR BOX ABOVE

neutral, neutrals **ADJECTIVE** ❶ People who are neutral do not support either side in a disagreement or war. ❷ D&T The neutral wire in an electric plug is the one that is not earth or live. ❸ ART A neutral colour is not definite or striking, for example pale grey. ❹ SCIENCE In chemistry, a neutral substance is neither acid nor alkaline ▷ **NOUN** ❺ HISTORY a person or country that does not support either side in a disagreement or war. ❻ D&T Neutral is the position between the gears of a vehicle in which the gears are not connected to the engine and so the vehicle cannot move. **neutrality NOUN**

neutralize, neutralizes, neutralizing, neutralized; also spelt **neutralise**
VERB ❶ To neutralize something means to prevent it from working or taking effect, especially by doing or applying something that has the opposite effect. ❷ SCIENCE If you

neutralize a substance, you make it neither acid nor alkaline.

neutron, neutrons **NOUN** an atomic particle that has no electrical charge.

never ADVERB at no time in the past, present, or future.
● USAGE NOTE: Do not use *never* to mean 'not' in writing. You should say *I didn't see her* not *I never saw her*

nevertheless ADVERB in spite of what has just been said • *They dress rather plainly but nevertheless look quite smart.*

new, newer, newest **ADJECTIVE** ❶ recently made, created, or discovered • *a new house* • *a new plan* • *a new virus.* ❷ not used or owned before • *We've got a new car.* ❸ different or unfamiliar • *a name which was new to me.*
● SIMILAR WORDS: ❶ latest, modern, recent

newborn ADJECTIVE born recently.

newcomer, newcomers **NOUN** someone who has recently arrived in a place.

newly ADVERB recently • *the newly born baby.*

new moon, new moons **NOUN** The moon is a new moon when it is a thin crescent shape at the start of its four-week cycle.

▷ SPELLING NOTE: *there's SAND in my SANDwich (sandwich)*

news NOUN News is information about things that have happened.

newsagent, newsagents NOUN a person or shop that sells newspapers and magazines.

newspaper, newspapers NOUN a publication, on large sheets of paper, that is produced regularly and contains news and articles.

newt, newts NOUN a small amphibious creature with a moist skin, short legs, and a long tail.
● WORD HISTORY: from a mistaken
● division of Middle English *an ewt*

New Testament NOUN The New Testament is the second part of the Bible, which deals with the life of Jesus Christ and with the early Church.

newton, newtons NOUN (SCIENCE) A newton is a unit of force. One newton causes one kilogram to have an acceleration of one metre per second. The newton is named after the English scientist Sir Isaac Newton (1643-1727).

New Year NOUN New Year is the time when people celebrate the start of a year.

New Zealander, New Zealanders NOUN someone who comes from New Zealand.

next ADJECTIVE ❶ coming immediately after something else • *Their next child was a girl.* ❷ in a position nearest to something • *in the next room.* ▷ ADVERB ❸ coming immediately after something else • *Steve arrived next.* ▷ PHRASE ❹ If one thing is **next to** another, it is at the side of it.

● SIMILAR WORDS: ❶ following,
● subsequent

next door ADJECTIVE OR ADVERB in the house next to yours.

NHS In Britain, an abbreviation for 'National Health Service'.

nib, nibs NOUN the pointed end of a pen.

nibble, nibbles, nibbling, nibbled VERB ❶ When you nibble something, you take small bites of it ▷ NOUN ❷ a small bite of something.

nice, nicer, nicest ADJECTIVE pleasant or attractive. **nicely** ADVERB

nicety, niceties *[Said nigh-se-tee]* NOUN a small detail • *the social niceties.*

niche, niches *[Said neesh]* NOUN ❶ a hollow area in a wall. ❷ If you say that you have found your niche, you mean that you have found a job or way of life that is exactly right for you.

nick, nicks, nicking, nicked VERB ❶ If you nick something, you make a small cut in its surface • *He nicked his chin.* ❷ INFORMAL To nick something also means to steal it ▷ NOUN ❸ a small cut in the surface of something.

nickel, nickels NOUN ❶ (SCIENCE) Nickel is a silver-coloured metallic element that is used in alloys. Its atomic number is 28 and its symbol is Ni. ❷ (GEOGRAPHY) A nickel is an American or Canadian coin worth five cents.

nickname, nicknames, nicknaming, nicknamed NOUN ❶ an informal name given to someone ▷ VERB ❷ If you nickname someone, you give

▷ SPELLING NOTE: On WEDNESday Wayne WED NESta (*Wednesday*)

them a nickname.
● **WORD HISTORY:** from Middle
● English *an ekename* meaning 'an
● additional name'

nicotine NOUN (SCIENCE) Nicotine
is an addictive substance found in
tobacco.

niece, nieces NOUN Someone's niece
is the daughter of their sister or
brother.

nifty ADJECTIVE neat and pleasing or
cleverly done.

Nigerian, Nigerians [Said nie-jeer-
ee-an] ADJECTIVE ❶ belonging or
relating to Nigeria ▷ NOUN
❷ someone from Nigeria.

niggle, niggles, niggling, niggled
VERB ❶ If something niggles you, it
worries you slightly ▷ NOUN ❷ a
small worry that you keep thinking
about.

night, nights NOUN Night is the time
between sunset and sunrise when it is
dark.

nightclub, nightclubs NOUN a
place where people go late in the
evening to drink and dance.

nightdress, nightdresses NOUN a
loose dress that a woman or girl wears
to sleep in.

nightfall NOUN Nightfall is the time
of day when it starts to get dark.

nightie, nighties NOUN INFORMAL a
nightdress.

nightingale, nightingales NOUN a
small brown European bird, the male
of which sings very beautifully,
especially at night.

nightly ADJECTIVE OR ADVERB
happening every night • *the nightly
news programme.*

nightmare, nightmares NOUN a
very frightening dream; also used of
any very frightening or unpleasant
situation • *The meal itself was a
nightmare.* **nightmarish** ADJECTIVE
● **WORD HISTORY:** from *night* +
● Middle English *mare* meaning 'evil
● spirit'

nil NOUN Nil means zero or nothing.
It is used especially in sports scores.

nimble, nimbler, nimblest
ADJECTIVE ❶ able to move quickly
and easily. ❷ able to think quickly and
cleverly. **nimbly** ADVERB

nimbus, nimbuses NOUN
(GEOGRAPHY) A nimbus is a dark cloud
bringing rain and snow.

nine the number 9. **ninth**
ADJECTIVE

nineteen the number 19.
nineteenth ADJECTIVE

ninety, nineties the number 90.
ninetieth ADJECTIVE

nip, nips, nipping, nipped VERB
❶ INFORMAL If you nip somewhere,
you go there quickly. ❷ To nip
someone or something means to
pinch or squeeze them slightly
▷ NOUN ❸ a light pinch.

nipple, nipples NOUN Your nipples
are the two small pieces of projecting
flesh on your chest. Babies suck milk
through the nipples on their mothers'
breasts.

nirvana [Said neer-*vah*-na] NOUN
Nirvana is the ultimate state of

spiritual enlightenment which can be achieved in the Hindu and Buddhist religions.

nit, nits **NOUN** Nits are the eggs of a kind of louse that sometimes lives in people's hair.

nitrate, nitrates **NOUN** (SCIENCE) A nitrate is a chemical compound that includes nitrogen and oxygen. Nitrates are used as fertilizers in agriculture.

nitrogen **NOUN** (SCIENCE) Nitrogen is a chemical element usually found as a gas. It forms about 78% of the earth's atmosphere. Nitrogen's atomic number is 7 and its symbol is N.

nitroglycerine **NOUN** (SCIENCE) Nitroglycerine is a dense oily liquid used as an explosive.

no **INTERJECTION** ❶ used to say that something is not true or to refuse something ▷ **ADJECTIVE** ❷ none at all or not at all • *She gave no reason* • *You're no friend of mine.* ▷ **ADVERB** ❸ used with a comparative to mean 'not' • *no later than 24th July.*

no. a written abbreviation for **number**.

nobility **NOUN** ❶ Nobility is the quality of being noble • *the unmistakable nobility of his character.* ❷ The nobility of a society are all the people who have titles and high social rank.

noble, nobler, noblest; nobles **ADJECTIVE** ❶ honest and brave, and deserving admiration. ❷ very impressive • *broad cheekbones which gave them a noble appearance.* ▷ **NOUN** ❸ a member of the nobility. **nobly** **ADVERB**

noble gas, noble gases **NOUN**

(SCIENCE) any of the gases which belong to group 18 of the periodic table and which do not react with other elements. Examples include helium, neon and argon.

nobleman, noblemen **NOUN** a man who is a member of the nobility. **noblewoman** **NOUN**

nobody, nobodies **PRONOUN** ❶ not a single person ▷ **NOUN** ❷ Someone who is a nobody is not at all important.
● **USAGE NOTE:** *Nobody* and *no-one* mean the same

nocturnal **ADJECTIVE** ❶ happening at night • *a nocturnal journey through New York.* ❷ active at night • *a nocturnal animal.*

nod, nods, nodding, nodded **VERB** ❶ When you nod, you move your head up and down, usually to show agreement ▷ **NOUN** ❷ a movement of your head up and down. **nod off** **VERB** If you nod off, you fall asleep.

node, nodes **NOUN** ❶ (SCIENCE) In biology, a node is the place on the stem of a plant from which a branch or leaf grows. ❷ (MATHS) A node is also a point where two lines intersect.
● **WORD HISTORY:** from Latin *nodus* meaning 'knot'

nodule, nodules [*Said nod-yool*] **NOUN** (SCIENCE) A nodule is a small, rounded lump, especially one on the root of a plant.

noise, noises **NOUN** a sound, especially one that is loud or unpleasant.
● **SIMILAR WORDS:** din, racket, sound

▷ SPELLING NOTE: *Elaine and Emily shout EE when they mEEt to grEEt each other (-ee-)*

noise pollution NOUN
(GEOGRAPHY) noise that is annoying
or harmful to people in the place
where they live or work and that they
have no control over.

noisy, noisier, noisiest ADJECTIVE
making a lot of noise or full of noise
• *a noisy crowd.* **noisily** ADVERB
noisiness NOUN

nomad, nomads NOUN a person
who belongs to a tribe which travels
from place to place rather than living
in just one place. **nomadic**
ADJECTIVE

nominal ADJECTIVE ❶ Something
that is nominal is supposed to have a
particular identity or status, but in
reality does not have it • *the nominal
leader of his party.* ❷ A nominal
amount of money is very small
compared to the value of something
• *I am prepared to sell my shares at a
nominal price.* **nominally** ADVERB

nominate, nominates, nominating,
nominated VERB If you nominate
someone for a job or position, you
formally suggest that they have it.
nomination NOUN
● SIMILAR WORDS: name, propose,
● suggest

non- PREFIX not • *non-smoking.*
● WORD HISTORY: from Latin

nonagon, nonagons NOUN (MATHS)
a shape with nine straight sides.

nonchalant [Said **non**-shal-nt]
ADJECTIVE seeming calm and not
worried. **nonchalance** NOUN
nonchalantly ADVERB

noncommissioned officer,
noncommissioned officers NOUN an

officer such as a sergeant or corporal
who has been promoted from the
lower ranks.

nondescript ADJECTIVE Someone
or something nondescript has no
special or interesting qualities or
details • *a nondescript coat.*

none PRONOUN not a single thing or
person, or not even a small amount of
something.

nonfiction NOUN (LIBRARY)
Nonfiction is writing that gives facts
and information rather than telling a
story.

nonplussed ADJECTIVE confused
and unsure about how to react.

non-renewable resources
PLURAL NOUN (SCIENCE) substances
such as coal and oil that occur
naturally and cannot be replaced once
they have been used up.

nonsense NOUN Nonsense is
foolish and meaningless words or
behaviour. **nonsensical** ADJECTIVE

non sequitur, non sequiturs [Said
non **sek**-kwit-ter] NOUN (ENGLISH) A
non sequitur is a remark that does not
follow logically from what has just
been said.
● WORD HISTORY: from Latin *non*
● *sequitur* meaning 'It does not
● follow'

nonstop ADJECTIVE OR ADVERB
continuing without any pauses or
breaks • *nonstop excitement.*

noodle, noodles NOUN Noodles are
a kind of pasta shaped into long, thin
pieces.

nook, nooks NOUN LITERARY a small

a
b
c
d
e
f
g
h
i
j
k
l
m
n
o
p
q
r
s
t
u
v
w
x
y
z

▷ SPELLING NOTE: 'i' before 'e' except after 'c'

A
B
C
D
E
F
G
H
I
J
K
L
M
N
O
P
Q
R
S
T
U
V
W
X
Y
Z

sheltered or hidden place.

noon NOUN Noon is midday.

no-one or **no one** PRONOUN not a single person.
● **USAGE NOTE:** *No-one* and *nobody*
● mean the same

noose, nooses NOUN a loop at the end of a piece of rope, with a knot that tightens when the rope is pulled.

nor CONJUNCTION used after 'neither' or after a negative statement, to add something else that the negative statement applies to • *They had neither the time nor the money for the sport.*

norm NOUN If something is the norm, it is the usual and expected thing • *cultures where large families are the norm.*
● **WORD HISTORY:** from Latin *norma*
● meaning 'carpenter's rule'

normal ADJECTIVE usual and ordinary • *I try to lead a normal life.*
normality NOUN
● **SIMILAR WORDS:** conventional,
● ordinary, usual

normally ADVERB ❶ usually • *I don't normally like dancing.* ❷ in a way that is normal • *The foetus is developing normally.*

north NOUN ❶ The north is the direction to your left when you are looking towards the place where the sun rises. ❷ The north of a place or country is the part which is towards the north when you are in the centre
▷ ADVERB OR ADJECTIVE ❸ North means towards the north • *The helicopter took off and headed north.*
▷ ADJECTIVE ❹ A north wind blows

from the north.

North America NOUN North America is the third largest continent, consisting of Canada, the United States, and Mexico. **North American** ADJECTIVE

north-east NOUN, ADVERB, OR ADJECTIVE North-east is halfway between north and east.

north-easterly ADJECTIVE ❶ North-easterly means to or towards the north-east. ❷ A north-easterly wind blows from the north-east.

north-eastern ADJECTIVE in or from the north-east.

northerly ADJECTIVE ❶ Northerly means to or towards the north • *travelling in a northerly direction.* ❷ A northerly wind blows from the north.

northern ADJECTIVE in or from the north • *the mountains of northern Italy.*

North Pole NOUN (GEOGRAPHY) The North Pole is the most northerly point of the earth's surface.

northward or **northwards** ADVERB ❶ Northward or northwards means towards the north • *We continued northwards.* ▷ ADJECTIVE ❷ The northward part of something is the north part.

north-west NOUN, ADVERB, OR ADJECTIVE North-west is halfway between north and west.

north-westerly ADJECTIVE ❶ North-westerly means to or towards the north-west. ❷ A north-westerly wind blows from the north-west.

north-western ADJECTIVE in or from the north-west.

Norwegian, Norwegians *[Said nor-__wee__-jn]* ADJECTIVE ❶ belonging or relating to Norway ▷ NOUN ❷ someone who comes from Norway. ❸ Norwegian is the main language spoken in Norway.

nose, noses NOUN ❶ the part of your face above your mouth which you use for smelling and breathing. ❷ the front part of a car or plane.

nostalgia *[Said nos-__tal__-ja]* NOUN Nostalgia is a feeling of affection for the past, and sadness that things have changed. **nostalgic** ADJECTIVE

nostril, nostrils NOUN Your nostrils are the two openings in your nose which you breathe through.

nosy, nosier, nosiest; *also spelt* **nosey** ADJECTIVE trying to find out about things that do not concern you.

not ADVERB used to make a sentence negative, to refuse something, or to deny something.
▶ SEE GRAMMAR BOX BELOW

notable ADJECTIVE important or interesting • *The production is notable for some outstanding performances.* **notably** ADVERB

notation, notations NOUN A notation is a set of written symbols, such as those used in music or mathematics.
● **WORD HISTORY:** from Latin *notare* meaning 'to note'

notch, notches NOUN a small V-shaped cut in a surface.
● **WORD HISTORY:** from a mistaken division of Middle English *an otch*

note, notes, noting, noted NOUN ❶ a short letter. ❷ a written piece of information that helps you to remember something • *You should make a note of that.* ❸ In music, a note is a musical sound of a particular pitch, or a written symbol that represents it. ❹ a banknote. ❺ an atmosphere, feeling, or quality • *There was a note of regret in his voice* • *I'm determined to close on an optimistic note.* ▷ VERB ❻ If you note a fact, you become aware of it or you mention it • *I noted that the rain had*

WHAT DOES NOT DO?

You can turn most sentences into negatives if you want to express the opposite meaning.

You can usually make a sentence into a negative by adding the word *not*: *Robbie was **not** feeling tired.*

If a sentence already contains an auxiliary verb, such as *have*, *will*, *be*, or *must*, the word *not* should go after this verb:

*She has **not** gone to the shops.*

If the sentence does not already contain an auxiliary verb, a form of the verb *do* is added, and the word *not* is placed after this:
*We **do not** expect to win.*

In spoken and informal English, the ending *-n't* may be added to an auxiliary verb in place of *not*:
*She **hasn't** gone to the shops.*

▷ SPELLING NOTE: *an ELegant angEL (angel)*

stopped. ▷ PHRASE **7** If you **take note** of something, you pay attention to it • *The world hardly took note of this crisis.*

note down VERB If you note something down, you write it down so that you will remember it.

notebook, notebooks **NOUN** a small book for writing notes in.

noted ADJECTIVE well-known and admired • *a noted Hebrew scholar.*

nothing PRONOUN not anything • *There was nothing to do.*

  ● USAGE NOTE: *Nothing* is usually
  ● followed by a singular verb: *nothing*
  ● *was in the bag.* If the expression
  ● *nothing but* is followed by a plural
  ● noun, the verb should be plural too:
  ● *a large room where nothing but*
  ● *souvenirs were sold*
  ● SIMILAR WORDS: nil, nought, zero

notice, notices, noticing, noticed **VERB ①** If you notice something, you become aware of it ▷ NOUN
② Notice is attention or awareness • *I'm glad he brought it to my notice.*
③ a written announcement.
④ Notice is also advance warning about something • *We were lucky to get you at such short notice.* ▷ PHRASE
⑤ If you **hand in your notice**, you tell your employer that you intend to leave your job after a fixed period of time.
  ● SIMILAR WORDS: **①** detect,
  ● observe, perceive

noticeable ADJECTIVE obvious and easy to see • *a noticeable improvement.* **noticeably ADVERB**

noticeboard, noticeboards **NOUN** a board for notices.

notify, notifies, notifying, notified **VERB** To notify someone of something means to officially inform them of it • *You must notify us of any change of address.* **notification NOUN**

notion, notions **NOUN** an idea or belief.

notorious ADJECTIVE well-known for something bad • *The area has become notorious for violence against tourists.* **notoriously ADVERB notoriety NOUN**

notwithstanding PREPOSITION FORMAL in spite of • *Notwithstanding his age, Sikorski had an important job.*

nougat *[Said noo-gah]* **NOUN** Nougat is a kind of chewy sweet containing nuts and sometimes fruit.
  ● WORD HISTORY: from Provençal
  ● *noga* meaning 'nut'

nought the number o.

noun, nouns **NOUN** (ENGLISH) a word which refers to a person, thing, or idea. Examples of nouns are 'president', 'table', 'sun', and 'beauty'.
▶ SEE GRAMMAR BOX ON PAGE 575

nourish, nourishes, nourishing, nourished *[Said nur-rish]* **VERB** To nourish people or animals means to provide them with food.

nourishing ADJECTIVE Food that is nourishing makes you strong and healthy.

nourishment NOUN Nourishment is food that your body needs in order to remain healthy • *poor nourishment.*

novel, novels **NOUN ①** (LIBRARY) a book that tells an invented story

---

▷ SPELLING NOTE: *LEt's measure the angLE (angle)*

a
b
c
d
e
f
g
h
i
j
k
l
m
n
o
p
q
r
s
t
u
v
w
x
y
z

WHAT IS A NOUN?

A noun is a word that labels a person, a thing or an idea. In any sentence, the nouns will tell you which people or things are involved. They are sometimes called 'naming words'.

Common nouns are words which indicate every example of a certain type of thing. They begin with small letters:

girl
city
picture

Proper nouns are words which give the name of a particular person, place, or object. They begin with capital letters:

Anna Jamieson
Los Angeles
The Mona Lisa

Some common nouns are **concrete nouns**. These are words that indicate things that you *can* touch:

cat
pen
apple

Other common nouns are **abstract nouns**. These are words that indicate things that you *cannot* touch:

beauty
ambition
popularity

Some common nouns are **collective nouns**. These are words that indicate a group or collection of things:

pack
bunch
flock

▷ ADJECTIVE **2** new and interesting • *a very novel experience.*

novelist, novelists NOUN a person who writes novels.

novelty, novelties NOUN **1** Novelty is the quality of being new and interesting • *The novelty had worn off.* **2** something new and interesting • *Steam power was still a bit of a novelty.* **3** a small, unusual object sold as a gift or souvenir.

November NOUN November is the eleventh month of the year. It has 30 days.

● **WORD HISTORY:** from Latin
● *November* meaning 'the ninth
● month'

novice, novices NOUN **1** someone who is not yet experienced at something. **2** someone who is preparing to become a monk or nun.

now ADVERB **1** at the present time or moment ▷ CONJUNCTION **2** as a result or consequence of a particular fact • *Things have got better now there is a new board.* ▷ PHRASE **3** **Just now** means very recently • *I drove Brenda back to the camp just now.* **4** If something happens **now and then**, it happens sometimes but not regularly.

nowadays ADVERB at the present time • *Nowadays most fathers choose to be present at the birth.*

nowhere ADVERB not anywhere.

noxious [Said **nok**-shus] ADJECTIVE harmful or poisonous • *a noxious gas.*

▷ SPELLING NOTE: A Rude Idiot Thought He Might Eat Toffee In Church (*arithmetic*)

A
B
C
D
E
F
G
H
I
J
K
L
M
N
O
P
Q
R
S
T
U
V
W
X
Y
Z

nozzle, nozzles **NOUN** a spout fitted onto the end of a pipe or hose to control the flow of a liquid.

nuance, nuances [Said **nyoo-ahnss**] **NOUN** a small difference in sound, colour, or meaning • *the nuances of his music.*

nubile [Said **nyoo-bile**] **ADJECTIVE** A woman who is nubile is young and sexually attractive.
● **WORD HISTORY:** from Latin *nubere* meaning 'to take a husband'

nuclear **ADJECTIVE** ❶ (SCIENCE) relating to the energy produced when the nuclei of atoms are split • *nuclear power* • *the nuclear industry.*
❷ relating to weapons that explode using the energy released by atoms • *nuclear war.* ❸ (SCIENCE) relating to the structure and behaviour of the nuclei of atoms • *nuclear physics.*

nuclear reactor, nuclear reactors **NOUN** A nuclear reactor is a device which is used to obtain nuclear energy.

nucleus, nuclei [Said **nyoo-klee-uss**] **NOUN** ❶ (SCIENCE) The nucleus of an atom is the central part of it. It is positively charged and is made up of protons and neutrons. ❷ (SCIENCE) The nucleus of a cell is the part that contains the chromosomes and controls the growth and reproduction of the cell. ❸ The nucleus of something is the basic central part of it to which other things are added.
● **WORD HISTORY:** from Latin *nucleus* meaning 'kernel'

nude, nudes **ADJECTIVE** ❶ naked ▷ **NOUN** ❷ a picture or statue of a naked person. **nudity NOUN**

nudge, nudges, nudging, nudged **VERB** ❶ If you nudge someone, you push them gently, usually with your elbow ▷ **NOUN** ❷ a gentle push.

nudist, nudists **NOUN** a person who believes in wearing no clothes.

nugget, nuggets **NOUN** a small rough lump of something, especially gold.

nuisance, nuisances **NOUN** someone or something that is annoying or inconvenient.
● **SIMILAR WORDS:** bother, inconvenience, problem

null **PHRASE** **Null and void** means not legally valid • *Other documents were declared to be null and void.*

nulla-nulla, nulla-nullas **NOUN** a thick heavy stick used as a weapon by Australian Aborigines.

numb, numbs, numbing, numbed **ADJECTIVE** ❶ unable to feel anything • *My legs felt numb* • *numb with grief.* ▷ **VERB** ❷ If something numbs you, it makes you unable to feel anything • *The cold numbed my fingers.*

numbat, numbats **NOUN** a small Australian marsupial with a long snout and tongue and strong claws which it uses for hunting and eating insects.

number, numbers, numbering, numbered **NOUN** ❶ a word or a symbol used for counting or calculating. ❷ Someone's number is the series of numbers that you dial when you telephone them. ❸ A number of things is a quantity of them • *Adrian has introduced me to a large number of people.* ❹ a song or piece of music ▷ **VERB** ❺ If things number a

▷ SPELLING NOTE: *Beautiful Elephants Are Usually Tiny (beautiful)*

a
b
c
d
e
f
g
h
i
j
k
l
m
n
o
p
q
r
s
t
u
v
w
x
y
z

WHAT DO NUMBERS DO?

Numbers tell you how many of a thing there are.

Cardinal numbers tell you the total number of a thing:
Three figures huddled in the doorway.

Ordinal numbers tell you the order of something. They often end with the letters -*th*:
*Her **sixth** novel was the most successful yet.*

---

particular amount, there are that many of them • *At that time London's population numbered about 460,000.* ❻ If you number something, you give it a number • *The picture is signed and numbered by the artist.* ❼ To be numbered among a particular group means to belong to it • *Only the best are numbered among their champions.*
- **SIMILAR WORDS:** ❶ digit, figure, numeral
- ▶ SEE GRAMMAR BOX ABOVE

numeral, numerals **NOUN** a symbol that represents a number • *a wristwatch with Roman numerals.*

numerate [Said *nyoo-mer-rit*] **ADJECTIVE** (MATHS) able to do arithmetic. **numeracy NOUN**

numerator, numerators **NOUN** (MATHS) In maths, the numerator is the top part of a fraction.

numerical ADJECTIVE expressed in numbers or relating to numbers • *a numerical value.*

numerous ADJECTIVE existing or happening in large numbers.

nun, nuns **NOUN** a woman who has taken religious vows and lives in a convent.

nurse, nurses, nursing, nursed **NOUN** ❶ a person whose job is to look after people who are ill ▷ **VERB** ❷ If you

nurse someone, you look after them when they are ill. ❸ If you nurse a feeling, you feel it strongly for a long time • *He nursed a grudge against the USA.*

nursery, nurseries **NOUN** ❶ a place where young children are looked after while their parents are working. ❷ a room in which young children sleep and play. ❸ a place where plants are grown and sold.

nursery rhyme, nursery rhymes **NOUN** (ENGLISH) A nursery rhyme is a short poem or song for young children.

nursery school, nursery schools **NOUN** a school for children from three to five years old.

nursing home, nursing homes **NOUN** a privately run hospital, especially for old people.

nurture, nurtures, nurturing, nurtured **VERB** FORMAL If you nurture a young child or a plant, you look after it carefully.

nut, nuts **NOUN** ❶ a fruit with a hard shell and an edible centre that grows on certain trees. ❷ a piece of metal with a hole in the middle which a bolt screws into.

nutmeg NOUN Nutmeg is a spice used for flavouring in cooking.

▷ SPELLING NOTE: *Betty Eats Cakes And Uses Seven Eggs (because)*

nutrient, nutrients NOUN
(SCIENCE) Nutrients are substances that help plants or animals to grow • *the nutrients in the soil.*

nutrition NOUN (D & T) Nutrition is the food that you eat, considered from the point of view of how it helps you to grow and remain healthy • *The effects of poor nutrition are evident.*
nutritional ADJECTIVE **nutritionist** NOUN

nutritious ADJECTIVE containing substances that help you to grow and remain healthy.

nutty, nuttier, nuttiest ADJECTIVE
❶ INFORMAL mad or very foolish.
❷ tasting of nuts.

nylon, nylons NOUN ❶ Nylon is a type of strong artificial material • *nylon stockings.* ❷ Nylons are stockings or tights.

nymph, nymphs *[Said nimf]* NOUN
❶ In Greek and Roman mythology, a nymph is a young goddess who lives in trees, rivers, or mountains.
❷ (SCIENCE) In biology, a nymph is the immature form of an insect, such as a dragonfly, which becomes an adult without passing through the stage of being a pupa. The nymph looks like the adult, but cannot fly or reproduce.

A
B
C
D
E
F
G
H
I
J
K
L
M
N
O
P
Q
R
S
T
U
V
W
X
Y
Z

▷ SPELLING NOTE: *there's a rAKE in the brAKEs (brake)*

Oo

oaf, oafs **NOUN** a clumsy and stupid person.
● **WORD HISTORY:** from Old Norse
● *alfr* meaning 'elf'

oak, oaks **NOUN** a large tree which produces acorns. It has a hard wood which is often used to make furniture.

OAP, OAPs **NOUN** In Britain, a man over the age of 65 or a woman over the age of 60 who receives a pension. OAP is an abbreviation for 'old age pensioner'.

oar, oars **NOUN** a wooden pole with a wide, flat end, used for rowing a boat.

oasis, oases [*Said oh-ay-siss*] **NOUN** a small area in a desert where water and plants are found.

oat, oats **NOUN** Oats are a type of grain.

oath, oaths **NOUN** a formal promise, especially a promise to tell the truth in a court of law.
● **SIMILAR WORDS:** pledge,
● promise, vow

oatmeal **NOUN** Oatmeal is a rough flour made from oats.

OBE, OBEs **NOUN** a British honour awarded by the King or Queen. OBE is an abbreviation for 'Officer of the Order of the British Empire'.

obedient **ADJECTIVE** If you are obedient, you do what you are told to do. **obediently** **ADVERB** **obedience** **NOUN**

obelisk, obelisks **NOUN** a stone pillar built in honour of a person or an event.

obese [*Said oh-bees*] **ADJECTIVE** extremely fat. **obesity** **NOUN**
● **WORD HISTORY:** from Latin
● *ob-* meaning 'much' and *edere*
● meaning 'to eat'

obey, obeys, obeying, obeyed **VERB** If you obey a person or an order, you do what you are told to do.

obituary, obituaries **NOUN** a piece of writing about the life and achievements of someone who has just died.

object, objects, objecting, objected **NOUN** ❶ anything solid that you can touch or see, and that is not alive. ❷ an aim or purpose. ❸ The object of your feelings or actions is the person that they are directed towards. ❹ In grammar, the object of a verb or preposition is the word or phrase which follows it and describes the person or thing affected ▷ **VERB** ❺ If you object to something, you dislike it or disapprove of it.
● **SIMILAR WORDS:** ❺ oppose,
● protest, take exception

objection, objections **NOUN** If you have an objection to something, you dislike it or disapprove of it.

▷ SPELLING NOTE: *you'll brEAK that Electrical Aerial, Kitty (break)*

objectionable ADJECTIVE
unpleasant and offensive.

objective, objectives NOUN ❶ an
aim • *The protection of the countryside
is their main objective.* ▷ ADJECTIVE
❷ If you are objective, you are not
influenced by personal feelings or
prejudices • *an objective approach.*
objectively ADVERB **objectivity**
NOUN

obligation, obligations NOUN
something that you must do because
it is your duty.

obligatory [Said ob-**lig**-a-tree]
ADJECTIVE required by a rule or law
• *Religious education was made
obligatory.*

oblige, obliges, obliging, obliged
VERB ❶ If you are obliged to do
something, you have to do it. ❷ If you
oblige someone, you help them.
obliging ADJECTIVE

oblique [Said o-**bleek**] ADJECTIVE
❶ An oblique remark is not direct, and
is therefore difficult to understand.
❷ An oblique line slopes at an angle.

obliterate, obliterates, obliterating,
obliterated VERB To obliterate
something is to destroy it completely.
obliteration NOUN

oblivion NOUN Oblivion is
unconsciousness or complete lack of
awareness of your surroundings.
oblivious ADJECTIVE **obliviously**
ADVERB

oblong, oblongs NOUN ❶ a
four-sided shape with two parallel
short sides, two parallel long sides,
and four right angles ▷ ADJECTIVE
❷ shaped like an oblong.

obnoxious [Said ob-**nok**-shuss]
ADJECTIVE extremely unpleasant.

oboe, oboes NOUN a woodwind
musical instrument with a double
reed. **oboist** NOUN
● **WORD HISTORY:** from French *haut*
● *bois* meaning literally 'high wood', a
● reference to the instrument's pitch

obscene ADJECTIVE indecent and
likely to upset people • *obscene
pictures.* **obscenely** ADVERB
obscenity NOUN
● **SIMILAR WORDS:** filthy, indecent,
● pornographic

obscure, obscures, obscuring,
obscured ADJECTIVE ❶ Something
that is obscure is known by only a few
people • *an obscure Mongolian dialect.*
❷ Something obscure is difficult to
see or to understand • *The news was
shrouded in obscure language.* ▷ VERB
❸ To obscure something is to make it
difficult to see or understand • *His
view was obscured by trees.* **obscurity**
NOUN
● **SIMILAR WORDS:** ❷ cryptic,
● unclear, vague

observance NOUN The observance
of a law or custom is the practice of
obeying or following it.

observant ADJECTIVE Someone
who is observant notices things that
are not easy to see.

observation, observations NOUN
❶ Observation is the act of watching
something carefully • *Success hinges
on close observation.* ❷ something
that you have seen or noticed. ❸ a
remark. ❹ Observation is the ability
to notice things that are not easy to
see.

▷ SPELLING NOTE: *I always visit my FRIend on a FRIday (Friday)*

observatory, observatories NOUN
An observatory is a room or building containing telescopes and other equipment for studying the sun, moon, and stars.

observe, observes, observing, observed VERB **❶** To observe something is to watch it carefully. **❷** To observe something is to notice it. **❸** If you observe that something is the case, you make a comment about it. **❹** To observe a law or custom is to obey or follow it. **observer** NOUN **observable** ADJECTIVE

obsession, obsessions NOUN If someone has an obsession about something, they cannot stop thinking about that thing. **obsessional** ADJECTIVE **obsessed** ADJECTIVE **obsessive** ADJECTIVE

obsolete ADJECTIVE out of date and no longer used.
 ● SIMILAR WORDS: outmoded,
 ● passé

obstacle, obstacles NOUN something which is in your way and makes it difficult to do something.
 ● SIMILAR WORDS: difficulty,
 ● stumbling block

obstetrics NOUN Obstetrics is the branch of medicine concerned with pregnancy and childbirth. **obstetrician** NOUN

obstinate ADJECTIVE Someone who is obstinate is stubborn and unwilling to change their mind. **obstinately** ADVERB **obstinacy** NOUN

obstruct, obstructs, obstructing, obstructed VERB If something obstructs a road or path, it blocks it.

obstruction NOUN **obstructive** ADJECTIVE

obtain, obtains, obtaining, obtained VERB If you obtain something, you get it. **obtainable** ADJECTIVE

obtrusive ADJECTIVE noticeable in an unpleasant way.

obtuse ADJECTIVE **❶** Someone who is obtuse is stupid or slow to understand things. **❷** (MATHS) An obtuse angle is an angle between 90° and 180°.

obvious ADJECTIVE easy to see or understand. **obviously** ADVERB
 ● SIMILAR WORDS: clear, evident,
 ● plain

occasion, occasions, occasioning, occasioned NOUN **❶** a time when something happens. **❷** an important event. **❸** An occasion for doing something is an opportunity for doing it ▷ VERB **❹** FORMAL To occasion something is to cause it • *damage occasioned by fire*.

occasional ADJECTIVE happening sometimes but not often • *an occasional outing*. **occasionally** ADVERB

occult NOUN The occult is the knowledge and study of supernatural and magical forces or powers.

occupancy NOUN The occupancy of a building is the act of living or working in it.

occupant, occupants NOUN The occupants of a building are the people who live or work in it.

occupation, occupations NOUN **❶** a job or profession. **❷** a hobby or

a
b
c
d
e
f
g
h
i
j
k
l
m
n
o
p
q
r
s
t
u
v
w
x
y
z

▷ SPELLING NOTE: *I want to see (C) your licenCe (licence)*

something you do for pleasure. ❸ The occupation of a country is the act of invading it and taking control of it. **occupational ADJECTIVE**

occupy, occupies, occupying, occupied **VERB** ❶ The people who occupy a building are the people who live or work there. ❷ When people occupy a place, they move into it and take control of it • *Demonstrators occupied the building.* ❸ To occupy a position in a system or plan is to have that position • *His phone-in show occupies a daytime slot.* ❹ If something occupies you, you spend your time doing it • *That problem occupies me night and day.* **occupier NOUN**

occur, occurs, occurring, occurred **VERB** ❶ If something occurs, it happens or exists • *The second attack occurred at a swimming pool.* ❷ If something occurs to you, you suddenly think of it.
- **USAGE NOTE:** If an event has been
- planned, you should not say that it
- *occurred* or *happened*: *the wedding
- took place on Saturday.* Only
- something unexpected *occurs* or
- *happens*: *an accident has occurred;
- the burglary happened last night*

occurrence, occurrences **NOUN** ❶ an event. ❷ The occurrence of something is the fact that it happens or exists • *the occurrence of diseases.*

ocean, oceans **NOUN** ❶ LITERARY the sea. ❷ The five oceans are the five very large areas of sea • *the Atlantic Ocean.* **oceanic ADJECTIVE**

o'clock ADVERB You use 'o'clock' after the number of the hour to say what the time is.

octagon, octagons **NOUN** a shape with eight straight sides. **octagonal ADJECTIVE**

octave, octaves **NOUN** ❶ [MUSIC] the difference in pitch between the first note and the eighth note of a musical scale. ❷ [ENGLISH] eight lines of poetry together.

octet, octets **NOUN** [MUSIC] An octet is a group of eight musicians who sing or play together; also a piece of music written for eight instruments or singers.

October NOUN October is the tenth month of the year. It has 31 days.
- **WORD HISTORY:** from Latin
- *october* meaning 'the eighth month'

octopus, octopuses **NOUN** a sea creature with eight long tentacles which it uses to catch food.
- **WORD HISTORY:** from Greek *okto*
- + *pous* meaning 'eight feet'

odd, odder, oddest **ADJECTIVE** ❶ Something odd is strange or unusual. ❷ Odd things do not match each other • *odd socks.* ❸ Odd numbers are numbers that cannot be divided exactly by two ▷ **ADVERB** ❹ You use 'odd' after a number to say that it is approximate • *I've written twenty odd plays.* **oddly ADVERB oddness NOUN**

oddity, oddities **NOUN** something very strange.

oddments PLURAL NOUN Oddments are things that are left over after other things have been used.

odds PLURAL NOUN In gambling, the probability of something happening is called the odds • *The* *odds are against the record being beaten.*

odds and ends PLURAL NOUN
You can refer to a collection of small unimportant things as odds and ends.

ode, odes NOUN (ENGLISH) a poem written in praise of someone or something.

odious ADJECTIVE extremely unpleasant.

odour, odours NOUN FORMAL a strong smell. **odorous** ADJECTIVE

odyssey, odysseys [Said *od-i-see*] NOUN a long and eventful journey.

oesophagus, oesophaguses [Said *ee-sof-fag-uss*] NOUN the tube that carries food from your throat to your stomach.

oestrogen another spelling of estrogen.

of PREPOSITION ❶ consisting of or containing • *a collection of short stories* • *a cup of tea.* ❷ used when naming something or describing a characteristic of something • *the city of Canberra* • *a woman of great power and influence.* ❸ belonging to or connected with • *a friend of Rachel* • *the cover of the book.*
  ● USAGE NOTE: Where *of* means 'belonging to', it can be replaced by an apostrophe: *the cover of the book* is the same as *the book's cover*

off PREPOSITION OR ADVERB
❶ indicating movement away from or out of a place • *They had just stepped off the plane* • *She got up and marched off.* ❷ indicating separation or distance from a place • *some islands off the coast of Australia* • *The whole*

crescent has been fenced off. ❸ not working • *It was Frank's night off.*
▷ ADVERB OR ADJECTIVE ❹ not switched on • *He turned the radio off* • *the off switch.* ▷ ADJECTIVE
❺ cancelled or postponed • *The concert was off.* ❻ Food that is off has gone sour or bad ▷ PREPOSITION
❼ not liking or not using something • *He went right off alcohol.*
  ● USAGE NOTE: Do not use *of* after *off*. You should say *he stepped off the bus* not *he stepped off of the bus*. It is very informal to use *off* where you mean 'from': *they bought milk of a farmer* instead of *they bought milk from a farmer*. Always use *from* in written work

offal NOUN Offal is liver, kidneys, and other parts of animals, which can be eaten.

offence, offences NOUN ❶ a crime • *a drink-driving offence.* ▷ PHRASES ❷ If something **gives offence**, it upsets people. If you **take offence**, you are upset by someone or something.

offend, offends, offending, offended VERB ❶ If you offend someone, you upset them. ❷ FORMAL To offend or to offend a law is to commit a crime. **offender** NOUN

offensive, offensives ADJECTIVE
❶ Something offensive is rude and upsetting • *offensive behaviour.*
❷ Offensive actions or weapons are used in attacking someone ▷ NOUN
❸ an attack • *a full-scale offensive against the rebels.* **offensively** ADVERB

offer, offers, offering, offered VERB
❶ If you offer something to someone,

a b c d e f g h i j k l m n **o** p q r s t u v w x y z

▷ SPELLING NOTE: have a pIEce of pIE (piece)

A
B
C
D
E
F
G
H
I
J
K
L
M
N
O
P
Q
R
S
T
U
V
W
X
Y
Z

you ask them if they would like it ▷ **NOUN** ❷ something that someone says they will give you or do for you if you want them to • *He refused the offer of a drink.* ❸ a specially low price for a product in a shop • *You will need a voucher to qualify for the special offer.*

offering, offerings **NOUN** something that is offered or given to someone.

offhand ADJECTIVE ❶ If someone is offhand, they are unfriendly and slightly rude ▷ **ADVERB** ❷ If you know something offhand, you know it without having to think very hard • *I couldn't tell you offhand how long he's been here.*

office, offices **NOUN** ❶ a room where people work at desks. ❷ a government department • *the Office of Fair Trading.* ❸ a place where people can go for information, tickets, or other services. ❹ Someone who holds office has an important job or position in government or in an organization.

officer, officers **NOUN** a person with a position of authority in the armed forces, the police, or a government organization.

official, officials **ADJECTIVE** ❶ approved by the government or by someone in authority • *the official figures.* ❷ done or used by someone in authority as part of their job • *official notepaper.* ▷ **NOUN** ❸ a person who holds a position of authority in an organization. **officially ADVERB**

officialdom NOUN You can refer to officials in government or other organizations as officialdom, especially when you find that they are

difficult to deal with.

officiate, officiates, officiating, officiated **VERB** To officiate at a ceremony is to be in charge and perform the official part of the ceremony.

offing PHRASE If something is **in the offing**, it is likely to happen soon • *A change is in the offing.*

off-licence, off-licences **NOUN** a shop which sells alcoholic drinks.

offline ADJECTIVE ❶ If a computer is offline, it is switched off or not connected to the Internet ▷ **ADVERB** ❷ If you do something offline, you do it while not connected to the Internet.

offset, offsets, offsetting, offset **VERB** If one thing is offset by another thing, its effect is reduced or cancelled out by that thing • *This tedium can be offset by watching the television.*

offshoot, offshoots **NOUN** something that has developed from another thing • *The technology we use is an offshoot of the motor industry.*

offshore ADJECTIVE OR ADVERB in or from the part of the sea near the shore • *an offshore wind* • *a wreck fifteen kilometres offshore.*

offside ADJECTIVE ❶ If a soccer, rugby, or hockey player is offside, they have broken the rules by moving too far forward ▷ **NOUN** ❷ the side of a vehicle that is furthest from the pavement.

offspring NOUN A person's or animal's offspring are their children.

often ADVERB happening many times or a lot of the time.

▷ SPELLING NOTE: *plaice the fish has a glittering 'EYE' (I) (plaice)*

ogle, ogles, ogling, ogled *[Said oh-gl]* **VERB** To ogle someone is to stare at them in a way that indicates a sexual interest.

ogre, ogres *[Said oh-gur]* **NOUN** a cruel, frightening giant in a fairy story.

ohm, ohms *[rhymes with home]* **NOUN** SCIENCE In physics, an ohm is a unit used to measure electrical resistance.

oil, oils, oiling, oiled **NOUN** ❶ Oil is a thick, sticky liquid used as a fuel and for lubrication. ❷ Oil is also a thick, greasy liquid made from plants or animals • *cooking oil* • *bath oil*. ▷ **VERB** ❸ If you oil something, you put oil in it or on it.

oil painting, oil paintings **NOUN** a picture that has been painted with thick paints made from coloured powder and a kind of oil.

oilskin, oilskins **NOUN** a piece of clothing made from a thick, waterproof material, worn especially by fishermen.

oily **ADJECTIVE** Something that is oily is covered with or contains oil • *an oily rag* • *oily skin*.

ointment, ointments **NOUN** a smooth, thick substance that you put on sore skin to heal it.

okay or **OK** **ADJECTIVE** INFORMAL Okay means all right • *Tell me if this sounds okay*.
● **SIMILAR WORDS:** acceptable, all
● right, satisfactory

old, older, oldest **ADJECTIVE** ❶ having lived or existed for a long time • *an old lady* • *old clothes*. ❷ 'Old' is used to give the age of

someone or something • *This photo is five years old*. ❸ 'Old' also means former • *my old art teacher*.

olden **PHRASE** In the olden days means long ago.

Old English **NOUN** Old English was the English language from the fifth century AD until about 1100. Old English is also known as Anglo-Saxon.

old-fashioned **ADJECTIVE** ❶ Something which is old-fashioned is no longer fashionable • *old-fashioned shoes*. ❷ Someone who is old-fashioned believes in the values and standards of the past.
● **SIMILAR WORDS:** ❶ dated,
● outmoded, passé

Old Norse **NOUN** Old Norse was a language spoken in Scandinavia and Iceland from about 700 AD to about 1350 AD. Many English words are derived from Old Norse.

Old Testament **NOUN** The Old Testament is the first part of the Christian Bible. It is also the holy book of the Jewish religion and contains writings which relate to the history of the Jews.

oleander, oleanders **NOUN** an evergreen shrub with fragrant white, pink, or purple flowers.

olive, olives **NOUN** ❶ a small green or black fruit containing a stone. Olives are usually pickled and eaten as a snack or crushed to produce oil ▷ **ADJECTIVE OR NOUN** ❷ dark yellowish-green.

-ology **SUFFIX** '-ology' is used to form words that refer to the study of something • *biology* • *geology*.

a
b
c
d
e
f
g
h
i
j
k
l
m
n
o
p
q
r
s
t
u
v
w
x
y
z

▷ SPELLING NOTE: *I went to see (C) the doctor's new practiCe (practice)*

● **WORD HISTORY:** from Greek *logos* meaning 'reason', 'speech', or 'discourse'

Olympic Games [Said ol-**lim**-pik] **PLURAL NOUN** The Olympic Games are a set of sporting contests held in a different city every four years.

ombudsman, ombudsmen **NOUN** The ombudsman is a person who investigates complaints against the government or a public organization.

omelette, omelettes [Said **om**-lit] **NOUN** a dish made by beating eggs together and cooking them in a flat pan.

omen, omens **NOUN** something that is thought to be a sign of what will happen in the future • *John saw this success as a good omen for his trip.*
● **SIMILAR WORDS:** portent, sign

ominous ADJECTIVE suggesting that something unpleasant is going to happen • *an ominous sign.* **ominously ADVERB**
● **SIMILAR WORDS:** sinister, threatening

omission, omissions **NOUN** ❶ something that has not been included or done • *There are some striking omissions in the survey.* ❷ Omission is the act of not including or not doing something • *controversy over the omission of female novelists.*

omit, omits, omitting, omitted **VERB** ❶ If you omit something, you do not include it. ❷ **FORMAL** If you omit to do something, you do not do it.

omnibus, omnibuses **NOUN** ❶ a book containing a collection of stories or articles by the same author or about the same subject ▷ **ADJECTIVE** ❷ An omnibus edition of a radio or television show contains two or more programmes that were originally broadcast separately.

omnipotent [Said om-**nip**-a-tent] **ADJECTIVE** having very great or unlimited power • *omnipotent emperors.* **omnipotence NOUN**

omniscient narrator, omniscient narrators **NOUN** (**ENGLISH**) A narrator who tells a story that he or she is not part of, and who knows everything about all the characters: their past, their future, and even what they think.

omnivore NOUN An omnivore is an animal that eats all kinds of food, including meat and plants. **omnivorous ADJECTIVE**

on PREPOSITION ❶ touching or attached to something • *The woman was sitting on the sofa.* ❷ If you are on a bus, plane, or train, you are inside it. ❸ If something happens on a particular day, that is when it happens • *It is his birthday on Monday.* ❹ If something is done on an instrument or machine, it is done using that instrument or machine • *He preferred to play on his computer.* ❺ A book or talk on a particular subject is about that subject ▷ **ADVERB** ❻ If you have a piece of clothing on, you are wearing it ▷ **ADJECTIVE** ❼ A machine or switch that is on is working. ❽ If an event is on, it is happening or taking place • *The race is definitely on.*

once ADVERB ❶ If something happens once, it happens one time only. ❷ If something was once true, it was true in the past, but is no longer true ▷ **CONJUNCTION** ❸ If something happens once another thing has happened, it happens immediately afterwards • *Once you get used to working for yourself, it's tough working for anybody else.* ▷ **PHRASES** ❹ If you do something **at once**, you do it immediately. If several things happen **at once**, they all happen at the same time.

one, ones ❶ One is the number 1 **ADJECTIVE** ❷ If you refer to the one person or thing of a particular kind, you mean the only person or thing of that kind • *My one aim is to look after the horses well.* ❸ One also means 'a'; used when emphasizing something • *They got one almighty shock.* ▷ **PRONOUN** ❹ One refers to a particular thing or person • *Alf Brown's business was a good one.* ❺ One also means people in general • *One likes to have the opportunity to chat.*

one-dimensional **ADJECTIVE** (MATHS) something that is one-dimensional has height or length or width, but not more than one of them, for example a line or a curve.

one-off, one-offs **NOUN** something that happens or is made only once.

onerous [*Said* **ohn**-er-uss] **ADJECTIVE** FORMAL difficult or unpleasant • *an onerous task.*

oneself **PRONOUN** 'Oneself' is used when you are talking about people in general • *One could hardly hear oneself talk.*

one-sided **ADJECTIVE** ❶ If an activity or relationship is one-sided, one of the people has a lot more success or involvement than the other

• *a one-sided contest.* ❷ A one-sided argument or report considers the facts or a situation from only one point of view.

one-way **ADJECTIVE** ❶ One-way streets are streets along which vehicles can drive in only one direction. ❷ A one-way ticket is one that you use to travel to a place, but not to travel back again.

ongoing **ADJECTIVE** continuing to happen • *an ongoing process of learning.*

onion, onions **NOUN** a small, round vegetable with a brown skin like paper and a very strong taste.

online **ADJECTIVE** ❶ If a computer is online, it is switched on or connected to the Internet ▷ **ADVERB** ❷ If you do something online, you do it while connected to the Internet.

onlooker, onlookers **NOUN** someone who is watching an event.

only **ADVERB** ❶ You use 'only' to indicate the one thing or person involved • *Only Keith knows whether he will continue.* ❷ You use 'only' to emphasize that something is unimportant or small • *He's only a little boy.* ❸ You can use 'only' to introduce something which happens immediately after something else • *She had thought of one plan, only to discard it for another.* ▷ **ADJECTIVE** ❹ If you talk about the only thing or person, you mean that there are no others • *their only hit single.* ❺ If you are an only child, you have no brothers or sisters ▷ **CONJUNCTION** ❻ 'Only' also means but or except • *He was like you, only blond.* ▷ **PHRASE** ❼ Only

a b c d e f g h i j k l m n o p q r s t u v w x y z

▷ SPELLING NOTE: *pAL up with the principAL and principAL staff (principal)*

A
B
C
D
E
F
G
H
I
J
K
L
M
N
O
P
Q
R
S
T
U
V
W
X
Y
Z

too means extremely • *I would be only too happy to swap places.*

onomatopoeia *[Said on-o-mat-o-pee-a]* NOUN (ENGLISH) the use of words which sound like the thing that they represent. 'Hiss' and 'buzz' are examples of onomatopoeia.
onomatopoeic ADJECTIVE
● **WORD HISTORY:** from Greek
● *onoma* meaning 'name' and *poiein* meaning 'to make'

onset NOUN The onset of something unpleasant is the beginning of it • *the onset of war.*

onslaught, onslaughts *[Said on-slawt]* NOUN a violent attack.

onto or **on to** PREPOSITION If you put something onto an object, you put it on it.

onus *[rhymes with bonus]* NOUN FORMAL If the onus is on you to do something, it is your duty to do it.

onwards or **onward** ADVERB
● continuing to happen from a particular time • *He could not speak a word from that moment onwards.*
● travelling forwards • *Duncliffe escorted the pair onwards to his own room.*

onyx *[Said on-iks]* NOUN Onyx is a semiprecious stone used for making ornaments and jewellery.

ooze, oozes, oozing, oozed VERB When a thick liquid oozes, it flows slowly • *The cold mud oozed over her new footwear.*

opal, opals NOUN a pale or whitish semiprecious stone used for making jewellery.

opaque *[Said oh-pake]* ADJECTIVE If something is opaque, you cannot see through it • *opaque glass windows.*

open, opens, opening, opened VERB
● When you open something, or when it opens, you move it so that it is no longer closed • *She opened the door.*
● When a shop or office opens, people are able to go in. ● To open something also means to start it • *He tried to open a bank account.*
▷ ADJECTIVE ● Something that is open is not closed or fastened • *an open box of chocolates.* ● If you have an open mind, you are willing to consider new ideas or suggestions. ● Someone who is open is honest and frank. ● When a shop or office is open, people are able to go in. ● An open area of sea or land is a large, empty area • *open country.* ● If something is open to you, it is possible for you to do it • *There is no other course open to us but to fight it out.* ● If a situation is still open, it is still being considered • *Even if the case remains open, the full facts may never be revealed.* ▷ PHRASE ● In the open means outside. ● In the open also means not secret. **openly** ADVERB

opening, openings ADJECTIVE
● Opening means coming first • *the opening day of the season.* ▷ NOUN
● The opening of a book or film is the first part of it. ● a hole or gap. ● an opportunity • *The two men circled, looking for an opening to attack.*
● **SIMILAR WORDS:** ● aperture,
● gap, hole

open-minded ADJECTIVE willing to consider new ideas and suggestions.

open-plan ADJECTIVE An open-plan office or building has very few dividing walls inside.

opera, operas NOUN a play in which the words are sung rather than spoken. **operatic** ADJECTIVE
● WORD HISTORY: from Latin *opera* meaning 'works'

operate, operates, operating, operated VERB ❶ To operate is to work • *We are shocked at the way that businesses operate.* ❷ When you operate a machine, you make it work. ❸ When surgeons operate, they cut open a patient's body to remove or repair a damaged part.

operation, operations NOUN ❶ a complex, planned event • *a full-scale military operation.* ❷ a form of medical treatment in which a surgeon cuts open a patient's body to remove or repair a damaged part. ❸ (MATHS) any process in which a number or quantity is operated on according to a set of rules, for example addition, subtraction, multiplication, and division ▷ PHRASE ❹ If something is **in operation**, it is working or being used • *The system is in operation from April to the end of September.*

operational ADJECTIVE working or able to be used • *an operational aircraft.*

operative ADJECTIVE Something that is operative is working or having an effect.

operator, operators NOUN ❶ someone who works at a telephone exchange or on a switchboard. ❷ someone who operates a machine • *a computer operator.* ❸ someone

who runs a business • *a tour operator.*

opinion, opinions NOUN a belief or view.
● SIMILAR WORDS: belief, judgment, view

opinionated ADJECTIVE Someone who is opinionated has strong views and refuses to accept that they might be wrong.

opium NOUN Opium is a drug made from the seeds of a poppy. It is used in medicine to relieve pain.
● WORD HISTORY: from Latin *opium* meaning 'poppy juice'

opponent, opponents NOUN someone who is against you in an argument or a contest.

opportune ADJECTIVE FORMAL happening at a convenient time • *The king's death was opportune for the prince.*

opportunism NOUN Opportunism is taking advantage of any opportunity to gain money or power for yourself. **opportunist** NOUN

opportunity, opportunities NOUN a chance to do something.

oppose, opposes, opposing, opposed VERB If you oppose something, you disagree with it and try to prevent it.

opposed ADJECTIVE ❶ If you are opposed to something, you disagree with it • *He was totally opposed to bullying in schools.* ❷ Opposed also means opposite or very different • *two opposed schools of thought.* ▷ PHRASE ❸ If you refer to one thing **as opposed to** another, you are emphasizing that it is the first thing rather than the second which

a
b
c
d
e
f
g
h
i
j
k
l
m
n
o
p
q
r
s
t
u
v
w
x
y
z

▷ SPELLING NOTE: *Psychiatrists Seldom Yell Callously Hard (psychiatrist)*

A
B
C
D
E
F
G
H
I
J
K
L
M
N
O
P
Q
R
S
T
U
V
W
X
Y
Z

concerns you • *Real spectators, as opposed to invited guests, were hard to spot.*

opposite, opposites **PREPOSITION OR ADVERB** ❶ If one thing is opposite another, it is facing it • *the shop opposite the station* • *the house opposite.* ▷ **ADJECTIVE** ❷ The opposite part of something is the part farthest away from you • *the opposite side of town.* ❸ If things are opposite, they are completely different • *I take the opposite view to you.* ▷ **NOUN** ❹ If two things are completely different, they are opposites.

● **SIMILAR WORDS:** ❹ antithesis,
● contrary, reverse

opposition NOUN ❶ If there is opposition to something, people disagree with it and try to prevent it. ❷ The political parties who are not in power are referred to as the Opposition. ❸ In a game or sports event, the opposition is the person or team that you are competing against.

oppressed ADJECTIVE People who are oppressed are treated cruelly or unfairly. **oppress VERB oppressor NOUN**

oppression NOUN cruel and unfair treatment of people.

oppressive ADJECTIVE ❶ If the weather is oppressive, it is hot and humid. ❷ An oppressive situation makes you feel depressed or concerned • *The silence became oppressive.* ❸ An oppressive system treats people cruelly or unfairly • *Married women were subject to oppressive laws.* **oppressively ADVERB**

opt, opts, opting, opted **VERB** If you opt for something, you choose it. If you opt out of something, you choose not to be involved in it.

optic ADJECTIVE (SCIENCE) relating to eyes • *the optic nerves.*
● **WORD HISTORY:** from Greek *optos*
● meaning 'seen' or 'visible'

optical ADJECTIVE ❶ (SCIENCE) concerned with vision, light, or images. ❷ relating to the appearance of things.

optician, opticians **NOUN** someone who tests people's eyes, and makes and sells glasses and contact lenses.

optics NOUN (SCIENCE) Optics is the study of vision, sight, and light.

optimism NOUN Optimism is a feeling of hopefulness about the future. **optimist NOUN**

optimistic ADJECTIVE hopeful about the future. **optimistically ADVERB**

optimum ADJECTIVE the best that is possible • *Six is the optimum number of participants for a good meeting.*

option, options **NOUN** a choice between two or more things. **optional ADJECTIVE**

opulent [Said **op**-*yool*-nt] **ADJECTIVE** grand and expensive-looking • *an opulent seafront estate.*

opus, opuses or opera **NOUN** ❶ (MUSIC) An opus is a musical composition. 'Opus' is often used with a number, indicating its position in a series of published works by the same composer. ❷ (ART) An opus is also a great artistic work, such as a piece of writing or a painting.

or CONJUNCTION ❶ used to link two different things • *I didn't know whether to laugh or cry.* ❷ used to introduce a warning • *Do what I say or else I will fire.*

-or SUFFIX '-or' is used to form nouns from verbs • *actor* • *conductor*.
● WORD HISTORY: from Latin

oracle, oracles NOUN ❶ In ancient Greece, an oracle was a place where a priest or priestess made predictions about the future. ❷ a prophecy made by a priest or other person with great authority or wisdom.

oral, orals ADJECTIVE ❶ spoken rather than written • *oral history*. ❷ Oral describes things that are used in your mouth or done with your mouth • *an oral vaccine*. ▷ NOUN ❸ an examination that is spoken rather than written. **orally** ADVERB
● SIMILAR WORDS: ❶ spoken, ● verbal

orange, oranges NOUN ❶ a round citrus fruit that is juicy and sweet and has a thick reddish-yellow skin ▷ ADJECTIVE OR NOUN ❷ reddish-yellow.
● WORD HISTORY: from Sanskrit ● *naranga* meaning 'orange'

orang-utan, orang-utans; *also spelt* **orang-utang** NOUN a large ape with reddish-brown hair.

orator, orators NOUN someone who is good at making speeches.

oratory NOUN Oratory is the art and skill of making formal public speeches.

orbit, orbits, orbiting, orbited NOUN ❶ the curved path followed by an object going round a planet or the sun ▷ VERB ❷ If something orbits a planet or the sun, it goes round and round it.

orchard, orchards NOUN a piece of land where fruit trees are grown.

orchestra, orchestras [*Said or-kess-tra*] NOUN (MUSIC) a large group of musicians who play musical instruments together. **orchestral** ADJECTIVE
● WORD HISTORY: from Greek ● *orkhestra* meaning 'the area in a ● theatre reserved for musicians'

orchestrate, orchestrates, orchestrating, orchestrated VERB ❶ To orchestrate something is to organize it very carefully in order to produce a particular result. ❷ To orchestrate a piece of music is to rewrite it so that it can be played by an orchestra. **orchestration** NOUN

orchid, orchids [*Said or-kid*] NOUN Orchids are plants with beautiful and unusual flowers.

ordain, ordains, ordaining, ordained VERB When someone is ordained, they are made a member of the clergy.

ordeal, ordeals NOUN a difficult and extremely unpleasant experience • *the ordeal of being arrested and charged with attempted murder*.
● SIMILAR WORDS: hardship, ● torture, tribulation

order, orders, ordering, ordered NOUN ❶ a command given by someone in authority. ❷ If things are arranged or done in a particular order, they are arranged or done in that sequence • *in alphabetical order*. ❸ Order is a situation in which

everything is in the correct place or done at the correct time.
4 something that you ask to be brought to you or sent to you.
5 (SCIENCE) An order is a division of living organisms that is smaller than a class and larger than a family ▷ **VERB**
6 To order someone to do something is to tell them firmly to do it. **7** When you order something, you ask for it to be brought or sent to you ▷ **PHRASE**
8 If you do something **in order to** achieve a particular thing, you do it because you want to achieve that thing.

orderly **ADJECTIVE** Something that is orderly is well organized or arranged.
● **SIMILAR WORDS:** methodical,
● well-organized

ordinal number, ordinal numbers **NOUN** An ordinal number is a number such as 'third' or 'fifth', which tells you what position something has in a group or series.

ordinarily **ADVERB** If something ordinarily happens, it usually happens.

ordinary **ADJECTIVE** Ordinary means not special or different in any way.
● **SIMILAR WORDS:** conventional,
● normal, usual

ordination **NOUN** When someone's ordination takes place, they are made a member of the clergy.

ordnance **NOUN** Weapons and other military supplies are referred to as ordnance.

ore, ores **NOUN** Ore is rock or earth from which metal can be obtained.

oregano [Said or-rig-**garh**-no]

NOUN Oregano is a herb used for flavouring in cooking.

organ, organs **NOUN** **1** Your organs are parts of your body that have a particular function, for example your heart or lungs. **2** a large musical instrument with pipes of different lengths through which air is forced. It has various keyboards which are played like a piano.

organic **ADJECTIVE** **1** Something that is organic is produced by or found in plants or animals • *decaying organic matter.* **2** Organic food is produced without the use of artificial fertilizers or pesticides. **organically** **ADVERB**

organic chemistry **NOUN** (SCIENCE) Organic chemistry is the branch of chemistry concerned with carbon compounds.

organic compound **NOUN** (SCIENCE) In chemistry, an organic compound is a compound that contains carbon.

organism, organisms **NOUN** (SCIENCE) any living animal, plant, fungus, or bacterium.

organist, organists **NOUN** someone who plays the organ.

organization, organizations; *also spelt* **organisation** **NOUN** **1** any group or business. **2** The organization of something is the act of planning and arranging it.
organizational **ADJECTIVE**
● **SIMILAR WORDS:** **1** body,
● company, group

organize, organizes, organizing, organized; *also spelt* **organise** **VERB**
1 If you organize an event, you plan

and arrange it. ❷ If you organize things, you arrange them in a sensible order. **organized** ADJECTIVE **organizer** NOUN

orgasm, orgasms NOUN the moment of greatest pleasure and excitement during sexual activity.

orgy, orgies [Said *or-jee*] NOUN ❶ a wild, uncontrolled party involving a lot of drinking and sexual activity. ❷ You can refer to a period of intense activity as an orgy of that activity • *an orgy of violence.*

● WORD HISTORY: from Greek *orgia*
● meaning 'nocturnal festival'

orient NOUN LITERARY The Orient is eastern and south-eastern Asia.

oriental ADJECTIVE relating to eastern or south-eastern Asia.

orientated ADJECTIVE If someone is interested in a particular thing, you can say that they are orientated towards it • *These men are very career-orientated.*

orientation NOUN You can refer to an organization's activities and aims as its orientation • *Poland's political and military orientation.*

oriented ADJECTIVE Oriented means the same as orientated.

orienteering NOUN Orienteering is a sport in which people run from one place to another in the countryside, using a map and compass to guide them.

origin, origins NOUN ❶ You can refer to the beginning or cause of something as its origin or origins. ❷ You can refer to someone's family background as their origin or origins

• *She was of Swedish origin.*

● SIMILAR WORDS: ❶ root, source

original, originals ADJECTIVE ❶ Original describes things that existed at the beginning, rather than being added later, or things that were the first of their kind to exist • *the original owner of the cottage.* ❷ Original means imaginative and clever • *a stunningly original idea.* ▷ NOUN ❸ a work of art or a document that is the one that was first produced, and not a copy. **originally** ADVERB **originality** NOUN

originate, originates, originating, originated VERB When something originates, or you originate it, it begins to happen or exist. **originator** NOUN

ornament, ornaments NOUN a small, attractive object that you display in your home or that you wear in order to look attractive.

ornamental ADJECTIVE designed to be attractive rather than useful • *an ornamental lake.*

ornamentation NOUN Ornamentation is decoration on a building, a piece of furniture, or a work of art.

ornate ADJECTIVE Something that is ornate has a lot of decoration on it.

ornithology NOUN Ornithology is the study of birds. **ornithologist** NOUN

● WORD HISTORY: from Greek *ornis*
● meaning 'bird' and *-logia* meaning
● 'study of'

orphan, orphans, orphaning, orphaned NOUN ❶ a child whose

a
b
c
d
e
f
g
h
i
j
k
l
m
n
o
p
q
r
s
t
u
v
w
x
y
z

parents are dead ▷ **VERB** ❷ If a child is orphaned, its parents die.

orphanage, orphanages **NOUN** a place where orphans are looked after.

orthodontics **NOUN** (SCIENCE) Orthodontics is the branch of dentistry concerned with straightening irregular teeth. **orthodontic ADJECTIVE orthodontist NOUN**

orthodox **ADJECTIVE** ❶ Orthodox beliefs or methods are the ones that most people have or use and that are considered standard. ❷ People who are orthodox believe in the older, more traditional ideas of their religion or political party. ❸ The Orthodox church is the part of the Christian church which separated from the western European church in the 11th century and is the main church in Greece and Russia. **orthodoxy NOUN**

oscillate, oscillates, oscillating, oscillated [Said **os**-sil-late] **VERB** ❶ (SCIENCE) If something oscillates, it moves repeatedly backwards and forwards. ❷ FORMAL If you oscillate between two moods, you keep changing from one to the other. **oscillation NOUN oscillatory ADJECTIVE**

osmosis [Said oz-**moh**-siss] **NOUN** TECHNICAL Osmosis is the process by which a liquid moves through a semipermeable membrane from a weaker solution to a more concentrated one.

osprey, ospreys [Said **oss**-pree] **NOUN** a large bird of prey which catches fish with its feet.

ostensibly **ADVERB** If something is done ostensibly for a reason, that seems to be the reason for it • Byrnes submitted his resignation, ostensibly on medical grounds.

ostentatious **ADJECTIVE** ❶ Something that is ostentatious is intended to impress people, for example by looking expensive • ostentatious sculptures. ❷ People who are ostentatious try to impress other people with their wealth or importance. **ostentatiously ADVERB ostentation NOUN**

ostinato, ostinatos (MUSIC) **NOUN** ❶ a musical phrase that is continuously repeated throughout a piece ▷ **ADJECTIVE** ❷ continuously repeated • an ostinato passage.
 ● **WORD HISTORY:** an Italian word
 ● meaning 'obstinate'

ostrich, ostriches **NOUN** The ostrich is the largest bird in the world. Ostriches cannot fly.

other, others **ADJECTIVE OR PRONOUN** ❶ Other people or things are different people or things • All the other children had gone home • One of the cabinets came from the palace; the other is a copy. ▷ **PHRASES** ❷ **The other day** or **the other week** means recently • She had bought four pairs of shoes the other day.

otherwise **ADVERB** ❶ You use 'otherwise' to say a different situation would exist if a particular fact or occurrence was not the case • You had to learn to swim pretty quickly, otherwise you sank. ❷ 'Otherwise' means apart from the thing mentioned • She had written to her daughter, but otherwise refused to take sides. ❸ 'Otherwise' also means in a different way • The majority voted otherwise.

▷ SPELLING NOTE: Eddy Ant thinks mEAt is a grEAt trEAt to EAt (-ea-)

otter, otters **NOUN** a small, furry animal with a long tail. Otters swim well and eat fish.

ouch INTERJECTION You say ouch when you suddenly feel pain.

ought [Said *awt*] **VERB** If you say that someone ought to do something, you mean that they should do it • *He ought to see a doctor.*
- **USAGE NOTE:** Do not use *did* and *had* with *ought*: He ought not to come is correct: he didn't ought to come is not correct

ounce, ounces **NOUN** a unit of weight equal to one sixteenth of a pound or about 28.35 grams.

our ADJECTIVE 'Our' refers to something belonging or relating to the speaker or writer and one or more other people • *We recently sold our house.*
- **USAGE NOTE:** Some people pronounce *our* and *are* in the same way, so do not confuse the spellings of these words

ours PRONOUN 'Ours' refers to something belonging or relating to the speaker or writer and one or more other people • *a friend of ours from Korea.*

ourselves PRONOUN
❶ 'Ourselves' is used when the same speaker or writer and one or more other people do an action and are affected by it • *We haven't damaged ourselves too badly.* **❷** 'Ourselves' is used to emphasize 'we'.

oust, ousts, ousting, ousted **VERB** If you oust someone, you force them out of a job or a place • *Cole was ousted from the board.*

out ADVERB **❶** towards the outside of a place • *Two dogs rushed out of the house.* **❷** not at home • *She was out when I rang last night.* **❸** in the open air • *They are playing out in bright sunshine.* **❹** no longer shining or burning • *The lights went out.*
▷ **ADJECTIVE** **❺** on strike • *1000 construction workers are out in sympathy.* **❻** unacceptable or unfashionable • *Miniskirts are out.* **❼** incorrect • *Logan's timing was out in the first two rounds.*

out- SUFFIX **❶** 'Out-' means 'exceeding' or 'going beyond'. • *outdo* • *outclass.* **❷** 'Out-' also means on the outside or away from the centre • *outback* • *outpost.*

out-and-out ADJECTIVE entire or complete • *an out-and-out lie.*

outback NOUN In Australia, the outback is the remote parts where very few people live.

outboard motor, outboard motors **NOUN** a motor that can be fixed to the back of a small boat.

outbreak, outbreaks **NOUN** If there is an outbreak of something unpleasant, such as war, it suddenly occurs.

outburst, outbursts **NOUN** **❶** a sudden, strong expression of an emotion, especially anger • *John broke into an angry outburst about how unfairly the work was divided.* **❷** a sudden occurrence of violent activity • *an outburst of gunfire.*

outcast, outcasts **NOUN** someone who is rejected by other people.

outclassed ADJECTIVE If you are

a b c d e f g h i j k l m n **o** p q r s t u v w x y z

outclassed, you are much worse than your opponent at a particular activity.

outcome, outcomes **NOUN** a result • *the outcome of the election.*

outcrop, outcrops **NOUN** a large piece of rock that sticks out of the ground.

outcry, outcries **NOUN** If there is an outcry about something, a lot of people are angry about it • *a public outcry over alleged fraud.*

outdated **ADJECTIVE** no longer in fashion.

outdo, outdoes, outdoing, outdid, outdone **VERB** If you outdo someone, you do a particular thing better than they do.

outdoor **ADJECTIVE** happening or used outside • *outdoor activities.*

outdoors **ADVERB** outside • *It was too chilly to sit outdoors.*

outer **ADJECTIVE** The outer parts of something are the parts furthest from the centre • *the outer door of the office.*

outer space **NOUN** Outer space is everything beyond the Earth's atmosphere.

outfit, outfits **NOUN** ❶ a set of clothes. ❷ **INFORMAL** an organization.

outgoing **ADJECTIVE** ❶ Outgoing describes someone who is leaving a job or place • *the outgoing President.* ❷ Someone who is outgoing is friendly and not shy.

outgoings **PLURAL NOUN** Your outgoings are the amount of money that you spend.

outgrow, outgrows, outgrowing,

outgrew, outgrown **VERB** ❶ If you outgrow a piece of clothing, you grow too big for it. ❷ If you outgrow a way of behaving, you stop it because you have grown older and more mature.

outhouse, outhouses **NOUN** a small building in the grounds of a house to which it belongs.

outing, outings **NOUN** a trip made for pleasure.

outlandish **ADJECTIVE** very unusual or odd • *outlandish clothes.*

outlaw, outlaws, outlawing, outlawed **VERB** ❶ If something is outlawed, it is made illegal ▷ **NOUN** ❷ In the past, an outlaw was a criminal.

outlay, outlays **NOUN** an amount of money spent on something • *a cash outlay of 300 dollars.*

outlet, outlets **NOUN** ❶ An outlet for your feelings or ideas is a way of expressing them. ❷ a hole or pipe through which water or air can flow away. ❸ a shop which sells goods made by a particular manufacturer.

outline, outlines, outlining, outlined **VERB** ❶ If you outline a plan or idea, you explain it in a general way. ❷ You say that something is outlined when you can see its shape because there is a light behind it ▷ **NOUN** ❸ a general explanation or description of something. ❹ The outline of something is its shape.

outlive, outlives, outliving, outlived **VERB** To outlive someone is to live longer than they do.

outlook **NOUN** ❶ Your outlook is your general attitude towards life.

A B C D E F G H I J K L M N O P Q R S T U V W X Y Z

❷ The outlook of a situation is the way it is likely to develop • *The Japanese economy's outlook is uncertain.*

outlying ADJECTIVE Outlying places are far from cities.

outmoded ADJECTIVE old-fashioned and no longer useful • *an outmoded form of transport.*

outnumber, outnumbers, outnumbering, outnumbered VERB If there are more of one group than of another, the first group outnumbers the second.

out of PREPOSITION ❶ If you do something out of a particular feeling, you are motivated by that feeling • *Out of curiosity she went along.* ❷ 'Out of' also means from • *old instruments made out of wood.* ❸ If you are out of something, you no longer have any of it • *I do hope we're not out of fuel again.* ❹ If you are out of the rain, sun, or wind, you are sheltered from it. ❺ You also use 'out of' to indicate proportion. For example, one out of five means one in every five.

out of date ADJECTIVE old-fashioned and no longer useful.

out of doors ADVERB outside • *Sometimes we eat out of doors.*

outpatient, outpatients NOUN Outpatients are people who receive treatment in hospital without staying overnight.

outpost, outposts NOUN a small collection of buildings a long way from a main centre • *a remote mountain outpost.*

output, outputs NOUN ❶ Output is the amount of something produced by a person or organization. ❷ ⟨ICT⟩ The output of a computer is the information that it produces.

outrage, outrages, outraging, outraged VERB ❶ If something outrages you, it angers and shocks you • *I was outraged at what had happened to her.* ▷ NOUN ❷ Outrage is a feeling of anger and shock. ❸ something very shocking or violent.
outrageous ADJECTIVE
outrageously ADVERB

outright ADJECTIVE ❶ absolute • *an outright rejection.* ▷ ADVERB ❷ in an open and direct way • *Have you asked him outright?* ❸ completely and totally • *I own the company outright.*

outset NOUN The outset of something is the beginning of it • *the outset of his journey.*

outshine, outshines, outshining, outshone VERB If you outshine someone, you perform better than they do.

outside NOUN ❶ The outside of something is the part which surrounds or encloses the rest of it ▷ PREPOSITION ❷ on or to the exterior of • *outside the house.* ❸ Outside also means not included in something • *outside office hours.* ▷ ADJECTIVE ❹ Outside means not inside • *an outside toilet.* ▷ ADVERB ❺ out of doors.
● USAGE NOTE: Do not use *of* after
● *outside.* You should write *she was*
● *waiting outside the school* and not
● *outside of the school*

outsider, outsiders NOUN

a
b
c
d
e
f
g
h
i
j
k
l
m
n
o
p
q
r
s
t
u
v
w
x
y
z

▷ SPELLING NOTE: *King IAn went to ParllAment in a carrIAge for his marrIAge (-ia-)*

❶ someone who does not belong to a particular group. **❷** a competitor considered unlikely to win in a race.

outsize or **outsized** ADJECTIVE much larger than usual • *outsize feet*.

outskirts PLURAL NOUN The outskirts of a city or town are the parts around the edge of it.

outspan, outspans, outspanning, outspanned VERB In South Africa, if you outspan, you relax.

outspoken ADJECTIVE Outspoken people give their opinions openly, even if they shock other people.

outstanding ADJECTIVE
❶ extremely good • *The collection contains hundreds of outstanding works of art*. **❷** Money that is outstanding is still owed • *an outstanding mortgage of 46,000 pounds*.

outstretched ADJECTIVE If your arms are outstretched, they are stretched out as far as possible.

outstrip, outstrips, outstripping, outstripped VERB If one thing outstrips another thing, it becomes bigger or more successful or moves faster than the other thing.

outward ADJECTIVE OR ADVERB
❶ Outward means away from a place or towards the outside • *the outward journey*. ▷ ADJECTIVE **❷** The outward features of someone are the ones they appear to have, rather than the ones they actually have • *He never showed any outward signs of emotion*.
outwardly ADVERB

outwards ADVERB away from a place or towards the outside • *The door opened outwards*.

outweigh, outweighs, outweighing, outweighed VERB If you say that the advantages of something outweigh its disadvantages, you mean that the advantages are more important than the disadvantages.

outwit, outwits, outwitting, outwitted VERB If you outwit someone, you use your intelligence to defeat them.

oval, ovals NOUN **❶** a round shape, similar to a circle but wider in one direction than the other ▷ ADJECTIVE **❷** shaped like an oval • *an oval table*.

ovary, ovaries [Said oh-var-ree] NOUN A woman's ovaries are the two organs in her body that produce eggs.

ovation, ovations NOUN a long burst of applause.

oven, ovens NOUN the part of a cooker that you use for baking or roasting food.

over, overs PREPOSITION **❶** Over something means directly above it or covering it • *the picture over the fireplace* • *He put his hands over his eyes*. **❷** A view over an area is a view across that area • *The pool and terrace look out over the sea*. **❸** If something is over a road or river, it is on the opposite side of the road or river. **❹** Something that is over a particular amount is more than that amount. **❺** 'Over' indicates a topic which is causing concern • *An American was arguing over the bill*. **❻** If something happens over a period of time, it happens during that period • *I went to New Zealand over Christmas*.
▷ ADVERB OR PREPOSITION **❼** If you lean over, you bend your body in a

particular direction • *He bent over and rummaged in a drawer* • *She was hunched over her typewriter.* ▷ **ADVERB** **8** 'Over' is used to indicate a position • *over by the window* • *Come over here.* **9** If something rolls or turns over, it is moved so that its other side is facing upwards • *He flipped over the envelope.* ▷ **ADJECTIVE** **10** Something that is over is completely finished ▷ **PHRASE** **11 All over** a place means everywhere in that place • *studios all over America.* ▷ **NOUN** **12** In cricket, an over is a set of six balls bowled by a bowler from the same end of the pitch.

over- **PREFIX** 'Over' means to too great an extent or too much • *overprotective* • *overindulge* • *overact.*

overall, overalls **ADJECTIVE** **1** Overall means taking into account all the parts or aspects of something • *The overall quality of pupils' work had shown a marked improvement.* ▷ **ADVERB** **2** taking into account all the parts of something • *Overall, things are not really too bad.* ▷ **NOUN** **3** IN PLURAL Overalls are a piece of clothing that looks like trousers and a jacket combined. You wear overalls to protect your other clothes when you are working **4** An overall is a piece of clothing like a coat that you wear to protect your other clothes when you are working.

overawed **ADJECTIVE** If you are overawed by something, you are very impressed by it and a little afraid of it.

overbearing **ADJECTIVE** trying to dominate other people • *Mozart had a difficult relationship with his overbearing father.*

overboard **ADVERB** If you fall overboard, you fall over the side of a ship into the water.

overcast **ADJECTIVE** If it is overcast, the sky is covered by cloud.

overcoat, overcoats **NOUN** a thick, warm coat.

overcome, overcomes, overcoming, overcame, overcome **VERB** **1** If you overcome a problem or a feeling, you manage to deal with it or control it ▷ **ADJECTIVE** **2** If you are overcome by a feeling, you feel it very strongly.

overcrowded **ADJECTIVE** If a place is overcrowded, there are too many things or people in it.

overdo, overdoes, overdoing, overdid, overdone **VERB** If you overdo something, you do it too much or in an exaggerated way • *It is important never to overdo new exercises.*

overdose, overdoses **NOUN** a larger dose of a drug than is safe.

overdraft, overdrafts **NOUN** an agreement with a bank that allows someone to spend more money than they have in their account.

overdrawn **ADJECTIVE** If someone is overdrawn, they have taken more money from their bank account than the account has in it.

overdrive **NOUN** Overdrive is an extra, higher gear in a vehicle, which is used at high speeds to reduce engine wear and save petrol.

overdue **ADJECTIVE** If someone or something is overdue, they are late • *The payments are overdue.*

overestimate, overestimates, overestimating, overestimated **VERB**

a
b
c
d
e
f
g
h
i
j
k
l
m
n
o
p
q
r
s
t
u
v
w
x
y
z

▷ SPELLING NOTE: *LEt's measure the angLE (angle)*

If you overestimate something, you think that it is bigger, more important, or better than it really is • *We had overestimated his popularity.*

overflow, overflows, overflowing, overflowed, overflown **VERB** If a liquid overflows, it spills over the edges of its container. If a river overflows, it flows over its banks.

overgrown ADJECTIVE A place that is overgrown is covered with weeds because it has not been looked after • *an overgrown path.*

overhang, overhangs, overhanging, overhung **VERB** If one thing overhangs another, it sticks out sideways above it • *old trees whose branches overhang a footpath.*

overhaul, overhauls, overhauling, overhauled **VERB** ❶ If you overhaul something, you examine it thoroughly and repair any faults ▷ **NOUN** ❷ If you give something an overhaul, you examine it and repair or improve it.

overhead ADJECTIVE ❶ Overhead means above you • *overhead cables.* ▷ **ADVERB** ❷ Overhead means above you • *seagulls flying overhead.*

overheads PLURAL NOUN The overheads of a business are the costs of running it.

overhear, overhears, overhearing, overheard **VERB** If you overhear someone's conversation, you hear what they are saying to someone else.

overjoyed ADJECTIVE extremely pleased • *Colm was overjoyed to see me.*
● **SIMILAR WORDS:** delighted, over the moon

overlaid ADJECTIVE If something is

overlaid by something else, it is covered by it.

overland ADJECTIVE OR ADVERB travelling across land rather than going by sea or air • *an overland trek to India* • *Wray was returning to England overland.*

overlander, overlanders **NOUN** In Australian history, an overlander was a man who drove cattle or sheep long distances through the outback.

overlap, overlaps, overlapping, overlapped **VERB** If one thing overlaps another, one part of it covers part of the other thing.

overleaf ADVERB on the next page • *Write to us at the address shown overleaf.*

overload, overloads, overloading, overloaded **VERB** If you overload someone or something, you give them too much to do or to carry.

overlook, overlooks, overlooking, overlooked **VERB** ❶ If a building or window overlooks a place, it has a view over that place. ❷ If you overlook something, you ignore it or do not notice it.

overly ADVERB excessively • *I'm not overly fond of jazz.*

overnight ADVERB ❶ for the duration of the night • *Further rain was forecast overnight.* ❷ suddenly • *Good players don't become bad ones overnight.* ❸ during the night. ▷ **ADJECTIVE** ❹ sudden • *an overnight success.* ❺ for use when you go away for one or two nights • *an overnight bag.*

▷ SPELLING NOTE: *A Rude Idiot Thought He Might Eat Toffee In Church (<u>arithmetic</u>)*

overpower, overpowers, overpowering, overpowered **VERB** ❶ If you overpower someone, you seize them despite their struggles, because you are stronger than them. ❷ If a feeling overpowers you, it affects you very strongly.
overpowering ADJECTIVE

overrate, overrates, overrating, overrated **VERB** If you overrate something, you think that it is better or more important than it really is.
overrated ADJECTIVE

overreact, overreacts, overreacting, overreacted **VERB** If you overreact, you react in an extreme way.

overriding ADJECTIVE more important than anything else • *an overriding duty.*

overrule, overrules, overruling, overruled **VERB** To overrule a person or their decisions is to decide that their decisions are incorrect.
● **SIMILAR WORDS:** countermand,
● override, reverse

overrun, overruns, overrunning, overran, overrun **VERB** ❶ If an army overruns a country, it occupies it very quickly. ❷ If animals or plants overrun a place, they spread quickly over it. ❸ If an event overruns, it continues for longer than it was meant to.

overseas ADVERB ❶ abroad • *travelling overseas.* ▷ **ADJECTIVE** ❷ abroad • *an overseas tour.* ❸ from abroad • *overseas students.*

oversee, oversees, overseeing, oversaw, overseen **VERB** To oversee a job is to make sure it is done properly.
overseer NOUN

overshadow, overshadows, overshadowing, overshadowed **VERB** If something is overshadowed, it is made unimportant by something else that is better or more important.

oversight, oversights **NOUN** something which you forget to do or fail to notice.

overspill NOUN OR ADJECTIVE Overspill refers to the moving of people from overcrowded cities to houses in smaller towns • *an East End overspill* • *overspill estates.*

overstate, overstates, overstating, overstated **VERB** If you overstate something, you exaggerate its importance.

overstep, oversteps, overstepping, overstepped **PHRASE** If you **overstep the mark**, you behave in an unacceptable way.

overt ADJECTIVE open and obvious • *overt signs of stress.* **overtly ADVERB**

overtake, overtakes, overtaking, overtook, overtaken **VERB** If you overtake someone, you pass them because you are moving faster than them.

overthrow, overthrows, overthrowing, overthrew, overthrown **VERB** If a government is overthrown, it is removed from power by force.

overtime NOUN ❶ Overtime is time that someone works in addition to their normal working hours ▷ **ADVERB** ❷ If someone works overtime, they do work in addition to their normal working hours.

overtones PLURAL NOUN If something has overtones of an

▷ SPELLING NOTE: *Beautiful Elephants Are Usually Tiny (beautiful)*

emotion or attitude, it suggests it without showing it openly • *the political overtones of the trial.*

overture, overtures NOUN ❶ a piece of music that is the introduction to an opera or play. ❷ If you make overtures to someone, you approach them because you want to start a friendly or business relationship with them.

overturn, overturns, overturning, overturned VERB ❶ To overturn something is to turn it upside down or onto its side. ❷ If someone overturns a legal decision, they change it by using their higher authority.

overview, overviews NOUN a general understanding or description of a situation.

overweight ADJECTIVE too fat, and therefore unhealthy • *overweight businessmen.*

overwhelm, overwhelms, overwhelming, overwhelmed VERB ❶ If you are overwhelmed by something, it affects you very strongly • *The priest appeared overwhelmed by the news.* ❷ If one group of people overwhelm another, they gain complete control or victory over them.
overwhelming ADJECTIVE
overwhelmingly ADVERB

overwork, overworks, overworking, overworked VERB If you overwork, you work too hard.

overwrought [Said oh-ver-**rawt**] ADJECTIVE extremely upset • *He didn't get angry or overwrought.*

oviparous [Said oh-**vip**-par-russ] ADJECTIVE SCIENCE Animals that

are oviparous produce eggs that hatch outside the mother's body. Fish, reptiles, and birds are oviparous.

ovulate, ovulates, ovulating, ovulated [Said ov-yool-late] VERB SCIENCE When a woman or female animal ovulates, she produces ova or eggs from her ovary.

ovule, ovules NOUN SCIENCE ❶ the part of a plant that develops into a seed. ❷ an immature ovum.

ovum, ova [Said oh-vum] NOUN SCIENCE a reproductive cell of a woman or female animal. The ovum is fertilized by a male sperm to produce young.
● WORD HISTORY: a Latin word
● meaning 'egg'

owe, owes, owing, owed VERB ❶ If you owe someone money, they have lent it to you and you have not yet paid it back. ❷ If you owe a quality or skill to someone, they are responsible for giving it to you • *He owes his success to his mother.* ❸ If you say that you owe someone gratitude or loyalty, you mean that they deserve it from you.

owl, owls NOUN Owls are birds of prey that hunt at night. They have large eyes and short, hooked beaks.

own, owns, owning, owned ADJECTIVE ❶ If something is your own, it belongs to you or is associated with you • *She stayed in her own house.* ▷ VERB ❷ If you own something, it belongs to you ▷ PHRASE ❸ On your own means alone.

owner, owners NOUN The owner of something is the person it belongs to.

ownership NOUN If you have ownership of something, you own it • *He shared the ownership of a sailing dinghy.*

ox, oxen NOUN Oxen are cattle which are used for carrying or pulling things.

oxide, oxides NOUN a compound of oxygen and another chemical element.

oxidize, oxidizes, oxidizing, oxidized; *also spelt* **oxidise** VERB (SCIENCE) When a substance oxidizes, it changes chemically by reacting with oxygen. **oxidation** NOUN

oxygen NOUN Oxygen is a chemical element in the form of a colourless gas. It makes up about 21% of the Earth's atmosphere. With an extremely small number of exceptions, living things need oxygen to live, and things cannot burn without it. Oxygen's atomic number is 8 and its symbol is O.

oxymoron, oxymora or oxymorons NOUN (ENGLISH) two words that contradict each other placed beside each other, for example 'deafening silence'.

oyster, oysters NOUN Oysters are large, flat shellfish. Some oysters can be eaten, and others produce pearls.
● **WORD HISTORY:** from Greek
● *ostrakon* meaning 'shell'

oz an abbreviation for 'ounces'.

ozone NOUN Ozone is a form of oxygen that is poisonous and has a strong smell. There is a layer of ozone high above the Earth's surface.

ozone layer NOUN The ozone layer is that part of the Earth's atmosphere that protects living things from the harmful radiation of the sun.

a
b
c
d
e
f
g
h
i
j
k
l
m
n
o
p
q
r
s
t
u
v
w
x
y
z

Pp

p ❶ p is an abbreviation for 'pence'. **❷** p is also a written abbreviation for 'page'. The plural is pp.

pa, pa or pas **NOUN** In New Zealand, a Maori village or settlement.

pace, paces, pacing, paced **NOUN** **❶** The pace of something is the speed at which it moves or happens. **❷** a step; also used as a measurement of distance ▷ **VERB** **❸** If you pace up and down, you continually walk around because you are anxious or impatient.

pacemaker, pacemakers **NOUN** a small electronic device put into someone's heart to control their heartbeat.

Pacific [Said pas-**sif**-ik] **NOUN** The Pacific is the ocean separating North and South America from Asia and Australia.

pacifist, pacifists **NOUN** someone who is opposed to all violence and war. **pacifism NOUN**

pacify, pacifies, pacifying, pacified **VERB** If you pacify someone who is angry, you calm them.
● **SIMILAR WORDS:** appease, calm, ● placate

pack, packs, packing, packed **VERB** **❶** If you pack, you put things neatly into a suitcase, bag, or box. **❷** If people pack into a place, it becomes crowded with them ▷ **NOUN** **❸** a bag or rucksack carried on your back. **❹** a packet or collection of something • *a pack of cigarettes.* **❺** A pack of playing cards is a complete set. **❻** A pack of dogs or wolves is a group of them.
pack up VERB If you pack up your belongings, you put them in a bag because you are leaving.

package, packages **NOUN** **❶** a small parcel. **❷** a set of proposals or offers presented as a whole • *a package of beauty treatments.*
packaged ADJECTIVE

packaging NOUN (D & T)
Packaging is the container or wrapping in which an item is sold or sent.

packed ADJECTIVE very full • *The church was packed with people.*

packet, packets **NOUN** a thin cardboard box or paper container in which something is sold.

pact, pacts **NOUN** a formal agreement or treaty.

pad, pads, padding, padded **NOUN** **❶** a thick, soft piece of material. **❷** a number of pieces of paper fixed together at one end. **❸** The pads of an animal such as a cat or dog are the soft, fleshy parts on the bottom of its paws. **❹** a flat surface from which helicopters take off or rockets are launched ▷ **VERB** **❺** If you pad

▷ SPELLING NOTE: *you'll br**EAK** that Electrical Aerial, Kitty (br**eak**)*

something, you put a pad inside it or over it to protect it or change its shape. ❻ If you pad around, you walk softly. **padding NOUN**

paddle, paddles, paddling, paddled **NOUN** ❶ a short pole with a broad blade at one or both ends, used to move a small boat or a canoe ▷ **VERB** ❷ If someone paddles a boat, they move it using a paddle. ❸ If you paddle, you walk in shallow water.

paddock, paddocks **NOUN** a small field where horses are kept.

paddy, paddies **NOUN** A paddy or paddy field is an area in which rice is grown.

padlock, padlocks, padlocking, padlocked **NOUN** ❶ a lock made up of a metal case with a U-shaped bar attached to it, which can be put through a metal loop and then closed. It is unlocked by turning a key in the lock on the case ▷ **VERB** ❷ If you padlock something, you lock it with a padlock.

padre, padres [Said **pah**-dray] **NOUN** a priest, especially a chaplain to the armed forces.
● **WORD HISTORY:** from Italian or ● Spanish padre meaning 'father'

paediatrician, paediatricians [Said pee-dee-ya-**trish**-n]; also spelt **pediatrician NOUN** a doctor who specializes in treating children.
● **WORD HISTORY:** from Greek pais ● meaning 'child' and iatros meaning ● 'physician'

paediatrics [Said pee-dee-ya-**triks**]; also spelt **pediatrics NOUN** Paediatrics is the area of medicine which deals with children's diseases.

paediatric ADJECTIVE

pagan, pagans [Said **pay**-gan] **ADJECTIVE** ❶ involving beliefs and worship outside the main religions of the world • pagan myths and cults. ▷ **NOUN** ❷ someone who believes in a pagan religion. **paganism NOUN**

page, pages, paging, paged **NOUN** ❶ one side of one of the pieces of paper in a book or magazine; also the sheet of paper itself. ❷ In medieval times, a page was a young boy servant who was learning to be a knight ▷ **VERB** ❸ To page someone is to send a signal or message to a small electronic device which they are carrying.

pageant, pageants [Said **paj**-jent] **NOUN** a grand, colourful show or parade.

pagoda, pagodas **NOUN** a tall, elaborately decorated Buddhist or Hindu temple.

pail, pails **NOUN** a bucket.

pain, pains, paining, pained **NOUN** ❶ Pain is an unpleasant feeling of physical hurt. ❷ Pain is also an unpleasant feeling of deep unhappiness ▷ **VERB** ❸ If something pains you, it makes you very unhappy. **painless ADJECTIVE painlessly ADVERB**
● **SIMILAR WORDS:** ❶ ache, hurt, ● pang, twinge

painful ADJECTIVE ❶ causing emotional pain. ❷ causing physical pain. **painfully ADVERB**

painkiller, painkillers **NOUN** a drug that reduces or stops pain.

painstaking ADJECTIVE very

a b c d e f g h i j k l m n o **p** q r s t u v w x y z

careful and thorough • *years of painstaking research.*

paint, paints, painting, painted NOUN
① (ART) Paint is a coloured liquid used to decorate buildings, or to make a picture ▷ VERB ② (ART) If you paint something or paint a picture of it, you make a picture of it using paint. ③ (D & T) When you paint something such as a wall, you cover it with paint. **painter** NOUN **painting** NOUN

pair, pairs, pairing, paired NOUN
① two things of the same type or that do the same thing • *a pair of earrings.*
② You use 'pair' when referring to certain objects which have two main matching parts • *a pair of scissors.*
▷ VERB ③ When people pair off, they become grouped in pairs. ④ If you pair up with someone, you agree to do something together.
● USAGE NOTE: The verb following
● *pair* can be singular or plural. If *pair*
● refers to a unit, the verb is singular:
● *a pair of good shoes is essential.* If
● *pair* refers to two individual things,
● the verb is plural: *the pair are said to*
● *dislike each other*

pakeha, pakeha or pakehas [Said *pa-ki-ha*] NOUN In New Zealand English, someone who is of European rather than Maori descent.

Pakistani, Pakistanis [Said *pah-kiss-tah-nee*] ADJECTIVE
① belonging or relating to Pakistan
▷ NOUN ② someone who comes from Pakistan.

pal, pals NOUN INFORMAL a friend.

palace, palaces NOUN a large, grand house, especially the official home of a king or queen.

palaeolithic [Said *pal-lee-oh-lith-ik*] ADJECTIVE (GEOGRAPHY) belonging or relating to the period about 2.5 to 3 million years ago when primitive man emerged and was making unpolished chipped stone tools.

palaeontology [Said *pal-lee-on-tol-loj-ee*] NOUN (SCIENCE) Palaeontology is the study of fossils.

palagi, palagi or palagis [Said *pa-lang-ee*] NOUN a Samoan name for a New Zealander of European descent.

palatable ADJECTIVE Palatable food tastes pleasant.

palate, palates [Said *pall-lat*] NOUN
① the top of the inside of your mouth.
② Someone's palate is their ability to judge good food and wine • *dishes to tempt every palate.*

pale, paler, palest ADJECTIVE rather white and without much colour or brightness.

Palestinian, Palestinians NOUN an Arab from the region formerly called Palestine situated between the River Jordan and the Mediterranean.

palette, palettes NOUN (ART) a flat piece of wood on which an artist mixes colours.

palindrome, palindromes NOUN (ENGLISH) A palindrome is a word or phrase that is the same whether you read it forwards or backwards; for example the word 'refer'.

pall, palls, palling, palled [rhymes with *fall*] VERB ① If something palls, it becomes less interesting or less enjoyable • *This record palls after ten* minutes. ▷ NOUN ❷ a thick cloud of smoke. ❸ a cloth covering a coffin.

palm, palms NOUN ❶ A palm or palm tree is a tropical tree with no branches and a crown of long leaves. ❷ the flat surface of your hand which your fingers bend towards.

Palm Sunday NOUN (RE) Palm Sunday is the Sunday before Easter.

palpable ADJECTIVE obvious and easily sensed • *Happiness was palpable in the air.* **palpably** ADVERB
● WORD HISTORY: from Latin
● *palpabilis* meaning 'able to be
● touched'

paltry [Said **pawl**-tree] ADJECTIVE A paltry sum of money is a very small amount.
● SIMILAR WORDS: insignificant,
● trifling, trivial

pamper, pampers, pampering, pampered VERB If you pamper someone, you give them too much kindness and comfort.

pamphlet, pamphlets NOUN
(ENGLISH) a very thin book in paper covers giving information about something.

pan, pans, panning, panned NOUN
❶ a round metal container with a long handle, used for cooking things in on top of a cooker ▷ VERB
❷ When a film camera pans, it moves in a wide sweep. ❸ INFORMAL To pan something is to criticize it strongly.

panacea, panaceas [Said pan-**nass**-see-ah] NOUN something that is supposed to cure everything.

panache [Said pan-**nash**] NOUN Something that is done with panache

is done confidently and stylishly.

pancake, pancakes NOUN a thin, flat piece of fried batter which can be served with savoury or sweet fillings.

pancreas, pancreases [Said **pang**-kree-ass] NOUN (SCIENCE) The pancreas is an organ in the body situated behind the stomach. It produces insulin and enzymes that help with digestion.

panda, pandas NOUN A panda or giant panda is a large animal rather like a bear that lives in China. It has black fur with large patches of white.

panda car, panda cars NOUN In Britain, a police patrol car.

pandemonium [Said pan-dim-**moan**-ee-um] NOUN Pandemonium is a state of noisy confusion • *scenes of pandemonium.*
● WORD HISTORY: from
● *Pandemonium*, the capital of Hell in
● Milton's 'Paradise Lost'

pander, panders, pandering, pandered VERB If you pander to someone, you do everything they want.

pane, panes NOUN a sheet of glass in a window or door.

panel, panels NOUN ❶ a small group of people who are chosen to do something • *a panel of judges.* ❷ a flat piece of wood that is part of a larger object • *door panels.* ❸ A control panel is a surface containing switches and instruments to operate a machine. **panelled** ADJECTIVE

panelling NOUN Panelling is rectangular pieces of wood covering an inside wall.

▷ SPELLING NOTE: *The government licenSes Schnapps (licenSes)*

a
b
c
d
e
f
g
h
i
j
k
l
m
n
o
p
q
r
s
t
u
v
w
x
y
z

pang, pangs **NOUN** a sudden strong feeling of sadness or pain.

panic, panics, panicking, panicked **NOUN** ❶ Panic is a sudden overwhelming feeling of fear or anxiety ▷ **VERB** ❷ If you panic, you become so afraid or anxious that you cannot act sensibly.

panorama, panoramas **NOUN** an extensive view over a wide area of land • *a fine panorama over the hills.*
panoramic ADJECTIVE

pansy, pansies **NOUN** a small garden flower with large round petals.

pant, pants, panting, panted **VERB** If you pant, you breathe quickly and loudly through your mouth.

panther, panthers **NOUN** a large wild animal belonging to the cat family, especially the black leopard.

pantomime, pantomimes **NOUN** a musical play, usually based on a fairy story and performed at Christmas.

pantry, pantries **NOUN** a small room where food is kept.
● **WORD HISTORY:** from Old French *paneterie* meaning 'bread store'

pants PLURAL NOUN ❶ Pants are a piece of underwear with holes for your legs and elastic around the waist or hips. ❷ Pants are also trousers.

papaya, papayas **NOUN** a fruit with sweet yellow flesh that grows in the West Indies and tropical Australia.

paper, papers, papering, papered **NOUN** ❶ Paper is a material made from wood pulp and used for writing on or wrapping things. ❷ a newspaper ❸ IN PLURAL Papers are official documents, for example a passport for identification ❹ part of a written examination ▷ **VERB** ❺ If you paper a wall, you put wallpaper on it.
● **WORD HISTORY:** from *papyrus*, the plant from which paper was made in ancient Egypt, Greece, and Rome

paperback, paperbacks **NOUN** a book with a thin cardboard cover.

paperwork NOUN Paperwork is the part of a job that involves dealing with letters and records.

papier-mâché [Said pap-yay mash-shay] **NOUN** Papier-mâché is a hard substance made from mashed wet paper mixed with glue and moulded when moist to make things such as bowls and ornaments.
● **WORD HISTORY:** from French *papier-mâché* meaning literally 'chewed paper'

paprika NOUN Paprika is a red powder made from a kind of pepper.
● **WORD HISTORY:** a Hungarian word

papyrus [Said pap-eye-russ] **NOUN** (HISTORY) Papyrus was a type of paper made in ancient Egypt, Greece, and Rome from the stems of a tall water plant which is also called papyrus.

par PHRASE ❶ Something that is on **a par** with something else is similar in quality or amount • *This match was on a par with the German Cup Final.* ❷ Something that is **below par** or **under par** is below its normal standard ▷ **NOUN** ❸ In golf, par is the number of strokes which it is thought a good player should take for an individual hole or all the holes on a particular golf course.

parable, parables NOUN (RE) a short story which makes a moral or religious point.

parabola, parabolas [Said par-**rab**-bol-la] NOUN (MATHS) A parabola is a regular curve like the path of something that is thrown up in the air and comes down in a different place. **parabolic** ADJECTIVE

parachute, parachutes [Said par-**rash**-oot] NOUN a circular piece of fabric attached by lines to a person or package so that they can fall safely to the ground from an aircraft.

parade, parades, parading, paraded NOUN ❶ a line of people or vehicles standing or moving together as a display ▷ VERB ❷ When people parade, they walk together in a group as a display.

Paradise NOUN According to some religions, Paradise is a wonderful place where good people go when they die.
● WORD HISTORY: from Greek
● *paradeisos* meaning 'garden'

paradox, paradoxes NOUN something that contains two ideas that seem to contradict each other • *the paradox of having to drink in order to stay sober.* **paradoxical** ADJECTIVE

paraffin NOUN Paraffin is a strong-smelling liquid which is used as a fuel.

paragon, paragons NOUN someone whose behaviour is perfect in some way • *a paragon of elegance.*

paragraph, paragraphs NOUN (ENGLISH) a section of a piece of writing. A new paragraph should

always begin on a new line.

parallel, parallels NOUN
❶ Something that is a parallel to something else has similar qualities or features to it ▷ ADJECTIVE
❷ (MATHS) If two lines are parallel, they are the same distance apart along the whole of their length.

parallelogram, parallelograms NOUN (MATHS) a four-sided shape in which each side is parallel to the opposite side.

paralyse, paralyses, paralysing, paralysed VERB If something paralyses you, it causes loss of feeling and movement in your body.
● SIMILAR WORDS: freeze,
● immobilize, numb

paralysis [Said par-**ral**-liss-iss] NOUN Paralysis is loss of the power to move.

paramedic, paramedics [Said par-ram-**med**-dik] NOUN a person who does some types of medical work, for example for the ambulance service.

parameter, parameters [Said par-**ram**-met-ter] NOUN a limit which affects the way something is done • *the general parameters set by the president.*

paramilitary ADJECTIVE A paramilitary organization has a military structure but is not the official army of a country.

paramount ADJECTIVE more important than anything else • *Safety is paramount.*

paranoia [Said par-ran-**noy**-ah] NOUN Paranoia is a mental illness in

a
b
c
d
e
f
g
h
i
j
k
l
m
n
o
p
q
r
s
t
u
v
w
x
y
z

▷ SPELLING NOTE: *plaice* the fish has a glittering 'EYE' (i) (plaice) which someone believes that other people are trying to harm them.

paranoid [Said **par-ran-noyd**] ADJECTIVE Someone who is paranoid believes wrongly that other people are trying to harm them.

parapet, parapets NOUN a low wall along the edge of a bridge or roof.
● WORD HISTORY: from Italian
● *parapetto* meaning 'chest-high wall'

paraphernalia [Said **par-raf-fan-ale-yah**] NOUN Someone's paraphernalia is all their belongings or equipment.
● WORD HISTORY: from Latin
● *parapherna* meaning 'personal
● property of a married woman'

paraphrase, paraphrases, paraphrasing, paraphrased NOUN ❶ A paraphrase of a piece of writing or speech is the same thing said in a different way • *a paraphrase of the popular song.* ▷ VERB ❷ If you paraphrase what someone has said, you express it in a different way.

parasite, parasites NOUN a small animal or plant that lives on or inside a larger animal or plant. **parasitic** ADJECTIVE
● WORD HISTORY: from Greek
● *parasitos* meaning 'someone who
● eats at someone else's table'

parasol, parasols NOUN an object like an umbrella that provides shelter from the sun.

paratroops or **paratroopers** PLURAL NOUN Paratroops are soldiers trained to be dropped by parachute.

parcel, parcels, parcelling, parcelled

NOUN ❶ something wrapped up in paper ▷ VERB ❷ If you parcel something up, you make it into a parcel.

parched ADJECTIVE ❶ If the ground is parched, it is very dry and in need of water. ❷ If you are parched, you are very thirsty.

parchment NOUN Parchment is thick yellowish paper of very good quality.

pardon, pardons, pardoning, pardoned INTERJECTION ❶ You say **pardon** or **beg your pardon** to express surprise or apology, or when you have not heard what someone has said ▷ VERB ❷ If you pardon someone, you forgive them for doing something wrong.

pare, pares, paring, pared VERB When you pare fruit or vegetables, you cut off the skin.

parent, parents NOUN Your parents are your father and mother. **parental** ADJECTIVE

parentage NOUN A person's parentage is their parents and ancestors.

parenthesis, parentheses [Said par-**renth**-iss-iss] NOUN (ENGLISH) ❶ A parenthesis is a phrase or remark inside brackets, dashes, or commas that is inserted into a piece of writing or speech. ❷ Parentheses are a pair of brackets put round a word or phrase. **parenthetical** ADJECTIVE

pariah, pariahs [Said par-**eye**-ah] NOUN A pariah is someone who is disliked and rejected by other people.

parish, parishes NOUN an area with

▷ SPELLING NOTE: *I went to see (C) the doctor's new practiCe (practice)*

its own church and clergyman, and often its own elected council.

parishioner, parishioners NOUN A clergyman's parishioners are the people who live in his parish and attend his church.

parity NOUN FORMAL If there is parity between things, they are equal • *By 1943 the USA had achieved a rough parity of power with the British.*

park, parks, parking, parked NOUN
❶ a public area with grass and trees.
❷ a private area of grass and trees around a large country house ▷ VERB
❸ When someone parks a vehicle, they drive it into a position where it can be left. **parked** ADJECTIVE **parking** NOUN

parliament, parliaments NOUN
(HISTORY) the group of elected representatives who make the laws of a country. **parliamentary** ADJECTIVE

parlour, parlours NOUN OLD-FASHIONED a sitting room.
● **WORD HISTORY:** from Old French *parleur* meaning 'room for talking to visitors (in a convent)'

parochial [Said par-roe-key-yal] ADJECTIVE concerned only with local matters • *narrow parochial interests.*

parody, parodies, parodying, parodied NOUN ❶ an amusing imitation of the style of an author or of a familiar situation ▷ VERB ❷ If you parody something, you make a parody of it.
● **SIMILAR WORDS:** ❶ send-up, spoof, takeoff

parole NOUN When prisoners are given parole, they are released early on condition that they behave well.
● **WORD HISTORY:** from French *parole d'honneur* meaning 'word of honour'

parrot, parrots NOUN a brightly coloured tropical bird with a curved beak.

parry, parries, parrying, parried VERB
❶ If you parry a question, you cleverly avoid answering it • *My searching questions are simply parried with evasions.* ❷ If you parry a blow, you push aside your attacker's arm to defend yourself.

parsley NOUN Parsley is a herb with curly leaves used for flavouring in cooking.

parsnip, parsnips NOUN a long, pointed, cream-coloured root vegetable.

parson, parsons NOUN a vicar or other clergyman.

part, parts, parting, parted NOUN
❶ one of the pieces or aspects of something. ❷ one of the roles in a play or film, played by an actor or actress. ❸ Someone's part in something is their involvement in it • *He was jailed for eleven years for his part in the plot.* ▷ PHRASE ❹ If you **take part** in an activity, you do it together with other people ▷ VERB
❺ If things that are next to each other part, they move away from each other.
❻ If two people part, they leave each other.
● **SIMILAR WORDS:** ❶ bit, component, constituent, piece

partake, partakes, partaking, partook, partaken VERB FORMAL If

A
B
C
D
E
F
G
H
I
J
K
L
M
N
O
P
Q
R
S
T
U
V
W
X
Y
Z

you partake of food, you eat it • *She partook of the refreshments offered.*

partial ADJECTIVE ❶ not complete or whole • *a partial explanation* • *partial success.* ❷ liking something very much • *I'm very partial to marigolds.* ❸ supporting one side in a dispute, rather than being fair and without bias. **partially** ADVERB

participate, participates, participating, participated VERB If you participate in an activity, you take part in it. **participant** NOUN **participation** NOUN
● SIMILAR WORDS: be involved in, ● join in, take part

participle, participles NOUN In grammar, a participle is a form of a verb used with an auxiliary verb in compound tenses and often as an adjective. English has two participles: the past participle, which describes a completed action, and the present participle, which describes a continuing action. For example in 'He has gone', 'gone' is a past participle and in 'She was winning', 'winning' is a present participle.

particle, particles NOUN
❶ (SCIENCE) a basic unit of matter, such as an atom, molecule or electron. ❷ a very small piece of something.

particular ADJECTIVE ❶ relating or belonging to only one thing or person • *That particular place is dangerous.* ❷ especially great or intense • *Pay particular attention to the forehead.* ❸ Someone who is particular has high standards and is not easily satisfied. **particularly** ADVERB

particulars PLURAL NOUN Particulars are facts or details.

parting, partings NOUN an occasion when one person leaves another.

partisan, partisans ADJECTIVE
❶ favouring or supporting one person or group • *a partisan crowd.* ▷ NOUN
❷ a member of an unofficial armed force fighting to free their country from enemy occupation • *Norwegian partisans.*

partition, partitions, partitioning, partitioned NOUN ❶ a screen separating one part of a room or vehicle from another. ❷ Partition is the division of a country into independent areas ▷ VERB ❸ To partition something is to divide it into separate parts.

partly ADVERB to some extent but not completely.

partner, partners, partnering, partnered NOUN ❶ Someone's partner is the person they are married to or are living with. ❷ Your partner is the person you are doing something with, for example in a dance or a game. ❸ Business partners are joint owners of their business ▷ VERB ❹ If you partner someone, you are their partner for a game or social occasion. **partnership** NOUN

part of speech, parts of speech NOUN a particular grammatical class of word, such as 'noun' or 'adjective'.
▶ SEE GRAMMAR BOX ON PAGE 613

partook the past tense of **partake**.

partridge, partridges NOUN a brown game bird with a round body and a short tail.

▷ SPELLING NOTE: *pAL up with the principAL and principAL staff (principal)*

WHAT IS A PART OF SPEECH?

Every word in the dictionary can be classified into a group. These groups are known as **parts of speech**. If we know which group a word belongs to, we can understand what sort of idea the word represents, and how it can be combined with other words to produce meaningful statements.

You can check the part of speech of any word by looking it up in the dictionary. The part of speech is given after the main entry word. The most common parts of speech in this dictionary are noun, verb, adjective, adverb, pronoun, preposition, interjection and conjunction. There are grammar boxes for all of these.

part-time ADJECTIVE involving work for only a part of the working day or week.

party, parties NOUN ❶ a social event held for people to enjoy themselves. ❷ an organization whose members share the same political beliefs and campaign for election to government. ❸ a group who are doing something together. ❹ FORMAL one of the people involved in a legal agreement or dispute.

pass, passes, passing, passed VERB ❶ To pass something is to move past it. ❷ To pass in a particular direction is to move in that direction • *We passed through the gate.* ❸ If you pass something to someone, you hand it to them or transfer it to them. ❹ If you pass a period of time doing something, you spend it that way • *He hoped to pass the long night in meditation.* ❺ When a period of time passes, it happens and finishes. ❻ If you pass a test, you are considered to be of an acceptable standard. ❼ When a new law or proposal is passed, it is formally approved. ❽ When a judge passes sentence on someone, the judge states what the

punishment will be. ❾ If you pass the ball in a ball game, you throw, kick, or hit it to another player in your team ▷ NOUN ❿ the transfer of the ball in a ball game to another player in the same team. ⓫ an official document that allows you to go somewhere. ⓬ a narrow route between mountains.

pass away or **pass on** VERB Someone who has passed away has died.

pass out VERB If someone passes out, they faint.

● SIMILAR WORDS: ❶ go past,
● overtake ❺ elapse, go by, lapse

passable ADJECTIVE of an acceptable standard • *a passable imitation of his dad.*

passage, passages NOUN ❶ a space that connects two places. ❷ a long narrow corridor. ❸ a section of a book or piece of music.

passé *[Said pas-say]* ADJECTIVE no longer fashionable.

passenger, passengers NOUN a person travelling in a vehicle, aircraft, or ship.

passer-by, passers-by NOUN

▷ SPELLING NOTE: *LEarn the principLEs (principle)*

someone who is walking past
someone or something.

passing ADJECTIVE lasting only for
a short time • *a passing phase.*
● SIMILAR WORDS: brief, fleeting,
momentary

passion, passions NOUN ❶ Passion
is a very strong feeling of physical
attraction. ❷ Passion is also any
strong emotion.
● SIMILAR WORDS: ❷ emotion,
fervour, intensity

passionate ADJECTIVE expressing
very strong feelings about something.
passionately ADVERB
● SIMILAR WORDS: emotional,
fervent, intense

passive ADJECTIVE ❶ remaining
calm and showing no feeling when
provoked ▷ NOUN ❷ (ENGLISH) In
grammar, the passive or passive voice
is the form of the verb in which the
person or thing to which an action is
being done is the grammatical subject
of the sentence, and is given more
emphasis as a result. For example, the
passive of *The committee rejected your
application* is *Your application was*

rejected by the committee. **passively**
ADVERB **passivity** NOUN
● SIMILAR WORDS: ❶ inactive,
submissive
▶ SEE GRAMMAR BOX BELOW

Passover NOUN The Passover is an
eight-day Jewish festival held in
spring.

passport, passports NOUN an
official identification document which
you need to show when you travel
abroad.

password, passwords NOUN ❶ a
secret word known to only a few
people. It allows people on the same
side to recognize a friend. ❷ (ICT) a
word you need to know to get into
some computers or computer files.

past NOUN ❶ The past is the period
of time before the present
▷ ADJECTIVE ❷ Past things are
things that happened or existed before
the present • *the past 30 years.*
❸ (ENGLISH) The past tense of a verb
is the form used to express something
that happened in the past
▷ PREPOSITION OR ADVERB ❹ You
use 'past' when you are telling the

THE PASSIVE VOICE

The **passive** voice and the **active**
voice are two different ways of
presenting information in a sentence.
The **passive** always uses a form of
the auxiliary verb *to be* with the past
participle of the verb. When a
sentence is in the passive voice, the
subject of the verb is affected by the
action, rather than doing it:
*The cat **is being fed** by Anna.*
*The mouse **was chased** by a cat.*

It usually sounds more natural to use
the active rather than the passive.
However, it is sometimes better to
use the passive if you want to avoid
giving blame or if the name of the
subject is not known:
The book has been mislaid.
We are being followed.

Also look at the grammar box at
active.

▷ SPELLING NOTE: *Psychiatrists Seldom Yell Callously Hard (psychiatrist)*

time • *It was ten past eleven.* ❺ If you go past something, you move towards it and continue until you are on the other side • *They drove rapidly past their cottage.* ▷ PREPOSITION ❻ Something that is past a place is situated on the other side of it • *It's just past the church there.*

pasta NOUN Pasta is a dried mixture of flour, eggs, and water, formed into different shapes.

paste, pastes, pasting, pasted NOUN ❶ Paste is a soft, rather sticky mixture that can be easily spread • *tomato paste.* ▷ VERB ❷ If you paste something onto a surface, you stick it with glue.

pastel, pastels ADJECTIVE ❶ Pastel colours are pale and soft ▷ NOUN ❷ (ART) Pastels are small sticks of coloured crayon, used for drawing pictures.

pasteurized [*Said past-yoor-ized*]; also spelt **pasteurised** ADJECTIVE Pasteurized milk has been treated with a special heating process to kill bacteria.

pastiche, pastiches [*Said pass-teesh*] NOUN (ART) FORMAL A pastiche is a work of art that contains a mixture of styles or that copies the style of another artist.

pastime, pastimes NOUN a hobby or something you do just for pleasure.
● SIMILAR WORDS: activity, hobby,
● recreation

pastor, pastors NOUN a clergyman in charge of a congregation.

pastoral ADJECTIVE
❶ characteristic of peaceful country

life and landscape • *pastoral scenes.*
❷ relating to the duties of the clergy in caring for the needs of their parishioners • *a pastoral visit.*

past participle, past participles NOUN (ENGLISH) In grammar, the past participle of an English verb is the form, usually ending in '-ed' or '-en', that is used to make some past tenses and the passive. For example 'killed' in 'She has killed the goldfish' and 'broken' in 'My leg was broken' are past participles.

pastry, pastries NOUN ❶ Pastry is a mixture of flour, fat, and water, rolled flat and used for making pies. ❷ a small cake.

past tense NOUN In grammar, the past tense is the tense of a verb that you use mainly to refer to things that happened or existed before the time of writing or speaking.
▶ SEE GRAMMAR BOX ON PAGE 616

pasture, pastures NOUN Pasture is an area of grass on which farm animals graze.

pasty, pasties ADJECTIVE ❶ [*rhymes with hasty*] Someone who is pasty looks pale and unhealthy ▷ NOUN ❷ [*Said pass-tee*] a small pie containing meat and vegetables.

pat, pats, patting, patted VERB ❶ If you pat something, you tap it lightly with your hand held flat ▷ NOUN ❷ a small lump of butter.

patch, patches, patching, patched NOUN ❶ a piece of material used to cover a hole in something. ❷ an area of a surface that is different in appearance from the rest • *a bald patch.* ▷ VERB ❸ If you patch

a b c d e f g h i j k l m n o **p** q r s t u v w x y z

▷ SPELLING NOTE: *the QUeen stood on the QUay (quay)*

A
B
C
D
E
F
G
H
I
J
K
L
M
N
O
P
Q
R
S
T
U
V
W
X
Y
Z

TALKING ABOUT THE PAST

You can talk about events that have already happened by using **simple past tenses** or **compound tenses**.

The **simple past tense** is formed without any auxiliary verbs. It is usually formed by taking the dictionary form of the verb and adding the ending -*ed*. (If the verb already ends in -*e*, then you only need to add -*d*.)
I **cooked** the dinner.
She **liked** fish.

You can also use **compound tenses** to talk about actions that have happened.

One compound past tense is formed by using *was* or *were* in front of the main verb, and adding the ending -*ing*. This shows that an action happening in the past was continuous:
I **was cooking** the dinner.
We **were dining**.

Notice that if the verb ends in *e*, the *e*

is dropped.

Another compound past tense is formed by using a form of the verb *to have* in front of the main verb, and adding the ending -*ed*. This shows that an action has been completed:
I **have cooked** the dinner.
We **have dined**.

Notice that if the verb already ends in *e* you don't need to add one.

Another compound past tense is formed by using *had* in front of the main verb, and adding the ending -*ed*. This form shows that an action in the past had been completed before something else took place:
I **had cooked** the dinner.
We **had dined**.

Another compound past tense is formed by using *did* in front of the basic form of the verb. This can add emphasis:
We **did enjoy** that!

---

something, you mend it by fixing a patch over the hole.
patch up VERB If you patch something up, you mend it hurriedly or temporarily.

patchwork ADJECTIVE ❶ A patchwork quilt is made from many small pieces of material sewn together ▷ **NOUN ❷** Something that is a patchwork is made up of many parts.

patchy, patchier, patchiest **ADJECTIVE** Something that is patchy is unevenly spread or incomplete in parts • *patchy fog on the hills*.

pâté [*Said pa-tay*] **NOUN** Pâté is a mixture of meat, fish, or vegetables blended into a paste and spread on bread or toast.

patella, patellae **NOUN** (SCIENCE) Your patella is your kneecap.

patent, patents, patenting, patented **NOUN ❶** an official right given to an inventor to be the only person or company allowed to make or sell a new product ▷ **VERB ❷** If you patent something, you obtain a patent for it ▷ **ADJECTIVE ❸** obvious • *This was patent nonsense*. **patently ADVERB**

▷ SPELLING NOTE: *Rhythmical Hounds Yap To Heavy Music (rhythm)*

paternal ADJECTIVE relating to a father • *paternal pride*.

paternity NOUN Paternity is the state or fact of being a father.

path, paths NOUN ❶ a strip of ground for people to walk on. ❷ Your path is the area ahead of you and the direction in which you are moving.

pathetic ADJECTIVE ❶ If something is pathetic, it makes you feel pity. ❷ Pathetic also means very poor or unsuccessful • *a pathetic attempt*. **pathetically** ADVERB
● SIMILAR WORDS: ❶ heart-
● rending, moving, sad

pathological ADJECTIVE extreme and uncontrollable • *a pathological fear of snakes*. **pathologically** ADVERB

pathology NOUN Pathology is the study of diseases and the way they develop. **pathologist** NOUN

pathos [*Said pay-thoss*] NOUN Pathos is a quality in literature or art that causes great sadness or pity.

pathway, pathways NOUN a path.

patience NOUN Patience is the ability to stay calm in a difficult or irritating situation.
● SIMILAR WORDS: forbearance,
● tolerance

patient, patients ADJECTIVE ❶ If you are patient, you stay calm in a difficult or irritating situation ▷ NOUN ❷ a person receiving medical treatment from a doctor or in a hospital. **patiently** ADVERB

patio, patios NOUN a paved area close to a house.

patois [*Said pat-twah*] NOUN A patois is an unwritten regional dialect, especially in France.

patriarch, patriarchs [*Said pay-tree-ark*] NOUN (GEOGRAPHY) the male head of a family or tribe. **patriarchal** ADJECTIVE

patrician ADJECTIVE FORMAL belonging to a family of high rank.

patriot, patriots NOUN someone who loves their country and feels very loyal towards it. **patriotic** ADJECTIVE **patriotism** NOUN

patrol, patrols, patrolling, patrolled VERB ❶ When soldiers, police, or guards patrol an area, they walk or drive around to make sure there is no trouble ▷ NOUN ❷ a group of people patrolling an area.
● WORD HISTORY: from French
● *patrouiller* meaning 'to flounder in
● mud'

patron, patrons NOUN ❶ a person who supports or gives money to artists, writers, or musicians. ❷ The patrons of a hotel, pub, or shop are the people who use it. **patronage** NOUN

patronize, patronizes, patronizing, patronized; *also spelt* **patronise** VERB ❶ If someone patronizes you, they treat you kindly, but in a way that suggests that you are less intelligent than them or inferior to them. ❷ If you patronize a hotel, pub, or shop, you are a customer there. **patronizing** ADJECTIVE

patron saint, patron saints NOUN The patron saint of a group of people or place is a saint who is believed to look after them.

a
b
c
d
e
f
g
h
i
j
k
l
m
n
o
p
q
r
s
t
u
v
w
x
y
z

▷ SPELLING NOTE: *there's SAND in my SANDwich (sandwich)*

patter, patters, pattering, pattered
VERB ❶ If something patters on a surface, it makes quick, light, tapping sounds ▷ **NOUN** ❷ a series of light tapping sounds • *a patter of light rain.*

pattern, patterns **NOUN** ❶ a decorative design of repeated shapes. ❷ The pattern of something is the way it is usually done or happens • *a perfectly normal pattern of behaviour.* ❸ a diagram or shape used as a guide for making something, for example clothes. **patterned ADJECTIVE**

paunch, paunches **NOUN** If a man has a paunch, he has a fat stomach.

pauper, paupers **NOUN** OLD-FASHIONED a very poor person.

pause, pauses, pausing, paused **VERB** ❶ If you pause, you stop what you are doing for a short time ▷ **NOUN** ❷ a short period when you stop what you are doing. ❸ a short period of silence.

pave, paves, paving, paved **VERB** When an area of ground is paved, it is covered with flat blocks of stone or concrete.

pavement, pavements **NOUN** a path with a hard surface at the side of a road.

pavilion, pavilions **NOUN** a building at a sports ground where players can wash and change.

paw, paws, pawing, pawed **NOUN** ❶ The paws of an animal such as a cat or bear are its feet with claws and soft pads ▷ **VERB** ❷ If an animal paws something, it hits it or scrapes at it with its paws.

pawn, pawns, pawning, pawned
VERB ❶ If you pawn something, you leave it with a pawnbroker in exchange for money ▷ **NOUN** ❷ the smallest and least valuable playing piece in chess.

pawnbroker, pawnbrokers **NOUN** a dealer who lends money in return for personal property left with him or her, which may be sold if the loan is not repaid on time.

pawpaw, pawpaws **NOUN** the same as a **papaya.**

pay, pays, paying, paid **VERB** ❶ When you pay money to someone, you give it to them because you are buying something or owe it to them. ❷ If it pays to do something, it is to your advantage to do it • *They say it pays to advertise.* ❸ If you pay for something that you have done, you suffer as a result. ❹ If you pay attention to something, you give it your attention. ❺ If you pay a visit to someone, you visit them ▷ **NOUN** ❻ Someone's pay is their salary or wages.
● **SIMILAR WORDS:** ❶ give, ● reimburse, settle

payable ADJECTIVE ❶ An amount of money that is payable has to be paid or can be paid • *All fees are payable in advance.* ❷ If a cheque is made payable to you, you are the person who should receive the money.

payment, payments **NOUN** ❶ Payment is the act of paying money. ❷ a sum of money paid.

payroll, payrolls **NOUN** Someone who is on an organization's payroll is employed and paid by them.

PC, PCs **NOUN** ❶ In Britain, a police

constable. ❷ a personal computer ▷ **ADJECTIVE** ❸ short for **politically correct**.

PE NOUN PE is a lesson in which gymnastics or sports are taught. PE is an abbreviation for 'physical education'.

pea, peas **NOUN** Peas are small round green seeds that grow in pods and are eaten as a vegetable.

peace NOUN ❶ Peace is a state of calm and quiet when there is no disturbance of any kind. ❷ When a country is at peace, it is not at war.
peaceable ADJECTIVE
● **SIMILAR WORDS:** ❶ stillness,
● tranquillity

peaceful ADJECTIVE quiet and calm. **peacefully ADVERB**
● **SIMILAR WORDS:** serene, tranquil

peach, peaches **NOUN** ❶ a soft, round fruit with yellow flesh and a yellow and red skin ▷ **ADJECTIVE** ❷ pale pink with a hint of orange.

peacock, peacocks **NOUN** a large bird with green and blue feathers. The male has a long tail which it can spread out in a fan.

peak, peaks, peaking, peaked **NOUN** ❶ The peak of an activity or process is the point at which it is strongest or most successful. ❷ the pointed top of a mountain ▷ **VERB** ❸ When something peaks, it reaches its highest value or its greatest level of success. **peaked ADJECTIVE**
● **SIMILAR WORDS:** ❶ climax,
● culmination, high point

peal, peals, pealing, pealed **NOUN** ❶ A peal of bells is the musical sound made by bells ringing one after another ▷ **VERB** ❷ When bells peal, they ring one after the other.

peanut, peanuts **NOUN** Peanuts are small oval nuts that grow under the ground.

pear, pears **NOUN** a fruit which is narrow at the top and wide and rounded at the bottom.

pearl, pearls **NOUN** a hard, round, creamy-white object used in jewellery. Pearls grow inside the shell of an oyster.

peasant, peasants **NOUN** a person who works on the land, especially in a poor country.

peat NOUN Peat is dark-brown decaying plant material found in cool, wet regions. Dried peat can be used as fuel.

pebble, pebbles **NOUN** a smooth, round stone.

peck, pecks, pecking, pecked **VERB** ❶ If a bird pecks something, it bites at it quickly with its beak. ❷ If you peck someone on the cheek, you give them a quick kiss ▷ **NOUN** ❸ a quick bite by a bird. ❹ a quick kiss on the cheek.

peculiar ADJECTIVE ❶ strange and perhaps unpleasant. ❷ relating or belonging only to a particular person or thing • *a gesture peculiar to her.* **peculiarly ADVERB peculiarity NOUN**

pedal, pedals, pedalling, pedalled **NOUN** ❶ a control lever on a machine or vehicle that you press with your foot ▷ **VERB** ❷ When you pedal a bicycle, you push the pedals round with your feet to move along.

a
b
c
d
e
f
g
h
i
j
k
l
m
n
o
p
q
r
s
t
u
v
w
x
y
z

▷ SPELLING NOTE: *Eddy Ant thinks mEAt is a grEAt trEAt to EAt (-ea-)*

pedantic ADJECTIVE If a person is pedantic, they are too concerned with unimportant details and rules.

peddle, peddles, peddling, peddled VERB Someone who peddles something sells it.

pedestal, pedestals NOUN a base on which a statue stands.

pedestrian, pedestrians NOUN ❶ someone who is walking ▷ ADJECTIVE ❷ Pedestrian means ordinary and rather dull • *a pedestrian performance.*

pedestrian crossing, pedestrian crossings NOUN a specially marked place where you can cross the road safely.

pediatrician another spelling of paediatrician.

pediatrics another spelling of paediatrics.

pedigree, pedigrees ADJECTIVE ❶ A pedigree animal is descended from a single breed and its ancestors are known and recorded ▷ NOUN ❷ Someone's pedigree is their background or ancestry.

peek, peeks, peeking, peeked VERB ❶ If you peek at something, you have a quick look at it • *I peeked round the corner.* ▷ NOUN ❷ a quick look at something.

peel, peels, peeling, peeled NOUN ❶ The peel of a fruit is the skin when it has been removed ▷ VERB ❷ When you peel fruit or vegetables, you remove the skin. ❸ If a surface is peeling, it is coming off in thin layers. **peelings** PLURAL NOUN

peep, peeps, peeping, peeped VERB ❶ If you peep at something, you have a quick look at it. ❷ If something peeps out from behind something else, a small part of it becomes visible • *a handkerchief peeping out of his breast pocket.* ▷ NOUN ❸ a quick look at something.

peer, peers, peering, peered VERB ❶ If you peer at something, you look at it very hard ▷ NOUN ❷ a member of the nobility. ❸ Your peers are the people who are of the same age and social status as yourself.

peerage, peerages NOUN ❶ The peers in a country are called the peerage. ❷ A peerage is also the rank of being a peer.

peer group, peer groups NOUN Your peer group is the people who are of the same age and social status as yourself.

peerless ADJECTIVE so magnificent that nothing can equal it • *peerless wines.*

peewee, peewees NOUN a small black-and-white Australian bird with long, thin legs.

peg, pegs, pegging, pegged NOUN ❶ a plastic or wooden clip used for hanging wet clothes on a line. ❷ a hook on a wall where you can hang things ▷ VERB ❸ If you peg clothes on a line, you fix them there with pegs. ❹ If a price is pegged at a certain level, it is fixed at that level.

peggy square, peggy squares NOUN In New Zealand, a small square of knitted wool which is sewn together with others to make a rug.

▷ SPELLING NOTE: *Elaine and Emily shout EE when they mEEt to grEEt each other (-ee-)*

pejorative *[Said pej-jor-ra-tiv]* **ADJECTIVE** A pejorative word expresses criticism.

pekinese, pekineses *[Said pee-kin-eez]; also spelt* **pekingese** **NOUN** a small long-haired dog with a flat nose.

pelican, pelicans **NOUN** a large water bird with a pouch beneath its beak in which it stores fish.

pellet, pellets **NOUN** a small ball of paper, lead, or other material.

pelt, pelts, pelting, pelted **VERB** ❶ If you pelt someone with things, you throw the things with force at them. ❷ If you pelt along, you run very fast ▷ **NOUN** ❸ the skin and fur of an animal.

pelvis, pelvises **NOUN** the wide, curved group of bones at hip-level at the base of your spine. **pelvic** **ADJECTIVE**

pen, pens, penning, penned **NOUN** ❶ a long, thin instrument used for writing with ink. ❷ a small fenced area in which farm animals are kept for a short time ▷ **VERB** ❸ LITERARY If someone pens a letter or article, they write it. ❹ If you are penned in or penned up, you have to remain in an uncomfortably small area.
● **WORD HISTORY:** from Latin *penna*
● meaning 'feather'; pens used to be
● made from feathers

penal **ADJECTIVE** relating to the punishment of criminals.

penalize, penalizes, penalizing, penalized; *also spelt* **penalise** **VERB** If you are penalized, you are made to suffer some disadvantage as a punishment for something.

penalty, penalties **NOUN** ❶ a punishment or disadvantage that someone is made to suffer. ❷ In soccer, a penalty is a free kick at goal that is given to the attacking team if the defending team have committed a foul near their goal.

penance **NOUN** If you do penance, you do something unpleasant to show that you are sorry for something wrong that you have done.

pence a plural form of **penny**.

penchant *[Said pon-shon]* **NOUN** FORMAL If you have a penchant for something, you have a particular liking for it • *a penchant for crime.*

pencil, pencils **NOUN** (ART) a long thin stick of wood with graphite in the centre, used for drawing or writing.

pendant, pendants **NOUN** a piece of jewellery attached to a chain and worn round the neck.

pending FORMAL **ADJECTIVE** ❶ Something that is pending is waiting to be dealt with or will happen soon ▷ **PREPOSITION** ❷ Something that is done pending a future event is done until the event happens • *The army should stay in the west pending a future war.*

pendulum, pendulums **NOUN** a rod with a weight at one end in a clock which swings regularly from side to side to control the clock.

penetrate, penetrates, penetrating, penetrated **VERB** To penetrate an area that is difficult to get into is to succeed in getting into it. **penetration** **NOUN**

a b c d e f g h i j k l m n o **p** q r s t u v w x y z

penetrating ADJECTIVE ❶ loud and high-pitched • *a penetrating voice.* ❷ having or showing deep understanding • *penetrating questions.*

pen friend, pen friends NOUN someone living in a different place or country whom you write to regularly, although you may never have met each other.

penguin, penguins NOUN a black and white bird with webbed feet and small wings like flippers.

penicillin NOUN Penicillin is a powerful antibiotic obtained from fungus and used to treat infections.

peninsula, peninsulas NOUN an area of land almost surrounded by water.

penis, penises NOUN A man's penis is the part of his body that he uses when urinating and having sexual intercourse.

penitent ADJECTIVE Someone who is penitent is deeply sorry for having done something wrong. **penitence** NOUN

penknife, penknives NOUN a small knife with a blade that folds back into the handle.

pennant, pennants NOUN a triangular flag, especially one used by ships as a signal.

penniless ADJECTIVE Someone who is penniless has no money.

penny, pennies or pence NOUN a unit of currency in Britain and some other countries. In Britain a penny is worth one-hundredth of a pound.

pension, pensions [Said **pen**-shn]

NOUN a regular sum of money paid to an old or retired person.

pensioner, pensioners NOUN an old or retired person who gets a pension paid by the state.

pensive ADJECTIVE deep in thought.
- SIMILAR WORDS: dreamy,
- meditative, thoughtful

pentagon, pentagons NOUN (MATHS) a shape with five straight sides; a **regular pentagon** is a shape with five straight sides of the same length.

pentameter, pentameters [Said pen-**tam**-e-ter] NOUN (ENGLISH) a line of verse made up of five metrical feet.

pentathlon, pentathlons [Said pen-**tath**-lon] NOUN a sports contest in which athletes compete in five different events.

penthouse, penthouses NOUN a luxurious flat at the top of a building.

pent-up ADJECTIVE Pent-up emotions have been held back for a long time without release.
- SIMILAR WORDS: bottled up,
- suppressed

penultimate ADJECTIVE The penultimate thing in a series is the one before the last.

peony, peonies [Said **pee**-yon-ee] NOUN a garden plant with large pink, white, or red flowers.

people, peoples, peopling, peopled PLURAL NOUN ❶ People are men, women, and children ▷ NOUN ❷ all the men, women, and children of a

A
B
C
D
E
F
G
H
I
J
K
L
M
N
O
P
Q
R
S
T
U
V
W
X
Y
Z

particular country or race ▷ **VERB**
❸ If an area is peopled by a particular group, that group of people live there.
- **SIMILAR WORDS: ❶** humanity,
- mankind, persons **❷** nation,
- population, race

pepper, peppers **NOUN ❶** a hot-tasting powdered spice used for flavouring in cooking. **❷** a hollow green, red, yellow, or orange fruit eaten as a vegetable, with sweet-flavoured flesh.

peppermint, peppermints **NOUN** Peppermint is a plant with a strong taste. It is used for making sweets and in medicine.

per PREPOSITION 'Per' is used to mean 'each' when expressing rates and ratios • *The class meets two evenings per week.*

perceive, perceives, perceiving, perceived **VERB** If you perceive something that is not obvious, you see it or realize it.
- **SIMILAR WORDS:** notice, see, spot

per cent PHRASE You use **per cent** to talk about amounts as a proportion of a hundred. An amount that is 10 per cent (10%) of a larger amount is equal to 10 hundredths of the larger amount • *86 per cent of Americans believe Presley is alive.*
- **WORD HISTORY:** from Latin *per*
- meaning 'each' and *centum*
- meaning 'hundred'

percentage, percentages **NOUN** (MATHS) a fraction expressed as a number of hundredths • *the high percentage of failed marriages.*

perceptible ADJECTIVE Something that is perceptible can be seen • *a barely perceptible nod.*

perception, perceptions **NOUN ❶** Perception is the recognition of things using the senses, especially the sense of sight. **❷** Someone who has perception realizes or notices things that are not obvious. **❸** Your perception of something or someone is your understanding of them.

perceptive ADJECTIVE Someone who is perceptive realizes or notices things that are not obvious.
perceptively ADVERB
- **SIMILAR WORDS:** astute,
- observant, sharp

perch, perches, perching, perched **VERB ❶** If you perch on something, you sit on the edge of it. **❷** When a bird perches on something, it stands on it ▷ **NOUN ❸** a short rod for a bird to stand on. **❹** an edible freshwater fish.

percolator, percolators **NOUN** a special pot for making and serving coffee.

percussion NOUN OR ADJECTIVE (MUSIC) Percussion instruments are musical instruments that you hit to produce sounds. **percussionist NOUN**

perennial ADJECTIVE continually occurring or never ending • *The damp cellar was a perennial problem.*

perfect, perfects, perfecting, perfected **ADJECTIVE ❶** of the highest standard and without fault • *His English was perfect.* **❷** complete or absolute • *They have a perfect right to say so.* **❸** (ENGLISH) In English grammar, the perfect tense of a verb is formed with the present tense of

▷ SPELLING NOTE: *an ELegant angEL (angel)*

a
b
c
d
e
f
g
h
i
j
k
l
m
n
o
p
q
r
s
t
u
v
w
x
y
z

'have' and the past participle of the main verb • *I have lost my home.*
▷ **VERB** ❹ If you perfect something, you make it as good as it can possibly be. **perfectly ADVERB perfection NOUN**

● **SIMILAR WORDS:** ❶ faultless,
● flawless ❹ improve, refine

perfectionist, perfectionists **NOUN** someone who always tries to do everything perfectly.

perforated ADJECTIVE Something that is perforated has had small holes made in it. **perforation NOUN**

perform, performs, performing, performed **VERB** ❶ To perform a task or action is to do it. ❷ (**DRAMA**) To perform is to act, dance, or play music in front of an audience. **performer NOUN**

performance, performances **NOUN** ❶ (**DRAMA**) an entertainment provided for an audience. ❷ The performance of a task or action is the doing of it. ❸ Someone's or something's performance is how successful they are • *the poor performance of the American economy.*

perfume, perfumes **NOUN** ❶ Perfume is a pleasant-smelling liquid which women put on their bodies. ❷ The perfume of something is its pleasant smell. **perfumed ADJECTIVE**

perfunctory ADJECTIVE done quickly without interest or care • *a perfunctory kiss.*

perhaps ADVERB You use 'perhaps' when you are not sure whether something is true or possible.

peril, perils **NOUN** FORMAL Peril is great danger. **perilous ADJECTIVE perilously ADVERB**

perimeter, perimeters **NOUN** (**MATHS**) The perimeter of an area or figure is the whole of its outer edge.

period, periods **NOUN** ❶ a particular length of time. ❷ one of the parts the day is divided into at school. ❸ A woman's period is the monthly bleeding from her womb
▷ **ADJECTIVE** ❹ relating to a historical period of time • *period furniture.* **periodic ADJECTIVE periodically ADVERB**

periodical, periodicals **NOUN** a magazine.

periodic table NOUN (**SCIENCE**) The periodic table is a table showing the chemical elements arranged according to their atomic numbers.

peripheral [Said per-**rif**-fer-ral] **ADJECTIVE** ❶ of little importance in comparison with other things • *a peripheral activity.* ❷ on or relating to the edge of an area.

periphery, peripheries **NOUN** The periphery of an area is its outside edge.

periscope, periscopes **NOUN** A periscope is a tube with mirrors which is used in a submarine to see above the surface of the water.

perish, perishes, perishing, perished **VERB** ❶ FORMAL If someone or something perishes, they are killed or destroyed. ❷ If fruit or fabric perishes, it rots. **perishable ADJECTIVE**

perjury NOUN FORMAL OR LEGAL If someone commits perjury, they tell a

▷ SPELLING NOTE: *LEt's measure the angLE (angle)*

lie in court while under oath. **perjure**
VERB

perk, perks, perking, perked **NOUN**
❶ an extra, such as a company car,
offered by an employer in addition to a
salary. Perk is an abbreviation of
'perquisite' ▷ **VERB** ❷ INFORMAL
When someone perks up, they
become more cheerful. **perky**
ADJECTIVE

perm, perms, perming, permed
NOUN ❶ If you have a perm, your
hair is curled and treated with
chemicals to keep the curls for several
months ▷ **VERB** ❷ To perm
someone's hair means to put a perm
in it.

permanent **ADJECTIVE** lasting for
ever, or present all the time.
permanently **ADVERB**
permanence **NOUN**

permeable [Said per-mee-a-bl]
ADJECTIVE FORMAL If something is
permeable, liquids are able to pass
through it • permeable rock.

permeate, permeates, permeating,
permeated **VERB** To permeate
something is to spread through it and
affect every part of it • The feeling of
failure permeates everything I do.

permissible **ADJECTIVE** allowed
by the rules.
● **SIMILAR WORDS:** allowable,
● permitted

permission **NOUN** If you have
permission to do something, you are
allowed to do it.
● **SIMILAR WORDS:** authorization,
● go-ahead

permissive **ADJECTIVE** A

permissive society allows things which
some people disapprove of, especially
freedom in sexual behaviour.
permissiveness **NOUN**

permit, permits, permitting,
permitted **VERB** ❶ To permit
something is to allow it or make it
possible ▷ **NOUN** ❷ an official
document which says that you are
allowed to do something.
● **SIMILAR WORDS:** ❶ allow, give
● permission, let

permutation, permutations
NOUN one possible arrangement of a
number of things.

pernicious **ADJECTIVE** FORMAL
very harmful • the pernicious influence
of television.

peroxide **NOUN** Peroxide is a
chemical used for bleaching hair or as
an antiseptic.

perpendicular **ADJECTIVE**
(MATHS) upright, or at right angles to
a horizontal line.
● **WORD HISTORY:** from Latin
● perpendiculum meaning 'plumb
● line'

perpetrate, perpetrates,
perpetrating, perpetrated **VERB**
FORMAL To perpetrate a crime is to
commit it. **perpetrator** **NOUN**

perpetual **ADJECTIVE** never ending
• a perpetual toothache. **perpetually**
ADVERB **perpetuity** **NOUN**

perpetuate, perpetuates,
perpetuating, perpetuated **VERB** To
perpetuate a situation or belief is to
cause it to continue • The television
series will perpetuate the myths.

perplexed **ADJECTIVE** If you are

a b c d e f g h i j k l m n o **P** q r s t u v w x y z

▷ SPELLING NOTE: A Rude Idiot Thought He Might Eat Toffee In Church (_arithmetic_)

A
B
C
D
E
F
G
H
I
J
K
L
M
N
O
P
Q
R
S
T
U
V
W
X
Y
Z

perplexed, you are puzzled and do not know what to do.

persecute, persecutes, persecuting, persecuted **VERB** To persecute someone is to treat them cruelly and unfairly over a long period of time. **persecution NOUN persecutor NOUN**
- **SIMILAR WORDS:** pick on,
- victimize

persevere, perseveres, persevering, persevered **VERB** If you persevere, you keep trying to do something and do not give up. **perseverance NOUN**
- **SIMILAR WORDS:** carry on,
- continue, keep going

Persian *[Said per-shn]* **ADJECTIVE OR NOUN** an old word for **Iranian**, especially referring to language.

persimmon, persimmons **NOUN** a sweet, red, tropical fruit.

persist, persists, persisting, persisted **VERB** ❶ If something undesirable persists, it continues to exist. ❷ If you persist in doing something, you continue in spite of opposition or difficulty. **persistence NOUN persistent ADJECTIVE**

person, people or persons **NOUN** ❶ a man, woman, or child. ❷ In grammar, the first person is the speaker (I), the second person is the person being spoken to (you), and the third person is anyone else being referred to (he, she, they).
- **USAGE NOTE:** The usual plural of
- *person* is *people*. *Persons* is much
- less common, and is used only in
- formal or official English
- **SIMILAR WORDS:** ❶ human
- being, individual

persona, personas or personae *[Said per-soh-na]* **NOUN** FORMAL Your persona is the image of yourself and your character that you choose to present to other people.

personal ADJECTIVE ❶ Personal means belonging or relating to a particular person rather than to people in general • *my personal feeling.* ❷ **PE** Personal matters relate to your feelings, relationships, and health which you may not wish to discuss with other people. **personally ADVERB**
- **SIMILAR WORDS:** ❶ individual,
- own, private

personality, personalities **NOUN** ❶ Your personality is your character and nature. ❷ a famous person in entertainment or sport.

personification NOUN ❶ **ENGLISH** Personification is a form of imagery in which something inanimate is described as if it has human qualities • *The trees sighed and whispered as the impatient breeze stirred their branches.* ❷ Someone who is the personification of some quality is a living example of that quality • *He was the personification of evil.*

personify, personifies, personifying, personified **VERB** Someone who personifies a particular quality seems to be a living example of it. If you personify a thing or concept, you write or speak of it as if it has human abilities or qualities, for example 'The sun is trying to come out' or 'the cruel sea'.

personnel *[Said per-son-nell]* **NOUN** The personnel of an organization are the people who work for it.

perspective, perspectives **NOUN** ❶ A particular perspective is one way of thinking about something. ❷ **ART** Perspective is a method artists use to make some people and things seem further away than others.

perspiration NOUN Perspiration is the moisture that appears on your skin when you are hot or frightened.

perspire, perspires, perspiring, perspired **VERB** If someone perspires, they sweat.

persuade, persuades, persuading, persuaded **VERB** If someone persuades you to do something or persuades you that something is true, they make you do it or believe it by giving you very good reasons. **persuasion NOUN persuasive ADJECTIVE**
● **SIMILAR WORDS:** convince, talk
● into

pertaining ADJECTIVE FORMAL If information or questions are pertaining to a place or thing, they are about that place or thing • *issues pertaining to women.*

pertinent ADJECTIVE especially relevant to the subject being discussed • *He asks pertinent questions.*

perturbed ADJECTIVE Someone who is perturbed is worried.

Peruvian, Peruvians [Said *per-roo-vee-an*] **ADJECTIVE** ❶ belonging or relating to Peru ▷ **NOUN** ❷ someone who comes from Peru.

pervade, pervades, pervading, pervaded **VERB** Something that pervades a place is present and noticeable throughout it • *a fear that pervades the community.* **pervasive ADJECTIVE**

perverse ADJECTIVE Someone who is perverse deliberately does things that are unreasonable or harmful. **perversely ADVERB perversity NOUN**

pervert, perverts, perverting, perverted **VERB** ❶ FORMAL To pervert something is to interfere with it so that it is no longer what it should be • *a conspiracy to pervert the course of justice.* ▷ **NOUN** ❷ a person whose sexual behaviour is disgusting or harmful. **perversion NOUN**
● **WORD HISTORY:** from Latin
● *pervertere* meaning 'to turn the
● wrong way'

perverted ADJECTIVE ❶ Someone who is perverted has disgusting or unacceptable behaviour or ideas, especially sexual behaviour or ideas. ❷ Something that is perverted is completely wrong • *a perverted sense of value.*

peso, pesos [Said *pay-soh*] **NOUN** the main unit of currency in several South American countries.

pessimism NOUN Pessimism is the tendency to believe that bad things will happen. **pessimist NOUN**

pessimistic ADJECTIVE believing that bad things will happen. **pessimistically ADVERB**

pest, pests **NOUN** ❶ an insect or small animal which damages plants or food supplies. ❷ someone who keeps

▷ SPELLING NOTE: *Betty Eats Cakes And Uses Seven Eggs (because)*

bothering or annoying you.

pester, pesters, pestering, pestered **VERB** If you pester someone, you keep bothering them or asking them to do something.
● **SIMILAR WORDS:** annoy, badger, hassle

pesticide, pesticides **NOUN** (SCIENCE) Pesticides are chemicals sprayed onto plants to kill insects and grubs.

pet, pets, petting, petted **NOUN** ❶ a tame animal kept at home ▷ **ADJECTIVE** ❷ Someone's pet theory or pet project is something that they particularly support or feel strongly about ▷ **VERB** ❸ If you pet a person or animal, you stroke them affectionately.

petal, petals **NOUN** The petals of a flower are the coloured outer parts.

peter out, peters out, petering out, petered out **VERB** If something peters out, it gradually comes to an end.

petite [Said pet-teet] **ADJECTIVE** A woman who is petite is small and slim.

petition, petitions, petitioning, petitioned **NOUN** ❶ a document demanding official action which is signed by a lot of people. ❷ an formal request to a court for legal action to be taken ▷ **VERB** ❸ If you petition someone in authority, you make a formal request to them • *I petitioned the Chinese government for permission to visit its country.*

Petri dish, Petri dishes **NOUN** (SCIENCE) A Petri dish is a flat, shallow dish used in laboratories. It is named after J. R. Petri (1852-1921), a German

bacteriologist.

petrified ADJECTIVE If you are petrified, you are very frightened.

petrol NOUN (SCIENCE) Petrol is a liquid obtained from petroleum and used as a fuel for motor vehicles.

petroleum NOUN (SCIENCE) Petroleum is thick, dark oil found under the earth or under the sea bed.
● **WORD HISTORY:** from Latin *petra* meaning 'rock' and *oleum* meaning 'oil'

petticoat, petticoats **NOUN** a piece of women's underwear like a very thin skirt.

petty, pettier, pettiest **ADJECTIVE** ❶ Petty things are small and unimportant. ❷ Petty behaviour consists of doing small things which are selfish and unkind.

petulant ADJECTIVE showing unreasonable and childish impatience or anger. **petulantly ADVERB petulance NOUN**

petunia, petunias [Said pit-yoon-nee-ah] **NOUN** a garden plant with large trumpet-shaped flowers.

pew, pews **NOUN** a long wooden seat with a back, which people sit on in church.

pewter NOUN Pewter is a silvery-grey metal made from a mixture of tin and lead.

pH NOUN The pH of a solution or of the soil is a measurement of how acid or alkaline it is. Acid solutions have a pH of less than 7 and alkaline solutions have a pH greater than 7. pH is an abbreviation for 'potential

▷ SPELLING NOTE: *there's a rAKE in the brAKEs (brake)*

hydrogen' • *not suitable for soils with a high pH.*

phalanger, phalangers [Said *fal-lan-jer*] NOUN an Australian marsupial with thick fur and a long tail. In Australia and New Zealand, it is also called a possum.

phallus, phalluses NOUN a penis or a symbolic model of a penis. **phallic** ADJECTIVE

phantom, phantoms NOUN ❶ a ghost ▷ ADJECTIVE ❷ imagined or unreal • *a phantom pregnancy.*

pharaoh, pharaohs [Said *fair-oh*] NOUN The pharaohs were kings of ancient Egypt.

pharmaceutical [Said *far-mass-yoo-tik-kl*] ADJECTIVE connected with the industrial production of medicines.

pharmacist, pharmacists NOUN a person who is qualified to prepare and sell medicines.

pharmacy, pharmacies NOUN a shop where medicines are sold.

phase, phases, phasing, phased NOUN ❶ a particular stage in the development of something ▷ VERB ❷ To phase something is to cause it to happen gradually in stages.

PhD, PhDs NOUN a degree awarded to someone who has done advanced research in a subject. PhD is an abbreviation for 'Doctor of Philosophy'.

pheasant, pheasants NOUN a large, long-tailed game bird.

phenomenal [Said *fin-nom-in-nal*] ADJECTIVE extraordinarily great or good. **phenomenally** ADVERB

phenomenon, phenomena NOUN something that happens or exists, especially something remarkable or something being considered in a scientific way • *a well-known geographical phenomenon.*
● USAGE NOTE: The word
● *phenomenon* is singular. The plural
● form is *phenomena*

philanthropist, philanthropists [Said *fil-lan-throp-pist*] NOUN someone who freely gives help or money to people in need. **philanthropic** ADJECTIVE **philanthropy** NOUN

philistine, philistines NOUN If you call someone a philistine, you mean that they do not like art, literature, or music.

philosophical or **philosophic** ADJECTIVE Someone who is philosophical does not get upset when disappointing things happen.

philosophy, philosophies NOUN ❶ Philosophy is the study or creation of ideas about existence, knowledge or beliefs. ❷ a set of beliefs that a person has. **philosopher** NOUN
● WORD HISTORY: from Greek
● *philosophos* meaning 'lover of
● wisdom'

phlegm [Said *flem*] NOUN Phlegm is a thick mucus which you get in your throat when you have a cold.

phobia, phobias NOUN a great fear or hatred of something • *The man had a phobia about flying.* **phobic** ADJECTIVE
● WORD HISTORY: from Greek
● *phobos* meaning 'fear'

-phobia SUFFIX '-phobia' means

a
b
c
d
e
f
g
h
i
j
k
l
m
n
o
p
q
r
s
t
u
v
w
x
y
z

▷ SPELLING NOTE: *you'll brEAK that Electrical Aerial, Kitty (break)*

'fear of' • *claustrophobia*.

phoenix, phoenixes *[Said fee-niks]*
NOUN an imaginary bird which,
according to myth, burns itself to
ashes every five hundred years and
rises from the fire again.

phone, phones, phoning, phoned
NOUN ❶ a piece of electronic
equipment which allows you to speak
to someone in another place by keying
in or dialling their number ▷ **VERB**
❷ If you phone someone, you key in
or dial their number and speak to
them using a phone.

-phone **SUFFIX** '-phone' means
'giving off sound' • *telephone*
• *gramophone*.
  ● **WORD HISTORY:** from Greek
  ● *phōnē* meaning 'voice' or 'sound'

phonetics **NOUN** (ENGLISH)
Phonetics is the study of speech
sounds. **phonetic** **ADJECTIVE**

phoney, phonier, phoniest; *also spelt*
phony **ADJECTIVE** INFORMAL false
and intended to deceive.

phosphorus **NOUN** (SCIENCE)
Phosphorus is a whitish, nonmetallic
element that burns easily and is used
in making fertilizers and matches. Its
atomic number is 15 and its symbol is
P.

photo, photos **NOUN** INFORMAL a
photograph.

photo- **PREFIX** 'Photo-' means
'light' or 'using light' • *photography*.

photocopier, photocopiers **NOUN**
a machine which makes instant copies
of documents by photographing them.

photocopy, photocopies,
photocopying, photocopied (LIBRARY)
NOUN ❶ a copy of a document
produced by a photocopier ▷ **VERB**
❷ If you photocopy a document, you
make a copy of it using a photocopier.

photogenic **ADJECTIVE** Someone
who is photogenic always looks nice in
photographs.

photograph, photographs,
photographing, photographed **NOUN**
❶ a picture made using a camera
▷ **VERB** ❷ When you photograph
someone, you take a picture of them
by using a camera. **photographer**
NOUN **photography** **NOUN**

photographic **ADJECTIVE**
connected with photography.

photosynthesis **NOUN** (SCIENCE)
Photosynthesis is the process by
which the action of sunlight on the
chlorophyll in plants produces the
substances that keep the plants alive.

phototropism *[Said foh-toh-troh-
pizm]* **NOUN** (SCIENCE) Phototropism
is the growth of a plant towards or
away from a source of light.

phrasal verb, phrasal verbs **NOUN**
a verb such as 'take over' or 'break in',
which is made up of a verb and an
adverb or preposition.

phrase, phrases, phrasing, phrased
NOUN ❶ a group of words
considered as a unit ▷ **VERB** ❷ If you
phrase something in a particular way,
you choose those words to express it
• *I should have phrased that better.*
▶ SEE GRAMMAR BOX ON PAGE 631

phylum, phyla **NOUN** (SCIENCE) A
phylum is a major division of living
organisms that is smaller than a

▷ SPELLING NOTE: *I always visit my FRIend on a FRIday (Friday)*

WHAT IS A PHRASE?

A **phrase** is a group of words which combine together but is not usually capable of standing on its own to describe an idea or situation. It requires additional words to form a meaningful sentence:
*She drank **a cup of tea**.*
*I **was reading** a book.*

Some phrases act as nouns:
***A stack of newspapers** lay on the floor.*
***My sister's friend** lives in Canada.*

Some phrases act as verbs. Verb phrases often contain an auxiliary verb. They may also contain adverbs:
*She **was always complaining** about the buses.*
*He **used to play** the piano.*

Some phrases act as adjectives. When words combine to act as an adjective,

they are usually hyphenated if they occur before the noun:
*The food here is **of the highest quality**.*
*He asked for an **up-to-the-minute** report.*

Some phrases act as adverbs. Adverb phrases often begin with a preposition:
*She disappeared **in the blink of an eye**.*
*They played **with great gusto**.*

Some phrases are acceptable as substitutes for sentences. Although they do not contain a subject and a verb, they can be understood on their own:
Happy Birthday!
Good morning.
All right?

kingdom and larger than a class. For example, the phylum *Anthropoda* includes insects, crustaceans, and spiders.

physical ADJECTIVE ❶ concerning the body rather than the mind. ❷ (GEOGRAPHY) relating to things that can be touched or seen, especially with regard to their size or shape • *the physical characteristics of their machinery* • *the physical world*.
physically ADVERB

physical education NOUN Physical education consists of the sport that you do at school.

physician, physicians NOUN a doctor.

physics NOUN Physics is the

scientific study of matter, energy, gravity, electricity, heat, and sound.
physicist NOUN

physio- PREFIX 'Physio-' means to do with the body or natural functions • *physiotherapy*.
● **WORD HISTORY:** from Greek *phusio*, from *phuein* meaning 'to make grow'

physiology NOUN Physiology is the scientific study of the way the bodies of living things work.

physiotherapy NOUN Physiotherapy is medical treatment which involves exercise and massage.
physiotherapist NOUN

physique, physiques *[Said fiz-**zeek**]* NOUN A person's physique is the

▷ SPELLING NOTE: *I want to see (C) your licenCe (licence)*

shape and size of their body.

pi [rhymes with **fly**] **NOUN** (MATHS) Pi is a number, approximately 3.142 and symbolized by the Greek letter Π. Pi is the ratio of the circumference of a circle to its diameter.

pianissimo [Said pee-an-**iss**-sim-moh] **ADJECTIVE AND ADVERB** (MUSIC) In music, pianissimo is an instruction to play or sing something very quietly.

piano, pianos (MUSIC) **NOUN** ① a large musical instrument with a row of black and white keys. When the keys are pressed, little hammers hit wires to produce the different notes. ② In music, piano is an instruction to play or sing something quietly. **pianist NOUN**

● **WORD HISTORY:** originally called
● 'pianoforte', from Italian
● *gravecembalo col piano e forte*
● meaning 'harpsichord with soft and
● loud (sounds)'

piccolo, piccolos **NOUN** a high-pitched wind instrument like a small flute.

● **WORD HISTORY:** from Italian
● *piccolo* meaning 'small'

pick, picks, picking, picked **VERB** ① To pick something is to choose it. ② If you pick a flower or fruit, or pick something from a place, you remove it with your fingers. ③ If someone picks a lock, they open it with a piece of wire instead of a key ▷ **NOUN** ④ The pick of a group of people or things are the best ones in it. ⑤ a pickaxe. **pick on VERB** If you pick on someone, you criticize them unfairly or treat them unkindly. **pick up VERB** If you pick someone

or something up, you collect them from the place where they are waiting.

pickaxe, pickaxes **NOUN** a tool consisting of a curved pointed iron bar attached in the middle to a long handle.

picket, pickets, picketing, picketed **VERB** ① When a group of people picket a place of work, they stand outside to persuade other workers to join a strike ▷ **NOUN** ② someone who is picketing a place.

pickings PLURAL NOUN Pickings are goods or money that can be obtained very easily • *rich pickings*.

pickle, pickles, pickling, pickled **NOUN** ① Pickle or pickles consists of vegetables or fruit preserved in vinegar or salt water ▷ **VERB** ② To pickle food is to preserve it in vinegar or salt water.

pickpocket, pickpockets **NOUN** a thief who steals from people's pockets or handbags.

picnic, picnics, picnicking, picnicked **NOUN** ① a meal eaten out of doors ▷ **VERB** ② People who are picnicking are having a picnic.

pictorial ADJECTIVE relating to or using pictures • *a pictorial record of the railway*.

picture, pictures, picturing, pictured **NOUN** ① a drawing, painting, or photograph of someone or something. ② If you have a picture of something in your mind, you have an idea or impression of it ③ IN PLURAL If you go to the pictures, you go to see a film at the cinema ▷ **VERB** ④ If someone is pictured in a newspaper or magazine,

▷ SPELLING NOTE: *The government licenSes Schnapps (licenSes)*

a photograph of them is printed in it.
❺ If you picture something, you think
of it and imagine it clearly • *That is
how I always picture him.*

picturesque [*Said pik-chur-**esk**]
ADJECTIVE A place that is
picturesque is very attractive and
unspoiled.

pie, pies **NOUN** a dish of meat,
vegetables, or fruit covered with
pastry.

piece, pieces, piecing, pieced **NOUN**
❶ a portion or part of something.
❷ something that has been written or
created, such as a work of art or a
musical composition. **❸** a coin • *a 50
pence piece.* ▷ **VERB** **❹** If you piece
together a number of things, you
gradually put them together to make
something complete.

**piecemeal ADVERB OR
ADJECTIVE** done gradually and at
irregular intervals • *a piecemeal
approach to career management.*

pie chart, pie charts **NOUN** (MATHS)
a circular graph divided into sections
to show the relative sizes of things.

pier, piers **NOUN** a large structure
which sticks out into the sea at a
seaside town, and which people can
walk along.

pierce, pierces, piercing, pierced
VERB If a sharp object pierces
something, it goes through it, making
a hole.
● **SIMILAR WORDS:** penetrate,
● puncture

piercing ADJECTIVE **❶** A piercing
sound is high-pitched and unpleasant.
❷ Someone with piercing eyes seems

to look at you very intensely.
● **SIMILAR WORDS:** **❶** penetrating,
● shrill

piety [*Said **pie**-it-tee*] **NOUN** Piety is
strong and devout religious belief or
behaviour.

pig, pigs **NOUN** a farm animal kept for
its meat. It has pinkish skin, short legs,
and a snout.

pigeon, pigeons **NOUN** a largish bird
with grey feathers, often seen in
towns.

pigeonhole, pigeonholes **NOUN**
one of the sections in a frame on a
wall where letters can be left.

piggyback, piggybacks **NOUN** If
you give someone a piggyback, you
carry them on your back, supporting
them under their knees.

piglet, piglets **NOUN** a young pig.

pigment, pigments **NOUN** a
substance that gives something a
particular colour. **pigmentation
NOUN**

pigsty, pigsties **NOUN** a hut with a
small enclosed area where pigs are
kept.

pigtail, pigtails **NOUN** a length of
plaited hair.

pike, pikes **NOUN** **❶** a large
freshwater fish of northern countries
with strong teeth. **❷** a medieval
weapon consisting of a pointed metal
blade attached to a long pole.

pilchard, pilchards **NOUN** a small
sea fish.

pile, piles, piling, piled **NOUN** **❶** a
quantity of things lying one on top of

a
b
c
d
e
f
g
h
i
j
k
l
m
n
o
p
q
r
s
t
u
v
w
x
y
z

▷ **SPELLING NOTE:** *have a pIEce of pIE (piece)*

another. ❷ the soft surface of a
carpet consisting of many threads
standing on end ❸ IN PLURAL Piles
are painful swellings that appear in
the veins inside or just outside a
person's anus ▷ VERB ❹ If you pile
things somewhere, you put them one
on top of the other.

pile-up, pile-ups NOUN INFORMAL a
road accident involving several
vehicles.

pilfer, pilfers, pilfering, pilfered VERB
Someone who pilfers steals small
things over a period of time.

pilgrim, pilgrims NOUN (RE) a
person who travels to a holy place for
religious reasons. **pilgrimage** NOUN

pill, pills NOUN ❶ a small, hard tablet
of medicine that you swallow. ❷ The
pill is a type of drug that women can
take regularly to prevent pregnancy.
● WORD HISTORY: from Latin *pilula*
● meaning 'little ball'

pillage, pillages, pillaging, pillaged
VERB If a group of people pillage a
place, they steal from it using
violence.

pillar, pillars NOUN ❶ a tall, narrow,
solid structure, usually supporting part
of a building. ❷ Someone who is
described as a pillar of a particular
group is an active and important
member of it • *a pillar of the Church*.

pillar box, pillar boxes NOUN a red
cylinder or box in which you post
letters.

pillory, pillories, pillorying, pilloried
VERB If someone is pilloried, they are
criticized severely by a lot of people.

pillow, pillows NOUN a rectangular

cushion which you rest your head on
when you are in bed.

pillowcase, pillowcases NOUN a
cover for a pillow which can be
removed and washed.

pilot, pilots, piloting, piloted NOUN
❶ a person who is trained to fly an
aircraft. ❷ a person who goes on
board ships to guide them through
local waters to a port ▷ VERB ❸ To
pilot something is to control its
movement or to guide it ▷ ADJECTIVE
❹ testing of a scheme or product,
done to see if it would be successful.

pimp, pimps NOUN a man who finds
clients for prostitutes and takes a large
part of their earnings.

pimple, pimples NOUN a small spot
on the skin. **pimply** ADJECTIVE

pin, pins, pinning, pinned NOUN ❶ a
thin, pointed piece of metal used to
fasten together things such as pieces
of fabric or paper ▷ VERB ❷ If you
pin something somewhere, you fasten
it there with a pin or a drawing pin.
❸ If someone pins you in a particular
position, they hold you there so that
you cannot move. ❹ If you try to pin
something down, you try to get or give
a clear and exact description of it or
statement about it.

PIN, PINs NOUN an abbreviation for
'personal identification number': a
number used by the holder of a cash
card or credit card.

pinafore, pinafores NOUN a dress
with no sleeves, worn over a blouse.

pincers PLURAL NOUN ❶ Pincers
are a tool used for gripping and pulling
things. They consist of two pieces of

▷ SPELLING NOTE: *plaice* the fish has a glittering 'EYE' (I) (*plaice*)

metal hinged in the middle. ❷ The pincers of a crab or lobster are its front claws.

pinch, pinches, pinching, pinched **VERB** ❶ If you pinch something, you squeeze it between your thumb and first finger. ❷ INFORMAL If someone pinches something, they steal it ▷ **NOUN** ❸ A pinch of something is the amount that you can hold between your thumb and first finger • *a pinch of salt*.

pinched ADJECTIVE If someone's face is pinched, it looks thin and pale.

pine, pines, pining, pined **NOUN** ❶ A pine or pine tree is an evergreen tree with very thin leaves ▷ **VERB** ❷ If you pine for something, you are sad because you cannot have it.

pineapple, pineapples **NOUN** a large, oval fruit with sweet, yellow flesh and a thick, lumpy brown skin.

ping-pong NOUN the same as table tennis.

pink, pinker, pinkest **ADJECTIVE** pale reddish-white.

pinnacle, pinnacles **NOUN** ❶ a tall pointed piece of stone or rock. ❷ The pinnacle of something is its best or highest level • *the pinnacle of his career*.

pinpoint, pinpoints, pinpointing, pinpointed **VERB** If you pinpoint something, you explain or discover exactly what or where it is.

pinstripe ADJECTIVE Pinstripe cloth has very narrow vertical stripes.

pint, pints **NOUN** a unit of liquid volume equal to one eighth of a gallon or about 0.568 litres.

pioneer, pioneers, pioneering, pioneered *[Said pie-on-ear]* **NOUN** ❶ Someone who is a pioneer in a particular activity is one of the first people to develop it ▷ **VERB** ❷ Someone who pioneers a new process or invention is the first person to develop it.

pious *[Said pie-uss]* **ADJECTIVE** very religious and moral.

pip, pips **NOUN** Pips are the hard seeds in a fruit.

pipe, pipes, piping, piped **NOUN** ❶ a long, hollow tube through which liquid or gas can flow. ❷ an object used for smoking tobacco. It consists of a small hollow bowl attached to a tube ▷ **VERB** ❸ To pipe a liquid or gas somewhere is to transfer it through a pipe.

pipeline, pipelines **NOUN** a large underground pipe that carries oil or gas over a long distance.

piper, pipers **NOUN** a person who plays the bagpipes.

piping NOUN Piping consists of pipes and tubes.

piranha, piranhas *[Said pir-rah-nah]* **NOUN** a small, fierce fish with sharp teeth.

pirate, pirates **NOUN** Pirates were sailors who attacked and robbed other ships.

pirouette, pirouettes *[Said pir-roo-et]* **NOUN** In ballet, a pirouette is a fast spinning step done on the toes.

Pisces *[Said pie-seez]* **NOUN** Pisces

a
b
c
d
e
f
g
h
i
j
k
l
m
n
o
p
q
r
s
t
u
v
w
x
y
z

▷ SPELLING NOTE: *I went to see (C) the doctor's new practiCe (practice)*

is the twelfth sign of the zodiac, represented by two fish. People born between February 19th and March 20th are born under this sign.
● **WORD HISTORY:** the plural of Latin *piscis* meaning 'a fish'

pistil, pistils **NOUN** in a flower, the pistil is the female reproductive part made up of the carpel or two or more carpels fused together.

pistol, pistols **NOUN** a small gun held in the hand.

piston, pistons **NOUN** a cylinder or disc that slides up and down inside a tube. Pistons make parts of engines move.

pit, pits **NOUN** ❶ a large hole in the ground. ❷ a small hollow in the surface of something. ❸ a coal mine.

pitch, pitches, pitching, pitched **NOUN** ❶ (PE) an area of ground marked out for playing a game such as football. ❷ (MUSIC) The pitch of a sound is how high or low it is. ❸ a black substance used in road tar and also for making boats and roofs waterproof ▷ **VERB** ❹ If you pitch something somewhere, you throw it with a lot of force. ❺ If you pitch something at a particular level of difficulty, you set it at that level • *Any film must be pitched at a level to suit its intended audience.* ❻ When you pitch a tent, you fix it in an upright position.

pitcher, pitchers **NOUN** a large jug.

pitfall, pitfalls **NOUN** The pitfalls of a situation are its difficulties or dangers.

pith **NOUN** the white substance between the outer skin and the flesh of an orange or lemon.

pitiful **ADJECTIVE** Someone or something that is pitiful is in such a sad or weak situation that you feel pity for them.

pittance **NOUN** a very small amount of money.

pitted **ADJECTIVE** covered in small hollows • *Nails often become pitted.*

pity, pities, pitying, pitied **VERB** ❶ If you pity someone, you feel very sorry for them ▷ **NOUN** ❷ Pity is a feeling of being sorry for someone. ❸ If you say that it is a pity about something, you are expressing your disappointment about it.

pivot, pivots, pivoting, pivoted **VERB** ❶ If something pivots, it balances or turns on a central point • *The keel pivots on a large stainless steel pin.* ▷ **NOUN** ❷ the central point on which something balances or turns. **pivotal** **ADJECTIVE**

pixie, pixies **NOUN** an imaginary little creature in fairy stories.

pizza, pizzas [Said *peet-sah*] **NOUN** a flat piece of dough covered with cheese, tomato, and other savoury food.

pizzicato [Said *pit-sik-kat-oh*] **ADVERB** (MUSIC) If a stringed instrument such as a violin is played pizzicato, it is played by plucking the strings.

placard, placards **NOUN** a large notice carried at a demonstration or displayed in a public place.

placate, placates, placating, placated **VERB** If you placate someone, you stop them feeling angry by doing something to please them.

▷ SPELLING NOTE: *You must practiSe your Ss (practise)*

place, places, placing, placed NOUN ❶ any point, building, or area. ❷ the position where something belongs • *She set the holder in its place on the table.* ❸ a space at a table set with cutlery where one person can eat. ❹ If you have a place in a group or at a college, you are a member or are accepted as a student. ❺ a particular point or stage in a sequence of things • *second place in the race.* ▷ PHRASE ❻ When something **takes place**, it happens ▷ VERB ❼ If you place something somewhere, you put it there. ❽ If you place an order, you order something.
● SIMILAR WORDS: ❶ location,
● site, spot

placebo, placebos [Said plas-*see-boh*] NOUN a substance given to a patient in place of a drug and from which, though it has no active ingredients, the patient may imagine they get some benefit.

placenta, placentas [Said plas-*sen-tah*] NOUN The placenta is the mass of veins and tissues in the womb of a pregnant woman or animal. It gives the foetus food and oxygen.

placid ADJECTIVE calm and not easily excited or upset. **placidly** ADVERB
● SIMILAR WORDS: even-tempered,
● unexcitable

plagiarism [Said play-*jer-rizm*] NOUN Plagiarism is copying someone else's work or ideas and pretending that it is your own. **plagiarist** NOUN **plagiarize** VERB
● WORD HISTORY: from Latin
● *plagiarus* meaning 'plunderer'

plague, plagues, plaguing, plagued [Said playg] NOUN ❶ Plague is a very infectious disease that kills large numbers of people. ❷ A plague of unpleasant things is a large number of them occurring at the same time • *a plague of rats.* ▷ VERB ❸ If problems plague you, they keep causing you trouble.

plaice NOUN an edible European flat fish.

plaid, plaids [Said plad] NOUN Plaid is woven material with a tartan design.

plain, plainer, plainest; plains ADJECTIVE ❶ very simple in style with no pattern or decoration • *plain walls.* ❷ obvious and easy to recognize or understand • *plain language.* ❸ A person who is plain is not at all beautiful or attractive ▷ ADVERB ❹ You can use 'plain' before a noun or adjective to emphasize it • *You were just plain stupid.* ▷ NOUN ❺ a large, flat area of land with very few trees. **plainly** ADVERB
● SIMILAR WORDS: ❶ bare, simple,
● unadorned

plaintiff, plaintiffs NOUN a person who has brought a court case against another person.

plait, plaits, plaiting, plaited VERB ❶ If you plait three lengths of hair or rope together, you twist them over each other in turn to make one thick length ▷ NOUN ❷ a length of hair that has been plaited.

plan, plans, planning, planned NOUN ❶ a method of achieving something that has been worked out beforehand. ❷ a detailed diagram or drawing of something that is to be made ▷ VERB

▷ SPELLING NOTE: *plaice the fish has a glittering 'EYE' (I) (pla*i*ce)*

A
B
C
D
E
F
G
H
I
J
K
L
M
N
O
P
Q
R
S
T
U
V
W
X
Y
Z

❸ If you plan something, you decide in detail what it is to be and how to do it. ❹ If you are planning to do something, you intend to do it • *They plan to marry in the summer.*
● **SIMILAR WORDS:** ❶ scheme,
● strategy ❸ devise, scheme, think
● out ❹ intend, mean, propose

plane, planes, planing, planed **NOUN**
❶ a vehicle with wings and engines that enable it to fly. ❷ a flat surface. ❸ You can refer to a particular level of something as a particular plane • *to take the rock and roll concert to a higher plane.* ❹ a tool with a flat bottom with a sharp blade in it. You move it over a piece of wood to remove thin pieces from the surface ▷ **VERB** ❺ If you plane a piece of wood, you smooth its surface with a plane.

planet, planets **NOUN** a round object in space which moves around the sun or a star and is lit by light from it.
planetary ADJECTIVE

plank, planks **NOUN** a long rectangular piece of wood.

plankton NOUN Plankton is a layer of tiny plants and animals that live just below the surface of a sea or lake.

plant, plants, planting, planted **NOUN**
❶ a living thing that grows in the earth and has stems, leaves, and roots. ❷ a factory or power station • *a giant bottling plant.* ▷ **VERB** ❸ When you plant a seed or plant, you put it into the ground. ❹ If you plant something somewhere, you put it there firmly or secretly.

plantation, plantations **NOUN** ❶ a large area of land where crops such as tea, cotton, or sugar are grown. ❷ a

large number of trees planted together.

plaque, plaques *[rhymes with **black**]*
NOUN ❶ a flat piece of metal which is fixed to a wall and has an inscription in memory of a famous person or event. ❷ Plaque is a substance which forms around your teeth and consists of bacteria, saliva, and food.

plasma *[Said plaz-mah]* **NOUN**
Plasma is the clear fluid part of blood.

plaster, plasters, plastering, plastered **NOUN** ❶ Plaster is a paste made of sand, lime, and water, which is used to form a smooth surface for inside walls and ceilings. ❷ a strip of sticky material with a small pad, used for covering cuts on your body
▷ **VERB** ❸ To plaster a wall is to cover it with a layer of plaster
▷ **PHRASE** ❹ If your arm or leg is **in plaster**, it has a plaster cast on it to protect a broken bone. **plasterer NOUN**

plastered ADJECTIVE ❶ If something is plastered to a surface, it is stuck there. ❷ If something is plastered with things, they are all over its surface.

plastic, plastics **NOUN** ❶ Plastic is a substance made by a chemical process that can be moulded when soft to make a wide range of objects
▷ **ADJECTIVE** ❷ made of plastic.

plastic surgery NOUN Plastic surgery is surgery to replace or repair damaged skin or to improve a person's appearance by changing the shape of their features.

plate, plates **NOUN** ❶ a flat dish used to hold food. ❷ a flat piece of metal or other hard material used for various purposes in machinery or building • *heavy steel plates used in shipbuilding.*

plateau, plateaus or plateaux [rhymes with **snow**] NOUN a large area of high and fairly flat land.

plated ADJECTIVE Metal that is plated is covered with a thin layer of silver or gold.

platform, platforms NOUN ❶ a raised structure on which someone or something can stand. ❷ the raised area in a railway station where passengers get on and off trains.

platinum NOUN Platinum is a valuable silver-coloured metal.

platitude, platitudes NOUN a statement made as if it were significant but which has become meaningless or boring because it has been used so many times before.

platonic ADJECTIVE A platonic relationship is simply one of friendship and does not involve sexual attraction.
● WORD HISTORY: from the name
● of the Greek philosopher Plato

platoon, platoons NOUN a small group of soldiers, commanded by a lieutenant.

platter, platters NOUN a large serving plate.

platypus, platypuses NOUN A platypus or duck-billed platypus is an Australian mammal which lives in rivers. It has brown fur, webbed feet, and a snout like a duck.
● WORD HISTORY: from Greek
● *platus* meaning 'flat' and *pous*
● meaning 'foot'

plaudits PLURAL NOUN FORMAL Plaudits are expressions of admiration.

plausible ADJECTIVE An explanation that is plausible seems likely to be true. **plausibility** NOUN

play, plays, playing, played VERB ❶ When children play, they take part in games or use toys. ❷ When you play a sport or match, you take part in it. ❸ If an actor plays a character in a play or film, he or she performs that role. ❹ If you play a musical instrument, you produce music from it. ❺ If you play a CD, you listen to it ▷ NOUN ❻ a piece of drama performed in the theatre or on television. **player** NOUN

playboy, playboys NOUN a rich man who spends his time enjoying himself.

playful ADJECTIVE ❶ friendly and light-hearted • *a playful kiss on the tip of his nose.* ❷ lively • *a playful puppy.* **playfully** ADVERB

playground, playgrounds NOUN a special area for children to play in.

playgroup, playgroups NOUN an informal kind of school for very young children where they learn by playing.

playing card, playing cards NOUN Playing cards are cards printed with numbers or pictures which are used to play various games.

playing field, playing fields NOUN an area of grass where people play sports.

playwright, playwrights NOUN (DRAMA AND ENGLISH) a person who writes plays.

plaza, plazas [Said **plah**-za] NOUN

an open square in a city.

plea, pleas **NOUN** ❶ an emotional request • *a plea for help.* ❷ In a court of law, someone's plea is their statement that they are guilty or not guilty.

plead, pleads, pleading, pleaded **VERB** ❶ If you plead with someone, you ask them in an intense emotional way to do something. ❷ When a person pleads guilty or not guilty, they state in court that they are guilty or not guilty of a crime.

pleasant ADJECTIVE ❶ enjoyable or attractive. ❷ friendly or charming. **pleasantly ADVERB**
● **SIMILAR WORDS:** agreeable, nice, pleasing

please, pleases, pleasing, pleased ❶ You say please when you are asking someone politely to do something **VERB** ❷ If something pleases you, it makes you feel happy and satisfied.
● **SIMILAR WORDS:** ❷ delight, gladden, satisfy

pleased ADJECTIVE happy or satisfied.

pleasing ADJECTIVE attractive, satisfying, or enjoyable • *a pleasing appearance.*

pleasure, pleasures **NOUN** ❶ Pleasure is a feeling of happiness, satisfaction, or enjoyment. ❷ an activity that you enjoy. **pleasurable ADJECTIVE**

pleat, pleats **NOUN** a permanent fold in fabric made by folding one part over another.

plebiscite, plebiscites [*Said pleb-iss-ite*] **NOUN** FORMAL a vote on

a matter of national importance in which all the voters in a country can take part.
● **WORD HISTORY:** from Latin *plebiscitum* meaning 'decree of the people'

pledge, pledges, pledging, pledged **NOUN** ❶ a solemn promise ▷ **VERB** ❷ If you pledge something, you promise that you will do it or give it.

plentiful ADJECTIVE existing in large numbers or amounts and readily available • *Fruit and vegetables were plentiful.* **plentifully ADVERB**

plenty NOUN If there is plenty of something, there is a lot of it.

plethora [*Said pleth-thor-ah*] **NOUN** A plethora of something is an amount that is greater than you need • *a plethora of styles.*

pleurisy [*Said ploor-ris-see*] **NOUN** Pleurisy is a serious illness in which a person's lungs become inflamed and breathing is difficult.

pliable ADJECTIVE ❶ If something is pliable, you can bend it without breaking it. ❷ Someone who is pliable can be easily influenced or controlled.
● **SIMILAR WORDS:** ❶ bendy, flexible, supple

pliers PLURAL NOUN Pliers are a small tool with metal jaws for holding small objects and bending wire.

plight NOUN Someone's plight is the very difficult or dangerous situation that they are in • *the plight of the refugees.*

plinth, plinths **NOUN** a block of stone on which a statue or pillar stands.

▷ SPELLING NOTE: *the QUeen stood on the QUay (quay)*

plod, plods, plodding, plodded **VERB**
If you plod somewhere, you walk there slowly and heavily.

plonk, plonks, plonking, plonked **VERB** If you plonk something down, you put it down heavily and carelessly.

plop, plops, plopping, plopped **NOUN**
❶ a gentle sound made by something light dropping into a liquid ▷ **VERB**
❷ If something plops into a liquid, it drops into it with a gentle sound.

plot, plots, plotting, plotted **NOUN**
❶ a secret plan made by a group of people. ❷ (ENGLISH) The plot of a novel or play is the story. ❸ a small piece of land ▷ **VERB** ❹ If people plot to do something, they plan it secretly
• *His family is plotting to disinherit him.*
❺ If someone plots the course of a plane or ship on a map, or plots a graph, they mark the points in the correct places.
● **SIMILAR WORDS:** ❶ conspiracy,
● scheme ❹ conspire, plan, scheme

plough, ploughs, ploughing, ploughed *[rhymes with **cow**]* **NOUN**
❶ a large farming tool that is pulled across a field to turn the soil over before planting seeds ▷ **VERB**
❷ When someone ploughs land, they use a plough to turn over the soil.

ploy, ploys **NOUN** a clever plan or way of behaving in order to get something that you want.

pluck, plucks, plucking, plucked **VERB** ❶ To pluck a fruit or flower is to remove it with a sharp pull. ❷ To pluck a chicken or other dead bird means to pull its feathers out before cooking it. ❸ When you pluck a stringed instrument, you pull the

strings and let them go ▷ **NOUN**
❹ Pluck is courage. **plucky ADJECTIVE**

plug, plugs, plugging, plugged **NOUN**
❶ a plastic object with metal prongs that can be pushed into a socket to connect an appliance to the electricity supply. ❷ a disc of rubber or metal with which you block up the hole in a sink or bath ▷ **VERB** ❸ If you plug a hole, you block it with something.

plum, plums **NOUN** a small fruit with a smooth red or yellow skin and a large stone in the middle.

plumage *[Said **ploom**-mage]* **NOUN**
A bird's plumage is its feathers.

plumber, plumbers **NOUN** a person who connects and repairs water pipes.
● **WORD HISTORY:** from Old French
● *plommier* meaning 'worker in lead'

plumbing NOUN The plumbing in a building is the system of water pipes, sinks, and toilets.

plume, plumes **NOUN** a large, brightly coloured feather.

plummet, plummets, plummeting, plummeted **VERB** If something plummets, it falls very quickly • *Sales have plummeted.*

plump, plumper, plumpest **ADJECTIVE** rather fat • *a small plump baby.*
● **SIMILAR WORDS:** chubby, podgy,
● tubby

plunder, plunders, plundering, plundered **VERB** If someone plunders a place, they steal things from it.

plunge, plunges, plunging, plunged **VERB** ❶ If something plunges, it falls

a
b
c
d
e
f
g
h
i
j
k
l
m
n
o
p
q
r
s
t
u
v
w
x
y
z

plunge | 642

WHAT IS A PLURAL?

Most nouns can exist in either the singular or plural.

The **singular** form of the noun is used to mean only one instance of a thing. This is the main form given in the dictionary:
one book
a raven

The **plural** form of the noun is used to mean more than one instance of a thing. The plural form is given in the dictionary in smaller type after the main form:
two books
some ravens

The plural form of the noun is usually formed by adding the letter -s to the singular:
book → books
raven → ravens

Words that end in -s, -z, -x, -ch, or -sh in the singular are made plural by adding the letters -es:
cross → crosses
box → boxes

Words that end in a consonant + -y in the singular are made plural by removing the -y and adding -ies:
pony → ponies
party → parties

Words that end in -ife in the singular are made plural by removing the -fe and adding -ves:
knife → knives
life → lives

Some words that end in -f in the singular are made plural by removing the -f and adding -ves. Other words

that end in -f in the singular are made plural by simply adding -s:
hoof → hooves
roof → roofs

BE CAREFUL not to use an apostrophe (') when you add an -s to make a plural.

IRREGULAR PLURALS

Some words that have come to English from a foreign language have plurals that do not end in -s.

Some words that came to English from French have plurals ending in -x:
bureau → bureaux
gateau → gateaux

Some words that came into English from Italian have plurals ending in -i:
paparazzo → paparazzi
graffito → graffiti

Some words that came into English from Hebrew have plurals ending in -im:
cherub → cherubim
kibbutz → kibbutzim

Some words that came into English from Latin have plurals ending in -i, -a, or -ae:
cactus → cacti
medium → media
formula → formulae

Some words that came into English from Ancient Greek have plurals ending in -a:
phenomenon → phenomena
criterion → criteria

The plural forms of a few words are not formed according to any regular

▷ SPELLING NOTE: *there's SAND in my SANDwich (sandwich)*

rule. However, there are very few words like this. Here are some of the most common ones:
child, children; deer, deer; fish, fish or

fishes; foot, feet; man, men; mouse, mice; ox, oxen; sheep, sheep; woman, women.

suddenly. ❷ If you plunge an object into something, you push it in quickly. ❸ If you plunge into an activity or state, you suddenly become involved in it or affected by it • *The United States had just plunged into the war.*
▷ **NOUN** ❹ a sudden fall.
● **SIMILAR WORDS:** ❶ dive, drop, ❶ fall, plummet

Plunket Society NOUN In New Zealand, the Plunket Society was an organization for the care of mothers and babies. It is now called the Royal New Zealand Society for the Health of Women and Children.

pluperfect NOUN (ENGLISH) In grammar, the pluperfect is the tense of a verb used to describe actions that were completed before another event in the past happened. In English the pluperfect is formed using 'had' followed by the past participle, as in 'She had eaten them before I arrived'.

plural, plurals **NOUN** (ENGLISH) the form of a word that is used to refer to two or more people or things, for example the plural of 'chair' is 'chairs', and the plural of 'mouse' is 'mice'.
▶ SEE GRAMMAR BOX ON PAGES 642–43

pluralism NOUN Pluralism is the belief that it is possible for different social and religious groups to live together peacefully while keeping their own beliefs and traditions.
pluralist ADJECTIVE OR NOUN

plural noun, plural nouns **NOUN**

In this dictionary, 'plural noun' is the name given to a noun that is normally used only in the plural, for example 'scissors' or 'police'.

plus ❶ You use 'plus' to show that one number is being added to another • *Two plus two equals four.* **ADJECTIVE** ❷ slightly more than the number mentioned • *a career of 25 years plus.*
▷ **PREPOSITION** ❸ You can use 'plus' when you mention an additional item • *He wrote a history of Scotland plus a history of British literature.*
● **USAGE NOTE:** Although you can use *plus* to mean 'additionally' in spoken language, you should avoid it in written work: *plus, you could win a holiday in Florida*

plush ADJECTIVE very expensive and smart • *a plush hotel.*

Pluto NOUN Pluto is the smallest planet in the solar system and the furthest from the sun.

ply, plies, plying, plied **VERB** ❶ If you ply someone with things or questions, you keep giving them things or asking them questions. ❷ To ply a trade is to do a particular job as your work
▷ **NOUN** ❸ Ply is the thickness of wool or thread, measured by the number of strands it is made from.

plywood NOUN Plywood is wooden board made from several thin sheets of wood glued together under pressure.

p.m. used to specify times between 12

▷ SPELLING NOTE: *On WEDNESday Wayne WED NESta (Wednesday)*

A
B
C
D
E
F
G
H
I
J
K
L
M
N
O
P
Q
R
S
T
U
V
W
X
Y
Z

noon and 12 midnight, eg *He went to bed at 9 p.m.* It is an abbreviation for the Latin phrase 'post meridiem', which means 'after noon'.

pneumatic [Said new-**mat**-ik] **ADJECTIVE** (D & T) operated by or filled with compressed air • *a pneumatic drill.*

● **WORD HISTORY:** from Latin
● *pneumaticus* meaning 'of air or
● wind'

pneumonia [Said new-**moan**-ee-ah] **NOUN** Pneumonia is a serious disease which affects a person's lungs and makes breathing difficult.

poach, poaches, poaching, poached **VERB** ❶ If someone poaches animals from someone else's land, they illegally catch the animals for food. ❷ When you poach food, you cook it gently in hot liquid. **poacher NOUN**

pocket, pockets **NOUN** ❶ a small pouch that forms part of a piece of clothing. ❷ A pocket of something is a small area of it • *There are still pockets of resistance.*

pocket money NOUN Pocket money is an amount of money given regularly to children by their parents.

pod, pods **NOUN** a long narrow seed container that grows on plants such as peas or beans.

poddy, poddies **NOUN** In Australian English, a calf or lamb that is being fed by hand.

podium, podiums **NOUN** a small platform, often one on which someone stands to make a speech.

poem, poems **NOUN** a piece of writing in which the words are

arranged in short rhythmic lines, often with a rhyme.

poet, poets **NOUN** a person who writes poems.

poetic ADJECTIVE ❶ very beautiful and expressive • *a pure and poetic love.* ❷ relating to poetry. **poetically ADVERB**

poetic licence NOUN (ENGLISH) If a writer or poet uses poetic licence, they change the facts or the usual rules to make what they are writing more powerful or interesting.

poetry NOUN Poetry is poems, considered as a form of literature.

poignant [Said **poyn**-yant] **ADJECTIVE** Something that is poignant has a strong emotional effect on you, often making you feel sad • *a moving and poignant moment.* **poignancy NOUN**

point, points, pointing, pointed **NOUN** ❶ an opinion or fact expressed by someone • *You've made a good point.* ❷ a quality • *Tact was never her strong point.* ❸ the purpose or meaning something has • *He completely missed the point in most of his argument.* ❹ a position or time • *At some point during the party, a fight erupted.* ❺ a single mark in a competition. ❻ the thin, sharp end of something such as a needle or knife. ❼ The points of a compass are the 32 directions indicated on it. ❽ The decimal point in a number is the dot separating the whole number from the fraction. ❾ On a railway track, the points are the levers and rails which enable a train to move from one track to another ▷ **VERB** ❿ If you point at something, you stick out your finger to show where it is. **11** If something points in a particular direction, it faces that way.

point-blank ADJECTIVE
1 Something that is shot at point-blank range is shot with a gun held very close to it ▷ ADVERB **2** If you say something point-blank, you say it directly without explanation or apology.

pointed ADJECTIVE **1** A pointed object has a thin, sharp end. **2** Pointed comments express criticism. **pointedly** ADVERB

pointer, pointers NOUN a piece of information which helps you to understand something • *Here are a few pointers to help you make a choice.*

pointless ADJECTIVE Something that is pointless has no purpose. **pointlessly** ADVERB

point of view, points of view NOUN Your point of view is your opinion about something or your attitude towards it.

poise NOUN Someone who has poise is calm and dignified.

poised ADJECTIVE If you are poised to do something, you are ready to do it at any moment.

poison, poisons, poisoning, poisoned NOUN **1** Poison is a substance that can kill people or animals if they swallow it or absorb it ▷ VERB **2** To poison someone is to try to kill them with poison.

poisonous ADJECTIVE containing something that causes death or illness.

poke, pokes, poking, poked VERB
1 If you poke someone or something, you push at them quickly with your finger or a sharp object. **2** Something that pokes out of another thing appears from underneath or behind it • *roots poking out of the earth.* ▷ NOUN **3** a sharp jab or prod.
● SIMILAR WORDS: **1** dig, jab, ● prod

poker, pokers NOUN **1** Poker is a card game in which the players make bets on the cards dealt to them. **2** a long metal rod used for moving coals or logs in a fire.

polar ADJECTIVE relating to the area around the North and South Poles.

polar bear, polar bears NOUN a large white bear which lives in the area around the North Pole.

polarize, polarizes, polarizing, polarized; *also spelt* **polarise** VERB If groups polarize, they form opposite opinions from each other. **polarization** NOUN

pole, poles NOUN **1** a long rounded piece of wood or metal. **2** The earth's poles are the two opposite ends of its axis • *the North Pole.*

Pole, Poles NOUN someone who comes from Poland.

pole vault NOUN The pole vault is an athletics event in which contestants jump over a high bar using a long flexible pole to lift themselves into the air.

police, polices, policing, policed PLURAL NOUN **1** The police are the people who are officially responsible for making sure that people obey the

▷ SPELLING NOTE: *Elaine and Emily shout EE when they mEEt to grEEt each other (-ee-)*

law ▷ **VERB** ❷ To police an area is to keep law and order there by means of the police or an armed force.

policeman, policemen **NOUN** a man who is a member of a police force. **policewoman NOUN**

policy, policies **NOUN** ❶ a set of plans, especially in politics or business • *the new economic policy.* ❷ An insurance policy is a document which shows an agreement made with an insurance company.

polio NOUN Polio is an infectious disease that is caused by a virus and often results in paralysis. Polio is short for 'poliomyelitis'.

polish, polishes, polishing, polished **VERB** ❶ If you polish something, you put polish on it or rub it with a cloth to make it shine. ❷ If you polish a skill or technique you have, you work on it in order to improve it ▷ **NOUN** ❸ Polish is a substance that you put on an object to clean it and make it shine • *shoe polish.* ❹ Something that has polish is elegant and of good quality. **polished ADJECTIVE**

Polish [*Said* **pole**-*ish*] **ADJECTIVE** ❶ belonging or relating to Poland ▷ **NOUN** ❷ Polish is the main language spoken in Poland.

polite ADJECTIVE ❶ Someone who is polite has good manners and behaves considerately towards other people. ❷ Polite society is cultivated and refined. **politely ADVERB**
● **SIMILAR WORDS:** civil,
● courteous, well-mannered

politeness NOUN the quality of having good manners and behaving considerately.

political ADJECTIVE (GEOGRAPHY) ❶ relating to the state, government, or public administration. ❷ relating to or interested in politics. **politically ADVERB**

politically correct ADJECTIVE careful not to offend or designed not to offend minority or disadvantaged groups.

politician, politicians **NOUN** a person involved in the government of a country.

politics NOUN (HISTORY) Politics is the activity and planning concerned with achieving power and control in a country or organization.

polka, polkas **NOUN** a fast dance in which couples dance together in circles around the room.

poll, polls, polling, polled **NOUN** ❶ a survey in which people are asked their opinions about something ❷ IN PLURAL A political election can be referred to as the polls. ▷ **VERB** ❸ If you are polled on something, you are asked your opinion about it as part of a survey.

pollen NOUN Pollen is a fine yellow powder produced by flowers in order to fertilize other flowers of the same species.

pollinate, pollinates, pollinating, pollinated **VERB** To pollinate a plant is to fertilize it with pollen. **pollination NOUN**

pollutant, pollutants **NOUN** a substance that causes pollution.

pollute, pollutes, polluting, polluted **VERB** To pollute water or air is to make it dirty and dangerous to use or

▷ SPELLING NOTE: *'i' before 'e' except after 'c'*

live in. **polluted** ADJECTIVE
  ● **SIMILAR WORDS:** contaminate,
  ● foul, poison

pollution NOUN (GEOGRAPHY)
Pollution of the environment happens
when dirty or dangerous substances
get into the air, water, or soil.

polo NOUN Polo is a game played
between two teams of players on
horseback. The players use wooden
hammers with long handles to hit a
ball.

polo-necked ADJECTIVE A
polo-necked jumper has a deep fold of
material at the neck.

polyester NOUN (D & T) a
man-made fibre, used especially to
make clothes.

polygamy [Said pol-**lig**-gam-ee]
NOUN Polygamy is having more than
one wife at the same time.
polygamous ADJECTIVE

polygon, polygons NOUN (MATHS)
any two-dimensional shape whose
sides are all straight; a **regular
polygon** has straight sides of the
same length.

polyhedron, polyhedrons or
polyhedra NOUN (MATHS) A
polyhedron is any three-dimensional
shape whose edges are all straight and
whose sides are all flat.

polymer, polymers NOUN (SCIENCE)
A polymer is a chemical compound
with large molecules made up of
many simple repeated units.

polystyrene NOUN Polystyrene is
a very light plastic, used especially as
insulating material or to make
containers.

polythene NOUN Polythene is a
type of plastic that is used to make
thin sheets or bags.

polyunsaturated ADJECTIVE
Polyunsaturated oils and margarines
are made mainly from vegetable fats
and are considered to be healthier
than saturated oils. **polyunsaturate**
NOUN

pomegranate, pomegranates
NOUN a round fruit with a thick
reddish skin. It contains a lot of small
seeds.
  ● **WORD HISTORY:** from Latin
  ● *pomum granatum* meaning 'apple
  ● full of seeds'

pomp NOUN Pomp is the use of
ceremony, fine clothes, and
decorations on special occasions • *Sir
Patrick was buried with much pomp.*

pompous ADJECTIVE behaving in a
way that is too serious and self-
important. **pomposity** NOUN

pond, ponds NOUN a small, usually
man-made area of water.

ponder, ponders, pondering,
pondered VERB If you ponder, you
think about something deeply • *He
was pondering the problem when
Phillipson drove up.*
  ● **SIMILAR WORDS:** consider, mull
  ● over, think

ponderous ADJECTIVE dull, slow,
and serious • *the ponderous
commentary.*

pong, pongs NOUN INFORMAL an
unpleasant smell.

pontiff, pontiffs NOUN FORMAL The
pontiff is the Pope.

▷ SPELLING NOTE: *King IAn went to ParlIAment in a carrIAge for his marrIAge (-ia-)*

pony, ponies **NOUN** a small horse.

ponytail, ponytails **NOUN** a hairstyle in which long hair is tied at the back of the head and hangs down like a tail.

pony trekking **NOUN** Pony trekking is a leisure activity in which people ride across country on ponies.

poodle, poodles **NOUN** a type of dog with curly hair.

pool, pools, pooling, pooled **NOUN**
❶ a small area of still water. **❷** Pool is a game in which players try to hit coloured balls into pockets around the table using long sticks called cues.
❸ A pool of people, money, or things is a group or collection used or shared by several people **❹** IN PLURAL The pools are a competition in which people try to guess the results of football matches. ▷ **VERB** **❺** If people pool their resources, they gather together the things they have so that they can be shared or used by all of them.

poor, poorer, poorest **ADJECTIVE**
❶ Poor people have very little money and few possessions. **❷** Poor places are inhabited by people with little money and show signs of neglect.
❸ You use 'poor' to show sympathy • *Poor you!* **❹** 'Poor' also means of a low quality or standard • *a poor performance.*
  ● **SIMILAR WORDS:**
  ● **❶** impoverished, penniless, poverty-stricken

poorly **ADJECTIVE** **❶** feeling unwell or ill ▷ **ADVERB** **❷** badly • *a poorly planned operation.*

pop, pops, popping, popped **NOUN**

❶ Pop is modern music played and enjoyed especially by young people.
❷ You can refer to fizzy, nonalcoholic drinks as pop. **❸** a short, sharp sound ▷ **VERB** **❹** If something pops, it makes a sudden sharp sound. **❺** If you pop something somewhere, you put it there quickly • *I'd just popped the pie in the oven.* **❻** If you pop somewhere, you go there quickly • *His mother popped out to buy him an ice cream.*

popcorn **NOUN** Popcorn is a snack consisting of grains of maize heated until they puff up and burst.

Pope, Popes **NOUN** The Pope is the head of the Roman Catholic Church.
  ● **WORD HISTORY:** from Latin *Papa*
  ● meaning 'bishop' or 'father'

poplar, poplars **NOUN** a type of tall thin tree.

poppy, poppies **NOUN** a plant with a large red flower on a hairy stem.

populace **NOUN** FORMAL The populace of a country is its people.

popular **ADJECTIVE** **❶** liked or approved of by a lot of people.
❷ involving or intended for ordinary people • *the popular press.* **popularly** **ADVERB** **popularity** **NOUN** **popularize** **VERB**
  ● **SIMILAR WORDS:** **❶** fashionable,
  ● well-liked

populate, populates, populating, populated **VERB** The people or animals that populate an area live there.

population, populations **NOUN** The population of a place is the people who live there, or the number of people living there.

population density NOUN
(GEOGRAPHY) a measure of the number of people living in a given area of land, usually expressed as the number of people per square kilometre.

population pyramid NOUN
(GEOGRAPHY) a pyramid-shaped diagram that shows the breakdown of a population by age. The youngest are represented by a rectangle at the base and the oldest by one at the top.

porcelain NOUN Porcelain is a delicate, hard material used to make crockery and ornaments.

porch, porches NOUN a covered area at the entrance to a building.

porcupine, porcupines NOUN a large rodent with long spines covering its body.
● **WORD HISTORY:** from Old French
● *porc d'espins* meaning 'pig with
● spines'

pore, pores, poring, pored NOUN
❶ The pores in your skin or on the surface of a plant are very small holes which allow moisture to pass through ▷ VERB ❷ If you pore over something, you study it carefully.

pork NOUN Pork is meat from a pig which has not been salted or smoked.

pornography NOUN Pornography refers to magazines and films that are designed to cause sexual excitement by showing naked people and sexual acts. **pornographic** ADJECTIVE
● **WORD HISTORY:** from Greek
● *pornos* meaning 'prostitute' and
● *graphein* meaning 'to write'

porous ADJECTIVE containing many holes through which water and air can pass • *The porous material that the jacket is made of cuts down sweating.*

porpoise, porpoises *[Said por-pus]*
NOUN a sea mammal related to the dolphin.
● **WORD HISTORY:** from Latin *porcus*
● meaning 'pig' and *piscis* meaning
● 'fish'

porridge NOUN Porridge is a thick, sticky food made from oats cooked in water or milk.

port, ports NOUN ❶ a town or area which has a harbour or docks. ❷ Port is a kind of strong, sweet red wine ▷ ADJECTIVE ❸ The port side of a ship is the left side when you are facing the front.

-port SUFFIX '-port' comes at the end of words that have something to do with 'carrying' in their meaning • *transport.*
● **WORD HISTORY:** from Latin
● *portāre* meaning 'to carry'

portable ADJECTIVE designed to be easily carried • *a portable television* • *a portable barbecue.*

porter, porters NOUN ❶ a person whose job is to be in charge of the entrance of a building, greeting and directing visitors. ❷ A porter in a railway station or hospital is a person whose job is to carry or move things.

portfolio, portfolios NOUN ❶ a thin, flat case for carrying papers. ❷ A portfolio is also a group of selected duties, investments, or items of artwork • *the education portfolio* • *Choose your share portfolio wisely.*

a
b
c
d
e
f
g
h
i
j
k
l
m
n
o
p
q
r
s
t
u
v
w
x
y
z

▷ SPELLING NOTE: *LEt's measure the angLE (angle)*

● **WORD HISTORY:** from Italian
portafoglio meaning 'carrier for
papers'

porthole, portholes **NOUN** a small
window in the side of a ship or aircraft.

portion, portions **NOUN** a part or
amount of something • *a portion of
fresh fruit.*
● **SIMILAR WORDS:** bit, part, piece

portrait, portraits **NOUN** (ART) a
picture or photograph of someone.

portray, portrays, portraying,
portrayed **VERB** When an actor, artist,
or writer portrays someone or
something, they represent or describe
them. **portrayal NOUN**

Portuguese [Said por-tyoo-**geez**]
ADJECTIVE ❶ belonging or relating
to Portugal ▷ **NOUN** ❷ someone
who comes from Portugal.
❸ Portuguese is the main language
spoken in Portugal and Brazil.

pose, poses, posing, posed **VERB**
❶ If something poses a problem, it is
the cause of the problem. ❷ If you
pose a question, you ask it. ❸ If you
pose as someone else, you pretend to
be that person in order to deceive
people ▷ **NOUN** ❹ a way of standing,
sitting, or lying • *Mr Clark assumes a
pose for the photographer.*
● **SIMILAR WORDS:** ❹ attitude,
posture

poser, posers **NOUN** ❶ someone
who behaves or dresses in an
exaggerated way in order to impress
people. ❷ a difficult problem.

posh, posher, poshest **ADJECTIVE**
❶ INFORMAL smart, fashionable, and
expensive • *a posh restaurant.*

❷ upper-class • *the man with the posh
voice.*

position, positions, positioning,
positioned **NOUN** ❶ (DRAMA) The
position of someone or something is
the place where they are or ought to
be • *Would the cast take their positions,
please.* ❷ When someone or
something is in a particular position,
they are sitting or lying in that way • *I
raised myself to a sitting position.* ❸ a
job or post in an organization. ❹ The
position that you are in at a particular
time is the situation that you are in
• *This puts the president in a difficult
position.* ▷ **VERB** ❺ To position
something somewhere is to put it
there • *Llewelyn positioned a cushion
behind Joanna's back.*

positive ADJECTIVE ❶ completely
sure about something • *I was positive
he'd known about that money.*
❷ confident and hopeful • *I felt very
positive about everything.* ❸ showing
approval or encouragement • *I
anticipate a positive response.*
❹ providing definite proof of the truth
or identity of something • *positive
evidence.* ❺ (MATHS) A positive
number is greater than zero.
❻ (SCIENCE) In physics, a positive
electric charge has an opposite charge
to that of an electron. **positively
ADVERB**
● **SIMILAR WORDS:** ❹ absolute,
certain, definite

possess, possesses, possessing,
possessed **VERB** ❶ If you possess a
particular quality, you have it. ❷ If
you possess something, you own it.
❸ If a feeling or belief possesses you,
it strongly influences you • *Absolute
terror possessed her.* **possessor NOUN**

▷ SPELLING NOTE: *A Rude Idiot Thought He Might Eat Toffee In Church* (<u>arithmetic</u>)

WHAT IS THE POSSESSIVE?

The possessive case is formed by adding an apostrophe (') and the letter *s* to the dictionary form of the word.

The **possessive** is used when a noun indicates a person or thing that owns another person or thing:
*The **cat's** fur was wet.*
*The **doctor's** cat was called Joey.*

If the noun is plural and already ends in *-s*, the possessive is formed by simply adding an apostrophe:
*The vet often trims **cats'** claws.*

***Doctors'** surgeries make me nervous.*

The possessive can also be shown by using the word *of* in front of the noun. This is usually used when you are talking about something that is not alive or cannot be touched:
*We climbed to the top **of the hill**.*
*He is a master **of disguise**.*

When a possessive is not followed by another noun, it refers to the place where that person lives or works:
*I am going to stay at my **aunt's**.*
*I bought a loaf at the **baker's**.*

possession, possessions NOUN
❶ If something is in your possession or if you are in possession of it, you have it. ❷ Your possessions are the things that you own or that you have with you.
● SIMILAR WORDS: ❷ belongings,
● property

possessive ADJECTIVE ❶ A person who is possessive about someone or something wants to keep them to themselves ▷ NOUN ❷ In grammar, the possessive is the form of a noun or pronoun used to show possession • *my car* • *That's hers.*
▶ SEE GRAMMAR BOX ABOVE

possibility, possibilities NOUN something that might be true or might happen • *the possibility of a ban.*
● SIMILAR WORDS: chance,
● likelihood, probability

possible ADJECTIVE ❶ likely to happen or able to be done. ❷ likely or capable of being true or correct. **possibly** ADVERB

● SIMILAR WORDS: ❶ feasible,
● practicable

possum, possums NOUN In Australian and New Zealand English, a possum is a phalanger, a marsupial with thick fur and a long tail.

post, posts, posting, posted NOUN
❶ The post is the system by which letters and parcels are collected and delivered. ❷ a job or official position in an organization. ❸ a strong upright pole fixed into the ground • *They are tied to a post.* ▷ VERB ❹ If you post a letter, you send it to someone by putting it into a postbox. ❺ If you are posted somewhere, you are sent by your employers to work there. **postal** ADJECTIVE

post- PREFIX after a particular time or event • *his postwar career.*
● WORD HISTORY: from Latin *post*
● meaning 'after'

postage NOUN Postage is the money that you pay to send letters and parcels by post.

▷ SPELLING NOTE: *Beautiful Elephants Are Usually Tiny (**beautiful**)*

A
B
C
D
E
F
G
H
I
J
K
L
M
N
O
P
Q
R
S
T
U
V
W
X
Y
Z

postal order, postal orders **NOUN** a piece of paper representing a sum of money which you can buy at a post office.

postbox, postboxes **NOUN** a metal box with a hole in it which you put letters into for collection by the postman.

postcard, postcards **NOUN** a card, often with a picture on one side, which you write on and send without an envelope.

postcode, postcodes **NOUN** a short sequence of letters and numbers at the end of an address which helps the post office to sort the mail.

poster, posters **NOUN** a large notice or picture that is stuck on a wall as an advertisement or for decoration.

posterior, posteriors **NOUN** HUMOROUS A person's posterior is their bottom.

posterity NOUN FORMAL You can refer to the future and the people who will be alive then as posterity • *to record the voyage for posterity.*
● **WORD HISTORY:** from Latin
● *posteritas* meaning 'future
● generations'

posthumous [Said **poss**-tyum-uss] **ADJECTIVE** happening or awarded after a person's death • *a posthumous medal.* **posthumously ADVERB**

postman, postmen **NOUN** someone who collects and delivers letters and parcels sent by post.

postmortem, postmortems **NOUN** A postmortem is a medical examination of a dead body to find out how the person died.

post office, post offices **NOUN**
❶ The Post Office is the national organization responsible for postal services. ❷ a building where you can buy stamps and post letters.

postpone, postpones, postponing, postponed **VERB** If you postpone an event, you arrange for it to take place at a later time than was originally planned. **postponement NOUN**
● **SIMILAR WORDS:** put off, shelve

posture, postures **NOUN** Your posture is the position or manner in which you hold your body.

posy, posies **NOUN** a small bunch of flowers.

pot, pots **NOUN** a deep round container; also used to refer to its contents.

potassium NOUN (SCIENCE) Potassium is a soft silver-coloured element used in making soap, detergents, fertilizers, and glass. Its atomic number is 19 and its symbol is K.

potassium nitrate NOUN a white chemical compound used to make gunpowder, fireworks and fertilizers. Potassium nitrate is also called saltpetre.

potato, potatoes **NOUN** a white vegetable that has a brown or red skin and grows underground.

potent ADJECTIVE effective or powerful • *a potent cocktail.* **potency NOUN**

potential ADJECTIVE ❶ capable of becoming the thing mentioned • *potential customers* • *potential sources of finance.* ▷ **NOUN** ❷ Your potential

▷ SPELLING NOTE: *Betty Eats Cakes And Uses Seven Eggs (because)*

is your ability to achieve success in the future. **potentially** ADVERB

potential energy NOUN
Potential energy is the energy stored in something.

pothole, potholes NOUN ❶ a hole in the surface of a road caused by bad weather or traffic. ❷ an underground cavern.

potion, potions NOUN a drink containing medicine, poison, or supposed magical powers.

potted ADJECTIVE Potted meat or fish is cooked and put into a small sealed container to preserve it.

potter, potters, pottering, pottered NOUN ❶ a person who makes pottery ▷ VERB ❷ If you potter about, you pass the time doing pleasant, unimportant things.

pottery NOUN ❶ Pottery is pots, dishes, and other items made from clay and fired in a kiln. ❷ Pottery is also the craft of making pottery.

potty, potties; pottier, pottiest NOUN ❶ a bowl which a small child can sit on and use instead of a toilet ▷ ADJECTIVE ❷ INFORMAL crazy or foolish.

pouch, pouches NOUN ❶ a small, soft container with a fold-over top • *a tobacco pouch.* ❷ Animals like kangaroos have a pouch, which is a pocket of skin in which they carry their young.

poultry NOUN Chickens, turkeys, and other birds kept for their meat or eggs are referred to as poultry.

pounce, pounces, pouncing, pounced VERB If an animal or person pounces on something, they leap and grab it.

pound, pounds, pounding, pounded NOUN ❶ The pound is the main unit of currency in Britain and in some other countries. ❷ a unit of weight equal to 16 ounces or about 0.454 kilograms ▷ VERB ❸ If you pound something, you hit it repeatedly with your fist • *Someone was pounding on the door.* ❹ If you pound a substance, you crush it into a powder or paste • *Wooden mallets were used to pound the meat.* ❺ If your heart is pounding, it is beating very strongly and quickly. ❻ If you pound somewhere, you run there with heavy noisy steps.

pour, pours, pouring, poured VERB ❶ If you pour a liquid out of a container, you make it flow out by tipping the container. ❷ If something pours somewhere, it flows there quickly and in large quantities • *Sweat poured down his face.* ❸ When it is raining heavily, you can say that it is pouring.

pout, pouts, pouting, pouted VERB If you pout, you stick out your lips or bottom lip.

poverty NOUN (GEOGRAPHY) the state of being very poor.
  ● SIMILAR WORDS: destitution,
  ● penurylessness, want

powder, powders, powdering, powdered NOUN ❶ Powder consists of many tiny particles of a solid substance ▷ VERB ❷ If you powder a surface, you cover it with powder. **powdery** ADJECTIVE

power, powers, powering, powered

a
b
c
d
e
f
g
h
i
j
k
l
m
n
o
p
q
r
s
t
u
v
w
x
y
z

▷ SPELLING NOTE: there's a rAKE in the brAKEs (*brake*)

NOUN ❶ Someone who has power has a lot of control over people and activities. ❷ Someone who has the power to do something has the ability to do it • *the power of speech.* ❸ Power is also the authority to do something • *the power of arrest.* ❹ The power of something is the physical strength that it has to move things. ❺ Power is energy obtained, for example, by burning fuel or using the wind or waves. ❻ (MATHS) In maths, a power is the product of a number multiplied by itself a certain number of times. For example, the third power of 10 is 1000. ❼ (SCIENCE) In physics, power is the energy transferred from one thing to another in one second. It is measured in watts ▷ **VERB** ❽ Something that powers a machine provides the energy for it to work.

● **SIMILAR WORDS:** ❸ force, ● strength

powerful **ADJECTIVE** ❶ able to control people and events. ❷ having great physical strength. ❸ having a strong effect. **powerfully** **ADVERB**

powerless **ADJECTIVE** unable to control or influence events • *I was powerless to save her.*

● **SIMILAR WORDS:** helpless, ● impotent, incapable

power station, power stations **NOUN** a place where electricity is generated.

practicable **ADJECTIVE** If a task or plan is practicable, it can be carried out successfully • *a practicable option.*

practical, practicals **ADJECTIVE** ❶ The practical aspects of something are those that involve experience and real situations rather than ideas or theories • *the practical difficulties of teaching science.* ❷ sensible and likely to be effective • *practical low-heeled shoes.* ❸ Someone who is practical is able to deal effectively and sensibly with problems ▷ **NOUN** ❹ an examination in which you make or perform something rather than simply write. **practicality** **NOUN**

● **SIMILAR WORDS:** ❷ functional, ● utilitarian

practically **ADVERB** ❶ almost but not completely or exactly • *The house was practically a wreck.* ❷ in a practical way • *practically minded.*

practice, practices **NOUN** ❶ You can refer to something that people do regularly as a practice • *the practice of kissing hands.* ❷ Practice is regular training or exercise • *I need more practice.* ❸ A doctor's or lawyer's practice is his or her business.

● **USAGE NOTE:** The noun *practice* ● ends in *ice*

practise, practises, practising, practised **VERB** ❶ If you practise something, you do it regularly in order to improve. ❷ People who practise a religion, custom, or craft regularly take part in the activities associated with it • *a practising Buddhist.* ❸ Someone who practises medicine or law works as a doctor or lawyer.

● **USAGE NOTE:** The verb *practise* ● ends in *ise*

practised **ADJECTIVE** Someone who is practised at doing something is very skilful at it • *a practised performer.*

practitioner, practitioners **NOUN** You can refer to someone who works in a particular profession as a practitioner • *a medical practitioner.*

▷ SPELLING NOTE: *I went to see (C) the doctor's new practiCe (practice)*

pragmatic ADJECTIVE A pragmatic way of considering or doing something is a practical rather than theoretical way • *He is pragmatic about the risks involved.* **pragmatically** ADVERB **pragmatism** NOUN

prairie, prairies NOUN a large area of flat, grassy land in North America.

praise, praises, praising, praised VERB ❶ If you praise someone or something, you express strong approval of their qualities or achievements ▷ NOUN ❷ Praise is what is said or written in approval of someone's qualities or achievements.
● SIMILAR WORDS: ❶ acclaim, approve, compliment ❷ acclaim, approval, commendation

pram, prams NOUN a baby's cot on wheels.

prance, prances, prancing, pranced VERB Someone who is prancing around is walking with exaggerated movements.

prank, pranks NOUN a childish trick.

prattle, prattles, prattling, prattled VERB If someone prattles on, they talk a lot without saying anything important.

prawn, prawns NOUN a small, pink, edible shellfish with a long tail.

pray, prays, praying, prayed VERB RE When someone prays, they speak to God to give thanks or to ask for help.

prayer, prayers NOUN RE ❶ Prayer is the activity of praying. ❷ the words said when someone prays.

pre- PREFIX 'Pre-' means before a particular time or event • *pre-war.*
● WORD HISTORY: from Latin *prae* meaning 'before'

preach, preaches, preaching, preached VERB When someone preaches, they give a short talk on a religious or moral subject as part of a church service. **preacher** NOUN

precarious ADJECTIVE ❶ If your situation is precarious, you may fail in what you are doing at any time. ❷ Something that is precarious is likely to fall because it is not well balanced or secured. **precariously** ADVERB
● SIMILAR WORDS: ❷ insecure, shaky, unsafe

precaution, precautions NOUN an action that is intended to prevent something from happening • *It's still worth taking precautions against accidents.* **precautionary** ADJECTIVE

precede, precedes, preceding, preceded VERB ❶ Something that precedes another thing happens or occurs before it. ❷ If you precede someone somewhere, you go in front of them. **preceding** ADJECTIVE

precedence [Said **press**-id-ens] NOUN If something takes precedence over other things, it is the most important thing and should be dealt with first.

precedent, precedents NOUN An action or decision that is regarded as a precedent is used as a guide in taking similar action or decisions later.

precinct, precincts NOUN ❶ A shopping precinct is a pedestrian shopping area ❷ IN PLURAL The precincts of a place are its buildings

a b c d e f g h i j k l m n o **p** q r s t u v w x y z

▷ SPELLING NOTE: *You must practiSe your Ss (practise)*

and the land around it.

precious ADJECTIVE Something that is precious is valuable or very important and should be looked after or used carefully.

precipice, precipices *[Said press-sip-piss]* NOUN a very steep rock face.

precipitate, precipitates, precipitating, precipitated VERB FORMAL If something precipitates an event or situation, it causes it to happen suddenly.

precipitation NOUN (GEOGRAPHY) FORMAL Precipitation is rain, snow, or hail; used especially when stating the amount that falls during a particular period.

precise ADJECTIVE exact and accurate in every detail • *precise measurements.* **precisely** ADVERB **precision** NOUN

preclude, precludes, precluding, precluded VERB FORMAL If something precludes an event or situation, it prevents it from happening • *The meal precluded serious conversation.*

precocious ADJECTIVE Precocious children behave in a way that seems too advanced for their age.

preconceived ADJECTIVE Preconceived ideas about something have been formed without any real experience or information. **preconception** NOUN

precondition, preconditions NOUN If something is a precondition for another thing, it must happen before the second thing can take place.

precursor, precursors NOUN A precursor of something that exists now is a similar thing that existed at an earlier time.

predator, predators *[Said pred-dat-tor]* NOUN (SCIENCE) an animal that kills and eats other animals. **predatory** ADJECTIVE

predecessor, predecessors NOUN Someone's predecessor is a person who used to do their job before.

predestination NOUN (RE) Belief in predestination is the belief that future events have already been decided by God or by fate. **predestined** ADJECTIVE

predetermined ADJECTIVE decided in advance or controlled by previous events rather than left to chance.

predicament, predicaments NOUN a difficult situation.
● SIMILAR WORDS: dilemma, fix,
● jam

predict, predicts, predicting, predicted VERB If someone predicts an event, they say that it will happen in the future.
● SIMILAR WORDS: forecast,
● foretell, prophesy

prediction, predictions NOUN something that is forecast in advance.

predominant ADJECTIVE more important or more noticeable than anything else in a particular set of people or things • *Yellow is the predominant colour in the house.* **predominantly** ADVERB
● SIMILAR WORDS: chief, main,
● prevailing

A B C D E F G H I J K L M N O P Q R S T U V W X Y Z

▷ SPELLING NOTE: *I want to see (C) your licenCe (licence)*

predominate, predominates, predominating, predominated **VERB** If one type of person or thing predominates, it is the most common, frequent, or noticeable • *Fresh flowers predominate in the bouquet.* **predominance NOUN**

pre-eminent ADJECTIVE recognized as being the most important in a particular group • *the pre-eminent experts in the area.* **pre-eminence NOUN**

pre-empt, pre-empts, pre-empting, pre-empted **VERB** FORMAL If you pre-empt something, you prevent it by doing something else which makes it pointless or impossible • *a wish to pre-empt any further publicity.*

preen, preens, preening, preened **VERB** When a bird preens its feathers, it cleans them using its beak • *a parrot preening itself.*

preface, prefaces [Said pref-fiss] **NOUN** an introduction at the beginning of a book explaining what the book is about or why it was written.

prefect, prefects **NOUN** a pupil who has special duties at a school.
● **WORD HISTORY:** from Latin
● *praefectus* meaning 'someone put
● in charge'

prefer, prefers, preferring, preferred **VERB** If you prefer one thing to another, you like it better than the other thing. **preferable ADJECTIVE preferably ADVERB**

preference, preferences [Said pref-fer-enss] **NOUN** ❶ If you have a preference for something, you like it more than other things • *a preference for white.* ❷ When making a choice, if you give preference to one type of person or thing, you try to choose that type.

preferential ADJECTIVE A person who gets preferential treatment is treated better than others.

prefix, prefixes **NOUN** (ENGLISH) a letter or group of letters added to the beginning of a word to make a new word, for example 'semi-', 'pre-', and 'un-'.

pregnant ADJECTIVE A woman who is pregnant has a baby developing in her womb. **pregnancy NOUN**

prehistoric ADJECTIVE existing at a time in the past before anything was written down.

prejudice, prejudices **NOUN** (RE) ❶ Prejudice is an unreasonable and unfair dislike or preference formed without carefully examining the facts. ❷ Prejudice is also an intolerance towards certain people or groups • *racial prejudice.* **prejudiced ADJECTIVE prejudicial ADJECTIVE**

preliminary ADJECTIVE Preliminary activities take place before something starts, in preparation for it • *the preliminary rounds of the competition.*
● **SIMILAR WORDS:** first, initial,
● preparatory

prelude, preludes **NOUN** Something that is an introduction to a more important event can be described as a prelude to that event.

premature ADJECTIVE happening too early, or earlier than expected

▷ SPELLING NOTE: *The government licenSes Schnapps (licenses)*

A
B
C
D
E
F
G
H
I
J
K
L
M
N
O
P
Q
R
S
T
U
V
W
X
Y
Z

WHAT IS A PREPOSITION?

A preposition is a word that is used before a noun or pronoun to relate it to other words.

Prepositions may tell you the **place** of something in relation to another thing:
*She saw the cat **in** the garden.*
*The cat was sheltering **under** a bench.*

Prepositions may also indicate **movement**:
*The train came **into** the station.*
*We pushed **through** the crowd.*

Prepositions may indicate **time**:
*They will arrive **on** Friday.*
*They will stay **for** two days.*

• *premature baldness.* **prematurely ADVERB**

premeditated ADJECTIVE
planned in advance • *a premeditated attack.*

premier, premiers **NOUN** ❶ The leader of a government is sometimes referred to as the premier. ❷ In Australia, the leader of a State government ▷ **ADJECTIVE** ❸ considered to be the best or most important • *Wellington's premier jewellers.*

premiere, premieres *[Said prem-mee-er]* **NOUN** the first public performance of a new play or film.

premise, premises *[Said prem-iss]* **NOUN** ❶ IN PLURAL The premises of an organization are all the buildings it occupies on one site ❷ a statement which you suppose is true and use as the basis for an idea or argument.

premium, premiums **NOUN** an extra sum of money that has to be paid • *Paying a premium for space is worthwhile.*

premonition, premonitions *[Said prem-on-ish-on]* **NOUN** a feeling that something unpleasant is going to

happen.
● **SIMILAR WORDS:** feeling,
● foreboding, presentiment

preoccupation, preoccupations **NOUN** If you have a preoccupation with something, it is very important to you and you keep thinking about it.

preoccupied ADJECTIVE
Someone who is preoccupied is deep in thought or totally involved with something.

preparatory ADJECTIVE
Preparatory activities are done before doing something else in order to prepare for it.

prepare, prepares, preparing, prepared **VERB** If you prepare something, you make it ready for a particular purpose or event • *He was preparing the meal.* **preparation NOUN**

prepared ADJECTIVE If you are prepared to do something, you are willing to do it.

preposition, prepositions **NOUN** (ENGLISH) a word such as 'by', 'for', 'into', or 'with', which usually has a noun as its object.
▶ SEE GRAMMAR BOX ABOVE

▷ SPELLING NOTE: *have a plEce of pIE (piece)*

preposterous ADJECTIVE
extremely unreasonable and ridiculous
• *a preposterous statement*.

prerequisite, prerequisites [Said
pree-**rek**-wiz-zit] NOUN FORMAL
Something that is a prerequisite for
another thing must happen or exist
before the other thing is possible
• *Self-esteem is a prerequisite for a
happy life*.

prerogative, prerogatives [Said
prir-**rog**-at-tiv] NOUN FORMAL
Something that is the prerogative of a
person is their special privilege or
right.

Presbyterian, Presbyterians
NOUN OR ADJECTIVE (RE) a member
of the Presbyterian Church, a
Protestant church in Scotland and
Northern Ireland.

prescribe, prescribes, prescribing,
prescribed VERB When a doctor
prescribes treatment, he or she states
what treatment a patient should have.

prescription, prescriptions NOUN
a piece of paper on which the doctor
has written the name of a medicine
needed by a patient.

presence NOUN ❶ Someone's
presence in a place is the fact of their
being there • *His presence made me
happy*. ❷ If you are in someone's
presence, you are in the same place as
they are. ❸ Someone who has
presence has an impressive
appearance or manner.

present, presents, presenting,
presented ADJECTIVE [Said **prez**-ent]
❶ If someone is present somewhere,
they are there • *He had been present at
the birth of his son*. ❷ A present

situation is one that exists now rather
than in the past or the future ▷ NOUN
[Said **prez**-ent] ❸ The present is the
period of time that is taking place
now. ❹ something that you give to
someone for them to keep.
❺ (ENGLISH) The present tense of a
verb is the form used to express
something that is happening in the
present ▷ VERB [Said pri-**zent**] ❻ If
you present someone with something,
you give it to them • *She presented a
bravery award to the girl*.
❼ Something that presents a
difficulty or a challenge causes it or
provides it. ❽ The person who
presents a radio or television show
introduces each part or each guest.
presenter NOUN
● SIMILAR WORDS:
● ❷ contemporary, current, existing

presentable ADJECTIVE neat or
attractive and suitable for people to
see.

presentation, presentations
NOUN ❶ the act of presenting or a
way of presenting something. ❷ The
presentation of a piece of work is the
way it looks or the impression it gives.
❸ (D & T) To give a presentation is to
give a talk or demonstration to an
audience of something you have been
studying or working on.

present-day ADJECTIVE existing
or happening now • *present-day
farming practices*.

presently ADVERB ❶ If something
will happen presently, it will happen
soon • *I'll finish the job presently*.
❷ Something that is presently
happening is happening now • *Some
progress is presently being made*.

▷ SPELLING NOTE: *plaice the fish has a glittering 'EYE' (I) (plaice)*

TALKING ABOUT THE PRESENT

You can talk about events that are happening now by using **simple tenses** or **compound tenses**.

The **simple present tense** is formed by using the verb on its own, without any auxiliary verbs. For the first and second person, and for all plural forms, the simple present tense of the verb is the same as the main form given in the dictionary:
*I **cook** the dinner.*

For the third person singular, however, you need to add an -s to the dictionary form to make the simple present tense:
*He **cooks** the dinner.*

You can also talk about an event that

is happening in the present by using **compound tenses**. Compound tenses are formed by adding an auxiliary verb to a form of the main verb.

The most common compound present tense is formed by putting a form of the verb *to be* in front of the main verb, and adding the ending -ing. This shows that the action is going on at the present time and is continuous:
*I **am listening** to the radio.*

You can also talk about the present using a form of the verb *to do* in front of the basic form of the verb. This can add emphasis:
*I **do like** fish.*

present participle, present participles NOUN (ENGLISH) In grammar, the present participle of an English verb is the form that ends in '-ing'. It is used to form some tenses, and can be used to form adjectives and nouns from a verb.

present tense NOUN (ENGLISH) In grammar, the present tense is the tense of a verb that you use mainly to talk about things that happen or exist at the time of writing or speaking.
▶ SEE GRAMMAR BOX ABOVE

preservative, preservatives NOUN a substance or chemical that stops things decaying.

preserve, preserves, preserving, preserved VERB ❶ If you preserve something, you take action so that it remains as it is. ❷ If you preserve

food, you treat it to prevent it from decaying ▷ NOUN ❸ Preserves are foods such as jam or chutney that have been made with a lot of sugar or vinegar. **preservation** NOUN

preside, presides, presiding, presided VERB A person who presides over a formal event is in charge of it.

president, presidents NOUN ❶ In a country which has no king or queen, the president is the elected leader • *the President of the United States of America.* ❷ The president of an organization is the person who has the highest position. **presidency** NOUN **presidential** ADJECTIVE

press, presses, pressing, pressed VERB ❶ If you press something, you push it or hold it firmly against something else • *Lisa pressed his hand*

▷ SPELLING NOTE: *I went to see (C) the doctor's new practiCe (practice)*

• *Press the blue button.* ❷ If you press clothes, you iron them. ❸ If you press for something, you try hard to persuade someone to agree to it • *She was pressing for improvements to the education system.* ❹ If you press charges, you make an accusation against someone which has to be decided in a court of law ▷ **NOUN** ❺ Newspapers and the journalists who work for them are called the press.

press conference, press conferences **NOUN** When someone gives a press conference, they have a meeting to answer questions put by reporters.

pressing ADJECTIVE Something that is pressing needs to be dealt with immediately • *pressing needs.*

pressure, pressures, pressuring, pressured **NOUN** ❶ (SCIENCE) Pressure is the force that is produced by pushing on something. ❷ (PSHE) If you are under pressure, you have too much to do and not enough time, or someone is trying hard to persuade you to do something ▷ **VERB** ❸ If you pressure someone, you try hard to persuade them to do something.

pressurize, pressurizes, pressurizing, pressurized; *also spelt* **pressurise VERB** If you pressurize someone, you try hard to persuade them to do something.

prestige [Said press-**teezh**] **NOUN** If you have prestige, people admire you because of your position. **prestigious ADJECTIVE**
● **SIMILAR WORDS:** honour,
● standing, status

presumably ADVERB If you say that something is presumably the case, you mean you assume that it is • *Your audience, presumably, are younger.*

presume, presumes, presuming, presumed [Said priz-**yoom**] **VERB** If you presume something, you think that it is the case although you have no proof. **presumption NOUN**
● **SIMILAR WORDS:** assume,
● believe, suppose

presumptuous ADJECTIVE Someone who behaves in a presumptuous way does things that they have no right to do.

pretence, pretences **NOUN** a way of behaving that is false and intended to deceive people.

pretend, pretends, pretending, pretended **VERB** If you pretend that something is the case, you try to make people believe that it is, although in fact it is not • *Latimer pretended not to notice.*
● **SIMILAR WORDS:** affect, feign,
● sham

pretender, pretenders **NOUN** A pretender to a throne or title is someone who claims it but whose claim is being questioned.

pretension, pretensions **NOUN** Someone with pretensions claims that they are more important than they really are.

pretentious ADJECTIVE Someone or something that is pretentious is trying to seem important when in fact they are not.

pretext, pretexts **NOUN** a false

▷ SPELLING NOTE: *You must practiSe your Ss (practise)*

A
B
C
D
E
F
G
H
I
J
K
L
M
N
O
P
Q
R
S
T
U
V
W
X
Y
Z

reason given to hide the real reason for doing something.

pretty, prettier, prettiest **ADJECTIVE**
① attractive in a delicate way
▷ **ADVERB** **②** INFORMAL quite or rather • *He spoke pretty good English.*
prettily ADVERB prettiness NOUN

prevail, prevails, prevailing, prevailed
VERB **①** If a custom or belief prevails in a particular place, it is normal or most common there • *This attitude has prevailed in Britain for many years.*
② If someone or something prevails, they succeed in their aims • *In recent years better sense has prevailed.*
prevailing ADJECTIVE

prevalent ADJECTIVE very common or widespread • *the hooliganism so prevalent today.*
prevalence NOUN

prevent, prevents, preventing, prevented **VERB** If you prevent something, you stop it from happening or being done.
preventable ADJECTIVE
prevention NOUN
● **SIMILAR WORDS:** avert, forestall,
● stop

preventive or **preventative**
ADJECTIVE intended to help prevent things such as disease or crime
• *preventive health care.*

preview, previews **NOUN** **①** an opportunity to see something, such as a film or exhibition, before it is shown to the public. **②** (ICT) a part of a computer program which allows you to look at what you have keyed or added to a document or spreadsheet as it will appear when it is printed.

previous ADJECTIVE happening or

existing before something else in time or position • *previous reports* • *the previous year.* **previously ADVERB**
● **SIMILAR WORDS:** earlier, former,
● preceding

prey, preys, preying, preyed [*rhymes with say*] **NOUN** **①** The creatures that an animal hunts and eats are called its prey ▷ **VERB** **②** An animal that preys on a particular kind of animal lives by hunting and eating it.

price, prices, pricing, priced **NOUN**
① The price of something is the amount of money you have to pay to buy it ▷ **VERB** **②** To price something at a particular amount is to fix its price at that amount.
● **SIMILAR WORDS:** **①** charge, cost,
● expense

priceless ADJECTIVE Something that is priceless is so valuable that it is difficult to work out how much it is worth.

pricey, pricier, priciest **ADJECTIVE**
INFORMAL expensive.

prick, pricks, pricking, pricked **VERB**
① If you prick something, you stick a sharp pointed object into it ▷ **NOUN**
② a small, sharp pain caused when something pricks you.

prickle, prickles, prickling, prickled
NOUN **①** Prickles are small sharp points or thorns on plants ▷ **VERB**
② If your skin prickles, it feels as if a lot of sharp points are being stuck into it. **prickly ADJECTIVE**

pride, prides, priding, prided **NOUN**
① Pride is a feeling of satisfaction you have when you have done something well. **②** Pride is also a feeling of being better than other people. **③** A pride of

▷ SPELLING NOTE: *pAL up with the principAL and principAL staff (principal)*

lions is a group of them ▷ **VERB ❹** If you pride yourself on a quality or skill, you are proud of it • *She prides herself on punctuality.*
● **SIMILAR WORDS: ❶** gratification,
● pleasure, satisfaction

priest, priests **NOUN** (RE) **❶** a member of the clergy in some Christian Churches. **❷** In many non-Christian religions, a priest is a man who has special duties in the place where people worship. **priestly ADJECTIVE**

priestess, priestesses **NOUN** a female priest in a non-Christian religion.

priesthood NOUN The priesthood is the position of being a priest.

prim, primmer, primmest **ADJECTIVE** Someone who is prim always behaves very correctly and is easily shocked by anything rude.
● **SIMILAR WORDS:** priggish,
● prudish, strait-laced

primaeval another spelling of primeval.

primarily ADVERB You use 'primarily' to indicate the main or most important feature of something • *I still rated people primarily on their looks.*

primary ADJECTIVE 'Primary' is used to describe something that is extremely important for someone or something • *the primary aim of his research.*

primary colour, primary colours **NOUN** In art, the primary colours are red, yellow, and blue, from which other colours can be obtained by

mixing them together.

primary school, primary schools **NOUN** a school for children aged up to 11.

primate, primates **NOUN ❶** an archbishop. **❷** a member of the group of animals which includes humans, monkeys, and apes.

prime, primes, priming, primed **ADJECTIVE ❶** main or most important • *a prime cause of brain damage.* **❷** of the best quality • *in prime condition.* ▷ **NOUN ❸** Someone's prime is the stage when they are at their strongest, most active, or most successful ▷ **VERB ❹** If you prime someone, you give them information about something in advance to prepare them • *We are primed for every lesson.*
● **SIMILAR WORDS: ❸** height,
● heyday, peak

prime minister, prime ministers **NOUN** The prime minister is the leader of the government.

primeval or **primaeval** *[Said pry-mee-vl]* **ADJECTIVE** belonging to a very early period in the history of the world.

primitive ADJECTIVE ❶ connected with a society that lives very simply without industries or a writing system • *the primitive peoples of the world.* **❷** very simple, basic, or old-fashioned • *a very small primitive cottage.*

primordial *[Said pry-mor-dee-al]* **ADJECTIVE** FORMAL existing at the beginning of time.

primrose, primroses **NOUN** A primrose is a small plant that has pale

a
b
c
d
e
f
g
h
i
j
k
l
m
n
o
p
q
r
s
t
u
v
w
x
y
z

▷ SPELLING NOTE: L*Earn* the princip*LEs* (princip*le*)

yellow flowers in spring.
- **WORD HISTORY:** from Latin *prima rosa* meaning 'first rose'

prince, princes **NOUN** a male member of a royal family, especially the son of a king or queen. **princely ADJECTIVE**

princess, princesses **NOUN** a female member of a royal family, usually the daughter of a king or queen, or the wife of a prince.

principal, principals **ADJECTIVE** ❶ main or most important • *the principal source of food.* ▷ **NOUN** ❷ the person in charge of a school or college. **principally ADVERB**
- **USAGE NOTE:** Do not confuse *principal* with *principle*: *my principal objection*

principality, principalities **NOUN** a country ruled by a prince.

principle, principles **NOUN** ❶ a belief you have about the way you should behave • *a woman of principle.* ❷ a general rule or scientific law which explains how something happens or works • *the principle of evolution in nature.*
- **USAGE NOTE:** Do not confuse *principle* with *principal*: *a man with no principles*
- **SIMILAR WORDS:** ❶ precept, standard, rule

print, prints, printing, printed **VERB** ❶ To print a newspaper or book is to reproduce it in large quantities using a mechanical or electronic copying process. ❷ If you print when you are writing, you do not join the letters together ▷ **NOUN** ❸ The letters and numbers on the pages of a book or

newspaper are referred to as the print. ❹ a photograph, or a printed copy of a painting. ❺ Footprints and fingerprints can be referred to as prints. **printer NOUN**

printing NOUN the process of producing printed material such as books and newspapers.

print-out, print-outs **NOUN** a printed copy of information from a computer.

prior, priors **ADJECTIVE** ❶ planned or done at an earlier time • *I have a prior engagement.* ▷ **PHRASE** ❷ Something that happens **prior to** a particular time or event happens before it ▷ **NOUN** ❸ a monk in charge of a small group of monks in a priory. **prioress NOUN**

prioritize, prioritizes, prioritizing, prioritized; *also spelt* **prioritise VERB** To prioritize things is to decide which is the most important and deal with it first.

priority, priorities **NOUN** something that needs to be dealt with first • *The priority is building homes.*

priory, priories **NOUN** a place where a small group of monks live under the charge of a prior.

prise, prises, prising, prised **VERB** If you prise something open or away from a surface, you force it open or away • *She prised his fingers loose.*

prism, prisms **NOUN** ❶ an object made of clear glass with many flat sides. It separates light passing through it into the colours of the rainbow. ❷ (MATHS) any polyhedron with two identical parallel ends and

▷ SPELLING NOTE: *pAL up with the principAL and principAL staff (principal)*

sides which are parallelograms.

prison, prisons NOUN a building where criminals are kept in captivity.

prisoner, prisoners NOUN someone who is kept in prison or held in captivity against their will.

pristine [Said **priss**-teen] ADJECTIVE FORMAL very clean or new and in perfect condition.

private, privates ADJECTIVE ❶ for the use of one person rather than people in general • *a private bathroom.* ❷ taking place between a small number of people and kept secret from others • *a private conversation.* ❸ owned or run by individuals or companies rather than by the state • *a private company.* ▷ NOUN ❹ a soldier of the lowest rank. **privacy** NOUN **privately** ADVERB

private school, private schools NOUN a school that does not receive money from the government, and parents pay for their children to attend.

privatize, privatizes, privatizing, privatized; *also spelt* **privatise** VERB If the government privatizes a state-owned industry or organization, it allows it to be bought and owned by a private individual or group.

privilege, privileges NOUN a special right or advantage given to a person or group • *the privileges of monarchy.* **privileged** ADJECTIVE

privy ADJECTIVE FORMAL If you are privy to something secret, you have been told about it.

prize, prizes, prizing, prized NOUN ❶ a reward given to the winner of a

competition or game ▷ ADJECTIVE ❷ of the highest quality or standard • *his prize dahlia.* ▷ VERB ❸ Something that is prized is wanted and admired for its value or quality.
● SIMILAR WORDS: ❶ award, ● reward, trophy

pro, pros NOUN ❶ INFORMAL a professional ▷ PHRASE ❷ The **pros and cons** of a situation are its advantages and disadvantages.

pro- PREFIX 'Pro-' means supporting or in favour of • *pro-democracy protests.*

probability, probabilities NOUN ❶ The probability of something happening is how likely it is to happen • *the probability of success.* ❷ If something is a probability, it is likely to happen • *The probability is that you will be feeling better.*
● SIMILAR WORDS: ❶ chances, ● likelihood, odds

probable ADJECTIVE Something that is probable is likely to be true or correct, or likely to happen • *the most probable outcome.*

probably ADVERB Something that is probably the case is likely but not certain.

probation NOUN Probation is a period of time during which a person convicted of a crime is supervised by a probation officer instead of being sent to prison. **probationary** ADJECTIVE

probe, probes, probing, probed VERB ❶ If you probe, you ask a lot of questions to discover the facts about something ▷ NOUN ❷ a long thin instrument used by doctors and dentists when examining a patient.

▷ SPELLING NOTE: *LEarn the principLEs (principle)*

a
b
c
d
e
f
g
h
i
j
k
l
m
n
o
p
q
r
s
t
u
v
w
x
y
z

problem, problems NOUN ❶ an unsatisfactory situation that causes difficulties. ❷ a puzzle or question that you solve using logical thought or mathematics. **problematic** ADJECTIVE
● SIMILAR WORDS: ❶ difficulty,
● predicament

procedure, procedures NOUN a way of doing something, especially the correct or usual way • *It's standard procedure.* **procedural** ADJECTIVE

proceed, proceeds, proceeding, proceeded VERB ❶ If you proceed to do something, you start doing it, or continue doing it • *She proceeded to tell them.* ❷ FORMAL If you proceed in a particular direction, you move in that direction • *The taxi proceeded along a lonely road.*

proceedings PLURAL NOUN ❶ You can refer to an organized and related series of events as the proceedings • *She was determined to see the proceedings from start to finish.* ❷ Legal proceedings are legal action taken against someone.

proceeds PLURAL NOUN The proceeds from a fund-raising event are the money obtained from it.

process, processes, processing, processed NOUN ❶ a series of actions intended to achieve a particular result or change ▷ PHRASE ❷ If you are **in the process** of doing something, you have started doing it but have not yet finished ▷ VERB ❸ When something such as food or information is processed, it is treated or dealt with.

procession, processions NOUN a group of people or vehicles moving in a line, often as part of a ceremony.

processor, processors NOUN ICT In computing, a processor is the central chip in a computer which controls its operations.

proclaim, proclaims, proclaiming, proclaimed VERB If someone proclaims something, they announce it or make it known • *You have proclaimed your innocence.* **proclamation** NOUN

procrastinate, procrastinates, procrastinating, procrastinated VERB FORMAL If you procrastinate, you put off doing something.

procure, procures, procuring, procured VERB FORMAL If you procure something, you obtain it.

prod, prods, prodding, prodded VERB If you prod something, you give it a push with your finger or with something pointed.

prodigal ADJECTIVE LITERARY Someone who is prodigal spends money freely and wastefully.

prodigy, prodigies *[Said prod-dij-ee]* NOUN someone who shows an extraordinary natural ability at an early age.

produce, produces, producing, produced VERB ❶ To produce something is to make it or cause it • *a white wine produced mainly from black grapes.* ❷ If you produce something from somewhere, you bring it out so it can be seen ▷ NOUN ❸ Produce is food that is grown to be sold • *fresh produce.*

producer, producers NOUN The

producer of a record, film, or show is the person in charge of making it or putting it on.

product, products NOUN ❶ something that is made to be sold • high-quality products. ❷ (MATHS) The product of two or more numbers or quantities is the result of multiplying them together. ❸ (SCIENCE) a substance formed in a chemical reaction.

production, productions NOUN (D & T) ❶ Production is the process of manufacturing or growing something in large quantities • modern methods of production. ❷ Production is also the amount of goods manufactured or food grown by a country or company • Production has fallen by 13.2%. ❸ A production of a play, opera, or other show is a series of performances of it.

productive ADJECTIVE ❶ To be productive means to produce a large number of things • Farms were more productive in these areas. ❷ If something such as a meeting is productive, good or useful things happen as a result of it.

● SIMILAR WORDS: ❷ beneficial, ● useful, worthwhile

productivity NOUN Productivity is the rate at which things are produced or dealt with.

profane ADJECTIVE FORMAL showing disrespect for a religion or religious things • profane language.

profess, professes, professing, professed VERB ❶ FORMAL If you profess to do or have something, you claim to do or have it. ❷ If you

profess a feeling or opinion, you express it • He professes a lasting affection for Trinidad.

profession, professions NOUN ❶ a type of job that requires advanced education or training. ❷ You can use 'profession' to refer to all the people who have a particular profession • the medical profession.

professional, professionals ADJECTIVE ❶ Professional means relating to the work of someone who is qualified in a particular profession • I think you need professional advice. ❷ Professional also describes activities when they are done to earn money rather than as a hobby • professional football. ❸ A professional piece of work is of a very high standard ▷ NOUN ❹ a person who has been trained in a profession. ❺ someone who plays a sport to earn money rather than as a hobby.

professor, professors NOUN the senior teacher in a department of a British university. **professorial** ADJECTIVE

proficient ADJECTIVE If you are proficient at something, you can do it well. **proficiency** NOUN

profile, profiles NOUN ❶ Your profile is the outline of your face seen from the side. ❷ A profile of someone is a short description of their life and character.
● WORD HISTORY: from Italian ● profilare meaning 'to sketch lightly'

profit, profits, profiting, profited NOUN ❶ When someone sells something, the profit is the amount they gain by selling it for more than it

▷ SPELLING NOTE: there's SAND in my SANDwich (sandwich)

cost them to buy or make ▷ **VERB**
❷ If you profit from something, you gain or benefit from it. **profitable ADJECTIVE**

● **SIMILAR WORDS:** ❶ gain,
● proceeds, return

profound ADJECTIVE ❶ great in degree or intensity • *a profound need to please.* ❷ showing great and deep intellectual understanding • *a profound question.* **profoundly ADVERB profundity NOUN**

profuse [Said prof-*yooss*] **ADJECTIVE** very large in quantity or number • *There were profuse apologies for his absence.* **profusely ADVERB**

program, programs, programming, programmed (ICT) **NOUN** ❶ a set of instructions that a computer follows to perform a particular task ▷ **VERB** ❷ When someone programs a computer, they write a program and put it into the computer. **programmer NOUN**

programme, programmes **NOUN** ❶ a planned series of events • *a programme of official engagements.* ❷ a particular piece presented as a unit on television or radio, such as a play, show, or discussion. ❸ a booklet giving information about a play, concert, or show that you are attending.
● **SIMILAR WORDS:** ❶ agenda,
● plan, schedule

progress, progresses, progressing, progressed **NOUN** ❶ Progress is the process of gradually improving or getting near to achieving something • *Gerry is now making some real progress towards fitness.* ❷ The progress of something is the way in which it develops or continues • *news*

on the progress of the war. ▷ **PHRASE**
❸ Something that is **in progress** is happening • *A cricket match was in progress.* ▷ **VERB** ❹ If you progress, you become more advanced or skilful.
❺ To progress is to continue • *As the evening progressed, sadness turned to rage.* **progression NOUN**
● **SIMILAR WORDS:** ❶ advance,
● headway ❷ course, movement

progressive ADJECTIVE ❶ having modern ideas about how things should be done. ❷ happening gradually • *a progressive illness.*

prohibit, prohibits, prohibiting, prohibited **VERB** If someone prohibits something, they forbid it or make it illegal. **prohibition NOUN**
● **USAGE NOTE:** You *prohibit* a
● person *from* doing something

prohibitive ADJECTIVE If the cost of something is prohibitive, it is so high that people cannot afford it.

project, projects, projecting, projected **NOUN** ❶ a carefully planned attempt to achieve something or to study something over a period of time ▷ **VERB** ❷ Something that is projected is planned or expected to happen in the future • *The population aged 65 or over is projected to increase.* ❸ To project an image onto a screen is to make it appear there using equipment such as a projector. ❹ Something that projects sticks out beyond a surface or edge. **projection NOUN**

projector, projectors **NOUN** a piece of equipment which produces a large image on a screen by shining light through a photographic slide or film strip.

▷ SPELLING NOTE: On WEDNESday Wayne WED NESta (Wednesday)

proletariat NOUN FORMAL
Working-class people are sometimes referred to as the proletariat. **proletarian** ADJECTIVE

proliferate, proliferates, proliferating, proliferated VERB If things proliferate, they quickly increase in number. **proliferation** NOUN

- **WORD HISTORY:** from Latin
- *prolifer* meaning 'having children'

prolific ADJECTIVE producing a lot of something • *this prolific artist.*

prologue, prologues NOUN a speech or section that introduces a play or book.

prolong, prolongs, prolonging, prolonged VERB If you prolong something, you make it last longer. **prolonged** ADJECTIVE

prom, proms NOUN INFORMAL a concert at which some of the audience stand.

promenade, promenades *[Said prom-min-ahd]* NOUN a road or path next to the sea at a seaside resort.

- **WORD HISTORY:** a French word,
- from *se promener* meaning 'to go for
- a walk'

prominent ADJECTIVE
❶ Prominent people are important.
❷ Something that is prominent is very noticeable • *a prominent nose.* **prominence** NOUN **prominently** ADVERB

promiscuous *[Said prom-misk-yoo-uss]* ADJECTIVE Someone who is promiscuous has sex with many different people. **promiscuity** NOUN

promise, promises, promising, promised VERB ❶ If you promise to do something, you say that you will definitely do it. ❷ Something that promises to have a particular quality shows signs that it will have that quality • *This promised to be a very long night.* ▷ NOUN ❸ a statement made by someone that they will definitely do something • *He made a promise to me.* ❹ Someone or something that shows promise seems likely to be very successful. **promising** ADJECTIVE

- **SIMILAR WORDS:** ❶ guarantee,
- pledge, vow ❸ guarantee, oath,
- vow

promontory, promontories *[Said prom-mon-tree]* NOUN an area of high land sticking out into the sea.

promote, promotes, promoting, promoted VERB ❶ If someone promotes something, they try to make it happen. ❷ If someone promotes a product such as a film or a book, they try to make it popular by advertising. ❸ If someone is promoted, they are given a more important job at work. **promoter** NOUN **promotion** NOUN

prompt, prompts, prompting, prompted VERB ❶ If something prompts someone to do something, it makes them decide to do it • *Curiosity prompted him to push at the door.* ❷ If you prompt someone when they stop speaking, you tell them what to say next or encourage them to continue ▷ ADVERB ❸ exactly at the time mentioned • *Wednesday morning at 10.40 prompt.* ▷ ADJECTIVE ❹ A prompt action is done without any delay • *a prompt reply.* **promptly** ADVERB

a
b
c
d
e
f
g
h
i
j
k
l
m
n
o
p
q
r
s
t
u
v
w
x
y
z

▷ SPELLING NOTE: *Eddy Ant thinks mEAt is a grEAt trEAt to EAt (-ea-)*

A
B
C
D
E
F
G
H
I
J
K
L
M
N
O
P
Q
R
S
T
U
V
W
X
Y
Z

WHAT IS A PRONOUN?

A **pronoun** is a word that is used in place of a noun. Pronouns may be used instead of naming a person or thing.

Personal pronouns replace the subject or object of a sentence:
She caught a fish.
The nurse reassured him.

Reflexive pronouns replace the object when it is the same person or thing as the subject:
Matthew saw himself in the mirror.

Demonstrative pronouns replace the subject or object when you want to show where something is:
That is a nice jacket.
Have you seen this?

Possessive pronouns replace the subject or object when you want to show who owns it:

The blue car is mine.
Hers is a strange story.

Relative pronouns replace a noun to link two different parts of the sentence:
Do you know the man who lives next door?
I watched a programme that I had recorded yesterday.

Interrogative pronouns ask questions:
What are you doing?

Indefinite pronouns replace a subject or object to talk about a broad or vague range of people or things:
Everybody knew the exercise was a waste of time.
Some say he cheats at cards.

Also look at the grammar box at **relative pronoun**.

prone ADJECTIVE ❶ If you are prone to something, you have a tendency to be affected by it or to do it • *She is prone to depression.* ❷ If you are prone, you are lying flat and face downwards • *lying prone on the grass.*
● SIMILAR WORDS: ❶ inclined,
● liable, subject

prong, prongs NOUN The prongs of a fork are the long, narrow, pointed parts.

pronoun, pronouns NOUN
[ENGLISH] In grammar, a pronoun is a word that is used to replace a noun. 'He', 'she', and 'them' are all pronouns.
▶ SEE GRAMMAR BOX ABOVE

pronounce, pronounces, pronouncing, pronounced VERB
[ENGLISH] When you pronounce a word, you say it.
● USAGE NOTE: There is an *o* before
● the *u* in *pronounce*. Compare this
● spelling with *pronunciation*

pronounced ADJECTIVE very noticeable • *He talks with a pronounced lowland accent.*

pronouncement,
pronouncements NOUN a formal statement • *the government's latest pronouncement on the economy.*

pronunciation, pronunciations
[Said pron-nun-see-**ay**-shn] NOUN the way a word is usually said.

▷ SPELLING NOTE: *Elaine and Emily shout EE when they mEEt to grEEt each other (-ee-)*

- **USAGE NOTE:** There is no *o* before the *u* in *pronunciation*. Compare this spelling with *pronounce*

proof NOUN If you have proof of something, you have evidence which shows that it is true or exists.
- **SIMILAR WORDS:** confirmation, evidence, verification

prop, props, propping, propped VERB ❶ If you prop an object somewhere, you support it or rest it against something • *The barman propped himself against the counter.* ▷ NOUN ❷ a stick or other object used to support something. ❸ The props in a play are all the objects and furniture used by the actors.

propaganda NOUN (HISTORY) Propaganda is exaggerated or false information that is published or broadcast in order to influence people.

propagate, propagates, propagating, propagated VERB ❶ If people propagate an idea, they spread it to try to influence many other people. ❷ If you propagate plants, you grow more of them from an original one. **propagation** NOUN

propane NOUN Propane is a gas found in petroleum and used as a fuel for cooking and heating.

propel, propels, propelling, propelled VERB To propel something is to cause it to move in a particular direction.

propeller, propellers NOUN a device on a boat or aircraft with rotating blades which make the boat or aircraft move.

propensity, propensities NOUN FORMAL A propensity is a tendency to behave in a particular way.

proper ADJECTIVE ❶ real and satisfactory • *He was no nearer having a proper job.* ❷ correct or suitable • *Put things in their proper place.* ❸ accepted or conventional • *a proper wedding.* **properly** ADVERB

proper noun, proper nouns NOUN the name of a person, place, or institution.

property, properties NOUN ❶ A person's property is the things that belong to them. ❷ a building and the land belonging to it. ❸ a characteristic or quality • *Mint has powerful healing properties.*

prophecy, prophecies NOUN a statement about what someone believes will happen in the future.
- **USAGE NOTE:** The noun *prophecy* ends in *cy*

prophesy, prophesies, prophesying, prophesied VERB If someone prophesies something, they say it will happen.
- **USAGE NOTE:** The verb *prophesy* ends in *sy*

prophet, prophets NOUN (RE) a person who predicts what will happen in the future.

prophetic ADJECTIVE correctly predicting what will happen • *It was a prophetic warning.*

proportion, proportions NOUN ❶ A proportion of an amount or group is a part of it • *a tiny proportion of the population.* ❷ The proportion of one amount to another is its size in comparison with the other amount • *the highest proportion of single women to men.* ❸ IN PLURAL You can refer to

a b c d e f g h i j k l m n o **p** q r s t u v w x y z

▷ SPELLING NOTE: 'i' before 'e' except after 'c'

A
B
C
D
E
F
G
H
I
J
K
L
M
N
O
P
Q
R
S
T
U
V
W
X
Y
Z

the size of something as its proportions • *a red umbrella of vast proportions.*

proportional or **proportionate** ADJECTIVE If one thing is proportional to another, it remains the same size in comparison with the other • *proportional increases in profit.* **proportionally** or **proportionately** ADVERB

proportional representation NOUN Proportional representation is a system of voting in elections in which the number of representatives of each party is in proportion to the number of people who voted for it.

proposal, proposals NOUN a plan that has been suggested • *business proposals.*

propose, proposes, proposing, proposed VERB ❶ If you propose a plan or idea, you suggest it. ❷ If you propose to do something, you intend to do it • *And how do you propose to do that?* ❸ When someone proposes a toast to a particular person, they ask people to drink a toast to that person. ❹ If someone proposes to another person, they ask that person to marry them.

proposition, propositions NOUN ❶ a statement expressing a theory or opinion. ❷ an offer or suggestion • *I made her a proposition.*

proprietor, proprietors NOUN The proprietor of a business is the owner.

propriety NOUN FORMAL Propriety is what is socially or morally acceptable • *a model of propriety.*

propulsion NOUN Propulsion is

the power that moves something.

prose NOUN Prose is ordinary written language in contrast to poetry.
● **WORD HISTORY:** from Latin *prosa*
● *oratorio* meaning 'straightforward
● speech'

prosecute, prosecutes, prosecuting, prosecuted VERB If someone is prosecuted, they are charged with a crime and have to stand trial. **prosecutor** NOUN

prosecution NOUN The lawyers who try to prove that a person on trial is guilty are called the prosecution.

prospect, prospects, prospecting, prospected NOUN ❶ If there is a prospect of something happening, there is a possibility that it will happen • *There was little prospect of going home.* ❷ Someone's prospects are their chances of being successful in the future ▷ VERB ❸ If someone prospects for gold or oil, they look for it. **prospector** NOUN

prospective ADJECTIVE 'Prospective' is used to say that someone wants to be or is likely to be something. For example, the prospective owner of something is the person who wants to own it.

prospectus, prospectuses NOUN a booklet giving details about a college or a company.

prosper, prospers, prospering, prospered VERB When people or businesses prosper, they are successful and make a lot of money. **prosperous** ADJECTIVE **prosperity** NOUN

prostitute, prostitutes NOUN a

person, usually a woman, who has sex with men in exchange for money.
prostitution NOUN

prostrate ADJECTIVE lying face downwards on the ground.

protagonist, protagonists **NOUN**
FORMAL ❶ Someone who is a protagonist of an idea or movement is a leading supporter of it. ❷ a main character in a play or story.
● **WORD HISTORY:** from Greek *prōtagōnistēs* meaning 'main actor in a play'

protea, proteas **NOUN** an evergreen African shrub with colourful flowers.

protect, protects, protecting, protected **VERB** ❶ To protect someone or something is to prevent them from being harmed or damaged. ❷ (SCIENCE) to prevent a particular animal, plant, or area of land from being harmed or damaged by making it illegal to do so • *a protected species.*
protection NOUN protective ADJECTIVE protector NOUN

protection, protections **NOUN** ❶ the act of preventing harm or damage. ❷ something that keeps a person or thing safe.

protégé, protégés [*Said proh-tij-ay*] **NOUN** Someone who is the protégé of an older, more experienced person is helped and guided by that person.

protein, proteins **NOUN** Protein is a substance that is found in meat, eggs, and milk and that is needed by bodies for growth.

protest, protests, protesting, protested **VERB** ❶ If you protest about something, you say or

demonstrate publicly that you disagree with it • *They protested against the killing of a teenager.*
▷ **NOUN** ❷ a demonstration or statement showing that you disagree with something.

Protestant, Protestants **NOUN OR ADJECTIVE** (RE) a member of one of the Christian Churches which separated from the Catholic Church in the sixteenth century.

protestation, protestations **NOUN** a strong declaration that something is true or not true • *his protestations of love.*

protocol NOUN Protocol is the system of rules about the correct way to behave in formal situations.

proton, protons **NOUN** a particle which forms part of the nucleus of an atom and has a positive electrical charge.

prototype, prototypes **NOUN** (D & T) a first model of something that is made so that the design can be tested and improved.

protracted ADJECTIVE lasting longer than usual • *a protracted dispute.*

protractor, protractors **NOUN** a flat, semicircular piece of plastic used for measuring angles.

protrude, protrudes, protruding, protruded **VERB** FORMAL If something is protruding from a surface or edge, it is sticking out. **protrusion NOUN**

proud, prouder, proudest **ADJECTIVE** ❶ feeling pleasure and satisfaction at something you own or have achieved • *I was proud of our players today.*

▷ SPELLING NOTE: *an ELegant angEL (angel)*

❷ having great dignity and self-respect • *too proud to ask for money.* **proudly** ADVERB

prove, proves, proving, proved or proven VERB ❶ To prove that something is true is to provide evidence that it is definitely true • *A letter from Kathleen proved that he lived there.* ❷ If something proves to be the case, it becomes clear that it is so • *His first impressions of her proved wrong.*
  ● SIMILAR WORDS: ❶ confirm, show, verify

proverb, proverbs NOUN a short sentence which gives advice or makes a comment about life. **proverbial** ADJECTIVE

provide, provides, providing, provided VERB ❶ If you provide something for someone, you give it to them or make it available for them. ❷ If you provide for someone, you give them the things they need.
  ● SIMILAR WORDS: ❶ furnish, supply

provided or **providing** CONJUNCTION If you say that something will happen provided something else happens, you mean that the first thing will happen only if the second thing does.
  ● USAGE NOTE: *Provided* is followed by *that*, but *providing* is not: *I'll come, providing he doesn't; You can go, provided that you phone as soon as you get there*

providence NOUN Providence is God or a force which is believed to arrange the things that happen to us.

province, provinces NOUN ❶ one of the areas into which some large countries are divided, each province having its own administration. ❷ IN PLURAL You can refer to the parts of a country which are not near the capital as the provinces.
  ● WORD HISTORY: from Latin *provincia* meaning 'a conquered territory'

provincial ADJECTIVE ❶ connected with the parts of a country outside the capital • *a provincial theatre.* ❷ narrow-minded and lacking sophistication.

provision, provisions NOUN (GEOGRAPHY) ❶ The provision of something is the act of making it available to people • *the provision of health care.* ❷ IN PLURAL Provisions are supplies of food.

provisional ADJECTIVE A provisional arrangement has not yet been made definite and so might be changed.

proviso, provisos [Said prov-*eye*-zoh] NOUN a condition in an agreement.

provocation, provocations NOUN an act done deliberately to annoy someone.

provocative ADJECTIVE ❶ intended to annoy people or make them react • *a provocative speech.* ❷ intended to make someone feel sexual desire • *provocative poses.*

provoke, provokes, provoking, provoked VERB ❶ If you provoke someone, you deliberately try to make them angry. ❷ If something provokes an unpleasant reaction, it causes it • *illness provoked by tension or worry.*

▷ SPELLING NOTE: *LEt's measure the angLE (angle)*

prow, prows NOUN the front part of a boat.

prowess NOUN Prowess is outstanding ability • *his prowess at tennis.*

prowl, prowls, prowling, prowled VERB If a person or animal prowls around, they move around quietly and secretly, as if hunting.

proximity NOUN FORMAL Proximity is nearness to someone or something.

proxy PHRASE If you do something by proxy, someone else does it on your behalf • *voting by proxy.*

prude, prudes NOUN someone who is too easily shocked by sex or nudity. **prudish** ADJECTIVE
● **WORD HISTORY:** from Old French
● *prode femme* meaning 'respectable
● woman'

prudent ADJECTIVE behaving in a sensible and cautious way • *It is prudent to plan ahead.* **prudence** NOUN **prudently** ADVERB

prune, prunes, pruning, pruned NOUN ❶ a dried plum ▷ VERB ❷ When someone prunes a tree or shrub, they cut back some of the branches.

pry, pries, prying, pried VERB If someone is prying, they are trying to find out about something secret or private.

PS PS is written before an additional message at the end of a letter. PS is an abbreviation for 'postscript'.

psalm, psalms [*Said sahm*] NOUN one of the 150 songs, poems, and prayers which together form the Book

of Psalms in the Bible.

pseudo- [*Said syoo-doh*] PREFIX 'Pseudo-' is used to form adjectives and nouns indicating that something is not what it is claimed to be • *pseudo-scientific theories.*
● **WORD HISTORY:** from Greek
● *pseudēs* meaning 'false'

pseudonym, pseudonyms [*Said syoo-doe-nim*] NOUN a name an author uses rather than their real name.

PSHE NOUN an abbreviation for 'Personal, Social, and Health Education': a lesson in which students are taught about social and personal issues.

psyche, psyches [*Said sigh-kee*] NOUN your mind and your deepest feelings.

psychiatry NOUN Psychiatry is the branch of medicine concerned with mental illness. **psychiatrist** NOUN **psychiatric** ADJECTIVE

psychic ADJECTIVE having unusual mental powers such as the ability to read people's minds or predict the future.

psychoanalysis NOUN Psychoanalysis is the examination and treatment of someone who is mentally ill by encouraging them to talk about their feelings and past events in order to discover the cause of the illness. **psychoanalyst** NOUN **psychoanalyse** VERB

psychology NOUN Psychology is the scientific study of the mind and of the reasons for people's behaviour. **psychological** ADJECTIVE **psychologist** NOUN

a b c d e f g h i j k l m n o **p** q r s t u v w x y z

▷ SPELLING NOTE: *Psychiatrists Seldom Yell Callously Hard* (psychiatrist)

psychopath, psychopaths **NOUN** a mentally ill person who behaves violently without feeling guilt. **psychopathic ADJECTIVE**

psychosis, psychoses [Said sigh-**koe**-siss] **NOUN** a severe mental illness. **psychotic ADJECTIVE**

pterodactyl, pterodactyls [Said ter-rod-**dak**-til] **NOUN** Pterodactyls were flying reptiles in prehistoric times.
- **WORD HISTORY:** from Greek
- *pteron* meaning 'wing' and *daktulos*
- meaning 'finger'

PTO PTO is an abbreviation for 'please turn over'. It is written at the bottom of a page to indicate that the writing continues on the other side.

pub, pubs **NOUN** a building where people go to buy and drink alcoholic or soft drinks and talk with their friends.

puberty [Said **pyoo**-ber-tee] **NOUN** Puberty is the stage when a person's body changes from that of a child into that of an adult.

pubic [Said pyoo-bik] **ADJECTIVE** relating to the area around and above a person's genitals.

public NOUN ❶ You can refer to people in general as the public ▷ **ADJECTIVE** ❷ relating to people in general • *There was some public support for the idea.* ❸ provided for everyone to use, or open to anyone • *public transport.* **publicly ADVERB**

publican, publicans **NOUN** a person who owns or manages a pub.

publication, publications **NOUN** ❶ The publication of a book is the act of printing it and making it available. ❷ a book or magazine • *an extensive*

range of medical publications.

publicity NOUN Publicity is information or advertisements about an item or event.

publicize, publicizes, publicizing, publicized; *also spelt* **publicise VERB** When someone publicizes a fact or event, they advertise it and make it widely known.

public school, public schools **NOUN** In Britain, a public school is a school that is privately run and that charges fees for the pupils to attend.

public servant, public servants **NOUN** In Australia and New Zealand, someone who works in the public service.

public service NOUN In Australia and New Zealand, the public service is the government departments responsible for the administration of the country.

publish, publishes, publishing, published **VERB** (LIBRARY) When a company publishes a book, newspaper, or magazine, they print copies of it and distribute it. **publishing NOUN**

publisher, publishers **NOUN** (LIBRARY) The publisher of a book, newspaper or magazine is the person or company that prints copies of it and distributes it.

pudding, puddings **NOUN** ❶ a sweet cake mixture cooked with fruit or other flavouring and served hot. ❷ You can refer to the sweet course of a meal as the pudding.

puddle, puddles **NOUN** a small shallow pool of liquid.

▷ SPELLING NOTE: *Beautiful Elephants Are Usually Tiny (beautiful)*

puerile [Said **pyoo**-rile] ADJECTIVE
Puerile behaviour is silly and childish.
- WORD HISTORY: from Latin
- *puerilis*, from *puer* meaning 'boy'

puff, puffs, puffing, puffed VERB
❶ To puff a cigarette or pipe is to
smoke it. ❷ If you are puffing, you are
breathing loudly and quickly with your
mouth open. ❸ If something puffs
out or puffs up, it swells and becomes
larger and rounder ▷ NOUN ❹ a
small amount of air or smoke that is
released.

puffin, puffins NOUN a black and
white sea bird with a large brightly
coloured beak.

pug, pugs NOUN a small, short-haired
dog with a flat nose.

puja [Said **poo**-jah] NOUN Puja is a
variety of practices which make up
Hindu worship.

puke, pukes, puking, puked VERB
INFORMAL If someone pukes, they vomit.

pull, pulls, pulling, pulled VERB
❶ When you pull something, you hold
it and move it towards you. ❷ When
something is pulled by a vehicle or
animal, it is attached to it and moves
along behind it • *Four oxen can pull a
single plough.* ❸ When you pull a
curtain or blind, you move it so that it
covers or uncovers the window. ❹ If
you pull a muscle, you injure it by
stretching it too far or too quickly.
❺ When a vehicle pulls away, pulls
out, or pulls in, it moves in that
direction ▷ NOUN ❻ The pull of
something is its attraction or influence
• *the pull of the past.*
pull down VERB When a building is
pulled down, it is deliberately

destroyed for some reason.
pull out VERB If you pull out of
something, you leave it or decide not
to continue with it • *The German
government has pulled out of the project.*
pull through VERB When someone
pulls through, they recover from a
serious illness.

pulley, pulleys NOUN ⟨D&T⟩ a
device for lifting heavy weights. The
weight is attached to a rope which
passes over a wheel or series of wheels.

pullover, pullovers NOUN a woollen
piece of clothing that covers the top
part of your body.

pulmonary ADJECTIVE MEDICAL
relating to the lungs or to the veins
and arteries carrying blood between
the lungs and the heart.

pulp NOUN If something is turned
into a pulp, it is crushed until it is soft
and moist.

pulpit, pulpits [Said **pool**-pit] NOUN
the small raised platform in a church
where a member of the clergy stands
to preach.

pulse, pulses, pulsing, pulsed NOUN
❶ Your pulse is the regular beating of
blood through your body, the rate of
which you can feel at your wrists and
elsewhere. ❷ The seeds of beans,
peas, and lentils are called pulses
when they are used for food ▷ VERB
❸ If something is pulsing, it is moving
or vibrating with rhythmic, regular
movements • *She could feel the blood
pulsing in her eardrums.*

puma, pumas [Said **pyoo**-mah]
NOUN a wild animal belonging to the
cat family.

a
b
c
d
e
f
g
h
i
j
k
l
m
n
o
p
q
r
s
t
u
v
w
x
y
z

▷ SPELLING NOTE: *Betty Eats Cakes And Uses Seven Eggs (because)*

pumice [Said **pum-miss**] **NOUN**
Pumice stone is very lightweight grey
stone that can be used to soften areas
of hard skin.

pummel, pummels, pummelling,
pummelled **VERB** If you pummel
something, you beat it with your fists.

pump, pumps, pumping, pumped
NOUN ❶ a machine that is used to
force a liquid or gas to move in a
particular direction. ❷ Pumps are
light shoes with flat soles which
people wear for sport or leisure
▷ **VERB** ❸ To pump a liquid or gas
somewhere is to force it to flow in that
direction, using a pump. ❹ If you
pump money into something, you put
a lot of money into it.

pumpkin, pumpkins **NOUN** a very
large, round, orange fruit eaten as a
vegetable.

pun, puns **NOUN** a clever and
amusing use of words so that what
you say has two different meanings,
such as *my dog's a champion boxer*.

punch, punches, punching, punched
VERB ❶ If you punch someone, you
hit them hard with your fist ▷ **NOUN**
❷ a hard blow with the fist. ❸ a tool
used for making holes. ❹ Punch is a
drink made from a mixture of wine,
spirits, and fruit.

punctual ADJECTIVE arriving at the
correct time. **punctually ADVERB**
punctuality NOUN
● **SIMILAR WORDS:** on time, prompt

punctuate, punctuates,
punctuating, punctuated **VERB**
❶ Something that is punctuated by a
particular thing is interrupted by it at
intervals • *a grey day punctuated by
bouts of rain.* ❷ (ENGLISH) When you
punctuate a piece of writing, you put
punctuation into it.

punctuation NOUN (ENGLISH)
The marks in writing such as full stops,
question marks, and commas are called
punctuation or punctuation marks.
▶ SEE GRAMMAR BOX BELOW

puncture, punctures, puncturing,
punctured **NOUN** ❶ If a tyre has a
puncture, a small hole has been made
in it and it has become flat ▷ **VERB**
❷ To puncture something is to make
a small hole in it.

pungent ADJECTIVE having a
strong, unpleasant smell or taste.
pungency NOUN

punish, punishes, punishing,
punished **VERB** To punish someone
who has done something wrong is to
make them suffer because of it.
● **SIMILAR WORDS:** chastise,
● discipline, penalize

WHAT DOES PUNCTUATION DO?

Punctuation marks are essential parts
of written language. They help the
reader to understand what is being
read.

Look at the grammar boxes at
apostrophe, bracket, colon,

**comma, dash, exclamation mark,
full stop, hyphen, inverted
comma, question mark,** and
semicolon.

▷ SPELLING NOTE: *there's a rAKE in the brAKEs (brake)*

punishment, punishments NOUN
something unpleasant done to
someone because they have done
something wrong.

punitive [Said *pyoo-nit-tiv*]
ADJECTIVE harsh and intended to
punish people • *punitive military action.*

Punjabi, Punjabis [Said *pun-jah-
bee*] ADJECTIVE ❶ belonging or
relating to the Punjab, a state in
north-western India ▷ NOUN
❷ someone who comes from the
Punjab. ❸ Punjabi is a language
spoken in the Punjab.

punk NOUN Punk or punk rock is an
aggressive style of rock music.

punt, punts NOUN a long, flat-
bottomed boat. You move it along by
pushing a pole against the river
bottom.

puny, punier, puniest ADJECTIVE
very small and weak.

pup, pups NOUN a young dog. Some
other young animals such as seals are
also called pups.

pupil, pupils NOUN ❶ The pupils at
a school are the children who go
there. ❷ Your pupils are the small,
round, black holes in the centre of
your eyes.

puppet, puppets NOUN a doll or toy
animal that is moved by pulling strings
or by putting your hand inside its
body.

puppy, puppies NOUN a young dog.

purchase, purchases, purchasing,
purchased VERB ❶ When you
purchase something, you buy it
▷ NOUN ❷ something you have

bought. **purchaser** NOUN

pure, purer, purest ADJECTIVE
❶ Something that is pure is not mixed
with anything else • *pure wool* • *pure
white.* ❷ Pure also means clean and
free from harmful substances • *The
water is pure enough to drink.*
❸ People who are pure have not done
anything considered to be sinful.
❹ Pure also means complete and
total • *a matter of pure luck.* **purity**
NOUN

● SIMILAR WORDS: ❷ clean,
● uncontaminated ❸ chaste,
● innocent, virtuous

purebred ADJECTIVE (SCIENCE) A
purebred animal has parents and
grandparents of the same breed.

purée, purées [Said *pyoo-ray*] NOUN
a food which has been mashed or
blended to a thick, smooth consistency.

purely ADVERB involving only one
feature and not including anything
else • *purely professional.*

Purgatory NOUN Roman Catholics
believe that Purgatory is a place where
spirits of the dead are sent to suffer for
their sins before going to Heaven.

purge, purges, purging, purged VERB
To purge something is to remove
undesirable things from it • *to purge
the country of criminals.*

purify, purifies, purifying, purified
VERB To purify something is to
remove all dirty or harmful substances
from it. **purification** NOUN

purist, purists NOUN someone who
believes that something should be
done in a particular, correct way • *a
football purist.*

▷ SPELLING NOTE: *you'll brEAK that Electrical Aerial, Kitty (break)*

puritan, puritans NOUN someone who believes in strict moral principles and avoids physical pleasures. **puritanical** ADJECTIVE **puritanism** NOUN

purple NOUN OR ADJECTIVE reddish-blue.

purport, purports, purporting, purported [Said pur-**port**] VERB FORMAL Something that purports to be or have a thing is claimed to be or have it • *a country which purports to disapprove of smokers.*

purpose, purposes NOUN ❶ The purpose of something is the reason for it • *the purpose of the meeting.* ❷ If you have a particular purpose, this is what you want to achieve • *To make music is my purpose in life.* ▷ PHRASE ❸ If you do something **on purpose**, you do it deliberately. **purposely** ADVERB **purposeful** ADJECTIVE

purr, purrs, purring, purred VERB When a cat purrs, it makes a low vibrating sound because it is contented.

purse, purses, pursing, pursed NOUN ❶ a small leather or fabric container for carrying money ▷ VERB ❷ If you purse your lips, you move them into a tight, rounded shape.

purser, pursers NOUN the officer responsible for the paperwork and the welfare of passengers on a ship.

pursue, pursues, pursuing, pursued VERB ❶ If you pursue an activity or plan, you do it or make efforts to achieve it • *I decided to pursue a career in photography.* ❷ If you pursue someone, you follow them to try to catch them. **pursuer** NOUN **pursuit** NOUN

purveyor, purveyors NOUN FORMAL A purveyor of goods or services is a person who sells them or provides them.

pus NOUN Pus is a thick yellowish liquid that forms in an infected wound.

push, pushes, pushing, pushed VERB ❶ When you push something, you press it using force in order to move it. ❷ If you push someone into doing something, you force or persuade them to do it • *His mother pushed him into auditioning for a part.* ❸ INFORMAL Someone who pushes drugs sells them illegally.

push off VERB INFORMAL If you tell someone to push off, you are telling them rudely to go away.

● SIMILAR WORDS: ❶ shove,
● thrust

pushchair, pushchairs NOUN a small folding chair on wheels in which a baby or toddler can be wheeled around.

pusher, pushers NOUN INFORMAL someone who sells illegal drugs.

pushing PREPOSITION Someone who is pushing a particular age is nearly that age • *pushing sixty.*

pushover NOUN INFORMAL ❶ something that is easy. ❷ someone who is easily persuaded or defeated.

pushy, pushier, pushiest ADJECTIVE INFORMAL behaving in a forceful and determined way.

pussy, pussies NOUN INFORMAL a cat.

put, puts, putting, put VERB ❶ When you put something somewhere, you move it into that place or position. ❷ If you put an idea or remark in a

a b c d e f g h i j k l m n o **p** q r s t u v w x y z

particular way, you express it that way
• *I think you've put that very well.* ❸ To
put someone or something in a
particular state or situation means to
cause them to be in it • *It puts us both
in an awkward position.* ❹ You can use
'put' to express an estimate of the size
or importance of something • *Her
wealth is now put at £290 million.*
put down VERB ❶ To put someone
down is to criticize them and make
them appear foolish. ❷ If an animal is
put down, it is killed because it is very
ill or dangerous.
put off VERB ❶ If you put
something off, you delay doing it.
❷ To put someone off is to discourage
them.
put out VERB ❶ If you put a fire out
or put the light out, you make it stop
burning or shining. ❷ If you are put
out, you are annoyed or upset.
put up VERB If you put up
resistance to something, you argue or
fight against it • *She put up a
tremendous struggle.*
put up with VERB If you put up
with something, you tolerate it even
though you disagree with it or dislike it.
● **SIMILAR WORDS:** ❶ place,
● position, set

putt, putts **NOUN** In golf, a putt is a
gentle stroke made when the ball is
near the hole.

putting NOUN Putting is a game
played on a small grass course with no
obstacles. You hit a ball gently with a
club so that it rolls towards one of a
series of holes around the course.

putty NOUN Putty is a paste used to
fix panes of glass into frames.

puzzle, puzzles, puzzling, puzzled

VERB ❶ If something puzzles you, it
confuses you and you do not
understand it • *There was something
about her that puzzled me.* ▷ **NOUN**
❷ A puzzle is a game or question that
requires a lot of thought to complete
or solve. **puzzled ADJECTIVE**
puzzlement NOUN
● **SIMILAR WORDS:** ❶ baffle,
● mystify, perplex

PVC NOUN PVC is a plastic used for
making clothing, pipes, and many
other things. PVC is an abbreviation
for 'polyvinyl chloride'.

pygmy, pygmies *[Said **pig**-mee]; also
spelt* **pigmy NOUN** a very small person,
especially one who belongs to a racial
group in which all the people are small.
● **WORD HISTORY:** from Greek
● *pugmaios* meaning 'undersized'

pyjamas PLURAL NOUN Pyjamas
are loose trousers and a jacket or top
that you wear in bed.
● **WORD HISTORY:** from Persian *pay
● jama* meaning 'leg clothing'

pylon, pylons **NOUN** a very tall metal
structure which carries overhead
electricity cables.

pyramid, pyramids **NOUN** ❶ a
three-dimensional shape with a flat
base and flat triangular sides sloping
upwards to a point. ❷ The Pyramids
are ancient stone structures built over
the tombs of Egyptian kings and
queens.

pyre, pyres **NOUN** a high pile of wood
on which a dead body or religious
offering is burned.

python, pythons **NOUN** a large
snake that kills animals by squeezing
them with its body.

▷ SPELLING NOTE: *I want to see (C) your licenCe (licence)*

Qq

quack, quacks, quacking, quacked **VERB** When a duck quacks, it makes a loud harsh sound.

quad, quads [Said kwod] **NOUN** Quad is the same as **quadruplet**.

quadrangle, quadrangles [Said kwod-rang-gl] **NOUN** a courtyard with buildings all round it.

quadri- **PREFIX** 'Quadri-' means 'four'.

quadriceps **NOUN** (PE) a large muscle in four parts at the front of your thigh.

quadrilateral, quadrilaterals [Said kwod-ril-lat-ral] **NOUN** (MATHS) a shape with four straight sides.

quadruped, quadrupeds [Said kwod-roo-ped] **NOUN** any animal with four legs.

quadruple, quadruples, quadrupling, quadrupled [Said kwod-roo-pl] **VERB** When an amount or number quadruples, it becomes four times as large as it was.

quadruplet, quadruplets [Said kwod-roo-plet] **NOUN** Quadruplets are four children born at the same time to the same mother.

quagmire, quagmires [Said kwag-mire] **NOUN** a soft, wet area of land which you sink into if you walk on it.

quail, quails, quailing, quailed **NOUN** ❶ a type of small game bird with a round body and short tail ▷ **VERB** ❷ If you quail, you feel or look afraid.

quaint, quainter, quaintest **ADJECTIVE** attractively old-fashioned or unusual • quaint customs. **quaintly ADVERB**

quake, quakes, quaking, quaked **VERB** If you quake, you shake and tremble because you are very frightened.

Quaker, Quakers **NOUN** a member of a Christian group, the Society of Friends.

qualification, qualifications **NOUN** ❶ Your qualifications are your skills and achievements, especially as officially recognized at the end of a course of training or study. ❷ something you add to a statement to make it less strong • It is a good novel and yet cannot be recommended without qualification.

qualify, qualifies, qualifying, qualified **VERB** ❶ (PE) When you qualify, you pass the examinations or tests that you need to pass to do a particular job or to take part in a sporting event. ❷ If you qualify a statement, you add a detail or explanation to make it less strong • I would qualify that by putting it into context. ❸ If you qualify for something, you become entitled to have it • *You qualify for a discount.* **qualified** ADJECTIVE

qualitative ADJECTIVE relating to the quality of something.

quality, qualities NOUN ❶ The quality of something is how good it is • *The quality of food is very poor.* ❷ a characteristic • *These qualities are essential for success.*

qualm, qualms [*Said kwahm*] NOUN If you have qualms about what you are doing, you worry that it might not be right.

quandary, quandaries [*Said kwon-dree*] NOUN If you are in a quandary, you cannot decide what to do.

quango, quangos NOUN a body responsible for a particular area of public administration, which is financed by the government but is outside direct government control. Quango is short for quasi-autonomous non-governmental organization.

quantitative ADJECTIVE relating to the size or amount of something.

quantity, quantities NOUN ❶ an amount you can measure or count • *a small quantity of alcohol.* ❷ Quantity is the amount of something that there is • *emphasis on quantity rather than quality.*

quarantine [*Said kwor-an-teen*] NOUN If an animal is in quarantine, it is kept away from other animals for a time because it might have an infectious disease.
● **WORD HISTORY:** from Italian
● *quarantina* meaning 'forty days'

quarrel, quarrels, quarrelling, quarrelled NOUN ❶ an angry argument ▷ VERB ❷ If people quarrel, they have an angry argument.
● **SIMILAR WORDS:** ❶ argument,
● disagreement, fight ❷ argue,
● disagree, fall out

quarry, quarries, quarrying, quarried [*Said kwor-ree*] NOUN ❶ a place where stone is removed from the ground by digging or blasting. ❷ A person's or animal's quarry is the animal that they are hunting ▷ VERB ❸ To quarry stone means to remove it from a quarry by digging or blasting.
● **WORD HISTORY:** sense 2 is from
● Middle English *quirre* meaning
● 'entrails given to the hounds to eat'

quart, quarts [*Said kwort*] NOUN a unit of liquid volume equal to two pints or about 1.136 litres.

quarter, quarters NOUN ❶ one of four equal parts. ❷ an American coin worth 25 cents. ❸ You can refer to a particular area in a city as a quarter • *the French quarter.* ❹ You can use 'quarter' to refer vaguely to a particular person or group of people • *You are very popular in certain quarters.* ❺ IN PLURAL A soldier's or a servant's quarters are the rooms that they live in.

quarterly, quarterlies ADJECTIVE OR ADVERB ❶ Quarterly means happening regularly every three months • *my quarterly report.* ▷ NOUN ❷ a magazine or journal published every three months.

quartet, quartets [*Said kwor-tet*] NOUN a group of four musicians who sing or play together; also a piece of music written for four instruments or

▷ SPELLING NOTE: *have a pIEce of pIE (piece)*

singers • *a string quartet.*

quartile, quartiles NOUN (MATHS)
When you divide data into quartiles,
you divide it into four equal groups.

quartz NOUN Quartz is a kind of
hard, shiny crystal used in making very
accurate watches and clocks.

quash, quashes, quashing, quashed
[Said kwosh] VERB To quash a
decision or judgment means to reject
it officially • *The judges quashed their
convictions.*

quasi- *[Said kway-sie]* PREFIX
'Quasi-' means resembling something
but not actually being that thing • *a
quasi-religious order.*
● WORD HISTORY: a Latin word
meaning 'as if'

quatrain, quatrains *[Said kwot-
rain]* NOUN (ENGLISH) A quatrain is a
verse of poetry with four lines.

quaver, quavers, quavering, quavered
[Said kway-ver] VERB ❶ If your voice
quavers, it sounds unsteady, usually
because you are nervous ▷ NOUN
❷ (MUSIC) a musical note (♪) that
has the time value of an eighth of a
semibreve. In the United States and
Canada, a quaver is known as an
eighth note.

quay, quays *[Said kee]* NOUN a place
where boats are tied up and loaded or
unloaded.

queasy, queasier, queasiest *[Said
kwee-zee]* ADJECTIVE feeling slightly
sick.

queen, queens NOUN ❶ a female
monarch or a woman married to a
king. ❷ a female bee or ant which can
lay eggs. ❸ In chess, the queen is the
most powerful piece, which can move
in any direction. ❹ In a pack of cards,
a queen is a card with a picture of a
queen on it.

queen mother, queen mothers
NOUN the widow of a king and the
mother of the reigning monarch.

queer, queerer, queerest ADJECTIVE
Queer means very strange.

quell, quells, quelling, quelled VERB
❶ To quell a rebellion or riot means to
put an end to it by using force. ❷ If
you quell a feeling such as fear or
grief, you stop yourself from feeling it
• *trying to quell the loneliness.*

quench, quenches, quenching,
quenched VERB If you quench your
thirst, you have a drink so that you are
no longer thirsty.

query, queries, querying, queried
[Said qweer-ree] NOUN ❶ a question
▷ VERB ❷ If you query something,
you ask about it because you think it
might not be right • *No-one queried my
decision.*

quest, quests NOUN a long search
for something.

question, questions, questioning,
questioned NOUN ❶ a sentence
which asks for information. ❷ If there
is some question about something,
there is doubt about it. ❸ a problem
that needs to be discussed • *Can we
get back to the question of the car?*
▷ VERB ❹ If you question someone,
you ask them questions. ❺ If you
question something, you express
doubts about it • *He never stopped
questioning his own beliefs.* ▷ PHRASE
❻ If something is **out of the
question**, it is impossible.

▷ SPELLING NOTE: *the QUeen stood on the QUay (quay)*

a b c d e f g h i j k l m n o p **q** r s t u v w x y z

WHAT IS A QUESTION?

Questions are used to ask for information.

A question has a question mark at the end of the sentence:
What is your name?

Questions are often introduced by a questioning word such as *what, who, where, when, why,* or *how*:
Where do you live?

If a sentence does not already contain an auxiliary verb, a form of the auxiliary verb *do* may be placed at the start to turn it into a question:
***Does** Anna have a sister?*

If there is already an auxiliary verb in the sentence, you can turn it into a question by reversing the word order so the auxiliary verb comes before the subject instead of after it:
***Are** you going to the swimming baths?*
***Must** they keep doing that?*

A question can also be made by adding a phrase, such as *isn't it?* or *don't you?*, on to the end of a statement:
*It is hot today, **isn't it?***
*You like chocolate, **don't you?***

● **SIMILAR WORDS: ❶** inquiry, query **❺** challenge, dispute
▶ SEE GRAMMAR BOX ABOVE

questionable ADJECTIVE possibly not true or not honest.

question mark, question marks NOUN the punctuation mark (?) which is used at the end of a question.
▶ SEE GRAMMAR BOX BELOW

questionnaire, questionnaires NOUN (MATHS) a list of questions which asks for information for a survey.

queue, queues, queuing or queueing, queued *[Said **kyoo**]* NOUN **❶** a line of people or vehicles waiting for

something ▷ VERB **❷** When people queue, they stand in a line waiting for something.

quibble, quibbles, quibbling, quibbled VERB **❶** If you quibble, you argue about something unimportant ▷ NOUN **❷** a minor objection.

quiche, quiches *[Said **keesh**]* NOUN a tart with a savoury filling.
● **WORD HISTORY:** a French word, originally from German *Kuchen* meaning 'cake'

quick, quicker, quickest ADJECTIVE **❶** moving with great speed. **❷** lasting only a short time • *a quick chat*. **❸** happening without any delay

---

WHAT DOES THE QUESTION MARK DO?

The **question mark (?)** marks the end of a question:
When is the train leaving?

After an indirect question or a polite request, a full stop is used rather than a question mark:
Anna asked when the train was leaving.
Will you please send me an application form.

▷ SPELLING NOTE: *I went to see (C) the doctor's new practiCe (practice)*

• *a quick response.* ❹ intelligent and able to understand things easily.

quickly ADVERB with great speed.

quicksand, quicksands **NOUN** an area of deep wet sand that you sink into if you walk on it.

quid NOUN INFORMAL In British English, a pound in money.

quiet, quieter, quietest **ADJECTIVE** ❶ Someone or something that is quiet makes very little noise or no noise at all. ❷ Quiet also means peaceful • *a quiet evening at home.* ❸ A quiet event happens with very little fuss or publicity • *a quiet wedding.* ▷ **NOUN** ❹ Quiet is silence.
quietly ADVERB
● USAGE NOTE: Do not confuse the
● spellings of *quiet* and the adverb
● *quite*

quieten, quietens, quietening, quietened **VERB** To quieten someone means to make them become quiet.

quill, quills **NOUN** ❶ a pen made from a feather. ❷ A bird's quills are the large feathers on its wings and tail. ❸ A porcupine's quills are its spines.

quilt, quilts **NOUN** A quilt for a bed is a cover, especially a cover that is padded.

quilted ADJECTIVE Quilted clothes or coverings are made of thick layers of material sewn together.

quin, quins **NOUN** Quin is the same as **quintuplet**.

quince, quinces **NOUN** an acid-tasting fruit used for making jam and marmalade.

quintessential ADJECTIVE

FORMAL A person or thing that is quintessential seems to represent the basic nature of something in a pure, concentrated form • *It was the quintessential Hollywood party.*

quintet, quintets *[Said kwin-**tet**]* **NOUN** a group of five musicians who sing or play together; also a piece of music written for five instruments or singers.

quintuplet, quintuplets *[Said kwin-**tyoo**-plit]* **NOUN** Quintuplets are five children born at the same time to the same mother.

quip, quips, quipping, quipped **NOUN** ❶ an amusing or clever remark ▷ **VERB** ❷ To quip means to make an amusing or clever remark.

quirk, quirks **NOUN** ❶ an odd habit or characteristic • *an interesting quirk of human nature.* ❷ an unexpected event or development • *a quirk of fate.*
quirky ADJECTIVE

quit, quits, quitting, quit **VERB** If you quit something, you leave it or stop doing it • *Leigh quit his job as a salesman.*

quite ADVERB ❶ fairly but not very • *quite old.* ❷ completely • *Jane lay quite still.* ▷ **PHRASE** ❸ You use **quite a** to emphasize that something is large or impressive • *It was quite a party.*
● USAGE NOTE: You should be
● careful about using *quite*. It can
● mean 'completely': *quite amazing*. It
● can also mean 'fairly but not very':
● *quite friendly*. Do not confuse the
● spellings of *quite* and the adjective
● *quiet*

quiver, quivers, quivering, quivered

▷ SPELLING NOTE: *You must practiSe your Ss (practise)*

A B C D E F G H I J K L M N O P **Q** R S T U V W X Y Z

WHAT IS A QUOTATION?

There are two ways of writing what people say. You can write down the exact words that are spoken. This is called **direct speech**. The second way is to write down the meaning of what they say without using the exact words. This is called **indirect speech** or **reported speech**.

When you use direct speech, the exact words spoken go into quotation marks:
Robbie said, 'Thank you very much for the prize.'

The sentence will contain a main verb which indicates speaking, such as *say, tell, ask,* or *answer*. The words contained in quotation marks begin with a capital letter. If there is no other punctuation, they are separated from the rest of the sentence by a comma:
'This is the best picture,' said the judge.

When you use indirect or reported speech, there is a subordinate clause which reports the meaning of what was said.
The judge said that Robbie's picture was the best.

When the reported words are a statement, the clause that reports them is usually introduced by *that*. The main clause usually contains a verb such as *say, tell, explain,* or *reply*:
The judge said that Robbie should win first prize.

Sometimes the word *that* can be left out.
The judge said Robbie should win first prize.

VERB ❶ If something quivers, it trembles ▷ **NOUN** ❷ a trembling movement • *a quiver of panic.*

quixotic [Said kwik-**sot**-ik] **ADJECTIVE** unrealistic and romantic.

quiz, quizzes, quizzing, quizzed **NOUN** ❶ a game in which the competitors are asked questions to test their knowledge ▷ **VERB** ❷ If you quiz someone, you question them closely about something.

quizzical [Said **kwiz**-ik-kl] **ADJECTIVE** amused and questioning • *a quizzical smile.*

quota, quotas **NOUN** a number or quantity of something which is officially allowed • *a quota of three foreign players allowed in each team.*

quotation, quotations **NOUN** an extract from a book or speech which is quoted.
▶ SEE GRAMMAR BOX ABOVE

quote, quotes, quoting, quoted **VERB** ❶ If you quote something that someone has written or said, you repeat their exact words. ❷ If you quote a fact, you state it because it supports what you are saying ▷ **NOUN** ❸ an extract from a book or speech. ❹ an estimate of how much a piece of work will cost.

Qur'an another spelling of **Koran**.

Rr

Some words which sound as if they should begin with letter *r* are spelt with *wr*, for example *wrangle*, *wretch*, *write*, and *wrong*. Other words which sound as if they ought to begin with letter *r* alone are actually spelt with *rh*, for example *rhapsody*, *rheumatism*, *rhino*, and *rhododendron*.

RAAF In Australia, an abbreviation for 'Royal Australian Air Force'.

rabbi, rabbis *[Said rab-by]* **NOUN** a Jewish religious leader.
● **WORD HISTORY:** from Hebrew *rabh* + *-i* meaning 'my master'

rabbit, rabbits **NOUN** a small animal with long ears.

rabble **NOUN** a noisy, disorderly crowd.

rabid **ADJECTIVE** ❶ used to describe someone with strong views that you do not approve of • *a rabid Nazi.* ❷ A rabid dog or other animal has rabies.

rabies *[Said ray-beez]* **NOUN** an infectious disease which causes people and animals, especially dogs, to go mad and die.

raccoon, raccoons; *also spelt* **racoon** **NOUN** a small North American animal with a long striped tail.

race, races, racing, raced **NOUN** ❶ a competition to see who is fastest, for example in running or driving. ❷ one of the major groups that human beings can be divided into according to their physical features ▷ **VERB** ❸ If you race someone, you compete with them in a race. ❹ If you race something or if it races, it goes at its greatest rate • *Her heart raced uncontrollably.* ❺ If you race somewhere, you go there as quickly as possible • *The hares raced away out of sight.* **racing** **NOUN**

racecourse, racecourses **NOUN** a grass track, sometimes with jumps, along which horses race.

racehorse, racehorses **NOUN** a horse trained to run in races.

racial **ADJECTIVE** relating to the different races that people belong to • *racial harmony.* **racially** **ADVERB**

racism or **racialism** **NOUN** (PSHE) Racism or racialism is the treatment of some people as inferior because of their race. **racist** **NOUN OR ADJECTIVE**

rack, racks, racking, racked **NOUN** ❶ a piece of equipment for holding things or hanging things on ▷ **VERB** ❷ If you are racked by something, you suffer because of it • *She was racked by guilt.* ▷ **INFORMAL PHRASE** ❸ If you **rack your brains**, you try hard to think of or remember something.

racket, rackets **NOUN** ❶ If someone

is making a racket, they are making a lot of noise. ❷ an illegal way of making money • *a drugs racket.* ❸ Racket is another spelling of **racquet.**

racquet, racquets; *also spelt* **racket NOUN** a bat with strings across it used in tennis and similar games.
  ● **WORD HISTORY:** from Arabic
  ● *rahat* meaning 'palm of the hand'

radar NOUN Radar is equipment used to track ships or aircraft that are out of sight by using radio signals that are reflected back from the object and shown on a screen.
  ● **WORD HISTORY:** from *RA(dio) D(etecting) A(nd) R(anging)*

radiant ADJECTIVE ❶ Someone who is radiant is so happy that it shows in their face. ❷ glowing brightly. **radiance NOUN**

radiate, radiates, radiating, radiated **VERB** ❶ If things radiate from a place, they form a pattern like lines spreading out from the centre of a circle. ❷ If you radiate a quality or emotion, it shows clearly in your face and behaviour • *He radiated health.*

radiation NOUN the stream of particles given out by a radioactive substance.

radiator, radiators **NOUN** ❶ a hollow metal device for heating a room, usually connected to a central heating system. ❷ the part of a car that is filled with water to cool the engine.

radical, radicals **NOUN** ❶ Radicals are people who think there should be great changes in society, and try to make them happen ▷ **ADJECTIVE**

❷ very significant, important, or basic • *a radical change in the law.* **radically ADVERB radicalism NOUN**

radii the plural of **radius.**

radio, radios, radioing, radioed **NOUN** ❶ Radio is a system of sending sound over a distance by transmitting electrical signals. ❷ Radio is also the broadcasting of programmes to the public by radio. ❸ a piece of equipment for listening to radio programmes ▷ **VERB** ❹ To radio someone means to send them a message by radio • *The pilot radioed that a fire had started.*

radioactive ADJECTIVE giving off powerful and harmful rays. **radioactivity NOUN**

radiotherapy NOUN the treatment of diseases such as cancer using radiation. **radiotherapist NOUN**

radish, radishes **NOUN** a small salad vegetable with a red skin and white flesh and a hot taste.

radium NOUN a radioactive element which is used in the treatment of cancer.

radius, radii **NOUN** (MATHS) The radius of a circle is the length of a straight line drawn from its centre to its circumference.

RAF In Britain, an abbreviation for 'Royal Air Force'.

raffia NOUN a material made from palm leaves and used for making mats and baskets.

raffle, raffles **NOUN** a competition in which people buy numbered tickets

a
b
c
d
e
f
g
h
i
j
k
l
m
n
o
p
q
r
s
t
u
v
w
x
y
z

▷ SPELLING NOTE: *Psychiatrists Seldom Yell Callously Hard (psychiatrist)*

and win a prize if they have the ticket that is chosen.

raft, rafts **NOUN** a floating platform made from long pieces of wood tied together.

rafter, rafters **NOUN** Rafters are the sloping pieces of wood that support a roof.

rag, rags **NOUN** ❶ a piece of old cloth used to clean or wipe things. ❷ If someone is dressed in rags, they are wearing old torn clothes.

rage, rages, raging, raged **NOUN** ❶ Rage is great anger ▷ **VERB** ❷ To rage about something means to speak angrily about it. ❸ If something such as a storm or battle is raging, it is continuing with great force or violence • *The fire still raged out of control.*
● **SIMILAR WORDS:** ❶ anger, fury, ● wrath

ragged ADJECTIVE Ragged clothes are old and torn.

raid, raids, raiding, raided **VERB** ❶ To raid a place means to enter it by force to attack it or steal something ▷ **NOUN** ❷ the raiding of a building or a place • *an armed raid on a bank.*

rail, rails **NOUN** ❶ a fixed horizontal bar used as a support or for hanging things on. ❷ Rails are the steel bars which trains run along. ❸ Rail is the railway considered as a means of transport • *I plan to go by rail.*

railing, railings **NOUN** Railings are a fence made from metal bars.

railway, railways **NOUN** a route along which trains travel on steel rails.

rain, rains, raining, rained **NOUN** ❶ water falling from the clouds in small drops ▷ **VERB** ❷ When it is raining, rain is falling. **rainy ADJECTIVE**

rainbird, rainbirds **NOUN** a bird whose call is believed to be a sign that it will rain.

rainbow, rainbows **NOUN** an arch of different colours that sometimes appears in the sky after it has been raining.

raincoat, raincoats **NOUN** a waterproof coat.

rainfall NOUN the amount of rain that falls in a place during a particular period.

rainforest, rainforests **NOUN** (GEOGRAPHY) a dense forest of tall trees in a tropical area where there is a lot of rain.

rainwater NOUN rain that has been stored.

raise, raises, raising, raised **VERB** ❶ If you raise something, you make it higher • *She went to the window and raised the blinds* • *a drive to raise standards of literacy.* ❷ If you raise your voice, you speak more loudly. ❸ To raise money for a cause means to get people to donate money towards it. ❹ To raise a child means to look after it until it is grown up. ❺ If you raise a subject, you mention it.

raisin, raisins **NOUN** Raisins are dried grapes.

rake, rakes, raking, raked **NOUN** a garden tool with a row of metal teeth and a long handle.
rake up VERB If you rake up

▷ SPELLING NOTE: *the QUeen stood on the QUay (quay)*

something embarrassing from the past, you remind someone about it.

rally, rallies, rallying, rallied **NOUN** ❶ a large public meeting held to show support for something. ❷ a competition in which vehicles are raced over public roads. ❸ In tennis or squash, a rally is a continuous series of shots exchanged by the players ▷ **VERB** ❹ When people rally to something, they gather together to continue a struggle or to support something.

ram, rams, ramming, rammed **VERB** ❶ If one vehicle rams another, it crashes into it. ❷ To ram something somewhere means to push it there firmly • *He rammed his key into the lock.* ▷ **NOUN** ❸ an adult male sheep.

RAM NOUN ICT a storage space which can be filled with data but which loses its contents when the machine is switched off. RAM stands for 'random access memory'.

Ramadan NOUN RE the ninth month of the Muslim year, during which Muslims eat and drink nothing during daylight.
● **WORD HISTORY:** from Arabic
● *Ramadan* meaning literally 'the hot
● month'

ramble, rambles, rambling, rambled **NOUN** ❶ a long walk in the countryside ▷ **VERB** ❷ To ramble means to go for a ramble. ❸ To ramble also means to talk in a confused way • *He then started rambling and repeating himself.*
rambler NOUN

ramification, ramifications **NOUN**

The ramifications of a decision or plan are all its consequences and effects.

ramp, ramps **NOUN** a sloping surface connecting two different levels.

rampage, rampages, rampaging, rampaged **VERB** ❶ To rampage means to rush about wildly causing damage ▷ **PHRASE** ❷ To go **on the rampage** means to rush about in a wild or violent way.
● **SIMILAR WORDS:** ❶ go berserk,
● run amok

rampant ADJECTIVE If something such as crime or disease is rampant, it is growing or spreading uncontrollably.

rampart, ramparts **NOUN** Ramparts are earth banks, often with a wall on top, built to protect a castle or city.

ramshackle ADJECTIVE A ramshackle building is in very poor condition.

ranch, ranches **NOUN** a large farm where cattle or horses are reared, especially in the USA.
● **WORD HISTORY:** from Mexican
● Spanish *rancho* meaning 'small
● farm'

rancid *[Said ran-sid]* **ADJECTIVE** Rancid food has gone bad.
● **WORD HISTORY:** from Latin
● *rancere* meaning 'to stink'

rancour *[Said rang-kur]* **NOUN** FORMAL Rancour is bitter hatred.
rancorous ADJECTIVE

rand NOUN The rand is the main unit of currency in South Africa.

random ADJECTIVE ❶ A random choice or arrangement is not based on any definite plan ▷ **PHRASE** ❷ If you

▷ SPELLING NOTE: *Rhythmical Hounds Yap To Heavy Music (rhythm)*

do something **at random**, you do it without any definite plan • *He chose his victims at random.* **randomly ADVERB**

● **SIMILAR WORDS:** ❶ chance, haphazard, incidental

range, ranges, ranging, ranged **NOUN**
❶ The range of something is the maximum distance over which it can reach things or detect things • *This mortar has a range of 15,000 metres.* ❷ a number of different things of the same kind • *A wide range of colours are available.* ❸ a set of values on a scale • *The average age range is between 35 and 55.* ❹ A range of mountains is a line of them. ❺ A rifle range or firing range is a place where people practise shooting at targets ▷ **VERB** ❻ When a set of things ranges between two points, they vary within these points on a scale • *prices ranging between 370 and 1200 pounds.*

● **SIMILAR WORDS:** ❷ series, variety

ranger, rangers **NOUN** someone whose job is to look after a forest or park.

rank, ranks, ranking, ranked **NOUN**
❶ Someone's rank is their official level in a job or profession. ❷ The ranks are the ordinary members of the armed forces, rather than the officers. ❸ The ranks of a group are its members • *We welcomed five new members to our ranks.* ❹ a row of people or things ▷ **VERB** ❺ To rank as something means to have that status or position on a scale • *His dismissal ranks as the worst humiliation he has ever known.* ▷ **ADJECTIVE**
❻ complete and absolute • *rank stupidity.* ❼ having a strong,

unpleasant smell • *the rank smell of unwashed clothes.*

ransack, ransacks, ransacking, ransacked **VERB** To ransack a place means to disturb everything and leave it in a mess, in order to search for or steal something.

● **WORD HISTORY:** from Old Norse *rann* meaning 'house' and *saka* meaning 'to search'

ransom, ransoms **NOUN** money that is demanded to free someone who has been kidnapped.

rant, rants, ranting, ranted **VERB** To rant means to talk loudly in an excited or angry way.

rap, raps, rapping, rapped **VERB** ❶ If you rap something, you hit it with a series of quick blows ▷ **NOUN** ❷ a quick knock or blow on something • *A rap on the door signalled his arrival.*
❸ Rap is a style of poetry spoken to music with a strong rhythmic beat • *He really likes rap.*

rape, rapes, raping, raped **VERB** ❶ If a man rapes a woman, he violently forces her to have sex with him against her will ▷ **NOUN** ❷ Rape is the act or crime of raping a woman • *victims of rape.* ❸ Rape is a plant with yellow flowers that is grown as a crop for oil and fodder. **rapist NOUN**

rapid ADJECTIVE happening or moving very quickly • *rapid industrial expansion* • *He took a few rapid steps.* **rapidly ADVERB rapidity NOUN**

rapids PLURAL NOUN An area of a river where the water moves extremely fast over rocks is referred to as rapids.

rapier, rapiers NOUN a long thin sword with a sharp point.

rapport [Said rap-*por*] NOUN FORMAL If there is a rapport between two people, they find it easy to understand each other's feelings and attitudes.

rapt ADJECTIVE If you are rapt, you are so interested in something that you are not aware of other things • *sitting with rapt attention in front of the screen.*

rapture NOUN Rapture is a feeling of extreme delight. **rapturous** ADJECTIVE **rapturously** ADVERB

rare, rarer, rarest ADJECTIVE ❶ Something that is rare is not common or does not happen often • *a rare flower* • *Such major disruptions are rare.* ❷ Rare meat has been lightly cooked. **rarely** ADVERB

rarefied [Said rare-*if-eyed*] ADJECTIVE seeming to have little connection with ordinary life • *He grew up in a rarefied literary atmosphere.*

raring ADJECTIVE If you are raring to do something, you are very eager to do it.

rarity, rarities NOUN ❶ something that is interesting or valuable because it is unusual. ❷ The rarity of something is the fact that it is not common.

rascal, rascals NOUN If you refer to someone as a rascal, you mean that they do bad or mischievous things.

rash, rashes ADJECTIVE ❶ If you are rash, you do something hasty and foolish ▷ NOUN ❷ an area of red

spots that appear on your skin when you are ill or have an allergy. ❸ A rash of events is a lot of them happening in a short time • *a rash of strikes.* **rashly** ADVERB

● SIMILAR WORDS: ❶ foolhardy,
● reckless

rasher, rashers NOUN a thin slice of bacon.

rasp, rasps, rasping, rasped VERB ❶ To rasp means to make a harsh unpleasant sound ▷ NOUN ❷ a coarse file with rows of raised teeth, used for smoothing wood or metal.

raspberry, raspberries NOUN a small soft red fruit that grows on a bush.

rat, rats NOUN a long-tailed animal which looks like a large mouse.

rate, rates, rating, rated NOUN ❶ The rate of something is the speed or frequency with which it happens • *New diet books appear at the rate of nearly one a week.* ❷ The rate of interest is its level • *a further cut in interest rates.* ❸ the cost or charge for something. ❹ Rates are a local tax paid by people who own buildings ▷ PHRASE ❺ If you say **at this rate** something will happen, you mean it will happen if things continue in the same way • *At this rate we'll be lucky to get home before six.* ❻ You say **at any rate** when you want to add to or amend what you have just said • *He is the least appealing character, to me at any rate.* ▷ VERB ❼ The way you rate someone or something is your opinion of them • *He was rated as one of England's top young players.*

rather ADVERB ❶ Rather means to

a certain extent • *We got along rather well* • *The reality is rather more complex.*
▷ **PHRASE** ❷ If you **would rather** do a particular thing, you would prefer to do it. ❸ If you do one thing **rather than** another, you choose to do the first thing instead of the second.
● **SIMILAR WORDS:** ❶ quite,
● relatively, somewhat ❷ preferably,
● sooner

ratify, ratifies, ratifying, ratified **VERB** FORMAL To ratify a written agreement means to approve it formally, usually by signing it. **ratification** NOUN

rating, ratings NOUN ❶ a score based on the quality or status of something. ❷ The ratings are statistics showing how popular each television programme is.

ratio, ratios NOUN a relationship which shows how many times one thing is bigger than another • *The adult to child ratio is 1 to 6.*

ration, rations, rationing, rationed NOUN ❶ Your ration of something is the amount you are allowed to have. ❷ Rations are the food given each day to a soldier or member of an expedition ▷ **VERB** ❸ When something is rationed, you are only allowed a limited amount of it, because there is a shortage.

rational ADJECTIVE When people are rational, their judgments are based on reason rather than emotion. **rationally** ADVERB **rationality** NOUN

rationale [Said rash-on-*nahl*] NOUN The rationale for a course of action or for a belief is the set of reasons on which it is based.

rattle, rattles, rattling, rattled **VERB** ❶ When something rattles, it makes short, regular knocking sounds. ❷ If something rattles you, it upsets you • *He was obviously rattled by events.* ▷ **NOUN** ❸ the noise something makes when it rattles. ❹ a baby's toy which makes a noise when it is shaken.

rattlesnake, rattlesnakes NOUN a poisonous American snake.

raucous [Said *raw*-kuss] ADJECTIVE A raucous voice is loud and rough.

ravage, ravages, ravaging, ravaged FORMAL **VERB** ❶ To ravage something means to seriously harm or damage it • *a country ravaged by floods.* ▷ **NOUN** ❷ The ravages of something are its damaging effects • *the ravages of two world wars.*

rave, raves, raving, raved **VERB** ❶ If someone raves, they talk in an angry, uncontrolled way • *He started raving about being treated badly.* ❷ INFORMAL If you rave about something, you talk about it very enthusiastically ▷ **ADJECTIVE** ❸ INFORMAL If something gets a rave review, it is praised enthusiastically ▷ **NOUN** ❹ INFORMAL a large party with electronic dance music.

raven, ravens NOUN ❶ a large black bird with a deep, harsh call ▷ **ADJECTIVE** ❷ Raven hair is black and shiny.

ravenous ADJECTIVE very hungry.

ravine, ravines NOUN a deep, narrow valley with steep sides.

raving, ravings ADJECTIVE ❶ If someone is raving, they are mad • *a* *raving lunatic.* ▷ **NOUN** ❷ Someone's ravings are crazy things they write or say.

ravioli [Said rav-ee-**oh**-lee] **NOUN** Ravioli consists of small squares of pasta filled with meat and served with a sauce.

ravishing ADJECTIVE Someone or something that is ravishing is very beautiful • *a ravishing landscape.*

raw ADJECTIVE ❶ Raw food has not been cooked. ❷ A raw substance is in its natural state • *raw sugar.* ❸ If part of your body is raw, the skin has come off or been rubbed away. ❹ Someone who is raw is too young or too new in a job or situation to know how to behave.

raw material, raw materials **NOUN** Raw materials are the natural substances used to make something.

ray, rays **NOUN** ❶ a beam of light or radiation. ❷ A ray of hope is a small amount that makes an unpleasant situation seem slightly better. ❸ a large sea fish with eyes on the top of its body, and a long tail.

raze, razes, razing, razed **VERB** To raze a building, town, or forest means to completely destroy it • *The town was razed to the ground during the occupation.*

razor, razors **NOUN** a tool that people use for shaving.

razor blade, razor blades **NOUN** a small, sharp, flat piece of metal fitted into a razor for shaving.

re- PREFIX ❶ 'Re-' is used to form nouns and verbs that refer to the repetition of an action or process

• *reread* • *remarry.* ❷ 'Re-' is also used to form verbs that refer to going back to a previous condition • *refresh* • *renew.*

● **WORD HISTORY:** from a Latin
● prefix

reach, reaches, reaching, reached **VERB** ❶ When you reach a place, you arrive there. ❷ When you reach for something, you stretch out your arm to it. ❸ If something reaches a place or point, it extends as far as that place or point • *She has a cloak that reaches to the ground.* ❹ If something or someone reaches a stage or level, they get to it • *Unemployment has reached record levels.* ❺ To reach an agreement or decision means to succeed in achieving it ▷ **PHRASE** ❻ If a place is **within reach**, you can get there • *a cycle route well within reach of most people.* ❼ If something is **out of reach**, you cannot get it to it by stretching out your arm • *Store out of reach of children.*

react, reacts, reacting, reacted **VERB** ❶ When you react to something, you behave in a particular way because of it • *He reacted badly to the news.* ❷ (SCIENCE) If one substance reacts with another, a chemical change takes place when they are put together.

reactant, reactants **NOUN** (SCIENCE) In a chemical reaction, a reactant is a substance that reacts with another one.

reaction, reactions **NOUN** ❶ Your reaction to something is what you feel, say, or do because of it • *Reaction to the visit is mixed.* ❷ Your reactions are your ability to move quickly in response to something that happens

a
b
c
d
e
f
g
h
i
j
k
l
m
n
o
p
q
r
s
t
u
v
w
x
y
z

▷ SPELLING NOTE: *Elaine and Emily shout EE when they mEEt to grEEt each other (-ee-)*

• *Squash requires fast reactions.* ❸ If there is a reaction against something, it becomes unpopular • *a reaction against Christianity.* ❹ SCIENCE In a chemical reaction, a chemical change takes place when two substances are put together.

reactionary, reactionaries **ADJECTIVE** ❶ Someone who is reactionary tries to prevent political or social change ▷ **NOUN** ❷ Reactionaries are reactionary people.

reactive ADJECTIVE SCIENCE a chemical substance that is reactive will react readily with another. **reactivity NOUN**

reactor, reactors **NOUN** a device which is used to produce nuclear energy.

read, reads, reading, read **VERB** ❶ When you read, you look at something written and follow it or say it aloud. ❷ If you can read someone's moods or mind, you can judge what they are feeling or thinking. ❸ When you read a meter or gauge, you look at it and record the figure on it. ❹ If you read a subject at university, you study it.

reader, readers **NOUN** ❶ The readers of a newspaper or magazine are the people who read it regularly. ❷ At a university, a reader is a senior lecturer just below the rank of professor.

readership NOUN The readership of a newspaper or magazine consists of the people who read it regularly.

readily ADVERB ❶ willingly and eagerly • *She readily agreed to see Alex.*

❷ easily done or quickly obtainable • *Help is readily available.*

reading, readings **NOUN** ❶ Reading is the activity of reading books. ❷ The reading on a meter or gauge is the figure or measurement it shows.

readjust, readjusts, readjusting, readjusted *[Said ree-aj-just]* **VERB** ❶ If you readjust, you adapt to a new situation. ❷ If you readjust something, you alter it to a different position.

ready ADJECTIVE ❶ having reached the required stage, or prepared for action or use • *In a few days time the plums will be ready to eat.* ❷ willing or eager to do something • *She says she's not ready for marriage.* ❸ If you are ready for something, you need it • *I'm ready for bed.* ❹ easily produced or obtained • *ready cash.* **readiness NOUN**

ready-made ADJECTIVE already made and therefore able to be used immediately.

reaffirm, reaffirms, reaffirming, reaffirmed **VERB** To reaffirm something means to state it again • *He reaffirmed his support for the campaign.*

real ADJECTIVE ❶ actually existing and not imagined or invented. ❷ genuine and not imitation • *Who's to know if they're real guns?* ❸ true or actual and not mistaken • *This was the real reason for her call.*
● **SIMILAR WORDS:** ❶ authentic,
● genuine, true

real estate NOUN Real estate is property in the form of land and buildings rather than personal

▷ SPELLING NOTE: *'i' before 'e' except after 'c'*

possessions • *invested in real estate.*

realism NOUN Realism is the recognition of the true nature of a situation • *a triumph of muddled thought over realism and common sense.* **realist** NOUN

realistic ADJECTIVE ❶ recognizing and accepting the true nature of a situation. ❷ representing things in a way that is true to real life • *His novels are more realistic than his short stories.* **realistically** ADVERB

reality NOUN (PSHE) ❶ Reality is the real nature of things, rather than the way someone imagines it • *Fiction and reality were increasingly blurred.* ❷ If something has become reality, it actually exists or is actually happening.
● SIMILAR WORDS: ❶ fact, truth

realize, realizes, realizing, realized; *also spelt* **realise** VERB ❶ If you realize something, you become aware of it. ❷ FORMAL If your hopes or fears are realized, what you hoped for or feared actually happens • *Our worst fears were realized.* ❸ To realize a sum of money means to receive it as a result of selling goods or shares. **realization** NOUN

really ADVERB ❶ used to add emphasis to what is being said • *I'm not really surprised.* ❷ used to indicate that you are talking about the true facts about something • *What was really going on?*
● USAGE NOTE: If you want to emphasize an adjective you should always use *really* rather than *real*: *really interesting*

realm, realms [*Said* **relm**] NOUN

FORMAL ❶ You can refer to any area of thought or activity as a realm • *the realm of politics.* ❷ a country with a king or queen • *defence of the realm.*

reap, reaps, reaping, reaped VERB ❶ To reap a crop such as corn means to cut and gather it. ❷ When people reap benefits or rewards, they get them as a result of hard work or careful planning. **reaper** NOUN

reappear, reappears, reappearing, reappeared VERB When people or things reappear, you can see them again, because they have come back • *The stolen ring reappeared three years later in a pawn shop.* **reappearance** NOUN

reappraisal, reappraisals NOUN FORMAL If there is a reappraisal, people think about something and decide whether they want to change it • *a reappraisal of the government's economic policies.*

rear, rears, rearing, reared NOUN ❶ The rear of something is the part at the back ▷ VERB ❷ To rear children or young animals means to bring them up until they are able to look after themselves. ❸ When a horse rears, it raises the front part of its body, so that its front legs are in the air.

rear admiral, rear admirals NOUN a senior officer in the navy.

rearrange, rearranges, rearranging, rearranged VERB To rearrange something means to organize or arrange it in a different way.

reason, reasons, reasoning, reasoned NOUN ❶ The reason for something is the fact or situation which explains

a b c d e f g h i j k l m n o p q **r** s t u v w x y z

▷ SPELLING NOTE: *King IAn went to ParlIAment in a carrIAge for his marrIAge (-ia-)*

why it happens or which causes it to happen. ❷ If you have reason to believe or feel something, there are definite reasons why you believe it or feel it • *He had every reason to be upset.* ❸ Reason is the ability to think and make judgments ▷ **VERB** ❹ If you reason that something is true, you decide it is true after considering all the facts. ❺ If you reason with someone, you persuade them to accept sensible arguments.
● **SIMILAR WORDS:** ❶ cause,
● motive ❸ rationality, sense,
● senses, understanding

reasonable ADJECTIVE
❶ Reasonable behaviour is fair and sensible. ❷ If an explanation is reasonable, there are good reasons for thinking it is correct. ❸ A reasonable amount is a fairly large amount. ❹ A reasonable price is fair and not too high. **reasonably ADVERB**

reasoning NOUN Reasoning is the process by which you reach a conclusion after considering all the facts.

reassess, reassesses, reassessing, reassessed **VERB** If you reassess something, you consider whether it still has the same value or importance. **reassessment NOUN**

reassure, reassures, reassuring, reassured **VERB** If you reassure someone, you say or do things that make them less worried. **reassurance NOUN**

rebate, rebates **NOUN** money paid back to someone who has paid too much tax or rent.

rebel, rebels, rebelling, rebelled

NOUN ❶ (HISTORY) Rebels are people who are fighting their own country's army to change the political system. ❷ Someone who is a rebel rejects society's values and behaves differently from other people ▷ **VERB** ❸ To rebel means to fight against authority and reject accepted values.

rebellion, rebellions **NOUN** (HISTORY) A rebellion is organized and often violent opposition to authority.
● **SIMILAR WORDS:** mutiny,
● revolution, uprising

rebellious ADJECTIVE unwilling to obey and likely to rebel against authority.

rebuff, rebuffs, rebuffing, rebuffed **VERB** ❶ If you rebuff someone, you reject what they offer • *She rebuffed their offers of help.* ▷ **NOUN** ❷ a rejection of an offer.

rebuild, rebuilds, rebuilding, rebuilt **VERB** When a town or building is rebuilt, it is built again after being damaged or destroyed.

rebuke, rebukes, rebuking, rebuked *[Said rib-yook]* **VERB** To rebuke someone means to speak severely to them about something they have done.

recall, recalls, recalling, recalled **VERB** ❶ To recall something means to remember it. ❷ If you are recalled to a place, you are ordered to return there. ❸ If a company recalls products, it asks people to return them because they are faulty.

recap, recaps, recapping, recapped **VERB** To recap means to repeat and summarize the main points of an explanation or discussion.

▷ SPELLING NOTE: *an ELegant angEL (angel)*

recapture, recaptures, recapturing, recaptured **VERB** ❶ When you recapture a pleasant feeling, you experience it again • *She may never recapture that past assurance.* ❷ When soldiers recapture a place, they capture it from the people who took it from them. ❸ When animals or prisoners are recaptured, they are caught after they have escaped.

recede, recedes, receding, receded **VERB** ❶ When something recedes, it moves away into the distance. ❷ If a man's hair is receding, he is starting to go bald at the front.

receipt, receipts [*Said ris-seet*] **NOUN** ❶ a piece of paper confirming that money or goods have been received. ❷ In a shop or theatre, the money received is often called the receipts • *Box-office receipts were down last month.* ❸ FORMAL The receipt of something is the receiving of it • *You have to sign here and acknowledge receipt.*

receive, receives, receiving, received **VERB** ❶ When you receive something, someone gives it to you, or you get it after it has been sent to you. ❷ To receive something also means to have it happen to you • *injuries she received in a car crash.* ❸ When you receive visitors or guests, you welcome them. ❹ If something is received in a particular way, that is how people react to it • *The decision has been received with great disappointment.*

receiver, receivers **NOUN** the part of a telephone you hold near to your ear and mouth.

recent **ADJECTIVE** Something recent

happened a short time ago. **recently ADVERB**

reception, receptions **NOUN** ❶ In a hotel or office, reception is the place near the entrance where appointments or enquiries are dealt with. ❷ a formal party. ❸ The reception someone or something gets is the way people react to them • *Her tour met with a rapturous reception.* ❹ If your radio or television gets good reception, the sound or picture is clear.

receptionist, receptionists **NOUN** The receptionist in a hotel or office deals with people when they arrive, answers the telephone, and arranges appointments.

receptive **ADJECTIVE** Someone who is receptive to ideas or suggestions is willing to consider them.

recess, recesses **NOUN** ❶ a period when no work is done by a committee or parliament • *the Christmas recess.* ❷ a place where part of a wall has been built further back than the rest.

recession, recessions **NOUN** a period when a country's economy is less successful and more people become unemployed.

recharge, recharges, recharging, recharged **VERB** To recharge a battery means to charge it with electricity again after it has been used.

recipe, recipes [*Said res-sip-ee*] **NOUN** ❶ D&T a list of ingredients and instructions for cooking something. ❷ If something is a recipe for disaster or for success, it is likely to result in disaster or success.

a
b
c
d
e
f
g
h
i
j
k
l
m
n
o
p
q
r
s
t
u
v
w
x
y
z

▷ SPELLING NOTE: *LEt's measure the angLE (angle)*

recipient, recipients NOUN The recipient of something is the person receiving it.

reciprocal ADJECTIVE A reciprocal agreement involves two people, groups, or countries helping each other in a similar way • *a reciprocal agreement on trade.*

reciprocate, reciprocates, reciprocating, reciprocated VERB If you reciprocate someone's feelings or behaviour, you feel or behave in the same way towards them.

recital, recitals NOUN a performance of music or poetry, usually by one person.

recite, recites, reciting, recited VERB If you recite a poem or something you have learnt, you say it aloud. **recitation** NOUN

reckless ADJECTIVE showing a complete lack of care about danger or damage • *a reckless tackle.* **recklessly** ADVERB **recklessness** NOUN

reckon, reckons, reckoning, reckoned VERB ① INFORMAL If you reckon that something is true, you think it is true • *I reckoned he was still fond of her.* ② INFORMAL If someone reckons to do something, they claim or expect to do it • *Officers on the case are reckoning to charge someone shortly.* ③ To reckon an amount means to calculate it. ④ If you reckon on something, you rely on it happening when making your plans • *He reckons on being world champion.* ⑤ If you had not reckoned with something, you had not expected it and therefore were unprepared when it happened • *Giles had not reckoned with the strength of Sally's feelings.*

reckoning, reckonings NOUN a calculation • *There were a thousand or so, by my reckoning.*

reclaim, reclaims, reclaiming, reclaimed VERB ① When you reclaim something, you collect it after leaving it somewhere or losing it. ② To reclaim land means to make it suitable for use, for example by draining it. **reclamation** NOUN

recline, reclines, reclining, reclined VERB To recline means to lie or lean back at an angle • *a photo of him reclining on his bed.*

recluse, recluses NOUN Someone who is a recluse lives alone and avoids other people. **reclusive** ADJECTIVE

recognize, recognizes, recognizing, recognized; *also spelt* recognise VERB ① If you recognize someone or something, you realize that you know who or what they are • *The receptionist recognized me at once.* ② To recognize something also means to accept and acknowledge it • *The RAF recognized him as an outstanding pilot.* **recognition** NOUN **recognizable** ADJECTIVE **recognizably** ADVERB
 SIMILAR WORDS: ① identify, know, place

recommend, recommends, recommending, recommended VERB If you recommend something to someone, you praise it and suggest they try it. **recommendation** NOUN

reconcile, reconciles, reconciling, reconciled VERB ① To reconcile two things that seem to oppose one another, means to make them work or exist together successfully • *The designs reconciled style with comfort.*

▷ SPELLING NOTE: *A Rude Idiot Thought He Might Eat Toffee In Church (arithmetic)*

❷ When people are reconciled, they become friendly again after a quarrel. ❸ If you reconcile yourself to an unpleasant situation, you accept it. **reconciliation** NOUN

reconnaissance [Said rik-kon-iss-sanss] NOUN Reconnaissance is the gathering of military information by soldiers, planes, or satellites.

reconsider, reconsiders, reconsidering, reconsidered VERB To reconsider something means to think about it again to decide whether to change it. **reconsideration** NOUN

reconstruct, reconstructs, reconstructing, reconstructed VERB ❶ To reconstruct something that has been damaged means to build it again. ❷ To reconstruct a past event means to get a complete description of it from small pieces of information. **reconstruction** NOUN

record, records, recording, recorded NOUN ❶ If you keep a record of something, you keep a written account or store information in a computer • *medical records.* ❷ a round, flat piece of plastic on which music has been recorded. ❸ an achievement which is the best of its type. ❹ Your record is what is known about your achievements or past activities ▷ VERB ❺ If you record information, you write it down or put it into a computer. ❻ To record sound means to put it on tape, record, or compact disc ▷ ADJECTIVE ❼ higher, lower, better, or worse than ever before • *Profits were at a record level.*
● **SIMILAR WORDS:** ❶ document, file, register ❺ note, register, write down

recorder, recorders NOUN a small woodwind instrument.

recording, recordings NOUN A recording of something is a record, CD, or DVD of it.

recount, recounts, recounting, recounted VERB ❶ If you recount a story, you tell it ▷ NOUN ❷ a second count of votes in an election when the result is very close.

recoup, recoups, recouping, recouped [Said rik-koop] VERB If you recoup money that you have spent or lost, you get it back.

recourse NOUN FORMAL If you have recourse to something, you use it to help you • *For once, the members settled their differences without recourse to war.*

recover, recovers, recovering, recovered VERB ❶ To recover from an illness or unhappy experience means to get well again or get over it. ❷ If you recover a lost object or your ability to do something, you get it back.
● **SIMILAR WORDS:** ❶ convalesce, get better, recuperate ❷ regain, retrieve

recovery NOUN ❶ the act of getting better again. ❷ the act of getting something back.

recreate, recreates, recreating, recreated VERB To recreate something means to succeed in making it happen or exist again • *a museum that faithfully recreates an old farmhouse.*

recreation, recreations [Said rek-kree-ay-shn] NOUN Recreation is all the things that you do for enjoyment in your spare time. **recreational** ADJECTIVE

recrimination, recriminations NOUN Recriminations are accusations made by people about each other.

recruit, recruits, recruiting, recruited VERB ❶ To recruit people means to get them to join a group or help with something ▷ NOUN ❷ someone who has joined the army or some other organization. **recruitment** NOUN

rectangle, rectangles NOUN a four-sided shape with four right angles. **rectangular** ADJECTIVE

rectify, rectifies, rectifying, rectified VERB FORMAL If you rectify something that is wrong, you put it right.

rector, rectors NOUN a Church of England priest in charge of a parish.

rectory, rectories NOUN a house where a rector lives.

rectum, rectums NOUN TECHNICAL the bottom end of the tube down which waste food passes out of your body. **rectal** ADJECTIVE

recuperate, recuperates, recuperating, recuperated VERB When you recuperate, you gradually recover after being ill or injured. **recuperation** NOUN

recur, recurs, recurring, recurred VERB If something recurs, it happens or occurs again • *His hamstring injury recurred after the first game.* **recurrence** NOUN **recurrent** ADJECTIVE

recurring ADJECTIVE ❶ happening or occurring many times

• *a recurring dream.* ❷ MATHS A recurring digit is one that is repeated over and over again after the decimal point in a decimal fraction.

recycle, recycles, recycling, recycled VERB GEOGRAPHY To recycle used products means to process them so that they can be used again • *recycled glass.*

red, redder, reddest; reds NOUN OR ADJECTIVE ❶ Red is the colour of blood or of a ripe tomato ▷ ADJECTIVE ❷ Red hair is between orange and brown in colour.

redback, redbacks NOUN a small Australian spider with a poisonous bite.

red blood cell, red blood cells NOUN SCIENCE Your red blood cells are the cells in your blood that carry oxygen, carbon dioxide, and haemoglobin to and from your tissues.

redcurrant, redcurrants NOUN Redcurrants are very small, bright red fruits that grow in bunches on a bush.

redeem, redeems, redeeming, redeemed VERB ❶ If a feature redeems an unpleasant thing or situation, it makes it seem less bad. ❷ If you redeem yourself, you do something that gives people a good opinion of you again. ❸ If you redeem something, you get it back by paying for it. ❹ RE In Christianity, to redeem someone means to free them from sin by giving them faith in Jesus Christ.

redemption NOUN Redemption is the state of being redeemed.

red-handed PHRASE To catch someone red-handed means to catch them doing something wrong.

red-hot ADJECTIVE Red-hot metal has been heated to such a high temperature that it has turned red.

redress, redresses, redressing, redressed FORMAL VERB ❶ To redress a wrong means to put it right ▷ NOUN ❷ If you get redress for harm done to you, you are compensated for it.

red tape NOUN Red tape is official rules and procedures that seem unnecessary and cause delay.

reduce, reduces, reducing, reduced VERB ❶ To reduce something means to make it smaller in size or amount. ❷ You can use 'reduce' to say that someone or something is changed to a weaker or inferior state • *The village was reduced to rubble.*
● SIMILAR WORDS: ❶ cut,
● decrease, lessen

reduction, reductions NOUN When there is a reduction in something, it is made smaller.

redundancy, redundancies NOUN ❶ Redundancy is the state of being redundant. ❷ The number of redundancies is the number of people made redundant.

redundant ADJECTIVE ❶ When people are made redundant, they lose their jobs because there is no more work for them or no money to pay them. ❷ When something becomes redundant, it is no longer needed.

reed, reeds NOUN ❶ Reeds are hollow stemmed plants that grow in shallow water or wet ground. ❷ a thin piece of cane or metal inside some wind instruments which vibrates when air is blown over it.

reef, reefs NOUN (GEOGRAPHY) a long line of rocks or coral close to the surface of the sea.

reek, reeks, reeking, reeked VERB ❶ To reek of something means to smell strongly and unpleasantly of it ▷ NOUN ❷ If there is a reek of something, there is a strong unpleasant smell of it.

reel, reels, reeling, reeled NOUN ❶ a cylindrical object around which you wrap something; often part of a device which you turn as a control. ❷ a fast Scottish dance ▷ VERB ❸ When someone reels, they move unsteadily as if they are going to fall. ❹ If your mind is reeling, you are confused because you have too much to think about.
reel off VERB If you reel off information, you repeat it from memory quickly and easily.

re-elect, re-elects, re-electing, re-elected VERB When someone is re-elected, they win an election again and are able to stay in power.

refer, refers, referring, referred VERB ❶ If you refer to something, you mention it. ❷ If you refer to a book or record, you look at it to find something out. ❸ When a problem or issue is referred to someone, they are formally asked to deal with it • *The case was referred to the European Court.*
● WORD HISTORY: from Latin *referre* meaning 'to carry back'
● USAGE NOTE: The word *refer* contains the sense 'back' in its meaning. Therefore, you should not use *back* after *refer*: this refers to what has already been said not refers back

▷ SPELLING NOTE: *there's a rAKE in the brAKEs (brake)*

A
B
C
D
E
F
G
H
I
J
K
L
M
N
O
P
Q
R
S
T
U
V
W
X
Y
Z

referee, referees **NOUN** ❶ the official who controls a football game or a boxing or wrestling match. ❷ someone who gives a reference to a person who is applying for a job • *She offered to be one of his referees.*

reference, references **NOUN** ❶ A reference to something or someone is a mention of them. ❷ Reference is the act of referring to something or someone for information or advice • *He makes that decision without reference to her.* ❸ a number or name that tells you where to find information or identifies a document. ❹ If someone gives you a reference when you apply for a job, they write a letter about your abilities.

referendum, referendums or referenda **NOUN** a vote in which all the people in a country are officially asked whether they agree with a policy or proposal • *a referendum on whether or not to join the European Community.*

refine, refines, refining, refined **VERB** To refine a raw material such as oil or sugar means to process it to remove impurities.

refined ADJECTIVE ❶ very polite and well-mannered. ❷ processed to remove impurities.

refinement, refinements **NOUN** ❶ Refinements are minor improvements. ❷ Refinement is politeness and good manners.

refinery, refineries **NOUN** a factory where substances such as oil or sugar are refined.

reflect, reflects, reflecting, reflected **VERB** ❶ If something reflects an attitude or situation, it shows what it is like • *His off-duty hobbies reflected his maritime interests.* ❷ If something reflects light or heat, the light or heat bounces off it. ❸ When something is reflected in a mirror or water, you can see its image in it. ❹ (MATHS) If something reflects, its direction is reversed. ❺ When you reflect, you think about something • *There's no time to reflect on the matter.*
reflective ADJECTIVE reflectively ADVERB

reflection, reflections **NOUN** ❶ If something is a reflection of something else, it shows what it is like • *This is a terrible reflection of the times.* ❷ an image in a mirror or water. ❸ Reflection is the process by which light and heat are bounced off a surface. ❹ (MATHS) In maths, reflection is also the turning back of something on itself • *reflection of an axis.* ❺ Reflection is also thought • *After days of reflection she decided to leave.*

reflex, reflexes **NOUN** ❶ A reflex or reflex action is a sudden uncontrollable movement that you make as a result of pressure or a blow. ❷ If you have good reflexes, you respond very quickly when something unexpected happens ▷ **ADJECTIVE** ❸ (MATHS) A reflex angle is between 180° and 360°.

reflexive, reflexives **ADJECTIVE OR NOUN** (ENGLISH) In grammar, a reflexive verb or pronoun is one that refers back to the subject of the sentence • *She washed herself* • *He positioned himself at the door.*

reform, reforms, reforming, reformed **NOUN** ❶ Reforms are major changes to laws or institutions • *a programme of economic reform.* ▷ VERB ② When laws or institutions are reformed, major changes are made to them. ③ When people reform, they stop committing crimes or doing other unacceptable things. **reformer** NOUN

Reformation NOUN (HISTORY) The Reformation was a religious and political movement in Europe in the 16th century that began as an attempt to reform the Roman Catholic Church, but ended in the establishment of the Protestant Churches.

refraction NOUN Refraction is the bending of a ray of light, for example when it enters water or glass.

refrain, refrains, refraining, refrained VERB ① FORMAL If you refrain from doing something, you do not do it • *Please refrain from smoking in the hall.* ▷ NOUN ② (MUSIC) The refrain of a song is a short, simple part, repeated many times.

refresh, refreshes, refreshing, refreshed VERB ① If something refreshes you when you are hot or tired, it makes you feel cooler or more energetic • *A glass of fruit juice will refresh you.* ▷ PHRASE ② To **refresh someone's memory** means to remind them of something they had forgotten.

refreshing ADJECTIVE You say that something is refreshing when it is pleasantly different from what you are used to • *She is a refreshing contrast to her father.*

refreshment, refreshments NOUN Refreshments are drinks and small amounts of food provided at an event.

refrigerator, refrigerators NOUN an electrically cooled container in which you store food to keep it fresh.

refuel, refuels, refuelling, refuelled VERB When an aircraft or vehicle is refuelled, it is filled with more fuel.

refuge, refuges NOUN ① a place where you go for safety. ② If you take refuge, you go somewhere for safety or behave in a way that will protect you • *They took refuge in a bomb shelter* • *Father Rowan took refuge in silence.*
  ● SIMILAR WORDS: ① haven,
  ● sanctuary, shelter

refugee, refugees NOUN Refugees are people who have been forced to leave their country and live elsewhere.

refund, refunds, refunding, refunded NOUN ① money returned to you because you have paid too much for something or because you have returned goods ▷ VERB ② To refund someone's money means to return it to them after they have paid for something with it.

refurbish, refurbishes, refurbishing, refurbished VERB FORMAL To refurbish a building means to decorate it and repair damage. **refurbishment** NOUN

refusal, refusals NOUN A refusal is when someone says firmly that they will not do, allow, or accept something.

refuse, refuses, refusing, refused [*Said* rif-**yooz**] VERB ① If you refuse to do something, you say or decide firmly that you will not do it. ② If someone refuses something, they do

a
b
c
d
e
f
g
h
i
j
k
l
m
n
o
p
q
r
s
t
u
v
w
x
y
z

A
B
C
D
E
F
G
H
I
J
K
L
M
N
O
P
Q
R
S
T
U
V
W
X
Y
Z

not allow it or do not accept it • *The United States has refused him a visa* • *He offered me a second drink which I refused.*

refuse [*Said* ref-**yoos**] NOUN Refuse is rubbish or waste.

refute, refutes, refuting, refuted VERB FORMAL To refute a theory or argument means to prove that it is wrong.
⬤ USAGE NOTE: *Refute* does not mean the same as *deny*. If you *refute* something, you provide evidence to show that it is not true. If you *deny* something, you say that it is not true

regain, regains, regaining, regained VERB To regain something means to get it back.

regal ADJECTIVE very grand and suitable for a king or queen • *regal splendour.* **regally** ADVERB

regard, regards, regarding, regarded VERB ❶ To regard someone or something in a particular way means to think of them in that way or have that opinion of them • *We all regard him as a friend* • *Many disapprove of the tax, regarding it as unfair.* ❷ LITERARY To regard someone in a particular way also means to look at them in that way • *She regarded him curiously for a moment.* ▷ NOUN ❸ If you have a high regard for someone, you have a very good opinion of them ▷ PHRASES ❹ **Regarding, as regards, with regard to,** and **in regard to** are all used to indicate what you are talking or writing about • *There was always some question regarding education* • *As regards the war, he believed in victory at any price.*

❺ 'Regards' is used in various expressions to express friendly feelings • *Give my regards to your husband.*

regardless PREPOSITION OR ADVERB done or happening in spite of something else • *He led from the front, regardless of the danger.*

regatta, regattas NOUN a race meeting for sailing or rowing boats.

regency, regencies NOUN a period when a country is ruled by a regent.

regenerate, regenerates, regenerating, regenerated VERB FORMAL To regenerate something means to develop and improve it after it has been declining • *a scheme to regenerate the docks area of the city.* **regeneration** NOUN

regent, regents NOUN someone who rules in place of a king or queen who is ill or too young to rule.

reggae NOUN Reggae is a type of music, originally from the West Indies, with a strong beat.

regime, regimes [*Said* ray-**jeem**] NOUN a system of government, and the people who are ruling a country • *a communist regime.*

regiment, regiments NOUN a large group of soldiers commanded by a colonel. **regimental** ADJECTIVE

regimented ADJECTIVE very strictly controlled • *the regimented life of the orphanage.* **regimentation** NOUN

region, regions NOUN ❶ (GEOGRAPHY) a large area of land. ❷ You can refer to any area or part as

▷ SPELLING NOTE: *I want to see (C) your licenCe (licence)*

a region • *the pelvic region.* ▷ PHRASE
❸ **In the region of** means
approximately • *The scheme will cost in
the region of six million.* **regional**
ADJECTIVE **regionally** ADVERB
● SIMILAR WORDS: ❶ area,
● district, territory

register, registers, registering,
registered NOUN ❶ an official list or
record of things • *the electoral register.*
❷ TECHNICAL a style of speaking or
writing used in particular
circumstances or social occasions
▷ VERB ❸ When something is
registered, it is recorded on an official
list • *The car was registered in my name.*
❹ If an instrument registers a
measurement, it shows it. ❺ If your
face registers a feeling, it expresses it.
registration NOUN

registrar, registrars NOUN ❶ a
person who keeps official records of
births, marriages, and deaths. ❷ At a
college or university, the registrar is a
senior administrative official. ❸ a
senior hospital doctor.

registration number,
registration numbers NOUN the
sequence of letters and numbers on
the front and back of a motor vehicle
that identify it.

registry, registries NOUN a place
where official records are kept.

registry office, registry offices
NOUN a place where births,
marriages, and deaths are recorded,
and where people can marry without a
religious ceremony.

regret, regrets, regretting, regretted
VERB ❶ If you regret something, you
are sorry that it happened. ❷ You can

say that you regret something as a
way of apologizing • *We regret any
inconvenience to passengers.* ▷ NOUN
❸ If you have regrets, you are sad or
sorry about something. **regretful**
ADJECTIVE **regretfully** ADVERB
● SIMILAR WORDS: ❶ repent, rue

regrettable ADJECTIVE
unfortunate and undesirable • *a
regrettable accident.* **regrettably**
ADVERB

regular, regulars ADJECTIVE
❶ even and equally spaced • *soft
music with a regular beat.* ❷ MATHS
A regular shape has equal angles and
equal sides • *a regular polygon.*
❸ Regular events or activities happen
often and according to a pattern, for
example each day or each week • *The
trains to London are fairly regular.* ❹ If
you are a regular customer or visitor
somewhere, you go there often.
❺ usual or normal • *I was filling in for
the regular bartender.* ❻ having a well
balanced appearance • *a regular
geometrical shape.* ▷ NOUN ❼ People
who go to a place often are known as
its regulars. **regularly** ADVERB
regularity NOUN
● SIMILAR WORDS: ❶ even,
● steady, uniform

regulate, regulates, regulating,
regulated VERB To regulate
something means to control the way it
operates • *Sweating helps to regulate
the body's temperature.* **regulator**
NOUN

regulation, regulations NOUN
❶ Regulations are official rules.
❷ Regulation is the control of
something • *regulation of the betting
industry.*

a b c d e f g h i j k l m n o p q **r** s t u v w x y z

▷ SPELLING NOTE: *The government licenSes Schnapps (licenses)*

regurgitate, regurgitates, regurgitating, regurgitated *[Said rig-**gur**-jit-tate]* **VERB** To regurgitate food means to bring it back from the stomach before it is digested.

rehabilitate, rehabilitates, rehabilitating, rehabilitated **VERB** To rehabilitate someone who has been ill or in prison means to help them lead a normal life. **rehabilitation NOUN**

rehearsal, rehearsals **NOUN** (DRAMA) a practice of a performance in preparation for the actual event.

rehearse, rehearses, rehearsing, rehearsed **VERB** (DRAMA) To rehearse a performance means to practise it in preparation for the actual event.

reign, reigns, reigning, reigned *[Said rain]* **VERB** ❶ When a king or queen reigns, he or she rules a country. ❷ You can say that something reigns when it is a noticeable feature of a situation or period of time • *Panic reigned after his assassination.* ▷ **NOUN** ❸ (HISTORY) The reign of a king or queen is the period during which he or she reigns.

rein, reins **NOUN** ❶ Reins are the thin leather straps which you hold when you are riding a horse ▷ **PHRASE** ❷ To **keep a tight rein on** someone or something means to control them firmly.

reincarnation NOUN People who believe in reincarnation believe that when you die, you are born again as another creature.

reindeer NOUN Reindeer are deer with large antlers, that live in northern regions.

reinforce, reinforces, reinforcing, reinforced **VERB** ❶ To reinforce something means to strengthen it • *a reinforced steel barrier.* ❷ If something reinforces an idea or claim, it provides evidence to support it.

reinforcement, reinforcements **NOUN** ❶ Reinforcements are additional soldiers sent to join an army in battle. ❷ Reinforcement is the reinforcing of something.

reinstate, reinstates, reinstating, reinstated **VERB** ❶ To reinstate someone means to give them back a position they have lost. ❷ To reinstate something means to bring it back • *Parliament voted against reinstating capital punishment.* **reinstatement NOUN**

reiterate, reiterates, reiterating, reiterated *[Said ree-**it**-er-ate]* **VERB** FORMAL If you reiterate something, you say it again. **reiteration NOUN**

reject, rejects, rejecting, rejected **VERB** ❶ If you reject a proposal or request, you do not accept it or agree to it. ❷ If you reject a belief, political system, or way of life, you decide that it is not for you ▷ **NOUN** ❸ a product that cannot be used, because there is something wrong with it. **rejection NOUN**

● **SIMILAR WORDS:** ❶ decline, ● refuse, turn down

rejoice, rejoices, rejoicing, rejoiced **VERB** To rejoice means to be very pleased about something • *The whole country rejoiced after his downfall.*

rejoin, rejoins, rejoining, rejoined **VERB** If you rejoin someone, you go back to them soon after leaving them

▷ SPELLING NOTE: *have a plEce of plE (pie̱ce)*

• *She rejoined her friends in the bar.*

rejuvenate, rejuvenates, rejuvenating, rejuvenated [*Said ree-joo-vin-ate*] **VERB** To rejuvenate someone means to make them feel young again. **rejuvenation NOUN**

relapse, relapses **NOUN** If a sick person has a relapse, their health suddenly gets worse after improving.

relate, relates, relating, related **VERB** ❶ If something relates to something else, it is connected or concerned with it • *The statistics relate only to western Germany.* ❷ If you can relate to someone, you can understand their thoughts and feelings. ❸ To relate a story means to tell it.

relation, relations **NOUN** ❶ If there is a relation between two things, they are similar or connected in some way • *This theory bears no relation to reality.* ❷ Your relations are the members of your family. ❸ Relations between people are their feelings and behaviour towards each other • *Relations between husband and wife had not improved.*

relationship, relationships **NOUN** (PSHE) ❶ The relationship between two people or groups is the way they feel and behave towards each other. ❷ a close friendship, especially one involving romantic or sexual feelings. ❸ The relationship between two things is the way in which they are connected • *the relationship between slavery and the sugar trade.*

relative, relatives **ADJECTIVE** ❶ compared to other things or people of the same kind • *The fighting resumed after a period of relative calm*

• *He is a relative novice.* ❷ You use 'relative' when comparing the size or quality of two things • *the relative strengths of the British and German forces.* ▷ **NOUN** ❸ Your relatives are the members of your family.

relative pronoun, relative pronouns **NOUN** a pronoun that replaces a noun that links two parts of a sentence.
▶ SEE GRAMMAR BOX ON PAGE 710

relax, relaxes, relaxing, relaxed **VERB** ❶ If you relax, you become calm and your muscles lose their tension. ❷ If you relax your hold, you hold something less tightly. ❸ To relax something also means to make it less strict or controlled • *The rules governing student conduct were relaxed.* **relaxation NOUN**
● SIMILAR WORDS: ❶ rest, take it easy, unwind ❷ lessen, loosen, slacken

relaxed **ADJECTIVE** ❶ calm and not worried or tense. ❷ If a place or situation is relaxed, it is calm and peaceful.

relay, relays, relaying, relayed **NOUN** ❶ (PE) A relay race or relay is a race between teams, with each team member running one part of the race ▷ **VERB** ❷ To relay a television or radio signal means to send it on. ❸ If you relay information, you tell it to someone else.

release, releases, releasing, released **VERB** ❶ To release someone or something means to set them free or remove restraints from them. ❷ To release something also means to issue it or make it available • *He is releasing an album of love songs.* ▷ **NOUN**

a b c d e f g h i j k l m n o p q **r** s t u v w x y z

▷ SPELLING NOTE: *plaice the fish has a glittering 'EYE' (I) (plaice)*

R

WHAT IS A RELATIVE PRONOUN?

Relative pronouns are used to replace a noun which links two different parts of a sentence. The relative pronouns are *who*, *whom*, *whose*, *which*, and *that*.

Relative pronouns always refer back to a word in the earlier part of the sentence. The word they refer to is called the **antecedent**. (In the examples that follow, the antecedents are underlined.)
*I have <u>a friend</u> **who** lives in Rome.*
*We could go to <u>a place</u> **that** I know.*

The forms *who*, *whom*, and *whose* are used when the antecedent is a person. *Who* indicates the subject of the verb, while *whom* indicates the object of the verb:
*It was <u>the same person</u> **who** saw me yesterday.*
*It was <u>the person</u> **whom** I saw yesterday.*

The distinction between *who* and *whom* is often ignored in everyday English, and *who* is often used as the object:

*It was <u>the person</u> **who** I saw yesterday.*

Whom is used immediately after a preposition. However, if the preposition is separated from the relative pronoun, *who* is usually used:
*He is <u>a man</u> **in whom** I have great confidence.*
*He is <u>a man</u> **who** I have great confidence **in**.*

Whose is the possessive form of the relative pronoun. It can refer to things as well as people:
*Anna has <u>a sister</u> **whose** name is Rosie.*
*I found <u>a book</u> **whose** pages were torn.*

Which is only used when the antecedent is not a person:
*We took <u>the road</u> **which** leads to the sea.*

That refers to things or people. It is never used immediately after a preposition, but it can be used if the preposition is separated from the relative pronoun:
*It was <u>a film</u> **that** I had little interest **in**.*

❸ When the release of someone or something takes place, they are set free. **❹** A press release or publicity release is an official written statement given to reporters. **❺** A new release is a new CD or DVD that has just become available.

relegate, relegates, relegating, relegated **VERB** To relegate something or someone means to give them a less important position or status • *relegated to a lower division.* **relegation NOUN**

relent, relents, relenting, relented **VERB** If someone relents, they agree to something they had previously not allowed.

relentless ADJECTIVE never stopping and never becoming less intense • *the relentless rise of business closures.* **relentlessly ADVERB**

relevant ADJECTIVE (LIBRARY) If something is relevant, it is connected with and is appropriate to what is being discussed • *We have passed all relevant information to the police.*

▷ SPELLING NOTE: *I went to see (C) the doctor's new practiCe (practice)*

relevance NOUN
● **SIMILAR WORDS:** appropriate,
● pertinent, significant

reliable ADJECTIVE ① Reliable
people and things can be trusted to do
what you want. **②** If information is
reliable, you can assume that it is
correct. **reliably ADVERB reliability
NOUN**

reliant ADJECTIVE If you are reliant
on someone or something, you
depend on them • *They are not wholly
reliant on charity.* **reliance NOUN**

relic, relics NOUN ① Relics are
objects or customs that have survived
from an earlier time. **②** an object
regarded as holy because it is thought
to be connected with a saint.

relief NOUN ① If you feel relief, you
are glad and thankful because a bad
situation is over or has been avoided.
② Relief is also money, food, or
clothing provided for poor or hungry
people.

relief map, relief maps NOUN a
map showing the shape of mountains
and hills by shading.

**relieve, relieves, relieving, relieved
VERB ①** If something relieves an
unpleasant feeling, it makes it less
unpleasant • *Drugs can relieve much of
the pain.* **②** FORMAL If you relieve
someone, you do their job or duty for a
period. **③** If someone is relieved of
their duties, they are dismissed from
their job. **④** If you relieve yourself, you
urinate.

religion, religions NOUN RE
① Religion is the belief in a god or
gods and all the activities connected
with such beliefs. **②** a system of

religious belief • *the Christian religion.*

religious ADJECTIVE ① HISTORY
connected with religion • *religious
worship.* **②** RE Someone who is
religious has a strong belief in a god or
gods.
● **SIMILAR WORDS: ②** devout,
● pious

religiously ADVERB If you do
something religiously, you do it
regularly as a duty • *He stuck religiously
to the rules.*

**relinquish, relinquishes,
relinquishing, relinquished** [Said
ril-ling-kwish] **VERB** FORMAL If you
relinquish something, you give it up.

**relish, relishes, relishing, relished
VERB ①** If you relish something, you
enjoy it • *He relished the idea of getting
some cash.* ▷ **NOUN ②** Relish is
enjoyment • *He told me with relish of
the wonderful times he had.* **③** Relish is
also a savoury sauce or pickle.

relive, relives, reliving, relived VERB
If you relive a past experience, you
remember it and imagine it happening
again.

**relocate, relocates, relocating,
relocated VERB** If people or
businesses are relocated, they are
moved to a different place.
relocation NOUN

reluctant ADJECTIVE If you are
reluctant to do something, you are
unwilling to do it. **reluctance NOUN**

reluctantly ADVERB If you do
something reluctantly, you do it
although you do not want to.

rely, relies, relying, relied VERB ① If
you rely on someone or something,

▷ SPELLING NOTE: *You must practiSe your Ss (practise)*

A
B
C
D
E
F
G
H
I
J
K
L
M
N
O
P
Q
R
S
T
U
V
W
X
Y
Z

you need them and depend on them • *She has to rely on hardship payments.* ❷ If you can rely on someone to do something, you can trust them to do it • *They can always be relied on to turn up.*

remain, remains, remaining, remained **VERB** ❶ If you remain in a particular place, you stay there. ❷ If you remain in a particular state, you stay the same and do not change • *The two men remained silent.* ❸ Something that remains still exists or is left over • *Huge amounts of weapons remain to be collected.*

remainder **NOUN** The remainder of something is the part that is left • *He gulped down the remainder of his coffee.*

remains **PLURAL NOUN** ❶ The remains of something are the parts that are left after most of it has been destroyed • *the remains of an ancient mosque.* ❷ You can refer to a dead body as remains • *More human remains have been unearthed today.*

● **SIMILAR WORDS:** debris,
● remnants

remand, remands, remanding, remanded **VERB** ❶ If a judge remands someone who is accused of a crime, the trial is postponed and the person is ordered to come back at a later date ▷ **PHRASE** ❷ If someone is **on remand**, they are in prison waiting for their trial to begin.

remark, remarks, remarking, remarked **VERB** ❶ If you remark on something, you mention it or comment on it • *She had remarked on the boy's improvement.* ▷ **NOUN** ❷ A remark is something you say, often in

a casual way • *a flippant remark.*

remarkable **ADJECTIVE** impressive and unexpected • *It was a remarkable achievement.* **remarkably** **ADVERB**
● **SIMILAR WORDS:** extraordinary,
● outstanding, wonderful

remarry, remarries, remarrying, remarried **VERB** If someone remarries, they get married again.

remedial **ADJECTIVE** ❶ Remedial activities are to help someone improve their health after they have been ill. ❷ Remedial exercises are designed to improve someone's ability in something • *the remedial reading class.*

remedy, remedies, remedying, remedied **NOUN** ❶ a way of dealing with a problem • *a remedy for colic.* ▷ **VERB** ❷ If you remedy something that is wrong, you correct it • *We have to remedy the situation immediately.*

remember, remembers, remembering, remembered **VERB** ❶ If you can remember someone or something from the past, you can bring them into your mind or think about them. ❷ If you remember to do something, you do it when you intended to • *Ben had remembered to book reservations.*
● **SIMILAR WORDS:** ❶ recall,
● recollect

remembrance **NOUN** If you do something in remembrance of a dead person, you are showing that they are remembered with respect and affection.

remind, reminds, reminding, reminded **VERB** ❶ If someone reminds you of a fact, they say

▷ SPELLING NOTE: *pAL up with the principAL and principAL staff (principal)*

something to make you think about it
• *Remind me to buy a bottle of wine, will you?* ❷ If someone reminds you of another person, they look similar and make you think of them.

reminder, reminders **NOUN** ❶ If one thing is a reminder of another, the first thing makes you think of the second • *a reminder of better times.* ❷ a note sent to tell someone they have forgotten to do something.

reminiscent **ADJECTIVE** Something that is reminiscent of something else reminds you of it.

remission **NOUN** When prisoners get remission for good behaviour, their sentences are reduced.

remit, remits **NOUN** FORMAL The remit of a person or committee is the subject or task they are responsible for • *Their remit is to research into a wide range of health problems.*

remittance, remittances **NOUN** FORMAL payment for something sent through the post.

remnant, remnants **NOUN** a small part of something left after the rest has been used or destroyed.

remorse **NOUN** FORMAL Remorse is a strong feeling of guilt. **remorseful** **ADJECTIVE**
   ● SIMILAR WORDS: contrition, regret, repentance

remote, remoter, remotest **ADJECTIVE** ❶ Remote areas are far away from places where most people live. ❷ far away in time • *the remote past.* ❸ If you say a person is remote, you mean they do not want to be friendly • *She is severe, solemn, and*

remote. ❹ If there is only a remote possibility of something happening, it is unlikely to happen. **remoteness** **NOUN**

remote control **NOUN** Remote control is a system of controlling a machine or vehicle from a distance using radio or electronic signals.

remotely **ADVERB** used to emphasize a negative statement • *He isn't remotely keen.*

removal **NOUN** ❶ The removal of something is the act of taking it away. ❷ A removal company transports furniture from one building to another.

remove, removes, removing, removed **VERB** ❶ If you remove something from a place, you take it off or away. ❷ If you are removed from a position of authority, you are not allowed to continue your job. ❸ If you remove an undesirable feeling or attitude, you get rid of it • *Most of her fears had been removed.* **removable** **ADJECTIVE**
   ● SIMILAR WORDS: ❶ extract, take away, withdraw

Renaissance [Said ren-**nay**-sonss] **NOUN** The Renaissance was a period from the 14th to 16th centuries in Europe when there was a great revival in the arts and learning.
   ● WORD HISTORY: a French word, meaning literally 'rebirth'

renal **ADJECTIVE** MEDICAL concerning the kidneys • *renal failure.*

rename, renames, renaming, renamed **VERB** If you rename something, you give it a new name.

▷ SPELLING NOTE: *LEarn the principLEs (principle)*

render, renders, rendering, rendered
VERB You can use 'render' to say that something is changed into a different state • *The bomb was quickly rendered harmless.*

rendezvous [*Said* **ron**-*day*-*voo*]
NOUN ❶ a meeting • *Baxter arranged a six o'clock rendezvous.* ❷ a place where you have arranged to meet someone • *The pub became a popular rendezvous.*

rendition, renditions **NOUN**
FORMAL a performance of a play, poem, or piece of music.

renew, renews, renewing, renewed
VERB ❶ To renew an activity or relationship means to begin it again. ❷ To renew a licence or contract means to extend the period of time for which it is valid. **renewal NOUN**

renewable, renewables **ADJECTIVE**
❶ able to be renewed ▷ **NOUN** ❷
(GEOGRAPHY) a renewable form of energy, such as wind power or solar power.

renewable resources PLURAL
NOUN (GEOGRAPHY) sources of energy, such as wind, sun, and water, which are constantly replaced so do not become used up.

renounce, renounces, renouncing, renounced **VERB** FORMAL If you renounce something, you reject it or give it up. **renunciation NOUN**

renovate, renovates, renovating, renovated **VERB** If you renovate an old building or machine, you repair it and restore it to good condition. **renovation NOUN**

renowned ADJECTIVE well-known

for something good • *He is not renowned for his patience.* **renown NOUN**

rent, rents, renting, rented **VERB**
❶ If you rent something, you pay the owner a regular sum of money in return for being able to use it ▷ **NOUN** ❷ Rent is the amount of money you pay regularly to rent land or accommodation.

rental ADJECTIVE ❶ concerned with the renting out of goods and services • *Scotland's largest video rental company.* ▷ **NOUN** ❷ the amount of money you pay when you rent something.

reorganize, reorganizes, reorganizing, reorganized; *also spelt* **reorganise VERB** To reorganize something means to organize it in a new way in order to make it more efficient or acceptable. **reorganization NOUN**

rep, reps **NOUN** INFORMAL a travelling salesman or saleswoman. Rep is an abbreviation for representative.

repair, repairs, repairing, repaired
NOUN ❶ something you do to mend something that is damaged or broken ▷ **VERB** ❷ If you repair something, you mend it.

repay, repays, repaying, repaid **VERB**
❶ To repay money means to give it back to the person who lent it. ❷ If you repay a favour, you do something to help the person who helped you. **repayment NOUN**

repeal, repeals, repealing, repealed
VERB If the government repeals a law, it cancels it so that it is no longer valid.

▷ SPELLING NOTE: *Psychiatrists Seldom Yell Callously Hard (psychiatrist)*

A B C D E F G H I J K L M N O P Q R S T U V W X Y Z

repeat, repeats, repeating, repeated
VERB ❶ If you repeat something, you say, write, or do it again. ❷ If you repeat what someone has said, you tell someone else about it • *I trust you not to repeat that to anyone.* ▷ **NOUN** ❸ something which is done or happens again • *the number of repeats shown on TV.* **repeated ADJECTIVE repeatedly ADVERB**

repel, repels, repelling, repelled **VERB** ❶ If something repels you, you find it horrible and disgusting. ❷ When soldiers repel an attacking force, they successfully defend themselves against it. ❸ When a magnetic pole repels an opposite pole, it forces the opposite pole away.
● **SIMILAR WORDS:** ❶ disgust,
● revolt, sicken

repellent, repellents **ADJECTIVE**
❶ FORMAL horrible and disgusting • *I found him repellent.* ▷ **NOUN**
❷ Repellents are chemicals used to keep insects or other creatures away.

repent, repents, repenting, repented **VERB** FORMAL If you repent, you are sorry for something bad you have done. **repentance NOUN repentant ADJECTIVE**

repercussion, repercussions **NOUN** The repercussions of an event are the effects it has at a later time.

repertoire, repertoires *[Said rep-et-twar]* **NOUN** A performer's repertoire is all the pieces of music or dramatic parts he or she has learned and can perform

repertory, repertories **NOUN**
❶ Repertory is the practice of performing a small number of plays in a theatre for a short time, using the same actors in each play. ❷ In Australian, New Zealand, and South African English, repertory is the same as **repertoire**.

repetition, repetitions **NOUN** ❶ If there is a repetition of something, it happens again • *We don't want a repetition of last week's fiasco.* ❷ (ENGLISH) Repetition is when a word, phrase, or sound is repeated, for example to emphasize a point or to make sure it is understood, or for poetic effect.

repetitive ADJECTIVE A repetitive activity involves a lot of repetition and is boring • *dull and repetitive work.*

replace, replaces, replacing, replaced **VERB** ❶ When one thing replaces another, the first thing takes the place of the second. ❷ If you replace something that is damaged or lost, you get a new one. ❸ If you replace something, you put it back where it was before • *She replaced the receiver.*
● **SIMILAR WORDS:** ❶ supersede,
● supplant

replacement, replacements **NOUN** ❶ The replacement for someone or something is the person or thing that takes their place. ❷ The replacement of a person or thing happens when they are replaced by another person or thing.

replay, replays, replaying, replayed **VERB** ❶ If a match is replayed, the teams play it again. ❷ If you replay a tape or film, you play it again • *Replay the first few seconds of the tape please.* ▷ **NOUN** ❸ a match that is played for a second time.

▷ SPELLING NOTE: *the QUeen stood on the QUay (quay)*

replenish, replenishes, replenishing, replenished VERB FORMAL If you replenish something, you make it full or complete again.

replica, replicas NOUN an accurate copy of something • *a replica of Columbus's ship.* **replicate** VERB

reply, replies, replying, replied VERB ❶ If you reply to something, you say or write an answer ▷ NOUN ❷ what you say or write when you answer someone.

report, reports, reporting, reported VERB ❶ If you report that something has happened, you tell someone about it or give an official account of it • *He reported the theft to the police.* ❷ To report someone to an authority means to make an official complaint about them. ❸ If you report to a person or place, you go there and say you have arrived ▷ NOUN ❹ an account of an event or situation.
● SIMILAR WORDS: ❹ account, description

reported speech NOUN a report of what someone said that gives the content of the speech without repeating the exact words.

reporter, reporters NOUN someone who writes news articles or broadcasts news reports.

repossess, repossesses, repossessing, repossessed VERB If a shop or company repossesses goods that have not been paid for, they take them back.

represent, represents, representing, represented VERB (PSHE) ❶ If you represent someone, you act on their behalf • *lawyers representing relatives*

of the victims. ❷ If a sign or symbol represents something, it stands for it. ❸ To represent something in a particular way means to describe it in that way • *The popular press tends to represent him as a hero.*

representation, representations NOUN ❶ Representation is the state of being represented by someone • *Was there any student representation?* ❷ You can describe a picture or statue of someone as a representation of them.

representative, representatives NOUN ❶ (PSHE) a person chosen to act on behalf of another person or a group ▷ ADJECTIVE ❷ A representative selection is typical of the group it belongs to • *The photos chosen are not representative of his work.*

repress, represses, repressing, repressed VERB ❶ If you repress a feeling, you succeed in not showing or feeling it • *I couldn't repress my anger any longer.* ❷ To repress people means to restrict their freedom and control them by force. **repression** NOUN

repressive ADJECTIVE Repressive governments use force and unjust laws to restrict and control people.

reprieve, reprieves, reprieving, reprieved *[Said rip-preev]* VERB ❶ If someone who has been sentenced to death is reprieved, their sentence is changed and they are not killed ▷ NOUN ❷ a delay before something unpleasant happens • *The zoo won a reprieve from closure.*

reprimand, reprimands,

reprimanding, reprimanded **VERB**
❶ If you reprimand someone, you
officially tell them that they should
not have done something ▷ **NOUN**
❷ something said or written by a
person in authority when they are
reprimanding someone.

reprisal, reprisals **NOUN** Reprisals
are violent actions taken by one group
of people against another group that
has harmed them.

reproach, reproaches, reproaching,
reproached **FORMAL NOUN** ❶ If you
express reproach, you show that you
feel sad and angry about what
someone has done • *a long letter of
reproach.* ▷ **VERB** ❷ If you reproach
someone, you tell them, rather sadly,
that they have done something wrong.
reproachful ADJECTIVE

reproduce, reproduces,
reproducing, reproduced **VERB** ❶ To
reproduce something means to make
a copy of it. ❷ (SCIENCE) When living
things reproduce, they produce more
of their own kind • *Bacteria reproduce
by splitting into two.*

reproduction, reproductions
NOUN ❶ a modern copy of a painting
or piece of furniture. ❷ (SCIENCE)
Reproduction is the process by which
a living thing produces more of its
kind • *the study of animal reproduction.*

reproductive ADJECTIVE
(SCIENCE) relating to the reproduction
of living things • *the female
reproductive system.*

reptile, reptiles **NOUN** a cold-
blooded animal, such as a snake or a
lizard, which has scaly skin and lays
eggs. **reptilian ADJECTIVE**

● **WORD HISTORY:** from Latin
● *reptilis* meaning 'creeping'

republic, republics **NOUN** a country
which has a president rather than a
king or queen. **republican NOUN OR
ADJECTIVE republicanism NOUN**
● **WORD HISTORY:** from Latin *res*
● *publica* meaning literally 'public
● thing'

repulse, repulses, repulsing,
repulsed **VERB** ❶ If you repulse
someone who is being friendly, you
put them off by behaving coldly
towards them • *He repulses friendly
advances.* ❷ To repulse an attacking
force means to fight it and cause it to
retreat. ❸ If something repulses you,
you find it horrible and disgusting and
you want to avoid it.

repulsion NOUN ❶ Repulsion is a
strong feeling of disgust. ❷ Repulsion
is a force separating two objects, such
as the force between two like electric
charges.

repulsive ADJECTIVE horrible and
disgusting.

reputable ADJECTIVE known to be
good and reliable • *a well-established
and reputable firm.*

reputation, reputations **NOUN** The
reputation of something or someone
is the opinion that people have of
them • *The college had a good
reputation.*
● **SIMILAR WORDS:** name, renown,
● standing

reputed ADJECTIVE If something is
reputed to be true, some people say
that it is true • *the reputed tomb of
Christ.* **reputedly ADVERB**

a b c d e f g h i j k l m n o p q **r** s t u v w x y z

request, requests, requesting, requested **VERB** ❶ If you request something, you ask for it politely or formally ▷ **NOUN** ❷ If you make a request for something, you request it.

requiem, requiems [Said **rek-wee-em**] **NOUN** ❶ A requiem or requiem mass is a mass celebrated for someone who has recently died. ❷ a piece of music for singers and an orchestra, originally written for a requiem mass • *Mozart's Requiem.*
● **WORD HISTORY**: from Latin *requies* meaning 'rest'

require, requires, requiring, required **VERB** ❶ If you require something, you need it. ❷ If you are required to do something, you have to do it because someone says you must • *The rules require employers to provide safety training.*

requirement, requirements **NOUN** something that you must have or must do • *A good degree is a requirement for entry.*

requisite, requisites FORMAL **ADJECTIVE** ❶ necessary for a particular purpose • *She filled in the requisite paperwork.* ▷ **NOUN** ❷ something that is necessary for a particular purpose.

rescue, rescues, rescuing, rescued **VERB** ❶ If you rescue someone, you save them from a dangerous or unpleasant situation ▷ **NOUN** ❷ Rescue is help which saves someone from a dangerous or unpleasant situation. **rescuer NOUN**

research, researches, researching, researched **NOUN** ❶ Research is work that involves studying something

and trying to find out facts about it ▷ **VERB** ❷ If you research something, you try to discover facts about it. **researcher NOUN**

resemblance **NOUN** If there is a resemblance between two things, they are similar to each other • *There was a remarkable resemblance between them.*
● **SIMILAR WORDS**: likeness, similarity

resemble, resembles, resembling, resembled **VERB** To resemble something means to be similar to it.

resent, resents, resenting, resented **VERB** If you resent something, you feel bitter and angry about it.

resentful **ADJECTIVE** bitter and angry • *He felt very resentful about losing his job.* **resentfully ADVERB**

resentment, resentments **NOUN** a feeling of anger or bitterness.

reservation, reservations **NOUN** ❶ If you have reservations about something, you are not sure that it is right. ❷ If you make a reservation, you book a place in advance. ❸ an area of land set aside for American Indian peoples • *a Cherokee reservation.*

reserve, reserves, reserving, reserved **VERB** ❶ If something is reserved for a particular person or purpose, it is kept specially for them ▷ **NOUN** ❷ a supply of something for future use. ❸ In sport, a reserve is someone who is available to play in case one of the team is unable to play. ❹ A nature reserve is an area of land where animals, birds, or plants are officially protected. ❺ If someone shows

reserve, they keep their feelings hidden. **reserved** ADJECTIVE
● **SIMILAR WORDS:** ❶ put by, save,
● set aside

reservoir, reservoirs *[Said rez-ev-wahr]* NOUN a lake used for storing water before it is supplied to people.

reshuffle, reshuffles NOUN a reorganization of people or things.

reside, resides, residing, resided *[Said riz-zide]* VERB FORMAL If a quality resides in something, the quality is in that thing.

residence, residences NOUN FORMAL a house.

resident, residents NOUN ❶ A resident of a house or area is someone who lives there ▷ ADJECTIVE ❷ If someone is resident in a house or area, they live there.

residential ADJECTIVE ❶ A residential area contains mainly houses rather than offices or factories. ❷ providing accommodation • *residential care for the elderly*.

residue, residues NOUN a small amount of something that remains after most of it has gone • *an increase in toxic residues found in drinking water.* **residual** ADJECTIVE

resign, resigns, resigning, resigned VERB ❶ If you resign from a job, you formally announce that you are leaving it. ❷ If you resign yourself to an unpleasant situation, you realize that you have to accept it. **resigned** ADJECTIVE

resignation, resignations NOUN ❶ Someone's resignation is a formal statement of their intention to leave a job. ❷ Resignation is the reluctant acceptance of an unpleasant situation or fact.

resilient ADJECTIVE able to recover quickly from unpleasant or damaging events. **resilience** NOUN

resin, resins NOUN ❶ Resin is a sticky substance produced by some trees. ❷ Resin is also a substance produced chemically and used to make plastics.

resist, resists, resisting, resisted VERB ❶ If you resist something, you refuse to accept it and try to prevent it • *The pay squeeze will be fiercely resisted by the unions.* ❷ If you resist someone, you fight back against them.
● **SIMILAR WORDS:** ❶ fight,
● oppose

resistance, resistances NOUN ❶ Resistance to something such as change is a refusal to accept it. ❷ Resistance to an attack consists of fighting back • *The demonstrators offered no resistance.* ❸ Your body's resistance to germs or disease is its power to not be harmed by them. ❹ Resistance is also the power of a substance to resist the flow of an electrical current through it.

resistant ADJECTIVE ❶ opposed to something and wanting to prevent it • *People were very resistant to change.* ❷ If something is resistant to a particular thing, it is not harmed or affected by it • *Certain insects are resistant to this spray.*

resolute *[Said rez-ol-loot]* ADJECTIVE FORMAL Someone who is

▷ SPELLING NOTE: Eddy Ant thinks mEAt is a grEAt trEAt to EAt (-ea-)

A
B
C
D
E
F
G
H
I
J
K
L
M
N
O
P
Q
R
S
T
U
V
W
X
Y
Z

resolute is determined not to change their mind. **resolutely** ADVERB

resolution, resolutions NOUN
❶ Resolution is determination. **❷** If you make a resolution, you promise yourself to do something. **❸** a formal decision taken at a meeting. **❹** (ENGLISH) The resolution of a problem is the solving of it.

resolve, resolves, resolving, resolved VERB **❶** If you resolve to do something, you firmly decide to do it. **❷** If you resolve a problem, you find a solution to it ▷ NOUN **❸** Resolve is absolute determination.

resonance, resonances NOUN
❶ Resonance is sound produced by an object vibrating as a result of another sound nearby. **❷** Resonance is also a deep, clear, and echoing quality of sound.

resonate, resonates, resonating, resonated VERB If something resonates, it vibrates and produces a deep, strong sound.

resort, resorts, resorting, resorted VERB **❶** If you resort to a course of action, you do it because you have no alternative ▷ NOUN **❷** a place where people spend their holidays ▷ PHRASE **❸** If you do something **as a last resort**, you do it because you can find no other way of solving a problem.

resounding ADJECTIVE **❶** loud and echoing • *a resounding round of applause.* **❷** A resounding success is a great success.

resource, resources NOUN The resources of a country, organization, or person are the materials, money, or skills they have • *We don't have the resources to fund the project.*

resourceful ADJECTIVE A resourceful person is good at finding ways of dealing with problems. **resourcefulness** NOUN

respect, respects, respecting, respected VERB **❶** If you respect someone, you have a good opinion of their character or ideas. **❷** If you respect someone's rights or wishes, you do not do things that they would not like, or would consider wrong • *It is about time they started respecting the law.* ▷ NOUN **❸** If you have respect for someone, you have a good opinion of them ▷ PHRASE **❹** You can say **in this respect** to refer to a particular feature • *At least in this respect we are equals.*

respectable ADJECTIVE
❶ considered to be acceptable and morally correct • *respectable families.* **❷** adequate or reasonable • *a respectable rate of economic growth.* **respectably** NOUN ADVERB

respectful ADJECTIVE showing respect for someone • *Our children are always respectful to their elders.* **respectfully** ADVERB

respective ADJECTIVE belonging or relating individually to the people or things just mentioned • *They went into their respective rooms to pack.*

respectively ADVERB in the same order as the items just mentioned • *They finished first and second respectively.*

respiration NOUN (SCIENCE) Your respiration is your breathing.

▷ SPELLING NOTE: *Elaine and Emily shout EE when they mEEt to grEEt each other (-ee-)*

respiratory ADJECTIVE [SCIENCE] relating to breathing • *respiratory diseases.*

respire, respires, respiring, respired VERB [SCIENCE] To respire is to breathe.

respite NOUN FORMAL a short rest from something unpleasant.

respond, responds, responding, responded VERB When you respond to something, you react to it by doing or saying something.

respondent, respondents NOUN ❶ a person who answers a questionnaire or a request for information. ❷ In a court case, the respondent is the defendant.

response, responses NOUN Your response to an event is your reaction or reply to it • *There has been no response to his remarks yet.*

responsibility, responsibilities NOUN ❶ If you have responsibility for something, it is your duty to deal with it or look after it • *The garden was to have been his responsibility.* ❷ If you accept responsibility for something that has happened, you agree that you caused it or were to blame • *We must all accept responsibility for our own mistakes.*

responsible ADJECTIVE ❶ If you are responsible for something, it is your job to deal with it. ❷ If you are responsible for something bad that has happened, you are to blame for it. ❸ If you are responsible to someone, that person is your boss and tells you what you have to do. ❹ A responsible person behaves properly and sensibly without needing to be supervised.

❺ A responsible job involves making careful judgments about important matters. **responsibly** ADVERB
● SIMILAR WORDS: ❶ accountable,
● answerable, liable

responsive ADJECTIVE ❶ quick to show interest and pleasure. ❷ taking notice of events and reacting in an appropriate way • *The course is responsive to students' needs.*

rest, rests, resting, rested NOUN ❶ The rest of something is all the remaining parts of it. ❷ If you have a rest, you sit or lie quietly and relax ▷ VERB ❸ If you rest, you relax and do not do anything active for a while.

restaurant, restaurants [Said *rest-ront*] NOUN a place where you can buy and eat a meal.
● WORD HISTORY: a French word;
● from *restaurer* meaning 'to restore'

restaurateur, restaurateurs [Said *rest-er-a-tur*] NOUN someone who owns or manages a restaurant.

restful ADJECTIVE Something that is restful helps you feel calm and relaxed.

restless ADJECTIVE finding it hard to remain still or relaxed because of boredom or impatience. **restlessness** NOUN **restlessly** ADVERB

restore, restores, restoring, restored VERB ❶ To restore something means to cause it to exist again or to return to its previous state • *He was anxious to restore his reputation.* ❷ To restore an old building or work of art means to clean and repair it. **restoration** NOUN
● SIMILAR WORDS: ❷ refurbish,
● renovate

a
b
c
d
e
f
g
h
i
j
k
l
m
n
o
p
q
r
s
t
u
v
w
x
y
z

▷ SPELLING NOTE: *'i' before 'e' except after 'c'*

A
B
C
D
E
F
G
H
I
J
K
L
M
N
O
P
Q
R
S
T
U
V
W
X
Y
Z

restrain, restrains, restraining, restrained **VERB** To restrain someone or something means to hold them back or prevent them from doing what they want to.

restrained **ADJECTIVE** behaving in a controlled way.

restraint, restraints **NOUN**
❶ Restraints are rules or conditions that limit something • *wage restraints*. ❷ Restraint is calm, controlled behaviour.

restrict, restricts, restricting, restricted **VERB** ❶ If you restrict something, you prevent it becoming too large or varied. ❷ To restrict people or animals means to limit their movement or actions. **restrictive ADJECTIVE**

restriction, restrictions **NOUN** a rule or situation that limits what you can do • *financial restrictions*.

result, results, resulting, resulted **NOUN** ❶ The result of an action or situation is the situation that is caused by it • *As a result of the incident he got a two-year suspension.* ❷ The result is also the final marks, figures, or situation at the end of an exam, calculation, or contest • *election results* • *The result was calculated to three decimal places.* ▷ **VERB** ❸ If something results in a particular event, it causes that event to happen. ❹ If something results from a particular event, it is caused by that event • *The fire had resulted from carelessness.* **resultant ADJECTIVE**
● SIMILAR WORDS:
● ❶ consequence, outcome, upshot

resume, resumes, resuming,
resumed *[Said riz-**yoom**]* **VERB** If you resume an activity or position, you return to it after a break. **resumption NOUN**

resurgence **NOUN** If there is a resurgence of an attitude or activity, it reappears and grows stronger. **resurgent ADJECTIVE**

resurrect, resurrects, resurrecting, resurrected **VERB** If you resurrect something, you make it exist again after it has disappeared or ended. **resurrection NOUN**

Resurrection **NOUN** (RE) In Christian belief, the Resurrection is the coming back to life of Jesus Christ three days after he had been killed.

resuscitate, resuscitates, resuscitating, resuscitated *[Said ris-**suss**-it-tate]* **VERB** If you resuscitate someone, you make them conscious again after an accident. **resuscitation NOUN**

retail **NOUN** The retail price is the price at which something is sold in the shops. **retailer NOUN**

retain, retains, retaining, retained **VERB** To retain something means to keep it. **retention NOUN**

retaliate, retaliates, retaliating, retaliated **VERB** If you retaliate, you do something to harm or upset someone because they have already acted in a similar way against you. **retaliation NOUN**

retarded **ADJECTIVE** If someone is retarded, their mental development is much less advanced than average.

rethink, rethinks, rethinking, rethought **VERB** If you rethink

▷ SPELLING NOTE: *King IAn went to ParlIAment in a carrIAge for his marrIAge (-ia-)*

something, you think about how it should be changed • *We have to rethink our strategy.*

reticent ADJECTIVE Someone who is reticent is unwilling to tell people about things. **reticence** NOUN

retina, retinas NOUN the light-sensitive part at the back of your eyeball, which receives an image and sends it to your brain.

retinue, retinues NOUN a group of helpers or friends travelling with an important person.

retire, retires, retiring, retired VERB ❶ When older people retire, they give up work. ❷ FORMAL If you retire, you leave to go into another room, or to bed • *She retired early with a good book.* **retired** ADJECTIVE **retirement** NOUN

retort, retorts, retorting, retorted VERB ❶ To retort means to reply angrily ▷ NOUN ❷ a short, angry reply.

retract, retracts, retracting, retracted VERB ❶ If you retract something you have said, you say that you did not mean it. ❷ When something is retracted, it moves inwards or backwards • *The undercarriage was retracted shortly after takeoff.* **retraction** NOUN **retractable** ADJECTIVE

retreat, retreats, retreating, retreated VERB ❶ To retreat means to move backwards away from something or someone. ❷ If you retreat from something difficult or unpleasant, you avoid doing it ▷ NOUN ❸ If an army moves away from the enemy, this is referred to as a retreat. ❹ a quiet

place that you can go to rest or do things in private.

retribution NOUN FORMAL Retribution is punishment • *the threat of retribution.*

retrieve, retrieves, retrieving, retrieved VERB If you retrieve something, you get it back. **retrieval** NOUN

retriever, retrievers NOUN a large dog often used by hunters to bring back birds and animals which have been shot.

retro- PREFIX 'Retro-' means 'back' or 'backwards' • *retrospective.*
● **WORD HISTORY:** from Latin *retrō*
● meaning 'behind' or 'backwards'

retrospect NOUN When you consider something in retrospect, you think about it afterwards and often have a different opinion from the one you had at the time • *In retrospect, I probably shouldn't have resigned.*

retrospective ADJECTIVE ❶ concerning things that happened in the past. ❷ taking effect from a date in the past. **retrospectively** ADVERB

return, returns, returning, returned VERB ❶ When you return to a place, you go back after you have been away. ❷ If you return something to someone, you give it back to them. ❸ When you return a ball during a game, you hit it back to your opponent. ❹ When a judge or jury returns a verdict, they announce it ▷ NOUN ❺ Your return is your arrival back at a place. ❻ The return on an investment is the profit or interest you get from it. ❼ a ticket for the journey

▷ SPELLING NOTE: *an ELegant angEL (angel)*

a
b
c
d
e
f
g
h
i
j
k
l
m
n
o
p
q
r
s
t
u
v
w
x
y
z

to a place and back again ▷ **PHRASE**
8 If you do something **in return** for a favour, you do it to repay the favour.

reunion, reunions **NOUN** a party or meeting for people who have not seen each other for a long time.

reunite, reunites, reuniting, reunited **VERB** If people are reunited, they meet again after they have been separated for some time.

rev, revs, revving, revved INFORMAL **VERB** **1** When you rev the engine of a vehicle, you press the accelerator to increase the engine speed ▷ **NOUN** **2** The speed of an engine is measured in revolutions per minute, referred to as revs • *I noticed that the engine revs had dropped.*

Rev or **Revd** abbreviations for Reverend.

revamp, revamps, revamping, revamped **VERB** To revamp something means to improve or repair it.

reveal, reveals, revealing, revealed **VERB** **1** To reveal something means to tell people about it • *They were not ready to reveal any of the details.* **2** If you reveal something that has been hidden, you uncover it.

revel, revels, revelling, revelled **VERB** If you revel in a situation, you enjoy it very much. **revelry NOUN**

revelation, revelations **NOUN** **1** a surprising or interesting fact made known to people. **2** If an experience is a revelation, it makes you realize or learn something.

revenge, revenges, revenging, revenged **NOUN** **1** Revenge involves

hurting someone who has hurt you ▷ **VERB** **2** If you revenge yourself on someone who has hurt you, you hurt them in return.
● **SIMILAR WORDS:** **1** retaliation, ● vengeance **2** avenge, retaliate

revenue, revenues **NOUN** Revenue is money that a government, company, or organization receives • *government tax revenues.*

revered **ADJECTIVE** If someone is revered, he or she is respected and admired • *He is still revered as the father of the nation.*

reverence **NOUN** Reverence is a feeling of great respect.

Reverend **NOUN** Reverend is a title used before the name of a member of the clergy • *the Reverend George Young.*

reversal, reversals **NOUN** If there is a reversal of a process or policy, it is changed to the opposite process or policy.

reverse, reverses, reversing, reversed **VERB** **1** When someone reverses a process, they change it to the opposite process • *They won't reverse the decision to increase prices.* **2** If you reverse the order of things, you arrange them in the opposite order. **3** When you reverse a car, you drive it backwards ▷ **NOUN** **4** The reverse is the opposite of what has just been said or done ▷ **ADJECTIVE** **5** Reverse means opposite to what is usual or to what has just been described.

reversible **ADJECTIVE** Reversible clothing can be worn with either side on the outside.

revert, reverts, reverting, reverted

▷ SPELLING NOTE: *LEt's measure the angLE (angle)*

VERB FORMAL To revert to a former state or type of behaviour means to go back to it.

review, reviews, reviewing, reviewed **NOUN ❶** an article or an item on television or radio, giving an opinion of a new book or play. **❷** When there is a review of a situation or system, it is examined to decide whether changes are needed ▷ **VERB ❸** To review a play or book means to write an account expressing an opinion of it. **❹** To review something means to examine it to decide whether changes are needed. **reviewer NOUN**
● SIMILAR WORDS:
● **❷** examination, survey
● **❹** reassess, reconsider, revise

revise, revises, revising, revised **VERB ❶** If you revise something, you alter or correct it. **❷** When you revise for an examination, you go over your work to learn things thoroughly. **revision NOUN**

revive, revives, reviving, revived **VERB ❶** When a feeling or practice is revived, it becomes active or popular again. **❷** When you revive someone who has fainted, they become conscious again. **revival NOUN**

revolt, revolts, revolting, revolted **NOUN ❶** (HISTORY) a violent attempt by a group of people to change their country's political system ▷ **VERB ❷** (HISTORY) When people revolt, they fight against the authority that governs them. **❸** If something revolts you, it is so horrible that you feel disgust.

revolting ADJECTIVE horrible and disgusting • *The smell in the cell was revolting.*

revolution, revolutions **NOUN ❶** (HISTORY) a violent attempt by a large group of people to change the political system of their country. **❷** an important change in an area of human activity • *the Industrial Revolution.* **❸** one complete turn in a circle.

revolutionary, revolutionaries **ADJECTIVE ❶** involving great changes • *a revolutionary new cooling system.* ▷ **NOUN ❷** a person who takes part in a revolution.

revolve, revolves, revolving, revolved **VERB ❶** If something revolves round something else, it centres on that as the most important thing • *My job revolves around the telephone.* **❷** When something revolves, it turns in a circle around a central point • *The moon revolves round the earth.*

revolver, revolvers **NOUN** a small gun held in the hand.

revulsion NOUN Revulsion is a strong feeling of disgust or disapproval.

reward, rewards, rewarding, rewarded (PSHE) **NOUN ❶** something you are given because you have done something good ▷ **VERB ❷** If you reward someone, you give them a reward.

rewarding ADJECTIVE Something that is rewarding gives you a lot of satisfaction.

rewind, rewinds, rewinding, rewound **VERB** If you rewind a tape on a tape recorder or video, you make the tape go backwards.

rhapsody, rhapsodies *[Said rap-sod-ee]* **NOUN** a short piece of

a b c d e f g h i j k l m n o p q r s t u v w x y z

▷ SPELLING NOTE: *A Rude Idiot Thought He Might Eat Toffee In Church (arithmetic)*

A
B
C
D
E
F
G
H
I
J
K
L
M
N
O
P
Q
R
S
T
U
V
W
X
Y
Z

music which is very passionate and flowing.

rhetoric NOUN Rhetoric is speech or writing that is intended to impress people.

rhetorical ADJECTIVE ❶ A rhetorical question is one which is asked in order to make a statement rather than to get an answer. ❷ Rhetorical language is intended to be grand and impressive.

rheumatism [Said room-at-izm] NOUN Rheumatism is an illness that makes your joints and muscles stiff and painful. **rheumatic** ADJECTIVE

rhino, rhinos NOUN INFORMAL a rhinoceros.

rhinoceros, rhinoceroses NOUN a large African or Asian animal with one or two horns on its nose.
● WORD HISTORY: from Greek *rhin* meaning 'of the nose' and *keras* meaning 'horn'

rhododendron, rhododendrons NOUN an evergreen bush with large coloured flowers.

rhombus, rhombuses or rhombi NOUN (MATHS) a shape with four equal sides and no right angles.

rhubarb NOUN Rhubarb is a plant with long red stems which can be cooked with sugar and eaten.

rhyme, rhymes, rhyming, rhymed (ENGLISH) VERB ❶ If two words rhyme, they have a similar sound • *Sally rhymes with valley.* ▷ NOUN ❷ a word that rhymes with another. ❸ a short poem with rhyming lines.

rhythm, rhythms NOUN ❶ (MUSIC)

Rhythm is a regular movement or beat. ❷ a regular pattern of changes, for example, in the seasons. **rhythmic** ADJECTIVE **rhythmically** ADVERB

rib, ribs NOUN Your ribs are the curved bones that go from your backbone to your chest. **ribbed** ADJECTIVE

ribbon, ribbons NOUN a long, narrow piece of cloth used for decoration.

ribcage, ribcages NOUN Your ribcage is the framework of bones made up of your ribs which protects your internal organs like your heart and lungs.

rice NOUN Rice is a tall grass that produces edible grains. Rice is grown in warm countries on wet ground.

rich, richer, richest; riches ADJECTIVE ❶ Someone who is rich has a lot of money and possessions. ❷ Something that is rich in something contains a large amount of it • *Liver is particularly rich in vitamin A.* ❸ Rich food contains a large amount of fat, oil, or sugar. ❹ Rich colours, smells, and sounds are strong and pleasant. **richness** NOUN

riches PLURAL NOUN Riches are valuable possessions or large amounts of money • *the oil riches of the Middle East.*

richly ADVERB ❶ If someone is richly rewarded, they are rewarded well with something valuable. ❷ If you feel strongly that someone deserves something, you can say it is richly deserved.

Richter scale [Said *rik-ter*] NOUN

▷ SPELLING NOTE: *Rhythmical Hounds Yap To Heavy Music (rhythm)*

(GEOGRAPHY) a scale which is used for describing how strong an earthquake is.

rick, ricks **NOUN** a large pile of hay or straw.

rickets **NOUN** Rickets is a disease that causes soft bones in children if they do not get enough vitamin D.

rickety **ADJECTIVE** likely to collapse or break • *a rickety wooden jetty*.

rickshaw, rickshaws **NOUN** a hand-pulled cart used in Asia for carrying passengers.

ricochet, ricochets, ricocheting or ricochetting, ricocheted or ricochetted [*Said* **rik-osh-ay**] **VERB** When a bullet ricochets, it hits a surface and bounces away from it.

rid, rids, ridding, rid **PHRASE** ❶ When you **get rid** of something you do not want, you remove or destroy it ▷ **VERB** ❷ FORMAL To rid a place of something unpleasant means to succeed in removing it.

riddle, riddles **NOUN** ❶ a puzzle which seems to be nonsense, but which has an entertaining solution. ❷ Something that is a riddle puzzles and confuses you.
  ● **SIMILAR WORDS:** ❷ enigma,
  ● mystery

riddled **ADJECTIVE** full of something undesirable • *The report was riddled with errors*.
  ● **WORD HISTORY:** from Old English
  ● *hriddel* meaning 'sieve'

ride, rides, riding, rode, ridden **VERB** ❶ When you ride a horse or a bike, you sit on it and control it as it moves along. ❷ When you ride in a car, you travel in it ▷ **NOUN** ❸ a journey on a horse or bike or in a vehicle.

rider, riders **NOUN** ❶ a person riding on a horse or bicycle. ❷ an additional statement which changes or puts a condition on what has already been said.

ridge, ridges **NOUN** ❶ a long, narrow piece of high land. ❷ a raised line on a flat surface.

ridicule, ridicules, ridiculing, ridiculed **VERB** ❶ To ridicule someone means to make fun of them in an unkind way ▷ **NOUN** ❷ Ridicule is unkind laughter and mockery.

ridiculous **ADJECTIVE** very foolish. **ridiculously** **ADVERB**

rife **ADJECTIVE** FORMAL very common • *Unemployment was rife*.

riff, riffs **NOUN** (MUSIC) in jazz or rock music, a riff is a short repeated tune.

rifle, rifles, rifling, rifled **NOUN** ❶ a gun with a long barrel ▷ **VERB** ❷ When someone rifles something, they make a quick search through it to steal things.

rift, rifts **NOUN** ❶ a serious quarrel between friends that damages their friendship. ❷ a split in something solid, especially in the ground.

rig, rigs, rigging, rigged **VERB** ❶ If someone rigs an election or contest, they dishonestly arrange for a particular person to succeed ▷ **NOUN** ❷ a large structure used for extracting oil or gas from the ground or sea bed. **rig up** **VERB** If you rig up a device or structure, you make it quickly and fix it in place • *They had even rigged up a makeshift aerial*.

right, rights, righting, righted
ADJECTIVE OR ADVERB ❶ correct and in accordance with the facts
• *That clock never tells the right time*
• *That's absolutely right.* ❷ 'Right' means on or towards the right side of something ▷ **ADJECTIVE** ❸ The right choice or decision is the best or most suitable one. ❹ The right people or places are those that have influence or are socially admired • *He was always to be seen in the right places.* ❺ The right side of something is the side intended to be seen and to face outwards
▷ **NOUN** ❻ 'Right' is used to refer to principles of morally correct behaviour • *At least he knew right from wrong.*
❼ If you have a right to do something, you are morally or legally entitled to do it. ❽ The right is one of the two sides of something. For example, when you look at the word 'to', the 'o' is to the right of the 't'. ❾ The Right refers to people who support the political ideas of capitalism and conservatism rather than socialism
▷ **ADVERB** ❿ 'Right' is used to emphasize a precise place • *I'm right here.* ⓫ 'Right' means immediately • *I had to decide right then.* ▷ **VERB** ⓬ If you right something, you correct it or put it back in an upright position.
rightly ADVERB
  SIMILAR WORDS: ❸ appropriate, proper, suitable ❼ prerogative, privilege

right angle, right angles **NOUN** an angle of 90°.

righteous ADJECTIVE Righteous people behave in a way that is morally good and religious.

rightful ADJECTIVE Someone's rightful possession is one which they

have a moral or legal right to.
rightfully ADVERB

right-handed ADJECTIVE OR ADVERB Someone who is right-handed does things such as writing and painting with their right hand.

right-wing ADJECTIVE believing more strongly in capitalism or conservatism, or less strongly in socialism, than other members of the same party or group. **right-winger NOUN**

rigid ADJECTIVE ❶ Rigid laws or systems cannot be changed and are considered severe. ❷ A rigid object is stiff and does not bend easily. **rigidly ADVERB rigidity NOUN**
  SIMILAR WORDS: ❶ inflexible, strict

rigorous ADJECTIVE very careful and thorough. **rigorously ADVERB**

rigour, rigours **NOUN** FORMAL The rigours of a situation are the things which make it hard or unpleasant • *the rigours of childbirth.*

rim, rims **NOUN** the outside or top edge of an object such as a wheel or a cup.

rimu, rimu or rimus [*Said* ree-*moo*] **NOUN** a New Zealand tree with narrow, pointed leaves, which produces wood used for furniture.

rind, rinds **NOUN** Rind is the thick outer skin of fruit, cheese, or bacon.

ring, rings, ringing, ringed, rang, rung **VERB** ❶ If you ring someone, you phone them. ❷ When a bell rings, it makes a clear, loud sound. ❸ To ring something means to draw a circle around it. ❹ If something is ringed

▷ SPELLING NOTE: there's a rAKE in the brAKEs (*brake*)

with something else, it has that thing all the way around it • *The courthouse was ringed with police.* ▷ **NOUN** ❺ the sound made by a bell. ❻ a small circle of metal worn on your finger. ❼ an object or group of things in the shape of a circle. ❽ At a boxing match or circus, the ring is the place where the fight or performance takes place. ❾ an organized group of people who are involved in an illegal activity • *an international spy ring.*

● **USAGE NOTE:** The past tense of *ring* is *rang*, and the past participle is *rung*. Do not confuse these words: *she rang the bell; I had rung the police*

ringbark, ringbarks, ringbarking, ringbarked **VERB** If you ringbark a tree, you kill it by cutting away a strip of bark from around its trunk

ringer, ringers **NOUN** ❶ a person or thing that is almost identical to another. ❷ In Australian English, someone who works on a sheep farm. ❸ In Australian and New Zealand English, the fastest shearer in a woolshed.

ring-in, ring-ins **NOUN** INFORMAL ❶ In Australian English, a person or thing that is not normally a member of a particular group. ❷ In Australian and New Zealand English, someone who is brought in at the last minute as a replacement for someone else.

ringleader, ringleaders **NOUN** the leader of a group of people who get involved in mischief or crime.

ring road, ring roads **NOUN** A ring road is a road that goes round the edge of a town, avoiding the centre.

ringworm **NOUN** (SCIENCE) Ringworm is a fungal infection of the skin that causes itching circular patches.

rink, rinks **NOUN** a large indoor area for ice-skating or roller-skating.

rinse, rinses, rinsing, rinsed **VERB** ❶ When you rinse something, you wash it in clean water ▷ **NOUN** ❷ a liquid you can put on your hair to give it a different colour.

riot, riots, rioting, rioted **NOUN** ❶ When there is a riot, a crowd of people behave noisily and violently ▷ **VERB** ❷ To riot means to behave noisily and violently ▷ **PHRASE** ❸ To **run riot** means to behave in a wild and uncontrolled way.

rip, rips, ripping, ripped **VERB** ❶ When you rip something, you tear it violently. ❷ If you rip something away, you remove it quickly and violently ▷ **NOUN** ❸ a long split in cloth or paper.

rip off **VERB** INFORMAL If someone rips you off, they cheat you by charging you too much money.

RIP RIP is an abbreviation often written on gravestones, meaning 'rest in peace'.

ripe, riper, ripest **ADJECTIVE** ❶ When fruit or grain is ripe, it is fully developed and ready to be eaten. ❷ If a situation is ripe for something to happen, it is ready for it. **ripeness** **NOUN**

ripen, ripens, ripening, ripened **VERB** When crops ripen, they become ripe.

ripper, rippers **NOUN** INFORMAL In Australia and New Zealand English, an

a
b
c
d
e
f
g
h
i
j
k
l
m
n
o
p
q
r
s
t
u
v
w
x
y
z

excellent person or thing.

ripple, ripples, rippling, rippled **NOUN**
❶ Ripples are little waves on the surface of calm water. ❷ If there is a ripple of laughter or applause, people laugh or applaud gently for a short time ▷ **VERB** ❸ When the surface of water ripples, little waves appear on it.

rise, rises, rising, rose, risen **VERB**
❶ If something rises, it moves upwards. ❷ **FORMAL** When you rise, you stand up. ❸ To rise also means to get out of bed. ❹ When the sun rises, it first appears. ❺ The place where a river rises is where it begins. ❻ If land rises, it slopes upwards. ❼ If a sound or wind rises, it becomes higher or stronger. ❽ If an amount rises, it increases. ❾ If you rise to a challenge or a remark, you respond to it rather than ignoring it • *He rose to the challenge with enthusiasm.* ❿ When people rise up, they start fighting against people in authority ▷ **NOUN**
⓫ an increase. ⓬ Someone's rise is the process by which they become more powerful or successful • *his rise to fame.*
● **SIMILAR WORDS:** ❶ ascend,
● climb, go up

riser, risers **NOUN** An early riser is someone who likes to get up early in the morning.

risk, risks, risking, risked **NOUN** ❶ a chance that something unpleasant or dangerous might happen ▷ **VERB**
❷ If you risk something unpleasant, you do something knowing that the unpleasant thing might happen as a result • *If he doesn't play, he risks losing his place in the team.* ❸ If you risk someone's life, you put them in a

dangerous situation in which they might be killed. **risky ADJECTIVE**
● **WORD HISTORY:** from Italian
● *rischiare* meaning 'to be in danger'

rite, rites **NOUN** a religious ceremony.

ritual, rituals **NOUN** ❶ a series of actions carried out according to the custom of a particular society or group • *This is the most ancient of the Buddhist rituals.* ▷ **ADJECTIVE** ❷ Ritual activities happen as part of a tradition or ritual • *fasting and ritual dancing.* **ritualistic ADJECTIVE**

rival, rivals, rivalling, rivalled **NOUN**
❶ Your rival is the person you are competing with ▷ **VERB** ❷ If something rivals something else, it is of the same high standard or quality • *As a holiday destination, South Africa rivals Kenya for weather.*
● **SIMILAR WORDS:** ❶ adversary,
● opponent

rivalry, rivalries **NOUN** Rivalry is active competition between people.

river, rivers **NOUN** a natural feature consisting of water flowing for a long distance between two banks.

rivet, rivets **NOUN** a short, round pin with a flat head which is used to fasten sheets of metal together.

riveting ADJECTIVE If you find something riveting, you find it fascinating and it holds your attention • *I find tennis riveting.*

road, roads **NOUN** a long piece of hard ground specially surfaced so that people and vehicles can travel along it easily.

road map, road maps **NOUN** ❶ a map intended for drivers. ❷ a plan or

▷ SPELLING NOTE: *I always visit my FRIend on a FRIday (Friday)*

guide for future actions • *a road map for peace.*

road rage NOUN Road rage is aggressive behaviour by a driver as a reaction to the behaviour of another driver.

road train, road trains NOUN In Australia, a line of linked trailers pulled by a truck, used for transporting cattle or sheep.

roadworks PLURAL NOUN Roadworks are repairs being done on a road.

roam, roams, roaming, roamed VERB If you roam around, you wander around without any particular purpose • *Hens were roaming around the yard.*

roar, roars, roaring, roared VERB ❶ If something roars, it makes a very loud noise. ❷ To roar with laughter or anger means to laugh or shout very noisily. ❸ When a lion roars, it makes a loud, angry sound ▷ NOUN ❹ a very loud noise.

roast, roasts, roasting, roasted VERB ❶ When you roast meat or other food, you cook it using dry heat in an oven or over a fire ▷ ADJECTIVE ❷ Roast meat has been roasted ▷ NOUN ❸ a piece of meat that has been roasted.

rob, robs, robbing, robbed VERB ❶ If someone robs you, they steal your possessions. ❷ If you rob someone of something they need or deserve, you deprive them of it • *He robbed me of my childhood.*

robber, robbers NOUN Robbers are people who steal money or property using force or threats • *bank robbers.* **robbery** NOUN

robe, robes NOUN a long, loose piece of clothing which covers the body • *He knelt in his white robes before the altar.*

robin, robins NOUN a small bird with a red breast.

robot, robots NOUN a machine which is programmed to move and perform tasks automatically.
● WORD HISTORY: from Czech
● *robota* meaning 'work'

robust ADJECTIVE very strong and healthy. **robustly** ADVERB

rock, rocks, rocking, rocked NOUN ❶ Rock is the hard mineral substance that forms the surface of the earth. ❷ a large piece of rock • *She picked up a rock and threw it into the lake.* ❸ Rock or rock music is music with simple tunes and a very strong beat. ❹ Rock is also a sweet shaped into long, hard sticks, sold in holiday resorts ▷ VERB ❺ When something rocks or when you rock it, it moves regularly backwards and forwards or from side to side • *She rocked the baby.* ❻ If something rocks people, it shocks and upsets them • *Palermo was rocked by a crime wave.* ▷ PHRASE ❼ If someone's marriage or relationship is **on the rocks**, it is unsuccessful and about to end.

rock and roll NOUN Rock and roll is a style of music with a strong beat that was especially popular in the 1950s.

rock cycle NOUN (GEOGRAPHY) the series of events in which a rock of one type is changed to one or more other types, and then back to the original type.

rocket, rockets, rocketing, rocketed

a
b
c
d
e
f
g
h
i
j
k
l
m
n
o
p
q
r
s
t
u
v
w
x
y
z

▷ SPELLING NOTE: *I want to see (C) your licenCe (licence)*

A
B
C
D
E
F
G
H
I
J
K
L
M
N
O
P
Q
R
S
T
U
V
W
X
Y
Z

NOUN ❶ a space vehicle, usually shaped like a long pointed tube. **❷** an explosive missile • *They fired rockets into a number of government buildings.* **❸** a firework that explodes when it is high in the air ▷ **VERB ❹** If prices rocket, they increase very quickly.

rocking chair, rocking chairs **NOUN** a chair on two curved pieces of wood that rocks backwards and forwards when you sit in it.

rock melon, rock melons **NOUN** In Australian, New Zealand, and American English, a rock melon is a cantaloupe, a melon with orange flesh and a hard, lumpy skin.

rocky ADJECTIVE covered with rocks.

rod, rods **NOUN** a long, thin pole or bar, usually made of wood or metal • *a fishing rod.*

rodent, rodents **NOUN** a small mammal with sharp front teeth which it uses for gnawing.
  ● **WORD HISTORY:** from Latin *rodere*
  ● meaning 'to gnaw'

rodeo, rodeos **NOUN** a public entertainment in which cowboys show different skills.

roe NOUN Roe is the eggs of a fish.

rogue, rogues **NOUN ❶** You can refer to a man who behaves dishonestly as a rogue ▷ **ADJECTIVE ❷** a vicious animal that lives apart from its herd or pack.

role, roles; also spelt **rôle NOUN ❶** Someone's role is their position and function in a situation or society. **❷** (DRAMA) An actor's role is the character that he or she plays • *She*

was appearing in her first leading role.

roll, rolls, rolling, rolled **VERB ❶** When something rolls or when you roll it, it moves along a surface, turning over and over. **❷** When vehicles roll along, they move • *Tanks rolled into the village.* **❸** If you roll your eyes, you make them turn up or go from side to side. **❹** If you roll something flexible into a cylinder or ball, you wrap it several times around itself • *He rolled up the bag with the money in it.* ▷ **NOUN ❺** A roll of paper or cloth is a long piece of it that has been rolled into a tube • *a roll of film.* **❻** a small, rounded, individually baked piece of bread. **❼** an official list of people's names • *the electoral roll.* **❽** A roll on a drum is a long, rumbling sound made on it.

roll-call, roll-calls **NOUN** If you take a roll-call, you call a register of names to see who is present.

roller, rollers **NOUN ❶** a cylinder that turns round in a machine or piece of equipment. **❷** Rollers are tubes which you can wind your hair around to make it curly.

Rollerblade, Rollerblades **NOUN** TRADEMARK Rollerblades are roller-skates which have the wheels set in one straight line on the bottom of the boot.

roller-coaster, roller-coasters **NOUN** a pleasure ride at a fair, consisting of a small railway that goes up and down very steep slopes.

roller-skate, roller-skates, roller-skating, roller-skated **NOUN ❶** Roller-skates are shoes with four small wheels underneath ▷ **VERB**

▷ **SPELLING NOTE:** *The government licenSes Schnapps (licenses)*

❷ If you roller-skate, you move along wearing roller-skates.

rolling pin, rolling pins **NOUN** a wooden cylinder used for rolling pastry dough to make it flat.

ROM **NOUN** (ICT) a storage device that holds data permanently and cannot be altered by the programmer. ROM stands for 'read only memory'.

Roman Catholic, Roman Catholics **ADJECTIVE** ❶ relating or belonging to the branch of the Christian church that accepts the Pope in Rome as its leader ▷ **NOUN** ❷ someone who belongs to the Roman Catholic church. **Roman Catholicism** **NOUN**

romance, romances **NOUN** ❶ a relationship between two people who are in love with each other. ❷ Romance is the pleasure and excitement of doing something new and unusual • *the romance of foreign travel.* ❸ (LIBRARY) a novel about a love affair.

Romanian, Romanians [Said *roe-may-nee-an*]; also spelt **Rumanian** **ADJECTIVE** ❶ belonging or relating to Romania ▷ **NOUN** ❷ someone who comes from Romania. ❸ Romanian is the main language spoken in Romania.

Roman numeral, Roman numerals **NOUN** (HISTORY) Roman numerals are the letters used by the Romans in ancient times to write numbers. For example, V means five, VI means six, X means ten, and IX means nine.

romantic, romantics **ADJECTIVE** **OR NOUN** ❶ A romantic person has

ideas that are not realistic, for example about love or about ways of changing society • *a romantic idealist.* ▷ **ADJECTIVE** ❷ connected with sexual love • *a romantic relationship.* ❸ Something that is romantic is beautiful in a way that strongly affects your feelings • *It is one of the most romantic ruins in Scotland.* ❹ Romantic describes a style of music, literature, and art popular in Europe in the late 18th and early 19th centuries, which emphasized feeling and imagination rather than order and form. **romantically** **ADVERB** **romanticism** **NOUN**

rondavel, rondavels **NOUN** In South Africa, a rondavel is a small circular building with a conical roof.

roo, roos **NOUN** INFORMAL In Australian English, a kangaroo.

roof, roofs **NOUN** ❶ The roof of a building or car is the covering on top of it. ❷ The roof of your mouth or of a cave is the highest part.

roofing **NOUN** Roofing is material used for covering roofs.

rooftop, rooftops **NOUN** the outside part of the roof of a building.

rook, rooks **NOUN** ❶ a large black bird. ❷ a chess piece which can move any number of squares in a straight but not diagonal line.

room, rooms **NOUN** ❶ a separate section in a building, divided from other rooms by walls. ❷ If there is plenty of room, there is a lot of space • *There wasn't enough room for his gear.*

roost, roosts, roosting, roosted **NOUN** ❶ a place where birds rest or build

a b c d e f g h i j k l m n o p q **r** s t u v w x y z

▷ SPELLING NOTE: *have a plEce of plE (piece)*

their nests ▷ **VERB ❷** When birds roost, they settle somewhere for the night.

root, roots, rooting, rooted **NOUN ❶** The roots of a plant are the parts that grow under the ground. **❷** The root of a hair is the part beneath the skin. **❸** You can refer to the place or culture that you grew up in as your roots. **❹** The root of something is its original cause or basis • *We got to the root of the problem.* ▷ **VERB ❺** To root through things means to search through them, pushing them aside • *She rooted through his bag.*
root out VERB If you root something or someone out, you find them and force them out • *a major drive to root out corruption.*

rooted ADJECTIVE developed from or strongly influenced by something • *songs rooted in traditional African music.*

root word, root words **NOUN** (ENGLISH) A root word is a word from which other words can be made by adding a suffix or a prefix. For example, *clearly* and *unclear* can be made from the root word *clear*.

rope, ropes, roping, roped **NOUN ❶** a thick, strong length of twisted cord ▷ **VERB ❷** If you rope one thing to another, you tie them together with rope.

rosary, rosaries **NOUN** a string of beads that Catholics use for counting prayers.

rose, roses **NOUN ❶** a large garden flower which has a pleasant smell and grows on a bush with thorns ▷ **NOUN OR ADJECTIVE ❷** reddish-pink.

rosella, rosellas **NOUN** a brightly coloured Australian parrot.

rosemary NOUN Rosemary is a herb with fragrant spiky leaves, used for flavouring in cooking.

rosette, rosettes **NOUN** a large badge of coloured ribbons gathered into a circle, which is worn as a prize in a competition or to support a political party.

Rosh Hashanah or **Rosh Hashana NOUN** (RE) the festival celebrating the Jewish New Year.
● **WORD HISTORY:** a Hebrew phrase
● meaning 'head of the year'

roster, rosters **NOUN** a list of people who take it in turn to do a particular job • *He put himself first on the new roster for domestic chores.*

rostrum, rostrums or rostra **NOUN** a raised platform on which someone stands to speak to an audience or conduct an orchestra.
● **WORD HISTORY:** from Latin
● *rostrum* meaning 'ship's prow';
● Roman orators' platforms were
● decorated with the prows of
● captured ships

rosy, rosier, rosiest **ADJECTIVE ❶** reddish-pink. **❷** If a situation seems rosy, it is likely to be good or successful. **❸** If a person looks rosy, they have pink cheeks and look healthy.

rot, rots, rotting, rotted **VERB ❶** When food or wood rots, it decays and can no longer be used. **❷** When something rots another substance, it causes it to decay • *Sugary drinks rot your teeth.* ▷ **NOUN ❸** Rot is the condition that affects things when they rot • *The timber frame was not protected against rot.*

● **SIMILAR WORDS: ❶** decay,
● decompose

rota, rotas **NOUN** a list of people who take turns to do a particular job.

rotate, rotates, rotating, rotated **VERB** MATHS When something rotates, it turns with a circular movement • *He rotated the camera 180°.* **rotation** **NOUN**

rotor, rotors **NOUN ❶** The rotor is the part of a machine that turns. **❷** The rotors or rotor blades of a helicopter are the four long flat pieces of metal on top of it which rotate and lift it off the ground.

rotten **ADJECTIVE ❶** decayed and no longer of use • *The front bay window is rotten.* **❷** INFORMAL of very poor quality • *I think it's a rotten idea.* **❸** INFORMAL very unfair, unkind, or unpleasant • *That's a rotten thing to say!*

rouble, roubles [*Said* **roo**-*bl*] **NOUN** the main unit of currency in Russia.
● **WORD HISTORY:** In Russian *rubl*
● means literally 'silver bar'

rough, rougher, roughest; roughs [*Said* **ruff**] **ADJECTIVE ❶** uneven and not smooth. **❷** not using enough care or gentleness • *Don't be so rough or you'll break it.* **❸** difficult or unpleasant • *Teachers have been given a rough time.* **❹** approximately correct • *At a rough guess it is five times more profitable.* **❺** If the sea is rough, there are large waves because of bad weather. **❻** A rough town or area has a lot of crime or violence ▷ **NOUN OR ADJECTIVE ❼** A rough or a rough

sketch is a drawing or description that shows the main features but does not show the details. ▷ **NOUN ❽** On a golf course, the rough is the part of the course next to a fairway where the grass has not been cut. **roughly** **ADVERB** **roughness** **NOUN**

roulette [*Said* roo-**let**] **NOUN** Roulette is a gambling game in which a ball is dropped onto a revolving wheel with numbered holes in it.

round, rounder, roundest; rounds, rounding, rounded **ADJECTIVE ❶** Something round is shaped like a ball or a circle. **❷** complete or whole • *round numbers.* ▷ **PREPOSITION OR ADVERB ❸** If something is round something else, it surrounds it. **❹** The distance round something is the length of its circumference or boundary • *I'm about two inches larger round the waist.* **❺** You can refer to an area near a place as the area round it • *There's nothing to do round here.* ▷ **PREPOSITION ❻** If something moves round you, it keeps moving in a circle with you in the centre. **❼** When someone goes to the other side of something, they have gone round it ▷ **ADVERB OR PREPOSITION ❽** If you go round a place, you go to different parts of it to look at it • *We went round the museum.* ▷ **ADVERB ❾** If you turn or look round, you turn so you are facing in a different direction. **❿** When someone comes round, they visit you • *He came round with a bottle of wine.* ▷ **NOUN ⓫** one of a series of events • *After round three, two Americans shared the lead.* **⓬** If you buy a round of drinks, you buy a drink for each member of the group you are with.

▷ SPELLING NOTE: *I went to see (C) the doctor's new practiCe (practice)*

a b c d e f g h i j k l m n o p q **r** s t u v w x y z

round up VERB If you round up people or animals, you gather them together.
● SIMILAR WORDS: ❶ globular, ● spherical

roundabout, roundabouts NOUN ❶ a meeting point of several roads with a circle in the centre which vehicles have to travel around. ❷ a circular platform which rotates and which children can ride on in a playground. ❸ the same as a merry-go-round.

round character, round characters NOUN ENGLISH a character in a story or play that is complicated and fully developed, like a real person, and often undergoes a significant change.

rounded ADJECTIVE curved in shape, without any points or sharp edges.

rounders NOUN a game played by two teams, in which a player scores points by hitting a ball and running around four sides of a square pitch.

round-the-clock ADJECTIVE happening continuously.

roundworm, roundworms NOUN SCIENCE A roundworm is a type of parasitic worm that lives in the intestines of dogs and cats.

rouse, rouses, rousing, roused VERB ❶ If someone rouses you, they wake you up. ❷ If you rouse yourself to do something, you make yourself get up and do it. ❸ If something rouses you, it makes you feel very emotional and excited.

rouseabout, rouseabouts NOUN In Australian and New Zealand English, an unskilled worker who does odd jobs, especially on a farm.

rout, routs, routing, routed [rhymes with out] VERB To rout your opponents means to defeat them completely and easily.

route, routes [Said root] NOUN a way from one place to another.

routine, routines ADJECTIVE ❶ Routine activities are done regularly ▷ NOUN ❷ the usual way or order in which you do things. ❸ a boring repetition of tasks. **routinely** ADVERB

roving ADJECTIVE ❶ wandering or roaming • *roving gangs of youths.* ❷ not restricted to any particular location or area • *a roving reporter.*

row, rows, rowing, rowed [rhymes with snow] NOUN ❶ A row of people or things is several of them arranged in a line ▷ VERB ❷ When you row a boat, you use oars to make it move through the water.

row, rows, rowing, rowed [rhymes with now] NOUN ❶ a serious argument. ❷ If someone is making a row, they are making too much noise ▷ VERB ❸ If people are rowing, they are quarrelling noisily.

rowdy, rowdier, rowdiest ADJECTIVE rough and noisy.

royal, royals ADJECTIVE ❶ belonging to or involving a queen, a king, or a member of their family. ❷ 'Royal' is used in the names of organizations appointed or supported by a member of a royal family ▷ NOUN ❸ INFORMAL Members of

▷ SPELLING NOTE: *You must practiSe your Ss (practise)*

the royal family are sometimes referred to as the royals.
● **SIMILAR WORDS:** ❶ imperial,
● regal

royalist, royalists **NOUN** someone who supports their country's royal family.

royalty, royalties **NOUN** ❶ The members of a royal family are sometimes referred to as royalty. ❷ Royalties are payments made to authors and musicians from the sales of their books or CDs.

rub, rubs, rubbing, rubbed **VERB** If you rub something, you move your hand or a cloth backwards and forwards over it.
rub out VERB To rub out something written means to remove it by rubbing it with a rubber or a cloth.

rubber, rubbers **NOUN** ❶ Rubber is a strong, elastic substance used for making tyres, boots, and other products. ❷ a small piece of rubber used to rub out pencil mistakes.

rubbish NOUN ❶ Rubbish is unwanted things or waste material. ❷ You can refer to nonsense or something of very poor quality as rubbish.
● **SIMILAR WORDS:** ❶ garbage,
● refuse, trash, waste ❷ garbage,
● nonsense, twaddle

rubble NOUN Bits of old brick and stone are referred to as rubble.

rubella [Said roo-**bell**-a] **NOUN** (SCIENCE) Rubella is German measles.

rubric, rubrics [Said roo-**brik**] **NOUN** FORMAL a set of instructions at the beginning of an official document.

ruby, rubies **NOUN** a type of red jewel.

rucksack, rucksacks **NOUN** a bag with shoulder straps for carrying things on your back.

rudder, rudders **NOUN** a piece of wood or metal at the back of a boat or plane which is moved to make the boat or plane turn.

rude, ruder, rudest **ADJECTIVE** ❶ not polite. ❷ embarrassing or offensive because of reference to sex or other bodily functions • *rude jokes.* ❸ unexpected and unpleasant • *a rude awakening.* **rudely ADVERB rudeness NOUN**
● **SIMILAR WORDS:**
● ❶ discourteous, ill-mannered,
● impolite, uncivil

rudimentary ADJECTIVE FORMAL very basic or not developed • *He had only a rudimentary knowledge of French.*

rudiments PLURAL NOUN When you learn the rudiments of something, you learn only the simplest and most basic things about it.
● **WORD HISTORY:** from Latin
● *rudimentum* meaning 'beginning'

ruff, ruffs **NOUN** ❶ a stiff circular collar with many pleats in it, worn especially in the 16th century. ❷ a thick band of fur or feathers around the neck of a bird or animal.

ruffle, ruffles, ruffling, ruffled **VERB** ❶ If you ruffle someone's hair, you move your hand quickly backwards and forwards over their head. ❷ If something ruffles you, it makes you annoyed or upset ▷ **NOUN** ❸ Ruffles are small folds made in a piece of material for decoration.

rug, rugs **NOUN** ❶ a small, thick carpet. ❷ a blanket which you can use to cover your knees or for sitting on outdoors.

rugby **NOUN** Rugby is a game played by two teams, who try to kick and throw an oval ball to their opponents' end of the pitch. Rugby League is played with 13 players in each side, Rugby Union is played with 15 players in each side.

rugged **ADJECTIVE** ❶ rocky and wild • *the rugged west coast of Ireland.* ❷ having strong features • *his rugged good looks.*

rugger **NOUN** INFORMAL Rugger is the same as rugby.

ruin, ruins, ruining, ruined **VERB** ❶ If you ruin something, you destroy or spoil it completely. ❷ If someone is ruined, they have lost all their money ▷ **NOUN** ❸ Ruin is the state of being destroyed or completely spoilt. ❹ A ruin or the ruins of something refers to the parts that are left after it has been severely damaged • *the ruins of a thirteenth-century monastery.*

rule, rules, ruling, ruled **NOUN** ❶ Rules are statements which tell you what you are allowed to do ▷ **VERB** ❷ To rule a country or group of people means to have power over it and be in charge of its affairs. ❸ FORMAL When someone in authority rules on a particular matter, they give an official decision about it ▷ **PHRASE** ❹ As a rule means usually or generally • *As a rule, I eat my meals in front of the TV.* **rule out VERB** ❶ If you rule out an idea or course of action, you reject it. ❷ If one thing rules out another, it prevents it from happening or being

possible • *The accident ruled out a future for him in football.*
● **SIMILAR WORDS:** ❶ law,
● regulation

ruler, rulers **NOUN** ❶ a person who rules a country. ❷ a long, flat piece of wood or plastic with straight edges marked in centimetres or inches, used for measuring or drawing straight lines.

rum **NOUN** Rum is a strong alcoholic drink made from sugar cane juice.

Rumanian [Said roo-**may**-nee-an] another spelling of **Romanian**.

rumble, rumbles, rumbling, rumbled **VERB** ❶ If something rumbles, it makes a continuous low noise • *Another train rumbled past the house.* ▷ **NOUN** ❷ a continuous low noise • *the distant rumble of traffic.*

rummage, rummages, rummaging, rummaged **VERB** If you rummage somewhere, you search for something, moving things about carelessly.

rumour, rumours, rumoured **NOUN** ❶ a story that people are talking about, which may or may not be true ▷ **VERB** ❷ If something is rumoured, people are suggesting that it has happened.
● **WORD HISTORY:** from Latin *rumor*
● meaning 'common talk'
● **SIMILAR WORDS:** ❶ gossip,
● hearsay, story

rump, rumps **NOUN** ❶ An animal's rump is its rear end. ❷ Rump or rump steak is meat cut from the rear end of a cow.

run, runs, running, ran, run **VERB**

▷ SPELLING NOTE: L*Earn* the princip*LEs* (principle)

❶ When you run, you move quickly, leaving the ground during each stride. ❷ If you run away from a place, you leave it suddenly and secretly. ❸ If you say that a road or river runs in a particular direction, you are describing its course. ❹ If you run your hand or an object over something, you move it over it. ❺ If someone runs in an election, they stand as a candidate • *He announced he would run for President.* ❻ If you run a business or an activity, you are in charge of it. ❼ If you run an experiment, a computer program, or tape, you start it and let it continue • *He ran a series of computer checks.* ❽ To run a car means to have it and use it. ❾ If you run someone somewhere in a car, you drive them there • *Could you run me up to town?* ❿ If you run water, you turn on a tap to make it flow • *We heard him running the kitchen tap.* ⓫ If your nose is running, it is producing a lot of mucus. ⓬ If the dye in something runs, the colour comes out when it is washed. ⓭ If a feeling runs through your body, it affects you quickly and strongly. ⓮ If an amount is running at a particular level, it is at that level • *Inflation is currently running at 2.6%.* ⓯ If someone or something is running late, they have taken more time than was planned. ⓰ If an event or contract runs for a particular time, it lasts for that time ▷ **NOUN** ⓱ If you go for a run, you run for pleasure or exercise. ⓲ a journey somewhere • *It was quite a run to the village.* ⓳ If a play or show has a run of a particular length of time, it is on for that time. ⓴ A run of success or failure is a series of successes or failures. ㉑ In cricket or baseball, a player scores one

run by running between marked places on the pitch after hitting the ball.
run out VERB If you run out of something, you have no more left.
run over VERB If someone is run over, they are hit by a moving vehicle.
● **SIMILAR WORDS:** ❶ dash, race, sprint ❷ bolt, flee

runaway, runaways **NOUN** a person who has escaped from a place or left it secretly and hurriedly.

rundown ADJECTIVE ❶ tired and not well. ❷ neglected and in poor condition ▷ **NOUN** ❸ **INFORMAL** If you give someone the rundown on a situation, you tell them the basic, important facts about it.

rung, rungs **NOUN** The rungs on a ladder are the bars that form the steps.

runner, runners **NOUN** ❶ a person who runs, especially as a sport. ❷ a person who takes messages or runs errands. ❸ A runner on a plant such as a strawberry is a long shoot from which a new plant develops. ❹ The runners on drawers and ice-skates are the thin strips on which they move.

runner bean, runner beans **NOUN** Runner beans are long green pods eaten as a vegetable, which grow on a climbing plant.

runner-up, runners-up **NOUN** a person or team that comes second in a race or competition.

running ADJECTIVE ❶ continuing without stopping over a period of time • *a running commentary.* ❷ Running water is flowing rather than standing still.

a b c d e f g h i j k l m n o p q **r** s t u v w x y z

▷ SPELLING NOTE: *Psychiatrists Seldom Yell Callously Hard (psychiatrist)*

runny, runnier, runniest ADJECTIVE
❶ more liquid than usual • *Warm the honey until it becomes runny.* ❷ If someone's nose or eyes are runny, liquid is coming out of them.

runt, runts NOUN The runt of a litter of animals is the smallest and weakest.

runway, runways NOUN a long strip of ground used by aeroplanes for taking off or landing.

rupee, rupees [Said roo-**pee**] NOUN the main unit of currency in India, Pakistan, and some other countries.

rupture, ruptures, rupturing, ruptured NOUN ❶ a severe injury in which part of your body tears or bursts open ❷ To rupture part of the body means to cause it to tear or burst • *a ruptured spleen.*

rural ADJECTIVE (GEOGRAPHY) relating to or involving the countryside.

ruse, ruses NOUN FORMAL an action which is intended to trick someone.

rush, rushes, rushing, rushed VERB
❶ To rush means to move fast or do something quickly. ❷ If you rush someone into doing something, you make them do it without allowing them enough time to think ▷ NOUN ❸ If you are in a rush, you are busy and do not have enough time to do things. ❹ If there is a rush for something, there is a sudden increase in demand for it • *There was a rush for tickets.* ❺ Rushes are plants with long, thin stems that grow near water.

rush hour, rush hours NOUN The rush hour is one of the busy parts of the day when most people are travelling to or from work.

rusk, rusks NOUN a hard, dry biscuit given to babies.

Russian, Russians ADJECTIVE
❶ belonging or relating to Russia ▷ NOUN ❷ someone who comes from Russia. ❸ Russian is the main language spoken in Russia.

rust, rusts, rusting, rusted NOUN
❶ Rust is a reddish-brown substance that forms on iron or steel which has been in contact with water and which is decaying gradually ▷ NOUN OR ADJECTIVE ❷ reddish-brown ▷ VERB ❸ When a metal object rusts, it becomes covered in rust.

rustic ADJECTIVE simple in a way considered to be typical of the countryside • *a rustic old log cabin.*

rustle, rustles, rustling, rustled VERB When something rustles, it makes soft sounds as it moves. **rustling** ADJECTIVE OR NOUN

rusty, rustier, rustiest ADJECTIVE
❶ affected by rust • *a rusty iron gate.* ❷ If someone's knowledge is rusty, it is not as good as it used to be because they have not used it for a long time • *My German is a bit rusty these days.*

rut, ruts NOUN ❶ a deep, narrow groove in the ground made by the wheels of a vehicle ▷ PHRASE ❷ If someone is **in a rut**, they have become fixed in their way of doing things.

ruthless ADJECTIVE very harsh or cruel • *a ruthless drug dealer.* **ruthlessness** NOUN **ruthlessly** ADVERB

rye NOUN a type of grass that produces light brown grain.

▷ SPELLING NOTE: *the QUeen stood on the QUay (quay)*

Ss

a
b
c
d
e
f
g
h
i
j
k
l
m
n
o
p
q
r
s
t
u
v
w
x
y
z

Some words which sound as if they begin with *s* actually begin with *c*, for example *city*. Some words which sound as if they begin with *sh* actually begin with *ch*, for example *chivalry*. Other words which sound as if they begin with *s* actually begin with the letters *ps*, for example *psychiatry* and *psychology*.

Sabbath NOUN (RE) The Sabbath is the day of the week when members of some religious groups, especially Jews and Christians, do not work.
  ● **WORD HISTORY:** from Hebrew
  ● *shabbath* meaning 'to rest'

sable, sables NOUN a very expensive fur used for making coats and hats; also the wild animal from which this fur is obtained.

sabotage, sabotages, sabotaging, sabotaged *[Said sab-ot-ahj]* NOUN
❶ the deliberate damaging of things such as machinery and railway lines
▷ VERB **❷** If something is sabotaged, it is deliberately damaged. **saboteur** NOUN
  ● **WORD HISTORY:** from French
  ● *saboter* meaning 'to spoil through
  ● clumsiness'

sabre, sabres NOUN **❶** a heavy curved sword. **❷** a light sword used in fencing.

saccharine or **saccharin** *[Said sak-er-rine]* NOUN a chemical used instead of sugar to sweeten things.

sachet, sachets *[Said sash-ay]* NOUN a small closed packet, containing a small amount of something such as sugar or shampoo.

sack, sacks, sacking, sacked NOUN
❶ a large bag made of rough material used for carrying or storing goods
▷ VERB **❷** If someone is sacked, they are dismissed from their job by their employer ▷ PHRASE
❸ INFORMAL If someone gets **the sack**, they are dismissed from their job by their employer.

sacrament, sacraments NOUN an important Christian ceremony such as communion, baptism, or marriage.

sacred *[Said say-krid]* ADJECTIVE holy, or connected with religion or religious ceremonies • *sacred ground*.

sacrifice, sacrifices, sacrificing, sacrificed *[Said sak-riff-ice]* VERB
❶ If you sacrifice something valuable or important, you give it up. **❷** To sacrifice an animal means to kill it as an offering to a god ▷ NOUN **❸** the killing of an animal as an offering to a god or gods. **❹** the action of giving something up. **sacrificial** ADJECTIVE
  ● **SIMILAR WORDS:** **❶** forfeit, give
  ● up

sacrilege *[Said sak-ril-ij]* NOUN

Sacrilege is behaviour that shows great disrespect for something holy. **sacrilegious** ADJECTIVE

sacrosanct [Said **sak**-roe-sangkt] ADJECTIVE regarded as too important to be criticized or changed • *Freedom of the press is sacrosanct.*

sad, sadder, saddest ADJECTIVE ❶ If you are sad, you feel unhappy. ❷ Something sad makes you feel unhappy • *a sad story.* **sadly** ADVERB
● SIMILAR WORDS: ❶ low, melancholy, unhappy

sadden, saddens, saddening, saddened VERB If something saddens you, it makes you feel sad.

saddle, saddles, saddling, saddled NOUN ❶ a leather seat that you sit on when you are riding a horse. ❷ The saddle on a bicycle is the seat ▷ VERB ❸ If you saddle a horse, you put a saddle on it.

sadism [Said **say**-diz-m] NOUN Sadism is the obtaining of pleasure, especially sexual pleasure, from making people suffer pain or humiliation. **sadist** NOUN **sadistic** ADJECTIVE
● WORD HISTORY: from the Marquis de *Sade* (1740–1814), who got his pleasure in this way

sadness NOUN the feeling of being unhappy.

safari, safaris NOUN an expedition for hunting or observing wild animals.
● WORD HISTORY: from Swahili *safari* meaning 'journey'

safari park, safari parks NOUN a large park where wild animals such as lions and elephants roam freely.

safe, safer, safest; safes ADJECTIVE ❶ Something that is safe does not cause harm or danger. ❷ If you are safe, you are not in any danger. ❸ If it is safe to say something, you can say it with little risk of being wrong ▷ NOUN ❹ a strong metal box with special locks, in which you can keep valuable things. **safely** ADVERB
● SIMILAR WORDS: ❷ out of danger, secure

safeguard, safeguards, safeguarding, safeguarded VERB ❶ To safeguard something means to protect it ▷ NOUN ❷ something designed to protect people or things.

safekeeping NOUN If something is given to you for safekeeping, it is given to you to look after.

safety NOUN the state of being safe from harm or danger.

sag, sags, sagging, sagged VERB When something sags, it hangs down loosely or sinks downwards in the middle. **sagging** ADJECTIVE

saga, sagas [Said **sah**-ga] NOUN a very long story, usually with many different adventures • *a saga of rivalry, honour and love.*
● WORD HISTORY: from Old Norse *saga* meaning 'story'

sage, sages NOUN ❶ LITERARY a very wise person. ❷ Sage is also a herb used for flavouring in cooking.
● WORD HISTORY: sense 1 is from Latin *sapere* meaning 'to be wise'; sense 2 is from Latin *salvus* meaning 'healthy', because of the supposed medicinal properties of the plant

Sagittarius [Said saj-it-**tair**-ee-uss]

▷ SPELLING NOTE: *there's SAND in my SANDwich (sandwich)*

NOUN Sagittarius is the ninth sign of the zodiac, represented by a creature half man, half horse holding a bow and arrow. People born between November 22nd and December 21st are born under this sign.
● **WORD HISTORY:** from Latin *sagittarius* meaning 'archer'

sail, sails, sailing, sailed **NOUN**
❶ Sails are large pieces of material attached to a ship's mast. The wind blows against the sail and moves the ship ▷ **VERB** ❷ When a ship sails, it moves across water. ❸ If you sail somewhere, you go there by ship.

sailor, sailors **NOUN** a member of a ship's crew.

saint, saints **NOUN** a person who after death is formally recognized by a Christian Church as deserving special honour because of having lived a very holy life.
● **WORD HISTORY:** from Latin *sanctus* meaning 'holy'

saintly ADJECTIVE behaving in a very good or holy way.

sake, sakes **PHRASE** ❶ If you do something **for someone's sake**, you do it to help or please them. ❷ You use **for the sake of** to say why you are doing something • *a one-off expedition for interest's sake.*

salad, salads **NOUN** a mixture of raw vegetables.
● **WORD HISTORY:** from Old Provençal *salar* meaning 'to season with salt'

salamander, salamanders **NOUN** (SCIENCE) A salamander is an amphibian that looks rather like a lizard.

salami *[Said sal-lah-mee]* **NOUN** Salami is a kind of spicy sausage.

salary, salaries **NOUN** a regular monthly payment to an employee.
● **WORD HISTORY:** from Latin *salarium* meaning 'money given to soldiers to buy salt'

salat, salats **NOUN** (RE) a prayer that Muslims say five times a day.

sale, sales **NOUN** ❶ The sale of goods is the selling of them. ❷ an occasion when a shop sells things at reduced prices ❸ IN PLURAL The sales of a product are the numbers that are sold.

salesman, salesmen **NOUN** someone who sells products for a company. **saleswoman NOUN**

salient *[Said say-lee-ent]* **ADJECTIVE** FORMAL The salient points or facts are the important ones.

saliva *[Said sal-live-a]* **NOUN** Saliva is the watery liquid in your mouth that helps you chew and digest food.

sallow ADJECTIVE Sallow skin is pale and unhealthy.

salmon, salmons or salmon *[Said sam-on]* **NOUN** a large edible silver-coloured fish with pink flesh.

salmonella *[Said sal-mon-nell-a]* **NOUN** Salmonella is a kind of bacteria which can cause severe food poisoning.

salon, salons **NOUN** a place where hairdressers work.

saloon, saloons **NOUN** ❶ a car with a fixed roof and a separate boot. ❷ In America, a place where alcoholic drinks are sold and drunk.

▷ SPELLING NOTE: *On WEDNESday Wayne WED NESta (Wednesday)*

salt, salts NOUN ❶ Salt is a white substance found naturally in sea water. It is used to flavour and preserve food. ❷ a chemical compound formed from an acid base.

salty, saltier, saltiest ADJECTIVE containing salt or tasting of salt.

salute, salutes, saluting, saluted NOUN ❶ a formal sign of respect. Soldiers give a salute by raising their right hand to their forehead ▷ VERB ❷ If you salute someone, you give them a salute.

salvage, salvages, salvaging, salvaged VERB ❶ If you salvage things, you save them, for example from a wrecked ship or a destroyed building ▷ NOUN ❷ You refer to things saved from a wrecked ship or destroyed building as salvage.

salvation NOUN ❶ When someone's salvation takes place, they are saved from harm or evil. ❷ To be someone's salvation means to save them from harm or evil.

salvo, salvos or salvoes NOUN the firing of several guns or missiles at the same time.

same ADJECTIVE (usually preceded by the) ❶ If two things are the same, they are like one another. ❷ Same means just one thing and not two different ones • They were born in the same town.

Samoan, Samoans ADJECTIVE ❶ belonging or relating to Samoa ▷ NOUN ❷ someone who comes from Samoa.

sample, samples, sampling, sampled NOUN ❶ A sample of something is a

small amount of it that you can try or test • a sample of new wine. ▷ VERB ❷ If you sample something, you try it • I sampled his cooking.

samsara NOUN ❶ RE in Hinduism, the endless cycle of birth, death, and rebirth. ❷ RE in Buddhism, someone's rebirth.

samurai [Said sam-oor-eye] NOUN A samurai was a member of an ancient Japanese warrior class.

sanctimonious [Said sank-tim-moan-ee-uss] ADJECTIVE pretending to be very religious and virtuous.

sanction, sanctions, sanctioning, sanctioned VERB PSHE ❶ To sanction something means to officially approve of it or allow it ▷ NOUN ❷ Sanction is official approval of something. ❸ a severe punishment or penalty intended to make people obey the law. ❹ Sanctions are sometimes taken by countries against a country that has broken international law.

sanctity NOUN If you talk about the sanctity of something, you are saying that it should be respected because it is very important • the sanctity of marriage.

sanctuary, sanctuaries NOUN ❶ a place where you are safe from harm or danger. ❷ a place where wildlife is protected • a bird sanctuary.

sand, sands, sanding, sanded NOUN ❶ Sand consists of tiny pieces of stone. Beaches are made of sand ▷ VERB ❷ If you sand something, you rub sandpaper over it to make it smooth.

▷ SPELLING NOTE: Eddy Ant thinks mEAt is a grEAt trEAt to EAt (-ea-)

sandal, sandals NOUN Sandals are light open shoes with straps, worn in warm weather.

sandpaper NOUN (D & T) Sandpaper is strong paper with a coating of sand on it, used for rubbing surfaces to make them smooth.

sandshoe, sandshoes NOUN In British, Australian, and New Zealand English, a light canvas shoe with a rubber sole.

sandstone NOUN Sandstone is a type of rock formed from sand, often used for building.

sandwich, sandwiches, sandwiching, sandwiched NOUN ❶ two slices of bread with a filling between them ▷ VERB ❷ If one thing is sandwiched between two others, it is in a narrow space between them • *a small shop sandwiched between a bar and an office.*

● WORD HISTORY: sense 1 is named after the 4th Earl of *Sandwich* (1718–1792), for whom they were invented so that he could eat and gamble at the same time

sandy, sandier, sandiest ADJECTIVE ❶ A sandy area is covered with sand. ❷ Sandy hair is light orange-brown.

sane, saner, sanest ADJECTIVE ❶ If someone is sane, they have a normal and healthy mind. ❷ A sane action is sensible and reasonable.

sanguine [Said *sang*-gwin] ADJECTIVE FORMAL cheerful and confident.

sanitary ADJECTIVE Sanitary means concerned with keeping things clean and hygienic • *improving the sanitary*

conditions in the hospital.

sanitary towel, sanitary towels NOUN Sanitary towels are pads of thick, soft material which women wear during their periods.

sanitation NOUN Sanitation is the process of keeping places clean and hygienic, especially by providing a sewage system and clean water supply.

sanity NOUN Your sanity is your ability to think and act normally and reasonably.

sap, saps, sapping, sapped VERB ❶ If something saps your strength or confidence, it gradually weakens and destroys it ▷ NOUN ❷ Sap is the watery liquid in plants.

sapling, saplings NOUN a young tree.

sapphire, sapphires NOUN a blue precious stone.

sarcastic ADJECTIVE saying or doing the opposite of what you really mean in order to mock or insult someone • *a sarcastic remark.*
sarcasm NOUN **sarcastically** ADVERB
● WORD HISTORY: from Greek *sarkazein* meaning 'to tear the flesh'

sarcophagus, sarcophagi or sarcophaguses [Said sar-*kof*-fag-uss] NOUN a stone coffin used in ancient times.

sardine, sardines NOUN a small edible sea fish.

sardonic ADJECTIVE mocking or scornful • *a sardonic grin.*
sardonically ADVERB

▷ SPELLING NOTE: *there's SAND in my SANDwich (sandwich)*

sari, saris [Said **sah**-ree] NOUN a piece of clothing worn especially by Indian women, consisting of a long piece of material folded around the body.

sarmie, sarmies NOUN SLANG In South African English, a sarmie is a sandwich.

sartorial ADJECTIVE FORMAL relating to clothes • *sartorial elegance.*

sash, sashes NOUN a long piece of cloth worn round the waist or over one shoulder.
- **WORD HISTORY:** from Arabic *shash* meaning 'muslin'

Satan NOUN Satan is the Devil.

satanic [Said sa-**tan**-ik] ADJECTIVE caused by or influenced by Satan • *satanic forces.*

satchel, satchels NOUN a leather or cloth bag with a long strap.

satellite, satellites NOUN ❶ an spacecraft sent into orbit round the earth to collect information or as part of a communications system. ❷ a natural object in space that moves round a planet or star.

satin, satins NOUN Satin is a kind of smooth, shiny silk.

satire, satires NOUN Satire is the use of mocking or ironical humour, especially in literature, to show how foolish or wicked some people are. **satirical** ADJECTIVE

satisfaction NOUN Satisfaction is the feeling of pleasure you get when you do something you wanted or needed to do.

satisfactory ADJECTIVE

acceptable or adequate • *a satisfactory explanation.* **satisfactorily** ADVERB

satisfied ADJECTIVE happy because you have got what you want.

satisfy, satisfies, satisfying, satisfied VERB ❶ To satisfy someone means to give them enough of something to make them pleased or contented. ❷ To satisfy someone that something is the case means to convince them of it. ❸ To satisfy the requirements for something means to fulfil them.
- **SIMILAR WORDS:** ❶ content, indulge, please

satisfying ADJECTIVE Something that is satisfying gives you a feeling of pleasure and fulfilment.

satsuma, satsumas [Said sat-**soo**-ma] NOUN a fruit like a small orange.

saturated ADJECTIVE ❶ very wet. ❷ If a place is saturated with things, it is completely full of them. **saturation** NOUN

Saturday, Saturdays NOUN the day between Friday and Sunday.
- **WORD HISTORY:** from Latin *Saturni dies* meaning 'day of Saturn'

Saturn NOUN Saturn is the planet in the solar system which is sixth from the sun.

sauce, sauces NOUN a liquid eaten with food to give it more flavour.
- **USAGE NOTE:** Do not confuse the spellings of *sauce* and *source*, which can sound very similar

saucepan, saucepans NOUN a deep metal cooking pot with a handle and a lid.

saucer, saucers NOUN a small

▷ SPELLING NOTE: *'i' before 'e' except after 'c'*

curved plate for a cup.

saucy, saucier, sauciest **ADJECTIVE** cheeky in an amusing way.

Saudi, Saudis [rhymes with **cloudy**] **ADJECTIVE** ❶ belonging or relating to Saudi Arabia ▷ **NOUN** ❷ someone who comes from Saudi Arabia.

sauna, saunas [Said **saw**-na] **NOUN** If you have a sauna, you go into a very hot room in order to sweat, then have a cold bath or shower.
  ● **WORD HISTORY:** a Finnish word

saunter, saunters, sauntering, sauntered **VERB** To saunter somewhere means to walk there slowly and casually.

sausage, sausages **NOUN** a mixture of minced meat and herbs formed into a tubular shape and served cooked.

sauté, sautés, sautéing or sautéeing, sautéed [Said **soh**-tay] **VERB** To sauté food means to fry it quickly in a small amount of oil or butter.

savage, savages, savaging, savaged **ADJECTIVE** ❶ cruel and violent • savage fighting. ▷ **NOUN** ❷ If you call someone a savage, you mean that they are violent and uncivilized ▷ **VERB** ❸ If an animal savages you, it attacks you and bites you. **savagely ADVERB**
  ● **SIMILAR WORDS:** ❶ brutal, cruel, vicious

savagery NOUN Savagery is cruel and violent behaviour.

save, saves, saving, saved **VERB** ❶ If you save someone, you rescue them • He saved my life. ❷ If you save someone or something, you keep them safe. ❸ If you save something,

you keep it so that you can use it later • He'd saved up enough money for the deposit. ❹ To save time, money, or effort means to prevent it from being wasted • You could have saved us the trouble. ▷ **PREPOSITION** ❺ FORMAL Save means except • I was alone in the house save for a very old woman.

saving, savings **NOUN** ❶ a reduction in the amount of time or money used ❷ IN PLURAL Your savings are the money you have saved.

saviour, saviours **NOUN** ❶ If someone saves you from danger, you can refer to them as your saviour ▷ **PROPER NOUN** ❷ In Christianity, the Saviour is Jesus Christ.

savour, savours, savouring, savoured **VERB** If you savour something, you take your time with it and enjoy it fully • These spirits should be sipped and savoured like fine whiskies.

savoury ADJECTIVE ❶ Savoury is salty or spicy. ❷ Something that is not very savoury is not very pleasant or respectable • the less savoury places.

saw, saws, sawing, sawed, sawn ❶ Saw is the past tense of **see**. **NOUN** ❷ a tool, with a blade with sharp teeth along one edge, for cutting wood ▷ **VERB** ❸ If you saw something, you cut it with a saw.

sawdust NOUN Sawdust is the fine powder produced when you saw wood.

saxophone, saxophones **NOUN** a curved metal wind instrument often played in jazz bands.
  ● **WORD HISTORY:** named after
  ● Adolphe Sax (1814–1994), who
  ● invented the instrument

say, says, saying, said **VERB** ❶ When you say something, you speak words. ❷ 'Say' is used to give an example • *a maximum fee of, say, a million.* ▷ **NOUN** ❸ If you have a say in something, you can give your opinion and influence decisions.
● **SIMILAR WORDS:** ❶ remark,
● speak, utter

saying, sayings **NOUN** a well-known sentence or phrase that tells you something about human life.
● **SIMILAR WORDS:** adage, proverb

scab, scabs **NOUN** a hard, dry covering that forms over a wound. **scabby ADJECTIVE**

scaffolding NOUN Scaffolding is a framework of poles and boards that is used by workmen to stand on while they are working on the outside structure of a building.

scald, scalds, scalding, scalded *[Said skawld]* **VERB** ❶ If you scald yourself, you burn yourself with very hot liquid or steam ▷ **NOUN** ❷ a burn caused by scalding.

scale, scales, scaling, scaled **NOUN** ❶ The scale of something is its size or extent • *the sheer scale of the disaster.* ❷ a set of levels or numbers used for measuring things. ❸ The scale of a map, plan, or model is the relationship between the size of something in the map, plan, or model and its size in the real world • *a scale of 1:10,000.* ❹ (MUSIC) an upward or downward sequence of musical notes. ❺ The scales of a fish or reptile are the small pieces of hard skin covering its body ❻ IN PLURAL Scales are a piece of equipment used for weighing things ▷ **VERB** ❼ If you scale something

high, you climb it.

scalene ADJECTIVE A scalene triangle has sides which are all of different lengths.

scallop, scallops **NOUN** Scallops are edible shellfish with two flat fan-shaped shells.

scalp, scalps, scalping, scalped **NOUN** ❶ Your scalp is the skin under the hair on your head. ❷ the piece of skin and hair removed when someone is scalped ▷ **VERB** ❸ To scalp someone means to remove the skin and hair from their head in one piece.

scalpel, scalpels **NOUN** a knife with a thin, sharp blade, used by surgeons.

scaly ADJECTIVE covered with scales.

scamper, scampers, scampering, scampered **VERB** To scamper means to move quickly and lightly.

scampi PLURAL NOUN Scampi are large prawns often eaten fried in breadcrumbs.

scan, scans, scanning, scanned **VERB** ❶ If you scan something, you look at all of it carefully • *I scanned the horizon to the north-east.* ❷ If a machine scans something, it examines it by means of a beam of light or X-rays. ❸ (ENGLISH) If the words of a poem scan, they fit into a regular, rhythmical pattern. ❹ (ENGLISH) If you scan a line of poetry you count the number of beats or metrical feet it has ▷ **NOUN** ❺ an examination or search by a scanner • *a brain scan.*

scandal, scandals **NOUN** a situation or event that people think is shocking and immoral. **scandalous ADJECTIVE**

▷ SPELLING NOTE: *an ELegant angEL (angel)*

Scandinavia [Said skan-din-**nay**-vee-a] NOUN Scandinavia is the name given to a group of countries in Northern Europe, including Norway, Sweden, Denmark, and sometimes Finland and Iceland. **Scandinavian** NOUN OR ADJECTIVE

scanner, scanners NOUN ❶ a machine which is used to examine, identify, or record things by means of a beam of light or X-rays. ❷ ICT a machine which converts text or images into a form that can be stored on a computer.

scansion NOUN ENGLISH Scansion is the analysis of the rhythmic arrangement of syllables in lines of poetry.

scant, scanter, scantest ADJECTIVE If something receives scant attention, it does not receive enough attention.

scapegoat, scapegoats NOUN If someone is made a scapegoat, they are blamed for something, although it may not be their fault.

scar, scars, scarring, scarred NOUN ❶ a mark left on your skin after a wound has healed. ❷ a permanent effect on someone's mind that results from a very unpleasant experience • *the scars of war.* ▷ VERB ❸ If an injury scars you, it leaves a permanent mark on your skin. ❹ If an unpleasant experience scars you, it has a permanent effect on you.

scarce, scarcer, scarcest ADJECTIVE If something is scarce, there is not very much of it • *Fresh water is scarce in the desert.* **scarcity** NOUN

scarcely ADVERB Scarcely means hardly • *I can scarcely hear her.*

● USAGE NOTE: As *scarcely* already has a negative sense, it is followed by *ever* or *any*, and not by *never* or *no*

scare, scares, scaring, scared VERB ❶ If something scares you, it frightens you ▷ NOUN ❷ If something gives you a scare, it scares you. ❸ If there is a scare about something, a lot of people are worried about it • *an AIDS scare.* **scared** ADJECTIVE
● SIMILAR WORDS: ❶ alarm, frighten, startle

scarecrow, scarecrows NOUN an object shaped like a person, put in a field to scare birds away.

scarf, scarfs or scarves NOUN a piece of cloth worn round your neck or head to keep you warm.

scarlet NOUN OR ADJECTIVE bright red.

scary, scarier, scariest ADJECTIVE INFORMAL frightening.

scathing [Said **skayth**-ing] ADJECTIVE harsh and scornful • *They were scathing about his job.*

scatter, scatters, scattering, scattered VERB ❶ To scatter things means to throw or drop them all over an area. ❷ If people scatter, they move away in different directions.
● SIMILAR WORDS: ❶ sprinkle, strew, throw about

scattering NOUN A scattering of things is a small number of them spread over a large area • *the scattering of islands.*

scavenge, scavenges, scavenging, scavenged VERB If you scavenge for

▷ SPELLING NOTE: *LEt's measure the angLE (angle)*

things, you search for them among waste and rubbish. **scavenger** NOUN

scenario, scenarios [Said sin-**nar**-ee-oh] NOUN ❶ (DRAMA) The scenario of a film or play is a summary of its plot. ❷ the way a situation could possibly develop in the future • *the worst possible scenario*.

scene, scenes NOUN ❶ (ENGLISH & DRAMA) part of a play or film in which a series of events happen in one place. ❷ Pictures and views are sometimes called scenes • *a village scene*. ❸ The scene of an event is the place where it happened. ❹ an area of activity • *the music scene*.

scenery NOUN ❶ In the countryside, you can refer to everything you see as the scenery. ❷ In a theatre, the scenery is the painted cloth on the stage which represents the place where the action is happening.

scenic ADJECTIVE A scenic place or route has nice views.

scent, scents, scenting, scented NOUN ❶ a smell, especially a pleasant one. ❷ Scent is perfume ▷ VERB ❸ When an animal scents something, it becomes aware of it by smelling it.

sceptic, sceptics [Said **skep**-tik] NOUN someone who has doubts about things that other people believe.

sceptical [Said **skep**-tik-kl] ADJECTIVE If you are sceptical about something, you have doubts about it. **sceptically** ADVERB **scepticism** NOUN

sceptre, sceptres [Said **sep**-ter]

NOUN an ornamental rod carried by a king or queen as a symbol of power.

schedule, schedules, scheduling, scheduled [Said **shed**-yool] NOUN ❶ a plan that gives a list of events or tasks, together with the times at which each thing should be done ▷ VERB ❷ If something is scheduled to happen, it has been planned and arranged • *Their journey was scheduled for the beginning of May*.

schema, schemata [Said **skee**-ma] NOUN ❶ TECHNICAL an outline of a plan or theory. ❷ a mental model which the mind uses to understand new experiences or to view the world.

scheme, schemes, scheming, schemed NOUN ❶ a plan or arrangement • *a five-year development scheme*. ▷ VERB ❷ When people scheme, they make secret plans.

schism, schisms [Said **skizm**] NOUN a split or division within a group or organization.

schizophrenia [Said skit-soe-**free**-nee-a] NOUN Schizophrenia is a serious mental illness which prevents someone relating their thoughts and feelings to what is happening around them. **schizophrenic** NOUN OR ADJECTIVE
● WORD HISTORY: from Greek
● *skhizein* meaning 'to split' and *phren*
● meaning 'mind'

scholar, scholars NOUN ❶ a person who studies an academic subject and knows a lot about it. ❷ In South African English, a scholar is a school pupil.

scholarly ADJECTIVE having or showing a lot of knowledge.

A B C D E F G H I J K L M N O P Q R S T U V W X Y Z

scholarship, scholarships NOUN
❶ If you get a scholarship to a school
or university, your studies are paid for
by the school or university or by some
other organization. ❷ Scholarship is
academic study and knowledge.

school, schools, schooling, schooled
NOUN ❶ a place where children are
educated. ❷ University departments
and colleges are sometimes called
schools • *My oldest son is in medical
school.* ❸ You can refer to a large
group of dolphins or fish as a school
▷ VERB ❹ When someone is
schooled in something, they are
taught it • *They were schooled in the
modern techniques.*

schoolchild, schoolchildren NOUN
Schoolchildren are children who go to
school. **schoolboy** NOUN **schoolgirl**
NOUN

schooling NOUN Your schooling is
the education you get at school.

schooner, schooners NOUN a
sailing ship.

science, sciences NOUN ❶ Science
is the study of the nature and
behaviour of natural things and the
knowledge obtained about them. ❷ a
branch of science, for example physics
or biology.

science fiction NOUN Stories
about events happening in the future
or in other parts of the universe are
called science fiction.

scientific ADJECTIVE ❶ relating to
science or to a particular science
• *scientific knowledge.* ❷ done in a
systematic way, using experiments or
tests • *this scientific method.*
scientifically ADVERB

scientist, scientists NOUN an
expert in one of the sciences who does
work connected with it.

scimitar, scimitars [Said *sim-mit-ar*]
NOUN (HISTORY) A scimitar is a
curved sword used in the past in some
Eastern countries.

scintillating [Said *sin-til-late-ing*]
ADJECTIVE lively and witty
• *scintillating conversation.*

scissors PLURAL NOUN (D & T)
Scissors are a cutting tool with two
sharp blades.

scoff, scoffs, scoffing, scoffed VERB
❶ If you scoff, you speak in a scornful,
mocking way about something.
❷ INFORMAL If you scoff food, you eat
it quickly and greedily.

scold, scolds, scolding, scolded VERB
If you scold someone, you tell them
off.
● SIMILAR WORDS: rebuke,
● reprimand, tell off

scone, scones [Said *skon* or *skoan*]
NOUN Scones are small cakes made
from flour and fat and usually eaten
with butter.

scoop, scoops, scooping, scooped
VERB ❶ If you scoop something up,
you pick it up using a spoon or the
palm of your hand ▷ NOUN ❷ an
object like a large spoon which is used
for picking up food such as ice cream.

scooter, scooters NOUN ❶ a small,
light motorcycle. ❷ a simple cycle
which a child rides by standing on it
and pushing the ground with one foot.

scope NOUN ❶ If there is scope for
doing something, the opportunity to
do it exists. ❷ The scope of

▷ SPELLING NOTE: *Beautiful Elephants Are Usually Tiny (beautiful)*

something is the whole subject area which it deals with or includes.

-scope SUFFIX '-scope' is used to form nouns meaning an instrument used for observing or detecting • *microscope* • *telescope*.
● WORD HISTORY: from Greek
● *skopein* meaning 'to look at'

scorching ADJECTIVE extremely hot • *another scorching summer*.

score, scores, scoring, scored VERB ❶ If you score in a game, you get a goal, run, or point. ❷ To score in a game also means to record the score obtained by the players. ❸ If you score a success or victory, you achieve it. ❹ To score a surface means to cut a line into it ▷ NOUN ❺ The score in a game is the number of goals, runs, or points obtained by the two teams. ❻ Scores of things means very many of them • *Ros entertained scores of celebrities.* ❼ OLD-FASHIONED A score is twenty. ❽ (MUSIC) The score of a piece of music is the written version of it. **scorer** NOUN

scorn, scorns, scorning, scorned NOUN ❶ Scorn is great contempt • *a look of scorn*. ▷ VERB ❷ If you scorn someone, you treat them with great contempt. ❸ FORMAL If you scorn something, you refuse to accept it.

scornful ADJECTIVE showing contempt • *his scornful comment*. **scornfully** ADVERB
● SIMILAR WORDS: contemptuous,
● disdainful, sneering

Scorpio NOUN Scorpio is the eighth sign of the zodiac, represented by a scorpion. People born between October 23rd and November 21st are

born under this sign.

scorpion, scorpions NOUN an animal that looks like a small lobster, with a long tail with a poisonous sting on the end.

Scot, Scots NOUN ❶ a person who comes from Scotland ▷ ADJECTIVE ❷ Scots means the same as **Scottish**.

scotch, scotches NOUN Scotch is whisky made in Scotland.

scot-free ADVERB If you get away scot-free, you get away without being punished.
● WORD HISTORY: from Old English
● *scot* meaning 'payment'; hence
● 'payment-free'

Scotsman, Scotsmen NOUN a man who comes from Scotland. **Scotswoman** NOUN

Scottish ADJECTIVE belonging or relating to Scotland.

scoundrel, scoundrels NOUN OLD-FASHIONED a man who cheats and deceives people.

scour, scours, scouring, scoured VERB ❶ If you scour a place, you look all over it in order to find something • *The police scoured the area.* ❷ If you scour something such as a pan, you clean it by rubbing it with something rough.

scourge, scourges [rhymes with urge] NOUN something that causes a lot of suffering • *hay fever, that scourge of summer*.

scout, scouts, scouting, scouted NOUN ❶ a boy who is a member of the Scout Association, an organization for boys which aims to develop

character and responsibility.
❷ someone who is sent to an area to find out the position of an enemy army ▷ **VERB ❸** If you scout around for something, you look around for it.

scowl, scowls, scowling, scowled
VERB ❶ If you scowl, you frown because you are angry • *They were scowling at me.* ▷ **NOUN ❷** an angry expression.

scrabble, scrabbles, scrabbling, scrabbled **VERB** If you scrabble at something, you scrape at it with your hands or feet.
● **WORD HISTORY:** from Old Dutch
● *schrabbelen* meaning 'to scrape
● repeatedly'

scramble, scrambles, scrambling, scrambled **VERB ❶** If you scramble over something, you climb over it using your hands to help you ▷ **NOUN ❷** a motorcycle race over rough ground.

scrap, scraps, scrapping, scrapped
NOUN ❶ A scrap of something is a very small piece of it • *a scrap of cloth.*
❷ IN PLURAL Scraps are pieces of leftover food ▷ **ADJECTIVE OR NOUN ❸** Scrap metal or scrap is metal from old machinery or cars that can be re-used ▷ **VERB ❹** If you scrap something, you get rid of it • *They considered scrapping passport controls.*

scrapbook, scrapbooks **NOUN** a book in which you stick things such as pictures or newspaper articles.

scrape, scrapes, scraping, scraped
VERB ❶ If you scrape a surface, you rub a rough or sharp object against it.
❷ If something scrapes, it makes a harsh noise by rubbing against

something • *his shoes scraping across the stone ground.*

scratch, scratches, scratching, scratched **VERB ❶** To scratch something means to make a small cut on it accidentally • *They were always getting scratched by cats.* **❷** If you scratch, you rub your skin with your nails because it is itching ▷ **NOUN ❸** a small cut.

scratchcard, scratchcards **NOUN** a ticket in a competition with a surface that you scratch off to show whether or not you have won a prize.

scrawl, scrawls, scrawling, scrawled
VERB ❶ If you scrawl something, you write it in a careless and untidy way ▷ **NOUN ❷** You can refer to careless and untidy writing as a scrawl.

scrawny, scrawnier, scrawniest
ADJECTIVE thin and bony • *a small scrawny man.*

scream, screams, screaming, screamed **VERB ❶** If you scream, you shout or cry in a loud, high-pitched voice ▷ **NOUN ❷** a loud, high-pitched cry.
● **SIMILAR WORDS:** cry, shriek, yell

screech, screeches, screeching, screeched **VERB ❶** To screech means to make an unpleasant high-pitched noise • *The car wheels screeched.* ▷ **NOUN ❷** an unpleasant high-pitched noise.

screen, screens, screening, screened
NOUN ❶ a flat vertical surface on which a picture is shown • *a television screen.* **❷** a vertical panel used to separate different parts of a room or to protect something ▷ **VERB ❸** To screen a film or television programme

a b c d e f g h i j k l m n o p q r **s** t u v w x y z

▷ SPELLING NOTE: there's a rAKE in the brAKEs (*brake*)

means to show it. ❹ If you screen someone, you put something in front of them to protect them.

screenplay, screenplays **NOUN** The screenplay of a film is the script.

screw, screws, screwing, screwed **NOUN** ❶ a small, sharp piece of metal for fixing things together or for fixing something to a wall ▷ **VERB** ❷ If you screw things together, you fix them together using screws. ❸ If you screw something onto something else, you fix it there by twisting it round and round • *He screwed the top on the ink bottle.*
screw up VERB If you screw something up, you twist it or squeeze it so that it no longer has its proper shape • *Amy screwed up her face.*

screwdriver, screwdrivers **NOUN** a tool for turning screws.

scribble, scribbles, scribbling, scribbled **VERB** ❶ If you scribble something, you write it quickly and roughly. ❷ To scribble also means to make meaningless marks • *When Caroline was five she scribbled on a wall.* ▷ **NOUN** ❸ You can refer to something written or drawn quickly and roughly as a scribble.

scrimp, scrimps, scrimping, scrimped **VERB** If you scrimp, you live cheaply and spend as little money as you can.

script, scripts **NOUN** (DRAMA) the written version of a play or film.

scripture, scriptures **NOUN** Scripture refers to sacred writings, especially the Bible. **scriptural ADJECTIVE**

scroll, scrolls **NOUN** a long roll of paper or parchment with writing on it.

scrounge, scrounges, scrounging, scrounged **VERB** INFORMAL If you scrounge something, you get it by asking for it rather than by earning or buying it. **scrounger NOUN**
● SIMILAR WORDS: cadge, sponge

scrub, scrubs, scrubbing, scrubbed **VERB** ❶ If you scrub something, you clean it with a stiff brush and water ▷ **NOUN** ❷ If you give something a scrub, you scrub it. ❸ Scrub consists of low trees and bushes.

scruff NOUN The scruff of your neck is the back of your neck or collar.

scruffy, scruffier, scruffiest **ADJECTIVE** dirty and untidy • *four scruffy youths.*
● SIMILAR WORDS: tatty, unkempt

scrum, scrums **NOUN** When rugby players form a scrum, they form a group and push against each other with their heads down in an attempt to get the ball.

scrunchie, scrunchies **NOUN** a loop of elastic loosely covered with material which is used to hold hair in a ponytail.

scruple, scruples [Said **skroo**-pl] **NOUN** Scruples are moral principles that make you unwilling to do something that seems wrong • *The West must drop its scruples and fight back.*

scrupulous ADJECTIVE ❶ always doing what is honest or morally right. ❷ paying very careful attention to detail • *a long and scrupulous search.* **scrupulously ADVERB**

scrutinize, scrutinizes, scrutinizing,

scrutinized; *also spelt* **scrutinise VERB** If you scrutinize something, you examine it very carefully.

scrutiny NOUN If something is under scrutiny, it is being observed very carefully.

scuba diving NOUN Scuba diving is the sport of swimming underwater while breathing from tanks of compressed air on your back.

scuff, scuffs, scuffing, scuffed **VERB ①** If you scuff your feet, you drag them along the ground when you are walking. **②** If you scuff your shoes, you mark them by scraping or rubbing them.

scuffle, scuffles, scuffling, scuffled **NOUN ①** a short, rough fight ▷ **VERB ②** When people scuffle, they fight roughly.

scullery, sculleries **NOUN** a small room next to a kitchen where washing and cleaning are done.

sculpt, sculpts, sculpting, sculpted **VERB** When something is sculpted, it is carved or shaped in stone, wood, or clay.

sculptor, sculptors **NOUN** someone who makes sculptures.

sculpture, sculptures **NOUN ①** a work of art produced by carving or shaping stone or clay. **②** Sculpture is the art of making sculptures.

scum NOUN Scum is a layer of a dirty substance on the surface of a liquid.

scungy, scungier, scungiest **ADJECTIVE** In Australia and New Zealand, a slang word for dirty or messy.

scurrilous *[Said **skur**-ril-luss]* **ADJECTIVE** abusive and damaging to someone's good name • *scurrilous stories.*

scurry, scurries, scurrying, scurried **VERB** To scurry means to run quickly with short steps.

scurvy NOUN Scurvy is a disease caused by a lack of vitamin C.

scuttle, scuttles, scuttling, scuttled **VERB ①** To scuttle means to run quickly. **②** To scuttle a ship means to sink it deliberately by making holes in the bottom ▷ **NOUN ③** a container for coal.

scythe, scythes **NOUN** a tool with a long handle and a curved blade used for cutting grass or grain.

sea, seas **NOUN ①** The sea is the salty water that covers much of the earth's surface. **②** A sea of people or things is a very large number of them • *a sea of red flags.*

seagull, seagulls **NOUN** Seagulls are common white, grey, and black birds that live near the sea.

seahorse, seahorses **NOUN** a small fish which swims upright, with a head that resembles a horse's head.

seal, seals, sealing, sealed **NOUN ①** an official mark on a document which shows that it is genuine. **②** a piece of wax fixed over the opening of a container. **③** a large mammal with flippers, that lives partly on land and partly in the sea ▷ **VERB ④** If you seal an envelope, you stick down the flap. **⑤** If you seal an opening, you cover it securely so that air, gas, or liquid cannot get through.

▷ SPELLING NOTE: *I always visit my FRIend on a FRIday (Friday)*

A
B
C
D
E
F
G
H
I
J
K
L
M
N
O
P
Q
R
S
T
U
V
W
X
Y
Z

sea lion, sea lions **NOUN** a type of large seal.

seam, seams **NOUN** ❶ a line of stitches joining two pieces of cloth. ❷ A seam of coal is a long, narrow layer of it beneath the ground.

seaman, seamen **NOUN** a sailor.

seance, seances [Said *say-ahnss*]; also spelt **séance NOUN** a meeting in which people try to communicate with the spirits of dead people.

search, searches, searching, searched **VERB** ❶ If you search for something, you look for it in several places. ❷ If a person is searched their body and clothing are examined to see if they are hiding anything ▷ **NOUN** ❸ an attempt to find something.
● **SIMILAR WORDS:** ❶ hunt, look,
● scour ❸ look, hunt, quest

search engine, search engines **NOUN** a service on the Internet which enables users to search for items of interest.

searching ADJECTIVE intended to discover the truth about something • *searching questions.*

searchlight, searchlights **NOUN** a powerful light whose beam can be turned in different directions.

searing ADJECTIVE A searing pain is very sharp.

seashore NOUN The seashore is the land along the edge of the sea.

seasick ADJECTIVE feeling sick because of the movement of a boat. **seasickness NOUN**

seaside NOUN The seaside is an area next to the sea.

season, seasons, seasoning, seasoned **NOUN** ❶ The seasons are the periods into which a year is divided and which have their own typical weather conditions. The seasons are spring, summer, autumn, and winter. ❷ a period of the year when something usually happens • *the football season* • *the hunting season.* ▷ **VERB** ❸ If you season food, you add salt, pepper, or spices to it.

seasonal ADJECTIVE happening during one season or one time of the year • *seasonal work.*

seasoned ADJECTIVE very experienced • *a seasoned professional.*

seasoning NOUN Seasoning is flavouring such as salt and pepper • *Add seasoning before serving.*

season ticket, season tickets **NOUN** a train or bus ticket that you can use as many times as you like within a certain period.

seat, seats, seating, seated **NOUN** ❶ something you can sit on. ❷ The seat of a piece of clothing is the part that covers your bottom. ❸ If someone wins a seat in parliament, they are elected ▷ **VERB** ❹ If you seat yourself somewhere, you sit down. ❺ If a place seats a particular number of people, it has enough seats for that number • *The theatre seats 570 people.*

seat belt, seat belts **NOUN** a strap that you fasten across your body for safety when travelling in a car or an aircraft.

seating NOUN The seating in a place is the number or arrangement of seats there.

▷ SPELLING NOTE: *I want to see (C) your licenCe (licence)*

seaweed NOUN Plants that grow in the sea are called seaweed.

secateurs [Said sek-at-**turz**] PLURAL NOUN Secateurs are small shears for pruning garden plants.

secluded ADJECTIVE quiet and hidden from view • *a secluded beach.* **seclusion** NOUN

second, seconds, seconding, seconded ADJECTIVE ❶ The second item in a series is the one counted as number two ▷ NOUN ❷ one of the sixty parts that a minute is divided into ❸ IN PLURAL Seconds are goods that are sold cheaply because they are slightly faulty ▷ VERB ❹ If you second a proposal, you formally agree with it so that it can be discussed or voted on ▷ VERB ❺ If you are seconded somewhere, you are sent there temporarily to work. **secondly** ADVERB

secondary ADJECTIVE ❶ Something that is secondary is less important than something else. ❷ Secondary education is education for pupils between the ages of eleven and eighteen.

secondary school, secondary schools NOUN a school for pupils between the ages of eleven and eighteen.

second-class ADJECTIVE ❶ Second-class things are regarded as less important than other things of the same kind • *He has been treated as a second-class citizen.* ▷ ADJECTIVE OR ADVERB ❷ Second-class services are cheaper and therefore slower or less comfortable than first-class ones.

second cousin, second cousins

NOUN Your second cousins are the children of your parents' cousins.

second-hand ADJECTIVE OR ADVERB ❶ Something that is second-hand has already been owned by someone else • *a second-hand car.* ❷ If you hear a story second-hand, you hear it indirectly, rather than from the people involved.

second person NOUN (ENGLISH) In grammar, the second person is the person being spoken to (*you*).

second-person narrator NOUN (ENGLISH) A second-person narrator addresses the reader directly using the pronoun *you* and tells a story as if the reader is the character whose thoughts and actions are being described. For example, a **second-person narrative** might begin 'You are standing in a dusty street, pretending to be doing nothing...'.

second-rate ADJECTIVE of poor quality • *a second-rate movie.*

secret, secrets ADJECTIVE ❶ Something that is secret is told to only a small number of people and hidden from everyone else • *a secret meeting.* ▷ NOUN ❷ a fact told to only a small number of people and hidden from everyone else. **secretly** ADVERB **secrecy** NOUN
  ● SIMILAR WORDS: ❶ confidential, ● concealed, hidden

secret agent, secret agents NOUN a spy.

secretary, secretaries NOUN ❶ a person employed by an organization to keep records, write letters, and do office work. ❷ Ministers in charge of some government departments are

▷ SPELLING NOTE: *The government licenSes Schnapps (licenSes)*

a
b
c
d
e
f
g
h
i
j
k
l
m
n
o
p
q
r
s
t
u
v
w
x
y
z

also called secretaries • *the Health Secretary.* **secretarial ADJECTIVE**

secrete, secretes, secreting, secreted [Said sik-**kreet**] **VERB** ❶ When part of a plant or animal secretes a liquid, it produces it. ❷ FORMAL If you secrete something somewhere, you hide it. **secretion NOUN**

secretive ADJECTIVE Secretive people tend to hide their feelings and intentions.

● SIMILAR WORDS: reticent,
● tight-lipped

secret service NOUN A country's secret service is the government department in charge of espionage.

sect, sects **NOUN** a religious or political group which has broken away from a larger group.

sectarian [Said sek-**tair**-ee-an] **ADJECTIVE** strongly supporting a particular sect • *sectarian violence.*

section, sections **NOUN** (LIBRARY) A section of something is one of the parts it is divided into • *this section of the motorway.*

● SIMILAR WORDS: part, portion,
● segment

sector, sectors **NOUN** ❶ A sector of something, especially a country's economy, is one part of it • *the private sector.* ❷ A sector of a circle is one of the two parts formed when you draw two straight lines from the centre to the circumference.

secular ADJECTIVE having no connection with religion • *secular education.*

secure, secures, securing, secured **VERB** ❶ FORMAL If you secure

something, you manage to get it • *They secured the rights to her story.* ❷ If you secure a place, you make it safe from harm or attack. ❸ To secure something also means to fasten it firmly • *One end was secured to the pier.* ▷ **ADJECTIVE** ❹ If a place is secure, it is tightly locked or well protected. ❺ If an object is secure, it is firmly fixed in place. ❻ If you feel secure, you feel safe and confident. **securely ADVERB**

security NOUN OR ADJECTIVE ❶ Security means all the precautions taken to protect a place • *Security forces arrested one member.* ▷ **NOUN** ❷ A feeling of security is a feeling of being safe.

sedate, sedates, sedating, sedated [Said sid-**date**] **ADJECTIVE** ❶ quiet and dignified ▷ **VERB** ❷ To sedate someone means to give them a drug to calm them down or make them sleep. **sedately ADVERB**

sedative, sedatives [Said **sed**-at-tiv] **NOUN** ❶ a drug that calms you down or makes you sleep ▷ **ADJECTIVE** ❷ having a calming or soothing effect • *antihistamines which have a sedative effect.* **sedation NOUN**

sedentary [Said **sed**-en-tree] **ADJECTIVE** A sedentary occupation is one in which you spend most of your time sitting down.

sediment NOUN ❶ Sediment is solid material that settles at the bottom of a liquid • *a bottle of beer with sediment in it is usually a guarantee of quality.* ❷ Sediment is also small particles of rock that have been worn down and deposited together by water, ice, and wind.

▷ SPELLING NOTE: *have a plEce of plE (piece)*

sedimentary ADJECTIVE
(GEOGRAPHY) Sedimentary rocks are formed from fragments of shells or rocks that have become compressed. Sandstone and limestone are sedimentary rocks.

seduce, seduces, seducing, seduced
VERB ❶ To seduce someone means to persuade them to have sex. ❷ If you are seduced into doing something, you are persuaded to do it because it seems very attractive.

seductive ADJECTIVE ❶ A seductive person is sexually attractive. ❷ Something seductive is very attractive and tempting. **seductively** ADVERB

see, sees, seeing, saw, seen VERB ❶ If you see something, you are looking at it or you notice it. ❷ If you see someone, you visit them or meet them • *I went to see my dentist.* ❸ If you see someone to a place, you accompany them there. ❹ To see something also means to realize or understand it • *I see what you mean.* ❺ If you say you will see what is happening, you mean you will find out. ❻ If you say you will see if you can do something, you mean you will try to do it. ❼ If you see that something is done, you make sure that it is done. ❽ If you see to something, you deal with it. ❾ 'See' is used to say that an event takes place during a particular period of time • *The next couple of years saw two momentous developments.* ▷ PHRASES ❿ INFORMAL **Seeing that** or **seeing as** means because • *I took John for lunch, seeing as it was his birthday.* ▷ NOUN ⓫ A bishop's see is his diocese.

● SIMILAR WORDS: ❶ notice, perceive, spot

seed, seeds NOUN ❶ The seeds of a plant are the small, hard parts from which new plants can grow. ❷ The seeds of a feeling or process are its beginning or origins • *the seeds of mistrust.*

seedling, seedlings NOUN a young plant grown from a seed.

seedy, seedier, seediest ADJECTIVE untidy and shabby • *a seedy hotel in a rundown area.*

seek, seeks, seeking, sought VERB
FORMAL ❶ To seek something means to try to find it, obtain it, or achieve it • *The police were still seeking information.* ❷ If you seek to do something, you try to do it • *De Gaulle sought to reunite the country.*

seem, seems, seeming, seemed
VERB If something seems to be the case, it appears to be the case or you think it is the case • *He seemed such a quiet chap.*

seeming ADJECTIVE appearing to be real or genuine • *this seeming disregard for human life.* **seemingly** ADVERB

seep, seeps, seeping, seeped VERB If a liquid or gas seeps through something, it flows through very slowly.

seesaw, seesaws NOUN a long plank, supported in the middle, on which two children sit, one on each end, and move up and down in turn.

seething ADJECTIVE If you are seething about something, you are very angry but it does not show.

a
b
c
d
e
f
g
h
i
j
k
l
m
n
o
p
q
r
s
t
u
v
w
x
y
z

▷ SPELLING NOTE: *plaice the fish has a glittering 'EYE' (I) (plaice)*

segment, segments NOUN ❶ A
segment of something is one part of
it. ❷ The segments of an orange or
grapefruit are the sections which you
can divide it into. ❸ A segment of a
circle is one of the two parts formed
when you draw a straight line across
it.

segmentation NOUN
Segmentation is the dividing of
something into segments.

segregate, segregates, segregating,
segregated VERB To segregate two
groups of people means to keep them
apart from each other. **segregated**
ADJECTIVE **segregation** NOUN

seismograph, seismographs [Said
size-moh-grahf] NOUN (GEOGRAPHY)
A seismograph is an instrument for
measuring the strength of
earthquakes.

seismology [Said *size-mol-loj-ee*]
NOUN (GEOGRAPHY) Seismology is
the scientific study of earthquakes.
seismic ADJECTIVE

seize, seizes, seizing, seized VERB
❶ If you seize something, you grab it
firmly • *He seized the phone.* ❷ To
seize a place or to seize control of it
means to take control of it quickly and
suddenly. ❸ If you seize an
opportunity, you take advantage of it.
❹ If you seize on something, you
immediately show great interest in it
• *MPs have seized on a new report.*

seizure, seizures [Said *seez-yer*]
NOUN ❶ a sudden violent attack of
an illness, especially a heart attack or
a fit. ❷ If there is a seizure of power, a
group of people suddenly take control
using force.

seldom ADVERB not very often
• *They seldom speak to each other.*

select, selects, selecting, selected
VERB ❶ If you select something, you
choose it ▷ ADJECTIVE ❷ of good
quality • *a select gentlemen's club.*
selector NOUN

selection, selections NOUN
❶ Selection is the choosing of people
or things • *the selection of
parliamentary candidates.* ❷ A
selection of people or things is a set of
them chosen from a larger group.
❸ The selection of goods in a shop is
the range of goods available • *a good
selection of wines.*

selective ADJECTIVE choosing
things carefully • *I am selective about
what I eat.* **selectively** ADVERB

selective breeding NOUN
(SCIENCE) taking control of breeding
in order to produce animals or plants
with or without particular
characteristics • *Selective breeding can
be used to develop plants that are
resistant to disease.*

self, selves NOUN Your self is your
basic personality or nature • *Hershey is
her normal dependable self.*

self- PREFIX ❶ done to yourself or
by yourself • *self-help* • *self-control.*
❷ doing something automatically • *a
self-loading rifle.*

self-assured ADJECTIVE behaving
in a way that shows confidence in
yourself.

self-centred ADJECTIVE thinking
only about yourself and not about
other people.

self-confessed ADJECTIVE

admitting to having bad habits or unpopular opinions • *a self-confessed liar.*

self-confident ADJECTIVE confident of your own abilities or worth. **self-confidence** NOUN

self-conscious ADJECTIVE nervous and easily embarrassed, and worried about what other people think of you. **self-consciously** ADVERB

self-control NOUN Self-control is the ability to restrain yourself and not show your feelings.

self-defence NOUN Self-defence is the use of special physical techniques to protect yourself when someone attacks you.

self-employed ADJECTIVE working for yourself and organizing your own finances, rather than working for an employer.

self-esteem NOUN Your self-esteem is your good opinion of yourself.

self-evident ADJECTIVE Self-evident facts are completely obvious and need no proof or explanation.

self-indulgent ADJECTIVE allowing yourself to do or have things you enjoy, especially as a treat.

self-interest NOUN If you do something out of self-interest, you do it for your own benefit rather than to help other people.

selfish ADJECTIVE caring only about yourself, and not about other people. **selfishly** ADVERB **selfishness** NOUN

selfless ADJECTIVE putting other people's interests before your own.

self-made ADJECTIVE rich and successful through your own efforts • *a self-made man.*

self-raising ADJECTIVE Self-raising flour contains baking powder to make it rise.

self-respect NOUN Self-respect is a feeling of confidence and pride in your own abilities and worth.

self-righteous ADJECTIVE convinced that you are better or more virtuous than other people. **self-righteousness** NOUN

- SIMILAR WORDS: holier-than-
- thou, sanctimonious

self-service ADJECTIVE A self-service shop or restaurant is one where you serve yourself.

self-sufficient ADJECTIVE ❶ producing or making everything you need, and so not needing to buy things. ❷ able to live in a way in which you do not need other people.

sell, sells, selling, sold VERB ❶ If you sell something, you let someone have it in return for money. ❷ If a shop sells something, it has it available for people to buy • *a tobacconist that sells stamps.* ❸ If something sells, people buy it • *This book will sell.*
sell out VERB If a shop has sold out of something, it has sold it all. **seller** NOUN

- SIMILAR WORDS: ❷ deal in,
- retail, stock

Sellotape NOUN TRADEMARK Sellotape is a transparent sticky tape.

semblance NOUN If there is a

A
B
C
D
E
F
G
H
I
J
K
L
M
N
O
P
Q
R
S
T
U
V
W
X
Y
Z

WHAT DOES THE SEMICOLON DO?

The **semicolon** (;) and the **colon** (:) are often confused and used incorrectly.

The **semicolon** is stronger than a comma, but weaker than a full stop. It can be used to mark the break between two main clauses, especially where there is balance or contrast between them:
I'm not that interested in jazz; I prefer classical music.

The semicolon can also be used instead of a comma to separate clauses or items in a long list:
They did not enjoy the meal: the food was cold; the service was poor; and the music was too loud.

Also look at the grammar box at **colon**.

---

semblance of something, it seems to exist, although it might not really exist • *an effort to restore a semblance of normality.*

semen [*Said* see-*men*] **NOUN** Semen is the liquid containing sperm produced by a man's or male animal's sex organs.

semi- PREFIX 'Semi-' means half or partly • *semiskilled workers.*
● **WORD HISTORY:** from Latin
● *semi-* meaning 'half' or 'partly'

semibreve, semibreves **NOUN** (MUSIC) a musical note (○) which can be divided by any power of 2 to give all other notes. In the United States and Canada, a semibreve is known as a whole note.

semicircle, semicircles **NOUN** a half of a circle, or something with this shape. **semicircular ADJECTIVE**

semicolon, semicolons **NOUN** the punctuation mark (;), used to separate different parts of a sentence or to indicate a pause.
▶ SEE GRAMMAR BOX ABOVE

semidetached ADJECTIVE A semidetached house is joined to another house on one side.

semifinal, semifinals **NOUN** The semifinals are the two matches in a competition played to decide who plays in the final. **semifinalist NOUN**

seminar, seminars **NOUN** a meeting of a small number of university students or teachers to discuss a particular topic.

semipermeable ADJECTIVE A semipermeable material is one that certain substances with small enough molecules can pass through but which others with larger molecules can not.

semiprecious ADJECTIVE Semiprecious stones are stones such as opals or turquoises that are used in jewellery. They are less valuable than precious stones.

semitone, semitones **NOUN** (MUSIC) an interval representing the difference in pitch between a note and its sharpened or flattened equivalent. Two semitones are equal to one tone.

Senate, Senates **NOUN** The Senate is the smaller, more important of the

---

▷ SPELLING NOTE: *pAL up with the principAL and principAL staff (principal)*

two councils in the government of some countries, for example Australia, Canada, and the USA.

senator, senators **NOUN** a member of a Senate.

send, sends, sending, sent **VERB** ❶ If you send something to someone, you arrange for it to be delivered to them. ❷ To send a radio signal or message means to transmit it. ❸ If you send someone somewhere, you tell them to go there or arrange for them to go. ❹ If you send for someone, you send a message asking them to come and see you. ❺ If you send off for something, you write and ask for it to be sent to you. ❻ To send people or things in a particular direction means to make them move in that direction • *It should have sent him tumbling from the saddle.*
● **SIMILAR WORDS:** ❶ direct,
● dispatch, forward

senile **ADJECTIVE** If old people become senile, they become confused and cannot look after themselves. **senility NOUN**

senior, seniors **ADJECTIVE** ❶ The senior people in an organization or profession have the highest and most important jobs ▷ **NOUN** ❷ Someone who is your senior is older than you. **seniority NOUN**

senior citizen, senior citizens **NOUN** an elderly person, especially one receiving an old-age pension.

sensation, sensations **NOUN** ❶ a feeling, especially a physical feeling. ❷ If something is a sensation, it causes great excitement and interest.

sensational **ADJECTIVE**

❶ causing great excitement and interest. ❷ **INFORMAL** extremely good • *a sensational party.* **sensationally ADVERB**

sense, senses, sensing, sensed **NOUN** ❶ Your senses are the physical abilities of sight, hearing, smell, touch, and taste. ❷ a feeling • *a sense of guilt.* ❸ A sense of a word is one of its meanings. ❹ Sense is the ability to think and behave sensibly ▷ **VERB** ❺ If you sense something, you become aware of it ▷ **PHRASE** ❻ If something **makes sense**, you can understand it or it seems sensible • *It makes sense to find out as much as you can.*

senseless **ADJECTIVE** ❶ A senseless action has no meaning or purpose • *senseless destruction.* ❷ If someone is senseless, they are unconscious.

sensibility, sensibilities **NOUN** Your sensibility is your ability to experience deep feelings • *a man of sensibility rather than reason.*

sensible **ADJECTIVE** showing good sense and judgment. **sensibly ADVERB**
● **SIMILAR WORDS:** prudent,
● rational, wise

sensitive **ADJECTIVE** ❶ If you are sensitive to other people's feelings, you understand them. ❷ If you are sensitive about something, you are worried or easily upset about it • *He was sensitive about his height.* ❸ A sensitive subject or issue needs to be dealt with carefully because it can make people angry or upset. ❹ Something that is sensitive to a particular thing is easily affected or

▷ SPELLING NOTE: *LEarn the principLEs (principle)*

harmed by it. **sensitively** ADVERB

sensitivity NOUN ❶ the quality of being sensitive. ❷ SCIENCE the ability of a plant or animal to respond to external stimuli such as light, sound, movement, or temperature.

sensor, sensors NOUN ICT an instrument which reacts to physical conditions such as light or heat.

sensual [Said **senss**-yool] ADJECTIVE ❶ showing or suggesting a liking for sexual pleasures • *He was a very sensual person.* ❷ giving pleasure to your physical senses rather than to your mind • *the sensual rhythm of his voice.* **sensuality** NOUN

sensuous ADJECTIVE giving pleasure through the senses. **sensuously** ADVERB

sentence, sentences, sentencing, sentenced NOUN ❶ a group of words which make a statement, question, or command. When written down a sentence begins with a capital letter and ends with a full stop. ❷ In a law court, a sentence is a punishment given to someone who has been found guilty ▷ VERB ❸ When a guilty person is sentenced, they are told officially what their punishment will be.
▶ SEE GRAMMAR BOX ON PAGE 765

sentiment, sentiments NOUN ❶ a feeling, attitude, or opinion • *I doubt my parents share my sentiments.* ❷ Sentiment consists of feelings such as tenderness or sadness • *There's no room for sentiment in business.*

sentimental ADJECTIVE ❶ feeling or expressing tenderness or sadness to an exaggerated extent • *sentimental love stories.* ❷ relating to

a person's emotions • *things of sentimental value.* ❸ ENGLISH Sentimental literature is intended to provoke an emotional response to the story, rather than relying on the reader's own natural response. **sentimentality** NOUN

● **SIMILAR WORDS:** ❶ emotional, romantic, slushy

sentinel, sentinels NOUN OLD-FASHIONED a sentry.

sentry, sentries NOUN a soldier who keeps watch and guards a camp or building.

separate, separates, separating, separated ADJECTIVE ❶ If something is separate from something else, the two things are not connected ▷ VERB ❷ To separate people or things means to cause them to be apart from each other. ❸ If people or things separate, they move away from each other. ❹ If a married couple separate, they decide to live apart • *They separated after two unhappy years.* **separately** ADVERB **separation** NOUN

● **SIMILAR WORDS:** ❷ divide, split, part ❸ diverge, part, part company

sepia [Said **see**-pee-a] ADJECTIVE OR NOUN deep brown, like the colour of old photographs.

● **WORD HISTORY:** from Latin *sepia* meaning 'cuttlefish', because the brown dye is obtained from the ink of this fish

September NOUN September is the ninth month of the year. It has 30 days.

● **WORD HISTORY:** from Latin *September* meaning 'the seventh month'

▷ SPELLING NOTE: *Psychiatrists Seldom Yell Callously Hard (psychiatrist)*

WHAT IS A SENTENCE?

Different types of word can go together to make sentences. A sentence is a group of words which expresses an idea or describes a situation.

Sentences begin with a **capital letter**:
The child was sleeping.

Sentences usually end with a **full stop**:
Anna lives in Lisbon.

If a sentence is a question, it ends with a **question mark** instead of a full stop:
Where is my purse?

If a sentence is an exclamation of surprise, anger, or excitement, it ends with an **exclamation mark** instead of a full stop:
You must be joking!

Sentences have a **subject**, which indicates a person or thing. The rest of the sentence usually says something about the subject. The subject is usually the first word or group of words in a sentence:
***Anna** laughed. **Robbie** likes bananas.*

Most sentences have a **verb**. The verb says what the subject of the sentence is doing or what is happening to the subject. The verb usually follows immediately after the subject:
*Matthew **smiled**.*

SIMPLE SENTENCES, COMPOUND SENTENCES, AND COMPLEX SENTENCES

Simple sentences consist of only one main clause, and no subordinate clause:
Anna fed the cat.

The **subject** of a simple sentence is the person or thing that the sentence is about. It usually comes at the start of the sentence. The subject may be a noun, a pronoun, or a noun phrase:
***We** often go to the cinema.*

The remaining part of the sentence is called the **predicate**. The predicate says something about the subject:
*Anna **likes to go swimming**.*
*She **is a strong swimmer**.*
*A ginger cat **was sitting on the stair**.*

Compound sentences consist of two or more main clauses joined together by a conjunction. Both clauses are equally important:
Anna likes to go swimming, but Matthew likes to go fishing.

Complex sentences consist of a main clause with one or more subordinate clauses joined to it.

Numerous subordinate clauses can be added to a main clause:
***After looking at all the pictures**, the judges gave the first prize, **which was a silver trophy**, to Robbie, **because his work was the best**.*

septic ADJECTIVE If a wound becomes septic, it becomes infected with poison.

sepulchre, sepulchres [Said *sep-pul-ka*] NOUN LITERARY a large tomb.

sequel, sequels NOUN **1** A sequel to a book or film is another book or film which continues the story. **2** The sequel to an event is a result or consequence of it • *There's a sequel to my egg story.*

sequence, sequences **NOUN** **1** A sequence of events is a number of them coming one after the other • *the whole sequence of events that had brought me to this place.* **2** The sequence in which things are arranged is the order in which they are arranged • *Do things in the right sequence.*

sequin, sequins **NOUN** Sequins are small, shiny, coloured discs sewn on clothes to decorate them.

Serbian, Serbians **ADJECTIVE** **1** belonging to or relating to Serbia ▷ **NOUN** **2** someone who comes from Serbia. **3** Serbian is the form of Serbo-Croat spoken in Serbia.

Serbo-Croat [Said ser-boh-*kroh*-at] **NOUN** Serbo-Croat is the main language spoken in Serbia and Croatia.

serenade, serenades, serenading, serenaded **VERB** **1** If you serenade someone you love, you sing or play music to them outside their window ▷ **NOUN** **2** a song sung outside a woman's window by a man who loves her.

serene **ADJECTIVE** peaceful and calm • *She had a serene air.* **serenely** **ADVERB** **serenity** **NOUN**

serf, serfs **NOUN** Serfs were servants in medieval Europe who had to work on their master's land and could not leave without his permission.

sergeant, sergeants **NOUN** **1** a noncommissioned officer of middle rank in the army or air force. **2** a

police officer just above a constable in rank.

sergeant major, sergeant majors **NOUN** a noncommissioned army officer of the highest rank.

serial, serials **NOUN** a story which is broadcast or published in a number of parts over a period of time • *a television serial.*

serial number, serial numbers **NOUN** An object's serial number is a number you can see on it which identifies it and distinguishes it from other objects of the same kind.

series **NOUN** **1** (LIBRARY) A series of things is a number of them coming one after the other • *a series of loud explosions.* **2** A radio or television series is a set of programmes with the same title.
  ● **SIMILAR WORDS:** **1** sequence,
  ● set, succession

serious **ADJECTIVE** **1** A serious problem or situation is very bad and worrying. **2** Serious matters are important and should be thought about carefully. **3** If you are serious about something, you are sincere about it • *You are really serious about having a baby.* **4** People who are serious are thoughtful, quiet, and do not laugh much. **seriousness** **NOUN**
  ● **SIMILAR WORDS:** **1** grave,
  ● severe **4** grave, solemn

seriously **ADVERB** **1** You say seriously to emphasize that you mean what you say • *Seriously, though, something must be done.* ▷ **PHRASE** **2** If you **take something seriously**, you regard it as important.

sermon, sermons **NOUN** a talk on a

A
B
C
D
E
F
G
H
I
J
K
L
M
N
O
P
Q
R
S
T
U
V
W
X
Y
Z

religious or moral subject given as part of a church service.

serpent, serpents **NOUN** LITERARY a snake.

serrated **ADJECTIVE** having a row of V-shaped points along the edge, like a saw • *green serrated leaves.*

servant, servants **NOUN** someone who is employed to work in another person's house.

serve, serves, serving, served **VERB** ❶ If you serve a country, an organization, or a person, you do useful work for them. ❷ To serve as something means to act or be used as that thing • *the room that served as their office.* ❸ If something serves people in a particular place, it provides them with something they need • *a recycling plant which serves the whole of the county.* ❹ If you serve food or drink to people, you give it to them. ❺ To serve customers in a shop means to help them and provide them with what they want. ❻ To serve a prison sentence or an apprenticeship means to spend time doing it. ❼ When you serve in tennis or badminton, you throw the ball or shuttlecock into the air and hit it over the net to start playing ▷ **NOUN** ❽ the act of serving in tennis or badminton.

server, servers **NOUN** (ICT) a computer or computer program which supplies information or resources to a number of computers on a network.

service, services, servicing, serviced **NOUN** ❶ a system organized to provide something for the public • *the bus service.* ❷ Some government organizations are called services • *the diplomatic service.* ❸ The services are the army, the navy, and the air force. ❹ If you give your services to a person or organization, you work for them or help them in some way • *services to the community.* ❺ In a shop or restaurant, service is the process of being served. ❻ a religious ceremony. ❼ When it is your service in a game of tennis or badminton, it is your turn to serve ❽ IN PLURAL Motorway services consist of a petrol station, restaurant, shop, and toilets ▷ **VERB** ❾ When a machine or vehicle is serviced, it is examined and adjusted so that it will continue working efficiently.

serviceman, servicemen **NOUN** a man in the army, navy, or air force. **servicewoman** **NOUN**

service station, service stations **NOUN** a garage that sells petrol, oil, spare parts, and snacks.

servile **ADJECTIVE** too eager to obey people. **servility** **NOUN**
● **SIMILAR WORDS:** obsequious,
● subservient

serving, servings **NOUN** ❶ a helping of food ▷ **ADJECTIVE** ❷ A serving spoon or dish is used for serving food.

session, sessions **NOUN** ❶ a meeting of an official group • *the emergency session of the Indiana Supreme Court.* ❷ a period during which meetings are held regularly • *the end of the parliamentary session.* ❸ The period during which an activity takes place can also be called a session • *a drinking session.*

set, sets, setting, set **NOUN** ❶ Several things make a set when they belong together or form a group • *a set of weights.* **2** (MATHS) In maths, a set is a collection of numbers or other things which are treated as a group. **3** A television set is a television. **4** The set for a play or film is the scenery or furniture on the stage or in the studio. **5** In tennis, a set is a group of six or more games. There are usually several sets in a match ▷ **VERB** **6** If something is set somewhere, that is where it is • *The house was set back from the beach.* **7** When the sun sets, it goes below the horizon. **8** When you set the table, you prepare it for a meal by putting plates and cutlery on it. **9** When you set a clock or a control, you adjust it to a particular point or position. **10** If you set someone a piece of work or a target, you give it to them to do or to achieve. **11** When something such as jelly or cement sets, it becomes firm or hard ▷ **ADJECTIVE** **12** Something that is set is fixed and not varying • *a set charge.* **13** If you are set to do something, you are ready or likely to do it. **14** If you are set on doing something, you are determined to do it. **15** If a play or story is set at a particular time or in a particular place, the events in it take place at that time or in that place.

set about VERB If you set about doing something, you start doing it.

set back VERB If something sets back a project or scheme, it delays it.

set off VERB **1** When you set off, you start a journey. **2** To set something off means to cause it to start.

set out VERB **1** When you set out, you start a journey. **2** If you set out to

do something, you start trying to do it.

set up VERB If you set something up, you make all the necessary preparations for it • *We have done all we can about setting up a system of communication.*

● **SIMILAR WORDS:** **12** fixed, hard
● and fast, inflexible

setback, setbacks **NOUN** something that delays or hinders you.

settee, settees **NOUN** a long comfortable seat for two or three people to sit on.

setter, setters **NOUN** a long-haired breed of dog originally used in hunting.

setting, settings **NOUN** **1** The setting of something is its surroundings or circumstances • *The Irish setting made the story realistic.* **2** The settings on a machine are the different positions to which the controls can be adjusted.

settle, settles, settling, settled **VERB** **1** To settle an argument means to put an end to it • *The dispute was settled.* **2** If something is settled, it has all been decided and arranged. **3** If you settle on something or settle for it, you choose it • *We settled for orange juice and coffee.* **4** When you settle a bill, you pay it. **5** If you settle in a place, you make it your permanent home. **6** If you settle yourself somewhere, you sit down and make yourself comfortable. **7** If something settles, it sinks slowly down and comes to rest • *A black dust settled on the walls.*

settle down VERB **1** When someone settles down, they start living a quiet life in one place,

especially when they get married.
❷ To settle down means to become quiet or calm.

settlement, settlements NOUN
❶ an official agreement between people who have been involved in a conflict • *the last chance for a peaceful settlement.* ❷ (GEOGRAPHY) a place where people have settled and built homes.

settler, settlers NOUN someone who settles in a new country • *the first settlers in Cuba.*

seven the number 7.

seventeen the number 17.
seventeenth ADJECTIVE

seventh, sevenths ADJECTIVE
❶ The seventh item in a series is the one counted as number seven
▷ NOUN ❷ one of seven equal parts.

seventy, seventies the number 70.
seventieth ADJECTIVE

sever, severs, severing, severed VERB
❶ To sever something means to cut it off or cut right through it. ❷ If you sever a connection with someone or something, you end it completely
• *She severed her ties with England.*

several ADJECTIVE Several people or things means a small number of them.

severe ADJECTIVE ❶ extremely bad or unpleasant • *severe stomach pains.*
❷ stern and harsh • *Perhaps I am too severe with that young man.* **severely**
ADVERB **severity** NOUN

sew, sews, sewing, sewed, sewn [Said so] VERB (D & T) When you sew things together, you join them using a needle and thread. **sewing** NOUN

sewage [Said soo-ij] NOUN Sewage is dirty water and waste which is carried away in sewers.

sewer, sewers NOUN an underground channel that carries sewage to a place where it is treated to make it harmless.

sewerage NOUN Sewerage is the system by which sewage is carried away and treated.

sex, sexes NOUN ❶ The sexes are the two groups, male and female, into which people and animals are divided.
❷ The sex of a person or animal is their characteristic of being either male or female. ❸ Sex is the physical activity by which people and animals produce young.

sex cell, sex cells NOUN (SCIENCE) a male or female cell with half the usual number of chromosomes that unites with a cell of the opposite sex during sexual reproduction. Ova and sperms are sex cells.

sexism NOUN (PSHE) Sexism is discrimination against the members of one sex, usually women. **sexist**
ADJECTIVE OR NOUN

sextet, sextets NOUN ❶ (MUSIC) a group of six musicians who sing or play together; also a piece of music written for six instruments or singers.
❷ (ENGLISH) six lines of poetry together, especially linked by a pattern of rhyme.

sextuplet, sextuplets NOUN
Sextuplets are six children born at the same time to the same mother.

sexual ADJECTIVE ❶ connected

a b c d e f g h i j k l m n o p q r **s** t u v w x y z

▷ SPELLING NOTE: *Eddy Ant thinks mEAt is a grEAt trEAt to Eat (-ea-)*

with the act of sex or with people's desire for sex • *sexual attraction.*
2 relating to the difference between males and females • *sexual equality.*
3 relating to the biological process by which people and animals produce young • *sexual reproduction.* **sexually ADVERB**

sexual intercourse NOUN
Sexual intercourse is the physical act of sex between two people.

sexuality [Said seks-yoo-**al**-it-ee] **NOUN** A person's sexuality is their ability to experience sexual feelings.

sexy, sexier, sexiest **ADJECTIVE**
sexually attractive or exciting • *these sexy blue eyes.*

sforzando, sforzandos [Said sfort-**san**-doh] **ADJECTIVE AND ADVERB** (MUSIC) **1** In music, sforzando is an instruction to sing or play something with sudden, strong emphasis ▷ **NOUN 2** a symbol, such as *fz*, written above a note to indicate that it should be played or sung in this way.
● **WORD HISTORY:** an Italian word

shabby, shabbier, shabbiest **ADJECTIVE 1** old and worn in appearance • *a shabby overcoat.*
2 dressed in old, worn-out clothes • *a shabby figure crouching in a doorway.* **3** behaving in a mean or unfair way • *shabby treatment.*
shabbily ADVERB
● **SIMILAR WORDS: 1** tatty,
2 threadbare, worn

shack, shacks **NOUN** a small hut.

shackle, shackles, shackling, shackled **NOUN 1** In the past, shackles were two metal rings joined by a chain fastened around a prisoner's wrists or ankles ▷ **VERB**
2 To shackle someone means to put shackles on them. **3** LITERARY If you are shackled by something, it restricts or hampers you.

shade, shades, shading, shaded **NOUN 1** Shade is an area of darkness and coolness which the sun does not reach • *The table was in the shade.* **2** a lampshade. **3** The shades of a colour are its different forms. For example, olive green is a shade of green ▷ **VERB 4** If a place is shaded by trees or buildings, they prevent the sun from shining on it. **5** If you shade your eyes, you put your hand in front of them to protect them from a bright light.

shadow, shadows, shadowing, shadowed **NOUN 1** the dark shape made when an object prevents light from reaching a surface. **2** Shadow is darkness caused by light not reaching a place ▷ **VERB 3** To shadow someone means to follow them and watch them closely.

shadow cabinet NOUN The shadow cabinet consists of the leaders of the main opposition party, each of whom is concerned with a particular policy.

shadowy ADJECTIVE 1 A shadowy place is dark and full of shadows. **2** A shadowy figure or shape is difficult to see because it is dark or misty.

shady, shadier, shadiest **ADJECTIVE**
A shady place is sheltered from sunlight by trees or buildings.

shaft, shafts **NOUN 1** a vertical passage, for example one for a lift or

a b c d e f g h i j k l m n o p q r s t u v w x y z

THE VERBS SHALL AND WILL

The verbs *shall* and *will* have only one form. They do not have a present form ending in -s, and they do not have a present participle, a past tense, or a past participle.

These verbs are used as auxiliary verbs to form the future tense:
*We **shall** arrive on Thursday.*
*She **will** give a talk about Chinese history.*

People used to use *shall* to indicate the first person, and *will* to indicate the second person and the third person. However, this distinction is often ignored now:

*I **shall** see you on Sunday.*
*I **will** see you on Sunday.*

Shall is always used in questions involving *I* and *we*. *Will* is avoided in these cases:
***Shall** I put the cat out?*
***Shall** we dance?*

Will is always used when making polite requests, giving orders, and indicating persistence. *Shall* is avoided in these cases:
***Will** you please help me?*
***Will** you be quiet!*
*She **will** keep going on about Al Pacino.*

one in a mine. **2** A shaft of light is a beam of light. **3** D & T A shaft in a machine is a rod which revolves and transfers movement in the machine • *the drive shaft.*

shaggy, shaggier, shaggiest
ADJECTIVE Shaggy hair or fur is long and untidy.

shahada NOUN RE the Islamic declaration of faith, repeated every day by Muslims. It begins 'There is no God but Allah and Mohammed is the prophet of Allah'.

shake, shakes, shaking, shook, shaken VERB **1** To shake something means to move it quickly from side to side or up and down. **2** If something shakes, it moves from side to side or up and down with small, quick movements. **3** If your voice shakes, it trembles because you are nervous or angry. **4** If something shakes you, it shocks and upsets you. **5** When you shake your head, you move it from

side to side in order to say 'no'
▷ NOUN **6** If you give something a shake, you shake it ▷ PHRASE **7** When you **shake hands** with someone, you grasp their hand as a way of greeting them.
● SIMILAR WORDS: **2** quiver, tremble, vibrate

shaky, shakier, shakiest ADJECTIVE rather weak and unsteady • *Confidence in the economy is still shaky.* **shakily** ADVERB

shall VERB **1** If I say I shall do something, I mean that I intend to do it. **2** If I say something shall happen, I am emphasizing that it will definitely happen, or I am ordering it to happen • *There shall be work and security!* **3** 'Shall' is also used in questions when you are asking what to do, or making a suggestion • *Shall we sit down? • Shall I go and check for you?*
▶ SEE GRAMMAR BOX ABOVE

shallow, shallower, shallowest

▷ SPELLING NOTE: *'i' before 'e' except after 'c'*

ADJECTIVE ❶ Shallow means not deep. ❷ Shallow also means not involving serious thought or sincere feelings • *a well-meaning but shallow man.*

shallows **PLURAL NOUN** The shallows are the shallow part of a river or lake.

sham, shams **NOUN** ❶ Something that is a sham is not real or genuine ▷ **ADJECTIVE** ❷ not real or genuine • *a sham display of affection.*

shambles **NOUN** If an event is a shambles, it is confused and badly organized.

shame, shames, shaming, shamed **NOUN** ❶ Shame is the feeling of guilt or embarrassment you get when you know you have done something wrong or foolish. ❷ Shame is also something that makes people lose respect for you • *the scenes that brought shame to English soccer.* ❸ If you say something is a shame, you mean you are sorry about it • *It's a shame you can't come round.* ▷ **INTERJECTION** ❹ **INFORMAL** In South African English, you say 'Shame!' to show sympathy ▷ **VERB** ❺ If something shames you, it makes you feel ashamed. ❻ If you shame someone into doing something, you force them to do it by making them feel ashamed not to • *Two children shamed their parents into giving up cigarettes.*

shameful **ADJECTIVE** If someone's behaviour is shameful, they ought to be ashamed of it. **shamefully** **ADVERB**

shameless **ADJECTIVE** behaving in an indecent or unacceptable way, but showing no shame • *shameless dishonesty.* **shamelessly** **ADVERB**
  ● **SIMILAR WORDS:** barefaced, brazen, flagrant

shampoo, shampoos, shampooing, shampooed **NOUN** ❶ Shampoo is a soapy liquid used for washing your hair ▷ **VERB** ❷ When you shampoo your hair, you wash it with shampoo.
  ● **WORD HISTORY:** from Hindi *champna* meaning 'to knead'

shamrock, shamrocks **NOUN** a plant with three round leaves on each stem which is the national emblem of Ireland.
  ● **WORD HISTORY:** from Irish Gaelic *seamrog* meaning 'little clover'

shanghai, shanghais, shanghaiing, shanghaied **INFORMAL** **VERB** ❶ If someone is shanghaied, they are kidnapped and forced to work on a ship. ❷ If you shanghai someone, you trick or force them into doing something ▷ **NOUN** ❸ In Australian and New Zealand English, a catapult.

shanty, shanties **NOUN** ❶ (GEOGRAPHY) a small, rough hut. ❷ A sea shanty is a song sailors used to sing.

shanty town, shanty towns **NOUN** (GEOGRAPHY) A shanty town is a collection of small rough huts in which poor people live.

shape, shapes, shaping, shaped **NOUN** ❶ The shape of something is the form or pattern of its outline, for example whether it is round or square. ❷ (MATHS) something with a definite form, for example a circle or triangle. ❸ The shape of something such as an organization is its structure and size

▷ SPELLING NOTE: *King IAn went to ParlIAment in a carrIAge for his marrIAge (-ia-)*

▷ **VERB** ❹ If you shape an object, you form it into a particular shape • *Shape the dough into an oblong.* ❺ To shape something means to cause it to develop in a particular way • *events that shaped the lives of some of the leading characters.*
● **SIMILAR WORDS:** ❶ figure, form, outline

shapeless ADJECTIVE not having a definite shape.

shapely, shapelier, shapeliest **ADJECTIVE** A shapely woman has an attractive figure.

shard, shards **NOUN** a small fragment of pottery, glass, or metal.

share, shares, sharing, shared **VERB** (DRAMA) ❶ If two people share something, they both use it, do it, or have it • *We shared a bottle of champagne.* ❷ If you share an idea or a piece of news with someone, you tell it to them ▷ **NOUN** ❸ A share of something is a portion of it. ❹ The shares of a company are the equal parts into which its ownership is divided. People can buy shares as an investment.
share out VERB If you share something out, you give it out equally among a group of people.
● **SIMILAR WORDS:** ❸ lot, part, portion

shareholder, shareholders **NOUN** a person who owns shares in a company.

share-milker, share-milkers **NOUN** In New Zealand, someone who works on a dairy farm and shares the profit from the sale of its produce.

shark, sharks **NOUN** ❶ Sharks are

large, powerful fish with sharp teeth. ❷ a person who cheats people out of money.

sharp, sharper, sharpest; sharps **ADJECTIVE** ❶ A sharp object has a fine edge or point that is good for cutting or piercing things. ❷ A sharp outline or distinction is easy to see. ❸ A sharp person is quick to notice or understand things. ❹ A sharp change is sudden and significant • *a sharp rise in prices.* ❺ If you say something in a sharp way, you say it firmly and rather angrily. ❻ A sharp sound is short, sudden, and quite loud. ❼ A sharp pain is a sudden pain. ❽ A sharp taste is slightly sour. ❾ A musical instrument or note that is sharp is slightly too high in pitch ▷ **ADVERB** ❿ If something happens at a certain time sharp, it happens at that time precisely • *You'll begin at eight o'clock sharp.* ▷ **NOUN** ⓫ In music, a sharp is a note or key a semitone higher than that described by the same letter. It is represented by the symbol (♯).
sharply ADVERB sharpness NOUN
● **SIMILAR WORDS:** ❸ astute, perceptive, quick-witted

sharpen, sharpens, sharpening, sharpened **VERB** ❶ To sharpen an object means to make its edge or point sharper. ❷ If your senses or abilities sharpen, you become quicker at noticing or understanding things.
sharpener NOUN

shatter, shatters, shattering, shattered **VERB** ❶ If something shatters, it breaks into a lot of small pieces. ❷ If something shatters your hopes or beliefs, it destroys them completely. ❸ If you are shattered by an event or piece of news, you are

▷ SPELLING NOTE: *an ELegant angEL (angel)*

shocked and upset by it.

shattered ADJECTIVE INFORMAL completely exhausted • *He must be absolutely shattered after all his efforts.*

shattering ADJECTIVE making you feel shocked and upset • *a shattering event.*

shave, shaves, shaving, shaved VERB ❶ When a man shaves, he removes hair from his face with a razor. ❷ If you shave off part of a piece of wood, you cut thin pieces from it ▷ NOUN ❸ When a man has a shave, he shaves.

shaven ADJECTIVE If part of someone's body is shaven, it has been shaved • *a shaven head.*

shaver, shavers NOUN an electric razor.

shavings PLURAL NOUN Shavings are small, very thin pieces of wood which have been cut from a larger piece.

shawl, shawls NOUN a large piece of woollen cloth worn round a woman's head or shoulders or used to wrap a baby in.

she PRONOUN 'She' is used to refer to a woman or girl whose identity is clear. 'She' is also used to refer to a country, a ship, or a car.

sheaf, sheaves NOUN ❶ A sheaf of papers is a bundle of them. ❷ A sheaf of corn is a bundle of ripe corn tied together.

shear, shearing, sheared, shorn VERB To shear a sheep means to cut the wool off it.

shearer, shearers NOUN someone

whose job is to shear sheep.

shears PLURAL NOUN Shears are a tool like a large pair of scissors, used especially for cutting hedges.

sheath, sheaths NOUN ❶ a covering for the blade of a knife. ❷ a condom.

shed, sheds, shedding, shed NOUN ❶ a small building used for storing things ▷ VERB ❷ When an animal sheds hair or skin, some of its hair or skin drops off. When a tree sheds its leaves, its leaves fall off. ❸ FORMAL To shed something also means to get rid of it • *The firm is to shed 700 jobs.* ❹ If a lorry sheds its load, the load falls off the lorry onto the road. ❺ If you shed tears, you cry.

sheen NOUN a gentle brightness on the surface of something.

sheep NOUN A sheep is a farm animal with a thick woolly coat. Sheep are kept for meat and wool.
● USAGE NOTE: The plural of *sheep* is *sheep*

sheep-dip, sheep-dips NOUN a liquid disinfectant used to keep sheep clean and free of pests.

sheepdog, sheepdogs NOUN a breed of dog often used for controlling sheep.

sheepish ADJECTIVE If you look sheepish, you look embarrassed because you feel shy or foolish. **sheepishly** ADVERB

sheepskin NOUN Sheepskin is the skin and wool of a sheep, used for making rugs and coats.

sheer, sheerer, sheerest ADJECTIVE

❶ Sheer means complete and total • *sheer exhaustion.* **❷** A sheer cliff or drop is vertical. **❸** Sheer fabrics are very light and delicate.

sheet, sheets **NOUN ❶** a large rectangular piece of cloth used to cover a bed. **❷** A sheet of paper is a rectangular piece of it. **❸** **D & T** A sheet of glass or metal is a large, flat piece of it.

sheik, sheiks *[Said shake]* ; also spelt **sheikh NOUN** an Arab chief or ruler.
● **WORD HISTORY:** from Arabic
● *shaykh* meaning 'old man'

shelf, shelves **NOUN** a flat piece of wood, metal, or glass fixed to a wall and used for putting things on.

shell, shells, shelling, shelled **NOUN ❶** The shell of an egg or nut is its hard covering. **❷** The shell of a tortoise, snail, or crab is the hard protective covering on its back. **❸** The shell of a building or other structure is its frame • *The room was just an empty shell.* **❹** a container filled with explosives that can be fired from a gun ▷ **VERB ❺** If you shell peas or nuts, you remove their natural covering. **❻** To shell a place means to fire large explosive shells at it.

shellfish, shellfish or shellfishes **NOUN** a small sea creature with a shell.

shelter, shelters, sheltering, sheltered **NOUN ❶** a small building made to protect people from bad weather or danger. **❷** If a place provides shelter, it provides protection from bad weather or danger ▷ **VERB ❸** If you shelter in a place, you stay there and are safe. **❹** If you shelter

someone, you provide them with a place to stay when they are in danger.

sheltered ADJECTIVE ❶ A sheltered place is protected from wind and rain. **❷** If you lead a sheltered life, you do not experience unpleasant or upsetting things. **❸** Sheltered accommodation is accommodation designed for old or handicapped people.

shelve, shelves, shelving, shelved **VERB** If you shelve a plan, you decide to postpone it for a while.

shepherd, shepherds, shepherding, shepherded **NOUN ❶** a person who looks after sheep ▷ **VERB ❷** If you shepherd someone somewhere, you accompany them there.

sheriff, sheriffs **NOUN ❶** In America, a sheriff is a person elected to enforce the law in a county. **❷** In Australia, an administrative officer of the Supreme Court who carries out writs and judgments.
● **WORD HISTORY:** from Old English
● *scir* meaning 'shire' and *gerefa*
● meaning 'reeve', an official

sherry, sherries **NOUN** Sherry is a kind of strong wine.
● **WORD HISTORY:** from the Spanish
● town *Jerez* where it was first made

shield, shields, shielding, shielded **NOUN ❶** a large piece of a strong material like metal or plastic which soldiers or policeman carry to protect themselves. **❷** If something is a shield against something, it gives protection from it ▷ **VERB ❸** To shield someone means to protect them from something.

shift, shifts, shifting, shifted **VERB**

a b c d e f g h i j k l m n o p q r s t u v w x y z

▷ SPELLING NOTE: *A Rude Idiot Thought He Might Eat Toffee In Church (arithmetic)*

A B C D E F G H I J K L M N O P Q R S T U V W X Y Z

❶ If you shift something, you move it. If something shifts, it moves • *to shift the rubble.* **❷** If an opinion or situation shifts, it changes slightly ▷ **NOUN** **❸** A shift in an opinion or situation is a slight change. **❹** a set period during which people work in a factory • *the night shift.*

shilling, shillings **NOUN** a former British, Australian, and New Zealand coin worth one-twentieth of a pound.

shimmer, shimmers, shimmering, shimmered **VERB** **❶** If something shimmers, it shines with a faint, flickering light ▷ **NOUN** **❷** a faint, flickering light.

shin, shins, shinning, shinned **NOUN** **❶** Your shin is the front part of your leg between your knee and your ankle ▷ **VERB** **❷** If you shin up a tree or pole, you climb it quickly by gripping it with your hands and legs.

shine, shines, shining, shone **VERB** **❶** When something shines, it gives out or reflects a bright light • *The stars shone brilliantly.* **❷** If you shine a torch or lamp somewhere, you point it there.

shingle, shingles **NOUN** **❶** Shingle consists of small pebbles on the seashore. **❷** Shingles are small wooden roof tiles. **❸** Shingles is a disease that causes a painful red rash, especially around the waist.

shining **ADJECTIVE** **❶** Shining things are very bright, usually because they are reflecting light • *shining stainless steel tables.* **❷** A shining example of something is a very good or typical example of that thing • *a shining example of courage.*

● **SIMILAR WORDS:** **❶** bright, ● gleaming

shiny, shinier, shiniest **ADJECTIVE** Shiny things are bright and look as if they have been polished • *a shiny brass plate.*

ship, ships, shipping, shipped **NOUN** **❶** a large boat which carries passengers or cargo ▷ **VERB** **❷** If people or things are shipped somewhere, they are transported there.

-ship **SUFFIX** '-ship' is used to form nouns that refer to a condition or position • *fellowship.*

shipment, shipments **NOUN** **❶** a quantity of goods that are transported somewhere • *a shipment of olive oil.* **❷** The shipment of goods is the transporting of them.

shipping **NOUN** **❶** Shipping is the transport of cargo on ships. **❷** You can also refer to ships generally as shipping • *Attention all shipping!*

shipwreck, shipwrecks **NOUN** When there is a shipwreck, a ship is destroyed in an accident at sea • *He was drowned in a shipwreck.*

shipyard, shipyards **NOUN** a place where ships are built and repaired.

shiralee, shiralees **NOUN** OLD-FASHIONED In Australian English, the bundle of possessions carried by a swagman

shire, shires **NOUN** **❶** OLD-FASHIONED In Britain, a county. **❷** In Australia, a rural district with its own local council.

shirk, shirks, shirking, shirked **VERB**

To shirk a task means to avoid doing it.

shirt, shirts **NOUN** a piece of clothing worn on the upper part of the body, having a collar, sleeves, and buttons down the front.

shiver, shivers, shivering, shivered **VERB** ❶ When you shiver, you tremble slightly because you are cold or scared ▷ **NOUN** ❷ a slight trembling caused by cold or fear.

shoal, shoals **NOUN** A shoal of fish is a large group of them swimming together.

shock, shocks, shocking, shocked **NOUN** ❶ If you have a shock, you have a sudden upsetting experience. ❷ Shock is a person's emotional and physical condition when something very unpleasant or upsetting has happened to them. ❸ In medicine, shock is a serious physical condition in which the blood cannot circulate properly because of an injury. ❹ a slight movement in something when it is hit by something else • *The straps help to absorb shocks.* ❺ A shock of hair is a thick mass of it ▷ **VERB** ❻ If something shocks you, it upsets you because it is unpleasant and unexpected • *I was shocked by his appearance.* ❼ You can say that something shocks you when it offends you because it is rude or immoral. **shocked ADJECTIVE**
■ **SIMILAR WORDS:** ❻ appal, horrify ❼ disgust, scandalize

shock absorber, shock absorbers **NOUN** Shock absorbers are devices fitted near the wheels of a vehicle. They help to prevent the vehicle from bouncing up and down.

shocking ADJECTIVE ❶ INFORMAL very bad • *It's been a shocking year.* ❷ rude or immoral • *a shocking video.*

shoddy, shoddier, shoddiest **ADJECTIVE** badly made or done • *a shoddy piece of work.*

shoe, shoes, shoeing, shod **NOUN** ❶ Shoes are strong coverings for your feet. They cover most of your foot, but not your ankle ▷ **VERB** ❷ To shoe a horse means to fix horseshoes onto its hooves.

shoestring NOUN If you do something on a shoestring, you do it using very little money.

Shomer Shabbat or **Shomer Shabbos** or Shomerei Shabbos **NOUN** ⟨RE⟩ someone who observes the Jewish Sabbath.

shoot, shoots, shooting, shot **VERB** ❶ To shoot a person or animal means to kill or injure them by firing a gun at them. ❷ To shoot an arrow means to fire it from a bow. ❸ If something shoots in a particular direction, it moves there quickly and suddenly • *They shot back into Green Street.* ❹ When a film is shot, it is filmed • *The whole film was shot in California.* ❺ In games such as football or hockey, to shoot means to kick or hit the ball towards the goal ▷ **NOUN** ❻ an occasion when people hunt animals or birds with guns. ❼ a plant that is beginning to grow, or a new part growing from a plant.

shooting, shootings **NOUN** an incident in which someone is shot.

shooting star, shooting stars **NOUN** a meteor.

▷ SPELLING NOTE: *Betty Eats Cakes And Uses Seven Eggs (because)*

A
B
C
D
E
F
G
H
I
J
K
L
M
N
O
P
Q
R
S
T
U
V
W
X
Y
Z

shop, shops, shopping, shopped
NOUN ❶ a place where things are
sold. ❷ a place where a particular
type of work is done • *a bicycle repair
shop.* ▷ VERB ❸ When you shop, you
go to the shops to buy things.
shopper NOUN

shopkeeper, shopkeepers NOUN
someone who owns or manages a
small shop.

shoplifting NOUN Shoplifting is
stealing goods from shops. **shoplifter**
NOUN

shopping NOUN Your shopping is
the goods you have bought from the
shops.

shop steward, shop stewards
NOUN a trade union member elected
to represent the workers in a factory or
office.

shore, shores, shoring, shored NOUN
❶ The shore of a sea, lake, or wide
river is the land along the edge of it
▷ VERB ❷ If you shore something
up, you reinforce it or strengthen it • *a
short-term solution to shore up the worst
defence in the League.*

shoreline, shorelines NOUN the
edge of a sea, lake, or wide river.

shorn ❶ Shorn is the past participle
of shear. ADJECTIVE ❷ Grass or hair
that is shorn is cut very short.

short, shorter, shortest; shorts
ADJECTIVE ❶ not lasting very long.
❷ small in length, distance, or height
• *a short climb* • *the short road.* ❸ not
using many words • *a short speech.*
❹ If you are short with someone, you
speak to them crossly. ❺ If you have a
short temper, you get angry very

quickly. ❻ If you are short of
something, you do not have enough of
it. ❼ If a name is short for another
name, it is a short version of it ❽ IN
PLURAL Shorts are trousers with short
legs ▷ ADVERB ❾ If you stop short of
a place, you do not quite reach it
▷ PHRASE ❿ **Short of** is used to say
that a level or amount has not quite
been reached • *a hundred votes short of
a majority.*
● SIMILAR WORDS: ❹ abrupt, curt,
● sharp

shortage, shortages NOUN If there
is a shortage of something, there is
not enough of it.

shortbread NOUN Shortbread is a
crumbly biscuit made from flour and
butter.
● WORD HISTORY: from an
● old-fashioned use of *short* meaning
● 'crumbly'

short circuit, short circuits NOUN
a fault in an electrical system when
two points accidentally become
connected and the electricity travels
directly between them rather than
through the complete circuit.

shortcoming, shortcomings
NOUN Shortcomings are faults or
weaknesses.

shortcut, shortcuts NOUN ❶ a
quicker way of getting somewhere
than the usual route. ❷ a quicker way
of doing something • *Stencils have
been used as a shortcut to hand
painting.*

shorten, shortens, shortening,
shortened VERB If you shorten
something or if it shortens, it becomes
shorter • *This might help to shorten the*

▷ SPELLING NOTE: there's a rAKE in the brAKEs (*brake*)

inevitable conversation.

shortfall, shortfalls NOUN If there is a shortfall in something, there is less than you need.

shorthand NOUN Shorthand is a way of writing in which signs represent words or syllables. It is used to write down quickly what someone is saying.

short-list, short-lists, short-listing, short-listed NOUN ❶ a list of people selected from a larger group, from which one person is finally selected for a job or prize ▷ VERB ❷ If someone is short-listed for a job or prize, they are put on a short-list.

shortly ADVERB ❶ Shortly means soon • *I'll be back shortly.* ❷ If you speak to someone shortly, you speak to them in a cross and impatient way.

short-sighted ADJECTIVE ❶ If you are short-sighted, you cannot see things clearly when they are far away. ❷ A short-sighted decision does not take account of the way things may develop in the future.

short-term ADJECTIVE happening or having an effect within a short time or for a short time.

shot, shots ❶ Shot is the past tense and past participle of **shoot**. NOUN ❷ the act of firing a gun. ❸ Someone who is a good shot can shoot accurately. ❹ In football, golf, and tennis, a shot is the act of kicking or hitting the ball. ❺ a photograph or short film sequence • *I'd like to get some shots of the river.* ❻ INFORMAL If you have a shot at something, you try to do it.

shotgun, shotguns NOUN a gun that fires a lot of small pellets all at once.

shot put NOUN In athletics, the shot put is an event in which the contestants throw a heavy metal ball called a shot as far as possible. **shot putter** NOUN

should VERB ❶ You use 'should' to say that something ought to happen • *Ward should have done better.* ❷ You also use 'should' to say that you expect something to happen • *He should have heard by now.* ❸ FORMAL You can use 'should' to announce that you are about to do or say something • *I should like to express my thanks to the Professor.* ❹ 'Should' is used in conditional sentences • *If they should discover the fact, what use would the knowledge be to them?* ❺ 'Should' is sometimes used in 'that' clauses • *It is inevitable that you should go.* ❻ If you say that you should think something, you mean that it is probably true • *I should think that's unlikely.*

shoulder, shoulders, shouldering, shouldered NOUN ❶ Your shoulders are the parts of your body between your neck and the tops of your arms ▷ VERB ❷ If you shoulder something heavy, you put it across one of your shoulders to carry it. ❸ If you shoulder the responsibility or blame for something, you accept it.

shoulder blade, shoulder blades NOUN Your shoulder blades are the two large, flat bones in the upper part of your back, below your shoulders.

shout, shouts, shouting, shouted NOUN ❶ a loud call or cry ▷ VERB ❷ If you shout something, you say it

a
b
c
d
e
f
g
h
i
j
k
l
m
n
o
p
q
r
s
t
u
v
w
x
y
z

▷ SPELLING NOTE: *you'll brEAK that Electrical Aerial, Kitty (break)*

A
B
C
D
E
F
G
H
I
J
K
L
M
N
O
P
Q
R
S
T
U
V
W
X
Y
Z

very loudly • *He shouted something to his brother.*

● **SIMILAR WORDS:** call, cry, yell

shove, shoves, shoving, shoved **VERB**
1 If you shove someone or something, you push them roughly • *He shoved his wallet into a back pocket.* ▷ **NOUN** **2** a rough push.
shove off VERB INFORMAL If you tell someone to shove off, you are telling them angrily and rudely to go away.

shovel, shovels, shovelling, shovelled
NOUN **1** a tool like a spade, used for moving earth or snow ▷ **VERB** **2** If you shovel earth or snow, you move it with a shovel.

show, shows, showing, showed, shown **VERB** **1** To show that something exists or is true means to prove it • *The survey showed that 29 per cent would now approve the treaty.* **2** If a picture shows something, it represents it • *The painting shows supporters and crowd scenes.* **3** If you show someone something, you let them see it • *Show me your passport.* **4** If you show someone to a room or seat, you lead them there. **5** If you show someone how to do something, you demonstrate it to them. **6** If something shows, it is visible. **7** If something shows a quality or characteristic, you can see that it has it • *Her sketches and watercolours showed promise.* **8** If you show your feelings, you let people see them • *She was flustered, but too proud to show it.* **9** If you show affection or mercy, you behave in an affectionate or merciful way • *the first person who showed me some affection.* **10** To show a film or television programme means to let the public see it ▷ **NOUN** **11** a form

of light entertainment at the theatre or on television. **12** an exhibition • *the Napier Antiques Show.* **13** A show of a feeling or attitude is behaviour in which you show it • *a show of optimism.* ▷ **PHRASE** **14** If something is **on show**, it is being exhibited for the public to see.
show off VERB INFORMAL If someone is showing off, they are trying to impress people.
show up VERB **1** INFORMAL If you show up, you arrive at a place. **2** If something shows up, it can be seen clearly • *Her bones were too soft to show up on an X-ray.*

● **SIMILAR WORDS:**
● **1** demonstrate, prove **7** display, indicate, reveal **12** display, exhibition

show business NOUN Show business is entertainment in the theatre, films, and television.

showdown, showdowns **NOUN** INFORMAL a major argument or conflict intended to end a dispute.

shower, showers, showering, showered **NOUN** **1** a device which sprays you with water so that you can wash yourself. **2** If you have a shower, you wash yourself by standing under a shower. **3** a short period of rain. **4** You can refer to a lot of things falling at once as a shower • *a shower of confetti.* ▷ **VERB** **5** If you shower, you have a shower. **6** If you are showered with a lot of things, they fall on you.

showing, showings **NOUN** A showing of a film or television programme is a presentation of it so that the public can see it.

▷ SPELLING NOTE: *I always visit my FRIend on a FRIday (Friday)*

showjumping NOUN
Showjumping is a horse-riding competition in which the horses jump over a series of high fences.

show-off, show-offs NOUN
INFORMAL someone who tries to impress people with their knowledge or skills.

showroom, showrooms NOUN a shop where goods such as cars or electrical appliances are displayed.

showy, showier, showiest
ADJECTIVE large or bright and intended to impress people • *a showy house.*
- SIMILAR WORDS: flamboyant, flashy, ostentatious

shrapnel NOUN Shrapnel consists of small pieces of metal scattered from an exploding shell.
- WORD HISTORY: named after General Henry *Shrapnel* (1761–1842), who invented it

shred, shreds, shredding, shredded
VERB ❶ If you shred something, you cut or tear it into very small pieces ▷ NOUN ❷ A shred of paper or material is a small, narrow piece of it. ❸ If there is not a shred of something, there is absolutely none of it • *He was left without a shred of self-esteem.*

shrew, shrews [Said **shroo**] NOUN a small mouse-like animal with a long pointed nose.

shrewd, shrewder, shrewdest
ADJECTIVE Someone who is shrewd is intelligent and makes good judgments. **shrewdly** ADVERB
shrewdness NOUN
- SIMILAR WORDS: astute, clever, sharp

shriek, shrieks, shrieking, shrieked
NOUN ❶ a high-pitched scream ▷ VERB ❷ If you shriek, you make a high-pitched scream.

shrift NOUN If you give someone or something short shrift, you pay very little attention to them.

shrill, shriller, shrillest ADJECTIVE A shrill sound is unpleasantly high-pitched and piercing. **shrilly** ADVERB

shrimp, shrimps NOUN a small edible shellfish with a long tail and many legs.

shrine, shrines NOUN (RE) a place of worship associated with a sacred person or object.

shrink, shrinks, shrinking, shrank, shrunk VERB ❶ If something shrinks, it becomes smaller. ❷ If you shrink from something, you move away from it because you are afraid of it.
shrinkage NOUN

shrivel, shrivels, shrivelling, shrivelled VERB When something shrivels, it becomes dry and withered • *crops shrivelling from lack of water.*

shroud, shrouds, shrouding, shrouded NOUN ❶ a cloth in which a dead body is wrapped before it is buried ▷ VERB ❷ If something is shrouded in darkness or fog, it is hidden by it.

shrub, shrubs NOUN a low, bushy plant.

shrug, shrugs, shrugging, shrugged
VERB ❶ If you shrug your shoulders, you raise them slightly as a sign of indifference ▷ NOUN ❷ If you give a shrug of your shoulders, you shrug them.

a
b
c
d
e
f
g
h
i
j
k
l
m
n
o
p
q
r
s
t
u
v
w
x
y
z

▷ SPELLING NOTE: *I want to see (C) your licenCe (licence)*

A
B
C
D
E
F
G
H
I
J
K
L
M
N
O
P
Q
R
S
T
U
V
W
X
Y
Z

shrunken ADJECTIVE FORMAL Someone or something that is shrunken has become smaller than it used to be • *a shrunken old man*.

shudder, shudders, shuddering, shuddered VERB ❶ If you shudder, you tremble with fear or horror. ❷ If a machine or vehicle shudders, it shakes violently ▷ NOUN ❸ a shiver of fear or horror.

shuffle, shuffles, shuffling, shuffled VERB ❶ If you shuffle, you walk without lifting your feet properly off the ground. ❷ If you shuffle about, you move about and fidget because you feel uncomfortable or embarrassed. ❸ If you shuffle a pack of cards, you mix them up before you begin a game ▷ NOUN ❹ the way someone walks when they shuffle.

shun, shuns, shunning, shunned VERB If you shun someone or something, you deliberately avoid them.

shunt, shunts, shunting, shunted VERB INFORMAL If you shunt people or things to a place, you move them there • *You are shunted from room to room*.

shut, shuts, shutting, shut VERB ❶ If you shut something, you close it. ❷ When a shop or pub shuts, it is closed and you can no longer go into it ▷ ADJECTIVE ❸ If something is shut, it is closed.
shut up VERB INFORMAL If you shut up, you stop talking.

shutter, shutters NOUN Shutters are hinged wooden or metal covers fitted on the outside or inside of a window.

shuttle, shuttles ADJECTIVE ❶ A shuttle service is an air, bus, or train service which makes frequent journeys between two places ▷ NOUN ❷ a plane used in a shuttle service.

shuttlecock, shuttlecocks NOUN the feathered object used like a ball in the game of badminton.

shy, shyer, shyest; shies, shying, shied ADJECTIVE ❶ A shy person is nervous and uncomfortable in the company of other people ▷ VERB ❷ When a horse shies, it moves away suddenly because something has frightened it. ❸ If you shy away from doing something, you avoid doing it because you are afraid or nervous.
shyly ADVERB **shyness** NOUN
● SIMILAR WORDS: ❶ bashful,
● self-conscious, timid

sibling, siblings NOUN FORMAL Your siblings are your brothers and sisters.

sick, sicker, sickest ADJECTIVE ❶ If you are sick, you are ill. ❷ If you feel sick, you feel as if you are going to vomit. If you are sick, you vomit. ❸ INFORMAL If you are sick of doing something, you feel you have been doing it too long. ❹ INFORMAL A sick joke or story deals with death or suffering in an unpleasantly frivolous way ▷ PHRASE ❺ If something **makes you sick**, it makes you angry.
sickness NOUN
● SIMILAR WORDS: ❷ nauseous,
● queasy

sicken, sickens, sickening, sickened VERB If something sickens you, it makes you feel disgusted. **sickening** ADJECTIVE

sickle, sickles NOUN a tool with a

▷ SPELLING NOTE: *The government licenSes Schnapps (licenses)*

short handle and a curved blade used for cutting grass or grain.

sickly, sicklier, sickliest **ADJECTIVE**
❶ A sickly person or animal is weak and unhealthy. ❷ Sickly also means very unpleasant to smell or taste.

side, sides, siding, sided **NOUN**
❶ Side refers to a position to the left or right of something • *the two armchairs on either side of the fireplace.*
❷ The sides of a boundary or barrier are the two areas it separates • *this side of the border.* ❸ Your sides are the parts of your body from your armpits down to your hips. ❹ The sides of something are its outside surfaces, especially the surfaces which are not its front or back. ❺ The sides of a hill or valley are the parts that slope. ❻ The two sides in a war, argument, or relationship are the two people or groups involved. ❼ A particular side of something is one aspect of it • *the sensitive, caring side of human nature.*
▷ **ADJECTIVE** ❽ situated on a side of a building or vehicle • *the side door.*
❾ A side road is a small road leading off a larger one. ❿ A side issue is less important than the main one ▷ **VERB**
⓫ If you side with someone in an argument, you support them.

sideboard, sideboards **NOUN** ❶ a long, low cupboard for plates and glasses ❷ IN PLURAL A man's sideboards are his sideburns.

sideburns **PLURAL NOUN** A man's sideburns are areas of hair growing on his cheeks in front of his ears.
- **WORD HISTORY:** from a 19th
- century US army general called
- *Burnside* who wore his whiskers like
- this

side effect, side effects **NOUN** The side effects of a drug are the effects it has in addition to its main effects.

sidekick, sidekicks **NOUN** INFORMAL Someone's sidekick is their close friend who spends a lot of time with them.

sideline, sidelines **NOUN** an extra job in addition to your main job.

sideshow, sideshows **NOUN** Sideshows are stalls at a fairground.

sidestep, sidesteps, sidestepping, sidestepped **VERB** If you sidestep a difficult problem or question, you avoid dealing with it.

sidewalk, sidewalks **NOUN** In American English, a sidewalk is a pavement.

sideways **ADVERB** from or towards the side of something or someone.

siding, sidings **NOUN** a short railway track beside the main tracks, where engines and carriages are left when not in use.

sidle, sidles, sidling, sidled **VERB** If you sidle somewhere, you walk there cautiously and slowly, as if you do not want to be noticed.

siege, sieges *[Said seej]* **NOUN**
(HISTORY) a military operation in which an army surrounds a place and prevents food or help from reaching the people inside.

sieve, sieves, sieving, sieved *[Said siv]*
NOUN ❶ a kitchen tool made of mesh, used for sifting or straining things ▷ **VERB** ❷ If you sieve a powder or liquid, you pass it through a sieve.

▷ SPELLING NOTE: *have a plEce of plE (piece)*

sift, sifts, sifting, sifted **VERB** ❶ If you sift a powdery substance, you pass it through a sieve to remove lumps. ❷ If you sift through something such as evidence, you examine it all thoroughly.

sigh, sighs, sighing, sighed **VERB** ❶ When you sigh, you let out a deep breath ▷ **NOUN** ❷ the breath you let out when you sigh.

sight, sights, sighting, sighted **NOUN** ❶ Sight is the ability to see • *His sight was so poor that he could not follow the cricket.* ❷ something you see • *It was a ghastly sight.* ❸ IN PLURAL Sights are interesting places which tourists visit ▷ **VERB** ❹ If you sight someone or something, you see them briefly or suddenly • *He had been sighted in Cairo.* ▷ **PHRASES** ❺ If something is **in sight**, you can see it. If it is **out of sight**, you cannot see it.

● USAGE NOTE: Do not confuse the ● spellings of *sight* and *site*

sighted **ADJECTIVE** Someone who is sighted can see.

sighting, sightings **NOUN** A sighting of something rare or unexpected is an occasion when it is seen.

sightseeing **NOUN** Sightseeing is visiting the interesting places that tourists usually visit. **sightseer** **NOUN**

sign, signs, signing, signed **NOUN** ❶ a mark or symbol that always has a particular meaning, for example in mathematics or music. ❷ a gesture with a particular meaning. ❸ A sign can also consist of words, a picture, or a symbol giving information or a warning. ❹ RE A sign is an event or happening that some people believe God has sent as a warning or instruction to an individual or to people in general. ❺ If there are signs of something, there is evidence that it exists or is happening • *We are now seeing the first signs of recovery.* ▷ **VERB** ❻ If you sign a document, you write your name on it • *He hurriedly signed the death certificate.* ❼ If you sign, you communicate by using sign language.

sign on **VERB** ❶ If you sign on for a job or course, you officially agree to do it by signing a contract. ❷ When people sign on, they officially state that they are unemployed and claim benefit from the state.

sign up **VERB** If you sign up for a job or course, you officially agree to do it by signing a contract.

● SIMILAR WORDS: ❷ gesture,
● signal

signal, signals, signalling, signalled **NOUN** ❶ a gesture, sound, or action intended to give a message to someone. ❷ A railway signal is a piece of equipment beside the track which tells train drivers whether to stop or not ▷ **VERB** ❸ If you signal to someone, you make a gesture or sound to give them a message.

signature, signatures **NOUN** If you write your signature, you write your name the way you usually write it.

significant **ADJECTIVE** large or important • *a significant amount* • *a significant victory.* **significance** **NOUN** **significantly** **ADVERB**

significant figure, significant figures **NOUN** MATHS each of the figures of a number that express its size to a particular degree of accuracy; for example, 4.271 expressed to three significant figures is 4.27.

signify, signifies, signifying, signified **VERB** A gesture that signifies something has a particular meaning • *They signified a desire to leave.*

sign language NOUN Sign language is a way of communicating using your hands, used especially by deaf people.

signpost, signposts **NOUN** a road sign with information on it such as the name of a town and how far away it is.

Sikh, Sikhs *[Said **seek**]* **NOUN** (RE) a person who believes in Sikhism, an Indian religion which separated from Hinduism in the sixteenth century and which teaches that there is only one God. **Sikhism NOUN**
● **WORD HISTORY:** from Hindi *sikh* meaning 'disciple'

silence, silences, silencing, silenced **NOUN** ❶ Silence is quietness. ❷ Someone's silence about something is their failure or refusal to talk about it ▷ **VERB** ❸ To silence someone or something means to stop them talking or making a noise.

silent ADJECTIVE ❶ If you are silent, you are not saying anything. ❷ If you are silent about something, you do not tell people about it. ❸ When something is silent, it makes no noise. ❹ A silent film has only pictures and no sound. **silently ADVERB**
● **SIMILAR WORDS:** ❶ dumb, mute, speechless

silhouette, silhouettes *[Said*

*sil-loo-**ett**]* **NOUN** the outline of a dark shape against a light background. **silhouetted ADJECTIVE**

silicon NOUN Silicon is an element found in sand, clay, and stone. It is used to make parts of computers.

silk, silks **NOUN** Silk is a fine, soft cloth made from a substance produced by silkworms.

silkworm, silkworms **NOUN** Silkworms are the larvae of a particular kind of moth.

silky, silkier, silkiest **ADJECTIVE** smooth and soft.

sill, sills **NOUN** a ledge at the bottom of a window.

silly, sillier, silliest **ADJECTIVE** foolish or childish.
● **SIMILAR WORDS:** daft, foolish stupid

silt NOUN Silt is fine sand or soil which is carried along by a river.

silver NOUN ❶ Silver is a valuable greyish-white metallic element used for making jewellery and ornaments. ❷ Silver is also coins made from silver or from silver-coloured metal ▷ **ADJECTIVE OR NOUN** ❸ greyish-white.

silver beet, silver beets **NOUN** a type of beet grown in Australia and New Zealand.

silver fern NOUN a tall fern that is found in New Zealand. It is the symbol of New Zealand national sports teams.

silverfish, silverfishes or silverfish **NOUN** A silverfish is a small insect with no wings that eats paper and clothing.

a
b
c
d
e
f
g
h
i
j
k
l
m
n
o
p
q
r
s
t
u
v
w
x
y
z

▷ SPELLING NOTE: *I went to see (C) the doctor's new practiCe (practice)*

silver jubilee, silver jubilees **NOUN** the 25th anniversary of an important event.

silver medal, silver medals **NOUN** a medal made from silver awarded to the competitor who comes second in a competition.

silver wedding, silver weddings **NOUN** A couple's silver wedding is the 25th anniversary of their wedding.

silvery **ADJECTIVE** having the appearance or colour of silver • *the silvery moon.*

similar **ADJECTIVE** **❶** If one thing is similar to another, or if two things are similar, they are like each other. **❷** In maths, two triangles are similar if the angles in one correspond exactly to the angles in the other. **similarly** **ADVERB**
- **USAGE NOTE:** Be careful when deciding whether to use *similar* or *same*. *Similar* means 'alike but not identical', and *same* means 'identical'. Do not put *as* after *similar*: her dress was similar to mine

similarity, similarities **NOUN** If there is a similarity between things, they are alike in some way.
- **SIMILAR WORDS:** likeness, resemblance

simile, similes [Said **sim**-ill-ee] **NOUN** (ENGLISH) an expression in which a person or thing is described as being similar to someone or something else. Examples of similes are She runs like a deer and He's as white as a sheet.

simmer, simmers, simmering, simmered **VERB** When food simmers, it cooks at just below boiling point.

simple, simpler, simplest **ADJECTIVE** **❶** Something that is simple is uncomplicated and easy to understand or do. **❷** Simple also means plain and not elaborate in style • *a simple coat.* **❸** A simple way of life is uncomplicated. **❹** Someone who is simple is mentally retarded. **❺** You use 'simple' to emphasize that what you are talking about is the only important thing • *His attitude was not so much conviction as simple stubbornness.* **simplicity** **NOUN**

simple-minded **ADJECTIVE** not very intelligent or sophisticated • *simple-minded pleasures.*

simplify, simplifies, simplifying, simplified **VERB** To simplify something means to make it easier to do or understand. **simplification** **NOUN**

simplistic **ADJECTIVE** too simple or naive • *a rather simplistic approach to the subject.*

simply **ADVERB** **❶** Simply means merely • *It was simply a question of making the decision.* **❷** You use 'simply' to emphasize what you are saying • *It is simply not true.* **❸** If you say or write something simply, you do it in a way that makes it easy to understand.

simulate, simulates, simulating, simulated **VERB** To simulate something means to imitate it • *The wood has been painted to simulate stone.* **simulation** **NOUN**

simultaneous **ADJECTIVE** Things that are simultaneous happen at the same time. **simultaneously** **ADVERB**

▷ SPELLING NOTE: *You must practiSe your Ss (practise)*

sin, sins, sinning, sinned **NOUN** ❶ Sin is wicked and immoral behaviour ▷ **VERB** ❷ To sin means to do something wicked and immoral.
● **SIMILAR WORDS:** ❶ evil, iniquity, ● wrongdoing ❷ lapse, transgress

since **PREPOSITION, CONJUNCTION, OR ADVERB**
❶ Since means from a particular time until now • *I've been waiting patiently since half past three.* ▷ **ADVERB**
❷ Since also means at some time after a particular time in the past • *They split up and he has since remarried.* ▷ **CONJUNCTION** ❸ Since also means because • *I'm forever on a diet, since I put on weight easily.*
● **USAGE NOTE:** Do not put *ago*
● before *since*, as it is not needed: *it is*
● *ten years since she wrote her book* not
● *ten years ago since*

sincere **ADJECTIVE** If you are sincere, you say things that you really mean • *a sincere expression of friendliness.* **sincerity** **NOUN**
● **SIMILAR WORDS:** genuine, honest

sincerely **ADVERB** ❶ If you say or feel something sincerely, you mean it or feel it genuinely ▷ **PHRASE** ❷ You write **Yours sincerely** before your signature at the end of a letter in which you have named the person you are writing to in the greeting at the beginning of the letter. For example, if you began your letter 'Dear Mr Brown' you would use 'Yours sincerely'.

sine, sines **NOUN** (MATHS) In mathematics, a sine is a function of an angle. If B is the right angle in a right-angled triangle ABC, the sine of the angle at A is BC divided by AC.

sinew, sinews [Said **sin**-yoo] **NOUN**

a tough cord in your body that connects a muscle to a bone.

sinful **ADJECTIVE** wicked and immoral.

sing, sings, singing, sang, sung **VERB**
❶ When you sing, you make musical sounds with your voice, usually producing words that fit a tune.
❷ When birds or insects sing, they make pleasant sounds. **singer NOUN**
● **USAGE NOTE:** The past tense of
● *sing* is *sang*, and the past participle
● is *sung*. Do not confuse these
● words: *the team sang the national*
● *anthem; we have sung together many*
● *times*

singe, singes, singeing, singed **VERB**
❶ To singe something means to burn it slightly so that it goes brown but does not catch fire ▷ **NOUN** ❷ a slight burn.

single, singles, singling, singled **ADJECTIVE** ❶ Single means only one and not more • *A single shot was fired.*
❷ People who are single are not married. ❸ A single bed or bedroom is for one person. ❹ A single ticket is a one-way ticket ▷ **NOUN** ❺ a recording of one or two short pieces of music on a small record, CD, or cassette. ❻ Singles is a game of tennis, badminton, or squash between just two players.
single out VERB If you single someone out from a group, you give them special treatment • *He'd been singled out for some special award.*

single-handed **ADVERB** If you do something single-handed, you do it on your own, without any help.

single-minded **ADJECTIVE** A

single-minded person has only one aim and is determined to achieve it.

singly ADVERB If people do something singly, they do it on their own or one by one.

singular NOUN ❶ In grammar, the singular is the form of a word that refers to just one person or thing ▷ ADJECTIVE ❷ FORMAL unusual and remarkable • *her singular beauty.* **singularity** NOUN **singularly** ADVERB

sinister ADJECTIVE seeming harmful or evil • *something cold and sinister about him.*

● **WORD HISTORY:** from Latin
● *sinister* meaning 'left-hand side',
● because the left side was
● considered unlucky

sink, sinks, sinking, sank, sunk NOUN ❶ a basin with taps supplying water, usually in a kitchen or bathroom ▷ VERB ❷ If something sinks, it moves downwards, especially through water • *An Indian cargo ship sank in icy seas.* ❸ To sink a ship means to cause it to sink by attacking it. ❹ If an amount or value sinks, it decreases. ❺ If you sink into an unpleasant state, you gradually pass into it • *He sank into black despair.* ❻ To sink something sharp into an object means to make it go deeply into it • *The tiger sank its teeth into his leg.*
sink in VERB When a fact sinks in, you fully understand it or realize it • *The truth was at last sinking in.*

sinner, sinners NOUN someone who has committed a sin.

sinus, sinuses NOUN Your sinuses are the air passages in the bones of your skull, just behind your nose.

sip, sips, sipping, sipped VERB ❶ If you sip a drink, you drink it by taking a small amount at a time ▷ NOUN ❷ a small amount of drink that you take into your mouth.

siphon, siphons, siphoning, siphoned [*Said sigh-fn*]; *also spelt* **syphon** VERB If you siphon off a liquid, you draw it out of a container through a tube and transfer it to another place.

sir NOUN ❶ Sir is a polite, formal way of addressing a man. ❷ Sir is also the title used in front of the name of a knight or baronet.

siren, sirens NOUN a warning device, for example on a police car, which makes a loud, wailing noise.

● **WORD HISTORY:** the Sirens in
● Greek mythology were sea nymphs
● who had beautiful voices and sang
● in order to lure sailors to their
● deaths on the rocks where the
● nymphs lived

sirloin NOUN Sirloin is a prime cut of beef from the lower part of a cow's back.

● **WORD HISTORY:** from Old French
● *sur* meaning 'above' and *longe*
● meaning 'loin'

sis or **sies** [*Said siss*] INTERJECTION INFORMAL In South African English, you say 'Sis!' to show disgust.

sister, sisters NOUN ❶ Your sister is a girl or woman who has the same parents as you. ❷ a member of a female religious order. ❸ In a hospital, a sister is a senior nurse who supervises a ward ▷ ADJECTIVE ❹ Sister means closely related to something or very similar to it

▷ SPELLING NOTE: L*Earn* the princip*LEs* (principle)

• *Citroen and its sister company Peugeot.*

sisterhood NOUN Sisterhood is a strong feeling of companionship between women.

sister-in-law, sisters-in-law NOUN Your sister-in-law is the wife of your brother, the sister of your husband or wife, or the woman married to your wife's or husband's brother.

sit, sits, sitting, sat VERB ❶ If you are sitting, your weight is supported by your buttocks rather than your feet. ❷ When you sit or sit down somewhere, you lower your body until you are sitting. ❸ If you sit an examination, you take it. ❹ FORMAL When a parliament, law court, or other official body sits, it meets and officially carries out its work.

sitcom, sitcoms NOUN INFORMAL a television comedy series which shows characters in amusing situations that are similar to everyday life.
● **WORD HISTORY:** shortened from *situation comedy*

site, sites, siting, sited NOUN ❶ a piece of ground where a particular thing happens or is situated • *a building site.* ▷ VERB ❷ If something is sited in a place, it is built or positioned there.
● **USAGE NOTE:** Do not confuse the spellings of *site* and *sight*

sitting, sittings NOUN ❶ one of the times when a meal is served. ❷ one of the occasions when a parliament or law court meets and carries out its work.

sitting room, sitting rooms NOUN

a room in a house where people sit and relax.

situated ADJECTIVE If something is situated somewhere, that is where it is • *a town situated 45 minutes from Geneva.*

situation, situations NOUN ❶ what is happening in a particular place at a particular time • *the political situation.* ❷ (GEOGRAPHY) The situation of a building or town is its surroundings • *a beautiful situation.*
● **SIMILAR WORDS:**
● ❶ circumstances, condition, state of affairs

Siva PROPER NOUN Siva is a Hindu god and is one of the Trimurti.

six Six is the number 6.

sixteen the number 16. **sixteenth** ADJECTIVE

sixth, sixths ADJECTIVE ❶ The sixth item in a series is the one counted as number six ▷ NOUN ❷ one of six equal parts.

sixth sense NOUN You say that someone has a sixth sense when they know something instinctively, without having any evidence of it.

sixty, sixties the number 60. **sixtieth** ADJECTIVE

sizable or **sizeable** ADJECTIVE fairly large • *a sizable amount of money.*

size, sizes NOUN ❶ The size of something is how big or small it is • *the size of the audience.* ❷ The size of something is also the fact that it is very large • *the sheer size of Australia.* ❸ one of the standard graded measurements of clothes and shoes.

a b c d e f g h i j k l m n o p q r **s** t u v w x y z

A
B
C
D
E
F
G
H
I
J
K
L
M
N
O
P
Q
R
S
T
U
V
W
X
Y
Z

● **SIMILAR WORDS:** ❶ dimensions,
● magnitude, proportions

sizzle, sizzles, sizzling, sizzled **VERB**
If something sizzles, it makes a hissing
sound like the sound of frying food.

sjambok, sjamboks *[Said sham-
bok]* **NOUN** In South African English, a
sjambok is a long whip made from
animal hide.

skate, skates, skating, skated **NOUN**
❶ Skates are ice skates or roller
skates. ❷ a flat edible sea fish
▷ **VERB** ❸ If you skate, you move
about on ice wearing ice skates. ❹ If
you skate round a difficult subject, you
avoid discussing it.

skateboard, skateboards **NOUN** a
narrow board on wheels which you
stand on and ride for fun.

skeleton, skeletons **NOUN** Your
skeleton is the framework of bones in
your body.

sketch, sketches, sketching,
sketched **NOUN** ❶ (ART) a quick,
rough drawing. ❷ A sketch of a
situation or incident is a brief
description of it. ❸ a short, humorous
piece of acting, usually forming part of
a comedy show ▷ **VERB** ❹ If you
sketch something, you draw it quickly
and roughly.

sketchy, sketchier, sketchiest
ADJECTIVE giving only a rough
description or account • *Details
surrounding his death are sketchy.*

skew or **skewed** *[Said skyoo]*
ADJECTIVE in a slanting position,
rather than straight or upright.

skewer, skewers, skewering,
skewered **NOUN** ❶ a long metal pin

used to hold pieces of food together
during cooking ▷ **VERB** ❷ If you
skewer something, you push a skewer
through it.

ski, skis, skiing, skied **NOUN** ❶ Skis
are long pieces of wood, metal, or
plastic that you fasten to special boots
so you can move easily on snow
▷ **VERB** ❷ When you ski, you move
on snow wearing skis, especially as a
sport.

skid, skids, skidding, skidded **VERB** If
a vehicle skids, it slides in an
uncontrolled way, for example
because the road is wet or icy.

skilful **ADJECTIVE** If you are skilful
at something, you can do it very well.
skilfully **ADVERB**
● **SIMILAR WORDS:** able, expert,
● proficient

skill, skills **NOUN** ❶ Skill is the
knowledge and ability that enables
you to do something well. ❷ a type of
work or technique which requires
special training and knowledge.
● **SIMILAR WORDS:** ❶ ability,
● expertise, proficiency

skilled **ADJECTIVE** ❶ A skilled
person has the knowledge and ability
to do something well. ❷ Skilled work
is work which can only be done by
people who have had special training
• *It's a skilled job.*

skim, skims, skimming, skimmed
VERB ❶ If you skim something from
the surface of a liquid, you remove it.
❷ If something skims a surface, it
moves along just above it • *seagulls
skimming the waves.*

skimmed milk **NOUN** Skimmed
milk has had the cream removed.

skin, skins, skinning, skinned **NOUN**
❶ Your skin is the natural covering of
your body. An animal skin is the skin
and fur of a dead animal. ❷ The skin
of a fruit or vegetable is its outer
covering. ❸ a solid layer which forms
on the surface of a liquid ▷ **VERB**
❹ If you skin a dead animal, you
remove its skin. ❺ If you skin a part of
your body, you accidentally graze it.

skinny, skinnier, skinniest
ADJECTIVE extremely thin.

skip, skips, skipping, skipped **VERB**
❶ If you skip along, you move along
jumping from one foot to the other.
❷ If you skip something, you miss it
out or avoid doing it • *It is all too easy
to skip meals.* ▷ **NOUN** ❸ Skips are
the movements you make when you
skip. ❹ a large metal container for
holding rubbish and rubble.

skipper, skippers **NOUN** INFORMAL
The skipper of a ship or boat is its
captain.
● **WORD HISTORY:** from Old Dutch
● *schipper* meaning 'shipper'

skirmish, skirmishes **NOUN** a short,
rough fight.

skirt, skirts, skirting, skirted **NOUN**
❶ A woman's skirt is a piece of
clothing which fastens at her waist
and hangs down over her legs ▷ **VERB**
❷ Something that skirts an area is
situated around the edge of it. ❸ If
you skirt something, you go around
the edge of it • *We skirted the town.*
❹ If you skirt a problem, you avoid
dealing with it • *He was skirting the
real question.*
● **WORD HISTORY:** from Old Norse
● *skyrta* meaning 'shirt'

skirting, skirtings **NOUN** A skirting
or skirting board is a narrow strip of
wood running along the bottom of a
wall in a room.

skite, skites, skiting, skited INFORMAL
VERB ❶ In Australian and New
Zealand English, to skite is to talk in a
boastful way about something that
you own or that you have done
▷ **NOUN** ❷ In Australian and New
Zealand English, someone who boasts.

skittle, skittles **NOUN** Skittles is a
game in which players roll a ball and
try to knock down wooden objects
called skittles.

skull, skulls **NOUN** Your skull is the
bony part of your head which
surrounds your brain.

skunk, skunks **NOUN** a small black
and white animal from North America
which gives off an unpleasant smell
when it is frightened.

sky, skies **NOUN** The sky is the space
around the earth which you can see
when you look upwards.
● **WORD HISTORY:** from Old Norse
● *sky* meaning 'cloud'

skylight, skylights **NOUN** a window
in a roof or ceiling.

skyline, skylines **NOUN** The skyline
is the line where the sky meets
buildings or the ground • *the New York
City skyline.*

skyscraper, skyscrapers **NOUN** a
very tall building.

slab, slabs **NOUN** a thick, flat piece of
something.

slack, slacker, slackest; slacks
ADJECTIVE ❶ Something that is

a b c d e f g h i j k l m n o p q r **s** t u v w x y z

slack is loose and not firmly stretched or positioned. ❷ A slack period is one in which there is not much work to do ▷ **NOUN** ❸ The slack in a rope is the part that hangs loose ❹ IN PLURAL Slacks are casual trousers. **slackness NOUN**

slacken, slackens, slackening, slackened **VERB** ❶ If something slackens, it becomes slower or less intense • *The rain had slackened to a drizzle.* ❷ To slacken also means to become looser • *Her grip slackened on Arnold's arm.*

slag, slags, slagging, slagged **NOUN** ❶ Slag is the waste material left when ore has been melted down to remove the metal • *a slag heap.* ▷ **VERB** ❷ INFORMAL To slag someone off means to criticize them in an unpleasant way, usually behind their back.

slalom, slaloms [Said **slah-lom**] **NOUN** a skiing competition in which the competitors have to twist and turn quickly to avoid obstacles.
● **WORD HISTORY:** from Norwegian *slad + lom* meaning 'sloping path'

slam, slams, slamming, slammed **VERB** ❶ If you slam a door or if it slams, it shuts noisily and with great force. ❷ If you slam something down, you throw it down violently • *She slammed the phone down and stormed out of the room.*

slander, slanders, slandering, slandered **NOUN** ❶ Slander is something untrue and malicious said about someone ▷ **VERB** ❷ To slander someone means to say untrue and malicious things about them. **slanderous ADJECTIVE**

● **SIMILAR WORDS:** ❶ defamation,
● smear

slang NOUN Slang consists of very informal words and expressions.

slant, slants, slanting, slanted **VERB** ❶ If something slants, it slopes • *The back can be adjusted to slant into the most comfortable position.* ❷ If news or information is slanted, it is presented in a biased way ▷ **NOUN** ❸ a slope. ❹ A slant on a subject is one way of looking at it, especially a biased one.

slap, slaps, slapping, slapped **VERB** ❶ If you slap someone, you hit them with the palm of your hand. ❷ If you slap something onto a surface, you put it there quickly and noisily ▷ **NOUN** ❸ If you give someone a slap, you slap them.
● **WORD HISTORY:** from German *Schlappe,* an imitation of the sound

slash, slashes, slashing, slashed **VERB** ❶ If you slash something, you make a long, deep cut in it. ❷ INFORMAL To slash money means to reduce it greatly • *slashing prices.* ▷ **NOUN** ❸ a diagonal line that separates letters, words, or numbers, for example in the number 340/21/K.

slat, slats **NOUN** Slats are the narrow pieces of wood or metal plastic in things such as Venetian blinds. **slatted ADJECTIVE**

slate, slates, slating, slated **NOUN** ❶ Slate is a dark grey rock that splits easily into thin layers. ❷ Slates are small, flat pieces of slate used for covering roofs ▷ **VERB** ❸ INFORMAL If critics slate a play, film, or book, they criticize it severely.

▷ SPELLING NOTE: *there's SAND in my SANDwich (sandwich)*

slaughter, slaughters, slaughtering, slaughtered **VERB** ❶ To slaughter a large number of people means to kill them unjustly or cruelly. ❷ To slaughter farm animals means to kill them for meat ▷ **NOUN** ❸ Slaughter is the killing of many people.

● **SIMILAR WORDS:** ❸ carnage,
● massacre, murder

slave, slaves, slaving, slaved **NOUN** ❶ someone who is owned by another person and must work for them ▷ **VERB** ❷ If you slave for someone, you work very hard for them • *slaving away for minimum wages.* **slavery NOUN**

● **WORD HISTORY:** from Latin
● *Sclavus* place name meaning 'a Slav', because
● the Slavonic races were frequently
● conquered and made into slaves

slay, slays, slaying, slew, slain **VERB** LITERARY To slay someone means to kill them.

sleazy, sleazier, sleaziest **ADJECTIVE** A sleazy place looks dirty, run-down, and not respectable.

sled, sleds **NOUN** a sledge.

sledge, sledges **NOUN** a vehicle on runners used for travelling over snow.

sledgehammer, sledgehammers **NOUN** a large, heavy hammer.

sleek, sleeker, sleekest **ADJECTIVE** ❶ Sleek hair is smooth and shiny. ❷ Someone who is sleek looks rich and dresses elegantly.

sleep, sleeps, sleeping, slept **NOUN** ❶ Sleep is the natural state of rest in which your eyes are closed and you are unconscious. ❷ If you have a sleep, you sleep for a while • *He'll be*

ready for a sleep soon. ▷ **VERB** ❸ When you sleep, you rest in a state of sleep ▷ **PHRASE** ❹ If a sick or injured animal **is put to sleep**, it is painlessly killed.

● **SIMILAR WORDS:** ❷ doze, nap,
● slumber

sleeper, sleepers **NOUN** ❶ You use 'sleeper' to say how deeply someone sleeps • *I'm a very heavy sleeper.* ❷ a bed on a train, or a train which has beds on it. ❸ Railway sleepers are the large beams that support the rails of a railway track.

sleeping bag, sleeping bags **NOUN** a large, warm bag for sleeping in, especially when you are camping.

sleeping pill, sleeping pills **NOUN** A sleeping pill or a sleeping tablet is a pill which you take to help you sleep.

sleepout, sleepouts **NOUN** ❶ In Australia, an area of veranda or porch which has been closed off to be used as a bedroom. ❷ In New Zealand, a small building outside a house, used for sleeping.

sleepover, sleepovers **NOUN** a gathering or party at which friends spend the night at another friend's house.

sleepwalk, sleepwalks, sleepwalking, sleepwalked **VERB** If you sleepwalk, you walk around while you are asleep.

sleepy, sleepier, sleepiest **ADJECTIVE** ❶ tired and ready to go to sleep. ❷ A sleepy town or village is very quiet. **sleepily ADVERB sleepiness NOUN**

sleet NOUN Sleet is a mixture of rain and snow.

sleeve, sleeves **NOUN** The sleeves of

a
b
c
d
e
f
g
h
i
j
k
l
m
n
o
p
q
r
s
t
u
v
w
x
y
z

A
B
C
D
E
F
G
H
I
J
K
L
M
N
O
P
Q
R
S
T
U
V
W
X
Y
Z

a piece of clothing are the parts that cover your arms. **sleeveless ADJECTIVE**

sleigh, sleighs *[Said slay]* NOUN a sledge.

slender ADJECTIVE ❶ attractively thin and graceful. **❷** small in amount or degree • *the first slender hopes of peace.*

● **SIMILAR WORDS: ❶** slim, willowy

sleuth, sleuths *[Said slooth]* NOUN OLD-FASHIONED a detective.
   ● **WORD HISTORY:** a shortened
   ● form of *sleuthhound*, a tracker dog,
   ● from Old Norse *sloth* meaning
   ● 'track'

slew, slews, slewing, slewed **❶** Slew is the past tense of *slay*. **VERB ❷** If a vehicle slews, it slides or skids • *The bike slewed into the crowd.*

slice, slices, slicing, sliced NOUN **❶** A slice of cake, bread, or other food is a piece of it cut from a larger piece. **❷** a kitchen tool with a broad, flat blade • *a fish slice.* **❸** In sport, a slice is a stroke in which the player makes the ball go to one side, rather than straight ahead ▷ **VERB ❹** If you slice food, you cut it into thin pieces. **❺** To slice through something means to cut or move through it quickly, like a knife • *The ship sliced through the water.*

slick, slicker, slickest; slicks **ADJECTIVE ❶** A slick action is done quickly and smoothly • *slick passing and strong running.* **❷** A slick person speaks easily and persuasively but is not sincere • *a slick TV presenter.* ▷ **NOUN ❸** An oil slick is a layer of oil floating on the surface of the sea or a lake.

slide, slides, sliding, slid **VERB ❶** When something slides, it moves smoothly over or against something else ▷ NOUN **❷** a small piece of photographic film which can be projected onto a screen so that you can see the picture. **❸** a small piece of glass on which you put something that you want to examine through a microscope. **❹** In a playground, a slide is a structure with a steep, slippery slope for children to slide down.

slight, slighter, slightest; slights, slighting, slighted **ADJECTIVE ❶** Slight means small in amount or degree • *a slight dent.* **❷** A slight person has a slim body ▷ **PHRASE ❸** **Not in the slightest** means not at all • *This doesn't surprise me in the slightest.* ▷ **VERB ❹** If you slight someone, you insult them by behaving rudely towards them ▷ NOUN **❺** A slight is rude or insulting behaviour. **slightly ADVERB**

slim, slimmer, slimmest; slims, slimming, slimmed **ADJECTIVE ❶** A slim person is attractively thin. **❷** A slim object is thinner than usual • *a slim book.* **❸** If there is only a slim chance that something will happen, it is unlikely to happen ▷ **VERB ❹** If you are slimming, you are trying to lose weight. **slimmer NOUN**

slime NOUN Slime is an unpleasant, thick, slippery substance.

slimy, slimier, slimiest **ADJECTIVE ❶** covered in slime. **❷** Slimy people are friendly and pleasant in an insincere way • *a slimy business partner.*

sling, slings, slinging, slung **VERB**

▷ SPELLING NOTE: *Eddy Ant thinks mEAt is a grEAt trEAt to EAt (-ea-)*

① INFORMAL If you sling something somewhere, you throw it there. **②** If you sling a rope between two points, you attach it so that it hangs loosely between them ▷ NOUN **③** a piece of cloth tied round a person's neck to support a broken or injured arm. **④** a device made of ropes or cloth used for carrying things.

slip, slips, slipping, slipped VERB **①** If you slip, you accidentally slide and lose your balance. **②** If something slips, it slides out of place • *One of the knives slipped from her grasp.* **③** If you slip somewhere, you go there quickly and quietly • *She slipped out of the house.* **④** If you slip something somewhere, you put it there quickly and quietly. **⑤** If something slips to a lower level or standard, it falls to that level or standard • *The shares slipped to an all-time low.* ▷ NOUN **⑥** a small mistake. **⑦** A slip of paper is a small piece of paper. **⑧** a piece of clothing worn under a dress or skirt.

slipped disc, slipped discs NOUN a painful condition in which one of the discs in your spine has moved out of its proper position.

slipper, slippers NOUN Slippers are loose, soft shoes that you wear indoors.

slippery ADJECTIVE **①** smooth, wet, or greasy, and difficult to hold or walk on. **②** You describe a person as slippery when they cannot be trusted • *She's a slippery customer.*

slippery dip, slippery dips NOUN INFORMAL In Australian English, a children's slide at a playground or funfair.

slip rail, slip rails NOUN In Australian and New Zealand English, a rail in a fence that can be slipped out of place to make an opening.

slipstream, slipstreams NOUN The slipstream of a car or plane is the flow of air directly behind it.

slit, slits, slitting, slit VERB **①** If you slit something, you make a long, narrow cut in it ▷ NOUN **②** a long, narrow cut or opening.

slither, slithers, slithering, slithered VERB To slither somewhere means to move there by sliding along the ground in an uneven way • *The snake slithered into the water.*

sliver, slivers NOUN a small, thin piece of something.

slob, slobs NOUN INFORMAL a lazy, untidy person.

slog, slogs, slogging, slogged VERB INFORMAL If you slog at something, you work hard and steadily at it • *They are still slogging away at algebra.*

slogan, slogans NOUN a short, easily-remembered phrase used in advertising or by a political party.
● **WORD HISTORY:** from Gaelic *sluagh-ghairm* meaning 'war cry'
● **SIMILAR WORDS:** catch-phrase, motto

slop, slops, slopping, slopped VERB **①** If a liquid slops, it spills over the edge of a container in a messy way. ▷ NOUN **②** IN PLURAL You can refer to dirty water or liquid waste as slops.

slope, slopes, sloping, sloped NOUN **①** a flat surface that is at an angle, so that one end is higher than the other. **②** The slope of something is the angle at which it slopes ▷ **VERB** ❸ If a surface slopes, it is at an angle. ❹ If something slopes, it leans to one side rather than being upright • *sloping handwriting*.

● **SIMILAR WORDS:** ❶ incline,
● slant, tilt ❷ gradient, inclination

sloppy, sloppier, sloppiest
ADJECTIVE INFORMAL ❶ very messy or careless • *two sloppy performances.*
❷ foolishly sentimental • *some sloppy love story.* **sloppily ADVERB**
sloppiness NOUN

slot, slots, slotting, slotted **NOUN**
❶ a narrow opening in a machine or container, for example for putting coins in ▷ **VERB** ❷ When you slot something into something else, you put it into a space where it fits.

sloth, sloths [rhymes with **growth**]
NOUN ❶ FORMAL Sloth is laziness.
❷ a South and Central American animal that moves very slowly and hangs upside down from the branches of trees.

slouch, slouches, slouching, slouched **VERB** If you slouch, you stand or sit with your shoulders and head drooping forwards.

slouch hat, slouch hats **NOUN** a hat with a wide, flexible brim, especially an Australian army hat with the left side of the brim turned up.

Slovak, Slovaks **ADJECTIVE**
❶ belonging to or relating to Slovakia
▷ **NOUN** ❷ someone who comes from Slovakia. ❸ Slovak is the language spoken in Slovakia.

slow, slower, slowest; slows, slowing, slowed **ADJECTIVE** ❶ moving, happening, or doing something with

very little speed • *His progress was slow.* ❷ Someone who is slow is not very clever. ❸ If a clock or watch is slow, it shows a time earlier than the correct one ▷ **VERB** ❹ If something slows, slows down, or slows up, it moves or happens more slowly.
slowness NOUN

slowly ADVERB not quickly or hurriedly.

slow motion NOUN Slow motion is movement which is much slower than normal, especially in a film • *It all seemed to happen in slow motion.*

sludge NOUN Sludge is thick mud or sewage.

slug, slugs **NOUN** ❶ a small, slow-moving creature with a slimy body, like a snail without a shell.
❷ INFORMAL A slug of a strong alcoholic drink is a mouthful of it.

sluggish ADJECTIVE moving slowly and without energy • *the sluggish waters.*

sluice, sluices, sluicing, sluiced [Said *sloose*] **NOUN** ❶ a channel which carries water, with an opening called a sluicegate which can be opened or closed to control the flow of water
▷ **VERB** ❷ If you sluice something, you wash it by pouring water over it
• *He had sluiced his hands under a tap.*
● **WORD HISTORY:** from Latin
● *exclusa aqua* meaning 'water shut
● out'

slum, slums **NOUN** a poor, run-down area of a city.

slumber, slumbers, slumbering, slumbered LITERARY **NOUN**
❶ Slumber is sleep ▷ **VERB** ❷ When

you slumber, you sleep.

slump, slumps, slumping, slumped
VERB ❶ If an amount or a value slumps, it falls suddenly by a large amount. ❷ If you slump somewhere, you fall or sit down heavily • *He slumped against the side of the car.* ▷ **NOUN** ❸ a sudden, severe drop in an amount or value • *the slump in house prices.* ❹ a time when there is economic decline and high unemployment.

slur, slurs, slurring, slurred **NOUN**
❶ an insulting remark ▷ **VERB**
❷ When people slur their speech, they do not say their words clearly, often because they are drunk or ill.

slurp, slurps, slurping, slurped **VERB**
If you slurp a drink, you drink it noisily.
● **WORD HISTORY:** from Old Dutch
● *slorpen* meaning 'to sip'

slush NOUN ❶ Slush is wet melting snow. ❷ INFORMAL You can refer to sentimental love stories as slush.
slushy ADJECTIVE

slut, sluts **NOUN** OFFENSIVE a dirty, untidy woman, or one considered to be immoral.

sly, slyer or slier, slyest or sliest
ADJECTIVE ❶ A sly expression or remark shows that you know something other people do not know • *a sly smile.* ❷ A sly person is cunning and good at deceiving people. **slyly ADVERB**
● **SIMILAR WORDS:** ❷ crafty,
● cunning, devious

smack, smacks, smacking, smacked
VERB ❶ If you smack someone, you hit them with your open hand. ❷ If something smacks of something else,

it reminds you of it • *His tale smacks of fantasy.* ▷ **NOUN** ❸ If you give someone a smack, you smack them.
❹ a loud, sharp noise • *He landed with a smack on the tank.*

small, smaller, smallest; smalls
ADJECTIVE ❶ Small means not large in size, number, or amount. ❷ Small means not important or significant • *small changes.* ▷ **NOUN** ❸ The small of your back is the narrow part where your back curves slightly inwards.
● **SIMILAR WORDS:** ❶ little, tiny
● ❷ insignificant, minor, trivial

smallpox NOUN Smallpox is a serious contagious disease that causes a fever and a rash.

small talk NOUN Small talk is conversation about unimportant things.

smart, smarter, smartest; smarts, smarting, smarted **ADJECTIVE** ❶ A smart person is clean and neatly dressed. ❷ Smart means clever • *a smart idea.* ❸ A smart movement is quick and sharp ▷ **VERB** ❹ If a wound smarts, it stings. ❺ If you are smarting from criticism or unkindness, you are feeling upset by it. **smartly ADVERB**

smarten, smartens, smartening, smartened **VERB** If you smarten something up, you make it look neater and tidier.

smash, smashes, smashing, smashed
VERB ❶ If you smash something, you break it into a lot of pieces by hitting it or dropping it. ❷ To smash through something such as a wall means to go through it by breaking it.

a
b
c
d
e
f
g
h
i
j
k
l
m
n
o
p
q
r
s
t
u
v
w
x
y
z

❸ To smash against something means to hit it with great force • *An immense wave smashed against the hull.* ▷ **NOUN** ❹ INFORMAL If a play or film is a smash or a smash hit, it is very successful. ❺ a car crash. ❻ In tennis, a smash is a stroke in which the player hits the ball downwards very hard.

smashing **ADJECTIVE** INFORMAL If you describe something as smashing, you mean you like it very much.

smattering **NOUN** A smattering of knowledge or information is a very small amount of it • *a smattering of Russian.*

smear, smears, smearing, smeared **NOUN** ❶ a dirty, greasy mark on a surface • *a smear of pink lipstick.* ❷ an untrue and malicious rumour ▷ **VERB** ❸ If something smears a surface, it makes dirty, greasy marks on it • *The blade was chipped and smeared.* ❹ If you smear a surface with a greasy or sticky substance, you spread a layer of the substance over the surface.

smell, smells, smelling, smelled or smelt **NOUN** ❶ The smell of something is a quality it has which you perceive through your nose • *a smell of damp wood.* ❷ Your sense of smell is your ability to smell things ▷ **VERB** ❸ If something smells, it has a quality you can perceive through your nose, especially an unpleasant quality. ❹ If you smell something, you become aware of it through your nose. ❺ If you can smell something such as danger or trouble, you feel it is present or likely to happen.

● **SIMILAR WORDS:** ❶ odour, scent

smelly, smellier, smelliest

ADJECTIVE having a strong, unpleasant smell.

smelt, smelts, smelting, smelted **VERB** To smelt a metal ore means to heat it until it melts, so that the metal can be extracted.

smile, smiles, smiling, smiled **VERB** ❶ When you smile, the corners of your mouth move outwards and slightly upwards because you are pleased or amused ▷ **NOUN** ❷ the expression you have when you smile.

smirk, smirks, smirking, smirked **VERB** ❶ When you smirk, you smile in a sneering or sarcastic way • *The boy smirked and turned the volume up.* ▷ **NOUN** ❷ a sneering or sarcastic smile.

smith, smiths **NOUN** someone who makes things out of iron, gold, or another metal.

smitten **ADJECTIVE** If you are smitten with someone or something, you are very impressed with or enthusiastic about them • *They were totally smitten with each other.*

smock, smocks **NOUN** a loose garment like a long blouse.

smog **NOUN** Smog is a mixture of smoke and fog which occurs in some industrial cities.

smoke, smokes, smoking, smoked **NOUN** ❶ Smoke is a mixture of gas and small particles sent into the air when something burns ▷ **VERB** ❷ If something is smoking, smoke is coming from it. ❸ When someone smokes a cigarette or pipe, they suck smoke from it into their mouth and blow it out again. ❹ To smoke fish or meat means to hang it over burning wood so that the smoke preserves it and gives it a pleasant flavour • *smoked bacon.* **smoker** NOUN **smoking** NOUN

smoky, smokier, smokiest
ADJECTIVE A smoky place is full of smoke.

smooth, smoother, smoothest; smooths, smoothing, smoothed
ADJECTIVE ❶ A smooth surface has no roughness and no holes in it. ❷ A smooth liquid or mixture has no lumps in it. ❸ A smooth movement or process happens evenly and steadily • *smooth acceleration.* ❹ Smooth also means successful and without problems • *staff responsible for the smooth running of the hall.* ▷ VERB ❺ If you smooth something, you move your hands over it to make it smooth and flat. **smoothly** ADVERB **smoothness** NOUN

smoothie, smoothies NOUN a thick type of drink made in an electric blender from milk, fruit and crushed ice.

smother, smothers, smothering, smothered VERB ❶ If you smother a fire, you cover it with something to put it out. ❷ To smother a person means to cover their face with something so that they cannot breathe. ❸ To smother someone also means to give them too much love and protection • *She loved her own children, almost smothering them with love.* ❹ If you smother an emotion, you control it so that people do not notice it • *They tried to smother their glee.*

smothered ADJECTIVE completely

covered with something • *a spectacular trellis smothered in climbing roses.*

smoulder, smoulders, smouldering, smouldered VERB ❶ When something smoulders, it burns slowly, producing smoke but no flames. ❷ If a feeling is smouldering inside you, you feel it very strongly but do not show it • *smouldering with resentment.*

smudge, smudges, smudging, smudged NOUN ❶ a dirty or blurred mark or a smear on something ▷ VERB ❷ If you smudge something, you make it dirty or messy by touching it or marking it.

smug, smugger, smuggest
ADJECTIVE Someone who is smug is very pleased with how good or clever they are. **smugly** ADVERB **smugness** NOUN

smuggle, smuggles, smuggling, smuggled VERB To smuggle things or people into or out of a place means to take them there illegally or secretly.

smuggler, smugglers NOUN someone who smuggles goods illegally into a country.

snack, snacks NOUN a light, quick meal.

snag, snags, snagging, snagged
NOUN ❶ a small problem or disadvantage • *There is one snag: it is not true.* ❷ In Australian and New Zealand English, a sausage. ▷ VERB ❸ If you snag your clothing, you damage it by catching it on something sharp.

snail, snails NOUN a small, slow-moving creature with a long,

a b c d e f g h i j k l m n o p q r **s** t u v w x y z

▷ SPELLING NOTE: *LEt's measure the angLE (angle)*

shiny body and a shell on its back.

snail mail NOUN INFORMAL the conventional postal system, as opposed to email.

snake, snakes, snaking, snaked NOUN **①** a long, thin, scaly reptile with no legs ▷ VERB **②** Something that snakes moves in long winding curves • *The queue snaked out of the shop.*

snap, snaps, snapping, snapped VERB **①** If something snaps or if you snap it, it breaks with a sharp cracking noise. **②** If you snap something into a particular position, you move it there quickly with a sharp sound. **③** If an animal snaps at you, it shuts its jaws together quickly as if to bite you. **④** If someone snaps at you, they speak in a sharp, unfriendly way. **⑤** If you snap someone, you take a quick photograph of them ▷ NOUN **⑥** the sound of something snapping. **⑦** INFORMAL a photograph taken quickly and casually ▷ ADJECTIVE **⑧** A snap decision or action is taken suddenly without careful thought.

snapper, snappers NOUN a fish with edible pink flesh, found in waters around Australia and New Zealand.

snapshot, snapshots NOUN a photograph taken quickly and casually.

snare, snares, snaring, snared NOUN **①** a trap for catching birds or small animals ▷ VERB **②** To snare an animal or bird means to catch it using a snare.

snarl, snarls, snarling, snarled VERB **①** When an animal snarls, it bares its teeth and makes a fierce growling noise. **②** If you snarl, you say

something in a fierce, angry way ▷ NOUN **③** the noise an animal makes when it snarls.

snatch, snatches, snatching, snatched VERB **①** If you snatch something, you reach out for it quickly and take it. **②** If you snatch an amount of time or an opportunity, you quickly make use of it ▷ NOUN **③** If you make a snatch at something, you reach out for it quickly to try to take it. **④** A snatch of conversation or song is a very small piece of it.

sneak, sneaks, sneaking, sneaked VERB **①** If you sneak somewhere, you go there quickly trying not to be seen or heard. **②** If you sneak something somewhere, you take it there secretly ▷ NOUN **③** INFORMAL someone who tells people in authority that someone else has done something wrong.

sneaker, sneakers Sneakers are casual shoes with rubber soles.

sneaking ADJECTIVE If you have a sneaking feeling about something or someone, you have this feeling rather reluctantly • *I had a sneaking suspicion that she was enjoying herself.*

sneaky, sneakier, sneakiest ADJECTIVE INFORMAL Someone who is sneaky does things secretly rather than openly.

sneer, sneers, sneering, sneered VERB **①** If you sneer at someone or something, you show by your expression and your comments that you think they are stupid or inferior ▷ NOUN **②** the expression on someone's face when they sneer.

sneeze, sneezes, sneezing, sneezed

▷ SPELLING NOTE: *A Rude Idiot Thought He Might Eat Toffee In Church* (<u>arithmetic</u>)

VERB ❶ When you sneeze, you suddenly take in breath and blow it down your nose noisily, because there is a tickle in your nose ▷ **NOUN ❷** an act of sneezing.

snide ADJECTIVE A snide comment or remark criticizes someone in a nasty and unfair way.

sniff, sniffs, sniffing, sniffed **VERB ❶** When you sniff, you breathe in air through your nose hard enough to make a sound. **❷** If you sniff something, you smell it by sniffing. **❸** You can say that a person sniffs at something when they do not think very much of it • *Bessie sniffed at his household arrangements.* ▷ **NOUN ❹** the noise you make when you sniff. **❺** A sniff of something is a smell of it • *a sniff at the flowers.*

snigger, sniggers, sniggering, sniggered **VERB ❶** If you snigger, you laugh in a quiet, sly way • *They were sniggering at her accent.* ▷ **NOUN ❷** a quiet, disrespectful laugh.

snip, snips, snipping, snipped **VERB ❶** If you snip something, you cut it with scissors or shears in a single quick action ▷ **NOUN ❷** a small cut made by scissors or shears.

snippet, snippets **NOUN** A snippet of something such as information or news is a small piece of it.

snob, snobs **NOUN ❶** someone who admires upper-class people and looks down on lower-class people. **❷** someone who believes that they are better than other people. **snobbery NOUN snobbish ADJECTIVE**

snooker NOUN Snooker is a game

played on a large table covered with smooth green cloth. Players score points by hitting different coloured balls into side pockets using a long stick called a cue.

snoop, snoops, snooping, snooped **VERB** INFORMAL Someone who is snooping is secretly looking round a place to find out things.
● **WORD HISTORY:** from Dutch *snoepen* meaning 'to eat furtively'

snooper NOUN a person who interferes in other people's business.

snooze, snoozes, snoozing, snoozed INFORMAL **VERB ❶** If you snooze, you sleep lightly for a short time, especially during the day ▷ **NOUN ❷** a short, light sleep.

snore, snores, snoring, snored **VERB ❶** When a sleeping person snores, they make a loud noise each time they breathe ▷ **NOUN ❷** the noise someone makes when they snore.

snorkel, snorkels **NOUN** a tube you can breathe through when you are swimming just under the surface of the sea. **snorkelling NOUN**
● **WORD HISTORY:** from German *Schnorchel*, originally an air pipe for a submarine

snort, snorts, snorting, snorted **VERB ❶** When people or animals snort, they force breath out through their nose in a noisy way • *Sarah snorted with laughter.* ▷ **NOUN ❷** the noise you make when you snort.

snout, snouts **NOUN** An animal's snout is its nose.

snow, snows, snowing, snowed **NOUN ❶** Snow consists of flakes of

a b c d e f g h i j k l m n o p q r **s** t u v w x y z

A
B
C
D
E
F
G
H
I
J
K
L
M
N
O
P
Q
R
S
T
U
V
W
X
Y
Z

ice crystals which fall from the sky in cold weather ▷ **VERB** ❷ When it snows, snow falls from the sky.

snowball, snowballs, snowballing, snowballed **NOUN** ❶ a ball of snow for throwing ▷ **VERB** ❷ When something such as a project snowballs, it grows rapidly.

snowdrift, snowdrifts **NOUN** a deep pile of snow formed by the wind.

snowdrop, snowdrops **NOUN** a small white flower which appears in early spring.

snowman, snowmen **NOUN** a large mound of snow moulded into the shape of a person.

snub, snubs, snubbing, snubbed **VERB** ❶ To snub someone means to behave rudely towards them, especially by making an insulting remark or ignoring them ▷ **NOUN** ❷ an insulting remark or a piece of rude behaviour ▷ **ADJECTIVE** ❸ A snub nose is short and turned-up.
  ● **SIMILAR WORDS:** ❷ affront, insult, slap in the face

snuff NOUN Snuff is powdered tobacco which people take by sniffing it up their noses.

snug, snugger, snuggest **ADJECTIVE** A snug place is warm and comfortable. If you are snug, you are warm and comfortable. **snugly ADVERB**

snuggle, snuggles, snuggling, snuggled **VERB** If you snuggle somewhere, you cuddle up more closely to something or someone.

SO ADVERB ❶ 'So' is used to refer back to what has just been mentioned • Had he locked the car? If so, where

were the keys? ❷ 'So' is used to mean also • He laughed, and so did Jarvis. ❸ 'So' can be used to mean 'therefore' • It's a bit expensive, so I don't think I will get one. ❹ 'So' is used when you are talking about the degree or extent of something • Why are you so cruel? ❺ 'So' is used before words like 'much' and 'many' to say that there is a definite limit to something • There are only so many questions that can be asked about the record.
▷ **CONJUNCTION** ❻ 'So that' and 'so as' are used to introduce the reason for doing something • to die so that you might live.

soak, soaks, soaking, soaked **VERB** ❶ To soak something or leave it to soak means to put it in a liquid and leave it there. ❷ When a liquid soaks something, it makes it very wet. ❸ When something soaks up a liquid, the liquid is drawn up into it.
  ● **SIMILAR WORDS:** ❷ saturate, wet

soaked ADJECTIVE extremely wet.

soaking ADJECTIVE If something is soaking, it is very wet.

soap, soaps **NOUN** Soap is a substance made of natural oils and fats and used for washing yourself. **soapy ADJECTIVE**

soap opera, soap operas **NOUN** a popular television drama serial about people's daily lives.

soar, soars, soaring, soared **VERB** ❶ If an amount soars, it quickly increases by a great deal • Property prices soared. ❷ If something soars into the air, it quickly goes up into the air. **soaring ADJECTIVE**

▷ SPELLING NOTE: Betty Eats Cakes And Uses Seven Eggs (<u>because</u>)

sob, sobs, sobbing, sobbed VERB
❶ When someone sobs, they cry in a
noisy way, breathing in short breaths
▷ NOUN ❷ the noise made when you
cry.

sober, soberer, soberest; sobers,
sobering, sobered ADJECTIVE ❶ If
someone is sober, they are not drunk.
❷ Sober also means serious and
thoughtful. ❸ Sober colours are plain
and rather dull ▷ VERB ❹ To sober
up means to become sober after being
drunk. **soberly** ADVERB

sobering ADJECTIVE Something
which is sobering makes you serious
and thoughtful • *the sobering lesson of
the last year.*

so-called ADJECTIVE You use
'so-called' to say that the name by
which something is called is incorrect
or misleading • *so-called
environmentally-friendly products.*

soccer NOUN Soccer is a game
played by two teams of eleven players
kicking a ball in an attempt to score
goals.
  ● WORD HISTORY: formed from
  Association Football

sociable ADJECTIVE Sociable
people are friendly and enjoy talking to
other people. **sociability** NOUN
  ● SIMILAR WORDS: friendly,
  gregarious, outgoing

social ADJECTIVE ❶ to do with
society or life within a society • *women
from similar social backgrounds.* ❷ to
do with leisure activities that involve
meeting other people. **socially**
ADVERB

socialism NOUN Socialism is the
political belief that the state should

own industries on behalf of the people
and that everyone should be equal.
socialist ADJECTIVE OR NOUN

socialize, socializes, socializing,
socialized; *also spelt* **socialise** VERB
When people socialize, they meet
other people socially, for example at
parties.

social security NOUN Social
security is a system by which the
government pays money regularly to
people who have no other income or
only a very small income.

social work NOUN Social work
involves giving help and advice to
people with serious financial or family
problems. **social worker** NOUN

society, societies NOUN ❶ Society
is the people in a particular country or
region • *a major problem in society.*
❷ an organization for people who
have the same interest or aim • *the
school debating society.* ❸ Society is
also rich, upper-class, fashionable
people.
  ● SIMILAR WORDS: ❶ civilization,
  culture

sociology NOUN Sociology is the
study of human societies and the
relationships between groups in these
societies. **sociological** ADJECTIVE
sociologist NOUN

sock, socks NOUN Socks are pieces of
clothing covering your foot and ankle
• *a pair of blue socks.*

socket, sockets NOUN ❶ a place on
a wall or on a piece of electrical
equipment into which you can put a
plug or bulb. ❷ Any hollow part or
opening into which another part fits
can be called a socket • *eye sockets.*

▷ SPELLING NOTE: there's a rAKE in the brAKEs (brake)

A
B
C
D
E
F
G
H
I
J
K
L
M
N
O
P
Q
R
S
T
U
V
W
X
Y
Z

sod NOUN LITERARY The sod is the surface of the ground, together with the grass and roots growing in it.

soda, sodas NOUN ❶ Soda is the same as **soda water**. ❷ Soda is also sodium in the form of crystals or a powder, and is used for baking or cleaning.

soda lime NOUN (SCIENCE) a solid mixture of sodium and calcium hydroxide used to absorb moisture and carbon dioxide.

soda water, soda waters NOUN Soda water is fizzy water used for mixing with alcoholic drinks or fruit juice.

sodden ADJECTIVE soaking wet.

sodium NOUN (SCIENCE) Sodium is a silvery-white chemical element which combines with other chemicals. Salt is a sodium compound. Sodium's atomic number is 11 and its symbol is Na.

sofa, sofas NOUN a long comfortable seat with a back and arms for two or three people.
● **WORD HISTORY:** from Arabic
● *suffah* meaning 'an upholstered
● raised platform'

soft, softer, softest ADJECTIVE
❶ Something soft is not hard, stiff, or firm. ❷ Soft also means very gentle • *a soft breeze.* ❸ A soft sound or voice is quiet and not harsh. ❹ A soft colour or light is not bright. **softly** ADVERB

soft drink, soft drinks NOUN any cold, nonalcoholic drink.

soften, softens, softening, softened VERB ❶ If something is softened or

softens, it becomes less hard, stiff, or firm. ❷ If you soften, you become more sympathetic and less critical • *Phillida softened as she spoke.*

software NOUN (ICT) Computer programs are known as software.

soggy, soggier, soggiest ADJECTIVE unpleasantly wet or full of water.

soil, soils, soiling, soiled NOUN ❶ Soil is the top layer on the surface of the earth in which plants grow ▷ VERB ❷ If you soil something, you make it dirty. **soiled** ADJECTIVE
● **SIMILAR WORDS:** ❶ earth,
● ground

solace NOUN LITERARY Solace is something that makes you feel less sad • *I found solace in writing.*

solar ADJECTIVE (SCIENCE)
❶ relating or belonging to the sun.
❷ using the sun's light and heat as a source of energy • *a solar-powered calculator.*

solar system NOUN The solar system is the sun and all the planets, comets, and asteroids that orbit round it.

solder, solders, soldering, soldered VERB ❶ To solder two pieces of metal together means to join them with molten metal ▷ NOUN ❷ Solder is the soft metal used for soldering.

soldier, soldiers NOUN a person in an army.

sole, soles, soling, soled ADJECTIVE
❶ The sole thing or person of a particular type is the only one of that type ▷ NOUN ❷ The sole of your foot or shoe is the underneath part. ❸ a flat sea-water fish which you can eat

▷ SPELLING NOTE: *you'll brEAK that Electrical Aerial, Kitty (break)*

▷ **VERB** ❹ When a shoe is soled, a sole is fitted to it.

solely ADVERB If something involves solely one thing, it involves that thing and nothing else.

solemn ADJECTIVE Solemn means serious rather than cheerful or humorous. **solemnly ADVERB solemnity NOUN**

solenoid, solenoids **NOUN** (SCIENCE) a cylindrical coil of wire which acts as a magnet when an electric current is passed through it.

solicitor, solicitors **NOUN** a lawyer who gives legal advice and prepares legal documents and cases.

solid, solids **ADJECTIVE** ❶ A solid substance or object is hard or firm, and not in the form of a liquid or gas. ❷ You say that something is solid when it is not hollow • solid steel. ❸ You say that a structure is solid when it is strong and not likely to fall down • solid fences. ❹ You use 'solid' to say that something happens for a period of time without interruption • I cried for two solid days. ▷ **NOUN** ❺ a solid substance or object. **solidly ADVERB**

solidarity NOUN If a group of people show solidarity, they show unity and support for each other.

soliloquy, soliloquies [Said sol-*lill*-ok-wee] **NOUN** (ENGLISH) a speech in a play made by a character who is alone on the stage.
  ● **WORD HISTORY:** from Latin solus
  ● meaning 'alone' and loqui meaning
  ● 'to speak'

solitary ADJECTIVE ❶ A solitary activity is one that you do on your own. ❷ A solitary person or animal spends a lot of time alone. ❸ If there is a solitary person or object somewhere, there is only one.

solitary confinement NOUN A prisoner in solitary confinement is being kept alone in a prison cell.

solitude NOUN Solitude is the state of being alone.
  ● **SIMILAR WORDS:** isolation,
  ● seclusion

solo, solos **NOUN** ❶ a piece of music played or sung by one person alone ▷ **ADJECTIVE** ❷ A solo performance or activity is done by one person alone • my first solo flight. ▷ **ADVERB** ❸ Solo means alone • to sail solo around the world.

soloist, soloists **NOUN** a person who performs a solo.

solstice, solstices **NOUN** one of the two times in the year when the sun is at its furthest point south or north of the equator.
  ● **WORD HISTORY:** from Latin sol
  ● meaning 'sun' and sistere meaning
  ● 'to stand still'

soluble ADJECTIVE (SCIENCE) A soluble substance is able to dissolve in liquid.

solution, solutions **NOUN** ❶ a way of dealing with a problem or difficult situation • a quick solution to our problem. ❷ The solution to a riddle or a puzzle is the answer. ❸ (SCIENCE) a liquid in which a solid substance has been dissolved.

solve, solves, solving, solved **VERB** (MATHS) If you solve a problem or a

question, you find a solution or
answer to it.
● **SIMILAR WORDS:** answer, resolve,
● work out

solvent, solvents **ADJECTIVE** ❶ If a
person or company is solvent, they
have enough money to pay all their
debts ▷ **NOUN** ❷ a liquid that can
dissolve other substances. **solvency**
NOUN

Somali, Somalis **ADJECTIVE**
❶ belonging or relating to Somalia
▷ **NOUN** ❷ The Somalis are a group
of people who live in Somalia.
❸ Somali is the language spoken by
Somalis.

sombre **ADJECTIVE** ❶ Sombre
colours are dark and dull. ❷ A sombre
person is serious, sad, or gloomy.

some ❶ You use 'some' to refer to a
quantity or number when you are not
stating the quantity or number exactly
• There's some money on the table.
❷ You use 'some' to emphasize that a
quantity or number is fairly large • She
had been there for some days. **ADVERB**
❸ You use 'some' in front of a
number to show that it is not exact • a
fishing village some seven miles north.

somebody **PRONOUN** Somebody
means someone.
● **USAGE NOTE:** Somebody and
● someone mean the same

some day **ADVERB** Some day
means at a date in the future that is
unknown or that has not yet been
decided.

somehow **ADVERB** ❶ You use
'somehow' to say that you do not
know how something was done or will
be done • You'll find a way of doing it

somehow. ❷ You use 'somehow' to
say that you do not know the reason
for something • Somehow it didn't feel
quite right.

someone **PRONOUN** You use
'someone' to refer to a person without
saying exactly who you mean.
● **USAGE NOTE:** Someone and
● somebody mean the same

somersault, somersaults **NOUN** a
forwards or backwards roll in which
the head is placed on the ground and
the body is brought over it.
● **WORD HISTORY:** from Old
● Provençal sobre meaning 'over' and
● saut meaning 'jump'

something **PRONOUN** You use
'something' to refer to anything that is
not a person without saying exactly
what you mean.

sometime **ADVERB** ❶ at a time in
the future or the past that is unknown
or that has not yet been fixed • He has
to find out sometime. ▷ **ADJECTIVE**
❷ FORMAL 'Sometime' is used to say
that a person had a particular job or
role in the past • a sometime actress,
dancer and singer.

sometimes **ADVERB** occasionally,
rather than always or never.

somewhat **ADVERB** to some
extent or degree • The future seemed
somewhat bleak.

somewhere **ADVERB**
❶ 'Somewhere' is used to refer to a
place without stating exactly where it
is • There has to be a file somewhere.
❷ 'Somewhere' is used when giving
an approximate amount, number, or
time • somewhere between the winter of
1989 and the summer of 1991.

▷ SPELLING NOTE: I want to see (C) your licenCe (licence)

son, sons NOUN Someone's son is their male child.

sonar NOUN Sonar is equipment on a ship which calculates the depth of the sea or the position of an underwater object using sound waves.
● WORD HISTORY: from So(und) Na(vigation) R(anging)

sonata, sonatas NOUN a piece of classical music, usually in three or more movements, for piano or for another instrument with or without piano.

song, songs NOUN a piece of music with words that are sung to the music.

songbird, songbirds NOUN a bird that produces musical sounds like singing.

son-in-law, sons-in-law NOUN Someone's son-in-law is the husband of their daughter.

sonnet, sonnets NOUN (ENGLISH) a poem with 14 lines, in which lines rhyme according to fixed patterns.
● WORD HISTORY: from Old Provençal sonet meaning 'little poem'

soon, sooner, soonest ADVERB If something is going to happen soon, it will happen in a very short time.

soot NOUN Soot is black powder which rises in the smoke from a fire.
sooty ADJECTIVE

soothe, soothes, soothing, soothed VERB ❶ If you soothe someone who is angry or upset, you make them calmer. ❷ Something that soothes pain makes the pain less severe.
soothing ADJECTIVE

sophisticated ADJECTIVE ❶ Sophisticated people have refined or cultured tastes or habits. ❷ A sophisticated machine or device is made using advanced and complicated methods.
sophistication NOUN
● SIMILAR WORDS: ❶ cultured, urbane

soppy, soppier, soppiest ADJECTIVE INFORMAL silly or foolishly sentimental.

soprano, sopranos NOUN a woman, girl, or boy with a singing voice in the highest range of musical notes.

sorcerer, sorcerers [Said sor-ser-er] NOUN a person who performs magic by using the power of evil spirits.

sorceress, sorceresses NOUN a female sorcerer.

sorcery NOUN Sorcery is magic that uses the power of evil spirits.

sordid ADJECTIVE ❶ dishonest or immoral • a rather sordid business. ❷ dirty, unpleasant, or depressing • the sordid guest house.
● SIMILAR WORDS: ❷ seedy, sleazy, squalid

sore, sorer, sorest; sores ADJECTIVE ❶ If part of your body is sore, it causes you pain and discomfort. ❷ LITERARY 'Sore' is used to emphasize something • The President is in sore need of friends. ▷ NOUN ❸ a painful place where your skin has become infected. **sorely** ADVERB **soreness** NOUN
● SIMILAR WORDS: ❶ painful, sensitive, tender

sorghum [Said saw-gum] NOUN a

type of tropical grass that is grown for hay, grain, and syrup.

sorrow, sorrows NOUN ❶ Sorrow is deep sadness or regret. ❷ Sorrows are things that cause sorrow • *the sorrows of this world.*

sorry, sorrier, sorriest ADJECTIVE ❶ If you are sorry about something, you feel sadness or regret about it. ❷ feeling sympathy for someone. ❸ 'Sorry' is used to describe people and things that are in a bad physical or mental state • *She was in a pretty sorry state when we found her.*
● SIMILAR WORDS: ❶ apologetic, ● contrite, regretful

sort, sorts, sorting, sorted NOUN ❶ The different sorts of something are the different types of it ▷ VERB ❷ To sort things means to arrange them into different groups or types.
sort out VERB If you sort out a problem or misunderstanding, you deal with it and find a solution to it.
● USAGE NOTE: When you use *sort* in its singular form, the adjective before it should also be singular: *that sort of car.* When you use the plural form *sorts*, the adjective before it should be plural: *those sorts of shop; those sorts of shops*
● SIMILAR WORDS: ❶ kind, type, ● variety

SOS NOUN An SOS is a signal that you are in danger and need help.

so-so ADJECTIVE neither good nor bad • *The food is so-so.*

soufflé, soufflés [*Said soo-flay*]; *also spelt* **souffle** NOUN a light, fluffy food made from beaten egg whites and other ingredients that is baked in the oven • *Did your soufflé rise?*

sought the past tense and past participle of **seek**.

soul, souls NOUN ❶ A person's soul is the spiritual part of them that is supposed to continue after their body is dead. ❷ People also use 'soul' to refer to a person's mind, character, thoughts, and feelings. ❸ 'Soul' can be used to mean person • *There was not a soul there.* ❹ Soul is a type of pop music.

sound, sounds, sounding, sounded; sounder, soundest NOUN ❶ (SCIENCE) Sound is everything that can be heard. It is caused by vibrations travelling through air or water to your ear. ❷ A particular sound is something that you hear. ❸ The sound of someone or something is the impression you have of them • *I like the sound of your father's grandfather.* ▷ VERB ❹ If something sounds or if you sound it, it makes a noise. ❺ To sound something deep, such as a well or the sea, means to measure how deep it is using a weighted line or sonar ▷ ADJECTIVE ❻ in good condition • *a guarantee that a house is sound.* ❼ reliable and sensible • *The logic behind the argument seems sound.*
soundly ADVERB

sound bite, sound bites NOUN a short and memorable sentence or phrase extracted from a longer speech for use on radio or television.

sound effect, sound effects NOUN Sound effects are sounds created artificially to make a play more realistic, especially a radio play.

soundproof ADJECTIVE If a room

is soundproof, sound cannot get into it or out of it.

soundtrack, soundtracks NOUN The soundtrack of a film is the part you hear.

soup, soups NOUN Soup is liquid food made by boiling meat, fish, or vegetables in water.

sour, sours, souring, soured
ADJECTIVE ❶ If something is sour, it has a sharp, acid taste. ❷ Sour milk has an unpleasant taste because it is no longer fresh. ❸ A sour person is bad-tempered and unfriendly ▷ VERB ❹ If a friendship, situation, or attitude sours or if something sours it, it becomes less friendly, enjoyable, or hopeful.

source, sources NOUN ❶ The source of something is the person, place, or thing that it comes from • *the source of his confidence.* ❷ (HISTORY) A source is a person or book that provides information for a news story or for research. ❸ The source of a river or stream is the place where it begins.

● **USAGE NOTE:** Do not confuse the
● spellings of *source* and *sauce*, which
● can sound very similar

sour grapes PLURAL NOUN You describe someone's behaviour as sour grapes when they say something is worthless but secretly want it and cannot have it.

south NOUN ❶ The south is the direction to your right when you are looking towards the place where the sun rises. ❷ The south of a place or country is the part which is towards the south when you are in the centre

▷ ADVERB OR ADJECTIVE ❸ South means towards the south • *The taxi headed south* • *the south end of the site.*
▷ ADJECTIVE ❹ A south wind blows from the south.

South America NOUN South America is the fourth largest continent. It has the Pacific Ocean on its west side, the Atlantic on the east, and the Antarctic to the south. South America is joined to North America by the Isthmus of Panama. **South American** ADJECTIVE

south-east NOUN, ADVERB, OR ADJECTIVE South-east is halfway between south and east.

south-easterly ADJECTIVE ❶ South-easterly means to or towards the south-east. ❷ A south-easterly wind blows from the south-east.

south-eastern ADJECTIVE in or from the south-east.

southerly ADJECTIVE ❶ Southerly means to or towards the south. ❷ A southerly wind blows from the south.

southern ADJECTIVE in or from the south.

Southern Cross NOUN The Southern Cross is a small group of stars which can be seen from the southern part of the earth, and which is represented on the national flags of Australia and New Zealand.

South Pole NOUN (GEOGRAPHY) The South Pole is the place on the surface of the earth that is farthest towards the south.

southward or **southwards**
ADVERB ❶ Southward or southwards

a
b
c
d
e
f
g
h
i
j
k
l
m
n
o
p
q
r
s
t
u
v
w
x
y
z

▷ SPELLING NOTE: *plaice the fish has a glittering 'EYE' (I) (plaice)*

means towards the south • *the dusty road which led southwards.*
▷ **ADJECTIVE** ❷ The southward part of something is the south part.

south-west NOUN, ADVERB, OR ADJECTIVE South-west is halfway between south and west.

south-westerly ADJECTIVE ❶ South-westerly means to or towards the south-west. ❷ A south-westerly wind blows from the south-west.

south-western ADJECTIVE in or from the south-west.

souvenir, souvenirs **NOUN** something you keep to remind you of a holiday, place, or event.
● **WORD HISTORY:** from French *se souvenir* meaning 'to remember'

sovereign, sovereigns [*Said* **sov**-rin] **NOUN** ❶ a king, queen, or royal ruler of a country. ❷ In the past, a sovereign was a British gold coin worth one pound ▷ **ADJECTIVE** ❸ A sovereign state or country is independent and not under the authority of any other country.

sovereignty [*Said* **sov**-rin-tee] **NOUN** Sovereignty is the political power that a country has to govern itself.

Soviet, Soviets [*Said* **soh**-vee-et] **ADJECTIVE** ❶ belonging or relating to the country that used to be the Soviet Union ▷ **NOUN** ❷ The people and the government of the country that used to be the Soviet Union were sometimes referred to as the Soviets.

sow, sows, sowing, sowed, sown [*Said* **soh**] **VERB** ❶ To sow seeds or sow an area of land with seeds means to plant them in the ground. ❷ To sow undesirable feelings or attitudes means to cause them • *You have sown discontent.*

sow, sows [*rhymes with* **now**] **NOUN** an adult female pig.

soya NOUN Soya flour, margarine, oil, and milk are made from soya beans.
● **WORD HISTORY:** from Chinese *chiang yu* meaning 'paste sauce'

soya bean, soya beans **NOUN** Soya beans are a type of edible Asian bean.

spa, spas **NOUN** a place where water containing minerals bubbles out of the ground, at which people drink or bathe in the water to improve their health.
● **WORD HISTORY:** from the Belgian town *Spa* where there are mineral springs

space, spaces, spacing, spaced **NOUN** ❶ Space is the area that is empty or available in a place, building, or container. ❷ Space is the area beyond the earth's atmosphere surrounding the stars and planets. ❸ a gap between two things • *the space between the tables.* ❹ Space can also refer to a period of time • *two incidents in the space of a week.* ▷ **VERB** ❺ If you space a series of things, you arrange them with gaps between them.

spacecraft NOUN a rocket or other vehicle that can travel in space.

spaceman, spacemen **NOUN** someone who travels in space.

spaceship, spaceships **NOUN** a spacecraft that carries people through space • *He and his brother claimed to have been abducted by an aliens.*

space shuttle, space shuttles
NOUN a spacecraft designed to be used many times for travelling out into space and back again.

spacious ADJECTIVE having or providing a lot of space • *the spacious living room.*
  ● SIMILAR WORDS: capacious, commodious, roomy

spade, spades NOUN ❶ a tool with a flat metal blade and a long handle used for digging. ❷ Spades is one of the four suits in a pack of playing cards. It is marked by a black symbol like a heart-shaped leaf with a stem.

spaghetti [Said spag-**get**-ee] NOUN Spaghetti consists of long, thin pieces of pasta.

spam NOUN unwanted e-mails, usually containing advertising.

span, spans, spanning, spanned
NOUN ❶ the period of time during which something exists or functions • *looking back today over a span of forty years.* ❷ The span of something is the total length of it from one end to the other ▷ VERB ❸ If something spans a particular length of time, it lasts throughout that time • *a career that spanned 50 years.* ❹ A bridge that spans something stretches right across it.

spangle, spangles, spangling, spangled VERB ❶ If something is spangled, it is covered with small, sparkling objects ▷ NOUN ❷ Spangles are small sparkling pieces of metal or plastic used to decorate clothing or hair.

Spaniard, Spaniards [Said span-yard] NOUN someone who comes from Spain.

spaniel, spaniels NOUN a dog with long drooping ears and a silky coat.
  ● WORD HISTORY: from Old French *espaigneul* meaning 'Spanish dog'

Spanish ADJECTIVE ❶ belonging or relating to Spain ▷ NOUN ❷ Spanish is the main language spoken in Spain, and is also spoken by many people in Central and South America.

spank, spanks, spanking, spanked
VERB If a child is spanked, it is punished by being slapped, usually on its leg or bottom.

spanner, spanners NOUN a tool with a specially shaped end that fits round a nut to turn it.

spar, spars, sparring, sparred VERB
❶ When boxers spar, they hit each other with light punches for practice. ❷ To spar with someone also means to argue with them, but not in an unpleasant or serious way ▷ NOUN ❸ a strong pole that a sail is attached to on a yacht or ship.

spare, spares, sparing, spared
ADJECTIVE ❶ extra to what is needed • *What does she do in her spare time?* ▷ NOUN ❷ a thing that is extra to what is needed ▷ VERB ❸ If you spare something for a particular purpose, you make it available • *Few troops could be spared to go abroad.* ❹ If someone is spared an unpleasant experience, they are prevented from suffering it • *The capital was spared the misery of an all-out train strike.*

sparing ADJECTIVE If you are

sparing with something, you use it in very small quantities. **sparingly** **ADVERB**

spark, sparks, sparking, sparked **NOUN** **①** a tiny, bright piece of burning material thrown up by a fire. **②** a small flash of light caused by electricity. **③** A spark of feeling is a small amount of it • *that tiny spark of excitement.* ▷ **VERB** **④** If something sparks, it throws out sparks. **⑤** If one thing sparks another thing off, it causes the second thing to start happening • *The tragedy sparked off a wave of sympathy among staff.*

sparkle, sparkles, sparkling, sparkled **VERB** **①** If something sparkles, it shines with a lot of small, bright points of light ▷ **NOUN** **②** Sparkles are small, bright points of light. **sparkling** **ADJECTIVE**
  ● **SIMILAR WORDS:** **①** gleam,
  ● glitter, twinkle

sparrow, sparrows **NOUN** a common, small bird with brown and grey feathers.

sparse, sparser, sparsest **ADJECTIVE** small in number or amount and spread out over an area • *the sparse audience.* **sparsely** **ADVERB**

spartan **ADJECTIVE** A spartan way of life is very simple with no luxuries • *spartan accommodation.*
  ● **WORD HISTORY:** from *Sparta*, a
  ● city in Ancient Greece, whose
  ● inhabitants were famous for their
  ● discipline, military skill, and stern
  ● and plain way of life

spasm, spasms **NOUN** **①** a sudden tightening of the muscles. **②** a sudden, short burst of something • *a*

sudden spasm of fear.

spasmodic **ADJECTIVE** happening suddenly for short periods of time at irregular intervals • *spasmodic movements.*

spastic, spastics **ADJECTIVE** **①** A spastic person is born with a disability which makes it difficult for them to control their muscles ▷ **NOUN** **②** a spastic person.
  ● **WORD HISTORY:** from Greek
  ● *spasmos* meaning 'cramp' or
  ● 'convulsion'

spate **NOUN** A spate of things is a large number of them that happen or appear in a rush • *a recent spate of first novels from older writers.*

spatial [Said *spay-shl*] **ADJECTIVE** to do with size, area, or position.

spatter, spatters, spattering, spattered **VERB** **①** If something spatters a surface, it covers the surface with drops of liquid ▷ **NOUN** **②** A spatter of something is a small amount of it in drops or tiny pieces.

spawn, spawns, spawning, spawned **NOUN** **①** Spawn is a jelly-like substance containing the eggs of fish or amphibians ▷ **VERB** **②** When fish or amphibians spawn, they lay their eggs. **③** If something spawns something else, it causes it • *The depressed economy spawned the riots.*

speak, speaks, speaking, spoke, spoken **VERB** **①** When you speak, you use your voice to say words. **②** If you speak a foreign language, you know it and can use it.
speak out **VERB** To speak out about something means to publicly state an opinion about it.

▷ SPELLING NOTE: *pAL up with the principAL and principAL staff (principal)*

● **SIMILAR WORDS:** ❶ say, talk,
● utter

speaker, speakers **NOUN** ❶ a
person who is speaking, especially
someone making a speech. ❷ A
speaker on a radio or hi-fi is a
loudspeaker.

spear, spears, spearing, speared
NOUN ❶ a weapon consisting of a
long pole with a sharp point ▷ **VERB**
❷ To spear something means to push
or throw a spear or other pointed
object into it.

spearhead, spearheads,
spearheading, spearheaded **VERB** If
someone spearheads a campaign,
they lead it.

spec PHRASE If you do something **on
spec**, you do it hoping for a result but
without any certainty • *He turned up at
the same event on spec.*

special ADJECTIVE (RE)
❶ Something special is more
important or better than other things
of its kind. ❷ Special describes
someone who is officially appointed,
or something that is needed for a
particular purpose • *Karen actually had
to get special permission to go there.*
❸ Special also describes something
that belongs or relates to only one
particular person, group, or place • *the
special needs of the chronically sick.*

specialist, specialists **NOUN**
❶ someone who has a particular skill
or who knows a lot about a particular
subject • *a skin specialist.*
▷ **ADJECTIVE** ❷ having a skill or
knowing a lot about a particular
subject • *a specialist teacher.*
specialism NOUN

speciality, specialities **NOUN** A
person's speciality is something they
are especially good at or know a lot
about • *Roses are her speciality.*

specialize, specializes, specializing,
specialized; *also spelt* **specialise**
VERB If you specialize in something,
you make it your speciality • *a shop
specializing in ceramics.*
specialization NOUN

specialized or **specialised**
ADJECTIVE developed for a particular
purpose or trained in a particular area
of knowledge • *a specialized sales team.*

specially ADVERB If something has
been done specially for a particular
person or purpose, it has been done
only for that person or purpose.

species [*Said* spee-sheez] **NOUN**
(SCIENCE) a division of plants or
animals whose members have the
same characteristics and are able to
breed with each other.

specific ADJECTIVE ❶ particular
• *specific areas of difficulty.* ❷ precise
and exact • *She will ask for specific
answers.* **specifically ADVERB**

specification, specifications
NOUN (D & T) a detailed description
of what is needed for something, such
as the necessary features in the design
of something • *I like to build it to my
own specifications.*

specify, specifies, specifying,
specified **VERB** To specify something
means to state or describe it precisely
• *In his will he specified that these
documents were never to be removed.*

specimen, specimens **NOUN** A
specimen of something is an example

▷ SPELLING NOTE: L**Earn** the princip**LEs** (princip**le**)

or small amount of it which gives an idea of what the whole is like • *a specimen of your writing.*

speck, specks NOUN a very small stain or amount of something.

speckled ADJECTIVE Something that is speckled is covered in very small marks or spots.

specs PLURAL NOUN INFORMAL Short for **spectacles**.

spectacle, spectacles NOUN ❶ a strange or interesting sight or scene • *an astonishing spectacle.* ❷ a grand and impressive event or performance.

spectacles PLURAL NOUN Someone's spectacles are their glasses.

spectacular, spectaculars ADJECTIVE ❶ Something spectacular is very impressive or dramatic ▷ NOUN ❷ a grand and impressive show or performance.
● SIMILAR WORDS: ❶ impressive, sensational, stunning

spectator, spectators NOUN a person who is watching something.
● SIMILAR WORDS: observer, onlooker, watcher

spectra the plural of **spectrum**.

spectre, spectres NOUN ❶ a frightening idea or image • *the spectre of war.* ❷ a ghost.

spectrum, spectra or spectrums NOUN ❶ (ART) The spectrum is the range of different colours produced when light passes through a prism or a drop of water. A rainbow shows the colours in a spectrum. ❷ A spectrum of opinions or emotions is a range of

them • *a wide spectrum of beliefs.*

speculate, speculates, speculating, speculated VERB If you speculate about something, you think about it and form opinions about it.
speculation NOUN

speculative ADJECTIVE ❶ A speculative piece of information is based on guesses and opinions rather than known facts. ❷ Someone with a speculative expression seems to be trying to guess something • *His mother regarded him with a speculative eye.*

speech, speeches NOUN ❶ Speech is the ability to speak or the act of speaking. ❷ a formal talk given to an audience. ❸ In a play, a speech is a group of lines spoken by one of the characters.
● SIMILAR WORDS: ❷ address, talk

speechless ADJECTIVE Someone who is speechless is unable to speak for a short time because something has shocked them.

speed, speeds, speeding, sped or speeded NOUN ❶ The speed of something is the rate at which it moves or happens. ❷ Speed is very fast movement or travel ▷ VERB ❸ If you speed somewhere, you move or travel there quickly. ❹ Someone who is speeding is driving a vehicle faster than the legal speed limit.
● SIMILAR WORDS: ❷ rapidity, swiftness, velocity

speedboat, speedboats NOUN a small, fast motorboat.

speed limit, speed limits NOUN The speed limit is the maximum speed at which vehicles are legally allowed to drive on a particular road.

speedway NOUN Speedway is the sport of racing lightweight motorcycles on special tracks.

speedy, speedier, speediest ADJECTIVE done very quickly. **speedily** ADVERB

spell, spells, spelling, spelt or spelled VERB ❶ When you spell a word, you name or write its letters in order. ❷ When letters spell a word, they form that word when put together in a particular order. ❸ If something spells a particular result, it suggests that this will be the result • *This haphazard method could spell disaster for you.* ▷ NOUN ❹ A spell of something is a short period of it • *a spell of rough weather.* ❺ a word or sequence of words used to perform magic. **spell out** VERB If you spell something out, you explain it in detail • *I don't have to spell it out, do I?*

spellbound ADJECTIVE so fascinated by something that you cannot think about anything else • *She had sat spellbound through the film.*

spelling, spellings NOUN The spelling of a word is the correct order of letters in it.

spend, spends, spending, spent VERB ❶ When you spend money, you buy things with it. ❷ To spend time or energy means to use it.

spent ADJECTIVE ❶ Spent describes things which have been used and therefore cannot be used again • *spent matches.* ❷ If you are spent, you are exhausted and have no energy left.

sperm, sperms NOUN a cell

produced in the sex organ of a male animal which can enter a female animal's egg and fertilize it.

spew, spews, spewing, spewed VERB ❶ When things spew from something or when it spews them out, they come out of it in large quantities. ❷ INFORMAL To spew something up means to vomit.

sphere, spheres NOUN ❶ a perfectly round object, such as a ball. ❷ An area of activity or interest can be referred to as a sphere of activity or interest. **spherical** ADJECTIVE

sphinx, sphinxes [Said **sfingks**] NOUN In mythology, the sphinx was a monster with a person's head and a lion's body.

spice, spices, spicing, spiced NOUN ❶ Spice is powder or seeds from a plant added to food to give it flavour. ❷ Spice is something which makes life more exciting • *Variety is the spice of life.* ▷ VERB ❸ To spice food means to add spice to it. ❹ If you spice something up, you make it more exciting or lively.

spicy, spicier, spiciest ADJECTIVE strongly flavoured with spices.

spider, spiders NOUN a small insect-like creature with eight legs that spins webs to catch insects for food.
  ● WORD HISTORY: from Old English
  ● *spinnan* meaning 'to spin'

spike, spikes NOUN ❶ a long pointed piece of metal. ❷ The spikes on a sports shoe are the pointed pieces of metal attached to the sole. ❸ Some other long pointed objects are called spikes • *beautiful pink flower* *spikes • spikes of gelled hair.*

spiky, spikier, spikiest **ADJECTIVE**
Something spiky has sharp points.

spill, spills, spilling, spilled or spilt
VERB ❶ If you spill something or if it
spills, it accidentally falls or runs out of
a container. ❷ If people or things spill
out of a place, they come out of it in
large numbers.

spillage, spillages **NOUN** the spilling
of something, or something that has
been spilt • *the oil spillage in the
Shetlands.*

spin, spins, spinning, spun **VERB**
❶ If something spins, it turns quickly
around a central point. ❷ When
spiders spin a web, they give out a
sticky substance and make it into a
web. ❸ When people spin, they make
thread by twisting together pieces of
fibre using a machine. ❹ If your head
is spinning, you feel dizzy or confused
▷ **NOUN** ❺ a rapid turn around a
central point • *a golf club which puts
more spin on the ball.*

spinach [*Said* **spin-ij**] **NOUN**
Spinach is a vegetable with large green
leaves.

spinal **ADJECTIVE** to do with the
spine.

spine, spines **NOUN** ❶ Your spine is
your backbone. ❷ Spines are long,
sharp points on an animal's body or
on a plant.

spinifex **NOUN** Spinifex is a coarse,
spiny Australian grass.

spinning wheel, spinning wheels
NOUN a wooden machine for
spinning flax or wool.

spin-off, spin-offs **NOUN** something
useful that unexpectedly results from
an activity.

spinster, spinsters **NOUN** a woman
who has never married.
- **WORD HISTORY:** originally a
- person whose occupation was
- spinning; later, the official label of
- an unmarried woman

spiny **ADJECTIVE** covered with
spines.

spiral, spirals, spiralling, spiralled
NOUN ❶ a continuous curve which
winds round and round, with each
curve above or outside the previous
one ▷ **ADJECTIVE** ❷ in the shape of
a spiral • *a spiral staircase.* ▷ **VERB**
❸ If something spirals, it moves up or
down in a spiral curve • *The aircraft
spiralled down.* ❹ If an amount or
level spirals, it rises or falls quickly at
an increasing rate • *Prices have
spiralled recently.*

spire, spires **NOUN** The spire of a
church is the tall cone-shaped
structure on top.

spirit, spirits, spiriting, spirited **NOUN**
❶ Your spirit is the part of you that is
not physical and that is connected
with your deepest thoughts and
feelings. ❷ **RE** The spirit of a dead
person is a nonphysical part that is
believed to remain alive after death.
❸ a supernatural being, such as a
ghost. ❹ Spirit is liveliness, energy,
and self-confidence • *a band full of
spirit.* ❺ Spirit can refer to an attitude
• *his old fighting spirit.* ❻ IN PLURAL
Spirits can describe how happy or
unhappy someone is • *in good spirits.*
❼ Spirits are strong alcoholic drinks
such as whisky and gin ▷ **VERB** ❽ If

you spirit someone or something into or out of a place, you get them in or out quickly and secretly.

spirited ADJECTIVE showing energy and courage.

spirit level, spirit levels NOUN a device for finding out if a surface is level, consisting of a bubble of air sealed in a tube of liquid in a wooden or metal frame.

spiritual, spirituals ADJECTIVE (RE) **①** to do with people's thoughts and beliefs, rather than their bodies and physical surroundings. **②** to do with people's religious beliefs • *spiritual guidance.* ▷ NOUN **③** a religious song originally sung by Black slaves in America. **spiritually** ADVERB **spirituality** NOUN

spit, spits, spitting, spat NOUN **①** Spit is saliva. **②** a long stick made of metal or wood which is pushed through a piece of meat so that it can be hung over a fire and cooked. **③** a long, flat, narrow piece of land sticking out into the sea ▷ VERB **④** If you spit, you force saliva or some other substance out of your mouth. **⑤** When it is spitting, it is raining very lightly.

spite, spites, spiting, spited PHRASE **①** In spite of is used to introduce a statement which makes the rest of what you are saying seem surprising • *In spite of all the gossip, Virginia stayed behind.* ▷ VERB **②** If you do something to spite someone, you do it deliberately to hurt or annoy them ▷ NOUN **③** If you do something out of spite, you do it to hurt or annoy someone.

spiteful ADJECTIVE A spiteful person does or says nasty things to people deliberately to hurt them.
● SIMILAR WORDS: malicious,
● nasty, vindictive

spitting image NOUN If someone is the spitting image of someone else, they look just like them.

splash, splashes, splashing, splashed VERB **①** If you splash around in water, your movements disturb the water in a noisy way. **②** If liquid splashes something, it scatters over it in a lot of small drops ▷ NOUN **③** A splash is the sound made when something hits or falls into water. **④** A splash of liquid is a small quantity of it that has been spilt on something.

splatter, splatters, splattering, splattered VERB When something is splattered with a substance, the substance is splashed all over it • *fur coats splattered with paint.*

spleen, spleens NOUN Your spleen is an organ near your stomach which controls the quality of your blood.

splendid ADJECTIVE **①** very good indeed • *a splendid career.* **②** beautiful and impressive • *a splendid old mansion.* **splendidly** ADVERB
● SIMILAR WORDS: **②** grand,
● magnificent

splendour, splendours NOUN **①** If something has splendour, it is beautiful and impressive **②** IN PLURAL The splendours of something are its beautiful and impressive features.

splint, splints NOUN a long piece of wood or metal fastened to a broken limb to hold it in place.

a
b
c
d
e
f
g
h
i
j
k
l
m
n
o
p
q
r
s
t
u
v
w
x
y
z

▷ SPELLING NOTE: *there's SAND in my SANDwich (sandwich)*

splinter, splinters, splintering, splintered **NOUN** ❶ a thin, sharp piece of wood or glass which has broken off a larger piece ▷ **VERB** ❷ If something splinters, it breaks into thin, sharp pieces.

split, splits, splitting, split **VERB** ❶ If something splits or if you split it, it divides into two or more parts. ❷ If something such as wood or fabric splits, a long crack or tear appears in it. ❸ If people split something, they share it between them ▷ **NOUN** ❹ A split in a piece of wood or fabric is a crack or tear. ❺ A split between two things is a division or difference between them • *the split between rugby league and rugby union.*
split up VERB If two people split up, they end their relationship or marriage.
● **SIMILAR WORDS:** ❶ break, divide, separate ❺ division, schism

split infinitive, split infinitives **NOUN** (ENGLISH) A split infinitive is an infinitive with a word between the 'to' and the verb, as in 'to boldly go'. This is often thought to be incorrect.

split second NOUN an extremely short period of time.

splitting ADJECTIVE A splitting headache is very painful.

splutter, splutters, spluttering, spluttered **VERB** ❶ If someone splutters, they speak in a confused way because they are embarrassed. ❷ If something splutters, it makes a series of short, sharp sounds.

spoil, spoils, spoiling, spoiled or spoilt **VERB** ❶ If you spoil something, you prevent it from being successful or

satisfactory. ❷ To spoil children means to give them everything they want, with harmful effects on their character. ❸ To spoil someone also means to give them something nice as a treat.
● **SIMILAR WORDS:** ❶ mess up, ruin, wreck ❷ overindulge, pamper

spoils PLURAL NOUN Spoils are valuable things obtained during war or as a result of violence • *the spoils of war.*

spoilsport, spoilsports **NOUN** someone who spoils people's fun.

spoke, spokes **NOUN** The spokes of a wheel are the bars which connect the hub to the rim.

spokesperson, spokespersons **NOUN** someone who speaks on behalf of another person or a group. **spokesman NOUN spokeswoman NOUN**

sponge, sponges, sponging, sponged **NOUN** ❶ a sea creature with a body made up of many cells. ❷ part of the very light skeleton of a sponge, used for bathing and cleaning. ❸ A sponge or sponge cake is a very light cake ▷ **VERB** ❹ If you sponge something, you clean it by wiping it with a wet sponge.

sponsor, sponsors, sponsoring, sponsored **VERB** ❶ To sponsor something, such as an event or someone's training, means to support it financially • *The visit was sponsored by the London Natural History Society.* ❷ If you sponsor someone who is doing something for charity, you agree to give them a sum of money for the charity if they manage to do it. ❸ If you sponsor a proposal or suggestion, you officially put it forward and support it • *the MP who sponsored the Bill.* ▷ NOUN ❹ a person or organization sponsoring something or someone. sponsorship NOUN

spontaneous ADJECTIVE
❶ Spontaneous acts are not planned or arranged, but are done because you feel like it. ❷ A spontaneous event happens because of processes within something rather than being caused by things outside it • *spontaneous bleeding.* spontaneously ADVERB spontaneity NOUN

spoof, spoofs NOUN something such as an article or television programme that seems to be about a serious matter but is actually a joke.

spooky, spookier, spookiest ADJECTIVE eerie and frightening.

spool, spools NOUN a cylindrical object onto which thread, tape, or film can be wound.

spoon, spoons NOUN an object shaped like a small shallow bowl with a long handle, used for eating, stirring, and serving food.

spoonful, spoonfuls or spoonsful NOUN the amount held by a spoon.

sporadic ADJECTIVE happening at irregular intervals • *a few sporadic attempts at keeping a diary.* sporadically ADVERB

spore, spores NOUN TECHNICAL Spores are cells produced by bacteria and nonflowering plants such as fungi which develop into new bacteria or plants.

sporran, sporrans NOUN a large purse made of leather or fur, worn by a Scotsman over his kilt.
● WORD HISTORY: from Scottish Gaelic *sporan* meaning 'purse'

sport, sports, sporting, sported NOUN
❶ Sports are games and other enjoyable activities which need physical effort and skill. ❷ You say that someone is a sport when they accept defeat or teasing cheerfully • *Be a sport, Minister!* ▷ VERB ❸ If you sport something noticeable or unusual, you wear it • *A German boy sported a ponytail.*

sporting ADJECTIVE ❶ relating to sport. ❷ behaving in a fair and decent way.

sports car, sports cars NOUN a low, fast car, usually with room for only two people.

sportsman, sportsmen NOUN a man who takes part in sports and is good at them.

sportswoman, sportswomen NOUN a woman who takes part in sports and is good at them.

sporty, sportier, sportiest ADJECTIVE ❶ A sporty car is fast and flashy. ❷ A sporty person is good at sports.

spot, spots, spotting, spotted NOUN
❶ Spots are small, round, coloured areas on a surface. ❷ Spots on a person's skin are small lumps, usually caused by an infection or allergy. ❸ A spot of something is a small amount of it • *spots of rain.* ❹ A place can be called a spot • *the most beautiful spot in the garden.* ▷ VERB ❺ If you spot something, you notice it ▷ PHRASE ❻ If you do something **on the spot**, you do it immediately.

a
b
c
d
e
f
g
h
i
j
k
l
m
n
o
p
q
r
s
t
u
v
w
x
y
z

▷ SPELLING NOTE: *Eddy Ant thinks mEAt is a grEAt trEAt to EAt (-ea-)*

spot check, spot checks **NOUN** a random examination made without warning on one of a group of things or people • *spot checks by road safety officers.*

spotless **ADJECTIVE** perfectly clean. **spotlessly** **ADVERB**
- **SIMILAR WORDS:** clean,
- immaculate, impeccable

spotlight, spotlights, spotlighting, spotlit or spotlighted **NOUN**
1 (DRAMA) a powerful light which can be directed to light up a small area ▷ **VERB** **2** If something spotlights a situation or problem, it draws the public's attention to it • *a national campaign to spotlight the problem.*

spot-on **ADJECTIVE** INFORMAL exactly correct or accurate.

spotted **ADJECTIVE** Something spotted has a pattern of spots on it.

spotter, spotters **NOUN** a person whose hobby is looking out for things of a particular kind • *a train spotter.*

spotty, spottier, spottiest **ADJECTIVE** Someone who is spotty has spots or pimples on their skin, especially on their face.

spouse, spouses **NOUN** Someone's spouse is the person they are married to.

spout, spouts, spouting, spouted **VERB** **1** When liquid or flame spouts out of something, it shoots out in a long stream. **2** When someone spouts what they have learned, they say it in a boring way ▷ **NOUN** **3** a tube with a lip-like end for pouring liquid • *a teapot with a long spout.*

sprain, sprains, spraining, sprained **VERB** **1** If you sprain a joint, you accidentally damage it by twisting it violently ▷ **NOUN** **2** the injury caused by spraining a joint.

sprawl, sprawls, sprawling, sprawled **VERB** **1** If you sprawl somewhere, you sit or lie there with your legs and arms spread out. **2** A place that sprawls is spread out over a large area • *a Monday market which sprawls all over town.* ▷ **NOUN** **3** anything that spreads in an untidy and uncontrolled way • *a sprawl of skyscrapers.* **sprawling** **ADJECTIVE**

spray, sprays, spraying, sprayed **NOUN** **1** Spray consists of many drops of liquid splashed or forced into the air • *The salt spray stung her face.* **2** Spray is also a liquid kept under pressure in a can or other container • *hair spray.* **3** a piece of equipment for spraying liquid • *a garden spray.* **4** A spray of flowers or leaves consists of several of them on one stem ▷ **VERB** **5** To spray a liquid over something means to cover it with drops of the liquid.

spread, spreads, spreading, spread **VERB** **1** If you spread something out, you open it out or arrange it so that it can be seen or used easily • *He spread the map out on his knees.* **2** If you spread a substance on a surface, you put a thin layer on the surface. **3** If something spreads, it gradually reaches or affects more people • *The news spread quickly.* **4** If something spreads over a period of time, it happens regularly or continuously over that time • *His four international appearances were spread over eight years.* **5** If something such as work is spread, it is distributed evenly

▷ **NOUN** **6** The spread of something is the extent to which it gradually reaches or affects more people • *the spread of Buddhism.* **7** A spread of ideas, interests, or other things is a wide variety of them. **8** soft food put on bread • *cheese spread.*

spread-eagled **ADJECTIVE** Someone who is spread-eagled is lying with their arms and legs spread out.

spreadsheet, spreadsheets **NOUN** (ICT) a computer program that is used for entering and arranging figures, used mainly for financial planning.

spree, sprees **NOUN** a period of time spent doing something enjoyable • *a shopping spree.*

sprig, sprigs **NOUN** **1** a small twig with leaves on it. **2** In Australian and New Zealand English, sprigs are studs on the sole of a football boot.

sprightly, sprightlier, sprightliest **ADJECTIVE** lively and active.

spring, springs, springing, sprang, sprung **NOUN** **1** Spring is the season between winter and summer. **2** a coil of wire which returns to its natural shape after being pressed or pulled. **3** a place where water comes up through the ground. **4** an act of springing • *With a spring he had opened the door.* ▷ **VERB** **5** To spring means to jump upwards or forwards • *Martha sprang to her feet.* **6** If something springs in a particular direction, it moves suddenly and quickly • *The door sprang open.* **7** If one thing springs from another, it is the result of it • *The failures sprang from three facts.*

springboard, springboards **NOUN** **1** a flexible board on which a diver or gymnast jumps to gain height. **2** If something is a springboard for an activity or enterprise, it makes it possible for it to begin.

springbok, springboks **NOUN** **1** a small South African antelope which moves in leaps. **2** A Springbok is a person who has represented South Africa in a sports team.

spring-clean, spring-cleans, spring-cleaning, spring-cleaned **VERB** To spring-clean a house means to clean it thoroughly throughout.

spring onion, spring onions **NOUN** a small onion with long green shoots, often eaten raw in salads.

sprinkle, sprinkles, sprinkling, sprinkled **VERB** If you sprinkle a liquid or powder over something, you scatter it over it.

sprinkling, sprinklings **NOUN** A sprinkling of something is a small quantity of it • *a light sprinkling of snow.*

sprint, sprints, sprinting, sprinted **NOUN** **1** a short, fast race ▷ **VERB** **2** To sprint means to run fast over a short distance.

sprinter, sprinters **NOUN** an athlete who runs fast over short distances.

sprite, sprites **NOUN** a type of fairy.

sprout, sprouts, sprouting, sprouted **VERB** **1** When something sprouts, it grows. **2** If things sprout up, they appear rapidly • *Their houses sprouted up in that region.* ▷ **NOUN** **3** Sprouts are the same as **brussels sprouts**.

▷ SPELLING NOTE: *'i' before 'e' except after 'c'*

A
B
C
D
E
F
G
H
I
J
K
L
M
N
O
P
Q
R
S
T
U
V
W
X
Y
Z

spruce, spruces; sprucer, sprucest; spruces, sprucing, spruced **NOUN** ❶ an evergreen tree with needle-like leaves ▷ **ADJECTIVE** ❷ Someone who is spruce is very neat and smart ▷ **VERB** ❸ To spruce something up means to make it neat and smart.

spunk, spunks **NOUN** INFORMAL ❶ OLD-FASHIONED Spunk is courage. ❷ In Australian and New Zealand English, someone who is good-looking.

spur, spurs, spurring, spurred **VERB** ❶ If something spurs you to do something or spurs you on, it encourages you to do it ▷ **NOUN** ❷ Something that acts as a spur encourages a person to do something. ❸ Spurs are sharp metal points attached to the heels of a rider's boots and used to urge a horse on ▷ **PHRASE** ❹ If you do something **on the spur of the moment**, you do it suddenly, without planning it.

spurious [Said spyoor-ee-uss] **ADJECTIVE** not genuine or real.

spurn, spurns, spurning, spurned **VERB** If you spurn something, you refuse to accept it • You spurned his last offer.

spurt, spurts, spurting, spurted **VERB** ❶ When a liquid or flame spurts out of something, it comes out quickly in a thick, powerful stream ▷ **NOUN** ❷ A spurt of liquid or flame is a thick powerful stream of it • a small spurt of blood. ❸ A spurt of activity or effort is a sudden, brief period of it.

spy, spies, spying, spied **NOUN** ❶ a person sent to find out secret information about a country or

organization ▷ **VERB** ❷ Someone who spies tries to find out secret information about another country or organization. ❸ If you spy on someone, you watch them secretly. ❹ If you spy something, you notice it.

squabble, squabbles, squabbling, squabbled **VERB** ❶ When people squabble, they quarrel about something trivial ▷ **NOUN** ❷ a quarrel.

squad, squads **NOUN** (PE) a small group chosen to do a particular activity • the fraud squad • the England football squad.

● **WORD HISTORY:** from Old Spanish escuadra meaning 'square', because of the square formation used by soldiers

squadron, squadrons **NOUN** a section of one of the armed forces, especially the air force.

● **WORD HISTORY:** from Italian squadrone meaning 'soldiers drawn up in a square formation'

squalid **ADJECTIVE** ❶ dirty, untidy, and in bad condition. ❷ Squalid activities are unpleasant and often dishonest.

squall, squalls **NOUN** a brief, violent storm.

squalor **NOUN** Squalor consists of bad or dirty conditions or surroundings.

squander, squanders, squandering, squandered **VERB** To squander money or resources means to waste them • They have squandered huge amounts of money.

square, squares, squaring, squared

NOUN ❶ (MATHS) a shape with four equal sides and four right angles. **❷** In a town or city, a square is a flat, open place, bordered by buildings or streets. **❸** The square of a number is the number multiplied by itself. For example, the square of 3, written 3², is 3 × 3 ▷ **ADJECTIVE ❹** shaped like a square • *her delicate square face.* **❺** 'Square' is used before units of length when talking about the area of something • *24m².* **❻** 'Square' is used after units of length when you are giving the length of each side of something square • *a towel measuring a foot square.* ▷ **VERB ❼** If you square a number, you multiply it by itself.

squarely ADVERB ❶ Squarely means directly rather than indirectly or at an angle • *I looked squarely in the mirror.* **❷** If you approach a subject squarely, you consider it fully, without trying to avoid unpleasant aspects of it.

square root, square roots **NOUN** A square root of a number is a number that makes the first number when it is multiplied by itself. For example, the square roots of 25 are 5 and -5.

squash, squashes, squashing, squashed **VERB ❶** If you squash something, you press it, so that it becomes flat or loses its shape ▷ **NOUN ❷** If there is a squash in a place, there are a lot of people squashed in it. **❸** Squash is a game in which two players hit a small rubber ball against the walls of a court using rackets. **❹** Squash is a drink made from fruit juice, sugar, and water.

squat, squats, squatting, squatted; squatter, squattest **VERB ❶** If you

squat down, you crouch, balancing on your feet with your legs bent. **❷** A person who squats in an unused building lives there as a squatter ▷ **NOUN ❸** a building used by squatters ▷ **ADJECTIVE ❹** short and thick.

squatter, squatters **NOUN ❶** a person who lives in an unused building without permission and without paying rent. **❷** In Australian English, someone who owns a large area of land for sheep or cattle farming. **❸** In Australia and New Zealand in the past, someone who rented land from the King or Queen.

squawk, squawks, squawking, squawked **VERB ❶** When a bird squawks, it makes a loud, harsh noise ▷ **NOUN ❷** a loud, harsh noise made by a bird.

squeak, squeaks, squeaking, squeaked **VERB ❶** If something squeaks, it makes a short high-pitched sound ▷ **NOUN ❷** a short, high-pitched sound. **squeaky ADJECTIVE**

squeal, squeals, squealing, squealed **VERB ❶** When things or people squeal, they make long, high-pitched sounds ▷ **NOUN ❷** a long, high-pitched sound.

squeamish ADJECTIVE easily upset by unpleasant sights or situations.

squeeze, squeezes, squeezing, squeezed **VERB ❶** When you squeeze something, you press it firmly from two sides. **❷** If you squeeze something into a small amount of time or space, you manage to fit it in ▷ **NOUN ❸** If you give something a squeeze, you squeeze it • *She gave my hand a quick squeeze.* ❹ If getting into something is a squeeze, it is just possible to fit into it • *It would take four comfortably, but six would be a squeeze.*

squelch, squelches, squelching, squelched **VERB** ❶ To squelch means to make a wet, sucking sound. ▷ **NOUN** ❷ a wet, sucking sound.

squid, squids **NOUN** a sea creature with a long soft body and many tentacles.

squiggle, squiggles **NOUN** a wriggly line.

squint, squints, squinting, squinted **VERB** ❶ If you squint at something, you look at it with your eyes screwed up ▷ **NOUN** ❷ If someone has a squint, their eyes look in different directions from each other.

squire, squires **NOUN** In a village, the squire was a gentleman who owned a large house with a lot of land.

squirm, squirms, squirming, squirmed **VERB** If you squirm, you wriggle and twist your body about, usually because you are nervous or embarrassed.

squirrel, squirrels **NOUN** a small furry animal with a long bushy tail.
● **WORD HISTORY:** from Greek *skia* meaning 'shadow' and *oura* meaning 'tail'

squirt, squirts, squirting, squirted **VERB** ❶ If a liquid squirts, it comes out of a narrow opening in a thin, fast stream ▷ **NOUN** ❷ a thin, fast stream of liquid.

Sri Lankan, Sri Lankans [Said sree-**lang**-kan] **ADJECTIVE** ❶ belonging or relating to Sri Lanka ▷ **NOUN** ❷ someone who comes from Sri Lanka.

stab, stabs, stabbing, stabbed **VERB** ❶ To stab someone means to wound them by pushing a knife into their body. ❷ To stab at something means to push at it sharply with your finger or with something long and narrow ▷ **PHRASE** ❸ INFORMAL If you **have a stab** at something, you try to do it ▷ **NOUN** ❹ You can refer to a sudden unpleasant feeling as a stab of something • *He felt a stab of guilt.*

stable, stables **ADJECTIVE** ❶ not likely to change or come to an end suddenly • *I am in a stable relationship.* ❷ firmly fixed or balanced and not likely to move, wobble, or fall ▷ **NOUN** ❸ a building in which horses are kept. **stability NOUN stabilize VERB**

staccato [Said stak-**kah**-toe] **ADJECTIVE** consisting of a series of short, sharp, separate sounds.

stack, stacks, stacking, stacked **NOUN** ❶ A stack of things is a pile of them, one on top of the other ❷ IN PLURAL, INFORMAL If someone has stacks of something, they have a lot of it ▷ **VERB** ❸ If you stack things, you arrange them one on top of the other in a pile.

stadium, stadiums **NOUN** a sports ground with rows of seats around it.
● **WORD HISTORY:** from Greek *stadion* meaning 'racecourse'

staff, staffs, staffing, staffed **NOUN** ❶ The staff of an organization are the people who work for it ▷ **VERB** ❷ To staff an organization means to find and employ people to work in it. ❸ If an organization is staffed by particular people, they are the people who work for it.

stag, stags **NOUN** an adult male deer.

stage, stages, staging, staged **NOUN**
❶ a part of a process that lasts for a period of time. ❷ (DRAMA) In a theatre, the stage is a raised platform where the actors or entertainers perform. ❸ (DRAMA) You can refer to the profession of acting as the stage ▷ **VERB** ❹ If someone stages a play or event, they organize it and present it or take part in it.
● **SIMILAR WORDS:** ❶ period,
● phase, point

stagecoach, stagecoaches **NOUN** a large carriage pulled by horses which used to carry passengers and mail.

stagger, staggers, staggering, staggered **VERB** ❶ If you stagger, you walk unsteadily because you are ill or drunk. ❷ If something staggers you, it amazes you. ❸ If events are staggered, they are arranged so that they do not all happen at the same time. **staggering ADJECTIVE**
● **SIMILAR WORDS:** ❶ lurch, reel,
● totter

stagnant ADJECTIVE Stagnant water is not flowing and is unhealthy and dirty.

stag night, stag nights **NOUN** a party for a man who is about to get married, which only men go to.

staid ADJECTIVE serious and dull.

stain, stains, staining, stained **NOUN**
❶ a mark on something that is difficult to remove ▷ **VERB** ❷ If a

substance stains something, the thing becomes marked or coloured by it.

stained glass NOUN Stained glass is coloured pieces of glass held together with strips of lead.

stainless steel NOUN Stainless steel is a metal made from steel and chromium which does not rust.

stair, stairs **NOUN** Stairs are a set of steps inside a building going from one floor to another.

staircase, staircases **NOUN** a set of stairs.

stairway, stairways **NOUN** a set of stairs.

stake, stakes, staking, staked **PHRASE** ❶ If something is **at stake**, it might be lost or damaged if something else is not successful • *The whole future of the company was at stake.* ▷ **VERB** ❷ If you say you would stake your money, life, or reputation on the success or truth of something, you mean you would risk it • *He is prepared to stake his own career on this.* ▷ **NOUN** ❸ If you have a stake in something such as a business, you own part of it and its success is important to you. ❹ a pointed wooden post that can be hammered into the ground and used as a support. ❺ IN PLURAL The stakes involved in something are the things that can be lost or gained.

stalactite, stalactites **NOUN** (GEOGRAPHY) A stalactite is a piece of rock like a huge icicle hanging from the roof of a cave.

stalagmite, stalagmites **NOUN** (GEOGRAPHY) A stalagmite is a large

a
b
c
d
e
f
g
h
i
j
k
l
m
n
o
p
q
r
s
t
u
v
w
x
y
z

pointed piece of rock sticking up from the floor of a cave.

stale, staler, stalest **ADJECTIVE** ❶ Stale food or air is no longer fresh. ❷ If you feel stale, you have no new ideas and are bored.
● **SIMILAR WORDS:** ❶ fusty, musty, old

stalemate NOUN ❶ Stalemate is a situation in which neither side in an argument or contest can win. ❷ In chess, stalemate is a situation in which a player cannot make any move permitted by the rules, so that the game ends and no-one wins.

stalk, stalks, stalking, stalked *[Said stawk]* **NOUN** ❶ The stalk of a flower or leaf is its stem ▷ **VERB** ❷ To stalk a person or animal means to follow them quietly in order to catch, kill, or observe them. ❸ If someone stalks into a room, they walk in a stiff, proud, or angry way.

stall, stalls, stalling, stalled **NOUN** ❶ a large table containing goods for sale or information ❷ IN PLURAL In a theatre, the stalls are the seats at the lowest level, in front of the stage ▷ **VERB** ❸ When a vehicle stalls, the engine suddenly stops. ❹ If you stall when someone asks you to do something, you try to avoid doing it until a later time.

stallion, stallions **NOUN** an adult male horse that can be used for breeding.

stamen, stamens **NOUN** (SCIENCE) The stamens of a flower are the small delicate stalks which grow inside the blossom and produce pollen.

stamina NOUN Stamina is the physical or mental energy needed to do something for a very long time.

stammer, stammers, stammering, stammered **VERB** ❶ When someone stammers, they speak with difficulty, repeating words and sounds and hesitating awkwardly ▷ **NOUN** ❷ Someone who has a stammer tends to stammer when they speak.

stamp, stamps, stamping, stamped **NOUN** ❶ a small piece of gummed paper which you stick on a letter or parcel before posting it. ❷ a small block with a pattern cut into it, which you press onto an inky pad and make a mark with it on paper; also the mark made by the stamp. ❸ If something bears the stamp of a particular quality or person, it shows clear signs of that quality or of the person's style or characteristics ▷ **VERB** ❹ If you stamp a piece of paper, you make a mark on it using a stamp. ❺ If you stamp, you lift your foot and put it down hard on the ground.
stamp out VERB To stamp something out means to put an end to it • *the battle to stamp out bullying in schools.*

stampede, stampedes, stampeding, stampeded **VERB** ❶ When a group of animals stampede, they run in a wild, uncontrolled way ▷ **NOUN** ❷ a group of animals stampeding.
● **WORD HISTORY:** from Spanish *estampida* meaning 'crash' or 'din'

stance, stances **NOUN** Your stance on a particular matter is your attitude and way of dealing with it • *He takes no particular stance on animal rights.*

stand, stands, standing, stood **VERB** ❶ If you are standing, you are upright,

A B C D E F G H I J K L M N O P Q R S T U V W X Y Z

your legs are straight, and your weight is supported by your feet. When you stand up, you get into a standing position. **②** If something stands somewhere, that is where it is • *The house stands alone on the top of a small hill.* **③** If you stand something somewhere, you put it there in an upright position • *Stand the containers on bricks.* **④** If a decision or offer stands, it is still valid • *My offer still stands.* **⑤** You can use 'stand' when describing the state or condition of something • *Youth unemployment stands at 35%.* **⑥** If a letter stands for a particular word, it is an abbreviation for that word. **⑦** If you say you will not stand for something, you mean you will not tolerate it. **⑧** If something can stand a situation or test, it is good enough or strong enough not to be damaged by it. **⑨** If you cannot stand something, you cannot bear it • *I can't stand that woman.* **⑩** If you stand in an election, you are one of the candidates ▷ **PHRASE** **⑪** When someone **stands trial**, they are tried in a court of law ▷ **NOUN** **⑫** a stall or very small shop outdoors or in a large public building. **⑬** a large structure at a sports ground, where the spectators sit. **⑭** a piece of furniture designed to hold something • *an umbrella stand.*

stand by VERB **①** If you stand by to provide help or take action, you are ready to do it if necessary. **②** If you stand by while something happens, you do nothing to stop it.

stand down VERB If someone stands down, they resign from their job or position.

stand in VERB If you stand in for someone, you take their place while they are ill or away.

stand out VERB If something stands out, it can be easily noticed or is more important than other similar things.

stand up VERB **①** If something stands up to rough treatment, it is not damaged or harmed. **②** If you stand up to someone who is criticizing or attacking you, you defend yourself.

standard, standards **NOUN** **①** a level of quality or achievement that is considered acceptable • *The work is not up to standard.* **②** IN PLURAL Standards are moral principles of behaviour ▷ **ADJECTIVE** **③** usual, normal, and correct • *The practice became standard procedure for most motor companies.*

standard English NOUN Standard English is the form of English taught in schools, used in text books and broadsheet newspapers, and spoken and written by most educated people.

standardize, standardizes, standardizing, standardized; *also spelt* **standardise VERB** To standardize things means to change them so that they all have a similar set of features • *We have decided to standardize our equipment.*

stand-by, stand-bys **NOUN** **①** something available for use when you need it • *a useful stand-by.* ▷ **ADJECTIVE** **②** A stand-by ticket is a cheap ticket that you buy just before a theatre performance or a flight if there are any seats left.

stand-in, stand-ins **NOUN** someone who takes a person's place while the person is ill or away • *The school had to*

a
b
c
d
e
f
g
h
i
j
k
l
m
n
o
p
q
r
s
t
u
v
w
x
y
z

▷ SPELLING NOTE: *Betty Eats Cakes And Uses Seven Eggs (because)*

employ a stand-in whilst the teacher was ill.

standing ADJECTIVE
❶ permanently in existence or used regularly • *a standing joke.* ▷ NOUN
❷ A person's standing is their status and reputation. ❸ Standing is used to say how long something has existed • *a friend of 20 years' standing.*

standpoint, standpoints NOUN If you consider something from a particular standpoint, you consider it from that point of view • *from a military standpoint.*

standstill NOUN If something comes to a standstill, it stops completely.

stanza, stanzas NOUN (ENGLISH) a verse of a poem.

staple, staples, stapling, stapled
NOUN ❶ Staples are small pieces of wire that hold sheets of paper firmly together ▷ VERB ❷ If you staple sheets of paper together, you fasten them together with staples ▷ ADJECTIVE
❸ A staple food forms a regular and basic part of someone's everyday diet.

star, stars, starring, starred NOUN
❶ a large ball of burning gas in space that appears as a point of light in the sky at night. ❷ a shape with four, five, or more points sticking out in a regular pattern. ❸ Famous actors, sports players, and musicians are referred to as stars ❹ IN PLURAL The horoscope in a newspaper or magazine can be referred to as the stars • *I'm a Virgo, but don't read my stars every day.*
▷ VERB ❺ If an actor or actress stars in a film or if the film stars that person, he or she has one of the most

important parts in it.

starboard ADJECTIVE OR NOUN
The starboard side of a ship is the right-hand side when you are facing the front.
● **WORD HISTORY:** from Old English *steorbord* meaning 'steering side', because boats were formerly steered with a paddle over the right-hand side

starch, starches, starching, starched
NOUN ❶ Starch is a substance used for stiffening fabric such as cotton and linen. ❷ Starch is a carbohydrate found in foods such as bread and potatoes ▷ VERB ❸ To starch fabric means to stiffen it with starch.

stare, stares, staring, stared VERB
❶ If you stare at something, you look at it for a long time ▷ NOUN ❷ a long fixed look at something.
● **SIMILAR WORDS:** ❶ gawp, gaze, goggle

starfish, starfishes or starfish NOUN
a flat, star-shaped sea creature with five limbs.

stark, starker, starkest ADJECTIVE
❶ harsh, unpleasant and plain • *the stark choice.* ▷ PHRASE ❷ If someone is **stark-naked**, they have no clothes on at all.

starling, starlings NOUN a common European bird with shiny dark feathers.

start, starts, starting, started VERB
❶ If something starts, it begins to take place or comes into existence • *When does the party start?* ❷ If you start to do something, you begin to do it • *Susie started to cry.* ❸ If you start something, you cause it to begin or to

come into existence • *as good a time as any to start a business.* ❹ If you start a machine or car, you operate the controls to make it work. ❺ If you start, your body suddenly jerks because of surprise or fear ▷ **NOUN** ❻ The start of something is the point or time at which it begins. ❼ If you do something with a start, you do it with a sudden jerky movement because of surprise or fear • *I awoke with a start.*

starter, starters **NOUN** a small quantity of food served as the first part of a meal.

startle, startles, startling, startled **VERB** If something sudden and unexpected startles you, it surprises you and makes you slightly frightened. **startled ADJECTIVE startling ADJECTIVE**

starve, starves, starving, starved **VERB** ❶ If people are starving, they are suffering from a serious lack of food and are likely to die. ❷ To starve a person or animal means to prevent them from having any food. ❸ INFORMAL If you say you are starving, you mean you are very hungry. ❹ If someone or something is starved of something they need, they are suffering because they are not getting enough of it • *The hospital was starved of cash.* **starvation NOUN**

stash, stashes, stashing, stashed **VERB** INFORMAL If you stash something away in a secret place, you store it there to keep it safe.

state, states, stating, stated **NOUN** ❶ The state of something is its condition, what it is like, or its circumstances. ❷ Countries are sometimes referred to as states • *the*

state of Denmark. ❸ Some countries are divided into regions called states which make some of their own laws • *the State of Vermont.* ❹ You can refer to the government or administration of a country as the state ▷ **PHRASE** ❺ If you are **in a state**, you are nervous or upset and unable to control your emotions ▷ **ADJECTIVE** ❻ A state ceremony involves the ruler or leader of a country ▷ **VERB** ❼ If you state something, you say it or write it, especially in a formal way.

state house, state houses **NOUN** In New Zealand, a house built and owned by the government and rented out.

stately home, stately homes **NOUN** In Britain, a very large old house which belongs to an upper-class family.

statement, statements **NOUN** ❶ something you say or write when you give facts or information in a formal way. ❷ a document provided by a bank showing all the money paid into and out of an account during a period of time.

state school, state schools **NOUN** a school maintained and financed by the government in which education is free.

statesman, statesmen **NOUN** an important and experienced politician.

static ADJECTIVE ❶ never moving or changing • *The temperature remains fairly static.* ▷ **NOUN** ❷ Static is an electrical charge caused by friction. It builds up in metal objects.

station, stations, stationing, stationed **NOUN** ❶ a building and

a
b
c
d
e
f
g
h
i
j
k
l
m
n
o
p
q
r
s
t
u
v
w
x
y
z

platforms where trains stop for passengers. ❷ A bus or coach station is a place where some buses start their journeys. ❸ A radio station is the frequency on which a particular company broadcasts. ❹ In Australian and New Zealand English, a large sheep or cattle farm. ❺ OLD-FASHIONED A person's station is their position or rank in society ▷ VERB ❻ Someone who is stationed somewhere is sent there to work or do a particular job • *Her husband was stationed in Vienna.*

stationary ADJECTIVE not moving • *a stationary car.*
  ● SIMILAR WORDS: fixed, motionless

stationery NOUN Stationery is paper, pens, and other writing equipment.

statistic, statistics NOUN
  ❶ Statistics are facts obtained by analysing numerical information.
  ❷ Statistics is the branch of mathematics that deals with the analysis of numerical information.
  statistical ADJECTIVE

statistician, statisticians [Said stat-iss-**tish-an**] NOUN a person who studies or works with statistics.

statue, statues NOUN a sculpture of a person.

stature NOUN ❶ Someone's stature is their height and size.
  ❷ Someone's stature is also their importance and reputation • *the desire to gain international stature.*

status, statuses [Said **stay**-tuss] NOUN ❶ A person's status is their position and importance in society.

❷ Status is also the official classification given to someone or something • *I am not sure what your legal status is.*
  ● SIMILAR WORDS: ❶ position, prestige, standing

status quo [Said stay-tuss **kwoh**] NOUN The status quo is the situation that exists at a particular time • *They want to keep the status quo.*
  ● WORD HISTORY: a Latin expression, meaning literally 'the state in which'

statute, statutes NOUN a law.
  statutory ADJECTIVE

staunch, stauncher, staunchest ADJECTIVE A staunch supporter is a strong and loyal supporter.

stave, staves, staving, staved NOUN ❶ In music, a stave is the five lines that music is written on ▷ VERB ❷ If you stave something off, you try to delay or prevent it.

stay, stays, staying, stayed VERB ❶ If you stay in a place, you do not move away from it • *She stayed in bed until noon.* ❷ If you stay at a hotel or a friend's house, you spend some time there as a guest or visitor. ❸ If you stay in a particular state, you continue to be in it • *I stayed awake the first night.* ❹ In Scottish and South African English, to stay in a place can also mean to live there ▷ NOUN ❺ a short time spent somewhere • *a very pleasant stay in Cornwall.*
  ● SIMILAR WORDS: ❶ linger, remain

stead NOUN FORMAL Something that will stand someone in good stead will be useful to them in the future.

▷ SPELLING NOTE: *I always visit my FRIend on a FRIday (Friday)*

steadfast ADJECTIVE refusing to change or give up.

steady, steadier, steadiest; steadies, steadying, steadied ADJECTIVE
❶ continuing or developing gradually without major interruptions or changes • *a steady rise in profits.*
❷ firm and not shaking or wobbling • *O'Brien held out a steady hand.* ❸ A steady look or voice is calm and controlled. ❹ Someone who is steady is sensible and reliable ▷ VERB
❺ When you steady something, you hold on to prevent it from shaking or wobbling. ❻ When you steady yourself, you control and calm yourself. **steadily** ADVERB
● SIMILAR WORDS: ❷ firm, secure,
● stable

steak, steaks NOUN ❶ Steak is good-quality beef without much fat.
❷ A fish steak is a large piece of fish.
● WORD HISTORY: from Old Norse
● *steik* meaning 'roast'

steal, steals, stealing, stole, stolen VERB ❶ To steal something means to take it without permission and without intending to return it. ❷ To steal somewhere means to move there quietly and secretively.
● SIMILAR WORDS: ❶ nick,
● purloin, take

stealth [*rhymes with* health] NOUN If you do something with stealth, you do it quietly and secretively. **stealthy** ADJECTIVE **stealthily** ADVERB

steam, steams, steaming, steamed NOUN ❶ Steam is the hot vapour formed when water boils ▷ ADJECTIVE ❷ Steam engines are operated using steam as a means of power ▷ VERB ❸ If something

steams, it gives off steam. ❹ To steam food means to cook it in steam. **steamy** ADJECTIVE

steam-engine, steam-engines NOUN any engine that uses the energy of steam to produce mechanical work.

steamer, steamers NOUN ❶ a ship powered by steam. ❷ a container with small holes in the bottom in which you steam food.

steed, steeds NOUN LITERARY a horse.

steel, steels, steeling, steeled NOUN ❶ Steel is a very strong metal containing mainly iron with a small amount of carbon ▷ VERB ❷ To steel yourself means to prepare to deal with something unpleasant.

steel band, steel bands NOUN a group of people who play music on special metal drums.

steep, steeper, steepest; steeps, steeping, steeped ADJECTIVE ❶ A steep slope rises sharply and is difficult to go up. ❷ larger than is reasonable • *a steep price increase.*
▷ VERB ❸ To steep something in a liquid means to soak it thoroughly. **steeply** ADVERB
● SIMILAR WORDS: ❶ precipitous,
● sheer

steeped ADJECTIVE If a person or place is steeped in a particular quality, they are deeply affected by it • *an industry steeped in tradition.*

steeple, steeples NOUN a tall pointed structure on top of a church tower.

steeplechase, steeplechases

abcdefghijklmnopqrstuvwxyz

NOUN a long horse race in which the horses jump over obstacles such as hedges and water jumps.

● **WORD HISTORY:** originally a race with a church steeple in sight as the goal

steer, steers, steering, steered **VERB**
❶ To steer a vehicle or boat means to control it so that it goes in the right direction. ❷ To steer someone towards a particular course of action means to influence and direct their behaviour or thoughts ▷ **NOUN** ❸ a castrated bull.

● **SIMILAR WORDS:** ❶ direct, guide, pilot

stem, stems, stemming, stemmed
NOUN ❶ The stem of a plant is the long thin central part above the ground that carries the leaves and flowers. ❷ The stem of a glass is the long narrow part connecting the bowl to the base ▷ **VERB** ❸ If a problem stems from a particular situation, that situation is the original starting point or cause of the problem. ❹ If you stem the flow of something, you restrict it or stop it from spreading • *to stem the flow of refugees.*

stench, stenches **NOUN** a very strong, unpleasant smell.

stencil, stencils, stencilling, stencilled **NOUN** ❶ a thin sheet with a cut-out pattern through which ink or paint passes to form the pattern on the surface below ▷ **VERB** ❷ To stencil a design on a surface means to create it using a stencil.

● **WORD HISTORY:** from Middle English *stanselen* meaning 'to decorate with bright colours'

step, steps, stepping, stepped **NOUN**

❶ If you take a step, you lift your foot and put it down somewhere else. ❷ one of a series of actions that you take in order to achieve something. ❸ a raised flat surface, usually one of a series that you can walk up or down ▷ **VERB** ❹ If you step in a particular direction, you move your foot in that direction. ❺ If someone steps down or steps aside from an important position, they resign.

step- **PREFIX** If a word like 'father' or 'sister' has 'step-' in front of it, it shows that the family relationship has come about because a parent has married again • *stepfather* • *stepsister.*

steppe, steppes *[Said step]* **NOUN** a large area of open grassland with no trees.

● **WORD HISTORY:** from Old Russian *step* meaning 'lowland'

stepping stone, stepping stones **NOUN** ❶ Stepping stones are a line of large stones that you walk on to cross a shallow river. ❷ a job or event that is regarded as a stage in your progress, especially in your career.

stereo, stereos **ADJECTIVE** ❶ A stereo recording or music system is one in which the sound is directed through two speakers ▷ **NOUN** ❷ a piece of equipment that reproduces sound from records, tapes, or CDs directing the sound through two speakers.

stereotype, stereotypes, stereotyping, stereotyped **(PSHE)** **NOUN** ❶ a fixed image or set of characteristics that people consider to represent a particular type of person or thing • *the stereotype of the polite, industrious Japanese.* ▷ **VERB** ❷ If you

▷ SPELLING NOTE: *The government licenSes Schnapps (licenses)*

stereotype someone, you assume they are a particular type of person and will behave in a particular way.

sterile ADJECTIVE ❶ Sterile means completely clean and free from germs. ❷ A sterile person or animal is unable to produce offspring. **sterility** NOUN
● SIMILAR WORDS: ❶ germ-free,
● sterilized

sterilize, sterilizes, sterilizing, sterilized; *also spelt* **sterilise** VERB
❶ To sterilize something means to make it completely clean and free from germs, usually by boiling it or treating it with an antiseptic. ❷ If a person or animal is sterilized, they have an operation that makes it impossible for them to produce offspring.

sterling NOUN ❶ Sterling is the money system of Great Britain
▷ ADJECTIVE ❷ excellent in quality
• *Volunteers are doing sterling work.*

stern, sterner, sternest; sterns
ADJECTIVE ❶ very serious and strict
• *a stern father* • *a stern warning.*
▷ NOUN ❷ The stern of a boat is the back part.

sternum, sternums or sterna NOUN
SCIENCE Your sternum is the flat bone in the centre of your chest that is joined to your ribs.

steroid, steroids NOUN Steroids are chemicals that occur naturally in your body. Sometimes sportsmen illegally take them as drugs to improve their performance.

stethoscope, stethoscopes NOUN a device used by doctors to listen to a patient's heart and breathing, consisting of earpieces connected to a hollow tube and a small disc.
● WORD HISTORY: from Greek
● *stēthos* meaning 'chest' and *skopein*
● meaning 'to look at'

stew, stews, stewing, stewed NOUN
❶ a dish of small pieces of savoury food cooked together slowly in a liquid
▷ VERB ❷ To stew meat, vegetables, or fruit means to cook them slowly in a liquid.
● WORD HISTORY: from Middle
● English *stuen* meaning 'to take a
● very hot bath'

steward, stewards NOUN ❶ a man who works on a ship or plane looking after passengers and serving meals. ❷ a person who helps to direct the public at a race, march, or other event.
● WORD HISTORY: from Old English
● *stigweard* meaning 'hall protector'

stewardess, stewardesses NOUN a woman who works on a ship or plane looking after passengers and serving meals.

stick, sticks, sticking, stuck NOUN
❶ a long, thin piece of wood. ❷ A stick of something is a long, thin piece of it • *a stick of celery.* ▷ VERB ❸ If you stick a long or pointed object into something, you push it in. ❹ If you stick one thing to another, you attach it with glue or sticky tape. ❺ If one thing sticks to another, it becomes attached and is difficult to remove. ❻ If a movable part of something sticks, it becomes fixed and will no longer move or work properly • *My gears keep sticking.* ❼ INFORMAL If you stick something somewhere, you put it there. ❽ If you stick by someone, you continue to help and support them. ❾ If you stick to something,

● a b c d e f g h i j k l m n o p q r **s** t u v w x y z

you keep to it and do not change to
something else • *He should have stuck
to the old ways of doing things.*
⑩ When people stick together, they
stay together and support each other.
stick out VERB ❶ If something
sticks out, it projects from something
else. ❷ To stick out also means to be
very noticeable.
stick up VERB ❶ If something
sticks up, it points upwards from a
surface. ❷ INFORMAL If you stick up
for a person or principle, you support
or defend them.

sticker, stickers **NOUN** a small piece
of paper or plastic with writing or a
picture on it, that you stick onto a
surface.

sticking plaster, sticking plasters
NOUN a small piece of fabric that you
stick over a cut or sore to protect it.

stick insect, stick insects **NOUN**
an insect with a long cylindrical body
and long legs, which looks like a twig.

sticky, stickier, stickiest **ADJECTIVE**
❶ A sticky object is covered with a
substance that can stick to other
things • *sticky hands.* ❷ Sticky paper
or tape has glue on one side so that
you can stick it to a surface.
❸ INFORMAL A sticky situation is
difficult or embarrassing to deal with.
❹ Sticky weather is unpleasantly hot
and humid.

stiff, stiffer, stiffest **ADJECTIVE**
❶ D&T Something that is stiff is
firm and not easily bent. ❷ If you feel
stiff, your muscles or joints ache when
you move. ❸ Stiff behaviour is formal
and not friendly or relaxed. ❹ Stiff
also means difficult or severe • *stiff
competition for places.* ❺ A stiff drink

contains a large amount of alcohol.
❻ A stiff breeze is blowing strongly
▷ **ADVERB** ❼ INFORMAL If you are
bored stiff or scared stiff, you are very
bored or very scared. **stiffly ADVERB**
stiffness NOUN

stiffen, stiffens, stiffening, stiffened
VERB ❶ If you stiffen, you suddenly
stop moving and your muscles
become tense • *I stiffened with tension.*
❷ If your joints or muscles stiffen,
they become sore and difficult to bend
or move. ❸ If fabric or material is
stiffened, it is made firmer so that it
does not bend easily.

stifle, stifles, stifling, stifled *[Said
sty-fl]* **VERB** ❶ If the atmosphere
stifles you, you feel you cannot
breathe properly. ❷ To stifle
something means to stop it from
happening or continuing • *Martin
stifled a yawn.* **stifling ADJECTIVE**

stigma, stigmas **NOUN** If something
has a stigma attached to it, people
consider it unacceptable or a disgrace
• *the stigma of mental illness.*

stile, stiles **NOUN** a step on either
side of a wall or fence to enable you to
climb over.

stiletto, stilettos **NOUN** Stilettos are
women's shoes with very high, narrow
heels.
  ● **WORD HISTORY:** from Italian *stilo*
  ● meaning 'dagger', because of the
  ● shape of the heels

still, stiller, stillest; stills **ADVERB**
❶ If a situation still exists, it has
continued to exist and it exists now.
❷ If something could still happen, it
might happen although it has not
happened yet. ❸ 'Still' emphasizes

▷ SPELLING NOTE: *plaice the fish has a glittering 'EYE' (i) (plaice)*

that something is the case in spite of other things • *Whatever you think of him, he's still your father.* ▷ **ADVERB OR ADJECTIVE** ❹ Still means staying in the same position without moving • *Sit still* • *The air was still.* ▷ **ADJECTIVE** ❺ A still place is quiet and peaceful with no signs of activity ▷ **NOUN** ❻ a photograph taken from a cinema film or video. **stillness NOUN**

stillborn ADJECTIVE A stillborn baby is dead when it is born.

stilt, stilts **NOUN** ❶ Stilts are long upright poles on which a building is built, for example on wet land. ❷ Stilts are also two long pieces of wood or metal on which people balance and walk.

stilted ADJECTIVE formal, unnatural, and rather awkward • *a stilted conversation.*

stimulant, stimulants **NOUN** a drug or other substance that makes your body work faster, increasing your heart rate and making it difficult to sleep.

stimulate, stimulates, stimulating, stimulated **VERB** ❶ To stimulate something means to encourage it to begin or develop • *to stimulate discussion.* ❷ If something stimulates you, it gives you new ideas and enthusiasm. **stimulating ADJECTIVE stimulation NOUN**
- **SIMILAR WORDS:** ❶ arouse,
- encourage, inspire

stimulus, stimuli **NOUN** something that causes a process or event to begin or develop.

sting, stings, stinging, stung **VERB**

❶ If a creature or plant stings you, it pricks your skin and injects a substance which causes pain. ❷ If a part of your body stings, you feel a sharp tingling pain there. ❸ If someone's remarks sting you, they make you feel upset and hurt ▷ **NOUN** ❹ A creature's sting is the part it stings you with.
- **SIMILAR WORDS:** ❷ hurt, smart

stink, stinks, stinking, stank, stunk **VERB** ❶ Something that stinks smells very unpleasant ▷ **NOUN** ❷ a very unpleasant smell.
- **SIMILAR WORDS:** ❷ pong,
- stench

stint, stints **NOUN** a period of time spent doing a particular job • *a three-year stint in the army.*

stipulate, stipulates, stipulating, stipulated **VERB** FORMAL If you stipulate that something must be done, you state clearly that it must be done. **stipulation NOUN**

stir, stirs, stirring, stirred **VERB** ❶ When you stir a liquid, you move it around using a spoon or a stick. ❷ To stir means to move slightly. ❸ If something stirs you, it makes you feel strong emotions • *The power of the singing stirred me.* ▷ **NOUN** ❹ If an event causes a stir, it causes general excitement or shock • *two books which have caused a stir.*

stirring, stirrings **ADJECTIVE** ❶ causing excitement, emotion, and enthusiasm • *a stirring account of the action.* ▷ **NOUN** ❷ If there is a stirring of emotion, people begin to feel it.

stirrup, stirrups **NOUN** Stirrups are two metal loops hanging by leather

▷ SPELLING NOTE: *I went to see (C) the doctor's new practiCe (practice)*

straps from a horse's saddle, which you put your feet in when riding.

stitch, stitches, stitching, stitched
VERB ❶ When you stitch pieces of material together, you use a needle and thread to sew them together. ❷ To stitch a wound means to use a special needle and thread to hold the edges of skin together ▷ **NOUN** ❸ one of the pieces of thread that can be seen where material has been sewn. ❹ one of the pieces of thread that can be seen where a wound has been stitched • *He had eleven stitches in his lip.* ❺ If you have a stitch, you feel a sharp pain at the side of your abdomen, usually because you have been running or laughing.

stoat, stoats **NOUN** a small wild animal with a long body and brown fur.

stock, stocks, stocking, stocked
NOUN ❶ Stocks are shares bought as an investment in a company; also the amount of money raised by the company through the issue of shares. ❷ A shop's stock is the total amount of goods it has for sale. ❸ If you have a stock of things, you have a supply ready for use. ❹ The stock an animal or person comes from is the type of animal or person they are descended from • *She was descended from Scots Highland stock.* ❺ Stock is farm animals. ❻ Stock is a liquid made from boiling meat, bones, or vegetables together in water. Stock is used as a base for soups, stews, and sauces ▷ **VERB** ❼ A shop that stocks particular goods keeps a supply of them to sell. ❽ If you stock a shelf or cupboard, you fill it with food or other things ▷ **ADJECTIVE** ❾ A stock

expression or way of doing something is one that is commonly used.
stock up VERB If you stock up with something, you buy a supply of it.

stockbroker, stockbrokers **NOUN** A stockbroker is a person whose job is to buy and sell shares for people who want to invest money.

stock exchange, stock exchanges
NOUN a place where there is trading in stocks and shares • *the New York Stock Exchange.*

stocking, stockings **NOUN** Stockings are long pieces of thin clothing that cover a woman's leg.

stockman, stockmen **NOUN** a man who looks after sheep or cattle on a farm.

stock market, stock markets
NOUN The stock market is the organization and activity involved in buying and selling stocks and shares.

stockpile, stockpiles, stockpiling, stockpiled **VERB** ❶ If someone stockpiles something, they store large quantities of it for future use ▷ **NOUN** ❷ a large store of something.

stocktaking NOUN Stocktaking is the counting and checking of all a shop's or business's goods.

stocky, stockier, stockiest
ADJECTIVE A stocky person is rather short, but broad and solid-looking.

stoke, stokes, stoking, stoked **VERB** To stoke a fire means to keep it burning by moving or adding fuel.

stomach, stomachs, stomaching, stomached **NOUN** ❶ Your stomach is the organ inside your body where food

▷ SPELLING NOTE: *You must practiSe your Ss (practise)*

is digested. ❷ You can refer to the front part of your body above your waist as your stomach ▷ **VERB** ❸ If you cannot stomach something, you strongly dislike it and cannot accept it.

stone, stones, stoning, stoned **NOUN** ❶ Stone is the hard solid substance found in the ground and used for building. ❷ a small piece of rock. ❸ The stone in a fruit such as a plum or cherry is the large seed in the centre. ❹ a unit of weight equal to 14 pounds or about 6.35 kilograms. ❺ You can refer to a jewel as a stone • *a diamond ring with three stones.* ▷ **VERB** ❻ To stone something or someone means to throw stones at them.

Stone Age NOUN (HISTORY) The Stone Age is the earliest known period of human history when people used stone to make weapons and tools. The Stone Age is often divided into three periods: the Palaeolithic, the Mesolithic, and the Neolithic.

stoned ADJECTIVE INFORMAL affected by drugs.

stony, stonier, stoniest **ADJECTIVE** ❶ Stony ground is rough and contains a lot of stones or rocks. ❷ If someone's expression is stony, it shows no friendliness or sympathy.

stool, stools **NOUN** ❶ a seat with legs but no back or arms. ❷ a lump of faeces.

stoop, stoops, stooping, stooped **VERB** ❶ If you stoop, you stand or walk with your shoulders bent forwards. ❷ If you would not stoop to something, you would not disgrace yourself by doing it.

stop, stops, stopping, stopped **VERB** ❶ If you stop doing something, you no longer do it. ❷ If an activity or process stops, it comes to an end or no longer happens. ❸ If a machine stops, it no longer functions or it is switched off. ❹ To stop something means to prevent it. ❺ If people or things that are moving stop, they no longer move. ❻ If you stop somewhere, you stay there for a short while ▷ **PHRASE** ❼ To **put a stop to** something means to prevent it from happening or continuing ▷ **NOUN** ❽ a place where a bus, train, or other vehicle stops during a journey. ❾ If something that is moving comes to a stop, it no longer moves.
● **SIMILAR WORDS:** ❶ cease,
● desist, halt

stoppage, stoppages **NOUN** If there is a stoppage, people stop work because of a disagreement with their employer.

stopper, stoppers **NOUN** a piece of glass or cork that fits into the neck of a jar or bottle.

stopwatch, stopwatches **NOUN** a watch that can be started and stopped by pressing buttons, which is used to time events.

storage NOUN The storage of something is the keeping of it somewhere until it is needed.

store, stores, storing, stored **NOUN** ❶ a shop. ❷ A store of something is a supply kept for future use. ❸ a place where things are kept while they are not used ▷ **VERB** ❹ When you store something somewhere, you keep it there until it is needed ▷ **PHRASE** ❺ Something that is **in store for** you

a
b
c
d
e
f
g
h
i
j
k
l
m
n
o
p
q
r
s
t
u
v
w
x
y
z

▷ SPELLING NOTE: *pAL up with the principAL and principAL staff (principal)*

is going to happen to you in the future.

● **SIMILAR WORDS:** ❶ hoard,
● stockpile, supply

storeroom, storerooms **NOUN** a room where things are kept until they are needed.

storey, storeys **NOUN** A storey of a building is one of its floors or levels.

stork, storks **NOUN** a very large white and black bird with long red legs and a long bill.

storm, storms, storming, stormed **NOUN** ❶ When there is a storm, there is heavy rain, a strong wind, and often thunder and lightning. ❷ If something causes a storm, it causes an angry or excited reaction • *His words caused a storm of protest.* ▷ **VERB** ❸ If someone storms out, they leave quickly, noisily, and angrily. ❹ To storm means to say something in a loud, angry voice • *'It's a fiasco!' he stormed.* ❺ If people storm a place, they attack it. **stormy ADJECTIVE**

story, stories **NOUN** (ENGLISH) ❶ a description of imaginary people and events written or told to entertain people. ❷ The story of something or someone is an account of the important events that have happened to them • *his life story.*

● **SIMILAR WORDS:** anecdote,
● tale, yarn

stout, stouter, stoutest **ADJECTIVE** ❶ rather fat. ❷ thick, strong, and sturdy • *stout walking shoes.* ❸ determined, firm, and strong • *He can outrun the stoutest opposition.* **stoutly ADVERB**

stove, stoves **NOUN** a piece of

equipment for heating a room or for cooking.

stow, stows, stowing, stowed **VERB** ❶ If you stow something somewhere or stow it, you store it until it is needed. ❷ If someone stows away in a ship or plane, they hide in it to go somewhere secretly without paying.

straddle, straddles, straddling, straddled **VERB** ❶ If you straddle something, you stand or sit with one leg on either side of it. ❷ If something straddles a place, it crosses it, linking different parts together • *The town straddles a river.*

straight, straighter, straightest **ADJECTIVE OR ADVERB** ❶ continuing in the same direction without curving or bending • *the straight path* • *Amy stared straight ahead of her.* ❷ upright or level rather than sloping or bent • *Keep your arms straight.* ▷ **ADVERB** ❸ immediately and directly • *We will go straight to the hotel.* ▷ **ADJECTIVE** ❹ neat and tidy • *Get this room straight.* ❺ honest, frank, and direct • *They wouldn't give me a straight answer.* ❻ A straight choice involves only two options.

straightaway ADVERB If you do something straightaway, you do it immediately.

straighten, straightens, straightening, straightened **VERB** ❶ To straighten something means to remove any bends or curves from it. ❷ To straighten something also means to make it neat and tidy. ❸ To straighten out a confused situation means to organize and deal with it.

straightforward ADJECTIVE

▷ SPELLING NOTE: *LEarn the principLEs (principle)*

❶ easy and involving no problems. **❷** honest, open, and frank.

strain, strains, straining, strained
NOUN ❶ Strain is worry and nervous tension. **❷** If a strain is put on something, it is affected by a strong force which may damage it. **❸** You can refer to an aspect of someone's character, remarks, or work as a strain • *There was a strain of bitterness in his voice.* **❹** You can refer to distant sounds of music as strains of music. **❺** A particular strain of plant is a variety of it • *strains of rose.* ▷ **VERB ❻** To strain something means to force it or use it more than is reasonable or normal. **❼** If you strain a muscle, you injure it by moving awkwardly. **❽** To strain food means to pour away the liquid from it.
● **SIMILAR WORDS: ❶** anxiety, ● stress **❻** overexert, tax

strained **ADJECTIVE ❶** worried and anxious. **❷** If a relationship is strained, people feel unfriendly and do not trust each other.

strait, straits **NOUN ❶** You can refer to a narrow strip of sea as a strait or the straits • *the Straits of Hormuz.* **❷** IN PLURAL If someone is in a bad situation, you can say they are in difficult straits.

straitjacket, straitjackets **NOUN** a special jacket used to tie the arms of a violent person tightly around their body.

strait-laced **ADJECTIVE** having a very strict and serious attitude to moral behaviour.

strand, strands **NOUN ❶** A strand of thread or hair is a single long piece of

it. **❷** You can refer to a part of a situation or idea as a strand of it • *the different strands of the problem.*

stranded **ADJECTIVE** If someone or something is stranded somewhere, they are stuck and cannot leave.

strange, stranger, strangest
ADJECTIVE ❶ unusual or unexpected. **❷** not known, seen, or experienced before • *alone in a strange country.* **strangely** **ADVERB** **strangeness** **NOUN**
● **SIMILAR WORDS: ❶** curious, ● odd, peculiar **❷** alien, new, ● unfamiliar

stranger, strangers **NOUN ❶** someone you have never met before. **❷** If you are a stranger to a place or situation, you have not been there or experienced it before.

strangle, strangles, strangling, strangled **VERB** To strangle someone means to kill them by squeezing their throat. **strangulation** **NOUN**

strangled **ADJECTIVE** A strangled sound is unclear and muffled.

stranglehold, strangleholds **NOUN** To have a stranglehold on something means to have control over it and prevent it from developing.

strap, straps, strapping, strapped **NOUN ❶** a narrow piece of leather or cloth, used to fasten or hold things together ▷ **VERB ❷** To strap something means to fasten it with a strap.

strapping **ADJECTIVE** tall, strong, and healthy-looking.

strata the plural of **stratum**.

▷ SPELLING NOTE: *Psychiatrists Seldom Yell Callously Hard (psychiatrist)*

stratagem, stratagems **NOUN** A stratagem is a plan or tactic.

strategic [Said strat-**tee**-jik] **ADJECTIVE** planned or intended to achieve something or to gain an advantage • a strategic plan.
strategically ADVERB

strategy, strategies **NOUN** ❶ a plan for achieving something. ❷ Strategy is the skill of planning the best way to achieve something, especially in war.
strategist NOUN

stratosphere NOUN (GEOGRAPHY) The stratosphere is the layer of the earth's atmosphere which lies between 10 and 50 kilometres above the earth.

stratum, strata **NOUN** The strata in the earth's surface are the different layers of rock.

straw, straws **NOUN** ❶ Straw is the dry, yellowish stalks from cereal crops. ❷ a hollow tube of paper or plastic which you use to suck a drink into your mouth ▷ **PHRASE** ❸ If something is **the last straw**, it is the latest in a series of bad events and makes you feel you cannot stand any more.

strawberry, strawberries **NOUN** a small red fruit with tiny seeds in its skin.

stray, strays, straying, strayed **VERB** ❶ When people or animals stray, they wander away from where they should be. ❷ If your thoughts stray, you stop concentrating ▷ **ADJECTIVE** ❸ A stray dog or cat is one that has wandered away from home. ❹ Stray things are separated from the main group of things of their kind • a stray

piece of lettuce. ▷ **NOUN** ❺ a stray dog or cat.

streak, streaks, streaking, streaked **NOUN** ❶ a long mark or stain. ❷ If someone has a particular streak, they have that quality in their character. ❸ A lucky or unlucky streak is a series of successes or failures ▷ **VERB** ❹ If something is streaked with a colour, it has lines of the colour in it. ❺ To streak somewhere means to move there very quickly. **streaky ADJECTIVE**

stream, streams, streaming, streamed **NOUN** ❶ a small river. ❷ You can refer to a steady flow of something as a stream • a constant stream of people. ❸ In a school, a stream is a group of children of the same age and ability ▷ **VERB** ❹ To stream somewhere means to move in a continuous flow in large quantities • Rain streamed down the windscreen.

streamer, streamers **NOUN** a long, narrow strip of coloured paper used for decoration.

streamline, streamlines, streamlining, streamlined **VERB** ❶ To streamline a vehicle, aircraft, or boat means to improve its shape so that it moves more quickly and efficiently. ❷ To streamline an organization means to make it more efficient by removing parts of it.

street, streets **NOUN** a road in a town or village, usually with buildings along it.

strength, strengths **NOUN** ❶ Your strength is your physical energy and the power of your muscles. ❷ Strength can refer to the degree of

someone's confidence or courage.
❸ You can refer to power or influence as strength • *The campaign against factory closures gathered strength.*
❹ Someone's strengths are their good qualities and abilities. **❺** The strength of an object is the degree to which it can stand rough treatment. **❻** The strength of a substance is the amount of other substances that it contains • *coffee with sugar and milk in it at the correct strength.* **❼** The strength of a feeling or opinion is the degree to which it is felt or supported. **❽** The strength of a relationship is its degree of closeness or success. **❾** The strength of a group is the total number of people in it ▷ **PHRASE**
❿ If people do something **in strength**, a lot of them do it together • *The press were here in strength.*
● **SIMILAR WORDS: ❶** might,
● muscle **❸** force, intensity, power

strengthen, strengthens, strengthening, strengthened **VERB**
❶ To strengthen something means to give it more power, influence, or support and make it more likely to succeed. **❷** To strengthen an object means to improve it or add to its structure so that it can withstand rough treatment.
● **SIMILAR WORDS:** fortify,
● reinforce

strenuous [Said *stren-yoo-uss*] **ADJECTIVE** involving a lot of effort or energy. **strenuously ADVERB**

stress, stresses, stressing, stressed **NOUN ❶** Stress is worry and nervous tension. **❷** Stresses are strong physical forces applied to an object. **❸** (ENGLISH) Stress is emphasis put on a word or part of a word when it is

pronounced, making it slightly louder ▷ **VERB ❹** If you stress a point, you emphasize it and draw attention to its importance. **stressful ADJECTIVE**
● **SIMILAR WORDS: ❶** anxiety,
● pressure, strain **❸** accent,
● emphasis **❹** accentuate,
● emphasize

stretch, stretches, stretching, stretched **VERB ❶** Something that stretches over an area extends that far. **❷** When you stretch, you hold out part of your body as far as you can. **❸** To stretch something soft or elastic means to pull it to make it longer or bigger ▷ **NOUN ❹** A stretch of land or water is an area of it. **❺** A stretch of time is a period of time.

stretcher, stretchers **NOUN** a long piece of material with a pole along each side, used to carry an injured person.

strewn ADJECTIVE If things are strewn about, they are scattered about untidily • *The costumes were strewn all over the floor.*

stricken ADJECTIVE severely affected by something unpleasant.

strict, stricter, strictest **ADJECTIVE**
❶ Someone who is strict controls other people very firmly. **❷** A strict rule must always be obeyed absolutely. **❸** The strict meaning of something is its precise and accurate meaning. **❹** You can use 'strict' to describe someone who never breaks the rules or principles of a particular belief • *a strict Muslim.*
● **SIMILAR WORDS: ❶** severe, stern
● **❷** stringent

strictly ADVERB ❶ Strictly means

a
b
c
d
e
f
g
h
i
j
k
l
m
n
o
p
q
r
s
t
u
v
w
x
y
z

▷ SPELLING NOTE: *Rhythmical Hounds Yap To Heavy Music (rhythm)*

A
B
C
D
E
F
G
H
I
J
K
L
M
N
O
P
Q
R
S
T
U
V
W
X
Y
Z

only for a particular purpose • *I was in it strictly for the money.* ▷ **PHRASE**
❷ You say **strictly speaking** to correct a statement or add more precise information • *Somebody pointed out that, strictly speaking, electricity was a discovery, not an invention.*

stride, strides, striding, strode, stridden **VERB** ❶ To stride along means to walk quickly with long steps ▷ **NOUN** ❷ a long step; also the length of a step.

strident [*Said* stry-*dent*] **ADJECTIVE** loud, harsh, and unpleasant.

strife **NOUN** *FORMAL* Strife is trouble, conflict, and disagreement.

strike, strikes, striking, struck **NOUN** ❶ If there is a strike, people stop working as a protest. ❷ A hunger strike is a refusal to eat anything as a protest. A rent strike is a refusal to pay rent. ❸ a military attack • *the threat of American air strikes.* ▷ **VERB** ❹ To strike someone or something means to hit them. ❺ If an illness, disaster, or enemy strikes, it suddenly affects or attacks someone. ❻ If a thought strikes you, it comes into your mind. ❼ If you are struck by something, you are impressed by it. ❽ When a clock strikes, it makes a sound to indicate the time. ❾ To strike a deal with someone means to come to an agreement with them. ❿ If someone strikes oil or gold, they discover it in the ground. ⓫ If you strike a match, you rub it against something to make it burst into flame.
strike off **VERB** If a professional person is struck off for bad behaviour, their name is removed from an official

register and they are not allowed to practise their profession.
strike up **VERB** To strike up a conversation or friendship means to begin it.

striker, strikers **NOUN** ❶ Strikers are people who are refusing to work as a protest. ❷ In soccer, a player whose function is to attack and score goals.

striking **ADJECTIVE** very noticeable because of being unusual or very attractive. **strikingly** **ADVERB**

string, strings, stringing, strung **NOUN** ❶ String is thin cord made of twisted threads. ❷ You can refer to a row or series of similar things as a string of them • *a string of islands* • *a string of injuries.* ❸ The strings of a musical instrument are tightly stretched lengths of wire or nylon which vibrate to produce the notes ❹ IN PLURAL The section of an orchestra consisting of stringed instruments is called the strings.
string along **VERB** *INFORMAL* To string someone along means to deceive them.
string out **VERB** ❶ If things are strung out, they are spread out in a long line. ❷ To string something out means to make it last longer than necessary.

stringed **ADJECTIVE** A stringed instrument is one with strings, such as a guitar or violin.

stringent **ADJECTIVE** Stringent laws conditions are very severe or are strictly controlled • *stringent financial checks.*

stringy-bark, stringy-barks **NOUN** any Australian eucalypt that has bark

▷ SPELLING NOTE: *there's SAND in my SANDwich (sandwich)*

that peels off in long, tough strands.

strip, strips, stripping, stripped NOUN
❶ A strip of something is a long, narrow piece of it. ❷ A comic strip is a series of drawings which tell a story. ❸ A sports team's strip is the clothes worn by the team when playing a match ▷ VERB ❹ If you strip, you take off all your clothes. ❺ To strip something means to remove whatever is covering its surface. ❻ To strip someone of their property or rights means to take their property or rights away from them officially.

stripe, stripes NOUN Stripes are long, thin lines, usually of different colours. **striped** ADJECTIVE

stripper, strippers NOUN an entertainer who does striptease.

striptease NOUN Striptease is a form of entertainment in which someone takes off their clothes gradually to music.

strive, strives, striving, strove, striven VERB If you strive to do something, you make a great effort to achieve it.

stroke, strokes, stroking, stroked VERB ❶ If you stroke something, you move your hand smoothly and gently over it ▷ NOUN ❷ If someone has a stroke, they suddenly lose consciousness as a result of a blockage or rupture in a blood vessel in the brain. A stroke can result in damage to speech and paralysis. ❸ The strokes of a brush or pen are the movements that you make with it. ❹ The strokes of a clock are the sounds that indicate the hour. ❺ A swimming stroke is a particular style of swimming ▷ PHRASE ❻ If you

have **a stroke of luck**, then you are lucky and something good happens to you.

stroll, strolls, strolling, strolled VERB
❶ To stroll along means to walk slowly in a relaxed way ▷ NOUN ❷ a slow, pleasurable walk.
● SIMILAR WORDS: amble,
● saunter, walk

stroller, strollers NOUN In Australian English, a stroller is a pushchair.

strong, stronger, strongest
ADJECTIVE ❶ Someone who is strong has powerful muscles. ❷ You also say that someone is strong when they are confident and have courage. ❸ Strong objects are able to withstand rough treatment. ❹ Strong also means great in degree or intensity • *a strong wind*. ❺ A strong argument or theory is supported by a lot of evidence. ❻ If a group or organization is strong, it has a lot of members or influence. ❼ You can use 'strong' to say how many people there are in a group • *The audience was about two dozen strong.* ❽ Your strong points are the things you are good at. ❾ A strong economy or currency is stable and successful. ❿ A strong liquid or drug contains a lot of a particular substance ▷ ADVERB ⓫ If someone or something is still going strong, they are still healthy or working well after a long time. **strongly** ADVERB
● SIMILAR WORDS: ❶ muscular,
● powerful ❹ acute, intense

stronghold, strongholds NOUN
❶ a place that is held and defended by an army. ❷ A stronghold of an attitude or belief is a place in which

the attitude or belief is strongly held • *Europe's last stronghold of male dominance.*

structure, structures, structuring, structured **NOUN** D&T ❶ The structure of something is the way it is made, built, or organized. ❷ something that has been built or constructed. ❸ ▷ **VERB** D&T To structure something means to arrange it into an organized pattern or system. **structural ADJECTIVE structurally ADVERB**
● **SIMILAR WORDS:**
● ❶ arrangement, construction,
● make-up

struggle, struggles, struggling, struggled **VERB** ❶ If you struggle to do something, you try hard to do it in difficult circumstances. ❷ When people struggle, they twist and move violently during a fight ▷ **NOUN** ❸ Something that is a struggle is difficult to achieve and takes a lot of effort. ❹ a fight • *After a brief struggle the suspect was taken away.*

strum, strums, strumming, strummed **VERB** To strum a guitar means to play it by moving your fingers backwards and forwards across all the strings.

strut, struts, strutting, strutted **VERB** ❶ To strut means to walk in a stiff, proud way with your chest out and your head high ▷ **NOUN** ❷ a piece of wood or metal which strengthens or supports part of a building or structure.

Stuart, Stuarts **NOUN** Stuart was the family name of the monarchs who ruled Scotland from 1371 to 1714 and England from 1603 to 1714.

stub, stubs, stubbing, stubbed **NOUN** ❶ The stub of a pencil or cigarette is the short piece that remains when the rest has been used. ❷ The stub of a cheque or ticket is the small part that you keep ▷ **VERB** ❸ If you stub your toe, you hurt it by accidentally kicking something.

stubble NOUN ❶ The short stalks remaining in the ground after a crop is harvested are called stubble. ❷ If a man has stubble on his face, he has very short hair growing there because he has not shaved recently.

stubborn ADJECTIVE ❶ Someone who is stubborn is determined not to change their opinion or course of action. ❷ A stubborn stain is difficult to remove. **stubbornly ADVERB stubbornness NOUN**
● **SIMILAR WORDS:** ❶ inflexible,
● obstinate, pig-headed

stuck ADJECTIVE ❶ If something is stuck in a particular position, it is fixed or jammed and cannot be moved • *His car's stuck in a snowdrift.* ❷ If you are stuck, you are unable to continue what you were doing because it is too difficult. ❸ If you are stuck somewhere, you are unable to get away.

stuck-up ADJECTIVE INFORMAL proud and conceited.

stud, studs **NOUN** ❶ a small piece of metal fixed into something. ❷ A male horse or other animal that is kept for stud is kept for breeding purposes.

studded ADJECTIVE decorated with small pieces of metal or precious stones.

student, students **NOUN** a person

studying at university or college.

studied ADJECTIVE A studied action or response has been carefully planned and is not natural • *She sipped her glass of white wine with studied boredom.*

studio, studios NOUN ❶ a room where a photographer or painter works. ❷ a room containing special equipment where records, films, or radio or television programmes are made.

studious [Said **styoo**-dee-uss] ADJECTIVE spending a lot of time studying.

studiously ADVERB carefully and deliberately • *She was studiously ignoring me.*

study, studies, studying, studied VERB ❶ If you study a particular subject, you spend time learning about it. ❷ If you study something, you look at it carefully • *He studied the map in silence.* ▷ NOUN ❸ Study is the activity of studying a subject • *the serious study of medieval archaeology.* ❹ Studies are subjects which are studied • *media studies.* ❺ a piece of research on a particular subject • *a detailed study of the world's most violent people.* ❻ a room used for writing and studying.

stuff, stuffs, stuffing, stuffed NOUN ❶ You can refer to a substance or group of things as stuff ▷ VERB ❷ If you stuff something somewhere, you push it there quickly and roughly. ❸ If you stuff something with a substance or objects, you fill it with the substance or objects.

stuffing NOUN Stuffing is a mixture

of small pieces of food put inside poultry or a vegetable before it is cooked.

stuffy, stuffier, stuffiest ADJECTIVE ❶ very formal and old-fashioned. ❷ If it is stuffy in a room, there is not enough fresh air.
● **SIMILAR WORDS:** ❷ airless, ● close, fusty

stumble, stumbles, stumbling, stumbled VERB ❶ If you stumble while you are walking or running, you trip and almost fall. ❷ If you stumble when speaking, you make mistakes when pronouncing the words. ❸ If you stumble across something or stumble on it, you find it unexpectedly.

stump, stumps, stumping, stumped NOUN ❶ a small part of something that is left when the rest has been removed • *the stump of a dead tree.* ❷ In cricket, the stumps are the three upright wooden sticks that support the bails, forming the wicket ▷ VERB ❸ If a question or problem stumps you, you cannot think of an answer or solution.

stun, stuns, stunning, stunned VERB ❶ If you are stunned by something, you are very shocked by it. ❷ To stun a person or animal means to knock them unconscious with a blow to the head.

stunning ADJECTIVE very beautiful or impressive • *a stunning first novel.*

stunt, stunts, stunting, stunted NOUN ❶ an unusual or dangerous and exciting action that someone does to get publicity or as part of a film ▷ VERB ❷ To stunt the growth or

a b c d e f g h i j k l m n o p q r s t u v w x y z

▷ SPELLING NOTE: *Elaine and Emily shout EE when they mEEt to grEEt each other (-ee-)*

development of something means to prevent it from developing as it should.

stupendous ADJECTIVE very large or impressive • *a stupendous amount of money.*

stupid, stupider, stupidest **ADJECTIVE** showing lack of good judgment or intelligence and not at all sensible. **stupidly ADVERB**
● **SIMILAR WORDS:** foolish, obtuse, unintelligent

stupidity NOUN a lack of intelligence or good judgment.

sturdy, sturdier, sturdiest **ADJECTIVE** strong and firm and unlikely to be damaged or injured • *a sturdy chest of drawers.*

sturgeon [Said **stur**-jon] **NOUN** a large edible fish, the eggs of which are also eaten and are known as caviar.

stutter, stutters, stuttering, stuttered **NOUN** ❶ Someone who has a stutter finds it difficult to speak smoothly and often repeats sounds through being unable to complete a word ▷ **VERB** ❷ When someone stutters, they hesitate or repeat sounds when speaking.

sty, sties **NOUN** a pigsty.

stye, styes **NOUN** a small red swelling on a person's eyelid caused by an infection.

style, styles, styling, styled **NOUN** ❶ The style of something is the general way in which it is done or presented, often showing the attitudes of the people involved. ❷ A person or place that has style is smart, elegant, and fashionable. ❸ The style

of something is its design • *new windows that fit in with the style of the house.* ▷ **VERB** ❹ To style a piece of clothing or a person's hair means to design and create its shape.
● **SIMILAR WORDS:** ❷ elegance, flair, panache

stylish ADJECTIVE smart, elegant, and fashionable. **stylishly ADVERB**
● **SIMILAR WORDS:** chic, smart

suave [Said swahv] **ADJECTIVE** charming, polite, and confident • *a suave Italian.*

sub- PREFIX ❶ 'Sub-' is used at the beginning of words that have 'under' as part of their meaning • *submarine.* ❷ 'Sub-' is also used to form nouns that refer to the parts into which something is divided • *Subsection 2 of section 49* • *a particular subgroup of citizens.*

subatomic ADJECTIVE (SCIENCE) A subatomic particle is a particle which is part of an atom.

subconscious NOUN ❶ Your subconscious is the part of your mind that can influence you without your being aware of it ▷ **ADJECTIVE** ❷ happening or existing in someone's subconscious and therefore not directly realized or understood by them • *a subconscious fear of rejection.* **subconsciously ADVERB**

subcontinent, subcontinents **NOUN** a large mass of land, often consisting of several countries, and forming part of a continent • *the Indian subcontinent.*

subdue, subdues, subduing, subdued **VERB** ❶ If soldiers subdue a group of people, they bring them

under control by using force • *It would be quite impossible to subdue the whole continent.* ❷ To subdue a colour, light, or emotion means to make it less bright or strong.
● SIMILAR WORDS: ❶ control, overcome, quell

subdued ADJECTIVE ❶ rather quiet and sad. ❷ not very noticeable or bright.

subject, subjects, subjecting, subjected NOUN ❶ The subject of writing or a conversation is the thing or person being discussed. ❷ In grammar, the subject is the word or words representing the person or thing doing the action expressed by the verb. For example, in the sentence 'My cat keeps catching birds', 'my cat' is the subject. ❸ an area of study. ❹ The subjects of a country are the people who live there ▷ VERB ❺ To subject someone to something means to make them experience it • *He was subjected to constant interruption.* ▷ ADJECTIVE ❻ Someone or something that is subject to something is affected by it • *He was subject to attacks at various times.*

subjective ADJECTIVE influenced by personal feelings and opinion rather than based on fact or rational thought.

subjunctive NOUN In grammar, the subjunctive or subjunctive mood is one of the forms a verb can take. It is used to express attitudes such as wishing and doubting.

sublime ADJECTIVE Something that is sublime is wonderful and affects people emotionally • *the sublime music of Mozart.*

submarine, submarines NOUN a ship that can travel beneath the surface of the sea.

submerge, submerges, submerging, submerged VERB ❶ To submerge means to go beneath the surface of a liquid. ❷ If you submerge yourself in an activity, you become totally involved in it.

submission, submissions NOUN ❶ Submission is a state in which someone accepts the control of another person • *Now he must beat us into submission.* ❷ The submission of a proposal or application is the act of sending it for consideration.

submissive ADJECTIVE behaving in a quiet, obedient way.

submit, submits, submitting, submitted VERB ❶ If you submit to something, you accept it because you are not powerful enough to resist it. ❷ If you submit an application or proposal, you send it to someone for consideration.

subordinate, subordinates, subordinating, subordinated NOUN ❶ A person's subordinate is someone who is in a less important position than them ▷ ADJECTIVE ❷ If one thing is subordinate to another, it is less important • *Non-elected officials are subordinate to elected leaders.* ▷ VERB ❸ To subordinate one thing to another means to treat it as being less important.

subordinate clause, subordinate clauses NOUN (ENGLISH) In grammar, a subordinate clause is a clause which adds details to the main clause of a sentence.

▷ SPELLING NOTE: *King IAn went to ParlIAment in a carrIAge for his marrIAge (-ia-)*

A
B
C
D
E
F
G
H
I
J
K
L
M
N
O
P
Q
R
S
T
U
V
W
X
Y
Z

subscribe, subscribes, subscribing, subscribed **VERB** ❶ If you subscribe to a particular belief or opinion, you support it or agree with it. ❷ If you subscribe to a magazine, you pay to receive regular copies. **subscriber NOUN**

subscription, subscriptions **NOUN** a sum of money that you pay regularly to belong to an organization or to receive regular copies of a magazine.

subsequent ADJECTIVE happening or coming into existence at a later time than something else • *the December uprising and the subsequent political violence.* **subsequently ADVERB**

subservient ADJECTIVE Someone who is subservient does whatever other people want them to do.

subset, subsets **NOUN** (MATHS) A subset of a larger set or group is a smaller set or group contained within it.

subside, subsides, subsiding, subsided **VERB** ❶ To subside means to become less intense or quieter • *Her excitement suddenly subsided.* ❷ If water or the ground subsides, it sinks to a lower level.

subsidence NOUN If a place is suffering from subsidence, parts of the ground have sunk to a lower level.

subsidiary, subsidiaries *[Said sub-sid-yer-ee]* **NOUN** ❶ a company which is part of a larger company ▷ **ADJECTIVE** ❷ treated as being of less importance and additional to another thing • *Drama is offered as a subsidiary subject.*

subsidize, subsidizes, subsidizing, subsidized; *also spelt* **subsidise VERB** To subsidize something means to provide part of the cost of it • *He feels the government should do much more to subsidize films.* **subsidized ADJECTIVE**

subsidy, subsidies **NOUN** a sum of money paid to help support a company or provide a public service.

substance, substances **NOUN** ❶ Anything which is a solid, a powder, a liquid, or a paste can be referred to as a substance. ❷ If a speech or piece of writing has substance, it is meaningful or important • *a good speech, but there was no substance.*
 ● **SIMILAR WORDS:** ❶ material,
 ● stuff

substantial ADJECTIVE ❶ very large in degree or amount • *a substantial pay rise.* ❷ large and strongly built • *a substantial stone building.*

substantially ADVERB Something that is substantially true is generally or mostly true.

substitute, substitutes, substituting, substituted **VERB** ❶ To substitute one thing for another means to use it instead of the other thing or to put it in the other thing's place. ❷ (MATHS) to replace one mathematical element with another of the same value ▷ **NOUN** ❸ If one thing is a substitute for another, it is used instead of it or put in its place. **substitution NOUN**
 ● **SIMILAR WORDS:** ❶ exchange,
 ● replace ❸ alternative,
 ● replacement, surrogate

▷ SPELLING NOTE: *an ELegant angEL (angel)*

subtend, subtends, subtending, subtended **VERB** (MATHS) to be opposite to and mark the limit of an angle or the side of a geometric shape. For exmple, a right angle is subtended by a hypotenuse.

subterfuge, subterfuges [Said sub-ter-fyooj] **NOUN** Subterfuge is the use of deceitful or dishonest methods.

subtitle, subtitles **NOUN** A film with subtitles has a printed translation of the dialogue at the bottom of the screen.

subtle, subtler, subtlest [Said sut-tl] **ADJECTIVE** ❶ very fine, delicate, or small in degree • a subtle change. ❷ using indirect methods to achieve something. **subtly ADVERB subtlety NOUN**

subtract, subtracts, subtracting, subtracted **VERB** If you subtract one number from another, you take away the first number from the second.

subtraction, subtractions **NOUN** (MATHS) Subtraction is subtracting one number from another, or a sum in which you do this.

suburb, suburbs **NOUN** an area of a town or city that is away from its centre.

suburban ADJECTIVE ❶ relating to a suburb or suburbs. ❷ dull and conventional.

suburbia NOUN You can refer to the suburbs of a city as suburbia.

subversive, subversives **ADJECTIVE** ❶ intended to destroy or weaken a political system • subversive activities. ▷ **NOUN** ❷ Subversives are

people who try to destroy or weaken a political system. **subversion NOUN**

subvert, subverts, subverting, subverted **VERB** FORMAL To subvert something means to cause it to weaken or fail • a cunning campaign to subvert the music industry.

subway, subways **NOUN** ❶ a footpath that goes underneath a road. ❷ an underground railway.

succeed, succeeds, succeeding, succeeded **VERB** ❶ To succeed means to achieve the result you intend. ❷ To succeed someone means to be the next person to have their job. ❸ If one thing succeeds another, it comes after it in time • The explosion was succeeded by a crash. **succeeding ADJECTIVE**
● **SIMILAR WORDS:** ❶ be
● successful, do well, make it

success, successes **NOUN** ❶ Success is the achievement of something you have been trying to do. ❷ Someone who is a success has achieved an important position or made a lot of money.

successful ADJECTIVE having achieved what you intended to do. **successfully ADVERB**

succession, successions **NOUN** ❶ A succession of things is a number of them occurring one after the other. ❷ When someone becomes the next person to have an important position, you can refer to this event as their succession to this position • his succession to the throne. ▷ **PHRASE** ❸ If something happens a number of weeks, months, or years **in succession**, it happens that number

▷ SPELLING NOTE: *LEt's measure the angLE (angle)*

A
B
C
D
E
F
G
H
I
J
K
L
M
N
O
P
Q
R
S
T
U
V
W
X
Y
Z

of times without a break • *Borg won Wimbledon five years in succession.*

successive ADJECTIVE occurring one after the other without a break • *three successive victories.*

successor, successors NOUN Someone's successor is the person who takes their job when they leave.

succinct [Said suk-**singkt**] ADJECTIVE expressing something clearly and in very few words. **succinctly** ADVERB

succulent ADJECTIVE Succulent food is juicy and delicious.

succumb, succumbs, succumbing, succumbed VERB If you succumb to something, you are unable to resist it any longer • *She never succumbed to his charms.*

such ADJECTIVE OR PRONOUN ❶ You use 'such' to refer to the person or thing you have just mentioned, or to someone or something similar • *Naples or Palermo or some such place.* ▷ PHRASE ❷ You can use **such as** to introduce an example of something • *herbal teas such as camomile.* ❸ You can use **such as it is** to indicate that something is not great in quality or quantity • *The action, such as it is, is set in Egypt.* ❹ You can use **such and such** when you want to refer to something that is not specific • *A good trick is to ask whether they have seen such and such a film.* ▷ ADJECTIVE ❺ 'Such' can be used for emphasizing • *I have such a terrible sense of guilt.*

suchlike ADJECTIVE OR PRONOUN used to refer to things similar to those already mentioned • *shampoos, talcs,*

toothbrushes, and suchlike.

suck, sucks, sucking, sucked VERB ❶ If you suck something, you hold it in your mouth and pull at it with your cheeks and tongue, usually to get liquid out of it. ❷ To suck something in a particular direction means to draw it there with a powerful force. ❸ INFORMAL To suck up to someone means to do things to please them in order to obtain praise or approval.

sucker, suckers NOUN ❶ INFORMAL If you call someone a sucker, you mean that they are easily fooled or cheated. ❷ Suckers are pads on the bodies of some animals and insects which they use to cling to a surface.

suckle, suckles, suckling, suckled VERB When a mother suckles a baby, she feeds it with milk from her breast.

sucrose [Said *syoo*-**kroze**] NOUN TECHNICAL Sucrose is sugar in crystalline form found in sugar cane and sugar beet.

suction NOUN ❶ Suction is the force involved when a substance is drawn or sucked from one place to another. ❷ Suction is the process by which two surfaces stick together when the air between them is removed • *They stay there by suction.*

Sudanese [Said *soo*-dan-**neez**] ADJECTIVE ❶ belonging or relating to the Sudan ▷ NOUN ❷ someone who comes from the Sudan.

sudden ADJECTIVE happening quickly and unexpectedly • *a sudden cry.* **suddenly** ADVERB **suddenness** NOUN

sudoku [Said *soo*-**doh**-koo] NOUN a

▷ SPELLING NOTE: *A Rude Idiot Thought He Might Eat Toffee In Church* (<u>arithmetic</u>)

puzzle in which you have to enter numbers in a square made up of nine three-by-three grids, so that every column, row, and grid contains the numbers one to nine.
- **WORD HISTORY:** Japanese for 'numbers singly'

sue, sues, suing, sued **VERB** To sue someone means to start a legal case against them, usually to claim money from them.

suede [*Said* **swayd**] **NOUN** Suede is a thin, soft leather with a rough surface.
- **WORD HISTORY:** from French *gants de Suède* meaning 'gloves from Sweden'

suffer, suffers, suffering, suffered **VERB** ❶ If someone is suffering pain, or suffering as a result of an unpleasant situation, they are badly affected by it. ❷ If something suffers as a result of neglect or a difficult situation, its condition or quality becomes worse • *The bus service is suffering.* **sufferer NOUN suffering NOUN**

suffice, suffices, sufficing, sufficed **VERB** FORMAL If something suffices, it is enough or adequate for a purpose.

sufficient ADJECTIVE If a supply or quantity is sufficient for a purpose, there is enough of it available. **sufficiently ADVERB**

suffix, suffixes **NOUN** (ENGLISH) a group of letters which is added to the end of a word to form a new word, for example '-ology' or '-itis'.

suffocate, suffocates, suffocating, suffocated **VERB** To suffocate means to die as a result of having too little air

or oxygen to breathe. **suffocation NOUN**

suffrage NOUN Suffrage is the right to vote in political elections.

suffragette, suffragettes **NOUN** a woman who, at the beginning of the 20th century, campaigned for women to be given the right to vote.

suffused ADJECTIVE LITERARY If something is suffused with light or colour, light or colour has gradually spread over it.

sugar NOUN Sugar is a sweet substance used to sweeten food and drinks.

suggest, suggests, suggesting, suggested **VERB** ❶ If you suggest a plan or idea to someone, you mention it as a possibility for them to consider. ❷ If something suggests a particular thought or impression, it makes you think in that way or gives you that impression • *Nothing you say suggests he is mentally ill.*
- **SIMILAR WORDS:** ❶ advocate, propose, recommend ❷ hint, imply

suggestion, suggestions **NOUN** ❶ a plan or idea that is mentioned as a possibility for someone to consider. ❷ A suggestion of something is a very slight indication or faint sign of it.
- **SIMILAR WORDS:** ❶ proposal, recommendation

suggestive ADJECTIVE ❶ Something that is suggestive of a particular thing gives a slight hint or sign of it. ❷ Suggestive remarks or gestures make people think about sex.
- **SIMILAR WORDS:** ❷ risqué, smutty

a
b
c
d
e
f
g
h
i
j
k
l
m
n
o
p
q
r
s
t
u
v
w
x
y
z

▷ SPELLING NOTE: *Beautiful Elephants Are Usually Tiny* (<u>beautiful</u>)

suicidal ADJECTIVE ❶ People who are suicidal want to kill themselves. ❷ Suicidal behaviour is so dangerous that it is likely to result in death • *a mad suicidal attack.*

suicide NOUN People who commit suicide deliberately kill themselves.
  ● **WORD HISTORY:** from Latin *sui* meaning 'of oneself' and *caedere* meaning 'to kill'

suicide bomber, suicide bombers NOUN a terrorist who carries out a bomb attack, knowing that he or she will be killed in the explosion. **suicide bombing** NOUN

suit, suits, suiting, suited NOUN ❶ a matching jacket and trousers or skirt. ❷ In a court of law, a suit is a legal action taken by one person against another. ❸ one of four different types of card in a pack of playing cards. The four suits are hearts, clubs, diamonds, and spades ▷ VERB ❹ If a situation or course of action suits you, it is appropriate or acceptable for your purpose. ❺ If a piece of clothing or a colour suits you, you look good when you are wearing it • *that new dress really suits her.* ❻ If you do something to suit yourself, you do it because you want to and without considering other people.

suitable ADJECTIVE right or acceptable for a particular purpose or occasion. **suitability** NOUN **suitably** ADVERB
  ● **SIMILAR WORDS:** appropriate, apt, fitting

suitcase, suitcases NOUN a case in which you carry your clothes when you are travelling.

suite, suites [*Said* **sweet**] NOUN ❶ In a hotel, a suite is a set of rooms. ❷ a set of matching furniture or bathroom fittings.

suited ADJECTIVE right or appropriate for a particular purpose or person • *He is well suited to be minister for the arts.*

suitor, suitors NOUN OLD-FASHIONED A woman's suitor is a man who wants to marry her.

Sukkoth or **Succoth** NOUN RE an eight-day Jewish harvest festival.

sulk, sulks, sulking, sulked VERB Someone who is sulking is showing their annoyance by being silent and moody.

sulky, sulkier, sulkiest ADJECTIVE showing annoyance by being silent and moody.

sullen ADJECTIVE behaving in a bad-tempered and disagreeably silent way • *a sullen and resentful workforce.*

sulphate, sulphates NOUN SCIENCE A sulphate is a salt or compound containing sulphuric acid.

sulphur NOUN SCIENCE Sulphur is a pale yellow nonmetallic element which burns with a very unpleasant smell. Its atomic number is 16 and its symbol is S.

sultan, sultans NOUN In some Muslim countries, the ruler of the country is called the sultan.

sultana, sultanas NOUN ❶ a dried grape. ❷ the wife of a sultan.

sum, sums, summing, summed NOUN ❶ an amount of money. ❷ In arithmetic, a sum is a calculation.

▷ SPELLING NOTE: Betty Eats Cakes And Uses Seven Eggs (*because*)

❸ The sum of something is the total amount of it.

sum up VERB If you sum something up, you briefly describe its main points.

summarize, summarizes, summarizing, summarized; *also spelt* **summarise** VERB (EXAM TERM) To summarize something means to give a short account of its main points.

summary, summaries NOUN ❶ A summary of something is a short account of its main points ▷ ADJECTIVE ❷ A summary action is done without delay or careful thought • *Summary executions are common.* **summarily** ADVERB
● SIMILAR WORDS: ❶ précis, ● résumé, synopsis

summer, summers NOUN Summer is the season between spring and autumn.

summit, summits NOUN ❶ The summit of a mountain is its top. ❷ a meeting between leaders of different countries to discuss particular issues.

summon, summons, summoning, summoned VERB ❶ If someone summons you, they order you to go to them. ❷ If you summon up strength or energy, you make a great effort to be strong or energetic.

summons, summonses NOUN ❶ an official order to appear in court. ❷ an order to go to someone • *The result was a summons to headquarters.*

sumptuous ADJECTIVE Something that is sumptuous is magnificent and obviously very expensive.

sum total NOUN The sum total of a number of things is all of them added or considered together.

sun, suns, sunning, sunned NOUN ❶ The sun is the star providing heat and light for the planets revolving around it in our solar system. ❷ You refer to heat and light from the sun as sun • *We need a bit of sun.* ▷ VERB ❸ If you sun yourself, you sit in the sunshine.

sunbathe, sunbathes, sunbathing, sunbathed VERB If you sunbathe, you sit in the sunshine to get a suntan.

sunburn NOUN Sunburn is sore red skin on someone's body due to too much exposure to the rays of the sun. **sunburnt** ADJECTIVE

sundae, sundaes *[Said **sun**-day]* NOUN a dish of ice cream with cream and fruit or nuts.

Sunday, Sundays NOUN Sunday is the day between Saturday and Monday.
● WORD HISTORY: from Old English ● *sunnandæg* meaning 'day of the ● sun'

Sunday school, Sunday schools NOUN Sunday school is a special class held on Sundays to teach children about Christianity.

sundial, sundials NOUN an object used for telling the time, consisting of a pointer which casts a shadow on a flat base marked with the hours.

sundry ADJECTIVE ❶ 'Sundry' is used to refer to several things or people of various sorts • *sundry journalists and lawyers.* ▷ PHRASE ❷ **All and sundry** means everyone.

sunflower, sunflowers NOUN a tall

a
b
c
d
e
f
g
h
i
j
k
l
m
n
o
p
q
r
s
t
u
v
w
x
y
z

plant with very large yellow flowers.

sunglasses PLURAL NOUN
Sunglasses are spectacles with dark lenses that you wear to protect your eyes from the sun.

sunken ADJECTIVE ❶ having sunk to the bottom of the sea, a river, or lake • *sunken ships*. ❷ A sunken object or area has been constructed below the level of the surrounding area • *a sunken garden*. ❸ curving inwards • *Her cheeks were sunken*.

sunlight NOUN Sunlight is the bright light produced when the sun is shining. **sunlit** ADJECTIVE

sunny, sunnier, sunniest ADJECTIVE When it is sunny, the sun is shining.

sunrise, sunrises NOUN Sunrise is the time in the morning when the sun first appears, and the colours produced in the sky at that time.

sunset, sunsets NOUN Sunset is the time in the evening when the sun disappears below the horizon, and the colours produced in the sky at that time.

sunshine NOUN Sunshine is the bright light produced when the sun is shining.

sunspot, sunspots NOUN (SCIENCE) Sunspots are dark cool patches that appear on the surface of the sun. Sunspots have a strong magnetic field.

sunstroke NOUN (SCIENCE) Sunstroke is an illness caused by spending too much time in hot sunshine.

suntan, suntans NOUN If you have a suntan, the sun has turned your skin brown. **suntanned** ADJECTIVE

super ADJECTIVE very nice or very good • *a super party*.

super- PREFIX 'Super-' is used to describe something that is larger or better than similar things • *a European superstate*.

superb ADJECTIVE very good indeed. **superbly** ADVERB

supercilious [Said soo-per-**sill**-ee-uss] ADJECTIVE If you are supercilious, you behave in a scornful way towards other people because you think they are inferior to you.

superego NOUN TECHNICAL Your superego is the part of your mind that controls your ideas of right and wrong and produces feelings of guilt.

superficial ADJECTIVE
❶ involving only the most obvious or most general aspects of something • *a superficial knowledge of music*. ❷ not having a deep, serious, or genuine interest in anything • *a superficial and rather silly woman*. ❸ Superficial wounds are not very deep or severe. **superficially** ADVERB

superfluous [Said soo-**per**-floo-uss] ADJECTIVE FORMAL unnecessary or no longer needed.

superhuman ADJECTIVE having much greater power or ability than is normally expected of humans • *superhuman strength*.

superimpose, superimposes, superimposing, superimposed VERB To superimpose one image on another means to put the first image on top of the other so that they are seen as one image.

superintendent, superintendents

▷ SPELLING NOTE: *you'll brEAK that Electrical Aerial, Kitty (brEAK)*

a b c d e f g h i j k l m n o p q r s t u v w x y z

WHAT IS A SUPERLATIVE?

Many adjectives have three different forms. These are known as the **positive**, the **comparative**, and the **superlative**. The comparative and superlative are used when you make comparisons.

The **positive** form of an adjective is given as the entry in the dictionary. It is used when there is no comparison between different objects: *Matthew is **tall**.*

The **superlative** form is usually made by adding the ending -*est* to the positive form of the adjective. It shows that something possesses a quality to a greater extent than all the others in its class or group: *Matthew is the **tallest** boy in his class.*

You can also express superlatives by using the words *most* or *least* with the positive (not the superlative) form of the adjective: *Matthew is the **most energetic** member of the family.*

Also look at the grammar box at **comparative**.

NOUN ❶ a police officer above the rank of inspector. **❷** a person whose job is to be responsible for a particular thing • *the superintendent of prisons.*

superior, superiors **ADJECTIVE ❶** better or of higher quality than other similar things. **❷** in a position of higher authority than another person. **❸** showing too much pride and self-importance • *Jerry smiled in a superior way.* ▷ **NOUN ❹** Your superiors are people who are in a higher position than you in society or an organization. **superiority NOUN**

superlative, superlatives *[Said soo-**per**-lat-tiv]* **NOUN ❶** In grammar, the superlative is the form of an adjective which indicates that the person or thing described has more of a particular quality than anyone or anything else. For example, 'quickest', 'best', and 'easiest' are all superlatives ▷ **ADJECTIVE ❷** FORMAL very good indeed • *a superlative performance.*
▶ SEE GRAMMAR BOX ABOVE

supermarket, supermarkets **NOUN** a shop selling food and household goods arranged so that you can help yourself and pay for everything at a till by the exit.

supernatural ADJECTIVE ❶ Something that is supernatural, for example ghosts or witchcraft, cannot be explained by normal scientific laws ▷ **NOUN ❷** You can refer to supernatural things as the supernatural.

supernova, supernovae or supernovas **NOUN** (SCIENCE) A supernova is a star that explodes and for a few days becomes very much brighter than the sun.

superpower, superpowers **NOUN** a very powerful and influential country such as the USA.

supersede, supersedes, superseding, superseded *[Said soo-per-**seed**]* **VERB** If something supersedes another thing, it replaces it because it is more modern • *New*

▷ SPELLING NOTE: *I always visit my FRIend on a FRIday (Friday)*

York superseded Paris as the centre for modern art.

supersonic ADJECTIVE A supersonic aircraft can travel faster than the speed of sound.

superstar, superstars **NOUN** You can refer to a very famous entertainer or sports player as a superstar.

superstition, superstitions **NOUN** Superstition is a belief in things like magic and powers that bring good or bad luck. **superstitious ADJECTIVE**
- **WORD HISTORY:** from Latin
- *superstitio* meaning 'dread of the
- supernatural'

supervise, supervises, supervising, supervised **VERB** To supervise someone means to check and direct what they are doing to make sure that they do it correctly. **supervision NOUN supervisor NOUN**
- **SIMILAR WORDS:** oversee,
- superintend

supper, suppers **NOUN** Supper is a meal eaten in the evening or a snack eaten before you go to bed.

supplant, supplants, supplanting, supplanted **VERB** FORMAL To supplant someone or something means to take their place • *By the 1930s the wristwatch had supplanted the pocket watch.*

supple ADJECTIVE able to bend and move easily.

supplement, supplements, supplementing, supplemented **VERB** ❶ To supplement something means to add something to it to improve it • *Many village men supplemented their wages by fishing for salmon.* ▷ **NOUN** ❷ something that is added to something else to improve it.

supplementary ADJECTIVE added to something else to improve it • *supplementary doses of vitamin E.*

supplementary angle, supplementary angles **NOUN** (MATHS) A supplementary angle is either of two angles that together make up 180°.

supplier, suppliers **NOUN** a firm which provides particular goods.

supply, supplies, supplying, supplied **VERB** ❶ To supply someone with something means to provide it or send it to them ▷ **NOUN** ❷ A supply of something is an amount available for use • *the world's supply of precious metals.* ❸ IN PLURAL Supplies are food and equipment for a particular purpose.

support, supports, supporting, supported **VERB** ❶ If you support someone, you agree with their aims and want them to succeed. ❷ If you support someone who is in difficulties, you are kind, encouraging, and helpful to them. ❸ If something supports an object, it is underneath it and holding it up. ❹ To support someone or something means to prevent them from falling by holding them. ❺ To support someone financially means to provide them with money ▷ **NOUN** ❻ an object that is holding something up. ❼ Moral support is encouragement given to someone to help them do something difficult. ❽ Financial support is money that is provided for someone or something. **supportable ADJECTIVE**

supporter, supporters **NOUN** a

A B C D E F G H I J K L M N O P Q R **S** T U V W X Y Z

person who agrees with or helps someone.

supportive ADJECTIVE A supportive person is encouraging and helpful to someone who is in difficulties.

suppose, supposes, supposing, supposed VERB **①** If you suppose that something is the case, you think that it is likely • *I supposed that would be too obvious.* ▷ PHRASE **②** You can say **I suppose** when you are not entirely certain or enthusiastic about something • *Yes, I suppose he could come.* ▷ CONJUNCTION **③** You can use 'suppose' or 'supposing' when you are considering or suggesting a possible situation or action • *Supposing he were to break down under interrogation?*

supposed ADJECTIVE **①** 'Supposed' is used to express doubt about something that is generally believed • *the supposed culprit.* **②** If something is supposed to be done or to happen, it is planned, expected, or required to be done or to happen • *You are supposed to report it to the police* • *It was supposed to be this afternoon.* **③** Something that is supposed to be the case is generally believed or thought to be so • *Wimbledon is supposed to be the best tournament of them all.* **supposedly** ADVERB

supposition, suppositions NOUN something that is believed or assumed to be true • *the supposition that science requires an ordered universe.*

suppress, suppresses, suppressing, suppressed VERB **①** If an army or government suppresses an activity, it prevents people from doing it. **②** If

someone suppresses a piece of information, they prevent it from becoming generally known. **③** If you suppress your feelings, you stop yourself expressing them.
suppression NOUN
● SIMILAR WORDS: **①** crush, quell, ● stop

supremacy [Said soo-**prem**-mass-ee] NOUN If a group of people has supremacy over others, it is more powerful than the others.

supreme ADJECTIVE **①** 'Supreme' is used as part of a title to indicate the highest level of an organization or system • *the Supreme Court.*
② 'Supreme' is used to emphasize the greatness of something • *the supreme achievement of the human race.*
supremely ADVERB
● SIMILAR WORDS: **②** greatest, ● highest, paramount

surcharge, surcharges NOUN an additional charge.

sure, surer, surest ADJECTIVE **①** If you are sure about something, you have no doubts about it. **②** If you are sure of yourself, you are very confident. **③** If something is sure to happen, it will definitely happen. **④** Sure means reliable or accurate • *a sure sign that something is wrong.*
▷ PHRASE **⑤** If you **make sure** about something, you check it or take action to see that it is done
▷ INTERJECTION **⑥** Sure is an informal way of saying 'yes' • *'Can I come too?' – 'Sure'.*

surely ADVERB 'Surely' is used to emphasize the belief that something is the case • *Surely these people here knew that?*

▷ SPELLING NOTE: *The government licenSes Schnapps (licenses)*

a
b
c
d
e
f
g
h
i
j
k
l
m
n
o
p
q
r
s
t
u
v
w
x
y
z

surf, surfs, surfing, surfed **VERB**
① When you surf, you go surfing.
② When you surf the Internet, you go from website to website reading the information ▷ **NOUN** **③** Surf is the white foam that forms on the top of waves when they break near the shore.

surface, surfaces, surfacing, surfaced **NOUN** **①** The surface of something is the top or outside area of it. **②** The surface of a situation is what can be seen easily rather than what is hidden or not immediately obvious ▷ **VERB** **③** If someone surfaces, they come up from under water to the surface.

surfboard, surfboards **NOUN** a long narrow lightweight board used for surfing.

surf club, surf clubs **NOUN** In Australia, a surf club is an organization of lifesavers in charge of safety on a particular beach, and which often provides leisure facilities.

surfeit [Said sur-fit] **NOUN** If there is a surfeit of something, there is too much of it.

surfing NOUN Surfing is a sport which involves riding towards the shore on the top of a large wave while standing on a surfboard.

surge, surges, surging, surged **NOUN**
① a sudden great increase in the amount of something • a surge of panic. ▷ **VERB** **②** If something surges, it moves suddenly and powerfully • The soldiers surged forwards.

surgeon, surgeons **NOUN** a doctor who performs operations.

surgery, surgeries **NOUN** **①** Surgery is medical treatment involving cutting open part of the patient's body to treat the damaged part. **②** The room or building where a doctor or dentist works is called a surgery. **③** A period of time during which a doctor is available to see patients is called surgery • evening surgery.

surgical ADJECTIVE used in or involving a medical operation • surgical gloves. **surgically ADVERB**

surly, surlier, surliest **ADJECTIVE** rude and bad-tempered. **surliness NOUN**

surmise, surmises, surmising, surmised **VERB** FORMAL To surmise something means to guess it • I surmised it was of French manufacture.

surmount, surmounts, surmounting, surmounted **VERB**
① To surmount a difficulty means to manage to solve it. **②** FORMAL If something is surmounted by a particular thing, that thing is on top of it • The island is surmounted by a huge black castle.

surname, surnames **NOUN** Your surname is your last name which you share with other members of your family.

surpass, surpasses, surpassing, surpassed **VERB** FORMAL To surpass someone or something means to be better than them.

surplus, surpluses **NOUN** If there is a surplus of something there is more of it than is needed.
● **SIMILAR WORDS:** excess, surfeit

surprise, surprises, surprising,

A B C D E F G H I J K L M N O P Q R **S** T U V W X Y Z

surprised NOUN **1** an unexpected event. **2** Surprise is the feeling caused when something unexpected happens ▷ VERB **3** If something surprises you, it gives you a feeling of surprise. **4** If you surprise someone, you do something they are not expecting. **surprising** ADJECTIVE

surreal ADJECTIVE very strange and dreamlike.

surrealism ADJECTIVE (ART) Surrealism began in the 1920s. It involves the putting together of strange images and things that are not normally seen together.

surrender, surrenders, surrendering, surrendered VERB **1** To surrender means to stop fighting and agree that the other side has won. **2** If you surrender to a temptation or feeling, you let it take control of you. **3** To surrender something means to give it up to someone else • *The gallery director surrendered his keys.* ▷ NOUN **4** Surrender is a situation in which one side in a fight agrees that the other side has won and gives in.
● SIMILAR WORDS: **1** give in, ● submit, yield **4** capitulation, ● submission

surreptitious [Said sur-rep-**tish**-uss] ADJECTIVE A surreptitious action is done secretly or so that no-one will notice • *a surreptitious glance.* **surreptitiously** ADVERB

surrogate, surrogates ADJECTIVE **1** acting as a substitute for someone or something ▷ NOUN **2** a person or thing that acts as a substitute.

surround, surrounds, surrounding,

surrounded VERB **1** To surround someone or something means to be situated all around them ▷ NOUN **2** The surround of something is its outside edge or border.
● SIMILAR WORDS: **1** encircle, ● enclose

surrounding, surroundings ADJECTIVE The surrounding area of a particular place is the area around it • *the surrounding countryside.*

surroundings PLURAL NOUN You can refer to the area and environment around a place or person as their surroundings • *very comfortable surroundings.*

surveillance [Said sur-**vay**-lanss] NOUN Surveillance is the close watching of a person's activities by the police or army.
● WORD HISTORY: from French ● *surveiller* meaning 'to watch over'

survey, surveys, surveying, surveyed VERB **1** To survey something means to look carefully at the whole of it. **2** To survey a building or piece of land means to examine it carefully in order to make a report or plan of its structure and features ▷ NOUN **3** A survey of something is a detailed examination of it, often in the form of a report.
● SIMILAR WORDS: **1** look over, ● scan, view

surveyor, surveyors NOUN a person whose job is to survey buildings or land.

survival, survivals NOUN Survival is being able to continue living or existing in spite of great danger or difficulties • *There was no hope of*

a b c d e f g h i j k l m n o p q r **s** t u v w x y z

▷ SPELLING NOTE: *plaice the fish has a glittering 'EYE' (I) (pla*i*ce)*

A
B
C
D
E
F
G
H
I
J
K
L
M
N
O
P
Q
R
S
T
U
V
W
X
Y
Z

survival for the missing diver.

survive, survives, surviving, survived
VERB To survive means to continue to
live or exist in spite of a great danger
or difficulties • *a German monk who
survived the shipwreck.* **survivor**
NOUN

sus- **PREFIX** `Sus-' is another form of
sub-.

susceptible **ADJECTIVE** If you are
susceptible to something, you are
likely to be influenced or affected by it
• *Elderly people are more susceptible to
infection.* **susceptibility** **NOUN**

suspect, suspects, suspecting,
suspected **VERB** [Said sus-**pekt**] **①** If
you suspect something, you think that
it is likely or is probably true • *I
suspected that the report would be sent.*
② If you suspect something, you have
doubts about its reliability • *He
suspected her intent.* **③** If you suspect
someone of doing something wrong,
you think that they have done it
▷ **NOUN** [Said **sus**-pekt] **④** someone
who is thought to be guilty of a crime
▷ **ADJECTIVE** **⑤** If something is
suspect, it cannot be trusted or relied
upon • *a rather suspect holy man.*

suspend, suspends, suspending,
suspended **VERB** **①** If something is
suspended, it is hanging from
somewhere • *the television set
suspended above the bar.* **②** To
suspend an activity or event means to
delay it or stop it for a while. **③** If
someone is suspended from their job,
they are told not to do it for a period of
time, usually as a punishment.

suspender, suspenders **NOUN**
Suspenders are fastenings which hold

up a woman's stockings.

suspense **NOUN** Suspense is a
state of excitement or anxiety caused
by having to wait for something.

suspension **NOUN** **①** The
suspension of something is the
delaying or stopping of it. **②** A
person's suspension is their removal
from a job for a period of time, usually
as a punishment. **③** The suspension
of a vehicle consists of springs and
shock absorbers which provide a
smooth ride. **④** a liquid mixture in
which very small bits of a solid
material are contained and are not
dissolved.

suspicion, suspicions **NOUN**
① Suspicion is the feeling of not
trusting someone or the feeling that
something is wrong. **②** a feeling that
something is likely to happen or is
probably true • *the suspicion that more
could have been achieved.*
● **SIMILAR WORDS:** **①** distrust,
● misgiving, scepticism

suspicious **ADJECTIVE** **①** If you
are suspicious of someone, you do not
trust them. **②** 'Suspicious' is used to
describe things that make you think
that there is something wrong with a
situation • *suspicious circumstances.*
suspiciously **ADVERB**
● **SIMILAR WORDS:** **②** dubious,
● questionable, suspect

sustain, sustains, sustaining,
sustained **VERB** **①** To sustain
something means to continue it for a
period of time • *Their team-mates were
unable to sustain the challenge.* **②** If
something sustains you, it gives you
energy and strength. **③** FORMAL To
sustain an injury or loss means to

▷ SPELLING NOTE: *I went to see (C) the doctor's new practiCe (practice)*

suffer it • *She sustained a broken toe.*

sustainable ADJECTIVE
❶ capable of being sustained. ❷ If economic development or energy resources are sustainable they are capable of being maintained at a steady level without exhausting natural resources or causing ecological damage • *sustainable forestry.*

sustenance NOUN FORMAL
Sustenance is food and drink.

swab, swabs, swabbing, swabbed
NOUN ❶ a small piece of cotton wool used for cleaning a wound ▷ VERB
❷ To swab something means to clean it using a large mop and a lot of water.
❸ To swab a wound means to clean it or take specimens from it using a swab.

swag, swags NOUN INFORMAL
❶ goods or valuables, especially ones which have been gained dishonestly.
❷ In Australian and New Zealand English, the bundle of possessions belonging to a tramp. ❸ In Australian and New Zealand English, swags of something is lots of it.

swagger, swaggers, swaggering, swaggered VERB ❶ To swagger means to walk in a proud, exaggerated way ▷ NOUN ❷ an exaggerated walk.

swagman, swagmen NOUN
INFORMAL In Australia and New Zealand in the past, a tramp who carried his possessions on his back.

swallow, swallows, swallowing, swallowed VERB ❶ If you swallow something, you make it go down your throat and into your stomach.
❷ When you swallow, you move your throat muscles as if you were swallowing something, especially when you are nervous ▷ NOUN ❸ a bird with pointed wings and a long forked tail.

swamp, swamps, swamping, swamped NOUN ❶ an area of permanently wet land ▷ VERB ❷ If something is swamped, it is covered or filled with water. ❸ If you are swamped by things, you have more than you are able to deal with • *She was swamped with calls.* **swampy** ADJECTIVE

swan, swans NOUN a large, usually white, bird with a long neck that lives on rivers or lakes.

swap, swaps, swapping, swapped
[rhymes with stop] VERB To swap one thing for another means to replace the first thing with the second, often by making an exchange with another person • *Webb swapped shirts with a Leeds player.*
  ● SIMILAR WORDS: exchange,
  ● switch, trade

swarm, swarms, swarming, swarmed NOUN ❶ A swarm of insects is a large group of them flying together ▷ VERB ❷ When bees or other insects swarm, they fly together in a large group. ❸ If people swarm somewhere, a lot of people go there quickly and at the same time • *the crowds of office workers who swarm across the bridge.* ❹ If a place is swarming with people, there are a lot of people there • *The town was swarming with visiting supporters.*

swarthy, swarthier, swarthiest
ADJECTIVE A swarthy person has a dark complexion.

a
b
c
d
e
f
g
h
i
j
k
l
m
n
o
p
q
r
s
t
u
v
w
x
y
z

▷ SPELLING NOTE: *You must practiSe your Ss (practise)*

swashbuckling ADJECTIVE
'Swashbuckling' is used to describe people who have the exciting behaviour or appearance of pirates.
● **WORD HISTORY:** from Middle English *swashbuckling* meaning 'making a noise by striking your sword against a shield'

swastika, swastikas [Said *swoss-tik-ka*] **NOUN** a symbol in the shape of a cross with each arm bent over at right angles. It was the official symbol of the Nazis in Germany, but in India it is a good luck sign.
● **WORD HISTORY:** from Sanskrit *svasti* meaning 'prosperity'

swat, swats, swatting, swatted **VERB** To swat an insect means to hit it sharply in order to kill it.

swathe, swathes [rhymes with *bathe*] **NOUN** ❶ a long strip of cloth that is wrapped around something • *swathes of white silk.* ❷ A swathe of land is a long strip of it.

swathed ADJECTIVE If someone is swathed in something, they are wrapped in it • *She was swathed in towels.*

sway, sways, swaying, swayed **VERB** ❶ To sway means to lean or swing slowly from side to side. ❷ If something sways you, it influences your judgment ▷ **NOUN** ❸ LITERARY Sway is the power to influence people • *under the sway of more powerful neighbours.*

swear, swears, swearing, swore, sworn **VERB** ❶ To swear means to say words that are considered to be very rude or blasphemous. ❷ If you swear to something, you state solemnly that you will do it or that it is true. ❸ If you swear by something, you firmly believe that it is a reliable cure or solution • *Some women swear by extra vitamins.*

swearword, swearwords **NOUN** a word which is considered to be rude or blasphemous, which people use when they are angry.

sweat, sweats, sweating, sweated **NOUN** ❶ Sweat is the salty liquid produced by your sweat glands when you are hot or afraid ▷ **VERB** ❷ When you sweat, sweat comes through the pores in your skin in order to lower the temperature of your body.

sweater, sweaters **NOUN** a knitted piece of clothing covering your upper body and arms.

sweatshirt, sweatshirts **NOUN** a piece of clothing made of thick cotton, covering your upper body and arms.

sweaty ADJECTIVE covered or soaked with sweat.

swede, swedes **NOUN** a large round root vegetable with yellow flesh and a brownish-purple skin.
● **WORD HISTORY:** from *Swedish turnip* because it was introduced from Sweden in the 18th century

Swede, Swedes **NOUN** someone who comes from Sweden.

Swedish ADJECTIVE ❶ belonging or relating to Sweden ▷ **NOUN** ❷ Swedish is the main language spoken in Sweden.

sweep, sweeps, sweeping, swept **VERB** ❶ If you sweep the floor, you use a brush to gather up dust or rubbish from it. ❷ To sweep things off a surface means to push them all off with a quick, smooth movement. ❸ If something sweeps from one place to another, it moves there very quickly • *A gust of wind swept over the terrace.* ❹ If an attitude or new fashion sweeps a place, it spreads rapidly through it • *a phenomenon that is sweeping America.* ▷ NOUN ❺ If you do something with a sweep of your arm, you do it with a wide curving movement of your arm.

sweeping ADJECTIVE ❶ A sweeping curve or movement is long and wide. ❷ A sweeping statement is based on a general assumption rather than on careful thought. ❸ affecting a lot of people to a great extent • *sweeping changes.*

sweet, sweeter, sweetest; sweets ADJECTIVE ❶ containing a lot of sugar • *a mug of sweet tea.* ❷ pleasant and satisfying • *sweet success.* ❸ A sweet smell is soft and fragrant. ❹ A sweet sound is gentle and tuneful. ❺ attractive and delightful • *a sweet little baby.* ▷ NOUN ❻ Things such as toffees, chocolates, and mints are sweets. ❼ a dessert. **sweetly** ADVERB **sweetness** NOUN
● SIMILAR WORDS: ❺ charming,
● cute, delightful

sweet corn NOUN Sweet corn is a long stalk covered with juicy yellow seeds that can be eaten as a vegetable.

sweeten, sweetens, sweetening, sweetened VERB To sweeten food means to add sugar or another sweet substance to it.

sweetener, sweeteners NOUN a very sweet, artificial substance that

can be used instead of sugar.

sweetheart, sweethearts NOUN ❶ You can call someone who you are very fond of 'sweetheart'. ❷ A young person's sweetheart is their boyfriend or girlfriend.

sweet pea, sweet peas NOUN Sweet peas are delicate, very fragrant climbing flowers.

sweet tooth NOUN If you have a sweet tooth, you like sweet food very much.

swell, swells, swelling, swelled, swollen VERB ❶ If something swells, it becomes larger and rounder • *It causes the abdomen to swell.* ❷ If an amount swells, it increases in number ▷ NOUN ❸ The regular up and down movement of the waves at sea can be called a swell.

swelling, swellings NOUN ❶ an enlarged area on your body as a result of injury or illness. ❷ The swelling of something is an increase in its size.

sweltering ADJECTIVE If the weather is sweltering, it is very hot.

swerve, swerves, swerving, swerved VERB To swerve means to suddenly change direction to avoid colliding with something.

swift, swifter, swiftest; swifts ADJECTIVE ❶ happening or moving very quickly • *a swift glance.* ▷ NOUN ❷ a bird with narrow crescent-shaped wings. **swiftly** ADVERB

swig, swigs, swigging, swigged INFORMAL VERB ❶ To swig a drink means to drink it in large mouthfuls, usually from a bottle ▷ NOUN ❷ If you have a swig of a drink, you take a

a b c d e f g h i j k l m n o p q r **s** t u v w x y z

▷ SPELLING NOTE: *LEarn the principLEs (principle)*

large mouthful of it.

swill, swills, swilling, swilled **VERB** ❶ To swill something means to pour water over it to clean it • *Swill the can out thoroughly.* ▷ **NOUN** ❷ Swill is a liquid mixture containing waste food that is fed to pigs.

swim, swims, swimming, swam, swum **VERB** ❶ To swim means to move through water using various movements with parts of the body. ❷ If things are swimming, it seems as if everything you see is moving and you feel dizzy ▷ **NOUN** ❸ If you go for a swim, you go into water to swim for pleasure. **swimmer NOUN**

swimming NOUN Swimming is the activity of moving through water using your arms and legs.

swimming bath, swimming baths **NOUN** a public swimming pool.

swimming costume, swimming costumes **NOUN** the clothing worn by a woman when she goes swimming.

swimming pool, swimming pools **NOUN** a large hole that has been tiled and filled with water for swimming.

swimming trunks PLURAL NOUN Swimming trunks are shorts worn by a man when he goes swimming.

swimsuit, swimsuits **NOUN** a swimming costume.

swindle, swindles, swindling, swindled **VERB** ❶ To swindle someone means to deceive them to obtain money or property ▷ **NOUN** ❷ a trick in which someone is cheated out of money or property. **swindler NOUN**

swine, swines **NOUN** ❶ OLD-FASHIONED Swine are pigs. ❷ INFORMAL If you call someone a swine, you mean they are nasty and spiteful.

swing, swings, swinging, swung **VERB** ❶ If something swings, it moves repeatedly from side to side from a fixed point. ❷ If someone or something swings in a particular direction, they turn quickly or move in a sweeping curve in that direction ▷ **NOUN** ❸ a seat hanging from a frame or a branch, which you sit in and move backwards and forwards. ❹ A swing in opinion is a significant change in people's opinion.

swipe, swipes, swiping, swiped **VERB** ❶ To swipe at something means to try to hit it making a curving movement with the arm. ❷ INFORMAL To swipe something means to steal it. ❸ To swipe a credit card means to pass it through a machine that electronically reads the information stored in the card ▷ **NOUN** ❹ To take a swipe at something means to swipe at it.

swirl, swirls, swirling, swirled **VERB** To swirl means to move quickly in circles • *The black water swirled around his legs.*

swish, swishes, swishing, swished **VERB** ❶ To swish means to move quickly through the air making a soft sound • *The curtains swished back.* ▷ **NOUN** ❷ the sound made when something swishes.

Swiss ADJECTIVE ❶ belonging or relating to Switzerland ▷ **NOUN** ❷ someone who comes from Switzerland.

switch, switches, switching, switched **NOUN** ❶ a small control for an electrical device or machine. ❷ a change • *a switch in routine.* ▷ **VERB** ❸ To switch to a different task or topic means to change to it. ❹ If you switch things, you exchange one for the other.
switch off VERB To switch off a light or machine means to stop it working by pressing a switch.
switch on VERB To switch on a light or machine means to start it working by pressing a switch.

switchboard, switchboards **NOUN** The switchboard in an organization is the part where all telephone calls are received.

swivel, swivels, swivelling, swivelled **VERB** ❶ To swivel means to turn round on a central point ▷ **ADJECTIVE** ❷ A swivel chair or lamp is made so that you can move the main part of it while the base remains in a fixed position.

swollen ADJECTIVE Something that is swollen has swelled up.
● **SIMILAR WORDS:** distended,
● enlarged, puffed up

swoon, swoons, swooning, swooned **VERB** LITERARY To swoon means to faint as a result of strong emotion.

swoop, swoops, swooping, swooped **VERB** To swoop means to move downwards through the air in a fast curving movement • *A flock of pigeons swooped low over the square.*

swop another spelling of **swap**.

sword, swords [*Said* **sord**] **NOUN** a weapon consisting of a very long blade with a short handle.

swordfish, swordfishes or swordfish **NOUN** a large sea fish with an upper jaw which sticks out like a sword.

sworn ADJECTIVE If you make a sworn statement, you swear that everything in it is true.

swot, swots, swotting, swotted INFORMAL **VERB** ❶ To swot means to study or revise very hard. ❷ If you swot up on a subject you find out as much about it as possible in a short time ▷ **NOUN** ❸ someone who spends too much time studying.

sycamore, sycamores [*Said sik-am-mor*] **NOUN** a tree that has large leaves with five points.

syllable, syllables **NOUN** (ENGLISH) a part of a word that contains a single vowel sound and is pronounced as a unit. For example, 'book' has one syllable and 'reading' has two.

syllabus, syllabuses or syllabi **NOUN** The subjects that are studied for a particular course or examination are called the syllabus.
● **USAGE NOTE:** The plural *syllabuses*
● is much more common than *syllabi*

symbiosis [*Said sim-bee-oh-siss*] **NOUN** (SCIENCE) FORMAL Symbiosis is a relationship between two organisms which benefits both. **symbiotic ADJECTIVE**

symbol, symbols **NOUN** (RE) a shape, design, or idea that is used to represent something • *The fish has long been a symbol of Christianity.*
● **SIMILAR WORDS:** emblem,
● representation, sign

symbolic ADJECTIVE Something that is symbolic has a special meaning

a b c d e f g h i j k l m n o p q r **s** t u v w x y z

▷ SPELLING NOTE: *the QUeen stood on the QUay (quay)*

that is considered to represent something else • *Six tons of ivory were burned in a symbolic ceremony.*

symbolize, symbolizes, symbolizing, symbolized; *also spelt* **symbolise** VERB If a shape, design, or idea symbolizes something, it is regarded as being a symbol of it • *In China and Japan the carp symbolizes courage.* **symbolism** NOUN

symmetrical ADJECTIVE (MATHS) If something is symmetrical, it could be split into two halves, one being the exact reflection of the other. **symmetrically** ADVERB

symmetry NOUN (MATHS) Something that has symmetry is symmetrical.

sympathetic ADJECTIVE ❶ A sympathetic person shows kindness and understanding to other people. ❷ If you are sympathetic to a proposal or an idea, you approve of it.

sympathize, sympathizes, sympathizing, sympathized; *also spelt* **sympathise** VERB To sympathize with someone who is in difficulties means to show them understanding and care.

sympathizer, sympathizers; *also spelt* **sympathiser** NOUN People who support a particular cause can be referred to as sympathizers.

sympathy, sympathies NOUN ❶ Sympathy is kindness and understanding towards someone who is in difficulties. ❷ If you have sympathy with someone's ideas or actions, you agree with them ▷ PHRASE ❸ If you do something **in sympathy** with someone, you do it to

show your support for them.
● SIMILAR WORDS: ❶ compassion, ● pity

symphony, symphonies NOUN a piece of music for an orchestra, usually in four movements.
● WORD HISTORY: from Greek *sumphōnos* meaning 'harmonious'

symptom, symptoms NOUN ❶ something wrong with your body that is a sign of an illness. ❷ Something that is considered to be a sign of a bad situation can be referred to as a symptom of it • *another symptom of the racism sweeping across the country.* **symptomatic** ADJECTIVE

synagogue, synagogues [*Said sin-a-gog*] NOUN (RE) a building where Jewish people meet for worship and religious instruction.
● WORD HISTORY: from Greek *sunagōgē* meaning 'meeting'

synchronize, synchronizes, synchronizing, synchronized [*Said sing-kron-nize*]; *also spelt* **synchronise** VERB ❶ (MUSIC) To synchronize two actions means to do them at the same time and speed. ❷ To synchronize watches means to set them to show exactly the same time as each other.

syncopation NOUN (MUSIC) Syncopation in rhythm is the stressing of weak beats instead of the usual strong ones.
● WORD HISTORY: from Greek *suncopē* meaning 'cutting off'

syndicate, syndicates NOUN an association of business people formed to carry out a particular project.

▷ SPELLING NOTE: *Rhythmical Hounds Yap To Heavy Music (rhythm)*

syndrome, syndromes **NOUN** ❶ a medical condition characterized by a particular set of symptoms • *Down's syndrome.* ❷ You can refer to a typical set of characteristics as a syndrome • *the syndrome of skipping from one wonder diet to the next.*

synecdoche [Said sin-**ek**-dok-kee] **NOUN** (ENGLISH) a figure of speech in which part of something is used to mean the whole. For example, in *Give us this day our daily bread*, bread means 'food'.

synod, synods **NOUN** a council of church leaders which meets regularly to discuss religious and moral issues.

synonym, synonyms **NOUN** (ENGLISH) If two words have the same or a very similar meaning, they are synonyms.

synonymous **ADJECTIVE** ❶ Two words that are synonymous have the same or very similar meanings. ❷ If two things are closely associated, you can say that one is synonymous with the other • *New York is synonymous with the Statue of Liberty.*

synopsis, synopses **NOUN** a summary of a book, play, or film.

syntax **NOUN** (ENGLISH) The syntax of a language is its grammatical rules and the way its words are arranged.

synthesis, syntheses **NOUN** ❶ A synthesis of different ideas or styles is a blended combination of them. ❷ (SCIENCE) The synthesis of a substance is its production by means of a chemical reaction. **synthesize**

VERB synthesizer NOUN

synthetic **ADJECTIVE** made from artificial substances rather than natural ones.

syphon another spelling of **siphon**.

Syrian, Syrians [Said **sirr**-ee-an] **ADJECTIVE** ❶ belonging or relating to Syria ▷ **NOUN** ❷ someone who comes from Syria.

syringe, syringes [Said sir-**rinj**] **NOUN** a hollow tube with a part which is pushed down inside and a fine hollow needle at one end, used for injecting or extracting liquids.

syrup, syrups **NOUN** a thick sweet liquid made by boiling sugar with water.
● **WORD HISTORY:** from Arabic
● *sharab* meaning 'drink'

system, systems **NOUN** ❶ (LIBRARY) an organized way of doing or arranging something according to a fixed plan or set of rules. ❷ People sometimes refer to the government and administration of the country as the system. ❸ You can also refer to a set of equipment as a system • *an old stereo system.* ❹ In biology, a system of a particular kind is the set of organs that perform that function • *the immune system.*
● **SIMILAR WORDS:** ❶ method,
● procedure, routine

systematic **ADJECTIVE** following a fixed plan and done in an efficient way • *a systematic study.* **systematically ADVERB**

a b c d e f g h i j k l m n o p q r **s** t u v w x y z

Tt

tab, tabs NOUN a small extra piece that is attached to something, for example on a curtain so it can be hung on a pole.

tabby, tabbies NOUN a cat whose fur has grey, brown, or black stripes.
● **WORD HISTORY:** from Old French
● *tabis* meaning 'striped silk cloth'

tabernacle, tabernacles [Said **tab-er-nak-kl**] NOUN ❶ a place of worship for certain Christian groups. ❷ a sanctuary in which the ancient Hebrews carried the Ark of the Covenant as they wandered from place to place. ❸ a Jewish temple.
● **WORD HISTORY:** from Latin
● *tabernaculum* meaning 'tent'

table, tables, tabling, tabled NOUN ❶ a piece of furniture with a flat horizontal top supported by one or more legs. ❷ a set of facts or figures arranged in rows or columns ▷ VERB ❸ If you table something such as a proposal, you say formally that you want it to be discussed.

tablecloth, tablecloths NOUN a cloth used to cover a table and keep it clean.

tablespoon, tablespoons NOUN a large spoon used for serving food; also the amount that a tablespoon contains.

tablet, tablets NOUN ❶ any small, round pill made of powdered medicine. ❷ a slab of stone with words cut into it.

table tennis NOUN Table tennis is a game for two or four people in which you use bats to hit a small hollow ball over a low net across a table.

tabloid, tabloids NOUN (ENGLISH) a newspaper with small pages, short news stories, and lots of photographs.

taboo, taboos NOUN ❶ a social custom that some words, subjects, or actions must be avoided because they are considered embarrassing or offensive • *We have a powerful taboo against boasting.* ❷ a religious custom that forbids people to do something ▷ **ADJECTIVE** ❸ forbidden or disapproved of • *Retirement has become a taboo subject.*

tacit [Said **tass**-it] ADJECTIVE understood or implied without actually being said or written. **tacitly** ADVERB

taciturn [Said **tass**-it-urn] ADJECTIVE Someone who is taciturn does not talk very much and so seems unfriendly.

tack, tacks, tacking, tacked NOUN ❶ a short nail with a broad, flat head. ❷ If you change tack, you start to use a different method for dealing with something ▷ VERB ❸ If you tack something to a surface, you nail it there with tacks. ❹ If you tack a piece

▷ SPELLING NOTE: *On WEDNESday Wayne WED NESta (Wednesday)*

of fabric, you sew it with long loose stitches.

tackies or **takkies** PLURAL NOUN INFORMAL In South African English, tackies are tennis shoes or plimsolls.

tackle, tackles, tackling, tackled VERB ❶ If you tackle a difficult task, you start dealing with it in a determined way. ❷ If you tackle someone in a game such as soccer, you try to get the ball away from them. ❸ If you tackle someone about something, you talk to them about it in order to get something changed or dealt with ▷ NOUN ❹ A tackle in sport is an attempt to get the ball away from your opponent. ❺ Tackle is the equipment used for fishing.
● SIMILAR WORDS: ❶ deal with,
● undertake

tacky, tackier, tackiest ADJECTIVE ❶ slightly sticky to touch • *The cream feels tacky to the touch.* ❷ INFORMAL badly made and in poor taste • *tacky furniture.*

tact NOUN Tact is the ability to see when a situation is difficult or delicate and to handle it without upsetting people. **tactless** ADJECTIVE **tactlessly** ADVERB
● SIMILAR WORDS: delicacy,
● diplomacy, discretion

tactful ADJECTIVE behaving with or showing tact. **tactfully** ADVERB

tactic, tactics NOUN ❶ PE Tactics are the methods you use to achieve what you want, especially to win a game. ❷ Tactics are also the ways in which troops and equipment are used in order to win a battle. **tactical**

ADJECTIVE **tactically** ADVERB

tactile ADJECTIVE involving the sense of touch.

tadpole, tadpoles NOUN Tadpoles are the larvae of frogs and toads. They are black with round heads and long tails and live in water.
● **WORD HISTORY:** from Middle
● English *tadde* meaning 'toad' and
● *pol* meaning 'head'

taffeta [Said *taf-fit-a*] NOUN Taffeta is a stiff, shiny fabric that is used mainly for making women's clothes.

tag, tags, tagging, tagged NOUN ❶ a small label made of cloth, paper, or plastic. ❷ If you tag along with someone, you go with them or behind them.

tail, tails, tailing, tailed NOUN ❶ The tail of an animal, bird, or fish is the part extending beyond the end of its body. ❷ Tail can be used to mean the end part of something • *the tail of the plane.* ❸ IN PLURAL If a man is wearing tails, he is wearing a formal jacket which has two long pieces hanging down at the back ▷ VERB ❹ INFORMAL If you tail someone, you follow them in order to find out where they go and what they do
▷ ADJECTIVE OR ADVERB ❺ The 'tails' side of a coin is the side which does not have a person's head.
tail off VERB If something tails off, it becomes gradually less.

tailback, tailbacks NOUN a long queue of traffic stretching back from whatever is blocking the road.

tailor, tailors, tailoring, tailored NOUN ❶ a person who makes, alters, and repairs clothes, especially for men

a
b
c
d
e
f
g
h
i
j
k
l
m
n
o
p
q
r
s
t
u
v
w
x
y
z

▷ SPELLING NOTE: *Eddy Ant thinks mEAt is a grEAt trEAt to Eat (-ea-)*

▷ **VERB** ❷ If something is tailored for a particular purpose, it is specially designed for it.

tailor-made ADJECTIVE suitable for a particular person or purpose, or specifically designed for them.

taint, taints, tainting, tainted **VERB**
❶ To taint something is to spoil it by adding something undesirable to it
▷ **NOUN** ❷ an undesirable quality in something which spoils it.

taipan, taipans **NOUN** a large and very poisonous Australian snake.

take, takes, taking, took, taken **VERB**
❶ 'Take' is used to show what action or activity is being done • *Amy took a bath* • *She took her driving test.* ❷ If something takes a certain amount of time, or a particular quality or ability, it requires it • *He takes three hours to get ready.* ❸ If you take something, you put your hand round it and hold it or carry it • *Here, let me take your coat.*
❹ If you take someone somewhere, you drive them there by car or lead them there. ❺ If you take something that is offered to you, you accept it
• *He had to take the job.* ❻ If you take the responsibility or blame for something, you accept responsibility or blame. ❼ If you take something that does not belong to you, you steal it. ❽ If you take pills or medicine, you swallow them. ❾ If you can take something painful, you can bear it
• *We can't take much more of this.* ❿ If you take someone's advice, you do what they say you should do. ⓫ If you take a person's temperature or pulse, you measure it. ⓬ If you take a car or train, or a road or route, you use it to go from one place to another.

take after VERB If you take after someone in your family, you look or behave like them.

take down VERB If you take down what someone is saying, you write it down.

take in VERB ❶ If someone is taken in, they are deceived. ❷ If you take something in, you understand it.

take off VERB ❶ When an aeroplane takes off, it leaves the ground and begins to fly. ❷ If you **take care of** someone or something, you look after them. ❸ If you **take care of** a problem or situation, you deal with it and get it sorted. **takeoff NOUN**

take over VERB To take something over means to start controlling it. **takeover NOUN**

take to VERB If you take to someone or something, you like them immediately.

takeaway, takeaways **NOUN** ❶ a shop or restaurant that sells hot cooked food to be eaten elsewhere.
❷ a hot cooked meal bought from a takeaway.

takings PLURAL NOUN Takings are the money that a shop or cinema gets from selling its goods or tickets.

talc NOUN Talc is the same as talcum powder.

talcum powder NOUN Talcum powder is a soft perfumed powder used for absorbing moisture on the body.

tale, tales **NOUN** a story.

talent, talents **NOUN** Talent is the natural ability to do something well. **talented ADJECTIVE**

▷ SPELLING NOTE: *Elaine and Emily shout EE when they mEEt to grEEt each other (-ee-)*

● **SIMILAR WORDS:** ability, flair, gift

talisman, talismans [*Said tal-iz-man*] **NOUN** an object which you believe has magic powers to protect you or bring luck.
● **WORD HISTORY:** from Greek *telesma* meaning 'holy object'

talk, talks, talking, talked **VERB** ❶ When you talk, you say things to someone. ❷ If people talk, especially about other people's private affairs, they gossip about them • *the neighbours might talk.* ❸ If you talk on or about something, you make an informal speech about it ▷ **NOUN** ❹ Talk is discussion or gossip. ❺ an informal speech about something.
talk down VERB If you talk down to someone, you talk to them in a way that shows that you think you are more important or clever than them.

talkative ADJECTIVE talking a lot.
● **SIMILAR WORDS:** chatty, garrulous, loquacious

tall, taller, tallest **ADJECTIVE** ❶ of more than average or normal height. ❷ having a particular height • *a wall ten metres tall.* ▷ **PHRASE** ❸ If you describe something as **a tall story**, you mean that it is difficult to believe because it is so unlikely.

tally, tallies, tallying, tallied **NOUN** ❶ an informal record of amounts which you keep adding to as you go along • *He ended with a reasonable goal tally last season.* ▷ **VERB** ❷ If numbers or statements tally, they are exactly the same or they give the same results or conclusions.

Talmud [*Said tal-mood*] **NOUN** The Talmud consists of the books containing the ancient Jewish ceremonies and civil laws.
● **WORD HISTORY:** a Hebrew word meaning literally 'instruction'

talon, talons **NOUN** Talons are sharp, hooked claws, especially of a bird of prey.

tambourine, tambourines **NOUN** a percussion instrument made of a skin stretched tightly over a circular frame, with small round pieces of metal around the edge that jingle when the tambourine is beaten or shaken.

tame, tamer, tamest; tames, taming, tamed **ADJECTIVE** ❶ A tame animal or bird is not afraid of people and is not violent towards them. ❷ Something that is tame is uninteresting and lacks excitement or risk • *The report was pretty tame.* ▷ **VERB** ❸ If you tame people or things, you bring them under control. ❹ To tame a wild animal or bird is to train it to be obedient and live with humans.

tamper, tampers, tampering, tampered **VERB** If you tamper with something, you interfere or meddle with it.

tampon, tampons **NOUN** a firm, specially shaped piece of cotton wool that a woman places inside her vagina to absorb the blood during her period.

tan, tans, tanning, tanned **NOUN** ❶ If you have a tan, your skin is darker than usual because you have been in the sun ▷ **VERB** ❷ To tan an animal's hide is to turn it into leather by treating it with chemicals ▷ **ADJECTIVE** ❸ Something that is

a b c d e f g h i j k l m n o p q r s **t** u v w x y z

▷ SPELLING NOTE: '*i*' before '*e*' except after '*c*'

tan is of a light yellowish-brown colour • *a tan dress.*

tandem, tandems **NOUN** a bicycle designed for two riders sitting one behind the other.

tang, tangs **NOUN** a strong, sharp smell or flavour • *the tang of lemon.*
tangy **ADJECTIVE**

tangata whenua [Said *tang-ah-tah feh-noo-ah*] **NOUN** Tangata whenua is a Maori term for the original Polynesian settlers in New Zealand, and their descendants.

tangent, tangents **NOUN** ❶ A tangent of a curve is any straight line that touches the curve at one point only ▷ **PHRASE** ❷ If you **go off at a tangent**, you start talking or thinking about something that is not completely relevant to what has gone before.

tangerine, tangerines **NOUN** ❶ a type of small sweet orange with a loose rind ▷ **NOUN OR ADJECTIVE** ❷ reddish-orange.

tangible [Said *tan-jib-bl*] **ADJECTIVE** clear or definite enough to be easily seen or felt • *tangible proof.*

tangle, tangles, tangling, tangled **NOUN** ❶ a mass of things such as hairs or fibres knotted or coiled together and difficult to separate ▷ **VERB** ❷ If you are tangled in wires or ropes, you are caught or trapped in them so that it is difficult to get free.

tango, tangos **NOUN** A tango is a Latin American dance using long gliding steps and sudden pauses; also a piece of music composed for this

dance • *They danced another tango.*

taniwha, taniwha or taniwhas [Said *tun-ee-fah*] **NOUN** In New Zealand, a monster of Maori legends that lives in water.

tank, tanks **NOUN** ❶ a large container for storing liquid or gas. ❷ an armoured military vehicle which moves on tracks and is equipped with guns or rockets.

tankard, tankards **NOUN** a large metal mug used for drinking beer.

tanker, tankers **NOUN** a ship or lorry designed to carry large quantities of gas or liquid • *a petrol tanker.*

tannin **NOUN** a brown or yellow substance found in plants and used in making leather.

tantalizing or **tantalising** **ADJECTIVE** Something that is tantalizing makes you feel hopeful and excited, although you know that you probably will not be able to have what you want • *a tantalizing glimpse of riches to come.*

tantamount **ADJECTIVE** If you say that something is tantamount to something else, you mean that it is almost the same as it • *That would be tantamount to treason.*

tantrum, tantrums **NOUN** a noisy and sometimes violent outburst of temper, especially by a child.

Tanzanian, Tanzanians [Said *tan-zan-nee-an*] **ADJECTIVE** ❶ belonging or relating to Tanzania ▷ **NOUN** ❷ someone who comes from Tanzania.

tap, taps, tapping, tapped **NOUN** ❶ a

A B C D E F G H I J K L M N O P Q R S **T** U V W X Y Z

▷ SPELLING NOTE: *King IAn went to ParlIAment in a carrIAge for his marrIAge (-ia-)*

device that you turn to control the flow of liquid or gas from a pipe or container. ❷ the action of hitting something lightly; also the sound that this action makes ▷ **VERB** ❸ If you tap something or tap on it, you hit it lightly. ❹ If a telephone is tapped, a device is fitted to it so that someone can listen secretly to the calls.

tap-dancing NOUN Tap-dancing is a type of dancing in which the dancers wear special shoes with pieces of metal on the toes and heels which click against the floor.

tape, tapes, taping, taped **NOUN** ❶ Tape is plastic ribbon covered with a magnetic substance and used to record sounds, pictures, and computer information. ❷ a cassette or spool with magnetic tape wound round it. ❸ Tape is a long, thin strip of fabric that is used for binding or fastening. ❹ Tape is also a strip of sticky plastic which you use for sticking things together ▷ **VERB** ❺ If you tape sounds or television pictures, you record them using a tape recorder or a video recorder. ❻ If you tape one thing to another, you attach them using sticky tape.

tape measure, tape measures **NOUN** a strip of plastic or metal that is marked off in inches or centimetres and used for measuring things.

taper, tapers, tapering, tapered **VERB** ❶ Something that tapers becomes thinner towards one end ▷ **NOUN** ❷ a thin candle.

tape recorder, tape recorders **NOUN** a machine used for recording sounds onto magnetic tape, and for playing these sounds back.

tapestry, tapestries **NOUN** a piece of heavy cloth with designs embroidered on it.

tar NOUN Tar is a thick, black, sticky substance which is used in making roads.

tarantula, tarantulas [Said tar-**rant**-yoo-la] **NOUN** a large, hairy poisonous spider.

target, targets **NOUN** ❶ something which you aim at when firing weapons. ❷ The target of an action or remark is the person or thing at which it is directed • *You become a target for our hatred.* ❸ Your target is the result that you are trying to achieve.

tariff, tariffs **NOUN** ❶ a tax that a government collects on imported goods. ❷ any list of prices or charges.

tarmac NOUN Tarmac is a material used for making road surfaces. It consists of crushed stones mixed with tar.

  ● **WORD HISTORY:** short for
  ● *tarmacadam*, from the name of
  ● John *McAdam*, the Scottish
  ● engineer who invented it

tarnish, tarnishes, tarnishing, tarnished **VERB** ❶ If metal tarnishes, it becomes stained and loses its shine. ❷ If something tarnishes your reputation, it spoils it and causes people to lose their respect for you.

tarot [Said **tar**-roh] **NOUN** A tarot card is one of a special pack of cards used for fortune-telling.

tarpaulin, tarpaulins **NOUN** a sheet of heavy waterproof material used as a protective covering.

tarragon NOUN Tarragon is a herb

a
b
c
d
e
f
g
h
i
j
k
l
m
n
o
p
q
r
s
t
u
v
w
x
y
z

with narrow green leaves used in cooking.

tarry, tarries, tarrying, tarried **VERB** OLD-FASHIONED To tarry is to wait, or to stay somewhere for a little longer.

tarseal **NOUN** In New Zealand English, tarseal is the tarmac surface of a road.

tart, tarts; tarter, tartest **NOUN** ❶ a pastry case with a sweet filling ▷ **ADJECTIVE** ❷ Something that is tart is sour or sharp to taste. ❸ A tart remark is unpleasant and cruel.

tartan, tartans **NOUN** Tartan is a woollen fabric from Scotland with checks of various colours and sizes, depending on which clan it belongs to.

tartar **NOUN** Tartar is a hard, crusty substance that forms on teeth.

tarwhine, tarwhines **NOUN** an edible Australian marine fish, especially a sea bream.

task, tasks **NOUN** any piece of work which has to be done.
● SIMILAR WORDS: chore, duty, job

Tasmanian devil, Tasmanian devils **NOUN** a black-and-white marsupial of Tasmania, which eats flesh.

tassel, tassels **NOUN** a tuft of loose threads tied by a knot and used for decoration.

taste, tastes, tasting, tasted **NOUN** ❶ Your sense of taste is your ability to recognize the flavour of things in your mouth. ❷ The taste of something is its flavour. ❸ If you have a taste of food or drink, you have a small amount of it to see what it is like. ❹ If

you have a taste for something, you enjoy it • *a taste for publicity*. ❺ If you have a taste of something, you experience it • *my first taste of defeat.* ❻ A person's taste is their choice in the things they like to buy or have around them • *His taste in music is great.* ▷ **VERB** ❼ When you can taste something in your mouth, you are aware of its flavour. ❽ If you taste food or drink, you have a small amount of it to see what it is like. ❾ If food or drink tastes of something, it has that flavour.

taste bud, taste buds **NOUN** Your taste buds are the little points on the surface of your tongue which enable you to taste things.

tasteful **ADJECTIVE** attractive and elegant. **tastefully** **ADVERB**

tasteless **ADJECTIVE** ❶ vulgar and unattractive. ❷ A tasteless remark or joke is offensive. ❸ Tasteless food has very little flavour.

tasty, tastier, tastiest **ADJECTIVE** having a pleasant flavour.

tatters **PLURAL NOUN** Clothes that are in tatters are badly torn. **tattered** **ADJECTIVE**

tattoo, tattoos, tattooing, tattooed **VERB** ❶ If someone tattoos you or tattoos a design on you, they draw it on your skin by pricking little holes and filling them with coloured dye ▷ **NOUN** ❷ a picture or design tattooed on someone's body. ❸ a public military display of exercises and music.

tatty, tattier, tattiest **ADJECTIVE** worn out or untidy and rather dirty.

taught the past tense and past participle of **teach**.

taunt, taunts, taunting, taunted **VERB** ❶ To taunt someone is to speak to them about their weaknesses or failures in order to make them angry or upset ▷ **NOUN** ❷ an offensive remark intended to make a person angry or upset.

Taurus NOUN Taurus is the second sign of the zodiac, represented by a bull. People born between April 20th and May 20th are born under this sign.
● **WORD HISTORY:** from Latin *taurus* meaning 'bull'

taut ADJECTIVE stretched very tight • *taut wires*.

tautology, tautologies **NOUN** (ENGLISH) Tautology is using different words to say the same thing twice in the same sentence.

tavern, taverns **NOUN** OLD-FASHIONED a pub.

tawdry, tawdrier, tawdriest *[Said taw-dree]* **ADJECTIVE** cheap, gaudy, and of poor quality.

tawny NOUN OR ADJECTIVE brownish-yellow.

tax, taxes, taxing, taxed **NOUN** ❶ Tax is an amount of money that the people in a country have to pay to the government so that it can provide public services such as health care and education ▷ **VERB** ❷ If a sum of money is taxed, a certain amount of it has to be paid to the government. ❸ If goods are taxed, a certain amount of their price has to be paid to the government. ❹ If a person or company is taxed, they have to pay a

certain amount of their income to the government. ❺ If something taxes you, it makes heavy demands on you • *They must be told not to tax your patience.* **taxation NOUN**

taxi, taxis, taxiing, taxied **NOUN** ❶ a car with a driver which you hire to take you to where you want to go ▷ **VERB** ❷ When an aeroplane taxis, it moves slowly along the runway before taking off or after landing.

taxonomy NOUN (SCIENCE) the process of naming and classifying animals and plants.

tea, teas **NOUN** ❶ Tea is the dried leaves of an evergreen shrub found in Asia. ❷ Tea is a drink made by brewing the leaves of the tea plant in hot water; also a cup of this. ❸ Tea is also any drink made with hot water and leaves or flowers • *peppermint tea.* ❹ Tea is a meal taken in the late afternoon or early evening.

tea bag, tea bags **NOUN** a small paper bag with tea leaves in it which is placed in boiling water to make tea.

teach, teaches, teaching, taught **VERB** ❶ If you teach someone something, you give them instructions so that they know about it or know how to do it. ❷ If you teach a subject, you help students learn about a subject at school, college, or university. **teaching NOUN**
● **SIMILAR WORDS:** ❶ educate, instruct, train, tutor

teacher, teachers **NOUN** a person who teaches other people, especially children.

teak NOUN Teak is a hard wood which comes from a large Asian tree.

a b c d e f g h i j k l m n o p q r s **t** u v w x y z

▷ SPELLING NOTE: *A Rude Idiot Thought He Might Eat Toffee In Church (arithmetic)*

team, teams, teaming, teamed **NOUN**
1 a group of people who work together or play together against another group in a sport or game
▷ **VERB** **2** If you team up with someone, you join them and work together with them.

teamwork NOUN Teamwork is the ability of a group of people to work well together.

teapot, teapots **NOUN** a round pot with a handle, a lid, and a spout, used for brewing and pouring tea.

tear, tears, tearing, tore, torn **NOUN**
1 a hole that has been made in something ▷ **VERB** **2** If you tear something, it is damaged by being pulled so that a hole appears in it.
3 If you tear somewhere, you rush there • *He tore through busy streets in a high-speed chase.*
● **SIMILAR WORDS:** **1** hole, rip,
● rupture

tearaway, tearaways **NOUN** someone who is wild and uncontrollable.

tearful ADJECTIVE about to cry or crying gently. **tearfully ADVERB**

tears PLURAL NOUN Tears are the drops of salty liquid that come out of your eyes when you cry.

tease, teases, teasing, teased **VERB**
1 If you tease someone, you deliberately make fun of them or embarrass them because it amuses you ▷ **NOUN** **2** someone who enjoys teasing people.

teaspoon, teaspoons **NOUN** a small spoon used for stirring drinks; also the amount that a teaspoon holds.

teat, teats **NOUN** **1** a nipple on a female animal. **2** a piece of rubber or plastic that is shaped like a nipple and fitted to a baby's feeding bottle.

tea tree, tea trees **NOUN** a tree found in Australia and New Zealand with leaves that contain tannin, like tea leaves.

tech, techs **NOUN** INFORMAL a technical college.

technical ADJECTIVE **1** involving machines, processes, and materials used in industry, transport, and communications. **2** skilled in practical and mechanical things rather than theories and ideas. **3** involving a specialized field of activity • *I never understood the technical jargon.*

technical college, technical colleges **NOUN** a college where you can study subjects like technology and secretarial skills.

technicality, technicalities **NOUN**
1 The technicalities of a process or activity are the detailed methods used to do it. **2** an exact detail of a law or a set of rules, especially one some people might not notice • *The verdict may have been based on a technicality.*

technically ADVERB If something is technically true or correct, it is true or correct when you consider only the facts, rules, or laws, but may not be important or relevant in a particular situation • *Technically, they were not supposed to drink on duty.*

technician, technicians **NOUN** someone whose job involves skilled practical work with scientific equipment.

▷ SPELLING NOTE: *Beautiful Elephants Are Usually Tiny (beautiful)*

technique, techniques NOUN **1** a particular method of doing something • *these techniques of manufacture*. **2** Technique is skill and ability in an activity which is developed through training and practice • *Jim's unique vocal technique*.

techno- PREFIX 'Techno-' means a craft or art • *technology*.
- WORD HISTORY: from Greek *tekhnē* meaning 'a skill'

technology, technologies NOUN **1** D & T Technology is the study of the application of science and scientific knowledge for practical purposes in industry, farming, medicine, or business. **2** a particular area of activity that requires scientific methods and knowledge • *computer technology*. **technological** ADJECTIVE **technologically** ADVERB

tectonic ADJECTIVE **1** relating to or involving the geological forces that shape the earth's crust. **2 tectonic plates** are large slowly moving pieces of the Earth's crust. The movement of tectonic plates against or away from one another is one of the main causes of earthquakes.

teddy, teddies NOUN A teddy or teddy bear is a stuffed toy that looks like a friendly bear.
- WORD HISTORY: named after the American President Theodore (*Teddy*) Roosevelt, who hunted bears

tedious [*Said* tee-dee-uss] ADJECTIVE boring and lasting for a long time • *the tedious task of clearing up*.

tedium [*Said* tee-dee-um] NOUN the quality of being boring and lasting for a long time • *the tedium of unemployment*.

tee, tees, teeing, teed NOUN **1** the small wooden or plastic peg on which a golf ball is placed before the golfer first hits it ▷ VERB **2** To tee off is to hit the golf ball from the tee, or to start a round of golf.

teem, teems, teeming, teemed VERB **1** If a place is teeming with people or things, there are a lot of them moving about. **2** If it teems, it rains very heavily • *The rain was teeming down*.

teenage ADJECTIVE **1** aged between thirteen and nineteen. **2** typical of people aged between thirteen and nineteen • *teenage fashion*. **teenager** NOUN

teens PLURAL NOUN Your teens are the period of your life when you are between thirteen and nineteen years old.

tee shirt another spelling of **T-shirt**.

teeter, teeters, teetering, teetered VERB To teeter is to shake or sway slightly in an unsteady way and seem about to fall over.

teeth the plural of **tooth**.

teethe, teethes, teething, teethed [*rhymes with* **breathe**] VERB When babies are teething, their teeth are starting to come through, usually causing them pain.

teetotal [*Said* tee-toe-tl] ADJECTIVE Someone who is teetotal never drinks alcohol. **teetotaller** NOUN

tele- PREFIX 'Tele-' means at or over

a b c d e f g h i j k l m n o p q r s **t** u v w x y z

A B C D E F G H I J K L M N O P Q R S **T** U V W X Y Z

a distance • *telegraph*.
● **WORD HISTORY:** from Greek *tele*
● meaning 'far'

telecommunications NOUN
Telecommunications is the science
and activity of sending signals and
messages over long distances using
electronic equipment.

telegram, telegrams NOUN a
message sent by telegraph.

telegraph NOUN The telegraph is a
system of sending messages over long
distances using electrical or radio
signals.

telepathy [Said til-**lep**-ath-ee]
NOUN Telepathy is direct
communication between people's
minds. **telepathic** ADJECTIVE

telephone, telephones,
telephoning, telephoned NOUN ❶ a
piece of electrical equipment for
talking directly to someone who is in a
different place ▷ VERB ❷ If you
telephone someone, you speak to
them using a telephone.

telephone box, telephone boxes
NOUN a small shelter in the street
where there is a public telephone.

telescope, telescopes NOUN a long
instrument shaped like a tube which
has lenses which make distant objects
appear larger and nearer.

teletext NOUN Teletext is an
electronic system that broadcasts
pages of information onto a television
set.

televise, televises, televising,
televised VERB If an event is
televised, it is filmed and shown on
television.

television, televisions NOUN a
piece of electronic equipment which
receives pictures and sounds by
electrical signals over a distance.

tell, tells, telling, told VERB ❶ If you
tell someone something, you let them
know about it. ❷ If you tell someone
to do something, you order or advise
them to do it. ❸ If you can tell
something, you are able to judge
correctly what is happening or what
the situation is • *I could tell he was
scared.* ❹ If an unpleasant or tiring
experience begins to tell, it begins to
have a serious effect • *The pressure
began to tell.*
● **SIMILAR WORDS:** ❶ inform,
● notify

teller, tellers NOUN a person who
receives or gives out money in a bank.

telling ADJECTIVE Something that is
telling has an important effect, often
because it shows the true nature of a
situation • *a telling account of the war.*

telltale ADJECTIVE A telltale sign
reveals information • *the sad, telltale
signs of a recent accident.*

telly, tellies NOUN INFORMAL a
television.

temerity [Said tim-**mer**-it-ee]
NOUN If someone has the temerity to
do something, they do it even though
it upsets or annoys other people • *She
had the temerity to call him Bob.*

temp, temps NOUN INFORMAL a
secretary who works for short periods
of time in different places.

temper, tempers, tempering,
tempered NOUN ❶ Your temper is
the frame of mind or mood you are in.

▷ SPELLING NOTE: there's a rAKE in the brAKEs (brake)

❷ a sudden outburst of anger
▷ **PHRASE** ❸ If you **lose your temper**, you become very angry
▷ **VERB** ❹ To temper something is to make it more acceptable or suitable
• *curiosity tempered with some caution.*

temperament, temperaments
[Said **tem**-pra-ment] **NOUN** Your temperament is your nature or personality, shown in the way you react towards people and situations
• *an artistic temperament.*

temperamental ADJECTIVE
Someone who is temperamental has moods that change often and suddenly.

temperate ADJECTIVE A temperate place has weather that is neither extremely hot nor extremely cold.

temperature, temperatures **NOUN**
❶ (SCIENCE) The temperature of something is how hot or cold it is.
❷ Your temperature is the temperature of your body ▷ **PHRASE**
❸ If you **have a temperature**, the temperature of your body is higher than it should be, because you are ill.

tempest, tempests **NOUN** LITERARY
a violent storm.

tempestuous [Said tem-**pest**-yoo-uss] **ADJECTIVE** violent or strongly emotional • *a tempestuous relationship.*

template, templates **NOUN** a shape or pattern cut out in wood, metal, plastic, or card which you draw or cut around to reproduce that shape or pattern.

temple, temples **NOUN** ❶ (RE) a building used for the worship of a god

in various religions • *a Buddhist temple.* ❷ Your temples are the flat parts on each side of your forehead.

tempo, tempos or tempi **NOUN**
❶ The tempo of something is the speed at which it happens • *the slow tempo of change.* ❷ (MUSIC) The tempo of a piece of music is its speed.

temporary ADJECTIVE lasting for only a short time. **temporarily ADVERB**

tempt, tempts, tempting, tempted
VERB ❶ If you tempt someone, you try to persuade them to do something by offering them something they want. ❷ If you are tempted to do something, you want to do it but you think it might be wrong or harmful
• *He was tempted to reply with sarcasm.*
● **SIMILAR WORDS:** ❶ entice, lure

temptation, temptations **NOUN**
❶ Temptation is the state you are in when you want to do or have something, even though you know it might be wrong or harmful.
❷ something that you want to do or have, even though you know it might be wrong or harmful

ten the number 10. **tenth ADJECTIVE**

tenacious [Said tin-**nay**-shuss]
ADJECTIVE determined and not giving up easily. **tenaciously ADVERB tenacity NOUN**

tenant, tenants **NOUN** someone who pays rent for the place they live in, or for land or buildings that they use. **tenancy NOUN**

tend, tends, tending, tended **VERB**
❶ If something tends to happen, it happens usually or often. ❷ If you

a
b
c
d
e
f
g
h
i
j
k
l
m
n
o
p
q
r
s
t
u
v
w
x
y
z

▷ SPELLING NOTE: *you'll brEAK that Electrical Aerial, Kitty (break)*

tendency | 880

tend someone or something, you look after them • *the way we tend our cattle.*
● **SIMILAR WORDS:** ❶ be apt to, be
● inclined to, be liable to

tendency, tendencies **NOUN** a trend or type of behaviour that happens very often • *a tendency to be critical.*

tender, tenderest; tenders, tendering, tendered **ADJECTIVE** ❶ Someone who is tender has gentle and caring feelings. ❷ If someone is at a tender age, they are young and do not know very much about life. ❸ Tender meat is easy to cut or chew. ❹ If a part of your body is tender, it is painful and sore ▷ **VERB** ❺ If someone tenders an apology or their resignation, they offer it ▷ **NOUN** ❻ a formal offer to supply goods or to do a job for a particular price.
● **SIMILAR WORDS:** ❶ affectionate,
● gentle, loving

tendon, tendons **NOUN** a strong cord of tissue which joins a muscle to a bone.

tendril, tendrils **NOUN** Tendrils are short, thin stems which grow on climbing plants and attach themselves to walls.

tenement, tenements *[Said ten-em-ent]* **NOUN** a large house or building divided into many flats.

tenet, tenets **NOUN** The tenets of a theory or belief are the main ideas it is based upon.

tenner, tenners **NOUN** INFORMAL a ten-pound or ten-dollar note.

tennis NOUN Tennis is a game played by two or four players on a

rectangular court in which a ball is hit by players over a central net.

tenor, tenors **NOUN** ❶ a man who sings in a fairly high voice. ❷ The tenor of something is the general meaning or mood that it expresses • *the whole tenor of his poetry had changed.* ▷ **ADJECTIVE** ❸ A tenor recorder, saxophone, or other musical instrument has a range of notes of a fairly low pitch.

tense, tenser, tensest; tenses, tensing, tensed **ADJECTIVE** ❶ If you are tense, you are nervous and cannot relax. ❷ A tense situation or period of time is one that makes people nervous and worried. ❸ If your body is tense, your muscles are tight ▷ **VERB** ❹ If you tense, or if your muscles tense, your muscles become tight and stiff ▷ **NOUN** ❺ The tense of a verb is the form which shows whether you are talking about the past, present, or future.
● **SIMILAR WORDS:** ❶ anxious,
● nervous, uptight
▶ SEE GRAMMAR BOX ON PAGE 881

tension, tensions **NOUN** ❶ Tension is the feeling of nervousness or worry that you have when something dangerous or important is happening. ❷ D&T The tension in a rope or wire is how tightly it is stretched.

tent, tents **NOUN** a shelter made of canvas or nylon held up by poles and pinned down with pegs and ropes.

tentacle, tentacles **NOUN** The tentacles of an animal such as an octopus are the long, thin parts that it uses to feel and hold things.

tentative ADJECTIVE acting or

▷ SPELLING NOTE: *I always visit my FRIend on a FRIday (Friday)*

WHAT IS A TENSE?

The "tense" of the verb tells us whether the action is in the past, the present or the future.

Some forms of the verb indicate that the action has already happened. These forms are **past tenses**:
*The captain **asked** Matthew for advice.*
*The captain **has asked** Matthew for advice.*
*The captain **was asking** Matthew for advice this morning.*
*The captain **had asked** Matthew for advice that morning.*

Some forms of the verb indicate that

the action is happening at the present time. These forms are **present tenses**:
*I **see** some cause for optimism.*
*I **do see** some cause for optimism.*

Some forms of the verb indicate that the action will happen in the future. These forms are **future tenses**:
*They **will go** to Fiji in September.*
*They **will have gone** to Fiji by the end of September.*

Also look at the grammar boxes at **future**, **past tense**, and **present tense**.

speaking cautiously because of being uncertain or afraid. **tentatively** ADVERB

tenterhooks PLURAL NOUN If you are on tenterhooks, you are nervous and excited about something that is going to happen.
- WORD HISTORY: from the hooks
- called *tenterhooks* which were used
- to stretch cloth tight while it was
- drying

tenuous [*Said* ten-yoo-uss] ADJECTIVE If an idea or connection is tenuous, it is so slight and weak that it may not really exist or may easily cease to exist • *a very tenuous friendship.*

tenure, tenures [*Said* ten-yoor] NOUN ❶ Tenure is the legal right to live in a place or to use land or buildings for a period of time. ❷ Tenure is the period of time during which someone holds an important job • *His tenure ended in 1998.*

tepee, tepees [*Said* tee-pee] NOUN a cone-shaped tent of animal skins used by North American Indians.

tepid ADJECTIVE Tepid liquid is only slightly warm.

term, terms, terming, termed NOUN ❶ a fixed period of time • *her second term of office.* ❷ one of the periods of time that each year is divided into at a school or college. ❸ a name or word used for a particular thing ❹ IN PLURAL The terms of an agreement are the conditions that have been accepted by the people involved in it. ❺ If you express something in particular terms, you express it using a particular type of language or in a way that clearly shows your attitude • *The young priest spoke of her in glowing terms.* ▷ PHRASE ❻ If you **come to terms with** something difficult or unpleasant, you learn to accept it ▷ VERB ❼ To term something is to give it a name or to describe it • *He termed my performance memorable.*

▷ SPELLING NOTE: *I want to see (C) your licenCe (licence)*

terminal, terminals **ADJECTIVE**
① A terminal illness or disease cannot be cured and causes death gradually ▷ **NOUN** **②** a place where vehicles, passengers, or goods begin or end a journey. **③** A computer terminal is a keyboard and a visual display unit that is used to put information into or get information out of a computer. **④** one of the parts of an electrical device through which electricity enters or leaves. **terminally ADVERB**

terminate, terminates, terminating, terminated **VERB** When you terminate something or when it terminates, it stops or ends. **termination NOUN**

terminology, terminologies **NOUN** The terminology of a subject is the set of special words and expressions used in it.

terminus, terminuses [Said *ter-min-uss*] **NOUN** a place where a bus or train route ends.

termite, termites **NOUN** Termites are small white insects that feed on wood.

tern, terns **NOUN** a small black and white sea bird with long wings and a forked tail.

ternary ADJECTIVE (MUSIC) Ternary form is a musical structure of three sections, the first and the second contrasting with each other and the third being a repetition of the first.

terrace, terraces **NOUN** **①** a row of houses joined together. **②** a flat area of stone next to a building where people can sit.

terracotta NOUN a type of brown pottery with no glaze.
● **WORD HISTORY:** from Italian *terra cotta* meaning 'baked earth'

terrain NOUN The terrain of an area is the type of land there • *the region's hilly terrain.*

terrapin, terrapins **NOUN** a small North American freshwater turtle.

terrestrial ADJECTIVE involving the earth or land.

terrible ADJECTIVE **①** serious and unpleasant • *a terrible illness.* **②** INFORMAL very bad or of poor quality • *Paddy's terrible haircut.*

terribly ADVERB very or very much • *I was terribly upset.*

terrier, terriers **NOUN** a small, short-bodied dog.

terrific ADJECTIVE **①** INFORMAL very pleasing or impressive • *a terrific film.* **②** great in amount, degree, or intensity • *a terrific blow on the head.* **terrifically ADVERB**

terrify, terrifies, terrifying, terrified **VERB** If something terrifies you, it makes you feel extremely frightened.

territorial ADJECTIVE involving or relating to the ownership of a particular area of land or water • *a territorial dispute.*

territory, territories **NOUN** **①** The territory of a country is the land that it controls. **②** An animal's territory is an area which it regards as its own and defends when other animals try to enter it.

terror, terrors **NOUN** **①** Terror is great fear or panic. **②** something that makes you feel very frightened.

terrorism NOUN Terrorism is the use of violence for political reasons. **terrorist** NOUN OR ADJECTIVE

terrorize, terrorizes, terrorizing, terrorized; *also spelt* **terrorise** VERB If someone terrorizes you, they frighten you by threatening you or being violent to you.

terse, terser, tersest ADJECTIVE A terse statement is short and rather unfriendly.

tertiary [Said **ter**-shar-ee] ADJECTIVE ❶ third in order or importance. ❷ Tertiary education is education at university or college level.

test, tests, testing, tested VERB ❶ When you test something, you try it to find out what it is, what condition it is in, or how well it works. ❷ If you test someone, you ask them questions to find out how much they know ▷ NOUN ❸ a deliberate action or experiment to find out whether something works or how well it works. ❹ a set of questions or tasks given to someone to find out what they know or can do.

testament, testaments NOUN ❶ LEGAL a will. ❷ a copy of either the Old or the New Testament of the Bible.

test case, test cases NOUN a legal case that becomes an example for deciding other similar cases.

testicle, testicles NOUN A man's testicles are the two sex glands beneath the penis that produce sperm.

testify, testifies, testifying, testified VERB ❶ When someone testifies, they make a formal statement, especially in a court of law • *Ismay later testified at the British inquiry.* ❷ To testify to something is to show that it is likely to be true • *a consultant's certificate testifying to her good health.*

testimonial, testimonials [Said tess-tim-**moh**-nee-al] NOUN a statement saying how good someone or something is.

testimony, testimonies NOUN A person's testimony is a formal statement they make, especially in a court of law.

testing ADJECTIVE Testing situations or problems are very difficult to deal with • *It is a testing time for his team.*

testis, testes NOUN A man's testes are his testicles.

test match, test matches NOUN one of a series of international cricket or rugby matches.

testosterone [Said tess-**toss**-ter-rone] NOUN Testosterone is a male hormone that produces male characteristics.

test tube, test tubes NOUN a small cylindrical glass container that is used in chemical experiments.

tetanus [Said **tet**-ah-nuss] NOUN Tetanus is a painful infectious disease caused by germs getting into wounds.

tether, tethers, tethering, tethered VERB ❶ If you tether an animal, you tie it to a post ▷ PHRASE ❷ If you are **at the end of your tether**, you are extremely tired and have no more patience or energy left to deal with

a
b
c
d
e
f
g
h
i
j
k
l
m
n
o
p
q
r
s
t
u
v
w
x
y
z

▷ SPELLING NOTE: *have a plEce of plE (piece)*

A
B
C
D
E
F
G
H
I
J
K
L
M
N
O
P
Q
R
S
T
U
V
W
X
Y
Z

your many problems.

tetrahedron, tetrahedrons or tetrahedra [Said tet-ra-**hee**-dron] NOUN (MATHS) A tetrahedron is any three-dimensional shape with six straight edges and four flat sides.

Teutonic [Said tyoo-**tonn**-ik] ADJECTIVE FORMAL involving or related to German people.

text, texts, texting, texted NOUN ❶ The text of a book is the main written part of it, rather than the pictures or index. ❷ Text is any written material. ❸ a book or other piece of writing used for study or an exam at school or college. ❹ Text is short for 'text message' ▷ VERB ❺ If you text someone, you send them a text message. **textual** ADJECTIVE

textbook, textbooks NOUN a book about a particular subject for students to use.

textile, textiles NOUN (D & T) a woven cloth or fabric.

text message, text messages NOUN a written message sent using a mobile phone.

texture, textures NOUN The texture of something is the way it feels when you touch it.
  ● SIMILAR WORDS: consistency,
  ● feel

Thai, Thais ADJECTIVE ❶ belonging or relating to Thailand ▷ NOUN ❷ someone who comes from Thailand. ❸ Thai is the main language spoken in Thailand.

than PREPOSITION OR CONJUNCTION ❶ You use 'than' to link two parts of a comparison • She

was older than me. ❷ You use 'than' to link two parts of a contrast • Players would rather play than train.

thank, thanks, thanking, thanked VERB When you thank someone, you show that you are grateful for something, usually by saying 'thank you'.

thankful ADJECTIVE happy and relieved that something has happened. **thankfully** ADVERB

thankless ADJECTIVE A thankless job or task involves doing a lot of hard work that other people do not notice or are not grateful for • Referees have a thankless task.

thanks PLURAL NOUN ❶ When you express your thanks to someone, you tell or show them how grateful you are for something ▷ PHRASE ❷ If something happened **thanks to** someone or something, it happened because of them • I'm as prepared as I can be, thanks to you.
  ▷ INTERJECTION ❸ You say 'thanks' to show that you are grateful for something.

thanksgiving NOUN ❶ Thanksgiving is an act of thanking God, especially in prayer or in a religious ceremony. ❷ In the United States, Thanksgiving is a public holiday in the autumn.

thank you INTERJECTION You say 'thank you' to show that you are grateful to someone for something.

that, those ADJECTIVE OR PRONOUN ❶ 'That' or 'those' is used to refer to things or people already mentioned or known about • That man was waving. ▷ CONJUNCTION

▷ SPELLING NOTE: plaice the fish has a glittering 'EYE' (I) (plaice)

WHAT DOES THAT DO?

That is a relative pronoun. A relative pronoun replaces a noun which links two different parts of a sentence.

Relative pronouns always refer back to a word in the earlier part of the sentence. The word they refer to is called the **antecedent**. (In the examples that follow, the antecedents are underlined.)
*I have <u>a friend</u> **who** lives in Rome.*

*We could go to <u>a place</u> **that** I know.*

That refers to things or people. It is never used immediately after a preposition, but it can be used if the preposition is separated from the relative pronoun:
*It was <u>a film</u> **that** I had little interest **in**.*

Also look at the grammar box at **relative pronoun**.

❷ 'That' is used to introduce a clause • *I said that I was coming home.*
▷ **PRONOUN** ❸ 'That' is also used to introduce a relative clause • *I followed Alex to a door that led inside.*
● **USAGE NOTE:** You can use either *that* or *which* in clauses known as defining clauses. These are clauses that identify the object you are talking about. In the sentence *The book that is on the table is mine*, 'that is on the table' is a defining clause which distinguishes the book from other books that are not on the table. Some people think these types of clause should only be introduced by *that*, and *which* should be kept for nondefining clauses. These nondefining clauses add extra information about the object, but do not identify it. In the sentence *The book, which is on the table, is mine*, 'which is on the table' is a nondefining clause which gives the reader extra detail about the book
▶ SEE GRAMMAR BOX ABOVE

thatch, thatches, thatching, thatched
NOUN ❶ Thatch is straw and reeds used to make roofs ▷ **VERB** ❷ To

thatch a roof is to cover it with thatch.

thaw, thaws, thawing, thawed **VERB**
❶ When snow or ice thaws, it melts.
❷ When you thaw frozen food, or when it thaws, it returns to its normal state in a warmer atmosphere.
❸ When people who are unfriendly thaw, they begin to be more friendly and relaxed ▷ **NOUN** ❹ a period of warmer weather in winter when snow or ice melts.

the **ADJECTIVE** The definite article 'the' is used when you are talking about something that is known about, that has just been mentioned, or that you are going to give details about.
▶ SEE GRAMMAR BOX ON PAGE 886

theatre, theatres [Said **thee**-uh-tuh]
NOUN ❶ (DRAMA) a building where plays and other entertainments are performed on a stage. ❷ Theatre is work such as writing, producing, and acting in plays. ❸ An operating theatre is a room in a hospital designed and equipped for surgical operations.
● **WORD HISTORY:** from Greek *theatron* meaning 'viewing place'

theatrical [Said thee-**at**-rik-kl]

▷ SPELLING NOTE: *I went to see (C) the doctor's new practiCe (practice)*

A
B
C
D
E
F
G
H
I
J
K
L
M
N
O
P
Q
R
S
T
U
V
W
X
Y
Z

THE DEFINITE ARTICLE

The word *the* is known as the **definite article**. You use it before a noun to refer to a specific example of that noun:
the kitchen table
the school I attend

The definite article *the* may be used before singular and plural nouns. However, you cannot use the indefinite article *a* or *an* before a plural noun. You need to use the word *some* in this case:
the tables
some tables
the schools
some schools

Also look at the grammar box at **a**.

ADJECTIVE ❶ (DRAMA) involving the theatre or performed in a theatre • *his theatrical career.* ❷ Theatrical behaviour is exaggerated, unnatural, and done for effect. **theatrically ADVERB**

thee PRONOUN OLD-FASHIONED Thee means you.

theft, thefts NOUN Theft is the crime of stealing.
● SIMILAR WORDS: robbery,
● stealing

their ADJECTIVE 'Their' refers to something belonging or relating to something or things, other than yourself or the person you are talking to, which have already been mentioned • *It was their fault.*
▷ USAGE NOTE: Be careful not to
● confuse *their* with *there*

theirs PRONOUN 'Theirs' refers to something belonging or relating to people or things, other than yourself or the person you are talking to, which have already been mentioned • *Amy had been Helen's friend, not theirs.*

them PRONOUN 'Them' refers to things or people, other than yourself or the people you are talking to, which have already been mentioned • *He picked up the pillows and threw them to the floor.*

theme, themes NOUN ❶ a main idea or topic in a piece of writing, painting, film, or music • *the main theme of the book.* ❷ a tune, especially one played at the beginning and end of a television or radio programme.

themselves PRONOUN
❶ 'Themselves' is used when people, other than yourself or the person you are talking to, do an action and are affected by it • *They think they've made a fool of themselves.* ❷ 'Themselves' is used to emphasize 'they' • *He was as excited as they themselves were.*

then ADVERB at a particular time in the past or future • *I'd left home by then.*

theologian, theologians [Said *thee-ol-loe-jee-an*] NOUN someone who studies religion and the nature of God.

theology NOUN Theology is the study of religion and God. **theological ADJECTIVE**

theorem, theorems [Said *thee-rem*] NOUN (MATHS) A theorem is a

---

▷ SPELLING NOTE: *You must practiSe your Ss (practise)*

statement in mathematics that can be proved to be true by reasoning.

theoretical ADJECTIVE ❶ based on or to do with ideas of a subject rather than the practical aspects. ❷ not proved to exist or be true. **theoretically** ADVERB

theory, theories NOUN ❶ an idea or set of ideas that is meant to explain something • *Darwin's theory of evolution.* ❷ Theory is the set of rules and ideas that a particular subject or skill is based upon ▷ PHRASE ❸ You use **in theory** to say that although something is supposed to happen, it may not in fact happen • *In theory, prices should rise by 2%.*

● SIMILAR WORDS: ❶ conjecture, ● hypothesis

therapeutic [Said ther-ap-**yoo**-tik] ADJECTIVE ❶ If something is therapeutic, it helps you to feel happier and more relaxed • *Laughing is therapeutic.* ❷ In medicine, therapeutic treatment is designed to treat a disease or to improve a person's health.

therapy NOUN Therapy is the treatment of mental or physical illness, often without the use of drugs or operations. **therapist** NOUN

there ADVERB ❶ in, at, or to that place, point, or case • *He's sitting over there.* ▷ PRONOUN ❷ 'There' is used to say that something exists or does not exist, or to draw attention to something • *There are flowers on the table.*

● USAGE NOTE: Be careful not to ● confuse *there* with *their*. A good way ● to remember that *there* is ● connected to the idea of place is by

● remembering the spelling of two ● other place words, *here* and *where*

thereby ADVERB FORMAL as a result of the event or action mentioned • *They had recruited 200 new members, thereby making the day worthwhile.*

therefore ADVERB as a result.

thermal ADJECTIVE ❶ to do with or caused by heat • *thermal energy.* ❷ Thermal clothes are specially designed to keep you warm in cold weather.

thermodynamics NOUN (SCIENCE) Thermodynamics is the branch of physics concerned with the relationship between heat and other forms of energy. **thermodynamic** ADJECTIVE

thermometer, thermometers NOUN (SCIENCE) an instrument for measuring the temperature of a room or a person's body.

thermostat, thermostats NOUN a device used to control temperature, for example on a central heating system.

thesaurus, thesauruses [Said this-**saw**-russ] NOUN (LIBRARY) a reference book in which words with similar meanings are grouped together.

● WORD HISTORY: from Greek ● *thēsauros* meaning 'treasure'

these the plural of **this**.

thesis, theses [Said **thee**-siss] NOUN a long piece of writing, based on research, that is done as part of a university degree.

they PRONOUN ❶ 'They' refers to

a
b
c
d
e
f
g
h
i
j
k
l
m
n
o
p
q
r
s
t
u
v
w
x
y
z

people or things, other than you or the people you are talking to, that have already been mentioned • *They married two years later.* ❷ 'They' is sometimes used instead of 'he' or 'she' where the sex of the person is unknown or unspecified. Some people consider this to be incorrect • *Someone could have a nasty accident if they tripped over that.*

thick, thicker, thickest **ADJECTIVE**
❶ Something thick has a large distance between its two opposite surfaces. ❷ If something is a particular amount thick, it measures that amount between its two sides. ❸ Thick means growing or grouped closely together and in large quantities • *thick dark hair.* ❹ Thick liquids contain little water and do not flow easily • *thick soup.* ❺ INFORMAL A thick person is stupid or slow to understand things.

thicken, thickens, thickening, thickened **VERB** If something thickens, it becomes thicker • *The clouds thickened.*

thicket, thickets **NOUN** a small group of trees growing closely together.

thief, thieves **NOUN** a person who steals.

thieving **NOUN** Thieving is the act of stealing.

thigh, thighs **NOUN** Your thighs are the top parts of your legs, between your knees and your hips.

thimble, thimbles **NOUN** a small metal or plastic cap that you put on the end of your finger to protect it when you are sewing.

thin, thinner, thinnest; thins, thinning, thinned **ADJECTIVE** ❶ Something that is thin is much narrower than it is long. ❷ A thin person or animal has very little fat on their body. ❸ Thin liquids contain a lot of water • *thin soup.* ▷ **VERB** ❹ If you thin something such as paint or soup, you add water or other liquid to it.
● **SIMILAR WORDS:** ❷ lean, skinny,
● slim

thing, things **NOUN** ❶ an object, rather than a plant, an animal, a human being ❷ IN PLURAL Your things are your clothes or possessions.
● **SIMILAR WORDS:** ❶ article,
● object

think, thinks, thinking, thought **VERB** ❶ When you think about ideas or problems, you use your mind to consider them. ❷ If you think something, you have the opinion that it is true or the case • *I think she has a secret boyfriend.* ❸ If you think of something, you remember it or it comes into your mind. ❹ If you think a lot of someone or something, you admire them or think they are good.

third, thirds **ADJECTIVE** ❶ The third item in a series is the one counted as number three ▷ **NOUN** ❷ one of three equal parts.

third person **NOUN** (ENGLISH) In grammar, the third person is anyone or anything being referred to which isn't a first or second person (*he, she, they,* or *it*).

third-person narrator **NOUN** (ENGLISH) A third-person narrator is either a minor character in the story or not a character at all and uses the pronouns *he, she, it,* and *they.*

▷ SPELLING NOTE: LEarn the principLEs (principle)

Third World NOUN The poorer countries of Africa, Asia, and South America can be referred to as the Third World.

thirst, thirsts NOUN ❶ If you have a thirst, you feel a need to drink something. ❷ A thirst for something is a very strong desire for it • *a thirst for money.* **thirsty** ADJECTIVE **thirstily** ADVERB

thirteen the number 13. **thirteenth** ADJECTIVE

thirty, thirties the number 30. **thirtieth** ADJECTIVE

this, these ADJECTIVE OR PRONOUN ❶ 'This' is used to refer to something or someone that is nearby or has just been mentioned • *This is Robert.* ❷ 'This' is used to refer to the present time or place • *this week.*

thistle, thistles NOUN a wild plant with prickly-edged leaves and purple flowers.

thong, thongs NOUN a long narrow strip of leather.

thorax, thoraxes or thoraces *[Said thor-raks]* NOUN SCIENCE ❶ In a human or animal, the thorax is the part of the body enclosing the ribs. ❷ In an insect, the thorax is the part of the body between the head and the abdomen where the wings and legs are.

thorn, thorns NOUN one of many sharp points growing on some plants and trees.

thorny, thornier, thorniest ADJECTIVE ❶ covered with thorns. ❷ A thorny subject or question is difficult to discuss or answer.

thorough *[Said thur-ruh]* ADJECTIVE ❶ done very carefully and completely • *a thorough examination.* ❷ A thorough person is very careful and makes sure nothing has been missed out. **thoroughly** ADVERB

thoroughbred, thoroughbreds NOUN an animal that has parents that are of the same high quality breed.

thoroughfare, thoroughfares NOUN a main road in a town.

those the plural of **that**.

thou PRONOUN OLD-FASHIONED Thou means you.

though *[rhymes with show]* CONJUNCTION ❶ despite the fact that • *Meg felt better, even though she knew it was the end.* ❷ if • *It looks as though you were right.*

thought, thoughts ❶ Thought is the past tense and past participle of **think**. NOUN ❷ an idea that you have in your mind. ❸ Thought is the activity of thinking • *She was lost in thought.* ❹ Thought is a particular way of thinking or a particular set of ideas • *this school of thought.*
  ● SIMILAR WORDS:
  ● ❸ consideration, reflection,
  ● thinking

thoughtful ADJECTIVE ❶ When someone is thoughtful, they are quiet and serious because they are thinking about something. ❷ A thoughtful person remembers what other people want or need, and tries to be kind to them. **thoughtfully** ADVERB
  ● SIMILAR WORDS: ❶ meditative,
  ● pensive, reflective ❷ caring,
  ● considerate, kind

a
b
c
d
e
f
g
h
i
j
k
l
m
n
o
p
q
r
s
t
u
v
w
x
y
z

▷ SPELLING NOTE: *Psychiatrists Seldom Yell Callously Hard (psychiatrist)*

thoughtless ADJECTIVE A thoughtless person forgets or ignores what other people want, need, or feel • *insulted by his thoughtless remark.* **thoughtlessly** ADVERB

thousand, thousands the number 1000. **thousandth** ADJECTIVE

thrash, thrashes, thrashing, thrashed VERB ❶ To thrash someone is to beat them by hitting them with something. ❷ To thrash someone in a contest or fight is to defeat them completely. ❸ To thrash out a problem or an idea is to discuss it in detail until a solution is reached.

thread, threads, threading, threaded NOUN ❶ a long, fine piece of cotton, silk, nylon, or wool. ❷ The thread on something such as a screw or the top of a container is the raised spiral line of metal or plastic round it. ❸ The thread of an argument or story is an idea or theme that connects the different parts of it ▷ VERB ❹ When you thread something, you pass thread, tape, or cord through it. ❺ If you thread your way through people or things, you carefully make your way through them.

threadbare ADJECTIVE Threadbare cloth or clothing is old and thin.

threat, threats NOUN ❶ a statement that someone will harm you, especially if you do not do what they want. ❷ anything or anyone that seems likely to harm you. ❸ If there is a threat of something unpleasant happening, it is very possible that it will happen.

threaten, threatens, threatening,

threatened VERB ❶ If you threaten to harm someone or threaten to do something that will upset them, you say that you will do it. ❷ If someone or something threatens a person or thing, they are likely to harm them.
● SIMILAR WORDS: ❷ endanger,
● jeopardize

three the number 3.

three-dimensional ADJECTIVE (MATHS) A three-dimensional object or shape is not flat, but has height or depth as well as length and width.

threesome, threesomes NOUN a group of three.

threshold, thresholds [Said *thresh-hold*] NOUN ❶ the doorway or the floor in the doorway of a building or room. ❷ The threshold of something is the lowest amount, level, or limit at which something happens or changes • *the tax threshold* • *His boredom threshold was exceptionally low.*

thrice ADVERB OLD-FASHIONED If you do something thrice, you do it three times.

thrift NOUN Thrift is the practice of saving money and not wasting things.

thrifty, thriftier, thriftiest ADJECTIVE A thrifty person saves money and does not waste things.

thrill, thrills, thrilling, thrilled NOUN ❶ a sudden feeling of great excitement, pleasure, or fear; also any event or experience that gives you such a feeling ▷ VERB ❷ If something thrills you, or you thrill to it, it gives you a feeling of great pleasure and excitement. **thrilled**

ADJECTIVE thrilling ADJECTIVE
● SIMILAR WORDS: ❶ buzz, kick

thriller, thrillers NOUN a book, film, or play that tells an exciting story about dangerous or mysterious events.

thrive, thrives, thriving, thrived or throve VERB When people or things thrive, they are healthy, happy, or successful. **thriving** ADJECTIVE

throat, throats NOUN ❶ the back of your mouth and the top part of the passages inside your neck. ❷ the front part of your neck.

throb, throbs, throbbing, throbbed VERB ❶ If a part of your body throbs, you feel a series of strong beats or dull pains. ❷ If something throbs, it vibrates and makes a loud, rhythmic noise • *The engines throbbed.*

throes PLURAL NOUN ❶ Throes are a series of violent pangs or movements • *death throes.* ▷ PHRASE ❷ If you are **in the throes of** something, you are deeply involved in it.

thrombosis, thromboses [Said *throm-boe-siss*] NOUN a blood clot which blocks the flow of blood in the body. Thromboses are dangerous and often fatal.

throne, thrones NOUN ❶ a ceremonial chair used by a king or queen on important official occasions. ❷ The throne is a way of referring to the position of being king or queen.

throng, throngs, thronging, thronged NOUN ❶ a large crowd of people ▷ VERB ❷ If people throng somewhere or throng a place, they go

there in great numbers • *Hundreds of city workers thronged the scene.*

throttle, throttles, throttling, throttled VERB To throttle someone is to kill or injure them by squeezing their throat.

through [Said *threw*] PREPOSITION ❶ moving all the way from one side of something to the other • *a path through the woods.* ❷ because of • *He had been exhausted through lack of sleep.* ❸ during • *He has to work through the summer.* ❹ If you go through an experience, it happens to you • *I don't want to go through that again.* ▷ ADJECTIVE ❺ If you are through with something, you have finished doing it or using it.
● USAGE NOTE: Do not confuse the spellings of *through* and *threw*, the past tense of *throw*

throughout PREPOSITION ❶ during • *I stayed awake throughout the night.* ▷ ADVERB ❷ happening or existing through the whole of a place • *The house was painted brown throughout.*

throve the past tense of **thrive**.

throw, throws, throwing, threw, thrown VERB ❶ When you throw something you are holding, you move your hand quickly and let it go, so that it moves through the air. ❷ If you throw yourself somewhere, you move there suddenly and with force • *We threw ourselves on the ground.* ❸ To throw someone into an unpleasant situation is to put them there • *It threw them into a panic.* ❹ If something throws light or shadow on something else, it makes that thing have light or shadow on it. ❺ If you

a b c d e f g h i j k l m n o p q r s **t** u v w x y z

▷ SPELLING NOTE: *Rhythmical Hounds Yap To Heavy Music (rhythm)*

throw yourself into an activity, you become actively and enthusiastically involved in it. ❻ If you throw a fit or tantrum, you suddenly begin behaving in an uncontrolled way.

● **SIMILAR WORDS:** ❶ chuck, fling,
● hurl

throwback, throwbacks **NOUN** something which has the characteristics of something that existed a long time ago • *Everything about her was a throwback to the fifties.*

thrush, thrushes **NOUN** ❶ a small brown songbird. ❷ Thrush is a disease of the mouth or of the vagina, caused by a fungus.

thrust, thrusts, thrusting, thrust **VERB** ❶ If you thrust something somewhere, you push or move it there quickly with a lot of force. ❷ If you thrust your way somewhere, you move along, pushing between people or things ▷ **NOUN** ❸ a sudden forceful movement. ❹ The main thrust of an activity or idea is the most important part of it • *the general thrust of his argument.*

thud, thuds, thudding, thudded **NOUN** ❶ a dull sound, usually made by a solid, heavy object hitting something soft ▷ **VERB** ❷ If something thuds somewhere, it makes a dull sound, usually by hitting something else.

thug, thugs **NOUN** a very rough and violent person.

● **WORD HISTORY:** from Hindi *thag*
● meaning 'thief'

thumb, thumbs, thumbing, thumbed **NOUN** ❶ the short, thick finger on the side of your hand ▷ **VERB** ❷ If

someone thumbs a lift, they stand at the side of the road and stick out their thumb until a driver stops and gives them a lift.

thump, thumps, thumping, thumped **VERB** ❶ If you thump someone or something, you hit them hard with your fist. ❷ If something thumps somewhere, it makes a fairly loud, dull sound, usually when it hits something else. ❸ When your heart thumps, it beats strongly and quickly ▷ **NOUN** ❹ a hard hit • *a great thump on the back.* ❺ a fairly loud, dull sound.

thunder, thunders, thundering, thundered **NOUN** ❶ Thunder is a loud cracking or rumbling noise caused by expanding air which is suddenly heated by lightning. ❷ Thunder is any loud rumbling noise • *the distant thunder of bombs.* ▷ **VERB** ❸ When it thunders, a loud cracking or rumbling noise occurs in the sky after a flash of lightning. ❹ If something thunders, it makes a loud continuous noise • *The helicopter thundered low over the trees.*

thunderbolt, thunderbolts **NOUN** a flash of lightning, accompanied by thunder.

thunderous **ADJECTIVE** A thunderous noise is very loud • *thunderous applause.*

Thursday, Thursdays **NOUN** Thursday is the day between Wednesday and Friday.

● **WORD HISTORY:** from Old English
● *Thursdæg* meaning 'Thor's day';
● Thor was the Norse god of thunder

thus **ADVERB** FORMAL ❶ in this way • *I sat thus for nearly half an hour.*

❷ therefore • *Critics were thus able to denounce him.*

thwart, thwarts, thwarting, thwarted **VERB** To thwart someone or their plans is to prevent them from doing or getting what they want.

thy **ADJECTIVE** OLD-FASHIONED Thy means your.

thyme [Said *time*] **NOUN** Thyme is a bushy herb with very small leaves.

thyroid gland, thyroid glands **NOUN** Your thyroid gland is situated at the base of your neck. It releases hormones which control your growth and your metabolism.

tiara, tiaras [Said *tee-ah-ra*] **NOUN** a semicircular crown of jewels worn by a woman on formal occasions.

Tibetan, Tibetans **ADJECTIVE** ❶ belonging or relating to Tibet ▷ **NOUN** ❷ someone who comes from Tibet.

tibia, tibias **NOUN** (SCIENCE) Your tibia is the inner and thicker of the two bones in your leg below your knee.

tic, tics **NOUN** a twitching of a group of muscles, especially the muscles in the face.

tick, ticks, ticking, ticked **NOUN** ❶ a written mark to show that something is correct or has been dealt with. ❷ The tick of a clock is the series of short sounds it makes when it is working. ❸ a tiny, blood-sucking, insect-like creature that usually lives on the bodies of people or animals ▷ **VERB** ❹ To tick something written on a piece of paper is to put a tick next to it • *Tick all boxes that apply.* ❺ When a clock ticks, it makes a regular series

of short sounds as it works.
tick off **VERB** INFORMAL If you tick someone off, you speak angrily to them because they have done something wrong. **ticking NOUN**

ticket, tickets **NOUN** a piece of paper or card which shows that you have paid for a journey or have paid to enter a place of entertainment.

tickle, tickles, tickling, tickled **VERB** ❶ When you tickle someone, you move your fingers lightly over their body in order to make them laugh. ❷ If something tickles you, it amuses you or gives you pleasure • *Simon is tickled by the idea.*

tidal **ADJECTIVE** to do with or produced by tides • *a tidal estuary.*

tidal wave, tidal waves **NOUN** (GEOGRAPHY) a very large wave, often caused by an earthquake, that comes over land and destroys things.

tide, tides, tiding, tided **NOUN** ❶ The tide is the regular change in the level of the sea on the shore, caused by the gravitational pull of the sun and the moon. ❷ The tide of opinion or fashion is what the majority of people think or do at a particular time. ❸ A tide of something is a large amount of it • *the tide of anger and bitterness.* **tide over** **VERB** If something will tide someone over, it will help them through a difficult period of time.

tidings **PLURAL NOUN** FORMAL Tidings are news.

tidy, tidier, tidiest; tidies, tidying, tidied **ADJECTIVE** ❶ Something that is tidy is neat and arranged in an orderly way. ❷ Someone who is tidy always keeps their things neat and

▷ SPELLING NOTE: *On WEDNESday Wayne WED NESta (Wednesday)*

arranged in an orderly way.
❸ INFORMAL A tidy amount of money is a fairly large amount of it ▷ **VERB**
❹ To tidy a place is to make it neat by putting things in their proper place.

tie, ties, tying, tied **VERB** ❶ If you tie one thing to another or tie it in a particular position, you fasten it using cord of some kind. ❷ If you tie a knot or a bow in a piece of cloth or cloth, you fasten the ends together to make a knot or bow. ❸ Something or someone that is tied to something else is closely linked with it • *40,000 jobs are tied to the project.* ❹ If you tie with someone in a competition or game, you have the same number of points ▷ **NOUN** ❺ a long, narrow piece of cloth worn around the neck under a shirt collar and tied in a knot at the front. ❻ a connection or feeling that links you with a person, place, or organization • *I had very close ties with the family.*
● SIMILAR WORDS: ❶ bind, fasten

tied up **ADJECTIVE** If you are tied up, you are busy.

tier, tiers **NOUN** one of a number of rows or layers of something • *Take the stairs to the upper tier.*

tiff, tiffs **NOUN** a small unimportant quarrel.

tiger, tigers **NOUN** a large meat-eating animal of the cat family. It comes from Asia and has an orange coloured coat with black stripes.

tiger snake, tiger snakes **NOUN** a fierce, very poisonous Australian snake with dark stripes across its back.

tight, tighter, tightest **ADJECTIVE**
❶ fitting closely • *The shoes are too tight.* ❷ firmly fastened and difficult to move • *a tight knot.* ❸ stretched or pulled so as not to be slack • *a tight cord.* ❹ A tight plan or arrangement allows only the minimum time or money needed to do something • *Our schedule tonight is very tight.*
▷ **ADVERB** ❺ held firmly and securely • *He held me tight.* **tightly** **ADVERB** **tightness** **NOUN**
● SIMILAR WORDS: ❸ stretched, ● taut

tighten, tightens, tightening, tightened **VERB** ❶ If you tighten your hold on something, you hold it more firmly. ❷ If you tighten a rope or chain, or if it tightens, it is stretched or pulled until it is straight. ❸ If someone tightens a rule or system, they make it stricter or more efficient.

tightrope, tightropes **NOUN** a tightly-stretched rope on which an acrobat balances and performs tricks.

tights **PLURAL NOUN** Tights are a piece of clothing made of thin stretchy material that fit closely round a person's hips, legs, and feet.

tiki, tiki or tikis **NOUN** In New Zealand, a small carving of an ancestor worn as a pendant in some Maori cultures.

tile, tiles, tiling, tiled **NOUN** ❶ a small flat square piece of something, for example slate or carpet, that is used to cover surfaces ▷ **VERB** ❷ To tile a surface is to fix tiles to it. **tiled** **ADJECTIVE**

till, tills, tilling, tilled **PREPOSITION OR CONJUNCTION** ❶ Till means the same as until ▷ **NOUN** ❷ a drawer or box in a shop where money is kept,

usually in a cash register ▷ **VERB**
❸ To till the ground is to plough it for raising crops.

tiller, tillers **NOUN** the handle fixed to the top of the rudder for steering a boat.

tilt, tilts, tilting, tilted **VERB** ❶ If you tilt an object or it tilts, it changes position so that one end or side is higher than the other ▷ **NOUN** ❷ a position in which one end or side of something is higher than the other.
● **SIMILAR WORDS:** ❶ incline, lean, ● tip

timber, timbers **NOUN** ❶ Timber is wood that has been cut and prepared ready for building and making furniture. ❷ The timbers of a ship or house are the large pieces of wood that have been used to build it.

time, times, timing, timed **NOUN**
❶ Time is what is measured in hours, days, and years • *What time is it?*
❷ 'Time' is used to mean a particular period or point • *I enjoyed my time in Durban.* ❸ If you say it is time for something or it is time to do it, you mean that it ought to happen or be done now • *It is time for a change.*
❹ 'Times' is used after numbers to indicate how often something happens • *I saw my father four times a year.* ❺ 'Times' is used after numbers when you are saying how much bigger, smaller, better, or worse one thing is compared to another • *The Belgians drink three times as much beer as the French.* ❻ 'Times' is used in arithmetic to link numbers that are multiplied together • *Two times three is six.* ▷ **VERB** ❼ If you time something for a particular time, you plan that it

should happen then • *We could not have timed our arrival better.* ❽ If you time an activity or action, you measure how long it lasts.
● **SIMILAR WORDS:** ❷ interval, ● period, spell

timeless ADJECTIVE Something timeless is so good or beautiful that it cannot be affected by the passing of time or by changes in fashion.

timely ADJECTIVE happening at just the right time • *a timely appearance.*
● **SIMILAR WORDS:** opportune, ● well-timed

timer, timers **NOUN** a device that measures time, especially one that is part of a machine.

timescale, timescales **NOUN** The timescale of an event is the length of time during which it happens.

time signature, time signatures **NOUN** (MUSIC) A time signature is a sign at the beginning of a line of music showing the number of beats in a bar.

timetable, timetables **NOUN** ❶ a plan of the times when particular activities or jobs should be done. ❷ a list of the times when particular trains, boats, buses, or aeroplanes arrive and depart.

timid ADJECTIVE shy and having no courage or self-confidence. **timidly ADVERB timidity NOUN**
● **SIMILAR WORDS:** fearful, shy, ● timorous

timing NOUN ❶ Someone's timing is their skill in judging the right moment at which to do something. ❷ The timing of an event is when it actually happens.

A
B
C
D
E
F
G
H
I
J
K
L
M
N
O
P
Q
R
S
T
U
V
W
X
Y
Z

timpani [*Said* **tim-pan-ee**] **PLURAL NOUN** Timpani are large drums with curved bottoms that are played in an orchestra.

tin, tins **NOUN** ❶ Tin is a soft silvery-white metal. ❷ a metal container which is filled with food and then sealed in order to preserve the food. ❸ a small metal container which may have a lid • *a cake tin*.

tinder **NOUN** Tinder is small pieces of dry wood or grass that burn easily and can be used for lighting a fire.

tinge, tinges **NOUN** a small amount of something • *a tinge of envy*. **tinged ADJECTIVE**

tingle, tingles, tingling, tingled **VERB** ❶ When a part of your body tingles, you feel a slight prickling feeling in it ▷ **NOUN** ❷ a slight prickling feeling. **tingling NOUN OR ADJECTIVE**

tinker, tinkers, tinkering, tinkered **NOUN** ❶ a person who travels from place to place mending metal pots and pans or doing other small repair jobs ▷ **VERB** ❷ If you tinker with something, you make a lot of small changes to it in order to repair or improve it • *All he wanted was to tinker with engines.*

tinkle, tinkles, tinkling, tinkled **VERB** ❶ If something tinkles, it makes a sound like a small bell ringing ▷ **NOUN** ❷ a sound like that of a small bell ringing.

tinned ADJECTIVE Tinned food has been preserved by being sealed in a tin.

tinsel NOUN Tinsel is long threads with strips of shiny paper attached,

used as a decoration at Christmas.

tint, tints, tinting, tinted **NOUN** ❶ a small amount of a particular colour • *a distinct tint of green*. ▷ **VERB** ❷ If a person tints their hair, they change its colour by adding a weak dye to it. **tinted ADJECTIVE**

tiny, tinier, tiniest **ADJECTIVE** extremely small.
● **SIMILAR WORDS:** diminutive,
● minute

tip, tips, tipping, tipped **NOUN** ❶ the end of something long and thin • *a fingertip*. ❷ a place where rubbish is dumped. ❸ If you give someone such as a waiter a tip, you give them some money to thank them for their services. ❹ a useful piece of advice or information ▷ **VERB** ❺ If you tip an object, you move it so that it is no longer horizontal or upright. ❻ If you tip something somewhere, you pour it there quickly or carelessly. **tipped ADJECTIVE**

tipple, tipples **NOUN** A person's tipple is the alcoholic drink that they normally drink.

tipsy, tipsier, tipsiest **ADJECTIVE** slightly drunk.

tiptoe, tiptoes, tiptoeing, tiptoed **VERB** If you tiptoe somewhere, you walk there very quietly on your toes.

tirade, tirades [*Said* **tie-rade**] **NOUN** a long, angry speech in which you criticize someone or something.
● **WORD HISTORY:** from Italian
● *tirata* meaning 'volley of shots'

tire, tires, tiring, tired **VERB** ❶ If something tires you, it makes you use a lot of energy so that you want to rest

or sleep. ❷ If you tire of something, you become bored with it.
  ● **SIMILAR WORDS:** ❶ exhaust, ● fatigue, weary

tired ADJECTIVE having little energy. **tiredness** NOUN

tireless ADJECTIVE Someone who is tireless has a lot of energy and never seems to need a rest.

tiresome ADJECTIVE A person or thing that is tiresome makes you feel irritated or bored.

tiring ADJECTIVE Something that is tiring makes you tired.

tissue, tissues [Said **tiss**-yoo] NOUN ❶ The tissue in plants and animals consists of cells that are similar in appearance and function • *scar tissue* • *dead tissue*. ❷ Tissue is thin paper that is used for wrapping breakable objects. ❸ a small piece of soft paper that you use as a handkerchief.

tit, tits NOUN a small European bird • *a blue tit*.

titanic ADJECTIVE very big or important.
  ● **WORD HISTORY:** in Greek legend, ● the *Titans* were a family of giants

titillate, titillates, titillating, titillated VERB If something titillates someone, it pleases and excites them, especially in a sexual way. **titillation** NOUN

title, titles NOUN ❶ the name of a book, play, or piece of music. ❷ a word that describes someone's rank or job • *My official title is Design Manager*. ❸ the position of champion in a sports competition • *the European featherweight title*.

titled ADJECTIVE Someone who is titled has a high social rank and has a title such as 'Princess', 'Lord', 'Lady', or 'Sir'.

titration NOUN (SCIENCE) a way of calculating the concentration of a solution by adding to it amounts of another substance which reacts with it, until the reaction between them is complete.

titter, titters, tittering, tittered VERB If you titter, you laugh in a way that shows you are nervous or embarrassed.

TNT NOUN TNT is a type of powerful explosive. It is an abbreviation for 'trinitrotoluene'.

to PREPOSITION ❶ 'To' is used to indicate the place that someone or something is moving towards or pointing at • *They are going to China*. ❷ 'To' is used to indicate the limit of something • *Goods to the value of 500 pounds*. ❸ 'To' is used in ratios and rates when saying how many units of one type there are for each unit of another • *I only get about 30 kilometres to the gallon from it*. ▷ ADVERB ❹ If you push or shut a door to, you close it but do not shut it completely.
  ● **USAGE NOTE:** The preposition *to* is ● spelt with one *o*, the adverb *too* has ● two *os*, and the number *two* is spelt ● with *wo*

toad, toads NOUN an amphibian that looks like a frog but has a drier skin and lives less in the water.

toadstool, toadstools NOUN a type of poisonous fungus.

toast, toasts, toasting, toasted NOUN ❶ Toast is slices of bread made brown

a
b
c
d
e
f
g
h
i
j
k
l
m
n
o
p
q
r
s
t
u
v
w
x
y
z

A
B
C
D
E
F
G
H
I
J
K
L
M
N
O
P
Q
R
S
T
U
V
W
X
Y
Z

and crisp by cooking at a high temperature. ❷ To drink a toast to someone is to drink an alcoholic drink in honour of them ▷ **VERB** ❸ If you toast bread, you cook it at a high temperature so that it becomes brown and crisp. ❹ If you toast yourself, you sit in front of a fire so that you feel pleasantly warm. ❺ To toast someone is to drink an alcoholic drink in honour of them.

● **WORD HISTORY:** from Latin *tostus* meaning 'parched'

toaster, toasters **NOUN** a piece of electrical equipment used for toasting bread.

tobacco NOUN Tobacco is the dried leaves of the tobacco plant which people smoke in pipes, cigarettes, and cigars.

tobacconist, tobacconists **NOUN** a shop where tobacco, cigarettes, and cigars are sold.

toboggan, toboggans **NOUN** a flat seat with two wooden or metal runners, used for sliding over the snow.

today ADVERB OR NOUN ❶ Today means the day on which you are speaking or writing. ❷ Today also means the present period of history • *the challenges of teaching in today's schools.*

toddle, toddles, toddling, toddled **VERB** To toddle is to walk in short, quick steps, as a very young child does.

toddler, toddlers **NOUN** a small child who has just learned to walk.

to-do, to-dos **NOUN** A to-do is a

situation in which people are very agitated or confused • *It's just like him to make such a to-do about a baby.*

toe, toes **NOUN** ❶ Your toes are the five movable parts at the end of your foot. ❷ The toe of a shoe or sock is the part that covers the end of your foot.

toff, toffs **NOUN** INFORMAL, OLD-FASHIONED a rich person or one from an aristocratic family.

toffee, toffees **NOUN** Toffee is a sticky, chewy sweet made by boiling sugar and butter together with water.

toga, togas **NOUN** a long loose robe worn in ancient Rome.

together ADVERB ❶ If people do something together, they do it with each other. ❷ If two things happen together, they happen at the same time. ❸ If things are joined or fixed together, they are joined or fixed to each other. ❹ If things or people are together, they are very near to each other.
● **USAGE NOTE:** Two nouns joined by *together with* do not make a plural subject, so the following verb is not plural: *Jones, together with his partner, has had great success*
● **SIMILAR WORDS:** ❶ collectively, jointly ❷ concurrently, simultaneously

togetherness NOUN Togetherness is a feeling of closeness and friendship.

toil, toils, toiling, toiled **VERB** ❶ When people toil, they work hard doing unpleasant, difficult, or tiring tasks or jobs ▷ **NOUN** ❷ Toil is unpleasant, difficult, or tiring work.

toilet, toilets NOUN ❶ a large bowl, connected by a pipe to the drains, which you use when you want to get rid of urine or faeces. ❷ a small room containing a toilet.

toiletries PLURAL NOUN Toiletries are the things you use when cleaning and taking care of your body, such as soap and talc.

token, tokens NOUN ❶ a piece of paper or card that is worth a particular amount of money and can be exchanged for goods • *record tokens*. ❷ a flat round piece of metal or plastic that can sometimes be used instead of money. ❸ If you give something to someone as a token of your feelings for them, you give it to them as a way of showing those feelings ▷ ADJECTIVE ❹ If something is described as token, it shows that it is not being treated as important • *a token contribution to your fees*.

told Told is the past tense and past participle of **tell**.

tolerable ADJECTIVE ❶ able to be put up with. ❷ fairly satisfactory or reasonable • *a tolerable salary*.

tolerance NOUN ❶ A person's tolerance is their ability to accept or put up with something which may not be enjoyable or pleasant for them. ❷ Tolerance is the quality of allowing other people to have their own attitudes or beliefs, or to behave in a particular way, even if you do not agree or approve • *religious tolerance*.

tolerant ADJECTIVE accepting of different views and behaviour.

tolerate, tolerates, tolerating,

tolerated VERB ❶ If you tolerate things that you do not approve of or agree with, you allow them. ❷ If you can tolerate something, you accept it, even though it is unsatisfactory and unpleasant. **toleration** NOUN
● SIMILAR WORDS: ❷ bear,
● endure, stand

toll, tolls, tolling, tolled NOUN ❶ The death toll in an accident is the number of people who have died in it. ❷ a sum of money that you have to pay in order to use a particular bridge or road ▷ VERB ❸ When someone tolls a bell, it is rung slowly, often as a sign that someone has died.

tom, toms NOUN a male cat.

tomahawk, tomahawks NOUN a small axe used by North American Indians.

tomato, tomatoes NOUN a small round red fruit, used as a vegetable and often eaten raw in salads.

tomb, tombs NOUN a large grave for one or more corpses.

tomboy, tomboys NOUN a girl who likes playing rough or noisy games.

tome, tomes NOUN FORMAL a very large heavy book.

tomorrow ADVERB OR NOUN ❶ Tomorrow means the day after today. ❷ You can refer to the future, especially the near future, as tomorrow • *The children of tomorrow will never know war*.

ton, tons NOUN ❶ a unit of weight equal to 2240 pounds or about 1016 kilograms ❷ IN PLURAL INFORMAL If you have tons of something, you have a lot of it.

a b c d e f g h i j k l m n o p q r s **t** u v w x y z

▷ SPELLING NOTE: *LEt's measure the angLE (angle)*

tonal ADJECTIVE involving the quality or pitch of a sound or of music.

tone, tones, toning, toned NOUN ❶ Someone's tone is a quality in their voice which shows what they are thinking or feeling. ❷ (MUSIC) The tone of a musical instrument or a singer's voice is the kind of sound it has. ❸ (ENGLISH) The tone of a piece of writing is its style and the ideas or opinions expressed in it • *I was shocked at the tone of your leading article.* ❹ (ART) a lighter, darker, or brighter shade of the same colour • *The whole room is painted in two tones of orange.*
tone down VERB If you tone down something, you make it less forceful or severe.

tone-deaf ADJECTIVE unable to sing in tune or to recognize different tunes.

tongs PLURAL NOUN Tongs consist of two long narrow pieces of metal joined together at one end. You press the pieces together to pick an object up.

tongue, tongues NOUN ❶ Your tongue is the soft part in your mouth that you can move and use for tasting, licking, and speaking. ❷ a language. ❸ Tongue is the cooked tongue of an ox. ❹ The tongue of a shoe or boot is the piece of leather underneath the laces.

tonic, tonics NOUN ❶ Tonic or tonic water is a colourless, fizzy drink that has a slightly bitter flavour and is often mixed with alcoholic drinks. ❷ a medicine that makes you feel stronger, healthier, and less tired. ❸ anything that makes you feel

stronger or more cheerful • *It was a tonic just being with her.*

tonight ADVERB OR NOUN Tonight is the evening or night that will come at the end of today.

tonne, tonnes [Said *tun*] NOUN (MATHS) a unit of weight equal to 1000 kilograms.

tonsil, tonsils NOUN Your tonsils are the two small, soft lumps in your throat at the back of your mouth.

tonsillitis [Said ton-sil-**lie**-tiss] NOUN Tonsillitis is a painful swelling of your tonsils caused by an infection.

too ADVERB ❶ also or as well • *You were there too.* ❷ more than a desirable, necessary, or acceptable amount • *a man who had taken too much to drink.*
● **USAGE NOTE:** The adverb *too* has two *o*s, the preposition *to* is spelt with one *o*, and the number *two* is spelt with *wo*

tool, tools NOUN ❶ any hand-held instrument or piece of equipment that you use to help you do a particular kind of work. ❷ an object, skill, or idea that is needed or used for a particular purpose • *You can use the survey as a bargaining tool in the negotiations.*
● **SIMILAR WORDS:** ❶ implement, instrument, utensil

toot, toots, tooting, tooted VERB If a car horn toots, it produces a short sound.

tooth, teeth NOUN ❶ Your teeth are the hard enamel-covered objects in your mouth that you use for biting and chewing food. ❷ The teeth of a comb, saw, or zip are the parts that stick out in a row on its edge.

toothpaste NOUN Toothpaste is a substance which you use to clean your teeth.

top, tops, topping, topped NOUN **1** The top of something is its highest point, part, or surface. **2** The top of a bottle, jar, or tube is its cap or lid. **3** a piece of clothing worn on the upper half of your body. **4** a toy with a pointed end on which it spins ▷ ADJECTIVE **5** The top thing of a series of things is the highest one • *the top floor of the building.* ▷ VERB **6** If someone tops a poll or popularity chart, they do better than anyone else in it • *It has topped the bestseller lists in almost every country.* **7** If something tops a particular amount, it is greater than that amount • *The temperature topped 90°.*

top up VERB To top something up is to add something to it in order to keep it at an acceptable or usable level.

top hat, top hats NOUN a tall hat with a narrow brim that men wear on special occasions.

topic, topics NOUN a particular subject that you write about or discuss.

topical ADJECTIVE involving or related to events that are happening at the time you are speaking or writing.

topography, topographies NOUN (GEOGRAPHY) **1** Topography is the study and description of the physical features of an area, for example the hills, valleys, or rivers. **2** The topography of a particular area is its physical shape.

topping, toppings NOUN food that is put on top of other food in order to decorate it or add to its flavour.

topple, topples, toppling, toppled VERB If something topples, it becomes unsteady and falls over.

top-secret ADJECTIVE meant to be kept completely secret.

topsy-turvy ADJECTIVE in a confused state • *My life was truly topsy-turvy.*

top-up card, top-up cards NOUN a card that you use to add credit to your mobile phone.

Torah NOUN The Torah is Jewish law and teaching.

torch, torches NOUN **1** a small electric light carried in the hand and powered by batteries. **2** a long stick with burning material wrapped around one end.

torment, torments, tormenting, tormented NOUN [Said *tor*-ment] **1** Torment is extreme pain or unhappiness. **2** something that causes extreme pain and unhappiness • *It's a torment to see them staring at me.* ▷ VERB [Said tor-**ment**] **3** If something torments you, it causes you extreme unhappiness.

torn **1** Torn is the past participle of **tear**. ADJECTIVE **2** If you are torn between two or more things, you cannot decide which one to choose and this makes you unhappy • *torn between duty and pleasure.*

tornado, tornadoes or tornados [Said tor-**nay**-doh] NOUN a violent

a
b
c
d
e
f
g
h
i
j
k
l
m
n
o
p
q
r
s
t
u
v
w
x
y
z

▷ SPELLING NOTE: *Beautiful Elephants Are Usually Tiny* (beautiful) storm with strong circular winds around a funnel-shaped cloud.

torpedo, torpedoes, torpedoing, torpedoed [Said tor-**pee**-doh] NOUN **1** a tube-shaped bomb that travels underwater and explodes when it hits a target ▷ VERB **2** If a ship is torpedoed, it is hit, and usually sunk, by a torpedo.

torrent, torrents NOUN **1** When a lot of water is falling very rapidly, it can be said to be falling in torrents. **2** A torrent of speech is a lot of it directed continuously at someone • *torrents of abuse*.

torrential ADJECTIVE Torrential rain pours down very rapidly and in great quantities.

torrid ADJECTIVE **1** Torrid weather is very hot and dry. **2** A torrid love affair is one in which people show very strong emotions.

torso, torsos NOUN the main part of your body, excluding your head, arms, and legs.

tortoise, tortoises NOUN a slow-moving reptile with a large hard shell over its body into which it can pull its head and legs for protection.

tortuous ADJECTIVE **1** A tortuous road is full of bends and twists. **2** A tortuous piece of writing is long and complicated.

torture, tortures, torturing, tortured NOUN **1** Torture is great pain that is deliberately caused to someone to punish them or get information from them ▷ VERB **2** If someone tortures another person, they deliberately cause that person great pain to punish

them or get information. **3** To torture someone is also to cause them to suffer mentally. **torturer** NOUN

Tory, Tories NOUN In Britain, a member or supporter of the Conservative Party.
● **WORD HISTORY:** from Irish
● *toraidhe* meaning 'outlaw'

toss, tosses, tossing, tossed VERB **1** If you toss something somewhere, you throw it there lightly and carelessly. **2** If you toss a coin, you decide something by throwing a coin into the air and guessing which side will face upwards when it lands. **3** If you toss your head, you move it suddenly backwards, especially when you are angry, annoyed, or want your own way. **4** To toss is to move repeatedly from side to side • *We tossed and turned and tried to sleep.*
● **SIMILAR WORDS:** **1** fling, sling,
● throw

tot, tots, totting, totted NOUN **1** a very young child. **2** a small amount of strong alcohol such as whisky ▷ VERB **3** To tot up numbers is to add them together.

total, totals, totalling, totalled NOUN **1** the number you get when you add several numbers together ▷ ADJECTIVE **2** Total means complete • *a total failure.* ▷ VERB **3** When you total a set of numbers or objects, you add them all together. **4** If several numbers total a certain figure, that is the figure you get when all the numbers are added together • *Their debts totalled over 300,000 dollars.* **totally** ADVERB
● **SIMILAR WORDS:** **1** aggregate,
● sum, whole

▷ SPELLING NOTE: *Betty Eats Cakes And Uses Seven Eggs (because)*

totalitarian [Said toe-tal-it-tair-ee-an] **ADJECTIVE** A totalitarian political system is one in which one political party controls everything and does not allow any other parties to exist. **totalitarianism NOUN**

tote, totes, toting, toted **VERB** INFORMAL To tote a gun is to carry it.

totem pole, totem poles **NOUN** a long wooden pole with symbols and pictures carved and painted on it. Totem poles are made by some North American Indians.

totter, totters, tottering, tottered **VERB** When someone totters, they walk in an unsteady way • She tottered away in her high-heeled shoes.

toucan, toucans [Said too-kan] **NOUN** a large tropical bird with a very large beak.

touch, touches, touching, touched **VERB** ❶ If you touch something, you put your fingers or hand on it. ❷ When two things touch, their surfaces come into contact • Their knees were touching. ❸ If you are touched by something, you are emotionally affected by it • I was touched by his thoughtfulness. ▷ **NOUN** ❹ Your sense of touch is your ability to tell what something is like by touching it. ❺ a detail which is added to improve something • finishing touches. ❻ a small amount of something • a touch of mustard. ▷ **PHRASE** ❼ If you are in touch with someone, you are in contact with them.

touchdown, touchdowns **NOUN** Touchdown is the landing of an aircraft.

touching **ADJECTIVE** causing feelings of sadness and sympathy.
● **SIMILAR WORDS:** moving, poignant, sad

touchy, touchier, touchiest **ADJECTIVE** ❶ If someone is touchy, they are easily upset or irritated. ❷ A touchy subject is one that needs to be dealt with carefully, because it might upset or offend people.

tough, tougher, toughest [Said tuff] **ADJECTIVE** ❶ A tough person is strong and independent and able to put up with hardship. ❷ A tough substance is difficult to break. ❸ A tough task, problem, or way of life is difficult or full of hardship. ❹ Tough policies or actions are strict and firm • tough measures against organized crime. **toughly ADVERB toughness NOUN toughen VERB**
● **SIMILAR WORDS:** ❷ durable, resilient, strong

toupee, toupees [Said too-pay] **NOUN** a small wig worn by a man to cover a bald patch on his head.

tour, tours, touring, toured **NOUN** ❶ a long journey during which you visit several places. ❷ a short trip round a place such as a city or famous building ▷ **VERB** ❸ If you tour a place, you go on a journey or a trip round it.

tourism **NOUN** (GEOGRAPHY) Tourism is the business of providing services for people on holiday, for example hotels and sightseeing trips.

tourist, tourists (GEOGRAPHY) **NOUN** a person who visits places for pleasure or interest.

tournament, tournaments **NOUN**

▷ SPELLING NOTE: *there's a rAKE in the brAKEs (brake)*

(PE) a sports competition in which players who win a match play further matches, until just one person or team is left.

tourniquet, tourniquets [Said *toor-nik-kay*] NOUN a strip of cloth tied tightly round a wound to stop it bleeding.

tousled ADJECTIVE Tousled hair is untidy.

tout, touts, touting, touted VERB ❶ If someone touts something, they try to sell it. ❷ If someone touts for business or custom, they try to obtain it in a very direct way • *volunteers who spend days touting for donations.* ▷ NOUN ❸ someone who sells tickets outside a sports ground or theatre, charging more than the original price.

tow, tows, towing, towed VERB ❶ If a vehicle tows another vehicle, it pulls it along behind it ▷ NOUN ❷ To give a vehicle a tow is to tow it ▷ PHRASE ❸ If you have someone **in tow**, they are with you because you are looking after them.

towards PREPOSITION ❶ in the direction of • *He turned towards the door.* ❷ about or involving • *My feelings towards Susan have changed.* ❸ as a contribution for • *a huge donation towards the new opera house.* ❹ near to • *We sat towards the back.*

towel, towels NOUN a piece of thick, soft cloth that you use to dry yourself with.

towelling NOUN Towelling is thick, soft cloth that is used for making towels.

tower, towers, towering, towered NOUN ❶ a tall, narrow building, sometimes attached to a larger building such as a castle or church ▷ VERB ❷ Someone or something that towers over other people or things is much taller than them. **towering** ADJECTIVE

town, towns NOUN ❶ a place with many streets and buildings where people live and work. ❷ Town is the central shopping and business part of a town rather than the suburbs • *She has gone into town.*

township, townships NOUN a small town in South Africa where only Black people or Coloured people were allowed to live.

towpath, towpaths NOUN a path along the side of a canal or river.

toxic ADJECTIVE poisonous • *toxic waste.*
• WORD HISTORY: from Greek *toxikon* meaning 'poison used on arrows' from *toxon* meaning 'arrow'.

toxin, toxins NOUN a poison, especially one produced by bacteria and very harmful to living creatures.

toy, toys, toying, toyed NOUN ❶ any object made to play with ▷ VERB ❷ If you toy with an idea, you consider it without being very serious about it • *She toyed with the idea of telephoning him.* ❸ If you toy with an object, you fiddle with it • *Jessica was toying with her glass.*

toyi-toyi or **toy-toy** NOUN In South Africa, a toyi-toyi is a dance performed to protest about something.

trace, traces, tracing, traced **VERB**
1 If you trace something, you find it after looking for it • *Police are trying to trace the owner.* **2** (EXAM TERM) To trace the development of something is to find out or describe how it developed. **3** If you trace a drawing or a map, you copy it by covering it with a piece of transparent paper and drawing over the lines underneath ▷ **NOUN** **4** a sign which shows you that someone or something has been in a place • *No trace of his father had been found.* **5** a very small amount of something. **tracing NOUN**

track, tracks, tracking, tracked **NOUN**
1 a narrow road or path. **2** a strip of ground with rails on it that a train travels along. **3** a piece of ground, shaped like a ring, which horses, cars, or athletes race around **4** **IN PLURAL** Tracks are marks left on the ground by a person or animal • *the deer tracks by the side of the path.* ▷ **ADJECTIVE** **5** In an athletics competition, the track events are the races on a running track ▷ **VERB** **6** If you track animals or people, you find them by following their footprints or other signs that they have left behind.
track down VERB If you track down someone or something, you find them by searching for them.

track record, track records **NOUN**
The track record of a person or a company is their past achievements or failures • *the track record of the film's star.*

tracksuit, tracksuits **NOUN** a loose, warm suit of trousers and a top, worn for outdoor sports.

tract, tracts **NOUN** **1** A tract of land or forest is a large area of it. **2** a pamphlet which expresses a strong opinion on a religious, moral, or political subject. **3** a system of organs and tubes in an animal's or person's body that has a particular function • *the digestive tract.*

traction NOUN Traction is a form of medical treatment given to an injured limb which involves pulling it gently for long periods of time using a system of weights and pulleys.

tractor, tractors **NOUN** a vehicle with large rear wheels that is used on a farm for pulling machinery and other heavy loads.

trade, trades, trading, traded **NOUN**
1 (HISTORY) Trade is the activity of buying, selling, or exchanging goods or services between people, firms, or countries. **2** Someone's trade is the kind of work they do, especially when it requires special training in practical skills • *a joiner by trade.* ▷ **VERB** **3** When people, firms, or countries trade, they buy, sell, or exchange goods or services. **4** If you trade things, you exchange them • *Their mother had traded her rings for a few potatoes.*
● **SIMILAR WORDS:** **1** business, commerce **3** deal, do business, traffic

trademark, trademarks **NOUN** a name or symbol that a manufacturer always uses on its products. Trademarks are usually protected by law so that no-one else can use them.

trader, traders **NOUN** a person whose job is to buy and sell goods • *a timber trader.*

▷ SPELLING NOTE: *I always visit my FRIend on a FRIday (Friday)*

A B C D E F G H I J K L M N O P Q R S T U V W X Y Z

tradesman, tradesmen NOUN a person, for example a shopkeeper, whose job is to sell goods.

trade union, trade unions NOUN an organization of workers that tries to improve the pay and conditions in a particular industry.

tradition, traditions NOUN a custom or belief that has existed for a long time without changing.
 ● SIMILAR WORDS: convention,
 ● custom

traditional ADJECTIVE
 ❶ Traditional customs or beliefs have existed for a long time without changing • *her traditional Indian dress.* ❷ A traditional organization or institution is one in which older methods are used rather than modern ones • *a traditional school.*
 traditionally ADVERB

traditionalist, traditionalists NOUN someone who supports the established customs and beliefs of their society, and does not want to change them.

traffic, traffics, trafficking, trafficked NOUN ❶ Traffic is the movement of vehicles or people along a route at a particular time. ❷ Traffic in something such as drugs is an illegal trade in them ▷ VERB ❸ Someone who traffics in drugs or other goods buys and sells them illegally.

traffic light, traffic lights NOUN Traffic lights are the set of red, amber, and green lights at a road junction which control the flow of traffic.

traffic warden, traffic wardens NOUN a person whose job is to make sure that cars are not parked in the wrong place or for longer than is allowed.

tragedy, tragedies [Said **traj-id-ee**] NOUN ❶ an event or situation that is disastrous or very sad. ❷ a serious story or play, that usually ends with the death of the main character.

tragic ADJECTIVE ❶ Something tragic is very sad because it involves death, suffering, or disaster • *a tragic accident.* ❷ Tragic films, plays, and books are sad and serious • *a tragic love story.* **tragically** ADVERB

trail, trails, trailing, trailed NOUN ❶ a rough path across open country or through forests. ❷ a series of marks or other signs left by someone or something as they move along ▷ VERB ❸ If you trail something or it trails, it drags along behind you as you move, or it hangs down loosely • *a small plane trailing a banner.* ❹ If someone trails along, they move slowly, without any energy or enthusiasm. ❺ If a voice trails away or trails off, it gradually becomes more hesitant until it stops completely.

trailer, trailers NOUN a small vehicle which can be loaded with things and pulled behind a car.

train, trains, training, trained NOUN ❶ a number of carriages or trucks which are pulled by a railway engine. ❷ A train of thought is a connected series of thoughts. ❸ A train of vehicles or people is a line or group following behind something or someone • *a train of wives and girlfriends.* ▷ VERB ❹ If you train someone, your teach them how to do something. ❺ If you train, you learn how to do a particular job • *She trained* *as a serious actress.* **❻** If you train for a sports match or a race, you prepare for it by doing exercises. **training NOUN**

trainee, trainees **NOUN** someone who is being taught how to do a job.

trainers PLURAL NOUN Trainers are special shoes worn for running or jogging.

trait, traits **NOUN** a particular characteristic or tendency. In literature, a trait is an aspect of a character in a story, for example, kind, greedy, funny, or stupid • *a very English trait.*

traitor, traitors **NOUN** (HISTORY) someone who betrays their country or the group which they belong to.

trajectory, trajectories *[Said traj-jek-tor-ee]* **NOUN** The trajectory of an object moving through the air is the curving path that it follows.

tram, trams **NOUN** a vehicle which runs on rails along the street and is powered by electricity from an overhead wire.

tramp, tramps, tramping, tramped **NOUN** ❶ a person who has no home, no job, and very little money. ❷ a long country walk • *I took a long, wet tramp through the fine woodlands.* ▷ **VERB** ❸ If you tramp from one place to another, you walk with slow, heavy footsteps.

trample, tramples, trampling, trampled **VERB** ❶ If you trample on something, you tread heavily on it so that it is damaged. ❷ If you trample on someone or on their rights or feelings, you behave in a way that shows you don't care about them.

trampoline, trampolines **NOUN** a piece of gymnastic equipment consisting of a large piece of strong cloth held taut by springs in a frame, on which a gymnast jumps to help them jump high.

trance, trances **NOUN** a mental state in which someone seems to be asleep but is conscious enough to be aware of their surroundings and to respond to questions and commands.

tranquil *[Said trang-kwil]* **ADJECTIVE** calm and peaceful • *tranquil lakes* • *I have a tranquil mind.* **tranquillity NOUN**

tranquillize, tranquillizes, tranquillizing, tranquillized; *also spelt* **tranquillise VERB** If people or animals are tranquillized, they are given a drug to make them become calm, sleepy, or unconscious.

tranquillizer, tranquillizers; *also spelt* **tranquilliser NOUN** a drug that makes people feel less anxious or nervous.

trans- PREFIX Trans- means across, through, or beyond • *transatlantic.*

transaction, transactions **NOUN** a business deal which involves buying and selling something.

transcend, transcends, transcending, transcended **VERB** If one thing transcends another, it goes beyond it or is superior to it • *Her beauty transcends all barriers.*

transcribe, transcribes, transcribing, transcribed **VERB** If you transcribe something that is spoken or written, you write it down, copy it, or change it into a different form of

▷ SPELLING NOTE: *The government licenSes Schnapps (licenses)*

A B C D E F G H I J K L M N O P Q R S **T** U V W X Y Z

writing • *These letters were often transcribed by his wife Patti.*

transcript, transcripts **NOUN** a written copy of of something that is spoken.

transfer, transfers, transferring, transferred **VERB** ❶ If you transfer something from one place to another, you move it • *They transferred the money to the Swiss account.* ❷ If you transfer to a different place or job, or are transferred to it, you move to a different place or job within the same organization ▷ **NOUN** ❸ the movement of something from one place to another. ❹ a piece of paper with a design on one side which can be ironed or pressed onto cloth, paper, or china. **transferable ADJECTIVE**

transfixed ADJECTIVE If a person is transfixed by something, they are so impressed or frightened by it that they cannot move • *Price stood transfixed at the sight of that tiny figure.*

transform, transforms, transforming, transformed **VERB** ❶ If something is transformed, it is changed completely • *The frown is transformed into a smile.* ❷ (MATHS) To transform a shape is to change how it looks, for example by translation, reflection, rotation, or enlargement. **transformation NOUN**

transfusion, transfusions **NOUN** A transfusion or blood transfusion is a process in which blood from a healthy person is injected into the body of another person who is badly injured or ill.

transient [Said **tran**-zee-ent] **ADJECTIVE** Something transient does

not stay or exist for very long • *transient emotions.* **transience NOUN**

transistor, transistors **NOUN** ❶ a small electrical device in something such as a television or radio which is used to control electric currents. ❷ A transistor or a transistor radio is a small portable radio.

transit NOUN ❶ Transit is the carrying of goods or people by vehicle from one place to another ▷ **PHRASE** ❷ People or things that are **in transit** are travelling or being taken from one place to another • *damage that had occurred in transit.*

transition, transitions **NOUN** a change from one form or state to another • *the transition from war to peace.*

transitional ADJECTIVE A transitional period or stage is one during which something changes from one form or state to another.

transition metal, transition metals **NOUN** (SCIENCE) one of a group of metals which includes chromium, copper and gold. Transition metals have an incomplete penultimate electron shell, can have more than one valency, and tend to form compounds.

transitive ADJECTIVE In grammar, a transitive verb is a verb which has an object.

transitory ADJECTIVE lasting for only a short time.

translate, translates, translating, translated **VERB** ❶ To translate something that someone has said or written is to say it or write it in a different language. **②** MATHS To translate a shape is to move it up or down, or from side to side, but not change it in any other way.

translation NOUN **translator** NOUN

translucent ADJECTIVE If something is translucent, light passes through it so that it seems to glow • *translucent petals.*

transmission, transmissions NOUN **①** The transmission of something involves passing or sending it to a different place or person • *the transmission of infectious diseases.* **②** The transmission of television or radio programmes is the broadcasting of them. **③** a broadcast.

transmit, transmits, transmitting, transmitted VERB **①** When a message or an electronic signal is transmitted, it is sent by radio waves. **②** To transmit something to a different place or person is to pass it or send it to the place or person • *the clergy's role in transmitting knowledge.*

transmitter NOUN

transparency, transparencies NOUN **①** a small piece of photographic film which can be projected onto a screen. **②** Transparency is the quality that an object or substance has if you can see through it.

transparent ADJECTIVE D & T If an object or substance is transparent, you can see through it. **transparently** ADVERB

- SIMILAR WORDS: clear, limpid,
- see-through

transpire, transpires, transpiring, transpired VERB **①** FORMAL When it transpires that something is the case, people discover that it is the case • *It transpired that he had flown off on holiday.* **②** When something transpires, it happens • *You start to wonder what transpired between them.*

- USAGE NOTE: Some people think
- that it is wrong to use *transpire* to
- mean 'happen'. However, it is very
- widely used in this sense, especially
- in spoken English

transplant, transplants, transplanting, transplanted NOUN **①** a process of removing something from one place and putting it in another • *a man who needs a heart transplant.* ▷ VERB **②** When something is transplanted, it is moved to a different place.

transport, transports, transporting, transported NOUN GEOGRAPHY **①** Vehicles that you travel in are referred to as transport • *public transport.* **②** Transport is the moving of goods or people from one place to another • *The prices quoted include transport costs.* ▷ VERB **③** When goods or people are transported from one place to another, they are moved there.

- SIMILAR WORDS: **③** carry,
- convey, transfer

transportation NOUN GEOGRAPHY Transportation is the transporting of people and things from one place to another.

transpose, transposes, transposing, transposed VERB **①** FORMAL If you transpose something to a different place or position, you move it there.

a
b
c
d
e
f
g
h
i
j
k
l
m
n
o
p
q
r
s
t
u
v
w
x
y
z

▷ SPELLING NOTE: *plaice the fish has a glittering 'EYE' (I) (plaice)*

② To transpose something also means to alter it to a different form, while keeping its essential features. **transposition NOUN**

transverse ADJECTIVE TECHNICAL Transverse is used to describe something that is at right angles to something else.

transvestite, transvestites **NOUN** a person who enjoys wearing clothes normally worn by people of the opposite sex.

trap, traps, trapping, trapped **NOUN** **①** a piece of equipment or a hole that is carefully positioned in order to catch animals or birds. **②** a trick that is intended to catch or deceive someone ▷ **VERB** **③** Someone who traps animals catches them using traps. **④** If you trap someone, you trick them so that they do or say something which they did not want to. **⑤** If you are trapped somewhere, you cannot move or escape because something is blocking your way or holding you down. **⑥** If you are trapped, you are in an unpleasant situation that you cannot easily change • *I'm trapped in an unhappy marriage.* **trapper NOUN**
● **SIMILAR WORDS:** **③** catch, snare
● **④** dupe, trick

trap door, trap doors **NOUN** a small horizontal door in a floor, ceiling, or stage.

trapeze, trapezes **NOUN** a bar of wood or metal hanging from two ropes on which acrobats and gymnasts swing and perform skilful movements.

trapezium, trapeziums or trapezia [*Said* trap-**pee**-zee-um] **NOUN** a

four-sided shape with two sides parallel to each other.

trappings PLURAL NOUN The trappings of a particular rank, position, or state are the clothes or equipment that go with it.

trash NOUN **①** Trash is rubbish • *He picks up your trash on Mondays.* **②** If you say that something such as a book, painting, or film is trash, you mean that it is not very good.

trauma, traumas [*Said* **traw**-ma] **NOUN** a very upsetting experience which causes great stress • *the trauma of his mother's death.*

traumatic ADJECTIVE A traumatic experience is very upsetting.

travel, travels, travelling, travelled **VERB** **①** To travel is to go from one place to another. **②** When something reaches one place from another, you say that it travels there • *Gossip travels fast.* ▷ **NOUN** **③** Travel is the act of travelling • *air travel.* **④** IN PLURAL Someone's travels are the journeys that they make to places a long way from their home • *my travels in the Himalayas.* **traveller NOUN** **travelling ADJECTIVE**
● **SIMILAR WORDS:** **①** go, journey

traveller's cheque, traveller's cheques **NOUN** Traveller's cheques are cheques for use abroad. You buy them at home and then exchange them when you are abroad for foreign currency.

traverse, traverses, traversing, traversed **VERB** FORMAL If you traverse an area of land or water, you go across it or over it • *They have traversed the island from the west coast.*

▷ SPELLING NOTE: *I went to see (C) the doctor's new practiCe (practice)*

travesty, travesties **NOUN** a very bad or ridiculous representation or imitation of something • *British salad is a travesty of freshness.*

trawl, trawls, trawling, trawled **VERB** When fishermen trawl, they drag a wide net behind a ship in order to catch fish.

trawler, trawlers **NOUN** a fishing boat that is used for trawling.

tray, trays **NOUN** a flat object with raised edges which is used for carrying food or drinks.

treacherous **ADJECTIVE** ❶ A treacherous person is likely to betray you and cannot be trusted. ❷ The ground or the sea can be described as treacherous when it is dangerous or unreliable • *treacherous mountain roads.* **treacherously ADVERB**
- **SIMILAR WORDS:** ❶ disloyal, untrustworthy

treachery **NOUN** Treachery is behaviour in which someone betrays their country or a person who trusts them.

treacle **NOUN** Treacle is a thick, sweet syrup used to make cakes and toffee • *treacle tart.*

tread, treads, treading, trod, trodden **VERB** ❶ If you tread on something, you walk on it or step on it. ❷ If you tread something into the ground or into a carpet, you crush it in by stepping on it • *bubblegum that has been trodden into the pavement.*
▷ **NOUN** ❸ A person's tread is the sound they make with their feet as they walk • *his heavy tread.* ❹ The tread of a tyre or shoe is the pattern of ridges on it that stops it slipping.

treadmill, treadmills **NOUN** Any task or job that you must keep doing even though it is unpleasant or tiring can be referred to as a treadmill • *My life is one constant treadmill of making music.*

treason **NOUN** Treason is the crime of betraying your country, for example by helping its enemies.

treasure, treasures, treasuring, treasured **NOUN** ❶ Treasure is a collection of gold, silver, jewels, or other precious objects, especially one that has been hidden • *buried treasure.* ❷ Treasures are valuable works of art • *the finest art treasures in the world.* ▷ **VERB** ❸ If you treasure something, you are very pleased that you have it and regard it as very precious • *He treasures his friendship with her.* **treasured ADJECTIVE**

treasurer, treasurers **NOUN** a person who is in charge of the finance and accounts of an organization.

Treasury **NOUN** The Treasury is the government department that deals with the country's finances.

treat, treats, treating, treated **VERB** ❶ If you treat someone in a particular way, you behave that way towards them. ❷ If you treat something in a particular way, you deal with it that way or see it that way • *We are now treating this case as murder.* ❸ When a doctor treats a patient or an illness, he or she gives them medical care and attention. ❹ If something such as wood or cloth is treated, a special substance is put on it in order to protect it or give it special properties • *The carpet's been treated with a stain protector.* ❺ If you treat someone, you

a b c d e f g h i j k l m n o p q r s **t** u v w x y z

▷ SPELLING NOTE: *You must practiSe your Ss (practise)*

buy or arrange something special for them which they will enjoy ▷ **NOUN** ❻ If you give someone a treat, you buy or arrange something special for them which they will enjoy • *my birthday treat.* **treatment NOUN**

treatise, treatises [Said *tree-tiz*] **NOUN** a long formal piece of writing about a particular subject.

treaty, treaties **NOUN** a written agreement between countries in which they agree to do something or to help each other.

treble, trebles, trebling, trebled **VERB** ❶ If something trebles or is trebled, it becomes three times greater in number or amount • *Next year we can treble that amount.* ▷ **ADJECTIVE** ❷ Treble means three times as large or three times as strong as previously. • *a treble dose.*

tree, trees **NOUN** a large plant with a hard woody trunk, branches, and leaves.

trek, treks, trekking, trekked **VERB** ❶ If you trek somewhere, you go on a long and difficult journey ▷ **NOUN** ❷ a long and difficult journey, especially one made by walking.
  ● **WORD HISTORY:** an Afrikaans
  ● word

trellis, trellises **NOUN** a frame made of horizontal and vertical strips of wood or metal and used to support plants.

tremble, trembles, trembling, trembled **VERB** ❶ If you tremble, you shake slightly, usually because you are frightened or cold. ❷ If something trembles, it shakes slightly. ❸ If your voice trembles, it sounds unsteady,

usually because you are frightened or upset. **trembling ADJECTIVE**

tremendous ADJECTIVE ❶ large or impressive • *a tremendous size.* ❷ INFORMAL very good or pleasing • *tremendous fun.* **tremendously ADVERB**

tremor, tremors **NOUN** ❶ a shaking movement of your body which you cannot control. ❷ an unsteady quality in your voice, for example when you are upset. ❸ a small earthquake.

trench, trenches **NOUN** a long narrow channel dug into the ground.

trenchant [Said *trent-shent*] **ADJECTIVE** Trenchant writings or comments are bold and firmly expressed.

trend, trends **NOUN** a change towards doing or being something different.

trendy, trendier, trendiest **ADJECTIVE** INFORMAL Trendy things or people are fashionable.

trepidation NOUN FORMAL Trepidation is fear or anxiety • *He saw the look of trepidation on my face.*

trespass, trespasses, trespassing, trespassed **VERB** If you trespass on someone's land or property, you go onto it without their permission. **trespasser NOUN**

tresses PLURAL NOUN OLD-FASHIONED A woman's tresses are her long flowing hair.

trestle, trestles **NOUN** a wooden or metal structure that is used as one of the supports for a table.

trevally, trevallies **NOUN** an

Australian and New Zealand fish that is caught for both food and sport.

tri- PREFIX three • *tricycle*.

triad, triads *[Said **try**-ad]* NOUN ❶ FORMAL a group of three similar things. ❷ (MUSIC) In music, a triad is a chord of three notes consisting of the tonic and the third and fifth above it.

trial, trials NOUN ❶ the legal process in which a judge and jury decide whether a person is guilty of a particular crime after listening to all the evidence about it. ❷ an experiment in which something is tested • *Trials of the drug start next month*.

triangle, triangles NOUN ❶ (MATHS) a shape with three straight sides. ❷ a percussion instrument consisting of a thin steel bar bent in the shape of a triangle. **triangular** ADJECTIVE

triangulation NOUN (GEOGRAPHY) Triangulation is a method of surveying land, in which the land is divided into triangles and the areas of the triangles are calculated. **triangulate** VERB

triathlon, triathlons *[Said tri-**ath**-lon]* NOUN a sports contest in which athletes compete in three different events.

tribe, tribes NOUN a group of people of the same race, who have the same customs, religion, language, or land, especially when they are thought to be primitive. **tribal** ADJECTIVE

tribulation, tribulations NOUN FORMAL Tribulation is trouble or

suffering • *the tribulations of a female football star*.

tribunal, tribunals *[Said try-**byoo**-nl]* NOUN a special court or committee appointed to deal with particular problems • *an industrial tribunal*.

tributary, tributaries NOUN a stream or river that flows into a larger river.

tribute, tributes NOUN ❶ A tribute is something said or done to show admiration and respect for someone • *Police paid tribute to her courage*. ❷ If one thing is a tribute to another, it is the result of the other thing and shows how good it is • *His success has been a tribute to hard work*.

trice NOUN If someone does something in a trice, they do it very quickly.

triceps *[Said **try**-seps]* NOUN (PE) Your triceps is the large muscle at the back of your upper arm that straightens your arm.

trick, tricks, tricking, tricked NOUN ❶ an action done to deceive someone. ❷ Tricks are clever or skilful actions done in order to entertain people • *magic tricks*. ▷ VERB ❸ If someone tricks you, they deceive you.

trickery NOUN Trickery is deception • *He accused the Serbs of trickery*.

trickle, trickles, trickling, trickled VERB ❶ When a liquid trickles somewhere, it flows slowly in a thin stream. ❷ When people or things trickle somewhere, they move there slowly in small groups or amounts ▷ NOUN ❸ a thin stream of liquid. ❹ A trickle of people or things is a

▷ SPELLING NOTE: L**Earn** the princip**LEs** (princip**le**)

A
B
C
D
E
F
G
H
I
J
K
L
M
N
O
P
Q
R
S
T
U
V
W
X
Y
Z

small number or quantity of them.

tricky, trickier, trickiest **ADJECTIVE** difficult to do or deal with.

tricycle, tricycles **NOUN** a vehicle similar to a bicycle but with two wheels at the back and one at the front.

trifle, trifles, trifling, trifled **NOUN** ❶ A trifle means a little • *He seemed a trifle annoyed.* ❷ Trifles are things that are not very important or valuable. ❸ a cold pudding made of layers of sponge cake, fruit, jelly, and custard ▷ **VERB** ❹ If you trifle with someone or something, you treat them in a disrespectful way • *He was not to be trifled with.*

trifling **ADJECTIVE** small and unimportant.

trigger, triggers, triggering, triggered **NOUN** ❶ the small lever on a gun which is pulled in order to fire it ▷ **VERB** ❷ If something triggers an event or triggers it off, it causes it to happen.
● **WORD HISTORY:** from Dutch
● *trekken* meaning 'to pull'

trigonometry [*Said trig-gon-nom-it-ree*] **NOUN** Trigonometry is the branch of mathematics that is concerned with calculating the angles of triangles or the lengths of their sides.

trill, trills, trilling, trilled **VERB** If a bird trills, it sings with short high-pitched repeated notes.

trillion, trillions **NOUN** INFORMAL Trillions of things means an extremely large number of them. Formerly, a trillion meant a million million million.

trilogy, trilogies **NOUN** a series of three books or plays that have the same characters or are on the same subject.

trim, trimmer, trimmest; trims, trimming, trimmed **ADJECTIVE** ❶ neat, tidy, and attractive ▷ **VERB** ❷ To trim something is to clip small amounts off it. ❸ If you trim off parts of something, you cut them off because they are not needed • *Trim off the excess marzipan.* ▷ **NOUN** ❹ If something is given a trim, it is cut a little • *All styles need a trim every six to eight weeks.* ❺ a decoration on something, especially along its edges • *a fur trim.* **trimmed ADJECTIVE**

trimming, trimmings **NOUN** Trimmings are extra parts added to something for decoration or as a luxury • *bacon and eggs with all the trimmings.*

Trimurti NOUN In the Hindu religion, the Trimurti are the three deities Brahma, Vishnu, and Siva.

trinity NOUN (RE) ❶ In the Christian religion, the Trinity is the joining of God the Father, God the Son, and God the Holy Spirit. ❷ LITERARY A trinity is a group of three things or people.

trinket, trinkets **NOUN** a cheap ornament or piece of jewellery.

trio, trios **NOUN** ❶ a group of three musicians who sing or play together; also a piece of music written for three instruments or singers. ❷ any group of three things or people together • *a trio of children's tales.*

trip, trips, tripping, tripped **NOUN** ❶ a journey made to a place ▷ **VERB**

❷ If you trip, you catch your foot on something and fall over. ❸ If you trip someone or trip them up, you make them fall over by making them catch their foot on something.

● **SIMILAR WORDS:** ❶ excursion,
● journey, outing

tripe NOUN Tripe is the stomach lining of a pig, cow, or ox, which is cooked and eaten.

triple, triples, tripling, tripled
ADJECTIVE ❶ consisting of three things or three parts • *the Triple Alliance.* ▷ VERB ❷ If you triple something or if it triples, it becomes three times greater in number or size.

triplet, triplets NOUN Triplets are three children born at the same time to the same mother.

tripod, tripods [*Said* **try-pod**] NOUN a stand with three legs used to support something like a camera or telescope.

tripper, trippers NOUN a tourist or someone on an excursion.

trite ADJECTIVE dull and not original • *his trite novels.*

triumph, triumphs, triumphing, triumphed NOUN ❶ a great success or achievement. ❷ Triumph is a feeling of great satisfaction when you win or achieve something ▷ VERB ❸ If you triumph, you win a victory or succeed in overcoming something.

triumphal ADJECTIVE done or made to celebrate a victory or great success • *a triumphal return to Rome.*

triumphant ADJECTIVE Someone who is triumphant feels very happy because they have won a victory or

have achieved something • *a triumphant shout.*

trivia PLURAL NOUN Trivia are unimportant things.

trivial ADJECTIVE Something trivial is unimportant.
● **WORD HISTORY:** from Latin
● *trivialis* meaning 'found
● everywhere'

troll, trolls NOUN an imaginary creature in Scandinavian mythology that lives in caves or mountains and is believed to turn to stone at daylight.

trolley, trolleys NOUN ❶ a small table on wheels. ❷ a small cart on wheels used for carrying heavy objects • *a supermarket trolley.*

trombone, trombones NOUN a brass wind instrument with a U-shaped slide which you move to produce different notes.

troop, troops, trooping, trooped NOUN ❶ Troops are soldiers. ❷ A troop of people or animals is a group of them ▷ VERB ❸ If people troop somewhere, they go there in a group.

trooper, troopers NOUN a low-ranking soldier in the cavalry.

trophy, trophies NOUN ❶ a cup or shield given as a prize to the winner of a competition. ❷ something you keep to remember a success or victory.
● **WORD HISTORY:** from Greek *tropē*
● meaning 'defeat of the enemy'

tropical ADJECTIVE belonging to or typical of the tropics • *a tropical island.*

tropics PLURAL NOUN The tropics are the hottest parts of the world between two lines of latitude, the

a
b
c
d
e
f
g
h
i
j
k
l
m
n
o
p
q
r
s
t
u
v
w
x
y
z

▷ SPELLING NOTE: *the QUeen stood on the QUay (quay)*

Tropic of Cancer, 23½° north of the equator, and the Tropic of Capricorn, 23½° south of the equator.

trot, trots, trotting, trotted **VERB** ❶ When a horse trots, it moves at a speed between a walk and a canter, lifting its feet quite high off the ground. ❷ If you trot, you run or jog using small quick steps ▷ **NOUN** ❸ When a horse breaks into a trot, it starts trotting.

trotter, trotters **NOUN** A pig's trotters are its feet.

trouble, troubles, troubling, troubled **NOUN** ❶ Troubles are difficulties or problems. ❷ If there is trouble, people are quarrelling or fighting • *There was more trouble after the match.* ▷ **PHRASE** ❸ If you are **in trouble**, you are in a situation where you may be punished because you have done something wrong ▷ **VERB** ❹ If something troubles you, it makes you feel worried or anxious. ❺ If you trouble someone for something, you disturb them in order to ask them for it • *Can I trouble you for some milk?* **troubling ADJECTIVE troubled ADJECTIVE**

● **SIMILAR WORDS:** ❶ difficulty,
● problem, worry ❺ bother,
● inconvenience

troublesome ADJECTIVE causing problems or difficulties • *a troublesome teenager.*

trough, troughs [Said *troff*] **NOUN** a long, narrow container from which animals drink or feed.

trounce, trounces, trouncing, trounced **VERB** If you trounce someone, you defeat them

completely • *trounced three-nil.*

troupe, troupes [Said *troop*] **NOUN** a group of actors, singers, or dancers who work together and often travel around together.

trousers PLURAL NOUN Trousers are a piece of clothing covering the body from the waist down, enclosing each leg separately.
● **WORD HISTORY:** from Gaelic
● *triubhas*

trout NOUN a type of freshwater fish.

trowel, trowels **NOUN** ❶ a small garden tool with a curved, pointed blade used for planting or weeding. ❷ a small tool with a flat blade used for spreading cement or plaster.

truant, truants **NOUN** ❶ a child who stays away from school without permission ▷ **PHRASE** ❷ If children **play truant**, they stay away from school without permission. **truancy NOUN**

truce, truces **NOUN** an agreement between two people or groups to stop fighting for a short time.

truck, trucks **NOUN** ❶ a large motor vehicle used for carrying heavy loads. ❷ an open vehicle used for carrying goods on a railway.

truculent [Said *truk-yoo-lent*] **ADJECTIVE** bad-tempered and aggressive. **truculence NOUN**

trudge, trudges, trudging, trudged **VERB** ❶ If you trudge, you walk with slow, heavy steps ▷ **NOUN** ❷ a slow tiring walk • *the long trudge home.*

true, truer, truest **ADJECTIVE** ❶ A true story or statement is based on facts and is not made up. ❷ 'True' is used to describe things or people that are genuine • *She was a true friend.* ❸ True feelings are sincere and genuine ▷ **PHRASE** ❹ If something **comes true**, it actually happens. **truly ADVERB**

● **SIMILAR WORDS:** ❶ accurate, ● correct, factual

truffle, truffles **NOUN** ❶ a soft, round sweet. ❷ a round mushroom-like fungus which grows underground and is considered very good to eat.

trump, trumps **NOUN** In a game of cards, trumps is the suit with the highest value.

trumpet, trumpets, trumpeting, trumpeted **NOUN** ❶ a brass wind instrument with a narrow tube ending in a bell-like shape ▷ **VERB** ❷ When an elephant trumpets, it makes a sound like a very loud trumpet.

truncated ADJECTIVE Something that is truncated is made shorter.

truncheon, truncheons [*Said trunt-shn*] **NOUN** a stick carried by police officers as a weapon, especially the short, thick kind formerly used by British police.

● **WORD HISTORY:** from Old French ● *tronchon* meaning 'stump'

trundle, trundles, trundling, trundled **VERB** If you trundle something or it trundles somewhere, it moves or rolls along slowly.

trunk, trunks **NOUN** ❶ the main stem of a tree from which the branches and roots grow. ❷ the main part of your body, excluding your head, neck, arms, and legs. ❸ the long flexible nose of an elephant. ❹ a

large, strong case or box with a hinged lid used for storing things ❺ **IN PLURAL** A man's trunks are his bathing pants or shorts.

truss, trusses, trussing, trussed **VERB** ❶ To truss someone or truss them up is to tie them up so that they cannot move ▷ **NOUN** ❷ a supporting belt with a pad worn by a man with a hernia.

trust, trusts, trusting, trusted **VERB** ❶ If you trust someone, you believe that they are honest and will not harm you. ❷ If you trust someone to do something, you believe they will do it successfully or properly. ❸ If you trust someone with something, you give it to them or tell it to them • *One member of the group cannot be trusted with the secret.* ❹ If you do not trust something, you feel that it is not safe or reliable • *I didn't trust my arms and legs to work.* ▷ **NOUN** ❺ Trust is the responsibility you are given to deal with or look after important or secret things • *He had built up a position of trust.* ❻ a financial arrangement in which an organization looks after and invests money for someone. **trusting ADJECTIVE**

trustee, trustees **NOUN** someone who is allowed by law to control money or property they are keeping or investing for another person.

trustworthy ADJECTIVE A trustworthy person is reliable and responsible and can be trusted.

trusty, trustier, trustiest **ADJECTIVE** Trusty things and animals are considered to be reliable because they have always worked well in the past • *a trusty black labrador.*

a
b
c
d
e
f
g
h
i
j
k
l
m
n
o
p
q
r
s
t
u
v
w
x
y
z

▷ **SPELLING NOTE:** there's SAND in my SANDwich (<u>sand</u>wich)

A
B
C
D
E
F
G
H
I
J
K
L
M
N
O
P
Q
R
S
T
U
V
W
X
Y
Z

truth, truths **NOUN** ❶ The truth is the facts about something, rather than things that are imagined or made up • *I know she was telling the truth.* ❷ an idea or principle that is generally accepted to be true • *the basic truths in life.*
● SIMILAR WORDS: ❶ fact, reality

truthful **ADJECTIVE** A truthful person is honest and tells the truth. **truthfully** **ADVERB**

try, tries, trying, tried **VERB** ❶ To try to do something is to make an effort to do it. ❷ If you try something, you use it or do it to test how useful or enjoyable it is • *Howard wanted me to try the wine.* ❸ When a person is tried, they appear in court and a judge and jury decide if they are guilty after hearing the evidence ▷ **NOUN** ❹ an attempt to do something. ❺ a test of something • *You gave it a try.* ❻ In rugby, a try is scored when someone carries the ball over the goal line of the opposing team and touches the ground with it.
● USAGE NOTE: You can use *try to* in speech and writing: *try to get here on time for once*. *Try and* is very common is speech, but you should avoid it in written work: *just try and stop me!*
● SIMILAR WORDS: ❶ attempt, endeavour, strive ❹ attempt, go, shot

trying **ADJECTIVE** Something or someone trying is difficult to deal with and makes you feel impatient or annoyed.

tryst, trysts [*Said* **trist**] **NOUN** an appointment or meeting, especially between lovers in a quiet, secret place.

tsar, tsars [*Said* **zar**]; *also spelt* **czar** **NOUN** a Russian emperor or king between 1547 and 1917.

tsarina, tsarinas [*Said* zah-**ree**-na]; *also spelt* **czarina** **NOUN** a female tsar or the wife of a tsar.

tsetse fly, tsetse flies [*Said* **tset**-*tsee*] **NOUN** an African fly that feeds on blood and causes serious diseases in people and animals.

T-shirt, T-shirts; *also spelt* **tee shirt** **NOUN** a simple short-sleeved cotton shirt with no collar.

tsunami, tsunamis **NOUN** (GEOGRAPHY) a large, often destructive sea wave, caused by an earthquake or volcanic eruption under the sea.
● WORD HISTORY: from Japanese *tsunami* meaning 'harbour wave'

tuatara, tuatara or tuataras [*Said* too-ah-**tah**-rah] **NOUN** a large, lizard-like reptile found on certain islands off the coast of New Zealand.

tub, tubs **NOUN** a wide circular container.

tuba, tubas **NOUN** a large brass musical instrument that can produce very low notes.

tubby, tubbier, tubbiest **ADJECTIVE** rather fat.

tube, tubes **NOUN** ❶ a round, hollow pipe. ❷ a soft metal or plastic cylindrical container with a screw cap at one end • *a tube of toothpaste.* **tubing** **NOUN**

tuberculosis [*Said* tyoo-ber-kyoo-**loe**-siss] **NOUN** Tuberculosis is a serious infectious disease affecting the lungs in particular.

tubular ADJECTIVE in the shape of a tube.

TUC In Britain, an abbreviation for 'Trades Union Congress', which is an association of trade unions.

tuck, tucks, tucking, tucked VERB ❶ If you tuck something somewhere, you put it there so that it is safe or comfortable • *She tucked the letter into her handbag.* ❷ If you tuck a piece of fabric into or under something, you push the loose ends inside or under it to make it tidy. ❸ If something is tucked away, it is in a quiet place where few people go • *a little house tucked away in a valley.*

tucker, tuckers, tuckering, tuckered INFORMAL NOUN ❶ In Australian and New Zealand English, tucker is food ▷ VERB ❷ In Australian and New Zealand English, if you are tuckered out you are tired out.

Tudor, Tudors NOUN Tudor was the family name of the English monarchs who reigned from 1485 to 1603.

Tuesday, Tuesdays NOUN Tuesday is the day between Monday and Wednesday.
● WORD HISTORY: from Old English *tiwesdæg* meaning 'Tiw's day'; Tiw was the Scandinavian god of war and the sky

tuft, tufts NOUN A tuft of something such as hair is a bunch of it growing closely together.

tug, tugs, tugging, tugged VERB ❶ To tug something is to give it a quick, hard pull ▷ NOUN ❷ a quick, hard pull • *He felt a tug at his arm.* ❸ a

small, powerful boat which tows large ships.

tug of war NOUN A tug of war is a sport in which two teams test their strength by pulling against each other on opposite ends of a rope.

tuition NOUN Tuition is the teaching of a subject, especially to one person or to a small group.

tulip, tulips NOUN a brightly coloured spring flower.
● WORD HISTORY: from Turkish *tulbend* meaning 'turban', because of its shape

tumble, tumbles, tumbling, tumbled VERB ❶ To tumble is to fall with a rolling or bouncing movement ▷ NOUN ❷ a fall.

tumbler, tumblers NOUN a drinking glass with straight sides.

tummy, tummies NOUN INFORMAL Your tummy is your stomach.

tumour, tumours [Said *tyoo*-mur] NOUN a mass of diseased or abnormal cells that has grown in a person's or animal's body.

tumultuous ADJECTIVE A tumultuous event or welcome is very noisy because people are happy or excited.

tuna [Said *tyoo*-na] NOUN Tuna are large fish that live in warm seas and are caught for food.

tundra NOUN The tundra is a vast treeless Arctic region.
● WORD HISTORY: a Russian word

tune, tunes, tuning, tuned NOUN ❶ a series of musical notes arranged in a particular way ▷ VERB ❷ To tune

a b c d e f g h i j k l m n o p q r s t u v w x y z

a musical instrument is to adjust it so that it produces the right notes. ❸ To tune an engine or machine is to adjust it so that it works well. ❹ If you tune to a particular radio or television station you turn or press the controls to select the station you want to listen to or watch ▷ **PHRASE** ❺ If your voice or an instrument is **in tune**, it produces the right notes.

tuneful ADJECTIVE having a pleasant and easily remembered tune.

tuner, tuners NOUN A piano tuner is a person whose job it is to tune pianos.

tunic, tunics NOUN a sleeveless garment covering the top part of the body and reaching to the hips, thighs, or knees.

Tunisian, Tunisians [Said tyoo-niz-ee-an] ADJECTIVE ❶ belonging or relating to Tunisia ▷ NOUN ❷ someone who comes from Tunisia.

tunnel, tunnels, tunnelling, tunnelled NOUN ❶ a long underground passage ▷ VERB ❷ To tunnel is to make a tunnel.

turban, turbans NOUN a head-covering worn by a Hindu, Muslim, or Sikh man, consisting of a long piece of cloth wound round his head.

turbine, turbines NOUN a machine or engine in which power is produced when a stream of air, gas, water, or steam pushes the blades of a wheel and makes it turn round.
   ● **WORD HISTORY:** from Latin *turbo* meaning 'whirlwind'

turbot [Said *tur-bot*] NOUN A turbot is a large European flat fish that is caught for food.

turbulent ADJECTIVE ❶ A turbulent period of history is one where there is much uncertainty, and possibly violent change. ❷ Turbulent air or water currents make sudden changes of direction. **turbulence** NOUN

tureen, tureens [Said *tur-reen*] NOUN a large dish with a lid for serving soup.

turf, turves; turfs, turfing, turfed NOUN Turf is short thick even grass and the layer of soil beneath it.
turf out VERB INFORMAL To turf someone out is to force them to leave a place.

turgid [Said *tur-jid*] ADJECTIVE LITERARY A turgid play, film, or piece of writing is difficult to understand and rather boring.

Turk, Turks NOUN someone who comes from Turkey.

turkey, turkeys NOUN a large bird kept for food; also the meat of this bird.

Turkish ADJECTIVE ❶ belonging or relating to Turkey ▷ NOUN ❷ Turkish is the main language spoken in Turkey.

turmoil NOUN Turmoil is a state of confusion, disorder, or great anxiety • *Europe is in a state of turmoil.*

turn, turns, turning, turned VERB ❶ When you turn, you move so that you are facing or going in a different direction. ❷ When you turn something or when it turns, it moves or rotates so that it faces in a different direction or is in a different position. ❸ If you turn your attention or

thoughts to someone or something, you start thinking about them or discussing them. ❹ When something turns or is turned into something else, it becomes something different • *A hobby can be turned into a career.* ▷ **NOUN** ❺ an act of turning something so that it faces in a different direction or is in a different position. ❻ a change in the way something is happening or being done • *Her career took a turn for the worse.* ❼ If it is your turn to do something, you have the right, chance, or duty to do it ▷ **PHRASE** ❽ **In turn** is used to refer to people, things, or actions that are in sequence one after the other.
turn down VERB If you turn down someone's request or offer, you refuse or reject it.
turn up VERB ❶ If someone or something turns up, they arrive or appear somewhere. ❷ If something turns up, it is found or discovered.
● **SIMILAR WORDS:** ❼ chance, go, ● opportunity

turncoat, turncoats **NOUN** a person who leaves one political party or group for an opposing one.

turning, turnings **NOUN** a road which leads away from the side of another road.

turning effect, turning effects **NOUN** (SCIENCE) the effect of a force to make something rotate around a point. For example, effort applied to a lever produces a turning effect to work on a load at the other end.

turning point, turning points **NOUN** the moment when decisions are taken and events start to move in a different direction.

turnip, turnips **NOUN** a round root vegetable with a white or yellow skin.

turnout, turnouts **NOUN** The turnout at an event is the number of people who go to it.

turnover, turnovers **NOUN** ❶ The turnover of people in a particular organization or group is the rate at which people leave it and are replaced by others. ❷ The turnover of a company is the value of the goods or services sold during a particular period.

turnstile, turnstiles **NOUN** a revolving mechanical barrier at the entrance to places like football grounds or zoos.

turpentine NOUN Turpentine is a strong-smelling colourless liquid used for cleaning and for thinning paint.

turps NOUN Turps is turpentine.

turquoise [Said *tur-kwoyz*] **NOUN OR ADJECTIVE** ❶ light bluish-green ▷ **NOUN** ❷ Turquoise is a bluish-green stone used in jewellery.

turret, turrets **NOUN** a small narrow tower on top of a larger tower or other buildings.

turtle, turtles **NOUN** a large reptile with a thick shell covering its body and flippers for swimming. It lays its eggs on land but lives the rest of its life in the sea.

tusk, tusks **NOUN** The tusks of an elephant, wild boar, or walrus are the pair of long curving pointed teeth it has.

tussle, tussles **NOUN** an energetic fight or argument between two

a b c d e f g h i j k l m n o p q r s **t** u v w x y z

▷ SPELLING NOTE: *'i' before 'e' except after 'c'*

people, especially about something they both want.

tutor, tutors, tutoring, tutored NOUN ❶ a teacher at a college or university. ❷ a private teacher ▷ VERB ❸ If someone tutors a person or subject, they teach that person or subject.

tutorial, tutorials NOUN a teaching session involving a tutor and a small group of students.

tutu, tutus [Said too-too] NOUN a short stiff skirt worn by female ballet dancers.

TV, TVs NOUN ❶ TV is television. ❷ a television set.

twang, twangs, twanging, twanged NOUN ❶ a sound like the one made by pulling and then releasing a tight wire. ❷ A twang is a nasal quality in a person's voice ▷ VERB ❸ If a tight wire or string twangs or you twang it, it makes a sound as it is pulled and then released.

tweak, tweaks, tweaking, tweaked VERB ❶ If you tweak something, you twist it or pull it ▷ NOUN ❷ a short twist or pull of something.

twee ADJECTIVE sweet and pretty but in bad taste or sentimental.

tweed, tweeds NOUN Tweed is a thick woollen cloth.

tweet, tweets, tweeting, tweeted VERB ❶ When a small bird tweets, it makes a short, high-pitched sound ▷ NOUN ❷ a short high-pitched sound made by a small bird.

tweezers PLURAL NOUN Tweezers are a small tool with two arms which can be closed together and are used

for pulling out hairs or picking up small objects.

twelve the number 12. **twelfth** ADJECTIVE

twenty, twenties the number 20. **twentieth** ADJECTIVE

twice ADVERB Twice means two times.

twiddle, twiddles, twiddling, twiddled VERB To twiddle something is to twist it or turn it quickly.

twig, twigs NOUN a very small thin branch growing from a main branch of a tree or bush.

twilight [Said twy-lite] NOUN ❶ Twilight is the time after sunset when it is just getting dark. ❷ The twilight of something is the final stages of it • the twilight of his career.

twin, twins NOUN ❶ If two people are twins, they have the same mother and were born on the same day. ❷ 'Twin' is used to describe two similar things that are close together or happen together • the little twin islands.

twine, twines, twining, twined NOUN ❶ Twine is strong smooth string ▷ VERB ❷ If you twine one thing round another, you twist or wind it round.

twinge, twinges NOUN a sudden, unpleasant feeling • a twinge of jealousy.

twinkle, twinkles, twinkling, twinkled VERB ❶ If something twinkles, it sparkles or seems to sparkle with an unsteady light • Her green eyes twinkled. ▷ NOUN ❷ a

A B C D E F G H I J K L M N O P Q R S T U V W X Y Z

sparkle or brightness that something has.

twirl, twirls, twirling, twirled **VERB** If something twirls, or if you twirl it, it spins or twists round and round.

twist, twists, twisting, twisted **VERB**
❶ When you twist something you turn one end of it in one direction while holding the other end or turning it in the opposite direction. **❷** When something twists or is twisted, it moves or bends into a strange shape. **❸** If you twist a part of your body, you injure it by turning it too sharply or in an unusual direction • *I've twisted my ankle.* **❹** If you twist something that someone has said, you change the meaning slightly ▷ **NOUN** **❺** a twisting action or motion. **❻** an unexpected development or event in a story or film, especially at the end • *Each day now seemed to bring a new twist to the story.*
  ● **SIMILAR WORDS:** **❶** coil, wind
  ● **❷** contort, distort

twisted **ADJECTIVE** **❶** Something twisted has been bent or moved into a strange shape • *a tangle of twisted metal.* **❷** If someone's mind or behaviour is twisted, it is unpleasantly abnormal • *He's bitter and twisted.*

twit, twits **NOUN** INFORMAL a silly person.

twitch, twitches, twitching, twitched **VERB** **❶** If you twitch, you make little jerky movements which you cannot control. **❷** If you twitch something, you give it a little jerk in order to move it ▷ **NOUN** **❸** a little jerky movement.

twitter, twitters, twittering, twittered **VERB** When birds twitter, they make short high-pitched sounds.

two the number 2.
  ● **USAGE NOTE:** Do not confuse the
  ● spelling of the preposition *to*, the
  ● adverb *too*, and the number *two*

two-dimensional **ADJECTIVE**
(MATHS) A two-dimensional shape has height and width but not depth.

two-faced **ADJECTIVE** A two-faced person is not honest in the way they behave towards other people.

twofold **ADJECTIVE** Something twofold has two equally important parts or reasons • *Their concern was twofold: personal and political.*

twosome, twosomes [Said *too*-sum] **NOUN** two people or things that are usually seen together.

two-time, two-times, two-timing, two-timed **VERB** INFORMAL If you two-time your boyfriend or girlfriend, you deceive them, by having a romantic relationship with someone else without telling them.

two-up **NOUN** In Australia and New Zealand, two-up is a popular gambling game in which two coins are tossed and bets are placed on whether they land heads or tails.

tycoon, tycoons **NOUN** a person who is successful in business and has become rich and powerful.
  ● **WORD HISTORY:** from Chinese *ta*
  ● + *chun* meaning 'great ruler'

type, types, typing, typed **NOUN** **❶** A type of something is a class of it that has common features and belongs to a larger group of related things • *What type of dog should we get?* **❷** A particular type of person has a

▷ SPELLING NOTE: *an ELegant angEL* (angel)

particular appearance or quality
• *Andrea is the type who likes to play safe.* ▷ **VERB** ❸ If you type something, you use a typewriter or word processor to write it.

typewriter, typewriters **NOUN** a machine with a keyboard with keys which are pressed to produce letters and numbers on a page.

typhoid [Said **tie**-foyd] **NOUN** Typhoid, or typhoid fever, is an infectious disease caused by dirty water or food. It produces fever and can kill.

typhoon, typhoons **NOUN** (GEOGRAPHY) a very violent tropical storm.
● **WORD HISTORY:** from Chinese *tai fung* meaning 'great wind'

typhus NOUN Typhus is an infectious disease transmitted by lice or mites. It results in fever, severe headaches, and a skin rash.

typical ADJECTIVE showing the most usual characteristics or behaviour. **typically ADVERB**
● **SIMILAR WORDS:** characteristic,
● standard, usual

typify, typifies, typifying, typified **VERB** If something typifies a situation or thing, it is characteristic of it or a typical example of it • *This story is one that typifies our times.*

typing NOUN Typing is the work or activity of producing something on a typewriter.

typist, typists **NOUN** a person whose job is typing.

tyrannosaurus, tyrannosauruses [Said tir-ran-oh-**saw**-russ] **NOUN** a very large meat-eating dinosaur which walked upright on its hind legs.
● **WORD HISTORY:** from Greek
● *turannos* meaning 'tyrant' and Latin
● *saurus* meaning 'lizard'

tyranny, tyrannies **NOUN** ❶ A tyranny is cruel and unjust rule of people by a person or group • *the evils of Nazi tyranny.* ❷ You can refer to something which is not human but is harsh as tyranny • *the tyranny of drugs.* **tyrannical ADJECTIVE**

tyrant, tyrants **NOUN** a person who treats the people he or she has authority over cruelly and unjustly.

tyre, tyres **NOUN** a thick ring of rubber fitted round each wheel of a vehicle and filled with air.

Uu

ubiquitous [Said yoo-**bik**-wit-tuss]
ADJECTIVE Something that is
ubiquitous seems to be everywhere at
the same time • *the ubiquitous jeans.*
● **WORD HISTORY:** from Latin
● *ubique* meaning 'everywhere'

udder, udders **NOUN** the baglike
organ that hangs below a cow's body
and produces milk.

UFO, UFOs **NOUN** a strange object
seen in the sky, which some people
believe to be a spaceship from another
planet. UFO is an abbreviation for
'unidentified flying object'.

Ugandan, Ugandans [Said
yoo-**gan**-dan] **ADJECTIVE**
❶ belonging or relating to Uganda
▷ **NOUN** ❷ someone who comes
from Uganda.

ugly, uglier, ugliest **ADJECTIVE** very
unattractive in appearance.
● **WORD HISTORY:** from Old Norse
● *uggligr* meaning 'terrifying'
● **SIMILAR WORDS:** unattractive,
● unsightly

UK an abbreviation for **United
Kingdom**.

ulcer, ulcers **NOUN** a sore area on
the skin or inside the body, which
takes a long time to heal • *stomach
ulcers.*

ulna, ulnas or ulnae **NOUN** (SCIENCE)
The ulna is the inner and longer bone

in the lower part of your arm.

ulterior [Said ul-**teer**-ee-or]
ADJECTIVE If you have an ulterior
motive for doing something, you have
a hidden reason for it.

ultimate **ADJECTIVE** ❶ final or
eventual • *Olympic gold is the ultimate
goal.* ❷ most important or powerful
• *the ultimate ambition of any player.*
▷ **NOUN** ❸ You can refer to the best
or most advanced example of
something as the ultimate • *This hotel
is the ultimate in luxury.* **ultimately**
ADVERB

ultimatum, ultimatums [Said
ul-tim-**may**-tum] **NOUN** a warning
stating that unless someone meets
your conditions, you will take action
against them.

ultra- **PREFIX** 'Ultra-' is used to form
adjectives describing something as
having a quality to an extreme degree
• *the ultra-competitive world of sport
today.*

ultramarine **NOUN OR**
ADJECTIVE bright blue.
● **WORD HISTORY:** from Latin
● *ultramarinus* meaning 'beyond the
● sea', because the pigment was
● imported from abroad

ultrasonic **ADJECTIVE** An
ultrasonic sound has a very high
frequency that cannot be heard by the
human ear.

▷ SPELLING NOTE: *A Rude Idiot Thought He Might Eat Toffee In Church* (*arithmetic*)

ultrasound NOUN sound which cannot be heard by the human ear because its frequency is too high.

ultraviolet ADJECTIVE Ultraviolet light is not visible to the human eye. It is a form of radiation that causes your skin to darken after being exposed to the sun.

umbilical cord, umbilical cords [Said um-*bil*-lik-kl] NOUN the tube of blood vessels which connects an unborn baby to its mother and through which the baby receives nutrients and oxygen.

umbrella, umbrellas NOUN a device that you use to protect yourself from the rain. It consists of a folding frame covered in cloth attached to a long stick.

umpire, umpires, umpiring, umpired NOUN ❶ The umpire in cricket or tennis is the person who makes sure that the game is played according to the rules and who makes a decision if there is a dispute ▷ VERB ❷ If you umpire a game, you are the umpire.

umpteen ADJECTIVE INFORMAL very many • *tomatoes and umpteen other plants.* **umpteenth** ADJECTIVE

un- PREFIX Un- is added to the beginning of many words to form a word with the opposite meaning • *an uncomfortable chair* • *He unlocked the door.*

unabashed ADJECTIVE not embarrassed or discouraged by something • *Samuel was unabashed.*

unabated ADJECTIVE OR ADVERB continuing without any reduction in intensity or amount • *The noise continued unabated all night.*

unable ADJECTIVE If you are unable to do something, you cannot do it.

unacceptable ADJECTIVE very bad or of a very low standard.

unaccompanied ADJECTIVE alone.

unaccustomed ADJECTIVE If you are unaccustomed to something, you are not used to it.

unaffected ADJECTIVE ❶ not changed in any way by a particular thing • *unaffected by the recession.* ❷ behaving in a natural and genuine way • *the most down-to-earth unaffected person I've ever met.*

unaided ADVERB OR ADJECTIVE without help • *He was incapable of walking unaided.*

unambiguous ADJECTIVE An unambiguous statement has only one meaning.

unanimous [Said yoon-*nan*-nim-mus] ADJECTIVE When people are unanimous, they all agree about something. **unanimously** ADVERB **unanimity** NOUN
● WORD HISTORY: from Latin
● *unanimus* meaning 'of one mind'

unannounced ADJECTIVE happening unexpectedly and without warning.

unarmed ADJECTIVE not carrying any weapons.

unassuming ADJECTIVE modest and quiet.

unattached ADJECTIVE An unattached person is not married and is not having a steady relationship with someone.

unattended ADJECTIVE not being watched or looked after • *an unattended handbag.*

unauthorized or **unauthorised** ADJECTIVE done without official permission • *unauthorized parking.*

unavoidable ADJECTIVE unable to be prevented or avoided • *an unavoidable delay.*

unaware ADJECTIVE If you are unaware of something, you do not know about it.
  ● USAGE NOTE: *Unaware* is usually followed by *of* or *that.* Do not confuse it with the adverb *unawares*

unawares ADVERB If something catches you unawares, it happens when you are not expecting it.
  ● USAGE NOTE: Do not confuse *unawares* with the adjective *unaware*

unbalanced ADJECTIVE ❶ with more weight or emphasis on one side than the other • *an unbalanced load* • *an unbalanced relationship.* ❷ slightly mad. ❸ made up of parts that do not work well together • *an unbalanced lifestyle.* ❹ An unbalanced account of something is an unfair one because it emphasizes some things and ignores others.

unbearable ADJECTIVE Something unbearable is so unpleasant or upsetting that you feel you cannot stand it • *The pain was unbearable.* **unbearably** ADVERB
  ● SIMILAR WORDS: insufferable, intolerable

unbeatable ADJECTIVE Something that is unbeatable is the best thing of its kind.

unbelievable ADJECTIVE ❶ extremely great or surprising • *unbelievable courage.* ❷ so unlikely that you cannot believe it. **unbelievably** ADVERB
  ● SIMILAR WORDS: ❶ astonishing, incredible ❷ far-fetched, implausible

unborn ADJECTIVE not yet born.

unbroken ADJECTIVE continuous or complete • *ten days of almost unbroken sunshine.*

uncanny ADJECTIVE strange and difficult to explain • *an uncanny resemblance.*
  ● WORD HISTORY: from Scottish *uncanny* meaning 'unreliable' or 'not safe to deal with'

uncertain ADJECTIVE ❶ not knowing what to do • *For a minute he looked uncertain.* ❷ doubtful or not known • *The outcome of the war was uncertain.* **uncertainty** NOUN

unchallenged ADJECTIVE accepted without any questions being asked • *an unchallenged decision.*

uncharacteristic ADJECTIVE not typical or usual • *My father reacted with uncharacteristic speed.*

uncivilized or **uncivilised** ADJECTIVE unacceptable, for example by being very cruel or rude • *the uncivilized behaviour of football hooligans.*

uncle, uncles NOUN the brother of your mother or father or the husband of your aunt.

a
b
c
d
e
f
g
h
i
j
k
l
m
n
o
p
q
r
s
t
u
v
w
x
y
z

▷ SPELLING NOTE: *Betty Eats Cakes And Uses Seven Eggs (because)*

unclean ADJECTIVE dirty • *unclean water*.

unclear ADJECTIVE confusing and not obvious.

uncomfortable ADJECTIVE ❶ If you are uncomfortable, you are not physically relaxed and feel slight pain or discomfort. ❷ Uncomfortable also means slightly worried or embarrassed. **uncomfortably** ADVERB

uncommon ADJECTIVE ❶ not happening often or not seen often. ❷ unusually great • *She had read Cecilia's last letter with uncommon interest*. **uncommonly** ADVERB

uncompromising ADJECTIVE determined not to change an opinion or aim in any way • *an uncompromising approach to life*. **uncompromisingly** ADVERB

unconcerned ADJECTIVE not interested in something or not worried about it.

unconditional ADJECTIVE with no conditions or limitations • *a full three-year unconditional guarantee*. **unconditionally** ADVERB

unconscious ADJECTIVE ❶ Someone who is unconscious is asleep or in a state similar to sleep as a result of a shock, accident, or injury. ❷ If you are unconscious of something, you are not aware of it. **unconsciously** ADVERB **unconsciousness** NOUN

uncontrollable ADJECTIVE If someone or something is uncontrollable, they or it cannot be controlled or stopped • *uncontrollable anger*. **uncontrollably** ADVERB

unconventional ADJECTIVE not behaving in the same way as most other people.

unconvinced ADJECTIVE not at all certain that something is true or right • *Some critics remain unconvinced by the plan*.

uncouth [Said un-**kooth**] ADJECTIVE bad-mannered and unpleasant.
  ● SIMILAR WORDS: boorish, coarse,
  ● vulgar

uncover, uncovers, uncovering, uncovered VERB ❶ If you uncover a secret, you find it out. ❷ To uncover something is to remove the cover or lid from it.

undaunted ADJECTIVE If you are undaunted by something disappointing, you are not discouraged by it.

undecided ADJECTIVE If you are undecided, you have not yet made a decision about something.

undemanding ADJECTIVE not difficult to do or deal with • *undemanding work*.

undeniable ADJECTIVE certainly true • *undeniable evidence*. **undeniably** ADVERB

under PREPOSITION ❶ below or beneath. ❷ You can use 'under' to say that a person or thing is affected by a particular situation or condition • *The country was under threat* • *Animals are kept under unnatural conditions*. ❸ If someone studies or works under a particular person, that person is their teacher or their boss.

▷ SPELLING NOTE: *there's a rAKE in the brAKEs (brake)*

④ less than • *under five kilometres* • *children under the age of 14.*
▷ **PHRASE ⑤ Under way** means already started • *A murder investigation is already under way.*

under- **PREFIX** 'Under-' is used in words that describe something as not being provided to a sufficient extent or not having happened to a sufficient extent.

underarm **ADJECTIVE ①** under your arm • *underarm hair.* ▷ **ADVERB ②** If you throw a ball underarm, you throw it without raising your arm over your shoulder.

undercarriage, undercarriages **NOUN** the part of an aircraft, including the wheels, that supports the aircraft when it is on the ground.

underclass **NOUN** The underclass is the people in society who are the most poor and whose situation is unlikely to improve.

underclothes **PLURAL NOUN** Your underclothes are the clothes that you wear under your other clothes and next to your skin.

undercover **ADJECTIVE** involving secret work to obtain information • *a police undercover operation.*

undercurrent, undercurrents **NOUN** a weak, partly hidden feeling that may become stronger later.

undercut, undercuts, undercutting, undercut **VERB ①** To undercut someone's prices is to sell a product more cheaply than they do. **②** If something undercuts your attempts to achieve something, it prevents them from being effective.

underdeveloped **ADJECTIVE** An underdeveloped country does not have modern industries, and usually has a low standard of living.

underdog, underdogs **NOUN** The underdog in a competition is the person who seems likely to lose.

underestimate, underestimates, underestimating, underestimated **VERB** If you underestimate something or someone, you do not realize how large, great, or capable they are.

underfoot **ADJECTIVE OR ADVERB** under your feet • *the icy ground underfoot.*

undergo, undergoes, undergoing, underwent, undergone **VERB** If you undergo something unpleasant, it happens to you.

underground **ADJECTIVE OR ADVERB ①** below the surface of the ground. **②** secret, unofficial, and usually illegal ▷ **NOUN ③** The underground is a railway system in which trains travel in tunnels below ground.

undergrowth **NOUN** Small bushes and plants growing under trees are called the undergrowth.

underhand **ADJECTIVE** secret and dishonest • *underhand behaviour.*

underlie, underlies, underlying, underlay, underlain **VERB** The thing that underlies a situation is the cause or basis of it. **underlying** **ADJECTIVE**

underline, underlines, underlining, underlined **VERB ①** If something underlines a feeling or a problem, it emphasizes it. **②** If you underline a

a
b
c
d
e
f
g
h
i
j
k
l
m
n
o
p
q
r
s
t
u
v
w
x
y
z

▷ SPELLING NOTE: *you'll brEAK that Electrical Aerial, Kitty (break)*

A
B
C
D
E
F
G
H
I
J
K
L
M
N
O
P
Q
R
S
T
U
V
W
X
Y
Z

word or sentence, you draw a line under it.

underling, underlings NOUN someone who is less important than someone else in rank or status.

undermine, undermines, undermining, undermined VERB To undermine an idea, feeling, or system is to make it less strong or secure • *You're trying to undermine my confidence again.*

- **WORD HISTORY:** from the practice in warfare of digging tunnels under enemy fortifications in order to make them collapse
- **SIMILAR WORDS:** subvert, weaken

underneath PREPOSITION
❶ below or beneath ▷ ADVERB OR PREPOSITION ❷ Underneath describes feelings and qualities that do not show in your behaviour • *Alex knew that underneath she was shattered.* ▷ ADJECTIVE ❸ The underneath part of something is the part that touches or faces the ground.

underpants PLURAL NOUN
Underpants are a piece of clothing worn by men and boys under their trousers.

underpass, underpasses NOUN a road or footpath that goes under a road or railway.

underpin, underpins, underpinning, underpinned VERB If something underpins something else, it helps it to continue by supporting and strengthening it • *Australian skill is usually underpinned by an immense team spirit.*

underprivileged ADJECTIVE
Underprivileged people have less

money and fewer opportunities than other people.

underrate, underrates, underrating, underrated VERB If you underrate someone, you do not realize how clever or valuable they are.

understand, understands, understanding, understood VERB
❶ If you understand what someone says, you know what they mean. ❷ If you understand a situation, you know what is happening and why. ❸ If you say that you understand that something is the case, you mean that you have heard that it is the case • *I understand that she's a lot better now.*

- **SIMILAR WORDS:**
- ❶ comprehend, follow, grasp, see

understandable ADJECTIVE If something is understandable, people can easily understand it.
understandably ADVERB

understanding, understandings NOUN ❶ If you have an understanding of something, you have some knowledge about it. ❷ an informal agreement between people ▷ ADJECTIVE ❸ kind and sympathetic.

- **SIMILAR WORDS:**
- ❶ comprehension, grasp, perception

understatement, understatements NOUN a statement that does not say fully how true something is • *To say I was pleased was an understatement.*

understudy, understudies NOUN someone who has learnt a part in a play so that they can act it if the main actor or actress is ill.

undertake, undertakes, undertaking, undertook, undertaken **VERB** When you undertake a task or job, you agree to do it.

undertaker, undertakers **NOUN** someone whose job is to prepare bodies for burial and arrange funerals.

undertaking, undertakings **NOUN** a task which you have agreed to do.

undertone, undertones **NOUN** **1** If you say something in an undertone, you say it very quietly. **2** If something has undertones of a particular kind, it indirectly suggests ideas of this kind • *unsettling undertones of violence.*

undervalue, undervalues, undervaluing, undervalued **VERB** If you undervalue something, you think it is less important than it really is.

underwater **ADVERB OR ADJECTIVE** **1** beneath the surface of the sea, a river, or a lake ▷ **ADJECTIVE** **2** designed to work in water • *an underwater camera.*

underwear **NOUN** Your underwear is the clothing that you wear under your other clothes, next to your skin.

underwent the past tense of undergo.

underworld **NOUN** You can refer to organized crime and the people who are involved in it as the underworld.

undesirable **ADJECTIVE** unwelcome and likely to cause harm • *undesirable behaviour.*

undid the past tense of undo.

undisputed **ADJECTIVE** definite and without any doubt • *the undisputed champion.*

undivided **ADJECTIVE** If you give something your undivided attention, you concentrate on it totally.

undo, undoes, undoing, undid, undone **VERB** **1** If you undo something that is tied up, you untie it. **2** If you undo something that has been done, you reverse the effect of it.

undoing **NOUN** If something is someone's undoing, it is the cause of their failure.

undoubted **ADJECTIVE** You use 'undoubted' to emphasize something • *The event was an undoubted success.* **undoubtedly** **ADVERB**

undress, undresses, undressing, undressed **VERB** When you undress, you take off your clothes.

undue **ADJECTIVE** greater than is reasonable • *undue violence.* **unduly** **ADVERB**

undulating **ADJECTIVE** FORMAL moving gently up and down • *undulating hills.*

undying **ADJECTIVE** lasting forever • *his undying love for his wife.*

unearth, unearths, unearthing, unearthed **VERB** If you unearth something that is hidden, you discover it.

unearthly **ADJECTIVE** strange and unnatural.

uneasy **ADJECTIVE** If you are uneasy, you feel worried that something may be wrong. **unease** **NOUN** **uneasily** **ADVERB** **uneasiness** **NOUN**

▷ SPELLING NOTE: *I want to see (C) your licenCe (licence)*

a
b
c
d
e
f
g
h
i
j
k
l
m
n
o
p
q
r
s
t
u
v
w
x
y
z

unemployed ADJECTIVE
❶ without a job • *an unemployed mechanic.* ▷ NOUN ❷ The unemployed are all the people who are without a job.

unemployment NOUN
Unemployment is the state of being without a job.

unending ADJECTIVE Something unending has continued for a long time and seems as if it will never stop • *unending joy.*

unenviable ADJECTIVE An unenviable situation is one that you would not like to be in.

unequal ADJECTIVE ❶ An unequal society does not offer the same opportunities and privileges to all people. ❷ Unequal things are different in size, strength, or ability.

uneven ADJECTIVE ❶ An uneven surface is not level or smooth. ❷ not the same or consistent • *six lines of uneven length.* **unevenly** ADVERB

uneventful ADJECTIVE An uneventful period of time is one when nothing interesting happens.

unexpected ADJECTIVE Something unexpected is surprising because it was not thought likely to happen. **unexpectedly** ADVERB

unfailing ADJECTIVE continuous and not weakening as time passes • *his unfailing cheerfulness.*

unfair ADJECTIVE not right or just. **unfairly** ADVERB

unfaithful ADJECTIVE If someone is unfaithful to their lover or the person they are married to, they have a sexual relationship with someone else.

unfamiliar ADJECTIVE If something is unfamiliar to you, or if you are unfamiliar with it, you have not seen or heard it before.

unfashionable ADJECTIVE Something that is unfashionable is not popular or is no longer used by many people.

unfavourable ADJECTIVE not encouraging or promising, or not providing any advantage.

unfit ADJECTIVE ❶ If you are unfit, your body is not in good condition because you have not been taking enough exercise. ❷ Something that is unfit for a particular purpose is not suitable for that purpose.

unfold, unfolds, unfolding, unfolded VERB ❶ When a situation unfolds, it develops and becomes known. ❷ If you unfold something that has been folded, you open it out so that it is flat.

unforeseen ADJECTIVE happening unexpectedly.

unforgettable ADJECTIVE Something unforgettable is so good or so bad that you are unlikely to forget it. **unforgettably** ADVERB

unforgivable ADJECTIVE Something unforgivable is so bad or cruel that it can never be forgiven or justified. **unforgivably** ADVERB

unfortunate ADJECTIVE ❶ Someone who is unfortunate is unlucky. ❷ If you describe an event as unfortunate, you mean that it is a pity that it happened • *an unfortunate accident.* **unfortunately** ADVERB

▷ SPELLING NOTE: *The government licenSes Schnapps (licenses)*

unfounded ADJECTIVE Something that is unfounded has no evidence to support it • *unfounded allegations*.

unfriendly ADJECTIVE ❶ A person who is unfriendly is not pleasant to you. ❷ A place that is unfriendly makes you feel uncomfortable or is not welcoming.

ungainly ADJECTIVE moving in an awkward or clumsy way.
● WORD HISTORY: from Old Norse
● *ungegn* meaning 'not straight'

ungrateful ADJECTIVE not appreciating the things you have.

unhappy, unhappier, unhappiest ADJECTIVE ❶ sad and depressed. ❷ not pleased or satisfied • *I am unhappy at being left out.* ❸ If you describe a situation as an unhappy one, you are sorry that it exists • *an unhappy state of affairs.* **unhappily** ADVERB **unhappiness** NOUN

unhealthy ADJECTIVE ❶ likely to cause illness • *an unhealthy lifestyle.* ❷ An unhealthy person is often ill.

unheard-of ADJECTIVE never having happened before and therefore surprising or shocking.

unhinged ADJECTIVE Someone who is unhinged is mentally ill.

unhurried ADJECTIVE Unhurried is used to describe actions or movements that are slow and relaxed.

unicellular ADJECTIVE (SCIENCE) consisting of only one cell.

unicorn, unicorns NOUN an imaginary animal that looks like a white horse with a straight horn growing from its forehead.

● WORD HISTORY: from Latin
● *unicornis* meaning 'having one
● horn'

unidentified ADJECTIVE You say that someone or something is unidentified when nobody knows who or what they are.

uniform, uniforms NOUN ❶ a special set of clothes worn by people at work or school ▷ ADJECTIVE ❷ Something that is uniform does not vary but is even and regular throughout. **uniformity** NOUN

unify, unifies, unifying, unified VERB If you unify a number of things, you bring them together. **unification** NOUN

unilateral ADJECTIVE A unilateral decision or action is one taken by only one of several groups involved in a particular situation. **unilaterally** ADVERB

unimaginable ADJECTIVE impossible to imagine or understand properly • *a fairyland of unimaginable beauty.*

unimportant ADJECTIVE having very little significance or importance.
● SIMILAR WORDS: insignificant,
● minor, trivial

uninhabited ADJECTIVE An uninhabited place is a place where nobody lives.

uninhibited ADJECTIVE If you are uninhibited, you behave freely and naturally and show your true feelings.

unintelligible ADJECTIVE FORMAL impossible to understand.

uninterested ADJECTIVE If you

a b c d e f g h i j k l m n o p q r s t **u** v w x y z

▷ SPELLING NOTE: *have a pIEce of pIE (piece)*

are uninterested in something, you are not interested in it.

uninterrupted ADJECTIVE continuing without breaks or interruptions • *uninterrupted views.*

union, unions NOUN ❶ an organization of people or groups with mutual interests, especially workers aiming to improve their pay and conditions. ❷ When the union of two things takes place, they are joined together to become one thing.

unique [Said yoo-**neek**] ADJECTIVE ❶ being the only one of its kind. ❷ If something is unique to one person or thing, it concerns or belongs to that person or thing only • *trees and vegetation unique to the Canary islands.* **uniquely** ADVERB **uniqueness** NOUN

⬤ USAGE NOTE: Something is either
⬤ *unique* or *not unique*, so you should
⬤ avoid saying things like *rather*
⬤ *unique* or *very unique*

unisex ADJECTIVE designed to be used by both men and women • *unisex clothing.*

unison NOUN If a group of people do something in unison, they all do it together at the same time.
⬤ WORD HISTORY: from Latin
⬤ *unisonus* meaning 'making the
⬤ same musical sound'

unit, units NOUN ❶ If you consider something as a unit, you consider it as a single complete thing. ❷ a group of people who work together at a particular job • *the Police Support Unit.* ❸ a machine or piece of equipment which has a particular function • *a remote control unit.* ❹ A unit of

measurement is a fixed standard that is used for measuring things.

unite, unites, uniting, united VERB If a number of people unite, they join together and act as a group.

United Kingdom NOUN The United Kingdom consists of Great Britain and Northern Ireland.

United Nations NOUN The United Nations is an international organization which tries to encourage peace, cooperation, and friendship between countries.

unity NOUN Where there is unity, people are in agreement and act together for a particular purpose.

universal ADJECTIVE concerning or relating to everyone in the world or every part of the universe • *Music and sports programmes have a universal appeal* • *universal destruction.* **universally** ADVERB

universe, universes NOUN The universe is the whole of space, including all the stars and planets.

university, universities NOUN a place where students study for degrees.

unjust ADJECTIVE not fair or reasonable. **unjustly** ADVERB

unjustified ADJECTIVE If a belief or action is unjustified, there is no good reason for it.

unkempt ADJECTIVE untidy and not looked after properly • *unkempt hair.*

unkind ADJECTIVE unpleasant and rather cruel. **unkindly** ADVERB **unkindness** NOUN

▷ SPELLING NOTE: *plaice the fish has a glittering 'EYE' (I) (plaice)*

● **SIMILAR WORDS:** cruel, nasty,
● uncharitable

unknown **ADJECTIVE** ❶ If
someone or something is unknown,
people do not know about them or
have not heard of them ▷ **NOUN**
❷ You can refer to the things that
people in general do not know about
as the unknown.

unlawful **ADJECTIVE** not legal • *the
unlawful use of drugs.*

unleaded **ADJECTIVE** Unleaded
petrol has a reduced amount of lead in
it in order to reduce the pollution from
cars.

unleash, unleashes, unleashing,
unleashed **VERB** When a powerful or
violent force is unleashed, it is
released.

unless **CONJUNCTION** You use
'unless' to introduce the only
circumstances in which something
will not take place or is not true
• *Unless it was raining, they played in
the little garden.*

unlike **PREPOSITION** You can use
'unlike' to show how two people,
things, or situations are different from
each other • *Unlike me, she enjoys
ballet.*

unlike **ADJECTIVE** If one thing is
unlike another, the two things are
different.

unlikely **ADJECTIVE** ❶ If
something is unlikely, it is probably
not true or probably will not happen.
❷ strange and unexpected • *There are
riches in unlikely places.*

unlimited **ADJECTIVE** If a supply of
something is unlimited, you can have

as much as you want or need.

unload, unloads, unloading,
unloaded **VERB** If you unload things
from a container or vehicle, you
remove them.

unlock, unlocks, unlocking, unlocked
VERB If you unlock a door or
container, you open it by turning a key
in the lock.

unlucky **ADJECTIVE** Someone who
is unlucky has bad luck. **unluckily**
ADVERB
● **SIMILAR WORDS:** hapless,
● unfortunate

unmarked **ADJECTIVE** ❶ with no
marks of damage or injury. ❷ with no
signs or marks of identification
• *unmarked police cars.*

unmistakable or
unmistakeable **ADJECTIVE**
Something unmistakable is so obvious
that it cannot be mistaken for
something else. **unmistakably**
ADVERB

unmitigated **ADJECTIVE** FORMAL
You use 'unmitigated' to describe a
situation or quality that is completely
bad • *an unmitigated disaster.*

unmoved **ADJECTIVE** not
emotionally affected • *He is unmoved
by criticism.*

unnatural **ADJECTIVE** ❶ strange
and rather frightening because it is
not usual • *There was an unnatural
stillness.* ❷ artificial and not typical
• *My voice sounded high-pitched and
unnatural.* **unnaturally** **ADVERB**

unnecessary **ADJECTIVE** If
something is unnecessary, there is no
need for it to happen or be done.

a b c d e f g h i j k l m n o p q r s t **u** v w x y z

▷ SPELLING NOTE: *I went to see (C) the doctor's new practiCe (practice)*

unnecessarily ADVERB

unnerve, unnerves, unnerving, unnerved VERB If something unnerves you, it frightens or startles you. **unnerving** ADJECTIVE

unobtrusive ADJECTIVE Something that is unobtrusive does not draw attention to itself.

unoccupied ADJECTIVE not occupied. For example, if a house is unoccupied, there is nobody living in it.

unofficial ADJECTIVE without the approval or permission of a person in authority • *unofficial strikes*. **unofficially** ADVERB

unorthodox ADJECTIVE unusual and not generally accepted • *an unorthodox theory*.

unpack, unpacks, unpacking, unpacked VERB When you unpack, you take everything out of a suitcase or bag.

unpaid ADJECTIVE ❶ If you do unpaid work, you do not receive any money for doing it. ❷ An unpaid bill has not yet been paid.

unpalatable ADJECTIVE ❶ Unpalatable food is so unpleasant that you can hardly eat it. ❷ An unpalatable idea is so unpleasant that it is difficult to accept.

unparalleled ADJECTIVE greater than anything else of its kind • *an unparalleled success*.

unpleasant ADJECTIVE ❶ Something unpleasant causes you to have bad feelings, for example by making you uncomfortable or upset.

❷ An unpleasant person is unfriendly or rude. **unpleasantly** ADVERB **unpleasantness** NOUN

unpopular ADJECTIVE disliked by most people • *an unpopular idea*.

unprecedented [Said un-**press**-id-en-tid] ADJECTIVE FORMAL Something that is unprecedented has never happened before or is the best of its kind so far.

unpredictable ADJECTIVE If someone or something is unpredictable, you never know how they will behave or react.

unprepared ADJECTIVE If you are unprepared for something, you are not ready for it and are therefore surprised or at a disadvantage when it happens.

unproductive ADJECTIVE not producing anything useful.
● SIMILAR WORDS: fruitless,
● useless

unqualified ADJECTIVE ❶ having no qualifications or not having the right qualifications for a particular job • *dangers posed by unqualified doctors*. ❷ total • *an unqualified success*.

unquestionable ADJECTIVE so obviously true or real that nobody can doubt it • *His devotion is unquestionable*. **unquestionably** ADVERB

unravel, unravels, unravelling, unravelled VERB ❶ If you unravel something such as a twisted and knotted piece of string, you unwind it so that it is straight. ❷ If you unravel a mystery, you work out the answer to it.

unreal ADJECTIVE so strange that

▷ SPELLING NOTE: *You must practiSe your Ss (practise)*

you find it difficult to believe.

unrealistic ADJECTIVE ❶ An unrealistic person does not face the truth about something or deal with it in a practical way. ❷ Something unrealistic is not true to life • *an unrealistic picture*.

unreasonable ADJECTIVE unfair and difficult to deal with or justify • *an unreasonable request*. **unreasonably** ADVERB

unrelated ADJECTIVE Things that are unrelated have no connection with each other.

unrelenting ADJECTIVE continuing in a determined way.

unreliable ADJECTIVE If people, machines, or methods are unreliable, you cannot rely on them.

unremitting ADJECTIVE never stopping.

unrest NOUN If there is unrest, people are angry and dissatisfied.

unrivalled ADJECTIVE better than anything else of its kind • *an unrivalled range of health and beauty treatments*.

unroll, unrolls, unrolling, unrolled VERB If you unroll a roll of cloth or paper, you open it up and make it flat.

unruly ADJECTIVE difficult to control or organize • *unruly children* • *unruly hair*.

unsatisfactory ADJECTIVE not good enough.

unscathed ADJECTIVE not injured or harmed as a result of a dangerous experience.

unscrew, unscrews, unscrewing,

unscrewed VERB If you unscrew something, you remove it by turning it or by removing the screws that are holding it.

unscrupulous ADJECTIVE willing to behave dishonestly in order to get what you want.

unseemly ADJECTIVE Unseemly behaviour is not suitable for a particular situation and shows a lack of control and good manners • *an unseemly squabble*.

unseen ADJECTIVE You use 'unseen' to describe things that you cannot see or have not seen.

unsettle, unsettles, unsettling, unsettled VERB If something unsettles you, it makes you restless or worried.

unshakable or **unshakeable** ADJECTIVE An unshakable belief is so strong that it cannot be destroyed.

unsightly ADJECTIVE very ugly • *an unsightly scar*.

unskilled ADJECTIVE Unskilled work does not require any special training or ability.

unsolicited ADJECTIVE given or happening without being asked for.

unsound ADJECTIVE ❶ If a conclusion or method is unsound, it is based on ideas that are likely to be wrong. ❷ An unsound building is likely to collapse.

unspeakable ADJECTIVE very unpleasant.

unspecified ADJECTIVE You say that something is unspecified when you are not told exactly what it is • *It*

a
b
c
d
e
f
g
h
i
j
k
l
m
n
o
p
q
r
s
t
u
v
w
x
y
z

▷ SPELLING NOTE: *pAL up with the principAL and principAL staff (principal)*

was being stored in some unspecified place.

unspoilt or **unspoiled**
ADJECTIVE If you describe a place as unspoilt or unspoiled, you mean it has not been changed and it is still in its natural or original state.

unspoken **ADJECTIVE** An unspoken wish or feeling is one that is not mentioned to other people.

unstable **ADJECTIVE** ❶ likely to change suddenly and create difficulty or danger • *The political situation in Moscow is unstable.* ❷ not firm or fixed properly and likely to wobble or fall.

unsteady **ADJECTIVE** ❶ having difficulty in controlling the movement of your legs or hands • *unsteady on her feet.* ❷ not held or fixed securely and likely to fall over. **unsteadily** **ADVERB**

unstuck **ADJECTIVE** separated from the thing that it was stuck to.

unsuccessful **ADJECTIVE** If you are unsuccessful, you do not succeed in what you are trying to do. **unsuccessfully** **ADVERB**

unsuitable **ADJECTIVE** not right or appropriate for a particular purpose. **unsuitably** **ADVERB**

unsuited **ADJECTIVE** not appropriate for a particular task or situation • *He's totally unsuited to the job.*

unsung **ADJECTIVE** You use 'unsung' to describe someone who is not appreciated or praised for their good work • *George is the unsung hero of the club.*

● **WORD HISTORY:** from the custom

● of celebrating in song the exploits
● of heroes

unsure **ADJECTIVE** uncertain or doubtful.

unsuspecting **ADJECTIVE** having no idea of what is happening or going to happen • *His horse escaped and collided with an unsuspecting cyclist.*

untangle, untangles, untangling, untangled **VERB** If you untangle something that is twisted together, you undo the twists.

untenable **ADJECTIVE** FORMAL A theory, argument, or position that is untenable cannot be successfully defended.

unthinkable **ADJECTIVE** so shocking or awful that you cannot imagine it to be true.

untidy, untidier, untidiest **ADJECTIVE** not neat or well arranged. **untidily** **ADVERB**

untie, unties, untying, untied **VERB** If you untie something, you undo the knots in the string or rope around it.

until **PREPOSITION OR CONJUNCTION** ❶ If something happens until a particular time, it happens before that time and stops at that time • *The shop stayed open until midnight* • *She waited until her husband was asleep.* ❷ If something does not happen until a particular time, it does not happen before that time and only starts happening at that time • *It didn't rain until the middle of the afternoon* • *It was not until they arrived that they found out who he was.*

untimely **ADJECTIVE** happening too soon or sooner than expected • *his*

A B C D E F G H I J K L M N O P Q R S T U V W X Y Z

▷ SPELLING NOTE: *LEarn the principLEs (principle)*

sudden untimely death.

unto PREPOSITION OLD-FASHIONED Unto means the same as to • *Nation shall speak peace unto nation.*

untold ADJECTIVE You use 'untold' to emphasize how great or extreme something is • *The island possessed untold wealth.*

untouched ADJECTIVE ❶ not changed, moved, or damaged • *a small village untouched by tourism.* ❷ If a meal is untouched, none of it has been eaten.

untoward ADJECTIVE unexpected and causing difficulties • *no untoward problems.*

untrue ADJECTIVE not true.

unused [*Said* un-**yoozd**] ADJECTIVE not yet used [*Said* un-**yoost**] ▷ ADJECTIVE If you are unused to something, you have not often done or experienced it.

unusual ADJECTIVE Something that is unusual does not occur very often. **unusually** ADVERB
● SIMILAR WORDS: exceptional,
● extraordinary, rare

unveil, unveils, unveiling, unveiled VERB When someone unveils a new statue or plaque, they draw back a curtain that is covering it.

unwanted ADJECTIVE Unwanted things are not desired or wanted, either by a particular person or by people in general • *He felt lonely and unwanted.*

unwarranted ADJECTIVE FORMAL not justified or not deserved • *unwarranted fears.*

unwelcome ADJECTIVE not wanted • *an unwelcome visitor* • *unwelcome news.*

unwell ADJECTIVE If you are unwell, you are ill.

unwieldy ADJECTIVE difficult to move or carry because of being large or an awkward shape.

unwilling ADJECTIVE If you are unwilling to do something, you do not want to do it. **unwillingly** ADVERB
● SIMILAR WORDS: averse, loath,
● reluctant

unwind, unwinds, unwinding, unwound VERB ❶ When you unwind after working hard, you relax. ❷ If you unwind something that is wrapped round something else, you undo it.

unwise ADJECTIVE foolish or not sensible.

unwitting ADJECTIVE Unwitting describes someone who becomes involved in something without realizing what is really happening • *her unwitting victims.* **unwittingly** ADVERB

unworthy ADJECTIVE FORMAL Someone who is unworthy of something does not deserve it.

unwrap, unwraps, unwrapping, unwrapped VERB When you unwrap something, you take off the paper or covering around it.

unwritten ADJECTIVE An unwritten law is one which is generally understood and accepted without being officially laid down.

up ADVERB OR PREPOSITION ❶ towards or in a higher place • *He*

a b c d e f g h i j k l m n o p q r s t **u** v w x y z

▷ SPELLING NOTE: *Psychiatrists Seldom Yell Callously Hard (*psychiatrist*)*

ran up the stairs • *high up in the mountains.* **2** towards or in the north • *I'm flying up to Darwin.*
▷ **PREPOSITION** **3** If you go up a road or river, you go along it. **4** You use 'up to' to say how large something can be or what level it has reached • *traffic jams up to 15 kilometres long.* **5** INFORMAL If someone is up to something, they are secretly doing something they should not be doing. **6** If it is up to someone to do something, it is their responsibility
▷ **ADJECTIVE** **7** If you are up, you are not in bed. **8** If a period of time is up, it has come to an end ▷ **ADVERB** **9** If an amount of something goes up, it increases.

up-and-coming **ADJECTIVE**
Up-and-coming people are likely to be successful.

upbringing **NOUN** Your upbringing is the way that your parents have taught you to behave.

update, updates, updating, updated **VERB** If you update something, you make it more modern or add new information to it • *He had failed to update his will.*

upgrade, upgrades, upgrading, upgraded **VERB** If a person or their job is upgraded, they are given more responsibility or status and usually more money.

upheaval, upheavals **NOUN** a big change which causes a lot of trouble.

uphill **ADVERB** **1** If you go uphill, you go up a slope ▷ **ADJECTIVE** **2** An uphill task requires a lot of effort and determination.

uphold, upholds, upholding, upheld **VERB** If someone upholds a law or a decision, they support and maintain it.

upholstery **NOUN** Upholstery is the soft covering on chairs and sofas that makes them comfortable.

upkeep **NOUN** The upkeep of something is the continual process and cost of keeping it in good condition.

upland, uplands **ADJECTIVE** **1** An upland area is an area of high land ▷ **NOUN** **2** Uplands are areas of high land.

uplifting **ADJECTIVE** making you feel happy.

upload, uploads, uploading, uploaded **VERB** If you upload a computer file or program, you transfer it from your computer into the memory of another computer.

up-market **ADJECTIVE** sophisticated and expensive.

upon **PREPOSITION** **1** FORMAL Upon means on • *I stood upon the stair.* **2** You use 'upon' when mentioning an event that is immediately followed by another • *Upon entering the hall he took a quick glance round.* **3** If an event is upon you, it is about to happen • *The football season is upon us once more.*

upper, uppers **ADJECTIVE** **1** referring to something that is above something else, or the higher part of something • *the upper arm.* ▷ **NOUN** **2** the top part of a shoe.

upper case **ADJECTIVE** (ENGLISH) Upper case letters are the capital letters used in printing or on a typewriter or computer.

▷ SPELLING NOTE: *the QUeen stood on the QUay (quay)*

upper class, upper classes NOUN
The upper classes are people who
belong to a very wealthy or aristocratic
group in a society.

uppermost ADJECTIVE OR
ADVERB ❶ on top or in the highest
position • *the uppermost leaves* • *Lay
your arms beside your body with the
palms turned uppermost.* ▷ ADJECTIVE
❷ most important • *His family is now
uppermost in his mind.*

upright ADJECTIVE OR ADVERB
❶ standing or sitting up straight,
rather than bending or lying down.
❷ behaving in a very respectable and
moral way.

uprising, uprisings NOUN If there is
an uprising, a large group of people
begin fighting against the existing
government to bring about political
changes.

uproar NOUN If there is uproar or an
uproar, there is a lot of shouting and
noise, often because people are angry.
● WORD HISTORY: from Dutch
oproer meaning 'revolt'
● SIMILAR WORDS: commotion,
furore, pandemonium

uproot, uproots, uprooting, uprooted
VERB ❶ If someone is uprooted, they
have to leave the place where they
have lived for a long time. ❷ If a tree
is uprooted, it is pulled out of the
ground.

upset, upsets, upsetting, upset
ADJECTIVE ❶ unhappy and
disappointed ▷ VERB ❷ If something
upsets you, it makes you feel worried
or unhappy. ❸ If you upset
something, you turn it over or spill it
accidentally ▷ NOUN ❹ A stomach

upset is a slight stomach illness
caused by an infection or by
something you have eaten.

upshot NOUN The upshot of a series
of events is the final result.

upside down ADJECTIVE OR
ADVERB the wrong way up.

upstage, upstages, upstaging,
upstaged VERB If someone upstages
you, they draw people's attention
away from you by being more
attractive or interesting.

upstairs ADVERB ❶ If you go
upstairs in a building, you go up to a
higher floor ▷ NOUN ❷ The upstairs
of a building is its upper floor or floors.

upstart, upstarts NOUN someone
who has risen too quickly to an
important position and is too arrogant.

upstream ADVERB towards the
source of a river • *They made their way
upstream.*

upsurge NOUN An upsurge of
something is a sudden large increase
in it.

uptake NOUN You can say that
someone is quick on the uptake if they
understand things quickly.

upthrust, upthrusts NOUN
(GEOGRAPHY) ❶ a block of rock that
has moved upwards during a violent
raising of part of the earth's crust.
❷ a violent raising of part of the
earth's crust.

uptight ADJECTIVE INFORMAL tense
or annoyed.

up-to-date ADJECTIVE ❶ being
the newest thing of its kind. ❷ having
the latest information.

▷ SPELLING NOTE: *Rhythmical Hounds Yap To Heavy Music (rhythm)*

A
B
C
D
E
F
G
H
I
J
K
L
M
N
O
P
Q
R
S
T
U
V
W
X
Y
Z

up-to-the-minute ADJECTIVE
Up-to-the-minute information is the
latest available information.

upturn, upturns NOUN an
improvement in a situation.

upturned ADJECTIVE ❶ pointing
upwards • *rain splashing down on her
upturned face.* ❷ upside down • *an
upturned bowl.*

upwards ADVERB ❶ towards a
higher place • *People stared upwards
and pointed.* ❷ to a higher level or
point on a scale • *The world population
is rocketing upwards.* **upward**
ADJECTIVE

uranium [Said yoo-**ray**-nee-um]
NOUN (SCIENCE) Uranium is a
radioactive metallic element used in
the production of nuclear power and
weapons. Its atomic number is 92 and
its symbol is U.

Uranus NOUN Uranus is the planet
in the solar system which is seventh
from the sun.

urban ADJECTIVE (GEOGRAPHY)
relating to a town or city • *She found
urban life very different to country life.*

urbane ADJECTIVE well-mannered,
and comfortable in social situations.

Urdu [Said **oor**-doo] NOUN Urdu is
the official language of Pakistan. It is
also spoken by many people in India.

urethra, urethras NOUN (SCIENCE)
The urethra is the tube in the body
that carries urine from the bladder out
of the body.

urge, urges, urging, urged NOUN ❶ If
you have an urge to do something,
you have a strong wish to do it

▷ VERB ❷ If you urge someone to do
something, you try hard to persuade
them to do it.
● **SIMILAR WORDS:** ❶ compulsion,
● desire, impulse ❷ beg, implore

urgent ADJECTIVE needing to be
dealt with as soon as possible.
urgently ADVERB **urgency** NOUN
● **SIMILAR WORDS:** crucial, pressing

urinal, urinals [Said yoor-**rye**-nl]
NOUN a bowl or trough fixed to the
wall in a public toilet for men to
urinate in.

urinate, urinates, urinating, urinated
[Said **yoor**-rin-ate] VERB When you
urinate, you go to the toilet and get rid
of urine from your body.

urine [Said **yoor**-rin] NOUN the
waste liquid that you get rid of from
your body when you go to the toilet.

URL, URLs NOUN an abbreviation for
'uniform resource locator': a technical
name for an Internet address.

urn, urns NOUN a decorated
container, especially one that is used
to hold the ashes of a person who has
been cremated.

us PRONOUN A speaker or writer uses
'us' to refer to himself or herself and
one or more other people • *Why don't
you tell us?*

US or **USA** an abbreviation for United
States (of America).

usage NOUN ❶ the degree to which
something is used, or the way in
which it is used. ❷ the way in which
words are actually used • *The terms
soon entered common usage.*

use, uses, using, used VERB [Said

yooz] ❶ If you use something, you do something with it in order to do a job or achieve something • *May I use your phone?* ❷ If you use someone, you take advantage of them by making them do things for you ▷ **NOUN** *[Said yoos]* ❸ The use of something is the act of using it • *the use of force.* ❹ If you have the use of something, you have the ability or permission to use it. ❺ If you find a use for something, you find a purpose for it. **usable** or **useable ADJECTIVE** **user NOUN**
  ● **SIMILAR WORDS:** ❶ application,
  ● employment, usage ❸ apply,
  ● employ, utilize

used *[Said yoost]* **VERB**
  ❶ Something that used to be done or used to be true was done or was true in the past ▷ **PHRASE** ❷ If you are **used to** something, you are familiar with it and have often experienced it *[Said yoozd]* ▷ **ADJECTIVE** A used object has had a previous owner.

useful ADJECTIVE If something is useful, you can use it in order to do something or to help you in some way. **usefully ADVERB usefulness NOUN**

useless ADJECTIVE ❶ If something is useless, you cannot use it because it is not suitable or helpful. ❷ If a course of action is useless, it will not achieve what is wanted.

username, usernames **NOUN** a name that someone uses when logging into a computer or website.

usher, ushers, ushering, ushered **VERB** ❶ If you usher someone somewhere, you show them where to go by going with them ▷ **NOUN** ❷ a person who shows people where to sit at a wedding or a concert.

USSR (HISTORY) an abbreviation for 'Union of Soviet Socialist Republics', a country which was made up of a lot of smaller countries including Russia, but which is now broken up.

usual ADJECTIVE ❶ happening, done, or used most often • *his usual seat.* ▷ **PHRASE** ❷ If you do something **as usual**, you do it in the way that you normally do it. **usually ADVERB**
  ● **SIMILAR WORDS:** ❶ customary,
  ● normal, regular

usurp, usurps, usurping, usurped *[Said yoo-zerp]* **VERB** FORMAL If someone usurps another person's job or title they take it when they have no right to do so.

ute, utes *[Said yoot]* **NOUN** INFORMAL In Australian and New Zealand English, a utility truck.

utensil, utensils *[Said yoo-ten-sil]* **NOUN** Utensils are tools • *cooking utensils.*
  ● **WORD HISTORY:** from Latin
  ● *utensilis* meaning 'available for use'

uterus, uteruses *[Said yoo-ter-russ]* **NOUN** FORMAL A woman's uterus is her womb.

utilitarian ADJECTIVE ❶ intended to produce the greatest benefit for the greatest number of people. ❷ designed to be useful rather than beautiful.

utility, utilities **NOUN** ❶ The utility of something is its usefulness. ❷ a service, such as water or gas, that is provided for everyone.

utility truck, utility trucks **NOUN** In Australian and New Zealand

---

▷ SPELLING NOTE: On WEDNESday Wayne WED NESta (Wednesday)

a b c d e f g h i j k l m n o p q r s t **u** v w x y z

English, a small motor vehicle with an open body and low sides.

utilize, utilizes, utilizing, utilized; *also spelt* **utilise** **VERB** FORMAL To utilize something is to use it. **utilization** **NOUN**

utmost **ADJECTIVE** used to emphasize a particular quality • *I have the utmost respect for Richard.*

utter, utters, uttering, uttered **VERB**
❶ When you utter sounds or words, you make or say them ▷ **ADJECTIVE**
❷ Utter means complete or total • *scenes of utter chaos.* **utterly** **ADVERB**

utterance, utterances **NOUN** something that is said • *his first utterance.*

uvula, uvulas or uvulae *[Said yoo-vyoo-la]* **NOUN** (SCIENCE) Your uvula is the small piece of flesh that hangs down above the back of your tongue.

Vv

v an abbreviation for **versus**.

vacant ADJECTIVE ❶ If something is vacant, it is not occupied or being used. ❷ If a job or position is vacant, no-one holds it at present. ❸ A vacant look suggests that someone does not understand something or is not very intelligent. **vacancy** NOUN **vacantly** ADVERB

vacate, vacates, vacating, vacated VERB FORMAL If you vacate a room or job, you leave it and it becomes available for someone else.

vacation, vacations NOUN ❶ the period between academic terms at a university or college • *the summer vacation.* ❷ a holiday.

vaccinate, vaccinates, vaccinating, vaccinated *[Said vak-sin-ate]* VERB To vaccinate someone means to give them a vaccine, usually by injection, to protect them against a disease. **vaccination** NOUN

vaccine, vaccines *[Said vak-seen]* NOUN a substance made from the germs that cause a disease, given to people to make them immune to that disease.
● WORD HISTORY: from Latin *vacca* meaning 'cow', because smallpox vaccine is based on cowpox, a disease of cows

vacuum, vacuums, vacuuming, vacuumed *[Said vak-yoom]* NOUN

❶ a space containing no air, gases, or other matter ▷ VERB ❷ If you vacuum something, you clean it using a vacuum cleaner.

vacuum cleaner, vacuum cleaners NOUN an electric machine which cleans by sucking up dirt.

vagina, vaginas *[Said vaj-jie-na]* NOUN A woman's vagina is the passage that connects her outer sex organs to her womb.
● WORD HISTORY: from Latin *vagina* meaning 'sheath'

vagrant, vagrants NOUN a person who moves from place to place, and has no home or regular job. **vagrancy** NOUN

vague, vaguer, vaguest *[Said vayg]* ADJECTIVE ❶ If something is vague, it is not expressed or explained clearly, or you cannot see or remember it clearly • *vague statements.*
❷ Someone looks or sounds vague if they are not concentrating or thinking clearly. **vaguely** ADVERB **vagueness** NOUN
● SIMILAR WORDS: ❶ imprecise, indefinite, unclear

vain, vainer, vainest ADJECTIVE ❶ A vain action or attempt is one which is not successful • *He made a vain effort to cheer her up.* ❷ A vain person is very proud of their looks, intelligence, or other qualities ▷ PHRASE ❸ If you

a b c d e f g h i j k l m n o p q r s t u **v** w x y z

A
B
C
D
E
F
G
H
I
J
K
L
M
N
O
P
Q
R
S
T
U
V
W
X
Y
Z

do something **in vain**, you do not succeed in achieving what you intend. **vainly ADVERB**

vale, vales **NOUN** LITERARY a valley.

valency NOUN (SCIENCE) The valency of an atom or chemical group is the number of atoms it has available to combine with atoms of hydrogen and so form compounds.

valentine, valentines **NOUN** **①** Your valentine is someone you love and send a card to on Saint Valentine's Day, February 14th. **②** A valentine or a valentine card is the card you send to the person you love on Saint Valentine's Day.

valet, valets [Said **val**-lit or **val**-lay] **NOUN** a male servant who is employed to look after another man.

valiant ADJECTIVE very brave. **valiantly ADVERB**

valid ADJECTIVE **①** Something that is valid is based on sound reasoning. **②** A valid ticket or document is one which is officially accepted. **validity NOUN**

validate, validates, validating, validated **VERB** If something validates a statement or claim, it proves that it is true or correct.

valley, valleys **NOUN** a long stretch of land between hills, often with a river flowing through it.

valour NOUN Valour is great bravery.

valuable ADJECTIVE **①** having great importance or usefulness. **②** worth a lot of money.
● **SIMILAR WORDS:** ② costly,
● expensive, precious

valuables PLURAL NOUN Valuables are things that you own that cost a lot of money.

valuation, valuations **NOUN** a judgment about how much money something is worth or how good it is.

value, values, valuing, valued **NOUN** **①** The value of something is its importance or usefulness • *information of great value.* **②** The value of something you own is the amount of money that it is worth. **③** The values of a group or a person are the moral principles and beliefs that they think are important • *the values of liberty and equality.* ▷ **VERB** **④** If you value something, you think it is important and you appreciate it. **⑤** When experts value something, they decide how much money it is worth. **valued ADJECTIVE valuer NOUN**

valve, valves **NOUN** **①** a part attached to a pipe or tube which controls the flow of gas or liquid. **②** a small flap in your heart or in a vein which controls the flow and direction of blood.

vampire, vampires **NOUN** In horror stories, vampires are corpses that come out of their graves at night and suck the blood of living people.

van, vans **NOUN** a covered vehicle larger than a car but smaller than a lorry, used for carrying goods.

Van Allen belt NOUN (SCIENCE) In astronomy, the Van Allen belt is the name used to describe either of two belts of charged particles which surround the Earth.

▷ SPELLING NOTE: *'i' before 'e' except after 'c'*

● **WORD HISTORY:** named after the
● American physicist, J.A. *Van Allen*
● (1914–2006), who discovered them.

vandal, vandals **NOUN** someone
who deliberately damages or destroys
things, particularly public property.
vandalize or **vandalise VERB**
vandalism NOUN

vane, vanes **NOUN** a flat blade that is
part of a mechanism for using the
energy of the wind or water to drive a
machine.

vanguard *[Said van-gard]* **NOUN** If
someone is in the vanguard of
something, they are in the most
advanced part of it.

vanilla NOUN Vanilla is a flavouring
for food such as ice cream, which
comes from the pods of a tropical
plant.

vanish, vanishes, vanishing, vanished
VERB ❶ If something vanishes, it
disappears • *The moon vanished behind
a cloud.* ❷ If something vanishes, it
ceases to exist • *a vanishing
civilization.*

vanity NOUN Vanity is a feeling of
excessive pride about your looks or
abilities.

vanquish, vanquishes, vanquishing,
vanquished *[Said vang-kwish]* **VERB**
LITERARY To vanquish someone means
to defeat them completely.

vapour NOUN (SCIENCE) Vapour is a
mass of tiny drops of water or other
liquids in the air which looks like mist.

variable, variables **ADJECTIVE**
❶ Something that is variable is likely
to change at any time ▷ **NOUN** ❷ In
any situation, a variable is something

in it that can change. ❸ (MATHS) In
maths, a variable is a symbol such as x
which can represent any value or any
one of a set of values. **variability**
NOUN

variance NOUN If one thing is at
variance with another, the two seem
to contradict each other.

variant, variants **NOUN** ❶ A variant
of something has a different form
from the usual one, for example *gaol*
is a variant of *jail* ▷ **ADJECTIVE**
❷ alternative or different • *a variant
form of the word.*

variation, variations **NOUN** ❶ a
change from the normal or usual
pattern • *a variation of the same route.*
❷ a change in level, amount, or
quantity • *There has been a large
variation in demand.*

varicose veins PLURAL NOUN
Varicose veins are swollen painful
veins in the legs.

varied ADJECTIVE of different types,
quantities, or sizes.

variety, varieties **NOUN** ❶ If
something has variety, it consists of
things which are not all the same.
❷ A variety of things is a number of
different kinds of them • *a wide variety
of readers.* ❸ A variety of something is
a particular type of it • *a new variety of
celery.* ❹ Variety is a form of
entertainment consisting of short
unrelated acts, such as singing,
dancing, and comedy.
● **SIMILAR WORDS:** ❷ assortment,
● mixture, range

various ADJECTIVE Various means
of several different types • *trees of
various sorts.* **variously ADVERB**

▷ SPELLING NOTE: *King IAn went to ParlIAment in a carrIAge for his marrIAge (-ia-)*

USAGE NOTE: You should avoid putting *different* after *various*: *the disease exists in various forms* not *various different forms*

SIMILAR WORDS: different, miscellaneous, sundry

varnish, varnishes, varnishing, varnished **NOUN** ❶ a liquid which when painted onto a surface gives it a hard clear shiny finish ▷ **VERB** ❷ If you varnish something, you paint it with varnish.

vary, varies, varying, varied **VERB** ❶ If things vary, they change • *Weather patterns vary greatly.* ❷ If you vary something, you introduce changes in it. **varied ADJECTIVE**

vascular ADJECTIVE relating to tubes or ducts that carry fluids within animals or plants.

vase, vases **NOUN** a glass or china jar for flowers.

vasectomy, vasectomies *[Said vas-sek-tom-ee]* **NOUN** an operation to sterilize a man by cutting the tube in his body that carries the sperm.

Vaseline NOUN TRADEMARK A soft clear jelly made from petroleum and used as an ointment or as grease.

vast ADJECTIVE extremely large. **vastly ADVERB vastness NOUN**

vat, vats **NOUN** a large container for liquids.

VAT NOUN In Britain, VAT is a tax which is added to the costs of making or providing goods and services. VAT is an abbreviation for 'value-added tax'.

vault, vaults, vaulting, vaulted *[rhymes with salt]* **NOUN** ❶ a strong secure room, often underneath a building, where valuables are stored, or underneath a church where people are buried. ❷ an arched roof, often found in churches ▷ **VERB** ❸ If you vault over something, you jump over it using your hands or a pole to help.

VCR an abbreviation for 'video cassette recorder'.

VDU, VDUs **NOUN** a monitor screen attached to a computer or word processor. VDU is an abbreviation for 'visual display unit'.

veal NOUN Veal is the meat from a calf.

vector, vectors **NOUN** (MATHS) In maths, a vector is a quantity, such as a force, which has magnitude and direction.

Veda, Vedas *[Said vay-da]* **NOUN** an ancient sacred text of the Hindu religion; also these texts as a collection. **Vedic ADJECTIVE**

veer, veers, veering, veered **VERB** If something which is moving veers in a particular direction, it suddenly changes course • *The aircraft veered sharply to one side.*

vegan, vegans *[Said vee-gn]* **NOUN** someone who does not eat any food made from animal products, such as meat, eggs, cheese, or milk.

vegetable, vegetables **NOUN** ❶ Vegetables are edible roots or leaves such as carrots or cabbage ▷ **ADJECTIVE** ❷ 'Vegetable' is used to refer to any plants in contrast to animals or minerals • *vegetable life.*

WORD HISTORY: from Latin *vegetabilis* meaning 'enlivening'

▷ SPELLING NOTE: *an ELegant angEL (angel)*

vegetarian, vegetarians **NOUN** a person who does not eat meat, poultry, or fish. **vegetarianism NOUN**

vegetation NOUN (GEOGRAPHY) Vegetation is the plants in a particular area.

vegetation cover NOUN (GEOGRAPHY) The vegetation cover of a particular area of land is the type and number of plants growing there.

vehement [Said vee-im-ent] **ADJECTIVE** Someone who is vehement has strong feelings or opinions and expresses them forcefully • He wrote a letter of vehement protest to the owner of the restaurant. **vehemence NOUN vehemently ADVERB**

vehicle, vehicles [Said vee-ik-kl] **NOUN** ① a machine, often with an engine, used for transporting people or goods. ② something used to achieve a particular purpose or as a means of expression • The play seemed an ideal vehicle for his music. **vehicular ADJECTIVE**

veil, veils [rhymes with male] **NOUN** a piece of thin, soft cloth that women sometimes wear over their heads.

vein, veins [rhymes with rain] **NOUN** ① Your veins are the tubes in your body through which your blood flows to your heart. ② Veins are the thin lines on leaves or on insects' wings. ③ A vein of a metal or a mineral is a layer of it in rock. ④ Something that is in a particular style is in that style or mood • in a more serious vein.

veld [Said felt] **NOUN** The veld is flat high grassland in Southern Africa.

veldskoen, veldskoens [Said felt-skoon] **NOUN** In South Africa, a veldskoen is a tough ankle-length boot.

velocity NOUN TECHNICAL Velocity is the speed at which something is moving in a particular direction.

velvet NOUN Velvet is a very soft material which has a thick layer of fine short threads on one side. **velvety ADJECTIVE**
- **WORD HISTORY:** from Latin villus meaning 'shaggy hair'

vendetta, vendettas **NOUN** a long-lasting bitter quarrel in which people try to harm each other.

vending machine, vending machines **NOUN** a machine which provides things such as drinks or sweets when you put money in it.

vendor, vendors **NOUN** a person who sells something.

veneer NOUN ① You can refer to a superficial quality that someone has as a veneer of that quality • a veneer of calm. ② Veneer is a thin layer of wood or plastic used to cover a surface.

venerable ADJECTIVE ① A venerable person is someone you treat with respect because they are old and wise. ② Something that is venerable is impressive because it is old or important historically.

venerate, venerates, venerating, venerated **VERB** FORMAL If you venerate someone, you feel great respect for them. **veneration NOUN**

vengeance NOUN ① Vengeance is the act of harming someone because they have harmed you ▷ **PHRASE** ② If something happens **with a**

vengeance, it happens to a much greater extent than was expected • *It began to rain again with a vengeance.*

venison NOUN Venison is the meat from a deer.
  ● **WORD HISTORY:** from Latin
  ● *venatio* meaning 'hunting'

Venn diagram, Venn diagrams NOUN (MATHS) a Venn diagram is a drawing which uses circles to show the relationships between different sets.
  ● **WORD HISTORY:** named after the
  ● English logician John *Venn*
  ● (1834–1923), who invented them.

venom NOUN ❶ The venom of a snake, scorpion, or spider is its poison. ❷ Venom is a feeling of great bitterness or spitefulness towards someone • *He was glaring at me with venom.* **venomous** ADJECTIVE

vent, vents, venting, vented NOUN ❶ a hole in something through which gases and smoke can escape and fresh air can enter • *air vents.* ▷ VERB ❷ If you vent strong feelings, you express them • *She wanted to vent her anger upon me.* ▷ PHRASE ❸ If you **give vent** to strong feelings, you express them • *Pamela gave vent to a lot of bitterness.*

ventilate, ventilates, ventilating, ventilated VERB To ventilate a room means to allow fresh air into it. **ventilated** ADJECTIVE

ventilation NOUN ❶ Ventilation is the process of breathing air in and out of the lungs. ❷ A ventilation system supplies fresh air into a building.

ventilator, ventilators NOUN a machine that helps people breathe

when they cannot breathe naturally, for example if they are very ill.

ventricle, ventricles NOUN (SCIENCE) ❶ A ventricle is a chamber of the heart that pumps blood to the arteries. ❷ A ventricle is also one of the four main cavities of the brain.

ventriloquist, ventriloquists [Said ven-**trill**-o-kwist] NOUN an entertainer who can speak without moving their lips so that the words seem to come from a dummy. **ventriloquism** NOUN
  ● **WORD HISTORY:** from Latin *venter*
  ● meaning 'belly' and *loqui* meaning
  ● 'to speak'

venture, ventures, venturing, ventured NOUN ❶ something new which involves the risk of failure or of losing money • *a successful venture in television films.* ▷ VERB ❷ If you venture something such as an opinion, you say it cautiously or hesitantly because you are afraid it might be foolish or wrong • *I would not venture to agree.* ❸ If you venture somewhere that might be dangerous, you go there.
  ● **SIMILAR WORDS:** ❶ enterprise,
  ● undertaking

venue, venues [Said ven-yoo] NOUN The venue for an event is the place where it will happen.

Venus NOUN Venus is the planet in the solar system which is second from the sun.

veranda, verandas [Said ver-**ran**-da]; also spelt **verandah** NOUN a platform with a roof that is attached to an outside wall of a house at ground level.

▷ SPELLING NOTE: *A Rude Idiot Thought He Might Eat Toffee In Church (*<u>arithmetic</u>*)*

WHAT IS A VERB?

A verb is a word that describes an action or a state of being. Verbs are sometimes called "doing words".

Verbs of state indicate the way things are:
*Robert **is** a Taurus. Anna **has** one sister.*

Verbs of action indicate specific events that happen, have happened or will happen:
*Anna **visits** the dentist.*
*The man **faxed** his order.*

Auxiliary verbs are used in combination with other verbs to allow the user to distinguish between different times, different degrees of completion, and different amounts of certainty:
*Anna **will** visit the dentist.*
*The man **is** faxing his order.*
*They **may** talk for up to three hours.*

A **phrasal verb** consists of a verb followed by either an adverb or a preposition. The two words taken together have a special meaning which could not be deduced from their literal meanings:
*The car **broke down** again.*
*When did you **take up** croquet?*

An **impersonal verb** is a verb that does not have a subject and is only used after *it* or *there*:

*It **rains** here every day.*

MODAL VERBS

Can, could, may, might, must, should, would, and *ought* are called "modal verbs". They are usually used as auxiliary verbs to change the tone of the meaning of another verb:
*I wonder if you **can come**.*

Even when they are used on their own, they *suggest* another verb:
*I certainly **can**. (i.e. I certainly **can come**)*

There is no difference between the third person present and the other forms of the present tense. No form of the verb ends in -s:
*I **can** speak German. She **can** speak German.*

These verbs do not have a present participle or a past participle.

The verb *could* may be used as the past tense of *can*:
*I **could** speak German when I was younger.*

You can talk about past time by using *could have, may have, might have, must have, should have, would have,* and *ought to have*:
*We **may have** taken a wrong turning.*
*She **must have** thought I was stupid.*

verb, verbs NOUN (ENGLISH) In grammar, a verb is a word that expresses actions and states, for example 'be', 'become', 'take', and 'run'.
▶ SEE GRAMMAR BOX ABOVE

verbal ADJECTIVE (ENGLISH) **❶** You use 'verbal' to describe things connected with words and their use • *verbal attacks on referees.* **❷** 'Verbal' describes things which are spoken rather than written • *a verbal agreement.* **verbally** ADVERB

verdict, verdicts NOUN **❶** In a law

a b c d e f g h i j k l m n o p q r s t u **v** w x y z

▷ SPELLING NOTE: *Beautiful Elephants Are Usually Tiny (beautiful)*

A
B
C
D
E
F
G
H
I
J
K
L
M
N
O
P
Q
R
S
T
U
V
W
X
Y
Z

court, a verdict is the decision which states whether a prisoner is guilty or not guilty. ❷ If you give a verdict on something, you give your opinion after thinking about it.

verge, verges, verging, verged **NOUN** ❶ The verge of a road is the narrow strip of grassy ground at the side ▷ **PHRASE** ❷ If you are **on the verge** of something, you are going to do it soon or it is likely to happen soon • *on the verge of crying.* ▷ **VERB** ❸ Something that verges on something else is almost the same as it • *dark blue that verged on purple.*

verify, verifies, verifying, verified **VERB** If you verify something, you check that it is true • *None of his statements could be verified.* **verifiable ADJECTIVE verification NOUN**

veritable ADJECTIVE You use 'veritable' to emphasize something • *a veritable jungle of shops.*

vermin PLURAL NOUN Vermin are small animals or insects, such as rats and cockroaches, which carry disease and damage crops.

vernacular, vernaculars *[Said ver-nak-yoo-lar]* **NOUN** The vernacular of a particular country or district is the language widely spoken there.

verruca, verrucas *[Said ver-roo-ka]* **NOUN** a small hard infectious growth rather like a wart, occurring on the sole of the foot.

versatile ADJECTIVE If someone is versatile, they have many different skills. **versatility NOUN**

verse, verses **NOUN** ❶ Verse is another word for poetry. ❷ one part

of a poem, song, or chapter of the Bible.

versed ADJECTIVE If you are versed in something, you know a lot about it.

version, versions **NOUN** ❶ A version of something is a form of it in which some details are different from earlier or later forms • *a cheaper version of the aircraft.* ❷ Someone's version of an event is their personal description of what happened.

versus PREPOSITION 'Versus' is used to indicate that two people or teams are competing against each other.

vertebra, vertebrae *[Said ver-tib-bra]* **NOUN** Vertebrae are the small bones which form a person's or animal's backbone.

vertebrate, vertebrates **NOUN** (SCIENCE) Vertebrates are any creatures which have a backbone.

vertex, vertexes or vertices **NOUN** (MATHS) The vertex of something such as a triangle or pyramid is the point opposite the base.

vertical ADJECTIVE (MATHS) Something that is vertical points straight up and forms a ninety-degree angle with the surface on which it stands. **vertically ADVERB**

vertigo NOUN Vertigo is a feeling of dizziness caused by looking down from a high place.

verve NOUN Verve is lively and forceful enthusiasm.

very ADVERB ❶ to a great degree • *very bad dreams.* ▷ **ADJECTIVE** ❷ 'Very' is used before words to emphasize them • *the very end of the book.* ▷ **PHRASE** ❸ You use **not very**

▷ SPELLING NOTE: *Betty Eats Cakes And Uses Seven Eggs (because)*

to mean that something is the case only to a small degree • *You're not very like your sister.*

● **SIMILAR WORDS:** ❶ extremely, greatly, really

vessel, vessels **NOUN** ❶ a ship or large boat. ❷ LITERARY any bowl or container in which a liquid can be kept. ❸ (SCIENCE) a thin tube along which liquids such as blood or sap move in animals and plants.

vest, vests **NOUN** a piece of underwear worn for warmth on the top half of the body.

vestige, vestiges [*Said* **vest**-ij] **NOUN** FORMAL If there is not a vestige of something, then there is not even a little of it left • *They have a vestige of strength left.*

vestry, vestries **NOUN** The vestry is the part of the church building where a priest or minister changes into their official clothes.

vet, vets, vetting, vetted **NOUN** ❶ a doctor for animals ▷ **VERB** ❷ If you vet someone or something, you check them carefully to see if they are acceptable • *He refused to let them vet his speeches.*

veteran, veterans **NOUN** ❶ someone who has served in the armed forces, particularly during a war. ❷ someone who has been involved in a particular activity for a long time • *a veteran of 25 political campaigns.*

veterinary [*Said* **vet**-er-in-ar-ee] **ADJECTIVE** 'Veterinary' is used to describe the work of a vet and the medical treatment of animals.

● **WORD HISTORY:** from Latin *veterinae* meaning 'animals used for

pulling carts and ploughs'

veterinary surgeon, veterinary surgeons **NOUN** the same as a **vet**.

veto, vetoes, vetoing, vetoed [*Said* **vee**-toh] **VERB** ❶ If someone in authority vetoes something, they say no to it ▷ **NOUN** ❷ Veto is the right that someone in authority has to say no to something • *Dr Baker has the power of veto.*

vexed ADJECTIVE If you are vexed, you are annoyed, worried, or puzzled.

VHF NOUN VHF is a range of high radio frequencies. VHF is an abbreviation for 'very high frequency'.

via PREPOSITION ❶ If you go to one place via another, you travel through that place to get to your destination • *He drove directly from Bonn via Paris.* ❷ Via also means done or achieved by making use of a particular thing or person • *to follow proceedings via newspapers or television.*

viable [*Said* **vy**-a-bl] **ADJECTIVE** Something that is viable is capable of doing what it is intended to do without extra help or financial support • *a viable business.* **viability NOUN**

viaduct, viaducts **NOUN** a long high bridge that carries a road or railway across a valley.

● **WORD HISTORY:** from Latin *via* meaning 'road' and *ducere* meaning 'to bring'

vibrant ADJECTIVE Something or someone that is vibrant is full of life, energy, and enthusiasm. **vibrantly ADVERB vibrancy NOUN**

vibrate, vibrates, vibrating, vibrated **VERB** (SCIENCE) If something

a b c d e f g h i j k l m n o p q r s t u **v** w x y z

vibrates, it moves a tiny amount backwards and forwards very quickly. **vibration** NOUN

vicar, vicars NOUN a priest in the Church of England.

vicarage, vicarages NOUN a house where a vicar lives.

vice, vices NOUN ❶ a serious moral fault in someone's character, such as greed, or a weakness, such as smoking. ❷ Vice is criminal activities connected with prostitution and pornography. ❸ a tool with a pair of jaws that hold an object tightly while it is being worked on.

vice- PREFIX 'Vice-' is used before a title or position to show that the holder is the deputy of the person with that title or position • *vice-president*.

viceregal ADJECTIVE ❶ of or concerning a viceroy. ❷ In Australia and New Zealand, viceregal means of or concerning a governor or governor-general.

viceroy, viceroys NOUN A viceroy is someone who has been appointed to govern a place as a representative of a monarch.

vice versa ADVERB 'Vice versa' is used to indicate that the reverse of what you have said is also true • *Wives often criticize their husbands, and vice versa.*

vicinity, vicinities [Said vis-**sin**-it-ee] NOUN If something is in the vicinity of a place, it is in the surrounding or nearby area.

vicious ADJECTIVE cruel and violent. **viciously** ADVERB **viciousness** NOUN

victim, victims NOUN someone who has been harmed or injured by someone or something.

victor, victors NOUN The victor in a fight or contest is the person who wins.

Victorian ADJECTIVE ❶ Victorian describes things that happened or were made during the reign of Queen Victoria (1837–1901). ❷ Victorian also describes people or things connected with the state of Victoria in Australia.

victory, victories NOUN a success in a battle or competition. **victorious** ADJECTIVE
● SIMILAR WORDS: conquest, triumph, win

video, videos, videoing, videoed NOUN ❶ Video is the recording and showing of films and events using a video recorder, video tape, and a television set. ❷ a sound and picture recording which can be played back on a television set. ❸ a video recorder ▷ VERB ❹ If you video something, you record it on magnetic tape for later viewing.

video recorder, video recorders NOUN A video recorder or video cassette recorder is a machine for recording and playing back programmes from television.

vie, vies, vying, vied VERB FORMAL If you vie with someone, you compete to do something sooner or better than they do.

Vietnamese [Said vyet-nam-**meez**] ADJECTIVE ❶ belonging or relating to Vietnam ▷ NOUN ❷ someone who comes from Vietnam. ❸ Vietnamese is the main language spoken in Vietnam.

▷ SPELLING NOTE: *you'll brEAK that Electrical Aerial, Kitty (break)*

view, views, viewing, viewed NOUN
❶ Your views are your personal
opinions • *his political views*.
❷ everything you can see from a
particular place ▷ VERB ❸ If you
view something in a particular way,
you think of it in that way • *They
viewed me with contempt.* ▷ PHRASE
❹ You use **in view of** to specify the
main fact or event influencing your
actions or opinions • *He wore a lighter
suit in view of the heat.* ❺ If something
is **on view**, it is being shown or
exhibited to the public.
● SIMILAR WORDS: ❷ prospect,
● scene, vista

viewer, viewers NOUN Viewers are
the people who watch television.

viewpoint, viewpoints NOUN
❶ Your viewpoint is your attitude
towards something. ❷ a place from
which you get a good view of an area
or event.

vigil, vigils *[Said vij-jil]* NOUN a
period of time, especially at night,
when you stay quietly in one place, for
example because you are making a
political protest or praying.

vigilant ADJECTIVE careful and alert
to danger or trouble. **vigilance** NOUN
vigilantly ADVERB

vigilante, vigilantes *[Said vij-il-ant-
ee]* NOUN Vigilantes are unofficially
organized groups of people who try to
protect their community and catch
and punish criminals.

vignette, vignettes *[Said vin-yet]*
NOUN (ENGLISH) A vignette is a short
description or piece of writing about a
particular subject or thing.

vigorous ADJECTIVE energetic or
enthusiastic. **vigorously** ADVERB
vigour NOUN

Viking, Vikings NOUN The Vikings
were seamen from Scandinavia who
raided parts of north-western Europe
from the 8th to the 11th centuries.

vile, viler, vilest ADJECTIVE
unpleasant or disgusting • *a vile
accusation* • *a vile smell*.

villa, villas NOUN a house, especially
a pleasant holiday home in a country
with a warm climate.

village, villages NOUN a collection of
houses and other buildings in the
countryside. **villager** NOUN

villain, villains NOUN ❶ someone
who harms others or breaks the law.
❷ the main evil character in a story.
villainous ADJECTIVE **villainy**
NOUN
● SIMILAR WORDS: ❶ criminal,
● evildoer, rogue

vindicate, vindicates, vindicating,
vindicated VERB FORMAL If someone
is vindicated, their views or ideas are
proved to be right • *My friend's
instincts have been vindicated by the
findings of the inquiry.*

vindictive ADJECTIVE Someone
who is vindictive is deliberately hurtful
towards someone, often as an act of
revenge. **vindictiveness** NOUN

vine, vines NOUN a trailing or
climbing plant which winds itself
around and over a support, especially
one which produces grapes.

vinegar NOUN Vinegar is a
sharp-tasting liquid made from sour
wine, beer, or cider, which is used for
salad dressing. **vinegary** ADJECTIVE

a
b
c
d
e
f
g
h
i
j
k
l
m
n
o
p
q
r
s
t
u
v
w
x
y
z

▷ SPELLING NOTE: *I always visit my FRIend on a FRIday (Friday)*

A
B
C
D
E
F
G
H
I
J
K
L
M
N
O
P
Q
R
S
T
U
V
W
X
Y
Z

● **WORD HISTORY:** from French *vin*
● meaning 'wine' and *aigre* meaning
● 'sour'

vineyard, vineyards [Said *vin-yard*]
NOUN an area of land where grapes
are grown.

vintage, vintages ADJECTIVE ❶ A
vintage wine is a good wine which has
been stored for a number of years to
improve its quality. ❷ Vintage
describes something which is the best
or most typical of its kind • *a vintage
guitar*. ❸ A vintage car is one made
between 1918 and 1930 ▷ NOUN ❹ a
grape harvest of one particular year
and the wine produced from it.

vinyl NOUN Vinyl is a strong plastic
used to make things such as furniture
and floor coverings.

viola, violas [Said *vee-oh-la*] NOUN a
musical instrument like a violin, but
larger and with a lower pitch.

violate, violates, violating, violated
VERB ❶ If you violate an agreement,
law, or promise, you break it. ❷ If you
violate someone's peace or privacy,
you disturb it. ❸ If you violate a place,
especially a holy place, you treat it
with disrespect or violence. **violation**
NOUN

violence NOUN ❶ Violence is
behaviour which is intended to hurt or
kill people. ❷ If you do or say
something with violence, you use a lot
of energy, often because you are angry.

violent ADJECTIVE ❶ If someone is
violent, they try to hurt or kill people.
❷ A violent event happens
unexpectedly and with great force.
❸ Something that is violent is said,
felt, or done with great force.

violently ADVERB

violet, violets NOUN ❶ a plant with
dark purple flowers ▷ NOUN OR
ADJECTIVE ❷ bluish purple.

violin, violins NOUN a musical
instrument with four strings that is
held under the chin and played with a
bow. **violinist** NOUN

VIP, VIPs NOUN VIPs are famous or
important people. VIP is an abbreviation
for 'very important person'.

viper, vipers NOUN Vipers are types
of poisonous snakes.

virgin, virgins NOUN ❶ someone
who has never had sexual intercourse
▷ PROPER NOUN ❷ The Virgin, or
the Blessed Virgin, is a name given to
Mary, the mother of Jesus Christ
▷ ADJECTIVE ❸ Something that is
virgin is fresh and unused • *virgin
land*. **virginity** NOUN

virginal, virginals ADJECTIVE
❶ Someone who is virginal looks
young and innocent. ❷ Something
that is virginal is fresh and clean and
looks as if it has never been used
▷ NOUN ❸ a keyboard instrument
popular in the 16th and 17th centuries.

Virgo NOUN Virgo is the sixth sign of
the zodiac, represented by a girl. People
born between August 23rd and
September 22nd are born under this sign.

virile ADJECTIVE A virile man has all
the qualities that a man is traditionally
expected to have, such as strength
and sexuality. **virility** NOUN

virtual [Said *vur-tyool*] ADJECTIVE
Virtual means that something has all
the characteristics of a particular
thing, but it is not formally recognized

▷ SPELLING NOTE: *I want to see (C) your licenCe (licen**c**e)*

as being that thing • *The country is in a virtual state of war.* **virtually ADVERB**

virtual reality NOUN Virtual reality is a situation or setting that has been created by a computer and that looks real to the person using it.

virtue, virtues **NOUN** ❶ Virtue is thinking and doing what is morally right and avoiding what is wrong. ❷ a good quality in someone's character. ❸ A virtue of something is an advantage • *The virtue of neatness is that you can always find things.* ▷ **A FORMAL PHRASE** ❹ **By virtue of** means because of • *The article stuck in my mind by virtue of one detail.*
● **SIMILAR WORDS:** ❶ goodness, integrity, morality

virtuoso, virtuosos or virtuosi *[Said vur-tyoo-oh-zoh]* **NOUN** someone who is exceptionally good at something, particularly playing a musical instrument.
● **WORD HISTORY:** from Italian *virtuoso* meaning 'skilled'

virtuous ADJECTIVE behaving with or showing moral virtue.
● **SIMILAR WORDS:** good, moral, upright

virus, viruses *[Said vie-russ]* **NOUN** ❶ SCIENCE a kind of germ that can cause disease. ❷ ICT a program that alters or damages the information stored in a computer system. **viral ADJECTIVE**

visa, visas **NOUN** an official stamp, usually put in your passport, that allows you to visit a particular country.

viscount, viscounts *[Said vie-kount]* **NOUN** a British nobleman. **viscountess NOUN**

viscous *[Said viss-kuss]* **ADJECTIVE** SCIENCE Something which is viscous is thick and sticky and does not flow easily.

Vishnu NOUN Vishnu is a Hindu god and is one of the Trimurti.

visibility NOUN You use 'visibility' to say how far or how clearly you can see in particular weather conditions.

visible ADJECTIVE ❶ able to be seen. ❷ noticeable or evident • *There was little visible excitement.* **visibly ADVERB**

vision, visions **NOUN** ❶ Vision is the ability to see clearly. ❷ a mental picture, in which you imagine how things might be different • *the vision of a possible future.* ❸ Vision is also imaginative insight • *a total lack of vision and imagination.* ❹ an unusual experience that you have, in which you see things that other people cannot see, as a result of madness, divine inspiration, or taking drugs. **visionary NOUN OR ADJECTIVE**

visit, visits, visiting, visited **VERB** ❶ If you visit someone, you go to see them and spend time with them. ❷ If you visit a place, you go to see it ▷ **NOUN** ❸ a trip to see a person or place. **visitor NOUN**

visor, visors *[Said vie-zor]* **NOUN** a transparent movable shield attached to a helmet, which can be pulled down to protect the eyes or face.

visual ADJECTIVE relating to sight • *a visual inspection.*

visualize, visualizes, visualizing, visualized *[Said viz-yool-eyes]*; *also spelt* **visualise VERB** If you visualize something, you form a mental picture of it.

vital ADJECTIVE ❶ necessary or very important • *vital evidence*.
❷ energetic, exciting, and full of life • *an active and vital life outside school*.
vitally ADVERB
● SIMILAR WORDS: ❶ essential,
● necessary

vitality NOUN People who have vitality are energetic and lively.

vitamin, vitamins NOUN D & T Vitamins are organic compounds which you need in order to remain healthy. They occur naturally in food.

vitriolic ADJECTIVE FORMAL Vitriolic language or behaviour is full of bitterness and hate.

vivacious [Said viv-**vay**-shuss] ADJECTIVE A vivacious person is attractively lively and high-spirited. **vivacity** NOUN

vivid ADJECTIVE very bright in colour or clear in detail • *vivid red paint* • *vivid memories*. **vividly** ADVERB **vividness** NOUN
● SIMILAR WORDS: intense,
● powerful

viviparous [Said viv-**vip**-par-uss] ADJECTIVE SCIENCE Viviparous animals give birth to live and fully-formed young, rather than to eggs.

vivisection NOUN Vivisection is the act of cutting open living animals for medical research.

vixen, vixens NOUN a female fox.

vocabulary, vocabularies NOUN ENGLISH ❶ Someone's vocabulary

is the total number of words they know in a particular language. ❷ The vocabulary of a language is all the words in it.

vocal ADJECTIVE ❶ You say that someone is vocal if they express their opinions strongly and openly.
❷ MUSIC Vocal means involving the use of the human voice, especially in singing. **vocalist** NOUN **vocally** ADVERB

vocal cords or **vocal chords** PLURAL NOUN SCIENCE Your vocal cords are the part of your throat which can be made to vibrate when you breathe out, making the sounds you use for speaking.

vocation, vocations NOUN ❶ a strong wish to do a particular job, especially one which involves serving other people. ❷ a profession or career.

vocational ADJECTIVE 'Vocational' is used to describe the skills needed for a particular job or profession • *vocational training*.

vociferous [Said voe-**sif**-fer-uss] ADJECTIVE FORMAL Someone who is vociferous speaks a lot, or loudly, because they want to make a point strongly • *vociferous critics*.
vociferously ADVERB

vodka, vodkas NOUN a strong clear alcoholic drink which originally came from Russia.

vogue [Said **vohg**] PHRASE If something is **the vogue** or **in vogue**, it is fashionable and popular • *Colour photographs became the vogue*.

voice, voices, voicing, voiced NOUN
❶ Your voice is the sounds produced

A B C D E F G H I J K L M N O P Q R S T U V W X Y Z

by your vocal cords, or the ability to make such sounds ▷ **VERB** ❷ If you voice an opinion or an emotion, you say what you think or feel • *A range of opinions were voiced.*

void, voids **NOUN** ❶ a situation which seems empty because it has no interest or excitement • *Cats fill a very large void in your life.* ❷ a large empty hole or space • *His feet dangled in the void.*

volatile **ADJECTIVE** liable to change often and unexpectedly • *The situation at work is volatile.*

volcanic **ADJECTIVE** A volcanic region has many volcanoes or was created by volcanoes.

volcano, volcanoes **NOUN** a hill with an opening through which lava, gas, and ash burst out from inside the earth onto the surface.
● **WORD HISTORY:** named after *Vulcan*, the Roman god of fire

vole, voles **NOUN** a small mammal like a mouse with a short tail, which lives in fields and near rivers.

volition **NOUN** FORMAL If you do something of your own volition, you do it because you have decided for yourself, without being persuaded by others • *He attended of his own volition.*

volley, volleys **NOUN** ❶ A volley of shots or gunfire is a lot of shots fired at the same time. ❷ In tennis, a volley is a stroke in which the player hits the ball before it bounces.

volleyball **NOUN** Volleyball is a game in which two teams hit a large ball back and forth over a high net with their hands. The ball is not allowed to bounce on the ground.

volt, volts **NOUN** (SCIENCE) A volt is a unit of electrical force. One volt produces one amp of electricity when the resistance is one ohm.
● **WORD HISTORY:** named after the Italian physicist Count Alessandro *Volta* (1745–1827).

voltage, voltages **NOUN** The voltage of an electric current is its force measured in volts.

volume, volumes **NOUN** ❶ (MATHS) The volume of something is the amount of space it contains or occupies. ❷ The volume of something is also the amount of it that there is • *a large volume of letters.* ❸ The volume of a radio, TV, or record player is the strength of the sound that it produces. ❹ a book, or one of a series of books.

voluminous [Said vol-**loo**-min-uss] **ADJECTIVE** very large or full in size or quantity • *voluminous skirts.*

voluntary **ADJECTIVE** ❶ Voluntary actions are ones that you do because you choose to do them and not because you have been forced to do them. ❷ Voluntary work is done by people who are not paid for what they do. **voluntarily** **ADVERB**

volunteer, volunteers, volunteering, volunteered **NOUN** ❶ someone who does work for which they are not paid • *a volunteer for Greenpeace.* ❷ someone who chooses to join the armed forces, especially during wartime ▷ **VERB** ❸ If you volunteer to do something, you offer to do it rather than being forced into it. ❹ If you volunteer information, you give it without being asked.

a b c d e f g h i j k l m n o p q r s t u **v** w x y z

voluptuous [Said vol-**lupt**-yoo-uss]
ADJECTIVE A voluptuous woman has
a figure which is considered to be
sexually exciting. **voluptuously**
ADVERB **voluptuousness NOUN**

vomit, vomits, vomiting, vomited
VERB ❶ If you vomit, food and drink
comes back up from your stomach
and out through your mouth ▷ **NOUN**
❷ Vomit is partly digested food and
drink that has come back up from
someone's stomach and out through
their mouth.

voodoo NOUN Voodoo is a form of
magic practised in the Caribbean,
especially in Haiti.

vortex, vortexes or vortices **NOUN**
(SCIENCE) A vortex is a mass of wind
or water which spins round so fast that
it pulls objects into its empty centre.

vote, votes, voting, voted **NOUN**
❶ Someone's vote is their choice in
an election, or at a meeting where
decisions are taken. ❷ When a group
of people have a vote, they make a
decision by allowing each person in
the group to say what they would
prefer. ❸ In an election, the vote is
the total number of people who have
made their choice • *the average Liberal
vote.* ❹ If people have the vote, they
have the legal right to vote in an
election ▷ **VERB** ❺ When people
vote, they indicate their choice or
opinion, usually by writing on a piece
of paper or by raising their hand. ❻ If
you vote that a particular thing should
happen, you are suggesting it should
happen • *I vote that we all go to
Holland.* **voter NOUN**

vouch, vouches, vouching, vouched
VERB ❶ If you say that you can

vouch for something, you mean that
you have evidence from your own
experience that it is true or correct.
❷ If you say that you can vouch for
someone, you mean that you are sure
that you can guarantee their good
behaviour or support • *Her employer
will vouch for her.*

voucher, vouchers **NOUN** a piece of
paper that can be used instead of
money to pay for something • *free
luncheon vouchers.*

vow, vows, vowing, vowed **VERB** ❶ If
you vow to do something, you make a
solemn promise to do it • *He vowed to
do better in future.* ▷ **NOUN** ❷ a
solemn promise.

vowel, vowels **NOUN** (ENGLISH) a
sound made without your tongue
touching the roof of your mouth or
your teeth, or one of the letters a, e, i,
o, u, which represent such sounds.

voyage, voyages **NOUN** a long
journey on a ship or in a spacecraft.
voyager NOUN

vulgar ADJECTIVE ❶ socially
unacceptable or offensive • *vulgar
language.* ❷ showing a lack of taste or
quality • *the most vulgar person who
ever existed.* **vulgarity NOUN**
vulgarly ADVERB

vulnerable ADJECTIVE weak and
without protection. **vulnerably**
ADVERB **vulnerability NOUN**
● SIMILAR WORDS: defenceless,
● susceptible, weak

vulture, vultures **NOUN** a large bird
which lives in hot countries and eats
the flesh of dead animals.

vying the present participle of **vie**.

▷ SPELLING NOTE: *I went to see (C) the doctor's new practiCe (practice)*

A B C D E F G H I J K L M N O P Q R S T U V W X Y Z

Ww

a
b
c
d
e
f
g
h
i
j
k
l
m
n
o
p
q
r
s
t
u
v
w
x
y
z

wacky, wackier, wackiest **ADJECTIVE**
INFORMAL odd or crazy • *wacky clothes.*

wad, wads **NOUN** ❶ A wad of papers
or banknotes is a thick bundle of
them. ❷ A wad of something is a
lump of it • *a wad of cotton wool.*

waddle, waddles, waddling, waddled
VERB When a duck or a fat person
waddles, they walk with short, quick
steps, swaying slightly from side to
side.

waddy, waddies **NOUN** a heavy,
wooden club used by Australian
Aborigines as a weapon in war.

wade, wades, wading, waded **VERB**
❶ If you wade through water or mud,
you walk slowly through it. ❷ If you
wade through a book or document,
you spend a lot of time and effort
reading it because you find it dull or
difficult.

wader, waders **NOUN** Waders are
long waterproof rubber boots worn by
fishermen.

wafer, wafers **NOUN** ❶ a thin, crisp,
sweet biscuit often eaten with ice
cream. ❷ a thin disc of special bread
used in the Christian service of Holy
Communion.

waffle, waffles, waffling, waffled
*[Said **wof**-fl]* **VERB** ❶ When
someone waffles, they talk or write a
lot without being clear or without
saying anything of importance
▷ **NOUN** ❷ Waffle is vague and
lengthy speech or writing. ❸ a thick,
crisp pancake with squares marked on
it often eaten with syrup poured over
it.

waft, wafts, wafting, wafted *[Said
wahft]* **VERB** If a sound or scent
wafts or is wafted through the air, it
moves gently through it.

wag, wags, wagging, wagged **VERB**
❶ When a dog wags its tail, it shakes
it repeatedly from side to side. ❷ If
you wag your finger, you move it
repeatedly up and down.

wage, wages, waging, waged **NOUN**
❶ A wage or wages is the regular
payment made to someone each week
for the work they do, especially for
manual or unskilled work ▷ **VERB**
❷ If a person or country wages a
campaign or war, they start it and
carry it on over a period of time.

wager, wagers **NOUN** a bet.

wagon, wagons; *also spelt* **waggon**
NOUN ❶ a strong four-wheeled
vehicle for carrying heavy loads,
usually pulled by a horse or tractor.
❷ Wagons are also the containers for
freight pulled by a railway engine.

waif, waifs **NOUN** a young, thin
person who looks hungry and
homeless.

▷ SPELLING NOTE: *You must practiSe your Ss (practise)*

A
B
C
D
E
F
G
H
I
J
K
L
M
N
O
P
Q
R
S
T
U
V
W
X
Y
Z

wail, wails, wailing, wailed **VERB**
❶ To wail is to cry loudly with sorrow or pain ▷ **NOUN** ❷ a long, unhappy cry.

waist, waists **NOUN** the middle part of your body where it narrows slightly above your hips.

waistcoat, waistcoats **NOUN** a sleeveless piece of clothing, often worn under a suit or jacket, which buttons up the front.

wait, waits, waiting, waited **VERB**
❶ If you wait, you spend time, usually doing little or nothing, before something happens. ❷ If something can wait, it is not urgent and can be dealt with later. ❸ If you wait on people in a restaurant, it is your job to serve them food ▷ **NOUN** ❹ a period of time before something happens ▷ **PHRASE** ❺ If you **can't wait** to do something, you are very excited and eager to do it.

waiter, waiters **NOUN** a man who works in a restaurant, serving people with food and drink.

waiting list, waiting lists **NOUN** a list of people who have asked for something which cannot be given to them immediately, for example medical treatment.

waitress, waitresses **NOUN** a woman who works in a restaurant, serving people with food and drink.

waive, waives, waiving, waived *[Said wave]* **VERB** If someone waives something such as a rule or a right, they decide not to insist on it being applied.

wake, wakes, waking, woke, woken

VERB ❶ When you wake or when something wakes you, you become conscious again after being asleep ▷ **NOUN** ❷ The wake of a boat or other object moving in water is the track of waves it leaves behind it. ❸ a gathering of people who have got together to mourn someone's death ▷ **PHRASE** ❹ If one thing follows **in the wake of** another, it follows it as a result of it, or in imitation of it • *a project set up in the wake of last year's riots.*

wake up VERB ❶ When you wake up or something wakes you up, you become conscious again after being asleep. ❷ If you wake up to a dangerous situation, you become aware of it.
● **SIMILAR WORDS:** ❶ awaken,
● rouse

waken, wakens, wakening, wakened **VERB** LITERARY When you waken someone, you wake them up.

walk, walks, walking, walked **VERB**
❶ When you walk, you move along by putting one foot in front of the other on the ground. ❷ If you walk away with or walk off with something such as a prize, you win it or achieve it easily ▷ **NOUN** ❸ a journey made by walking • *We'll have a quick walk.*
❹ Your walk is the way you walk • *his rolling walk.*
walk out VERB ❶ If you walk out on someone, you leave them suddenly. ❷ If workers walk out, they go on strike.

walkabout, walkabouts **NOUN**
❶ an informal walk amongst crowds in a public place by royalty or by some other well-known person.
❷ Walkabout is when an Australian

▷ SPELLING NOTE: *pAL up with the principAL and principAL staff (principal)*

Aborigine goes off to live and wander in the bush for a period of time.

walker, walkers NOUN a person who walks, especially for pleasure or to keep fit.

walking stick, walking sticks NOUN a wooden stick which people can lean on while walking.

walk of life, walks of life NOUN The walk of life that you come from is the position you have in society and the kind of job you have.

walkover, walkovers NOUN INFORMAL a very easy victory in a competition or contest.

walkway, walkways NOUN a passage between two buildings for people to walk along.

wall, walls NOUN ❶ one of the vertical sides of a building or a room. ❷ a long, narrow vertical structure made of stone or brick that surrounds or divides an area of land. ❸ a lining or membrane enclosing a bodily cavity or structure • *the wall of the womb*.

wallaby, wallabies NOUN an Australian animal like a small kangaroo.
● WORD HISTORY: from *wolaba*, an Australian Aboriginal word

wallaroo, wallaroos NOUN a large, stocky kangaroo that lives in rocky or mountainous regions of Australia.

wallet, wallets NOUN a small, flat case made of leather or plastic, used for keeping paper money and sometimes credit cards.

wallop, wallops, walloping, walloped VERB INFORMAL If you wallop

someone, you hit them very hard.

wallow, wallows, wallowing, wallowed VERB ❶ If you wallow in an unpleasant feeling or situation, you allow it to continue longer than is reasonable or necessary because you are getting a kind of enjoyment from it • *We're wallowing in misery.* ❷ When an animal wallows in mud or water, it lies or rolls about in it slowly for pleasure.

wallpaper, wallpapers NOUN Wallpaper is thick coloured or patterned paper for pasting onto the walls of rooms in order to decorate them.

walnut, walnuts NOUN ❶ an edible nut with a wrinkled shape and a hard, round, light-brown shell. ❷ Walnut is wood from the walnut tree which is often used for making expensive furniture.
● WORD HISTORY: from Old English *walh-hnutu* meaning 'foreign nut'

walrus, walruses NOUN an animal which lives in the sea and which looks like a large seal with a tough skin, coarse whiskers, and two tusks.

waltz, waltzes, waltzing, waltzed NOUN ❶ a dance which has a rhythm of three beats to the bar ▷ VERB ❷ If you waltz with someone, you dance a waltz with them. ❸ INFORMAL If you waltz somewhere, you walk there in a relaxed and confident way.
● WORD HISTORY: from Old German *walzen* meaning 'to revolve'

wan [rhymes with **on**] ADJECTIVE pale and tired-looking.

wand, wands NOUN a long, thin rod

that magicians wave when they are performing tricks and magic.

wander, wanders, wandering, wandered **VERB** ❶ If you wander in a place, you walk around in a casual way. ❷ If your mind wanders or your thoughts wander, you lose concentration and start thinking about other things. **wanderer NOUN**
  ● **SIMILAR WORDS:** ❶ ramble,
  ● roam, stroll

wane, wanes, waning, waned **VERB** If a condition, attitude, or emotion wanes, it becomes gradually weaker.

wangle, wangles, wangling, wangled **VERB** INFORMAL If you wangle something that you want, you manage to get it by being crafty or persuasive.

want, wants, wanting, wanted **VERB** ❶ If you want something, you feel a desire to have it. ❷ If something is wanted, it is needed or needs to be done. ❸ If someone is wanted, the police are searching for them • *John was wanted for fraud.* ▷ **NOUN** ❹ FORMAL A want of something is a lack of it.

wanting ADJECTIVE If you find something wanting or if it proves wanting, it is not as good in some way as you think it should be.

wanton ADJECTIVE A wanton action deliberately causes unnecessary harm or waste • *wanton destruction.*

war, wars, warring, warred **NOUN** ❶ a period of fighting between countries or states when weapons are used and many people may be killed. ❷ a competition between groups of people, or a campaign against

something • *a trade war* • *the war against crime.* ▷ **VERB** ❸ When two countries war with each other, they are fighting a war against each other. **warring ADJECTIVE**
  ● **SIMILAR WORDS:** ❶ battle,
  ● fighting, hostilities ❸ battle, fight

waratah, waratahs *[Said wor-ra-tah]* **NOUN** an Australian shrub with dark green leaves and large clusters of crimson flowers.

warble, warbles, warbling, warbled **VERB** When a bird warbles, it sings pleasantly with high notes.

ward, wards, warding, warded **NOUN** ❶ a room in a hospital which has beds for several people who need similar treatment. ❷ an area or district which forms a separate part of a political constituency or local council. ❸ A ward or a ward of court is a child who is officially put in the care of an adult or a court of law, because their parents are dead or because they need protection ▷ **VERB** ❹ If you ward off a danger or an illness, you do something to prevent it from affecting or harming you.

-ward or **-wards SUFFIX** -ward and -wards form adverbs or adjectives that show the way something is moving or facing • *homeward* • *westwards.*

warden, wardens **NOUN** ❶ a person in charge of a building or institution such as a youth hostel or prison. ❷ an official who makes sure that certain laws or rules are obeyed in a particular place or activity • *a traffic warden.*

warder, warders **NOUN** a person

who is in charge of prisoners in a jail.

wardrobe, wardrobes NOUN ❶ a tall cupboard in which you can hang your clothes. ❷ Someone's wardrobe is their collection of clothes.

ware, wares NOUN ❶ Ware is manufactured goods of a particular kind • *kitchenware*. ❷ Someone's wares are the things they sell, usually in the street or in a market.

warehouse, warehouses NOUN a large building where raw materials or manufactured goods are stored.

warfare NOUN Warfare is the activity of fighting a war.

warhead, warheads NOUN the front end of a bomb or missile, where the explosives are carried.

warlock, warlocks NOUN a male witch.

warm, warmer, warmest; warms, warming, warmed ADJECTIVE ❶ Something that is warm has some heat, but not enough to be hot • *a warm day*. ❷ Warm clothes or blankets are made of a material which protects you from the cold. ❸ Warm colours or sounds are pleasant and make you feel comfortable and relaxed. ❹ A warm person is friendly and affectionate ▷ VERB ❺ If you warm something, you heat it up gently so that it stops being cold. **warmly** ADVERB
warm up VERB If you warm up for an event or an activity, you practise or exercise gently to prepare for it.

warm-blooded ADJECTIVE ❶ (SCIENCE) An animal that is warm-blooded has a relatively high

body temperature which remains constant and does not change with the surrounding temperature. ❷ If you describe a person as warm-blooded, you mean that they are passionate.

warmth NOUN ❶ Warmth is a moderate amount of heat. ❷ Someone who has warmth is friendly and affectionate.

warn, warns, warning, warned VERB ❶ If you warn someone about a possible problem or danger, you tell them about it in advance so that they are aware of it • *I warned him what it would be like.* ❷ If you warn someone not to do something, you advise them not to do it, in order to avoid possible danger or punishment • *I have warned her not to train for 10 days.*
warn off VERB If you warn someone off, you tell them to go away or to stop doing something.
● SIMILAR WORDS: ❶ alert, ● caution, notify

warning, warnings NOUN something said or written to tell people of a possible problem or danger.

warp, warps, warping, warped VERB ❶ If something warps or is warped, it becomes bent, often because of the effect of heat or water. ❷ If something warps someone's mind or character, it makes them abnormal or corrupt. ❸ The warp in a piece of cloth is the stronger lengthwise threads.

warrant, warrants, warranting, warranted VERB ❶ FORMAL If something warrants a particular action, it makes the action seem

▷ SPELLING NOTE: *the QUeen stood on the QUay (quay)*

necessary • *no evidence to warrant a murder investigation.* ▷ **NOUN ②** an official document which gives permission to the police to do something • *a warrant for his arrest.*

warranty, warranties **NOUN** a guarantee • *a three-year warranty.*

warren, warrens **NOUN** a group of holes under the ground connected by tunnels, which rabbits live in.

warrigal, warrigals *[Said wor-rih-gl]* **NOUN ①** In Australian English, a dingo. **②** In Australian English, a wild horse or other wild creature ▷ **ADJECTIVE ③** In Australian English, wild.

warrior, warriors **NOUN** a fighting man or soldier, especially in former times.

warship, warships **NOUN** a ship built with guns and used for fighting in wars.

wart, warts **NOUN** a small, hard piece of skin which can grow on someone's face or hands.

wartime NOUN Wartime is a period of time during which a country is at war.

wary, warier, wariest **ADJECTIVE** cautious and on one's guard • *Michelle is wary of marriage.* **warily ADVERB**

was a past tense of **be**.

wash, washes, washing, washed **VERB ①** If you wash something, you clean it with water and soap. **②** If you wash, you clean yourself using soap and water. **③** If something is washed somewhere, it is carried there gently by water • *The infant Arthur was*

washed ashore. ▷ **NOUN ④** The wash is all the clothes and bedding that are washed together at one time • *a typical family's weekly wash.* **⑤** The wash in water is the disturbance and waves produced at the back of a moving boat ▷ **PHRASE ⑥** If you **wash your hands of** something, you refuse to have anything more to do with it.

wash up VERB ① If you wash up, you wash the dishes, pans, and cutlery used in preparing and eating a meal. **②** If something is washed up on land, it is carried by a river or sea and left there • *A body had been washed up on the beach.*

washbasin, washbasins **NOUN** a deep bowl, usually fixed to a wall, with taps for hot and cold water.

washer, washers **NOUN ①** a thin, flat ring of metal or plastic which is placed over a bolt before the nut is screwed on, so that it is fixed more tightly. **②** In Australian English, a small piece of towelling for washing yourself.

washing NOUN Washing consists of clothes and bedding which need to be washed or are in the process of being washed and dried.

washing machine, washing machines **NOUN** a machine for washing clothes in.

washing-up NOUN If you do the washing-up, you wash the dishes, pans, and cutlery which have been used in the cooking and eating of a meal.

wasp, wasps **NOUN** an insect with yellow and black stripes across its body, which can sting like a bee.

wastage NOUN Wastage is loss and misuse of something • *wastage of resources*.

waste, wastes, wasting, wasted
VERB ❶ If you waste time, money, or energy, you use too much of it on something that is not important or necessary. ❷ If you waste an opportunity, you do not take advantage of it when it is available. ❸ If you say that something is wasted on someone, you mean that it is too good, too clever, or too sophisticated for them • *This book is wasted on us.*
▷ NOUN ❹ If an activity is a waste of time, money, or energy, it is not important or necessary. ❺ Waste is the use of more money or some other resource than is necessary. ❻ Waste is also material that is no longer wanted, or material left over from a useful process • *nuclear waste*.
▷ ADJECTIVE ❼ unwanted in its present form • *waste paper*. ❽ Waste land is land which is not used or looked after by anyone.
waste away VERB If someone is wasting away, they are becoming very thin and weak because they are ill or not eating properly.
● SIMILAR WORDS: ❶ fritter away,
● misuse, squander ❺ misuse,
● squandering

wasted ADJECTIVE unnecessary • *a wasted journey*.

wasteful ADJECTIVE extravagant or causing waste by using something in a careless and inefficient way.
● SIMILAR WORDS: extravagant,
● prodigal, spendthrift

wasteland, wastelands NOUN A

wasteland is land which is of no use because it is infertile or has been misused.

wasting ADJECTIVE A wasting disease is one that gradually reduces the strength and health of the body.

watch, watches, watching, watched
NOUN ❶ a small clock usually worn on a strap on the wrist. ❷ a period of time during which a guard is kept over something ▷ VERB ❸ If you watch something, you look at it for some time and pay close attention to what is happening. ❹ If you watch someone or something, you take care of them. ❺ If you watch a situation, you pay attention to it or are aware of it • *I had watched Jimmy's progress with interest.*
watch out VERB ❶ If you watch out for something, you keep alert to see if it is near you • *Watch out for more fog and ice.* ❷ If you tell someone to watch out, you are warning them to be very careful.

watchdog, watchdogs NOUN ❶ a dog used to guard property. ❷ a person or group whose job is to make sure that companies do not act illegally or irresponsibly.

watchful ADJECTIVE careful to notice everything that is happening • *the watchful eye of her father.*

watchman, watchmen NOUN a person whose job is to guard property.

water, waters, watering, watered
NOUN ❶ (SCIENCE) Water is a clear, colourless, tasteless, and odourless liquid that is necessary for all plant and animal life. ❷ You use water or waters to refer to a large area of water,

a b c d e f g h i j k l m n o p q r s t u v **w** x y z

▷ SPELLING NOTE: *there's SAND in my SANDwich (sandwich)*

such as a lake or sea • *the black waters
of the lake.* ▷ **VERB** ❸ If you water a
plant or an animal, you give it water to
drink. ❹ If your eyes water, you have
tears in them because they are
hurting. ❺ If your mouth waters, it
produces extra saliva, usually because
you think of or can smell something
appetizing.
water down VERB If you water
something down, you make it weaker.

watercolour, watercolours **NOUN**
❶ Watercolours are paints for
painting pictures, which are diluted
with water or put on the paper using a
wet brush. ❷ a picture which has
been painted using watercolours.

watercress NOUN Watercress is a
small plant which grows in streams
and pools. Its leaves taste hot and are
eaten in salads.

water cycle NOUN (GEOGRAPHY)
The water cycle is the continuous
process in which water evaporates
from the sea, forming clouds. The
clouds break as rain, which makes its
way back to the sea, where the
process starts again.

waterfall, waterfalls **NOUN**
(GEOGRAPHY) A waterfall is water from
a river or stream as it flows over the
edge of a steep cliff in hills or
mountains and falls to the ground
below.

waterfront, waterfronts **NOUN** a
street or piece of land next to an area
of water such as a river or harbour.

watering can, watering cans
NOUN a container with a handle and
a long spout, which you use to water
plants.

waterlogged ADJECTIVE Land
that is waterlogged is so wet that the
soil cannot contain any more water, so
that some water remains on the
surface of the ground.

watermelon, watermelons **NOUN**
a large, round fruit which has a hard
green skin and red juicy flesh.

waterproof, waterproofs
ADJECTIVE ❶ not letting water pass
through • *waterproof clothing.*
▷ **NOUN** ❷ a coat which keeps water
out.

water quality NOUN
(GEOGRAPHY) a measurement of how
pure a body of water is.

watershed, watersheds **NOUN** an
event or period which marks a turning
point or the beginning of a new way of
life • *a watershed in European history.*

watersider, watersiders **NOUN** In
Australian and New Zealand English, a
person who loads and unloads the
cargo from ships.

water-skiing NOUN Water-skiing
is the sport of skimming over the
water on skis while being pulled by a
boat.

water table, water tables **NOUN**
(GEOGRAPHY) The water table is the
level below the surface of the ground
at which water can be found.

watertight ADJECTIVE
❶ Something that is watertight does
not allow water to pass through.
❷ An agreement or an argument that
is watertight has been so carefully put
together that nobody should be able
to find a fault in it.

waterway, waterways **NOUN** a

canal, river, or narrow channel of sea which ships or boats can sail along.

waterworks NOUN A waterworks is the system of pipes, filters, and tanks where the public supply of water is stored and cleaned, and from where it is distributed.

watery ADJECTIVE ❶ pale or weak • *a watery smile.* ❷ Watery food or drink contains a lot of water or is thin like water.

watt, watts [*Said wot*] NOUN a unit of measurement of electrical power.

wattle, wattles [*Said wot-tl*] NOUN an Australian acacia tree with spikes of brightly coloured flowers.

wave, waves, waving, waved VERB ❶ If you wave your hand, you move it from side to side, usually to say hello or goodbye. ❷ If you wave someone somewhere or wave them on, you make a movement with your hand to tell them which way to go. ❸ If you wave something, you hold it up and move it from side to side • *The doctor waved a piece of paper at him.* ▷ NOUN ❹ a ridge of water on the surface of the sea caused by wind or by tides. ❺ A wave is the form in which some types of energy such as heat, light, or sound travel through a substance. ❻ A wave of sympathy, alarm, or panic is a steady increase in it which spreads through you or through a group of people. ❼ an increase in a type of activity or behaviour • *the crime wave.*
● SIMILAR WORDS: ❸ brandish, ● flourish

wave-cut notch, wave-cut notches NOUN (GEOGRAPHY) a place

where a cliff is eroded by the sea at the high-water mark.

wave-cut platform, wave-cut platforms NOUN (GEOGRAPHY) a flat surface at the base of a cliff formed after erosion by the sea has created a wave-cut notch which eventually causes the cliff above it to fall away.

wavelength, wavelengths NOUN ❶ the distance between the same point on two adjacent waves of energy. ❷ the size of radio wave which a particular radio station uses to broadcast its programmes.

waver, wavers, wavering, wavered VERB ❶ If you waver or if your confidence or beliefs waver, you are no longer as firm, confident, or sure in your beliefs • *Ben has never wavered from his belief.* ❷ If something wavers, it moves slightly • *The gun did not waver in his hand.*

wavy, wavier, waviest ADJECTIVE having waves or regular curves • *wavy hair.*

wax, waxes, waxing, waxed NOUN ❶ Wax is a solid, slightly shiny substance made of fat or oil and used to make candles and polish. ❷ Wax is also the sticky yellow substance in your ears ▷ VERB ❸ If you wax a surface, you treat it or cover it with a thin layer of wax, especially to polish it. ❹ FORMAL If you wax eloquent, you talk in an eloquent way.

way, ways NOUN ❶ A way of doing something is the manner of doing it • *an excellent way of cooking meat.* ❷ The ways of a person or group are their customs or their normal behaviour • *Their ways are certainly*

▷ SPELLING NOTE: *Eddy Ant thinks mEAt is a grEAt trEAt to EAt (-ea-)*

different. ❸ The way you feel about something is your attitude to it or your opinion about it. ❹ If you have a way with people or things, you are very skilful at dealing with them. ❺ The way to a particular place is the route that you take to get there. ❻ If you go or look a particular way, you go or look in that direction • *She glanced the other way.* ❼ If you divide something a number of ways, you divide it into that number of parts. ❽ 'Way' is used with words such as 'little' or 'long' to say how far off in distance or time something is • *They lived a long way away.* ▷ **PHRASE** ❾ If something or someone is **in the way**, they prevent you from moving freely or seeing clearly. ❿ You say **by the way** when adding something to what you are saying • *By the way, I asked Brad to drop in.* ⓫ If you **go out of your way** to do something, you make a special effort to do it.
● **SIMILAR WORDS:** ❺ course, ● path, route

wayside **PHRASE** If someone or something **falls by the wayside**, they fail in what they are trying to do, or become forgotten and ignored.

wayward **ADJECTIVE** difficult to control and likely to change suddenly • *your wayward husband.*

WC, WCs **NOUN** a toilet. WC is an abbreviation for 'water closet'.

we **PRONOUN** A speaker or writer uses 'we' to refer to himself or herself and one or more other people • *We are going to see Eddie.*

weak, weaker, weakest **ADJECTIVE**
❶ not having much strength • *weak from lack of sleep.* ❷ If something is

weak, it is likely to break or fail • *Russia's weak economy.* ❸ If you describe someone as weak, you mean they are easily influenced by other people. **weakly** **ADVERB**
● **SIMILAR WORDS:** ❶ feeble, frail, ● puny

weaken, weakens, weakening, weakened ❶ If someone weakens something, they make it less strong or certain. ❷ If someone weakens, they become less certain about something.

weakling, weaklings **NOUN** a person who lacks physical strength or who is weak in character or health.

weakness, weaknesses **NOUN**
❶ Weakness is lack of moral or physical strength. ❷ If you have a weakness for something, you have a great liking for it • *a weakness for whisky.*

wealth **NOUN** ❶ (GEOGRAPHY) Wealth is the large amount of money or property which someone owns. ❷ A wealth of something is a lot of it • *a wealth of information.*
● **SIMILAR WORDS:** ❶ fortune, ● prosperity, riches

wealthy, wealthier, wealthiest **ADJECTIVE** having a large amount of money, property, or other valuable things.
● **SIMILAR WORDS:** affluent, rich, ● well-off

wean, weans, weaning, weaned **VERB** To wean a baby or animal is to start feeding it food other than its mother's milk.

weapon, weapons **NOUN** ❶ an object used to kill or hurt people in a

fight or war. ❷ anything which can be used to get the better of an opponent • *Surprise was his only weapon.*
weaponry NOUN

wear, wears, wearing, wore, worn
VERB ❶ When you wear something such as clothes, make-up, or jewellery, you have them on your body or face. ❷ If you wear a particular expression, it shows on your face. ❸ If something wears, it becomes thinner or worse in condition ▷ **NOUN ❹** You can refer to clothes that are suitable for a particular time or occasion as a kind of wear • *beach wear.* ❺ Wear is the amount or type of use that something has and which causes damage or change to it • *signs of wear.*
wear down VERB If you wear people down, you weaken them by repeatedly doing something or asking them to do something.
wear off VERB If a feeling such as pain wears off, it gradually disappears.
wear out VERB ❶ When something wears out or when you wear it out, it is used so much that it becomes thin, weak, and no longer usable. ❷ INFORMAL If you wear someone out, you make them feel extremely tired.

wear and tear NOUN Wear and tear is the damage caused to something by normal use.

wearing ADJECTIVE Someone or something that is wearing makes you feel extremely tired.

weary, wearier, weariest; wearies, wearying, wearied **ADJECTIVE ❶** very tired ▷ **VERB ❷** If you weary of something, you become tired of it.
wearily ADVERB weariness NOUN

weasel, weasels **NOUN** a small wild animal with a long, thin body and short legs.

weather, weathers, weathering, weathered **NOUN ❶** (GEOGRAPHY) The weather is the condition of the atmosphere at any particular time and the amount of rain, wind, or sunshine occurring ▷ **VERB ❷** (GEOGRAPHY) If something such as rock or wood weathers, it changes colour or shape as a result of being exposed to the wind, rain, or sun. ❸ If you weather a problem or difficulty, you come through it safely ▷ **PHRASE ❹** If you are **under the weather**, you feel slightly ill.

weather forecast, weather forecasts **NOUN** a statement saying what the weather will be like the next day or for the next few days.

weather vane, weather vanes **NOUN** a metal object on the roof of a building which turns round in the wind and shows which way the wind is blowing.

weave, weaves, weaving, wove, woven **VERB ❶** To weave cloth is to make it by crossing threads over and under each other, especially by using a machine called a loom. ❷ If you weave your way somewhere, you go there by moving from side to side through and round the obstacles ▷ **NOUN ❸** The weave of cloth is the way in which the threads are arranged and the pattern that they form • *a tight weave.*

weaver, weavers **NOUN** a person who weaves cloth.

web, webs **NOUN ❶** a fine net of

a b c d e f g h i j k l m n o p q r s t u v **w** x y z

threads that a spider makes from a sticky substance which it produces in its body. ❷ something that has a complicated structure or pattern • *a web of lies.* ❸ The Web is the same as the World Wide Web.

webbed ADJECTIVE Webbed feet have the toes connected by a piece of skin.

weblog, weblogs NOUN a person's online diary or journal that he or she puts on the Internet so that other people can read it. It is also shortened to **blog**.

website, websites NOUN a publication on the World Wide Web which contains information about a particular subject.

wed, weds, wedding, wedded or wed VERB OLD-FASHIONED If you wed someone or if you wed, you get married.

wedding, weddings NOUN (RE) a marriage ceremony.

wedge, wedges, wedging, wedged VERB ❶ If you wedge something, you force it to remain there by holding it there tightly, or by fixing something next to it to prevent it from moving • *I shut the shed door and wedged it with a log of wood.* ▷ NOUN ❷ a piece of something such as wood, metal, or rubber with one pointed edge and one thick edge which is used to wedge something. ❸ a piece of something that has a thick triangular shape • *a wedge of cheese.*

wedlock NOUN OLD-FASHIONED Wedlock is the state of being married.

Wednesday, Wednesdays NOUN Wednesday is the day between Tuesday and Thursday.

● **WORD HISTORY:** from Old English
● *Wodnes dæg* meaning 'Woden's
● day'

wee, weer, weest ADJECTIVE In Scotland, a term for very small.

weed, weeds, weeding, weeded NOUN ❶ a wild plant that prevents cultivated plants from growing properly ▷ VERB ❷ If you weed a place, you remove the weeds from it. **weed out** VERB If you weed out unwanted things, you get rid of them.

weedkiller, weedkillers NOUN (SCIENCE) a chemical used for killing weeds.

week, weeks NOUN ❶ a period of seven days, especially one beginning on a Sunday and ending on a Saturday. ❷ A week is also the number of hours you spend at work during a week • *a 35-hour week.* ❸ The week can refer to the part of a week that does not include Saturday and Sunday • *They are working during the week.*

weekday, weekdays NOUN any day except Saturday and Sunday.

weekend, weekends NOUN Saturday and Sunday.

weekly, weeklies ADJECTIVE OR ADVERB ❶ happening or appearing once a week ▷ NOUN ❷ a newspaper or magazine that is published once a week.

weep, weeps, weeping, wept VERB ❶ If someone weeps, they cry. ❷ If something such as a wound weeps, it oozes blood or other liquid.

weevil, weevils NOUN a type of

▷ SPELLING NOTE: On WEDNESday Wayne WED NESta (Wed*nes*day)

beetle which eats grain, seeds, or plants.

weft NOUN The weft of a piece of woven material is the threads which are passed sideways in and out of the threads held in a loom.

weigh, weighs, weighing, weighed VERB ❶ If something weighs a particular amount, that is how heavy it is. ❷ If you weigh something, you measure how heavy it is using scales. ❸ If you weigh facts or words, you think about them carefully before coming to a decision or before speaking. ❹ If a problem weighs on you or weighs upon you, it makes you very worried.

weigh down VERB ❶ If a load weighs you down, it stops you moving easily. ❷ If you are weighed down by a difficulty, it is making you very worried.

weigh up VERB If you weigh up a person or a situation, you make an assessment of them.

weight, weights, weighting, weighted NOUN ❶ (MATHS) The weight of something is its heaviness. ❷ a metal object which has a certain known heaviness. Weights are used with sets of scales in order to weigh things. ❸ any heavy object. ❹ The weight of something is its large amount or importance which makes it hard to fight against or contradict • *the weight of the law.* ▷ VERB ❺ If you weight something or weight it down, you make it heavier, often so that it cannot move ▷ PHRASE ❻ If you **pull your weight**, you work just as hard as other people involved in the same activity • *We won't succeed unless everyone pulls their weight.*

weighted ADJECTIVE A system that is weighted in favour of a particular person or group is organized in such a way that this person or group will have an advantage.

weightless ADJECTIVE (SCIENCE) Something that is weightless has no weight or very little weight, for example because it is in space and not affected by the Earth's gravity. **weightlessness**

weightlifting NOUN Weightlifting is the sport of lifting heavy weights in competition or for exercise. **weightlifter** NOUN

weighty, weightier, weightiest ADJECTIVE serious or important • *a weighty problem.*

weir, weirs [rhymes with **near**] NOUN a low dam which is built across a river to raise the water level, control the flow of water, or change its direction.

weird, weirder, weirdest [Said **weerd**] ADJECTIVE strange or odd. **weirdly** ADVERB
● SIMILAR WORDS: bizarre, odd, strange

weirdo, weirdos [Said **weer-doe**] NOUN INFORMAL If you call someone a weirdo, you mean they behave in a strange way.

welcome, welcomes, welcoming, welcomed VERB ❶ If you welcome a visitor, you greet them in a friendly way when they arrive. ❷ 'Welcome' can be said as a greeting to a visitor who has just arrived. ❸ If you welcome something, you approve of it and support it • *He welcomed the decision.* ▷ NOUN ❹ a greeting to a visitor • *a warm welcome.*

▷ **ADJECTIVE** ❺ If someone is welcome at a place, they will be warmly received there. ❻ If something is welcome, it brings pleasure or is accepted gratefully • *a welcome rest.* ❼ If you tell someone they are welcome to something or welcome to do something, you mean you are willing for them to have or to do it. **welcoming ADJECTIVE**

weld, welds, welding, welded **VERB** To weld two pieces of metal together is to join them by heating their edges and fixing them together so that when they cool they harden into one piece. **welder NOUN**

welfare NOUN ❶ The welfare of a person or group is their general state of health and comfort. ❷ Welfare services are provided to help with people's living conditions and financial problems • *welfare workers.*

welfare state NOUN The welfare state is a system in which the government uses money from taxes to provide health care and education services, and to give benefits to people who are old, unemployed, or sick.

well, better, best; wells, welling, welled **ADVERB** ❶ If something goes well, it happens in a satisfactory way • *The interview went well.* ❷ in a good, skilful, or pleasing way • *He draws well.* ❸ thoroughly and completely • *well established.* ❹ kindly • *We treat our employees well.* ❺ If something may well or could well happen, it is likely to happen. ❻ You use 'well' to emphasize an adjective, adverb, or phrase • *He was well aware of that.* ▷ **ADJECTIVE** ❼ If you are well, you are healthy ▷ **PHRASE** ❽ As well

means also • *He was a bus driver as well.* ❾ **As well as** means in addition to • *a meal which includes meat or fish, as well as rice.* ❿ If you say you **may as well** or **might as well** do something, you mean you will do it although you are not keen to do it ▷ **NOUN** ⓫ a hole drilled in the ground from which water, oil, or gas is obtained ▷ **VERB** ⓬ If tears well or well up, they appear in someone's eyes.

well-advised ADJECTIVE sensible or wise • *Bill would be well-advised to retire.*

well-balanced ADJECTIVE sensible and without serious emotional problems • *a well-balanced happy teenager.*

wellbeing NOUN Someone's wellbeing is their health and happiness.

well-earned ADJECTIVE thoroughly deserved.

well-heeled ADJECTIVE INFORMAL wealthy.

well-informed ADJECTIVE having a great deal of knowledge about a subject or subjects.

wellington, wellingtons **NOUN** Wellingtons or wellington boots are long waterproof rubber boots.

well-meaning ADJECTIVE A well-meaning person tries to be helpful but is often unsuccessful.

well-off ADJECTIVE INFORMAL quite wealthy.

well-to-do ADJECTIVE quite wealthy.

▷ SPELLING NOTE: *LEt's measure the angLE (angle)*

well-worn ADJECTIVE ❶ A well-worn expression or saying has been used too often and has become boring. ❷ A well-worn object or piece of clothing has been used and worn so much that it looks old and shabby.

welly, wellies NOUN INFORMAL Wellies are wellingtons.

Welsh ADJECTIVE ❶ belonging or relating to Wales ▷ NOUN ❷ Welsh is a language spoken in parts of Wales.

Welshman, Welshmen NOUN a man who comes from Wales. **Welshwoman** NOUN

welt, welts NOUN a raised mark on someone's skin made by a blow from something like a whip or a stick.

welter NOUN FORMAL A welter of things is a large number of them that happen or appear together in a state of confusion • *a welter of rumours*.

wench, wenches NOUN OLD-FASHIONED a woman or young girl.

wept the past tense and past participle of **weep**.

were a past tense of **be**.

werewolf, werewolves NOUN In horror stories, a werewolf is a person who changes into a wolf.
- **WORD HISTORY:** from Old English *wer* + *wulf* meaning 'man wolf'

Wesak [Said wess-suck] NOUN Wesak is the Buddhist festival celebrating the Buddha, held in May.

west NOUN ❶ The west is the direction in which you look to see the sun set. ❷ The west of a place or country is the part which is towards the west when you are in the centre

• *the west of America*. ❸ The West refers to the countries of North America and western and southern Europe ▷ ADVERB OR ADJECTIVE ❹ West means towards the west ▷ ADJECTIVE ❺ A west wind blows from the west.

westerly (GEOGRAPHY) ADJECTIVE ❶ When talking about a place, westerly means situated in the west • *France's most westerly region*. ❷ coming from the west • *a westerly wind*.

western, westerns ADJECTIVE ❶ in or from the west. ❷ coming from or associated with the countries of North America and western and southern Europe • *western dress*. ▷ NOUN ❸ a book or film about life in the west of America in the nineteenth century.

West Indian, West Indians NOUN someone who comes from the West Indies.

westward or **westwards** ADVERB Westward or westwards means towards the west • *He stared westwards towards the clouds*.

wet, wetter, wettest; wets, wetting, wet or wetted ADJECTIVE ❶ If something is wet, it is covered in water or another liquid. ❷ If the weather is wet, it is raining. ❸ If something such as paint, ink, or cement is wet, it is not yet dry or solid. ❹ INFORMAL If you say someone is wet, you mean they are weak and lacking confidence • *Don't be so wet!* ▷ NOUN ❺ In Australia, the wet is the rainy season ▷ VERB ❻ To wet something is to put water or some other liquid over it. ❼ If people wet

▷ SPELLING NOTE: *A Rude Idiot Thought He Might Eat Toffee In Church (arithmetic)*

A
B
C
D
E
F
G
H
I
J
K
L
M
N
O
P
Q
R
S
T
U
V
W
X
Y
Z

themselves or wet their beds, they urinate in their clothes or bed because they cannot control their bladder. **wetness NOUN**

wet suit, wet suits **NOUN** a close-fitting rubber suit which a diver wears to keep his or her body warm.

whack, whacks, whacking, whacked **VERB** If you whack someone or something, you hit them hard.

whale, whales **NOUN** a very large sea mammal which breathes through a hole on the top of its head.

whaling NOUN Whaling is the work of hunting and killing whales for oil or food.

wharf, wharves [Said **worf**] **NOUN** a platform beside a river or the sea, where ships load or unload.

what PRONOUN ❶ 'What' is used in questions • What time is it? ❷ 'What' is used in indirect questions and statements • I don't know what you mean. ❸ 'What' can be used at the beginning of a clause to refer to something with a particular quality • It is impossible to decide what is real and what is invented. ▷ **ADJECTIVE** ❹ 'What' can be used at the beginning of a clause to show that you are talking about the whole amount that is available to you • Their spouses try to earn what money they can. ❺ You say 'what' to emphasize an opinion or reaction • What nonsense! ▷ **PHRASE** ❻ You say **what about** at the beginning of a question when you are making a suggestion or offer • What about a drink?

whatever PRONOUN ❶ You use 'whatever' to refer to anything or

everything of a particular type • He said he would do whatever he could. ❷ You use 'whatever' when you do not know the precise nature of something • Whatever it is, I don't like it. ▷ **CONJUNCTION** ❸ You use 'whatever' to mean no matter what • Whatever happens, you have to behave decently. ▷ **ADVERB** ❹ You use 'whatever' to emphasize a negative statement or a question • You have no proof whatever • Whatever is wrong with you?

whatsoever ADVERB You use 'whatsoever' to emphasize a negative statement • I have no memory of it whatsoever.

wheat NOUN Wheat is a cereal plant grown for its grain which is used to make flour.

wheel, wheels, wheeling, wheeled **NOUN** ❶ (D & T) a circular object which turns on a rod attached to its centre. Wheels are fixed underneath vehicles so that they can move along. ❷ (D & T) The wheel of a car is its steering wheel ▷ **VERB** ❸ If you wheel something such as a bicycle, you push it. ❹ If someone or something wheels, they move round in the shape of a circle • Cameron wheeled around and hit him.

wheelbarrow, wheelbarrows **NOUN** a small cart with a single wheel at the front, used for carrying things in the garden.

wheelchair, wheelchairs **NOUN** a chair with wheels in which sick, injured, or disabled people can move around.

wheeze, wheezes, wheezing,

▷ SPELLING NOTE: Beautiful Elephants Are Usually Tiny (_beautiful_)

wheezed VERB If someone wheezes, they breathe with difficulty, making a whistling sound, usually because they have a chest complaint such as asthma. **wheezy ADJECTIVE**

whelk, whelks **NOUN** a snail-like shellfish with a strong shell and a soft edible body.

when ADVERB ❶ You use 'when' to ask what time something happened or will happen • *When are you leaving?* ▷ **CONJUNCTION** ❷ You use 'when' to refer to a time in the past • *I met him when I was sixteen.* ❸ You use 'when' to introduce the reason for an opinion, comment, or question • *How did you pass the exam when you hadn't studied for it?* ❹ 'When' is used to mean although • *He drives when he could walk.*

whence ADVERB OR CONJUNCTION OLD-FASHIONED Whence means from where.
● **USAGE NOTE:** You should not
● write *from whence* because *whence*
● already means 'from where'

whenever CONJUNCTION Whenever means at any time, or every time that something happens • *I still go on courses whenever I can.*

where ADVERB ❶ You use 'where' to ask which place something is in, is coming from, or is going to • *Where is Philip?* ▷ **CONJUNCTION, PRONOUN, OR ADVERB** ❷ You use 'where' when asking about or referring to something • *I hardly know where to begin.* ▷ **CONJUNCTION** ❸ You use 'where' to refer to the place in which something is situated or happening • *I don't know where we are.* ❹ 'Where' can introduce a clause that contrasts

with the other part of the sentence • *A teacher will be listened to, where a parent might not.*

whereabouts NOUN ❶ The whereabouts of a person or thing is the place where they are ▷ **ADVERB** ❷ You use 'whereabouts' when you are asking more precisely where something is • *Whereabouts in Canada are you from?*

whereas CONJUNCTION Whereas introduces a comment that contrasts with the other part of the sentence • *Her eyes were blue, whereas mine were brown.*

whereby PRONOUN FORMAL Whereby means by which • *a new system whereby you pay the bill quarterly.*

whereupon CONJUNCTION FORMAL Whereupon means at which point • *His enemies rejected his message, whereupon he tried again.*

wherever CONJUNCTION ❶ 'Wherever' means in every place or situation • *Alex heard the same thing wherever he went.* ❷ You use 'wherever' to show that you do not know where a place or person is • *the nearest police station, wherever that is.*

wherewithal NOUN If you have the wherewithal to do something, you have enough money to do it.

whet, whets, whetting, whetted **PHRASE** To **whet someone's appetite** for something, means to increase their desire for it.

whether CONJUNCTION You use 'whether' when you are talking about two or more alternatives • *I don't know*

▷ SPELLING NOTE: Betty Eats Cakes And Uses Seven Eggs (*because*)

a
b
c
d
e
f
g
h
i
j
k
l
m
n
o
p
q
r
s
t
u
v
w
x
y
z

WHAT DOES WHICH DO?

Which is a relative pronoun. A relative pronoun replaces a noun which links two different parts of a sentence.

Relative pronouns always refer back to a word in the earlier part of the sentence. The word they refer to is called the **antecedent**. (In the examples that follow, the antecedents are underlined.)

*I have <u>a friend</u> **who** lives in Rome.*
*We could go to <u>a place</u> **that** I know.*

Which is only used when the antecedent is not a person:
*We took <u>the road</u> **which** leads to the sea.*

Also look at the grammar box at **relative pronoun**.

whether that's true or false.

whey [rhymes with **day**] NOUN Whey is the watery liquid that is separated from the curds in sour milk when cheese is made.

which ADJECTIVE OR PRONOUN
❶ You use 'which' to ask about alternatives or to refer to a choice between alternatives • *Which room are you in?* ▷ PRONOUN ❷ 'Which' at the beginning of a clause identifies the thing you are talking about or gives more information about it • *certain wrongs which exist in our society.*
● USAGE NOTE: See the usage note at *that*
▶ SEE GRAMMAR BOX ABOVE

whichever ADJECTIVE OR PRONOUN You use 'whichever' when you are talking about different alternatives or possibilities • *Make your pizzas round or square, whichever you prefer.*

whiff, whiffs NOUN ❶ a slight smell of something. ❷ a slight sign or trace of something • *a whiff of criticism.*

while, whiles, whiling, whiled
CONJUNCTION ❶ If something

happens while something else is happening, the two things happen at the same time. ❷ While also means but • *Men tend to gaze more, while women dart quick glances.* ▷ NOUN ❸ a period of time • *a little while earlier.* ▷ PHRASE ❹ If an action or activity is **worth your while**, it will be helpful or useful to you if you do it.
while away VERB If you while away the time in a particular way, you pass the time that way because you have nothing else to do.

whilst CONJUNCTION Whilst means the same as while.

whim, whims NOUN a sudden desire or fancy.
● SIMILAR WORDS: fancy, impulse

whimper, whimpers, whimpering, whimpered VERB ❶ When children or animals whimper, they make soft, low, unhappy sounds. ❷ If you whimper something, you say it in an unhappy or frightened way, as if you are about to cry.

whimsical ADJECTIVE unusual and slightly playful • *an endearing, whimsical charm.*

▷ SPELLING NOTE: *there's a rAKE in the brAKEs (brake)*

whine, whines, whining, whined
VERB ❶ To whine is to make a long, high-pitched noise, especially one which sounds sad or unpleasant. **❷** If someone whines about something, they complain about it in an annoying way ▷ **NOUN ❸** A whine is the noise made by something or someone whining.

whinge, whinges, whinging or whingeing, whinged **VERB** If someone whinges about something, they complain about it in an annoying way.

whinny, whinnies, whinnying, whinnied **VERB** When a horse whinnies, it neighs softly.

whip, whips, whipping, whipped
NOUN ❶ a thin piece of leather or rope attached to a handle, which is used for hitting people or animals ▷ **VERB ❷** If you whip a person or animal, you hit them with a whip. **❸** When the wind whips something, it strikes it. **❹** If you whip something out or off, you take it out or off very quickly • *She had whipped off her glasses.* **❺** If you whip cream or eggs, you beat them until they are thick and frothy or stiff.
whip up VERB If you whip up a strong emotion, you make people feel it • *The thought of her unfairness whipped up his temper.*

whip bird, whip birds **NOUN** an Australian bird whose cry ends with a sound like the crack of a whip.

whiplash injury, whiplash injuries **NOUN** a neck injury caused by your head suddenly jerking forwards and then back again, for example in a car accident.

whippet, whippets **NOUN** a small, thin dog used for racing.

whirl, whirls, whirling, whirled **VERB ❶** When something whirls, or when you whirl it round, it turns round very fast ▷ **NOUN ❷** You can refer to a lot of intense activity as a whirl of activity.

whirlpool, whirlpools **NOUN** a small circular area in a river or the sea where the water is moving quickly round and round so that objects floating near it are pulled into its centre.

whirlwind, whirlwinds **NOUN ❶** a tall column of air which spins round and round very fast ▷ **ADJECTIVE ❷** more rapid than usual • *a whirlwind tour.*

whirr, whirrs, whirring, whirred; *also spelt* **whir** **VERB ❶** When something such as a machine whirrs, it makes a series of low sounds so fast that it sounds like one continuous sound ▷ **NOUN ❷** the noise made by something whirring.

whisk, whisks, whisking, whisked **VERB ❶** If you whisk someone or something somewhere, you take them there quickly • *We were whisked away into a private room.* **❷** If you whisk eggs or cream, you stir air into them quickly ▷ **NOUN ❸** a kitchen tool used for quickly stirring air into eggs or cream.

whisker, whiskers **NOUN** The whiskers of an animal such as a cat or mouse are the long, stiff hairs near its mouth.

whisky, whiskies; **NOUN** Whisky is a strong alcoholic drink made from grain such as barley.

a b c d e f g h i j k l m n o p q r s t u v **w** x y z

▷ SPELLING NOTE: *you'll brEAK that Electrical Aerial, Kitty (break)*

WORD HISTORY: from Scottish Gaelic *uisge beatha* meaning 'water of life'

whisper, whispers, whispering, whispered **VERB** ① When you whisper, you talk to someone very quietly, using your breath and not your throat ▷ **NOUN** ② If you talk in a whisper, you whisper.

whist NOUN Whist is a card game for four players in which one pair of players tries to win more tricks than the other pair.

whistle, whistles, whistling, whistled **VERB** ① When you whistle a tune or whistle, you produce a clear musical sound by forcing your breath out between your lips. ② If something whistles, it makes a loud, high sound • *The kettle whistled.* ▷ **NOUN** ③ A whistle is the sound something or someone makes when they whistle. ④ a small metal tube that you blow into to produce a whistling sound.

whit NOUN FORMAL You say 'not a whit' or 'no whit' to emphasize that something is not the case at all • *It does not matter one whit to the customer.*

white, whiter, whitest; whites **NOUN OR ADJECTIVE** ① White is the lightest possible colour. ② Someone who is white has a pale skin and is of European origin ▷ **ADJECTIVE** ③ If someone goes white, their face becomes very pale because they are afraid, shocked, or ill. ④ White coffee contains milk or cream ▷ **NOUN** ⑤ The white of an egg is the transparent liquid surrounding the yolk which turns white when it is cooked. **whiteness NOUN**

white blood cell, white blood cells **NOUN** (SCIENCE) Your white blood cells are the cells in your blood that cannot carry oxygen.

white-collar ADJECTIVE White-collar workers work in offices rather than doing manual work • *a white-collar union.*

white lie, white lies **NOUN** a harmless lie, especially one told to prevent someone's feelings from being hurt.

white paper, white papers **NOUN** A white paper is an official report published by the British Government, which gives the policy of the Government on a particular subject.

whitewash NOUN ① Whitewash is a mixture of lime and water used for painting walls white. ② an attempt to hide unpleasant facts • *the refusal to accept official whitewash in the enquiry.*

whither ADVERB OR CONJUNCTION OLD-FASHIONED Whither means to what place • *Whither shall I wander?*

whiting NOUN a sea fish related to the cod.

whittle, whittles, whittling, whittled **VERB** If you whittle a piece of wood, you shape it by shaving or cutting small pieces off it. **whittle away** or **whittle down VERB** To whittle away at something or to whittle it down means to make it smaller or less effective • *The 250 entrants had been whittled down to 34.*

whizz, whizzes, whizzing, whizzed; *also spelt* whiz **VERB** INFORMAL If you whizz somewhere, you move there

a b c d e f g h i j k l m n o p q r s t u v w x y z

WHAT DOES WHO DO?

Who is a relative pronoun. A relative pronoun replaces a noun which links two different parts of a sentence.

Relative pronouns always refer back to a word in the earlier part of the sentence. The word they refer to is called the **antecedent**. (In the examples that follow, the antecedents are underlined.)
*I have <u>a friend</u> **who** lives in Rome.*
*We could go to <u>a place</u> **that** I know.*

The forms *who*, *whom*, and *whose* are used when the antecedent is a

person. *Who* indicates the subject of the verb:
*It was <u>the same person</u> **who** saw me yesterday.*
*It was <u>the person</u> **whom** I saw yesterday.*

The distinction between *who* and *whom* is often ignored in everyday English, and *who* is often used as the object:
*It was <u>the person</u> **who** I saw yesterday.*

Also look at the grammar box at **relative pronoun**.

extremely quickly.

who PRONOUN ❶ You use 'who' when you are asking about someone's identity • *Who gave you that black eye?* ❷ 'Who' at the beginning of a clause refers to the person or people you are talking about • *a shipyard worker who wants to be a postman.*
▶ SEE GRAMMAR BOX ABOVE

whoa [Said woh] INTERJECTION Whoa is a command used to slow down or stop a horse.

whoever PRONOUN ❶ 'Whoever' means the person who • *Whoever bought it for you has to make the claim.* ❷ 'Whoever' also means no matter who • *I pity him, whoever he is.* ❸ 'Whoever' is used in questions give emphasis to who • *Whoever thought of such a thing?*

whole, wholes ADJECTIVE ❶ indicating all of something • *Have the whole cake.* ▷ NOUN ❷ the full amount of something • *the whole of Africa.* ▷ ADVERB ❸ in one piece

• *He swallowed it whole.* ▷ PHRASE ❹ You use **as a whole** to emphasize that you are talking about all of something • *The country as a whole is in a very odd mood.* ❺ You say **on the whole** to mean that something is generally true • *On the whole, we should be glad they are gone.*
wholeness NOUN

wholehearted ADJECTIVE enthusiastic and totally sincere.
wholeheartedly ADVERB

wholemeal ADJECTIVE Wholemeal flour is made from the complete grain of the wheat plant.

wholesale ADJECTIVE OR ADVERB ❶ Wholesale refers to the activity of buying goods cheaply in large quantities and selling them again, especially to shopkeepers • *We buy fruit and vegetables wholesale.* ▷ ADJECTIVE ❷ Wholesale also means done to an excessive extent • *the wholesale destruction of wild plant species.* **wholesaler** NOUN

A
B
C
D
E
F
G
H
I
J
K
L
M
N
O
P
Q
R
S
T
U
V
W
X
Y
Z

WHAT DOES WHOM DO?

Whom is a relative pronoun. A relative pronoun replaces a noun which links two different parts of a sentence.

Relative pronouns always refer back to a word in the earlier part of the sentence. The word they refer to is called the **antecedent**. (In the examples that follow, the antecedents are underlined.)
I have <u>a friend</u> who lives in Rome.
We could go to <u>a place</u> that I know.

The forms *who*, *whom*, and *whose* are used when the antecedent is a person. *Whom* indicates the object of the verb:
It was <u>the same person</u> who saw me yesterday.

It was <u>the person</u> whom I saw yesterday.

The distinction between *who* and *whom* is often ignored in everyday English, and *who* is often used as the object:
It was <u>the person</u> who I saw yesterday.

Whom is used immediately after a preposition. However, if the preposition is separated from the relative pronoun, *who* is usually used:
He is <u>a man</u> in whom I have great confidence.
He is <u>a man</u> who I have great confidence in.

Also look at the grammar box at **relative pronoun**.

---

wholesome ADJECTIVE good and likely to improve your life, behaviour, or health.

wholly [Said **hoe**-lee] **ADVERB** completely.

whom PRONOUN Whom is the object form of 'who' • *the girl whom Albert would marry.*
▶ SEE GRAMMAR BOX ABOVE

whoop, whoops, whooping, whooped **VERB** ❶ If you whoop, you shout loudly in a happy or excited way ▷ **NOUN** ❷ a loud cry of happiness or excitement • *whoops of delight.*

whooping cough [Said **hoop**-ing] **NOUN** an acute infectious disease which makes people cough violently and produce a loud sound when they breathe.

whore, whores [Said **hore**] **NOUN** OFFENSIVE a prostitute.

whose PRONOUN ❶ You use 'whose' to ask who something belongs to • *Whose gun is this?* ❷ You use 'whose' at the beginning of a clause which gives information about something relating or belonging to the thing or person you have just mentioned • *a wealthy gentleman whose marriage is breaking up.*
● **USAGE NOTE:** Many people are
● confused about the difference
● between *whose* and *who's*. *Whose* is
● used to show possession in a
● question or when something is
● being described: *whose bag is this?*
● *the person whose car is blocking the*
● *exit.* *Who's*, with the apostrophe, is
● a short form of *who is* or *who has*:
● *who's that girl? who's got my*
● *ruler?*
▶ SEE GRAMMAR BOX ON PAGE 983

▷ SPELLING NOTE: *The government licenSes Schnapps (licenses)*

WHAT DOES WHOSE DO?

Whose is a relative pronoun. A relative pronoun replaces a noun which links two different parts of a sentence.

Relative pronouns always refer back to a word in the earlier part of the sentence. The word they refer to is called the **antecedent**. (In the examples that follow, the antecedents are underlined.) *I have a friend who lives in Rome. We could go to a place that I know.*

The forms *who*, *whom*, and *whose* are used when the antecedent is a person.

Whose is the possessive form of the relative pronoun. It can refer to things as well as people: *Anna has a sister whose name is Rosie. I found a book whose pages were torn.*

Also look at the grammar box at **relative pronoun**.

a b c d e f g h i j k l m n o p q r s t u v **w** x y z

why ADVERB OR PRONOUN You use 'why' when you are asking about the reason for something, or talking about it • *Why did you do it?* • *He wondered why she suddenly looked happier.*

wick, wicks NOUN A wick is the cord in the middle of a candle, which you set alight • *Trim the wicks of these candles.*

wicked ADJECTIVE ❶ very bad • *a wicked thing to do.* ❷ mischievous in an amusing or attractive way • *His mother has a wicked sense of humour.* **wickedly** ADVERB **wickedness** NOUN

● **WORD HISTORY:** from Old English *wicce* meaning 'witch'
● **SIMILAR WORDS:** ❶ bad, evil, sinful

wicker ADJECTIVE A wicker basket or chair is made from twigs, canes, or reeds that have been woven together.

wicket, wickets NOUN ❶ In cricket, the wicket is one of the two sets of stumps and bails at which the bowler aims the ball. ❷ The grass between

the wickets on a cricket pitch is also called the wicket • *Covers were used to keep rain off the wicket.*

wide, wider, widest ADJECTIVE ❶ measuring a large distance from one side to the other. ❷ If there is a wide variety, range, or selection of something, there are many different kinds of it • *a wide range of colours.* ▷ ADVERB ❸ If you open or spread something wide, you open it to its fullest extent • *The dentist asked him to open his mouth wide.* **widely** ADVERB
● **SIMILAR WORDS:** ❷ broad,
● extensive, large

wide-awake ADJECTIVE completely awake.

widen, widens, widening, widened VERB ❶ If something widens or if you widen it, it becomes bigger from one side to the other. ❷ You can say that something widens when it becomes greater in size or scope • *This language course gives you the opportunity to widen your outlook.*

wide-ranging ADJECTIVE

▷ SPELLING NOTE: have a plEce of plE (*piece*)

A
B
C
D
E
F
G
H
I
J
K
L
M
N
O
P
Q
R
S
T
U
V
W
X
Y
Z

extending over a variety of different things or over a large area • *a wide-ranging survey.*

widespread **ADJECTIVE** existing or happening over a large area or to a great extent • *the widespread use of chemicals.*
   ● **SIMILAR WORDS:** common,
   ● general, universal

widow, widows **NOUN** a woman whose husband has died.

widowed **ADJECTIVE** If someone is widowed, their husband or wife has died.

widower, widowers **NOUN** a man whose wife has died.

width, widths **NOUN** The width of something is the distance from one side or edge to the other.

wield, wields, wielding, wielded *[Said weeld]* **VERB** ❶ If you wield a weapon or tool, you carry it and use it. ❷ If someone wields power, they have it and are able to use it.

wife, wives **NOUN** A man's wife is the woman he is married to.

Wi-Fi **NOUN** a system of accessing the Internet from machines such as laptop computers that aren't physically connected to a network.

wig, wigs **NOUN** a false head of hair worn to cover someone's own hair or to hide their baldness.

wiggle, wiggles, wiggling, wiggled **VERB** ❶ If you wiggle something, you move it up and down or from side to side with small jerky movements ▷ **NOUN** ❷ a small jerky movement.

wigwam, wigwams **NOUN** a kind of

tent used by North American Indians.
   ● **WORD HISTORY:** from American
   ● Indian *wikwam* meaning 'their
   ● house'

wiki, wikis **NOUN** a website (or page within one) that can be edited by anyone who looks it up on the Internet.

wild, wilder, wildest; wilds **ADJECTIVE** ❶ Wild animals, birds, and plants live and grow in natural surroundings and are not looked after by people. ❷ Wild land is natural and has not been cultivated • *wild areas of countryside.* ❸ Wild weather or sea is stormy and rough. ❹ Wild behaviour is excited and uncontrolled. ❺ A wild idea or scheme is original and crazy ▷ **NOUN** ❻ The wild is a free and natural state of living • *There are about 200 left in the wild.* ❼ The wilds are remote areas where few people live, far away from towns. **wildly** **ADVERB**

wilderness, wildernesses **NOUN** an area of natural land which is not cultivated.

wildfire **NOUN** If something spreads like wildfire, it spreads very quickly.

wild-goose chase, wild-goose chases **NOUN** a hopeless or useless search.

wildlife **NOUN** (SCIENCE) Wildlife means wild animals and plants.

Wild West **NOUN** The Wild West was the western part of the United States when it was first being settled by Europeans.

wiles **PLURAL NOUN** Wiles are clever or crafty tricks used to persuade

THE VERBS WILL AND SHALL

The verbs *will* and *shall* have only one form. They do not have a present form ending in -s, and they do not have a present participle, a past tense, or a past participle.

These verbs are used as auxiliary verbs to form the future tense:
She **will** give a talk about Chinese history.
We **shall** arrive on Thursday.

People used to use *shall* to indicate the first person, and *will* to indicate the second person and the third person. However, this distinction is often ignored now:

I **will** see you on Sunday.
I **shall** see you on Sunday.

Shall is always used in questions involving *I* and *we*. *Will* is avoided in these cases:
Shall I put the cat out?
Shall we dance?

Will is always used when making polite requests, giving orders, and indicating persistence. *Shall* is avoided in these cases:
Will you please help me?
Will you be quiet!
She **will** keep going on about Al Pacino.

a
b
c
d
e
f
g
h
i
j
k
l
m
n
o
p
q
r
s
t
u
w
x
y
z

people to do something.

wilful ADJECTIVE ❶ Wilful actions or attitudes are deliberate and often intended to hurt someone • *wilful damage.* ❷ Someone who is wilful is determined to get their own way • *a wilful little boy.* **wilfully** ADVERB
● SIMILAR WORDS: ❷ headstrong
● stubborn

will VERB ❶ You use 'will' to form the future tense • *Robin will be quite annoyed.* ❷ You use 'will' to say that you intend to do something • *I will not deceive you.* ❸ You use 'will' when inviting someone to do or have something • *Will you have another coffee?* ❹ You use 'will' when asking or telling someone to do something • *Will you do me a favour?* • *You will do as I say.* ❺ You use 'will' to say that you are assuming something to be the case • *As you will have gathered, I was surprised.*
▶ SEE GRAMMAR BOX ABOVE

will, wills, willing, willed VERB ❶ If you will something to happen, you try to make it happen by mental effort • *I willed my eyes to open.* ❷ If you will something to someone, you leave it to them when you die • *Penbrook Farm is willed to her.* ▷ NOUN ❸ Will is the determination to do something • *the will to win.* ❹ If something is the will of a person or group, they want it to happen • *the will of the people.* ❺ Your will is a legal document in which you say what you want to happen to your money and property when you die ▷ PHRASE ❻ If you can do something **at will**, you can do it whenever you want • *You can come and go at will.*

willing ADJECTIVE ready and eager to do something • *a willing helper.* **willingly** ADVERB **willingness** NOUN
● SIMILAR WORDS: game, prepared,
● ready

▷ SPELLING NOTE: *I went to see (C) the doctor's new practiCe (practice)*

willow, willows **NOUN** A willow or willow tree is a tree with long, thin branches and narrow leaves that often grows near water.

wilt, wilts, wilting, wilted **VERB** ❶ If a plant wilts, it droops because it needs more water or is dying. ❷ If someone wilts, they gradually lose strength or confidence • *James visibly wilted under pressure.*

wily, wilier, wiliest *[Said* **wie***-lee]* **ADJECTIVE** clever and cunning.

wimp, wimps **NOUN** INFORMAL someone who is feeble and timid.

win, wins, winning, won **VERB** ❶ If you win a fight, game, or argument, you defeat your opponent. ❷ If you win something, you succeed in obtaining it ▷ **NOUN** ❸ a victory in a game or contest.
win over VERB If you win someone over, you persuade them to support you.

wince, winces, wincing, winced **VERB** When you wince, the muscles of your face tighten suddenly because of pain, fear, or distress.

winch, winches, winching, winched **NOUN** ❶ a machine used to lift heavy objects. It consists of a cylinder around which a rope or chain is wound ▷ **VERB** ❷ If you winch an object or person somewhere, you lift, lower, or pull them using a winch.

wind, winds *[rhymes with* **tinned***]* **NOUN** ❶ a current of air moving across the earth's surface. ❷ Your wind is the ability to breathe easily • *Brown had recovered her wind.* ❸ Wind is air swallowed with food or drink, or gas produced in your

stomach, which causes discomfort. ❹ MUSIC The wind section of an orchestra is the group of musicians who play wind instruments.

wind, winds, winding, wound *[rhymes with* **mind***]* **VERB** ❶ If a road or river winds in a particular direction, it twists and turns in that direction. ❷ When you wind something round something else, you wrap it round it several times. ❸ When you wind a clock or machine or wind it up, you turn a key or handle several times to make it work.
wind up VERB ❶ When you wind up something such as an activity or a business, you finish it or close it. ❷ If you wind up in a particular place, you end up there.

windfall, windfalls **NOUN** a sum of money that you receive unexpectedly.

wind instrument, wind instruments **NOUN** an instrument you play by using your breath, for example a flute, an oboe, or a trumpet.

windmill, windmills **NOUN** a machine for grinding grain or pumping water. It is driven by vanes or sails turned by the wind.

window, windows **NOUN** a space in a wall or roof or in the side of a vehicle, usually with glass in it so that light can pass through and people can see in or out.

window box, window boxes **NOUN** a long, narrow container on a windowsill in which plants are grown.

windowsill, windowsills **NOUN** a ledge along the bottom of a window, either on the inside or outside of a

A
B
C
D
E
F
G
H
I
J
K
L
M
N
O
P
Q
R
S
T
U
V
W
X
Y
Z

▷ SPELLING NOTE: *You must practiSe your Ss (practise)*

building • *painting the windowsills red.*

windpipe, windpipes NOUN the tube which carries air into your lungs when you breathe.

windscreen, windscreens NOUN the glass at the front of a vehicle through which the driver looks.

windsurfing NOUN Windsurfing is the sport of moving along the surface of the sea or a lake standing on a board with a sail on it.

windswept ADJECTIVE A windswept place is exposed to strong winds • *a windswept beach.*

windward ADJECTIVE OR ADVERB ❶ facing the direction from which the wind is blowing, or moving in that direction ▷ NOUN ❷ NAUTICAL the direction from which the wind is blowing.

windy, windier, windiest ADJECTIVE If it is windy, there is a lot of wind.

wine, wines NOUN Wine is the red or white alcoholic drink which is normally made from grapes.
- **WORD HISTORY:** from Latin *vinum* meaning 'wine'

wing, wings NOUN ❶ A bird's or insect's wings are the parts of its body that it uses for flying. ❷ An aeroplane's wings are the long, flat parts on each side that support it while it is in the air. ❸ A wing of a building is a part which sticks out from the main part or which has been added later. ❹ A wing of an organization, especially a political party, is a group within it with a particular role or particular beliefs • *the left wing of the party.* ❺ IN

PLURAL The wings in a theatre are the sides of the stage which are hidden from the audience. **winged** ADJECTIVE

wink, winks, winking, winked VERB ❶ When you wink, you close one eye briefly, often as a signal that something is a joke or a secret ▷ NOUN ❷ the closing of your eye when you wink.

winkle, winkles NOUN a small sea-snail with a hard shell and a soft edible body.

winner, winners NOUN The winner of a prize, race, or competition is the person or thing that wins it.
- **SIMILAR WORDS:** champion, victor

winning ADJECTIVE ❶ The winning team or entry in a competition is the one that has won. ❷ attractive and charming • *a winning smile.*

winnings PLURAL NOUN Your winnings are the money you have won in a competition or by gambling.

winter, winters NOUN Winter is the season between autumn and spring.

wintry ADJECTIVE Something wintry has features that are typical of winter • *the wintry dawn.*

wipe, wipes, wiping, wiped VERB ❶ If you wipe something, you rub its surface lightly to remove dirt or liquid. ❷ If you wipe dirt or liquid off something, you remove it using a cloth or your hands • *Anne wiped the tears from her eyes.*
wipe out VERB To wipe out people or places is to destroy them

a b c d e f g h i j k l m n o p q r s t u v **w** x y z

▷ SPELLING NOTE: *pAL up with the principAL and principAL staff (principal)*

completely • *The tribe was wiped out.*

wire, wires, wiring, wired NOUN
1 (SCIENCE) Wire is metal in the form of a long, thin, flexible thread which can be used to make or fasten things or to conduct an electric current ▷ VERB **2** If you wire one thing to another, you fasten them together using wire. **3** (D & T) If you wire something or wire it up, you connect it so that electricity can pass through it. **wired** ADJECTIVE

wireless, wirelesses NOUN
OLD-FASHIONED a radio.

wiring NOUN The wiring in a building is the system of wires that supply electricity to the rooms.

wiry, wirier, wiriest ADJECTIVE
1 Wiry people are thin but with strong muscles. **2** Wiry things are stiff and rough to the touch • *wiry hair.*

wisdom NOUN **1** Wisdom is the ability to use experience and knowledge in order to make sensible decisions or judgments. **2** If you talk about the wisdom of an action or a decision, you are talking about how sensible it is.

wisdom tooth, wisdom teeth NOUN Your wisdom teeth are the four molar teeth at the back of your mouth which grow much later than other teeth.

wise, wiser, wisest ADJECTIVE
1 Someone who is wise can use their experience and knowledge to make sensible decisions and judgments ▷ PHRASE **2** If you say that someone is **none the wiser** or **no wiser**, you mean that they know no more about something than they did

before • *I left the conference none the wiser.*
● SIMILAR WORDS: **1** judicious,
● prudent, sensible

wisecrack, wisecracks NOUN a clever remark, intended to be amusing but often unkind.

wish, wishes, wishing, wished NOUN
1 a longing or desire for something, often something difficult to achieve or obtain. **2** something desired or wanted • *That wish came true two years later.* **3** IN PLURAL Good wishes are expressions of hope that someone will be happy or successful • *best wishes on your birthday.* ▷ VERB **4** If you wish to do something, you want to do it • *We wished to return.* **5** If you wish something were the case, you would like it to be the case, but know it is not very likely • *I wish I were tall.*

wishbone, wishbones NOUN a V-shaped bone in the breast of most birds.

wishful thinking NOUN If someone's hope or wish is wishful thinking, it is unlikely to come true.

wishy-washy ADJECTIVE
INFORMAL If a person or their ideas are wishy-washy, then their ideas are not firm or clear • *We need more than these wishy-washy reasons.*

wisp, wisps NOUN **1** A wisp of grass or hair is a small, thin, untidy bunch of it. **2** A wisp of smoke is a long, thin streak of it. **wispy** ADJECTIVE

wistful ADJECTIVE sadly thinking about something, especially something you want but cannot have • *A wistful look came into her eyes.* **wistfully** ADVERB

▷ SPELLING NOTE: L*Earn* the princip*LEs* (princip*le*)

wit, wits NOUN ❶ Wit is the ability to use words or ideas in an amusing and clever way. ❷ Wit means sense • *They haven't got the wit to realize what they're doing.* ❸ IN PLURAL Your wits are the ability to think and act quickly in a difficult situation • *the man who lived by his wits.* ▷ PHRASE ❹ If someone is **at their wits' end**, they are so worried and exhausted by problems or difficulties that they do not know what to do.

witch, witches NOUN a woman claimed to have magic powers and to be able to use them for good or evil.

witchcraft NOUN Witchcraft is the skill or art of using magic powers, especially evil ones.
● SIMILAR WORDS: black magic,
● sorcery, wizardry

witch doctor, witch doctors NOUN a man in some societies, especially in Africa, who appears to have magic powers.

witchetty grub, witchetty grubs NOUN a large Australian caterpillar that is eaten by Aborigines as food.

with PREPOSITION ❶ 'With' someone means in their company • *He was at home with me.* ❷ 'With' is used to show who your opponent is in a fight or competition • *next week's game with Brazil.* ❸ 'With' can mean using or having • *Apply the colour with a brush* • *a bloke with a moustache.* ❹ 'With' is used to show how someone does something or how they feel • *She looked at him with hatred.* ❺ 'With' can mean concerning • *a problem with her telephone bill.* ❻ 'With' is used to show support • *Are you with us or against us?*

withdraw, withdraws, withdrawing, withdrew, withdrawn VERB ❶ If you withdraw something, you remove it or take it out • *He withdrew the money from his bank.* ❷ If you withdraw to another place, you leave where you are and go there • *He withdrew to his study.* ❸ If you withdraw from an activity, you back out of it • *They withdrew from the conference.*

withdrawal, withdrawals NOUN ❶ The withdrawal of something is the act of taking it away • *the withdrawal of Russian troops.* ❷ The withdrawal of a statement is the act of saying formally that you wish to change or deny it. ❸ an amount of money you take from your bank or building society account.

withdrawal symptoms PLURAL NOUN Withdrawal symptoms are the unpleasant effects suffered by someone who has suddenly stopped taking a drug to which they are addicted.

withdrawn ❶ Withdrawn is the past participle of **withdraw**. ADJECTIVE ❷ unusually shy or quiet.

wither, withers, withering, withered VERB ❶ When something withers or withers away, it becomes weaker until it no longer exists. ❷ If a plant withers, it wilts or shrivels up and dies.

withering ADJECTIVE A withering look or remark makes you feel ashamed, stupid, or inferior.

withhold, withholds, withholding, withheld VERB FORMAL If you withhold something that someone wants, you do not let them have it.

within PREPOSITION OR ADVERB

▷ SPELLING NOTE: Psychiatrists Seldom Yell Callously Hard (*psychiatrist*)

A
B
C
D
E
F
G
H
I
J
K
L
M
N
O
P
Q
R
S
T
U
V
W
X
Y
Z

❶ 'Within' means in or inside ▷ **PREPOSITION** ❷ 'Within' can mean not going beyond certain limits • *Stay within the budget.* ❸ 'Within' can mean before a period of time has passed • *You must write back within fourteen days.*

without PREPOSITION
❶ 'Without' means not having, feeling, or showing • *Didier looked on without emotion.* ❷ 'Without' can mean not using • *You can't get in without a key.* ❸ 'Without' can mean not in someone's company • *He went without me.* ❹ 'Without' can indicate that something does not happen when something else happens • *Stone signalled the ship, again without response.*

withstand, withstands, withstanding, withstood **VERB** When something or someone withstands a force or action, they survive it or do not give in to it • *ships designed to withstand the North Atlantic winter.*

witness, witnesses, witnessing, witnessed **NOUN** ❶ someone who has seen an event such as an accident and can describe what happened. ❷ someone who appears in a court of law to say what they know about a crime or other event. ❸ someone who writes their name on a document that someone else has signed, to confirm that it is really that person's signature ▷ **VERB** ❹ FORMAL If you witness an event, you see it.
● **SIMILAR WORDS:** ❶ bystander,
● observer, onlooker

witticism, witticisms [*Said wit-tiss-izm*] **NOUN** a clever and amusing remark or joke.

witty, wittier, wittiest **ADJECTIVE** amusing in a clever way • *this witty novel.* **wittily ADVERB**

wives the plural of **wife**.

wizard, wizards **NOUN** a man in a fairy story who has magic powers.

wizened [*Said wiz-nd*] **ADJECTIVE** having a wrinkled skin, especially with age • *a wizened old man.*

WMD NOUN an abbreviation for 'weapon(s) of mass destruction'.

wobbegong, wobbegongs [*Said wob-bi-gong*] **NOUN** an Australian shark with a richly patterned brown-and-white skin.

wobble, wobbles, wobbling, wobbled **VERB** If something wobbles, it shakes or moves from side to side because it is loose or unsteady • *a cyclist who wobbled into my path.*

wobbly, wobblier, wobbliest **ADJECTIVE** unsteady • *a wobbly table.*

woe, woes LITERARY **NOUN** ❶ Woe is great unhappiness or sorrow ❷ IN PLURAL Someone's woes are their problems or misfortunes.

wok, woks **NOUN** a large bowl-shaped metal pan used for Chinese-style cooking.

woke the past tense of **wake**.

woken the past participle of **wake**.

wolf, wolves; wolfs, wolfing, wolfed **NOUN** ❶ a wild animal related to the dog. Wolves hunt in packs and kill other animals for food ▷ **VERB** ❷ INFORMAL If you wolf food or wolf it down, you eat it up quickly and greedily.

▷ SPELLING NOTE: *the QUeen stood on the QUay (quay)*

woman, women **NOUN** ❶ an adult female human being. ❷ Woman can refer to women in general • *man's inhumanity to woman.*

womanhood **NOUN** Womanhood is the state of being a woman rather than a girl • *on the verge of womanhood.*

womb, wombs [*Said* **woom**] **NOUN** A woman's womb is the part inside her body where her unborn baby grows.

wombat, wombats [*Said* **wom-bat**] **NOUN** a short-legged furry Australian animal which eats plants.

wonder, wonders, wondering, wondered **VERB** ❶ If you wonder about something, you think about it with curiosity or doubt. ❷ If you wonder at something, you are surprised and amazed at it • *He wondered at her anger.* ▷ **NOUN** ❸ Wonder is a feeling of surprise and amazement. ❹ something or someone that surprises and amazes people • *the wonders of science.*
  ● **SIMILAR WORDS:** ❹ marvel,
  ● miracle, phenomenon

wonderful **ADJECTIVE** ❶ making you feel very happy and pleased • *It was wonderful to be together.* ❷ very impressive • *Nature is a wonderful thing.* **wonderfully** **ADVERB**
  ● **SIMILAR WORDS:** ❷ amazing,
  ● magnificent, remarkable

wondrous **ADJECTIVE** LITERARY amazing and impressive.

wont [*rhymes with* **don't**] **ADJECTIVE** OLD-FASHIONED If someone is wont to do something, they do it often • *This was a term of endearment she was wont*

to use when speaking to him.

woo, woos, wooing, wooed **VERB** ❶ If you woo people, you try to get them to help or support you • *attempts to woo the women's vote.* ❷ OLD-FASHIONED When a man woos a woman, he tries to get her to marry him.

wood, woods **NOUN** ❶ Wood is the substance which forms the trunks and branches of trees. ❷ a large area of trees growing near each other.

wooded **ADJECTIVE** covered in trees • *a wooded area nearby.*

wooden **ADJECTIVE** made of wood • *a wooden box.*

woodland, woodlands **NOUN** Woodland is land that is mostly covered with trees.

woodpecker, woodpeckers **NOUN** a climbing bird with a long, sharp beak that it uses to drill holes into trees to find insects.

woodwind **ADJECTIVE** Woodwind instruments are musical instruments such as flutes, oboes, clarinets, and bassoons, that are played by being blown into.

woodwork **NOUN** ❶ Woodwork refers to the parts of a house, such as stairs, doors or window-frames, that are made of wood. ❷ Woodwork is the craft or skill of making things out of wood.

woodworm, woodworm or woodworms **NOUN** ❶ Woodworm are the larvae of a kind of beetle. They make holes in wood by feeding on it. ❷ Woodworm is damage caused to wood by woodworm making holes in it

a
b
c
d
e
f
g
h
i
j
k
l
m
n
o
p
q
r
s
t
u
w
x
y
z

▷ SPELLING NOTE: *Rhythmical Hounds Yap To Heavy Music (*rhythm*)*

ABCDEFGHIJKLMNOPQRSTUVWXYZ

• holes made by woodworm.

woody, woodier, woodiest
ADJECTIVE ❶ Woody plants have hard tough stems. ❷ A woody area has a lot of trees in it.

woof, woofs **NOUN** the sound that a dog makes when it barks.

wool, wools **NOUN** ❶ Wool is the hair that grows on sheep and some other animals. ❷ Wool is also yarn spun from the wool of animals which is used to knit, weave, and make such things as clothes, blankets, and carpets.

woollen, woollens **ADJECTIVE**
❶ made from wool ▷ **NOUN**
❷ Woollens are clothes made of wool.

woolly, woollier, woolliest
ADJECTIVE ❶ made of wool or looking like wool • *a woolly hat.* ❷ If you describe people or their thoughts as woolly, you mean that they seem confused and unclear.

woolshed, woolsheds **NOUN** In Australian and New Zealand English, a large building in which sheep are sheared.

woomera, woomeras **NOUN** a stick with a notch at one end used by Australian Aborigines to help fire a dart or spear.

word, words, wording, worded **NOUN**
❶ a single unit of language in speech or writing which has a meaning. ❷ a remark • *a word of praise.* ❸ a brief conversation • *Could I have a word?*
❹ A word can also be a message • *The word is that Sharon is exhausted.*
❺ Your word is a promise • *He gave me his word.* ❻ The word can be a

command • *I gave the word to start.*
❼ IN PLURAL The words of a play or song are the spoken or sung text ▷ **VERB** ❽ When you word something, you choose your words in order to express your ideas accurately or acceptably • *the best way to word our invitations.*

word equation, word equation **NOUN** (SCIENCE) A word equation describes a chemical reaction using words instead of chemical symbols.

wording NOUN The wording of a piece of writing or a speech is the words used in it, especially when these words have been carefully chosen to have a certain effect.

wordplay NOUN (ENGLISH) Wordplay is the making of jokes by clever use of words.

word processor, word processors **NOUN** an electronic machine which has a keyboard and a visual display unit and which is used to produce, store, and organize printed material.

work, works, working, worked **VERB**
❶ People who work have a job which they are paid to do • *My husband works for a national newspaper.* ❷ When you work, you do the tasks that your job involves. ❸ To work the land is to cultivate it. ❹ If someone works a machine, they control or operate it.
❺ If a machine works, it operates properly and effectively • *The radio doesn't work.* ❻ If something such as an idea or a system works, it is successful • *The housing benefit system is not working.* ❼ If something works its way into a particular position, it gradually moves there • *The cable had worked loose.* ▷ **NOUN** ❽ People who

▷ SPELLING NOTE: there's SAND in my SANDwich (*sandwich*)

have work or who are in work have a job which they are paid to do • *She's trying to find work.* **9** Work is the tasks that have to be done. **10** something done or made • *a work of art.* **11** In physics, work is transfer of energy. It is calculated by multiplying a force by the distance moved by the point to which the force has been applied. Work is measured in joules **12** IN PLURAL A works is a place where something is made by an industrial process • *the old steel works.* **13** Works are large scale building, digging, or general construction activities • *building works.*

work out VERB **1** If you work out a solution to a problem, you find the solution. **2** If a situation works out in a particular way, it happens in that way.

work up VERB **1** If you work up to something, you gradually progress towards it. **2** If you work yourself up or work someone else up, you make yourself or the other person very upset or angry about something. **worked up** ADJECTIVE

● **SIMILAR WORDS: 4** control, ● handle, operate **5** function, go, ● run

workable ADJECTIVE Something workable can operate successfully or can be used for a particular purpose • *a workable solution* • *This plan simply isn't workable.*

workaholic, workaholics NOUN a person who finds it difficult to stop working and do other things.

worker, workers NOUN a person employed in a particular industry or business • *During the war, her grandmother was a defence worker.*

workforce, workforces NOUN The workforce is all the people who work in a particular place.

workhouse, workhouses NOUN In the past a workhouse was a building to which very poor people were sent and made to work in return for food and shelter.

working, workings ADJECTIVE **1** Working people have jobs which they are paid to do. **2** Working can mean related to, used for, or suitable for work • *the working week* • *working conditions.* **3** Working can mean sufficient to be useful or to achieve what is required • *a working knowledge of Hebrew.* **4** IN PLURAL The workings of a piece of equipment, an organization, or a system are the ways in which it operates • *the workings of the European Union.*

working class, working classes NOUN The working class or working classes are the group of people in society who do not own much property and who do jobs which involve physical rather than intellectual skills.

workload, workloads NOUN the amount of work that a person or a machine has to do.

workman, workmen NOUN a man whose job involves using physical rather than intellectual skills.

workmanship NOUN Workmanship is the skill with which something is made or a job is completed.

workmate, workmates NOUN Someone's workmate is the fellow worker with whom they do their job.

▷ SPELLING NOTE: *On WEDNESday Wayne WED NESta (Wednesday)*

workout, workouts **NOUN** a session of physical exercise or training.

workplace NOUN Your workplace is the building or company where you work.

workshop, workshops **NOUN** ❶ a room or building that contains tools or machinery used for making or repairing things • *an engineering workshop.* ❷ a period of discussion or practical work in which a group of people learn about a particular subject • *a theatre workshop.*

world, worlds **NOUN** ❶ The world is the earth, the planet we live on. ❷ You can use 'world' to refer to people generally • *The eyes of the world are upon me.* ❸ Someone's world is the life they lead and the things they experience • *We come from different worlds.* ❹ A world is a division or section of the earth, its history, or its people, such as the Arab World, or the Ancient World. ❺ A particular world is a field of activity and the people involved in it • *the world of football.* ▷ **ADJECTIVE** ❻ 'World' is used to describe someone or something that is one of the best or most important of its kind • *a world leader.* ▷ **PHRASE** ❼ If you **think the world** of someone, you like or admire them very much.
  ● **WORD HISTORY:** from Old English
  ● *weorold* from *wer* meaning 'man'
  ● and *ald* meaning 'age'

worldly, worldlier, worldliest **ADJECTIVE** ❶ relating to the ordinary activities of life rather than spiritual things • *opportunities for worldly pleasures.* ❷ experienced and knowledgeable about life.

world war, world wars **NOUN** a war that involves countries all over the world.

worldwide ADJECTIVE throughout the world • *a worldwide increase in skin cancers.*

World Wide Web NOUN The World Wide Web is another name for the Internet, the worldwide communication system which people use through computers.

worm, worms, worming, wormed **NOUN** ❶ a small thin animal without bones or legs, which lives in the soil or off other creatures. ❷ an insect such as a beetle or moth at a very early stage in its life. ❸ a computer program that makes many copies of itself within a network, usually harming the system ▷ **VERB** ❹ If you worm an animal, you give it medicine in order to kill the worms that are living as parasites in its intestines. ❺ **worm out VERB** If you worm information out of someone, you gradually persuade them to give you it.

worn ❶ Worn is the past participle of wear. **ADJECTIVE** ❷ damaged or thin because of long use. ❸ looking old or exhausted • *Her husband looks frail and worn.*

worn-out ADJECTIVE ❶ used until it is too thin or too damaged to be of further use • *a worn-out cardigan.* ❷ extremely tired • *You must be worn-out after the drive.*

worried ADJECTIVE unhappy and anxious about a problem or about something unpleasant that might happen.

▷ SPELLING NOTE: *Eddy Ant thinks mEAt is a grEAt trEAt to EAt (-ea-)*

● **SIMILAR WORDS:** anxious,
● concerned, troubled

worry, worries, worrying, worried
VERB ❶ If you worry, you feel
anxious and fearful about a problem
or about something unpleasant that
might happen. ❷ If something
worries you, it causes you to feel
uneasy or fearful • *a puzzle which had
worried her all her life.* ❸ If you worry
someone with a problem, you disturb
or bother them by telling them about
it • *I didn't want to worry the boys with
this.* ❹ If a dog worries sheep or other
animals, it frightens or harms them by
chasing them or biting them ▷ **NOUN**
❺ Worry is a feeling of unhappiness
and unease caused by a problem or by
thinking of something unpleasant that
might happen • *the major source of
worry.* ❻ a person or thing that causes
you to feel anxious or uneasy
• *Inflation is the least of our worries.*
worrying ADJECTIVE
● **WORD HISTORY:** from Old English
● *wyrgan* meaning 'strangle'
● **SIMILAR WORDS:** ❶ be anxious,
● fret ❷ bother, perturb, trouble
● ❺ anxiety, concern

worse ADJECTIVE OR ADVERB
❶ Worse is the comparative form of
bad and **badly.** ❷ If someone who is
ill gets worse, they become more ill
than before ▷ **PHRASE** ❸ If someone
or something is **none the worse** for
something, they have not been
harmed by it • *He appeared none the
worse for the accident.*

worsen, worsens, worsening,
worsened **VERB** If a situation
worsens, it becomes more difficult or
unpleasant • *My relationship with my
mother worsened.*

● **SIMILAR WORDS:** decline,
● deteriorate, get worse

worse off ADJECTIVE If you are
worse off, you have less money or are
in a more unpleasant situation than
before • *There are people much worse
off than me.*

worship, worships, worshipping,
worshipped **VERB** ❶ RE If you
worship a god, you show your love and
respect by praying or singing hymns.
❷ If you worship someone or
something, you love them or admire
them very much ▷ **NOUN** ❸ Worship
is the feeling of respect, love, or
admiration you feel for something or
someone. **worshipper NOUN**
● **SIMILAR WORDS:** ❷ adore,
● idolize, love ❸ adoration, devotion

worst ADJECTIVE OR ADVERB
Worst is the superlative of **bad** and
badly.

worth PREPOSITION ❶ If
something is worth a sum of money, it
has that value • *a house worth 85,000
dollars.* ❷ If something is worth
doing, it deserves to be done ▷ **NOUN**
❸ A particular amount of money's
worth of something is the quantity of
it that you can buy for that money
• *five pound's worth of petrol.*
❹ Someone's worth is the value or
usefulness they are considered to
have.

worthless ADJECTIVE having no
real value or use • *a worthless piece of
junk.*

worthwhile ADJECTIVE important
enough to justify the time, money, or
effort spent on it • *a worthwhile career.*

worthy, worthier, worthiest

a
b
c
d
e
f
g
h
i
j
k
l
m
n
o
p
q
r
s
t
u
v
w
x
y
z

A
B
C
D
E
F
G
H
I
J
K
L
M
N
O
P
Q
R
S
T
U
V
W
X
Y
Z

ADJECTIVE If someone or something is worthy of something, they deserve it • *a worthy champion.*

would VERB ❶ You use 'would' to say what someone thought was going to happen • *We were sure it would be a success.* ❷ You use 'would' when you are referring to the result or effect of a possible situation • *If readers can help I would be most grateful.* ❸ You use 'would' when referring to someone's willingness to do something • *I wouldn't change places with him if you paid me.* ❹ You use 'would' in polite questions • *Would you like some lunch?*

would-be ADJECTIVE wanting to be or claiming to be • *a would-be pop singer.*

wound, wounds, wounding, wounded NOUN ❶ an injury to part of your body, especially a cut in your skin and flesh ▷ VERB ❷ If someone wounds you, they damage your body using a gun, knife, or other weapon. ❸ If you are wounded by what someone says or does, your feelings are hurt. **wounded** ADJECTIVE

WOW INTERJECTION Wow is an expression of admiration or surprise.

WPC, WPCs NOUN In Britain, a female member of the police force. WPC is an abbreviation for 'woman police constable'.

wrangle, wrangles, wrangling, wrangled VERB ❶ If you wrangle with someone, you argue noisily or angrily, often about something unimportant ▷ NOUN ❷ an argument that is difficult to settle. **wrangling** NOUN

wrap, wraps, wrapping, wrapped

VERB ❶ If you wrap something or wrap something up, you fold a piece of paper or cloth tightly around it to cover or enclose it. ❷ If you wrap paper or cloth round something, you put or fold the paper round it. ❸ If you wrap your arms, fingers, or legs round something, you coil them round it.

wrap up VERB If you wrap up, you put warm clothes on.

wrapped up ADJECTIVE INFORMAL If you are wrapped up in a person or thing, you give that person or thing all your attention.

wrapper, wrappers NOUN a piece of paper, plastic, or foil which covers and protects something that you buy • *sweet wrappers.*

wrapping, wrappings NOUN Wrapping is the material used to cover and protect something.

wrath [Said *roth*] NOUN LITERARY Wrath is great anger • *the wrath of his father.*

wreak, wreaks, wreaking, wreaked [Said *reek*] VERB To wreak havoc or damage is to cause it.

wreath, wreaths [Said *reeth*] NOUN an arrangement of flowers and leaves, often in the shape of a circle, which is put on a grave as a sign of remembrance for the dead person.

wreck, wrecks, wrecking, wrecked VERB ❶ If someone wrecks something, they break it, destroy it, or spoil it completely. ❷ If a ship is wrecked, it has been so badly damaged that it can no longer sail ▷ NOUN ❸ a vehicle which has been badly damaged in an accident. ❹ If

▷ SPELLING NOTE: *'i' before 'e' except after 'c'*

you say someone is a wreck, you mean that they are in a very poor physical or mental state of health and cannot cope with life. **wrecked ADJECTIVE**

wreckage NOUN Wreckage is what remains after something has been badly damaged or destroyed • *searching the wreckage for survivors.*

wren, wrens NOUN a very small brown songbird.

wrench, wrenches, wrenching, wrenched VERB ❶ If you wrench something, you give it a sudden and violent twist or pull • *Nick wrenched open the door.* ❷ If you wrench a limb or a joint, you twist and injure it ▷ NOUN ❸ a metal tool with parts which can be adjusted to fit around nuts or bolts to loosen or tighten them. ❹ a painful parting from someone or something.

wrest, wrests, wresting, wrested *[Said rest]* FORMAL If you wrest something from someone else you take it from them violently or with effort • *to try and wrest control of the island from the Mafia.*

wrestle, wrestles, wrestling, wrestled VERB ❶ If you wrestle someone or wrestle with them, you fight them by holding or throwing them, but not hitting them. ❷ When you wrestle with a problem, you try to deal with it. **wrestler NOUN**

wrestling NOUN Wrestling is a sport in which two people fight and try to win by throwing or holding their opponent on the ground.

wretch, wretches NOUN OLD-FASHIONED someone who is thought to be wicked or very unfortunate.

● **WORD HISTORY:** from Old English *wrecca* meaning 'exile' or 'despised person'

wretched *[Said ret-shid]* ADJECTIVE ❶ very unhappy or unfortunate • *a wretched childhood.* ❷ INFORMAL You use wretched to describe something or someone you resent or dislike • *a wretched bully.*

wriggle, wriggles, wriggling, wriggled VERB ❶ If someone wriggles, they twist and turn their body or a part of their body using quick movements • *He wriggled his arms and legs.* ❷ If you wriggle somewhere, you move there by twisting and turning • *I wriggled out of the van.* **wriggly ADJECTIVE**

wring, wrings, wringing, wrung VERB ❶ When you wring a wet cloth or wring it out, you squeeze the water out of it by twisting it. ❷ If you wring your hands, you hold them together and twist and turn them, usually because you are worried or upset. ❸ If someone wrings a bird's neck, they kill the bird by twisting and breaking its neck.

wrinkle, wrinkles, wrinkling, wrinkled NOUN ❶ Wrinkles are lines in someone's skin, especially on the face, which form as they grow old ▷ VERB ❷ If something wrinkles, folds or lines develop on it. ❸ When you wrinkle your nose, forehead, or eyes, you tighten the muscles in your face so that the skin folds into lines. **wrinkled ADJECTIVE wrinkly ADJECTIVE**

● **WORD HISTORY:** from Old English *wrinclian* meaning 'to wind around'
● **SIMILAR WORDS:** ❶ crease, fold

a b c d e f g h i j k l m n o p q r s t u v **w** x y z

▷ SPELLING NOTE: *King IAn went to ParlIAment in a carrIAge for his marrIAge (-ia-)*

A
B
C
D
E
F
G
H
I
J
K
L
M
N
O
P
Q
R
S
T
U
V
W
X
Y
Z

wrist, wrists **NOUN** the part of your body between your hand and your arm which bends when you move your hand.

writ, writs **NOUN** a legal document that orders a person to do or not to do a particular thing.

write, writes, writing, wrote, written **VERB** ❶ When you write something, you use a pen or pencil to form letters, words, or numbers on a surface. ❷ If you write something such as a poem, a book, or a piece of music, you create it. ❸ When you write to someone or write them a letter, you express your feelings in a letter. ❹ When someone writes something such as a cheque, they put the necessary information on it and sign it. ❺ When you write data you transfer it to a computer's memory.
write down VERB If you write something down, you record it on a piece of paper.
write up VERB If you write up something, you write a full account of it, often using notes that you have made.

writer, writers **NOUN** ❶ a person who writes books, stories, or articles as a job. ❷ The writer of something is the person who wrote it • *contact the writer of the report.*

writhe, writhes, writhing, writhed **VERB** If you writhe, you twist and turn your body, often because you are in pain.

writing, writings **NOUN** ❶ Writing is something that has been written or printed • *Apply in writing for the information.* ❷ Your writing is the way you write with a pen or pencil. ❸ Writing is also a piece of written work, especially the style of language used • *witty writing.* ❹ An author's writings are his or her written works.

written ❶ Written is the past participle of **write. ADJECTIVE** ❷ taken down in writing • *a written agreement.*

wrong, wrongs, wronging, wronged **ADJECTIVE** ❶ not working properly or unsatisfactory • *There was something wrong with the car.* ❷ not correct or truthful • *the wrong answer.* ❸ bad or immoral • *It is wrong to kill people.* ▷ **NOUN** ❹ an unjust action or situation • *the wrongs of our society.* ▷ **VERB** ❺ If someone wrongs you, they treat you in an unfair or unjust way. **wrongly ADVERB**
● **SIMILAR WORDS:** ❷ erroneous,
● inaccurate, incorrect

wrongful ADJECTIVE A wrongful act is regarded as illegal, unfair, or immoral • *wrongful imprisonment.*

wrought iron NOUN Wrought iron is a pure type of iron that is formed into decorative shapes.

wry ADJECTIVE A wry expression shows that you find a situation slightly amusing because you know more about it than other people. **wryly ADVERB wryness NOUN**

▷ SPELLING NOTE: *an ELegant angEL (angel)*

Xx

X or **x** ❶ 'X' is used to represent the name of an unknown or secret person or place • *The victim was referred to as Mr X throughout Tuesday's court proceedings.* ❷ People sometimes write 'X' on a map to mark a precise position. ❸ 'X' is used to represent a kiss at the bottom of a letter, a vote on a ballot paper, or the signature of someone who cannot write.

X chromosome, X chromosomes **NOUN** SCIENCE In biology, an X chromosome is one of an identical pair of chromosomes found in a woman's cells, or one of a nonidentical pair found in a man's cells. X chromosomes are associated with female characteristics.

xenon *[Said zen-non]* **NOUN** (SCIENCE) Xenon is a chemical element in the form of a colourless, odourless gas found in very small quantities in the atmosphere. It is used in radio valves and in some lamps. Its atomic number is 54 and its symbol is Xe.

xenophobia *[Said zen-nof-foe-bee-a]* **NOUN** a fear or strong dislike of people from other countries. **xenophobic ADJECTIVE**

● **WORD HISTORY:** from Greek *xenos* meaning 'stranger' and *phobos* meaning 'fear'

Xerox, Xeroxes *[Said zeer-roks]* **NOUN** TRADEMARK ❶ a machine that makes photographic copies of sheets of paper with writing or printing on them. ❷ a copy made by a Xerox machine.

Xmas NOUN INFORMAL Xmas means the same as Christmas.

X-ray, X-rays, X-raying, X-rayed **NOUN** ❶ a stream of radiation of very short wavelength that can pass through some solid materials. X-rays are used by doctors to examine the bones or organs inside a person's body. ❷ a picture made by sending X-rays through someone's body in order to examine the inside of it ▷ **VERB** ❸ If you are X-rayed, a picture is made of the inside of your body by passing X-rays through it.

xylem *[Said zy-lem]* **NOUN** TECHNICAL Xylem is a plant tissue that conducts water and mineral salts from the roots and carries them through the plant. It forms the wood in trees and shrubs.

xylophone, xylophones *[Said zy-lo-fone]* **NOUN** a musical instrument made of a row of wooden bars of different lengths. It is played by hitting the bars with special hammers.

▷ SPELLING NOTE: *LEt's measure the angLE (angle)*

Yy

-y suffix '-y' forms nouns • *anarchy*.

yabby, yabbies noun a small edible Australian crayfish.

yacht, yachts [*Said* **yot**] noun a boat with sails or an engine, used for racing or for pleasure trips.

yachting noun Yachting is the sport or activity of sailing a yacht.

yachtsman, yachtsmen noun a man who sails a yacht. **yachtswoman** noun

yak, yaks noun a type of long-haired ox with long horns, found mainly in Tibet.

yakka or **yacker** noun INFORMAL In Australian and New Zealand English, yakka or yacker is work.

yam, yams noun a root vegetable which grows in tropical regions.

yank, yanks, yanking, yanked verb ❶ If you yank something, you pull or jerk it suddenly with a lot of force ▷ noun ❷ INFORMAL A Yank is an American.
● USAGE NOTE: When *Yank* means
● 'an American' it starts with a capital
● letter

Yankee, Yankees noun the same as a Yank.

yap, yaps, yapping, yapped verb If a dog yaps, it barks with a high-pitched sound.

yard, yards noun ❶ a unit of length equal to 36 inches or about 91.4 centimetres. ❷ an enclosed area that is usually next to a building and is often used for a particular purpose • *a ship repair yard*.

yardstick, yardsticks noun someone or something you use as a standard against which to judge other people or things • *He had no yardstick by which to judge university.*

yarn, yarns noun ❶ D & T Yarn is thread used for knitting or making cloth. ❷ INFORMAL a story that someone tells, often with invented details to make it more interesting or exciting • *fishermen's yarns*.

yashmak, yashmaks noun a veil that some Muslim women wear over their faces when they are in public.

yawn, yawns, yawning, yawned verb When you yawn, you open your mouth wide and take in more air than usual. You often yawn when you are tired or bored.

yawning adjective A yawning gap or opening is very wide.

Y chromosome, Y chromosomes noun SCIENCE In biology, a Y chromosome is the single chromosome in a man's cells which will produce a male baby if it joins with an X chromosome during reproduction.

▷ SPELLING NOTE: *A Rude Idiot Thought He Might Eat Toffee In Church* (<u>arithmetic</u>)

ye OLD PRONOUN ❶ Ye used to mean 'you' ▷ ADJECTIVE ❷ Ye also used to mean 'the'.

yeah INTERJECTION INFORMAL Yeah means 'yes'.

year, years NOUN ❶ a period of twelve months or 365 days (366 days in a leap year), which is the time taken for the earth to travel once around the sun. ❷ a period of twelve consecutive months, not always January to December, on which administration or organization is based • *the current financial year.* ▷ PHRASE ❸ If something happens **year in, year out**, it happens every year • *a tradition kept up year in, year out.* **yearly** ADJECTIVE OR ADVERB

yearling, yearlings NOUN an animal between one and two years old.

yearn, yearns, yearning, yearned [rhymes with **learn**] VERB If you yearn for something, you want it very much indeed • *He yearned to sleep.* **yearning** NOUN

yeast, yeasts NOUN Yeast is a kind of fungus which is used to make bread rise, and to make liquids ferment in order to produce alcohol.

yell, yells, yelling, yelled VERB ❶ If you yell, you shout loudly, usually because you are angry, excited, or in pain ▷ NOUN ❷ a loud shout.

yellow, yellower, yellowest; yellows, yellowing, yellowed NOUN OR ADJECTIVE ❶ Yellow is the colour of buttercups, egg yolks, or lemons ▷ VERB ❷ When something yellows or is yellowed, it becomes yellow, often because it is old ▷ ADJECTIVE ❸ INFORMAL If you say someone is

yellow, you mean they are cowardly. **yellowish** ADJECTIVE

yellow box, yellow boxes NOUN a large spreading Australian tree which is a source of honey.

yellow fever NOUN Yellow fever is a serious infectious disease that is found in tropical countries. It causes fever and jaundice.

yelp, yelps, yelping, yelped VERB ❶ When people or animals yelp, they give a sudden, short cry ▷ NOUN ❷ a sudden, short cry.

yen NOUN ❶ The yen is the main unit of currency in Japan. ❷ If you have a yen to do something, you have a strong desire to do it • *Mike had a yen to try cycling.*

yes INTERJECTION You use 'yes' to agree with someone, to say that something is true, or to accept something.

yesterday NOUN OR ADVERB ❶ Yesterday is the day before today. ❷ You also use 'yesterday' to refer to the past • *Leave yesterday's sadness behind you.*

yet ADVERB ❶ If something has not happened yet, it has not happened up to the present time • *It isn't quite dark yet.* ❷ If something should not be done yet, it should not be done now, but later • *Don't switch off yet.* ❸ 'Yet' can mean there is still a possibility that something can happen • *We'll make a soldier of you yet.* ❹ You can use 'yet' when you want to say how much longer a situation will continue • *The service doesn't start for an hour yet.* ❺ 'Yet' can be used for emphasis • *She'd changed her mind yet again.*

▷ SPELLING NOTE: *Beautiful Elephants Are Usually Tiny (**beautiful**)*

a
b
c
d
e
f
g
h
i
j
k
l
m
n
o
p
q
r
s
t
u
v
w
x
y
z

▷ **CONJUNCTION** ⑥ You can use 'yet' to introduce a fact which is rather surprising • *He isn't a smoker yet he always carries a lighter.*

yeti, yetis *[Said **yet**-tee]* **NOUN** A yeti, or abominable snowman, is a large hairy apelike animal which some people believe exists in the Himalayas.

yew, yews **NOUN** An evergreen tree with bright red berries.

Yiddish NOUN Yiddish is a language derived mainly from German, which many Jewish people of European origin speak.
● **WORD HISTORY:** from German
○ *jüdisch* meaning 'Jewish'

yield, yields, yielding, yielded **VERB**
① If you yield to someone or something, you stop resisting and give in to them • *Russia recently yielded to US pressure.* ② If you yield something that you have control of or responsibility for, you surrender it • *They refused to yield control of their weapons.* ③ If something yields, it breaks or gives way • *The handle would yield to her grasp.* ④ To yield something is to produce it • *One season's produce yields food for the following year.* ▷ **NOUN** ⑤ A yield is an amount of food, money, or profit produced from a given area of land or from an investment.

yippee INTERJECTION 'Yippee!' is an exclamation of happiness or excitement.

yob, yobs **NOUN** INFORMAL a noisy, badly behaved boy or young man.

yodel, yodels, yodelling, yodelled *[Said **yoe**-dl]* **VERB** When someone yodels, they sing normal notes with

high quick notes in between. This style of singing is associated with the Swiss and Austrian Alps.

yoga *[Said **yoe**-ga]* **NOUN** Yoga is a Hindu method of mental and physical exercise or discipline.
● **WORD HISTORY:** from Sanskrit
○ *yoga* meaning 'union'

yogurt, yogurts; *also spelt* yoghurt *[Said **yog**-gurt or **yoe**-gurt]* **NOUN** Yogurt is a slightly sour thick liquid made from milk that has had bacteria added to it.

yoke, yokes **NOUN** ① a wooden bar attached to two collars which is laid across the necks of animals such as oxen to hold them together, and to which a plough or other tool may be attached. ② LITERARY If people are under a yoke of some kind, they are being oppressed • *the story of two women who escape the yoke of insensitive men.*

yokel, yokels *[Said **yoe**-kl]* **NOUN** someone who lives in the country and is regarded as being rather stupid and old-fashioned.

yolk, yolks *[rhymes with **joke**]* **NOUN** the yellow part in the middle of an egg.
● **WORD HISTORY:** from Old English
○ *geoloca*, from *geolu* meaning
○ 'yellow'

Yom Kippur *[Said yom kip-**poor**]* **NOUN** Yom Kippur is an annual Jewish religious holiday, which is a day of fasting and prayers. It is also called the Day of Atonement.

yonder ADVERB OR ADJECTIVE OLD over there • *There's an island yonder.*

▷ SPELLING NOTE: *Betty Eats Cakes And Uses Seven Eggs (because)*

yore AN OLD-FASHIONED PHRASE
Of yore means existing a long time
ago • *nostalgia for the days of yore.*

Yorkshire pudding, Yorkshire
puddings NOUN In Britain, Yorkshire
pudding is a kind of baked batter
made of flour, milk, and eggs, and
usually eaten with roast beef.

you PRONOUN ❶ 'You' refers to the
person or group of people that a
person is speaking or writing to.
❷ 'You' also refers to people in
general • *You can get a two-bedroom
villa quite cheaply.*

young, younger, youngest
ADJECTIVE ❶ A young person,
animal, or plant has not lived very long
and is not yet mature ▷ NOUN ❷ The
young are young people in general.
❸ The young of an animal are its
babies.
● SIMILAR WORDS: ❶ immature,
● undeveloped ❸ babies, offspring,
● progeny

youngster, youngsters NOUN a
child or young person.

your ADJECTIVE ❶ 'Your' means
belonging or relating to the person or
group of people that someone is
speaking to • *I do like your name.*
❷ 'Your' is used to show that
something belongs or relates to
people in general • *Your driving ability
is affected by just one or two drinks.*

yours PRONOUN 'Yours' refers to
something belonging or relating to the
person or group of people that

someone is speaking to • *His hair is
longer than yours.*

yourself, yourselves PRONOUN
❶ 'Yourself' is used when the person
being spoken to does the action and is
affected by it • *Why can't you do it
yourself?* ❷ 'Yourself' is used to
emphasize 'you' • *Do you yourself want
a divorce?*

youth, youths NOUN ❶ Someone's
youth is the period of their life before
they are a fully mature adult. ❷ Youth
is the quality or condition of being
young and often inexperienced. ❸ a
boy or young man. ❹ The youth are
young people thought of as a group
• *the youth of today.* youthful
ADJECTIVE

youth hostel, youth hostels NOUN
a place where young people can stay
cheaply when they are on holiday.

yo-yo, yo-yos NOUN a round wooden
or plastic toy attached to a piece of
string. You play by making the yo-yo
rise and fall on the string.

Yule NOUN OLD Yule means
Christmas.
● WORD HISTORY: from Old English
● *geola* a pagan winter feast

yuppie, yuppies NOUN If you say
people are yuppies, you think they are
young, middle-class, and earn a lot of
money which they spend on
themselves.
● WORD HISTORY: from y(oung)
● u(rban) or up(wardly mobile)
● p(rofessional) + -ie

a
b
c
d
e
f
g
h
i
j
k
l
m
n
o
p
q
r
s
t
u
v
w
x
y
z

▷ SPELLING NOTE: *there's a rAKE in the brAKEs (brake)*

Zz

A B C D E F G H I J K L M N O P Q R S T U V W X Y Z

Many words which sound as if they begin with letter z actually begin with letter x, for example *Xerox*, *xylem* and *xylophone*.

zakat NOUN (RE) a tax that all Muslims must pay which is used to help the poor in their community.

Zambian, Zambians *[Said zam-bee-an]* ADJECTIVE
1 belonging or relating to Zambia ▷ NOUN **2** someone who comes from Zambia.

zany, zanier, zaniest ADJECTIVE odd and ridiculous • *zany humour.*
● WORD HISTORY: from Italian
● *zanni* meaning 'clown'

zap, zaps, zapping, zapped VERB INFORMAL **1** To zap someone is to kill them, usually by shooting. **2** To zap also is to move somewhere quickly • *I zapped over to Paris.*

zeal NOUN Zeal is very great enthusiasm. **zealous** ADJECTIVE

zealot, zealots *[Said zel-lot]* NOUN a person who acts with very great enthusiasm, especially in following a political or religious cause.

zebra, zebras NOUN a type of African wild horse with black and white stripes over its body.

zebra crossing, zebra crossings NOUN a place where people can cross

the road safely. The road is marked with black and white stripes.

Zen or **Zen Buddhism** NOUN Zen is a form of Buddhism that concentrates on learning through meditation and intuition.

zenith NOUN LITERARY The zenith of something is the time when it is at its most successful or powerful • *the zenith of his military career.*

zero, zeros or zeroes, zeroing, zeroed **1** nothing or the number 0. **2** Zero is freezing point, 0° Centigrade ADJECTIVE **3** Zero means there is none at all of a particular thing • *His chances are zero.* ▷ VERB **4** To zero in on a target is to aim at or to move towards it • *The headlines zeroed in on the major news stories.*
● WORD HISTORY: from Arabic *sifr*
● meaning 'cipher' or 'empty'

zest NOUN **1** Zest is a feeling of pleasure and enthusiasm • *zest for life.* **2** Zest is a quality which adds extra flavour or interest to something • *brilliant ideas to add zest to your wedding list.* **3** The zest of an orange or lemon is the outside of the peel which is used to flavour food or drinks.

zigzag, zigzags, zigzagging, zigzagged NOUN **1** a line which has a series of sharp, angular turns to the right and left in it, like a continuous series of 'W's ▷ VERB **2** To zigzag is to move forward by going at an angle first right and then left • *He zigzagged his way across the racecourse.*

Zimbabwean, Zimbabweans *[Said zim-**bahb**-wee-an]* **ADJECTIVE**
❶ belonging or relating to Zimbabwe
▷ **NOUN** ❷ someone who comes from Zimbabwe.

zinc NOUN Zinc is a bluish-white metal used in alloys and to coat other metals to stop them rusting.

zing NOUN INFORMAL Zing is a quality in something that makes it lively or interesting • *There's a real zing around the studio.*

Zionism *[Said zie-on-izm]* **NOUN**
(RE) Zionism is a political movement which was originally concerned with the establishment of a state in Palestine for Jewish people. It is now concerned with the development of the modern state of Israel. **Zionist NOUN**

zip, zips, zipping, zipped **NOUN** ❶ a long narrow fastener with two rows of teeth that are closed or opened by a small clip pulled between them
▷ **VERB** ❷ When you zip something or zip it up, you fasten it using a zip.

zipper, zippers **NOUN** the same as a zip.

zodiac *[Said zoe-dee-ak]* **NOUN** The zodiac is an imaginary strip in the sky which contains the planets and stars which astrologers think are important influences on people. It is divided into 12 sections, each with a special name and symbol.
● **WORD HISTORY:** from Greek *zōidiakos kuklos* meaning 'circle of signs'

zombie, zombies **NOUN**
❶ INFORMAL If you refer to someone as a zombie, you mean that they seem to be unaware of what is going on around them and to act without thinking about what they are doing.
❷ In voodoo, a zombie is a dead person who has been brought back to life by witchcraft.
● **WORD HISTORY:** from an African word *zumbi* meaning 'good-luck charm'

zone, zones **NOUN** an area that has particular features or properties • *a war zone.*

zoo, zoos **NOUN** a place where live animals are kept so that people can look at them.

zoology *[Said zoo-ol-loj-jee]* **NOUN** Zoology is the scientific study of animals. **zoological ADJECTIVE zoologist NOUN**

zoom, zooms, zooming, zoomed
VERB ❶ To zoom is to move very quickly • *They zoomed to safety.* ❷ If a camera zooms in on something, it gives a close-up picture of it.

zucchini *[Said zoo-**keen**-nee]* **PLURAL NOUN** Zucchini are small vegetable marrows with dark green skin. They are also called **courgettes**.

Zulu, Zulus *[Said **zoo**-loo]* **NOUN**
❶ The Zulus are a group of Black people who live in southern Africa.
❷ Zulu is the language spoken by the Zulus.

zygote, zygotes *[Said **zye**-goat]* **NOUN** (SCIENCE) A zygote is an egg that has been fertilized by sperm and which could develop into an embryo.

▷ SPELLING NOTE: there's a rAKE in the brAKES (*brake*)

Spelling Rules

❶ ie or ei The rule is: *i* before *e*, except after *c*:

achieve	brief	chief
fierce	grieve	niece
relief	siege	thief
ceiling	conceit	deceit
deceive	receipt	receive

There are some exceptions:

seize
protein

❷ -ize or -ise In this dictionary, only the *-ize* (and *-ization*) endings are shown for verbs (and their nouns) such as *emphasize*, *organize* (*organization*) and *patronize*. Many of these words can also be spelled with the endings *-ise* (and *-isation*), and this is quite acceptable in British English. Care should be taken, however, because some words can only be spelled with *-ize* and others only with *-ise*.

Verbs (and nouns) only spelled with *-ize*:

capsize
prize [= *value highly*]

Verbs (and nouns) only spelled with *-ise*:

advertise	advise	chastise	comprise
compromise	despise	devise	disguise
excise	exercise	franchise	improvise
prise [= *force open*]	revise	supervise	surprise
televise			

❸ a. A final silent *e* is dropped when an ending that begins with a vowel is added:

servile + ity	=	servility
response + ible	=	responsible
tolerate + ing	=	tolerating
value + able	=	valuable
excuse + ed	=	excused

3 **b**. But the *e* is kept if an ending beginning with a vowel is added to a word that ends in *-ce* or *-ge*:

change + able	=	changeable
notice + able	=	noticeable
outrage + ous	=	outrageous
peace + able	=	peaceable

4 When an ending beginning with a vowel is added to a word that ends in a single vowel + a consonant, the consonant is doubled if the stress is on the end of the word:

admit + ance	=	admittance
begin + ing	=	beginning
occur + ence	=	occurrence
equip + ed	=	equipped

5 When an ending beginning with a vowel is added to a word that ends in a vowel + *l* or *p*, the *l* or *p* is usually doubled:

cancel + ation	=	cancellation
dial + ing	=	dialling
fulfil + ed	=	fulfilled
kidnap + er	=	kidnapper
slip + ing	=	slipping

6 When the adverb suffix *-ly* is added to an adjective that ends in a consonant followed by *-le*, the *-le* in the adjective is usually dropped:

gentle + ly	=	gently
idle + ly	=	idly
subtle + ly	=	subtly

7 When the adjective suffix *-ous* or *-ary* is added to a word that ends in *-our*, the *u* of the *-our* is dropped:

glamour + ous	=	glamorous
honour + ary	=	honorary
humour + ous	=	humorous

spelling rules

8 When an ending beginning with *e*, *i* or *y* is added to a word that ends in *c*, a *k* is added to the *c* to keep its hard sound:

mimic + ed	=	mimic**k**ed
picnic + ing	=	picnic**k**ing

9 a. When an ending is added to a word that ends in a consonant + *y*, the *y* changes to *i*:

beauty + ful	=	beaut**i**ful
crazy + ly	=	craz**i**ly
woolly + er	=	wooll**i**er

9 b. But, with certain short adjectives that end in a consonant + *y*, the *-ly* ending to make an adverb is added after the *y*:

shy + ly	=	shy**ly**
wry + ly	=	wry**ly**

10 The plural of a word that ends in a consonant + *y* is made by changing the *y* to *i* and adding *-es*:

story + es	=	stor**ies**
quality + es	=	qualit**ies**
spy + es	=	sp**ies**

11 The plural of a word that ends in a vowel plus *y* is made by adding *-s*:

donkey + s	=	donkey**s**
holiday + s	=	holiday**s**
boy + s	=	boy**s**
buoy + s	=	buoy**s**

12 The plural of a word that ends in *s*, *x*, *z*, *sh* or *ch* is made by adding *-es*:

bus + es	=	bus**es**
mass + es	=	mass**es**
fox + es	=	fox**es**
buzz + es	=	buzz**es**
rash + es	=	rash**es**
match + es	=	match**es**

13 The plural of a word that ends in *-eau* is made by adding *-x*:

---

gateau + x   =   gateaux
bureau + x   =   bureaux
(bureaus is also allowable)

---

14 The suffix *-ful* is always spelt with one *l*:

---

grateful   faithful   cupful

But *-fully* is always spelt with two:

---

gratefully   faithfully   beautifully

---

spelling rules

Commonly Confused Words and Spellings

accept = VERB	*Please accept my apologies.*
except = PREP	*He works every day except Tuesday.*

affect = VERB	*Tiredness affects concentration.*
effect = NOUN	*the beneficial effects of the medicine*

allude = VERB	*She alluded to the recent reports in the newspapers.*
elude = VERB	*I recognized his face, but his name eluded me.*

altar = NOUN	*The couple stood before the altar to take their marriage vows.*
alter = VERB	*His tone altered suddenly.*

ascent = NOUN	*the ascent of Everest by Edmund Hillary and Tenzing Norgay*
assent = NOUN	*The king gave his assent to the government's revised bill.*

aural = ADJECTIVE	*high- and low-pitched sounds which test aural function*
oral = ADJECTIVE	*He stumbled over his words in the oral examination.*

breath = NOUN	*There wasn't a breath of wind.*
breathe = VERB	*Breathe deeply a couple of times.*

broach = VERB	*She didn't dare broach the subject of a pay rise.*
brooch = NOUN	*a gold brooch set with emeralds and diamonds*

canvas = NOUN	*a hammock made from heavy canvas*
canvass = VERB	*TV reporters canvassing opinion*

coarse = ADJECTIVE **course** = NOUN	a coarse cloth which scratched the skin The river widens along its course.
complement = NOUN **compliment** = NOUN	Rice is a good complement to curry. My compliments to the chef.
council = NOUN **counsel** – VERB & NOUN	the local council • a council of war He counsels victims of crime. • give good counsel
cue – NOUN **queue** – NOUN	That's the leading lady's cue. a long queue at the post office
curb – VERB **kerb** – NOUN	trying hard to curb her appetite for chocolate The taxi drew up at the kerb.
currant – NOUN **current** – NOUN & ADJECTIVE	raisins, sultanas and currants ocean currents • current affairs.
dependant – NOUN **dependent** – ADJECTIVE	Do you have children or other dependants? The flood victims are dependent on international aid.
desert – NOUN & VERB **dessert** – NOUN	the Gobi Desert • The sentry deserted his post. Would you like ice-cream or fresh fruit for dessert?
draft – NOUN & VERB **draught** – NOUN	a first draft of the report • He's drafting a letter to his MP. There's a draught coming under that door.

commonly confused words and spellings

dual = ADJECTIVE	*Their children have dual citizenship of Britain and France.*
duel = NOUN	*The two men fought a duel with pistols at dawn.*

dyeing = VERB	*Have you been dyeing your hair again?*
dying = VERB	*The weakest are dying first, of hunger and cold.*

envelop = VERB	*A greenish haze seemed to envelop the landscape.*
envelope = NOUN	*Send a stamped addressed envelope.*

flair = NOUN	*a flair for design*
flare = NOUN & VERB	*The fishermen lit a flare to attract attention.* • *The horse's nostrils flared.*

forth – ADV	*They rode forth from the black gates in a great mass.*
fourth – ADJECTIVE	*the fourth day of July*

gilt – NOUN	*a clock decorated with silver gilt*
guilt – NOUN	*The evidence proves his guilt.*

hoard – NOUN & VERB	*a hoard of treasure* • *Many people hoard cooking ingredients years past their sell-by date.*
horde – NOUN	*hordes of noisy football fans*

its – ADJECTIVE	*The dog broke free of its lead and ran off.*
it's – SHORT FORM	*It's rude to stare.*

lead – VERB & NOUN	*You lead the way.* • *pipes made of lead*
led – VERB	*He was led astray by the other children.*

leant – VERB	*He leant against the tree.*
lent – VERB	*She lent me her bike.*

commonly confused words and spellings

licence = NOUN **license** = VERB	a driver's licence licensed to drive heavy goods vehicles
loath = ADJECTIVE **loathe** = VERB	I'm loath to ask him for money. We loathe each other.
loose = ADJECTIVE **lose** = VERB	His front tooth is loose. Be careful not to lose your pocket money.
miner = NOUN **minor** = ADJECTIVE & NOUN	a coal miner a minor inconvenience • a 14-year-old minor
practice – NOUN **practise** – VERB	a common practice • a dental practice He has a law degree but has never practised.
precede – VERB **proceed** – VERB	Summer precedes autumn. Let's proceed with the meeting.
principal – ADJECTIVE & NOUN **principle** – NOUN	the principal reason • the school principal Telling fibs is against my principles.
stationary – ADJECTIVE **stationery** – NOUN	The bus skidded and hit a stationary vehicle. paper, envelopes and other office stationery
their – ADJECTIVE **they're** = SHORT FORM **there** = ADV	It's not their fault. They're not to blame. She is standing there.
vain = ADJECTIVE **vein** = NOUN	He's vain and self-opinionated. Veins carry blood back to the heart.

commonly confused words and spellings

Commonly Misspelled Words

The English language is notorious for its difficult spelling rules. In the first place, we often have more than one way to spell one sound. *mete*, *meet*, and *meat* are pronounced identically, and the same sound is found in *deceit*. While groups like the Spelling Society and even a university professor or two have advocated a simpler approach to English spelling, the rules are unlikely to change in the near future. So in the meantime, we had better learn to spell words in the traditional way. Here is a list of words that are particularly tricky to get right. These will be especially useful for anyone preparing for a spelling competition such as *The Times* Spelling Bee.

achieve	cinnamon	euthanasia
address	commemorate	exaggerate
advertise	commitment	excellent
amateur	committee	excerpt
anaesthetic	comparative	exist
analysis	compatible	extraordinary
anoint	connoisseur	extrovert
apartment	conscience	facetious
appal	consensus	fascinate
appalling	contemporary	February
aqueduct	curriculum	fluorescent
archaeology	deceive	foreign
argument	definite	freight
artefact	despair	fulfil
beautiful	desperate	gauge
beige	detach	glamorous
believe	disappear	gorgeous
besiege	disappoint	government
biased	disastrous	guarantee
blatant	dissatisfied	guard
broccoli	ecstasy	guardian
budget	eighth	haemorrhage
business	embarrass	hamster
camouflage	enthral	handkerchief
cappuccino	environment	harass
Caribbean	espresso	height

honorary	minuscule	sausage
humorous	mischievous	schedule
hygiene	mortgage	seize
hypocrisy	necessary	separate
idiosyncrasy	niece	sergeant
independent	occasion	siege
indict	occurrence	sieve
innocuous	omit	silhouette
inoculate	parallel	skilful
instalment	peculiar	sovereign
integrate	perceive	successful
intelligent	permanent	supersede
introvert	pharaoh	suppress
irritable	phlegm	surprise
itinerary	piece	temperature
jealousy	pigeon	threshold
jeopardy	playwright	tomorrow
jewellery	possession	truly
knight	prejudice	unconscious
knowledge	privilege	usual
label	professor	until
laboratory	pronunciation	unwieldy
liaison	psychology	vacuum
lieutenant	query	vague
maintenance	questionnaire	vegetable
manoeuvre	queue	vehicle
margarine	receipt	veil
mathematician	receive	veterinary
mayonnaise	recommend	weight
medieval	reconnaissance	weird
Mediterranean	refrigerator	whinge
memento	rhinoceros	wilful
millennium	rhythm	withhold
millionaire	sacrilege	xylophone
miniature	satellite	yield

commonly misspelled words